D1440904

Heuristics and Biases

Is our case strong enough to go to trial? Will interest rates go up? Can I trust this person? Such questions – and the judgments required to answer them – are woven into the fabric of everyday experience. This book examines how people make such judgments. The study of human judgment was transformed in the 1970s, when Kahneman and Tversky introduced their "heuristics and biases" approach and challenged the dominance of strictly rational models. Their work highlighted the reflexive mental operations used to make complex problems manageable, and illuminated how the same processes can lead both to accurate and to dangerously flawed judgments. The heuristics and biases framework generated a torrent of influential research in psychology – research that reverberated widely and affected scholarship in economics, law, medicine, management, and political science. This book compiles the most influential research in the heuristic and biases tradition since the initial collection of 1982 (by Kahneman, Slovic, and Tversky). The various contributions develop and critically analyze the initial work on heuristics and biases, supplement these initial statements with emerging theory and empirical findings, and extend the reach of the framework to new real-world applications.

Thomas Gilovich is Professor of Psychology at Cornell University and a member of the Cornell Center for Behavioral Economics and Decision Research.

Dale Griffin is Associate Professor at the Graduate School of Business, Stanford University.

Daniel Kahneman is Eugene Higgins Professor of Psychology and Professor of Public Affairs at the Woodrow Wilson School of Public Affairs, Princeton University.

HEURISTICS AND BIASES

The Psychology of Intuitive Judgment

Edited by

THOMAS GILOVICH
Cornell University

DALE GRIFFIN
Stanford University

DANIEL KAHNEMAN
Princeton University

CAMBRIDGE
UNIVERSITY PRESS

PUBLISHED BY THE PRESS SYNDICATE OF THE UNIVERSITY OF CAMBRIDGE
The Pitt Building, Trumpington Street, Cambridge, United Kingdom

CAMBRIDGE UNIVERSITY PRESS
The Edinburgh Building, Cambridge CB2 2RU, UK
40 West 20th Street, New York, NY 10011-4211, USA
477 Williamstown, Port Melbourne, VIC 3207, Australia
Ruiz de Alarcón 13, 28014, Madrid, Spain
Dock House, The Waterfront, Cape Town 8001, South Africa

http://www.cambridge.org

© Cambridge University Press 2002

First published 2002
Reprinted with corrections 2003

Printed in the United States of America

Typeface Palatino 9.75/12.5 pt.   *System* LATEX 2$_\varepsilon$ [TB]

A catalog record for this book is available from the British Library.

Library of Congress Cataloging in Publication data
Heuristics and biases : the psychology of intuitive judgment / edited by Thomas
  Gilovich, Dale Griffin, Daniel Kahneman.
     p.   cm.
   Includes bibliographical references and index.
   ISBN 0-521-79260-6 – ISBN 0-521-79679-2 (pbk.)
    1. Judgment.   2. Reasoning (Psychology)   3. Critical thinking.   I. Gilovich,
  Thomas.   II. Griffin, Dale   III. Kahneman, Daniel, 1934–
  BF447 .H48   2002
  153.4 – dc21   2001037860

ISBN 0 521 79260 6 hardback
ISBN 0 521 79679 2 paperback

To the memory of Amos Tversky

Contents

List of Contributors

David A. Armor
Department of Psychology
Yale University

Maya Bar-Hillel
Department of Psychology
Hebrew University

Dale J. Barr
Department of Psychology
University of Chicago

Stephen J. Blumberg
National Institutes of Health

Nancy Brekke
Department of Psychology
Lake Forest College

Lyle Brenner
School of Management
University of Florida

Roger Buehler
Psychology Department
Wilfrid Laurier University

David B. Centerbar
Department of Psychology
University of Virginia

Gretchen Chapman
Psychology Department
Rutgers University

Incheol Choi
Department of Psychology
Seoul National University

Robert B. Cialdini
Department of Psychology
Arizona State University

Jean Czerlinski
Max Planck Institute for Human
    Development

Robyn Dawes
Department of Social & Decision
    Sciences
Carnegie Mellon University

Werner De Bondt
Department of Finance, Investment
    & Banking
University of Wisconsin – Madison

David Dunning
Department of Psychology
Cornell University

Nicholas Epley
Department of Psychology
Harvard University

David Faust
Department of Psychology
University Rhode Island

Melissa Finucane
Decision Research

Baruch Fischhoff
Department of Social & Decision
    Sciences
Carnegie Mellon University

Shane Frederick
Sloan School of Management
Massachusetts Institute of Technology

Gerd Gigerenzer
Max Planck Institute for Human
    Development

Thomas Gilovich
Psychology Department
Cornell University

Dale Griffin
Department of Commerce
University of British Columbia

Max Henrion
Decision Laboratory
Ask Jeeves!

Amy D. Holzberg
Department of Psychology
Cornell University

Christopher Jepson
Department of Psychology
University of Michigan

Eric Johnson
Graduate School of Business
Columbia University

Daniel Kahneman
Department of Psychology and
  Woodrow Wilson School
  of Public Policy
Princeton University

Boaz Keysar
Department of Psychology
University of Chicago

William M. Klein
Department of Psychology
Colby College

Derek J. Koehler
Department of Psychology
University of Waterloo

David H. Krantz
Department of Psychology
Columbia University

Ziva Kunda
Department of Psychology
University of Waterloo

Ju-Whei Lee
Department of Psychology
Chung Yuan University

Donald G. MacGregor
Decision Research

Scott Madey
Psychology Department
Shippensburg University

Laura F. Martignon
Max Planck Institute for Human
  Development

V. H. Medvec
Kellogg Graduate School
  of Management
Northwestern University

Paul E. Meehl
Psychology Department
University of Minnesota

Judith A. Meyerowitz
Department of Psychology
Cornell University

Dale T. Miller
Department of Psychology
Princeton University

Carol Nemeroff
Department of Psychology
Arizona State University

Efrat Neter
Department of Psychology
Hebrew University

Richard E. Nisbett
Department of Psychology
University of Michigan

Ellen Peters
Decision Research

Elizabeth C. Pinel
Department of Psychology
Penn State University

Paul C. Price
Department of Psychology
California State University – Fresno

Emily Pronin
Department of Psychology
Stanford University

Carolyn Puccio
Department of Psychology
Stanford University

Kim D. Reynolds
Department of Psychology
Arizona State University

Lee Ross
Department of Psychology
Stanford University

Michael Ross
Department of Psychology
University of Waterloo

Yuval Rottenstreich
Graduate School of Business
University of Chicago

Paul Rozin
Department of Psychology
University of Pennsylvania

Kenneth Savitsky
Department of Psychology
Williams College

Norbert Schwarz
Institute for Social Research
University of Michigan

Donna F. Schwartzman
Department of Psychology
Arizona State University

Stephen J. Sherman
Department of Psychology
Indiana University

Winston R. Sieck
Department of Psychology
University of Michigan

Steven A. Sloman
Department of Cognitive and Linguistic
   Sciences
Brown University

Paul Slovic
Decision Research

Keith E. Stanovich
Department of Human Development
   and Applied Psychology
University of Toronto

Brian R. Taylor
Albert Einstein College of Medicine

Shelley E. Taylor
Department of Psychology
UCLA

Philip E. Tetlock
Department of Psychology
The Ohio State University

Richard H. Thaler
Graduate School of Business
University of Chicago

Amos Tversky
1937–1996
Late of Department of Psychology
Stanford University

Leigh A. Vaughn
Institute for Social Research
University of Michigan

Neil D. Weinstein
Department of Psychology
Rutgers University

Richard F. West
School of Psychology
James Madison University

Thalia P. Wheatley
Department of Psychology
University of Virginia

Timothy D. Wilson
Department of Psychology
University of Virginia

J. Frank Yates
Department of Psychology
University of Michigan

Preface

Judgment pervades human experience. "Is it worth it?" "Would he be a good father to my children?" "Is our case strong enough to go to court?" "Is our left flank adequately protected?" How – and how well – do people make such judgments? It is to these questions that this book is devoted.

This book addresses these questions by presenting a number of contributions – some preexisting, some new – to the understanding of everyday judgment. Each of these contributions is connected to what has been called the *heuristics and biases* approach to the study of judgment under uncertainty. Indeed, this book is intended as an update or successor to the influential 1982 book on the subject by Kahneman, Slovic, and Tversky, *Judgment under Uncertainty: Heuristics and Biases*. Much has happened in the field of judgment since that book appeared, and in this work we attempt to capture many of the most important contributions and developments.

The core idea of the heuristics and biases program is that judgment under uncertainty is often based on a limited number of simplifying heuristics rather than more formal and extensive algorithmic processing. These heuristics typically yield accurate judgments but can give rise to systematic error. Kahneman and Tversky originally identified three such general purpose heuristics – availability, representativeness, and anchoring and adjustment. This book accordingly begins with twelve chapters dealing with more recent research on these heuristics. It continues with an examination of empirical and conceptual extensions of the ideas present in the 1982 book, with seven chapters on forecasting, overconfidence, and optimism, and two chapters on norms and counterfactual thinking.

We then turn to an examination of complementary views on everyday judgment that were put forward after 1982. Since that time, for example, a great deal of effort has gone into the development and investigation of various *dual processing* accounts of human judgment. Among these are accounts of how judgments are made through the interaction of one mental system akin to "intuition" and another akin to "reason." We thus begin our coverage of complementary perspectives with three chapters that examine such a "two-systems" perspective on human judgment. We then present three chapters on Support Theory, Amos Tversky's last comprehensive theoretical contribution to the understanding of judgment under uncertainty. These three chapters illustrate the broad ramifications of Support Theory's insight that judgments are not based on events themselves, but on descriptions of events. The examination of complementary perspectives on heuristics ends with four chapters on specific heuristics beyond those originally proposed by Kahneman and Tversky, and one chapter that examines the implications of considering alternative metaphors of the human judge.

The book concludes with ten chapters on various applications of the heuristics and biases approach to judgment. Four of these deal with judgments made by "the average person" in various aspects of everyday life and six are concerned with the judgments rendered by experts in a number of applied domains. These chapters are significant because they illustrate that the processes of judgment revealed by psychological research are not restricted to the psychological laboratory or to unfamiliar and unimportant tasks. These heuristics – and the biases that are associated with them – have implications for some of the most consequential judgments that life requires people to make.

On a procedural front, we should note that the source of each preexisting piece is indicated by a footnote on the opening page. All preexisting pieces have been edited to some degree. Deletions from the original are indicated by elipses (...). In nearly all cases, such deletions (and the concomitant renumbering of tables, figures, etc.) constitute the only changes from the original. Exceptions are noted in the opening footnote of the pertinent chapters. Readers interested in the full statement of any author are encouraged to consult the original work. Note also that all references are contained in an overall reference list at the back of the book, and that references to other chapters in the book are indicated by chapter number.

Our work in preparing this book was supported by NSF grants 9809262 and 0091416 to Cornell University, a Social Sciences and Humanities Research Council of Canada research grant to the University of British Columbia, and NSF grant 2556558 to Princeton University.

We wish to thank Zachary Dorsey, Richard Gonzalez, Michael Griffin, and Phil Laughlin for their help in the preparation of this book.

Thomas Gilovich
Dale Griffin
Daniel Kahneman

Introduction – Heuristics and Biases: Then and Now

Thomas Gilovich and Dale Griffin

In the late 1960s and early 1970s, a series of papers by Amos Tversky and Daniel Kahneman revolutionized academic research on human judgment. The central idea of the "heuristics and biases" program – that judgment under uncertainty often rests on a limited number of simplifying heuristics rather than extensive algorithmic processing – soon spread beyond academic psychology, affecting theory and research across a range of disciplines including economics, law, medicine, and political science. The message was revolutionary in that it simultaneously questioned the descriptive adequacy of ideal models of judgment and offered a cognitive alternative that explained human error without invoking motivated irrationality. The initial papers and a variety of related work were collected in a 1982 volume, *Judgment under Uncertainty: Heuristics and Biases* (Kahneman, Slovic, & Tversky, 1982). In the time since, research in the heuristics and biases tradition has prospered on a number of fronts, each represented by a section of the current volume. In this opening chapter, we wish to put the heuristics and biases approach in historical context and discuss some key issues that have been raised since the 1982 book appeared.

HISTORICAL OVERVIEW

Any discussion of the modern history of research on everyday judgment must take note of the large shadow cast by the classical model of rational choice. The model has been applied most vigorously in the discipline of economics, but its considerable influence can be felt in all the behavioral and social sciences and in related policy fields such as law and medicine. According to this model, the "rational actor" (i.e., the typical person) chooses what options to pursue by assessing the probability of each possible outcome, discerning the utility to be derived from each, and combining these two assessments. The option pursued is the one that offers the optimal combination of probability and utility.

Calculations of probability and multiattribute utility can be rather formidable judgments to make, but the theory of rational choice assumes that people make them and make them well. Proponents of the theory do not insist that people never make mistakes in these calculations; but they do insist that the mistakes are unsystematic. The model assumes, for example, that the rational actor will follow the elementary rules of probability when calculating, say, the likelihood of a given candidate winning an election or the odds of surviving a surgical intervention.

But is the average person as attuned to the axioms of formal rationality as this stance demands? Much of the modern history of judgment research can be summarized as follows. First, evidence is collected indicating that people's assessments of likelihood and risk do not conform to the laws of probability. Second, an argument ensues about the significance of these demonstrations between proponents of human rationality and those responsible for the empirical demonstrations. Three early contributions to this debate – one empirical, one methodological, and one theoretical – have been especially influential.

The empirical contribution was provided by Paul Meehl (1954), who compiled evidence comparing expert clinical prediction with actuarial methods and found that the actuarial methods, or formulas, almost always did better. His research also uncovered a sharp discrepancy between clinicians' assessments of their performance and their actual record of success (see Chapter 40 by Dawes, Faust, & Meehl for a modern summary of this literature). The juxtaposition of modest performance and robust confidence inspired research on faulty processes of reasoning that yield compelling but mistaken inferences.

Ward Edwards made a key methodological contribution by introducing Bayesian analyses to psychology, thus providing a normative standard with which everyday judgments could be compared (Edwards, Lindman, & Savage, 1963). From Edwards' own research (Edwards, 1968) and much that followed, it was clear that intuitive judgments of likelihood did not exactly correspondent with this "ideal" normative standard. This led, in turn, to an interest in the causes of suboptimal performance and strategies for improvement.

The most significant theoretical development in this field was Herbert Simon's contention that the "full" rationality implied by the rational choice model was an unrealistic standard for human judgment. He proposed a more limited criterion for actual performance, famously dubbed *bounded rationality*, that acknowledged the inherent processing limitations of the human mind. People reason and choose rationally, but only within the constraints imposed by their limited search and computational capacities. Simon (1957) also discussed the simplifying heuristics that people could employ to cope effectively with these limitations. Note that Simon did not reject the normative appeal of the full-information rational models, referring to them as "jewels of intellectual accomplishment" (Simon, 1983). (Two of the present contributions are strongly influenced by the Simonian perspective on heuristics: Frederick, Chapter 30; and Gigerenzer, Czerlinski, & Martignon, Chapter 31).

The Heuristics and Biases Approach
Inspired by the examples of biased real-world judgments of the sort identified by Meehl and his peers, and guided by the clear normative theory explicated by

Edwards and others, Kahneman and Tversky developed their own perspective on bounded rationality. Although acknowledging the role of task complexity and limited processing capacity in erroneous judgment, Kahneman and Tversky were convinced that the processes of intuitive judgment were not merely simpler than rational models demanded, but were categorically different in kind. Kahneman and Tversky described three general-purpose heuristics – availability, representativeness, and anchoring and adjustment – that underlie many intuitive judgments under uncertainty. These heuristics, it was suggested, were simple and efficient because they piggybacked on basic computations that the mind had evolved to make. Thus, when asked to evaluate the relative frequency of cocaine use in Hollywood actors, one may assess how easy it is to retrieve examples of celebrity drug-users – the availability heuristic piggybacks on highly efficient memory retrieval processes. When evaluating the likelihood that a given comic actor is a cocaine user, one may assess the similarity between that actor and the prototypical cocaine user (the representativeness heuristic piggybacks on automatic pattern-matching processes). Either question may also be answered by starting with a salient initial value (say, 50%) and adjusting downward to reach a final answer (the anchoring and adjustment heuristic, whose underlying mechanisms are debated in Chapters 6 and 7).

In the early experiments that defined this work, each heuristic was associated with a set of *biases*: departures from the normative rational theory that served as markers or signatures of the underlying heuristics. Use of the availability heuristic, for example, leads to error whenever memory retrieval is a biased cue to actual frequency because of an individual's tendency to seek out and remember dramatic cases or because of the broader world's tendency to call attention to examples of a particular (restricted) type. Some of these biases were defined as deviations from some "true" or objective value, but most by violations of basic laws of probability. (For elegant examples, see Chapter 1 by Tversky and Kahneman).

Several aspects of this program are important to note at the outset because they set the stage for a discussion of the criticisms it aroused. First, although the heuristics are distinguished from normative reasoning processes by patterns of biased judgments, the heuristics themselves are sensible estimation procedures that are by no measure "irrational." Second, although heuristics yield "quick and dirty" solutions, they draw on underlying processes (e.g., feature matching, memory retrieval) that are highly sophisticated. Finally, note that these heuristic processes are not exceptional responses to problems of excessive complexity or an overload of information, but normal intuitive responses to even the simplest questions about likelihood, frequency, and prediction.

The Positive and Negative Agendas. As the preceding discussion implies, Kahneman and Tversky distinguished between two messages or agendas for the heuristics and biases program, one "positive" and one "negative." The positive agenda is to elucidate the processes through which people make a variety of important and difficult real world judgments. Is a corporation's explosive growth likely to continue? Is a coup more likely in Ecuador or Indonesia? What is a reasonable estimate of next year's GNP? Thus, representativeness, availability, and anchoring and adjustment were proposed as a set of highly efficient mental shortcuts that provide subjectively compelling and often quite serviceable solutions to such judgmental problems.

But, the solutions were just that – serviceable, not exact or perfectly accurate. Thus the second, negative, agenda of the heuristics and biases program was to specify the conditions under which intuitive judgments were likely to depart from the rules of probability. When, in other words, are everyday judgments likely to be biased? Kahneman and Tversky's experience teaching statistics and their observations of predictions made in applied settings led them to conclude that people often fail to anticipate regression to the mean, fail to give adequate weight to sample size in assessing the import of evidence, and fail to take full advantage of base rates when making predictions. Their three (now familiar) heuristics were offered as an explanation of the when and why of such errors. Thus the two agendas blend together: Identifying particular biases is important in its own right, but doing so also sheds light on the underlying processes of judgment. (Kahneman & Tversky, 1982b, also offered positive and negative approaches to judgment errors, a perspective that is taken up by Kahneman & Frederick, Chapter 2.)

Automatic or Deliberate? There is another dichotomous aspect of the heuristics and biases approach that warrants discussion. Heuristics have often been described as something akin to strategies that people use deliberately in order to simplify judgmental tasks that would otherwise be too difficult for the typical human mind to solve. This use of the term fits with the "cognitive miser" metaphor that proved popular in the field of social cognition (Fiske & Taylor, 1991). The metaphor suggests, perhaps unfortunately and unwisely, that the biases documented in the heuristics and biases tradition are the product of lazy and inattentive minds. The implication is unfortunate and potentially misleading because the biases identified in this tradition have not been appreciably reduced by incentives for participants to sit straight, pay attention, and devote their full cognitive resources to the task (Camerer & Hogarth, 1999; Grether & Plott, 1979; Wilson, Houston, Etling, & Brekke, 1996; see Chapters 37 through 42 for descriptions of real-world judgments characterized by a high level of domain-specific expertise and motivation that nonetheless fit the patterns described by the heuristics and biases program). After reviewing 74 studies, Camerer and Hogarth (1999) concluded that incentives can reduce self-presentation effects, increase attention and effort, and reduce thoughtless responding, but noted that "no replicated study has made rationality violations disappear purely by raising incentives" (p. 7).

Imperviousness to incentives is just what one would expect from considering the other half of the dichotomy, or the other way that heuristics have been described. In particular, Tversky and Kahneman (1983; see Chapter 1) tied heuristics to "natural assessments" elicited by the task at hand that can influence judgment without being used deliberately or strategically. When deciding whether an elegantly-dressed lawyer is more likely to be a public defender or a member of a large corporate firm, for example, one cannot help computing the similarity between the individual and the prototype of each professional niche. This assessment then informs the judgment of likelihood in the absence of deliberative intent.

It seems to us that both uses of the term are valid and have their place. When deciding whether there are more coups in Ecuador or Indonesia, for example, one automatically searches for known instances of each (availability). Yet one can also deliberately recruit such instances and use the ease with which they come to mind as an explicit strategy – as when deciding to bet on one team over another after explicitly considering the number of star players on each. Similarly, existing research on anchoring makes it clear that many anchoring effects occur in the absence of any explicit adjustment (Mussweiler & Strack, 1999; see Chapman & Johnson, Chapter 6). Often people's estimates are automatically contaminated by previously mentioned values. Sometimes, however, the anchoring and adjustment heuristic is deliberately employed. If asked when George Washington was first elected president, most people do not know the answer; but they do know it was after 1776 and they adjust from that year (Epley & Gilovich, Chapter 7). Anchoring and adjustment is thus sometimes used as an explicit strategy of judgment.

For reasons that have to do with what was going on elsewhere in psychology, the "cognitive miser" view of heuristics took hold more pervasively than the "natural assessments" view, a result that still holds true today. With the rise of "two system" models of reasoning, however (described in Chapter 2 and Chapters 22 through 24), we predict this will change. The two systems view is consistent with the idea of rapid, automatic assessments that may or may not be overridden by deliberate processes, and the emergence of such a perspective should provide a boost to this relatively neglected statement of how heuristics work. Indeed, one of the objectives of this book is to reassert the natural assessments view of heuristics, a stance laid out most forcefully in the opening chapter by Tversky and Kahneman, and discussed extensively in Chapter 2 by Kahneman and Frederick.

Why The Heuristics and Biases Program Had (and Has) Such Influence and Appeal

The impact of any idea is a product of the quality of the idea itself and the intellectual zeitgeist at the time it is offered. Successful ideas must not only be good, but timely – even lucky. So it has been with the heuristics and biases approach to judgment. The popularity and impact of the approach were enhanced by elements of the prevailing atmosphere at the time it was launched, several of which still hold true today. Most important, perhaps, is the very strength and resilience of the rational choice model that motivated much of the heuristics and biases research. Although the model is most entrenched in the field of economics, it has had a profound impact on theoretical development in sociology, political science, law, and psychology as well. The very reach of the rational choice model thus opens up terrain for any systematic critique that offers an alternative perspective. Wherever the rational choice model shall go, in other words, the heuristics and biases program – or something much like it – must follow. And follow it did, as the heuristics and biases program has reshaped both explicit and implicit assumptions about human thought in all of these areas and a few more.

Models of spending and investment behavior have been particularly influenced by the heuristics and biases program, thanks partly to the deft translations offered by economist Richard Thaler (see DeBondt and Thaler, Chapter 38). Thaler's work is an example of how the heuristics and biases program has become a "full-circle" paradigm: insights that were sparked by observations in the classroom, battlefield, and conference room, then sharpened and tested in the experimental laboratory, are ultimately used to predict and explain behavior in the stock market, housing market, and employment market. The influence has also extended beyond applied economics to the fundamental core of theoretical economics. A recent review in a prominent economics journal, for example, advised economists to broaden their theories beyond the assumptions associated with "Chicago man" (the rational actor associated with the free-market economic theories developed at the University of Chicago) to incorporate the constraints associated with "K-T man" (McFadden, 1999).

A second boost to the heuristics and biases program is one we have already mentioned, the set of theories and metaphors associated with the "cognitive revolution" that dominated psychology when Kahneman and Tversky advanced their initial set of heuristics. The set of analogies associated with conceptualizing the mind as a computer is congenial to the idea of subroutines devoted to assessments of similarity, availability, and adjustment from some handy starting point. The fit is even tighter, of course, if one conceptualizes the mind (as was quite common in the 1970s) as a computer with limited processing capacity. Such a view makes the idea of effort-saving subroutines that sometimes provide reasonable but imperfect solutions seem particularly appealing and compelling. Sloman (1996) discusses the even closer fit of the heuristics and biases approach with the more modern conception of the mind as a connectionist computer, characterized by massively parallel processing and coherence-based computation (Sloman, Chapter 22, focuses on psychological evidence rather than computational principles).

The heuristics and biases message also fit well with – and was reinforced by – the pragmatic agenda of much of the field of social psychology. Social psychologists have had an enduring interest in social problems and their alleviation. Research on such topics as persuasion, conformity, and cognitive consistency has been fueled by a concern with the dark side of each – sinister propaganda, mindless conformity, and the biases to which rationalization gives rise. But the social evil with the greatest fascination for social psychologists has always been the combination of stereotyping, prejudice, and discrimination, topics to which the heuristics and biases agenda was seen as highly relevant. Anyone interested in the false beliefs that characterize many stereotypes is likely to be receptive to new ideas about sources of error and bias in everyday judgment.

The field of social psychology was thus receptive to Kahneman and Tversky's ideas from the very beginning and the field's enthusiasm provided another boost to their approach. This is exemplified most powerfully by Nisbett and Ross's (1980) influential treatment of the difficulties people confront in trying to negotiate the complexities of everyday social life, and the nonoptimal strategies they often pursue in the attempt to do so. Their work, which has been called the "errors and biases" perspective in social psychology, was different from Kahneman and Tversky's in an important respect. Nisbett and Ross and their school have been primarily concerned with the causes and consequences of nonoptimal reasoning in social life. Thus, the "fundamental attribution error" (Ross, 1977), the self-serving bias in attribution (Miller & Ross, 1975), and the confirmation bias in social interaction (Snyder & Swann, 1978; Word, Zanna, & Cooper, 1974) have been studied because of their implications for such problems as intergroup conflict and discrimination. In this case, the errors and biases are central; they are not studied first and foremost as a cue to the underlying processes of judgment. (This tradition is developed further by Pronin, Puccio, and Ross in Chapter 36.)

The heuristics and biases message was not only lucky with its supporters, it was also well packaged. Demonstration studies were designed as much like cocktail party anecdotes as traditional cognitive psychology studies, making them magnets for academic lecturers and textbook writers alike. Scenarios involving feminist bank tellers and African countries in the United Nations made the lessons of the heuristics and biases tradition memorable for students at all levels. It is difficult to overestimate the impact of style in the program's success – although the message would not have spread without substance as well. A medium of communication that included stories and personality sketches was well-suited to the message that people think more naturally in terms of narratives and stereotypes than set-theoretic concepts.

CRITIQUES AND CONTROVERSIES

The profile of any intellectual idea is also raised by the controversies it inspires, and the heuristics and biases tradition has inspired many. People, particularly academics, do not accept new ideas and approaches easily, nor should they. As Galbraith noted, "Faced with the choice between changing one's mind and proving that there is no need to do so, almost everyone gets busy on the proof." So it has been with the reaction to the heuristics and biases program – many minds have been busy defending the rationality of everyday judgment and proving that the core ideas of the heuristics and biases program are misguided. Here are the central ideas of some of those proofs.

The "We Cannot Be That Dumb" Critique. The most common critique of the research on heuristics and biases is that it offers an overly pessimistic assessment of the average person's ability to make sound and effective judgments. People by and large manage their lives satisfactorily, something they would be unlikely to accomplish, the argument goes, if their judgments were so prone to bias. Indeed, working collectively, humans have split the atom, recombined DNA, and traveled to the moon. Critics see the heuristics and biases program as denigrating "human decision makers as systematically flawed bumblers" (Ortmann & Hertwig, 2000) because "actual human reasoning has been described as 'biased,' 'fallacious,' or 'indefensible'" (Gigerenzer, 1991a, p. 259). As an outraged team of psychologists queried, "Are heuristics-and-biases experiments cases of cognitive misers' underachieving, or of their receiving a Bayesian hazing by statistical sophisticates?" (Barone, Maddux, & Snyder 1997, p. 143).

This critique owes much of its pervasiveness and appeal to the fanfare that the negative message of the heuristics and biases program has generated at the expense of its positive counterpart. There is, of course, some inevitability to this: Negative information typically dominates the positive. Just as there is a "bad news bias" in media reporting ("if it bleeds, it leads"), it is hardly surprising that the negative message of the heuristics and biases program would capture more attention, inspire more like-minded research, and serve as the focal point of disagreement and controversy. Nonetheless, the common belief that examples of human error are disproportionately cited in the scholarly literature turns out to be an oversimplification; the prominence of such demonstrations is accounted for by the prominence of the journals in which they are found (Robins & Craik, 1993).

There is, however, one version of this critique to which researchers in the heuristics and biases tradition must plead "no contest" or even "guilty." This is the criticism that studies in this tradition have paid scant attention to assessing the overall ecological validity of heuristic processes. Ecological validity (Brunswik, 1955) corresponds to the correlation of the actual outcome in the world with the cue available to the perceiver across a universe of situations. Thus, assessing the ecological validity of the representativeness heuristic would involve identifying a universe of relevant objects (e.g., every scholar in the engineering and law faculties at a given university), and then correlating the outcome value for each object (e.g., membership in either faculty) with the value of the cue variable for each object (e.g., relative similarity to the prototype of each faculty). This correlation, then, would provide a measure for the given universe of how well the representativeness cue performed. This Herculean task has not attracted researchers in the heuristics and biases tradition; the focus has been on identifying the cues that people use, not on evaluating the overall value of those cues. Nevertheless, researchers in this tradition clearly share a set of assumptions: the ecological validities are probably high, the heuristics are generally useful, but common and profoundly important exceptions are to be found. (Note how this summary could be applied to the "fast and frugal" decision heuristics discussed in Chapter 31 by Gigerenzer et al., despite the apparent opposition between the ecological rationality movement and the heuristics and biases perspective.)

Thus, although there is doubtless some scorekeeping with respect to instances of sound and unsound judgment, it is not of the "box score" sort in which a tally is kept of the number of instances in which people exhibit biased and unbiased judgments. Such a tally is beside the point. A meaningful overall characterization of the quality of human judgment is neither possible nor sought after. To the extent that any such characterization is possible, it would be hard to resist the conclusion that the glass is both half full and half empty. People make a great many judgments with surpassing skill and accuracy, but evidence of dubious belief, questionable judgment, and faulty reasoning is not hard to find (Dawes, 1988; Gilovich, 1991; Schick & Vaughn, 1999; Stanovich, 1986).

Note that there is more than a little irony in the strong form of this critique, one that advances the rather Panglossian notion that people's judgments are hardly ever biased (see Stanovich & West, 2000; Chapter 24, for a consideration of this view). The same scientists who advance this claim use a variety of methodological safeguards such as double-blind experimental designs to make sure their own observations are not contaminated by bias. Are the observations of scientists so much more prone to bias than the individuals they study?

Advocates of the "people are not that dumb" critique have found their voice among evolutionary psychologists for whom it is axiomatic that people perform all tasks critical for survival and reproduction extremely well. According to this school, ancestors who could not reliably make judgments important to survival did not survive long, and therefore the biological basis of their judgmental tendencies have been driven from the gene pool. There is, of course, considerable merit to this perspective. Only a creationist would maintain that our mental faculties were sculpted by something other than evolution. It is also the case that some judgments strike us as hard and others easy, and it is a good bet that the ones that strike us as hard were not subject to the same intense evolutionary pressures as those that strike us as easy. The problems our ancestors absolutely had to solve offer little challenge to us now because of the mental mechanisms we inherited to solve them.

But this logic hardly implies that there is no room for systematic error in judgment. Evolutionary pressures acting on the bulk of human judgments are neither sufficiently direct nor intense to sculpt the kind of mental machinery that would guarantee error-free or bias-free judgment. As Simon pointed out long ago (1956, 1957), evolutionary pressures only lead to local ("better than"), not global ("best possible") optimization. Evolutionary pressures lead to adaptations that are as good or better than a rival's; they do not lead to adaptations that are optimal. If they did, warblers would not rear cuckoo chicks (which they do even though the cuckoo chick is much bigger than the adult warbler), lions would not stalk upwind of their prey (which they do despite greater success stalking downwind), and people would not probability match in so many different domains (which they do despite paying a high price in foregone gains).

It is ironic that the heuristics and biases approach would be criticized as inconsistent with the dictates of evolution because it *is* an evolutionary account (see Chapter 2 in particular). It is an evolutionary account that recognizes the constraints imposed by an organism's evolutionary history, constraints that yield noteworthy imperfections in function. As Gould (1997, p. 52) argued, "even the strictest operation of pure Darwinism builds organisms full of nonadaptive parts and behaviors. . . . All organisms evolve as complex and interconnected wholes, not as loose alliances of separate parts, each independently optimized by natural selection." The heuristics and biases approach takes the notion of such historical constraints seriously and examines the imperfections that both reveal that history and illuminate current mechanisms.

Kahneman and Tversky's frequent analogies between perceptual and cognitive processes highlight this historical emphasis and reflect an important recognition that cognition evolved after (and out of) perception. Organisms must perceive and act before – or more pressingly than – they need to think, and this doubtless has implications for the quality with which these functions are carried out. Compare, for example, the quality of your motor memory with the quality of your semantic memory. Compare how easy it is to remember how to ski decades after last doing so with how easy it is to recall the trigonometric functions you learned in high school, the foreign language you learned as a teenager, or even all of your childhood romances.

It is clear, then, that there is no deep-rooted conflict between an evolutionary perspective on human cognition and the heuristics and biases approach (Samuels, Stich, & Bishop, in press). Both are concerned with understanding the psychological mechanisms people employ to solve a variety of important real-life problems. Both acknowledge that many cognitive problems essential to survival are typically solved with efficiency and precision. And both can accept the existence of pockets of (particularly informative) bias and error in human judgment.

Indeed, even one of the more popular metaphors of the evolutionary approach to reasoning – that of the mind as a Swiss Army knife – is entirely consistent with the heuristics and biases approach. Although psychologists and neuroscientists have no handle on just how modular the mind might be (Fodor, 2000), it is certainly not unreasonable to suppose that many higher-order cognitive functions are indeed performed by discrete modules. There might be, for example, a module that computes similarity between entities, another that performs basic counting and frequency functions, another that handles causal relations, and so on. Such a mind – one that used different "tools" to perform its various tasks – would produce a pattern of judgments that corresponds perfectly to that documented in the heuristics and biases tradition. At some times and in some contexts, tasks are performed by just the right module and sound judgments are made. At other times and in other contexts, however, specific tasks are coopted by the wrong module and systematically biased judgments are the result. On still other occasions, of course, the mind might not have the right module to handle the problem (no Swiss Army knife does everything an outdoorsman needs done) and so the task is assigned to a "next best" module, and imperfections in judgment should once again be the result. A modular mind should also produce a pattern of judgments whereby a problem described or structured in one way yields one type of response, whereas the same problem described or structured another way yields a vastly different response – exactly the pattern of results reported countless times in the heuristics and biases literature.

The "It's All Parlor Games" Critique. Another common critique of the heuristics and biases tradition has been to dismiss the reported findings as mere laboratory curiosities – as demonstrations that people cannot readily solve tricky "word problems." The implication is that judgment outside the laboratory is likely to look far superior to that exhibited within.

This critique overlooks that it was the existence of biased judgments in the real world that motivated the heuristics and biases research program. Recall that an important impetus for this research was the work by Paul Meehl on the problems inherent in expert clinical judgment. Recall also that it was the observation of faulty reasoning among students trying to learn statistics (e.g., the gambler's fallacy, the regression fallacy, insensitivity to sample size) that gave the research its initial shape. This critique also flies in the face of the influence that the heuristics and biases research program has had across a wide range of applied disciplines, something it could not do if it dealt only with contrived, artificial problems. As we have noted, the heuristics and biases program has influenced scholarship and curricula in political science, medicine, law, and management.

One particularly persistent form of this critique is the claim that the biases revealed in this research are merely the product of fiendish (or clueless) experimenters who ask misleading questions. Participants are not responding incorrectly, in other words; they are giving the right answer to a different question than the one the experimenter believes he or she is asking.

There is doubtless some merit to this claim, at least as applied to some individual experiments that purport to demonstrate a given bias or shortcoming of human judgment. There is a complex psychology – a subtle set of tacit assumptions and implicit demands – that accompanies participation in a psychology experiment. Even investigators attuned to this psychology can sometimes fail to anticipate correctly how a stimulus is likely to be construed or a question interpreted by a given participant. It is no small task for experimenters to "get it right," which is why psychological research requires so much pretesting.

But just as it is clear that some individual experiments are open to this critique, it is equally clear that the main biases uncovered in this research tradition (e.g., availability biases in likelihood estimates, insensitivity to sample size and prior probability, the conjunction fallacy, anchoring, packing and unpacking effects) are not. These have all been demonstrated in countless contexts and with varied paradigms and dependent measures, and with domain experts as well as student volunteers. Although an isolated demonstration of some of these biases may be open to this critique, the overall body of evidence in support of them is not. For example, in one of the original demonstrations of the conjunction fallacy using the famous "Linda problem," it is entirely possible that participants interpreted the option "is a bank teller" to mean "is a bank teller who is *not* active in the feminist movement" given that one of the other options was "is a bank teller who is active in the feminist movement." Participants who construed the former this way can hardly be faulted for ranking it lower in likelihood than the latter. But this alternative interpretation simply cannot handle the observation that when participants in a between-subjects design rated (rather than ranked) the likelihood of only one of these options, those evaluating Linda the feminist bank employee offered higher likelihood ratings than those evaluating Linda the bank employee. In such a between-subjects format, of course, there is no artifactual basis for participants to conclude that "bank teller" is to be interpreted as "nonfeminist bank teller." To the extent that any participants did so, it was because their mental model of bank teller crowded out the possibility of feminism, not because they could infer that the experimenter intended "bank teller" to mean "nonfeminist bank teller." (Chapters 1 and 2 contain more detailed discussions of alternative interpretations of the conjunction fallacy.)

This example raises the important point that certain misconstruals on the part of participants are not artifacts, they *are* the phenomena of interest. There is a long tradition of research in social psychology illustrating that people actively construe the meaning of a given task or stimulus (Griffin & Ross, 1991) and that their own chronically accessible categories, habits, and experiences powerfully influence their construals (Higgins, King, & Mavin, 1982; Higgins, Rholes, & Jones, 1977; Srull & Wyer, 1979, 1980). Consider Kahneman and Tversky's well-known engineer/lawyer problem. When asked whether a given description is likely to belong to an engineer or lawyer, one cannot fail to compute the similarity between the description and each professional stereotype. Both the immediacy and relevance of this assessment of similarity, then, make it highly likely that one's very definition of what the task is about will be hijacked. A question about likelihood is construed as a question about "fit." And there is nothing artifactual about the switch (on this point, see Kahneman & Frederick, Chapter 2; Bar-Hillel and Neter, Chapter 3, this volume). It happens both inside and outside the laboratory, and, just as one would expect if people were active interpreters of the tasks that confront them, various changes in the presentation of stimuli or the description of the task influence what participants interpret their task to be (e.g., Koehler, 1996; Macchi, 1995).

The "It's Not an Error" Critique. Another common accusation against the heuristics and biases tradition is that researchers hold experimental participants to an inappropriately high or even misguided standard of rationality. Jonathan

Cohen, for example, contends that rationality does not exist apart from human intuition (Cohen, 1981) – in fact, standards of rationality are the "distillation of our best intuitions about rationality" (Papineau, 2000, p. 173). Thus, how can the source of our standards of rationality prove to be irrational? Perhaps people – especially people participating in unfamiliar or otherwise misleading experimental games – make performance mistakes that mask their underlying rational competence, but by definition, human intuition must be rational.

This critique usefully points out two aspects of the "rationality problem." First, it has a distinct "Alice in Wonderland" flavor: People can and do define rationality in many contradictory ways (see Evans and Over, 1996, for an attempt to deal with the definitional problem). Second, it brings to the fore the crucial role of axioms in justifying a normative theory. Probability theory is built from a few fundamental rules or axioms that reflect people's considered opinions in the abstract. These axioms include the claim that the probability of an event *A* and its complement *not-A* sum to 1. This is an example of a coherence axiom that constrains the relation between the probabilities of events. Axioms have force only if people agree with them – it is possible to opt out and agree not to be bound, but most people find such rules to be compelling. In fact, it is the tension between the general agreement with the abstract rules of probability and the violation of those rules in richer contexts that give the heuristics and biases demonstrations their power (a point explored more deeply in Chapters 1, 2, and 22).

A number of prominent statisticians and philosophers have opted out from any version of probability theory that deals with unique or "one-shot" events. Supporters of the "objective frequency" or "relative frequency" approach (e.g., von Mises, 1928) restrict the domain of probability theory to events that can be repeated in an infinite series. According to this perspective, probability is defined as the relative frequency of an event in an infinite series. Other types of events – such as predictions, beliefs, or statements about a single case – cannot be evaluated by the rules of probability theory. There is no denying the appeal of dividing the domain of uncertainty into the "objective" (like the spin of a roulette wheel or the toss of a coin) and "subjective" (like a prediction of tomorrow's weather). However, as Keynes (1921) argued, a strict frequentist view entails that beliefs about unique events such as the coming of war, the end of a recession, and the outcome of a medical operation cannot be evaluated. And even those who take the frequentist stance in their professional lives act like subjectivists in their day-to-day affairs. An honest frequentist must concede that meaningful probabilistic statements can be made about unique events, such as the Yankees being more likely to win the World Series this year than, say, the Kansas City Royals or Montreal Expos, or that either author of this chapter is likely to lose a prize fight with the reigning champion in his weight class.

Such consideration notwithstanding, at some point one is thrown back to the level of axioms: Is one willing, for example, to subscribe to the rule that a set of predictions made with 80% probability should come true 80% of the time?

For those willing to opt in to such a "correspondence axiom," the demonstrations found within this book should be particularly relevant. However, even those readers who by personal taste or ideological alliance reject the correspondence axiom might be swayed by the "expected value" argument as characterized by the statistician De Finetti. "The formal rules normally used in probability calculations are also valid, as conditions of consistency for subjective probabilities. You must obey them, not because of any logical, empirical or metaphysical meaning of probability, but simply to avoid throwing money away"(De Finetti, 1970, p. 137). Finally, those frequentists who are unwilling to have their own beliefs evaluated by the coherence or correspondence axioms may still be curious to find out how well the classical rational actor model – incorporating the axioms of subjective probability – stands up to empirical test.

The "Frequencies, Good; Probabilities, Bad" Critique. Given the controversy surrounding the normative status of frequencies and subjective probabilities, it is not surprising that those who favor an evolutionary defense of rationality ("ecological rationality") should throw in their lot with the frequentists. Evolutionary psychologists (e.g., Pinker, 1997) maintain that success in our ancestral environment required only a talent for working with frequencies, not probabilities. This argument, precisely because it cannot be tested empirically, remains a matter of faith and ideology. However, the frequentist argument for evolutionary rationality contains a component that can be tested empirically: The evidence for heuristics and biases, it is claimed, "disappears" when stimuli are presented and questions are asked in terms of frequencies (Gigerenzer, 1991b; 1994).

This was a bold argument when first introduced and it is even bolder to maintain now (e.g., Gigerenzer, 1998; Cosmides & Tooby, 1996) when a score of studies have indicated that it simply does not hold up empirically. In fact, presenting frequencies rather than probabilities sometimes makes judgment distinctly worse (e.g., Griffin & Buehler, 1999; Treadwell & Nelson, 1996), sometimes makes judgments distinctly better (e.g., Tversky & Kahneman, 1983; Koehler, Brenner, & Tversky, 1997) and quite often leaves the quality of judgment largely unchanged (Brenner, Koehler, Liberman, & Tversky, 1996; Griffin & Buehler, 1999). Even more troublesome for the evolution/frequency argument, Kahneman and Tversky's original explanation of the probability–frequency discrepancy (Kahneman & Tversky, 1982a; Tversky & Kahneman, 1983) provides a unified account of when frequency formats improve judgments and when they do not (e.g., Sloman, Slovak, & Over, 2000).

Critics claim that assessments of single-event probabilities are unnatural, and that only a frequency format is consistent with how the mind works (Cosmides & Tooby, 1996; Gigerenzer, 1991b, 1994; Pinker, 1997). Kahneman and Tversky argued, in contrast, that representing problems in terms of frequencies tends to evoke mental models that facilitate the detection of set inclusion relations and thus improves judgment – and this view has received considerable support from the studies of Sloman and others (e.g., Evans, Handley, Perham, Over, &

Thompson, 2000; Girotto & Gonzalez, 2001; Sloman & Over, in press; Sloman et al., 2000).

Note that even some scholars who are sympathetic to the heuristics and biases tradition have concluded that its lessons are limited to "problems with probabilities." "While we have had the intellectual resources to pursue truth for at least 100,000 years, and quite possibly a lot longer, the notion of probability has only been around since 1654. . . . It is no accident that most of the 'irrationality' experiments trade in probabilities" (Papineau, 2000, p. 182). Thus, it is important to point out that although frequentistic formats – for whatever reason – sometimes induce more effective processes of judgment, it is simply not the case that the biases uncovered by Kahneman, Tversky, and others "disappear" if people are allowed to think in terms of frequencies rather than probabilities. Numerous studies in the heuristics and biases tradition make this clear, any one of which is sufficient to make the point. For example, in one of the earliest of Kahneman and Tversky's experiments, participants were asked to estimate either the number of possible committees of 2 people from a group of 10, or the number of possible committees of 8 from a group of 10. Here, as in many other studies, the participants were given no information in a probabilistic format nor was a probabilistic response required (or even possible). Nevertheless, even though the actual number of possible committees of 2 and 8 are the same, those estimating the number of 2-person committees gave estimates that were an average two and a half times higher than those estimating the number of 8-person committees (Tversky & Kahneman, 1973). There is clearly more to biased judgment than an inability to handle probabilities.

Recent Perspectives

As this book demonstrates, the heuristics and biases program has weathered its various critiques and remains a vigorous and still developing perspective on human judgment. Part of its vigor stems from parallel developments in psychology that have both influenced and been influenced by the work on heuristics and biases. Most significant in this regard has been the broad interest in effortless or "automatic" mental processes that play an important role in a wide variety of everyday phenomena. Work on the rapid, automatic assessments of the affective system is a good example (Slovic, Finucane, Peters, & MacGregor, Chapter 23; Zajonc, 1980). The idea that a quick, affective, yes/no, approach/avoid reaction precedes extensive cognitive elaboration has certainly been around for a long time and predates the heuristics and biases program. Current thinking about the way such a process operates, however, has been shaped by the heuristics and biases program, a result seen most clearly in the use of such terms as Slovic and colleagues' "affect heuristic" (Chapter 23) and Pratkanis's "attitude heuristic" (Pratkanis, 1989). Contemporary research on magical thinking also fits well with the heuristics and biases perspective (see Chapter 11 by Rozin & Nemeroff). This research, like that in the heuristics and biases tradition, highlights the conflict between an initial, reflexive evaluation and a more considered, rational assessment. The idea that heuristics often operate automatically is also compatible with current research on "automaticity" (Bargh, 1997; Bargh & Chartrand, 1999). This work, like the heuristic and biases program, stresses the fact that much of mental life is not the product of deliberate processing, but of quicker, more reflexive processes that are less available to conscious intervention.

Much of the work on relatively effortless, reflexive mental processes that followed in the wake of the research on the heuristics of judgment has been advanced as part of various "dual process" models of cognition. The advocates of each of these models postulate one set of mental processes that are quick and effortless, and another that are more deliberate and taxing. There are two types of dual process models. One advances the claim that people deliberately use less effortful procedures when the judgment is relatively unimportant and motivation is low. The more effortful procedures are reserved for occasions in which the stakes are high. The "Elaboration Likelihood" (Petty & Caccioppo, 1986) and "heuristic–systematic" models of persuasion (Chaiken, Liberman, & Eagly, 1989), and various perspectives on stereotyping (Bodenhausen, 1990; Fiske & Neuberg, 1990) fit this template. This work fits the "cognitive miser" perspective on heuristic processing.

There is another set of dual-process models that do not conform to the cognitive miser perspective. These models, often referred to as "two systems" models, postulate the existence of two mental systems that operate in parallel. (See Kahneman & Frederick, Chapter 2; Sloman, Chapter 22; Stanovich & West, Chapter 24.) An associationist, parallel-processing system ("System 1") that renders quick, holistic judgments is always in operation – not just when motivation is low and judgments are made on the cheap. The assessments made by the associationist system are then supplemented – and sometimes overridden – by the output of a more deliberate, serial, and rule-based system ("System 2"). These models fit the cognitive miser perspective less well because they do not postulate two different "routes" of information processing that operate in either–or fashion according to the motivation of the information processor (although they too can account for motivational influences through variation in the effort applied to the rule-based system, e.g., Tetlock, Chapter 32).

As we alluded to earlier, the heuristics and biases program has most often been seen through the cognitive miser lens. People are thought to employ various heuristics to save effort. But the idea of heuristics as "natural assessments" (Tversky & Kahneman, 1983; see Chapter 1) is clearly much more consistent with the two-systems perspective, and we expect this book to consolidate that view of what the heuristics and biases program is really about. The two-systems view also helps to clarify the differences and similarities between the heuristics of the "heuristics and biases" program and those of the "fast and frugal heuristics" program (Gigerenzer et al., Chapter 31; Gigerenzer, Todd, & the ABC Research Group, 1999). The prototypical fast and frugal heuristics studied by the ABC group are System 2 heuristics: strategies or rules that are deliberately chosen to ease computational burden (Kahneman & Frederick, Chapter 2; Griffin & Kahneman, in press). The "Take the Best" heuristic, for example, simplifies multiattribute choice by using an ordinal comparison on the most important dimension.

Some of these System 2 heuristics, however, rest on more basic System 1 processes that are subject to the kinds of errors associated with the heuristics and biases approach. Consider the "recognition heuristic," by which people choose the option that is most familiar. Familiarity appears to rely on the computation of fluency – how easily an object is identified or a word is read (Kelley & Jacoby, 1996) – which is an automatically computed natural assessment closely related to availability (Schwarz, Chapter 29). Thus the accuracy of the (System 2) decision rule rests on the validity of a System 1 computation, which is sensitive to a wide variety of environmental manipulations that lead to robust and systematic biases (e.g., Kelley & Jacoby, 1996; Reber, Winkielman, & Schwarz, 1998). It seems that System 1 heuristics, and the biases that arise from them, are difficult to avoid even in the context of deliberate choice (Frederick, Chapter 30; Over, 2000).

What are the natural assessments that are automatically elicited by certain stimuli or certain judgment contexts? In addition to the computations of similarity and availability that were the basis of the original research in this tradition, people typically make quick assessments of their affective reactions (Schwarz, Chapter 29; Slovic et al., Chapter 23), the ease or fluency of their perceptual experience (Kelley & Jacoby, 1996; Reber, Winkielman, & Schwarz, 1998), the causal structure of the pertinent environment (Heider, 1958; Michotte, 1963; Tversky & Kahneman, 1982) and whether a given event is abnormal or surprising (Kahneman & Miller, Chapter 20; Kahneman & Varey, 1990). There may very well be other natural assessments that constitute additional general-purpose heuristics that have yet to be empirically documented. In addition, there are certain assessments that are only "natural" in some contexts and therefore serve as the basis of various special-purpose heuristics. In some contexts, for example, a person is likely to compute how hard she has worked to get something, and then use the output of that computation to infer how much she values it (Aronson & Mills, 1959; Bem, 1972; Gerard & Mathewsen, 1966).

The assessments underlying the six general purpose heuristics identified (affect, availability, causality, fluency, similarity, and surprise) are different from the two discussed most actively in 1982 when the predecessor of this book was published. The notion of special-purpose heuristics, absent from the heuristics and biases landscape at that time, is even more novel (Kahneman & Frederick, Chapter 2; Frederick, Chapter 30). We view these new developments as a sign of the vigor and, to use the other sense of the term, heuristic value of the heuristics and biases perspective. Part I of this book presents papers that develop classic themes in this perspective, revealing how the original roots of the research continue to deepen. Part II presents papers that provide new theoretical approaches to heuristics and biases, revealing how the roots continue to spread. Finally, Part III presents papers that describe judgment in everyday life and by domain experts, showing how the heuristics and biases research has branched out into applied settings. At every level, research inspired by this program is flourishing, and we look forward to seeing what will grow out of the work summarized in this book.

PART ONE

THEORETICAL AND EMPIRICAL EXTENSIONS

1. Extensional versus Intuitive Reasoning:
The Conjunction Fallacy in Probability Judgment

Amos Tversky and Daniel Kahneman

Uncertainty is an unavoidable aspect of the human condition. Many significant choices must be based on beliefs about the likelihood of such uncertain events as the guilt of a defendant, the result of an election, the future value of the dollar, the outcome of a medical operation, or the response of a friend. Because we normally do not have adequate formal models for computing the probabilities of such events, intuitive judgment is often the only practical method for assessing uncertainty.

The question of how lay people and experts evaluate the probabilities of uncertain events has attracted considerable research interest. (See, e.g., Einhorn & Hogarth, 1981; Kahneman, Slovic, & Tversky, 1982; Nisbett & Ross, 1980.) Much of this research has compared intuitive inferences and probability judgments to the rules of statistics and the laws of probability. The student of judgment uses the probability calculus as a standard of comparison much as a student of perception might compare the perceived size of objects to their physical sizes. Unlike the correct size of objects, however, the "correct" probability of events is not easily defined. Because individuals who have different knowledge or hold different beliefs must be allowed to assign different probabilities to the same event, no single value can be correct for all people. Furthermore, a correct probability cannot always be determined, even for a single person. Outside the domain of random sampling, probability theory does not determine the probabilities of uncertain events – it merely imposes constraints on the relations among them. For example, if A is more probable than B, then the complement of A must be less probable than the complement of B.

The laws of probability derive from extensional considerations. A probability measure is defined on a family of events, and each event is construed as a set of possibilities, such as the three ways of getting a 10 on a throw of a pair of dice. The probability of an event equals the sum of the probabilities of its disjoint outcomes. Probability theory has traditionally been used to analyze repetitive chance processes, but the theory has also been applied to essentially unique events for which probability is not reducible to the relative frequency of "favorable" outcomes. The probability that the man who sits next to you

This is an edited version of a paper that originally appeared in *Psychological Review*, 91, 293–315.

on the plane is unmarried equals the probability that he is a bachelor plus the probability that he is either divorced or widowed. Additivity applies even when probability does not have a frequentistic interpretation and when the elementary events are not equiprobable.

The simplest and most fundamental qualitative law of probability is the *extension rule*: If the extension of A includes the extension of B (i.e., $A \supset B$), then $P(A) \geq P(B)$. Because the set of possibilities associated with a conjunction $A \& B$ is included in the set of possibilities associated with B, the same principle can also be expressed by the conjunction rule $P(A \& B) \leq P(B)$: A conjunction cannot be more probable than one of its constituents. This rule holds regardless of whether A and B are independent and is valid for any probability assignment on the same sample space. Furthermore, it applies not only to the standard probability calculus, but also to nonstandard models such as upper and lower probability (Dempster, 1967; Suppes, 1975), belief function (Shafer, 1976), Baconian probability (Cohen, 1977), rational belief (Kyburg, 1983), and possibility theory (Zadeh, 1978).

In contrast to formal theories of beliefs, intuitive judgments of probability are generally not extensional. People do not normally analyze daily events into exhaustive lists of possibilities or evaluate compound probabilities by aggregating elementary ones. Instead, they commonly use a limited number of heuristics, such as representativeness and availability (Kahneman et al., 1982). Our conception of judgmental heuristics is based on natural assessments that are routinely carried out as part of the perception of events and the comprehension of messages. Such natural assessments include computations of similarity and representativeness, attributions of causality, and evaluations of the availability of associations and exemplars. These assessments, we propose, are performed even in the absence of a specific task set, although their results are used to meet task demands as they arise. For example, the mere mention of "horror movies" activates instances of horror movies and evokes an assessment of their availability. Similarly, the statement that Woody Allen's aunt had hoped that he would be a dentist elicits a comparison of the character to the stereotype and an assessment of representativeness. It is presumably the mismatch between Woody Allen's personality and our stereotype of a dentist that makes the thought mildly amusing. Although these assessments are not tied to the estimation of frequency or probability, they are likely to play a dominant role when such judgments are required. The availability of horror movies may be used to answer the question, "What proportion of the movies produced last year were horror movies?", and representativeness may control the judgment that a particular boy is more likely to be an actor than a dentist.

The term *judgmental heuristic* refers to a strategy – whether deliberate or not – that relies on a natural assessment to produce an estimation or a prediction. One of the manifestations of a heuristic is the relative neglect of other considerations. For example, the resemblance of a child to various professional stereotypes may be given too much weight in predicting future vocational choice at the expense of other pertinent data, such as the base rate frequencies of occupations. Hence, the use of judgmental heuristics gives rise to predictable biases. Natural assessments can affect judgments in other ways for which the term *heuristic* is less apt. First, people sometimes misinterpret their task and fail to distinguish the required judgment from the natural assessment that the problem evokes. Second, the natural assessment may act as an anchor to which the required judgment is assimilated, even when the judge does not intend to use the one to estimate the other.

Previous discussions of errors of judgment have focused on deliberate strategies and misinterpretations of tasks. The present treatment calls special attention to the processes of anchoring and assimilation, which are often neither deliberate nor conscious. An example from perception may be instructive: If two objects in a picture of a three-dimensional scene have the same picture size, the one that appears more distant is not only seen as "really" larger, but also as larger in the picture. The natural computation of real size evidently influences the (less natural) judgment of picture size, although observers are unlikely to confuse the two values or use the former to estimate the latter.

The natural assessments of representativeness and availability do not conform to the extensional logic of probability theory. In particular, a conjunction can be more representative than one of its constituents, and instances of a specific category can be easier to retrieve than instances of a more inclusive category. The following demonstration illustrates the point. When they were given 60 seconds to list seven-letter words of a specified form, students at the University of British Columbia (UBC) produced many more words of the form _ _ _ _ ing than of the form _ _ _ _ _ n _, although the latter class includes the former. The average numbers of words produced in the two conditions were 6.4 and 2.9, respectively, $t(44) = 4.70$, $p < .01$. In this test of availability, the increased efficacy of memory search suffices to offset the reduced extension of the target class.

Our (Tversky & Kahneman, 1973) treatment of the availability heuristic suggests that the differential availability of *ing* words and of _ _ _ n _ _ _ words should be reflected in judgments of frequency. The following question tests this prediction:

In four pages of a novel (about 2,000 words), how many words would you expect to find that have the form _ _ _ _ _ ing (seven-letter words that end with "ing")? Indicate your best estimate by circling one of the values below: 0 1–2 3–4 5–7 8–10 11–15 16+.

A second version of the question requested estimates for words of the form _ _ _ _ _ n _. The median estimates were 13.4 for *ing* words ($n = 52$), and 4.7 for _ n _ words ($n = 53$, $p < .01$, by median test), contrary to the extension rule. Similar results were obtained for the comparison of words of the form _ _ _ _ _ ly with words of the form _ _ _ _ _ _ l _; the median estimates were 8.8 and 4.4, respectively.

This example illustrates the structure of the studies reported in this chapter. We constructed problems in which a reduction of extension was associated with an increase in availability or representativeness, and we tested the conjunction rule in judgments of frequency or probability. In the next section we discuss the representativeness heuristic and contrast it with the conjunction rule in the context of person perception. The third section describes conjunction fallacies in medical prognoses, sports forecasting, and choice among bets. In the fourth section, we investigate probability judgments for conjunctions of causes and effects and describe conjunction errors in scenarios of future events. Manipulations that enable respondents to resist the conjunction fallacy are explored in the fifth section, and the implications of the results are discussed in the final section.

REPRESENTATIVE CONJUNCTIONS

Modern research on categorization of objects and events (Mervis & Rosch, 1981; Rosch, 1978; Smith & Medin, 1981) has shown that information is commonly stored and processed in relation to mental models, such as prototypes and schemata. It is therefore natural and economical for the probability of an event to be evaluated by the degree to which that event is representative of an appropriate mental model (Kahneman & Tversky, 1972, 1973; Tversky & Kahneman, 1971, 1982). Because many of the results reported here are attributed to this heuristic, we first briefly analyze the concept of representativeness and illustrate its role in probability judgment.

Representativeness is an assessment of the degree of correspondence between a sample and a population, an instance and a category, an act and an actor or, more generally, between an outcome and a model. The model may refer to a person, a coin, or the world economy, and the respective outcomes could be marital status, a sequence of heads and tails, or the current price of gold. Representativeness can be investigated empirically by asking people, for example, which of two sequences of heads and tails is more representative of a fair coin or which of two professions is more representative of a given personality. This relation differs from other notions of proximity in that it is distinctly directional. It is natural to describe a sample as more or less representative of its parent population or a species (e.g., robin, penguin) as more or less representative of a superordinate category (e.g., bird). It is awkward to describe a population as representative of a sample or a category as representative of an instance.

When the model and the outcomes are described in the same terms, representativeness is reducible to similarity. Because a sample and a population, for example, can be described by the same attributes (e.g., central tendency and variability), the sample appears representative if its salient statistics match the corresponding parameters of the population. In the same manner, a person seems representative of a social group if his or her personality resembles the stereotypical member of that group. Representativeness, however, is not always reducible to similarity; it can also reflect causal and correlational beliefs (see, e.g., Chapman & Chapman, 1967; Jennings, Amabile, & Ross, 1982; Nisbett &

Ross, 1980). A particular act (e.g., suicide) is representative of a person because we attribute to the actor a disposition to commit the act, not because the act resembles the person. Thus, an outcome is representative of a model if the salient features match or if the model has a propensity to produce the outcome.

Representativeness tends to covary with frequency: Common instances and frequent events are generally more representative than unusual instances and rare events. The representative summer day is warm and sunny, the representative American family has two children, and the representative height of an adult male is about 5 feet 10 inches. However, there are notable circumstances in which representativeness is at variance with both actual and perceived frequency. First, a highly specific outcome can be representative but infrequent. Consider a numeric variable, such as weight, that has a unimodal frequency distribution in a given population. A narrow interval near the mode of the distribution is generally more representative of the population than a wider interval near the tail. For example, 68% of a group of Stanford University undergraduates ($N = 105$) stated that it is more representative for a female Stanford student "to weigh between 124 and 125 pounds" than "to weigh more than 135 pounds." However, 78% of a different group ($N = 102$) stated that among female Stanford students, there are more "women who weigh more than 135 pounds" than "women who weigh between 124 and 125 pounds." Thus, the narrow modal interval (124–125 pounds) was judged to be more representative but less frequent than the broad tail interval (above 135 pounds).

Second, an attribute is representative of a class if it is very diagnostic; that is, if the relative frequency of this attribute is much higher in that class than in a relevant reference class. For example, 65% of the subjects ($N = 105$) stated that it is more representative for a Hollywood actress "to be divorced more than 4 times" than "to vote Democratic." Multiple divorce is diagnostic of Hollywood actresses because it is part of the stereotype that the incidence of divorce is higher among Hollywood actresses than among other women. However, 83% of a different group ($N = 102$) stated that, among Hollywood actresses, there are more "women who vote Democratic" than "women who are divorced more than 4 times." Thus, the more diagnostic attribute was judged to be more representative but less frequent than an attribute (voting Democratic) of lower diagnosticity. Third, an unrepresentative instance of a category can be fairly representative of a superordinate category. For example, chicken is a worse exemplar of a bird than of an animal, and rice is an unrepresentative vegetable, although it is a representative food.

The preceding observations indicate that representativeness is nonextensional: It is not determined by frequency and is not bound by class inclusion. Consequently, the test of the conjunction rule in probability judgments offers the sharpest contrast between the extensional logic of probability theory and the psychological principles of representativeness. Our first set of studies of the conjunction rule were conducted in 1974, using occupation and political affiliation as target attributes to be predicted singly or in conjunction from brief personality sketches (see Tversky & Kahneman, 1982, for a brief summary). The studies described in the present section replicate and extend our earlier work. We used the following personality sketches of two fictitious individuals, Bill and Linda, followed by a set of occupations and avocations associated with each of them.

> Bill is 34 years old. He is intelligent but unimaginative, compulsive, and generally lifeless. In school, he was strong in mathematics but weak in social studies and humanities.
> Bill is a physician who plays poker for a hobby.
> Bill is an architect.
> Bill is an accountant. (A)
> Bill plays jazz for a hobby. (J)
> Bill surfs for a hobby.
> Bill is a reporter.
> Bill is an accountant who plays jazz for a hobby. (A&J)
> Bill climbs mountains for a hobby.
> Linda is 31 years old, single, outspoken and very bright. She majored in philosophy. As a student, she was deeply concerned with issues of discrimination and social justice, and also participated in anti-nuclear demonstrations.
> Linda is a teacher in elementary school.
> Linda works in a bookstore and takes Yoga classes.
> Linda is active in the feminist movement. (F)
> Linda is a psychiatric social worker.
> Linda is a member of the League of Women Voters.
> Linda is a bank teller. (T)
> Linda is an insurance salesperson.
> Linda is a bank teller and is active in the feminist movement. (T&F)

As the reader has probably guessed, the description of Bill was constructed to be representative of an accountant (A) and unrepresentative of a person who plays jazz for a hobby (J). The description of Linda was constructed to be representative of an active feminist (F) and unrepresentative of a bank teller (T). We also expected the ratings of representativeness to be higher for the classes defined by a conjunction of attributes (A&J for Bill, T&F for Linda) than for the less representative constituent of each conjunction (J and T, respectively).

A group of 88 undergraduates at the University of British Columbia (UBC) ranked the eight statements associated with each description by "the degree to which Bill [Linda] resembles the typical member of that class." The results confirmed our expectations. The percentages of respondents who displayed the predicted order (A > A&J > J for Bill; F > T&F > T for Linda) were 87% and 85%, respectively. This finding is neither surprising nor objectionable. If, like similarity and prototypicality, representativeness depends on both common and distinctive features (Tversky, 1977), it should be enhanced by the addition of shared features. Adding eyebrows to a schematic face makes it more similar to another schematic face with eyebrows (Gati & Tversky, 1982). Analogously, the addition of feminism to the profession of bank teller improves the match of Linda's current activities to her personality. More surprising and less acceptable is the finding that the great majority of subjects also rank the conjunctions ($A\&J$ and $T\&F$) as more probable than their less representative constituents (J & T). The following sections describe and analyze this phenomenon.

INDIRECT AND SUBTLE TESTS

Experimental tests of the conjunction rule can be divided into three types: *indirect* tests, *direct–subtle* tests, and *direct–transparent* tests. In the indirect tests, one group of subjects evaluates the probability of the conjunction, and another group of subjects evaluates the probability of its constituents. No subject is required to compare a conjunction (e.g., "Linda is a bank teller and a feminist") to its constituents. In the direct–subtle tests, subjects compare the conjunction to its less-representative constituent, but the inclusion relation between the events is not emphasized. In the direct–transparent tests, the subjects evaluate or compare the probabilities of the conjunction and its constituent in a format that highlights the relation between them.

The three experimental procedures investigate different hypotheses. The indirect procedure tests whether probability judgments conform to the conjunction rule; the direct–subtle procedure tests whether people will take advantage of an opportunity to compare the critical events; and the direct–transparent procedure tests whether people will obey the conjunction rule when they are compelled to compare the critical events. This sequence of tests also describes the course of our investigation, which began with the observation of violations of the conjunction rule in indirect tests and proceeded – to our increasing surprise – to the finding of stubborn failures of that rule in several direct–transparent tests. . . .

Subjects in the main study received one problem (either Bill or Linda) first in the format of a direct test. They were asked to rank all eight statements associated with that problem (including the conjunction, its separate constituents, and five filler items) according to their probability, using 1 for the most probable and 8 for the least probable. The subjects then received the remaining problem in the format of an indirect test, in which the list of alternatives included either the conjunction or its separate constituents. The same five filler items were used in both the direct and indirect versions of each problem.

Table 1.1 presents the average ranks (R) of the conjunction $R(A\&B)$ and its less-representative constituents $R(B)$, relative to the set of five filler items. The percentage of violations of the conjunction rule in the direct test is denoted by V. The results can be summarized as follows: (a) the conjunction is ranked higher than its less-likely constituents in all 12 comparisons; (b) there is no consistent difference between the ranks of the alternatives in the direct and indirect tests;

Table 1.1. Tests of the Conjunction Rule in Likelihood Rankings

Subjects	Problem	Direct Test				Indirect Test		
		V	R(A&B)	R(B)	N	R(A&B)	R(B)	Total N
Naive	Bill	92	2.5	4.5	94	2.3	4.5	88
	Linda	89	3.3	4.4	88	3.3	4.4	86
Informed	Bill	86	2.6	4.5	56	2.4	4.2	56
	Linda	90	3.0	4.3	53	2.9	3.9	55
Sophisticated	Bill	83	2.6	4.7	32	2.5	4.6	32
	Linda	85	3.2	4.3	32	3.1	4.3	32

Note: V = percentage of violations of the conjunction rule; $R(A\&B)$ and $R(B)$ = mean rank assigned to $A\&B$ and B, respectively; N = number of subjects in the direct test; Total N = total number of subjects in the indirect test, who were about equally divided between the two groups.

(c) the overall incidence of violations of the conjunction rule in direct tests is 88%, which virtually coincides with the incidence of the corresponding pattern in judgments of representativeness; and (d) there is no effect of statistical sophistication in either indirect or direct tests.

The violation of the conjunction rule in a direct comparison of B to $A\&B$ is called the *conjunction fallacy*. Violations inferred from between-subjects comparisons are called *conjunction errors*. Perhaps the most surprising aspect of Table 1.1 is the lack of any difference between indirect and direct tests. We had expected the conjunction to be judged more probable than the less likely of its constituents in an indirect test, in accord with the pattern observed in judgments of representativeness. However, we also expected that even naive respondents would notice the repetition of some attributes, alone and in conjunction with others, and that they would then apply the conjunction rule and rank the conjunction below its constituents. This expectation was violated, not only by statistically naive undergraduates, but even by highly sophisticated respondents. In both direct and indirect tests, the subjects apparently ranked the outcomes by the degree to which Bill (or Linda) matched the respective stereotypes. The correlation between the mean ranks of probability and representativeness was .96 for Bill and .98 for Linda. Does the conjunction rule hold when the relation of inclusion is made highly transparent? The studies described in the next section abandon all subtlety in an effort to compel the subjects to detect and appreciate the inclusion relation between the target events.

Transparent Tests

This section describes a series of increasingly desperate manipulations designed to induce subjects to obey the conjunction rule. We first presented the description of Linda to a group of 142 undergraduates at UBC and asked them to check which of two alternatives was more probable:

Linda is a bank teller. (*T*)
Linda is a bank teller and is active in the feminist movement. (*T&F*)

The order of alternatives was inverted for half of the subjects, but this manipulation had no effect. Overall, 85% of respondents indicated that *T&F* was more probable than *T*, in a flagrant violation of the conjunction rule. . . .

Although subjects do not spontaneously apply the conjunction rule, perhaps they can recognize its validity. We presented another group of UBC undergraduates with the description of Linda, followed by the two statements, *T* and *T&F*, and asked them to indicate which of the following two arguments they found more convincing:

Argument 1. Linda is more likely to be a bank teller than she is to be a feminist bank teller, because every feminist bank teller is a bank teller, but some women bank tellers are not feminists, and Linda could be one of them.
Argument 2. Linda is more likely to be a feminist bank teller than she is likely to be a bank teller, because she resembles an active feminist more than she resembles a bank teller.

The majority of subjects (65%, *n* = 58) chose the invalid resemblance argument (Argument 2) over the valid extensional argument (Argument 1). Thus, a deliberate attempt to induce a reflective attitude did not eliminate the appeal of the representativeness heuristic.

We made a further effort to clarify the inclusive nature of the event *T* by representing it as a disjunction. [Note that the conjunction rule can also be expressed as a disjunction rule $P(A \text{ or } B) \geq P(B)$.] The description of Linda was used again, with a 9-point rating scale for judgments of probability, but the statement *T* was replaced by

Linda is a bank teller whether or not she is active in the feminist movement. (*T**)

This formulation emphasizes the inclusion of *T&F* in *T*. Despite the transparent relation between the statements, the mean ratings of likelihood were 5.1 for *T&F* and 3.8 for *T** (*p* < .01, by *t* test). Furthermore, 57% of the subjects (*n* = 75) committed the conjunction fallacy by rating *T&F* higher than *T**, and only 16% gave a lower rating to *T&F* than to *T**.

The violations of the conjunction rule in direct comparisons of *T&F* to *T** are remarkable because the extension of "Linda is a bank teller whether or not she is active in the feminist movement" clearly includes the extension of "Linda is a bank teller and is active in the feminist movement." Many subjects evidently failed to draw extensional inferences from the phrase "whether or not," which may have been taken to indicate a weak disposition. This interpretation was supported by a between-subjects comparison, in which different subjects evaluated *T*, *T**, and *T&F* on a 9-point scale after evaluating the common filler statement, "Linda is a psychiatric social worker." The average ratings were 3.3

for T, 3.9 for T^*, and 4.5 for $T\&F$, with each mean significantly different from both others. The statements T and T^* are, of course, extensionally equivalent, but they are assigned different probabilities. Because feminism fits Linda, the mere mention of this attribute makes T^* more likely than T, and a definite commitment to it makes the probability of $T\&F$ even higher!

Modest success in loosening the grip of the conjunction fallacy was achieved by asking subjects to choose whether to bet on T or on $T\&F$. The subjects were given Linda's description, with the following instruction:

> If you could win \$10 by betting on an event, which of the following would you choose to bet on? (Check one).

The percentage of violations of the conjunction rule in this task was "only" 56% ($n = 60$), much too high for comfort but substantially lower than the typical value for comparisons of the two events in terms of probability. We conjecture that the betting context draws attention to the conditions in which one bet pays off whereas the other does not, allowing some subjects to discover that a bet on T dominates a bet on $T\&F$.

The respondents in the studies described in this section were statistically naive undergraduates at UBC. Does statistical education eradicate the fallacy? To answer this question, 64 graduate students of social sciences at the University of California, Berkeley, and at Stanford University, all with credit for several statistics courses, were given the rating-scale version of the direct test of the conjunction rule for the Linda problem. For the first time in this series of studies, the mean rating for $T\&F$ (3.5) was lower than the rating assigned to T (3.8), and only 36% of respondents committed the fallacy. Thus, statistical sophistication produced a majority who conformed to the conjunction rule in a transparent test, although the incidence of violations was fairly high even in this group of intelligent and sophisticated respondents.

Elsewhere (Kahneman & Tversky, 1982a), we distinguished between positive and negative accounts of judgments and preferences that violate normative rules. A positive account focuses on the factors that produce a particular response; a negative account seeks to explain why the correct response was not made. The positive analysis of the Bill and Linda problems invokes the representativeness heuristic. The stubborn persistence of the conjunction fallacy in highly transparent problems, however, lends special interest to the characteristic question of a negative analysis: Why do intelligent and reasonably well-educated people fail to recognize the applicability of the conjunction rule in transparent problems? Postexperimental interviews and class discussions with many subjects shed some light on this question. Naive as well as sophisticated subjects generally noticed the nesting of the target events in the direct–transparent test, but the naive, unlike the sophisticated, did not appreciate its significance for probability assessment. However, most naive subjects did not attempt to defend their responses. As one subject said after acknowledging the validity of the conjunction rule, "I thought you only asked for my opinion."

The interviews and the results of the direct–transparent tests indicate that naive subjects do not spontaneously treat the conjunction rule as decisive. Their attitude is reminiscent of children's responses in a Piagetian experiment. The child in the preconservation stage is not altogether blind to arguments based on conservation of volume and typically expects quantity to be conserved (Bruner, 1966). What the child fails to see is that the conservation argument is decisive and should overrule the perceptual impression that the tall container holds more water than the short one. Similarly, naive subjects generally endorse the conjunction rule in the abstract, but their application of this rule to the Linda problem is blocked by the compelling impression that $T\&F$ is more representative of her than T is. In this context, the adult subjects reason as if they had not reached the stage of formal operations. A full understanding of a principle of physics, logic, or statistics requires knowledge of the conditions under which it prevails over conflicting arguments, such as the height of the liquid in a container or the representativeness of an outcome. The recognition of the decisive nature of rules distinguishes different developmental stages in studies of conservation; it also distinguishes different levels of statistical sophistication in the present series of studies.

MORE REPRESENTATIVE CONJUNCTIONS

The preceding studies revealed massive violations of the conjunction rule in the domain of person perception and social stereotypes. Does the conjunction rule fare better in other areas of judgment? Does it hold when the uncertainty regarding the target events is attributed to chance rather than to partial ignorance? Does expertise in the relevant subject matter protect against the conjunction fallacy? Do financial incentives help respondents see the light? The following studies were designed to answer these questions.

Medical Judgment

In this study, we asked practicing physicians to make intuitive predictions on the basis of clinical evidence. We chose to study medical judgment because physicians possess expert knowledge and because intuitive judgments often play an important role in medical decision making. Two groups of physicians took part in the study. The first group consisted of 37 internists from the greater Boston area who were taking a postgraduate course at Harvard University. The second group consisted of 66 internists with admitting privileges in the New England Medical Center. They were given problems of the following type:

A 55-year-old woman had pulmonary embolism documented angiographically 10 days after a cholecystectomy. Please rank order the following in terms of the probability that they will be among the conditions experienced by the patient (use 1 for the most likely and 6 for the least likely). Naturally, the patient could experience more than one of these conditions.

Dyspnea and hemiparesis ($A\&B$)	Syncope and tachycardia
Calf pain	Hemiparesis (B)
Pleuritic chest pain	Hemoptysis

The symptoms listed for each problem included one, denoted B, that was judged by our consulting physicians to be nonrepresentative of the patient's condition, and the conjunction of B with another highly representative symptom denoted A. In the above example of pulmonary embolism (blood clots in the lung), dyspnea (shortness of breath) is a typical symptom, whereas hemiparesis (partial paralysis) is very atypical. Each participant first received three (or two) problems in the indirect format in which the list included either B or the conjunction $A\&B$, but not both, followed by two (or three) problems in the direct format illustrated above. The design was balanced so that each problem appeared about an equal number of times in each format. An independent group of 32 physicians from Stanford University were asked to rank each list of symptoms "by the degree to which they are representative of the clinical condition of the patient."

The design was essentially the same as in the Bill and Linda study. The results of the two experiments were also very similar. The correlation between mean ratings by probability and by representativeness exceeded .95 in all five problems. For every one of the five problems, the conjunction of an unlikely symptom with a likely one was judged more probable than the less-likely constituent. The ranking of symptoms was the same in direct and indirect tests: The overall mean ranks of $A\&B$ and of B, respectively, were 2.7 and 4.6 in the direct tests and 2.8 and 4.3 in the indirect tests. The incidence of violations of the conjunction rule in direct tests ranged from 73% to 100%, with an average of 91%. Evidently, substantive expertise does not displace representativeness and does not prevent conjunction errors.

Can the results be interpreted without imputing to these experts a consistent violation of the conjunction rule? The instructions used in the present study were especially designed to eliminate the interpretation of Symptom B as an exhaustive description of the relevant facts, which would imply the absence of Symptom A. Participants were instructed to rank symptoms in terms of the probability "that they will be among the conditions experienced by the patient." They were also reminded that "the patient could experience more than one of these conditions." To test the effect of these instructions, the following question was included at the end of the questionnaire:

In assessing the probability that the patient described has a particular symptom X, did you assume that (check one):
X is the *only* symptom experienced by the patient?
X is *among* the symptoms experienced by the patient?

Sixty of the 62 physicians who were asked this question checked the second answer, rejecting an interpretation of events that could have justified an apparent violation of the conjunction rule.

An additional group of 24 physicians, mostly residents at Stanford Hospital, participated in a group discussion in which they were confronted with their conjunction fallacies in the same questionnaire. The respondents did not defend their answers, although some references were made to "the nature of clinical experience." Most participants appeared surprised and dismayed to have made an elementary error of reasoning. Because the conjunction fallacy is easy to expose, people who committed it are left with the feeling that they should have known better.

Predicting Wimbledon

The uncertainty encountered in the previous studies regarding the prognosis of a patient or the occupation of a person is normally attributed to incomplete knowledge rather than to the operation of a chance process. Recent studies of inductive reasoning about daily events, conducted by Nisbett, Krantz, Jepson, and Kunda (1983), indicated that statistical principles (e.g., the law of large numbers) are commonly applied in domains such as sports and gambling, which include a random element. The next two studies test the conjunction rule in predictions of the outcomes of a sports event and of a game of chance, where the random aspect of the process is particularly salient.

A group of 93 subjects, recruited through an advertisement in the University of Oregon newspaper, were presented with the following problem in October 1980:

> Suppose Bjorn Borg reaches the Wimbledon finals in 1981. Please rank order the following outcomes from most to least likely.
> A. Borg will win the match (1.7).
> B. Borg will lose the first set (2.7).
> C. Borg will lose the first set but win the match (2.2).
> D. Borg will win the first set but lose the match (3.5).

The average rank of each outcome (1 = most probable, 2 = second-most probable, etc.) is given in parentheses. The outcomes were chosen to represent different levels of strength for the player, Borg, with A indicating the highest strength; C, a rather lower level because it indicates a weakness in the first set; B, lower still because it only mentions this weakness; and D, lowest of all.

After winning his fifth Wimbledon title in 1980, Borg seemed extremely strong. Consequently, we hypothesized that Outcome C would be judged more probable than Outcome B, contrary to the conjunction rule, because C represents a better performance for Borg than does B. The mean rankings indicate that this hypothesis was confirmed: 72% of the respondents assigned a higher rank to C than to B, violating the conjunction rule in a direct test.

Is it possible that the subjects interpreted the target events in a nonextensional manner that could justify or explain the observed ranking? It is well-known that connectives (e.g., and, or, if) are often used in ordinary language in ways that depart from their logical definitions. Perhaps the respondents interpreted the conjunction (A *and* B) as a disjunction (A *or* B), an implication (A *implies* B), or a conditional statement (A *if* B). Alternatively, the event B could be interpreted in the presence of the conjunction as B *and not* A. To investigate these possibilities, we presented to another group of 56 naive subjects at Stanford University the hypothetical results of the relevant tennis match, coded as sequences of wins and losses. For example, the sequence LWWLW denotes a five-set match in which Borg lost (L) the first and the fourth sets but won (W) the other sets and the match. For each sequence, the subjects were asked to examine the four target events of the original Borg problem and indicate, by marking + or −, whether the given sequence was consistent or inconsistent with each of the events.

With very few exceptions, all of the subjects marked the sequences according to the standard (extensional) interpretation of the target events. A sequence was judged consistent with the conjunction "Borg will lose the first set but win the match" when both constituents were satisfied (e.g., LWWLW), but not when either one or both constituents failed. Evidently, these subjects did not interpret the conjunction as an implication, a conditional statement, or a disjunction. Furthermore, both LWWLW and LWLWL were judged consistent with the inclusive event, "Borg will lose the first set," contrary to the hypothesis that the inclusive event B is understood in the context of the other events as, "Borg will lose the first set and the match." The classification of sequences therefore indicated little or no ambiguity regarding the extension of the target events. In particular, all sequences that were classified as instances of $B\&A$ were also classified as instances of B, but some sequences that were classified as instances of B were judged inconsistent with $B\&A$, in accord with the standard interpretation in which the conjunction rule should be satisfied.

Another possible interpretation of the conjunction error maintains that instead of assessing the probability $P(B|E)$ of Hypothesis B (e.g., that Linda is a bank teller) in light of evidence E (Linda's personality), subjects assess the inverse probability $P(E|B)$ of the evidence given to the hypothesis in question. Because $P(E|A\&B)$ may well exceed $P(E|B)$, the subjects' responses could be justified under this interpretation. Whatever plausibility this account may have in the case of Linda, it is surely inapplicable to the present study, in which it makes no sense to assess the conditional probability that Borg will reach the finals given the outcome of the final match.

Risky Choice

If the conjunction fallacy cannot be justified by a reinterpretation of the target events, can it be rationalized by a nonstandard conception of probability? On this hypothesis, representativeness is treated as a legitimate nonextensional interpretation of probability rather than as a fallible heuristic. The conjunction fallacy, then, may be viewed as a misunderstanding regarding the meaning of the word *probability*. To investigate this hypothesis, we tested the conjunction rule in the following decision problem, which provides an incentive to choose the most probable event, although the word *probability* is not mentioned.

Consider a regular six-sided die with four green faces and two red faces. The die will be rolled 20 times and the sequence of greens (G) and reds (R) will be recorded. You are asked to select one sequence, from a set of three, and you will win $25 if the sequence you chose appears on successive rolls of the die. Please check the sequence of greens and reds on which you prefer to bet.

1. RGRRR
2. GRGRRR
3. GRRRRR

Note that Sequence 1 can be obtained from Sequence 2 by deleting the first G. By the conjunction rule, therefore, Sequence 1 must be more probable than Sequence 2. Note also that all three sequences are rather unrepresentative of the die because they contain more Rs than Gs. However, Sequence 2 appears to be an improvement over Sequence 1 because it contains a higher proportion of the more likely color. A group of 50 respondents were asked to rank the events by the degree to which they are representative of the die; 88% ranked Sequence 2 highest and Sequence 3 lowest. Thus, Sequence 2 is favored by representativeness, although it is dominated by Sequence 1.

A total of 260 students at UBC and Stanford University were given the choice version of the problem. There were no significant differences between the populations, and their results were pooled. The subjects were run in groups of 30 to 50 in a classroom setting. About one half of the subjects ($N = 125$) actually played the gamble with real payoffs. The choice was hypothetical for the other subjects. The percentages of subjects who chose the dominated option of Sequence 2 were 65% with real payoffs and 62% in the hypothetical format. Only 2% of the subjects in both groups chose Sequence 3.

To facilitate the discovery of the relation between the two critical sequences, we presented a new group of 59 subjects with a (hypothetical) choice problem in which Sequence 2 was replaced by RGRRRG. This new sequence was preferred over Sequence 1, RGRRR, by 63% of the respondents, although the first five elements of the two sequences were identical. These results suggest that subjects coded each sequence in terms of the proportion of Gs and Rs and ranked the sequences by the discrepancy between the proportions in the two sequences (1/5 and 1/3) and the expected value of 2/3.

It is apparent from these results that conjunction errors are not restricted to misunderstandings of the word *probability*. Our subjects followed the representativeness heuristic even when the word was not mentioned and even in choices involving substantial payoffs. The results further show that the conjunction fallacy is not restricted to esoteric interpretations of the connective *and*, because that connective was also absent from the problem. The present test of the conjunction rule was direct, in the sense defined earlier, because the subjects were required to compare two events, one of which included the other. However, informal interviews with some of the respondents suggest that the test was subtle:

The relation of inclusion between sequences 1 and 2 was apparently noted by only a few of the subjects. Evidently, people are not attuned to the detection of nesting among events, even when these relations are clearly displayed.

Suppose that the relation of dominance between sequences 1 and 2 is called to the subject's attention. Do they immediately appreciate its force and treat it as a decisive argument for Sequence 1? The original choice problem (without Sequence 3) was presented to a new group of 88 subjects at Stanford University. These subjects, however, were not asked to select the sequence on which they preferred to bet, but only to indicate which of the following two arguments, if any, they found correct.

> *Argument 1:* The first sequence (RGRRR) is more probable than the second (GRGRRR) because the second sequence is the same as the first with an additional G at the beginning. Hence, every time the second sequence occurs, the first sequence must also occur. Consequently, you can win on the first and lose on the second, but you can never win on the second and lose on the first.
>
> *Argument 2:* The second sequence (GRGRRR) is more probable than the first (RGRRR) because the proportions of R and G in the second sequence are closer than those of the first sequence to the expected proportions of R and G for a die with four green and two red faces.

Most of the subjects (76%) chose the valid extensional argument over an argument that formulates the intuition of representativeness. Recall that a similar argument in the case of Linda was much less effective in combating the conjunction fallacy. The success of the present manipulation can be attributed to the combination of a chance setup and a gambling task, which promotes extensional reasoning by emphasizing the conditions under which the bets will pay off.

FALLACIES AND MISUNDERSTANDINGS

We have described violations of the conjunction rule in direct tests as a fallacy. The term *fallacy* is used here as a psychological hypothesis, not an evaluative epithet. A judgment is appropriately labeled a fallacy when most of the people who make it are disposed, after suitable explanation, to accept the following propositions: (a) They made a nontrivial error, which they would probably have repeated in similar problems; (b) the error was conceptual, not merely verbal or technical; and (c) they *should* have known the correct answer or a procedure to find it. Alternatively, the same judgment could be described as a failure of communication if the subject misunderstands the question or if the experimenter misinterprets the answer. Subjects who have erred because of a misunderstanding are likely to reject the propositions listed above and claim (as students often do after an examination) that they knew the correct answer all along, and that their error, if any, was verbal or technical rather than conceptual.

A psychological analysis should apply interpretive charity and avoid treating genuine misunderstandings as if they were fallacies. It should also avoid the temptation to rationalize any error of judgment by *ad hoc* interpretations that the respondents themselves would not endorse. The dividing line between fallacies and misunderstandings, however, is not always clear. In one of our earlier studies, for example, most respondents stated that a particular description is more likely to belong to a physical education teacher than to a teacher. Strictly speaking, the latter category includes the former, but it could be argued that teacher was understood in this problem in a sense that excludes physical education teacher, much as animal is often used in a sense that excludes insects. Hence, it was unclear whether the apparent violation of the extension rule in this problem should be described as a fallacy or as a misunderstanding. A special effort was made in the present studies to avoid ambiguity by defining the critical event as an intersection of well-defined classes, such as bank tellers and feminists. The comments of the respondents in postexperimental discussions supported the conclusion that the observed violations of the conjunction rule in direct tests are genuine fallacies, not just misunderstandings.

CAUSAL CONJUNCTIONS

The problems discussed in previous sections included three elements: a causal model M (Linda's personality); a basic target event B, which is unrepresentative of M (she is a bank teller); and an added event A, which is highly representative of the model M (she is a feminist). In these problems, the model M is positively associated with A and is negatively associated with B. This structure, called the $M \rightarrow A$ *paradigm*, is depicted on the left side of Fig. 1.1. We found that when the sketch of Linda's personality was omitted and she was identified merely as a "31-year-old woman," almost all respondents obeyed the conjunction rule and ranked the conjunction (bank teller and active feminist) as less probable than its constituents. The conjunction error in the original problem is therefore attributable to the relation between M and A, not to the relation between A and B.

The conjunction fallacy was common in the Linda problem despite the fact that the stereotypes of bank teller and feminist are mildly incompatible. When the constituents of a conjunction are highly incompatible, the incidence of conjunction errors is greatly reduced. For example, the conjunction "Bill is bored by

Figure 1.1. Schematic representation of two experimental paradigms used to test the conjunction rule. (Solid and broken arrows denote strong positive and negative associations, respectively, between the model M, the basic target B, and the added target A.)

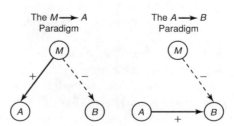

music and plays jazz for a hobby" was judged as less probable (and less representative) than its constituents, although "bored by music" was perceived as a probable (and representative) attribute of Bill. Quite reasonably, the incompatibility of the two attributes reduced the judged probability of their conjunction.

The effect of compatibility on the evaluation of conjunctions is not limited to near contradictions. For instance, it is more representative (as well as more probable) for a student to be in the upper half of the class in both mathematics and physics or to be in the lower half of the class in both fields than to be in the upper half in one field and in the lower half in the other. Such observations imply that the judged probability (or representativeness) of a conjunction cannot be computed as a function (e.g., product, sum, minimum, weighted average) of the scale values of its constituents. This conclusion excludes a large class of formal models that ignore the relation between the constituents of a conjunction. The viability of such models of conjunctive concepts has generated a spirited debate (Jones, 1982; Osherson & Smith, 1981, 1982; Zadeh, 1982; Lakoff, 1982).

The preceding discussion suggests a new formal structure, called the $A \rightarrow B$ *paradigm*, which is depicted on the right side of Fig. 1.1. Conjunction errors occur in the $A \rightarrow B$ paradigm because of the direct connection between A and B, although the added event A is not particularly representative of the model M. In this section, we investigate problems in which the added event A provides a plausible cause or motive for the occurrence of B. Our hypothesis is that the strength of the causal link, which has been shown in previous work to bias judgments of conditional probability (Tversky & Kahneman, 1980), will also bias judgments of the probability of conjunctions (see Beyth-Marom, 1982). Just as the thought of a personality and a social stereotype naturally evokes an assessment of their similarity, the thought of an effect and a possible cause evokes an assessment of causal impact (Ajzen, 1977). The natural assessment of propensity is expected to bias the evaluation of probability.

To illustrate this bias in the $A \rightarrow B$ paradigm, consider the following problem, which was presented to 115 undergraduates at Stanford University and UBC:

> A health survey was conducted in a representative sample of adult males in British Columbia of all ages and occupations. Mr. F. was included in the sample. He was selected by chance from the list of participants. Which of the following statements is more probable? (check one)
> Mr. F. has had one or more heart attacks.
> Mr. F. has had one or more heart attacks, and he is over 55 years old.

This seemingly transparent problem elicited a substantial proportion (58%) of conjunction errors among statistically naive respondents. To test the hypothesis that these errors are produced by the causal (or correlational) link between advanced age and heart attacks, rather than by a weighted average of the component probabilities, we removed this link by uncoupling the target events without changing their marginal probabilities.

A health survey was conducted in a representative sample of adult males in British Columbia of all ages and occupations. Mr. F. and Mr. G. were both included in the sample. They were unrelated and were selected by chance from the list of participants. Which of the following statements is more probable? (check one)

Mr. F. has had one or more heart attacks.

Mr. F. has had one or more heart attacks, and Mr. G. is over 55 years old.

Assigning the critical attributes to two independent individuals eliminates in effect the $A \rightarrow B$ connection by making the events (conditionally) independent. Accordingly, the incidence of conjunction errors dropped to 29% ($N = 90$).

The $A \rightarrow B$ paradigm can give rise to dual conjunction errors in which $A\&B$ is perceived as more probable than each of its constituents, as illustrated in the next problem.

Peter is a junior in college who is training to run the mile in a regional meet. In his best race, earlier this season, Peter ran the mile in 4:06 min. Please rank the following outcomes from most to least probable.

Peter will run the mile under 4:06 min.

Peter will run the mile under 4 min.

Peter will run the second half-mile under 1:55 min.

Peter will run the second half-mile under 1:55 min and will complete the mile under 4 min.

Peter will run the first half-mile under 2.05 min.

The critical event (a sub-1:55 minute second half *and* a sub-4 minute mile) is clearly defined as a conjunction and not as a conditional. Nevertheless, 76% of a group of undergraduate students from Stanford University ($N = 96$) ranked it above one of its constituents, and 48% of the subjects ranked it above both constituents. The natural assessment of the relation between the constituents apparently contaminated the evaluation of their conjunction. In contrast, no one violated the extension rule by ranking the second outcome (a sub-4 minute mile) above the first (a sub-4:06 minute mile). The preceding results indicate that the judged probability of a conjunction cannot be explained by an averaging model because in such a model $P(A\&B)$ lies between $P(A)$ and $P(B)$. An averaging process, however, may be responsible for some conjunction errors, particularly when the constituent probabilities are given in a numeric form.

Motives and Crimes

A conjunction error in a motive–action schema is illustrated by the following problem – one of several of the same general type administered to a group of 171 students at UBC:

John P. is a meek man, 42 years old, married, with two children. His neighbors describe him as mild-mannered, but somewhat secretive. He owns an import–export company based in New York City, and he travels frequently to Europe and the Far East. Mr. P. was convicted once for smuggling

precious stones and metals (including uranium) and received a suspended
sentence of 6 months in jail and a large fine.

Mr. P. is currently under police investigation.

Please rank the following statements by the probability that they will be
among the conclusions of the investigation. Remember that other possibilities exist and that more than one statement may be true. Use 1 for the
most probable statement, 2 for the second, etc.

Mr. P. is a child molester.

Mr. P. is involved in espionage and the sale of secret documents.

Mr. P. is a drug addict.

Mr. P. killed one of his employees.

One-half of the subjects ($n = 86$) ranked the events above. Other subjects
($n = 85$) ranked a modified list of possibilities in which the last event was
replaced by

Mr. P. killed one of his employees to prevent him from talking to the police.

Although the addition of a possible motive clearly reduces the extension of
the event (Mr. P. might have killed his employee for other reasons, such as
revenge or self-defense), we hypothesized that the mention of a plausible but
nonobvious motive would increase the perceived likelihood of the event. The
data confirmed this expectation. The mean rank of the conjunction was 2.90,
whereas the mean rank of the inclusive statement was 3.17 ($p < .05$, by t test).
Furthermore, 50% of the respondents ranked the conjunction as more likely
than the event that Mr. P. was a drug addict, but only 23% ranked the more
inclusive target event as more likely than drug addiction. In other problems of
the same type, we found that the mention of a cause or motive tends to increase
the judged probability of an action when the suggested motive (a) offers a
reasonable explanation of the target event, (b) appears fairly likely on its own,
and (c) is nonobvious, in the sense that it does not immediately come to mind
when the outcome is mentioned.

We have observed conjunction errors in other judgments involving criminal
acts in both the $A \rightarrow B$ and the $M \rightarrow A$ paradigms. For example, the hypothesis
that a policeman described as violence-prone was involved in the heroin trade
was ranked less likely (relative to a standard comparison set) than a conjunction
of allegations – that he is involved in the heroin trade and that he recently
assaulted a suspect. In that example, the assault was not causally linked to the
involvement in drugs, but it made the combined allegation more representative
of the suspect's disposition. The implications of the psychology of judgment to
the evaluation of legal evidence deserve careful study because the outcomes
of many trials depend on the ability of a judge or a jury to make intuitive
judgments on the basis of partial and fallible data (see Rubinstein, 1979; Saks &
Kidd, 1981).

Forecasts and Scenarios

The construction and evaluation of scenarios of future events are not only a favorite pastime of reporters, analysts, and news watchers. Scenarios are often used in the context of planning, and their plausibility influences significant decisions. Scenarios for the past are also important in many contexts, including criminal law and the writing of history. It is of interest, then, to evaluate whether the forecasting or reconstruction of real-life events is subject to conjunction errors. Our analysis suggests that a scenario that includes a possible cause and an outcome could appear more probable than the outcome on its own. We tested this hypothesis in two populations: statistically naive students and professional forecasters.

In April 1982, a sample of 245 UBC undergraduates were requested to evaluate the probability of occurrence of several events in 1983. A 9-point scale was used, defined by the following categories: less than 0.01, 0.1, 0.5, 1, 2, 5, 10, 25, and 50% or more. Each problem was presented to different subjects in two versions: one that included only the basic outcome and another that included a more detailed scenario leading to the same outcome. For example, one-half of the subjects evaluated the probability of

> A massive flood somewhere in North America in 1983, in which more than 1,000 people drown.

The other half of the subjects evaluated the probability of

> An earthquake in California sometime in 1983, causing a flood in which more than 1,000 people drown.

The estimates of the conjunction (earthquake and flood) were significantly higher than the estimates of the flood ($p < .01$, by a Mann–Whitney test). The respective geometric means were 3.1% and 2.2%. Thus, a reminder that a devastating flood could be caused by the anticipated California earthquake made the conjunction of an earthquake and a flood appear more probable than a flood. The same pattern was observed in other problems.

The subjects in the second part of the study were 115 participants in the Second International Congress on Forecasting held in Istanbul, Turkey, in July 1982. Most of the subjects were professional analysts employed by industry, universities, or research institutes. They were professionally involved in forecasting and planning, and many had used scenarios in their work. The research design and the response scales were the same as before. One group of forecasters evaluated the probability of

> A complete suspension of diplomatic relations between the USA and the Soviet Union, sometime in 1983.

The other respondents evaluated the probability of the same outcome embedded in the following scenario:

A Russian invasion of Poland, and a complete suspension of diplomatic relations between the USA and the Soviet Union, sometime in 1983.

Although *suspension* is necessarily more probable than *invasion and suspension*, a Russian invasion of Poland offered a plausible scenario leading to the breakdown of diplomatic relations between the superpowers. As expected, the estimates of probability were low for both problems but significantly higher for the conjunction *invasion and suspension* than for *suspension* ($p < .01$, by a Mann–Whitney test). The geometric means of estimates were 0.47 percent and 0.14 percent, respectively. A similar effect was observed in the comparison of the following outcomes:

A 30% drop in the consumption of oil in the US in 1983.
A dramatic increase in oil prices and a 30% drop in the consumption of oil in the US in 1983.

The geometric means of the estimated probability of the first and the second outcomes, respectively, were 0.22% and 0.36%. We speculate that the effect is smaller in this problem (although still statistically significant) because the basic target event (a large drop in oil consumption) makes the added event (a dramatic increase in oil prices) highly available, even when the latter is not mentioned.

Conjunctions involving hypothetical causes are particularly prone to error because it is more natural to assess the probability of the effect given the cause than the joint probability of the effect and the cause. We do not suggest that subjects deliberately adopt this interpretation; rather, we propose that the higher conditional estimate serves as an anchor that makes the conjunction appear more probable.

Attempts to forecast events such as a major nuclear accident in the United States or an Islamic revolution in Saudi Arabia typically involve the construction and evaluation of scenarios. Similarly, a plausible story of how the victim might have been killed by someone other than the defendant may convince a jury of the existence of reasonable doubt. Scenarios can usefully serve to stimulate the imagination, to establish the feasibility of outcomes, or to set bounds on judged probabilities (Kirkwood & Pollock, 1982; Zentner, 1982). However, the use of scenarios as a prime instrument for the assessment of probabilities can be highly misleading. First, this procedure favors a conjunctive outcome produced by a sequence of likely steps (e.g., the successful execution of a plan) over an equally probable disjunctive outcome (e.g., the failure of a careful plan), which can occur in many unlikely ways (Bar-Hillel, 1973; Tversky & Kahneman, 1973). Second, the use of scenarios to assess probability is especially vulnerable to conjunction errors. A detailed scenario consisting of causally linked and representative events may appear more probable than a subset of these events (Slovic, Fischhoff, & Lichtenstein, 1976). This effect contributes to the appeal of scenarios and the illusory insight that they often provide. The attorney who fills in guesses regarding unknown facts, such as motive or mode of operation, may strengthen a case by improving its coherence, although such additions can only lower probability. Similarly, a political analyst can improve scenarios by adding plausible causes and representative consequences. As Pooh-Bah in *The Mikado* explains, such additions provide "corroborative details intended to give artistic verisimilitude to an otherwise bald and unconvincing narrative."

EXTENSIONAL CUES

The numerous conjunction errors reported in this article illustrate people's affinity for nonextensional reasoning. It is nonetheless obvious that people can understand and apply the extension rule. What cues elicit extensional considerations and what factors promote conformity to the conjunction rule? In this section, we focus on a single estimation problem and report several manipulations that induce extensional reasoning and reduce the incidence of the conjunction fallacy. The participants in the studies described in this section were statistically naive students at UBC. Mean estimates are given in parentheses.

> A health survey was conducted in a sample of adult males in British Columbia, of all ages and occupations. Please give your best estimate of the following values:
> What percentage of the men surveyed have had one or more heart attacks? (18%)
> What percentage of the men surveyed are both over 55 years old and have had one or more heart attacks? (30%)

This version of the health-survey problem produced a substantial number of conjunction errors among statistically naive respondents: 65% of the respondents ($N = 147$) assigned a strictly higher estimate to the second question than to the first [the incidence of the conjunction fallacy was considerably lower (28%) for a group of advanced undergraduates at Stanford University ($N = 62$) who had completed one or more courses in statistics]. Reversing the order of the constituents did not significantly affect the results.

The observed violations of the conjunction rule in estimates of relative frequency are attributed to the $A \rightarrow B$ paradigm. We propose that the probability of the conjunction is biased toward the natural assessment of the strength of the causal or statistical link between age and heart attacks. Although the statement of the question appears unambiguous, we considered the hypothesis that the respondents who committed the fallacy had actually interpreted the second question as a request to assess a conditional probability. A new group of UBC undergraduates received the same problem, with the second question amended as follows:

> Among the men surveyed who are over 55 years old, what percentage have had one or more heart attacks?

The mean estimate was 59% ($N = 55$). This value is significantly higher than the mean of the estimates of the conjunction (45%) given by those subjects who had committed the fallacy in the original problem. Subjects who violate the conjunction rule therefore do not simply substitute the conditional $P(B|A)$ for the conjunction $P(A\&B)$.

A seemingly inconsequential change in the problem helps many respondents avoid the conjunction fallacy. A new group of subjects ($N = 159$) were given the original questions but were also asked to assess the "percentage of the men surveyed who are over 55 years old" prior to assessing the conjunction. This manipulation reduced the incidence of conjunction error from 65% to 31%. It appears that many subjects were appropriately cued by the requirement to assess the relative frequency of both classes before assessing the relative frequency of their intersection.

The following formulation also facilitates extensional reasoning:

> A health survey was conducted in a sample of 100 adult males in British Columbia, of all ages and occupations. Please give your best estimate of the following values:
> How many of the 100 participants have had one or more heart attacks?
> How many of the 100 participants are both over 55 years old and have had one or more heart attacks?

The incidence of the conjunction fallacy was only 25% in this version ($N = 117$). Evidently, an explicit reference to the number of individual cases encourages subjects to set up a representation of the problems in which class inclusion is readily perceived and appreciated. We have replicated this effect in several other problems of the same general type. The rate of errors was further reduced to a record 11% for a group ($N = 360$) who also estimated the number of participants over 55 years of age prior to the estimation of the conjunctive category. The present findings agree with the results of Beyth-Marom (1981), who observed higher estimates for conjunctions in judgments of probability than in assessments of frequency.

The results of this section show that nonextensional reasoning sometimes prevails even in simple estimates of relative frequency in which the extension of the target event and the meaning of the scale are completely unambiguous. However, we found that the replacement of percentages by frequencies and the request to assess both constituent categories markedly reduced the incidence of the conjunction fallacy. It appears that extensional considerations are readily brought to mind by seemingly inconsequential cues. A contrast worthy of note exists between the effectiveness of extensional cues in the health-survey problem and the relative inefficacy of the methods used to combat the conjunction fallacy in the Linda problem (argument, betting, "whether or not"). The force of the conjunction rule is more readily appreciated when the conjunctions are defined by the intersection of concrete classes than by a combination of properties. Although classes and properties are equivalent from a logical standpoint, they give rise to different mental representations in which different relations and rules are transparent. The formal equivalence of properties to classes is apparently not programmed into the lay mind.

DISCUSSION

In the course of this project we studied the extension rule in a variety of domains; we tested more than 3,000 subjects on dozens of problems, and we examined numerous variations of these problems. The results reported in this article constitute a representative though not exhaustive summary of this work.

The data revealed widespread violations of the extension rule by naive and sophisticated subjects in both indirect and direct tests. These results were interpreted within the framework of judgmental heuristics. We proposed that a judgment of probability or frequency is commonly biased toward the natural assessment that the problem evokes. Thus, the request to estimate the frequency of a class elicits a search for exemplars, the task of predicting vocational choice from a personality sketch evokes a comparison of features, and a question about the cooccurrence of events induces an assessment of their causal connection. These assessments are not constrained by the extension rule. Although an arbitrary reduction in the extension of an event typically reduces its availability, representativeness, or causal coherence, there are numerous occasions in which these assessments are higher for the restricted event than for the inclusive event. Natural assessments can bias probability judgment in three ways: The respondents (a) may use a natural assessment deliberately as a strategy of estimation, (b) may be primed or anchored by it, or (c) may fail to appreciate the difference between the natural and required assessments.

Logic versus Intuition

The conjunction error demonstrates with exceptional clarity the contrast between the extensional logic that underlies most formal conceptions of probability and the natural assessments that govern many judgments and beliefs. However, probability judgments are not always dominated by nonextensional heuristics. Rudiments of probability theory have become part of the culture, and even statistically naive adults can enumerate possibilities and calculate odds in simple games of chance (Edwards, 1975). Furthermore, some real-life contexts encourage the decomposition of events. The chances of a team to reach the playoffs, for example, may be evaluated as follows: "Our team will make it if we beat team B, which we should be able to do since we have a better defense, or if team B loses to both C and D, which is unlikely since neither one has a strong offense." In this example, the target event (reaching the playoffs) is decomposed into more elementary possibilities that are evaluated in an intuitive manner.

Judgments of probability vary in the degree to which they follow a decompositional or holistic approach and in the degree to which the assessment and aggregation of probabilities are analytic or intuitive (see, e.g., Hammond &

Brehmer, 1973). At one extreme, there are questions (e.g., What are the chances of beating a given hand in poker?) that can be answered by calculating the relative frequency of "favorable" outcomes. Such an analysis possesses all the features associated with an extensional approach: It is decompositional, frequentistic, and algorithmic. At the other extreme, there are questions (e.g., What is the probability that the witness is telling the truth?) that are normally evaluated in a holistic, singular, and intuitive manner (Kahneman & Tversky, 1982b). Decomposition and calculation provide some protection against conjunction errors and other biases, but the intuitive element cannot be entirely eliminated from probability judgments outside the domain of random sampling.

A direct test of the conjunction rule pits an intuitive impression against a basic law of probability. The outcome of the conflict is determined by the nature of the evidence, the formulation of the question, the transparency of the event structure, the appeal of the heuristic, and the sophistication of the respondents. Whether people obey the conjunction rule in any particular direct test depends on the balance of these factors. For example, we found it difficult to induce naive subjects to apply the conjunction rule in the Linda problem, but minor variations in the health-survey question had a marked effect on conjunction errors. This conclusion is consistent with the results of Nisbett et al. (1983), who showed that lay people can apply certain statistical principles (e.g., the law of large numbers) to everyday problems and that the accessibility of these principles varied with the content of the problem and increased significantly with the sophistication of the respondents. We found, however, that sophisticated and naive respondents answered the Linda problem similarly in indirect tests and only parted company in the most transparent versions of the problem. These observations suggest that statistical sophistication did not alter intuitions of representativeness, although it enabled the respondents to recognize in direct tests the decisive force of the extension rule.

Judgment problems in real life do not usually present themselves in the format of a within-subjects design or of a direct test of the laws of probability. Consequently, subjects' performance in a between-subjects test may offer a more realistic view of everyday reasoning. In the indirect test it is very difficult even for a sophisticated judge to ensure that an event has no subset that would appear more probable than it does and no superset that would appear less probable. The satisfaction of the extension rule could be ensured, without direct comparisons of $A\&B$ to B, if all events in the relevant ensemble were expressed as disjoint unions of elementary possibilities. In many practical contexts, however, such analysis is not feasible. The physician, judge, political analyst, or entrepreneur typically focuses on a critical target event and is rarely prompted to discover potential violations of the extension rule.

Studies of reasoning and problem solving have shown that people often fail to understand or apply an abstract logical principle even when they can use it properly in concrete familiar contexts. Johnson-Laird and Wason (1977), for example, showed that people who err in the verification of *if–then* statements in an abstract format often succeed when the problem evokes a familiar schema. The present results exhibit the opposite pattern: People generally accept the conjunction rule in its abstract form (B is more probable than $A\&B$) but defy it in concrete examples, such as the Linda and Bill problems, in which the rule conflicts with an intuitive impression.

The violations of the conjunction rule were not only prevalent in our research, they were also sizable. For example, subjects' estimates of the frequency of seven-letter words ending with *ing* were three times as high as their estimates of the frequency of seven-letter words ending with __ *n* __. A correction by a factor of three is the smallest change that would eliminate the inconsistency between the two estimates. However, the subjects surely know that there are many __ *n* __ words that are not *ing* words (e.g., present, content). If they believe, for example, that only one-half of the __ *n* __ words end with *ing*, then a 6:1 adjustment would be required to make the entire system coherent. The ordinal nature of most of our experiments did not permit an estimate of the adjustment factor required for coherence. Nevertheless, the size of the effect was often considerable. In the rating-scale version of the Linda problem, for example, there was little overlap between the distributions of ratings for $T\&F$ and for T. Our problems, of course, were constructed to elicit conjunction errors, and they do not provide an unbiased estimate of the prevalence of these errors. Note, however, that the conjunction error is only a symptom of a more general phenomenon: People tend to overestimate the probabilities of representative (or available) events and/or underestimate the probabilities of less-representative events. The violation of the conjunction rule demonstrates this tendency even when the "true" probabilities are unknown or unknowable. The basic phenomenon may be considerably more common than the extreme symptom by which it was illustrated.

Previous studies of the subjective probability of conjunctions (e.g., Bar-Hillel, 1973; Cohen & Hansel, 1957; Goldsmith, 1978; Wyer, 1976; Beyth-Marom, 1981) focused primarily on testing the multiplicative rule $P(A\&B) = P(B)P(A/B)$. This rule is strictly stronger than the conjunction rule; it also requires cardinal rather than ordinal assessments of probability. The results showed that people generally overestimate the probability of conjunctions in the sense that $P(A\&B) > P(B)P(A/B)$. Some investigators, notably Wyer and Beyth-Marom, also reported data that are inconsistent with the conjunction rule.

Conversing under Uncertainty

The representativeness heuristic generally favors outcomes that make good stories or good hypotheses. The conjunction *feminist bank teller* is a better hypothesis about Linda than *bank teller*, and the scenario of a Russian invasion of Poland followed by a diplomatic crisis makes a better story than simply *diplomatic crisis*. The notion of a good story can be illuminated by extending the Gricean concept of cooperativeness (Grice, 1975) to conversations under uncertainty. The standard analysis of conversation rules assumes that the speaker knows the truth. The maxim of quality enjoins him or her to say only the truth. The maxim of quantity enjoins the speaker to say all of it, subject to the maxim of relevance, which restricts the message to what the listener needs to know. What rules of cooperativeness apply to an uncertain speaker – that is, one who is uncertain of the truth? Such a speaker can guarantee absolute quality only for tautological statements (e.g., "Inflation will continue so long as prices rise"), which are unlikely to earn high marks as contributions to the conversation. A useful contribution must convey the speaker's relevant beliefs even if they are not certain. The rules of cooperativeness for an uncertain speaker must therefore allow for a trade-off of quality and quantity in the evaluation of messages. The expected value of a message can be defined by its information value if it is true, weighted by the probability that it is true. An uncertain speaker may wish to follow the maxim of value: Select the message that has the highest expected value.

The expected value of a message can sometimes be improved by increasing its content, although its probability is thereby reduced. The statement, "Inflation will be in the range of 6% to 9% by the end of the year" may be a more valuable forecast than, "Inflation will be in the range of 3% to 12%," although the latter is more likely to be confirmed. A good forecast is a compromise between a point estimate, which is sure to be wrong, and a 99.9% credible interval, which is often too broad. The selection of hypotheses in science is subject to the same trade-off. A hypothesis must risk refutation to be valuable, but its value declines if refutation is nearly certain. Good hypotheses balance informativeness against probable truth (Good, 1971). A similar compromise obtains in the structure of natural categories. The basic level category *dog* is much more informative than the more inclusive category *animal* and only slightly less informative than the narrower category *beagle*. Basic-level categories have a privileged position in language and thought, presumably because they offer an optimal combination of scope and content (Rosch, 1978). Categorization under uncertainty is a case in point. A moving object dimly seen in the dark may be appropriately labeled *dog* whereas the subordinate *beagle* would be rash and the superordinate *animal* far too conservative.

Consider the task of ranking possible answers to the question, "What do you think Linda is up to these days?" The maxim of value could justify a preference for $T\&F$ over T in this task, because the added attribute *feminist* considerably enriches the description of Linda's current activities at an acceptable cost in probable truth. Thus, the analysis of conversation under uncertainty identifies a pertinent question that is legitimately answered by ranking the conjunction above its constituent. We do not believe, however, that the maxim of value provides a fully satisfactory account of the conjunction fallacy. First, it is unlikely that our respondents interpret the request to rank statements by their probability as a request to rank them by their expected (informational) value. Second, conjunction fallacies have been observed in numeric estimates and in choices of bets, to which the conversational analysis simply does not apply. Nevertheless, the preference for statements of high expected (informational) value could hinder the appreciation of the extension rule. As we suggested in the discussion of the interaction of picture size and real size, the answer to a question can be biased by the availability of an answer to a cognate question – even when the respondent is well aware of the distinction between them.

The same analysis applies to other conceptual neighbors of probability. The concept of surprise is a case in point. Although surprise is closely tied to expectations, it does not follow the laws of probability (Kahneman & Tversky, 1982b). For example, the message that a tennis champion lost the first set of a match is more surprising than the message that she lost the first set but won the match, and a sequence of four consecutive heads in a coin toss is more surprising than four heads followed by two tails. It would be patently absurd, however, to bet on the less-surprising event in each of these pairs. Our discussions with subjects provided no indication that they interpreted the instruction to judge probability as an instruction to evaluate surprise. Furthermore, the surprise interpretation does not apply to the conjunction fallacy observed in judgment of frequency. We conclude that surprise and informational value do not properly explain the conjunction fallacy, although they may well contribute to the ease with which it is induced and to the difficulty of eliminating it.

Cognitive Illusions

Our studies of inductive reasoning have focused on systematic errors because they are diagnostic of the heuristics that generally govern judgment and inference. In the words of Helmholtz (1881/1903), "It is just those cases that are not in accordance with reality which are particularly instructive for discovering the laws of the processes by which normal perception originates." The focus on bias and illusion is a research strategy that exploits human error, although it neither assumes nor entails that people are perceptually or cognitively inept. Helmholtz's position implies that perception is not usefully analyzed into a normal process that produces accurate percepts and a distorting process that produces errors and illusions. In cognition, as in perception, the same mechanisms produce both valid and invalid judgments. Indeed, the evidence does not seem to support a "truth plus error" model, which assumes a coherent system of beliefs that is perturbed by various sources of distortion and error. Hence, we do not share Dennis Lindley's optimistic opinion that "inside every incoherent person there is a coherent one trying to get out," (Lindley, 1980, personal communication) and we suspect that incoherence is more than skin deep (Tversky & Kahneman, 1981).

It is instructive to compare a structure of beliefs about a domain, (e.g., the political future of Central America) to the perception of a scene (e.g., the view of Yosemite Valley from Glacier Point). We have argued that intuitive judgments of all relevant marginal, conjunctive, and conditional probabilities are not likely to be coherent – that is, to satisfy the constraints of probability theory. Similarly, estimates of distances and angles in the scene are unlikely to satisfy the laws of geometry. For example, there may be pairs of political events for which $P(A)$ is judged greater than $P(B)$ but $P(A/B)$ is judged less than $P(B/A)$ (see Tversky and Kahneman, 1980). Analogously, the scene may contain a triangle ABC for which the A angle appears greater than the B angle, although the BC distance appears to be smaller than the AC distance.

The violations of the qualitative laws of geometry and probability in judgments of distance and likelihood have significant implications for the interpretation and use of these judgments. Incoherence sharply restricts the inferences that can be drawn from subjective estimates. The judged ordering of the sides of a triangle cannot be inferred from the judged ordering of its angles, and the ordering of marginal probabilities cannot be deduced from the ordering of the respective conditionals. The results of the present study show that it is even unsafe to assume that $P(B)$ is bounded by $P(A\&B)$. Furthermore, a system of judgments that does not obey the conjunction rule cannot be expected to obey more complicated principles that presuppose this rule, such as Bayesian updating, external calibration, and the maximization of expected utility. The presence of bias and incoherence does not diminish the normative force of these principles, but it reduces their usefulness as descriptions of behavior and hinders their prescriptive applications. Indeed, the elicitation of unbiased judgments and the reconciliation of incoherent assessments pose serious problems that presently have no satisfactory solution (Lindley, Tversky, & Brown, 1979; Shafer & Tversky, 1983).

The issue of coherence has loomed larger in the study of preference and belief than in the study of perception. Judgments of distance and angle can readily be compared to objective reality and can be replaced by objective measurements when accuracy matters. In contrast, objective measurements of probability are often unavailable, and most significant choices under risk require an intuitive evaluation of probability. In the absence of an objective criterion of validity, the normative theory of judgment under uncertainty has treated the coherence of belief as the touchstone of human rationality. Coherence has also been assumed in many descriptive analyses in psychology, economics, and other social sciences. This assumption is attractive because the strong normative appeal of the laws of probability makes violations appear implausible. Our studies of the conjunction rule show that normatively inspired theories that assume coherence are descriptively inadequate, whereas psychological analyses that ignore the appeal of normative rules are, at best, incomplete. A comprehensive account of human judgment must reflect the tension between compelling logical rules and seductive nonextensional intuitions.

2. Representativeness Revisited: Attribute Substitution in Intuitive Judgment

Daniel Kahneman and Shane Frederick

The program of research now known as the *heuristics and biases approach* began with a survey of 84 participants at the 1969 meetings of the Mathematical Psychology Society and the American Psychological Association (Tversky & Kahneman, 1971). The respondents, including several authors of statistics texts, were asked realistic questions about the robustness of statistical estimates and the replicability of research results. The article commented tongue-in-cheek on the prevalence of a belief that the law of large numbers applies to small numbers as well: Respondents placed too much confidence in the results of small samples, and their statistical judgments showed little sensitivity to sample size.

The mathematical psychologists who participated in the survey not only should have known better – they did know better. Although their intuitive guesses were off the mark, most of them could have computed the correct answers on the back of an envelope. These sophisticated individuals apparently had access to two distinct approaches for answering statistical questions: one that is spontaneous, intuitive, effortless, and fast; and another that is deliberate, rule-governed, effortful, and slow. The persistence of large biases in the guesses of experts raised doubts about the educability of statistical intuitions. Moreover, it was known that the same biases affect choices in the real world, where researchers commonly select sample sizes that are too small to provide a fair test of their hypotheses (Cohen, 1969, 1992). Tversky and Kahneman (1971) therefore concluded that intuitions should be regarded "with proper suspicion" and that researchers should "replace impression formation by computation whenever possible" (p. 31).

To explain the judgments they had observed, Tversky and Kahneman conjectured that observers expect the statistics of a sample to closely resemble (or "represent") the corresponding population parameters, even when the sample is small. This "representation hypothesis" soon led to the idea of a "representativeness heuristic," according to which some probability judgments (the likelihood that X is a Y) are mediated by assessments of resemblance (the

We thank Maya Bar-Hillel, Tom Gilovich, Dale Griffin, Ralph Hertwig, Denis Hilton, David Krantz, Barbara Mellers, Greg Pogarsky, Ilana Ritov, Norbert Schwarz, and Philip Tetlock for helpful comments.

49

degree to which X "looks like" a Y). This was the origin of the idea of heuristics in which a difficult question is answered by substituting an answer to an easier one – a theme that we develop further in this chapter.

From its earliest days, the heuristics and biases program was guided by the idea that intuitive judgments occupy a position – perhaps corresponding to evolutionary history – between the automatic parallel operations of perception and the controlled serial operations of reasoning. The boundary between perception and judgment is fuzzy and permeable: The *perception* of a stranger as menacing is inseparable from a *prediction* of future harm. Intuitive thinking extends perception-like processing from current sensations to judgment objects that are not currently present, including mental representations that are evoked by language. However, the representations on which intuitive judgments operate retain some features of percepts: They are concrete and specific, and they carry causal propensities and an affective charge.

A slower and more controlled mode of thinking governs the performance of unfamiliar tasks, the processing of abstract concepts, and the deliberate application of rules. A comprehensive psychology of intuitive judgment cannot ignore such controlled thinking, because intuition can be overridden or corrected by self-critical operations, and because intuitive answers are not always available. But this sensible position seemed irrelevant in the early days of research on judgment heuristics. The authors of the "law of small numbers" saw no need to examine correct statistical reasoning. They believed that including easy questions in the design would insult the participants and bore the readers. More generally, the early studies of heuristics and biases displayed little interest in the conditions under which intuitive reasoning is preempted or overridden – controlled reasoning leading to correct answers was seen as a default case that needed no explaining. A lack of concern for boundary conditions is typical of young research programs, which naturally focus on demonstrating new and unexpected effects, not on making them disappear. However, the topic of boundary conditions must eventually be faced as a program develops. The question of how biases are avoided was first addressed some time ago (Kahneman & Tversky, 1982; Tversky & Kahneman, 1983); we expand on it here.

The first section introduces a distinction between two families of cognitive operations, called *System 1* and *System 2*. The second section presents an attribute-substitution model of heuristic judgment, which elaborates and extends earlier treatments of the topic (Kahneman & Tversky, 1982; Tversky & Kahneman, 1974, 1983). The third section introduces a research design for studying attribute substitution. The fourth section discusses the controversy over the representativeness heuristic. The last section situates representativeness within a broad family of prototype heuristics, in which properties of a prototypical exemplar dominate global judgments concerning an entire set.

TWO FAMILIES OF COGNITIVE OPERATIONS

The ancient idea that cognitive processes can be partitioned into two main families – traditionally called *intuition* and *reason* – is now widely embraced under the general label of *dual-process theories* (Chaiken & Trope, 1999; Hammond, 1996; Sloman, 1996, Chapter 22, this volume). Dual-process models come in many flavors, but all distinguish cognitive operations that are quick and associative from others that are slow and rule-governed (Gilbert, 1999). We adopt the generic labels *System 1* and *System 2* from Stanovich and West (Chapter 24). These terms may suggest the image of autonomous homunculi, but such a meaning is not intended. We use *systems* as a label for collections of processes that are distinguished by their speed, controllability, and the contents on which they operate (Table 2.1.)

Although System 1 is more primitive than System 2, it is not necessarily less capable. On the contrary, complex cognitive operations eventually migrate from System 2 to System 1 as proficiency and skill are acquired. A striking demonstration of the intelligence of System 1 is the ability of chess masters to perceive the strength or weakness of chess positions instantly. For those experts, pattern matching has replaced effortful serial processing. Similarly, prolonged cultural exposure eventually produces a facility for social judgments – for example, an ability to recognize quickly that "a man whose dull writing is occasionally enlivened by corny puns" is more similar to a stereotypical computer programmer than to a stereotypical accountant.

In the particular dual-process model we assume, System 1 quickly proposes intuitive answers to judgment problems as they arise, and System 2 monitors the quality of these proposals, which it may endorse, correct, or override. The judgments that are eventually expressed are called *intuitive* if they retain the hypothesized initial proposal without much modification. The roles of the two systems in determining stated judgments depend on features of the task and of the individual, including the time available for deliberation (Finucane et al., 2000), the respondent's mood (Isen, Nygren, & Ashby, 1988; Bless et al., 1996), intelligence (Stanovich & West, Chapter 24), and exposure to statistical thinking (Nisbett et al., 1983; Agnoli & Krantz, 1989; Agnoli, 1991). We assume that System 1 and System 2 can be active concurrently, that automatic and controlled cognitive operations compete for the control of overt responses, and that deliberate

Table 2.1. Two Cognitive Systems

System 1 (Intuitive)	System 2 (Reflective)
Process Characteristics	
Automatic	Controlled
Effortless	Effortful
Associative	Deductive
Rapid, parallel	Slow, serial
Process opaque	Self-aware
Skilled action	Rule application
Content on Which Processes Act	
Affective	Neutral
Causal propensities	Statistics
Concrete, specific	Abstract
Prototypes	Sets

judgments are likely to remain anchored on initial impressions. Our views in these regards are similar to the "correction model" proposed by Gilbert and colleagues (1989, 1991) and to other dual-process models (Epstein, 1994; Hammond, 1996; Sloman, 1996).

In the context of a dual-system view, errors of intuitive judgment raise two questions: "What features of System 1 created the error?" and "Why was the error not detected and corrected by System 2?" (cf. Kahneman & Tversky, 1982). The first question is more basic, of course, but the second should not be neglected, as illustrated next.

The notions of heuristic and bias were introduced by Tversky and Kahneman (1974; Kahneman, Slovic and Tversky, 1982, p. 3) in the following paragraph:

The subjective assessment of probability resembles the subjective assessment of physical quantities such as distance or size. These judgments are all based on data of limited validity, which are processed according to heuristic rules. For example, the apparent distance of an object is determined in part by its clarity. The more sharply the object is seen, the closer it appears to be. This rule has some validity, because in any given scene the more distant objects are seen less sharply than nearer objects. However, the reliance on this rule leads to systematic errors in the estimation of distance. Specifically, distances are often overestimated when visibility is poor because the contours of objects are blurred. On the other hand, distances are often underestimated when visibility is good because the objects are seen sharply. Thus, the reliance on clarity as an indication leads to common biases. Such biases are also found in intuitive judgments of probability.

This statement was intended to extend Brunswik's (1943) analysis of the perception of distance to the domain of intuitive thinking and to provide a rationale for using biases to diagnose heuristics. However, the analysis of the effect of haze is flawed: It neglects the fact that an observer looking at a distant mountain possesses two relevant cues, not one. The first cue is the blur of the contours of the target mountain, which is positively correlated with its distance, when all else is equal. This cue should be given positive weight in a judgment of distance, and it is. The second relevant cue, which the observer can readily assess by looking around, is the ambient or general haziness. In an optimal regression model for estimating distance, general haziness is a suppressor variable, which must be weighted negatively because it contributes to blur but is uncorrelated with distance. Contrary to the argument made in 1974, using blur as a cue does not inevitably lead to bias in the judgment of distance – the illusion could just as well be described as a *failure to assign adequate negative weight to ambient haze*. The effect of haziness on *impressions* of distance is a failing of System 1; the perceptual system is not designed to correct for this variable. The effect of haziness on *judgments* of distance is a separate failure of System 2. Although people are capable of consciously correcting their impressions of distance for the effects of ambient haze, they commonly fail to do so. A similar analysis applies to some of the judgmental biases we discuss later, in which errors and biases only occur when both systems fail.

ATTRIBUTE SUBSTITUTION

Early research on the representativeness and availability heuristics was guided by a simple and general hypothesis: When confronted with a difficult question people often answer an easier one instead, usually without being aware of the substitution. A person who is asked "What proportion of long-distance relationships break up within a year?" may answer as if she had been asked "Do instances of swift breakups of long-distance relationships come readily to mind?" This would be an application of the availability heuristic. A professor who has heard a candidate's job talk and now considers the question "How likely is it that this candidate could be tenured in our department?" may answer the much easier question: "How impressive was the talk?" This would be an example of the representativeness heuristic.

The heuristics and biases research program has focused primarily on representativeness and availability – two versatile attributes that are automatically computed and can serve as candidate answers to many different questions. It has also focused on thinking under uncertainty. However, the restriction to particular heuristics and to a specific context is largely arbitrary. We will say that judgment is mediated by a heuristic when an individual assesses a specified *target attribute* of a judgment object by substituting another property of that object – the *heuristic attribute* – which comes more readily to mind. Many judgments are made by this process of *attribute substitution*. For an example, consider the well-known study by Strack, Martin, & Schwarz (1988), in which college students answered a survey that included these two questions: "How happy are you with your life in general?" and "How many dates did you have last month?" The correlation between the two questions was negligible when they occurred in the order shown, but it rose to 0.66 when the dating question was asked first. We suggest that thinking about the dating question automatically evokes an affectively charged evaluation of one's satisfaction in that domain of life, which lingers to become the heuristic attribute when the happiness question is subsequently encountered. The observed value of 0.66 certainly underestimates the true correlation between the target and heuristic attributes, because dating frequency is not a perfect proxy for romantic satisfaction and because of measurement error in all variables. The results suggest that respondents had little besides love on their mind when they evaluated their overall well-being.

Biases

Because the target attribute and the heuristic attribute are different, the substitution of one for the other inevitably introduces systematic biases. In this chapter we are mostly concerned with *weighting biases*, which arise when cues available to the judge are given either too much or too little weight. Criteria for determining optimal weights can be drawn from several sources. In the classic lens model, the optimal weights associated with different cues are the regression weights that optimize the prediction of an external criterion, such as physical distance or the GPA that a college applicant will attain (Brunswik, 1943; Hammond, 1955). Our analysis of weighting biases applies to such cases, but it also extends to attributes for which no objective criterion is available, such as an individual's overall happiness or the probability that a particular patient will survive surgery. Normative standards for these attributes must be drawn from the constraints of ordinary language, and they are often imprecise. For example, the conventional meaning of *overall happiness* does not specify how much weight ought to be given to various life domains. However, it certainly does require that substantial weight be given to every important domain of life, and that no weight at all be given to the current weather, or to the recent consumption of a cookie. Similar rules of common sense apply to judgments of probability. For example, the statement "John is more likely to survive a week than a month" is a true statement in ordinary usage, which implies a rule that people would wish their judgments to follow. Accordingly, neglect of duration in assessments of survival probabilities would be properly described as a weighting bias, even if there is no way to establish a normative probability for individual cases (Kahneman & Tversky, 1996).

In some judgmental tasks, information that could serve to supplement or correct the heuristic is not neglected or underweighted, but simply lacking. If asked to judge the relative frequency of words beginning with k or r (Tversky and Kahneman, 1973) or to compare the population of a familiar foreign city with one that is unfamiliar (Gigerenzer and Goldstein, 1996), respondents have little recourse but to base such judgments on ease of retrieval or recognition. The necessary reliance on these heuristic attributes renders such judgements susceptible to biasing factors (e.g., the amount of media coverage). However, unlike weighting biases, such biases of insufficient information cannot be described as errors of judgment, because there is no way to avoid them.

Accessibility and Substitution

The intent to judge a target attribute initiates a search for a reasonable value. Sometimes this search terminates almost immediately because the required value can be read from a stored memory (e.g., the question, "How tall are you?") or current experience ("How much do you like this cake?"). For other judgments, however, the target attribute does not come to mind immediately, but the search for it evokes the value of other attributes that are conceptually and associatively related (e.g., a question about overall happiness may retrieve the answer to a related question about satisfaction with a particular domain of life). Attribute substitution occurs when the target attribute is assessed by mapping the value of some other attribute on the target scale. This process will control judgment when three conditions are satisfied: (1) the target attribute is relatively inaccessible; (2) a semantically and associatively related attribute is highly accessible; and (3) the substitution of the heuristic attribute in the judgment is not rejected by the critical operations of System 2.

Some attributes are permanent candidates for the heuristic role because they are routinely evaluated as part of perception and comprehension, and therefore always accessible (Tversky and Kahneman, 1983). These natural assessments include physical properties such as size and distance, and more abstract properties such as similarity (e.g., Tversky & Kahneman, 1983), cognitive fluency in perception and memory (e.g., Jacoby and Dallas, 1991; Schwarz & Vaughn, Chapter 5, this volume; Tversky & Kahneman, 1973), causal propensity (Kahneman & Varey, 1990; Heider, 1944; Michotte, 1963), surprisingness (Kahneman & Miller, 1986), affective valence (e.g., Bargh, 1997; Cacioppo, Priester, & Berntson, 1993; Kahneman, Ritov, & Schkade, 1999; Slovic, Finucane, Peters, & MacGregor, Chapter 23, this volume; Zajonc, 1980), and mood (Schwarz & Clore, 1983). Other attributes are accessible only if they have been recently evoked or primed (see, e.g., Bargh et al., 1986; Higgins & Brendl, 1995). The 'romantic satisfaction heuristic' for judging happiness illustrates the effect of temporary accessibility. The same mechanism of attribute substitution is involved, whether the heuristic attribute is accessible chronically or only temporarily.

There is sometimes more than one candidate for the role of heuristic attribute. For an example borrowed from Anderson (1991), consider the question, "Are more deaths caused by rattlesnakes or bees?" A respondent who read recently about someone who died from a snakebite or bee sting may use the relative availability of instances of the two categories as a heuristic. If no instances come to mind, the respondent might consult impressions of the "dangerousness" of the typical snake or bee, an application of representativeness. Indeed, it is quite possible that the question initiates both a search for instances and an assessment of dangerousness, and that a contest of accessibility determines the role of the two heuristics in the final response. As Anderson observed, it is not always possible to determine *a priori* which heuristic governs the response to a particular problem.

Cross-Dimensional Mapping

The process of attribute substitution involves the mapping of the heuristic attribute of the judgment object onto the scale of the target attribute. Our notion of cross-dimensional mapping extends Stevens' (1975) concept of cross-modality matching. Stevens postulated that intensive attributes (e.g., brightness, loudness, the severity of crimes) can be mapped onto a common scale of sensory strength, allowing direct matching of intensity across modalities. Indeed, observers find it quite possible to match the loudness of sounds to the severity of crimes. Our conception allows other ways of comparing values across dimensions, such as matching relative positions (e.g., percentiles) in the frequency distributions or ranges of different attributes (Parducci, 1965). An impression of a student's position in the distribution of aptitude may be mapped directly onto a corresponding position in the distribution of academic achievement and then translated into a letter grade. Note that cross-dimensional matching is inherently nonregressive: A judgment or prediction is just as extreme as the impression mapped onto it. Ganzach and Krantz (1990) applied the term *univariate matching* to a closely related notion.

Cross-dimensional mapping presents special problems when the scale of the target attribute has no upper bound. Kahneman, Ritov, and Schkade (1999) discussed two situations in which an attitude (or affective valuation) is mapped onto an unbounded scale of dollars: Respondents in surveys may be required to indicate how much money they would contribute for a cause, and jurors are sometimes required to specify an amount of punitive damages against a negligent firm. The mapping of attitudes onto dollars is a variant of direct scaling in psychophysics, where respondents assign numbers to indicate the intensity of sensations (Stevens, 1975). The normal practice of direct scaling is for the experimenter to provide a *modulus* – a specified number that is to be associated to a standard stimulus. For example, respondents may be asked to assign the number 10 to the loudness of a standard sound and judge the loudness of other sounds relative to that standard. Stevens (1975) observed that when the experimenter fails to provide a modulus, respondents spontaneously adopt one. The judgments of each respondent are therefore internally coherent but the overall level of these judgments reflects the individual's modulus. Because different respondents may pick moduli that differ greatly (sometimes varying by a factor of 100 or more), the variability in judgments of particular stimuli is dominated by arbitrary individual differences in the size of the modulus. A similar analysis applies to situations in which respondents are required to use the dollar scale to express affection for a species or outrage toward a defendant. Just as Stevens' observers had no principled way to assign a number to a moderately loud sound, survey participants and jurors have no principled way to scale affection or outrage onto dollars. The analogy of scaling without a modulus has been used to explain the notorious variability of dollar responses in surveys of willingness to pay and in jury awards (Kahneman, Ritov, & Schkade, 1999; Kahneman, Schkade, & Sunstein, 1998).

The Affect Heuristics

The article that defined the heuristics and biases approach (Tversky and Kahneman, 1974) included anchoring and adjustment as a heuristic, along with representativeness and availability. However *anchoring* does not fit the definition of judgment heuristic we have adopted here because it does not work through the substitution of one attribute for another, but by increasing the plausibility of a particular value of the target attribute (Chapman & Johnson, Chapter 6, this volume).

It has become evident that an *affect heuristic* (Slovic et al., Chapter 23, this volume) should replace anchoring in the list of major general-purpose heuristics. In hindsight, the failure to identify this heuristic earlier reflects the narrowly cognitive focus that characterized psychology for some decades. There is now compelling evidence for the proposition that every stimulus evokes an affective evaluation, and that this evaluation can occur outside of awareness (see reviews by Zajonc, 1980, 1997; Bargh, 1997). *Affective valence* is a natural assessment, and therefore a candidate for substitution in the numerous situations in which an affectively loaded response is required. The affect heuristic fits the model of attribute substitution. Slovic and colleagues (Chapter 23, this volume) discuss how a basic affective reaction can be used as the heuristic attribute for a wide variety of more complex evaluations, such as the costs and benefit ratio of various technologies, the safe level of chemicals, or even the predicted economic performance of various industries. In the same vein, Kahneman and Ritov (1994) and Kahneman, Ritov, and Schkade (1999) proposed that an automatic affective valuation is the principal determinant of willingness to pay for public goods, and Kahneman, Schkade, and Sunstein (1998) interpreted jurors' assessments of punitive awards as a mapping of outrage onto a dollar scale of punishments.

The idea of a single affect heuristic should be treated as a useful oversimplification because good and bad come in many distinctive flavors. The semantic differential task illustrates both the basic unity and the diversity of valuation. Participants in this task rate objects and concepts on bipolar scales defined by pairs of adjectives, such as GOOD–BAD, KIND–CRUEL, LARGE–SMALL, STRONG–WEAK, WARM–COLD, and others. The main finding of this research is that adjectives such as KIND, PLEASANT, BEAUTIFUL, CUDDLY, and SAFE are all highly correlated measures of a single evaluation factor, which has its highest loading on GOOD. However, the adjectives also retain their distinctive meanings: "Justice," for example, is GOOD, but not especially KIND. Thus, "goodness," "kindness," "ugliness," and "outrageousness" are best viewed as closely related but distinguishable evaluative attributes that can give rise to closely related but distinguishable heuristics.

System 2: The Supervision of Intuitive Judgments

Our model assumes that an intuitive judgment is expressed overtly only if it is endorsed by System 2. The Stroop task illustrates this two-system structure. Observers who are instructed to report the color in which words are printed tend to stumble when the word is the name of another color (e.g., the word *BLUE* printed in green). The difficulty arises because the word is automatically read, and activates a response ("blue" in this case) that competes with the required response. Errors are rare in the Stroop test, indicating generally successful monitoring and control of the overt response, but the conflict produces delays and hesitations. The successful suppression of erroneous responses is effortful, and its efficacy is reduced by stress and distraction.

Gilbert (1989) described a correction model in which initial impulses are often wrong and normally overridden. He argues that people initially believe whatever they are told (e.g., "Whitefish love grapes") and that it takes some time and mental effort to "unbelieve" such dubious statements. Here again, cognitive load disrupts the controlling operations of System 2, increasing the rate of errors and revealing aspects of intuitive thinking that are normally suppressed. In an ingenious extension of this approach, Bodenhausen (1990) exploited natural temporal variability in alertness. He found that "morning people" were substantially more susceptible to a judgment bias (the conjunction fallacy) in the evening and that "evening people" were more likely to commit the fallacy in the morning.

Because System 2 is relatively slow, its operations can be disrupted by time pressure. Finucane et al. (2000) reported a study in which respondents judged the risks and benefits of various products and technologies (e.g., nuclear power, chemical plants, cellular phones). When participants were forced to respond within 5 seconds, the correlations between their judgments of risks and their judgments of benefits were strongly negative. The negative correlations were much weaker (although still pronounced) when respondents were given more time to ponder a response. When time is short, the same affective evaluation apparently serves as a heuristic attribute for assessments of both benefits and risks. Respondents can move beyond this simple strategy, but they need more than 5 seconds to do so. As this example illustrates, judgment by heuristic often yields simplistic assessments, which System 2 sometimes corrects by bringing additional considerations to bear.

Schwarz and his colleagues have shown that attribute substitution can be prevented by alerting respondents to the possibility that their judgment could be contaminated by an irrelevant variable (Schwarz & Clore, 1983; Schwarz, 1996). For example, sunny or rainy weather typically affects reports of well-being, but Schwarz and Clore (1983) found that merely asking respondents about the weather just before the well-being question eliminates the effect – apparently by reminding respondents that their current mood (a candidate heuristic attribute) is influenced by a factor (current weather) that is obviously irrelevant to the requested target attribute (overall well-being). Schwarz (1996) also found that the weight of any aspect of life on judgments of happiness is actually reduced by asking people to describe their satisfaction with that particular aspect of life just before the global question. As these examples illustrate, the effects of a variable on judgment are normally increased by priming (a System 1 effect), but can be reduced by an explicit reminder that brings the self-critical operations of System 2 into play.

We suspect that System 2 endorsements of intuitive judgments are granted quite casually under normal circumstances. Consider the puzzle: "A bat and a ball cost $1.10 in total. The bat costs $1 more than the ball. How much does the ball cost?" Almost everyone we ask reports an initial tendency to answer "10 cents" because the sum $1.10 separates naturally into $1 and 10 cents, and 10 cents is about the right magnitude. Many people yield to this immediate impulse. The surprisingly high rate of errors in this easy problem illustrates how lightly System 2 monitors the output of System 1: people are not accustomed to thinking hard, and are often content to trust a plausible judgment that quickly comes to mind.

The ball and bat problem elicits many errors, although it is not really difficult and certainly not ambiguous. A moral of this example is that people often make quick intuitive judgments to which they are not deeply committed. A related moral is that we should be suspicious of analyses that explain apparent errors by attributing to respondents a bizarre interpretation of the question. Consider someone who answers a question about happiness by reporting her satisfaction with her romantic life. The respondent is surely not committed to the absurdly narrow interpretation of *happiness* that her response seemingly implies. More likely, at the time of answering she thinks that she *is* reporting happiness: A judgment comes quickly to mind and is not obviously mistaken; end of story. Similarly, we propose that respondents who judge probability by representativeness do not seriously believe that the questions, "How likely is X to be a Y?" and "How much does X resemble the stereotype of Y?" are synonymous. People who make a casual intuitive judgment normally know little about how their judgment came about, and know even less about its logical entailments. Attempts to reconstruct the meaning of intuitive judgments by interviewing respondents (see e.g., Hertwig and Gigerenzer, 1999) are therefore unlikely to succeed because such probes require better introspective access and more coherent beliefs than people can normally muster.

Heuristics: Deliberate or Automatic?

So far, we have described judgment by heuristic as an intuitive and unintentional process of attribute substitution, which we attribute to System 1. However, attribute substitution can also be a deliberate System 2 strategy, as when a voter decides to evaluate candidates solely by their stance on a particular issue. In other cases, a heuristic is both initiated spontaneously by System 1 and deliberately adopted by System 2. The *recognition heuristic* proposed by Gigerenzer and his colleagues appears to fall in that class.

Experiments described by Gigerenzer and Goldstein (1996; see also Gigerenzer et al., 1999) show that respondents rely on feelings of familiarity and unfamiliarity to compare uncertain quantities, such as the relative size of two cities. For example, 78% of a sample of German students recognized San Diego as an American city, but only 4% recognized San Antonio, and every student who recognized San Diego but not San Antonio concluded (correctly) that San Diego is larger. Though far from perfect (the correlation between actual population and recognition was only 0.60 in that experiment), the recognition heuristic is surely a reasonable strategy for that task. Indeed, when students were given pairs of the 22 most populous cities in the United States or Germany, Americans slightly outperformed Germans when comparing the size of German cities, and Germans did slightly better than Americans when judging American cities (Gigerenzer & Goldstein, 1996).

Gigerenzer and his colleagues have described the recognition heuristic as a deliberate strategy, which in our terms is an operation of System 2. This description seems highly plausible. In addition, however, we have proposed that familiarity is an attribute that System 1 evaluates routinely, regardless of the current judgment goal. On this view, the recognition heuristic has an automatic component, which could be studied by varying tasks and by measuring reaction times. Imagine a reaction-time study in which respondents on each trial see a question such as "Which city name is printed in larger font?" or "Which city name contains more vowels?" immediately followed by a pair of cities that differ in familiarity. Research on conceptual Stroop effects (e.g., Keysar, 1989) suggests that the more familiar city name will be the favored answer to any question that is associatively related to prominence, size or quantity. On this hypothesis, errors will be systematic, and response times will be faster for compatible than for incompatible responses. An even more radical possibility, arising from the work of Gilbert (1989), Begg (see. e.g., Begg & Armour, 1991; Begg, Anas, & Farinacci, 1992), and Mandler (see, e.g., Mandler, Hamson, & Dorfman, 1990) is that there will be a bias favoring the familiar item as an answer to *any* question – perhaps even "Which city is *smaller*?" or "Which city has *fewer* dentists?" If either of these hypotheses is correct, the recognition heuristic belongs to the family of heuristics that we consider here. Like many other members of that family, the recognition heuristic for judging city sizes (1) draws on a "natural assessment" of recognition or familiarity, (2) may be endorsed as a deliberate strategy, (3) makes people look smart under some conditions, and (4) will produce systematic errors and biases, because impressions of familiarity and recognition are systematically correlated with factors other than city size, such as number of mentions in the media.

IDENTIFYING A HEURISTIC

Hypotheses about judgment heuristics have most often been studied by examining weighting biases and deviations from normative rules. However, the hypothesis that one attribute is substituted for another in a judgment task – for example, representativeness for probability – can also be tested more directly. In the *heuristic elicitation design*, one group of respondents provides judgments of a target attribute for a set of objects and another group evaluates the hypothesized heuristic attribute for the same objects. The substitution hypothesis implies that the judgments of the two groups, when expressed in comparable units (e.g., percentiles), will be identical. This section examines several applications of heuristic elicitation.

Eliciting Representativeness

Figure 2.1 displays the results of two experiments in which a measure of representativeness was elicited. These results were published long ago, but we repeat them here because they still provide the most direct evidence for both attribute substitution and the representativeness heuristic. For a more recent application of a similar design, see Bar-Hillel and Neter (1993, Chapter 3, this volume).

The object of judgment in the study from which Figure 2.1A is drawn (Kahneman & Tversky, 1973; p. 49 in Kahneman, Slovic and Tversky, 1982) was

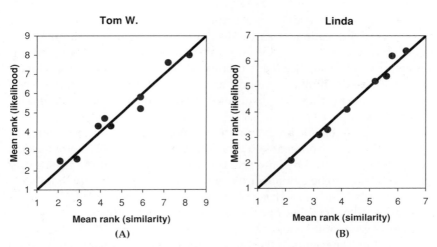

Figure 2.1. (A) Plot of average ranks for nine outcomes for Tom W., ranked by probability and similarity to stereotypes of graduate students in various fields (from Kahneman & Tversky, 1973) (B) Plot of average ranks for eight outcomes for Linda, ranked by probability and representativeness (from Tversky & Kahneman, 1982, p. 94).

the following description of a fictitious graduate student, which was shown along with a list of nine fields of graduate specialization:

Tom W. is of high intelligence, although lacking in true creativity. He has a need for order and clarity, and for neat and tidy systems in which every detail finds its appropriate place. His writing is rather dull and mechanical, occasionally enlivened by somewhat corny puns and by flashes of imagination of the sci-fi type. He has a strong drive for competence. He seems to have little feel and little sympathy for other people and does not enjoy interacting with others. Self-centered, he nonetheless has a deep moral sense. (p. 49)

Participants in a representativeness group ranked the nine fields of specialization by the degree to which Tom W. "resembles a typical graduate student." Participants in the probability group ranked the nine fields according to the likelihood of Tom W.'s specializing in each. Figure 2.1A plots the mean judgments of the two groups. The correlation between representativeness and probability is nearly perfect (.97). No stronger support for attribute-substitution could be imagined. The interpretation of the relationship between the attributes rests on two assumptions, both of which seem plausible: that representativeness is more accessible than probability, and that there is no third attribute that could explain both judgments.

The Tom W. study was also intended to examine the effect of the base rates of outcomes on categorical prediction. For that purpose, respondents in a third group estimated the proportion of graduate students enrolled in each of the nine fields. By design, some outcomes were defined quite broadly, whereas others were defined more narrowly. As intended, estimates of base-rates varied markedly across fields, ranging from 3% for Library Science to 20% for Humanities and Education. Also by design, the description of Tom W. included characteristics (e.g., introversion) that were intended to make him fit the stereotypes of the smaller fields (library science, computer science) better than the larger fields (humanities and social sciences). As intended, the correlation between the average judgments of representativeness and of base rates was strongly negative (−.65).

The logic of probabilistic prediction in this task suggests that the ranking of outcomes by their probabilities should be intermediate between their rankings by representativeness and by base rate frequencies. Indeed, if the personality description is taken to be a poor source of information, probability judgments should stay quite close to the base-rates. The description of Tom W. was designed to allow considerable scope for judgments of probability to diverge from judgments of representativeness, as this logic requires. Figure 2.1 shows no such divergence. Thus, the results of the Tom W. study simultaneously demonstrate the substitution of representativeness for probability and the neglect of known (but not explicitly mentioned) base rates.

Figure 2.1B is drawn from an early study of the Linda problem, the best known and most controversial example in the representativeness literature (Tversky & Kahneman, 1982, p. 92), in which a woman named Linda was described as follows:

Linda is 31 years old, single, outspoken, and very bright. She majored in philosophy. As a student, she was deeply concerned with issues of discrimination and social justice and also participated in antinuclear demonstrations.

As in the Tom W. study, separate groups of respondents were asked to rank a set of eight outcomes by representativeness and by probability. The results are shown in Fig. 2.1B. Again, the correlation between these rankings was almost perfect (.99).

Six of the eight outcomes that subjects were asked to rank were fillers (e.g., elementary school teacher, psychiatric social worker). The two critical outcomes were No. 6 (bank teller) and the so-called conjunction item No. 8 (bank teller and active in the feminist movement). Most subjects ranked the conjunction higher than its constituent, both in representativeness (85%) and probability (89%). The observed ranking of the two items is quite reasonable for judgments of similarity, but not for probability: Linda may resemble a feminist bank teller more than she resembles a bank teller, but she cannot be more likely to be a feminist bank teller than to be a bank teller. In this problem, reliance on representativeness yields probability judgments that violate a basic logical rule. As in the Tom W. study, the results make two points: they support the hypothesis of attribute substitution and also illustrate a predictable judgment error.

The entries plotted in Fig. 2.1 are averages of multiple judgments and the correlations are computed over a set of judgment objects. It should be noted that correlations between averages are generally much higher than corresponding correlations within the data of individual respondents (Nickerson, 1995). Indeed, group results may even be unrepresentative, if they are dominated by a few individuals who produce more variance than others and have an atypical pattern of responses. Fortunately, this particular hypothesis is not applicable to the experiments of Fig. 2.1, in which all responses were ranks.

Exploring the Outrage Heuristic

The results of Fig. 2.1 could be scored as a perfect hit for the hypothesis of attribute substitution in general and for the representativeness heuristic in particular. Next, we describe another study in the same design that yielded an instructive near-miss. One hypothesis of that study (Kahneman, Schkade, & Sunstein, 1998) couched in the language of the present treatment was that the setting of punitive damages in civil cases is mediated by an outrage heuristic. The heuristic elicitation procedure was used to test that hypothesis.

Participants drawn from a jury roll in Texas were shown vignettes of legal cases in which a plaintiff had suffered a personal injury while using a product. Respondents were told that the plaintiff had already been awarded compensatory damages, and that their next task as mock jurors was to determine whether punitive damages were also appropriate, and if so in what amount.

The study involved 28 variants of 10 basic scenarios. One of these scenarios concerned a child who had been burned when his pajamas caught fire as he was playing with matches. The pajamas were made of fabric that was not adequately fire-resistant, and the defendant firm had been aware of the problem. Each participant rated one version of each of the 10 scenarios. Two variables were manipulated experimentally as follows: For 4 of the 10 scenarios, 2 versions were constructed that differed in the severity of harm. In the high-harm version of the pajamas case, for example, the child was "severely burned over a significant portion of his body and required several weeks in the hospital and months of physical therapy." In the low-harm version, "the child's hands and arms were badly burned, and required professional medical treatment for several weeks." In addition, each of the 14 resulting vignettes was presented in two versions: one in which the defendant firm was large (annual profits in the range of $100–$200 million), and one in which it was of medium size ($10–$20 million). Each individual read vignettes involving firms of both sizes.

Respondents in a dollar punishment group were asked to indicate whether punitive damages were appropriate, and if so in what amount (the target attribute in this study). Respondents in the outrage group rated the outrageousness of the defendant's behavior (the hypothesized heuristic attribute). The mean outrageousness ratings and the median dollar awards were computed for each vignette. For the purpose of the present analysis, we also obtained (from 16 Princeton students) mean ratings of the severity of the harm suffered in each of the 14 vignettes. Lawsuits were not mentioned in these descriptions of harm.

Because the "pain" that a given financial penalty inflicts on a firm obviously varies with its annual profits, the relation between outrage and dollar awards was evaluated separately for large and small firms. Because dollar responses are known to be a very noisy measure, there was reason to expect that the fit of dollar awards to rated outrageousness would not be as impressive as the relationship between probability ranks and similarity ranks in Figs. 2.1A and 2.1B. Even with this allowance for noisy data, the correlations between the median punitive damages in dollars and the means of outrageousness ratings were disappointingly low: .77 for large firms and .87 for small firms. The main reason for the low correlations was an unanticipated discrepancy between the two measures in their sensitivity to the harm suffered by the plaintiff. Harm had no effect on outrageousness ratings, but did strongly affect dollar awards. When we reconsidered these data for this chapter, we concluded that the instructions to "judge the outrageousness of the defendant's *actions*" (italics ours) may have led many respondents to discount the harm resulting from these actions (Kahneman, Schkade, & Sunstein, 1998, offered a slightly different view). To test this interpretation, we defined a new variable for each case: the product of the average ratings of outrageousness and of harm. The data shown in Fig. 2.2 plot dollar punishments against this new variable. The correlations are still not as high as in Fig. 2.1, but they are now respectable: .90 for large firms and .94 for medium-sized firms.

We do not intend to suggest that respondents separately assessed outrageousness and harm and then computed their product; rather, we propose that the feeling of outrage is ordinarily sensitive to both the recklessness of the culprit and the suffering of the victim, but that the instructions to judge the outrageousness of the defendant's *actions* encouraged respondents to report something other than their immediate emotional response. In our view, the judgment of outrageousness is psychologically more complex than the emotion

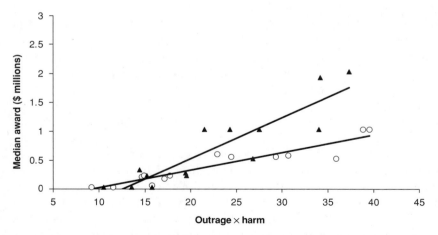

Figure 2.2. Median punitive awards (in dollars) for 14 cases, plotted against the product of average ratings of outrageousness and of severity of harm for each case, for large firms (filled triangles) and for medium-size firms (circles).

of outrage. This interpretation is *post hoc*, but testable in at least two ways: (1) The heuristic elicitation procedure could be repeated, with instructions that simply require a report of the respondent's anger or indignation rather than an evaluation of the defendant's behavior, or (2) the original heuristic elicitation procedure could be replicated under time pressure or cognitive load – manipulations that would interfere with discounting and thereby make outrageousness sensitive to harm.

Even when the heuristic elicitation procedure does demonstrate perfect correspondence (as it did for representativeness), the naming of a heuristic remains a judgment call. The analogy of naming factors in factor analysis is instructive: in both cases the appropriate label is rarely unique, although competing candidates are bound to have much in common. The *outrage heuristic* could just as well have been named the *indignation heuristic*, or perhaps just the *anger heuristic*. As is also the case in factor analysis, the label that is chosen for a heuristic may take on a life of its own in subsequent theorizing. We speculate that the course of research on heuristics could have been somewhat different if the *representativeness heuristic* had been named more simply the *similarity heuristic*.

THE REPRESENTATIVENESS CONTROVERSY

The experiments summarized in Fig. 2.1 provided direct evidence for the representativeness heuristic and two concomitant biases: neglect of base-rates and conjunction errors. In the terminology introduced by Tversky and Kahneman (1983), the design of these experiments was "subtle": adequate information was available for participants to avoid the error, but no effort was made to call their attention to that information. For example, participants in the Tom W. experiment had general knowledge of the relative base-rates of the various fields of specialization, but these base-rates were not explicitly mentioned in the problem. Similarly, both critical items in the Linda experiment were included in the list of outcomes, but they were separated by a filler so that respondents would not feel compelled to compare them. In the anthropomorphic language used here, System 2 was given a chance to correct the judgment, but was not prompted to do so.

In view of the confusing controversy that followed, it is perhaps unfortunate that the articles documenting base-rate neglect and conjunction errors did not stop with subtle tests. Each article also contained an experimental flourish – a demonstration in which the error occurred in spite of a manipulation that called participants' attention to the critical variable. The engineer–lawyer problem (Kahneman & Tversky, 1973) included special instructions to ensure that respondents would notice the base-rates of the outcomes. The brief personality descriptions shown to respondents were reported to have been drawn from a set containing descriptions of 30 lawyers and 70 engineers (or vice versa), and respondents were asked, "What is the probability that this description belongs to one of the 30 lawyers in the sample of 100?" To the authors' surprise, base rates were largely neglected in the responses, despite their salience in the instructions. Similarly, the authors were later shocked to discover that more than 80% of undergraduates committed a conjunction error even when asked point blank whether Linda was more likely to be "a bank teller" or "a bank teller who is active in the feminist movement" (Tversky & Kahneman, 1983). The novelty of these additional direct or "transparent" tests was the finding that respondents continued to show the biases associated with representativeness even in the presence of strong cues pointing to the normative response. The errors that people make in transparent judgment problems are analogous to observers' failure to allow for ambient haze in estimating distances: A correct response is within reach, but not chosen, and the failure involves an unexpected weakness of the corrective operations of System 2.

Discussions of the heuristics and biases approach have focused almost exclusively on the direct conjunction fallacy and on the engineer–lawyer problems. These are also the only studies that have been extensively replicated with varying parameters. The amount of critical attention is remarkable, because the studies were not, in fact, essential to the authors' central claim. In the terms of the present treatment, that claim was that intuitive prediction is an operation of System 1, which is susceptible both to base-rate neglect and conjunction fallacies. There was no intent to deny the possibility of System 2 interventions that would modify or override intuitive predictions. Thus, the articles in which these studies appeared would have been substantially the same, although far less provocative, if respondents had overcome base-rate neglect and conjunction errors in transparent tests.

To appreciate why the strong forms of base-rate neglect and of the conjunction fallacy sparked so much controversy, it is useful to distinguish two conceptions of human rationality (Kahneman, 2000b). *Coherence rationality* is the strict conception, which requires the agent's entire system of beliefs and preferences to be internally consistent, and immune to effects of framing and context. For example, an individual's probability P ("Linda is a bank teller") should be the sum of the probabilities P ("Linda is a bank teller and is a feminist"), and P ("Linda is a bank teller and not a feminist"). A subtle test of coherence rationality could be conducted by asking individuals to assess these three probabilities on separate occasions under circumstances that minimize recall. Coherence can also be tested in a between-groups design. Assuming random assignment, the sum of the average probabilities assigned to the two component events should equal the average judged probability of "Linda is a bank teller." If this prediction fails, then at least some individuals are incoherent. Demonstrations of incoherence present a significant challenge to important models of decision theory and economics, which attribute to agents a very strict form of rationality (Tversky & Kahneman, 1986). Failures of perfect coherence are less provocative to psychologists, who have a more realistic view of human capabilities.

A more lenient concept, *reasoning rationality*, only requires an ability to reason correctly about the information currently at hand, without demanding perfect consistency among beliefs that are not simultaneously evoked. The best known violation of reasoning rationality is the famous "four-card" problem (Wason, 1960). The failure of intelligent adults to reason their way through this problem is surprising because the problem is "easy," in the sense of being easily understood once explained. What everyone learns, when first told that intelligent people fail to solve the four-card problem, is that one's expectations about human reasoning abilities had not been adequately calibrated. There is, of course, no well-defined metric of reasoning rationality, but whatever metric one uses, the Wason problem calls for a downward adjustment. The surprising results of the Linda and engineer–lawyer problems led Tversky and Kahneman to a similar realization: The reasoning of their subjects was less proficient than they had anticipated. Many readers of the work shared this conclusion, but many others strongly resisted it.

The implicit challenge to reasoning rationality was met by numerous attempts to dismiss the findings of the engineer–lawyer and the Linda studies as artifacts of ambiguous language, confusing instructions, conversational norms, or inappropriate normative standards. Doubts have been raised about the proper interpretation of almost every word in the conjunction problem, including *bank teller, probability,* and even *and* (see, e.g., Dulany & Hilton, 1991; Hilton & Slugoski, 2001). These claims are not discussed in detail here. We suspect that most of them have some validity, and that they identified mechanisms that may have made the results in the engineer–lawyer and Linda studies exceptionally strong. However, we note a significant weakness shared by all these critical discussions: They provide no explanation of the essentially perfect consistency of the judgments observed in direct tests of the conjunction rule and in three other types of experiments: (1) subtle comparisons; (2) between-Ss comparisons; and, most importantly, (3) judgments of representativeness (see also Bar-Hillel and Neter, 1993, Chapter 3, this volume). Interpretations of the conjunction fallacy as an artifact implicitly dismiss the results of Fig. 2.1B as a coincidence (for an exception, see Ayton, 1998). The story of the engineer–lawyer problem is similar. Here again, multiple demonstrations in which base rate information was used (see Koehler, 1996, for a review) invite the inference that there is no general problem of base-rate neglect. Again, the data of prediction by representativeness in Fig. 2.1A (and related results reported by Kahneman & Tversky, 1973) were ignored.

The demonstrations that under some conditions people avoid the conjunction fallacy in direct tests, or use explicit base-rate information, led some scholars to the blanket conclusion that judgment biases are artificial and fragile, and that there is no need for judgment heuristics to explain them. This position was promoted most vigorously by Gigerenzer (1991). Kahneman and Tversky (1996) argued in response that the heuristics and biases position does not preclude the possibility of people performing flawlessly in particular variants of the Linda and of the lawyer–engineer problems. Because laypeople readily acknowledge the validity of the conjunction rule and the relevance of base-rate information, the fact that they sometimes obey these principles is neither a surprise nor an argument against the role of representativeness in routine intuitive prediction. However, the study of conditions under which errors are avoided can help us understand the capabilities and limitations of System 2. We develop this argument further in the next section.

Making Biases Disappear: A Task for System 2

Much has been learned over the years about variables and experimental procedures that reduce or eliminate the biases associated with representativeness. We next discuss conditions under which errors of intuition are successfully overcome, and some circumstances under which intuitions may not be evoked at all.

Statistical Sophistication. The performance of statistically sophisticated groups of respondents in different versions of the Linda problem illustrates the effects of both expertise and research design (Tversky and Kahneman, 1983). Statistical expertise provided no advantage in the eight-item version, in which the critical items were separated by a filler and were presumably considered separately. In the two item-version, in contrast, respondents were effectively compelled to compare "bank teller" to "bank teller and is active in the feminist movement." The incidence of conjunction errors dropped dramatically for the statistically sophisticated in this condition, but remained essentially unchanged among the statistically naïve. Most of the experts followed logic rather than intuition when they recognized that one of the categories contained the other. In the absence of a prompt to compare the items, however, the statistically sophisticated made their predictions in the same way as everyone else does – by representativeness. As Stephen Jay Gould (1991, p. 469) noted, knowledge of the truth does not dislodge the *feeling* that Linda is a feminist bank teller: "I know [the right answer], yet a little homunculus in my head continues to jump up and down, shouting at me – 'but she can't just be a bank teller; read the description.'"

Intelligence. Stanovich and West (Chapter 24, this volume) and Stanovich (1999) observed a generally negative correlation between conventional measures of intelligence and susceptibility to judgment biases. They used transparent versions of the problems, which provide adequate cues to the correct answer and therefore provide a test of reasoning rationality. Not surprisingly, intelligent people are more likely to possess the relevant logical rules and also to recognize the applicability of these rules in particular situations. In the terms of the present analysis, high-IQ respondents benefit from relatively efficient System 2 operations that enable them to overcome erroneous intuitions when adequate information is available. When a problem is too difficult for everyone, however, the correlation is likely to reverse because the more intelligent respondents are more likely to agree on a plausible error than to respond randomly (Kahneman, 2000b).

Frequency Format. Relative frequencies (e.g., 1 in 10) are more vividly represented and more easily understood than equivalent probabilities (.10) or percentages (10%). For example, the emotional impact of statements of risk is enhanced by the frequency format: "1 person in 1000 will die" is more frightening than a probability of .001 (Slovic et al., Chapter 23, this volume). The frequency representation also makes it easier to visualize partitions of sets and detect that one set is contained in another. As a consequence, the conjunction fallacy is generally avoided in direct tests, in which the frequency format makes it easy to recognize that feminist bank tellers are a subset of bank tellers (Gigerenzer & Hoffrage, 1995; Tversky & Kahneman, 1983). For similar reasons, some base-rate problems are more easily solved when couched in frequencies than in probabilities or percentages (Cosmides & Tooby, 1996). However, there is little support for the more general claims about the evolutionary adaptation of the mind to deal with frequencies (Evans et al., 2000). Furthermore, the ranking of outcomes by predicted relative frequency is very similar to the ranking of the same outcomes by representativeness (Mellers, Hertwig, & Kahneman, 2001). We conclude that the frequency format affects the corrective operations of System 2, not the intuitive operations of System 1; the language of frequencies improves respondents' ability to impose the logic of set inclusion on their considered judgments, but does not reduce the role of representativeness in their intuitions.

Manipulations of Attention. The weight of neglected variables can be increased by drawing attention to them, and experimenters have devised many ingenious ways to do so. Schwarz et al. (1991) found that respondents pay more attention to base-rate information when they are instructed to think as statisticians rather than clinical psychologists. Krosnick, Li, and Lehman (1990), exploited conversational conventions about the sequencing of information and confirmed that the impact of base-rate information was enhanced by presenting that information *after* the personality description rather than before it. Attention to the base-rate is also enhanced when participants observe the drawing of descriptions from an urn (Gigerenzer, Hell, & Blank, 1988), perhaps because watching the draw induces conscious expectations that reflect the known proportions of possible outcomes. The conjunction fallacy can also be reduced or eliminated by manipulations that increase the accessibility of the relevant rule, including some linguistic variations (Macchi, 1995), and practice with logical problems (Agnoli, 1991; Agnoli & Krantz, 1989).

The interpretation of these attentional effects is straightforward. We assume that most participants in judgment studies know, at least vaguely, that the base-rate is relevant and that the conjunction rule is valid (Kahneman & Tversky, 1982). Whether they apply this knowledge to override an intuitive judgment depends on their cognitive skills (education, intelligence) and on formulations that make the applicability of a rule apparent (frequency format) or a relevant factor more salient (manipulations of attention). We assume that intuitions are less sensitive to these factors, and that the appearance or disappearance of biases mainly reflects variations in the efficacy of corrective operations. This conclusion would be circular, of course, if the corrective operations were both inferred from the observation of correct performance and used to explain that performance. Fortunately, the circularity can be avoided – because the role of System 2 can be verified, for example, by using manipulations of time pressure, cognitive load, or mood to interfere with its operations.

Within-Subjects Factorial Designs. The relative virtues of between-subjects and within-subjects designs in studies of judgment are a highly contentious issue. Factorial designs have their dismissive critics (e.g., Poulton, 1989) and their vigorous defenders (e.g., Birnbaum, 1999). We do not attempt to adjudicate this controversy here. Our narrower point is that between-subjects designs are more appropriate for the study of heuristics of judgment. The following arguments favor this conclusion:

- Factorial designs are transparent. Participants are likely to identify the variables that are manipulated – especially if there are many trials and especially in a fully factorial design, in which the same stimulus attributes are repeated in varying combinations. The message that the design conveys to the participants is that the experimenter expects to find effects of every factor that is manipulated (Bar-Hillel & Fischhoff, 1981; Schwarz, 1996).
- Studies that apply a factorial design to judgment tasks commonly involve schematic and impoverished stimuli. The tasks are also highly repetitive. These features encourage participants to adopt simple mechanical rules that will allow them to respond quickly, without forming an individuated impression of each stimulus. For example, Ordóñez and Benson (1997) required respondents to judge the attractiveness of gambles on a 100-point scale. They found that under time pressure many respondents computed or estimated the expected values of the gambles and used the results as attractiveness ratings (e.g., a rating of 15 for a 52% chance to win $31.50).
- Factorial designs often yield judgments that are linear combinations of the manipulated variables. This is a central conclusion of a massive research effort conducted by Anderson and colleagues (see Anderson, 1996), who observed that people often average or add where they should multiply.

In summary, the factorial design is not appropriate for testing hypotheses about biases of neglect, because it effectively guarantees that no manipulated factor is neglected. Figure 2.3 illustrates this claim by several examples of an additive extension effect discussed further in the next section. The experiments summarized in the different panels share three important features: (1) In each case, the quantitative variable plotted on the abscissa was completely neglected in similar experiments conducted in a between-subjects or subtle design; (2) in each case, the quantitative variable combines additively with other information; (3) in each case, a compelling normative argument can be made for a quasi-multiplicative rule in which the lines shown in Fig. 2.3 should fan out. For example, Fig. 2.3C presents a study of categorical prediction (Novemsky & Kronzon, 1999) in which the respondent judged the relative likelihood that a person was a member of one occupation rather than another (e.g., computer

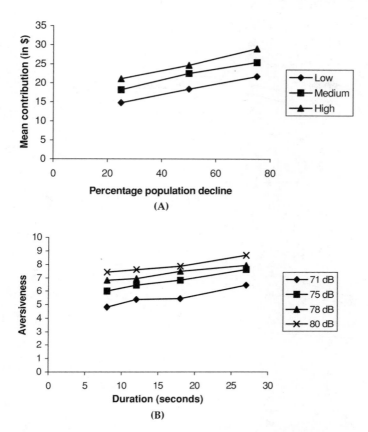

Figure 2.3. (A) Willingness to pay to restore damage to species that differ in popularity as a function of the damage they have suffered (from Kahneman, Ritov, & Schkade, 1999); (B) Global evaluations of aversive sounds of different loudness as a function of duration for subjects selected for their high sensitivity to duration (from Schreiber & Kahneman, 2000).

programmer vs. flight attendant) on the basis of short personality sketches (e.g., "shy, serious, organized, and sarcastic") and one of three specified base rates (10%, 50%, or 90%). Representativeness and base-rate were varied factorially within subjects. The effect of base-rate is clearly significant in this design (see also Birnbaum and Mellers, 1983). Furthermore, the effects of representativeness and base-rate are strictly additive. As Anderson (1996) argued, averaging (a special case of additive combination) is the most obvious way to combine the effects of two variables that are recognized as relevant, e.g., "she looks like a bank teller, but the base-rate is low." Additivity is not normatively appropriate in this case – any Bayes-like combination would produce curves that initially fan out from the origin and converge again at high values. Similar considerations apply to the other three panels of Fig. 2.3 (discussed later).

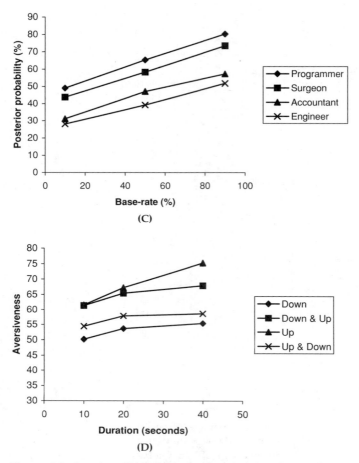

Figure 2.3. *(continued)* (C) Ratings of probability for predictions that differ in representativeness as a function of base-rate frequency (from Novemsky & Kronzon, 1999); (D) Global evaluations of episodes of painful pressure that differ in temporal profile as a function of duration (Ariely, 1998).

Between-subjects and factorial designs often yield different results in studies of intuitive judgment. Why should we believe one design rather than the other? The main argument against the factorial design is its poor ecological validity. Rapidly successive encounters with objects of rigidly controlled structure are unique to the laboratory, and the solutions that they evoke are not likely to be typical. Direct comparisons among concepts that differ in only one variable – such as *bank teller* and *feminist bank tellers* – also provide a powerful hint and a highly unusual opportunity to overcome intuitions. The between-subjects design in contrast, mimics the haphazard encounters in which most judgments

are made and is more likely to evoke the casually intuitive mode of judgment that governs much of mental life in routine situations (e.g., Langer,
1978).

PROTOTYPE HEURISTICS AND THE NEGLECT OF EXTENSION

In this section, we offer a common account of three superficially dissimilar
judgmental tasks: (1) categorical prediction (e.g., "In a set of 30 lawyers and
70 engineers, what is the probability that someone described as 'charming,
talkative, clever, and cynical' is one of the lawyers?"); (2) summary evaluations
of past events (e.g., "Overall, how aversive was it to be exposed for 30 minutes to your neighbor's car alarm?"); and (3) economic valuations of public
goods (e.g.,"What is the most you would be willing to pay to prevent 200,000
migrating birds from drowning in uncovered oil ponds?"). We propose that a
generalization of the representativeness heuristic accounts for the remarkably
similar biases that are observed in these diverse tasks.

The original analysis of categorical prediction by representativeness
(Kahneman & Tversky 1973; Tversky & Kahneman, 1983) invoked two assumptions in which the word *representative* was used in different ways: (1) a prototype
(a *representative exemplar*) is used to represent categories (e.g. bank tellers) in the
prediction task; (2) the probability that the individual belongs to a category is
judged by the degree to which the individual resembles (is *representative* of) the
category stereotype. Thus, categorical prediction by representativeness involves
two separate acts of substitution – the substitution of a prototypical exemplar
for a category, and the substitution of the heuristic attribute of similarity for
the target attribute of probability. Perhaps because they share a label, the two
processes have not been distinguished in discussions of the representativeness
heuristic. We separate them here by describing *prototype heuristics*, in which a
prototype is substituted for its category, but in which *representativeness* is not
necessarily the heuristic attribute.

The target attributes to which prototype heuristics are applied are extensional. An *extensional attribute* pertains to an aggregated property of a set or category for which an extension is specified – the probability that a set of lawyers
includes Jack; the overall unpleasantness of a set of moments of hearing a car
alarm; and the personal value of saving a certain number of birds from drowning
in oil ponds. Normative judgments of extensional attributes are governed by
a general principle of *conditional adding*, which dictates that each element of
the set adds to the overall judgment an amount that depends on the elements
already included. In simple cases, conditional adding is just regular adding –
the total weight of a collection of chairs is the sum of their individual weights.
In other cases, each element of the set contributes to the overall judgment, but
the combination rule is not simple addition and is typically subadditive. For
example, the economic value of protecting X birds should be increasing in X,

but the value of saving 2,000 birds is for most people less than twice as large as the value of saving 1,000 birds.

The logic of categorical prediction entails that the probability of membership in a category should vary with its relative size, or base-rate. In prediction by representativeness, however, the representation of outcomes by prototypical exemplars effectively discards base-rates, because the prototype of a category (e.g., lawyers) contains no information about the size of its membership. Next, we show that phenomena analogous to the neglect of base-rate are observed in other prototype heuristics: the monetary value attached to a public good is often insensitive to its *scope* and the global evaluations of a temporally extended experience is often insensitive to its *duration*. These various instantiations of *extension neglect* (neglect of base rates, scope, and duration) have been discussed in separate literatures, but all can be explained by the two-part process that defines prototype heuristics: (1) a category is represented by a prototypical exemplar, and (2) a (nonextensional) property of the prototype is then used as a heuristic attribute to evaluate an extensional target attribute of the category. As might be expected from the earlier discussion of base-rate neglect, extension neglect in all its forms is most likely to be observed in between-subjects experiments. Within-subject factorial designs consistently yield the *additive extension effect* illustrated in Fig. 2.3.

Scope Neglect in Willingness to Pay

The contingent valuation method (CVM) was developed by resource economists (see Mitchell & Carson, 1989) as a tool for assessing the value of public goods for purposes of litigation or cost–benefit analysis. Participants in contingent valuation (CV) surveys are asked to indicate their willingness to pay (WTP) for specified public goods, and their responses are used to estimate the total amount that the community would pay to obtain these goods. The economists who design contingent valuation surveys interpret WTP as a valid measures of economic value and assume that statements of WTP conform to the extensional logic of consumer theory. The relevant logic has been described by a critic of CVM (Diamond, 1996), who illustrates the conditional adding rule by the following example: in the absence of income effects, WTP for saving X birds should equal WTP for saving (X-k) birds, plus WTP to save k birds, where the last value is contingent on the costless prior provision of safety for (X-k) birds (Diamond, 1996).

Strict adherence to Bayes' rule may be an excessively demanding standard for intuitive predictions; similarly, it would be too much to ask for WTP responses that strictly conform to the "add-up rule." In both cases, however, it seems reasonable to expect *some* sensitivity to extension – to the base rate of outcomes in categorical prediction and to the scope of the good in WTP. In fact, several studies have documented nearly complete neglect of scope in CV surveys. The best-known demonstration of scope neglect is an experiment by Desvouges et al. (1993), who used the scenario of migratory birds that drown in oil ponds. The number of birds said to die each year was varied across groups. The WTP responses were completely insensitive to this variable, as the mean WTPs for saving 2,000, 20,000, or 200,000 birds were $80, $78, and $88, respectively.

A straightforward interpretation of this result involves the two acts of substitution that characterize prototype heuristics. The deaths of numerous birds are first represented by a prototypical instance, perhaps an image of a bird soaked in oil and drowning. The prototype automatically evokes an affective response, and the intensity of that emotion is then mapped onto the dollar scale – substituting the readily accessible heuristic attribute of affective intensity for the more complex target attribute of economic value. Other examples of radical insensitivity to scope lend themselves to a similar interpretation. Among others, Kahneman and Knetsch (see Kahneman, 1986) found that Toronto residents were willing to pay almost as much to clean up polluted lakes in a small region of Ontario as to clean up all the polluted lakes in Ontario, and McFadden and Leonard (1993) reported that residents in four western states were willing to pay only 28% more to protect 57 wilderness area than to protect a single area (for more discussion of scope insensitivity, see Frederick & Fischhoff, 1998).

The similarity between WTP statements and categorical predictions is not limited to such demonstrations of almost complete extension neglect. The two responses also yield similar results when extension and prototype information are varied factorially within subjects. Fig. 2.3A shows the results of a study of WTP for programs that prevented different levels of damage to species of varying popularity (Ritov and Kahneman, unpublished observations; cited in Kahneman, Ritov & Schkade, 1999). As in the case of base-rate (Fig. 2.3 C), extensional information (levels of damage) combines additively with nonextensional information. This rule of combination is unreasonable; in any plausible theory of value the lines would fan out.

Finally, the role of the emotion evoked by a prototypical instance was also examined directly in the same experiment, using the heuristic elicitation paradigm introduced earlier. Some respondents were asked to imagine that they saw a television program documenting the effect of adverse ecological circumstances on individual members of different species. The respondents indicated, for each species, how much concern they expected to feel while watching such a documentary. The correlation between this measure of affect and willingness to pay, computed across species, was .97.

Duration Neglect in the Evaluation of Experiences

We next discuss experimental studies of the global evaluation of experiences that extend over some time, such as a pleasant or a horrific film clip (Fredrickson & Kahneman, 1993), a prolonged unpleasant noise (Schreiber & Kahneman, 2000), pressure from a vise (Ariely, 1998), or a painful medical procedure (Redelmeier & Kahneman, 1996). Participants in these studies provided

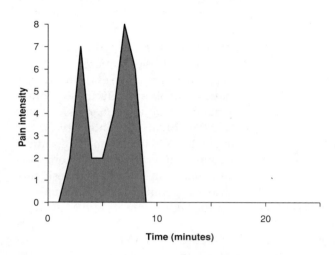

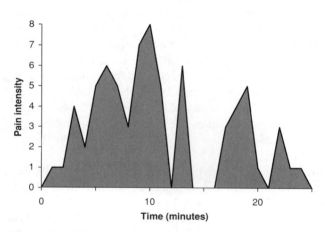

Figure 2.4. Pain intensity reported by two colonoscopy patients.

a continuous or intermittent report of hedonic or affective state, using a designated scale of momentary affect (Fig. 2.4). When the episode had ended, they indicated a global evaluation of "the *total* pain or discomfort" associated with the entire episode.

We first examine the normative rules that apply to this task. The global evaluation of a temporally extended outcome is an extensional attribute, which is governed by a distinctive logic. The most obvious rule is temporal monotonicity: there is a compelling intuition that adding an extra period of pain to an episode of discomfort can only make it worse overall. Thus, there are two ways of making a bad episode worse – making the discomfort more intense or prolonging it. It must therefore be possible to trade off intensity against duration. Formal analyses have identified conditions under which the total utility of an episode is equal to the temporal integral of a suitably transformed measure of the instantaneous utility associated with each moment (Kahneman, 2000d; Kahneman, Wakker, & Sarin, 1997).

Next, we turn to the psychology. Fredrickson and Kahneman (1993) proposed a "snapshot model" for the retrospective evaluation of episodes, which again involves two acts of substitution: first, the episode is represented by a prototypical moment; next, the affective value attached to the representative moment is substituted for the extensional target attribute of global evaluation. The snapshot model was tested in an experiment in which participants provided continuous ratings of their affect while watching plotless films that varied in duration and affective value (e.g., fish swimming in coral reefs; pigs being beaten to death with clubs), and later reported global evaluations of their experiences. The central finding was that the retrospective evaluations of these observers were predicted with substantial accuracy by a simple average of the Peak Affect recorded during a film and the End Affect reported as the film was about to end. This has been called the *Peak/End Rule*. However, the correlation between retrospective evaluations and the duration of the films was negligible, a finding that Fredrickson and Kahneman labeled *duration neglect*. The resemblance of duration neglect to the neglect of scope and base-rate is striking, and unlikely to be accidental. In the present analysis, all three are manifestations of extension neglect, caused by the use of a prototype heuristic.

The Peak/End Rule and duration neglect have both been confirmed on multiple occasions. Figure 2.4 presents raw data from a study reported by Redelmeier and Kahneman (1996), in which patients undergoing colonoscopy reported their current level of pain every 60 seconds throughout the procedure. Here again, an average of Peak/End pain quite accurately predicted subsequent global evaluations and choices. The duration of the procedure varied considerably among patients (from 4 to 69 minutes), but these differences were not reflected in subsequent global evaluations, in accord with duration neglect. The implications of these psychological rules of evaluation are paradoxical. In Fig. 2.4, for example, it appears evident that patient B had a worse colonoscopy than patient A (assuming that they used the scale similarly). However, it is also apparent that the Peak/End average was worse for patient A, whose procedure ended at a moment of relatively intense pain. The Peak/End rule prediction for these two profiles is that A would evaluate the procedure more negatively than B, and would be more more likely to prefer to undergo a barium enema rather than a repeat colonoscopy. The prediction was correct for these two individuals, and confirmed by the data of a large group of patients.

The effects of substantial variations of duration remained small (though statistically robust) even in studies conducted in a factorial design. Figure 2.3D is drawn from a study of responses to ischemic pain (Ariely, 1998) in which duration varied by a factor of 4. The Peak/End average accounted for 98% of the systematic variance of global evaluations in that study and 88% of the variance in a similar factorial study of responses to loud unpleasant sounds (Schreiber & Kahneman, 2000, panel 3b). Contrary to the normative standard for an extensional attribute, the effects of duration and other determinants of evaluation were additive (see panels b and d in Figure 3).

The participants in these studies were well aware of the relative duration of their experiences and did not consciously decide to ignore duration in their evaluations. As Fredrickson and Kahneman (1993, p. 54) noted, duration neglect is an attentional phenomenon:

[D]uration neglect does not imply that duration information is lost, nor that people believe that duration is unimportant. . . . people may be aware of duration and consider it important in the abstract [but] what comes most readily to mind in evaluating episodes are the salient moments of those episodes and the affect associated with those moments. Duration neglect might be overcome, we suppose, by drawing attention more explicitly to the attribute of time.

This comment applies equally well to other instances of extension neglect: the neglect of base-rate in categorical prediction, the neglect of scope in willingness to pay, the neglect of sample size in evaluations of evidence (Griffin & Tversky, 1992; Tversky & Kahneman, 1971), and the neglect of probability of success in evaluating a program of species preservation (DeKay & McClelland, 1995). More generally, inattention plays a similar role in any situation in which the intuitive judgments generated by System 1 violate rules that would be accepted as valid by the more deliberate reasoning that we associate with System 2. As we noted earlier, the responsibility for these judgmental mishaps is properly shared by the two systems: System 1 produces the initial error, and System 2 fails to correct it, although it could.

Violations of Dominance

The conjunction fallacy observed in the Linda problem is an example of a dominance violation in judgment: Linda must be at least as likely to be a bank teller as to be a feminist bank teller, but people believe the opposite. Insensitivity to extension (in this case, base-rate) effectively guarantees the existence of such dominance violations. For another illustration, consider the question, "How many murders were there last year in [Detroit/Michigan]?" Although there cannot be more murders in Detroit than in Michigan because Michigan contains Detroit, the word *Detroit* evokes a more violent image than the word *Michigan* (except, of course, for people who immediately think of Detroit when Michigan is mentioned). If people use an impression of violence as a heuristic and neglect geographic extension, their estimates of murders in the city may exceed their estimates for the state. In a large sample of University of Arizona students, this hypothesis was confirmed – the median estimate of the number of murders was 200 for Detroit, and 100 for Michigan.

Violations of dominance akin to the conjunction fallacy have been observed in several other experiments, involving both indirect (between-subjects) and direct tests. In a clinical experiment reported by Redelmeier, Katz, and Kahneman (2001), half of a large group of patients ($N = 682$) undergoing a colonoscopy were randomly assigned to a condition that made the actual experience strictly worse. Unbeknownst to the patient, the physician deliberately delayed the removal of the colonoscope for approximately 1 minute beyond the normal time. For many patients, the mild discomfort of that extra period was an improvement relative to the pain than they had just experienced. For these patients, of course, prolonging the procedure reduced the Peak/End average of discomfort. As expected, retrospective evaluations were less negative in the experimental group. Remarkably, a 5-year follow-up showed that participants in that group were also somewhat more likely to comply with recommendations to undergo a repeat colonoscopy (Redermeier, Katz, & Kahneman, 2001).

In an experiment that is directly analogous to the demonstrations of the conjunction fallacy, Kahneman et al. (1993) exposed participants to two cold-pressor experiences, one with each hand: a short episode (immersion of one hand in 14°C water for 60 seconds), and a long episode (the short episode plus an additional 30 seconds during which the water was gradually warmed to 15°C). The participants indicated the intensity of their pain throughout the experience. When they were later asked which of the two experiences they preferred to repeat, a substantial majority chose the long trial. These choices violate dominance, because after 60 seconds in cold water most people prefer the immediate experience of a warm towel to 30 extra seconds of slowly diminishing pain. In a replication, Schreiber and Kahneman (2000, Exp. 2) exposed participants to pairs of unpleasant noises in immediate succession. The participants listened to both sounds and chose one to be repeated at the end of the session. The short noise lasted 8 seconds at 77 db. The long noise consisted of the short noise plus an extra period (of up to 24 sec) at 66 db (less aversive, but still unpleasant and certainly worse than silence). Here again, the longer noise was preferred most of the time, and this unlikely preference persisted over a series of five choices.

The violations of dominance in these direct tests are particularly surprising because the situation is completely transparent. The participants in the experiments could easily retrieve the durations of the two experiences between which they had to choose, but the results suggest that they simply ignored duration. A simple explanation is that the results reflect "choosing by liking" (see Frederick, Chapter 30, this volume). The participants in the experiments simply followed the normal strategy of choice: "When choosing between two familiar options, consult your retrospective evaluations and choose the one that you like most (or dislike least)." *Liking* and *disliking* are products of System 1 that do not conform to the rules of extensional logic. System 2 could have intervened, but in these experiments, it generally did not. Kahneman et al. (1993) described a participant in their study who chose to repeat the long cold-pressor experience. Soon after the choice was recorded, the participant was asked which of the two experiences was longer. As he correctly identified the long trial, the participant was heard to mutter, "The choice I made doesn't seem to make much sense." *Choosing by liking* is a form of mindlessness (Langer, 1978) that illustrates the casual governance of System 2.

Like the demonstrations of the conjunction fallacy in direct tests (discussed earlier), violations of temporal monotonicity in choices should be viewed as an expendable flourish. Because the two aversive experiences occurred within a few minutes of each other, and because respondents could recall accurately the duration of the two events, System 2 had enough information to override choosing by liking. Its failure to do so is analogous to the failure of people to appreciate the set inclusion rule in direct tests of the conjunction fallacy. In both cases, the violations of dominance tell us nothing new about System 1; they only illustrate an unexpected weakness of System 2. Just as the theory of intuitive categorical prediction would have remained intact if the conjunction fallacy had not "worked" in a direct test, the model of evaluation by moments would have survived even if violations of dominance had been eliminated in highly transparent situations. The same methodological issues arise in both contexts. Between-subjects experiments or subtle tests are most appropriate for studying the basic intuitive evaluations of System 1, and also most likely to reveal complete extension neglect. Factorial designs in which extension is manipulated practically guarantee an effect of this variable, and almost guarantee that it will be additive, as in Figures 2.3B and 2.3D (Ariely, 1998; Ariely, Kahneman, & Loewenstein, 2000; Schreiber and Kahneman, 2000). Finally, although direct choices sometimes yield systematic violations of dominance, these violations can be avoided by manipulations that prompt System 2 to take control.

In our view, the similarity of the results obtained in diverse contexts is a compelling argument for a unified interpretation, and a significant challenge to critiques that pertain only to selected subsets of this body of evidence. A number of commentators have offered competing interpretations of base-rate neglect (Cosmides & Tooby, 1996; Koehler, 1996), insensitivity to scope in WTP (Kopp, 1992), and duration neglect (Ariely & Loewenstein, 2000). However, these interpretations are generally specific to a particular task and would not carry over to analogous findings in other domains. Similarly, the various attempts to explain the conjunction fallacy as an artifact do not explain analogous violations of dominance in the cold-pressor experiment. The account we offer is, in contrast, equally applicable to all three contexts and possibly others as well (see also Kahneman, Ritov, & Schkade, 1999). We attribute extension neglect and violations of dominance to a lazy System 2 and a prototype heuristic that combines two processes of System 1: the representation of categories by prototypes and the substitution of a nonextensional heuristic attribute for an extensional target attribute. We also propose that people have some appreciation of the role of extension in the various judgment tasks. Consequently, they incorporate extension in their judgments when their attention is drawn to this factor – most reliably in factorial experiments and sometimes (although not always) in direct tests. The challenge for competing interpretations is to provide a unified account of the diverse phenomena that have been considered in this section.

FINAL COMMENTS

The goal of the heuristics and biases program in its early days was to understand intuitive judgment under uncertainty, not develop a unified theory of it. *Judgment heuristics* were described as a collection of disparate cognitive procedures that are bound together by their common function in a particular domain. In contrast, we argue here that heuristics share a common process of attribute substitution and are not limited to questions about uncertain events. Our treatment is otherwise firmly anchored in previous work. The substitution of one question for another, the representation of categories by prototypes, the view of erroneous intuitions as easy to override but almost impossible to eradicate – all these ideas are quite old (Kahneman, Slovic, & Tversky, 1982). We show here that the same ideas apply to a diverse class of difficult judgments, including retrospective evaluations of colonoscopies and decisions about saving birds from drowning in oil.

Ironically, the original research program might have been less interesting, and less influential, if the scope of its central concept had been appreciated and made explicit at the outset. The attention that the program attracted was due in no small part to an expository style in which illustrative examples embedded in the text turn readers into observers. A more general treatment could not have exploited this style because broad categories, in the classic Roschian sense, do not have 'good' exemplars. Just as a robin is a good bird but a mediocre animal, the Linda problem is a compelling illustration of a conjunction fallacy, but a less obvious example of a violation of dominance. The restriction of the original treatment of judgment heuristics to the domain of uncertainty was therefore as fortunate as it was arbitrary. We believe that the interpretation of representativeness and of other heuristics that we have offered here is both more complete and more general than earlier versions. But the original concepts, at least for us, had a charm that this more elaborate analysis cannot match.

3. How Alike Is It? versus How Likely Is It?: A Disjunction Fallacy in Probability Judgments

Maya Bar-Hillel and Efrat Neter

The extension rule in probability theory states that if *A* is a subset of *B*, then the probability of *A* cannot exceed that of *B*. A special case of the extension rule is the conjunction rule, which states that the probability of *A&B* can exceed the probability of neither *A* nor *B* because it is contained in both.

Tversky and Kahneman (1983) demonstrated that under certain circumstances, people predictably and systematically violate the conjunction rule. In one study, they gave subjects the following description:

Linda is 31 years old, single, outspoken, and very bright. She majored in philosophy. As a student, she was deeply concerned with issues of discrimination and social justice, and also participated in anti-nuclear demonstrations (p. 297).

This was followed by a list of eight possible outcomes, each describing possible activities of Linda at the present time (her job, her interests, or both). Subjects were asked to rank order the outcomes by the probability that they describe Linda's current activities. Of the eight, one was representative of Linda ("Linda is active in the feminist movement"), one was unrepresentative of Linda ("Linda is a bank teller"), and one was a conjunction of these two ("Linda is a bank teller and is active in the feminist movement"). A large majority of the subjects (85%) rated the conjunctive outcome, "Linda is a bank teller and is active in the feminist movement," more probable than "Linda is a bank teller."

This result was predicted from the representativeness hypothesis: "Representativeness is an assessment of the degree of correspondence between a sample and a population, an instance and a category, an act and an actor or, more generally, between an outcome and a model" (Tversky & Kahneman, 1983, p. 295). Kahneman and Tversky (1972, 1973) provided much evidence that people often judge the probability of an outcome given a model by the extent to which the outcome represents the model. In addition, Tversky (1977) showed that adding to an outcome (*O*) a feature (*F*) that matches a model (*M*) enhances the match between the outcome and the model. In other words, the match of *O&F* to *M* can be greater than the match of *O* to *M*. Hence, insofar as people judge the probability of outcomes by their representativeness, being a bank teller and active

This is an edited and condensed version of a paper that first appeared in the *Journal of Personality and Social Psychology, 65,* 1119–1131. Copyright © 1986 by the American Psychological Association. Adapted with permission.

in the feminist movement would be judged more likely an outcome for Linda than being a bank teller, due to the addition of a feature that is representative of Linda (feminism) to her unrepresentative job. Whereas there is nothing logically wrong with the judgment that being a feminist bank teller is more *representative* of Linda than being a bank teller, judging the conjunctive outcome to be more *probable* than its constituent violates the logically necessary conjunction rule.

Another special case of the extension rule is the disjunction rule, according to which the probability of *A*-or-*B* can be smaller than neither the probability of *A* nor the probability of *B* because it contains both. Formally speaking, there is no difference between the three rules (conjunction, disjunction, and extension) because for any pair of events *A* and *B* in which *B* is a subset of *A*, *A* can always be represented as a disjunction, one of whose constituents is *B*, and *B* can always be represented as a conjunction, one of whose constituents is *A*. For example, one can argue that the set of bank tellers is a disjunction – of bank tellers who are active feminists with bank tellers who are not. Viewed in this way, Tversky and Kahneman's (1983) results could just as well have been labeled the *disjunction fallacy*. Why, then, are they regarded as a *conjunction fallacy*? Is this just a matter of arbitrary choice?

Formally speaking, the answer is yes, but psychological considerations favor one view over another. Consider the category *parent* and its subcategory *mother*. One can just as well choose to view *mother* as the conjunction of *parent* with *female* as to view *parent* as the disjunction of *mother* with *father*. In contrast, the category *bank teller* does not naturally evoke a representation as a union, and certainly not as a union of bank tellers who are active feminists with bank tellers who are not. At the same time, the subcategory of bank tellers who are active feminists can hardly be described except by resort to the conjunction of these two constituents. Indeed, the language does not even contain a single-word label to designate this category. In that sense, the categories *bank teller* and *bank teller and active feminist* are more naturally viewed, respectively, as a unitary category and a conjunction of two categories than as a disjunction of two categories and a unitary category.

How, then, might one create a category that would be naturally viewed as disjunctive? The simplest possibility to come to mind is to replace the connective *and* used to create conjunctive categories with the connective *or*. This idea must be implemented with caution, however, because the English words *and* and *or* do not always quite correspond to the logical connectives *and* and *or*. First, the English *or* is often understood in its exclusive sense of "*A* or *B*, but not both," as in, "The party will take place next week or the week after." Second, the English *and* can be used to create a union as well as an intersection – the sentences, "She invited colleagues *or* relatives" and "She invited colleagues *and* relatives" could be used to describe the same guest list. Third, and most pertinent to present concerns, not all categories that can be joined meaningfully by one of these connectives lend themselves to as meaningful a joining by the other. For example, whereas putting *and* between *bank teller* and *active in the feminist movement* creates a meaningful category, putting *or* between these two category names creates a rather odd one. Similarly, whereas the question, "Is Linda more likely to be a bank teller, or a bank teller and active in the feminist movement?" makes some sense, the question, "Is Linda more likely to be a bank teller, or a bank teller or active in the feminist movement?" sounds to us rather confusing. . . .

STUDY 1

For this study, we sought categories that would be disjunctive in character, yet defined without the connective *or*. Our solution derived from Rosch's work on categorization (e.g., Rosch, 1978). Recall that the classification of objects into categories is not unique. Thus, the same object can be classified as "artifact," "furniture," "chair," "office chair," or "Eleanor's black leather office chair," to mention but a few possibilities. Yet most people would usually think of it as just "chair." In the hierarchy of nested categories, the level at which objects are commonly classified is known as "the basic level category" (Rosch, 1978).

We capitalized on the observation that basic level categories are typically unitary (i.e., standardly thought of as neither conjunctive nor disjunctive categories), whereas higher levels are often disjunctive (e.g., "furniture" is the union set of "chairs," "tables," "beds," "cupboards"), and lower levels are often conjunctive (e.g., "leather chair"). However, superordinate categories often enjoy a name or label of their own, and are not explicitly defined as compound sets. If a described instance were to match a unitary category more than it matched its superordinate, a disjunction error could potentially arise.

Table 3.1 shows the five types of questions that we devised: (1) the instance is a brief personality description of a student, and the options are fields of university study (Danielle and Oded); (2) the instance is a brief personality description, and the options are places of residence (Gidi and Eldar); (3) the instance is a description of a place, and the options are countries or continents (Gila and Na'ama); (4) the instance is a brief personality description, and the options are sociopolitical movements (Eli and Ze'ev); and (5) the instance is a brief personality description, and the options are causes of death (Yaron and Y.C.).

The target option (i.e., the one designed to be most representative of the instance) was selected to be a basic level category name. The superordinate categories are natural ones, designated by familiar proper names or labels. To strengthen the tendency to view them as a union, their names were prefaced by the words *one of the* or *some kind of*. For example, the basic level cause of death "car accident" was paired with the superordinate "some kind of unnatural cause."

All questions were accompanied by seven options. To give a typical example, the list of fields of university studies provided with the description of Danielle was: literature, humanities, physics, natural sciences, geography or geology, statistics, and political science (not in this order). It is important to note that the lists always included two pairs of a basic level category and its superordinate category (here, literature, humanities, physics, and natural sciences). Also, there was an option defined with the connective *or* (here, geography or geology). The actual ordering of the various options varied from problem to problem.

Israeli university students taking summer courses (about 60 in advanced economics, 40 in elementary economics, 40 in statistics, 60 in mathematics, 35 in accounting, 15 in sociology) were given from one to four prediction problems, but never two of the same type. On the whole, this subject population is comparable to the populations identified in other studies (e.g., Tversky & Kahneman, 1983; Wolford, Taylor, & Beck, 1990) as "informed," although subject sophistication was not one of the variables studied here.

There are several concerns a disjunction fallacy might raise. First, we were concerned that subjects who see a disjunctive category listed alongside one of its constituents would interpret the disjunctive category in the subtractive sense. For example, given "one of the European countries" alongside "Switzerland," some subjects might implicitly exclude Switzerland from the European countries. Even though Tversky and Kahneman (1983) and Morier and Borgida (1984) ruled out this account of the conjunction fallacy, and it seems unlikely altogether with our natural categories, we thought it prudent to explicitly discourage the possibility....

Our approach was simply to include in the subjects' instructions the following explicit cautionary note:

It is quite possible for something to be included in more than one option listed. For example, suppose the list is of foodstuffs, and one option is "frozen foods" while another is "desserts." In this case, do not interpret "frozen foods" as "frozen foods excluding desserts," nor interpret "desserts" as "desserts which are not frozen" – "ice cream" qualifies as both "frozen food" and "dessert."

The second concern has to do with linguistic conventions. With respect to the assertion of disjunctions, it is "*misleading* (though not false) for a speaker to make a disjunctive assertion where he is in a position to assert one of the disjuncts. Thus, when a speaker asserts A or B he cannot assert A by itself since it is too uncertain" (Adams, 1975, pp. 19–20). For example, I am uncertain when I saw you last, and I assert that "it was either at last year's Psychonomics or when I was in Boston this summer." A listener who assumes Gricean cooperativeness would be justified in inferring from this assertion that I believe the disjunction is fairly likely, but neither of its constituents is sufficiently likely to be asserted by itself.

Applying the value maxim to our problems, a cooperative speaker under uncertainty would only assert, "Danielle is majoring in the humanities" if he or she is not in a position to assert the more informative "Danielle is a literature major." If, however, one can assert, "Danielle is a literature major," one would not assert, "Danielle is majoring in the humanities" because that would mislead a listener into thinking, counterfactually, that one could not have asserted,

Table 3.1. Stimuli Used in Experiment 1

Character	Target Category	Target Superordinate Category	Foil Category	Foil Superordinate Category	Description
Danielle	Literature	Humanities	Physics	Natural sciences	Sensitive and introspective. In high school she wrote poetry secretly. Did her military service as a teacher. Though beautiful, she has little social life, since she prefers to spend her time reading quietly at home rather than partying. What does she study?
Oded	Physics	Natural sciences	Literature	Humanities	Did his military service as a combat pilot. Was a brilliant high school student, whose teachers predicted for him an academic career. Independent and original, diligent and honest. His hobbies are shortwave radio and Astronomy. What does he study?
Gidi	Tel Aviv	Dan metropolitan area	Hadar Ha'Carmel	The North of Israel	23 years old, he wears the latest fashions, and drives a new sportscar. He spends time in discotheques and expensive pubs, and is a social butterfly. He is occasionally mentioned in the gossip columns. Where does he live?
Eldar	Kibbutz Rosh Ha'Nikra	The North of Israel	North Tel Aviv	Dan metropolitan area	23 years old, he dresses modestly, and wears sandals year-round, even in winter. He is tanned from outdoor work. He spends his leisure time hiking in the countryside. Where does he live?

Name					
Gila	Japan	Asia	North America	Canada	Writes letter home describing a densely populated country, in which modern technology coexists with an ancient local culture. The people, hardworking and competitive, are not inclined to invite strangers into their homes. Where was the letter written?
Na'ama	Switzerland	Europe	Latin America	Brazil	Writes letter home describing a country with snowy wild mountains, clean streets, and flower decked porches. Where was the letter written?
Eli	Peace Now	A peace movement	A national movement	Gush Emunim	39 years old, a professor of Greek Philosophy and Ethics, he holds socialist views. Following the Lebanon War he became politically active, while remaining a "bleeding heart." Where is he active?
Ze'ev	Gush Emunim	A national movement	A peace movement	Peace Now	39 years old, with a red beard and fiery eyes. Married, and a devoted father of five, he teaches Holy Studies in a West Bank settlement. He immigrated from the US 18 years ago. He spends his leisure time hiking in the countryside. Where is he active?
Yaron	Road accident	Unnatural cause	Disease	Cancer	Till he died suddenly at 27, was full of gaiety and life. A womanizer, he often drank, and acted wildly in parties and on the road. To his concerned friends he always said, "It couldn't happen to me." What did he die of?
Y.C.	Lung cancer	Cancer	Unnatural cause	Road accident	A woman who smoked over a packet a day for over 10 years. What did she die of?

"Danielle is a literature major." Hence, the disjunctive assertion, rather than following logically from the more specific assertion, is actually incompatible with it, in the sense that the two would be made under non-overlapping conditions. The rules of conversational implicature differ from those of logical entailment.

In a betting paradigm (as well as in some legal contexts, most notably contracts), however, logical entailment overrides conversational implicatures. The proposition that "Danielle is majoring in the humanities" is undeniably verified on learning that "Danielle is a literature major." Even a cooperative speaker, who in everyday conversation would not assert that "Danielle is majoring in the humanities" when "Danielle is a literature major" could be asserted, can legitimately prefer to bet that "Danielle is majoring in the humanities" than that "Danielle is a literature major." The conditions for asserting propositions do not coincide with the conditions for betting on them. In particular, one might sometimes legitimately prefer to assert A than B, yet prefer to bet on B than on A.

To address this concern, we ran two variants of our problems. In the first, subjects were asked to rank the listed categories by the probability that they included the described case as a member. In the second, a different group of subjects ranked the categories by their willingness to bet that the described case was a member in these categories. In this task, no mention whatsoever was made of the word *probability* (thus excluding any confusions this term might engender). In a betting paradigm, the question of why particular outcomes were chosen to be stated and not others is not as relevant as it is for the original task. There may be conditions under which one would be more likely to assert A than A-or-B, but there are no conditions under which a bet on A is more likely to win than a bet on A-or-B.

Results and Discussion

The results are shown in Table 3.2. The top row shows the rates of violation of the disjunction rule for the "rank the outcomes by your willingness-to-bet on them" formulation, the middle row shows the rates for the "rank the outcomes by their probability" formulation, and the bottom row combines the two conditions, which, of course, are normatively equivalent.

Table 3.2. Disjunction Fallacy Rates for the Target (Foil) Pairs in Experiment 1

Condition	Danielle	Oded	Gidi	Eldar	Gila	Na'ama	Eli	Ze'ev	Yaron	Y.C.	Overall
Betting	50(18)	65(24)	74(77)	61(3)	68(23)	71(32)	57(30)	63(29)	71(39)	52(54)	61(32)
N	66	66	35	31	40	31	63	51	28	65	476
Probability	56(31)	67(27)	83(51)	79(15)	78(40)	79(24)	57(28)	68(41)	69(37)	58(61)	66(37)
N	68	70	35	33	36	33	85	56	29	90	535
Combined	53(25)	66(26)	79(64)	70(9)	73(31)	75(28)	57(29)	66(35)	70(38)	55(58)	64(35)
N	134	132	70	64	76	64	148	107	58	155	1011

There are small but systematic differences between the probability version and willingness-to-bet version. The rate of the disjunction fallacy is lower under the betting formulation in 8 of the 10 cases (the exceptions being Gidi and Y.C.). However, the decrease averages less than 10% (even the most extreme difference, obtained for Eldar, and the overall difference, fall just short of significance; $z = 1.57$, $z = 1.65$, respectively). The rates of the disjunction fallacy never fall below 50% in either task. We conclude that the disjunction fallacy cannot be accounted for only by conversational implicatures.

The rate of the disjunction fallacy in our problems averaged .64, and never exceeded .83 (Gidi). This is less than the typical rates reported for the conjunction fallacy. Why might this be the case? Perhaps the disjunction rule simply is somehow more compelling than the conjunction rule, although this explanation has a distinct ad hoc flavor. More likely, note that Tversky and Kahneman's (1983) inclusive categories were highly nonrepresentative (e.g., "bank teller" as an occupation for Linda), whereas the representativeness of the conjunctive category was much enhanced by conjoining a representative feature (e.g., being an active feminist). In contrast, both levels of our target categories were representative. For example, Oded sounds much like a physics student, but because physics is a typical department in the natural sciences, he also sounds much like a student in the natural sciences (this is demonstrated explicitly in Study 2). . . .

If a basic level category and its superordinate are both representative of some description, why does the subcategory rank as more probable? Perhaps this is a mere reflection of people's predisposition to answer categorization questions at a basic level. To test this possibility, each list in our study contained, in addition to the target category and its superordinate disjunctive category, a foil basic-level category accompanied by its superordinate disjunctive category. The foil pair was designed to be unrepresentative of the instance (e.g., physics and natural sciences for Danielle, literature and humanities for Oded; see Table 3.1). We can compare the disjunction rate for these pairs to the disjunction rate for the target pair.

The parenthetical numbers in Table 3.2 show the disjunction fallacy rates for the foil pairs alongside those for the target pairs. In 8 of the 10 descriptions (the exceptions are Gidi and Y.C.), these rates are smaller for the foil pair than for the target pair, and even smaller than 50%. On average, the rates for the foil pair are just over one-half of those for the target pair (35% versus 64%, respectively). Moreover, in two category types (*a* and *d*), we can compare exactly the same two pairs in reversed roles. The pair literature–humanities is target for Danielle and foil for Oded, whereas the pair physics–natural sciences is target for Oded and foil for Danielle; the target-foil pairs are similarly reversed with regard to the Peace Now–peace movement versus Gush Emunim–nationalistic movement for Eli and Ze'ev. The disjunction fallacy rate is about twice as high in each of these pairs when they serve as target pairs as when the same pair is a foil pair.

The preference for predicting a basic level category over its superordinate category clearly interacts with whether the pair of nested categories is representative or not. When a category is highly likely, people seem to prefer the narrower possibility ("Oded studies physics") over the broader one ("Oded studies one of the natural sciences"). However, when the category is an unlikely one, they prefer the broader possibility ("Danielle studies one of the natural sciences") to the narrower one ("Danielle studies physics").

This is compatible with hypotheses put forth by Tversky (1977). Recall that, according to Rosch (e.g., 1978), superordinate categories (e.g., furniture) have fewer features in common than basic level ones (e.g., chairs). Recall also that the addition of similar features increases similarity, whereas the addition of dissimilar features decreases it. Thus physics, being richer in details that are compatible with Oded's description, is more like Oded than is natural sciences, whereas literature, being richer in details that are incompatible with Oded's description, is less like Oded than is humanities. The probability ranking, quite in accordance with the representativeness hypothesis, follows the similarity ranking. In Study 2, we subjected this hypothesis to a direct test.

STUDY 2

The second study had three purposes. In ascending order of importance these were (a) to extend and replicate the earlier study with new and more powerful stimuli; (b) to explore, in addition to the criteria of probability and willingness-to-bet, a third criterion for ranking options that is related to these two but is not normatively obligated to coincide with them; and (c) to directly test some of the speculations set forth to account for the results of the first study. We consider these in turn.

Increasing Power. In Study 2 we used five new stimuli, shown in Table 3.3.

1. The instance is a brief personality description of a student and the options are areas of university study (Yossi).
2. The instance is a brief personality description and the options are sports (Doron).
3. The instance is a description of a place and the options are countries or continents (Dorit and Alon).
4. The instance is a brief personality description and the options are Israeli political parties (Asher).

As before, the target option was designed to be a basic-level category name, and questions were accompanied by seven options, including two pairs of nested categories. A new set of Israeli university students (about 100 in advanced economics, 50 in elementary economics, 120 in social work, and 70 in law school) were given either three or four of these problems. The instructions were as in Study 1.

Table 3.3. Stimuli Used in Experiment 2

Character	Target Category	Target Superordinate Category	Foil Category	Foil Superordinate Category	Description
Yossi	Statistics	Social sciences	Hebrew language	Humanities	Recently discharged from service in Intelligence. Outstanding high school student, who once won a national math competition. Pedantic and careful, with a good head for numbers. A computer nut. Shy and reserved, a loner. What does he study?
Doron	Tennis	A ball game	Fast walking	A track and field sport	A successful Jerusalem attorney. Colleagues say his whims prevent him from being a team worker, attributing his success to competitiveness and drive. Slim and not tall, he watches his body and is vain. Spends several hours a week on his favorite sport. What sport is that?
Dorit	South Africa	Africa	Holland	Europe	Writes letter home describing an English-speaking country, where a modern Western technological society coexists with primal landscape and free-roaming wildlife. Where was the letter written?
Alon	Yugoslavia	Europe	Canada	North America	Writes letter home describing a multination country in constant strife, not very advanced economically, but outstanding in its beaches. Where was the letter written?
Asher	Meimad	A religious party	Mapam	A left-wing party	Very religious, but yet a liberal. Attended a religious high school, where he started a group for enhancing tolerance and understanding between the religious and the secular. Today he is more into foreign affairs and security issues, defining himself as a dove. What party does he vote for?

The main difference between the new set of descriptions and the previous set is that we attempted to choose target category pairs such that, although the basic level category would seem to be a very representative possibility, its superordinate would not seem so. We did this by either picking an unrepresentative subset of its superordinate category (e.g., tennis is an atypical ball game; South Africa is an atypical African country) or constructing a description that picks on features of the subset that the subset does not share with its superordinate (e.g., mathematical skill is required in statistics much more than in the typical social science; during its brief existence, Meimad was the only dovish and liberal–humanistic religious party in Israel). This attempt was intended to boost the rates of the disjunction fallacy.

A New Criterion for Ranking. Recall Tversky and Kahneman's (1983) suggestion that cooperative speakers "may wish to follow the maxim of value: Select the message that has the highest expected value" in which "the expected value of a message can be defined as its information value if it is true, weighted by the probability that it is true" (p. 312). We argued that in a rank by probability or rank by willingness-to-bet task, cooperativeness is beside the point, normatively speaking, and the information value of a statement should be totally subjugated to its probability of being true. However, if the task were to rank the options according to how inclined you would be to predict them, the value maxim is quite relevant. In other words, there is nothing normatively inappropriate in being more inclined to predict that "Danielle is a literature major" than the less informative, even if more likely to be correct, "Danielle is majoring in the humanities."

Just as the betting task was expected to make it harder for people to violate the disjunction rule by suggesting truth conditions and rewarding correctness alone rather than informativeness or cooperativeness as well, so a prediction task was expected to make it easier for them to violate the rule. Indeed, Yaniv and Foster (1990) showed that in a numeric prediction task in which subjects could choose at will the "graininess" of numeric estimates (i.e., the size of interval within which they choose to place their estimate), subjects naturally produce predictions that have a probability close to 50% of being correct – not one close to 90% or 95%. Similarly, subjects often evaluate as better others' finely grained estimates over more coarsely grained ones, even if the latter but not the former includes the true answer. For example, given the question, "What amount of money was spent on education by the U.S. federal government in 1987?" and the correct answer, $22.5 billion, 80% of Yaniv and Foster's subjects said that "$18 to $20 billion" was a better estimate than "$20 to $40 billion," although only the latter included the correct answer. Thus, in this study, we added a rank by tendency to predict task to the two tasks of the first study. Each subject ranked according to a single one of four criteria (see below for the fourth).

Testing the Representativeness Hypothesis Directly. In Study 1, we observed a simultaneous tendency to rank the basic-level category higher than its superordinate when both were likely options (the target pair) and to rank the basic-level category lower than its superordinate when both were not (the foil pair). We speculated that because basic-level categories are typically richer in common features than their superordinate categories, moving from the latter to the former typically increases similarity if they are similar to a description (by adding common features), and typically decreases similarity if they are dissimilar to the description (by adding features that are distinctive from the description). This speculation can be tested directly by asking subjects to rank options according to how suitable they seem to be for the described person. This, then, is the fourth criterion by which options were ranked in Study 2. It allowed us to test directly whether the probability rankings, in accordance with the representativeness hypothesis, indeed follow the suitability rankings.

Results and Discussion

Following Shafir, Smith, and Osherson (1990), we called the ranking of the superordinate category higher than its subset a *disjunction fallacy* when it is normatively inappropriate to rank them as such (as in the probability and the willingness-to-bet tasks) and a *disjunction effect* when there is no such normative constraint (as in the suitability and inclination-to-predict tasks). The results of Study 2 are shown in Table 3.4. The rows show the rates of the disjunction fallacy by the four tasks, as well as by some task combinations – betting plus probability for a disjunction fallacy rate, prediction plus suitability for a disjunction effect rate.

First, the overall rate of the disjunction fallacy is significantly higher here than in Study 1 (.77 versus .64, $z = 4.49$). We attribute this rise to the fact that the basic category and its superordinate were, on average, farther apart in this study than they had been in Study 1....

Second, the magnitude of the disjunction fallacy for the foil categories is again consistently lower than .50 (with two exceptions: Yossi under probability and Alon under prediction), and about one-half the magnitude of the rate for the target categories (the overall rate is .36 for the foils versus .74 for the targets).

However, the small but systematic differences between the probability version and willingness-to-bet version (found in Study 1) is no longer evident. Indeed, it seems to have slightly reversed itself – now the betting rates are higher than the probability rates for four of the five stories (the exception is Alon) as well as on average (.79 versus .75, $z = .90$, *ns*).

Is the disjunction effect rate in the prediction task, in which we argued that it was not fallacious, higher than in either the betting or probability tasks? No systematic pattern emerges: The prediction rates are sometimes higher (Doron, Dorit, Alon) and sometimes lower (Yossi, Asher) than the rates in the betting and probability tasks. The overall disjunction effect rate in the prediction task is .77, exactly like the overall disjunction fallacy rate (of the combined probability and betting tasks).

What about the suitability results? In the suitability task there is no normative reason whatsoever to rank superordinate categories higher (or, for that matter, lower) than their subsets. Thus, we might expect the disjunction effect to be largest in this task. Actually, however, it was most often (Doron, Alon, Asher) smallest, and on average (.68) smallest.

Finally, we combined the two conditions in which the disjunction rule is normatively necessary (betting and probability) and the two conditions in which it is not (prediction and suitability) and compared the combined rates. Contrary to normative expectation, the overall disjunction fallacy rate (.77) was higher than the overall disjunction effect rate (.72), although the difference is not significant ($z = 1.57$). A similar picture emerges with respect to the foil categories: Here too the effect is, if anything, higher where it is fallacious (.36, probability and betting) than where it is not (.35, predicting and suitability) and is at its lowest for suitability (.32). Table 3.4 shows no evidence for any normative effects of task.

In contrast to the absence of a task effect, there does seem to be a story effect. Some of our stories (e.g., Yossi) simply "worked better" (i.e., elicited higher disjunction fallacy rates) than others (e.g., Asher). Insofar as this is a reflection of our uneven success in designing appropriate stimuli, this effect is of little interest. It becomes more interesting if we interpret it in light of the representativeness hypothesis. This hypothesis says that people judge probability by similarity, suitability, or representativeness. If so, the similarity between the results we obtained under the different sets of instructions simply reflects the fact that all subjects were essentially doing the same thing. Regardless of the formal criterion they were asked to rank the options by, they were all ranking the options by representativeness. We computed the correlation between the disjunction effect rates for the suitability task and the combined disjunction fallacy rates (i.e., between the rates reported on lines 4 and 5 of Table 3.4). This correlation was $r = .97. . . .$

Table 3.4. Disjunction Fallacy Rates for Target (Foil) Pairs in Experiment 2, by Task, and by Combined Tasks

Task	Yossi	Doron	Dorit	Alon	Asher	Overall
Betting	87(47)	81(19)	80(37)	74(43)	70(21)	79(34)
N	38	36	35	35	33	177
Probability	84(61)	78(16)	74(43)	79(32)	59(41)	75(39)
N	38	37	35	34	34	178
Prediction	84(44)	82(17)	83(34)	82(55)	55(45)	77(39)
N	37	34	35	33	33	172
Suitability	85(49)	37(6)	83(33)	73(35)	50(33)	68(32)
N	39	36	40	41	76	232
Disjunction fallacy	86(54)	79(18)	77(40)	77(38)	64(31)	77(36)
N	76	73	70	69	67	355
Disjunction effect	84(47)	74(11)	83(34)	77(44)	51(37)	72(35)
N	76	70	75	74	109	404

Additional evidence for the representativeness hypothesis can be found in an analysis that is based on the rankings of all seven options in our lists, not just the critical four (target pair + foil pair). For each of our five stories, we correlated the mean rankings of all seven options as elicited by the suitability criterion with the mean rankings elicited by each of the other criteria. The median correlation is .91, and the combined correlation across all stories is in excess of .96. In comparison, Tversky and Kahneman (1983) found a correlation of .98 between mean rank by resemblance and mean rank by probability for Linda.

To be sure, correlations between mean ranks should be treated with circumspection, and even correlations as high as those reported here are not incompatible with large variability of individual rankings. However, they support the interpretation that options were ranked much the same by all four criteria. . . .

STUDY 3

In Study 1, subjects who ranked the options by their willingness to bet on them committed the disjunction fallacy at somewhat lower rates than those who ranked them by their probability. This minor but systematic effect disappeared in Study 2. Study 3 repeated the rank by willingness-to-bet task, but this time the bet was for real. Although we did not expect the move from betting for hypothetical money to betting for real money to have much impact, one clear advantage of betting for real money is that subjects are given a genuine incentive to suit themselves, not the experimenter, to do what they think is best for their interests rather than to try to guess what the experiment is about. Even if they believe that the experiment is about stereotypes, for example, or that they are really being asked for what is most reasonable to say rather than for what is most probably true, they can nonetheless exploit the options to their own benefit by ranking superordinate categories higher than their subsets. It may not make the experimenter happy, but it gives them a better shot at the reward.

The instructions were similar to those given in Studies 1 and 2, except for explicitly addressing themselves to the conditions under which the bet could be won, as follows:

After you ranked all the options, we will check the option you ranked number 1 (namely, your first choice for betting). If you were right, you will immediately be awarded 100NS. If not, you will neither win, nor lose, anything. Unfortunately, we do not have the means to offer this bet to all of you, but at the end, we shall draw several people (according to the class size) who will actually bet for real. Each one of you has an equal chance of being drawn.

The questions in this study were administered in a class setting. The participants in this study were 25 seniors in philosophy and 65 seniors in economics. Each received two questions. After answering the questions, 2 subjects in the first class and 3 in the second class were drawn by lottery to bet for real money (at the time, 100NS was a large sum, considering that it was more than 10 times the hourly rate paid to students for a task that took only about 10 minutes).

In another group of 36 subjects (about equally divided between social science and education majors), a monetary reward was promised to every subject whose bet turned out correct. For obvious budgetary reasons, this group was rewarded only 10NS each. . . .

The 10NS group responded only to the original version of Gidi, who was the most effective of the Study 1 stimuli.

Results and Discussion

We gave Gidi's description to 36 subjects, of whom 72% committed the disjunction fallacy on the target category pair. The disjunction fallacy rate in Study 1's hypothetical betting condition was 74% – a small and nonsignificant difference ($z = .19$).

Yossi elicited the disjunction fallacy at a rate of .74 and Doron at a rate of .72. These rates are lower by less than 15% than those reported for these stories in the betting task in Study 2. This effect is not significant ($z = 1.59$ for Yossi, $z = 1.03$ for Doron). Moreover, because we selected the two most extreme stimuli from Study 2, some regression to the mean was to be expected. . . .

GENERAL DISCUSSION

The extension rule is perhaps the simplest and most transparent rule of probability theory, one whose validity even untrained and unsophisticated people accept and endorse. Hence, its violation is one of the most startling and dramatic errors of probabilistic reasoning. In Tversky and Kahneman's (1983) classic study, a single and powerful device was used to induce the fallacy: A representative feature was conjoined to an unrepresentative one. This addition increased the judged representativeness of the conjunction over that of its unrepresentative component, but the probability of the conjunction could, of course, only reduce the probability of each component. Thus, the modal judgment that $P(A\&B)$ is greater than $P(A)$ provided striking and highly diagnostic evidence for the representativeness hypothesis.

The initial motivation behind the present study was to create a disjunction fallacy. It is well-known that, when categorizing things under conditions of certainty, people prefer basic level categories to their superordinate categories. If categorization under conditions of uncertainty were to exhibit the same preference, then disjunction fallacies might ensue. This would not only be an extension of the conjunction fallacy, but also would rely on an altogether different cognitive device than that evoked by representativeness.

To that end, the option lists we gave our subjects included a representative basic level category as well as its superordinate. We labeled this nested pair the *target pair*. To test whether the disjunction fallacy, if exhibited, actually results from a general tendency to categorize at a basic-level, the list also included an unrepresentative basic-level category along with its superordinate. We labeled this nested pair the *foil pair*.

The two nested pairs elicited markedly different rankings. Whereas for the target pair the majority of subjects ranked the narrower category more likely than its superordinate, for the foil pair it was the reverse. This pattern rules out an overall preference for basic-level categories, but it could be compatible with the representativeness hypothesis. The rationale of representativeness does not require that conjunction fallacies be the only form of extension fallacies. Whenever an ordering of events by representativeness differs from their ordering by set inclusion, there is a potential for an extension fallacy to occur. To explain our results by representativeness, we need only show that the target basic level category was more representative than its superordinate, whereas the foil basic level category was less representative than its superordinate.

Rather than rely on our own *a priori* judgments of representativeness, in Study 2 we collected suitability rankings alongside probability and willingness-to-bet rankings for all the stories we used. Although some previous studies elicited the occasional representativeness judgment (e.g., Kahneman & Tversky, 1973; Tversky & Kahneman, 1983), this study correlated representativeness judgments with probability judgments systematically. Table 3.4 shows that the probability judgments, as well as the normatively equivalent willingness-to-bet judgments, followed closely the pattern exhibited by the suitability judgments, in conformity with the representativeness hypothesis. In particular, irrespective of the type of judgment rendered, the target basic-level category was ranked above its superordinate for the target pair, and below it for the foil pair, just as required for a representativeness-based account of our results. Moreover, the disjunction fallacy rates are not merely correlated with the suitability disjunction effect rates, they are also quite similar to them.

Indeed, given the interaction we found between the disjunction fallacy rates and the type of nested pair, it seems not to matter whether the superordinate category really is disjunctive, or even whether it is at the Roschian superordinate level. Which of two events – even nested events – seems more probable is better predicted by their representativeness than by their scope, or by the level in the category hierarchy in which they are located. Colleagues often ask us questions such as, What would have happened had you included subordinate categories in your option lists (e.g., "clay court tennis" for Doron, "Bayesian statistics" for Yossi)? What if one option had overlapped with another, or if there had been two subsets of a single superordinate? The representativeness hypothesis suggests a general answer for such speculative questions: If you want to predict how such manipulations would affect probability judgments, find out how they would affect representativeness judgments. . . .

4. Imagining Can Heighten or Lower the Perceived Likelihood of Contracting a Disease: The Mediating Effect of Ease of Imagery

Steven J. Sherman, Robert B. Cialdini, Donna F. Schwartzman, and Kim D. Reynolds

Findings from a number of studies (Anderson, 1983; Anderson, Lepper, & Ross, 1980; Carroll, 1978; Gregory, Cialdini, & Carpenter, 1982; Ross, Lepper, Strack, & Steinmetz, 1977; Sherman, Zehner, Johnson, & Hirt, 1983) indicate that when a hypothetical outcome is imagined and/or explained, it becomes subjectively more likely to occur. For example, Gregory et al. (1982) asked subjects to imagine winning a contest or being arrested for a crime. In each case, subjects came to believe more strongly that the event could happen to them. Furthermore, the imagination procedure influenced later compliance behavior as well as probability estimates. Homeowners who imagined watching and enjoying the benefits of a cable television service were subsequently more likely to subscribe to such a service when given the opportunity to do so.

What process underlies these dramatic judgmental and behavioral effects of explaining and imagining hypothetical future events? The work to date indicates an interpretation based on the operation of one of the cognitive heuristics used in judgments under uncertainty, the *availability heuristic* (Tversky & Kahneman, 1973). According to this heuristic principle, one basis for the judgment of the likelihood of an uncertain outcome is cognitive availability; that is, the ease with which this outcome can be pictured or constructed. The more available an outcome is, the more likely it is perceived to be. . . .

What might one expect, however, if the event in question could be imagined only with great difficulty, or if subjects failed in their attempts to imagine or explain it? According to the availability heuristic, hypothetical events that defy easy explanation and for which images are difficult to construct should appear as improbable. Subjects may not simply use the availability of an already constructed scenario to judge its likelihood, but may instead directly use their assessment of the ease or difficulty in constructing explanations and images as an index of the likelihood of such an event. Because unlikely events are typically difficult to retrieve or explain, subjects may infer that if an event is difficult to explain or imagine, then it must be unlikely. To date, no study has investigated the effects of generating difficult-to-imagine scenarios on subsequent judgments. In addition, no work has been done that has directly manipulated the ease or

This is a revised and condensed version of a paper that first appeared in the *Personality and Social Psychology Bulletin, 11,* 118–127. Copyright © 1985, Sage Publications. Reprinted by permission.

difficulty of imagining an event to test the notion that only easy-to-imagine scenarios lead to increased likelihood estimates, whereas difficult-to-imagine scenarios might even render the event subjectively less likely. Such a demonstration would provide a rather direct test of the judgmental mechanism proposed to underlie the effects of imagination.

Our study was designed to test this proposition. Subjects were asked to imagine and describe events that varied in their ease or difficulty of imaginability. Compared to a group that does not imagine a particular event, those who imagine an easy-to-construct outcome should increase their subjective likelihood for that event, whereas those who imagine a difficult-to-construct outcome should decrease their subjective probability for that event.

METHOD

Subjects
The subjects were 120 female students enrolled in introductory psychology courses at Arizona State University. Up to four subjects were tested at each session, with each subject in a separate room. Each individual was assigned randomly to condition so that various conditions were represented within each session.

Procedure
Subjects received a booklet at the start of the experimental session that contained all relevant tasks and instructions. All subjects were told that the experiment concerned human thought and judgment.

Control (Reading Only) Subjects. Subjects in the control (reading only) conditions read that an illness (Hyposcenia-B) was becoming increasingly prevalent on the Arizona State University campus. They then read about the symptoms of this disease. In the easy-to-imagine condition, these symptoms were concrete and had probably been experienced by most subjects. The symptoms included low energy level, muscle aches, and frequent severe headaches. In the difficult-to-imagine condition, the symptoms were far less concrete – a vague sense of disorientation, a malfunctioning nervous system, and an inflamed liver. Pretesting with separate groups of subjects had shown that these sets of symptoms were rated easy and difficult to imagine, respectively. After reading about the disease, control subjects were asked to judge how likely it was that they would contract Hyposcenia-B in the future. This was done on a 10-point scale, ranging from very likely (1) to very unlikely (10). In addition, to ensure that any effects were specific to the event described, subjects were asked to estimate the likelihood of other events: failing a class (a negative outcome), becoming involved in a new romantic relationship (a positive outcome), and donating blood (a neutral event).

Experimental (Imagining) Subjects. Experimental (imagining) subjects also read either the easy-to-imagine or the difficult-to-imagine version of the disease. However, in addition, experimental subjects were told before they read the description that they would be reading it with an eye toward imagining a 3-week period during which they contracted and experienced the symptoms of the disease. To ensure that these subjects would actively imagine as requested, they were asked to write a detailed description of what they imagined their feelings and reactions would be during each of the 3 weeks. Following this, these subjects rated the likelihood of contracting the disease as well as the likelihood of the other events (e.g., failing a course). As a manipulation check, these subjects also rated how difficult it was to imagine the disease symptoms. . . .

Overview

The experiment involved a 2 (task-imagination vs. reading only) × 2 (accessibility of symptoms – easy-to-imagine versus difficult-to-imagine) factorial design. It was expected that the judgment of the likelihood of an event would be mediated by the ease or difficulty of imagining that event for subjects whose task was to imagine it. Thus we predicted that subjects in the imagination task, who were given easy-to-imagine symptoms, would judge the disease as more likely to be contracted than controls, who merely read about the easy-to-imagine symptoms. Similarly, we predicted that imagination-task subjects who had to imagine a difficult-to-imagine disease would judge it as more unlikely than comparable controls.

RESULTS

An initial analysis was performed to determine whether the accessibility of symptoms manipulation had been successful, as measured by the manipulation check item. As intended, subjects found the difficult-to-imagine symptoms more difficult to generate than the easy-to-imagine symptoms, 2.50 versus 4.15, respectively, $F(1, 38) = 5.29$, $p < .03$.

The major analysis of the study was a 2 (task) × 2 (symptom accessibility) analysis of variance of subjects' responses to the personal likelihood item, "How likely is it that you would contract Hyposcenia-B in the future?" The means are displayed in Table 4.1. As expected, there was a main effect for symptom accessibility, indicating that subjects encountering the difficult-to-imagine symptoms rated themselves as less likely to contract the disease than subjects

Table 4.1. Judgments of Disease Likelihood for Self

Task	Accessibility of Symptoms	
	Easy-to-Imagine	Difficult-to-Imagine
Imagine	5.25	7.70
Read only (control)	6.20	6.55

Note: $N = 20$ per cell. 1 = very likely; 10 = very unlikely.

encountering the easy-to-imagine symptoms, $F(1, 76) = 7.34$, $p < .01$. More important support for our hypothesis, however, came from the second major finding of the analysis: A task × symptom accessibility interaction indicating that the main effect occurred principally among the imagination task subjects, $F(1, 76) = 4.13$, $p < .05$. Furthermore, an examination of the interaction pattern in Table 4.1 shows that it is composed of two separate effects working in combination: A tendency for subjects imagining easy-to-imagine symptoms to rate their probability of contracting the disease as greater than it was for control subjects, and a tendency for subjects imagining difficult-to-imagine symptoms to rate their probability of getting the disease as smaller than control subjects.

DISCUSSION

The current findings lend support to past research showing that imagining hypothetical future events may render those events subjectively more likely (Carroll, 1978; Gregory et al., 1982). In our study, subjects who actively constructed images of experiencing a disease with easy-to-imagine symptoms judged themselves as more likely to contract that disease than did any other group of subjects. More important, the present study adds uniquely to the previous literature in demonstrating that when the event to be imagined is difficult to imagine and the image is arrived at with relatively great effort, the subjective likelihood of that event decreases rather than increases. Thus our subjects, who were asked to generate their own images of experiencing a disease with difficult-to-imagine symptoms, judged the likelihood of contracting the disease as smaller than did any other group. This experiment is the first to demonstrate these opposite effects of ease or difficulty of imagination on likelihood estimates and, in so doing, to support the availability heuristic interpretation of imagination–explanation effects directly. The results support the notion that the effect of imagining events or outcomes on judgments of likelihood is mediated by the ease or difficulty of initially making the image available. Subjects appear to use their assessments of the ease of constructing the required scenario as a direct cue to the probability of such an event....

The use of the availability or unavailability of a scenario as an indication of probability is of course consistent with the general use of availability for estimates of frequency or likelihood. Because likely events are typically easy to retrieve, imagine, or explain, whereas unlikely events are difficult to retrieve, imagine, or explain, subjects take the ease of imaginability as an indicator of likelihood. The problem with such a simple decision rule is, of course, that ease of imaginability may not always be caused by or even related to likelihood. Things other than frequency or likelihood may affect the ease with which a scenario may be constructed. For example, particularly vivid and striking events may easily spring to mind, and it is their vividness that causes the ease of imaginability rather than the likelihood of occurrence. Nevertheless, this implies that vivid events will be overestimated in terms of likelihood, and recent evidence is certainly consistent with this idea (Kahneman & Tversky, 1972; Lichtenstein et al., 1978; Rothbart et al., 1978).

The current findings serve to show the important effects of thinking about and considering possible future events and outcomes. As people are induced to think about the future and to imagine events in that future, judgments and even the course of that future may be altered. Whether the thinking involves predictions of future events (Sherman, 1980), explanations of hypothetical events (Ross et al., 1977; Sherman et al., 1983), or, as in the present study, imagination of future occurrences (Carroll, 1978; Gregory et al., 1982), such thoughts clearly alter later judgments and behavior. Thinking about the future and imagining events that could happen have been shown to bring about dramatic effects. Cognitive rehearsal and planning have been used in clinical settings to change the behavior of impulsive children (Meichenbaum & Goodman, 1971), reduce the relapse rate among alcoholics (Marlatt, 1978), and decrease the rate of early termination of therapy (Sherman, 1982). In the realm of sport psychology, imagination and mental rehearsal of upcoming performance have been shown to enhance performance (Suinn, 1976)....

Because the present study dealt with estimates of disease likelihood, it might have practical implications for the health behavior area in particular. One of the major problems in the health field has been in the area of medical compliance (DiMatteo & DiNicola, 1982; Haynes, Taylor, & Sackett, 1979). People are especially unwilling to comply with appropriate preventive regimens such as immunization shots (Masur, 1981). Health professionals have been giving increasing attention to social psychological theory and practice in the hope of increasing medical compliance (Sensenig & Cialdini, 1984). Perhaps one of the problems in this area is that the diseases involved or the medical consequences of noncompliance are difficult to imagine, and thus the likelihood of such consequences is judged as extremely low. Note, for example, the traditionally low compliance rates associated with such disorders as hypertension (Sackett & Snow, 1979), in which symptoms are difficult for sufferers to detect and, consequently, to imagine. This suggests that the health profession might increase patient compliance and preventative compliance by making vivid presentations of the medical problems and by describing symptoms and consequences, as well as effective countersteps (Leventhal, 1970; Rogers & Mewbom, 1976), in easy-to-imagine terms.

5. The Availability Heuristic Revisited: Ease of Recall and Content of Recall as Distinct Sources of Information

Norbert Schwarz and Leigh Ann Vaughn

According to Tversky and Kahneman's (1973, p. 208) availability heuristic, individuals estimate the frequency of an event or the likelihood of its occurrence "by the ease with which instances or associations come to mind." Although this heuristic has stimulated an enormous amount of research (see Sherman & Corty, 1984; Taylor, 1982, for reviews), the classic studies on the issue are ambiguous with regard to the underlying process. For example, in one of the better known studies, Tversky and Kahneman (1973, Experiment 3) observed that participants overestimated the number of words that begin with the letter r, but underestimated the number of words that have r as the third letter. They presumably did so because words that begin with a certain letter can be brought to mind more easily than words that have a certain letter in the third position. Note, however, that this differential ease of recall may influence participants' frequency estimates in two different ways. On one hand, participants may use the subjective experience of ease or difficulty of recall as a basis of judgment, as suggested by Tversky and Kahneman's (1973) description of the availability heuristic. If so, they would estimate a higher frequency if the recall task is experienced as easy rather than difficult. On the other hand, they may recall as many words of each type as possible within the time allotted to them and may base their judgment on the recalled sample of words. If it is easier to recall words that begin with a certain letter, these words would be overrepresented in the recalled sample, again resulting in an estimate of higher frequency. In the latter case, the estimate would be based on recalled *content* rather than on the *subjective experience* of ease of recall. In a related study, Gabrielcik and Fazio (1984) observed that exposing participants to subliminally presented words containing the letter t increased participants' estimates of the frequency of words beginning with t. Again, this finding may indicate either that participants could generate *more* words including a t if primed, or that participants relied on the *ease* with which relevant exemplars could be called to mind.

Completion of this chapter was supported by a fellowship from the Center for Advanced Study in the Behavioral Sciences to Norbert Schwarz.

Similar ambiguities apply to other experimental procedures. For example, in another well-known Tversky and Kahneman study (1973, Experiment 8), participants were read two lists of names, one presenting 19 famous men and 20 less famous women, and the other presenting 19 famous women and 20 less famous men. When asked, participants reported that there were more men than women in the first list, but more women than men in the second list, even though the opposite was the case (by a difference of one name). Again, the famous names were presumably easier to recall than the nonfamous ones, resulting in an overestimate. In fact, participants were able to recall about 50% more of the famous than of the nonfamous names. This difference in actual recall again highlights the ambiguity underlying most tests of the availability heuristic: Are participants' judgments indeed based on the phenomenal *experience* of ease or difficulty of recall, as Tversky and Kahneman's description of the availability heuristic suggests, or are their judgments based on the *content* of recall, with famous names being overrepresented in the recalled sample?

As these examples illustrate, manipulations intended to increase the subjective experience of ease of recall are also likely to affect the amount of recall. In most real-world situations, these two factors are naturally confounded. Unfortunately, this confound renders it difficult to determine if the obtained estimates of frequency, likelihood, or typicality are based on participants' phenomenal experiences or on a biased sample of recalled information. As Taylor (1982, p. 199) noted, the latter possibility would render the availability heuristic rather trivial; after all, "one's judgments are always based on *what* comes to mind" (emphasis added). In fact, some textbooks have chosen the latter interpretation in introducing the availability heuristic, as a quote from Medin and Ross (1997, p. 522) illustrates:

The availability heuristic refers to a tendency to form a judgment on the basis of what is readily brought to mind. For example, a person who is asked whether there are more English words that begin with the letter t or the letter k might try to think of words that begin with each of these letters. Since a person can probably think of more words beginning with t, he or she would (correctly) conclude that t is more frequent than k as the first letter of English words.

THE INTERPLAY OF DECLARATIVE AND EXPERIENTIAL INFORMATION

This chapter addresses the ambiguity of whether the *subjective experience* of ease or difficulty of recall has an impact on our judgments distinct from the impact of the *content* that comes to mind. The answer to this ambiguity has important implications for two different programs of research. On the one hand, Tversky and Kahneman's (1973) conceptualization of the availability heuristic emphasized the role of experiential information, specifically the phenomenal experience of ease or difficulty of recall. On the other hand, a large body of research in social cognition demonstrated that judgments are based on the declarative information that is most accessible at the time of judgment (for reviews, see Bodenhausen & Wyer, 1987; Higgins, 1996; Schwarz, 1995; Wyer & Srull, 1989). When asked to form a judgment, people rarely retrieve all information that may bear on the task, but truncate the search process as soon as enough information has come to mind to form a judgment with sufficient subjective certainty. Accordingly, the judgment is based on the information most accessible at the time. More important, the ambiguity noted previously cuts both ways: Much as one may wonder if the apparent impact of experienced ease of recall actually reflects reliance on a biased sample of recalled content, one may also wonder if the apparent impact of the most accessible information actually reflects reliance on the experienced ease with which the initial pieces of information came to mind.

We first review research that explored whether the phenomenal experience of ease or difficulty of recall is informative in its own right. If so, the impact of experienced ease of recall should be attenuated when the informational value of the experience is called into question. Studies that used misattribution manipulations support this hypothesis (e.g., Haddock, Rothman, Reber, & Schwarz, 1999; Schwarz, Bless, Strack, Klumpp, Rittenauer-Schatka, & Simons, 1991; Wänke, Schwarz, & Bless, 1995). Following a discussion of these studies, we address the interplay of declarative and experiential information and review research that introduced conditions under which reliance on experienced ease of recall and reliance on recalled content lead to different judgmental outcomes. This research suggests that individuals rely on ease of recall when the informational value of their subjective experiences is not called into question, but turn to content of recall when the experiential information is deemed uninformative (e.g., Schwarz et al., 1991). Finally, we identify some conditions that influence whether people are more likely to rely on experiential or declarative information in arriving at a judgment when *both* sources of information are considered informative (e.g., Grayson & Schwarz, 1999; Rothman & Schwarz, 1998; Vaughn, 1997). The chapter concludes with an integrative discussion of the interplay of experiential and declarative information in judgment formation.

EXPERIENCED EASE OF RECALL AS A SOURCE OF INFORMATION

If subjective experiences of ease or difficulty of recall serve as a source of information in their own right, their impact should vary as a function of the perceived diagnosticity of the experience, as has been observed for other types of experiential information, such as moods (e.g., Schwarz & Clore, 1983; Schwarz, Chapter 29, this volume) or arousal (e.g., Zillman, 1978). According to the availability heuristic, we should infer, for example, that there are many words that begin with the letter *t* if we find it easy to bring relevant examples to mind. This inference is based on the generally correct assumption that it is easier to recall exemplars of a frequent than of an infrequent category. Suppose, however, that you have reason to assume that a temporary situational factor renders words beginning with t more accessible than might otherwise be the case. If so, the experienced ease of recall may reflect this irrelevant influence rather than the actual frequency of words beginning with t. Hence, you may discount the subjective experience as a relevant source of information. Conversely, if you had reason to assume that a temporary situational factor inhibits the recall of words beginning with t but you find them easy to bring to mind nevertheless, the experienced ease of recall should seem particularly diagnostic. The emergence of such discounting and augmentation effects (Kelley, 1972) would provide compelling evidence for the role of experiential information in frequency judgments.

Manipulating the Perceived Diagnosticity of Recall Experiences

To test these predictions, Wänke et al. (1995) conducted a modified replication of Tversky and Kahneman's (1973, Experiment 3) letter experiment, described previously. In the control condition, participants received a blank sheet of paper and were asked to first write down 10 words that have t as the third letter, and subsequently words that begin with the letter t. Following this listing task, they rated the extent to which words beginning with a t are more or less frequent than words that have t as the third letter. As in Tversky and Kahneman's (1973) study, participants estimated that words that begin with a t are much more frequent than words having a t in the third position, as shown in Table 5.1 ("control condition").

As in the original study, this inference may either be based on the experience that words beginning with t came to mind more easily, or on the observation that they could recall a larger number of these words (although they were only asked to record 10). To isolate the role of experienced ease, the diagnosticity of the experience was manipulated in two experimental conditions. Specifically, participants had to record 10 words that begin with t on a sheet of paper that was imprinted with pale but visible rows of ts. Some participants were told that this background would make it easy to recall words beginning with t ("facilitating condition"), whereas others were told that this background would interfere with the recall task ("inhibiting condition"). As expected, participants who could attribute the experienced ease of recall to the impact of their work sheet assumed that there are fewer words beginning with t than participants in the control condition. Conversely, participants who expected their worksheet to interfere with recall but found recall easy nevertheless estimated that there are more words beginning with t than did participants in the control condition.

Table 5.1. Frequency of Words Having t as the First or Third Letter

Alleged Contextual Influence		
Facilitating	Control	Inhibiting
3.8	5.4	6.1

Note: N is 9 or 10 per condition. Shown are mean ratings along an 8-point scale, with 1 = "many more third-letter words than first-letter words" and 8 = "many more first-letter words than third-letter words." Adapted from Wänke, Schwarz, and Bless (1995).

In combination, the obtained discounting and augmentation effects indicate that participants did indeed base their frequency estimates on the *subjective experience* of ease of recall, rather than on the number of words they could bring to mind. Moreover, the misattribution effects obtained here have been replicated in other domains addressed later (e.g., Haddock et al., 1999; Schwarz et al., 1991). Hence, we may conclude that recall experiences are informative in their own right, much as has been observed for other types of experiential information (for reviews see Clore, 1992; Schwarz, Chapter 29, this volume; Schwarz & Clore, 1996; Strack, 1992).

Facial Feedback as an Indicator of Recall Difficulty

If subjective recall experiences are informative in their own right, any variable that leads people to *experience* a recall task as easy or difficult should influence subsequent judgments, even when the subjective experience is not due to the actual recall task itself. To address this issue, Stepper and Strack (1993, Experiment 2) asked all participants to recall six examples of either assertive or unassertive behavior, thus holding actual recall demands constant. To manipulate the subjective experience of ease of recall, they induced participants to adopt different facial expressions. In related research, specific facial expressions and body postures have been shown to be associated with emotions such as amusement, happiness, pride, sadness, and anger (e.g., Stepper & Strack, 1993, Experiment 1; for reviews, see Adelmann & Zajonc, 1989; Izard, 1990). Merely adopting such an expression facilitates the experience of the relevant emotion, even if one does not interpret the expression as an emotional response.

Extending this reasoning to ease of recall, Stepper and Strack induced participants to contract either their corrugator or their zygomaticus muscle during the recall task. Contraction of the corrugator muscle produces a furrowed brow, an expression commonly associated with a feeling of effort. Contraction of the zygomaticus muscle produces a light smile, an expression associated with a feeling of ease. The researchers predicted that participants might take such proprioceptive feedback as indications of ease or difficulty of recall, regardless of the actual number of examples they brought to mind.

The results were consistent with these predictions. Among participants who recalled six examples of assertive behavior, participants who adopted a light smile while bringing examples to mind subsequently judged themselves as more assertive than participants who had adopted a furrowed brow. Apparently, the experience of difficulty conveyed by a furrowed brow led the latter participants to conclude that they cannot be that assertive if it is so difficult to bring assertive behaviors to mind. Similarly, among participants who recalled six examples of unassertive behavior, participants who adopted a light smile while recalling examples subsequently judged themselves as less assertive than participants who had adopted a furrowed brow. These findings again indicate that subjective ease or difficulty of recall constitutes a source of information that is distinct from the declarative information that has been brought to mind: In this study, the amount of recalled declarative information was the same for all participants, yet the conclusions that participants drew from this information depended on the ease or difficulty of recall signalled by the proprioceptive feedback.

DIFFERENTIAL IMPLICATIONS OF EXPERIENCED EASE OF RECALL AND RECALLED CONTENT

As noted previously, the conditions under which a recall task is experienced as easy are often conditions under which we are also likely to recall a large number of instances. Under these conditions, reliance on recalled content leads to the same conclusions as reliance on ease of recall. It is possible, however, to create conditions under which reliance on these different sources of information leads to different judgments. Suppose that some individuals are asked to recall 6 examples of situations in which they behaved assertively, whereas others are asked to recall 12 examples. Suppose further that recalling 6 examples is experienced as easy, whereas recalling 12 examples is experienced as difficult. In this case, a judgment strategy that is based on recalled content would lead individuals to infer higher assertiveness when the recall task brought 12 rather than 6 examples to mind. In contrast, a strategy based on experienced ease or difficulty of recall would reverse this pattern: Finding it difficult to recall 12 examples of assertive behaviors, individuals may conclude that they cannot be that assertive after all, or else bringing 12 examples to mind would not be that difficult. Several studies bear on this differential impact of recalled content and ease of recall.

Recalled Content versus Ease of Recall

In an initial test of this possibility, Schwarz et al. (1991, Experiment 1) asked participants to report either 6 or 12 situations in which they behaved either assertively or unassertively. Although all participants could complete this task, pretests had shown that recalling 6 examples was experienced as easy, whereas recalling 12 examples was experienced as difficult. Following their reports, participants had to evaluate their own assertiveness. Table 5.2 shows the results.

Table 5.2. Self-Reports of Assertiveness as a Function of Valence and Number of Recalled Behaviors

Number of Recalled Examples	Type of Behavior	
	Assertive	Unassertive
6	6.3	5.2
12	5.2	6.2

Note: N is 9 or 10 per condition. Mean score of three questions is given; possible range is 1 to 10, with higher values reflecting higher assertiveness. Adapted from Schwarz, Bless, Strack, Klumpp, Rittenauer-Schatka, and Simons (1991, Experiment 1).

As expected, participants reported higher assertiveness after recalling 6 examples of assertive behaviors than after recalling 6 examples of unassertive behaviors. However, this difference did not increase as participants had to recall more examples. To the contrary – participants who had to recall assertive behaviors reported lower assertiveness after recalling 12 rather than 6 examples. Similarly, participants who had to recall unassertive behaviors reported higher assertiveness after recalling 12 rather than 6 examples. In fact, they reported higher assertiveness after recalling 12 unassertive behaviors rather than 12 assertive behaviors, in contrast to what one would expect on the basis of recalled content. Apparently, the experience that it was difficult to bring 12 examples to mind suggested to them that they cannot be that assertive (or unassertive) after all. Thus, the experienced difficulty of recall induced participants to draw inferences opposite to the implications of recalled content.

However, a possible alternative explanation deserves attention. Although all participants who were asked to do so did in fact report 12 examples, it is conceivable that the quality of their examples changed over the course of the recall task: They may have been able to recall some examples of clearly assertive behavior early on, but as the requested number increased, they had to include less convincing examples of assertiveness. If so, these less convincing examples, reported toward the end of the list may have been more accessible later on than the examples reported earlier. Hence, if participants based their judgments on the last few examples generated, one would obtain the same pattern of results. Schwarz et al. (1991, Experiment 1) tested this possibility by analyzing the examples that participants reported. This content analysis provided no evidence that the extremity of the examples decreased toward the end. If anything, the last two examples reported were somewhat more extreme than the first two examples reported. Thus, this alternative explanation can be discarded. Nevertheless, more direct evidence for the assumed role of subjective experiences would be welcome.

Undermining the Diagnosticity of the Recall Experience

To provide this evidence, Schwarz et al. (1991, Experiment 3) manipulated the perceived informational value of the experienced ease or difficulty of recall through misattribution manipulations. Specifically, they had participants listen to new-age music played at half-speed while they worked on the recall task. Some participants were told that this music would facilitate the recall of situations in which they behaved assertively and felt at ease, whereas others were told that it would facilitate the recall of situations in which they behaved unassertively and felt insecure. These manipulations render participants' recall experiences uninformative whenever the experience matches the alleged impact of the music; after all, it may simply be easy or difficult because of the music. In contrast, experiences that are opposite to the alleged impact of the music should be considered highly informative. Table 5.3 shows the results.

Table 5.3. Self-Reports of Assertiveness as a Function of Valence, Number
of Recalled Behaviors, and Diagnosticity of Ease of Recall

	Diagnosticity of Recall Experience			
	High		Low	
	Type of Behavior			
Number of Examples	Assertive	Unassertive	Assertive	Unassertive
6	5.6	3.1	3.9	5.1
12	4.5	4.4	4.8	4.0

Note: N is 9 or 10 per condition. Mean score of two questions is given; possible range is 1 to 9,
with higher values reflecting higher assertiveness. Adapted from Schwarz, Bless, Strack, Klumpp,
Rittenauer-Schatka, and Simons (1991, Experiment 3).

When the informational value of participants' experienced ease or difficulty
of recall was *not* called into question, the previously obtained results replicated.
As shown in the left panel (high diagnosticity), these participants evaluated
themselves as less assertive after recalling 12 rather than 6 examples of assertive behavior, and as more assertive after recalling 12 rather than 6 examples
of unassertive behavior. As in the previous study, they apparently concluded
from the experienced difficulty of recall that they cannot be that assertive
(or unassertive) if it is so difficult to recall 12 relevant examples.

Not so, however, when their subjective experiences of ease or difficulty of
recall matched the alleged side effects of the music. In this case, the meaning
of the subjective experience is ambiguous, and participants turned to a more
informative source of information: the content they had just recalled. As shown
in the right panel (low diagnosticity), these participants reported higher assertiveness after recalling 12 rather than 6 examples of assertive behavior, and
lower assertiveness after recalling 12 rather than 6 examples of unassertive
behavior, thus reversing the otherwise obtained pattern.

Perceived Expertise and the Informational Value
of Recall Experiences

In the preceding studies, the informational value of recall experiences was
manipulated by drawing participants' attention to an external source that al-
legedly facilitated or inhibited recall. The same logic, however, applies to an
individual difference variable, namely one's perceived expertise in the respective content domain. Suppose you are asked to list 12 famous Spanish matadors
and find this task difficult. Chances are that you would not conclude that there
are not many famous Spanish matadors; instead, you would blame your own
lack of expertise for the experienced difficulty, thus undermining its informational value. As this example illustrates, individuals may only rely on recall

experiences when they consider themselves at least moderately knowledgeable in the relevant content domain. Experimental data support this conclusion.

For example, Biller, Bless, and Schwarz (1992) had participants recall either 3 (easy) or 9 (difficult) examples of chronic diseases and subsequently asked them to estimate the percentage of Germans who suffer from chronic diseases. As expected, they estimated the prevalence of chronic diseases to be higher after recalling 3 ($M = 38.3\%$) rather than 9 ($M = 25.2\%$) examples, reflecting that they based their judgments on experienced ease of recall. To explore the role of perceived expertise, other participants were first asked to indicate how much they know about chronic diseases before they were asked to provide a prevalence estimate. The knowledge question was expected to draw their attention to their general lack of knowledge in this domain, thus undermining the informational value of their recall experiences. In this case, participants estimated the prevalence of chronic diseases to be lower after recalling 3 ($M = 23.1\%$) rather than 9 ($M = 33.0\%$) examples, reflecting that they based their judgments on the number of examples recalled.

These findings suggest that people rely on their subjective recall experiences only when they consider themselves knowledgeable, but turn to recalled content when they do not (see also Schwarz & Schuman, 1997). Extending this line of research, Vaughn (1997) explored the role of a particular kind of expertise, namely schematicity with regard to a personality trait (Markus, 1977). Specifically, she asked assertiveness schematics (who are considered experts on this trait) and aschematics (nonexperts) to recall either 3 or 8 examples of their own assertive behavior. As expected, assertiveness schematics based their self-assessments on their subjective recall experience and reported higher assertiveness after recalling 3 (easy) rather than 8 (difficult) examples. Conversely, assertiveness aschematics discounted their subjective accessibility experience and based their self-assessments on recalled information, reporting higher assertiveness after recalling 8 rather than 3 examples.

In combination, these studies indicate that perceived knowledgeability is a crucial prerequisite for reliance on experienced ease of recall as a source of information. When people are aware, or are made aware, of a lack of knowledge in the respective domain, the diagnostic value of recall experiences is called into question, much as is the case when their attention is drawn to external factors likely to influence their recall experience.

Conclusions
The reviewed studies demonstrate that recall tasks render two distinct sources of information available: the recalled content and the ease or difficulty with which it can be brought to mind. Depending on which source judges draw on, they may arrive at *opposite* conclusions. Hence, we cannot predict their judgments on the basis of recalled content alone, but must take into account if the content was easy or difficult to bring to mind and whether this subjective

experience is deemed diagnostic. When the diagnosticity of recall experiences is called into question, either due to external factors or a perceived lack of knowledge, judges turn to recalled content as the more informative source of information. These contingencies have important implications for judgment and decision making, as research into debiasing hindsight may illustrate.

WHEN DEBIASING HINDSIGHT BACKFIRES: THE INTERPLAY OF CONTENT AND EXPERIENCE

As Fischhoff (1982a, p. 428) noted, once people know the outcome of an event, they "not only tend to view what has happened as has having been inevitable, but also tend to view it as having been 'relatively inevitable' before it happened." As a result, they believe that they, and others, should have been able to anticipate the event and they even "misremember their own predictions so as to exaggerate in hindsight what they knew in foresight" (Fischhoff, 1982a, p. 428). Theoretically, the emergence of hindsight biases has been attributed to the high accessibility of outcome-related knowledge and its integration into the mental representation of the event (see Hawkins & Hastie, 1989, for a comprehensive review). Accordingly, attempts to debias hindsight have focused on strategies that increase the accessibility of factors that might have led to a different outcome, following Fischhoff's (1982b, p. 343) suggestion "to force oneself to argue against the inevitability of the reported outcome, that is, to try to convince oneself that it might have turned out otherwise." Even this strategy, however, has been found to only attenuate hindsight effects, not eliminate them (e.g., Koriat, Lichtenstein, & Fischhoff, 1980; Slovic & Fischhoff, 1977). Worse, the research reviewed previously suggests that this strategy may backfire. To the extent that attempts to "argue against the inevitability of the outcome" are experienced as difficult, they may only succeed in convincing us *even more* that the outcome was, indeed, inevitable.

To test this possibility, Sanna, Schwarz, and Stocker (2001, Experiment 2) presented participants with a description of the British – Gurkha War (taken from Fischhoff, 1975). Depending on conditions, participants were told either that the British or the Gurkha had won the war, or received no outcome information. Subsequently, they were asked, "If we hadn't already told you who had won, what would you have thought the probability of the British (Gurkhas, respectively) winning would be?" (0–100%). Replicating earlier findings, participants with outcome knowledge thought in hindsight that they would have predicted the alleged outcome in foresight; they assigned the outcome a probability of $M = 58.2\%$, which is significantly higher than the probability assigned by participants without outcome knowledge ($M = 48.3\%$). More important, other participants were asked to list either 2 (easy) or 10 (difficult) thoughts on how the war might have turned out otherwise; that is, how the Gurkha (British, respectively) might have won when they were told about a British (Gurkha, respectively) victory. Generating 2 reasons for an alternative outcome did not significantly attenuate hindsight ($M = 54.3\%$), whereas generating 10 reasons backfired: The latter participants considered the alleged outcome even more likely, $M = 68.0\%$, presumably because the counterfactual thoughts were difficult to bring to mind. Consistent with this interpretation, participants in the thought-listing conditions provided higher likelihood ratings, the more difficult they found the thought listing, $r(38) = .78$.

As these results demonstrate, debiasing hindsight is a tricky business: The more people think about why things could have turned out otherwise, the more they may convince themselves that the actual outcome was, indeed, inevitable. Note, however, that the misattribution research reviewed earlier suggests a potential remedy for these "backfire" effects of debiasing. When the informational value of experienced difficulty is undermined through (mis)attribution procedures, people rely on their thought content despite the fact that it was difficult to bring to mind. If so, generating many reasons for why things may have turned out otherwise may indeed eliminate hindsight, provided that the experienced difficulty of thought generation is discounted. Yet, this elimination of hindsight may come at the price of a bias in the opposite direction.

Exploring these issues, Sanna et al. (2001, Experiment 4) asked participants prior to the 2000 presidential elections in the United States to predict the percentage of the popular vote the major candidates would receive. Due to voting irregularities in Florida and an extended legal battle, the official outcome of the election remained uncertain for several weeks. Following the announcement of the official result, participants were asked to recall the predictions they had made 5 weeks earlier. Depending on conditions, participants did or did not list thoughts about how the election could have turned out otherwise. Table 5.4 shows the key results. The top panel shows that the Democratic candidate Gore achieved a minute lead of 0.32% over the Republican candidate Bush, although Bush was declared president. Prior to the election, participants in the zero-thoughts condition predicted a Gore lead of 4.45%, but after the election they recalled this prediction as a lead of merely 0.58%, indicating a significant hindsight bias. This replicates similar findings in previous research (e.g., Leary, 1982; Powell, 1988). Of interest is the extent to which the thought listing task affects the size of this hindsight bias.

Some participants were asked to list 12 thoughts about how the election could have turned out otherwise, which they experienced as difficult. As shown in the third panel, this intervention did not attenuate the hindsight effect, nor did it result in a backfire effect. In this present case, the absence of a backfire effect is probably due to a floor problem. Given Gore's minute lead in the actual results, a backfire effect would have required that participants erroneously recall that they actually predicted a Bush victory, thus reversing the ordinal placement of the candidates. More important, other participants were led to attribute the experienced difficulty to their own lack of knowledge. Prior to recalling their

Table 5.4. Recalled Election Predictions as a Function of Outcome Knowledge and Counterfactual Thoughts

Outcome Knowledge	
Candidate	Official Election Result
Bush	47.99
Gore	48.31
Difference	0.32

	Participants' Estimates	
	Pre-election Prediction	Postelection Recall
No Thought Listing		
Bush	45.08	47.54
Gore	49.54	48.22
Difference	4.45	0.58
12 Thoughts Listed		
Bush/Cheney	44.42	48.19
Gore/Lieberman	49.69	48.80
Difference	5.26	0.61
12 Thoughts Listed, Attribution to Lack of Expertise		
Bush/Cheney	45.14	44.57
Gore/Lieberman	49.85	52.09
Difference	4.71	7.52

Note: Shown are the predicted percentages of each candidate's share of the popular vote and the recalled predictions. Adapted from Sanna, Schwarz, and Stocker (2001, Experiment 4).

prediction, they were asked, "We realize that this was an extremely difficult task that only people with a good knowledge of politics may be able to complete. As background information, may we therefore ask you how knowledgeable you are about politics?" Following a rating of their political expertise, these participants recalled their pre-election predictions. The bottom panel of Table 5.4 shows the results. Whereas these participants had predicted a Gore lead of 4.71% prior to the election, they now recalled that they had predicted a lead of 7.52%. Thus, generating counterfactual thoughts not only eliminated the hindsight bias, but also introduced a significant bias in the opposite direction, once the informational value of the experienced difficulty was undermined.

In combination, these findings indicate that forcing oneself "to argue against the inevitability of the reported outcome" (Fischhoff, 1982b, p. 343) is a fallible strategy for debiasing hindsight. The more we try to do so, the more difficult we may find the task, leaving us all the more convinced that the outcome was inevitable. Moreover, once we discount our subjective experience of difficulty and rely on thought content, the successful elimination of hindsight may come at the price of a bias in the opposite direction.

RELYING ON EASE OF RECALL VERSUS RECALLED CONTENT: THE INFLUENCE OF PROCESSING MOTIVATION

So far, we have seen that experiential information is not used when its informational value is called into question, either due to a self-perceived lack of knowledge in the respective content domain or due to misattribution manipulations. In many cases, however, both sources of information may seem similarly diagnostic. What determines which source of information is preferred under these conditions? This is the issue to which we turn next.

Consistent with the notion of an availability *heuristic*, we may consider reliance on ease of recall a heuristic strategy, suggesting that variables known to determine the degree of heuristic processing should influence the extent to which individuals rely on this source of information. As a large body of research in social cognition has demonstrated, individuals' judgment strategies depend, *ceteris paribus*, on the motivation they bring to the task. The more self-relevant and involving the task is, the more likely they are to adopt a systematic processing strategy, paying attention to the specific implications of the information that comes to mind. In contrast, heuristic processing strategies are preferred for less-relevant and less-involving tasks (see the contributions in Chaiken & Trope, 1999, for variations on this theme). If so, the self-relevance of the material addressed in the recall task may determine if individuals rely on recalled content or experienced ease of recall in forming a judgment.

Assessing One's Vulnerability to Heart Disease

To explore this possibility, Rothman and Schwarz (1998) asked male undergraduates to list either 3 or 8 behaviors that they personally engage in that may either increase or decrease their risk of heart disease. Pretests indicated that listing 3 behaviors was experienced as easy, whereas listing 8 was experienced as difficult. The personal relevance of the task was assessed via a background characteristic; namely, whether participants had a family history of heart disease. Supposedly, assessing their own risk of heart disease is a more relevant task for males whose family history puts them at higher risk than for males without a family history of heart disease. Hence, participants with a family history of heart disease should be likely to adopt a systematic processing strategy, paying attention to the specific behaviors brought to mind by the recall task. In contrast, participants without a family history may rely on a heuristic strategy, drawing on the subjective experience of ease or difficulty of recall.

As shown in Table 5.5, the results supported these predictions. The top panel shows participants' self-reported vulnerability to heart disease. As expected, males with a family history of heart disease drew on the relevant behavioral information they recalled. Hence, they reported higher vulnerability after recalling 8 rather than 3 risk-increasing behaviors, and lower vulnerability after recalling 8 rather than 3 risk-decreasing behaviors. In contrast, males without a family history of heart disease drew on the experience of ease or difficulty of

Table 5.5. Vulnerability to Heart Disease as a Function of Type
and Number of Recalled Behaviors and Family History

	Type of Behavior	
	Risk-increasing	Risk-decreasing
Vulnerability Judgments		
With family history		
3 examples	4.6	5.8
8 examples	5.4	3.8
Without family history		
3 examples	3.9	3.1
8 examples	3.2	4.3
Need for Behavior Change		
With family history		
3 examples	3.6	5.2
8 examples	6.3	4.7
Without family history		
3 examples	3.4	3.0
8 examples	2.8	5.6

Note: N is 8 to 12 per condition. Judgments of vulnerability and the need to change current behavior were made on 9-point scales, with higher values indicating greater vulnerability and need to change, respectively. Adapted from Rothman and Schwarz (1998).

recall, resulting in the opposite pattern. They reported lower vulnerability after recalling 8 (difficult) rather than 3 (easy) risk-increasing behaviors, and higher vulnerability after recalling 8 rather than 3 risk-decreasing behaviors.

In addition, participants' perceived need for behavior change paralleled their vulnerability judgments, as shown in the bottom panel of Table 5.5. Note that participants with a family history of heart disease reported the highest need for behavior change after recalling 8 risk-increasing behaviors, whereas participants without a family history report the lowest need for behavior change under this condition, again illustrating a reversal in the judgmental outcome.

Assessing One's Vulnerability to Sexual Assault

Supporting the robustness of these findings, Grayson and Schwarz (1999) observed a parallel pattern when women were asked to assess their vulnerability to sexual assault. In their study, women had to recall 4 or 8 behaviors they personally engaged in that may either increase or decrease their risk of sexual assault. Some of these women assumed that sexual assault only happens to women who "ask for it," thus reducing the personal relevance of the recall task. These women relied on ease of recall and inferred higher vulnerability after recalling 4 rather than 8 risk-increasing behaviors, or 8 rather than 4 risk-decreasing behaviors. Other women assumed that sexual assault may happen to any woman, thus increasing the personal relevance of the recall task. These women relied on content of recall and inferred lower vulnerability after recalling 4 rather than 8 risk-increasing behaviors, or 8 rather than 4 risk-decreasing behaviors. Thus, women's beliefs about sexual assault determined the judgment strategy used, as did a family history of heart disease in Rothman and Schwarz's (1998) study.

Conclusions

In combination, these findings again illustrate that the same recall task renders two distinct sources of information available: recalled content and experienced ease of recall. Depending on which source individuals draw on, they arrive at *opposite* conclusions. In fact, analyses of the Rothman and Schwarz data shown in Table 5.5 did not reveal a main effect of the content of the re-call task, nor did analyses of the Grayson and Schwarz data. In neither study could one predict the impact of thinking about risk-increasing or -decreasing behaviors without knowing if individuals found it easy or difficult to bring the respective behaviors to mind, and which judgmental strategy they were likely to use.

Note also that the observed impact of personal involvement on individuals' processing strategy contradicts the common assumption that reliance on the availability heuristic is independent of judges' motivation. In several studies, researchers offered participants incentives for arriving at the correct answer, yet such incentives rarely attenuated reliance on the availability heuristic (see Nisbett & Ross, 1980; Payne, Bettman, & Johnson, 1993, for discussions). Unfortunately, these studies could not observe a change in processing strategy, even if it occurred. To see why, suppose that one presented participants with a list of the names of 19 famous females and 20 nonfamous males (Tversky & Kahneman, 1973). Suppose further that some participants are offered an incentive to arrive at the correct estimate of the proportion of female names on the list, whereas others are not. Without an incentive, individuals may rely on a heuristic strategy, drawing on experienced ease of recall. This would lead them to conclude that there were more female than male names on the list. With a successful incentive, however, they may be motivated to invest more effort. If so, they may recall as many names as they can and may count the number of female names in the recalled sample. Unfortunately, this systematic strategy would lead them to the same conclusion because the famous female names would be overrepresented in the recalled sample. As this example illustrates, we can distinguish only between heuristic and systematic strategies when we introduce conditions under which both strategies lead to different outcomes. When this is done, we are likely to observe the expected impact of processing motivation, as these findings illustrate.

SUMMARY

In summary, the reviewed research highlights that recall tasks render two distinct sources of information available: the recalled content and the ease or difficulty with which it could be brought to mind. In most situations, these two sources of information are naturally confounded and the experience of ease of recall goes along with a greater amount of recall. This confound rendered many of the classic tests of the availability heuristic nondiagnostic. When this confound is disentangled, however, the available evidence supports the original formulation of the availability heuristic: Individuals estimate the frequency of an event, the likelihood of its occurrence, and its typicality "by the ease with which instances or associations come to mind" (Tversky & Kahneman, 1973, p. 208). In this chapter, we reviewed several sources of evidence for this conclusion and addressed some of the complications that arise from the dual informativeness of recall tasks.

First, individuals only rely on their recall experiences as a source of information when their informational value is not called into question. When they attribute their experiences to an external influence (e.g., Haddock et al., 1999; Schwarz et al., 1991; Wänke et al., 1995) or are aware that they may not be knowledgeable about the content domain (e.g., Biller et al., 1992; Sanna et al., 2001), the otherwise observed influence of recall experiences is eliminated. This parallels the use of other sources of experiential information, such as moods, emotions, or bodily states (see Schwarz, Chapter 29, this volume; Schwarz & Clore, 1996; Strack, 1992, for reviews).

Second, when subjective recall experiences are considered nondiagnostic, individuals turn to the content of recall as an alternate source of information (e.g., Schwarz et al., 1991). Under unconstrained conditions, reliance on recalled content is likely to lead to the same outcome as reliance on ease of recall, reflecting that recall is experienced as easy when a large number of examples can be brought to mind. When people are induced to recall a few versus many examples, however, these two sources of information have opposite implications: Whereas the experienced ease (or difficulty) suggests that there are many (few) examples, the actual examples recalled lead to the opposite conclusion.

Finally, individuals are likely to rely on ease of recall when the judgment task is of low personal relevance, but draw on recalled content when the task is of high personal relevance (e.g., Grayson & Schwarz, 1999; Rothman & Schwarz, 1998). This influence of processing motivation is consistent with dual-process models of judgment (Chaiken & Trope, 1999). However, it could not be observed in previous studies that confounded ease and content of recall.

In addition to bearing on the availability heuristic (Tversky & Kahneman, 1973) and the conditions of its use, the reviewed work bears on research into knowledge accessibility effects in social judgment (see Higgins, 1996, for a review). One of the truisms of social cognition research holds that judgments are based on the information that is most accessible at the time of judgment. Yet the reviewed findings indicate that this is the case only when the respective information is easy to bring to mind. When recall is experienced as difficult, judges arrive at conclusions that contradict the accessible declarative information – inferring, for example, that they are not assertive despite the fact that the recall task rendered 12 examples highly accessible (Schwarz et al., 1991). This suggests that knowledge accessibility effects may often reflect reliance on subjective recall experiences, rather than reliance on the accessible declarative information per se. Complicating things further, which source of information individuals draw on depends on their processing motivation, as seen here (Grayson & Schwarz, 1999; Rothman & Schwarz, 1998). As a result, it is not sufficient to know *what* is accessible at the time of judgment; instead, we must consider the ease with which the accessible information comes to mind and the processing strategy that judges are likely to apply (Schwarz, 1998). Understanding this interplay of processing motivation, experiential information, and declarative information provides a promising avenue for future research, with potentially important implications for social cognition and decision making.

6. Incorporating the Irrelevant: Anchors in Judgments of Belief and Value

Gretchen B. Chapman and Eric J. Johnson

Imagine walking down a supermarket aisle and passing an end-of-aisle display of canned tomato soup. A sign on the display says, "Limit 12 per customer." Would such a sign influence the number of cans you would buy? Would you buy more cans than if the sign said "No limit per customer"? Our intuitions say no, but empirical evidence indicates that purchase behaviors are influenced by such a sign (Wansink, Kent, & Hoch, 1998). Consider another example: A wheel of fortune is spun and stops at the number 65. You are then asked if the percentage of African countries in the United Nations is above or below that number. Could this exercise influence your estimate of the relevant percentage? Although it may seem unlikely, the evidence is that such anchors have an effect: Groups who received larger numbers determined by a wheel of fortune gave higher estimates than groups who received lower numbers, demonstrating that irrelevant anchors influenced these estimates (Tversky & Kahneman, 1974).

"Anchoring and adjustment" is one of three well-known heuristics described by Tversky and Kahneman (1974) in a classic paper that also describes the representativeness and availability heuristics. Like the other heuristics, anchoring and adjustment can be a useful way of making judgments. Imagine that you are trying to set a value on an antique chair that you have inherited from a distant aunt. You might recall seeing a very similar chair in slightly better condition at a local antique dealer. You might start with that price as an anchor, and incorporate the difference in quality. This seems to be a useful and effort-saving use of the anchoring and adjustment heuristic. Now, however, imagine that you had seen (on Public Television's *Antiques Road Show*) a not-so-similar chair that, unlike yours, is signed by the designer and worth, as a result, many thousands of dollars more. If you were to use this as an anchor, and if you did not properly incorporate the fact that your chair did not have a signature, you might end up with an estimate that was too high, or biased. Thus anchoring can be a useful heuristic, but it can also result in biased answers.

Research suggests that people use an anchor-and-adjust strategy to solve a variety of estimation problems. For example, Rottenstreich and Tversky (1997) proposed that when judging the likelihood of a disjunctive event

This work was supported in part by NSF grant SBR97-96042 to the first author.

(e.g., the likelihood of being a chemistry or biology major), people anchor on an estimate for one event (e.g., chemistry major) and adjust to take into account the other event as well. Similarly, Kruger (1999) suggested that when answering questions such as, "How does your driving ability compare to that of your peers?" people first anchor on their own abilities, and then adjust for the skills of their peers. Griffin and Tversky (1992) proposed that when making confidence judgments, people anchor on the extremeness of the evidence confronting them and then adjust for the credibility of the evidence. In all these cases, adjustment is often insufficient, resulting in a bias.

Tversky and Kahneman (1974, p. 1128) presented anchoring as a process in which "people make estimates by starting from an initial value that is adjusted to yield a final answer [and] . . . adjustments are typically insufficient." Notions of anchoring were first introduced to decision-making research in early descriptions of preference reversals (Slovic, 1967; Slovic & Lichtenstein, 1968; Lichtenstein & Slovic, 1971). In judging the attractiveness of a gamble, the gamble attribute most compatible with the response mode seemed to be an anchor. For example, in pricing a gamble, subjects would anchor on the monetary outcome of the gamble and make adjustments from there.

The concept of anchoring and adjustment has had widespread impact. However, the mechanisms of anchoring have been systematically explored only recently. In this chapter, we review what is currently known about the causes and effects of anchoring. We start by offering some definitions, and then identify some stylized facts about this heuristic. We next examine two families of causes of anchoring. We close by reviewing other phenomena related to anchoring and potential applications.

ANCHORING DEFINITIONS

Because it has been used in many different areas, the term *anchoring* has been used to mean somewhat different things. We group these definitions into three types: One refers to an *anchoring procedure* in which a salient but uninformative number is presented to subjects. A second meaning is an *experimental result*, in which the uninformative number influences the judgments. Finally, anchoring and adjustment is sometimes used to refer to the *psychological process* by which the uninformative number has its effect.

Our discussion of anchoring might benefit from some standardized nomenclature that emphasizes these distinctions. We define an *anchoring procedure* as one in which a salient but uninformative number is presented to subjects before they make a numeric judgment. Most anchoring studies follow a two-step procedure introduced by Tversky and Kahneman (1974). Subjects are first asked to compare the anchor to the target value, stating whether the anchor is higher or lower than the target. For example, subjects are asked whether the percentage of African countries in the United Nations is more or less than 10%. Second, subjects are asked to give a numeric estimate of the target – for example, to state the percentage of African countries in the United Nations. Some anchoring studies (e.g., Wilson, Houston, Brekke, & Etling, 1996) use other procedures that do not include the initial comparison judgment. Differences in procedure may be important, because similar effects obtained with different procedures may not necessarily represent the same phenomenon or underlying mechanism.

All anchoring procedures involve presentation of an anchor. We concentrate on numeric anchors that are uninformative but salient to the decision maker. Thus, a number can be identified as an anchor before looking to see whether it influences judgment. There are two reasons for focusing on uninformative anchors. First, the influence of uninformative anchors is clearly a bias. If respondents report that an anchor is irrelevant to the judgment at hand, yet it influences their judgment, it is hard to argue that this reflects the rational use of relevant information. A second reason for focusing on uninformative anchors is to rule out one potentially uninteresting cause of anchoring effects. Subjects might attend to anchors and incorporate them into their judgments because they reason that the experimenter would not have mentioned the anchor were it not informative or relevant (Grice, 1975). This reduces the anchoring effect to a sort of demand effect (e.g., Schwarz, 1994; Schwarz & Bless, 1992; Sudman, Bradburn, & Schwarz, 1996). In order to avoid this type of explanation, a number of investigators use anchors that are obviously uninformative. For example, Russo and Shoemaker (1989, p. 90) asked participants to estimate the year Attila the Hun was defeated in Europe after considering an anchor constructed from their phone numbers. Because these numbers are in no plausible way related to the year of Attila's defeat, any influence is clearly an unwanted bias. Similarly, the output of a wheel of fortune is not plausibly predictive of the membership of African countries in the United Nations.

Informative numbers might be anchors. When anchors are informative, experiments that show anchoring often rely on demonstrating order effects – specifically, that earlier items of information receive more weight. For example, Kahneman and Tversky (1974) used a multiplication problem and contrasted estimates of two orders of the same product: $8 \times 7 \times 6 \times 5 \times 4 \times 3 \times 2 \times 1$ and $1 \times 2 \times 3 \times 4 \times 5 \times 6 \times 7 \times 8$. Here, the product of the first few numbers is relevant information with respect to the final estimate. However, the disparity of the two estimates, which depends on the order in which the sequences are presented, indicates that the earlier numbers receive too much weight in the estimation of the final product. Demonstrations that use meaningful information as anchors often raise a number of important but auxiliary questions, such as the appropriate weighting of a sequence of information and differences between sequential and simultaneous presentation. Therefore, we concentrate on cases in which anchors are irrelevant to the task at hand. As shown later, even when judges agree that the numbers are irrelevant, they do have an impact.

We define *anchoring* as an experimental result or outcome; the influence of an anchor that renders the final judgment too close to the anchor. Thus, *anchoring* is defined as assimilation rather than contrast (Sherif, Sherif, & Nebergall, 1965;

Sherif & Hovland, 1961). The vast majority of decision-making studies on anchoring have found a positive relation between anchors and judgments. We reserve discussion of the cognitive process underlying anchoring effects for a later section. First, we review key results about the anchoring effect.

NECESSARY CONDITIONS FOR ANCHORING

Not all uninformative numbers produce anchoring effects. Instead, certain features of the anchor, target, and judgment task are required.

Attention to the Anchor

As described earlier, the vast majority of anchoring studies follow a two-step procedure in which an initial comparison task is followed by numeric estimation of the target. This procedure assures that subjects attend to the anchor and compare it to the target. In fact, the initial comparative judgment is not necessary to produce anchoring. Wilson et al. (1996) found that anchoring could be achieved without the comparative judgment, provided that subjects devoted sufficient attention to the anchor. For example, doing five pages of computations on large numbers increased a later target judgment about cancer incidence (relative to a no-anchor control condition), but doing one page of computations did not. Thus, anchoring occurred even when subjects did not explicitly compare the anchor to the target value, but the anchor had to be made very salient by extensive processing. Wilson et al. (1996) suggest that it is necessary for the irrelevant anchor to come to mind as a potential response to the target question.

Anchor–Target Compatibility

In most studies of anchoring, the anchor is an arbitrary number on the same scale as the target response. Several studies have examined whether this condition is necessary for anchoring to occur. For example, Chapman and Johnson (1994) asked subjects to judge the value of various consumer items by indicating the amount of money or additional life expectancy they would demand in exchange for giving up the item. Before specifying an amount, subjects first considered an anchor expressed in dollars or years of life expectancy. Anchoring occurred if the anchor and response were on the same scale (e.g., both life expectancy) but not if they were on different scales (e.g., monetary anchor and life expectancy response). Kahneman and Knetsch (1993) report a similar result. They asked Toronto residents whether they would pay $25 (low anchor) or $200 (high anchor) to clean up specified lakes to maintain fish populations. Some subjects were then asked to estimate the amount the average Toronto resident would contribute. These subjects showed an anchoring effect, giving mean estimates of $14 and $36 in the low and high anchor conditions, respectively. Other subjects were instead asked to estimate the percentage of Toronto residents who would pay $100. These subjects did not show an anchoring effect (estimating 24% and 29% in the low and high anchor conditions, respectively). Thus, anchoring occurred when anchors and responses were both expressed on a dollar scale, but not when anchors were expressed as dollars but responses as percentages.

Strack and Mussweiler (1997) found that it is not sufficient for the anchor and response to be on the same numeric scale; to achieve strong anchoring, anchor and response must also express the same underlying dimension. They asked subjects to estimate the height or width of the Brandenburg Gate after considering a numeric anchor described as the height or width of the gate. Anchoring was much stronger if both the anchor and the target judgment represented the height (or both the width); it was weaker if one was height and the other was width. All anchors and responses were expressed as meters, but this agreement alone did not determine the size of the anchoring effect. To obtain a large anchoring effect, the anchor had to represent the same dimension (width or height) as the target.

In a similar experiment (Wilson et al., 1996, Experiment 1) subjects were asked to estimate the number of countries in the United Nations (UN). Before making this judgment, some subjects were asked to judge whether a high anchor was more or less than the number of countries in the UN, whereas other subjects were asked whether the same anchor was more or less than the number of physicians and surgeons in the phone book. Anchoring occurred both when the anchor had been compared to the target question (about the UN) and when compared to the irrelevant question (about physicians). The switch in questions (UN to physicians) produced an anchoring effect that was numerically but not statistically smaller than the anchoring effect in the no-switch condition. In this study, the anchor and target were both expressed on the same numeric scale (counting numbers), but not the same dimension or quantity (number of physicians or number of countries). The change in dimensions tended to reduce the anchoring effect, but the reduction was not as large as in the Strack and Mussweiler (1997) study.

Extreme Anchors

Several studies have found that anchoring occurs even when the anchors are extreme or represent implausible responses to the target question. Strack and Mussweiler (1997) asked subjects, for example, to estimate the year that Einstein first visited the United States after considering anchors of 1215 or 1992. These implausible anchors produced anchoring effects just as large as more plausible anchors (e.g., 1905, 1939). Similarly, Chapman and Johnson (1994) asked subjects to indicate minimum selling prices for monetary lotteries after considering a monetary anchor. Some of the anchors were higher than the most one could win or less than the least one could win in the lottery. Although they were implausible responses for the selling price question, they nevertheless produced an anchoring effect. In a second experiment, anchors of up to 28 times the lottery expected value (EV) also produced anchoring, but at the far extremes these anchors had a smaller proportional effect. Quattrone, Lawrence, Finkel, and Andrus (1981) found similar results. Thus, even extreme anchors produce anchoring effects, although it is possible that plausible and implausible anchors have their effects via different mechanisms (Strack & Mussweiler, 1997).

Awareness

Given that anchoring seems to be pervasive, it seems natural to ask if subjects are aware of its influence. Wilson et al. (1996) asked their participants whether they were influenced by the anchor. There was a moderate and significant correlation between reported awareness and the size of the anchoring effect. Nevertheless, the vast majority of subjects reported that they were not influenced by the anchor but still showed an anchoring effect. Thus, the relationship between anchoring and awareness of the anchor's effect was weak, and awareness was not necessary for anchoring. Making participants aware of the anchor's effect does not decrease anchoring. Both Wilson et al. (1996) and Quattrone et al. (1981) found that warning participants not to be influenced by the anchor was unsuccessful. Related to the issue of awareness is whether anchoring occurs even when subjects view the anchor as uninformative. Chapman and Johnson (1999, Experiments 3 and 4) found conflicting results on perceived informativeness. In one study, participants who perceived the randomly generated anchor to be informative showed a larger anchoring effect; whereas in a second study, they showed a smaller effect. In both studies, however, a significant anchoring effect was achieved even among participants who reported that the anchor was uninformative.

Incentives

By many accounts (e.g., Petty & Wegener, 1993; Wilson & Brekke, 1994), subjects cannot avoid judgment biases unless they are aware of them. Thus, given the modest relationship between anchoring and awareness, it would not be surprising if incentives did not reduce anchoring. In fact, the evidence about the influence of incentives on anchoring is mostly negative. Chapman and Johnson (unpublished data) used a procedure in which half the subjects were paid according to the preferences implied by their judgments of simple lotteries. There was no reduction in anchoring when subjects' payoffs depended on their responses. Wilson et al. (1996) found that offering an accuracy prize decreased subjects' ratings of the anchor's influence without actually decreasing the anchoring effect. Tversky and Kahneman (1974) also report that payment for accuracy did not reduce anchoring. Wright and Anderson (1989), however, did find a marginal ($p < .09$) reduction in anchoring due to incentives. Their incentive manipulation included both monetary payment for accuracy and public posting of accuracy scores, which may explain their greater success. Three negative findings and one marginal finding, however, lead to an overall conclusion that incentives reduce anchoring very little if at all.

Summary

In summary, anchoring effects are common when the anchor has received sufficient attention. This effect occurs even for extreme anchors and even when respondents are unaware of the effect, have been warned to avoid the effect, or are motivated to be accurate. Anchors are most influential if they are relevant to the target judgment; that is, if they are expressed on the response scale and represent the same underlying dimension, thus comprising a potential answer to the target question.

CAUSES OF ANCHORING

What are the psychological mechanisms that cause anchoring? Figure 6.1 illustrates three stages at which an anchoring process might occur. First, information regarding the target is retrieved through search of memory or the environment. The presence of the anchor could influence what information is retrieved; for example, information similar to the anchor might be primed selectively. Second, the information must be integrated to form an overall target judgment. The anchor may affect that integration process, for example, by giving greater weight to information compatible with the anchor. Or perhaps the anchor itself is included as one of the pieces of information to be integrated. Finally, the judgment must be expressed on an external scale (e.g., dollars, meters). The anchor might influence how the internal judgment is expressed on the external scale. For example, the anchor might facilitate use of the portion of the scale closest to the anchor. Of course, anchoring may have multiple causes, and the relevant mechanisms may occur at more than one stage. An understanding of the locus

Figure 6.1. Three stages at which an anchoring mechanism could occur. The bottom of the figure shows classification of several potential anchoring processes.

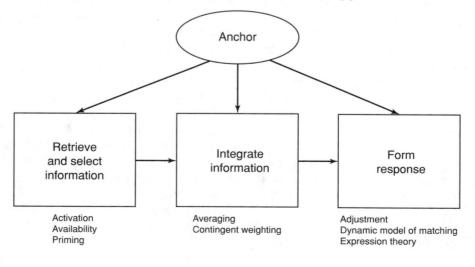

of anchoring effects is important in understanding how to debias this effect. For example, if anchoring occurs at the retrieval stage, then debiasing efforts aimed at later stages are likely to be unsuccessful.

ANCHORING AS ADJUSTMENT

Anchoring effects have most often been explained in conjunction with the idea of insufficient adjustment away from the anchor. The name *anchoring and adjustment* implies a particular cognitive process whereby decision makers first focus on the anchor and then make a series of dynamic adjustments toward their final estimate. Because these adjustments are insufficient, the final answer is biased toward the anchor. Tversky and Kahneman (1974) described this type of adjustment process as occurring when subjects answered the United Nations question. This type of account raises a central question: Why are adjustments insufficient (Lopes, 1982)? Most accounts focus either on uncertainty for the true value or a lack of cognitive effort.

The first class of explanations uses the idea that judges are uncertain about the value they want to report. For example, Quattrone et al. (1981) proposed that subjects adjust the anchor until shortly after it enters a range of plausible values for the target item. Thus, when adjusting from a high anchor, decision makers stop at the high end of plausible values, but stop at the low end when adjusting from low anchors. Their study showed a larger anchoring effect for questions judged to have a broad range of plausible values.

A more formal model with a similar underlying idea was developed by Busemeyer and Goldstein (1992; see also Busemeyer & Townsend, 1993) as an anchoring and adjustment account of preference reversals. This dynamic model of matching is not a proposed mechanism of anchoring per se, but rather an anchoring account of preference reversals. (The relation between anchoring and preference reversals is discussed in a later section.) This model is similar to that put forward by Quattrone et al. (1981) in that it posits a process in which decision makers test for a match between the anchor and the target and make adjustments if a match is not achieved. Premature matches lead to insufficient adjustment.

A second class of explanations for insufficient adjustment follow from the notion that adjustment is effortful. Consequently, lack of effort or lack of cognitive resources cause adjustment to be terminated too soon, resulting in a final response that is too close to the anchor. One line of evidence supporting such an adjustment process comes from studies that use cognitive load or busyness manipulations. These paradigms examine situations in which judges place too much weight on one type of information, much like an anchor in our description (Gilbert, Miller, & Ross, 1998). These include the overreliance on information about behavior, as opposed to situational constraints (i.e. the correspondence bias; Gilbert, Pelham, & Krull, 1988), and overreliance on one's own knowledge, as opposed to information available to others (i.e. the "curse of knowledge";

Keysar & Barr, Chapter 8, this volume). These phenomena can be understood as instances of anchoring on one piece of information and consequently underweighting subsequent knowledge by a process of insufficient adjustment.

For example, Kruger (1999) proposed an anchoring account of the "above average" effect – the result that, when asked to compare themselves with their peers, people tend to judge themselves as above average. Kruger argues that people anchor on their own abilities and then make adjustments to account for their peers' abilities. Whereas focusing on an anchor is an automatic process, adjustment is more effortful, and consequently tends to be insufficient. Kruger found that increasing cognitive load (by asking subjects to rehearse a string of digits) increased the above-average bias, suggesting that limiting cognitive resources makes adjustment more insufficient.

Other studies (e.g., Gilbert et al., 1988) provide similar evidence that increases in cognitive load affect the second stage (adjustment) of the process, and not the first stage (anchoring), suggesting that the second stage is more effortful and less automatic than the first. These studies do not use the traditional anchoring procedure (Tversky & Kahneman, 1974), so their relationship to other anchoring demonstrations is unclear. In addition, Gilbert et al. (1988, p. 738) point out, "The resource metaphor is only one way to describe such effects, and unfortunately, no critical experiment seems capable of distinguishing between resource and other viable interpretations (e.g., structure or skill)." We agree, and take these findings to be evidence that the first stage of the process is different in some ways from a second integration or expression stage, and that a difference in automaticity appears to be a likely candidate. It is less clear, however, whether this evidence requires an adjustment account of anchoring effects.

In evaluating whether adjustment is insufficient because of lack of effort or resources, another line of relevant research concerns the effect of incentives. If insufficient adjustment were the result of lack of effort or allocation of cognitive resources, we might expect individuals to exhibit less anchoring (that is, more sufficient adjustment) when the stakes are high. Busemeyer and Goldstein's (1992) adjustment account makes just this prediction. As discussed previously, evidence about the effect of incentives is mixed but mostly negative. More broadly, several judgment phenomena that are attributed to anchoring, most notably preference reversals, do not diminish in the face of incentives (see Slovic and Lichtenstein, 1983, for a review). If anchoring were due to lack of cognitive resources, we might also find that experts show less anchoring because they make greater use of specialized task heuristics that conserve cognitive effort. However, this does not appear to be the case (Northcraft & Neale, 1987). Finally, we might expect that warning people about anchoring would diminish anchoring biases. However, Wilson et al. (1996) as well as Quattrone et al. (1981) found that warning participants to avoid the anchoring effect was unsuccessful.

In addition to asking *why* adjustment is insufficient, one might also look for more direct evidence as to whether the anchoring effect does, in fact, result from a cognitive process that involves adjustment. Several studies have tested directly for adjustment processes. Following a suggestion by Lopes (1982), one type of study uses process-tracing measures to look for evidence of adjustment. A preference reversal study conducted by Schkade and Johnson (1989) asked subjects to price lotteries or to rate them on a 100-point scale. They hypothesized that the lottery attribute (dollars or probability) most similar to the response scale served as an anchor, causing the evaluation to be overly influenced by that attribute. They used process measures by, for example, asking subject to indicate a response by pointing or dragging a cursor along a response scale while the computer recorded the amount of movement. The point at which the subject first touched the cursor to the scale could be an indication of an anchor. These starting points on pricing scales were correlated with the amount to win in the lottery; starting points for rating judgments were correlated with probability information. However, although these starting points may indicate the beginning of an adjustment process, they might also be just an indication of subjects' final answers and an anchoring effect, rather than a specific anchoring process. This latter interpretation is bolstered by the fact that subjects' adjustments along the response scale did not correspond to an adjustment process. For example, larger adjustments should be associated with a smaller anchoring effect because anchoring results from insufficient adjustment, according to this view. However, Schkade and Johnson's data did not show this pattern. Chapman and Johnson (unpublished data) conducted a similar experiment in which subjects considered monetary anchors before evaluating lotteries. Using the same process measures, they likewise did not find an association between adjustments along the response scale and size of the anchoring effect.

A second type of study testing whether anchoring involves adjustment uses tasks where no adjustment could occur. For example, Jacowitz and Kahneman (1995) first presented trivia questions (e.g., the height of Mount Everest) to a calibration group. The 15th and 85th percentiles of the estimates from this group were used as anchors for a second group of subjects. These subjects were presented with a high or low anchor and asked whether it was higher or lower than the target value (e.g., the height of Mount Everest); they then provided their own target estimate. Subjects' estimates showed an anchoring effect, as expected. Of greater interest, the comparison judgments themselves showed an anchoring effect. Although 15% of the calibration subjects had given target estimates lower than the low anchor (or higher than the high anchor), a much larger percentage of the experimental subjects said that the target value was lower (or higher) than the anchor. That is, the comparison question influenced judgments of the target value even before subjects were actually asked to estimate the target. Green, Jacowitz, Kahneman, and McFadden (1998) found a similar result. It may be reasonable to posit that adjustment is involved in estimating the target, but not in judging whether the anchor is higher or lower than the target. Thus, anchoring occurred prior to any possible adjustment, indicating that an adjustment process is certainly not necessary for an anchoring effect.

In sum, although anchoring and adjustment have been close traveling companions since the 1970s, there is only limited evidence that the origins of anchoring lie in an insufficient adjustment process. Although research on increases in cognitive load suggests that an effortful adjustment process may underlie some anchoring-based biases, research using incentives and process tracing methods do not implicate an adjustment bias. In addition, the work by Jacowitz and Kahneman (1995) indicates that adjustment is not necessary for the anchoring effect. Thus, although the anchoring phenomenon is well established, an adjustment mechanism is more questionable. Because at least some conceptions of adjustment characterize it as occurring in response expression, the limited support for an adjustment mechanism suggests that the third stage in Fig. 6.1 may not be well supported.

ANCHORING AS ACTIVATION

In recent years, several authors have suggested that the origin of anchoring lies in the influence of anchors on the first, retrieval stage (see Fig. 6.1). Jacowitz and Kahneman (1995), Chapman and Johnson (1994, 1999), Stack and Mussweiler (1997) and Musseiler and Strack (1999, 2000) all suggest that the anchor acts as a suggestion, making information consistent with the anchor more available, either in memory through priming mechanisms or because of a biased external search. Because the anchor is considered as a candidate response that subjects entertain, at least as a transient belief, it influences the target value. This account is consistent with work by Gilbert (1990, 1991) and Gilbert, Tafarodi, and Malone, (1993) showing that comprehension includes an initial belief in the assertion presented, followed only later by rejection of false information.

Strack and Mussweiler (1997) examined the idea that anchoring is a special case of semantic priming. They propose that information retrieved in order to compare the anchor to the target is consequently more available for use when estimating the target value. This selective accessibility account (Mussweiler & Strack, 1999, 2000) predicts that the primed information will influence the target judgment only if it is relevant. As described above, Strack and Mussweiler (1997) found just this result. Anchors representing the width of the Brandenburg Gate had only a small influence on judgments of its height, although they had a large influence on judgments of its width. In a further experiment, Strack and Mussweiler (1997) found that extreme anchors resulted in shorter response times for the comparative judgment but longer response time for the absolute judgment (target estimation). This result indicates that comparisons to implausibly extreme anchors do not require relevant target information to be retrieved, yielding a faster comparative judgment. Because this target information has not been primed, however, the absolute judgment takes longer. The implication is that for less extreme anchors, the information primed during the comparative judgment is used in the absolute judgment.

Kahneman and Knetsch (1993) proposed that the target question acts as a memory probe that retrieves the anchor mentioned earlier. The anchor is then treated as a candidate response. This priming is in some ways shallow, however, because the anchor does not always influence the target judgment, even when it primes relevant information. For example, information primed in the course a comparative judgment about whether one would pay $200 to clean up Canadian lakes is relevant to an absolute judgment about the amount an average Toronto resident would pay, but it should also be relevant to a judgment about the percentage of Toronto residents who would pay $100. Nevertheless, the anchor influences responses to the first question but not the second, presumably because the first shares more surface features with the anchor.

Jacowitz and Kahneman's (1995) finding that anchoring occurs in response to the comparative judgment (and not just in target estimation) implies that the retrieval of target information primed by the anchor is biased, such that target features similar to the anchor are disproportionately retrieved. This biased retrieval explains why an unexpectedly large number of subjects judge that the target value is lower than the low anchor (or higher than the high anchor). In other words, the comparison between anchor and target results in the anchor appearing too similar to the target. Chapman and Johnson (1999) point to this biased retrieval or asymmetric priming of target features as the key process that produces anchoring. Specifically, they hypothesize that the presence of an anchor increases the availability of features that the anchor and target hold in common while reducing the availability of features of the target that differ from the anchor.

There is evidence from process measures that decision makers concentrate their attention on target features similar to the anchor. Schkade and Johnson (1989) report that subjects spent proportionally more time looking at payoffs in a pricing task (in which they posit a monetary anchor) than in a choice task. In addition, they spent more time looking at probabilities in a 100-point rating task (in which they posit a probability anchor) than in a pricing task. Although there was no explicit anchor used in these studies, Chapman and Johnson (1999) found similar results in a task that did use explicit anchors. Subjects compared apartments described on three attributes. When a provided anchor value was high, they spent more time looking at positive features of the apartment; when the anchor was low, they spent more time looking at negative features.

Mussweiler and Strack (1999, Experiment 4) found similar evidence. In their study, some subjects answered an anchoring question (e.g., about the length of the River Elbe) and were instructed to list the features of the target that came to mind. Subjects given a high anchor tended to list thoughts that implied a high target value, whereas subjects given a low anchor tended to list thoughts that implied a low target value. Mussweiler and Strack also found evidence that the presence of an anchor primes target features that are similar to the anchor. In this study (described in Mussweiler & Strack, 2000), subjects answered the anchoring question, "Is the annual mean temperature in Germany higher or lower than 5°C (or 20°C)?" and then participated in a lexical decision task. Subjects given the low anchor were faster at identifying words such as "cold" and "snow," whereas subjects given the high anchor were faster at identifying words such as "hot" and "sun." This result shows that the anchor primed consistent information in memory.

This activation account of anchoring suggests methods for reducing the anchoring bias. Chapman and Johnson (1999) asked subjects to make predictions (e.g., the likelihood of a Republican winning the presidential election) after considering a numeric anchor. Subjects who were prompted to think of a reason opposing the implications of the anchor value (e.g., for subjects with a low anchor, reasons why a Republican would win) showed less anchoring than a control group given no prompt. In contrast, subjects prompted to think of a similar reason (e.g., for subjects with a low anchor, reasons why a Republican would not win) showed no more anchoring than did the control group. Mussweiler, Strack, and Pfeiffer (2000) replicated this finding. These results suggest that subjects ordinarily retrieve target features or reasons that are similar to the anchor (as evidenced by no effect of the similar prompt) but not those different from the anchor (unless prompted).

Mussweiler and Strack (1999, Experiment 4) also reduced anchoring in a manner consistent with this activation account. Participants in one group were asked to report the target features that came to mind when answering the comparative question. Each participant in a second group was presented with a list of thoughts generated by one of the subjects in the first group. Members of a control group were asked to list target-irrelevant thoughts. The first (own-thoughts) group showed anchoring that was no different than the third (control) group; however, the second (others'-thoughts) group showed less anchoring. The authors proposed that thoughts generated by another subject are more likely to be viewed as suspect or biased than self-generated thoughts, and consequently subjects are more like to correct for their influence by generating alternative thoughts. Thus, a subject who is presented with a thought suggesting a high target value may counter by retrieving information supporting a low target value. Such a correction would cause the information activated to be less selective and more balanced.

Manipulations of information activation could be used not only to debias anchoring but also to augment it. If anchoring occurs because the anchor facilitates retrieval of target features similar to the anchor, then anything that enhances this selective facilitation should strengthen the anchoring effect. If a large pool of target features exists, the anchor has more opportunity to enhance the similar features selectively. Chapman and Johnson (1999, Experiment 5) asked half their subjects to list actions they undertook that affected their health, a task hypothesized to increase the pool of health-related information. All subjects then estimated the number of Americans who would die of heart disease or cancer in the next 10 years after considering a numeric anchor. Anchoring was stronger among subjects who had first elaborated on the health topic by listing their health-related actions. Making all target features more accessible through elaboration expanded the pool of features, thereby enhancing the anchor's ability to facilitate retrieval of similar features.

Thus, evidence from a number of studies points to anchors as a type of memory prompt or prime to activate target information similar to the anchor. Anchoring is reduced if subjects are explicitly prompted to consider the anchor's irrelevance (Chapman & Johnson, 1999; Mussweiler et al., 2000) or if the information primed by the anchor is irrelevant to the target judgment (Chapman & Johnson, 1994; Kahneman & Knetsch, 1993; Strack & Mussweiler, 1997). Strack and Mussweiler (1997) point out that the primed information has an effect only if the decision maker is uncertain of the target's value, a prediction consistent with data from Quattrone et al. (1981), Wilson et al. (1996), and Chapman and Johnson (unpublished). Kahneman and Knetsch (1993) describe the priming process as automatic, which may explain why anchoring is largely unaffected by incentives (Wilson et al., 1996). The accounts of anchoring described in this section, although highly similar, are not identical. Further research is needed to specify more precisely the activation processes that produce the anchoring effect. The evidence is mounting, however, that anchoring involves a constructive process of priming or memory retrieval that influences judgments of preference (Payne, Bettman, & Johnson, 1992) and belief.

Phenomena Related to Anchoring

Parallels have been drawn between anchoring and a number of other phenomena. The characterization of anchoring as activation suggests that the effect of anchors is related to judgments of similarity. In judging whether the value of a target object is above or below an anchor, people consider how the anchor and target are similar (Tversky, 1977). As a result, according to the activation view, anchors have their effect because decision makers consider reasons why their value for the target item is like the anchor, but show relative neglect for reasons why their value for the item is unlike the anchor.

This bias toward attending to similarities is analogous to a number of phenomena often labeled collectively as *confirmation bias*. In a variety of tasks, people tend to seek information that if consistent with the current hypothesis would yield positive feedback (e.g., Wason, 1960), and to interpret evidence as consistent with the hypothesis (e.g., Lord, Lepper, & Preston, 1984). Although this strategy is often effective (Klayman & Ha, 1987), it occurs even if the information sought is not diagnostic because it is consistent with many alternative hypotheses. In contrast, hypothesis testers are unlikely to seek information expected to be inconsistent with the target hypothesis, even if that information is quite diagnostic (e.g, Beattie & Baron, 1988; Skov & Sherman, 1986; Snyder & Swann, 1978). The confirmation bias is similar to our proposed model of anchoring in that decision makers examine evidence expected to confirm the hypothesis rather than evidence that could disconfirm the hypothesis. Similarly, Mussweiler and Strack's (2000) Selective Accessibility Model draws a parallel between confirmation bias and anchoring by positing that decision makers compare the target to the anchor by selectively generating information consistent with the hypothesis that the target's value is equal to the anchor.

A number of authors have noted parallels between anchoring and overconfidence (Block & Harper, 1991; Griffin & Tversky, 1992). Koriat, Lichtenstein, and Fischhoff (1980), for example, argued that overconfidence is due to a failure to consider why the selected answer might be wrong. They demonstrated that a prompt to list counter-reasons was effective in debiasing overconfidence. Using a similar manipulation, Koehler (1994) found that subjects who generated a hypothesis were less overconfident than those who merely evaluated the hypothesis, presumably because generation involves considering alternative hypotheses. This finding suggests that self-generated anchors lead to less bias than experimenter-generated anchors. Block and Harper (1991) found just this result. Subjects gave more accurate confidence intervals if they generated their own anchor (a point estimate) than if they were given another subject's point estimate.

Another phenomenon related to anchoring is the *hindsight bias*, or the tendency for decision makers with outcome knowledge to exaggerate the chances that they would have predicted the outcome in advance (Fischhoff, 1975). Anchoring has been suggested as a possible explanation of this bias (Hawkins & Hastie, 1990); specifically, knowledge of the outcome acts as an anchor that influences judgments of the predictability of the outcome. In hindsight bias experiments, evidence consistent with the outcome is more easily recalled than facts that contradict the outcome (Dellarosa & Bourne, 1984). Thus, the outcome knowledge draws attention to reasons why that outcome was predictable, but not reasons why alternative outcomes were predictable. Hindsight bias is reduced by asking subjects how they would explain alternate outcomes if they had occurred (Arkes, Faust, Guilmette, & Hart, 1988; Slovic & Fischhoff, 1977), in a manner similar to the attentional prompt manipulations used in anchoring studies (Chapman & Johnson, 1999; Mussweiler et al., 2000).

Shafir (1993) provided a demonstration of how the goal of a decision task can shift attention. He found that when asked to accept one of two options, decision makers appear to focus on the positive features of the options. In contrast, when asked to reject one of two options, decision makers focus on the negative features of the options. Consequently, an option with both many positive and many negative features can be both accepted and rejected over a second option with only average features. These results are consistent with the interpretation that the "accept" or "reject" instruction acts as an anchor by increasing the availability of features consistent with the instruction.

Anchoring has been used to explain preference reversals (Busemeyer & Goldstein, 1992; Ganzach, 1996; Lichtenstein & Slovic, 1971; Schkade & Johnson, 1989; Slovic & Lichtenstein, 1983). When Lichtenstein and Slovic (1971) first drew a link between anchoring and preference reversals, they presupposed an adjustment process. In light of more recent anchoring studies suggesting that anchors increase activation and salience, one might ask whether such an activation process might also underlie preference reversals. Anchors, acting as a prime, may contribute to response mode compatibility effects.

According to a compatibility account of preference reversals (Tversky, Sattath, & Slovic, 1988), the weight given to each attribute of a target item depends on the response mode. Specifically, those attributes that are compatible with the response scale are given more weight. Thus, in pricing lotteries, the dollar outcomes of the lotteries receive relatively more weight. Conversely, in rating lotteries on a 0–100 scale, the probabilities receive relatively more weight, and these weight shifts are accompanied by an increase in the attention paid to the probabilities relative to the dollar outcomes (Schkade & Johnson, 1989).

Anchoring itself also shows compatibility effects (Chapman & Johnson, 1994; Kahneman & Knetsch, 1993; Strack & Mussweiler, 1997). For example, monetary anchors influenced monetary judgments but not life expectancy judgments (Chapman & Johnson, 1994). In anchoring, the anchor draws attention to similar features of the target, which then influence target judgments. In preference reversals, it is the response scale that draws attention to similar features of the target, influencing the preference judgment.

The numerous phenomena related to anchoring suggest that anchoring mechanisms such as activation may underlie many judgments and judgmental biases. Baron (1994) described the tendency to search for evidence that favors a target possibility as one of the major biases leading to poor decisions, and Arkes (1991) described association-based errors as one of three main causes of judgment biases (along with strategy-based and psychophysically based errors). Association-based errors result from considering evidence that is primed by the decision task. Studies of anchoring place it in this class of phenomena. Arkes concludes that such errors cannot be corrected by increasing incentives but can be reduced by instructions or cues to perform a debiasing behavior, such as considering opposing evidence.

Although anchoring shares features with a variety of judgmental effects, it is sometimes improperly categorized with reference point effects, a distinct class of phenomena (Kahneman, 1992). Reference points are values that define the subjective neutral point and thus divide a scale of values into "gains" and "losses." Changes in the neutral reference point alter evaluations of a target value, especially if what could be perceived as a relative gain is instead perceived as a relative loss. Given that reference points and anchors both involve the presentation of a comparison stimulus (usually irrelevant to the judgment at hand), there is a tendency to confuse the two effects (Kahneman, 1992). In fact, they differ in process and outcome. As argued previously, anchoring occurs primarily through priming and attentional mechanisms; that is, anchoring is an associative error (Arkes, 1991). In contrast, reference point effects occur primarily through perceptual or psychophysical mechanisms (Arkes, 1991). That is, the position of the reference point alters the slope of the utility function or indifference curve (Sen & Johnson, 1997). Furthermore, anchoring generally leads to judgmental assimilation effects (outcomes too near the anchor), whereas reference points lead to evaluative contrast effects (higher evaluations with lower reference points) and changes in risk-aversion (greater risk-seeking when a given outcome is framed as a loss than as a gain).

Applications of Anchoring

Anchors have been found to influence many judgment tasks, including answers to factual knowledge questions (Jacowitz & Kahneman, 1995; Tversky & Kahneman, 1974), estimation of risks and uncertainty (Plous, 1989; Wright & Anderson, 1989; Yamagishi, 1994), statistical inferences (Lovie, 1985), evaluation of monetary lotteries (Carlson, 1990; Chapman & Johnson, 1994; Johnson & Schkade, 1989; Schkade & Johnson, 1989), judgments of self-efficacy (Cervone & Peake, 1986), judgments of spousal preferences (Davis, Hoch, & Ragsdale, 1986), and predictions of future performance (Czaczkes & Ganzach, 1996; Switzer & Sniezek, 1991).

Anchoring is also a key theoretical concept used to explain other judgment phenomena, such as egocentric biases (Kruger, 1999), attribution (Gilbert et al., 1988; Quattrone, 1982), and overconfidence (Griffin & Tversky, 1992). Anchoring has also been offered as a cause of preference reversals (Lichtenstein & Slovic, 1971; Schkade & Johnson, 1989), biases in utility assessment (Hershey & Schoemaker, 1985; Johnson & Schkade, 1989), information framing effects (Levin, Schnittjer, & Thee, 1988), and biased causal attribution (Gilbert, Chapter 8, this volume; Quattrone, 1982). Finally, anchoring and adjustment serves as a central theoretical component of explanations of the effect of ambiguity on probability judgments (Einhorn & Hogarth, 1985), of belief updating (Hogarth & Einhorn, 1992), and the expression of values (Goldstein & Einhorn, 1987; Busemeyer & Goldstein, 1992).

Many everyday tasks require numerical judgments and thus may be prone to anchoring effects. Northcraft and Neale (1987), for example, asked students and real estate agents to tour a house and appraise it. Appraisal values assigned by both experts (real estate appraisers) and amateurs (students) were positively related to the provided anchor – the listing price of the house. As is the case in many applied settings, one might argue that the anchors were not uninformative, as listing prices are generally correlated with real estate value. However, the participants in this study reported that list price should be irrelevant to the appraised value, yet they were nonetheless influenced by it. Similarly, Caverni and Pris (1990) found that secondary school teachers were influenced by the past records of their students when they graded a new assignment. Evaluation of the current assignment should, of course, be based on its own merits rather than the student's record.

Anchoring in personal injury verdicts was examined in Chapman and Bornstein's (1996) study of mock jurors. The anchors, which took the form of the plaintiff's requested compensation (or *ad damnum*), influenced both judgments of whether the defendant was liable and the amount of monetary compensation awarded. Anchoring occurred even for implausibly low ($100) or high ($1 billion) anchors (see also Chapman & Johnson, 1994; Quatrone et al., 1981; Strack & Musweiler, 1997). Legally, the *ad damnum* is irrelevant to both liability and compensation judgments because plaintiffs can request as large an amount as they wish. Englich and Mussweiler (in press) found similar anchoring effects in criminal sentencing.

A potentially important applied context for the measurement of preferences and value is the use of survey research in the area of "contingent evaluation." Green, Jacowitz, Kahneman, and McFadden (1998), for example, examined anchoring effects using respondents' answers to such questions as how much they would be willing to pay to save 50,000 offshore seabirds per year, as well as answers to objective estimation questions such as the height in feet of the tallest redwood in California. They demonstrated strong anchoring effects for both types of questions, and argued that such anchoring effects are much larger in size than the biasing effects typically ascribed to a lack of incentives in contingent valuation surveys.

Hurd et al. (1997) found that anchors influenced reports older adults gave of their monthly expenditures and savings account balances. This result is surprising because one might expect such figures to be well known to the respondents. In addition, the unfolding bracket sequence used as the anchoring manipulation in this study is a common survey technique, suggesting that the initial bracket or anchor may have a large biasing effect on many survey results.

Additional applications of anchoring include demonstration of this bias in group decision making (e.g., Rutledge, 1993) and in individual judgments of group decision outcomes (Allison & Beggan, 1994). Ritov (1996) examined anchoring in a competitive market simulation. In a negotiation between a buyer and seller, initial offers can act as an anchor, and Ritov found that these values affected final profit. Anchoring can also influence consumer behavior (e.g., Biswas & Burton, 1993). For example, Yadav (1994) found that when consumers evaluate two or more items bundled together, the most important item acts as an anchor, which affects the overall evaluation of the entire bundle.

Conclusions

A useful analogy might be drawn between the anchoring effect and the Stroop effect. In the classic Stroop effect, subjects are asked to name the ink color in which a word is printed. Reaction times are longer for color words that do not match the ink color (e.g., the word *red* printed in green ink) than for unrelated words (see MacLeod, 1991, for a review). The meaning of the word is irrelevant information, yet it influences performance. In a similar fashion, an irrelevant anchor influences judgment, even when decision makers are instructed to ignore it (e.g., Quattrone et al., 1981; Wilson et al., 1996).

Like the Stroop effect, anchoring appears to be both prevalent and robust, as research has yielded scores of demonstrations of this bias. The contaminating effects of irrelevant anchors can be observed in numerous real-world contexts. Understanding the causes of anchoring and what they tell us about the efficacy of various potential debiasing techniques is thus of considerable practical importance.

7. Putting Adjustment Back in the Anchoring and Adjustment Heuristic

Nicholas Epley and Thomas Gilovich

In what year was George Washington elected President? What is the freezing point of vodka? Few people know the answers to these questions, but most can arrive at a reasonable estimate by tinkering with a value they know is wrong. Most know that the United States declared its independence in 1776, so Washington must have been elected sometime after that. And most people also know that alcohol freezes at a lower temperature than water, so vodka must freeze at something colder than 32°F. To answer questions like these, in other words, people may spontaneously anchor on information that readily comes to mind and adjust their responses in a direction that seems appropriate, using what Tversky and Kahneman (1974) called the *anchoring and adjustment heuristic*. Although this heuristic is often helpful, adjustments tend to be insufficient, leaving people's final estimates biased toward the initial anchor value.

To examine this heuristic, Tversky and Kahneman (1974) developed a paradigm in which participants are given an irrelevant number and asked if the answer to a question is greater or less than that value. After this comparative assessment, participants provide an absolute answer. Countless experiments have shown that people's absolute answers are influenced by the initial comparison with the irrelevant anchor. People estimate that Gandhi lived to be roughly 67 years old, for example, if they first decided whether he died before or after the age of 140, but only 50 years old if they first decided whether he died before or after the age of 9 (Strack & Mussweiler, 1997).

Anchoring effects have been demonstrated in numerous contexts, including the evaluation of gambles (Carlson, 1990; Chapman & Johnson, 1994; Schkade & Johnson, 1989), estimates of risk and uncertainty (Plous, 1989; Wright & Anderson, 1989), perceptions of self-efficacy (Cervone & Peake, 1986), anticipations of future performance (Switzer & Sniezek, 1991), and answers to general knowledge questions (Jacowitz & Kahneman, 1995). Anchoring and adjustment has also figured prominently as an explanatory mechanism underlying such diverse phenomena as preference reversals (Lichtenstein & Slovic, 1971; Schkade & Johnson, 1989), probability estimates (Fischhoff & Beyth, 1975; Hawkins & Hastie, 1991), trait inference (Gilbert, 1989; Kruger, 1999), language

Originally published in *Psychological Science, 12*, 391–396. Copyright © 2001 by the American Psychological Society, reprinted by permission.

production and comprehension (Keysar & Barr, Chapter 8, this volume), and various egocentric biases such as the "spotlight effect" (Gilovich, Medvec, & Savitsky, 2000) and the "illusion of transparency" (Gilovich, Savitsky, & Medvec, 1998).

Anchoring effects have traditionally been interpreted as a result of insufficient adjustment from an irrelevant value (Tversky & Kahneman, 1974), but recent evidence casts doubt on this account. Instead, anchoring effects observed in the standard paradigm appear to be produced by the increased accessibility of anchor consistent information (Chapman & Johnson, Chapter 6, this volume; Mussweiler & Strack, 1999, 2000; Strack & Mussweiler, 1997). The attempt to answer the comparative question – say, whether Gandhi lived to be 140 – leads an individual to test the hypothesis that the irrelevant anchor value is correct – Did Gandhi live to be 140? Because people evaluate hypotheses by attempting to confirm them (Crocker, 1982; Snyder & Swann, 1978; Trope & Bassok, 1982), such a search generates evidence disproportionately consistent with the anchor. The absolute judgment is then biased by the evidence recruited in this confirmatory search. This alternative account, accompanied by failures to demonstrate a process of adjustment, has led some researchers to conclude that anchoring results from biased retrieval of target features, and not because of insufficient adjustment.

We believe this conclusion is premature. In particular, we suggest that just as memory research was sidetracked by an overly persistent analysis of people's ability to recall nonsense syllables, so too has anchoring research been sidetracked by an overly persistent analysis of people's responses in the standard anchoring paradigm. Outside this paradigm, anchors are often self-generated rather than provided by an experimenter or other external source. Most people know George Washington was elected after 1776, but how long after? Or that vodka freezes at less than 32°F, but how much less? Externally provided anchors, even outrageous ones, differ from self-generated anchors because they have to be taken seriously, if only for a moment. Self-generated anchors, in contrast, are known – from the beginning – to be wrong. There is thus no cause to consider whether the anchor value is correct, and thus no engine of heightened accessibility of anchor-consistent information. This difference leads us to propose that anchoring effects are produced by insufficient adjustment rather than selective accessibility when the anchor is self-generated. We investigate this possibility in three experiments.

STUDY 1

As an initial exploration, participants verbalized their thoughts when answering questions involving self-generated and experimenter-provided anchors. We predicted that participants would describe a process of anchoring and adjustment only when anchors were self-generated. In these cases, we expected that the verbal reports would typically begin with a reference to the anchor value,

Table 7.1. Percentage of Participants Describing a Process of Anchoring
and Adjustment in Their Verbal Reports, for Self-Generated
and Experimenter-Provided Anchoring Items

Question	n	Participantes Describing "Anchoring and Adjustment" (%)
Self-generated		
Washington elected president	42	64
Second European explorer	37	89
Experimenter-provided		
Mean length of whale	50	12
Mean winter temperature in Antarctica	50	14

Note: There were 50 participants in this experiment. The number of participants varies for
the self-generated anchoring items because not all participants knew the relevant anchor
(i.e., the date of Columbus' arrival in the West Indies or the date of the Declaration of
Independence). The anchor value provided for the mean length of a whale was 69 feet,
and was 1°F for the mean winter temperature in Antarctica.

followed by a statement describing adjustment away from it: "The United States
declared its independence in 1776, and it probably took a few years to elect
a president, so Washington was elected in . . . 1779." In contrast, we expected
experimenter-provided anchors to produce little or no mention of either the
anchor or adjustment, consistent with the selective accessibility account of anchoring effects in the standard paradigm (Strack & Mussweiler, 1997).

Method

Fifty Cornell undergraduates were each asked four questions, two of which
involved questions to which most participants could be counted on to generate a particular anchor value [(e.g., "When did the second European explorer
land in the West Indies?" (anchor-1492)], and two involved anchors provided
by the experimenter (one high and one low value) (Table 7.1).

Participants were asked to explain how they arrived at the answer to each
question. Their responses were recorded, transcribed, and evaluated by two
raters who were unaware of our hypotheses. The raters evaluated whether the
participant appeared to know the anchor value, whether they used the anchor
as a basis of their answer, and whether they mentioned adjustment from the
anchor to arrive at a final estimate. Interrater agreement was .94. A third rater
who was also unaware of our hypotheses resolved disagreements. Participants
were considered to have used anchoring and adjustment only if their verbal
reports referred to the anchor *and* a process of adjustment.

Results and Discussion

As predicted, participants were more likely to describe a process of anchoring and adjustment when the anchor values were self-generated than when
they were provided by the experimenter. Of those who appeared to know both

self-generated anchors ($n = 34$), 94% made reference to anchoring and adjustment in response to at least one of the self-generated items, and 65% did so in response to both. In contrast, only 22% ($n = 50$) described anchoring and adjustment in response to at least one of the experimenter-provided anchors, and only 4% did so in response to both (see Table 7.1).

To assess the statistical significance of these results, we calculated the percentage of items for which participants reported a process of anchoring and adjustment for the self-generated and experimenter-provided items. Four participants were excluded from this analysis because they knew neither of the self-generated anchors. As predicted, participants were far more likely to report using anchoring and adjustment when considering self-generated anchors ($M = 73.9\%$) than when considering experimenter-provided anchors ($M = 13.0\%$), paired t (45) = 8.56, $p < .0001$.

These results indicate that self-generated anchors activate different mental processes than experimenter-provided anchors. One might be concerned, however, about relying on participants' self-reports given the widespread doubts about whether people can report accurately on their own mental processes (Nisbett & Wilson, 1977). One might also be concerned about a Gricean alternative interpretation of these findings. That is, participants may be less likely to mention the experimenter-provided anchor value and how they adjusted from it because the anchor value was already mentioned in the initial comparative question. Note that this interpretation is rendered less plausible by the fact that the same pattern of results is obtained if we score participants' responses for statements of adjustment only, rather than statements of the initial anchor value and adjustment. Nevertheless, we conducted the following studies – which manipulate rather than assess the process of adjustment – to rule it out completely.

STUDY 2

When people adjust from self-generated anchors, they may do so in one of two ways. One possibility is that people "slide" along some mental scale continuously testing until they arrive at a satisfactory final estimate. More plausible, we believe, is that they may "jump" some amount from the anchor – analogous to a saccade in reading – to a more reasonable value and assess its plausibility. If the new value seems plausible, adjustment stops. If not, a new jump or saccade is made, the new value assessed, and so on.

Regardless of the continuous or discrete nature of adjustment, anything that influences participants' thresholds for accepting or denying values that come to mind should influence the amount of adjustment. If a participant is more willing to accept values, he or she will terminate the adjustment process more quickly and provide a final estimate closer to the original anchor value. If a participant is less accepting, he or she should continue to adjust and arrive at a final estimate further from the anchor.

We sought to influence participants' thresholds for acceptance or denial by using the tried-and-true influence of motor movements on attitudes and persuasion (Cacioppo, Priester, & Berntson, 1993; Forster & Strack, 1996, 1997; Martin, Harlow, & Strack, 1992; Priester, Cacioppo, & Petty, 1996). Previous research has demonstrated that people are more likely to accept propositions when they are nodding their heads up and down than when shaking them from side to side (Wells & Petty, 1980). We reasoned that asking participants to nod their heads would make them more willing to accept values that initially came to mind, and thus produce less adjustment from self-generated anchors. Shaking their heads from side to side, in contrast, should make participants more willing to reject values, and thus produce more adjustment from self-generated anchors. As a result of this difference in adjustment, we also predicted that participants would generate an answer more quickly when nodding than when shaking their heads.

Because nodding and shaking should not systematically influence the selective accessibility of anchor-consistent information, we predicted these head movements would not influence answers to externally provided anchoring questions.

Method

Participants ($n = 50$) were told that the experiment was a study of product evaluations, and that they would be asked to evaluate a set of headphones while moving their heads from side to side or up and down in order to assess the headphones under everyday use.

All participants listened to a tape containing 16 anchoring questions. To justify this procedure and reduce suspicion, the experimenter explained that she wished to examine "implicit evaluations" that people "form without conscious intention or effort." She thus needed to busy participants with another task while they were evaluating the headphones, in this case by answering the questions on the tape.

Depending on a random schedule, participants were then asked to nod their heads up and down, shake their heads from side to side, or hold their heads still. The experimenter, who was unaware of our hypotheses, provided brief demonstrations of the desired head movement, situated herself behind the participant, readied a stopwatch, and began the tape. The experimenter recorded the answer to each question as well as the time required to generate each answer.

Materials. The 16 anchoring questions were divided into blocks of 4. In order to maintain the cover story, the experimenter stopped the tape after each block and asked participants to evaluate the headphones. The first three blocks contained all self-generated anchoring items [e.g., "How long does it take Mars to orbit the sun?" (anchor = 365 days)], with participants completing one block while performing each of the head movements.

The last block contained four anchoring questions taken from Jacowitz and Kahneman (1995). Participants repeated the head movement made during Block 1, and the experimenter recorded both their answers and reaction times to the comparative and absolute components of each question. Because we were interested in adjustment and not anchoring effects per se, we did not manipulate the experimental anchor for each question. We selected the four items that produced the largest anchoring effects in the study by Jacowitz and Kahneman (1995), and provided high anchor values for two questions and low anchor values for two others (e.g., "Is the population of Chicago more or less than 200,000? What is Chicago's population?").

Following this procedure, participants completed a questionnaire that asked directly about the intended anchor value for each self-generated anchoring item (e.g., "In what year did the United States declare its independence?") and whether they had considered this value when generating their answer.

Results and Discussion

Two preconditions had to be met for an adequate test of our hypotheses about self-generated anchors. First, participants had to know the self-generated anchor. Second, they had to report considering the anchor when making their estimate. Participants who did not meet these preconditions were excluded on an item-by-item basis. On three questions, fewer than 30% of participants met both preconditions, generally because they did not know the intended anchor value. In some cases this left no participants in one or more of the experimental conditions. We therefore dropped from the analyses three questions (about the fastest mile, death of the first apostle, and orbit of Io). This left nine self-generated anchoring questions (three in the first block, four in the second, and two in the third).

To determine whether head movements influenced participants' responses, answers to each question were converted to standard scores and then averaged across all items within each block (i.e., within each head movement condition). Reaction times were logarithmically transformed to reduce skew, then standardized and averaged in the same fashion. Answers to the four items that required downward adjustment were reverse scored so that, like the other questions, higher scores on this index reflected a larger discrepancy between the anchor and final answer. As can be seen in Table 7.2, a repeated

Table 7.2. Mean Standardized Answers and Reaction Times to the Self-Generated and Experimenter-Provided Anchoring Items Given While Participants Were Nodding, Shaking, or Holding Their Heads Still (Study 2)

	Head Movement			
	Nodding	Still	Shaking	$F(p)$
Self-generated anchors ($n = 43$)				
Answer	−.21	−.07	.15	3.89 (.02)
Reaction time	−.27	−.10	.17	5.67 (.005)
Experimenter-provided anchors ($n = 50$)				
Answer	.16	−.25	.07	3.10 (.05)
Reaction Time	.01	−.03	.02	.03 (ns)

Table 7.3. Mean Responses to Self-Generated Anchoring Items Given While Participants Were Nodding, Shaking, or Holding Their Heads Still (Study 2)

Question	n	Anchor	Head Movement		
			Nodding	Still	Shaking
Washington elected president	37	1776	1777.60	1779.10	1788.10
Boiling point of water on Mt. Everest	32	212	189.31	173.99	141.41
Second European explorer	46	1492	1501.88	1514.36	1548
U.S. states in 1840	38	50	36.75	30.42	31.64
Freezing point of vodka	38	32	17.36	1.75	−9.55
Highest Body Temperature	40	98.6	108.34	110.17	107.47
Lowest Body Temperature	44	98.6	75.18	83.17	77.65
Orbit of Mars (days)[a]	37	365	127.89	99.36	202.60
Gestation Period of Elephant[a]	45	9	8.50	6.06	5.54

[a] The data presented for this item are adjustment scores, or the absolute difference between the participant's answer and their reported anchor. This was done because adjustment was common in both directions from the self-generated anchor on this item. Lower numbers indicate a smaller discrepancy between the final answer and the original anchor (i.e., less adjustment).

measures ANOVA on this composite measure indicated that participants' head movements significantly influenced their answers to the self-generated anchoring items, $F(2, 84) = 3.89$, $p < .05$. A follow-up contrast showed that participants provided answers closer to the self-generated anchor (i.e., they adjusted less) when they were nodding their heads than when they were shaking their heads, $F(1, 42) = 6.44$, $p < .05$. Participants gave responses in between those in these two conditions when they were holding their heads still. Responses to individual items, in raw scores, are presented in Table 7.3.

Participants' head movements also influenced the speed with which they generated their answers to the self-generated anchoring items, $F(2, 84) = 5.67$, $p < .05$. As predicted, participants answered more quickly when nodding than when shaking their heads, $F(1, 42) = 11.76$, $p < .01$. Again, the latency of participants' responses fell in between those in these two conditions when they were holding their heads still.

We contend that participants adjust in a serial fashion from self-generated anchors and that head movements influenced their responses by altering their willingness to accept values that came initially to mind. Participants were more willing to accept values that initially came to mind while nodding their heads, producing less adjustment and faster reaction times than when they were shaking them. This mechanism differs considerably from the selective accessibility model that appears to explain anchoring effects in response to experimenter-provided anchors, suggesting that different psychological processes may be operating in these two contexts. Consistent with this contention, Table 7.2 shows that participants' head movements did not have the same influence on responses to the experimenter-provided anchoring items.

STUDY 3

Because the strikingly different impact of head movements on self-generated versus experimenter-provided anchors is the only evidence of its kind of which we are aware, we thought it prudent to replicate these results. We thus conducted a close replication with two changes: (1) we used equal numbers of self-generated and experimenter-provided anchoring items, and (2) we counterbalanced the order in which these items were presented. These changes permitted us to conduct a direct statistical test of the differential effect of head movements on self-generated versus experimenter-provided anchors.

Method

Thirty-two Cornell students participated in a procedure identical to that of Study 2, except that only 8 questions were used instead of 16 and there was no control ("no head movement") condition. Of the 8 questions, 4 were self-generated anchoring questions from Study 2, and 4 were experimenter-provided anchoring questions from Jacowitz and Kahneman (1995) – two holdovers from Study 2 and two new items.

The four items within each anchor type were split into pairs, producing two self-generated pairs and two experimenter-provided pairs. Participants answered one pair of each item type while nodding their head, and the other while shaking it. The order in which questions were presented was counterbalanced and did not influence any of the results. After each pair, participants evaluated the headphones as part of the cover story. As in Study 2, participants completed a questionnaire at the end of the session to ascertain their knowledge of the self-generated anchors, and whether they had considered the anchor when making their estimate.

Results and Discussion

Individual responses were excluded and data transformed in the same manner as in Study 2. Two participants failed to satisfy the inclusion criteria on at least one item type, leaving 30 participants in the final analysis.

To test our predictions, participants' responses to each item were standardized and averaged across item type. Participants' scores were submitted to a 2 (anchor: self-generated versus experimenter-provided) × 2 (head movement: nodding versus shaking) repeated measures ANOVA. This analysis yielded a marginally significant main effect of head movement, $F(1, 29) = 3.89, p = .06$, qualified by the predicted significant interaction, $F(1, 29) = 9.38, p < .01$. As

Table 7.4. Mean Standardized Answers and Reaction Times to Both Self-Generated and Experimenter-Provided Anchors Given While Participants Were Nodding or Shaking Their Heads (Study 3)

	Head Movement		
	Nodding	Shaking	$t\,(p)$
Self-generated anchors ($n = 30$)			
Answer	−.27	.33	3.61 (.001)
Reaction time	−.16	.07	1.52 (.14)
Experimenter-provided anchors ($n = 32$)			
Answer	.04	−.07	<1 (ns)
Reaction time	−.04	.02	<1 (ns)

can be seen in Table 7.4, participants provided answers that were more discrepant from a self-generated anchor when they were shaking versus nodding their heads, paired $t\,(29) = 3.61$, $p < .005$. Responses to specific items, in raw scores, are presented in Table 7.5.

In contrast to the results for the self-generated items, head movements did not influence responses to the experimenter-provided items, paired $t < 1$, ns.

A similar, although considerably weaker pattern emerged in an analysis of participants' response latencies. As can be seen in the lower portion of Table 7.4, participants were somewhat faster to provide an answer to the self-generated items when they were nodding their heads than when they were shaking them, paired $t\,(29) = 1.52$, $p = .14$. Head movements had no influence on reaction times to experimenter-provided anchors, paired $t < 1$. The overall interaction between the type of question and the total amount of time required to generate an answer, however, was nonsignificant, $F\,(1, 29) < 1.77$, $p = .19$.

These data replicate those of Study 2 and demonstrate more conclusively that self-generated anchors activate a different set of mental operations than experimenter-provided anchors. Head movements influenced responses

Table 7.5. Answers to Self-Generated Anchoring Items Given While Participants Were Nodding or Shaking Their Heads (Study 3)

Question	n	Anchor	Head Movement	
			Nodding	Shaking
Washington elected president	28	1776	1783.50	1788.25
Second European explorer	30	1492	1508.72	1534.42
Boiling point of water on Mt. Everest	21	212	192.50	176.90
Freezing point of vodka	28	32	12.47	−19.09

when anchors were self-generated but not when they were provided by the experimenter.

GENERAL DISCUSSION

The results of these experiments reestablish the existence of anchoring *and* adjustment in some judgments under uncertainty. When questions activate self-generated anchors, people adjust from those anchors to arrive at final estimates. This process differs considerably from those involved when anchors are provided by an experimenter or other external source, demonstrating that there are distinct anchoring effects produced by different mechanisms. We therefore second Jacowitz and Kahneman's (1995) call for a careful taxonomy of the varieties of anchoring effects in order to advance psychologists' understanding of this pervasive element of judgment under uncertainty.

The present experiments have identified the anchor's source as one important feature of that taxonomy – a feature that allows us to distinguish those anchoring effects that are produced by a process of adjustment and those that are not. It is noteworthy in this regard that the numeric estimates we investigate here share this feature with a number of phenomena that have been explained through a process of anchoring and adjustment – phenomena such as trait inference (Gilbert, Chapter 9, this volume), interpersonal communication (Keysar & Barr, Chapter 8, this volume), comparative ability estimates (Kruger, 1999), and various egocentric biases (Gilovich et al., 1998, 2000; Keysar & Bly, 1995; Van Boven, Dunning, & Loewenstein, 2000). Trait inferences begin with a dispositional attribution that observers generate themselves; similarly, communication, comparative ability estimates, and the processes involved in a host of egocentric judgments begin with a spontaneous consideration of one's own comprehension, skills, or perspective on the world. Final judgments in these cases are thus likely the product of insufficient adjustment from these self-generated anchors. Note that many of these phenomena are amplified by cognitive load manipulations designed to hinder any underlying process of adjustment (Gilbert, Chapter 9, this volume; Kruger, 1999) – manipulations that have no effect on responses in the standard anchoring paradigm (Epley & Gilovich, 2001a).

Do adjustments from self-generated anchors tend to be insufficient? Research on trait inference suggests that although people try to adjust their impressions to accommodate situational influences, they adjust too little and are left inferring more about a person's disposition than is logically warranted (Gilbert, Chapter 9, this volume). Research on comparative ability estimates paints a similar picture: Although people try to adjust for others' ability level, they adjust too little and are left feeling systematically above average in domains in which absolute skill tends to be high, such as driving, and below average in domains in which it tends to be low, such as juggling (Kruger, 1999). Results from the control condition of Study 2 suggest that adjustments in numeric estimates also tend to be insufficient. Participants in that experiment estimated that George Washington, for example, was elected president in 1779 when he was actually elected in 1788. They also estimated that vodka froze at 1.75°F when it actually freezes closer to −20°F. Indeed, we report elsewhere that people tend to systematically fall short of the actual answer when adjusting from self-generated anchors (Epley & Gilovich, 2001b).

This research provides the first compelling evidence that anchoring effects can be produced by a process of adjustment. Although the adjustment process is anything but fully understood, its existence now seems apparent.

8. Self-Anchoring in Conversation: Why Language Users Do Not Do What They "Should"

Boaz Keysar and Dale J. Barr

An old story about J. Edgar Hoover illustrates the miscommunication of intentions. When Hoover noticed that the text of a memo his secretary typed had spilled into the page margins, he scribbled a note to her: "Watch the borders." The next day agents were on high alert on the border with Mexico. The question we'd like to address in this paper is this: Why did Hoover miscommunicate?

We propose that much miscommunication is systematic. It results from the nature of language use. We attempt to demonstrate our point by noting the similarities between the way people make decisions and the way they use language. As in decision making, uncertainty is inherent in the way people use language. The way language users overcome this uncertainty leads to systematic errors.

When we attempt to understand what speakers mean, we must infer what they mean from what they say. This is because all utterances are ambiguous. "Borders" is lexically ambiguous, but ambiguity in language goes beyond lexical ambiguity. In fact, everything people say is ambiguous because it can convey more than one intention. To overcome this inherent ambiguity, we propose that language users rely on certain heuristics of language use. As with other heuristics, they are generally successful but they occasionally lead to systematic error.

In this chapter, we propose that speakers, addressees, and overhearers reduce the uncertainty of linguistic utterances by using an anchoring and adjustment heuristic. We review evidence that language users tend to anchor on their own perspective and attempt to adjust to the perspective of others. These adjustments are typically insufficient, and can occasionally cause miscommunication.

COOPERATION AND PERSPECTIVE TAKING

Research on language use makes strong normative assumptions. It assumes that people adhere to certain normative rules of conversation to avoid misunderstanding. Grice (1975) argued that language users follow these rules and assume that others do too because conversation is governed by a "cooperative

The research described here was supported by PHS, grant R29 MH49685 to Boaz Keysar, and an NSF graduate fellowship to Dale Barr. We thank Linda Ginzel and Carmen Marti for their comments.

principle." Clark and colleagues (e.g., Clark, 1996; Clark & Carlson, 1981; Clark & Marshall, 1981; Greene, Gerrig, McKoon & Ratcliff, 1994) argue that for conversation to be truly cooperative, the production and comprehension of linguistic utterances should be governed by mutual knowledge – by information that interlocutors know they share. Thus, cooperative speakers should design utterances bearing in mind the other's thoughts, beliefs, assumptions, and so on. This is known as the *principle of optimal design*. Addressees, in turn, should assume that speakers' utterances are optimally designed for them in this way. In short, the cooperative interlocutor should take into account the other's perspective.

For example, when your annoyed friend says to you, "Nice job," after you wrecked her car, you interpret her utterance with respect to information that is mutually known: You both know that you wrecked her car, that a car is an expensive item, that people are rarely happy when they lose their means of transportation, and so on. Together with the principle of optimal design, these mutually held beliefs are the "context" for understanding her intended meaning. They allow you to make the inference that "Nice job" is intended as sarcasm rather than praise.

Rather than pursuing a technical discussion of "mutual knowledge," we discuss the more general notion of perspective taking. By *perspective taking*, we refer to people's attempts to take into account not only what they know to be mutually held beliefs, but also what they assume their partner believes from his or her perspective.

If everyone held the exact same beliefs and assumptions about the world, all perspectives would be identical and there would be no reason to assume that interlocutors should observe the principle of optimal design. Every piece of information would already be mutual by definition. The only reason to assume that interlocutors should follow this principle is because perspectives differ.

The realization that other perspectives differ from our own develops early in life. Between the ages of 3 and 4, children realize that although they might have a certain belief, others might have a different belief – which is false – about the same state of affairs. The ability of children to distinguish between their own true beliefs and others' false beliefs has been demonstrated in the now classic "false belief" paradigm (e.g., Astington, Harris, & Olson, 1988; Gopnik, & Wellman, 1992; Leslie, 1987; Perner, Leekam, & Wimmer, 1987; Wellman, 1990). In a typical false-belief task, a child is presented with a box that contains candy. The child sees the candy and also sees that Sally sees the candy in the box. Then Sally leaves. In front of the child, the experimenter then replaces the candy with pencils and closes the box so one cannot tell what it contains. Sally returns to the room. The child is asked what Sally thinks is in the box. Children younger than 3 years tend to say that Sally will think the box contains pencils. Once they develop a more adult-like understanding of the other's mind, they realize that

Sally will probably falsely believe the box has candy, not pencils. What they develop is an appreciation of differences in perspective.

Because this ability to distinguish between one's own perspective and the perspectives of others emerges early in life, it makes sense that people would use it in conversation, as the principle of optimal design suggests they should. However, the mere fact that people *have* the ability does not mean that they necessarily *use* it. In fact, in laboratory studies we find that this principle is violated across the board in the use of language – by speakers, addressees, and overhearers alike. We show that instead of following this normative principle, people use heuristic processing to resolve ambiguity.

SELF-ANCHORING AND ADJUSTMENT

When making judgments under uncertainty, people often anchor their responses to particular values – even irrelevant values – and adjust as needed (Kahneman, Slovic, & Tversky, 1982; Tversky & Kahneman, 1974; see also a review in Griffin, Gonzalez, & Varey, 2001). Such anchoring has been demonstrated in a variety of content domains with a variety of tasks. Anchoring occurs even when the exposure to the anchor value is completely incidental to the main task (e.g., Wilson, Houston, Brekke, & Etling, 1996). People show anchoring in diverse tasks, from the evaluation of utilities, to the prediction of future performance, to the attribution of causes of behavior (e.g., Gilbert & Osborne, 1989; Gilbert, Pelham, & Krull, 1988; Hershey & Schoemaker, 1985; Switzer & Sniezek, 1991; Quattrone, 1982). Anchoring coupled with insufficient adjustment typically results in a biased judgment (e.g., Slovic & Lichtenstein, 1971). Griffin and Tversky (1992), for example, used an anchoring and adjustment theory to explain why people are often over- or underconfident in their judgments. They found that people tend to anchor on the strength of evidence while insufficiently adjusting for what they know about the weight of the evidence.

Faced with the uncertainty of language, we propose that interlocutors also use such anchoring and adjustment. Instead of using information that is shared with their conversational partner, they anchor on their egocentric perspective and then attempt to adjust to their partner's perspective (Keysar, Barr, & Horton, 1998). We call this the *perspective adjustment theory* of language use. Thus, when addressees attempt to understand what speakers mean, they use an egocentric perspective. They also monitor for egocentric interpretations that violate the assumption that interpretations should rely on mutual knowledge. For example, if the egocentric interpretation uses information that is inaccessible to the speaker, the addressee detects the violation and readjusts the interpretation to align with the speaker's perspective. This adjustment, however, is often insufficient, resulting in egocentrically anchored interpretation errors. We demonstrate the value of this theory with studies on understanding and then show similar self-anchoring effects with speakers and observers.

SELF-ANCHORING WHILE UNDERSTANDING INTENTION

Consider the following situation as an illustration. Suppose you are taking a tour of the University of Chicago campus, and the guide stops next to Frank Lloyd Wright's Robie House. As the tour guide is talking about the Robie House, another building catches your attention because it is particularly unattractive, an unusual sight on that campus. At that point, you hear the guide say, "This building used to be a dormitory." In order to understand this phrase you must successfully identify the intended referent of "this building." The referent is most likely the Robie House because it is the topic of conversation and the focus of the group's attention. Indeed, when the Robie House was operated by the Chicago Theological Seminary between 1926 and 1963, it was used as a dormitory and dining hall. Assume also that you know that the guide is not looking at the other, unattractive building you just saw. One possiblity is that you interpret "This building used to be a dormitory," by considering your knowledge of what the guide is focused on, the topic, and so on. In other words, you would assume that the phrase has been optimally designed with respect to mutual knowledge. This information would immediately lead you to the conclusion that the guide is referring to the Robie House. However, the perspective adjustment theory makes a different prediction.

Instead of restricting your interpretation to what you know about the perspective of the speaker, your initial interpretation is anchored egocentrically – that is, in information available to you. This would lead you to identify quickly the unattractive building you were looking at as the intended referent of the guide's utterance, "This building used to be a dormitory." However, given that you know the perspective of the guide, you attempt to adjust to the guide's perspective. In general, then, the theory suggests a systematically egocentric error pattern, although the error might sometimes only be momentary. Such an interpretation error would occur whenever available, egocentric information suggests a different interpretation than the shared perspective.

To test between these two alternatives, Keysar, Barr, Balin, and Paek (1998) created a situation analogous to the Robie House case, except the participants in the experiment conversed about pictures of objects such as buildings, not the objects themselves. Unknown to the participants, we controlled critical moments during the experiment when we diverted the attention of the addressee to a picture that was not part of mutual focus. Immediately following this diversion, addressees heard an utterance from a confederate director that referred to the picture in mutual focus. Each critical moment was analogous to the example of looking at the unattractive building, which was not the topic of conversation, and then hearing, "This building used to be a dormitory."

We reasoned that if addressees interpret this utterance egocentrically, then the picture of the unattractive building should be identified as the referent. This temporary error should delay the identification of the picture of the Robie House as the actual referent. Indeed, participants in our experiment took longer to identify the Robie House as the referent when their attention was diverted to the unattractive building (which also could be a referent of "this building"), compared to a control condition when they were looking at a picture of a truck (which could not be a referent of "this building.") Such interference is a direct result of the egocentric anchor that picks the unattractive building as a temporary referent of the utterance.

If understanding is guided by the principle of optimal design, then differences in perspectives should not matter. Instead, we found that differences in perspective lead to a systematic pattern of errors, even when the differences are well known. In the case of the Robie House, the unattractive building was not the topic of the conversation, but it was physically present. The perspective of the tour guide was different to the extent that the guide was not focused on that building. In one sense, perspectives always diverge as individuals have private thoughts about things that are not present. We also explored the possibility that addressees search even their private thoughts for potential referents.

Consider the use of pronouns: Pronouns can be used to make definite reference to specific entities in the world, just as the demonstrative reference in "this building." When a speaker says, "He is courageous," the speaker is using the pronoun "he" to refer to a specific individual. The use of pronouns, like other definite descriptions, presupposes that the referent is readily identifiable by the listener (Chafe, 1976). Therefore, when a speaker is using a pronoun appropriately, the referent of that pronoun should be selected from among entities that are mutually known. Because the perspective adjustment theory suggests differently, we investigated how people understand pronouns.

The experiments were modeled after the following situation: Suppose that a history professor and a student are discussing topics for a term paper. After considering several options, the student proposes to write about Niccolo Machiavelli. The mention of Machiavelli reminds the professor of John Smith, a colleague whose political intrigues had recently been revealed. As the thought of John Smith crosses the professor's mind, the student comments: "I think he has been greatly misunderstood." Who would the professor take the pronoun "he" to refer to? Our experiments show that the professor indeed interprets the utterance egocentrically, and in some cases identifies the referent of "he" to be John Smith instead of Machiavelli. The participants in our experiment made incorrect interpretations three times as often when the professor was reminded of an intrigue-related colleague whose name was John compared to a colleague whose name was Mary. In addition, when the participants correctly identified the referent of "he" to be Machiavelli, there was evidence that they had to adjust their perspective: They took longer to identify Machiavelli as the referent of "he" when they were thinking of a colleague named John rather than a colleague named Mary. So when the private thought was about a person whose gender fit the pronoun, that person was considered as the referent. The fact that the thought is private and not shared by the other person is not sufficient to preempt anchoring in an egocentric interpretation.

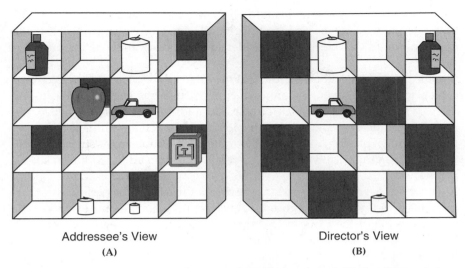

Addressee's View   Director's View
(A)   (B)

Figure 8.1. The array of objects from (A) the addressee's and (B) the director's perspectives. The two views are distinct because of the occluded slots. The critical instruction ("Put the small candle next to the truck") picks out a different candle from the director's perspective (the shared candle) than from the addressee's perspective (the occluded candle).

Perhaps the most dramatic demonstration of egocentric interpretation plus adjustment comes from an experiment that we recently conducted using an eyetracking system (Keysar, Barr, Balin, & Brauner, 2000). One participant sat in front of an array of objects as shown in Fig. 8.1. Another participant, who was actually a confederate, sat on the other side of the array. They played a simple game: The confederate (the "director") received a picture that included objects from the array but in different locations. The director then instructed the participant, the addressee, to rearrange objects to match the picture. Although most objects were mutually visible, some objects were occluded so that only the addressee could see them. They did not appear in the director's photograph and were therefore not part of the game.

Using an eyetracking device, we tracked the addressee's eye movements as they followed the director's instructions. It has been demonstrated that as soon as people identify an object as a referent, their eye fixates on that object as a precursor to the reach of the hand (Tanenhaus, Spivey-Knowlton, Eberhard, & Sedivy, 1995). Therefore, the eye movement information in our experiment indicated which objects addressees were considering as referents at any given moment.

Figure 8.1 illustrates how we tested the theory. At a critical point, the director told the addressee, "Put the small candle next to the truck." The only candles that are relevant here are those that are visible from the *director's* perspective: a large candle on the top row and a smaller one on the bottom row. Clearly, the director is talking about the mutually visible candle on the bottom row. The addressee, however, can also see a third candle that is obviously invisible to the director. Would the addressees consider the occluded candle as the intended candle?

Our data unambiguously show that they do. Addressees take the occluded candle to be the referent before correcting themselves and adjusting to the director's perspective. In 25% of the cases, the addressee actually reached for the occluded candle, sometimes correcting in midair, sometimes lifting it briefly, returning it, then picking up the correct candle. This demonstrates strikingly how addressees egocentrically identify a referent and then adjust to the speaker's perspective.

However, even when the addressee did not reach for the occluded candle, there was evidence for an egocentric anchor and adjustment. As soon as the addressees heard the expression "the small candle," their eye was fastest to fixate on the occluded candle – suggesting that they initially identified it as the intended candle. In most cases, one could see the adjustment as the eye moved from the occluded candle and eventually fixated on the candle next to it, the one intended by the director. Such adjustment delayed the identification of the intended candle: The addressees fixated on the intended object much later when the occluded slot contained a small candle than in a control condition, when the occluded slot contained an entirely different object that could not be a referent (e.g., a small toy monkey).

The robustness of the effects, along with the fact that participants reached for objects that the director could not see at all, made us somewhat concerned. We suspected that participants might not have paid attention to the difference between visible and occluded objects. It seemed possible that participants simply did not notice which objects were actually occluded from the director's perspective. To test this possibility, we asked participants to hide the occluded objects themselves. In spite of this, the experiment demonstrated the same interference effects and the same tendency to reach for those objects that could only be referents from the participant's egocentric perspective.

These experiments demonstrate that even when people have full knowledge of the other's perspective – even when it is very clear that the director cannot see certain objects, and that the objects should not be relevant to their interpretation – addressees do not routinely use that knowledge to constrain comprehension initially. They do not assume that speakers' utterances are optimally designed to match the shared perspective. Instead, they comprehend utterances from their own perspective, and then adjust to correct any error that arises.

Self Anchoring and Adjustment in Speaking

Although addressees do not follow the principle of optimal design, speakers' behavior implies they do. People speak differently to different audiences (e.g., Fussell, & Krauss, 1989; Krauss & Fussell, 1991). For example, one study demonstrated such "audience design" by asking New Yorkers to describe pictures of New York City to other people (Isaacs & Clark, 1987). When they were talking to other New Yorkers, they tended to use proper names such as "the Citicorp building." However, when New Yorkers addressed people who were not as familiar with the city, they were more likely to provide a longer description, such as "the building with the slanted roof." Such audience design suggests that speakers are following the principle of optimal design. Nevertheless, we discovered that speakers, like addressees, use an egocentric anchoring and adjustment mechanism.

What would seem to be an easy action – generating a sentence – requires complex mental machinery (Levelt, 1989). The production of a sentence involves several steps: planning a message (what the speaker intends to say); putting the plan into linguistic form (determining how to say it); and finally articulating it. There is also a monitoring system that triggers revisions when it detects errors.

At what point in this complex process does the speaker design the utterance for the specific addressee? One possibility is that audience design occurs at the outset, so that when speakers plan their messages, they already tailor the plan to their particular addressee. Another possibility is that planning a message is a relatively "egocentric" process – a process that does not take the other's perspective into account at all – but that the monitoring system is "in charge" of audience design. It could monitor for utterance plans that violate the perspective of the addressee, and then trigger a revision of these plans to make them more sensitive to the mutual knowledge with the addressee.

Horton and Keysar (1996) tested these two models of utterance generation by asking participants to describe various line drawings. The figures were displayed in the context of other figures, and the speakers could use the context in their descriptions. For example, when they described a circle in the context of a larger circle they could say the "small" circle. To test when audience design is employed, two kinds of contexts were used – context figures that were shared with the addressee and context figures that were privileged to the speaker. As optimal design would predict, speakers tended to make reference to the shared context more than to the context that was inaccessible to their addressee. This shows that indeed speakers in the experiment took their addressee's perspective into account when they described the figures.

Then we asked speakers to start their descriptions quickly, as soon as they saw the figures. It is important to note that the speakers were hurried only in the sense that they had to initiate their utterance immediately; they did not speak at a faster pace than normal. When speakers were hurried, their descriptions were no longer tailored to the perspective of their addressees – they used shared and privileged context to the exact same degree.

These results make sense if one assumes that before people speak, they monitor and correct their utterance plans for violations of their addressee's perspective. When speakers are under pressure, they do not have sufficient time and resources to monitor and adjust, and so they fall back on the unmonitored utterance plans. Given that speakers did not use the perspective of their addressees when they were hurried, their descriptions reflected egocentric planning. Although this experiment shows that speakers adjust to their addressee's perspective following an egocentric plan, it does not tell us if the adjustment is sufficient. Later, we describe a study that shows that the adjustments are often insufficient.

These findings suggest an intriguing solution to the audience design goal of speaking: Speakers do not design utterances for their audience from the outset; instead, utterances seem to be tailored specifically for certain addressees only because initial utterance plans that violate the principle of optimal design are monitored, detected and adjusted. Presumably, such a process saves time and effort because in many cases there might not be a need to adjust.

THE ILLUSION OF TRANSPARENCY: SYSTEMATIC CONSTRAINTS ON COMMUNICATION

Taking the perspective of others in conversation involves interpreting an utterance from the others' perspective: Given the context available to them – what they know and believe – how would they interpret the utterance? Such assessments appear superficially easy. However, when we know the intention behind an utterance, this knowledge affects our ability to appreciate its ambiguity. Keysar (1994) has shown that when we possess knowledge of the intended meaning of a speaker's utterance, we no longer are able to accurately judge how uninformed others would perceive that same utterance. Instead, we perceive the utterance as less ambiguous than it really is – as if the intention behind it is obvious or transparent.

This phenomenon is related to hindsight bias, which has been documented in a variety of domains (Fischhoff, 1975; Fischhoff & Beyth, 1975). For example, historical events seem almost inevitable in hindsight and people claim that they could have predicted these events. However, people's ability to predict uncertain future events without the benefit of hindsight is notoriously poor. Once people know the outcome of events, they perceive the outcome as inevitable. We describe how in a similar fashion, the perception of both meaning and intention is taken as inevitable. They are taken as transparent through the utterance.

Construal and the Illusory Transparency of Meaning
Consider the case of idioms. *Idioms* are expressions whose meaning is typically not a direct function of their constituent words. Knowing the meaning of the words "kick," "the," and "bucket," and the rules of English, is not sufficient to determine that the meaning of "kick the bucket" is to die. However, not all idioms are as opaque; some feel relatively transparent (Cacciari, & Tabossi, 1993). For example, "spill the beans" seems less arbitrary because spilling corresponds to the act of revealing and the beans stand for the revealed secrets. This idiom appears to be relatively transparent because one can see a relationship between

its elements and its meaning. We suggest that this feeling of transparency is exaggerated by the very knowledge of the meaning of the idiom. Once idioms are interpreted, the meaning and the idiom's ambiguous wording become one and the same in our mind.

If an idiom seems overly transparent to us because we already know its meaning, then we should expect people who do not know the meaning to be able to figure it out. After all, it seems that the meaning is "in" the idiom. For example, native speakers of a language might expect nonnative speakers to understand their use of idioms just because their meanings seem relatively transparent.

Keysar and Bly (1995, 1999) tested the illusory transparency of meaning using a variety of archaic English idioms that are no longer familiar to English speakers. For example, the expression "the goose hangs high" used to be an English idiom that meant that the future looks good; however, most English speakers today are unacquainted with this meaning. We told some students that "the goose hangs high" meant the future looks good, and others that it meant the future looks gloomy. We then asked them to judge what uninformed overhearers would take the idiom to mean. The students who believed it meant something good predicted that uninformed peers were more likely to think the idiom meant that the future looks good rather than gloomy. The students who believed the opposite predicted that the overhearers would think that it was gloomy rather than good. Thus, the very knowledge of the intended meaning colors the ambiguous expression and makes the meaning seem more transparent than it really is.

Illusory Transparency of Intention

The illusory transparency of meaning is the feeling that the meaning of what is really a relatively opaque linguistic expression is somehow transparent. Consider now a related but different illusion of transparency. David Olson and colleagues showed that 5-year-old children are subject to the illusion of the transparency of speakers' intentions (Olson, & Torrance, 1987). In that experiment, children were told that Lucy had two pairs of red shoes: one new and one old. Then Lucy, who wanted the new pair, asked Linus to bring her "the red shoes." Linus, who did not know that she wanted the new shoes, guessed and brought the wrong pair. The children in the study were surprised that he did not bring her the shoes that she had in mind. They behaved as if the ambiguous phrase "the red shoes" uniquely identified the shoes she intended him to bring. They behaved as if Lucy's intention was transparent.

As it turns out, adults tend to behave precisely like Olson's children (Keysar, 1993; 1994). Imagine that June recommends a restaurant for dinner to her friend Mark. He goes there and hates the food. He then calls June and leaves a recorded message: "June, I just finished dinner at the restaurant you recommended, and I must say, it was marvelous, just marvelous." Mark is clearly being sarcastic, but what would June think he meant? You know what he meant because you know he hated the dinner, but she does not have this information. You would experience an illusion of transparency if you attribute the perception of sarcasm to June because *you* know that Mark was sarcastic.

To test this, we presented people with the story about Mark and June and then played back the message he supposedly left on her answering machine (Keysar, 1994; Keysar & Baldwin, under review). However, the story was of two kinds. Mark either hated the food or he really liked it; other than that, the information in the story was identical and everyone heard exactly the same answering machine message. Although Mark had different intentions in the two versions, people's evaluation of *June's* perception should not vary. If they really take June's perspective – if they consider information that is available to *her* – then they should give the same answer in both cases. Instead, people were more likely to say that June perceived sarcasm when they knew he was being sarcastic than when they knew he was being sincere. This is precisely what one would expect if people take utterances as transparent – they behave as if the intention is obvious from what the speaker says.

As it turns out, the reason readers took Mark's intention as transparent is that he wanted June to perceive that intention. Keysar (1998) added a condition where the speaker's attitude was negative but he wanted to *conceal* it. In this case, Mark hated the restaurant, but he did not want June to know that. He wanted to spare her feelings because she recommended the restaurant. So he left her the same message, ". . . , it was marvelous, just marvelous." With this condition, participants no longer thought that June would perceive sarcasm, even though the event was negative. They were just as likely to predict that she would perceive sarcasm when he attempted to conceal his negative experience as when he had a positive experience and was truly sincere. So participants took Mark's *communicative intention* as transparent. It was as if they assumed that June would perceive whatever intention Mark wanted her to perceive.

Such an illusion of transparency could result from construal (e.g., Ross, 1990). Once we interpret an ambiguous behavior, we construe the behavior in terms of the interpretation and eventually we perceive it as unambiguous. When people knew Mark intended to be sarcastic, they reported that the repetition of "marvelous" clearly conveyed his sarcasm. When they knew he was being sincere, they reported that the repetition only underscored how much he really enjoyed it. Similarly, pauses in Mark's message were interpreted as either pregnant with sarcasm in one case or merely breathing breaks in the other. Clearly, when one construes the utterance in a particular way, it appears to include sufficient cues for the intended meaning, so that even the uninformed should be able to figure it out. The way the cognitive system construes ambiguity is a particular constraint that gives rise to an illusion of transparency in language use.

We further suggest that the illusory transparency we documented results from an anchoring and adjustment similar to the one we documented for speakers and addressees. We assume that observers anchor in the intention of the speaker (Mark) and then insufficiently adjust to the uninformed addressee's perspective. To test this, we manipulated the amount of time participants were allotted to respond. Indeed, when participants answered at their leisure, the illusion of transparency was smaller than when they were hurried. Because adjustment takes time, the less time people have to complete the task, the more anchored they would be in the speaker's actual intention.

Similarly, the experiment provided another source of evidence for an anchoring and adjustment mechanism. It showed that responses that reflect a more complete adjustment take longer than those that are closer to the anchor points. According to an anchoring and adjustment account, if participants attribute to June the perception of sincerity when Mark is sarcastic, they must have adjusted. Indeed, addressees' response times were delayed when they indicated that June would not perceive intended sarcasm than when they indicated that she would. The opposite was true when Mark was being sincere. It took longer to attribute the perception of sarcasm to June than the perception of a sincere intent. Precisely those responses that we predict would require adjustment took longer.

Our studies converge with Gilovich, Savitsky, and Medvec's (1998) and Gilovich and Savitsky's (1999) studies that documented a related illusion of transparency – the illusion that one's own internal states, such as private preferences or emotions, are accessible to uninformed others. They showed that the illusion results from anchoring on one's own internal states and not adjusting sufficiently to the perspective of others. Unlike the illusion of transparency we demonstrated for overhearers (i.e., June), in which people thought others' intentions shone through, these studies show that people perceive their *own* internal states as relatively transparent. We now describe how speakers experience the same illusion of transparency about their own intentions.

The Speaker's Illusion of Transparency

The task of speakers is to translate their intentions into linguistic forms. To ensure they have conveyed their intentions successfully, speakers monitor their own utterances. Sometimes they recognize an utterance as ambiguous and attempt a repair or correction. However, if speakers anchor in their own intention in the process of monitoring and evaluating their own utterances, the intended meaning of their own ambiguous utterances might seem relatively transparent to them. If this is true, then the illusion of transparency is an inherent element in communication that stems from the heuristic processing of language.

One implication of the illusion of transparency is that people do not fully realize the ambiguity of their own utterances. It is particularly surprising to find such ambiguities in written text because writing can be edited. The day in September 1997 when the rock band the Rolling Stones performed in Chicago's Soldier Field, the city put up a large sign on the highway that said, "AVOID LSD TONIGHT." The city authorities were not attempting to provide advice about drug use, but instead to advise against using Lake Shore Drive in the vicinity of Soldier Field. Likewise, the owner of a pharmacy in Bethlehem, Pennsylvania, adamantly rejected the idea that the sign above his store had dual meaning. The sign read: "Lyon's Pharmacy: We dispense with accuracy."

Part of the difficulty of writing is that when we write we are engrossed in a specific physical, emotional and mental context. It is difficult to take into account the variety of contexts that a future reader could have, contexts which might alter the meaning of what we write. More than 400 years ago, in his essay "Man Can Have No Knowledge," Montaigne described how even the same reader can interpret the same text differently on separate occasions (Frame, 1943):

When I pick up books, I will have perceived in such-and-such a passage surpassing charms which will have struck my soul; let me come upon it another time, in vain I turn it over and over, in vain I twist it and manipulate it, to me it is a shapeless and unrecognizable mass. (p. 425)

Montaigne then goes on to describe how even the meaning of one's own text can be lost:

Even in my own writing I do not always find again the sense of my first thought; I do not know what I meant to say, and often I get burned by correcting and putting in a new meaning, because I have lost the first one, which was better. (pp. 425–426)

Montaigne's experience demonstrates the role that his intention played at the time of writing. The text made sense to him only when he had the intention in mind, which in turn suggests that one needed the intention to make sense of the text.

Montaigne's experience might be a symptom of the way we evaluate the clarity of our own utterances. If we anchor in our own intentions when we evaluate the utterances that attempt to convey these same intentions, we might underestimate how ambiguous these utterances really are. Keysar and Henly (1998; in press) tested this idea with speakers, modeling the experiments on a study that investigated a similar phenomenon in a nonlinguistic domain (Griffin & Ross, 1991; Newton, 1990), in which participants finger-tapped a popular song so that an audience would be able to identify the song. Then they estimated how many people in the audience recognized the song. People consistently overestimated their success. Apparently, having the song in mind makes the tapping seem much less ambiguous than it really is.

In an analogous manner, might knowing our own intention when producing an utterance lead us to overestimate its effectiveness? To test this possibility, we asked people to read aloud syntactically ambiguous sentences such as, "The man is chasing a woman on a bicycle." The sentence could mean either that the man is chasing a woman who is riding a bike, or that the man is using a bike to chase the woman. We provided the speakers with a picture that disambiguated the sentence; for example, the picture showed a man running after a cycling woman. The speakers said the sentence to addressees, trying to convey the meaning expressed in the picture and then they predicted which of the two meanings the addressee would actually understand. The addressee, who did not have the picture, chose the meaning they thought the speaker intended.

In estimating the effectiveness of their utterances for addressees, there could be three possible outcomes: (1) calibrated estimation; (2) underestimation; or (3) overestimation.

Of all our speakers, only two were perfectly calibrated; one of these was an actor and the other a linguist. None of our speakers underestimated their effectiveness – they never thought that listeners did not understand them when they did. The rest of the speakers overestimated; they tended to think that they were understood when they were not. They demonstrated an illusion of transparency.

After we recorded the speakers' utterances, we asked them to judge whether they thought they would be able to understand their own intentions when they listened to the recordings the next day. The next day, when they returned to hear the recording, they were not as accurate as they had predicted. Again, they overestimated their effectiveness. They were in the same position as Montaigne when he was trying to understand his own intention.

One might want to know how often speakers experience an illusion of transparency outside the laboratory. The experiments used sentences that were syntactically ambiguous, and perhaps real-world sentences are often syntactically unambiguous. When a sentence is unambiguous, speakers cannot have an illusion of transparency by definition, because addressees can only interpret the sentence the way it was intended. In contrast to syntactic ambiguity, however, pragmatic ambiguity is the rule. *All* utterances can convey more than one intention. Therefore, the conditions in real life are even more likely to give rise to this phenomenon than the conditions in our experiments.

COMMUNICATION AND MISCOMMUNICATION OF INTENTIONS

Systematic Reasons for Miscommunication

Reasons for miscommunication are many, ranging from random error to the systematic operation of motivational and cognitive processes. Nickerson (1999) demonstrates how miscommunication can result from people's mistaken assessment of what others know and their tendency to overimpute their own knowledge to others. We have shown that even when language users are well informed about what others know, they still anchor egocentrically when taking the other's perspective. Although people might be quite good at taking into account differences in perspective when they use language, they only do so through this effortful and time-consuming process of adjustment. When people are overly busy and cognitively occupied, they might not be able to adjust sufficiently from the egocentric anchor. This has clear consequences in our overly busy world.

Inherent Limits on Adjustment

The degree of cognitive overload depends on changing circumstances; yet the studies we described indicate that even when speakers are completely at ease, perspective taking is systematically constrained. Speakers attempting to convey their intentions anchor in those same intentions, and believe their utterances to be more transparent than they really are. Consequently, speakers might not perceive a need to make further adjustments to the addressee's perspective. In the following anecdote, the mother of the 2-year-old Ely thought that what she was saying was unambiguous:

Linda: Ely, go get me your shoes.
    [Ely brings a white shoe]
Linda: Get the other shoe.
    [Ely brings a black shoe]

Unlike Olson's study, where it is the child who takes Lucy's intention as transparent, in this example, it is the adult who does. For Linda, "the other shoe" had only one meaning, and her very attempt to convey this meaning inhibited her ability to perceive other possible meanings.

The Challenge of Multiple Causes

Specific instances of miscommunication are very difficult to predict. One reason is that the meaning of an utterance is often overdetermined – addressees can disambiguate utterances using multiple contextual cues. Another reason is that there are multiple root causes for miscommunication. One of the challenges is to explain how different causes of miscommunication make their unique and interactive contributions.

It is especially interesting to see how sometimes conflicting forces determine whether communication will be successful. Consider the role of motivation. When the stakes are high, a speaker is motivated to communicate effectively; however, the higher the stakes, the greater the pressure – the higher the burden on the cognitive system, leaving fewer resources for monitoring and adjustment. In the 1991 British movie "Let Him Have It," a pivotal scene tragically demonstrates how resource-depleting pressure can triumph over the motivation to communicate effectively. Derek, a basically good lad, admires and seeks to emulate his criminal friend, Chris. When the two teenagers attempt to break into a store, the police show up. An officer captures Derek and then approaches Chris, who is carrying a gun. In a tense moment, the officer demands that Chris surrender the gun. At that point Derek yells: "Let him have it, Chris!" Chris turns, shoots and wounds the officer. Later, he shoots and kills another policeman. Chris is tried for murder and found guilty. Derek is also tried for murder, because the prosecution argues that he incited Chris to shoot at the officers by yelling, "Let him have it!" The defense argues that Derek actually meant the opposite – that he meant, "Let him have the gun!" Because Chris is only 16 years old, he serves 10 years in a juvenile prison. Derek, who is 19, is convicted of murder and hanged. The movie was based on the true story of Derek Bentley.

HEURISTICS IN LANGUAGE USE

The belief that language users rely on mutual knowledge when they communicate stems from the assumption that in order to communicate successfully they *should* rely on what they know about the other's perspective. Therefore, the general assumption has been that error-free communication is the optimal and desired goal of language users, and that in order to achieve this goal, they should focus on a mutual perspective.

This normative-optimality assumption does not take into account the way the mind deals with uncertainty, of which language use is a particular case. As in the domain of decision making, the behavior of language users reflects an important tradeoff between optimality and efficiency. When solving problems, the mind takes shortcuts and uses heuristics (e.g., Tversky, & Kahneman, 1974). In this way, mental resources are conserved and solutions are reached in a short amount of time. Given that the solutions are not always optimal, they show a systematic error pattern. The benefit of such a system, though, might generally outweigh its cost – except in extreme cases such as that of Derek Bentley.

What we consistently find is that language users do not do what they "should" do according to common sense and current theory. For example, they do not routinely use readily available information about the perspective of the other. The reason is twofold. First, information about perspective is not only knowledge, it is metaknowledge: It is knowledge about who knows what. Such higher-level information typically takes more cognitive resources and more time to use. By relying on an egocentric interpretation in the case of understanding, and an egocentric plan in the case of speaking, the language user is taking a shortcut that is cheap in mental resources and relatively fast.

The second reason we rely on an egocentric process is that it is typically successful. In many cases, the overlap between the foci of the speaker and the addressee is such that an egocentric process would be sufficient for successful communication. Information that is in mutual focus is also in the egocentric focus of each interlocutor. Consider as an example the small candle in Fig. 8.1. In our experiment, we distinguished between the two perspectives by preventing the director from seeing the smallest candle. However, when people normally sit around a small table, they typically share access to all the objects that are on the table. When perspectives overlap in this way, the metaknowledge about perspective becomes superfluous. One no longer need evaluate perspective because information about who knows what would be redundant. In these cases, it is most cost effective to have a system that does not take perspective into account at all. In the typical case of perspective overlap, then, the more "expensive" monitoring and adjustment process would play no role, reaping the benefits of the quick egocentric process without paying the price of correction.

A heuristic approach to language use has another advantage. It accounts for the systematicity of errors. The normative assumption that language users rely on mutual knowledge can only explain miscommunication as a result of random errors, noise, and unpredictable failures of attention or memory. In contrast, the perspective adjustment model predicts that when perspectives diverge or the cognitive system is overtaxed, errors will be systematically egocentric. It explains these errors as a result of insufficient adjustment. In many cases, then, miscommunication is not random and unpredictable; rather, it reflects directly the heuristic processing that underlies both how we speak and how we understand language.

BROADER IMPLICATIONS: WATCHING THE BORDER

The communication of intentions is fundamental to all social interaction. In order to navigate the social world, people are constantly inferring the motivation underlying the observable actions of others. Inferring intentions communicated through language is a ubiquitous and fundamental part of this process. Therefore, understanding the mental mechanisms of linguistic communication and understanding the conditions for their success and failure could be relevant to models in *game theory*, which is studied in a variety of the social sciences, from economics to international relations (e.g., Kreps, 1990; Laitin, 1993). A typical "game" is a situation in which the cost and benefit of people's actions depend not only on what they do, but also on what others do. For example, unsatisfied employees would want to express their concerns only if they believed that other employees were going to do the same. The risk of losing one's job would inhibit a sole complainer, but a complaint *en masse* could trigger a change in the system. In order to coordinate action, then, people can signal their intentions in a variety of ways, thereby making communication critical to people's ability to coordinate and cooperate (e.g., Chwe, 1998; Cooper, DeJong, Forsythe, & Ross, 1992, 1994).

International relations are also beset with problems of the credible communication of intentions. Communicating intentions is fundamental to the process of making decisions in international politics. In his classic book *Perception and Misperception in International Politics*, Jervis (1976) describes how two days before Germany's attack on Poland, Chamberlain sent a letter that was supposed to deter such an attack by making it clear that Britain intends to fight. The politely phrased letter was completely misunderstood as conciliatory, thus encouraging an attack.

However, such misperception of intentions occurs even when the relationship between the parties is friendly. Jervis describes how, on November 27, the Pentagon warned the commanding general in Pearl Harbor to expect "hostile action." Although the Pentagon was referring to hostile action from outside, the general interpreted it as a danger of internal sabotage. Such systematic misunderstanding can result from the way that intentions are signaled in such international games. If we understand the type of heuristics used in communication, it would allow a better understanding of how the constraints of the mind and the environment lead to successful signaling or systematic failure.

9. Inferential Correction

Daniel T. Gilbert

It is sometimes said that Tversky and Kahneman (1974) described two-and-a-half heuristics. Although the bulk of the research inspired by their seminal paper has indeed focused on the representativeness and availability heuristics, the remaining half-heuristic may well be the one that psychologists not yet born will consider the most important. Why? Because whereas the celebrity heuristics describe processes by which people make particular kinds of judgments (i.e., frequency and probability judgments on the one hand; categorical identity judgments on the other), their obscure sibling – anchoring and adjustment – describes the process by which the human mind does virtually all of its inferential work. Indeed, one of psychology's fundamental insights is that judgments are generally the products of nonconscious systems that operate quickly, on the basis of scant evidence, and in a routine manner, and then pass their hurried approximations to consciousness, which slowly and deliberately adjusts them. In this sense, anchoring and adjustment is a fundamental description of mental life. This chapter reviews some work on adjustment – or what my collaborators and I call *correction processes* – in the domain of dispositional inference.

A CORRECTION MODEL OF DISPOSITIONAL INFERENCE

We care about what others do, but we care more about why they do it. Two equally rambunctious nephews may break two equally expensive crystal vases at Aunt Sofia's house, but the one who did so by accident gets the reprimand and the one who did so by design gets the thumbscrews. Aunts are in the business of understanding what makes nephews act as they do, and for some time, social psychologists have been in the in the business of explaining how aunts achieve those understandings (e.g., Bem, 1967; Heider, 1958; Hilton & Slugoski, 1986; Jones & Davis, 1965; Kelley, 1967; Medcof, 1990; Reeder & Brewer, 1979; Trope, 1986; Weiner, Frieze, Kukla, Reed, Rest, & Rosenbaum, 1972). These so-called

I thank my collaborators, whose work is described herein: Eric Benson, Brian Giesler, Mike Gill, Traci Giuliano, Ned Jones, Doug Krull, Pat Malone, Shawn McNulty, Kate Morris, Randy Osborne, Brett Pelham, and Romin Tafarodi.

Portions of this manuscript are borrowed from Gilbert and Malone (1995) and Gilbert, Tafarodi, and Malone (1993).

attribution theories differ in both focus and detail, but most are grounded in a metaphor that construes the human skin as a special boundary that separates one set of causal forces from another. On the sunny side of the epidermis are the external or situational forces that press inward on the person, and on the meaty side are the internal or personal forces that exert pressure outward. Sometimes these forces press in conjunction, sometimes in opposition, and their dynamic interplay manifests itself as observable behavior. As such, aunts can determine the causes of behavior in much the same way that they determine the causes of physical movement: By observing the motion of an object ("The balloon rose rapidly in the morning sky") and then subtracting out the contribution of the external forces ("A light wind nudged the balloon ever upward"), an observer can estimate the magnitude and direction of the internal forces ("The balloon must have contained helium that contributed to the speed of its ascent"). According to attribution theories, aunts think of nephews as they think of balloons – objects whose behavioral motions are partially determined by the prevailing winds and partially determined by the rare and noble gasses with which genes and experience have inflated them.

Attribution theories suggest that because the psychological world is a mirror of the physical world, the two may be penetrated by the same logic. People behave as they do because of the kinds of people they are and because of the kinds of situations in which their behaviors unfold; thus, when we "make an attribution" about another, we attempt to determine which of these factors – the person or the person's situation – played the more significant role in shaping the person's behavior. Is the basketball player a graceless shooter, or did poor lighting cause him to miss the free throw? Did the senator speak in favor of abortion rights because she truly believes in freedom of choice, or was she merely pandering to the desires of her liberal audience? Did the student appear sad because he is chronically depressed, or had he just received word of a failing grade? Each of these is a question about the relative contributions to behavior of situational and dispositional factors, and this distinction is the defining feature of attribution theory.

Attribution theory's fundamental distinction leads quite naturally to its fundamental rule: When a behavior occurs in the presence of a sufficiently strong, facilitative force, an observer should not infer that the actor is predisposed to perform that behavior. Just as one should not confidently conclude that a balloon that rises on a windy day is filled with helium, one cannot make confident inferences about the abilities of an athlete, the convictions of a politician, or the mental health of a student when poor lighting, a roomful of opinionated voters, or sudden bad news may have induced their behaviors. In other words, we should not explain with dispositions that which has already been explained by the situation. This logical rule was first formalized by Jones and Davis (1965) as the *law of noncommon effects* and later extended and codified by Kelley (1967) as the *discounting principle*, which warns us not to attribute an effect to any one causal agent (e.g., a disposition) when another plausible causal agent (e.g., a situational force) is simultaneously present. When people do precisely what the physical environment or the social situation demands, dispositional inferences are logically unwarranted.

This simple rule is eminently reasonable but, as with the interstate speed limit, someone seems to have neglected to tell the drivers. Although ordinary people may acknowledge the logical validity of the discounting principle when it is stated in the abstract, in practice they are sometimes willing to abandon it. People may make inferences about the dispositions of others even when situational forces explain the behavior quite nicely. In scores of experiments, participants have violated attribution theory's logical canon by concluding that an actor was predisposed to certain behaviors, when in fact, those behaviors were demanded by the situations in which they occurred. Basketball players who are randomly assigned to shoot free throws in badly lighted gyms may, on average, be judged as less capable than players who are randomly assigned to shoot free throws on a well-lighted court (e.g., Ross, Amabile, & Steinmetz, 1977); politicians who are randomly assigned to read pro-choice speeches may, on average, be judged as more pro-choice than politicians who are randomly assigned to read pro-life speeches (e.g., Jones & Harris, 1967); students who are randomly assigned to receive bad news may, on average, be judged as more chronically depressed than students who are randomly assigned to receive good news (e.g., Gilbert, Pelham, & Krull, 1988). And so on. This logical error has been called "as robust and reliable a phenomenon as any in the literature on person perception" (Quattrone, 1982a, p. 376). So what causes it?

Building on the work of Tversky and Kahneman (1974), Quattrone (1982), and Trope (1986), my collaborators and I developed a model of the process by which enduring, unobservable, internal states are inferred from observable actions. We argued that dispositional inference comprises three sequential stages, which we dubbed *categorization, characterization*, and *correction*. According to this model, perceivers *categorize* or identify the actor's behavior ("Gee, my classmate sure is acting nervous"), *characterize* the actor in terms of enduring behavioral predispositions ("He must be an anxious sort of fellow"), and finally, *correct* these inferences with information about external influences on the actor's behavior ("Of course, the professor is really putting him on the spot, so maybe he's not such an anxious guy after all").

The evidence we offered for our model was grounded in a popular conceptualization of conscious attention as a scant resource. According to this view, people's attempts to, say, solve a crossword puzzle and recite the alphabet backwards do not cooccur successfully because each task requires the same limited resource – namely, conscious attention, size small (see Kahneman, 1973; Norman & Bobrow, 1975). However, two simple or well-practiced tasks, such as driving one's car from home to office while whistling a tune, may be performed simultaneously precisely because neither requires much of this attentional resource (Hasher & Zacks, 1979; Posner & Snyder, 1975; Schneider & Shiffrin, 1977; Wegner & Bargh, 1998). We suggested that categorization and characterization were less effortful than correction, and thus predicted that people whose attentional resources had been commandeered temporarily by an extraneous task (such as an experimenter's request that they recite the alphabet backwards) should be perfectly capable of performing the first two of these operations but should have considerable trouble performing the last. As such, these "cognitively busy" observers should draw dispositional inferences about actors whose behaviors are clearly the products of situational constraints.

Drawing Dispositional Inferences about Others

The Effects of Cognitive Busyness. We sought to demonstrate that cognitive busyness disables the perceiver's ability to use information about aspects of the situation that might have facilitated or impeded a target's behavior (Gilbert, Pelham, & Krull, 1988). We showed participants clips from a videotape of a female target discussing a variety of experimenter-assigned topics with a stranger, and asked them to estimate the target's level of trait anxiety. In most of the clips, the target appeared extremely anxious. Participants were told that to protect the privacy of the target person, the videotape would be shown without any sound. However, participants were told that they would be able to tell which topic the target was discussing in a given clip because the topic would appear in subtitles at the bottom of the screen. For participants in the *anxious topics condition*, most of the subtitles indicated that the target was discussing anxiety-provoking topics (e.g., her sexual fantasies), whereas for participants in the *relaxing topics condition*, most of the subtitles indicated that the target was discussing mundane topics (e.g., world travel). Under normal conditions, one would expect participants in the anxious topics condition to attribute the target's apparent anxiety to the nature of the topics she was being asked to discuss, and thus to make less extreme ratings of the target's trait anxiety than participants in the relaxing topics condition.

However, the circumstances were not normal. Half the participants in each condition were required to perform an extra task while watching the video clips. Specifically, participants in the *busy condition* were instructed to memorize the discussion topics in their proper sequence while viewing the tape, whereas participants in the *non-busy condition* were given no such instruction. Memorization requires rehearsal, and rehearsal requires resources. As such, the unique prediction derived from our model was that those participants who were asked to memorize the discussion topics would be the least likely to use them when drawing inferences about the target. After viewing the videotape, participants rated the target's trait-anxiety on scales that were anchored at the endpoints with such phrases as, "She is probably comfortable (uncomfortable) in social situations" and "She is a calm (nervous) sort of person." We stressed that participants should indicate what kind of person the target is "in her day-to-day life," and not just "how she was acting" in the video clips. Finally, we asked all participants to recall the discussion topics.

Table 9.1. The Effects of Busyness on Inferences
of Dispositional Anxiety

Discussion Topic	Busyness	
	Busy (Memorize Subtitles)	Non-Busy (Do Not Memorize Subtitles)
Anxious	8.88[a]	7.79
Relaxing	9.28	10.31
Difference	−0.40	−2.52

[a] Larger values indicate greater anxiety.
Source: Adapted from Gilbert, D. T., Pelham, B. W., & Krull, D. S. (1988).

As Table 9.1 shows, nonbusy participants used the situational constraint information (i.e., their knowledge of the topics) when estimating the target's trait anxiety, but busy participants did not. Although busy participants were less likely than nonbusy participants to use this information, they were actually *more* likely to recall it. In short, participants who were asked to memorize the topics that a target was discussing drew more dispositional inferences about that target than did participants who were not asked to memorize this information. This finding is consistent with our suggestion that initial characterizations require fewer resources than do subsequent corrections.

In a set of follow-up studies (Gilbert, McNulty, Giuliano, & Benson, 1992), we showed that a wide variety of manipulations could produce the same "undercorrection effect" that the rehearsal of word strings produced. For example, in one study, participants viewed the "anxious woman video" just described. As before, half were assigned to the anxious topics condition and half were assigned to the relaxing topics condition. However, in this study we manipulated cognitive busyness in a rather unusual way. Our model suggested that people effortlessly categorize behavior ("She looks anxious") before they go on to characterize the actor ("She's an anxious person") and then correct that inference ("But she was discussing her sex life, so she's probably not such an anxious person after all"). We reasoned that if the categorization stage were for some reason to become cognitively demanding, then resources that might normally be devoted to correction would be usurped by categorization, thus producing the undercorrection effect. In other words, the more difficulty observers had categorizing an action, the more likely they should be to draw dispositional inferences about the actor who performed it. To demonstrate this, participants in the non-busy condition were shown a normal version of the anxious woman video, while participants in the busy condition were shown a version of the video that had been visually degraded by misadjusting the tracking mechanisms on two videocassette recorders and then using those machines to make successive copies of the master tape. The final fourth-generation tape had a great deal of visual noise (streaking, blurring, color dropout, and snow) that interrupted the flow of the action and obscured some of its details. Indeed, participants who viewed the sloppy copy drew more dispositional inferences about the actor than did participants who viewed a pristine copy of the tape.

The foregoing research suggests that busy perceivers fail to correct their characterizations because they are too busy to use information about situational constraints, but *not* because they fail to notice, gather, or recall that information. Memory data support this suggestion. However, if busy perceivers really do have in memory all the information they require to correct their characterizations, then they should be perfectly able to do so at some later "unbusy" time. We examined this possibility in a series of studies (Gilbert & Osborne, 1989) that began by replicating our original demonstration of the undercorrection effect. For example, in one study we asked participants to watch the anxious woman video. As before, half were assigned to the anxious topics condition and half were assigned to the relaxing topics condition. In addition, half were assigned to rehearse an eight-digit number as they watched the video (busy condition) and the remaining half were not (nonbusy condition). After watching the videotape, participants rated the actor's trait anxiety and then stopped rehearsing the number. These formerly busy participants then spent a few minutes writing an essay about the actor's personality, and then rerated the actor. As Table 9.2 shows, ratings made while participants were busy showed the typical undercorrection effect; but ratings made after the participants had become unbusy did not. Apparently, formerly busy participants were able to use information stored in memory to correct their characterizations when later they had sufficient resources to do so.

Table 9.2. The Effects of Digit Rehearsal on Immediate and Delayed Inferences of Dispositional Anxiety

Discussion Topic	Busyness	
	Busy (Rehearsal)	Non-Busy (No Rehearsal)
Anxious		
Immediate rating	9.4[a]	6.8
Delayed rating	6.9	6.5
Relaxing		
Immediate rating	9.0	11.3
Delayed rating	10.4	11.1
Difference		
Immediate rating	0.4	−4.5
Delayed rating	−3.5	−4.6

[a] Larger values indicate greater anxiety.

Source: Adapted from Gilbert, D. T., & Osborne, R. E. (1989). Thinking backward: some curable and incurable consequences of cognitive busyness. *Journal of Personality and Social Psychology, 57,* 940–949.

As it turns out, not all of the consequences of busyness-induced undercorrection are so easily undone. Another study (Gilbert & Osborne, 1989) made use of the well-known fact that when observers draw dispositional inferences about an actor ("She's anxious"), those inferences can color the observers' view of new information such that the new information seems to confirm the observer's initial inference ("Look at those earrings – just the kind that an anxious person would wear"). We began by replicating a critical portion of the study just described. As usual, participants watched the anxious woman video. In this case, all were led to believe that the actor was discussing anxiety-provoking topics, and all were assigned to rehearse an eight-digit number as they watched the video. After watching the video, participants stopped rehearsing the number, and encountered some new information about the actor. Specifically, they heard a relatively uninformative audiotaped interview with the actor in which she described her major, her hometown, and so on. Participants rated the actor again.

Now, some participants were assigned to the *interlude condition*. These participants were allowed to spend a few minutes (after they watched the videotape but before they listened to the interview) thinking about the actor. The previous study led us to expect that during this time, these participants would use the information they had in memory to recover from the original undercorrection effect. Because they no longer considered the actor to be an anxious person, they should not have been inclined to "hear anxiety" in the actor's voice as she discussed her major and her hometown during the interview. On the other hand, participants in the *no-interlude condition* watched the videotape and then immediately heard the interview. We reasoned that because these participants did not have time to recover from the initial undercorrection effect, they would consider the actor an anxious person, and this belief would color their perception of her behavior during the interview. All of this suggested that when the interview was over and they had some time to reflect, the no interlude participants would find themselves in an unusual position. They would realize that they had failed to consider the situational constraint information and that their original impressions were mistaken ("I initially thought she was an anxious person, but now that I think about it, I realize she was discussing some pretty intense topics"). However, they would also be struck by the anxiety that they heard in her voice during the interview ("But regardless of what I saw in the video, she was definitely anxious when answering questions about her major") and would thus continue to consider the actor dispositionally anxious. As Table 9.3 shows, this is just what happened. Participants in the no-interlude condition continued to believe the actor to be dispositionally anxious, despite the fact that they had had time to recover from the initial undercorrection effect, and they did so because they believed the target had behaved anxiously during the interview. Apparently, people can recover from some – but not all – of the effects of busyness-induced undercorrection.

The Effects of Self-Regulation. The undercorrection effect makes some suggestions about the architecture of the dispositional inference process, but it also

Table 9.3. The Effects of Inferences of Dispositional Anxiety on Perception of Subsequent Behavior

	Time	
	Interlude	No Interlude
Target's dispositional anxiety	6.8[a]	11.3
Target's behavior during interview	3.77	10.23
Target's tone of voice during interview	1.40	3.20

[a] Larger values indicate greater anxiety.
Source: Adapted from Gilbert, D. T., & Osborne, R. E. (1989).

offers a picture of the way in which dispositional inference is likely to unfold in everyday life. In the laboratory, people have the luxury of observing others without being observed in return; but outside the laboratory, people are normally concerned with planning, conducting, and evaluating their own actions as well as with understanding the actions of others. Our attempts to find the meaning of the actions of our spouses, teachers, children, friends, and employees generally occur while we are interacting with them, and during those interactions, we are usually as concerned with the regulation of our own behavior ("What should I say next? Time to smile. Maybe I should offer him tea?") as we are with understanding the behavior of the other. Our model suggested that perceivers who devote substantial cognitive resources to the regulation of their own behavior should be unable to devote these same resources to the task of understanding those with whom they are interacting. As such, self-regulating perceivers should be able to categorize their partners' behavior and characterize their partners in terms of that behavior, but they should be unable to use situational constraint information to correct those characterizations.

In our initial investigation of the effects of self-regulation on dispositional inference, we asked participants to regulate nothing but their gaze (Gilbert, Krull, & Pelham, 1988). Participants watched silent clips from a videotape of an interview in which a female interviewee appeared depressed and unhappy. Participants in the *sad-questions condition* learned that the interviewee had been answering primarily sadness-inducing questions during the interview (e.g., "Describe a time when your parents made you feel unloved"), whereas participants in the *happy-questions condition* learned that she had been answering primarily happiness-inducing questions (e.g., "What is the nicest thing your parents ever did for you?"). All participants were told that their primary task was to form an impression of the target with particular emphasis on how dispositionally happy or sad she was. Under normal circumstances, we would expect participants in the sad questions condition to attribute the target's apparent sadness to the nature of the questions she was answering, and thus to make less extreme inferences about her dispositional unhappiness than participants in the happy questions condition.

Once again, however, circumstances were not normal. In each participant's booth was a camera that participants were told was "a parafoveal optiscope which will be recording your eye movements as you watch the film." Participants were told that as they watched the video, they would notice a series of words appearing and disappearing on the monitor. Participants in the *unregulated condition* were told that they should not concern themselves with these words "because they are not relevant to the condition of the experiment that you are in." Participants in the *self-regulated condition* were told this too, but they were also told that the device would not work if the participant moved her eyes too much. "Keep your eyes focused on the woman's face during the film clips," we told them, "and do not under any circumstances look down at the words that are appearing and disappearing at the bottom of the screen. If you do accidentally look at one of the words, look away as quickly as possible so that the optiscope can readjust its alignment." Thus, participants in the unregulated condition were told that they *could* ignore the words, whereas participants in the self-regulated condition were told that they *should* ignore the words. After viewing the video, participants rated the target's dispositional sadness on a series of bipolar scales that were anchored at the endpoints with such phrases as, "She is generally a happy (unhappy) sort of person" and "She probably has an optimistic (pessimistic) outlook on life."

We assumed that this simple act of self-regulation would usurp cognitive resources, thus leaving self-regulated participants unable to use the situational constraint information (i.e., the happiness- or sadness-inducing questions) when drawing inferences about the interviewee; this is precisely what happened. Whereas unregulated participants used the situational constraint information and considered the actor to be dispositionally happier when she was answering sad questions ($M = 9.95$) rather than happy questions ($M = 8.51$), self-regulated participants considered her just as happy when she was answering sad questions ($M = 8.64$) as when she was answering happy questions ($M = 9.09$). It is worth noting that although self-regulated participants were less likely than unregulated participants to use the situational constraint information, they were equally likely to recall it. In short, participants who were asked to regulate their gaze drew more dispositional inferences about an actor whose behavior was situationally induced than did participants who were allowed to gaze where they wished.

In another series of studies (Osborne & Gilbert, 1992), we demonstrated that the mere prospect of having to regulate one's behavior can make people cognitively busy and hence impair their attempts to draw accurate inferences about others. For example, in one study, busy and not-busy participants viewed the anxious woman video with anxiety-provoking or relaxing subtitles. After viewing the video, participants were told that they would interact with the actor

Table 9.4. The Effects of Prospective Interaction on Immediate and Delayed Inferences of Dispositional Anxiety

Discussion Topic	Busyness	
	Busy (Rehearsal)	Non-Busy (No Rehearsal)
Prospective interviewer (active)		
Anxious		
Immediate rating	9.71[a]	7.24
Delayed rating	9.13	7.19
Relaxing		
Immediate rating	9.00	11.62
Delayed rating	9.13	10.95
Difference		
Immediate rating	0.71	−4.38
Delayed rating	0.00	−3.76
Prospective interviewee (passive)		
Anxious		
Immediate rating	9.43	7.19
Delayed rating	7.46	6.86
Relaxing		
Immediate rating	9.43	11.29
Delayed rating	10.62	11.19
Difference		
Immediate rating	0.20	4.10
Delayed rating	3.16	4.33

[a] Larger values indicate greater anxiety.

Source: Adapted from Osborne, R. E., & Gilbert. D. T. (1992).

whom they had just seen. Some participants (active condition) were told that they would interview the actor, whereas others were told that they would be interviewed by her (passive condition). We reasoned that the role of interviewer was more active than the role of interviewee, and that participants who were assigned to the interviewer role would immediately begin thinking about how they should behave during the interaction ("Should I ask about her childhood?") whereas participants who were assigned to the interviewee role would not. As such, prospective interviewees should have been able to spend their time recovering from the busyness-induced undercorrection effect, whereas prospective interviewers should not. The results, shown in Table 9.4, confirmed that prediction. Apparently, the prospect of taking an active role in a social interaction is enough to prevent recovery from busyness-induced undercorrection.

Drawing Dispositional Inferences about Ourselves

Social psychologists have quite a bit to say about how self-knowledge is represented in memory (e.g., Klein & Loftus, 1993; Markus, 1977), activated by circumstance (e.g., Bargh, 1982; Jones, Rhodewalt, Berglas, & Skelton, 1981;

Tice, 1992), influenced by others (e.g., Tesser & Campbell, 1983; Wood, 1989), and modified by feedback (e.g., Swann & Predmore, 1985). But they have had relatively little to say about the mental operations by which self-knowledge originates in the first place. How do people learn about their own traits, characteristics, attitudes, and abilities? Ryle (1949) was the first to suggest that people draw inferences about themselves from observations of their own behavior, and Bem (1972) suggested that they do so by using attributional logic. If knowledge of self and knowledge of others are indeed achieved by identical processes, then the former should be susceptible to busyness-induced undercorrection.

We investigated this possibility in a series of studies (Gill & Gilbert, 1999). In one, participants listened to music that was designed to elevate their mood (*happy-music condition*) or depress their mood (*sad-music condition*). They were then asked to rate the extent to which each of 44 adjectives described their personalities. Participants in the *hurried condition* were told to respond to these items "as quickly as you can," whereas participants in the *unhurried condition* were told to "take your time and think carefully about your answers." (Research has shown that time pressure produces the same effects on dispositional inference as does cognitive load.) Our model predicted that all participants would use their current mood to draw dispositional inferences about themselves ("I'm tapping my toes and feeling pretty happy, so I guess I'm generally a happy person"), but that unhurried participants would then correct those characterizations ("Of course, I've just been listening to samba music, so maybe that's why I can't stop moving"). As Table 9.5 shows, this is just what happened. Hurried participants drew dispositional inferences about themselves that corresponded to their current moods, but unhurried participants did not. These results are consistent with the notion that people observe their own states (thoughts, feelings, and actions), draw dispositional inferences about themselves, and then correct those inferences with information about situational constraints if and when they can.

In the foregoing study, participants experienced a situation that altered their behavior, and either did or did not take that situation into account when drawing dispositional inferences about themselves. But situations do not always affect behavior per se; rather, they sometimes affect one's interpretation of one's behavior. For example, an English teacher may interpret his classroom performance as poor when he thinks about the teaching award that the drama coach just won, and he may go on to conclude that he has little talent for teaching. Conversely, he may interpret the same

Table 9.5. The Effects of Time Pressure on Inferences of One's Own Dispositional Happiness

	Busyness	
Time Pressure	Hurried	Unhurried
Happy[a]	38.4	33.3
Unhappy	34.7	36.2
Difference	3.7	−2.9

[a] The measure ranges from 10 to 50, and larger values indicate greater self-perceived dispositional happiness.

Source: Adapted from Gill, M. & Gilbert, D. T. (1999).

performance as outstanding when he thinks about the catcalls the math teacher received earlier that morning, and he may go on to conclude that he is indeed a natural communicator. In either case, the English teacher may need to remind himself that these colleagues teach different subjects than he does, and that they are therefore inappropriate standards for comparison.

We examined the possibility that people do indeed draw dispositional inferences about themselves from their own behaviors, and only subsequently consider the possibility that their interpretation of their action was inappropriately influenced by the behavior of another (Gilbert, Giesler, & Morris, 1995). In one study, participants expected to take a test of their "schizophrenia detection ability." Before taking the test, they watched an instructional video in which a model took the same test. The model saw 18 pairs of photographs and was asked to guess which of the people in the photographs was schizophrenic. In the *poor model condition*, the model responded correctly on just 4 trials, and in the *good model condition*, the model responded correctly on 16 trials. In both instances, participants knew that the model's performance was staged, and hence not a meaningful standard for comparison with their own. After viewing the instructional video, participants in the busy condition began rehearsing an eight-digit number, whereas participants in the non-busy condition did not. All participants then performed the schizophrenia-detection task themselves and were given bogus feedback indicating that they had responded correctly on 10 of the 18 trials. Participants then rated their competence at the task. As Table 9.6 shows, only busy participants were affected by the model's performance. Apparently, all participants believed they performed poorly or well and inferred their abilities from their own performances ("I suck at this"), but non-busy participants then went on to correct those inferences ("Now that I think about it, the model's performance was meaningless, and hence I really didn't do that badly after all").

Yet Is It Correction?

The studies described so far suggest that people initially take action as an index of the actor's dispositions and then, under some circumstances, correct

Table 9.6. The Effects of Busyness on Self-Inferences Drawn from Social Comparisons

Effect of Confederate's Performance	Busyness	
	Busy (Rehearsal)	Non-Busy (No Rehearsal)
Good	0.13[a]	−0.06
Poor	1.23	0.35
Difference	−1.36	−0.41

[a] Larger values indicate greater self-perceived competence.
Source: Adapted from Gilbert, D. T., Giesler, R. B., & Morris, K. A. (1995).

those inferences. Although the data are congenial with a correction account, high level accounts of what happens inside people's heads are sometimes useful but always fanciful stories, of which inventive theorists can usually spin any number (see Gilbert, 1999). For example, whereas a correction account suggests that people draw dispositional inferences and then correct them when they can, a selection account suggests that people draw dispositional inferences when they are busy, but not when they are non-busy. According to the selection account, non-busy perceivers never "pass through" one stage on their way to another; that is, there is no moment in time during which the non-busy observer has drawn anything like a dispositional inference. This account is a perfectly reasonable *post hoc* description of the effects of busyness on inference that cannot be refuted by the kinds of evidence described so far. However, it can be refuted by another kind of evidence.

We all know that beliefs can be changed in a moment ("Yikes – a monster! Oh, wait, its just Uncle Tim in his Halloween costume"), but that emotions subside rather more slowly ("Gosh, my palms are still sticky"). This suggests that if nonbusy observers do draw dispositional inferences that last for just a moment before they are corrected, then the emotional reactions that those inferences generate should linger even after the inferences have been undone. In a follow-up to the study just described (Gilbert, Giesler, & Morris, 1995), participants took a test of their schizophrenia detection ability and then watched a model perform very well or very poorly, knowing all the while that the model's performance was not a meaningful standard for comparison with their own. The results of the dispositional inference measures were very much like those shown in Table 9.6, suggesting that only busy participants took the model's performance as an index of the model's ability (and hence a positive or negative reflection on their own abilities). But in addition to measuring participants' inferences, we also measured their emotional reactions at various points in time, and the results were striking. Although busy participants did, and non-busy participants did not, report drawing dispositional inferences, both groups experienced identical changes in their emotional states. Those who saw the model perform poorly felt a brief jolt of positive affect whereas those who saw the model perform well felt a brief jolt of negative affect – and this happened just as strongly and reliably for non-busy as for busy participants. In other words, non-busy participants experienced precisely the emotions one would expect them to have experienced had they briefly drawn a dispositional inference about the model. These findings provide compelling support for the correction account, and are simply unexplainable by the selection account. This does not mean that the account will go away, of course; it merely means that it should.

A MORE GENERAL CORRECTION MODEL

The busyness-induced undercorrection of dispositional inferences is now a well-established and widely replicated phenomenon. However, as our work on this problem proceeded, we became convinced that each of our studies was but an instance of a more general phenomenon – namely, the tendency for people to initially believe *any* notion that they entertained, and to doubt that notion subsequently if at all. If this suggestion sounds odd, it is only because most of us hear it with a Cartesian ear. René Descartes (1644/1984) was the first to suggest that *understanding* and *believing* are separate and sequential psychological operations. Three centuries later, the notion that "considering an idea" is different from and prior to "embracing an idea" infuses most modern psychological theorizing. Zimbardo and Lieppe (1991, p. 135) summarized the conventional wisdom as follows:

> Learning requires that the audience pay *attention* to the message and, in turn, gain some *comprehension* of it, understanding the new beliefs it proposes. Then, if the message has compelling arguments, *acceptance* of its conclusion and a change in attitude will follow. (italics in original)

What could be more obvious? First, a person comprehends a message, and then later may accept it – which is to say that understanding and believing are the separate and sequential operations that Descartes described.

But Descartes' contemporary, Benedict Spinoza (1672/1982), did not accept this doctrine, and argued that understanding and believing are a single mental operation. Spinoza suggested that human beings believe assertions as part of understanding them, and that they then "unbelieve" those assertions that are found to be at odds with other established facts. According to Spinoza, people immediately and inevitably accept that which they comprehend, understand, or entertain, and they are incapable of withholding that acceptance. They may change their minds *after* accepting an assertion, but they cannot stop their minds from being changed by initial contact with it (see Gilbert, 1991, 1992).

Acceptance, then, is a passive and inevitable act, whereas *rejection* is an active operation that undoes the initial acceptance. The most basic prediction of this Spinozan hypothesis is that when something prevents a person from "undoing" the initial acceptance, then she should continue to believe whatever she is considering – even when what she is considering is patently false. For example, if a person is told that lead pencils are a health hazard, the Spinozan hypothesis suggests that she must immediately believe that assertion and only then take active measures to unbelieve it. These active measures may require cognitive work (i.e., the search for or generation of contravening evidence), and if something impairs the person's ability to perform such work, then the person should continue to believe in the danger of lead pencils until the cognitive work can be done. The Cartesian hypothesis, however, makes no such predictions. That hypothesis suggests that both acceptance and rejection of an assertion are the results of cognitive work that *follows* comprehension of the assertion. As such, a shortage of resources should make both of these options impossible, thus leaving the person in a state of *non*-belief, rather than a state of belief or disbelief.

In a series of studies (Gilbert, Krull, & Malone, 1990), we attempted to provide direct evidence for the Spinozan hypothesis by presenting participants with assertions whose veracity they could not assess because one word of the assertion was in a foreign language. Participants read 28 propositions, one at a time, of the form *An X is a Y*, where *X* was ostensibly a Hopi noun and *Y* was its ostensible English equivalent. Participants were told that at the end of the session their knowledge of the Hopi vocabulary would be tested. After seeing each proposition on the computer screen, the participants saw the word *true* or *false*, which indicated that the preceding proposition had been either accurate or inaccurate. In addition, participants occasionally heard a tone during the experiment, and when this happened they were instructed to press a response button as quickly as possible. This tone-detection task was designed to interrupt participants' processing of the proposition that was currently being presented on the computer screen.

The Spinozan hypothesis (but not the Cartesian hypothesis) predicted that interruption would (1) prevent participants from unbelieving the assertions that they automatically accepted on comprehension and would thus cause participants to report that false assertions were true, but (2) would not cause participants to report that true assertions were false. As Table 9.7 shows, precisely this asymmetry emerged – an asymmetry that is not easily explained by the Cartesian hypothesis. The Spinozan hypothesis was also unique in suggesting that the processing of a false proposition should require more time and cognitive capacity than the processing of a true proposition, simply because false propositions must be accepted and then unaccepted (see also Carpenter & Just, 1975; Clark & Chase, 1972, 1974; Gough, 1965, 1966; Trabasso, Rollins, & Shaughnessey, 1971). An analysis of the time it took participants to respond to the interrupting tone revealed that they responded significantly more slowly to interruptions that occurred immediately after the presentation of a false proposition than to those that occurred immediately after the presentation of a true proposition. Supplementary data and studies ruled out the possibilities that interruption merely kept participants from remembering false propositions, or led them to feel uncertain about the veracity of propositions and thus led them to guess that the items were true.

Table 9.7. The Effects of Interruption on Identification of the Veracity of Propositions

	Interruption	
	Uninterrupted (No Tone)	Interrupted (Tone)
True propositions identified as		
True	55%	58%
False	22%	17%
False propositions identified as		
True	21%	33%
False	55%	35%

Source: Adapted from Gilbert, D. T., Krull, D. S. & Malone, P. S. (1990).

182 Daniel T. Gilbert

Of course, remembering that a proposition was labeled as true is not exactly the same as believing the proposition oneself, and in another set of studies (Gilbert, Tafarodi, & Malone, 1993) we sought to show that interruption of the processing of false items influenced belief as the Spinozan hypothesis suggested it would. We asked participants to read a pair of crime reports that contained both true and false statements. The crime reports "crawled" across the screen of a color video monitor (much like an emergency weather bulletin "crawls" across the bottom of a television screen), and participants were told that statements printed in black were true statements, but that statements printed in red were false statements. One report contained false statements that exacerbated the severity of the crime (e.g., the perpetrator verbally abused the victim after he robbed him), and the other report contained false statements that extenuated the severity of the crime (e.g., the perpetrator asked for the victim's forgiveness after he robbed him). Participants were told that as the crime report crawled across the screen, a string of digits would occasionally crawl across the screen on a line just beneath the text. Participants in the busy condition were told to press a button whenever the digit 5 appeared in the number line, and participants in the non-busy condition were told to ignore the numbers. Finally, participants recommended the length of prison terms for each criminal, rated the criminal on several related dimensions, and completed a recognition memory test for some of the statements contained in the reports.

We expected the false statements to influence the prison terms recommended by busy participants, but not by non-busy participants; this is, in fact, what happened. Busy participants recommended that perpetrators serve nearly twice as much time when the false statements contained in the police reports exacerbated the severity of the crime (11.15 years) as when the police reports extenuated the severity of the crimes (5.83 years). Non-busy participants showed no such tendency (7.03 versus 6.03 years, respectively). The memory test revealed that busy participants were, as predicted, more likely than non-busy participants to misremember the false statements as true. These data suggest that when people are prevented from unbelieving the assertions they comprehend, they act as though they believe them. Follow-up studies ruled out a variety of alternative interpretations.

What do these studies tell us about belief? Spinoza knew that people do have the power assent, reject, and suspend their judgment – but he thought they could do this only *after* they had briefly believed any information to which they were exposed. We performed six experiments to examine this notion, and each provided support for Spinoza's account. Of course, a wide range of other evidence is also commensurate with the Spinozan position (see Gilbert, 1991, for a full review). For example, research on human lie detection has consistently uncovered a truthfulness bias; that is, a tendency for people to conclude that others are telling the truth when they are not (DePaulo, Stone, & Lassiter, 1985; Zuckerman, Depaulo, & Rosenthal, 1981). If we assume that verbal claims "assert" their speaker's beliefs (i.e., that the claim "Abortion is evil" is taken to imply the claim "I believe that abortion is evil"), then this truthfulness bias is just the sort of mistake that a Spinozan system should make. Research on persuasive communications has shown that distraction can increase the persuasive impact of a message (Festinger & Maccoby, 1964; Petty, Wells, & Brock, 1976), and the Spinozan hypothesis provides a representational account that is consistent with high-level accounts of this effect (e.g., Chaiken, 1987; Petty & Cacioppo, 1986). Research on hypothesis testing shows that people often seek information that confirms the possibilities they are entertaining (Snyder & Swann, 1978; Wason & Johnson-Laird, 1972). The Spinozan hypothesis suggests that people may not be inept hypothesis testers, but rather may tend to believe the possibilities they are asked to entertain, in which case a confirmatory strategy may be quite rational (see Klayman & Ha, 1987). Research on the processing of linguistic denials shows that people often develop positive beliefs in assertions that are being denied (Wegner, Coulton, & Wenzlaff, 1985; Wegner, Wenzlaff, Kerker, & Beattie, 1981). This phenomenon is also explicable in Spinozan terms: A denial is both an assertion and its negation, and the act of understanding the assertion includes a belief in the very thing that is being negated or denied. Even research on visual perception suggests that people believe their visual representations of an object's spatial orientation ("The chair is laying on its side") and only later correct for the tilt of their own heads ("But wait – I'm bent, so the chair must be rightside up"; Rock & Nijhawan, 1989). This, too, is explicable in Spinozan terms.

The Spinozan model has clear implications for the problem of dispositional inference: If behaviors "assert" dispositions – that is, if a friendly behavior is taken as equivalent to the claim "I am a friendly person" – then the Spinozan model subsumes the correction model described earlier. In that sense, dispositional inference is merely an instance of belief, and the failure to consider situational constraints is merely the failure to doubt. The nice thing about the Spinozan interpretation of this work is that it provides a general framework within which numerous phenomena (including dispositional inference) may be similarly understood. However, thinking of dispositional inference as an instance of belief does not instantly solve all the problems that surround it. For example, the Spinozan model does not explain why observers tend to take behaviors as claims about the actor's dispositions ("I'm an anxious person") rather than as claims about the actor's situation ("I'm in a dreadful situation"; see Krull, 1993; Krull & Erickson, 1995). In other words, it may tell us why people believe the claims they consider, but it does not tell us why they consider the claims they do.

CODA

Proust (1923/1949, p. 253) wrote that "the stellar universe is not so difficult of comprehension as the real actions of other people." He was right, of course; human behavior is the most complex natural phenomenon in the known universe, and yet, without any special instruments or any special schooling, each of us analyzes it every day, drawing credible and confident conclusions about what the people who performed it must be like deep down inside. We make mistakes, but given the complexity of the problem, it is rather remarkable that we ever get it right. How do we perform these analyses so easily, so often, and (at least sometimes) so well? Social psychologists have been asking this question for more than half a century and the accumulated wisdom on the topic is substantial (see Gilbert, 1998). One small piece of the answer – the small piece reviewed here – is that we readily believe the claims that actions make about actors, and only later, with time and attention, consider the possibility that these claims were unfounded. There is still much to be learned about this small piece, and even more about the larger question to which it is a partial reply. But if we can chart the stellar universe by attending carefully to cold pinpricks of distant light, then perhaps with just a bit more time and effort we can map the inner world of the social perceiver as well.

10. Mental Contamination and the Debiasing Problem

Timothy D. Wilson, David B. Centerbar, and Nancy Brekke

People do not have access to or control over the recipe of their impressions, feelings, and attitudes. There exists a vast, adaptive unconscious that does much of the work of sizing up and evaluating the world (Nisbett & Wilson, 1977b; Wilson, 2001); people often know the final product with no awareness of exactly how it was formed. Consider Ms. Green, a partner in a prestigious law firm, who is interviewing candidates for the position of associate in her firm. When she interviews Mr. Jones, a young African-American attorney, she has an immediate negative impression, finding him to be arrogant and lacking the kind of brilliance she looks for in new associates. Ms. Green decides that her impression of Mr. Jones was accurate and at a meeting of the partners, argues against hiring him. She wonders, however, whether her negative evaluation was influenced by Mr. Jones' race.

Ms. Green may have suffered from mental contamination, which Wilson and Brekke (1994) defined as unconscious or uncontrollable mental processing that results in unwanted judgments, emotions, or behavior. Her dilemma illustrates the difficulty of knowing whether one's responses are contaminated, and if so, how to correct them. In this chapter, we review and update the arguments made by Wilson and Brekke (1994) concerning mental contamination, and also address several questions about the ways in which people try to protect their minds from unwanted influences.

THE WILSON AND BREKKE MODEL

The Wilson and Brekke model of contamination is illustrated in Fig. 10.1. Contamination begins when an unwanted mental process is triggered, such as a negative evaluation of a person based on his or her race. There are many other examples of unwanted influences on people's judgments and emotions, such as the effects of advertising (e.g., buying a product based on exaggerated claims about its value), halo effects (e.g., a professor giving a student a bad grade because he/she does not like the student), and misattribution (e.g., confusing romantic attraction and fear).

In order to avoid contamination, people must first detect that it exists. This is often quite difficult, because people have poor access to the processes by which they form their judgments (Nisbett & Wilson, 1977b). Ms. Green could

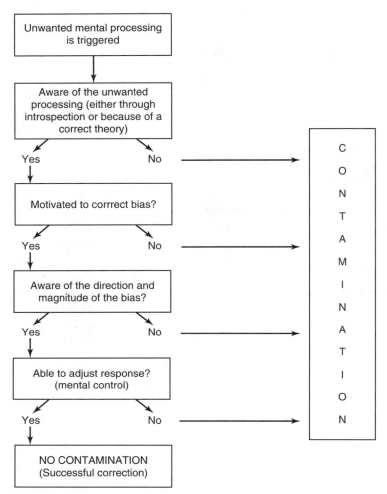

Figure 10.1. The process of mental contamination and debiasing (from Wilson & Brekke, 1984).

not observe directly whether her negative evaluation of Mr. Jones was tainted by prejudice. Unlike many examples of physical contamination, such as spoiled milk, there are no overt signs that a final judgment is tainted. In the words of Wilson and Brekke (1994), "Human judgments – even very bad ones – do not smell" (p. 121).

There may sometimes be indirect clues that a judgment is contaminated. For example, an unexpected reaction to a stimulus (e.g., disliking a highly touted job candidate) might trigger thoughts about bias (e.g., "Maybe I'm racist"). Furthermore, a potential contaminant might be so salient that people cannot fail to wonder if it biased their judgment (Stapel, Martin, & Schwarz, 1998). More commonly, we have no direct way of knowing whether our judgment is biased.

As noted by Wilson and Brekke (1994), Petty and Wegener (1993), and Wegener and Petty (1997), people often are at the mercy of their lay theories about bias. An unexpected reaction, for example, is likely to be attributed to bias only if people have an applicable theory about the cause of the bias, such as racism. If the job candidate were a white male from Des Moines, it is unlikely that white male supervisors would conclude that they were prejudiced against white males or Iowans, even if their evaluation were unexpectedly negative.

Once people decide that mental contamination has occurred, how easily can they correct for it? As seen in Fig. 10.1, several conditions must be satisfied. First, people must be motivated to correct the error. Ms. Green may know that her impression was biased and prefer that it not be biased, but believe that it is not worth the time and energy to try to correct it. Second, even if motivated to correct the error, people must be aware of the direction and magnitude of the bias. Ms. Green may know that her impression of Mr. Jones is unfairly negative and want to avoid this bias, but have no idea of the extent of the bias. Should she change her evaluation from "Should not be hired" to "Barely acceptable" or to "Best applicant I've seen in years"? Finally, people must have sufficient control over their responses to be able to correct the bias. Ms. Green might strongly suspect that biased processing has led to a lower impression of Mr. Jones, but find it very hard to disregard this impression at the partners' meeting.

The main causes of mental contamination, then, are (1) a lack of awareness of one's mental processes (e.g., the extent to which a negative evaluation of a job candidate was due to race); (2) a lack of control over one's mental processes (e.g., an inability to prevent a person's race from influencing an impression of him or her); (3) inaccurate theories about unwanted influences on judgments (e.g., a failure to appreciate how a person's race can influence impressions nonconsciously); and (4) inadequate motivation to correct for contamination (e.g., an insufficient desire to avoid a racist response; see Fig. 10.1). Numerous biases can be viewed as examples of mental contamination, as long as the individual would prefer not to exhibit the bias. Examples include automatic stereotyping and prejudice; unwanted effects of accessible information, whereby a judgment is influenced by irrelevant information that happens to have been primed; unwanted effects of persuasive communications, such as advertising; and misattribution, whereby a person's emotions and judgments are based on erroneous inferences about the causes of their arousal (see Wilson & Brekke, 1994, for other examples).

In this chapter, we discuss the consequences of unwanted judgments and ways they might be avoided, with an emphasis on issues that have arisen since Wilson and Brekke's (1994) article was published.

ARE ALL CORRECTION EFFORTS DELIBERATIVE AND THEORY-DRIVEN? IMPLICIT ADJUSTMENT VERSUS DEBIASING

There has been some controversy over the manner in which people attempt to correct their psychological responses. Some theorists, such as Wilson and

Brekke (1994) and Wegener and Petty (1997), stress the importance of deliberative applications of lay theories. Wegener and Petty's (1997) flexible correction model, for example, argues that correction is driven by the conscious belief that bias has occurred and a naive theory about the direction and magnitude of the bias. Other theorists, such as Martin (1986) and Martin and Stapel (1998), argue that correction can also be a spontaneous and automatic response to the nature of the situation and stimulus.

We suggest that both camps in this debate are correct because there are different levels and types of correction. We agree with Martin and Stapel (1998), who state that a great deal of mental processing occurs at an automatic and implicit level, and that some of this processing involves a correction for information deemed inappropriate or irrelevant to the judgment at hand. In fact, a number of such automatic correction processes have been documented in the social cognition literature, such as research on self-attribution, in which people observe their behavior and, under some circumstances, infer that this behavior reflects their internal states (e.g., Bem, 1972). The attribution about the cause of one's behavior or physiological responses sometimes involves a correction process, whereby people discount the role of one potential cause if another plausible one is present. These corrections occur automatically and nonconsciously.

Consider a classic misattribution study by Dutton and Aron (1974), in which male participants encountered an attractive woman while crossing a flimsy footbridge spanning a 200-ft gorge. The participants had to decide how much of their arousal was due to fear from the bridge versus attraction to the woman. This decision can be characterized as a correction process; people had to partial out the effects of one plausible cause from another. As it happened, people who encountered the woman on the bridge misattributed some of their arousal to attraction to the woman.

It seems clear that this correction process did not occur consciously and deliberatively. The men did not stand on the bridge scratching their heads thinking, "Hmm, is she beautiful or am I scared? Or a little of both? I'd say I'm feeling 37% fear and 63% attraction." Rather, their phenomenal experience was attraction to the woman with no conscious recognition of the processes that produced it. Although the issue of how aware people are of attribution processes was seldom discussed in the original literature on this topic, Nisbett and Wilson (1977b) later documented that participants in these studies rarely are able to verbalize the attribution processes hypothesized to have occurred.

The broader point is that mental correction occurs on a continuum of implicit and nonconscious adjustments of a response to explicit and deliberative adjustment, and researchers should keep in mind that when they use the term *correction*, they are sometimes referring to quite different mental processes. To help clear up this confusion, researchers should use different terms for the different ends of this continuum. We suggest that *implicit adjustment* be used to refer to rapid and nonconscious correction discussed by attribution theorists and Martin (1986), and *debiasing* (Fischhoff, 1982) be used to refer to deliberative and theory-driven correction discussed by Wilson and Brekke (1994) and Wegener and Petty (1997). In the interest of promoting these terms, we use them as defined here in the remainder of this chapter.

As noted by Wilson and Brekke (1994), the very fact that implicit adjustment is so common is a major source of bias. They discussed two subcategories of contamination: (1) unwanted consequences of automatic processing, whereby people process information automatically in undesired ways; and (2) source confusion, whereby people confuse two or more sources of a judgment, memory, or feeling. These types of contamination can involve implicit adjustment, such as the kind of misattribution errors just discussed.

The existence of implicit adjustment puts people in a difficult position to know whether a particular response is biased because they do not know whether a phenomenal judgment has already been "corrected." Suppose that Michael finds Donald to be slightly aggressive. How accurate is this impression? Was it biased by irrelevant information, such as the fact that Michael had just read a newspaper article about spousal abuse, which primed the construct of aggression? There are three possibilities:

1. The newspaper article did not prime aggression, thus Michael's impression of Donald was unbiased.
2. The newspaper articled primed the construct of aggression and produced assimilation, such that Michael finds Donald to be *more* aggressive than he would have if he had not read the newspaper article.
3. The newspaper article primed the construct of aggression, but Michael already corrected for this fact nonconsciously. This resulted in a contrast effect, such that Michael finds Donald to be *less* aggressive than he would have if he had not read the newspaper article.

Obviously, the extent to which Michael attempts to consciously adjust his impression depends on which of these processes he believes has occurred. Because he has no direct access to this process, he is at the mercy of his naive theories, which might well be wrong.

WHAT TRIGGERS DELIBERATIVE DEBIASING EFFORTS?

The previous discussion indicates that there are two stages of the debiasing process: The decision that bias has occurred and attempts to correct it. Naive theories can come into play at both stages. Because people do not have good access to their cognitive processes, they must rely on their theories when deciding whether a judgment is biased. Once this decision is made, people must again rely on their theories to inform them how to correct for the bias.

As noted by Martin and Stapel (1998), researchers have paid more attention to the second stage of the process (debiasing) than to the initial, bias-detection stage. In most of the research in this area, people are specifically instructed to avoid bias, which begs the question of when and how they invoke debiasing processes on their own (for exceptions, see Petty & Wegener, 1993; Stapel, Martin, & Schwarz, 1998).

How likely are people, in the absence of blatant warnings, to invoke a theory that their judgments are biased? Although this question is difficult to answer, our hunch is similar to Martin and Stapel's (1998) that people's default response is to assume that their judgments are uncontaminated. One source of evidence for this conclusion comes from studies showing that people are more willing to attribute bias to other people's judgments than to their own (Kruger & Gilovich, 1999; Pronin, Puccio, & Ross, ch. 36, this volume; Wilson & Brekke, 1994; Wilson, Gilbert, & Wheatley, 1998).

The reason for people's faith in their own judgments can be traced to both motivational and cognitive factors. On the motivational side, it can be disquieting to conclude that one's own judgments are biased, and functional to overestimate the validity of these judgments (Taylor & Brown, 1988). On the cognitive side, the immediacy and inescapability of a phenomenal judgment probably contributes to its perceived validity. The phenomenal experience of one's own judgment has a compellingness that is absent from the knowledge that someone else feels differently, which probably contributes to the greater faith in one's own judgment.

Although the question of how often people detect bias and try to correct for it in everyday life is difficult to answer, we are not optimistic. If there were any group of people who would be particularly sensitive to mental contamination, one would think it would be research psychologists familiar with the extensive literature on biases in social cognition and the difficulty of avoiding these biases. We offer two anecdotes suggesting that psychologists are no more likely than others to take steps to avoid unwanted influences. The first is a colleague who said that when he grades his students' papers and exams, he does so with full knowledge of the students' identity and past performance, even though he is aware of studies showing that halo effects can color one's impressions of papers and exams. "I don't want to be biased by how much I like the students or how well they did on a previous test," he said, "so I simply keep a close watch on myself to make sure this doesn't happen." Although this colleague is aware of research showing that people do not have direct access to how much they are biased by halo effects (Nisbett & Wilson, 1977a), he believes that he is an exception.

The second anecdote concerns the validity of the interview in predicting job performance of a job candidate. Despite evidence for the extremely low validity of the interview (e.g., Hunter & Hunter, 1984), the members of most departments of psychology are as confident in their impressions of a candidate after meeting him or her for half an hour as anyone else would be, and are as willing to let this impression override information known to be more valid (e.g., letters of recommendation, publication record). We confess that we often feel the same way. A strong impression of a person is so compelling and *odorless*, in

Wilson and Brekke's terms, that it is difficult to acknowledge that it might be tainted by unwanted influences, despite the fact that we are quite willing to see other people's impressions as rather smelly.

WHEN PEOPLE TRY TO CORRECT, HOW SUCCESSFUL ARE THEY?

Even in the rare instances in which people believe that their judgments are biased, they may not successfully debias these judgments. In fact, their corrected judgments might be worse than their uncorrected ones.

The dilemma people face is similar to the predicament of a hiker who arrives at the intersection of several trails. There is a sign pointing toward one of the paths indicating that it leads to the hiker's destination. However, the hiker has been told that a mischievous boy often moves the sign so that it points in the wrong direction, and she has just seen a boy running away from the sign, laughing gleefully. She is pretty sure that the sign is pointing to the wrong path (i.e., that it is "contaminated"), but how should she correct for this fact? Given that the sign is pointing to the trail on the far left, should she take the one on the far right? Or should she assume that the boy only had time to move the sign a little, and therefore take the middle trail? Or that he is a clever boy who tried to convince her that he moved the sign, when in fact he did not? Just as people are at the mercy of their theories when deciding whether a response is biased, so are they at the mercy of their theories when deciding how to correct for this bias.

Unfortunately, people's theories about debiasing do not appear to be particularly accurate. People who are exposed to contaminating information and engage in debiasing rarely end up with judgments similar to people who were not exposed to the contaminant. Three kinds of errors have been found: *insufficient correction* (debiasing in the direction of accuracy that does not go far enough), *unnecessary correction* (debiasing when there was no bias to start with), and *overcorrection* (too much debiasing, such that judgments end up biased in the opposite direction).

A number of studies found evidence for insufficient correction, which is the best of the three types of errors (because the corrected judgment is more accurate than the uncorrected one). Petty and Wegener (1993, Study 4), for example, found that rating the desirability of vacations in very appealing locations, such as Hawaii, lowered people's ratings of vacations in American cities such as Indianapolis and Kansas City. Giving people a subtle cue that their initial ratings might bias their later ones led to some, but not complete, debiasing. People in the subtle cue condition formed judgments that were still biased, but not as biased as people who did not receive the subtle cue. These results suggest that some debiasing is better than no debiasing.

However, this same study found evidence for unnecessary correction in another condition. Some participants received a more blatant cue that their ratings of the American cities might be biased. People in the control condition, who did not first rate vacations in Hawaii but received the blatant warning, engaged in unnecessary correction. That is, they seem to have assumed that their evaluations of the American cities were biased when in fact they were not. They became more negatively disposed toward vacations in these cities, even though their evaluations had not been biased in the first place.

Stapel, Martin, and Schwarz (1998) found evidence for overcorrection. Similar to the Petty and Wegener (1993) study, people first rated the desirability of the weather in tropical locations and then rated the desirability of the weather in midwestern cities. In the absence of any warnings, this lead to a contrast effect: Compared to a control group who did not first rate the tropical locations, people rated the weather in the midwestern cities as less desirable. When people were warned to avoid unwanted influences on their ratings, they overcorrected such that they showed an assimilation effect: Compared to the control group, they rated the weather in the midwestern cities as more desirable.

In sum, just because people attempt to correct a judgment they perceive to be biased is no guarantee that their result will be a more accurate judgment. Either unnecessary correction or overcorrection might occur, resulting in judgments that are more biased than they were before they were "corrected."

A CLOSER LOOK AT LAY THEORIES OF MENTAL PROTECTION

Our discussion thus far has focused on biased judgments, such as beliefs about the weather in various locations or the merits of a job candidate. Wilson and Brekke (1994) defined *mental contamination* quite broadly, including cases in which any response is biased in an unwanted way (i.e., emotions as well as beliefs).

Wilson, Gilbert, and Wheatley (1998) examined the manner in which people manage emotions versus beliefs. They also took a closer look at the specific strategies people believe they can take to avoid unwanted influences on these responses. As seen in Fig. 10.2, there are five strategies people believe they can adopt at different points of the contamination process. The left side of this figure shows a time line of actual contamination, from people's anticipation that a state might become contaminated, to exposure to a contaminant, to unwanted changes in a psychological state. The right side of the figure shows the different strategies people think they can adopt at each time point to avoid or undo the contamination.

The first line of defense is what Gilbert (1993) termed *exposure control*, which is the decision whether to allow a potentially contaminating stimulus to enter our minds. If we are concerned that our liking for a student will bias the grade we give his or her paper, we can grade the papers blindly to avoid any bias. Exposure control, to the extent that it is feasible, is the most effective defense against contamination. A stimulus that never enters our minds cannot bias our judgments or feelings.

The second line of defense is *preparation*. If we know in advance that we will be exposed to potentially contaminating information, we can take steps in advance

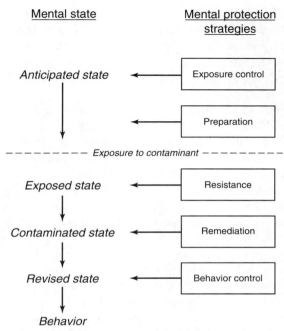

Figure 10.2. Lay beliefs about debiasing (from Wilson et al., 1998).

to blunt its impact. A person about to hear a speech from an untrustworthy source, for example, can try to strengthen her mental defenses by engaging in anticipatory counterarguing.

Once we are exposed to a contaminant – we hear the speech or know the author of the term paper we are grading – there are three steps people can take to try to avoid or undo contamination. The first of these steps is *resistance*, which occurs after a stimulus is encoded but before it has had an unwanted effect on our beliefs or emotions, resulting in what Wilson et al. (1998) called an *exposed state*. Resistance involves any mental operation that attempts to prevent an encoded stimulus from having an adverse effect, similar to an immunologic response that kills a virus after it enters the body but before the it causes disease.

If resistance fails, people end up with a contaminated state. The next line of defense is *remediation*, defined as any mental operation that attempts to undo the damage done by a contaminant. People end up with a revised state, which, if remediation is completely successful, is the same as the original mental state. If remediation fails or is insufficient to correct the damage, then people's last line of defense is *behavior control*. This is the attempt to prevent one's contaminated state from influencing behavior. If our beliefs have changed in an unwanted way (e.g., a lowered evaluation of a job candidate due to his or her race), we can try to stop ourselves from acting on that belief.

We should stress that these stages are meant to capture people's beliefs about how to avoid or undo bias and are not necessarily a portrayal of effective strategies. In terms of effectiveness, it is clear that the earlier the defense, the better. The most effective defense is preventing exposure to contaminating information, and the least effective is trying to undo or ignore contamination once it has occurred.

People seem to appreciate this point when it comes to managing their affect and emotions. Much of our lives is spent arranging environments in ways that maximize our pleasure, with the recognition that once we are exposed to negative stimuli, the game is mostly lost. Given the choice of encountering an unpleasant and argumentative colleague who always manages to spoil our mood, or taking a longer route to our office that avoids the colleague, most of us choose the latter option. Just as it is better to avoid the flu by avoiding exposure to the virus, so is it better to maintain a good mood by avoiding contact with stimuli that will ruin it – a fact that people generally appreciate.

When it comes to avoiding contaminated beliefs, however, people seem to have more faith in the later defenses of resistance and remediation and are thus less likely to engage in exposure control. People seem to believe that there is little danger in being exposed to information that might bias their beliefs because they think they have the ability to resist or remediate any unwanted influences. As noted by Gilbert (1991), people assume that belief formation occurs according to a process outlined by Descartes: First we comprehend a proposition (e.g., "the moon is made of blue cheese"), then we freely decide whether to accept it as true (e.g., whether it fits with our belief system). Gilbert (1991) argues persuasively that belief formation actually operates according to a process described by Spinoza, whereby we initially accept as true every proposition we comprehend, and then decide whether to "unbelieve" it.

One implication of Gilbert's Spinozan model is that people have a misplaced belief in resistance (see Fig. 10.2). To be able to resist unwanted influences on our beliefs before they change our minds, we would have to be able to encode a message without it influencing us, placing it in a kind of mental holding pattern. We would then have to neutralize the message in some way, such as by thinking of counterarguments. There is no such thing as a mental holding pattern, Gilbert argues, because people initially believe all propositions. According to this view, people cannot encode something without believing it; thus, mental resistance is impossible.

People's faith in remediation is also misplaced, we suggest, because of the difficulty of recognizing that contamination has taken place. Even if we correctly guess that it has, we have to know how to correct for the bias. As we have seen, people often get it wrong, either failing to detect bias or failing to correct for it. As also seen, people appreciate that other people are not very good at avoiding biased influences on their beliefs, but have a misplaced faith in their own ability to control their beliefs and avoid unwanted influences.

Why are people's strategies for managing their beliefs less effective than their strategies for managing their emotions? One reason, we suggest, is the ease of detecting contamination in these different realms. As discussed earlier, there are seldom any phenomenological signs that a belief is biased in an unwanted way – contaminated judgments do not smell. It is much easier to tell whether our emotions are "contaminated" – we feel lousy. Consequently, we have developed better strategies for avoiding contaminated emotions, namely exposure control (avoiding exposure to possibly contaminating information).

RECOMMENDATIONS

The lesson from our discussion so far should be clear: The best way to avoid biased judgments and emotions is exposure control, whereby we avoid stimuli that might influence our responses in unwanted ways. Although exposure control is the most effective prophylactic, Wilson and Brekke (1994) noted four problems with this strategy. First, we cannot control exposure to all possible contaminating information. When deciding which employees should be promoted, for example, we already know their gender, age, and race. Second, we do not always know in advance whether information will bias our judgments; therefore, excessive exposure control will result in the failure to receive information that is diagnostic and useful. Third, the excessive use of an exposure control strategy might cause people to examine only information that confirms their views, thereby fostering narrow-mindedness. Fourth, in order to avoid exposure to biasing information, people would have to be extremely vigilant, ready to shut their eyes and cover their ears whenever they suspected that potentially unwanted information was in the vicinity. Is such vigilance worth the effort it entails? As noted by William James (1897): "Our errors are surely not such awfully solemn things. In a world where we are so certain to incur them in spite of all our caution, a certain lightness of heart seems healthier than this excessive nervousness on their behalf" (p. 19).

We agree with James – people should not be in a state of constant nervousness, ever alert for contaminating information. However, we believe that mental errors can be "awfully solemn things" that are quite costly to ourselves and others. Some personal decisions, such as which brand of laundry detergent to buy or what to order in a restaurant, are relatively inconsequential. Other choices have much bigger consequences, such as whether to buy the $100,000 house on a busy street or the $150,000 house on the cul-de-sac, or whether to seek medical treatment for a mole on our forearm. For consequential decisions such as these, a dose of "excessive nervousness" might not be such a bad thing. Moreover, because our judgments often influence the lives of others, the costs of mental contamination can extend well beyond the personal realm. When we are in positions of power, such as professors assigning grades to students, or employers screening job applicants, we should be especially humble about the potential for bias.

Furthermore, the failure to appreciate the perils of mental contamination may lead people to design decision-making systems that are destined to produce biased judgments. The American legal system, for example, has overestimated people's ability to detect and correct for unwanted biases, such as jurors' ability to discount inadmissible evidence (Tanford, 1990). As a result, legal procedures often rely too much on defenses such as remediation and too little on preemptive strategies such as exposure control. At an institutional or societal level, the cumulative negative effects of such contaminated systems can be quite substantial.

Strategies for Dealing with Mental Contamination in Everyday Life

Exposure control is sometimes possible and can be considered to be a preventive strategy. As professors, we might choose to grade student papers without knowing the identity of each student so as to avoid the halo effect. Similar strategies are occasionally feasible in the realm of employment. When many professional orchestras audition new musicians, they ask the musician to play behind a screen, so that the decision maker is unaware of the person's gender, age, race, and any other potentially biasing information.

What if exposure control is not possible or is not desirable? Although we remain pessimistic about people's abilities to detect and correct for contamination once it enters their minds, we offer three suggestions for strategies that can help.

Examining the Test–Retest Reliability of One's Judgments. When it comes to debiasing a judgment of a specific stimulus, it can be useful to observe one's reactions over time under different circumstances – essentially, to observe the test–retest reliability of the evaluation. Doing so may allow one to tease apart whether the evaluation is a reliable reaction to the stimulus or a spurious, contaminated reaction to something about the circumstances under which it is evaluated.

Consider an example: One of us adopts such an approach when grading students' final papers. Because this activity takes place over the course of several days, she knows that her judgments might be affected by order and contrast effects as well as various situational factors (e.g., whether she reads a paper at the office between appointments or at home in front of the fireplace with a glass of wine in hand and classical music in the background). Accordingly, after reading each paper, she writes a tentative grade and some comments on a separate sheet. Then, after reading all of the papers, she looks at each paper again and gives it another grade. If the two grades she assigns do not match, she suspects contamination and gives the paper further scrutiny (e.g., she compares it to other papers in the same grade ranges).

Such a strategy is not perfect, of course. Although it can help us detect contamination, it does not tell us how to correct for it. The professor who determines that her evaluations were biased by the setting must still decide whether the paper grades were artificially inflated by the fireplace, music, and wine, or whether they were artificially deflated by the hectic, noisy office. Moreover, the test–retest strategy does not allow people to tease apart contaminants that are present at both times. For example, we have a friend who has a closet full of clothes she never wears that she ordered from a catalog. Each time she looks at the catalog she loves the way the clothes look, but she underestimates how much this is due to the fact that beautiful models are wearing them. When the clothes arrive, she is invariably disappointed at how they look on her.

Examining the Covariation of One's Responses with Potential Contaminants. It can be useful to examine our general patterns of response to different subgroups of stimuli. A faculty colleague of ours, for instance, once noted a suspicious trend in his evaluations of student papers: Heavy smokers tended to receive lower grades than nonsmokers. As it turned out, the papers that reeked of stale cigarette smoke gave him a headache as he read them, which then caused him to evaluate the work more negatively. The test–retest strategy would not have helped him here (because smokers' papers reliably reeked and reliably elicited headaches), yet by comparing his evaluations of smokers' and nonsmokers' work, he was able to identify a contaminant.

This strategy can be useful in the workplace. Recall Ms. Green from the prestigious law firm. If she notices that, in general, her reactions to African-American candidates are less favorable than her reactions to European-American candidates, this should give her reason to pause. Indeed, this is precisely the logic behind some affirmative action guidelines. Employers are required to keep records of group-related employment patterns (e.g., the percentages of women and minorities who apply, are interviewed, are hired) so that group-linked disparities can be more readily detected (Crosby & Cordova, 1996). The existence of group disparities does not prove that discrimination has occurred, but it should prompt further investigation by the employer. In other words, even though individual contaminated judgments are unscented, certain patterns of judgment do smell "fishy," thereby alerting us to the possibility of unwanted bias.

Once again, we must point out that this strategy is limited. Perceivers are not terribly adept at covariation assessment (Nisbett & Ross, 1980), and therefore may fail to detect suspicious patterns. When they do succeed, the patterns may be open to multiple interpretations and the implications of global trends for individual cases may be unclear.

Considering the Opposite. Some kinds of mental biases can be undone by asking people to "consider the opposite," whereby they imagine different outcomes than the ones they had been thinking about. Simply thinking about whether a specific hypothesis is true, for example, increases people's beliefs in its validity because the person focuses more on explanations as to why it could be true than why it could be false. Several studies have found that asking people to consider the possibility that the opposite hypothesis is true is sufficient to undo the bias of one-sided thinking (Lord, Lepper, & Preston, 1984).

For this strategy to work, however, people must be able to mentally simulate alternative outcomes or hypotheses (Hirt & Markman, 1995). In many everyday cases of contamination, people may be so locked into one way of looking at something that it is difficult for them to imagine alternatives. This is especially likely to be true, we suspect, when people have contaminated affective reactions. The affect may anchor their judgments to the extent that it is difficult for them to imagine they could feel otherwise. Suppose Ms. Green tried to imagine how she would have evaluated Mr. Jones if he were White. Her negative feelings might anchor her thinking to the point where it is difficult to perform this mental simulation.

Furthermore, people do not always know what aspect of a situation to mentally undo. Consider the men in the Dutton and Aron (1974) experiment who were approached by the woman on the scary bridge. Presumably, they had little idea that they were misattributing fear to attraction to the woman. Even if it occurred to them to consider the opposite, they might not know which aspect of the situation to transform. Should they imagine that they had met the woman at a different time of day or season of the year? Without some idea about the source of contamination, people do not know which mental simulation to run.

Legal Implications: Should People Be Held Responsible for Mental Contamination?

Given the difficulty of avoiding many forms of mental contamination, is it reasonable to expect people to try to avoid mental contamination? If a person in power acts on a contaminated judgment and harms another person as a result, should he or she be held liable for that harm? An interesting discussion of this issue has arisen among legal scholars in the area of employment discrimination.

Consider again our example of the law partner, Ms. Green, and the decision-making processes leading to her recommendation against hiring the young African-American attorney, Mr. Jones. Let us assume, for the sake of argument, that Ms. Green's negative decision was biased by Mr. Jones's race. Let us further suppose that Ms. Green is a well-meaning person who would be aghast to know that race influenced her decision not to hire Mr. Jones. If Mr. Jones were to file a racial discrimination suit, could Ms. Green or her firm be held legally liable under current antidiscrimination laws?

Because Ms. Green's decision was affected by Mr. Jones's race, she seems to be in violation of the law. Title VII of the Civil Rights Act (1964, amended 1994) prohibits discrimination in employment on the basis of race, color, sex, national origin, and religion. Krieger (1995) points out, however, that Title VII is based on an antiquated view of prejudice in which all discrimination is assumed to be conscious, deliberate, and intentional. In essence, antidiscrimination law was written to prevent blatant, conscious racism, and does not take into account the possibility that discrimination can be unintentional and nonconscious. More generally, the law assumes that people are fully aware of the mental processes leading to their decisions; in Krieger's words, that they possess "transparency of mind"(p. 1185).

Thus, under current law, it would be very difficult for Mr. Jones to prevail in a lawsuit against Ms. Green. Mr. Jones would be required to prove not only that Ms. Green had taken his race into consideration, but also that Ms. Green was motivated by deliberate discriminatory intent. The jury would be forced to choose between two extreme positions: a verdict of "no discrimination," which implies that race played no role in Ms. Green's decision, or the opposite verdict, which brands Ms. Green as a conscious discriminator who lied in court about her real reasons for not hiring Mr. Jones (Krieger, 1995). Clearly, the law is ill-equipped to deal with the kinds of bias we discuss here, in which discrimination may be unintended and nonconscious.

Krieger (1995) makes a number of recommendations to redress this lack of fit. For example, she suggests that a clear distinction in interpreting motivation and intent be made, such that unintentional forms of contamination and its consequences may be considered as legal evidence. She also argues that a two-tiered liability system be adopted such that there would exist a first tier for equitable relief for unintentional discrimination, and a second, higher tier providing compensatory and punitive damages for intentionally motivated discrimination (similar to the criminal justice system, in which there is a distinction between manslaughter and first-degree murder).

Other legal scholars appreciate the fact that nonconscious discrimination can exist, but are less sanguine about ways in which the legal system can be changed to prevent it. Wax (1999) suggests that in many cases, the unintentional and unconscious forms of bias are sporadic and unpredictable and that the financial and social costs of attempting to remedy such forms of discrimination would be prohibitive. Much of her argument hinges on the apparent difficulty of detecting unconscious discrimination and our lack of knowledge concerning how to prevent or combat it. As she puts it, "That we cannot know another mind is a problem that plagues discrimination law generally. The dilemma is even more acute when the other mind cannot know itself nor effectively control itself nor be effectively controlled by others" (Wax, 1999, p. 1226).

Wax argues that attaching liability to acts that are outside the realm of conscious control will have little deterrent effect and may actually produce undesirable outcomes. For example, employers may invest scarce resources in activities that protect them from lawsuits but do little to reduce the actual incidence of workplace discrimination.

CONCLUSION

This legal debate underscores the challenges of dealing with mental contamination in the real world and points to some important directions for future research. It is clear, for example, that techniques for detecting individual cases of mental contamination are sorely needed. In applied settings, the question of whether contamination has actually occurred is critical, and perceivers are unable to make this determination on their own. In this regard, it is interesting

that a number of researchers have devised techniques to measure an individual's level of implicit racial prejudice (e.g., Dovidio, Kawakami, Johnson, &
Johnson, 1997; Fazio, Jackson, Dunton, & Williams, 1995; Greenwald, McGhee,
& Schwartz, 1998). Might these measures index an individual's propensity to
engage in unconscious discrimination? Might they also be used some day in
the legal arena?

Such a day is clearly not yet here because these techniques are in their infancy and their reliability, validity, and controllability are still an open question.
Quite possibly these tests will have the same status as the polygraph, a tool of
some interest to psychological researchers but of little use in courts of law. It
is not inconceivable, however, that some day experts will administer implicit
tests to a defendant to determine his or her level of implicit prejudice, just as
clinicians now administer psychological tests to assess a defendant's mental
health. Whether such a day will be a welcome one depends, of course, on the
construct and predictive validity of the tests.

Even if valid implicit tests are developed, it may be that the nature of the
human cognitive system precludes complete decontamination. If so, the best
hope may lie in educating people about the causes of mental contamination
so that they are able to (1) identify, after the fact, those cases in which contamination has most likely occurred; and (2) when possible, structure their
decision-making environments so as to reduce the likelihood of contamination
in the first place. This strategy has been met with some success in the domain
of eyewitness identification (see Wells, 1993, for a review). Researchers have
determined, for example, that some lineup procedures and configurations produce more mistaken identifications than others. By using this information when
devising lineups, the police are able to reduce the number of "contaminated"
identifications that occur. Of course, not all factors that influence the accuracy
of eyewitness identification are amenable to control. The police cannot manipulate the quality of the viewing conditions under which the witness saw the
perpetrator or whether the suspect looks familiar because the witness saw him
earlier that day at the bus stop. In such cases, educating people – jurors, the
police, attorneys, and perhaps even the witnesses themselves – about potential
contaminants can help them determine the appropriate weight to give to an
individual eyewitness' identification.

In sum, although we are pessimistic about people's natural ability to willfully control and correct their judgments, we are by no means suggesting that
reducing mental contamination is a lost cause. Researchers are making promising advances in the detection of nonconscious biases and may ultimately devise
some effective debiasing strategies. The challenges of eliminating contamination are great, but so may be the personal and societal costs of ignoring the
problem.

11. Sympathetic Magical Thinking: The Contagion and Similarity "Heuristics"

Paul Rozin and Carol Nemeroff

THE LAWS OF SYMPATHETIC MAGIC

The *laws of sympathetic magic* constitute a small but central subset of what might be called *magical thinking*. They share with the larger category that they promote beliefs about the world that are generally contrary to current scientific beliefs. However, unlike most other examples of magic, the laws of sympathetic magic do not necessarily invoke a sense of human or animate agency as a device to account for events in the world (see Nemeroff & Rozin, 2000; Tambiah, 1990, for a discussion of magical thinking in a broader context). In contrast to the larger category of magical thinking, the laws of sympathetic magic may be more tractable to experimental study for three reasons: (1) they are clearly defined; (2) they are present in abundance as modes of thought among contemporary people in developed societies; and (3) they invoke principles (e.g., contact, resemblance) that are easy to manipulate in the laboratory.

Edwin Tylor (1879), James Frazer (1895), and Marcel Mauss (1902) proposed three laws of sympathetic magic that they took to be universal principles of thinking. The *law of contagion* holds that "once in contact, always in contact"; when objects make physical contact, essences may be permanently transferred. Thus, fingernail parings contain the "essence" of the person to whom they were previously attached, and foods carry the "essence" of those who prepared them. The *law of similarity* holds either that like causes like (causes resemble their effects) or appearance equals reality. A prototypical example of similarity is the voodoo practice of burning a representation of an enemy to cause the enemy harm; action on the image is believed to result in effects on the object it represents. The *law of opposites*, which is not discussed further in this chapter, is the opposite of the first reading of the law of similarity, and holds that causes are the opposite of their effects.

On some important dimensions, contagion is the opposite of similarity. Similarity bears a relation to the principle of generalization, and surely is manifested in nonhuman animals; "appearance equals reality" is a very useful heuristic.

Preparation of this paper was assisted by NIDA grant R21- DA10858-0 to Paul Rozin, and grant #H8-038 from the Arizona Department of Health Services funded through the Centers for Disease Control and Prevention to Carol Nemeroff.

Contagion, however, holds that things may not be what they seem. Their history, which may not be represented in their appearance, endows them with important properties.

Recent psychological research on these laws dates from their involvement in the analysis of disgust. For Americans, harmless replicas of disgusting objects are treated as disgusting (similarity), and brief contact with a disgusting entity renders an edible food unacceptable (contagion) (Rozin, Millman, & Nemeroff, 1986). Subsequent work (e.g., Rozin, Nemeroff, Wane, & Sherrod, 1989) established that the laws of sympathetic magic characterize some types of cognitions, even among educated, Western adults. Thus, what has been generally interpreted as a peculiar feature of the thought of "traditional peoples" now appears to be a basic feature of human thinking.

The two laws we discuss qualify as cognitive heuristics; they are rules of thumb that generally work to make sense of the world and promote adaptive behaviors. Generally, causes do resemble their effects, appearance is usually a very good indicator of reality ("If it looks like a tiger, it *is* a tiger"), and some important entities, such as germs, do pass along some of their nature by virtue of physical contact. However, the laws differ from most of the now classic heuristics, such as availability and anchoring, in two critical ways: (1) invocation of sympathetic magical intuitions is typically associated with a substantial affective component; and (2) people are usually either aware, or can be easily made aware, of the "irrational" aspects of these laws. Thus, when educated Americans refuse to eat chocolate shaped into realistic-looking dog feces, or refuse to eat a food touched by a sterilized cockroach, they are acutely aware that this "makes no sense," yet acknowledge their feeling of aversion. They can often overcome this aversion and "be rational," but their preference is not to. They willingly acknowledge their feelings and respond to them, unless pressed. For instance, if the issue of avoiding a harmlessly contaminated object (as with a sterilized cockroach) or a similarity based aversion (e.g., reluctance to use sugar from a bottle labeled cyanide when the individual is certain the bottle contains sugar and never contained cyanide) is tied to money (e.g., "How much would you pay to avoid doing this?"), some college students who acknowledge uncomfortable feelings will perform the act rather than pay anything at all (Rozin, Grant, Weinberg, & Parker, 2000). In other words, money promotes leading with the head as opposed to the heart. Similarly, if one asks a question in an affective way (e.g., "How worried are you?") as opposed to a cognitive way (e.g., "How likely is it?"), one can either elicit magical thinking or not (e.g., Nemeroff, 1995; Nemeroff, Brinkman & Woodward, 1994). Thus, Nemeroff (1995) found that participants think a disliked person's germs are more virulent than a loved one's germs when asked an experiential question, such as, "How sick do you think you would get [from contact]?" However, the effect is not significant if they are asked instead, "How likely would you be to get sick?"

In Western developed cultures, there is more conflict than in traditional cultures between magical thinking and prevailing cultural beliefs, and perhaps a greater inclination to support feelings or beliefs with a logical/rational account. Thus, educated and less-educated Westerners and more traditional folk all experience disgust at the prospect of consuming road-kill dog meat. However, educated Westerners, after careful consideration of the situation, overrule their feelings to the extent that they hold that the feelings of disgust do not require a negative moral judgment (because no organism was hurt in this process), whereas less-educated folk are more inclined to move from the emotion or feeling to a moral judgment (Haidt, Koller, & Dias, 1993).

In one form or another, the laws of sympathetic magic have appeared in the theories of a number of scholars. Freud (1950) saw them as part of the primitive, intuitive mode of thought that he called the *primary process*. For example, Freud claimed that the primary process does not distinguish between hallucination and reality, somewhat akin to the law of similarity. Piaget (1983) identifies *magical thinking* as a feature of childhood, and describes the principle of *realism*, in which the symbol of something is confused with what it represents (similarity).

In line with both Freud and Piaget is the more general position that sympathetic magical thinking is an example of a set of natural and intuitive modes of thought. This idea has been developed in important ways in the contributions of Shweder (1977), Nisbett and Ross (1980), and the very productive line of research on heuristics and biases stimulated by Kahneman and Tversky (1979, 1984) and Kahneman, Slovic, and Tversky (1982). Along with this tradition and in keeping with Simon's (1982) principle of satisficing (using shortcuts that usually approximate ideal analyses), it is recognized that these intuitions, or *heuristics*, may be adaptive and function well in a wide variety of situations. Perhaps the shortcomings of these intuitive modes of thought have become highlighted by the creation of the modern world, laden as it is with images (two- and three-dimensional representations/imitations) that challenge the law of similarity, or scientific accomplishments that are hard to understand intuitively (e.g., who could ever imagine the speed of light, or risks of 1 in 1,000,000?).

THE LAW OF SIMILARITY

Two Versions of the Law of Similarity
Like causes Like. As described by Tylor (1879), Frazer (1895), and Mauss (1902), the law of similarity essentially holds that causes resemble their effects. For instance, the treatment for a disease should have some surface relation to the presumed cause of the disease, or the cause of the disease should have a surface relation to the symptoms of the disease. Thus, the Zande people of Africa believe that fowl excrement cures ringworm because fowl excrement and ringworm are similar in appearance. The modern medical predilection to assume (with little evidence) that dietary cholesterol is a causative factor in

accumulation of cholesterol-containing plaques in arteries might be considered another example of like causes like. This cause–effect likeness principle is at the foundation of the tradition of homeopathic medicine.

Shweder (1977) notes that the distinction between likeness and cooccurrence likelihood is frequently absent not only in magical thought, but also in "our own mundane intellectual activities" and concluded that "magical thinking is an expression of a universal disinclination of normal adults to draw correlational lessons from their experience, coupled with a universal inclination to seek symbolic and meaningful connections (likenesses) among objects and events." (p. 637).

"Like causes like" is related to the representativeness heuristic (Kahneman & Tversky, 1972). In accordance with "representativeness," an event or entity is assigned to a category based on the similarity of its principle features to other members of that category. If the category in question is causes and their effects, this reduces to like causes like. Thus, one manifestation of representativeness is the tendency to expect a cause to resemble its effects. For example, in current lay thought, it is believed by many that because AIDS is lethal and extremely resistant to attempts at cure, the infectious agent (HIV) should have the same potent and indestructible qualities. In fact, the virus itself is generally very fragile outside of an appropriate host, and usually not especially potent (a substantial dose is required to induce a high likelihood of infection).

Appearance Equals Reality.   Another, perhaps even more basic realization of the law of similarity is that "appearance equals reality" – If it looks like a tiger, it *is* a tiger. Here, similarity promotes categorization rather than cause–effect inference, but as in the case of like causes like, surface properties are used to infer deeper properties. Thus, in the voodoo practice of harming the image to effect the object, the action on the image is taken as acting on the actual object, because at a deep level they are seen as one. Piaget (1983) described the child's tendency to presume that words or names embody the properties they refer to as *nominal realism*. This can be construed as an extension of appearance equals reality; the label "poison" is neither poisonous itself, nor does it necessarily imply that the entity labeled is poisonous. For example, in some of our studies, subjects were reluctant to consume a bottle of sugar labeled as "Poison," even though they knew the label was meaningless (see page 205 for more details; Rozin, Millman, & Nemeroff, 1986; Rozin, Markwith, & Ross, 1990).

Adaptive Value of Similarity

The idea that appearance equals reality is eminently reasonable because, in the world we evolved in, causes often do resemble effects, and most things that look like tigers *are* tigers. In the natural world, of course, mimicry takes advantage of this general tendency as a way to induce misidentification of a species. However, this generally useful heuristic becomes more of a bias in the worlds created by cultures, which invariably include art, symbolic language, and images. With images and words to represent objects, extensions of the law of similarity would cause us to fear a picture of a tiger or a toy gun.

Domains and Range of Operation of the Law of Similarity

Similarity is a general principle that came to the attention of modern psychologists in the framework of responses by educated Americans (undergraduates) to disgusting stimuli. Rozin, Millman, and Nemeroff (1986) showed that most students preferred a round piece of chocolate fudge to a piece with the same content, but realistically shaped to look like "dog doo." Similarly, most undergraduates were disinclined to put in their mouth a fake vomit, clearly made of rubber, in comparison to their willingness to put in their mouth a flat rubber sink stopper of about the same size.

Similar effects can be observed with the willingness to eat things that only appear to be harmful. This was demonstrated most clearly in the context of nominal realism. Subjects observed sugar from a commercial container being poured into two bottles, and then placed a "sugar" label on one, and "cyanide" on the other, at random (Rozin, Millman, & Nemeroff, 1986; Rozin, Markwith, & Ross, 1990). Undergraduate subjects were reluctant to consume sugar taken from the bottle labeled "Sodium Cyanide, Poison" even though *they* had arbitrarily placed that label on it. This effect was even observed when the label read "Not Sodium Cyanide," supporting Freud's (1966) contention that the unconscious does not process negatives. In these studies, subjects realized that their negative feelings were unfounded, but felt and acknowledged them anyway.

As noted previously, a common exemplification of similarity in traditional cultures occurs in voodoo practices, in which one does harm to an image (effigy) of a person, and presumes that this harms the actual person (like causes like). We have demonstrated this type of effect in the laboratory, with undergraduates (Rozin, Millman, & Nemeroff, 1986). Students showed poorer accuracy in throwing darts at a picture of John F. Kennedy's face (with the "desired" target the spot between the eyes) than they showed for a plain target or a picture of Adolph Hitler's face. Furthermore, when a dart did hit near the target on Kennedy's face, subjects would sometimes cringe. Finally, it is common knowledge, which we have confirmed in unpublished studies in our laboratory, that people are reluctant to throw out or tear up duplicate photographs of loved ones.

Development of Similarity

The principle of similarity, at least in its expression as "appearance equals reality," is undoubtedly a useful heuristic in animals as well as humans. It is related to the principle of generalization in learning, and is almost certainly part of the our genetic endowment and present at birth. Flavell (1986) showed that a confusion of appearance and reality characterizes the thinking of young children.

Summary
The law of similarity is fairly straightforward, primitive, and reasonable. There is little that need be said about the mechanism, when the law is viewed as an extension of the widespread feature of animal learning that we call *generalization*. The law of contagion, discussed next, is much more complex and apparently absent in animals and in young children. It seems to have been created by humans in the course of their cultural evolution.

THE LAW OF CONTAGION

A Framework for Discussing the Law of Contagion
Explication of the law of contagion requires some definitions. One object, usually of an animate nature, is a *source*; a second object, usually human, is a *target* or *recipient*. The law of contagion holds that *physical contact* between *source* and *target* results in the transfer of some effect or quality, which we call *essence*, from source to target. The source and target may mutually influence each other (exchange essence). The qualities exchanged may be physical, mental, or moral in nature, and negative or positive in valence. The contact between source and target may be direct, or may be mediated by a third object, or *vehicle*, that makes simultaneous or successive contact with both source and target. Common vehicles are food, clothing, and other possessions.

Characteristics of Contagion
Unlike similarity, contagion involves a rich set of assumptions and properties. Beginning with the idea of transfer of essence through physical contact, we proceed to explicate these features. We provide examples in each case, typically referring to modern, Western reactions to contact with AIDS. The basic phenomenon, very salient in American culture, is that objects (vehicles) that have contacted someone with AIDS, including a house formerly lived in by someone with AIDS, acquire negative properties (Nemeroff, Brinkman, & Woodward, 1994; Rozin, Markwith, & Nemeroff, 1992).

Physical Contact Is Critical. In magical contagion, actual physical contact (as opposed to mere proximity) – whether direct or indirect – is critical in accomplishing transmission of essence. People are more concerned about wearing a sweater that had been worn but was not owned by someone with AIDS (and then washed) than about a sweater owned but never worn by someone with AIDS (Nemeroff et al., 1994; Rozin et al., 1992). A cockroach that runs near one's plate is not nearly as contaminating as one that runs over one's food.

Once in Contact, Always in Contact. A core feature of the law of contagion is that once joined through direct or indirect physical contact, a transfer of essence occurs that is often permanent; hence "once in contact, always in contact." Consider a bowl of mashed potatoes that a cockroach briefly runs across. If the potatoes are placed in a freezer for 1 year, they are still inedible (assuming the person in question remembers their history). With respect to

AIDS, 92% of the negative 1-day effect remains after 1 year. Similar results are obtained with a piece of silverware that had been used 1 day or 1 year ago by someone with AIDS (Nemeroff et al., 1994; Rozin et al., 1992).

The Holographic or Metonymic Nature of Essence. All of the properties of the source pervade the entire source and are contained in its essence. Magical contagion is "holographic" in the metonymic sense of the whole being equivalent to the part ("the part equals the whole"). As a result, contact with any part of the source transfers essence, including fingernail parings or a lock of hair. Hitler's fingernails are as contaminating as his brains. This property, which can be called *route insensitivity*, is illustrated by the fact that 43% of subjects reported that there was no place at all on the body of a person with AIDS (including elbow and lock of hair) that they would feel as comfortable touching as the corresponding place on the body of a healthy stranger (Nemeroff et al., 1994).

Dose insensitivity. Minimal contact is usually sufficient to transmit near maximal amounts of essence. A sweater worn for 5 minutes by a person with AIDS (and then washed) yields a drop in desirability that is 71% of the effect of use for 1 full year; similar results hold for a fork vehicle (Rozin et al., 1992). We have also found that, in the view of 68% of our subjects, the function relating the probability of contracting AIDS to the number of viruses entering the body is flat (dose independence). According to these subjects, a single live AIDS virus that enters the body has a potency of infection (measured as probability of induction of AIDS) that is the same as 10,000 or 1,000,000 viruses (Nemeroff, Brinkman, & Woodward, 1994). Depending on the way the holographic principle is construed, one might consider dose insensitivity a consequence of the holographic nature of essence. Even a fraction of a hologram contains information sufficient to recreate the whole image.

Negativity bias. We argued for a general principle, applying across many human domains, that negative effects are stronger than positive effects; we call this general phenomenon *negativity bias* (Rozin & Royzman, 2001; see also Baumeister, Bratslavsky, Finkenauer, & Vohs, 2000). In one manifestation of negativity bias, which we call *negativity potency* (related to loss aversion), negative events are more negative than corresponding positive events are positive. This principle is illustrated with particular clarity in the domain of contagion. There is no positive entity that is as strongly positive as a cockroach, poison, or Hitler is negative. That is, contact with a butterfly, vitamin, or Mother Theresa does not produce positive effects as strong or reliable as the negative effects produced by the previously mentioned negative entities (Nemeroff & Rozin, 1994; Rozin, Nemeroff, Wane, & Sherrod, 1989). Furthermore, in what we describe as *negativity dominance*, combinations of contact with negative and positive entities (e.g., touching the target with a cockroach and an antibiotic or a valued object; touching of the target by a disliked and a liked person) result in a net effect more negative than would be expected from the sum of the negativity and positivity of the sources (Rozin et al., 1989; Rozin & Royzman, 2001).

Ethnographic reports corroborate this claim. Even among the Hua of Papua New Guinea (Meigs, 1984), who are among the world champions in contagion sensitivity and have many instances of positive contagion, negative contagion is clearly more potent and dominant than positive; in Hindu India, contact with a lower caste is polluting, whereas contact with a higher caste has no purifying effect, all of which relate to Stevenson's (1954, p. 50) claim that "pollution overcomes purity" (see also Appadurai, 1981). In studies of American undergraduates and a general sample of American adults, although almost everyone showed negative contagion effects, only about one-third showed positive contagion effects (Rozin et al., 1989, Nemeroff & Rozin, 1994).

A Wide Range of Properties of the Source Are Potentially Contagious. Questionnaire (e.g., Rozin et al. 1986, Rozin et al., 1989; Nemeroff & Rozin, 1994), laboratory (Rozin et al., 1986, 1999) and ethnographic data (e.g., Meigs, 1984) indicate that physical attributes (e.g., size, growth rate, color, illness), abilities (strength, coordination, visual acuity), dispositions (personality characteristics), and moral qualities are believed to be subject to transmission by contact. Intentions may also be thought to be transmitted in the sense that contact with a source person who has a harmful intent toward the target can bring bad luck to the target.

Backwards Action. In what has been described up to this point, influence flows from a contagious source to a recipient in much the same way that germs are transmitted from one individual to another. *Backward contagion* reverses the causal arrow, and challenges the normal sense of causation. Thus, in traditional magic, a target may cause harm to a source by burning a lock of the source's hair or fingernail parings from the source, or may attract a source by placing these same entities in a love potion. We obtained substantial evidence for such backward contagion in American college students. A substantial number (approximately one-third, but not the virtual unanimity of response we get for forward contagion) were uncomfortable about the prospect that their hairbrush or a lock of their hair (neither to be seen again) came into the possession of a personal enemy (Rozin et al., 1989). The reluctance of many Americans to *donate* blood since the beginning of the AIDS epidemic might conceivably be accounted for by backward contagion.

We envision two types of explanation of backward contagion: One is that the same types of transferred essence analysis holds in both types of contagion. On this view, backward contagion would require an additional assumption: that essence remains unitary in contact, even when physically separated. Thus, the essence in the cut lock of hair remains forever connected with its source, allowing action on the hair to affect its source. Alternatively, it is possible that an important component of contagion is mere association, in time or space, between target and source. In forward contagion, this association is supplemented by the forward transmission of essence by contact. However, in backward contagion, it could just be the association. This would account for the fact that backward contagion is weaker and less frequent than forward contagion, but leaves many questions unanswered. One, of course, is why contact is so important in backward contagion?

Domains, Evolution and Origins of Contagion

Contagion effects appear in domains as diverse as food transactions, contact with microbially contaminated entities, contact with other (especially unfamiliar) persons, contact with morally tainted entities, and contact with loved or greatly admired persons (positive contagion). This breadth raises questions about the evolutionary origin of contagion and the cultural history of expansion of the domain of contagion. We briefly consider four accounts of the origin of contagion, keeping in mind that it appears to be uniquely human. Two accounts are based on an origin of contagion as an adaptive means of avoiding microbial contamination, which shares with contagion the fundamental properties of importance of physical contact, the ability to produce a major effect with a minimal dose, and negativity bias (there is no potent positive opposite to germs).

According to the first account, contagion originated in association with disgust, the rejection of a set of potential foods as offensive. On this view, contagion arose as a means of avoiding microbial contamination from foods. Pinker (1997) notes that animal foods are much more likely than plant foods to be vehicles for the transmission of potentially harmful microorganisms. The principal risk from plant foods is toxins; toxins do not have contaminating properties, in the sense that they cannot multiply, and microbes in plants are much less likely to find a compatible host in animals. Almost all potential food elicitors of disgust are of animal origin (Rozin & Fallon, 1987), and almost all examples of negative food contagion effects involve foods of animal origin. Interpersonal contagion is often manifested in the domain of food because food is a highly social entity that is typically procured, handled, prepared, or eaten and shared by others. These multiple other-contacts with one's food allow for widespread interpersonal contagion influences, no doubt enhanced by the particular intimacy of the act of ingestion. There is evidence for a widespread traditional belief in "You are what you eat" – that is, the idea that one takes on the physical, behavioral, intentional, and moral properties of what one consumes (Nemeroff & Rozin, 1989; Stein & Nemeroff, 1995). This belief is a very concrete form of contagion. In the interpersonal domain, taken literally, it would apply only to other humans for the rare cases of cannibalism. However, when coupled with the principle of contagion, "You are what you eat" promises an enormous range for passage of personal influence by food (Rozin, 1990). Now, the food someone has raised or prepared becomes a vehicle for their essence.

A second account locates the origin of contagion in the interpersonal as opposed to the food domain. Illness transfer in humans usually involves a human vector, and therefore is interpersonal. Common vehicles are food, air, physical contact with infected persons, and shared objects and residues. On this account, there is no reason to specially privilege the food vehicle as the original source of contagion. Widespread avoidance of physical contact with or close proximity to ill or dead people suggests the possibility that the core issue in the origin of contagion is microbial contamination, whatever the source.

The third account does not attribute the origin of contagion to negative, microbial effects, but rather to positive effects. Although the relative weakness of positive contagion suggests that it might be an accidental overextension of the negative contagion principle, it is also possible that positive contagion has its own origin or adaptive value. An obvious function for positive contagion is in the support of kin relations and love bonds. It could well function to strengthen important blood bonds, with their obvious link to fitness. Sharing food is a particularly common behavior that centers on kin-related groups, and sexual intimacy involves highly contagious contact. Positive contagion includes valuing objects that belonged to and were in contact with ancestors, living loved ones, or greatly admired persons; Grandmother's ring, food prepared by a loved one, or Princess Diana's clothing are salient examples.

The relative weakness of positive contagion could be simply a result of the negativity dominance discussed previously. Alternatively, it could be a result of the fact that positive contagion virtually always competes with illness risk and disgust. The microbial risks of intercourse are well illustrated by sexually transmitted diseases. A deep kiss involves exchange of saliva, which is both a disgusting body fluid and a potential disease vector, when examined out of the context of love or lust (Nemeroff, 1988; Nemeroff & Rozin, 1994, 2000).

A final account of the origins of contagion is based in the work of Johnson and Lakoff (e.g., Johnson, 1987; Lakoff, 1987; Lakoff & Johnson, 1980), who write about the "embodied" nature of cognition. Our bodies, they say, provide us with preconceptual structures that shape our abstract thoughts. Body movements and perceptual interactions with the world, which are fundamentally based in the experience of having a human body, give rise to "image-schemata" that are "metaphorically projected" to structure our domains of thought. By this account, the contagion principle would arise from our phenomenological experience of our bodies as containers (having an inside, a boundary, and an outside), combined with other schemas such as trajectory, force, links, and so on. This account easily explains the breadth of magical contagion, although it does not address the negativity bias.

Given some initial locus for the origin of contagion, an account is still needed for the great breadth of contagion in contemporary humans. The problem of the spread of contagion is paralleled by the spread of disgust from its likely original food origin to a wide range of elicitors, including interpersonal contacts and especially contacts with ill or immoral persons. The range of disgust in contemporary humans overlaps substantially with the range of contagion. Indeed, our definition of disgust invokes contagion as a critical feature: Contact with a disgusting substance renders an otherwise acceptable entity (e.g., a food) unacceptable (Rozin & Fallon, 1987). Our account of the cultural evolution of disgust invokes the process of *preadaptation*; that is, the application of an adaptation that evolved for one purpose to a new purpose. We trace the cultural evolution of disgust as an expansion of elicitors from its origin as a response to distasteful foods through reactions to offensive foods, other animal properties of our existence (e.g., sex, death), interpersonal contacts, and certain types of moral offenses (Rozin, Haidt, & McCauley, 1993; Rozin, Haidt, McCauley, & Imada, 1997). The extension of contagion could have occurred by this same type of process, whatever its origins. Of course, once contagion became linked to disgust, either in origin or later on, its domain could have spread as the domain of disgust spread.

We commonly ask people why they reject juice that had brief contact with a cockroach. The answer almost always refers to toxins and microbes; the disease-generating properties of the roach. This, of course, relates to some of the views we have expressed about the microbial origins of contagion. However, in the laboratory, we often follow up this response by repeating the process with a new glass of juice, now contaminated by a sterilized roach – that is, a germ-free roach just removed from an autoclave. This roach, we point out, is safer than the average fork, such that juice that touched it should be totally safe to drink. Subjects almost always continue to reject the juice, while admitting, in an embarrassed way, that their initial microbial harm account must have been invalid or at least incomplete. It is the offensive roach properties that have been passed into the juice, somewhat independent of any physical threat of harm. We find the same sort of results with hypothetical sweaters (on questionnaires) that have been worn by someone with an infectious disease. They are rejected even after sterilization (Nemeroff & Rozin, 1994; Rozin, Markwith, & McCauley, 1994). Furthermore, the pattern of rejection is quite similar to the rejection of sweaters previously worn by morally tainted but healthy individuals. Also, those who are most inclined to reject "hepatitis sweaters" are generally the same as those most inclined to reject "healthy murderer sweaters."

Mental Models of Contagion

What are the properties that the mind attributes to the contagious entity? We enumerated the principles of contagion previously; these constrain but do not fully dictate the manner in which the contagious entity is conceived. Furthermore, given the wide range of contagious entities, from germs to individuals with compromised morals, it is likely that there might be different mental models, varying within individuals across domains of contagious entities, among individuals within a culture, and between cultures. We explored this possibility in an in-depth interview study with 36 more or less representative American adults (Nemeroff, 1988; Nemeroff & Rozin, 1994). Participants were asked to imagine various source people coming into contact with a sweater (and various other objects), and then imagine their reaction to wearing this sweater. We then asked them to further imagine a set of "purifications" of that sweater (such as laundering or changing its color or appearance) and asked participants to estimate their willingness to wear the sweater after each of the designated "purifications." Our logic was that one could deduce the nature of the contagious entity by discovering how it could be neutralized.

The source people were one's lover, a good person, and a sex symbol (positive interpersonal sources); one's enemy and an evil person (negative interpersonal sources); a person with contagious hepatitis and a person with AIDS (physical illness sources); and an imperceptible amount of dog feces on the sweater (physical disgust). Purification methods included physical cleansing (e.g., deodorizing, washing by hand, sterilizing); physical/symbolic transformations (e.g., unraveling the sweater and reknitting it into a scarf; gashing it); and spiritual "opposite-contacts" (i.e., having an opposite-valenced source wear the sweater, such as Mother Theresa wearing Hitler's sweater). Templates were devised for five possible models of contagion:

1. A physical germ model, in which contagion is seen as carried by a living invisible entity (particularly vulnerable to boiling, and to a lesser degree to washing).
2. A physical residue model, in which contagion is dependent on residues such as sweat, dandruff, and so on (particularly vulnerable to washing).
3. A symbolic interaction model, in which contagion is the result of the meaning implied by interaction with an object (symbolic actions like gashing or otherwise destroying or reconstituting should be effective).
4. An associative model, in which the reminding value of an object is the key to effects (change in appearance cues rather than substance, which would be expected to be moderately efficacious).
5. A spiritual essence model, in which the source's "nonmaterial essence" or "soul-stuff" are believed to be in the object (here, the only effective purifier might be an opposite force of the same type; that is, Mother Theresa's positive essence neutralizing Hitler's negative essence).

We had a separate set of subjects read a description of each model and rank order the set of purifications in terms of their effectiveness for/within each of the models. We then tested these template orders against the actual rank orders provided by participants in the study to determine the best-fitting model for each subject and each source.

The predicted purification potency for the two physical models (germ and physical residue) turned out to be highly similar, as did the potency ordering for the three nonphysical models (associative, spiritual, and symbolic interactional). Because of this relative similarity and the small sample size, we combined the models into two broad classes, henceforth termed *physical* (material) and *nonphysical* (spiritual).

On average, the nonphysical models were the best match for all interpersonal sources, both positive and negative, and the physical models were the best match for physical sources (illness and disgust). Thus, the idea of at least two broad models of contagious essence was supported. One is material/physical and is effectively moderated by washing; the other is spiritual/nonphysical, is reduced much less by washing, is very difficult to erase, and is most effectively reduced by opposite valence contact. Because positive contagion sources are almost entirely interpersonal, positive contagious essence is typically spiritual/nonphysical.

The associative model of contagion, which we have included in the nonphysical category, is problematic. It does not capture many of the properties of contagion, particularly the physical contact principle. Although physical contact may promote association, it is hardly necessary, and unlike the symbolic and spiritual essence models with which it is grouped, there is no "spiritual" aspect to it. In a sense, the association model is an alternative to contagion because it does not depend on physical contact and the transfer of essence. Unfortunately, it is a difficult model to distinguish from other nonphysical models. Two observations support the claim that there is something besides association going on in cases of non-physical contagion. First, ownership without contact, although heavy on association, seems less potent in transferring negativity than brief contact without ownership (Nemeroff, 1988; Rozin et al., 1992). Along the same lines, similarity, based on images or representations, and hence on association, is generally less potent than contagion, in which reminding cues are less salient. In the extreme, a book about Hitler's life with his photograph on the cover and quotes of his words inside is less offensive to many people than his worn sweater would be, even though the sweater is not uniquely linked to Hitler in its sensory properties.

Managing Contagion with Framing: Inattention and Ritual Rules

Unlike other heuristics, the contagion heuristic or principle is potentially crippling on the negative (as opposed to positive) side. One is continuously faced with abundant situations that present the possibility of negative contagion: the air breathed out by others around us; the necessarily shared objects, such as doorknobs, plates, and silverware in restaurants; money; and seats in public places. We propose that negative contagion is generally managed under the general aegis of framing, with two particular strategies: inattention and ritual rules.

Inattention. *Inattention* is like the Freudian defense mechanism of denial, except that it may be much more passive. We simply do not think much about the interpersonal history of most objects we deal with. When we receive change in the store, we do not think of the long string of humans, no doubt some unsavory, who handled it previously; likewise for the interpersonal history of a public bathroom doorknob or a seat on a train. The domains of inattention vary across individuals (see later) and across cultures. For example, the contamination produced by the bottoms of shoes bringing outside filth into the home is salient for most Japanese, but not attended to by most Americans. However,

Japanese traditionally sequentially share their bath water with family members and guests, while Americans find that offensive.

Ritual rules. Typically in religious systems, problems of contagion may be handled by establishing rituals to decontaminate and setting limits on the range of contamination. Such rules seem most prevalent in Judaism and Hinduism; not accidentally, these are arguably the two most contagion-sensitive religions, and the only two major world religions in which membership is primarily determined by biology; that is, by blood rather than beliefs (Morris, 1997). A particularly clear example of a ritual boundary is the 1/60th rule of Kashrut, relating to contamination of kosher foods by non-kosher entities (Nemeroff & Rozin, 1992). According to this rule, if contamination occurs by accident and the contaminant is less than 1/60th of the total volume of the contaminated entity, the food remains kosher. We have shown, however, that for a majority of Jews, the ritual boundary does not align with feelings; that is, although such people understand that a food accidentally contaminated at a level of less than 1/60th remains kosher, they find it offensive and reject it. There was a weak indication in the results from this study that the more kosher/orthodox Jews were more likely to be willing to consume technically kosher contaminations (less than 1/60th contaminant). This suggests that deep commitment to the Jewish dietary laws may successfully aid in the alignment of ritual boundaries and feelings, and set limits on emotional/magical contagion reactions.

The Development of Contagion

We know little about the development of contagion, or of other heuristics and biases for that matter. Contagion is a sophisticated idea. Because the history of an entity is important, contagion often holds that appearance is not equal to reality (the opposite of similarity). It frequently invokes invisible entities and abstract conceptions that are not available to young children (Au, 1993; Rosen & Rozin, 1993). Most work on contagion in children involves insect contaminants and food vehicles – that is, negative contagion in the food domain. Early work suggested that contagion became an active principle, at least in the domain of food and disgust for American children, at 6 to 8 years of age (Fallon, Rozin, & Pliner, 1984; Rozin, Fallon, & Augustoni-Ziskind, 1985, 1986). More recent work on Australian preschoolers using more sensitive measures, suggests that children as young as 4 years of age may show negative contagion sensitivity in the food domain (Siegal, 1988; Siegal & Share, 1990).

We do not yet know much about the development of the child's mental models of contagion. However, it is clear that association and true contagion are less differentiated in young children than they are in adults (Springer & Belk, 1994; Hejmadi, Rozin, & Siegal, 2000), and that in both the Hindu Indian and the American cultures, the earliest models of contagion seem to be material essence (Hejmadi, Rozin, & Siegal, 2000).

Individual Differences in Sympathetic Magical Beliefs

There are large individual differences in the extent of sympathetic magical thinking both within and between cultures. Of the 36 participants in the study on the nature of contagious essence (Nemeroff & Rozin, 1994), 24 displayed dual models-material essence for illness contaminants, and spiritual essence for interpersonal and moral contaminants. However, 6 of subjects seemed to have a material essence model for everything, including moral contagion; for these subjects, washing was generally effective. Another 6 subjects used a spiritual essence model for everything, so washing or boiling were quite ineffective, even for illness sources.

As well as differences in the quality of contagion, there are large individual variations in contagion sensitivity. Wide variations were demonstrated in American college students and their parents on a scale designed to measure disgust responses to neutral entities after contact with disgusting entities (Rozin, Fallon, & Mandell, 1984).

Another study exploring individual differences examined contagion and similarity thinking about kosher-relevant and -irrelevant contaminations in a sample of Jews of varying levels of orthodoxy (Nemeroff & Rozin, 1992). Generally, it was found that sensitivity to contagion items intercorrelated quite highly with each other, and the same for similarity items, but the two did not correlate substantially with each other. Some individuals were sensitive to contagion but not similarity such that, for example, they would reject a meat dish into which less than 1/60th volume of milk fell, but have no problem eating beef stroganoff made with non-dairy creamer (a similarity item in that the combination appeared nonkosher, but was, in fact, kosher). Other individuals were sensitive to similarity but not contagion. We also developed a series of questionnaire measures of the combined action of both contagion and similarity; for example, a drop of non-dairy creamer falling into a beef stew ("contagion via similarity"). A surprising number of people were put off by even this very weakened magical effect.

More recently, we created a scale of disgust sensitivity, in a more orthodox psychometric framework, including a number of items that deal with similarity and contagion (Haidt, McCauley, & Rozin, 1994). There is very wide variation in sensitivity to disgust, similarity, and contagion in both American and Japanese cultures (Haidt, McCauley, & Rozin, 1994; Imada, Haidt, McCauley, & Rozin, 2000, unpublished data). At extremes in American culture are persons who feel uncomfortable blowing their nose in a piece of brand-new toilet paper, handling money, or sleeping on a laundered pillowcase in a hotel, versus persons who are incredulous that anyone would have such concerns. We created a hands-on validation of this paper-and-pencil disgust scale, using college students (Rozin, Haidt, McCauley, Dunlop, & Ashmore, 1999). These students spent over an hour in the laboratory in a situation in which they were simply asked to indicate whether they would be willing to do 30 tasks; if they agreed, they actually performed the task. An example for similarity magic related to disgust was to present students with a brand-new bed pan, into which the experimenter poured some apple juice from a commercial apple juice bottle. Participants were asked if they would be willing to drink some of the apple juice: only 28% complied. For a typical contagion item, subjects were asked if they would be willing to drink water from a glass after it had been stirred by a used but washed comb; 30% complied. Norms for college students were established for a wide range of negative contagion and similarity situations.

There has been little attention paid to individuals who show minimal sensitivity to magical principles. However, there is a clinical entity, the cleaning variety of obsessive–compulsive disorder (OCD), that seems to represent excessive concern about negative contagion. Appropriately, persons with OCD show high scores on the disgust scale (Tolin, Brigidi, & Foa, 1999), and obsessive–compulsive tendencies in normal persons correlate positively with disgust scale scores (Rozin, Taylor, Ross, Bennett, & Hejmadi, 2000).

CONCLUSION

Magical thinking generally provides a way to promote meaning and understanding of the many baffling events that occur in the world of any human. In this respect, it serves some of the same functions as religion and science. For the sympathetic magical principles, a case can be made that these are useful heuristics that guide behavior adaptively in at least some domains. Before germ theory, although the medical profession held that contact with infected individuals was not threatening, lay persons behaved as if it was. The material essence of some aspects of contagion has a basis in fact; the spiritual essence does not, according to current doctrine, but we must be humble about things like this. "Action at a distance," a hallmark of magical thinking in the past, is a scientifically accepted aspect of modern physics, and "mind over matter," another such hallmark, is now recognized in areas such as psychoneuroimmunology. The contagion principle represents a truth about microbial contamination. The extension of this to moral contagion may have important and adaptive consequences for the establishment or maintenance of society and the social order.

12. Compatibility Effects in Judgment and Choice

Paul Slovic, Dale Griffin, and Amos Tversky

One of the main ideas that has emerged from behavioral decision research is a constructive conception of judgment and choice. According to this view, preferences and beliefs are actually constructed – not merely revealed – in the elicitation process. This conception is entailed by findings that normatively equivalent methods of elicitation often give rise to systematically different responses (e.g., Slovic, Fischhoff, & Lichtenstein, 1982; Tversky, Sattath, & Slovic, 1988). To account for these data within a constructive framework, we seek explanatory principles that relate the characteristics of the task to the attributes of the objects under study. One such notion is the compatibility hypothesis, which states that the weight of a stimulus attribute is enhanced by its compatibility with the response.

The rationale for this hypothesis is twofold. First, noncompatibility between the input and the output requires additional mental operations, which often increase effort and error and may reduce impact. Second, a response mode may prime or focus attention on the compatible features of the stimulus. Common features, for example, are weighted more heavily in judgments of similarity than in judgments of dissimilarity, whereas distinctive features are weighted more heavily in judgments of dissimilarity (Tversky, 1977). Consequently, entities with many common and many distinctive features (e.g., East and West Germany) are judged as both more similar to each other and as more different from each other than entities with relatively fewer common and fewer distinctive features (e.g., Sri Lanka and Nepal).

The significance of the compatibility between input and output has long been recognized by students of human performance. Engineering psychologists have discovered that responses to visual displays of information, such an instrument panel, are faster and more accurate if the response structure is compatible with the arrangement of the stimuli (Fitts & Seeger, 1953; Wickens, 1984). For example, the response to a pair of lights is faster and more accurate if the left light is assigned to the left key and the right light to the right key. Similarly, a square array of four burners on a stove is easier to control with a matching square array of knobs than with a linear array. The concept of compatibility has been extended beyond spatial organization. The reaction time to a stimulus light is faster with a pointing response than with vocal response, but the vocal response is faster than pointing if the stimulus is presented in an auditory mode (Brainard et al., 1962).

This chapter investigates the role of compatibility in judgment and choice. As in the study of perceptual–motor performance, we do not have an independent procedure for assessing the compatibility between stimulus elements and response modes. This hinders the development of a general theory, but does not render the concept meaningless or circular, provided that compatibility can be manipulated experimentally. For example, it seems reasonable to assume that a turn signal in which a left movement indicates a left turn and a right movement indicates a right turn is more compatible than the opposite design. By comparing people's performance with the two turn signals, it is possible to test whether the more compatible design yields better performance. Similarly, it seems reasonable to assume that the monetary payoffs of a bet are more compatible with pricing than with choice because both the payoffs and the prices are expressed in dollars. By comparing choice and pricing, therefore, we can test the hypothesis that the payoffs of a bet loom larger in pricing than in choice. . . .

PREDICTION

Study 1: Prediction of Market Value

In our first study, 77 Stanford students were presented with a list of 12 well-known U.S. companies taken from the 1987 *Business Week Top 100*. For each company, students were given two items of information: 1986 *market value* (the total value of the outstanding shares in billions of dollars) and 1987 *profit standing* (rank of the company in terms of its 1987 earnings among the Top 100). Half the subjects were asked to predict 1987 market value (in billions of dollars). They were informed that, among the Top 100, the highest market value in 1987 was $68.2 billion and that the lowest was $5.1 billion, so their predictions should fall within that range. The remaining subjects were asked to predict each company's rank (from 1 to 100) in market value for 1987. Thus, both groups of subjects received identical information and predicted the same criterion using a different response scale. Although the two response scales differ in units (dollar versus rank) and direction (low rank means high market value), the two dependent variables should yield the same ordering of the 12 companies. To encourage careful consideration, a $75 prize was offered for the person whose predictions most nearly matched the actual values.

The compatibility hypothesis states that a predictor is weighted more heavily when it matches the response scale than when it does not. That is, 1986 market value in dollars (D) should be weighted more heavily by the subjects who predict in dollars (d) than by those who predict in rank (r). By the same token,

1987 profit rank (R) should be weighted more heavily by the subjects who predict in rank than by those who predict in dollars. To investigate this hypothesis, we correlated the criteria with the predictors, estimated the relative weights of the two predictors, and devised a statistical test based on reversals of order.

The product-moment correlations of d with D and R were .93 and .77, respectively, whereas the correlations of r with D and R were .74 and .94, respectively. Thus, the correlation between the matched variables was higher than that between the nonmatched variables. It is instructive to examine the compatibility effect in terms of the relative weights of the two predictors in a multiple-regression equation. These values can be computed directly or derived from the correlations between the predictors and the criterion together with the correlation between the predictors. (To make the regression weights positive, the ranking order was reversed.) The multiple regressions for both dollars and ranks fit the average data very well with multiple correlations of .99. Let c and r denote the mean observed predictions of 1987 dollar value and rank, respectively, for a company whose 1986 dollar value is D_i and whose 1987 profit rank is R_i. The multiple-regression equations, then, take the form

$$d_i = \alpha_d D_i + \beta_d R_i$$
$$r_i = \alpha_r D_i + \beta_r R_i,$$

when the independent variables are expressed in standardized units. Thus, α_d and α_r are the regression weights for the 1986 market value (D_i) estimate from the predicted dollars and ranks, respectively. Similarly, β_d and β_r are the corresponding weights for the second predictor, 1987 profit rank. The relative weights for the first predictor in each of the two response modes are

$$A_d = \alpha_d / (\alpha_d + \beta_d)$$
$$A_r = \alpha_r / (\alpha_r + \beta_r).$$

These values measure the relative contribution of D_i in the prediction of dollars and rank, respectively. If the weighting of the dimensions is independent of the response scale, A_d and A_r are expected to be equal, except for minor perturbations due to a nonlinear relation between d and r. As we argue next, the compatibility hypothesis implies $A_d > A_r$. Note that A_d is the relative weight of the 1986 market value in dollars, estimated from the prediction of dollars, whereas A_r is the relative weight of the same variable estimated from the prediction of rank. The first index reflects the impact of D_i in a compatible condition (i.e., when the predictions are made in dollars), whereas A_r reflects the impact of D_i in the less compatible condition (i.e., when the predictions are made in ranks). If the compatibility between the predictor and the criterion enhances the weight of that variable, then A_d should exceed A_r.

The values estimated from the regression equations were $A_d = .64$ and $A_r = .32$, in accord with the compatibility hypothesis. Thus, D_i was weighted more than R_i in the prediction of dollars, whereas R_i was weighted more than D_i in the prediction of rank. Moreover, each predictor was weighted about twice as much in the compatible condition as it was in the noncompatible condition. When interpreting the relative weights, here and in later studies, we should keep in mind that they are based on aggregate data, that the predictors (D and R) are correlated, and that the relation between the two criteria (d and r) should be monotone but not necessarily linear. Although these factors do not account for the discrepancy between A_d and A_r, it is desirable to obtain a purely ordinal test of the compatibility hypothesis within the data of each subject that is not open to these objections. The following analysis of order reversals provides a basis for such a test.

The change in the relative weights induced by the response mode could produce reversals in the order of the predictions. In the present study, there were 21 pairs of companies (i, j) in which $D_i > D_j$ and $R_j > R_i$. If D is weighted more heavily than R in the subject's prediction of dollars and R is weighted more heavily than D in the subject's prediction of rank, we would expect $d_i > d_j$ and $r_j > r_i$. The data confirmed this hypothesis. Subjects who predicted dollars favored the company with the higher D 72% of the time, whereas subjects who predicted rank favored the company with the higher D only 39% of the time. (Ties were excluded from this analysis.) This difference is highly significant ($p < .001$). Note that the subjects did not directly compare the companies; the ordering was inferred from their predictions. . . .

Study 2: Prediction of Academic Performance

Our second test of the compatibility hypothesis involves the prediction of a student's grade in a course. We asked 258 subjects from the University of Oregon to predict the performance of 10 target students in a history course on the basis of the students' performance in two other courses: English literature and philosophy. For each of the 10 targets, the subjects were given a letter grade (from A+ to D) in one course and a class rank (from 1 to 100) in the other course. Half the subjects predicted the students' grade in history, whereas the other half predicted the students' class rank in history. Each of the four combinations of performance measures (grade/rank) and courses (literature/philosophy) was presented to a different group of subjects.

The compatibility hypothesis implies that a given predictor (e.g., grade in philosophy) will be given more weight when the criterion is expressed on the same scale (e.g., grade in history) than when it is expressed on a different scale (e.g., rank in history). The relative weight of grades to ranks, then, will be higher in the group that predicts grades than in the group that predicts ranks.

As in the previous study, we first correlated the criteria with the predictors. The (zero-order) correlations of g with G and R were .83 and .82, respectively, whereas the correlations of r with G and R were .70 and .91, respectively, in accord with the compatibility hypothesis. We next regressed the mean predictions of grades and ranks onto the two predictors. The letter grades were coded $D = 1$, $C- = 2$, ... $A+ = 10$. (To make the regression weights positive, the ranking order was reversed.) The multiple regression for both grades and ranks fit the average data very well with multiple correlations of .99. Let g_i and r_i denote the mean observed predictions of grade and rank, respectively, for a student with a grade G_i in one course and a rank R_i the other course. There was no significant interaction between the scale (rank/grade) and the course (literature/philosophy); therefore, the data for the two courses were pooled. The multiple-regression equations, then, take the form

$$g_i = \alpha_g G_i + \beta_g R_i$$
$$r_i = \alpha_r G_i + \beta_r R_i,$$

when the independent variables are expressed in standardized units. Thus, α_g and α_r are the regression weights for the grades (G_i) estimated from the predicted grades and ranks, respectively. Similarly, β_g and β_r are the corresponding weights for the second predictor, class rank. The relative weights for the first predictor in each of the two response modes are

$$A_g = \alpha_g / (\alpha_g + \beta_g)$$
$$A_r = \alpha_p / (\alpha_r + \beta_r).$$

These values measure the relative contribution of G_i in the prediction of grade and rank, respectively. Because the grades and ranks are monotonically related, A_g and A_r should be approximately equal if the weighting of the dimensions is independent of the response scale. However, if the match between the predictor and the criterion enhances the weight of the more compatible predictor, then A_g should exceed A_r.

The values estimated from the regression equations were $A_g = .51$ and $A_r = .40$, in accord with the compatibility hypothesis. Thus, grade in philosophy was weighted more heavily in the prediction of grade in history than in prediction of rank in history. Similarly, rank in philosophy was weighted more heavily in the prediction of rank in history than in the prediction of grade history.

To obtain an ordinal test of the compatibility hypothesis within the data for each subject, we analyzed the reversals of order induced by the change weights. There were 21 pairs of students (i, j) in which $G_i > G_j$ and $R_j > R_i$. If G is weighted more heavily than R in the prediction of grades and r is weighted more heavily than G in the prediction of rank, we would expect $g_i > g_j$ and $r_j > r_i$. Indeed, subjects who predicted grades favored the student with the higher G 58% of the time, whereas subjects who predicted rank favored the student with the higher G only 42% of the time. (Ties were excluded from this analysis.) This difference is statistically significant ($p < .001$). Recall that subjects did not compare students directly; the ordering was inferred from their predictions.

The compatibility effects observed in the previous two studies may be mediated by a process of anchoring and adjustment. Subjects may use the score on the compatible variable (the attribute that matches the criterion) as an anchor and then adjust this number up or down according to the value of the noncompatible variable. Because adjustments of an anchor are generally insufficient (Slovic & Lichtenstein, 1971; Tversky & Kahneman, 1974), the compatible attribute would be overweighted. An anchoring and adjustment process, therefore, provides a natural mechanism for generating compatibility effects. To test whether compatibility effects occur in the absence of anchoring, we replaced the prediction task described previously with a choice task in which the subject is no longer required to make a numerical prediction that would invoke anchoring. The following study, then, investigates the compatibility hypothesis in a context in which anchoring and adjustment are unlikely to play a significant role.

Seventy-eight Stanford undergraduates were presented with 20 pairs of students taken from the stimuli used in Study 2. In each pair, one student had a higher grade and the other a higher rank. Half the subjects were asked to predict, for each pair, which student would achieve a higher grade in history, whereas the remaining subjects were asked to predict, for each pair, which student would achieve a higher rank in history. Because both groups were asked to predict only which of two students would do better in history and not to make a numeric prediction, their tasks were virtually identical. Nevertheless, the student with the higher grade was selected 56% of the time by the grade group and only 49% of the time by the rank group ($p < .05$), indicating that the compatibility effect is present even in a choice task that does not require a quantitative response and is, therefore, unlikely to involve an adjustment of a numeric anchor. The strategy of anchoring and adjustment, however, probably contributes to the compatibility effect observed in numeric predictions.

PREFERENCE

The previous section investigated compatibility effects in prediction and judgment; this section is concerned with the role of compatibility in decision making in general and preference reversals in particular. A reversal of preference is a pattern of choices in which normatively equivalent elicitation procedures give rise to inconsistent preferences. A well-known example of preference reversal (PR) was discovered by Lichtenstein and Slovic (1971; see also Slovic & Lichtenstein, 1968). This phenomenon involves pairs of bets with comparable expected values: an H bet that offers a high probability of winning a relatively small amount of money (e.g., a 35/36 chance to win $4) and an L bet that offers a low probability of winning a moderate amount of money (e.g., an 11/36 chance to win $16). When offered a choice between such bets, most people choose the H bet over the L bet, but, when asked to state the lowest selling price of each bet, the majority state a higher price for the L bet than for the H bet. In general, about half the subjects state prices that are inconsistent with their choices, thereby exhibiting a PR. This pattern of preferences, which violates the standard theory of rational choice, has been observed in numerous experiments, including a study conducted on the floor of a Las Vegas casino (Lichtenstein & Slovic, 1973), and it persists even in the presence of monetary incentives designed to promote consistent responses (see, e.g., Grether & Plott, 1979; Slovic & Lichtenstein, 1983). . . .

Study 3: Monetary versus Nonmonetary Outcomes

If preference reversals are due primarily to the compatibility of prices and payoffs, their frequency should be substantially reduced when the outcomes of the bets are not expressed in monetary terms. To test this prediction, we constructed six pairs of H and L bets: three with monetary outcomes (as in the usual PR studies) and three with nonmonetary outcomes. Two hundred forty-eight students from the University of Oregon participated in this study. Half the subjects first chose between all six pairs of bets and later assigned a cash equivalent to each bet. The other half of the subjects performed these tasks in the opposite order. There was no significant order effect; therefore, the data for the two groups were combined.

The data show that the percentage of choices of H over L was roughly the same in the monetary and the nonmonetary bets (63% versus 66%), but that the percentage of cases in which C_H exceeds C_L was substantially smaller in the monetary than in the nonmonetary bets (33% versus 54%). Consequently, the overall incidence of predicted PR decreased significantly, from 41% to 24% ($p < .01$). Naturally, the pricing response is more compatible with monetary than with nonmonetary payoffs. Hence, the observed reduction in PR with nonmonetary outcomes underscores the role of compatibility in the evaluation of options. Because even the nonmonetary payoffs can be evaluated in monetary terms, albeit with some difficulty, we do not expect the complete elimination of preference reversals in this case.

Study 4: Time Preferences

The compatibility hypothesis entails that preference reversals should not be restricted to risky prospects and that they should also be found in riskless choice. The present study investigates this hypothesis using delayed payoffs that differ in size and length of delay (see Tversky, Slovic, & Kahneman, 1990). Consider a delayed payoff of the form (X, T) that offers a payment of X dollars T years from now.

One hundred sixty-nine students from the University of Oregon participated in a study of choice between delayed payoffs. Half the subjects first chose between S and L in each pair and later priced all eight options by stating "the smallest immediate cash payment for which you would be willing to exchange the delayed payment." The other subjects performed the choice and pricing tasks in the opposite order. There were no systematic differences between the groups, so their data were combined.

Because both the given payoffs and the stated prices are expressed in dollars, the compatibility hypothesis implies that the payoffs will be weighted more heavily in pricing than in choice. As a consequence, the preference for the short-term option (S) over the long-term option (L) should be greater in choice than in pricing. Overall, S was chosen over L 74% of the time, but S was priced higher than L only 25% of the time, yielding 52% preference reversals, as compared with 3% reversals in the opposite direction. The application of the diagnostic analysis described in Tversky, Slovic, and Kahneman (1990) revealed that, as in the case of choice between simple bets, the major determinant of PR was overpricing of the long-term option, as suggested by compatibility.

In the pricing task, each option is evaluated singly, whereas choice involves a direct comparison between options. The standard demonstrations of PR, therefore, are consistent with the alternative hypothesis that payoffs are weighted more heavily in a singular than in a comparative evaluation. To test this hypothesis against compatibility, we replicated the study presented previously with a new group of 184 students from the University of Oregon, with one change. Instead of pricing the options, the subjects were asked to rate the attractiveness of each option on a scale from 0 (not at all attractive) to 20 (extremely attractive). If PR is controlled, in part at least, by the nature of the task (singular versus comparative), we should expect L to be more popular in rating than in choice. However, if PR is produced by scale compatibility, there is no obvious reason why rating should differ from choice. Indeed, no discrepancy between choice and rating was observed. Overall, S was chosen over L 75% of the time (as in the original study), and the rating of S exceeded the rating of L in 76% of the cases. Only 11% of the patterns exhibited PR between choice and rating, as compared to 52% between choice and pricing.

Study 3 showed that the use of nonmonetary prizes greatly reduced the amount of PR, whereas Study 4 demonstrated substantial PR in the absence of risk. Evidently, preference reversals are controlled primarily by the compatibility between the price and the payoffs, regardless of the presence or absence of risk.

Study 5: Matching versus Pricing

In addition to pricing and choice, options can be evaluated through a matching procedure, in which a decision maker is required to fill in a missing value so as to equate a pair of options. Considerations of compatibility suggest that the attribute on which the match is made will be overweighted relative to another attribute. This hypothesis is tested in the following study, using 12 pairs of H and L bets (displayed in Table 12.1). In each pair, one value – either a probability or a payoff – was missing, and the subjects were asked to set the missing value so that they would be indifferent between the two bets. Consider, for example, the bets H (33/36, $50) and L (18/36, $125). If we replace the 18/36 probability in L by a question mark, the subject is asked in effect, "What chance to win $125 is equally attractive as a 33/36 chance to win $50?" The value set by the subject implies a preference between the original bets. If the value exceeds 1/2, we infer that the subject prefers H to L, and if the value is less than 1/2,

Table 12.1. Percentage of Responses Favoring the *H* Bet over the *L* Bet for Four Different Elicitation Procedures

	Choice	Probability Matching	Payoff Matching	Pricing
Small bets ([*H*], [*L*])				
(35/36, $4), (11/36, $16)	80	79	54	29
(29/36, $2), (7/36, $9)	75	62	44	26
(34/36, $3), (18/36, $6.50)	73	76	70	39
(32/36, $4), (4/36, $40)	69	70	26	42
(34/36, $2.50), (14/36, $8.50)	71	80	43	22
(33/36, $2), (18/36, $5)	56	66	69	18
Mean	**71**	**72**	**50**	**29**
Large bets ([*H*], [*L*])				
(35/36, $100), (11/36, $400)	88	76	69	65
(29/36, $50), (7/36, $225)	83	64	31	55
(34/36, $75), (18/36, $160)	77	79	65	55
(32/36, $100), (4/36, $1,000)	84	68	28	61
(34/36, $65), (14/36, $210)	78	80	36	57
(33/36, $50), (18/36, $125)	68	75	58	46
Mean	**80**	**74**	**48**	**56**
Overall mean	**76**	**73**	**49**	**37**

we infer that the subject prefers *L* to *H*. Using all four components as missing values, we can infer the preferences from matching either the probability or the payoff of each bet. If the compatibility hypothesis applies to matching, then the attribute on which the match is made will be overweighted relative to the other attribute. As a consequence, the inferred percentage of preferences for *H* over *L* should be higher for probability matches than for payoff matches.

Two hundred subjects from the University of Oregon participated in this study. Each subject saw 12 pairs, each consisting of a high-probability bet (*H*) and a low-probability bet (*L*). Six of these pairs consisted of bets with relatively small payoffs; the other six pairs consisted of bets with large payoffs, constructed by multiplying the payoffs in the first six pairs by a factor of 25 (see Table 12.1). Each pair of bets was evaluated in four ways: direct choice, pricing of each bet individually, matching by providing a missing payoff, and matching by providing a missing probability. Every subject performed both choice and pricing tasks and matched either probabilities or payoffs (no subject matched both probabilities and payoffs). The order in which these tasks were performed was counterbalanced.

The dependent variable of interest is the percentage of responses favoring the *H* bet over the *L* bet. These values are presented in Table 12.1 for all four tasks. Note that these percentages are observed directly in the choice task and inferred from the stated prices and the probability and payoff matches in other tasks. Under procedure invariance, all these values should coincide. The overall means showed that the tendency to favor the *H* bet over the *L* bet was highest in choice (76%) and in probability matching (73%), and substantially smaller in payoff matching (49%) and in pricing (37%). These results demonstrate two types of preference reversals: choice versus pricing and probability matching versus payoff matching.

Choice versus Pricing. The comparison of the results of choice and pricing in Table 12.1 reveals the familiar PR pattern. Subjects preferred the H bet, but assigned a higher cash equivalent to the L bet. This effect is due primarily to the overpricing of L bets implied by compatibility.

Probability Matching versus Payoff Matching. The major new result of this study concerns the discrepancy between probability matching and payoff matching. By compatibility, the dimension on which the match is made should be overweighted relative to the other dimension. Probability matching, therefore, should favor the H bet, whereas payoff matching should favor the L bet. Indeed, the tendency to favor the H bet over the L bet was much more pronounced in probability matching than in payoff matching.

Table 12.1 contains two other comparisons of interest: pricing versus payoff matching and choice versus matching. Although the pricing of a bet can be viewed as a special case of payoff matching in which the matched bet has $P = 1$, it appears that the monetary dimension looms even larger in pricing than in payoff matching. This conclusion, however, may not be generally valid because it holds for the small but not for the large bets.

Finally, the least expected feature of Table 12.1 concerns the relation between choice and matching. If, relative to choice, probability matching biases the responses in favor of the H bets and payoff matching biases the responses in favor of the L bets, then the choice data should lie between the two matching conditions. The finding that the tendency to favor the H bet is about the same in direct choice and in probability matching suggests that an additional effect beyond scale compatibility is involved.

The missing factor, we propose, is the prominence effect demonstrated by Tversky, Sattath, and Slovic (1988). In an extensive study of preference, these investigators showed that the more important attribute of an option is weighted more heavily in choice than in matching. In other words, the choice ordering is more lexicographic than that induced by matching. We originally interpreted PR in terms of compatibility rather than prominence (Tversky, Sattath, & Slovic, 1988) because we saw no *a priori* reason to hypothesize that probability is more important than money. The results of Study 5, however, forced us to reconsider the hypothesis that probability is more prominent than money, which is further supported by the finding that the rating of bets is dominated by probability (see Goldstein & Einhorn, 1987; Slovic & Lichtenstein, 1968; Tversky, Sattath, & Slovic, 1988). It appears to us now that the data of Table 12.1 represent the combination of two effects: a compatibility effect that is responsible for the difference between probability matching and payoff matching (including pricing), and a prominence effect that contributes to the relative attractiveness of H bets in choice. This account is illustrated in Fig. 12.1, which characterizes each of

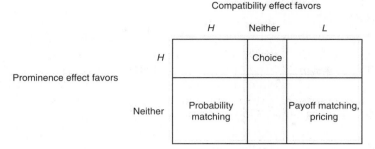

Figure 12.1. Compatibility and prominence effects for four elicitation procedures

the four elicitation procedures in terms of their compatibility and prominence effects.

Let us examine first the columns of Fig. 12.1, which represent the effects of the compatibility factor. Recall that the probability matching procedure enhances the significance of P and thereby favors the H bet. Analogously, the compatibility of the payoff matching and pricing procedures with the monetary outcomes enhances the significance of the payoffs and thereby favors the L bet. The choice procedure, however, is neutral with respect to the compatibility factor; hence, it would be expected to lie between the two matching procedures – if compatibility alone were involved. Now consider the rows of Fig. 12.1. In terms of the prominence factor, the more important dimension (i.e., probability) is expected to loom larger in choice than in either matching procedure. Thus, the tendency to choose the H bet should be greater in choice than in matching if prominence alone were involved. Table 12.1 suggests that both compatibility and prominence are present in the data. The finding that choice and probability matching yield similar results suggests that the two effects have roughly the same impact. It follows from this analysis that compatibility and prominence contribute jointly to the discrepancy between choice and pricing, which may help explain both the size and the robustness of the standard PR. It is noteworthy that each of these effects has been established independently. The demonstrations of compatibility reported in the first part of this chapter do not involve prominence, and the prominence effects demonstrated by Tversky, Sattath, and Slovic (1988) do not depend on scale compatibility.

DISCUSSION

Although the notion of compatibility has long been suggested as a possible cause of elicitation effects (e.g., Lichtenstein & Slovic, 1971; Slovic & MacPhillamy, 1974), this hypothesis has not heretofore been tested directly. The present investigations tested several implications of the compatibility hypothesis in studies of prediction and preference. In each of these studies, enhancing the compatibility between a stimulus attribute and the response mode led to increased weighting of that attribute. These findings indicate that compatibility plays an important role in judgment and choice.

The testing and application of the compatibility principle require auxiliary hypotheses about the characteristics of a stimulus attribute that make it more or less compatible with a given response mode. Many features of stimulus attributes and response scales could enhance their compatibility. These include the use of the same units (e.g., grades, ranks), the direction of relations (e.g., whether the correlations between input and output variables are positive or negative), and the numeric correspondence (e.g., similarity) between the values of input and output variables. Although we do not have a general procedure for assessing compatibility, there are many situations in which the compatibility ordering could be assumed with a fair degree of confidence. For example, it seems evident that the prediction of market value in dollars is more compatible with a predictor expressed in dollars than with a predictor expressed in ranks. The same situation exists in the domain of perceptual motor performance. There is no general theory for assessing the compatibility between an information display and a control panel, yet it is evident that some input–output configurations are much more compatible than others and therefore yield better performance. . . .

The compatibility notion discussed in this chapter concerns the correspondence between the scales in which the inputs and the outputs are expressed. In a previous paper (Tversky, Sattath, & Slovic, 1988), we explored a more abstract notion of compatibility that was later called *strategy compatibility* by Fischer and Hawkins (1988). To introduce this concept, we distinguished between qualitative and quantitative choice strategies. Qualitative strategies (e.g., dominance and min–max) are based on purely ordinal criteria, whereas quantitative strategies (e.g., multiattribute utility theory) are based on tradeoffs or weighting of the dimensions. We proposed that the qualitative strategy of selecting the option that is superior on the more important dimension is more likely to be used in the qualitative method of choice, whereas a quantitative strategy based on the tradeoffs between the dimensions is more likely to be used in the quantitative method of matching. In this sense, the prominence effect may be attributed to the compatibility between the nature of the task and the nature of the strategy it invokes. (For further discussion of strategy compatibility and its relation to scale compatibility, see Fischer & Hawkins, 1988.)

Although compatibility, like anchoring, has a powerful effect on prediction and preference, people are generally unaware of this phenomenon. Such a bias seems to operate at a very elementary level of information processing, and it is doubtful whether it can be eliminated by careful instructions or by monetary payoffs. Indeed, the use of incentives to promote careful responses has had little influence on the prevalence of preference reversals (Slovic & Lichtenstein, 1983).

The effects of compatibility described in this chapter represent a major source of violations of procedure invariance – namely, the requirement that normatively equivalent elicitation procedures should yield the same ordering of options or events. The failure of procedure invariance complicates the task of the practitioner and the theorist alike. From a practical perspective, the present findings underscore the lability of judgments and choices and make the elicitation task quite problematic. If the decision-maker's response depends critically on the method of elicitation, which method should be used, and how can it be justified? At the very least, we need to use multiple procedures (e.g., choice, pricing, rating) and compare their results. If they are consistent, we may have some basis for trusting the judgment; if they are not, further analysis is required. . . .

13. The Weighing of Evidence and the Determinants of Confidence

Dale Griffin and Amos Tversky

The weighing of evidence and the formation of belief are basic elements of human thought. The question of how to evaluate evidence and assess confidence has been addressed from a normative perspective by philosophers and statisticians; it has also been investigated experimentally by psychologists and decision researchers. One of the major findings that has emerged from this research is that people are often more confident in their judgments than is warranted by the facts. Overconfidence is not limited to lay judgment or laboratory experiments. The well-publicized observation that more than two-thirds of small businesses fail within 4 years (Dun & Bradstreet, 1967) suggests that many entrepreneurs overestimate their probability of success (Cooper, Woo, & Dunkelberg, 1988). With some notable exceptions, such as weather forecasters (Murphy & Winkler, 1977), who receive immediate frequentistic feedback and produce realistic forecasts of precipitation, overconfidence has been observed in judgments of physicians (Lusted, 1977), clinical psychologists (Oskamp, 1965), lawyers (Wagenaar & Keren, 1986), negotiators (Neale & Bazerman, 1990), engineers (Kidd, 1970), and security analysts (Staël von Holstein, 1972). As one critic described expert prediction, "often wrong, but rarely in doubt."

Overconfidence is common, but not universal. Studies of calibration have found that with very easy items, overconfidence is eliminated and underconfidence is often observed (Lichtenstein, Fischhoff, & Phillips, 1982). Furthermore, studies of sequential updating have shown that posterior probability estimates commonly exhibit conservatism or underconfidence (Edwards, 1968). In this chapter, we investigate the weighting of evidence and propose an account that explains the pattern of overconfidence and underconfidence observed in the literature.

THE DETERMINANTS OF CONFIDENCE

The assessment of confidence or degree of belief in a given hypothesis typically requires the integration of different kinds of evidence. In many problems, it is possible to distinguish between the strength, or extremeness, of the evidence

This is an edited version of a paper that first appeared in *Cognitive Psychology, 24*, 411–435. Copyright © 1992 by Academic Press. Reprinted by permission.

and its weight, or predictive validity. When we evaluate a letter of recommendation for a graduate student written by a former teacher, we may wish to consider two separate aspects of the evidence: (1) How positive or warm is the letter? and (2) How credible or knowledgeable is the writer? The first question refers to the strength or extremeness of the evidence, whereas the second question refers to its weight or credence. Similarly, suppose we wish to evaluate the evidence for the hypothesis that a coin is biased in favor of heads rather than tails. In this case, the proportion of heads in a sample reflects the strength of evidence for the hypothesis in question, and the size of the sample reflects the credence of these data. The distinction between the strength of evidence and its weight is closely related to the distinction between the size of an effect (e.g., a difference between two means) and its reliability (e.g., the standard error of the difference). Although it is not always possible to decompose the impact of evidence into the separate contributions of strength and weight, there are many contexts in which they can be varied independently. A strong or a weak recommendation may come from a reliable or unreliable source, and the same proportion of heads can be observed in a small or large sample.

Statistical theory and the calculus of chance prescribe rules for combining strength and weight. For example, probability theory specifies how sample proportion and sample size combine to determine posterior probability. The extensive experimental literature on judgment under uncertainty indicates that people do not combine strength and weight in accord with the rules of probability and statistics. Rather, intuitive judgments are overly influenced by the degree to which the available evidence is representative of the hypothesis in question (Dawes, 1988; Kahneman, Slovic, & Tversky, 1982; Nisbett & Ross, 1980). If people were to rely on representativeness alone, their judgments (e.g., that a person being interviewed will be a successful manager) would depend only on the strength of their impression (e.g., the degree to which the individual in question "looks like" a successful manager) with no regard for other factors that control predictive validity. In many situations, however, it appears that people do not neglect these factors altogether. We propose instead that people focus on the strength of the evidence – at least, as they perceive it – and then make some adjustment in response to its weight.

In evaluating a letter of recommendation, we suggest, people first attend to the warmth of the recommendation and then make allowance for the writer's limited knowledge. Similarly, when judging whether a coin is biased in favor of heads or tails, people focus on the proportion of heads in the sample and then adjust their judgment according to the number of tosses. Because such an adjustment is generally insufficient (Slovic & Lichtenstein, 1971; Tversky & Kahneman, 1974), the strength of the evidence tends to dominate its weight in comparison to an appropriate statistical model. Furthermore, the tendency to focus on the strength of the evidence leads people to underutilize other variables that control predictive validity, such as base rate and discriminability. This treatment combines judgment by representativeness, which is based entirely on the strength of an impression, with an anchoring and adjustment process that takes the weight of the evidence into account, albeit insufficiently.

This hypothesis implies a distinctive pattern of overconfidence and underconfidence. If people are highly sensitive to variations in the extremeness of evidence and not sufficiently sensitive to variations in its credence or predictive validity, then judgments will be overconfident when strength is high and weight is low, and they will be underconfident when weight is high and strength is low. As shown later, this hypothesis serves to organize and summarize much experimental evidence on judgment under uncertainty.

Consider the prediction of success in graduate school on the basis of a letter of recommendation. If people focus primarily on the warmth of the recommendation with insufficient regard for the credibility of the writer, or the correlation between the predictor and the criterion, they will be overconfident when they encounter a glowing letter based on casual contact, and they will be underconfident when they encounter a moderately positive letter from a highly knowledgeable source. Similarly, if people's judgments regarding the bias of a coin are determined primarily by the proportion of heads and tails in the sample with insufficient regard for sample size, then they will be overconfident when they observe an extreme proportion in a small sample, and underconfident when they observe a moderate proportion in a large sample. . . .

EVALUATING STATISTICAL HYPOTHESES

Study 1: Sample Size

We first investigate the relative impact of sample proportion (strength) and sample size (weight) in an experimental task involving the assessment of posterior probability. We presented 35 students with the following instructions:

Imagine that you are spinning a coin, and recording how often the coin lands heads and how often the coin lands tails. Unlike tossing, which (on average) yields an equal number of heads and tails, spinning a coin leads to a bias favoring one side or the other because of slight imperfections on the rim of the coin (and an uneven distribution of mass). Now imagine that you know that this bias is 3/5. It tends to land on one side 3 out of 5 times. But you do not know if this bias is in favor of heads or in favor of tails.

Subjects were then given various samples of evidence differing in sample size (from 3 to 33) and in the number of heads (from 2 to 19). All samples contained a majority of heads, and subjects were asked to estimate the probability (from .5 to 1) that the bias favored heads (H) rather than tails (T). Subjects received all 12 combinations of sample proportion and sample size shown in Table 13.1. They were offered a prize of $20 for the person whose judgments most closely matched the correct values.

Table 13.1 also presents, for each sample of data (D), the posterior probability for hypothesis H (a 3:2 bias in favor of heads) computed according to Bayes'

Table 13.1. Stimuli and Responses for Study 1

Number of Heads (H)	Number of Tails (T)	Sample Size (n)	Posterior Probability P(H|D)	Median Confidence (%)
2	1	3	.60	63.0
3	0	3	.77	85.0
3	2	5	.60	60.0
4	1	5	.77	80.0
5	0	5	.88	92.5
5	4	9	.60	55.0
6	3	9	.77	66.9
7	2	9	.88	77.0
9	8	17	.60	54.5
10	7	17	.77	59.5
11	6	17	.88	64.5
19	14	33	.88	60.0

rule. Assuming equal prior probabilities, Bayes' rule yields

$$\log\left(\frac{P(H|D)}{P(T|D)}\right) = n\left(\frac{h-t}{n}\right)\log\left(\frac{.6}{.4}\right),$$

where h and t are the number of heads and tails, respectively, and $n = h + t$ denotes sample size. The first term on the right side, n, represents the weight of evidence. The second term, the difference between the proportion of heads and tails in the sample, represents the strength of the evidence for H against T. The third term, which is held constant in this study, is the discriminability of the two hypotheses, corresponding to d' in signal detection theory. Plotting equal-support lines for strength and weight in logarithmic coordinates yields a family of parallel straight lines with a slope of -1, as illustrated by the dotted lines in Fig. 13.1. [To facilitate interpretation, the strength dimension is defined as h/n, which is linearly related to $(h - t)/n$.] Each line connects all data sets that provide the same support for hypothesis H. For example, a sample size of 9 with 6 heads and 3 tails and a sample size of 17 with 10 heads and 7 tails yields the same posterior probability (.77) for H over T. Thus, both point (9, 6/9) and point (17, 10/17) lie on the upper line. Similarly, the lower line connects the data sets that yield a posterior probability of .60 in favor of H (see Table 13.1).

To compare the observed judgments with Bayes' rule, we first transformed each probability judgment into log odds; then, for each subject as well as the median data, regressed the logarithm of these values against the logarithms of strength, $(h - t)/n$, and of weight, n, separately for each subject. The regressions fit the data quite well: multiple R was .95 for the median data and .82 for the median subject. According to Bayes' rule, the regression weights for strength and weight in this metric are equal (see Fig. 13.1). In contrast, the regression coefficient for strength was larger than the regression coefficient for weight for

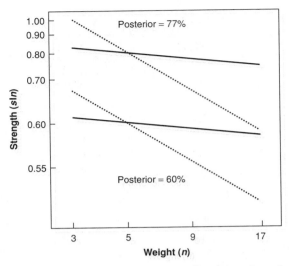

Figure 13.1. Equal support lines for strength and sample size.

30 out of 35 subjects ($p < .001$ by sign test). Across subjects, the median ratio of these coefficients was 2.2 to 1 in favor of strength. For the median data, the observed regression weight for strength (.81) was almost three times larger than that for weight.

The equal-support lines obtained from the regression analysis are plotted in Fig. 13.1 as solid lines. The comparison of the two sets of lines highly reveal two noteworthy observations. First, the intuitive lines are much shallower than the Bayesian lines, indicating that the strength of evidence dominates its weight. Second, for a given level of support (e.g., 60% or 77%), the Bayesian and the intuitive lines cross, indicating overconfidence when strength is high and weight is low, and underconfidence when strength is low and weight is high. As is seen later, the crossing point is determined primarily by the discriminability of the competing hypotheses (d').

Figure 13.2. plots the median confidence for a given sample of evidence as a function of the (Bayesian) posterior probability for two separate sample sizes. The best-fitting lines were calculated using the log odds metric. If the subjects were Bayesian, the solid lines would coincide with the dotted line. Instead, intuitive judgments based on the small sample ($n = 5$) were overconfident, whereas the judgments based on the larger sample ($n = 17$) were underconfident.

The results described in Table 13.1 are in general agreement with previous results that document the non-normative nature of intuitive judgment (for reviews, see, e.g., Kahneman, Slovic, & Tversky, 1982; von Winterfeld & Edwards, 1986). Moreover, they help reconcile apparently inconsistent findings. Edwards and his colleagues (e.g., Edwards, 1968), who used a sequential updating paradigm, argued that people are conservative in the sense that they

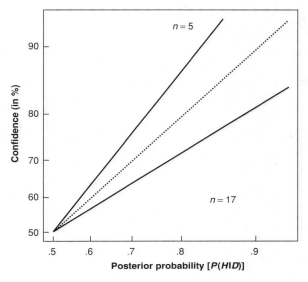

Figure 13.2. Sample size and confidence.

do not extract enough information from sample data. However, Tversky and Kahneman (1971), who investigated the role of sample size in researchers' confidence in the replicability of their results, concluded that people (even those trained in statistics) make radical inferences on the basis of small samples. Figures 13.1 and 13.2 suggest how the dominance of sample proportion over sample size could produce both findings. In some updating experiments conducted by Edwards, subjects were exposed to large samples of data typically of moderate strength. This is the context in which we expect underconfidence or conservatism. The situations studied by Tversky and Kahneman, however, involve moderately strong effects based on fairly small samples. This is the context in which overconfidence is likely to prevail. Both conservatism and overconfidence, therefore, can be generated by a common bias in the weighting of evidence; namely, the dominance of strength over weight.

As noted earlier, the tendency to focus on the strength of the evidence leads people to neglect or underweight other variables, such as the prior probability of the hypothesis in question or the discriminability of the competing hypotheses. These effects are demonstrated in the following two studies. All three studies reported in this section use a within-subject design, in which both the strength of the evidence and the mitigating variable (e.g., sample size) are varied within subjects. This procedure may underestimate the dominance of strength because people tend to respond to whatever variable is manipulated within a study whether or not it is normative to do so (Fischhoff & Bar-Hillel, 1984). Indeed, the neglect of sample size and base rate information has been most pronounced in between-subject comparisons (Kahneman & Tversky, 1972).

Study 2: Base Rate

Considerable research has demonstrated that people tend to neglect background data (e.g., base rates) in the presence of specific evidence (Kahneman, Slovic, & Tversky, 1982; Bar-Hillel, 1983). This neglect can lead either to underconfidence or overconfidence, as shown later. We asked 40 students to imagine that they had three different foreign coins, each with a known bias of $3:2$. As in Study 1, subjects did not know if the bias of each coin was in favor of heads (H) or tails (T). The subjects' prior probabilities of the two hypotheses (H and T) were varied. For one-half of the subjects, the probability of H was .50 for one type of coin, .67 for a second type of coin, and .90 for a third type of coin. For the other half of the subjects, the prior probabilities of H were .50, .33, and .10. Subjects were presented with samples of size 10, which included from 5 to 9 heads. They were then asked to give their confidence (in percentages) that the coin under consideration was biased in favor of heads. Again, a \$20 prize was offered for the person whose judgments most closely matched the correct values. Table 13.2 summarizes the sample data, the posterior probability for each

Table 13.2. Stimuli and Responses for Study 2

Number of Heads (Out of 10)	Prior Probability (Base rate)	Posterior Probability $P(H|D)$	Median Confidence (%)
5	9:1	.90	60.0
6	9:1	.95	70.0
7	9:1	.98	85.0
8	9:1	.99	92.5
9	9:1	.996	98.5
5	2:1	.67	55.0
6	2:1	.82	65.0
7	2:1	.91	71.0
8	2:1	.96	82.5
9	2:1	.98	90.0
5	1:1	.50	50.0
6	1:1	.69	60.0
7	1:1	.84	70.0
8	1:1	.92	80.0
9	1:1	.96	90.0
5	1:2	.33	33.0
6	1:2	.53	50.0
7	1:2	.72	57.0
8	1:2	.85	77.0
9	1:2	.93	90.0
5	1:9	.10	22.5
6	1:9	.20	45.0
7	1:9	.36	60.0
8	1:9	.55	80.0
9	1:9	.74	85.0

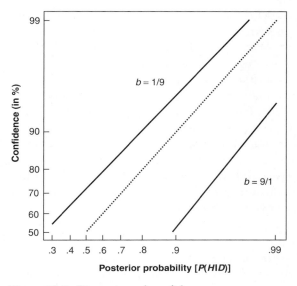

Figure 13.3. Base rate and confidence.

sample, and subjects' median confidence judgments. It is clear that our subjects overweighted strength of evidence and underweighted the prior probability.

Figure 13.3 plots median judgments of confidence as a function of (Bayesian) posterior probability for high (.90) and low (.10) prior probabilities of *H*. Again, if subjects were Bayesian, the solid lines of best fit would coincide with the dotted Bayesian line. It is evident from the figure that subjects were overconfident in the low base-rate condition and underconfident in the high base-rate condition.

These results are consistent with Grether's (1980, 1992) studies concerning the role of the representativeness heuristic in judgments of posterior probability. Unlike the present study, in which both prior probabilities and data were presented in numeric form, Grether's procedure involved random sampling of numbered balls from a bingo cage. He found that subjects overweighted the likelihood ratio relative to prior probability, as implied by representativeness, and that monetary incentives reduced but did not eliminate base-rate neglect. Grether's results, like those found by Camerer (1990) in an extensive study of market trading, contradict the claim of Gigerenzer, Hell, and Blank (1988) that explicit random sampling eliminates base-rate neglect.

Our analysis implies that people are prone to overconfidence when the base rate is low and to underconfidence when the base rate is high. Dunning, Griffin, Milojkovic, and Ross (1990) observed this pattern in a study of social prediction. In their study, each subject interviewed a target person before making predictions about the target's preferences and behavior (e.g., "If this person were offered a free subscription, which magazine would he choose: *Playboy* or the *New York Review of Books*?"). The authors presented each subject with the empirically

238   Dale Griffin and Amos Tversky

derived estimates of the base-rate frequency of the responses in question (e.g., that 68% of prior respondents preferred *Playboy*). To investigate the effect of empirical base rates, Dunning and colleagues analyzed separately the predictions that agreed with the base rate (i.e., "high" base rate predictions) and the predictions that went against the base-rate (i.e., "low" base rate predictions). Overconfidence was much more pronounced when base-rates were low (confidence = 72%, accuracy = 49%) than when base rates were high (confidence = 79%, accuracy = 75%). Moreover, for items with base rates that exceeded 75%, subjects' predictions were actually underconfident. This is exactly the pattern implied by the hypothesis that subjects evaluate the probability that a given person would prefer *Playboy* over the *New York Review of Books* on the basis of their impression of that person with little or no regard for the empirical base rate; that is, the relative popularity of the two magazines in the target population.

Study 3: Discriminability

When we consider the question of which of two hypotheses is true, confidence should depend on the degree to which the data fit one hypothesis better than the other. However, people seem to focus on the strength of evidence for a given hypothesis and neglect how well the same evidence fits an alternate hypothesis. The Barnum effect is a case in point. It is easy to construct a personality sketch that will impress many people as a fairly accurate description of their own characteristics because they evaluate the description by the degree to which it fits their personality with little or no concern for whether it fits others just as well (Forer, 1949). To explore this effect in a chance setup, we presented 50 students with evidence about two types of foreign coins. Within each type of coin, the strength of evidence (sample proportion) varied from 7/12 heads to 10/12 heads. The two types of coins differed in their characteristic biases. Subjects were instructed as follows:

Imagine that you are spinning a foreign coin called a *quinta*. Suppose that half of the quintas (the "X" type) have a .6 bias towards Heads (that is, Heads comes up on 60% of the spins for X-quintas) and half of the quintas (the "Y" type) have a .75 bias toward Tails (that is, Tails comes up on 75% of the spins for Y-quintas). Your job is to determine if this is an X-quinta or a Y-quinta.

They then received the samples of evidence displayed in Table 13.3. After they gave their confidence that each sample came from an *X*-quinta or a *Y*-quinta, subjects were asked to make the same judgments for *A* libnars (which have a .6 bias toward heads) and *B* libnars (which have a .5 chance of heads). The order of presentation of coins was counterbalanced.

Table 13.3 summarizes the sample data, the posterior probability for each sample, and subjects' median confidence judgments. The comparison of the confidence judgments to the Bayesian posterior probabilities indicates that our subjects focused primarily on the degree to which the data fit the favored hypothesis with insufficient regard for how well they fit the alternate hypothesis

Table 13.3. Stimuli and Responses for Study 3

Number of Heads (Out of 12)	Separation of Hypotheses (d')	Posterior Probability $P(B \mid D)$	Median Confidence (%)
7	.6 vs. .5	.54	55.0
8	.6 vs. .5	.64	66.0
9	.6 vs. .5	.72	75.0
10	.6 vs. .5	.80	85.0
7	.6 vs. .25	.95	65.0
8	.6 vs. .25	.99	70.0
9	.6 vs. .25	.998	80.0
10	.6 vs. .25	.999	90.0

(Fischhoff & Beyth-Marom, 1983). Figure 13.4 plots subjects' median confidence judgments against the Bayesian posterior probability both for low and high discriminability comparisons. When the discriminability between the hypotheses was low (when the coin's bias was either .6 or .5), subjects were slightly overconfident; when the discriminability between the hypotheses was high (when the bias was either .6 or .25), subjects were grossly underconfident.

In the early experimental literature on judgments of posterior probability, most studies (e.g., Peterson, Schneider, & Miller, 1965) examined symmetric hypotheses that were highly discriminable (e.g., 3:2 versus 2:3) and found consistent underconfidence. In accord with our hypothesis, however, studies that included pairs of hypotheses of low discriminability found overconfidence.

Figure 13.4. Discriminability and confidence.

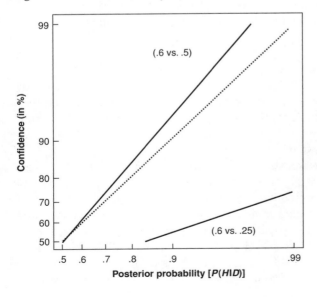

For example, Peterson and Miller (1965) found overconfidence in posterior probability judgments when the respective ratios were 3 : 2 and 3 : 4, and Phillips and Edwards (1966) found overconfidence when the ratios were 11 : 9 and 9 : 11.

CONFIDENCE IN KNOWLEDGE

The preceding section shows that people are more sensitive to the strength of evidence than to its weight. Consequently, people are overconfident when strength is high and weight is low, and underconfident when strength is low and weight is high. This conclusion, we propose, applies not only to judgments about chance processes such as coin spinning, but also to judgments about uncertain events such as who will win an upcoming election, or whether a given book will make the best-seller list. When people assess the probability of such events, we suggest that they evaluate their impression of the candidate or the book. These impressions may be based on a casual observation or on extensive knowledge of the preferences of voters and readers. In an analogy to a chance setup, the extremeness of an impression may be compared to sample proportion, and the credence of an impression may correspond to the size of the sample, or to the discriminability of the competing hypotheses. If people focus on the strength of the impression with insufficient appreciation of its weight, then the pattern of overconfidence and underconfidence observed in the evaluation of chance processes should also be present in evaluations of nonstatistical evidence.

In this section, we extend this hypothesis to complex evidential problems in which strength and weight cannot be readily defined. We first compare the prediction of self and of others. Next, we show how the present account gives rise to the "difficulty effect." Finally, we explore the determinants of confidence in general-knowledge questions, and relate the confidence-frequency discrepancy to the illusion of validity.

Study 4: Self versus Other

In this study, we ask people to predict their own behavior, about which they presumably know a great deal, and the behavior of others, about which they know less. If people base their confidence primarily on the strength of their impression with insufficient regard for its weight, we expect more overconfidence in the prediction of others than in the prediction of self.

Fourteen pairs of same-sex students, who did not know each other, were asked to predict each other's behavior in a task involving risk. They were first given 5 min to interview each other, and then they sat at individual computer terminals where they predicted their own and their partner's behavior in a Prisoner's Dilemma–type game called "The Corporate Jungle." On each trial, participants had the option of "merging" their company with their partner's company (i.e, cooperating), or "taking over" their partner's company (i.e., competing). If one partner tried to merge and the other tried to take over, the cooperative merger took a steep loss and the corporate raider made a substantial gain. However, if both partners tried a takeover on the same trial, they both suffered a loss. There were 20 payoff matrices, some designed to encourage cooperation and some designed to encourage competition.

Subjects were asked to predict their own behavior for 10 of the payoff matrices and the behavior of the person they had interviewed for the other 10. The order of the two tasks was counterbalanced, and each payoff matrix appeared an equal number of times in each task. In addition to predicting cooperation or competition for each matrix, subjects indicated their confidence in each prediction (on a scale from 50% to 100%). Shortly after the completion of the prediction task, subjects played 20 trials against their opponents, without feedback, and received payment according to the outcomes of the 20 trials.

The analysis is based on 25 subjects who completed the entire task. Overall, subjects were almost equally confident in their self predictions ($M = 84\%$) and in their predictions of others ($M = 83\%$), but they were considerably more accurate in predicting their own behavior ($M = 81\%$) than in predicting the behavior of others ($M = 68\%$). Thus, people exhibited considerable overconfidence in predictions of others, but were relatively well calibrated in predicting themselves (Fig. 13.5).

In some circumstances, in which the strength of evidence is not extreme, the prediction of one's own behavior may be underconfident. In the case of a job choice, for example, underconfidence may arise if a person has good reasons for taking job A and good reasons for taking job B, but fails to appreciate that even a small advantage for job A over B would generally lead to the choice of

Figure 13.5. Predicting self and other.

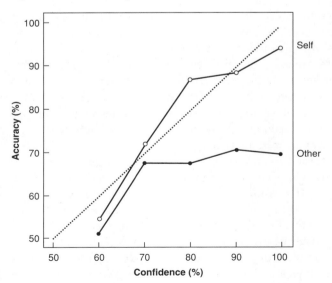

A. If confidence in the choice of A over B reflects the balance of arguments for the two positions (Koriat, Lichtenstein, & Fischhoff, 1980), then a balance of 2 to 1 would produce confidence of about 2/3, although the probability of choosing A over B is likely to be higher. Over the past few years, we have discreetly approached colleagues faced with a choice between job offers, and asked them to estimate the probability that they will choose one job over another.

The average confidence in the predicted choice was a modest 66%, but only 1 of the 24 respondents chose the opinion to which he or she initially assigned a lower probability, yielding an overall accuracy rate of 96%. It is noteworthy that there are situations in which people exhibit overconfidence even in predicting their own behavior (Vallone, Griffin, Lin, & Ross, 1990). The key variable, therefore, is not the target of prediction (self versus other), but rather the relation between the strength and the weight of the available evidence.

The tendency to be confident about the prediction of the behavior of others but not of one's own behavior has intriguing implications for the analysis of decision making. Decision analysts commonly distinguish between decision variables that are controlled by the decision maker and state variables that are not under his or her control. The analysis proceeds by determining the values of decision variables (i.e., decide what you want) and assigning probabilities to state variables (e.g., the behavior of others). Some decision analysts have noted that their clients often wish to follow an opposite course: determine or predict (with certainty) the behavior of others and assign probabilities to their own choices. After all, the behavior of others should be predictable from their traits, needs, and interests, whereas our own behavior is highly flexible and contingent on changing circumstances (Jones & Nisbett, 1972).

The Effect of Difficulty

The preceding analysis suggests that people assess their confidence in one of two competing hypotheses on the basis of their balance of arguments for and against this hypothesis, with insufficient regard for the quality of the data. This mode of judgment gives rise to overconfidence when people form a strong impression on the basis of limited knowledge and underconfidence when people form a moderate impression on the basis of extensive data.

The application of this analysis to general-knowledge questions is complicated by the fact that strength and weight cannot be experimentally controlled as in Studies 1–3. However, in an analogy to a chance setup, let us suppose that the balance of arguments for a given knowledge problem can be represented by the proportion of red and white balls in a sample. The difficulty of the problem can be represented by the discriminability of the two hypotheses; that is, the difference between the probability of obtaining a red ball under each of the two competing hypotheses. Naturally, the greater the difference, the easier the task; that is, the higher the posterior probability of the more likely hypothesis on the basis of any given sample. Suppose confidence is given by the balance of arguments; that is, the proportion of red balls in the sample. What is the pattern of results predicted by this model?

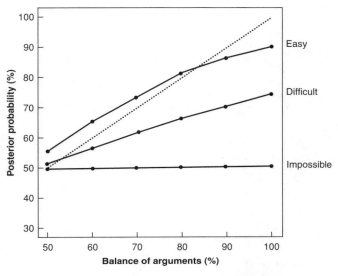

Figure 13.6. Predicted calibration for item difficulty.

Figure 13.6 displays the predicted results (for a sample of size 10) for three pairs of hypotheses that define three levels of task difficulty: an "easy" task where the probability of getting red balls under the competing hypotheses are .50 and .40, respectively; a "difficult" task, in which the probabilities are .50 and .45; and an "impossible" task, in which the probability of drawing a red ball is .5 under both hypotheses. We have chosen nonsymmetric hypotheses for our example to allow for an initial bias that is often observed in calibration data.

It is instructive to compare the predictions of this model to the results of Lichtenstein and Fischhoff (1977) who investigated the effect of task difficulty (Fig. 13.7). Their "easy" items (accuracy = 85%) produced underconfidence through much of the confidence range, their "difficult" items (accuracy = 61%) produced overconfidence through most of the confidence range, and their "impossible" task (discriminating European from American handwriting, accuracy = 51%) showed dramatic overconfidence throughout the entire range.

A comparison of Figs. 13.6 and 13.7 reveals that our simple chance model reproduces the pattern of results observed by Lichtenstein and Fischhoff (1977): slight underconfidence for very easy items, consistent overconfidence for difficult items, and dramatic overconfidence for "impossible" items. This pattern follows from the assumption that judged confidence is controlled by the balance of arguments for the competing hypotheses. The present account, therefore, can explain the observed relation between task difficulty and overconfidence (see Ferrell & McGoey, 1980).

The difficulty effect is one of the most consistent findings in the calibration literature (Lichtenstein & Fischhoff, 1977; Lichtenstein, Fischhoff, & Phillips, 1982; Yates, 1990). It is observed not only in general-knowledge questions, but also in clinical diagnoses (Oskamp, 1962), predictions of future events (contrast

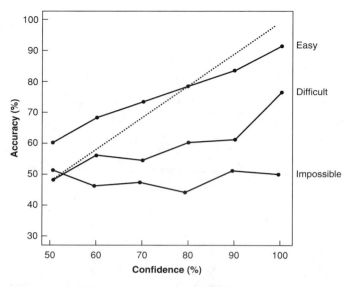

Figure 13.7. Calibration plots for item difficulty.

Fischhoff & MacGregor, 1982, versus Wright & Wisudha, 1982), and letter identification (Keren, 1988). Moreover, the difficulty effect may contribute to other
findings that have been interpreted in different ways. For example, Keren (1987)
showed that world-class bridge players were well calibrated, whereas amateur
players were overconfident. Keren interpreted this finding as an optimism bias
on the part of the amateur players. In addition, however, the professionals
were significantly more accurate than the amateurs in predicting the outcome
of bridge hands and the difference in difficulty could have contributed to the
difference in overconfidence.

The difficulty effect can also explain the main finding of a study by
Gigerenzer, Hoffrage, and Kleinbolting (1991). In this study, subjects in one
group were presented with pairs of cities and asked to choose the city with the
larger population and indicate their confidence in each answer. The items were
randomly selected from a list of all large West German cities. Subjects in a second group were presented with general-knowledge questions (e.g., "Was the
zipper invented before or after 1920?"), instructed to choose the correct answer,
and to assess their confidence in that answer. Judgments about the population
of cities were fairly well calibrated, but responses to the general-knowledge
questions exhibited overconfidence. However, the two tasks were not equally
difficult: average accuracy was 72% for the city judgments and only 53% for the
general-knowledge questions. Hence, the presence of overconfidence in the
latter but not in the former could be entirely due to the difficulty effect,
documented by Lichtenstein and Fischhoff (1977). Indeed, when Gigerenzer
et al. (1991) selected a set of city questions that were matched in difficulty to
the general-knowledge questions, the two domains yielded the same degree
of overconfidence. The authors did not acknowledge the fact that their study

confounded item generation (representative versus selective) with task difficulty (easy versus hard). Instead, they interpreted their data as confirmation for their theory that overconfidence in individual judgments is a consequence of item selection and that it disappears when items are randomly sampled from some natural environment. This prediction is tested in the following study.

Study 5: The Illusion of Validity

In this experiment, subjects compared pairs of American states on several attributes reported in the *1990 World Almanac*. To ensure representative sampling, we randomly selected 30 pairs of American states from the set of all possible pairs of states. Subjects were presented with pairs of states (e.g., Alabama, Oregon) and asked to choose the state that was higher on a particular attribute and assess the probability that their answer was correct. According to Gigerenzer et al. (1991), there should be no overconfidence in these judgments because the states were randomly selected from a natural reference class. In contrast, our account suggests that the degree of overconfidence depends on the relation between the strength and weight of the evidence. More specifically, overconfidence will be most pronounced when the weight of evidence is low and the strength of evidence is high. This is likely to arise in domains in which people can readily form a strong impression even though these impressions have low predictive validity. For example, an interviewer can form a strong impression of the quality of the mind of a prospective graduate student even though these impressions do not predict the candidate's performance (Dawes, 1979).

The use of natural stimuli precludes the direct manipulation of strength and weight. Instead, we used three attributes that vary in terms of the strength of impression that subjects are likely to form and the amount of knowledge they are likely to have. The three attributes were the number of people in each state (Population), the high-school graduation rate in each state (Education), and the difference in voting rates between the last two presidential elections in each state (Voting). We hypothesized that the three attributes would yield different patterns of confidence and accuracy. First, we expected people to be more knowledgeable about Population than about either Education or Voting. Second, we expected greater confidence in the prediction of Education than in the prediction of Voting because people's images or stereotypes of the various states are more closely tied to the former than the latter. For example, people are likely to view one state as more "educated" than another if it has more famous universities or if it is associated with more cultural events. Because the correlations between these cues and high-school graduation rates are very low, however, we expected greater overconfidence for Education than for Population or Voting. Thus, we expected high accuracy and high confidence for Population, low accuracy and low confidence for Voting, and low accuracy and higher confidence for Education.

To test these hypotheses, 298 subjects each evaluated half (15) of the pairs of states on one of the attributes. After subjects had indicated their confidence

Table 13.4. Confidence and Accuracy for Study 6

	Population ($N = 93$)	Voting ($N = 77$)	Education ($N = 118$)
Confidence	74.7	59.7	65.6
Accuracy	68.2	51.2	49.8
Conf–Acc	6.5	8.5	15.8
Frequency	51.3	36.1	41.2

for each of the 15 questions, they were asked to estimate how many of the 15 questions they had answered correctly. They were reminded that by chance alone, the expected number of correct answers was 7.5.

Table 13.4 presents mean judgments of confidence, accuracy, and estimated frequency of correct answers for each of the three attributes. Judgments of confidence exhibited significant overconfidence ($p < .01$) for all three attributes, contradicting the claim that, "If the set of general knowledge tasks is randomly sampled from a natural environment, we expect overconfidence to be zero" (Gigerenzer et al., 1991, p. 512). Evidently, there is a great deal more to overconfidence than the biased selection of items.

The observed pattern of confidence and accuracy is consistent with our hypothesis, as can be seen in Fig. 13.8. This figure plots average accuracy against average confidence, across all subjects and items, for each of the three attributes. For Population, people exhibited considerable accuracy and moderate overconfidence. For Voting, accuracy was at chance level, but overconfidence was again

Figure 13.8. Confidence and accuracy for three attributes.

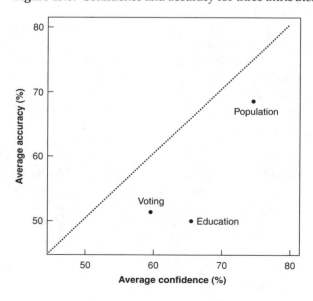

moderate. For Education, too, accuracy was at chance level, but overconfidence was massive.

The present results indicate that overconfidence cannot be fully explained by the effect of difficulty. Population and Voting produced comparable levels of overconfidence (6.5 versus 8.5, $t < 1$, ns) despite a large difference in accuracy (68.2 versus 51.2, $p < .001$). However, there is much greater overconfidence in judgments about Education than about Voting (15.8 versus 8.5, $p < .01$), even though their level of accuracy was nearly identical (49.8 versus 51.2, $t < 1$, ns).

This analysis may shed light on the relation between overconfidence and expertise. When predictability is reasonably high, experts are generally better calibrated than lay people. Studies of race oddsmakers (Griffith, 1949; Hausch, Ziemba, & Rubinstein, 1981; McGlothlin, 1956) and expert bridge players (Keren, 1987) are consistent with this conclusion. When predictability is very low, however, experts may be more prone to overconfidence than novices. If the future state of a mental patient, the Russian economy, or the stock market cannot be predicted from present data, then experts who have rich models of the system in question are more likely to exhibit overconfidence than lay people who have a very limited understanding of these systems. Studies of clinical psychologists (e.g., Oskamp, 1965) and stock market analysts (e.g., Yates, 1990) are consistent with this hypothesis.

Frequency versus Confidence

We now turn to the relation between people's confidence in the validity of their individual answers and their estimates of the overall hit rate. A sportscaster, for example, can be asked to assess his confidence in the prediction of each game as well as the number of games he expects to predict correctly. According to the present account, these judgments are not expected to coincide because they are based on different evidence. A judgment of confidence in a particular case, we propose, depends primarily on the balance of arguments for and against a specific hypothesis; for example, the relative strength of two opposing teams. Estimated frequency of correct prediction, however, is likely to be based on a general evaluation of the difficulty of the task, the knowledge of the judge, or past experience with similar problems. Thus, the overconfidence observed in average judgments of confidence need not apply to global judgments of expected accuracy. Indeed, Table 13.4 shows that estimated frequencies were substantially below the actual frequencies of correct prediction. In fact, the latter estimates were below chance for two of the three attributes. One possible explanation for this puzzling observation is that subjects reported the number of items they knew with certainty, without correction for guessing. Similar results have been observed by other investigators (e.g., Gigerenzer et al., 1991; May, 1986; Sniezek & Switzer, 1989). Evidently, people can maintain a high degree of confidence in the validity of specific answers even when they know that their overall hit rate is not very high. (This is the statistical version of the paradoxical statement "I believe in all of my beliefs, but I believe that some of my beliefs are false.") This phenomenon has been called the *illusion of validity* (Kahneman & Tversky, 1973): People often make confident predictions about individual cases on the basis of fallible data (e.g., personal interviews or projective tests), even when they know that these data have low predictive validity (Dawes, Faust, & Meehl, 1989).

The discrepancy between estimates of frequency and judgments of confidence is an interesting finding, but it does not undermine the significance of overconfidence in individual items. The latter phenomenon is important because people's decisions are commonly based on their confidence in their assessment of individual events, not on their estimates of their overall hit rate. For example, an extensive survey of new business owners (Cooper, Woo, & Dunkelberg, 1988) revealed that entrepreneurs were, on average, highly optimistic (i.e., overconfident) about the success of their specific new ventures even when they were reasonably realistic about the general rate of failure for ventures of that kind. We suggest that decisions to undertake new ventures are based primarily on beliefs about individual events, rather than about overall base rates. The tendency to prefer an individual or "inside" view rather than a statistical or "outside" view represents one of the major departures of intuitive judgment from normative theory (Kahneman & Lovallo, 1991; Kahneman & Tversky, 1982).

Finally, note that people's performance on the frequency task leaves much to be desired. The degree of underestimation in judgments of frequency was comparable, on average, to the degree of overconfidence in individual judgments of probability (see Table 13.4). Furthermore, the correlation across subjects between estimated and actual frequency was negligible for all three attributes (+ .10 for Population, − .10 for Voting, and + .15 for Education). These observations do not support the view that people estimate their hit rate correctly, and that the confidence-frequency discrepancy is merely a manifestation of their inability to evaluate the probability of unique events. . . .

CONCLUDING REMARKS

The preceding study demonstrated that the overconfidence observed in calibration experiments is not an artifact of item selection or a by-product of test difficulty. Furthermore, overconfidence is not limited to the prediction of discrete events; it has been observed consistently in the assessment of uncertain quantities (Alpert & Raiffa, 1982).

The significance of overconfidence to the conduct of human affairs can hardly be overstated. Although overconfidence is not universal, it is prevalent, often massive, and difficult to eliminate (Fischhoff, 1982). This phenomenon is significant not only because it demonstrates the discrepancy between intuitive judgments and the laws of chance, but primarily because confidence controls action (Heath & Tversky, 1991). It has been argued (see, e.g., Taylor & Brown, 1988) that overconfidence – like optimism – is adaptive because it makes people feel good and moves them to do things that they would not have done otherwise. These benefits, however, may be purchased at a high price. Overconfidence in the diagnosis of a patient, the outcome of a trial, or the projected interest rate could lead to inappropriate medical treatment, bad legal advice, and regrettable financial investments. It can be argued that people's willingness to engage in military, legal, and other costly battles would be reduced if they had a more realistic assessment of their chances of success. We doubt that the benefits of overconfidence outweigh its costs.

14. Inside the Planning Fallacy: The Causes and Consequences of Optimistic Time Predictions

Roger Buehler, Dale Griffin, and Michael Ross

Individuals, organizations, and governments all commonly plan projects and estimate when they will be completed. Kahneman and Tversky (1979) suggested that such estimates tend to be optimistic because planners rely on their best-case plans for a current project even though similar tasks in the past have typically run late. As a result of this planning fallacy, predicted completion times for specific future tasks tend to be more optimistic than can be justified by the actual completion times or by the predictors' general beliefs about the amount of time such tasks usually take.

Anecdotal evidence of the planning fallacy abounds. The history of grand construction projects is rife with optimistic and even unrealistic predictions (Hall, 1980), yet current planners seem to be unaffected by this bleak history. One recent example is the Denver International Airport, which opened 16 months late in 1995 with a construction-related cost overrun of $3.1 billion; when interest payments are added, the total cost is 300% greater than initially projected. The Eurofighter, a joint defense project of a number of European countries, was scheduled to go into service in 1997 with a total project cost of 20 billion Eurodollars; it is currently expected to be in service in 2002 with a total cost of some 45 billion Eurodollars. One of the most ambitious regional mega-projects is Boston's Central Artery/Tunnel expressway project, originally scheduled to open in 1999. The project is currently forecast to open 5 years late and double the original budget. Many consider the Sydney Opera House to be the champion of all planning disasters. According to original estimates in 1957, the opera house would be completed early in 1963 for $7 million. A scaled-down version of the opera house finally opened in 1973 at a cost of $102 million.

Granted, such mega-projects are often undertaken by governments and proponents of these schemes may deliberately provide overly optimistic assessments of cost and time to win political approval for the projects. In addition, some involve new technologies that turn out to be much more complex and expensive than their advocates envisioned (Hall, 1980). The phenomenon is not limited to commercial mega-projects, however, and its occurrence does not depend on deliberate deceit or untested technologies. From a psychological

This program of research has been supported by grants from the Social Sciences and Humanities Research Council of Canada.

perspective, the planning fallacy can perhaps be studied most profitably at the level of daily activities. Consider one familiar example: Academics who carry home a stuffed briefcase full of work on Fridays, fully intending to complete every task, are often aware that they have never gone beyond the first one or two jobs on any previous weekend. The intriguing aspect of this phenomenon is the ability of people to hold two seemingly contradictory beliefs: Although aware that most of their previous predictions were overly optimistic, they believe that their current forecasts are realistic. In the case of planning for projects, it seems, as George Bernard Shaw quipped, "We learn from history that man can never learn anything from history."

Our research focuses on the mechanisms by which people segregate their general theories about their predictions (i.e., that they are usually unrealistic) from their specific expectations for an upcoming task. Unlike the optimistic or self-enhancing biases documented by many researchers (e.g., Taylor & Brown, 1988; Weinstein, 1980), the planning fallacy features the intriguing combination of relatively pessimistic general theories with optimistic specific judgments. Our work has been guided by two questions that have surely puzzled many people: Why is the underestimation of task times so common? Why don't people learn from past experience and adjust their predictions accordingly? We begin by documenting the ubiquity of optimistic predictions in everyday tasks.

EVIDENCE OF THE PLANNING FALLACY IN EVERYDAY LIFE

In our initial study (Buehler, Griffin, & Ross, 1994, Study 1), we assessed the accuracy of university students' time estimates for an important academic project, their psychology honors thesis. We waited until most students were approaching the end of this year-long project, and then asked them to predict when they realistically expected to submit their thesis, as well as when they would submit it if "everything went as poorly as it possibly could." The students' "realistic" predictions were overly optimistic: Only 30% of the students finished the project by the predicted time. On average, the students took 55 days to complete their thesis, 22 days longer than they had anticipated, and 7 days longer than the average worst-case prediction.

Despite the optimistic bias, the students' forecasts were by no means devoid of information: The predicted completion times were highly correlated with actual completion times ($r = .77$). Compared to others in the sample, then, the students who predicted that they would take more time to finish actually did take more time. Predictions can be informative even in the presence of a marked optimistic bias.

In subsequent studies (Buehler et al., 1994; Buehler, Griffin, & Macdonald, 1997, Buehler & Griffin, 2000a), we examined students' ability to predict when they would finish a wide variety of tasks, such as school assignments; everyday tasks around their homes; and personal projects, including holiday shopping and completing income tax forms. In each study, respondents took, on average, substantially longer to finish their projects than they had predicted, and a majority of respondents failed to complete their tasks by the time they predicted (a basic result replicated by a number of other researchers, including Byram, 1997; and Taylor, Pham, Rivkin, & Armor, 1998). For example, when students were asked to complete a computer-based tutorial for Introductory Psychology, they reported that they usually completed such academic tasks about 1 day before the deadline; when asked to predict when they would complete the current tutorial project, students estimated that they would be finished, on average, about 4 days in advance of the deadline (Buehler et al., 1994). In fact, only about 30% completed by their predicted date; most finished, as usual, considerably closer to the deadline than they expected.

We obtained further evidence that our student participants really believed in their forecasts by assessing their confidence (Buehler et al., 1994, Studies 2 and 3; 1995). First, participants reported how certain they were that they would finish by the time they had predicted, on a scale ranging from 0% (not at all certain) to 100% (completely certain). The 50% or half-way mark on this scale indicated that respondents felt that it was a "toss-up" whether they would finish by the time they predicted. For the most part, participants were quite confident that they would meet their predictions: Confidence in meeting a predicted date and time was 74% for school assignments in one study, 84% in a second study, and 70% for household tasks. In each case, approximately 40% of the participants actually finished by the predicted time. As well as assessing judges' confidence in their "best guess" predictions, we used a fractile procedure (Lichtenstein, Fischhoff, & Phillips, 1982; Yates, 1990): Participants indicated times by which they were 50% certain they would finish their projects, 75% certain they would finish, and 99% certain they would finish (Buehler et al., 1995). Again, overconfidence was marked: Only 13% of the participants finished their academic projects by the time they reported as their 50% probability level, 19% finished by the time of their 75% probability level, and 45% finished by the time of their 99% probability level. The results for the 99% probability level are especially striking: Even when asked to make a highly conservative forecast, a prediction that they felt virtually certain that they would fulfill, students' confidence in their time estimates far exceeded their accomplishments.

Recall that the signature of the planning fallacy is the coincidence of an optimistic specific prediction with a more realistic general theory about past experiences and even other people's experiences. The same student participants who confidently believed that they would complete their current assignments well before the required date reported that they typically finished assignments later than they expected (68% of students admitted this) and generally just before the due date. A random telephone survey of Canadian taxpayers revealed that this pattern was not limited to students and their school assignments (Buehler et al., 1997). Those who were surveyed expected to mail their tax returns about a week earlier than they usually did; however, in accord with the planning fallacy, history repeated itself: on average, their reports of typical behavior in the past accurately matched present behavior, whereas their current predictions were markedly optimistic.

A COGNITIVE MODEL OF THE PLANNING FALLACY

The Inside versus the Outside View

What are the psychological mechanisms that underlie people's optimistic forecasts? And how do people segregate their general theories about their predictions (i.e., that they are usually unrealistic) from their specific expectations for an upcoming task? Our analysis begins with an anecdote about a group-authored textbook that was completed years later than expected – each of its authors was aware that such projects typically took years longer than planned, but nonetheless felt confident that the current project would be a pleasant exception. This ill-fated project was in many ways unexceptional, but has become famous as the initial case study for Kahneman and Tversky's (1979) inside versus outside analysis of the planning fallacy. This analysis builds on a perceptual metaphor of how people view a planned project. In the textbook example, the group of authors focused on the specific qualities of the current task, and seemed to look inside their representation of the developing project to assess its time course and likelihood of completion. The group of authors neglected, however, to look outside the specific project to evaluate the relevant distribution of comparable projects. More broadly, an inside or internal view of a task focuses on singular information: specific aspects of the target task that might lead to longer or shorter completion times. An outside or external view of the task focuses on distributional information: how the current task fits into the set of related tasks. Thus, the two general approaches to prediction differ primarily in whether individuals treat the target task as a unique case or as an instance of a category of similar problems.

For a number of reasons, people favor the inside perspective when developing plans and predictions (Kahneman & Lovallo, 1993; Kahneman & Tversky, 1979). People tend to generate their predictions by considering the unique features of the task at hand and constructing a scenario of their future progress on that task. This is, by and large, what *planning* means to most people: develop a series of steps that lead from the beginning to a successful conclusion of the project. In deciding how much work to take home for the weekend, for example, individuals may try to imagine when they will start a particular project and how many hours of actual working time they will require. They may also consider the other activities they have planned for the weekend and try to determine precisely when, where, and how they will find time to work on the project. They may even try to envision potential obstacles to completing the project, and how these obstacles will be overcome. Essentially, this internal approach to prediction involves sketching out a scenario that captures how the future project is likely to unfold. Several theorists have similarly noted the tendency to construct scenarios, narratives, or mental simulations as a basis for predicting the future (Dawes, 1988; Griffin, Dunning, & Ross, 1990; Johnson & Sherman,

1990; Kahneman & Lovallo, 1993; Kahneman & Tversky, 1982a; Klayman & Schoemaker, 1993; Ross & Buehler, 2001; Zukier, 1986).

People's completion estimates are likely to be overly optimistic if their forecasts are based exclusively on plan-based, future scenarios. A problem with the scenario approach is that people generally fail to appreciate the vast number of ways in which the future may unfold (Arkes, Faust, Guilmette, & Hart, 1988; Fischhoff, Slovic, & Lichtenstein, 1978; Hoch, 1985; Shaklee & Fischhoff, 1982). For instance, expert auto mechanics typically consider only a small subset of the possible faults that can occur in a car, and hence underestimate the probability of a breakdown (Fischhoff et al., 1978). Similarly, when individuals forecast personal events they often fail to consider alternatives to their favored scenario (Griffin et al., 1990; Hoch, 1985). Focusing on the target event (the successful completion of a set of plans) may lead a predictor to ignore or underweight the chances that some other event will occur. Indeed, developing a scenario leading to a given outcome seems to interfere with people's ability to generate scenarios that would yield alternative outcomes (Hoch, 1984; Koehler, 1991). When individuals are asked to predict based on realistic "best guess" scenarios, their forecasts are generally indistinguishable from those generated by "best case" scenarios (Griffin et al., 1990; Newby-Clark, Ross, Buehler, Koehler, & Griffin, 2000).

The act of scenario construction itself may lead people to exaggerate the likelihood of the scenario unfolding as envisioned. Individuals instructed to imagine hypothetical outcomes for events ranging from football games to presidential elections subsequently regard these outcomes as more likely (for reviews, see Johnson & Sherman, 1990; Koehler, 1991). In one study, for example, individuals who explained why they might succeed on an upcoming anagram task predicted that they would perform better than those who explained why they might fail (Sherman, Skov, Hervitz, & Stock, 1981). The implication of this research is straightforward: If people focus almost exclusively on their plans for successful task completion while generating predictions, they may convince themselves that an optimistic forecast is warranted.

One way to reduce the biases associated with scenario thinking (or the inside approach) is to incorporate relevant distributional information into prediction (Kahneman & Tversky, 1979). When individuals make predictions about everyday activities, the distributional information could either be their own past experiences (personal base rates) or the experiences of others (population base rates). The value of attending to both personal base rates (Osberg & Shrauger, 1986; Shrauger & Osberg, 1981) and population base rates (Dunning, Griffin, Milojkovic, & Ross, 1990; Epley & Dunning, 2000; Hoch, 1985; Vallone, Griffin, Lin, & Ross, 1990) has been demonstrated in several studies examining the accuracy and confidence of people's predictions about their own future behavior. In the Osberg and Shrauger (1986) study, for example, individuals who were instructed to focus on their own previous experiences forecast their activities during the next 2 months (e.g., whether they would skip a class, get high on drugs, change their hairstyle, go to a movie) more accurately than control subjects. Attending to past experience is particularly useful when base rates are extreme; that is, when the behaviors have been either very frequent or very infrequent in the past (Dunning et al., 1990; Shrauger, Mariano, & Walter, 1998; Shrauger, Ram, Greninger, & Mariano, 1996).

Obstacles to Using Past Experiences

Despite the predictive value of past experiences, our findings suggest that people neglect them while forming predictions. Why might this be so? One answer was suggested previously: prediction, by its very nature, elicits a focus on the future rather than the past, and this future orientation may prevent individuals from looking backward. However, a failure to use personal base rates need not always result from inattention to the past. People may sometimes attend to their past, but nevertheless fail to incorporate this information into their predictions because it doesn't seem relevant. People may have difficulty extracting an appropriate set of past experiences; the various instances seem so different from each other that individuals cannot compare them meaningfully (Kahneman & Lovallo, 1993; Kahneman & Tversky, 1979). As a British rugby-player-turned-commentator noted, "Each game is unique, and this one is no different [than] any other."

We suggest that people often make attributions that diminish the relevance of past experiences to their current task (Ross & Fletcher, 1985). People are probably most inclined to deny the significance of their personal history when they dislike its apparent implications (e.g., that a project will take longer than they hope). If they are reminded of a past episode that could challenge their optimistic plans, they may invoke attributions that render the experience uninformative for the present forecast. This analysis is consistent with evidence that individuals are inclined to explain away negative personal outcomes (for reviews, see Miller & Ross, 1975; Snyder & Higgins, 1988; Taylor & Brown, 1988). People's use of others' experiences (population base rates) is also limited by perceptual and attributional factors: A focus on the future reduces the salience of others' experiences, and the tendency to attribute others' outcomes to their own dispositions (Jones & Nisbett, 1972) limits the inferential value of others' experiences. Furthermore, our understanding of other people's experiences is typically associated with uncertainty about what actually happened; consequently, we can readily cast doubt on the generalizability of those experiences. To quote Douglas Adams, "Human beings, who are almost unique in having the ability to learn from the experience of others, are also remarkable for their apparent disinclination to do so."

EXAMINING COGNITIVE PROCESSES

In our studies, we have included "think-aloud" procedures to record the "on-line" narratives of participants as they estimated their completion times for various tasks, most of which had specific deadlines. We instructed respondents to say aloud every thought or idea that came to mind while predicting when they would finish an upcoming project. We later analyzed the verbal protocols for evidence that people focus on plan-based scenarios for the task at hand, rather than distributional information such as their previous experiences. In a typical study of academic and home projects (Buehler et al., 1994, Study 3), the majority of respondents' thoughts were directed toward the future ($M = 74\%$). The participants focused overwhelmingly on their plans for the current project, for the most part describing scenarios in which they finished the task without problems arising (only 3% of respondents' thoughts included potential impediments); their verbal protocols revealed an almost total neglect of other kinds of information, including their own past experiences (7% of thoughts) or others' experiences with similar projects (1%). We replicated this pattern of results a number of times using written thought listing measures instead of think-aloud procedures, and collecting retrospective rather than on-line measures of thoughts.

In another experiment (Buehler et al., 1994, Study 4), we examined the impact of asking people to focus on memories of relevant past experiences. Participants predicted when they would finish a standard, 1-hour computer assignment. Participants in the Recall condition reported on their previous experiences with similar assignments just before making their predictions. They indicated how far before the deadlines they had typically finished school assignments similar to the present one. Control participants were not asked any questions concerning their past experiences until after they had reported their predictions. In both conditions, participants remembered finishing the majority of their previous projects very close to the relevant deadlines. Participants underestimated their actual completion times in the Recall condition as well as in the standard Control condition, and the degree of underestimation did not differ between conditions. Even in the Recall condition, only 12% of participants reported thinking about past experiences when making their current plans (versus 2% in the Control condition). Again, this pattern has been replicated in several other studies, indicating that attention to and awareness of the past is not enough to make the past relevant to the future.

If an inside or scenario-based approach to prediction leads to an optimistic bias, then an even greater focus on detailed planning should exacerbate this bias. In two recent studies, participants identified tasks they intended to complete in the near future (school assignments in one study and Christmas shopping in another) and predicted when they would finish (Buehler & Griffin, 2000a). In both studies we instructed a subset of the participants, those in the "implemental condition" to formulate highly specific plans for completing their target task. These participants considered and described in detail when, where, and how they would carry out the task. This implemental focus produced highly optimistic predictions. In the Christmas shopping study, for example, participants, in the "implemental condition" predicted they would complete their designated shopping list more than a week before Christmas Day, whereas control participants expected to finish approximately 4 days before Christmas. Follow-up interviews revealed that participants in both conditions finished their designated shopping list only 3 days before Christmas. A similar pattern was obtained for the study involving school assignments. Participants in the implemental condition expected to finish their target school assignment, on average, approximately 2 full days before the deadline, whereas control participants expected to finish approximately 1 full day before the deadline. In both conditions, however, participants finished their assignments, on average, less than half a day before the deadline. In accord with the assumption that the planning fallacy is due in part to an over-reliance on scenario-based planning, increasing the focus on specific plans produced more optimistic forecasts; because this focus did not affect actual completion times it exacerbated the optimistic bias in prediction

A second implication of the inside–outside perceptual metaphor is that predictors who are not personally involved in the task are more likely to see the project from an outside perspective. Indeed, anecdotally it seems that the planning fallacy vanishes when individuals forecast other people's task completions. We are not surprised when our colleagues' journal reviews are late or when their house renovations take twice the time that they predicted. When explaining failures to meet previous predictions, observers may see actors as authors of their own misfortune whereas actors see themselves as the victims of circumstances. Furthermore, it may be difficult for observers to imagine exactly how and when another individual will complete a task. If observers cannot construct future scenarios with confidence, they may rely on available sources of distributional information, including the other individual's previous performance.

In our initial study of actor–observer differences in planning (Buehler et al., 1994, Study 5), observers were each yoked to a participant (actor) who predicted the time to completion for a computer-based tutorial assignment. Observers received the following items of information concerning their target actor: demographic information provided by the actor (sex, age, academic major), the instructions the actor received for completing the computer assignment, the actor's deadline for the assignment (1 or 2 weeks), and the actor's self-predicted completion time. Two additional sources of information that had been available to the actors at the time of prediction were (1) their thoughts about completing the assignment and (2) their memories of relevant previous experiences. In one condition (Thoughts), observers received the thoughts reported by the actor as he or she generated a completion estimate. In a second condition (Memories), observers received the actor's reports of previous completion times. In a third condition (Thoughts and Memories Combined) observers received both sources of information in counterbalanced order. After reviewing the information, observers tried to estimate as accurately as possible when the target actor would finish the assignment and also wrote their thoughts as they arrived at their predictions.

Whereas the actors' predictions were optimistically biased (by about $1\frac{1}{2}$ days), the observers' predictions were pessimistically biased (by about the same amount); the pessimistic bias was marginally stronger for participants exposed to the actors' past experiences (i.e., the Memories and Combined conditions) presumably because the actors' recollections of the past were more pessimistic than their current outcomes in this particular study. Furthermore, the observers' predictions were much more sensitive to differing deadlines than were the actors'. Finally, the observers were much less likely to report using the actors' plans to create their own estimate (even in the Thoughts condition, only 37% of observers described the actors' plans compared to 93% of actors who described their plans in their thought listing), and much more likely to report thinking about potential future problems, the actors' past problems, and the actors' dispositions.

Recall that a second reason that people may fail to incorporate the lessons of past experiences into their future predictions is that people may "fence off" the past through attributional means. To test the role of attributional processes in the planning fallacy, we asked participants to recall an occasion when they had failed to complete a task by the time they had originally anticipated, and then to recall a similar prediction failure experienced by a close acquaintance (Buehler et al., 1994, Study 3). Next, we asked them to explain why each of the two tasks was not finished by the expected time. The reasons participants reported for their own lateness were more external (environmentally caused), transitory (time limited), and specific (limited to the specific task) than the reasons they provided for similar tardiness by close acquaintances. Participants attributed their own lateness to such rare events as their computer monitor "frying" while they were typing their final English essay whereas others' failures seemed to reflect enduring personal problems with time management. In a related study (Buehler et al., 1994, Study 4), participants who either succeeded or failed in meeting their predictions rated their own reasons for the success or failure. Participants who finished late rated their reasons as significantly more transitory and specific than participants who finished on time. Both studies reveal that people interpret their own tardiness in a manner that makes it seem unique and unlikely to recur.

THE GENERALITY OF THE PLANNING FALLACY

Individual Differences Research

Ambrose Bierce, in the Devil's Dictionary, defined the future as "that period of time in which our affairs prosper, our friends are true, and happiness is assured." Samuel Johnson noted that marrying a second time represented the "triumph of hope over experience". Both witticisms capture a certain quality of human nature: people – at least, some people – look at the future through rose-colored glasses. Daily life and psychological studies provide plenty of reasons to believe that optimism about the future is one important dimension along which people differ. Some people seem to awaken each day with the firm belief that every problem encountered hides an opportunity; other people awaken with the equally firm belief that every opportunity encountered hides a problem. Perhaps, then, the planning fallacy is not a general phenomenon, but limited only to the most optimistic and hopeful of our participants. We explored this possibility using a number of well-known individual difference measures to assess our participants' levels of dispositional optimism (Scheier & Carver, 1985), self-esteem (Rosenberg, 1965), and non-clinical depression (Beck, Ward, Mendelson, Mock, & Erbaugh, 1961). In a number of student samples, we related such well-validated individual difference measures to recollections of past completion times, predictions for and thoughts about future tasks, and the actual completion times for those tasks (Buehler & Griffin, 2000a). We have been surprised by the lack of relation between any of these measures and our measures of recall, prediction, or thought focus.

In the same studies, we also measured participants' level of dispositional *procrastination*, the tendency to delay starting projects (Ferrari, Johnson, & McGown, 1995; Lay, 1986). Procrastination is relevant to studies of the planning fallacy for two somewhat contradictory reasons: Procrastinators typically finish their projects later than non-procrastinators, and they are aware they have problems with time management. Thus, whether procrastination moderates the planning fallacy depends on the relative effect of procrastination on behavior and prediction. In the domains of academic predictions and Christmas shopping predictions, we discovered that behavior and prediction were equally affected by personal tendencies: Procrastinators (Lay, 1986) reported typical completion times that were later than non-procrastinators, made less optimistic predictions than non-procrastinators, and completed the tasks later than non-procrastinators. As a result, the optimistic bias was equal between groups. The costs were not equal, however; procrastinators suffered more because the average procrastinator completed the academic projects after the official deadline. Unique among the various groups we have studied, the procrastinators also showed a much reduced tendency to focus exclusively on the future when making predictions; almost 40% of their thoughts were on the past, presumably because of the salience and consistency of their past failures to initiate projects promptly. However, even self-admitted chronic procrastinators do not fully achieve the outside viewpoint. We succeeded in obtaining an outside viewpoint only by turning to real outsiders – observer participants. Recall that when we asked observers to predict actors' outcomes, they evidenced a complete lack of future focus and no optimistic bias.

Cross-Cultural Research

The cognitive analysis of the planning fallacy implies that the phenomenon may also be robust across cultures. Japanese culture provides a particularly interesting test case for studying the optimistic prediction bias. Research to date suggests that Japanese adults show little or no self-enhancing biases in self-evaluation (and in fact, sometimes show a self-effacing bias) (Heine & Lehman, 1995). However, the level of "cognitive" overconfidence, as revealed in studies using general knowledge questions, is as great in Japan as in the United States (Lee, Yates, Shinotsuka, Singh, Onglatco, Yen, Gupta, & Bhatnagar, 1995).

We (Buehler, Griffin, Otsubo, Lehman, & Heine, 2000) distributed identical questionnaires (except for the Japanese translation) to participants at two universities: one Japanese and one Canadian. Participants named a school assignment that was due in the next 4 weeks, reported best-guess predictions for that project, described their thoughts while they made their predictions, reported when they typically finished similar assignments in the past, and later reported when they actually finished the target assignment. Both Japanese and Canadian participants showed the prototypical dissociation between their current predictions and their reports of typical completion times. Participants from both universities expected to finish the assignment nearly 2 full days before its deadline, despite reporting that they typically finished similar assignments less than 1 day before deadline. In fact the target assignments for this study were finished, on average, about half a day before the deadline. The resulting optimistic bias in prediction was slightly (although not significantly) greater for the Japanese than for the Canadian students. Furthermore, in a longer-term pilot study of summer-long research essays, the Japanese students were markedly optimistic – predicting that their essays would be finished 10 days before the deadline, but completing the assigments only 1 day beforehand (and recalling that similar tasks had been completed about 1 day before the deadline).

The thought listing measure also showed a very similar pattern across cultures. Consistent with previous findings, most participants (70%) focused on their plans for completing the task, whereas only about one-quarter of the participants (26%) referred to their past experiences (which implied that a more conservative prediction was in order), and very few participants contemplated the potential problems and delays they might encounter. The Canadian and Japanese samples did not differ significantly in their use of any of the thought categories.

Finally, to examine attributional processes, we asked participants to describe a past prediction failure of their own and that of a school friend and then explain why each of these had occurred. Once again, we found a moderate self-serving bias in Canadians' attributions for failures to complete tasks by the expected time: They reported causes that were more external, transitory, and specific than the causes they reported for a friend's late completion. For the Japanese students, however, the opposite pattern emerged: They attributed their own prediction failures to causes that were more internal, stable, and global than those of a friend. Thus, for Japanese students, there was no evidence of self-serving attribution biases that might "explain away" past prediction failures; in fact, the Japanese students seemed to take more responsibility for their own past failures than they assigned to others. This difference in attributional response raises the intriguing possibility that Japanese participants may be more influenced by reminders of past failures than Western participants.

MOTIVATION AND THE PLANNING FALLACY

The Role of Incentives

The Japanese data indicate that the planning fallacy can occur even when people are not motivated to deny their responsibility for past prediction failures. However, the findings do not eliminate the possibility that motivated reasoning (Kunda, 1990) could contribute to the phenomenon – that is, when finishing early is desirable, people may strive to convince themselves of the plausibility of that outcome. To the extent that the motivation to finish early affects prediction more than it affects actual completion, the planning fallacy may be accentuated. Consider, for example, the Canadian taxpayers surveyed by Buehler et al. (1997). Respondents with an incentive to submit their returns early (i.e., who were expecting refunds) predicted that they would send in their tax returns about 10 days earlier than non-motivated participants, but managed to mail them in only about 3 days earlier. As a result, the optimistic bias was markedly greater for the motivated respondents. Furthermore, the participants expecting a refund appeared to give less weight to their past experiences in making their predictions: reports of past completion times were less related to predicted completion times for participants who expected a refund than for participants who did not.

A follow-up laboratory experiment using a word-generation task replicated the incentive effect on prediction and shed further light on the mediating cognitive mechanisms: Monetary incentives for early completion of the task led to more optimistically biased predictions, increased attention to detailed future plans, and reduced attention to relevant past experiences. In other words, the incentives appeared to elicit the very pattern of cognitive processes that constitute the planning fallacy – a focus on singular information (plan-based scenarios) at the expense of relevant distributional information (past experiences).

We also examined whether incentives for a speedy finish lead observers to abandon their usual outside view and embrace an inside perspective on planning and prediction. In recent studies (Buehler & Griffin, 2000b), we offered observers cash incentives based directly on a target individuals' ability to complete a task (a take-home project that we assigned to them in one study and an upcoming school assignment in another study) quickly. These motivated observers made predictions that were as optimistically biased as the predictions generated by the target individuals themselves, and more biased than the predictions generated by observers without an incentive. Furthermore, thought-listing data revealed that the incentives affected observers' predictions, in part, because they prompted observers to rely more heavily on the target individuals' future plans for the task and less heavily on the targets' (or their own)

262   Roger Buehler, Dale Griffin, and Michael Ross

past experiences. These findings again suggest that the cognitive mechanisms underlying the planning fallacy can operate in the service of motivational forces.

When Optimistic Predictions Are Adaptive

We suggest that people overweight their specific plans about a given future project and underweight more general or distributional information, leading to a strong tendency toward overly optimistic predictions. We find that planning processes are often more directly related to predictions than to actual behavior. This does not mean that planning processes are unrelated to behavior – in the limit, the complete absence of plans would make project completion impossible. Completion times can be influenced through any of three mechanisms: planning (determining the series of steps necessary to achieve a goal), mental simulation (vividly imagining a coherent scenario or story about how the steps will unfold), and the very act of making the prediction (privately or publicly estimating a completion time). Plans are useful, even necessary, in guiding behavior but tend to be overweighted relative to other sources of information in prediction. Mental simulations may increase the overweighting of future plans, but they may also work to bring behavior more in line with people's goals (Gollwitzer, 1999; Gollwitzer & Brandstatter, 1997; Roese, 1994; Taylor et al., 1998). Optimistic predictions themselves may also affect behavior, either through self-fulfilling prophecy effects (e.g., Johnson & Sherman, 1990; Sherman, 1980), or because the predictions serve as guiding goals and standards (Locke & Latham, 1990). Even if projects are typically completed later than predicted, they may be completed earlier than if no detailed plans or predictions were made.

We suggest that whether (or when) the planning fallacy is adaptive depends on the reason for the past failure of similar projects. If a class of projects typically runs late because of relatively controllable factors (e.g., lack of organization, attention, or motivation), then the current effort may well benefit from an optimistic prediction. The presence of an optimistic standard or goal (Heath, Larrick, & Wu, 1999; Locke & Latham, 1990) may increase motivation to at least come close to the goal, leading to an earlier outcome. However, if a class of projects typically runs late because of relatively uncontrollable factors (e.g., the mechanical failure of a needed computer or photocopier, the sudden arrival of a visiting relative or influenza epidemic, an unexpected delay because of a different project running late), then the current effort will be unlikely to benefit from an optimistic prediction.

In a series of experiments we manipulated participants' predictions by anchoring them on more or less optimistic values and thus explored whether – or more precisely, when – optimistic predictions in themselves are functional (Buehler & Griffin, 1996). The specific anchoring manipulations varied across studies, from drawing a card to sliding a pointer along a numbered time line, but each one provided participants with an ostensibly random starting point that was either optimistic or pessimistic. Participants were then asked to adjust from this starting point to communicate their predictions for a particular project. In each study, the anchoring manipulation yielded a strong effect on predictions, allowing us to investigate whether the completion times would follow predictions. Studies also varied in the complexity of the target task. For example, in our initial study we asked participants to predict when they would complete a 1-hour computer tutorial required for their Introductory Psychology classes. This defined the simple and controllable end of the task dimension: Once participants showed up for the tutorial, it was entirely under their control whether they stayed to complete it within the hour. On the other end of the task dimension were more complex tasks such as completing income tax returns or school assignments that were vulnerable to outside influences and hence not completely under the actor's control.

We expected that participants induced to make particularly optimistic predictions would take these predictions to heart. Using these predictions as guiding standards, they would tend to start their assignments earlier. However, according to our analysis, the link between predictions and behavior should decrease as the task becomes longer and more complex. In fact, for the simplest task (the computer tutorial), participants exposed to the optimistic anchor predicted that they would finish their assignments 5 days earlier than those exposed to the pessimistic anchor, and did finish about 5 days earlier (although both groups showed a substantial optimistic bias). For the tax return task, participants exposed to the optimistic anchor predicted that they would send in their returns almost 20 days earlier than those exposed to the pessimistic anchor, started the task some 18 days earlier, but completed the task only 5 days earlier (a non-significant difference between conditions). In other complex tasks we examined (e.g., a library research project, a class assignment), the effects of prediction anchoring on completion times averaged about zero. It seems that the beneficial effects of optimistic predictions on completion times may be limited to tasks that are self-contained, temporally compact, and isolated from outside interruptions. Although optimistic predictions may provide the impetus to get action started, their impact appears to diminish over the course of extensive, long-term projects that are vulnerable to interruptions and delays caused by external influences.

The problem of identifying conditions under which optimistic expectations to complete a project determine completion times is reminiscent of the classic social psychological problem of identifying when attitudes and associated behavioral intentions affect behavior (Ajzen, 1991; Eagley & Chaiken, 1993; Fishbein & Ajzen, 1975). Two points of contact between research on attitudes and our analysis of the planning fallacy are especially noteworthy. First, an active but still controversial question in attitude research is when and how often past behavior predicts future behavior independent of attitudes and intentions (Oulette & Wood, 1998; Sheeran, Orbell, & Trafimow, 1999). Second, both the actual and perceived controllability of the task have been identified as determinants of intention–behavior consistency (Ajzen, 1991; Ajzen & Madden, 1986; Schifter & Ajzen, 1985). Thus, for some kinds of personal projects, lessons from attitude research may help to distinguish situations in which optimistic biases are "self-correcting" – that is, when strong intentions to finish early actually lead to early completions – from situations in which past experiences are the best predictors of completion times. However, for large-scale organizational projects, such as the mega-projects we began with, a forecaster cannot control the outcome unless he or she can fully dictate the resources available to the project. Similarly, many personal projects are subject to factors that are beyond the control of a person's best intentions and efforts. For such projects, bias reduction techniques ("debiasing") must target the optimistic predictions themselves. We next sketch out some particular barriers to intention–behavior consistency in personal projects, and then describe a series of studies on debiasing optimistic predictions that indicate the difficulty of reducing the planning fallacy in intuitive prediction.

The Rocky Road from Intentions to Task Completion

Attitude researchers long ago identified the match between the predicted and actual "object of judgment" to be a key determinant of attitude–behavior consistency (LaPiere, 1934; Lord, Lepper, & Mackie, 1984). The construal problem faced by a planner is even more daunting. What will the target task actually look like day by day? What goals and values will be most salient? How will the planner's emotions and motivations change over the course of the project? What other tasks might intervene, and how will they affect the perceived importance of the target task?

The analysis of temporal construal offered by Liberman and Trope (1998; Trope & Liberman, 2000) suggests that distant tasks (in time) are analyzed at a higher level of abstraction than are tasks close at hand. Thus, a student considering an honors' research project from a year's distance may construe the task as a problem of finding a good problem, getting to work on collecting data, and budgeting plenty of time for statistical analysis. In contrast, a student considering the same project from the distance of only 1 or 2 weeks may be more likely to construe the task as competing for a professor's attention, searching for appropriate reference material, and booking laboratory rooms at a convenient time. In general, a more detailed and low-level construal of the task highlights difficulties, and so predictions and judgments made at a more distant time should tend to be more optimistic. Both the tendency to construe distant events at a high level of abstraction and the associated relation between temporal distance and optimism has been confirmed in a number of experiments (Liberman & Trope, 1998). This suggests an intriguing avenue of investigation for debiasing through encouraging more detailed, lower-level construals of projects.

Another difficulty in matching predicted intentions and actual behavior is the problem of emotional construal. A planner faces a double inference problem:

(1) How to account for the effect of emotional states during the project period; and (2) How to adjust for the contaminating effects of current moods and emotions on the planning process. A person may anticipate that as the promised completion date looms, she or he will feel strongly committed to the goal of finishing early, give the project high priority, and so forth. Over time, however, people are likely to experience unforeseen changes in their hedonic states as a result of such basic hedonic processes as adaptation. Thus, the feeling of urgency associated with anticipated failure becomes less intense as the days go by, and a delayed completion – at first treated as a painful "loss" – gradually becomes the status quo. For example, an author may initially believe that he will be terribly embarrassed if his manuscript is not completed by a promised date; however, as he slips further and further behind his predicted pace, his frame of reference may change so that he feels only relief when his manuscript is completed within a year of the suggested day. That people may experience such unanticipated hedonic shifts is consistent with demonstrations of the problems people have in anticipating how their own feelings, preferences, and desires will change over time (Kahneman & Snell, 1992; Gilbert, Pinel, Wilson, Blumber, & Wheatley, Chapter 16, 2001, this volume; Wilson, Wheatley, Meyers, Gilbert, & Axsom, 2000; Loewenstein & Frederick, 1997; for a review, see also Loewenstein & Schkade, 1999).

Consider Loewenstein's (1996) concept of the "empathy gap" that exists between different hedonic states. People with a full stomach underestimate the difficulty of dieting when hungry, presumably because their intention to diet is very strong when they are sated. Despite having considerable experience with failed diets, people do not adjust for the low validity of these predictions due to the empathy gap. Similarly, people who are not sexually aroused underestimate the likelihood of failing to use condoms, presumably because their intentions are strong and they do not realize that fluctuating levels of sexual arousal can lower the validity of such intentions. We suspect that people possess general theories about how their task-relevant hedonic experiences change over time (e.g., "By the time the kids are in bed, I'm often too exhausted to finish the things I want to do"; "I usually spend too much time on the fun parts and avoid the unpleasant parts"; "Once I start browsing the newsgroup, I'm lost for the evening"), but this "set-based" information about the effect of hedonic states on the predictive validity of plans is ignored in favor of a "case-based" evaluation of current feelings and intentions.

Elster and Loewenstein (1992) liken people's future selves to their children at college; although people believe that such selves will continue to behave in accordance with present priorities and values, they tend to be less predictable and more open to temptation than we imagine. This analogy fits some additional findings from our comparison of planning biases in Japanese and Canadian students (Buehler et al., 2000). Participants in both cultures were asked to rate the strength of the emotional reactions they would feel if they failed to complete the task by the time they predicted; later, we asked the tardy members of those groups (the majority) how they actually felt. Members of both cultural groups significantly overestimated how badly they would feel about their prediction failure, consistent with a general "intensity bias" in affective forecasting (Buehler & McFarland, in press).

A key aspect of the intensity bias in affective prediction, like the planning fallacy itself, is that people know *about* but do not learn *from* the past. Why should students with poor grades overpredict how bad they will feel, and why should students with good grades overpredict how good they will feel – given that people have experienced the same type of outcomes many times in the past? More poignantly, why should people expect winter holidays to produce warmer feelings than they actually do, given a rich past diet of disappointment (Buehler & MacFarland, in press)? Why should both our Japanese and Canadian students overestimate how sad and guilty they will feel if they fail to complete a task by a predicted date (Buehler et al., 2000)? If one reason is that people neglect the lessons of the past when making case-specific predictions in the "inside mode," then encouraging them to think more distributionally may reduce the extremity bias in hedonic prediction. Consistent with this reasoning, Buehler and McFarland (in press) found that the intensity bias was reduced in participants who were encouraged to think about a set of relevant past experiences.

The "inside–outside perspective" account of the planning fallacy implies that people focus on the task at hand and neglect background factors. People may also exaggerate the emotional impact of a future event (such as failing to complete a task when promised) because their predictions are focused on that event alone and fail to account for the mitigating effects of the many other events, internal and external, that affect a person at any given time. Wilson et al. (2000) term this a *focalism bias*, and Schkade and Kahneman (1998) describe a similar phenomenon they call a *focusing illusion*. Focalism may play a dual role in the planning fallacy: First, the focus on a single case may prevent recognition of the time taken up by rival activities; second, the neglect of the background distractions created by competing activities may lead the predictor to exaggerate both the pleasure that results from completing the task on time and the pain that results from missing the predicted date. When background factors are made salient by asking participants to consider the entire field of events that might occur at a given point in their lives, affective forecasts become less extreme and thus more realistic (Wilson et al., 2000). Such manipulations might similarly improve task-completion forecasts. It is not clear whether the manipulation truly induces an outside perspective, but it does broaden the planner's field of view to include a wider range of background information and thus may weaken the reliance on specific plans for the task at hand.

Focalism undoubtedly causes as many problems with predictions of task motivation as with predictions of emotional or hedonic response. The act of task prediction necessarily leads the planner to focus on one particular task among many, and this may lead the planner to exaggerate the ongoing importance of the target task. When people make plans to lose weight, improve their grades in college, or complete their income tax returns early this year, they may well overestimate how much their current motivation to complete the task will be present throughout the project period, and may also overestimate how salient their plans and intentions will remain throughout the project period.

This analysis suggests two ways to bring behavior in line with predictions: ensure that the original level of motivation is maintained throughout the project period and enhance the salience of goal-directed plans throughout the same period. Pham and Taylor (1999) instructed participants to imagine when, where, and how they would study for an upcoming exam in order to achieve a high grade, and carry out this exercise of imagination every morning during the week leading up to the exam. Naturally, most students are motivated to do well, plan to do well, and intend to act in ways that allow them to do well. Carrying out the imagination exercise served to link students' motivations, plans, and intentions to their actual everyday behavior, and therefore led to improved exam performance. Similarly, in an investigation of the planning fallacy students were trained to envision themselves performing each of the steps needed to complete a school-related project by the time they had predicted (Taylor et al., 1998). Again participants rehearsed these simulations each day of the week during which they carried out the project. The exercise increased the proportion of students who finished by the predicted time from 14% (in a control condition) to 41%.

Gollwitzer (1999) has used similar manipulations at the time of prediction to make goal-related intentions and plans more mentally accessible in the relevant environments. He demonstrated that participants with a challenging goal (e.g., to finish a writing project during the winter vacation) were more likely to meet that goal if they were prompted to generate implementation intentions that specified precisely when, where, and how they would accomplish the goal. When the specified opportunity to act on their plans is encountered, people are more likely to initiate and carry out the actions required to meet their goals. Gollwitzer also reviewed a number of related studies in the area of health promotion showing that making vivid, detailed plans can increase the likelihood of self-protective behaviors such as breast self-examination (e.g., Orbell, Hodgkins, & Sheeran, 1997). Note that in such studies, the relative effect of an implemental focus on prediction versus behavior is not important; as long as the outcome is more likely to occur, the manipulation is successful. In the planning fallacy studies, in contrast, virtually all participants complete the task – the critical phenomenon is the match between predictions and completion times. As noted previously, our studies on school projects and holiday shopping found that requiring participants to generate detailed implementation intentions affected only predictions without bringing behavior into line. A challenge for future research is to identify factors that alter the impact of plans and mental simulations on behavior relative to their impact on prediction.

DEBIASING THE PLANNING FALLACY

Although the motivating effects of optimism may be worth the cost of mis-prediction in at least some situations (Armor & Taylor, 1998), there are many cases when accurate prediction is vital to success, such as when a new release of software is promised by a certain date. DeMarco (1982), a respected consultant in the software engineering industry, defines an *estimate* as "the most optimistic prediction that has a non-zero probability of coming true" (p. 14). In his field of specialty, optimistic predictions are the norm despite well-known rules of thumb such as the 90% rule (the last 10% of a project takes 90% of the resources). DeMarco estimates that 15% of software projects are never completed (justifying the term *vaporware*), and completed projects commonly cost two or three times as much as originally budgeted. For example, a recent General Accounting Office report on U.S. military equipment procurement concluded that only 1% of major military purchases involving high technology were delivered on time and on budget. What does our analysis offer in the way of suggestions for debiasing optimistic predictions themselves? We have investigated three approaches that follow from the analyses offered here: (1) reducing the dominance of the singular over the distributional approach by eliciting predictions for aggregate sets of events rather than single cases; (2) reducing the impact of "planning for success" by encouraging the consideration of alternative, more pessimistic scenarios; and (3) linking the past to the future by requiring participants to explain how past experiences might be relevant to the current task.

The first debiasing approach, eliciting aggregate frequencies rather than single-case estimates, enjoys a substantial track record of success. Cumulative representations and responses reduce the conjunction fallacy in within-subject designs (Tversky & Kahneman, 1983) and the unpacking effect predicted by support theory (Tversky & Koehler, 1994), perhaps because the aggregate set serves as a reminder of the set-inclusion relationships that are the foundation of logic and probability theory (Griffin & Tversky, 1992; Kahneman & Tversky, 1982b). Thus, when predicting a set of future tasks, people may be attentive to their own set of past experiences or to the set of others' experiences – that is, people may take a more outside perspective on the prediction process.

In our first two studies examining aggregate frequency judgments (Griffin & Buehler, 1999), participants listed 10 upcoming projects, provided best-guess completion times for each, estimated the *probability* that each project would be completed by the relevant best-guess date, and estimated how *many* of the 10 tasks would be completed by the relevant dates. In the third study, participants described a single project, estimated the probability that the project would be completed by the relevant best-guess date, and estimated how many of 10 similar tasks would be completed by relevant best-guess dates. In each study, the single-case probability and aggregate frequency estimates were counterbalanced for order. The results of all three studies failed to support the claim that frequency judgments are unbiased and follow normative principles (Cosmides & Tooby, 1996; Gigerenzer, 1991, 1994, 1998). Predictions, whether made for items or aggregates, were markedly over-optimistic and failed to discriminate between people who were more or less successful in task completion. The average item-specific confidence rating (73%) was almost identical to the expected aggregate frequency (7.2 out of 10), and the on-time completion rate was equally poor in both conditions (about 40% overall). Across all studies, only about 8% of the participants met or exceeded their predictions for the number of tasks they would complete.

Why was this manipulation such a failure? In accord with our analysis of the planning fallacy, the rich real-world prediction problems involved in these studies (e.g., "When will I buy a new bike? " "When will I get my car repaired?") may have masked the essentially statistical nature of such predictions. It takes a rather sophisticated view of the prediction process to see how a given task is like a "sample" from a population of tasks, and how the weight given to one's plans must be moderated by considerations of the "predictive validity" of one's plans in general (cf. Nisbett, Krantz, Jepson, & Kunda, 1983, Chapter 28, this volume). Instead, it seems that participants assessed the average "plan strength" for each problem, an inside estimation, and then calculated the average strength of all the plans in the set rather than starting with an outside view of the set of tasks.

The second debiasing manipulation, which involved the consideration of alternative scenarios (Newby-Clark et al., 2000), might look like a "sure thing" given the successful use of related techniques to reduce other judgmental biases such as overconfidence in knowledge and prediction (Koriat, Lichtenstein, & Fischhoff, 1980; Griffin et al., 1990; Hoch, 1985; Lord, Lepper, & Preston, 1984). Indeed, in many business and organizational contexts, where uncertain and uncontrollable events present serious difficulties for long-term planning, techniques involving multiple scenarios have become popular forecasting tools (for reviews, see Bunn, & Salo, 1993; Schoemaker, 1993). However, the failure of this technique in our studies bears testimony to the robustness of the planning fallacy and of the intuitive appeal of using best-case scenarios to guide time prediction. Participants' best-guess predictions closely resembled predictions based on their most optimistic scenarios and were far more optimistic than those based on their pessimistic scenarios; furthermore, participants generally rated their optimistic scenarios as much more plausible than pessimistic ones, presumably justifying their neglect of the pessimistic scenarios. Even when participants were instructed to create pessimistic scenarios that were highly plausible, they continued to neglect these scenarios despite the fact that they could have resulted in increased accuracy. These findings also highlight, once again, the costs of basing forecasts on the plausibility of an imagined scenario: In this research, the very scenarios that seemed most plausible (the optimistic ones) were also the least accurate.

Our third debiasing manipulation required participants to link their past experiences with their specific plans for an upcoming task. In this "recall-relevance" manipulation, participants first indicated the date and time they would finish a computer assignment if they finished it as far before its deadline as they typically completed assignments (Buehler et al., 1994, Study 4). Second, they described a plausible scenario – based on their past experiences – that would result in their completing the computer assignment at their typical time. This procedure should prevent participants from either ignoring past experiences with similar tasks or discounting the relevance of those experiences. After writing the hypothetical scenario, participants made predictions for the computer assignment. For this task, at least, the recall-relevance manipulation successfully eliminated the usual optimistic bias. Although this effect may have been an artifact of the relatively heavy-handed manipulation, it is worth remembering that the similarly heavy-handed demand for participants to construct a pessimistic scenario (Newby-Clark et al., 2000) utterly failed to reduce optimistic predictions. Although the mechanism is not entirely clear, the recall-relevance manipulation serves as our current debiasing champion and deserves a trial in applied fields.

CONCLUDING REMARKS

Everyone makes predictions about the future, paupers and princes alike. Tony Blair, British Prime Minister, illustrated this in his own paradoxical manner, proclaiming "I don't make predictions. I never have, and I never will." Problems of planning and prediction are fascinating to research because of their relevance to our own daily lives. Beyond this, there are at least three important reasons why this area of research is so close to our hearts. First, it provides a clear and simple testing ground for many of the theoretical statements developed in the heuristics and biases tradition. Here, there is no need to import any theory of probability or logic – accuracy and bias can be measured by the calendar and the clock. Second, improving the accuracy of project forecasting has the potential to provide huge applied benefits. Third, and most generally, the problem of integrating the memories of the past into our understanding of the present and our expectations for the future is a central human challenge that we all face in every domain of our social lives. Inside the planning fallacy we can discover insights about how hope, fear, disappointment, and reason combine to shape predictions and many other expectations for the future.

15. Probability Judgment across Cultures

J. Frank Yates, Ju-Whei Lee, Winston R. Sieck, Incheol Choi, and Paul C. Price

Consider the following general knowledge question:

Is jute (circle one):
   (a) a cereal crop
   or
   (b) a fiber crop?
Now indicate the probability (50–100%) that your chosen answer is correct:
_____ %

In a series of studies, George Wright and Lawrence Phillips, along with several collaborators, posed questions like these to respondents in Britain and in various Southeast Asian sites, including Hong Kong, Malaysia, and Indonesia. Figure 15.1 displays illustrative results from one of those studies (Wright et al., 1978) in the form of *calibration curves* (see also Phillips & Wright, 1977; Wright & Phillips, 1980). The abscissa shows the various probability judgments the participants rendered, rounded to the nearest 10%. The ordinate displays the corresponding proportions of correct answers. Consider, for example, the open point on the British curve above assessed probability 0.7. It indicates that, when the British respondents reported that they were 70% sure that their chosen answers were correct, about 62% of the time those answers really were correct. When judged probabilities tend to exceed proportions correct, the judgments are said to be *overconfident*. Overconfidence is the most common and frequently discussed finding in general-knowledge studies (Lichtenstein, Fischhoff, & Phillips, 1982). The phenomenon is manifested in general-knowledge question calibration curves when the curves are displaced to the right of the 1:1 diagonal. What is immediately evident in Fig. 15.1 is that in the Wright et al. (1978) study, overconfidence was markedly and consistently greater among the respondents in Asia than among those in Britain.

Preparation of this article and several of the studies described in it were supported in part by grants SES92-10027 and SBR96-17912 from the U.S. National Science Foundation to the University of Michigan and grants NSC81-0301-H033-02 and NSC85-2413-H033-004 from the R.O.C. National Science Council to Chung Yuan University. We deeply appreciate the helpful comments by George Wright, Lawrence Phillips, and Dale Griffin on a previous version of this chapter.

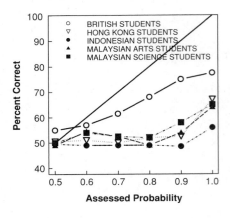

Figure 15.1. Calibration curves for respondents in Britain, Hong Kong, Indonesia, and Malaysia. Redrawn from Wright et al. (1978), Fig. 1, with permission.

It is useful to have a simple summary measure of overconfidence. The *bias* or *over/underconfidence index* serves that purpose:

$$Bias = Over/Underconfidence\ Index$$
$$= Mean\ Judgment - Proportion\ Correct \qquad (1)$$

Bias is the now-standard measure of the strength of overconfidence (when positive) or underconfidence (when negative). It would not be atypical to observe that, on average, a respondent says there is a 73% chance that his chosen answers are correct, but only 65% of those answers really are correct, implying a bias of 8%. Although Wright et al. (1978) did not actually report bias statistics, an inspection of Fig. 15.1 makes it obvious that the average bias would have been much higher for their Asian respondents than for their British counterparts. After all, every point on the calibration curves for the former is lower than the corresponding point on the curve for the latter.

Results like those depicted in Fig. 15.1 challenge people's intuitive beliefs about cultural differences. Yates, Lee, and Shinotsuka (1996) explained the general knowledge question paradigm to respondents in the United States and Taiwan, much the way we described it previously. Respondents were then asked to indicate whether they would expect overconfidence to be greater in the United States, in Taiwan, or the same in both places. A significant majority of the respondents (~62%) expected stronger overconfidence among Americans than among Chinese in Taiwan; fewer than 14% anticipated the reverse. This expectation of greater American overconfidence held regardless of whether respondents were in the United States or in Taiwan and whether or not the expression *overconfidence* was used when the concept was introduced.

Why are people's intuitions about Asian–Western differences in overconfidence so far off the mark? What do the findings in Fig. 15.1 mean? The purpose of this chapter is to summarize what we and others have learned about these issues. The sections of the chapter are organized according to the various questions that have been addressed:

- Are indications of greater Asian overconfidence mere artifacts of research procedure?
- Do the previously observed cross-cultural variations generalize – to other cultures, other target events besides the correctness of answers to categorical general-knowledge questions, and aspects of accuracy other than overconfidence?
- What explains the variations that exist?
- Finally, what do these variations imply for our understanding of fundamental principles of judgment and decision making and for practical affairs in arenas such as intercultural collaborations and commerce?

ARTIFACTS?

Is it possible that the kinds of differences observed by Wright, Phillips, and their colleagues were due to peculiarities of the techniques used in establishing them? Were they, effectively, methodological artifacts?

Item Difficulty

Lichtenstein and Fischhoff (1977) established what is now called the *hard–easy effect*, or sometimes simply the *difficulty effect*, that general-knowledge question overconfidence tends to be stronger when the questions considered by respondents are hard (in the sense that few people answer them correctly) than when the questions are easy. Indeed, when questions are extremely easy, overconfidence gives way to underconfidence. Now, suppose that the items used by Wright, Phillips, and their collaborators were more difficult for their Asian respondents than for their British counterparts, perhaps because of their cultural focus. Then the greater overconfidence exhibited by the Asian respondents could be nothing more than a manifestation of the hard–easy effect. There are indications that the item samples used in the Wright and Phillips studies were indeed more difficult for the Asian than for the British respondents (e.g., the fact that the Asian groups' calibration curves in Fig. 15.1 were uniformly lower than that for the British group).

Yates and colleagues (1989) deliberately assembled a pool of items that, on the basis of their content, were expected to be equally difficult in the cultures of both their mainland Chinese and American respondents. After the responses were collected, steps were taken to assure that the item pools analyzed really were equally difficult for the two groups. Even under these conditions, the same kinds of overconfidence differences established previously were observed once more: The Chinese respondents exhibited significantly greater overconfidence than did the Americans. Thus, although it remains plausible that item difficulty contributed to the Asian–British differences in overconfidence reported by the Wright and Phillips group, it is unlikely that they could have explained those differences fully.

Response Biases

Cultures sometimes differ in how they tend to use response scales (e.g., Pope, 1991; Zax & Takahashi, 1967). This suggests that cross-cultural variations in overconfidence might be simply another demonstration of differences in response biases. Here, the proposition would be that Asians, relative to Westerners, are more inclined to report probability judgments that are more extreme than they really feel are warranted. Yates, Lee, and Bush (1997) tested the response bias hypothesis using an approach that extended and refined one used by Fischhoff, Slovic, and Lichtenstein (1977). They had American and Chinese respondents state selling prices for real bets that paid respondents $2.20 (or its equivalent in Taiwan) if their answers to general-knowledge questions were right and no payment if their answers were wrong. Respondents' prices did indeed agree with the overconfident probability judgments they had stated for those answers, providing evidence against the response bias proposition.

Proper scoring rules are procedures for compensating people for the accuracy of their probability judgments (cf. Yates, 1990, Chap. 8). The more closely a person's judgments correspond to the events that actually occur, the better the score; the better the score, the more money, for instance, that an evaluator awards to the person. What makes a scoring rule "proper" is that, given certain reasonable assumptions, it is in the person's material interests to be candid in reporting what his or her true judgments really are. Put another way, reporting judgments that differ from true judgments leads to the expectation of worse compensation. Yates, Lee, Shinotsuka, and Sieck (2000) used a proper scoring rule to provide another test of the response bias proposal. They promised their Chinese, Japanese, and American respondents financial bonuses for the accuracy of their general-knowledge probability judgments, bonuses tied to a proper scoring rule whose properness had been explained to the respondents. Yates et al. observed the same pattern of cross-cultural variations in overconfidence as had been seen previously. Thus, once again, there was no support for the hypothesis that such variations are due to response biases.

In summary, then, there is no evidence that previous indications of cross-cultural variations in probability judgment are merely artifacts of research procedures. Instead, there appears to be something substantial to explain.

GENERALITY

The first part of such an accounting concerns generality: Where and under what circumstances should we expect to see variations like those initially observed? Also, do those variations extend beyond overconfidence?

Generalization to Other Cultures

In view of results such as those in Fig. 15.1, it is tempting to hazard a generalization that respondents everywhere in Asia tend to be more overconfident than respondents in the West. However, is this generalization justified? Yates et al. (1989) found that their mainland Chinese respondents exhibited substantially greater overconfidence than their American respondents. Whereas, on average, the over/underconfidence index for the Americans was 7.2%, it was considerably higher for the Chinese, 13.4%. The studies by the Wright and Phillips group included Chinese respondents in Hong Kong and Malaysia. The Wright and Phillips results, along with those of Yates et al. (1989), suggest that Chinese cultures might be distinctive in exhibiting high degrees of overconfidence. To evaluate this possibility, Yates, Lee, Levi, and Curley (1990) compared the general-knowledge overconfidence of American respondents to that of respondents in Taiwan, another Chinese culture. Consistent with the earlier comparisons, they found greater overconfidence among the Chinese in Taiwan. A similar result was found in another Taiwan–United States comparison reported by Lee et al. (1995).

The Lee et al. (1995) study actually involved respondents in several other sites besides Taiwan and the United States. Of particular interest is that it included respondents in India, a South Asian culture (actually, myriad subcultures) that differs in many ways from any of the cultures considered in earlier overconfidence studies. Nevertheless, consistent with the earlier findings, the Indian respondents' judgments were markedly more overconfident than those of the Americans who participated in the same investigation. In a previously unpublished study, we compared the general-knowledge judgments of Koreans and Americans using the same approach as has become standard. When we controlled for question difficulty, we found that the over/underconfidence index was 5.1% for the Korean respondents but only 2.4% for the American participants ($p = .027$). That is, once again, overconfidence was greater for the Asian group. Whitcomb, Önkal, Curley, and Benson (1995) broadened the picture even further in a comparison of general knowledge judgments by Americans and Turks. The pattern was the same: The overconfidence evident in the Turkish respondents' assessments was greater than that in the opinions of the Americans. Most recently, Price and Murphy (in press) sought to complete the picture further still by including consideration of Latin cultures. In a comparison of Brazilian and American judgments, they found substantially greater overconfidence among the Brazilians. Whereas the over/underconfidence index for the Americans was 5.1%, it was 12.1% for the respondents in Brazil.

The evidence reviewed so far seems consistent with the generalization that overconfidence really is greater in Asian (and, indeed, in Latin-American) than in Western cultures. Other evidence, however, indicates that the story is more complicated. Lee et al. (1995), for instance, found that their Singaporean respondents exhibited essentially the same degree of overconfidence as their

American respondents. Particularly intriguing is the case of the Japanese. Yates et al. (1989) found that the overconfidence of the Japanese was essentially the same as that of the Americans and, thus, substantially weaker than that revealed by the Chinese. Since that initial examination of Japanese judgments, there have been several others, most of them indicating that Japanese exhibit even less overconfidence than Americans. For instance, in the Lee et al. (1995) study, whereas the over/underconfidence index of the American respondents was about 7%, it was only about 3% for the Japanese.

Generalization Beyond "Discrete-Fact" General-Knowledge Questions

All the studies discussed to this point have dealt with cases in which respondents stated how sure they were about their knowledge concerning miscellaneous "discrete facts" (e.g., whether copper is denser than iron; whether Mexico City is more populous than Cairo). Understanding people's judgments about their own knowledge of such facts is nontrivial (despite the resemblance of the research items to the questions used in so-called trivia parlor games). After all, many of the practical decisions that people make in everyday life are predicated in part on what they assume to be true about the world in general. This seems to be especially the case when people are confronted with nonroutine decisions, such as a request for a change in some organizational policy. There is also the potential significance of such judgments for guiding or motivating people's attempts to learn more about particular topics. Depending on its foundations, we should expect overconfidence to discourage people from seeking to improve their knowledge in circumstances in which that knowledge is sorely deficient. Even given considerations like these, it is apparent that many of the other practical decisions that people face every day rest on judgments about facts or events different from those examined in previous general-knowledge studies. So the following question naturally arises: What is the character of cross-cultural variations in those other kinds of judgments, if such variations exist at all?

Preexisting Quantities

Another type of general knowledge concerns the values of preexisting quantitative variables (e.g., the average price of a hotel room in a city one is considering visiting). Judgments about such quantities have been the subject of a different stream of general-knowledge overconfidence studies initiated by the work of Alpert and Raiffa (1982). Suppose the focal quantity is the average price for a hotel room in a certain city. Then by some suitable means, we should be able to elicit the 1st and 99th percentiles of the person's subjective probability distribution for price; for example, $60 and $130, respectively. Thus, the person believes that there is only a 1% chance that the actual average room rate will be less than $60 and only a 1% chance that it will be more than $130. Of course, this also implies a belief that there is 98% chance that the average rate lies somewhere between those amounts. Expressed another way, the range from $60 to $130 constitutes a 98% *credible interval* for price (cf. Yates, 1990, Chap. 3).

Now, suppose that a person provides 98% credible intervals for a large number of quantities (e.g., hotel room rates in cities all over the world). If that person's judgments are "well calibrated" in the distribution sense, then those intervals should capture the actual values of the respective quantities about 98% of the time. Equivalently, the true values should fall outside those intervals only rarely, approximately 2% of the time. Those unexpected extreme values are called *surprises*, more specifically, "2% surprises" in our current illustration. Suppose a person's 98% credible intervals capture the true values of the pertinent quantities less often than 98%, say, in only about 80% of the instances. This would be taken as a case of "distribution overconfidence." One rationale for this interpretation is that the person has expressed great confidence (98% certainty) in a class of events (capturing true quantity values within 98% credible intervals) that actually occurs much less often than anticipated (80% of the time). A *surprise index* is simply the proportion of times that true values occur outside the bounds of specified credible intervals. Accordingly, in our example, our target person's 2% surprise index would be 20% rather than the 2% that ought to be observed for 98% credible intervals.

Massive distribution overconfidence has been the norm in studies of people's quantity judgments (e.g., Alpert & Raiffa, 1982). Yates et al. (1989) sought to determine whether, generalizing Wright and Phillips's findings with discrete facts, distribution overconfidence for quantitative facts would be significantly stronger among Chinese respondents than among American ones. That is indeed what they observed, for quantities such as "the area of Australia." Whereas the 2% surprise index for the American respondents was an enormous 53.8%, it was even larger for the Chinese – 59.8%.

Future Events

As we argued previously, many of the decisions people make routinely rest on their beliefs about facts as they currently exist (e.g., decisions about cities to include in an itinerary predicated in part on assumptions about how expensive are accommodations in those cities right now). However, many other decisions are driven by people's judgments about future occurrences (e.g., investment decisions contingent on anticipated sales of some product). Do the usual cross-cultural variations in overconfidence observed in judgments about currently knowable facts extend to judgments about the future?

Yates et al. (1989) addressed this question as it applied to quantity judgments. In one item, their Chinese participants were asked for distribution judgments about the low temperature the next day in the southern China city of Guangzhou. Their American counterparts were asked for the same kinds of judgments applying to the southern U.S. city of Miami. The overall 2% surprise index for the American respondents was 41.4%, which was greatly surpassed by the corresponding Chinese 2% surprise index of 53.2%. Zhang (1992) conducted a similar distribution judgment study with professional economists in Beijing. Their task was to make probabilistic distribution judgments of economic indexes for the Chinese economy. Their normal professional duties required them to make such forecasts routinely, although only in a deterministic, "single-value" way (i.e., making point forecasts equivalent to saying, "My best estimate is X," termed *striking numbers* by the economists themselves). Unfortunately, Zhang did not have a comparison group of economists performing a similar task in some Western culture, so he used the results of Yates et al. (1989) as a point of reference. Zhang observed that the overconfidence of the Chinese economists was at least as great as that of the Chinese respondents in the Yates et al. study, and therefore much stronger than that of the Americans in that investigation.

Wright and Wisudha (1982) examined British and Indonesian judgments about future discrete events rather than quantified variables. An illustrative item (p. 221): "At least one national leader (president or prime minister, etc.) (a) will (b) will not die during the next 30 days." The future-event judgments of the Indonesian respondents were far less overconfident than their judgments about currently knowable discrete facts (e.g., whether the Black Sea is larger than the Caspian Sea). Yet those judgments were still much more overconfident than the future-event judgments of the British respondents. So, once again, we see the same generalization of the prior general knowledge findings: Asian overconfidence is greater than Western overconfidence.

A significant feature of the future events used by Yates et al. (1989), Wright and Wisudha (1982), and, to some extent, those used by Zhang (1992) is their heterogeneity. Thus, in a quantity judgment study modeled after that of Yates et al., a given respondent could be asked to make judgments about temperatures, prices of goods and services, and average test scores. The very heterogeneity of the focal events limits our ability to learn much about the details of a person's underlying judgment processes, and this constrains the potential for improving those processes. Considerations such as these are among those that motivate studies focusing on people's judgments about homogeneous event classes. Another is that homogeneous events often have such great practical significance that acquiring accurate judgments about them is widely recognized as a priority. Therefore, the task of providing these judgments is often assigned to professionals who render them over and over again and are expected to develop great expertise at doing so. Weather forecasting provides familiar examples, such as forecasting precipitation or the kinds of severe storms that can create an airline tragedy in an instant. Medicine offers plenty of other illustrations (e.g., making cancer diagnoses). Will previously documented cross-cultural variations in overconfidence be observed in judgments about homogeneous event classes also?

Yates, Lee, Shinotsuka, Patalano, and Sieck (1998) pursued this issue in their studies within a simulated medical environment. Participants in Taiwan, Japan, and the United States each assumed the role of a physician who was confronted with two new (fictional) diseases in the community, Trebitis and Philiosis. On each trial, the "physician" must indicate whether it is more likely that the patient has Trebitis or Philiosis and then record a 50% to 100% probability judgment that that selection is indeed the patient's true condition. After each trial, the "physician" is told of the actual illness. The "physician" makes each diagnosis on the basis of a profile of "symptoms" (technically, *signs and symptoms* in real-life medical parlance) displayed on a computer screen (e.g., the presence or absence of earache, nausea, and rash). The symptoms for a given patient represent a random sample from an underlying "artificial ecology" for the target diseases that, as in the real life being simulated, is initially completely unknown to the participant as physician. That ecology is comprised of variables corresponding to the symptoms as well as the diseases. It entails statistical associations between the symptoms on the one hand and Trebitis and Philiosis, on the other hand, ranging from moderately strong to none. At the start of the experiment, being ignorant of the ecology, the participant can achieve no more than chance-level diagnostic accuracy. However, after inducing the nature of the ecology through feedback, quite respectable diagnostic accuracy is attainable, in principle, at least.

In the first study, the computer automatically displayed to the "physician" all of the known symptoms for any given patient. In the second study, though, the participant had the discretion to display as many or as few of the cues as desired. However, uncovering cues "cost" the participant points against the accuracy bonus that the participant was eligible to receive. This distinction did not affect conclusions about overconfidence. In both studies, the same basic pattern emerged. Mimicking what had been found in earlier studies, the Chinese participants displayed substantially more overconfidence than the Americans or the Japanese. Furthermore, in each study, Japanese overconfidence was weaker than American overconfidence, but not significantly so in either instance. So, even for judgments about a homogeneous class of events under well-controlled conditions, we see the same, now-familiar pattern.

The "medical practice" for each participant in the Yates et al. (1998) studies extended for 120 patients, distributed over 2 days separated by 1 week. This feature of the design allowed for an assessment of learning effects. Bias, or overconfidence, was essentially unchanged from one week to the next for the Japanese and American participants. Importantly, however, overconfidence diminished significantly over that time for the Chinese in both studies. Focused opportunities to learn relative frequencies as well as contingencies, like those in the Yates et al. (1998) study, might be the foundations for one other result reported by Zhang (1992). Modeling his study after that of Keren (1987), Zhang had Chinese bridge-club members make probability judgments that final contracts would be made during bridge card games. Zhang found almost no difference between the calibration curve for the Chinese participants in his study and that for Keren's Dutch bridge players. If anything, the Chinese players seemed to be slightly less extreme in their judgments than the Dutch. We return to the learning issues that might be implicated in findings like these when we discuss in earnest the "whys" of cross-cultural variations.

GENERALIZATION TO ASPECTS OF ACCURACY OTHER THAN OVERCONFIDENCE

Overconfidence is a particular variety of "miscalibration" in probability judgments. *Calibration* refers to the degree of matching that exists between the numbers people report as their probability judgments and the relative frequencies with which the events assigned those numbers actually occur. Suppose that, for each of 50 different days, a weather forecaster says there is a 70% chance of precipitation. If the forecaster is perfectly calibrated, then precipitation will be observed on exactly 35 of those days, a relative frequency of 70%. The match between the overall average judgment and the overall relative frequency is an indication of *calibration-in-the-large*, a special case of the more general notion of calibration. Suppose the target event is, "My chosen answer is correct," as in general-knowledge studies. Then the difference between the overall average judgment and the corresponding relative frequency is the "bias" measure we discussed previously, the over/underconfidence index. Virtually everyone intuitively accepts that people should seek good calibration – including minimal overconfidence – in their probability judgments. However, there is much more to probability judgment accuracy than calibration. This motivates our final generality question: Are there reliable cross-cultural variations in other aspects of probability judgment accuracy, and if so, what is their nature?

Overall Accuracy

Overall accuracy in probability judgments can be conceptualized as follows (Murphy, 1973; see also Yates, 1990, 1994):

$$\text{Overall Accuracy} = f(\text{Calibration, Discrimination, Base rate}) \qquad (2)$$

In this conceptual functional equation, Base Rate refers to the overall relative frequency of the focal, target event in a judgment situation (e.g., proportion correct in a general-knowledge study). (We discuss *discrimination* later.) For the moment, the key point highlighted by Eq. 2 is that calibration is only one of several contributors to overall judgment accuracy. This then directs our attention to a now-obvious question: What, if any, are the cross-cultural variations in overall accuracy for probability judgments? The *mean probability score*, denoted $\overline{PS}$ (sometimes called the *Brier (1950) score*), is the most common means of indexing overall accuracy, and thus provides a means of addressing this question. (See Yates, 1990, Chap. 3, 1984, 1998, for discussions of the details of accuracy measures like $\overline{PS}$.)

Recall that the mainland Chinese respondents in Yates et al. (1989) exhibited much greater general-knowledge overconfidence than their American and Japanese counterparts. Yet overall accuracy, as indexed by $\overline{PS}$, was essentially the same across all three groups. In the general-knowledge study by Yates et al. (1999), the mean values of $\overline{PS}$ for judgments by respondents from Taiwan, Japan, and the United States were, .2375, .1971, and .2286 respectively. ($\overline{PS}$ ranges between 0 and 1, with 0 being ideal.) The Japanese versus Chinese and Japanese versus American comparisons were statistically significant by the usual standards, whereas the Chinese versus American comparison was not. Yates et al. (1998) also examined overall accuracy, but in the context of judgments about a homogeneous class of externally defined focal events (diseases in a fictional medical ecology) rather than general knowledge. In that context, the overall accuracy of the Chinese participants was significantly worse than that of the Japanese and American participants. We are thus left with something of a muddled picture. Sometimes cross-cultural differences in overall probability judgment accuracy are observed, but sometimes not.

Discrimination

Discrimination is the extent to which – irrespective of their numeric labels, which are central to the calibration notion – the judgments in a given collection sharply distinguish instances in which the target event occurs from those in which it does not (Yates, 1990, 1994, 1998). Roughly, discrimination corresponds to d' or the area under an ROC curve in ROC or signal detection theory analyses (cf. Swets, 1986). Consistent with Eq. 2, overall accuracy is a compensatory function entailing both calibration and discrimination, as made precise in Murphy's (1973) decomposition of $\overline{PS}$ (see also Yates, 1982). Thus, a weakness in calibration can be offset by a strength in discrimination, and vice versa. There is a compelling case, however, that one should prefer good discrimination over good calibration when given the choice. For example, whereas good calibration often can be achieved by simple mathematical transformations (e.g., adding a constant to every probability judgment), good discrimination demands access to solid, predictive evidence and skill at exploiting that evidence, which are difficult to find in any real-life, practical situation. Such arguments make cross-cultural comparisons especially interesting. In particular, in the Yates et al. (1989) study, the weak calibration of the Chinese participants' judgments coupled with their overall accuracy being equivalent to that of the Americans and Japanese suggested that their discrimination might be especially good. If this were so, it might suggest that elements of Chinese culture are somehow able to foster judgment customs that facilitate this most appealing strength. Yates et al. (1989) did indeed observe that the discrimination of their Chinese respondents' general knowledge judgments was superior to that of their American and Japanese participants, even though the comparison with the latter group was not statistically significant.

Interpreting the strong Chinese discrimination in the Yates et al. (1989) study is complicated by the fuzzy meaning of the discrimination concept for judgments about general knowledge (see Yates, 1982, for an elaboration of the difficulties). This ambiguity was a primary reason Yates et al. (1998) undertook their artificial medical ecology study involving the fictitious diseases Trebitis and Philiosis. They were able to define the target event as $A =$ "The patient has Trebitis (rather than Philiosis)." The meaning of discrimination is completely straightforward when target events are defined externally this way rather than internally as in general knowledge studies (i.e., "My chosen answer is correct"). This permitted a cleaner test of the possibility of especially strong Chinese discrimination skills. However, such strength did not emerge. Recall that, in the first study by Yates et al. (1998), the computer automatically provided the participant as "physician" with all the available symptoms for every patient. In that study, the discrimination of the Chinese participants' judgments was significantly weaker, not stronger, than that of the American and Japanese participants. Also recall that in the second study, the participants themselves determined which symptoms they saw for each patient. Importantly, this discretion wiped out all differences in discrimination among the participant groups, a result to which we will return.

Noise

Yates (1982) described a "covariance decomposition" of $\overline{PS}$ that differs from Murphy's (1973) decomposition. In broad conceptual terms, it says the following:

$$\text{Overall Accuracy} = f(\text{Bias, Slope, Noise, Base Rate}) \qquad (3)$$

The "Bias" in Eq. 3 entails the same idea we have seen before (e.g., over- or underconfidence in the case of responses to general-knowledge questions). The same holds true for the "Base Rate." We will not discuss "Slope" here. What is of interest, however, is the remaining factor – "Noise." Probability judgments are said to be "noisy" to the degree that variation in those judgments is unrelated to the occurrence versus nonoccurrence of the target event (see Yates, 1994, 1998). Noise can arise from two main sources. The first noise contributor is reliance on information the person (at least implicitly) believes to be related statistically to the target event but really is not. Suppose, for instance, that a physician thinks that fever is associated with Disease D and therefore takes fever into account when trying to diagnose that disease. That is, the physician faithfully increases her probability judgments for Disease D whenever she observes fever and decreases those judgments when fever is absent. If fever and Disease D are independent, then by necessity those judgment variations will be unrelated to patients' true medical states and, thus, accuracy will suffer. The other major noise contributor is inconsistency or unreliability on the part of the person rendering judgments. What *inconsistency* means here is that the person tends to report different judgments for cases in which the available information is identical. Continuing our example, suppose that our physician is presented with Patient 15 and reports a probability for Disease D of 35%. Some time later, the physician sees Patient 183, who has the very same symptoms as Patient 15. To the extent that in such situations the diagnosis for Patient 183 would tend to differ from 35% in a nonsystematic, random way, this contributes to noise and thereby degrades accuracy.

In their study of general-knowledge judgments, Yates et al. (1989) found that the judgments of their Chinese participants were significantly noisier than the judgments of their American and Japanese counterparts. However, the noise levels in the judgments of the latter groups were essentially the same. In their study of diagnoses for the fictional diseases Trebitis and Philiosis, Yates et al. (1998) were able to examine directly the inconsistency contributor to the noisiness of participants' assessments. In agreement with the prior findings for general knowledge, the Chinese respondents' judgments were markedly more unreliable than those of the Americans and Japanese. Japanese consistency was typically much the same as American consistency.

At least one skeptic has openly wondered whether the kind of reasoning we observed among Chinese respondents and the resulting strong indications of overconfidence might be due to our use of psychology students as subjects. The rationale offered by such skeptics is that, in Chinese universities, the "brighter" students tend to pursue scientific and technical fields of study, in which, moreover, they are likely to be taught to think in a fashion that is more "Western." To test this idea, we performed a general-knowledge study with participants drawn from a psychology department ($N = 88$) and a mechanical engineering department ($N = 62$) in universities in Taiwan. As usual, we controlled for item difficulty across the two groups. The median over/underconfidence indexes were 10.8% and 11.0% for the psychology and engineering students, respectively, a nonsignificant difference. Thus, there was no evidence for the proposed artifact.

In sum, initial indications of cross-cultural variations in general-knowledge question overconfidence among respondents in Britain and in various sites in Southeast Asia appear to generalize in several ways. Similar general-knowledge variations distinguish a variety of cultures. Such differences are paralleled in judgments for other kinds of target events, too, among them events that emerge in the future. Additional variations apply to aspects of probability judgment accuracy beyond overconfidence, including overall accuracy.

EXPLANATIONS

What explains the various cross-cultural variations in judgments we reviewed? Probability judgment is a high-level cognitive process. This suggests that, more like social behavior and less like neurological activity, such judgments are unlikely to result from a single process. There are almost certainly a host of contributors to cross-cultural variations in probability judgment, all functioning at the same time. Thus, there is no reason to believe that the following accounts are mutually exclusive.

Ego Inflation

Why are people so surprised when they learn, for instance, that Wright et al. (1978) found more overconfidence among the Chinese than among the British? Recall that few respondents in Taiwan or the United States expected greater overconfidence among Chinese than among Americans (Yates et al., 1996). The most common rationale participants offered for this expectation rested on the presumed relation between overconfidence and self-enhancement or self-esteem. This lay "theory" says that when a person is confronted with a general-knowledge question such as, "Which metal is denser, (a) iron or (b) copper?" the person reasons as follows after selecting, for example, (a):

Fact 1: "I picked (a) as the right answer."
Fact 2: "I am an exceptionally bright person."
Conclusion: "Therefore, there is an exceptionally high probability that (a) really is the correct answer."

Overconfidence is attributed to "Fact 2," the self-appraisal stage of the argument. The claim is that people's self-appraisals are typically inflated and furthermore, that inflation is greater in some cultures than in others. In particular, Westerners – and especially Americans, with their media-fed reputations for arrogance – are expected to have distinctively outsized egos. In contrast, Asians are thought to possess a high degree of personal modesty.

Suppose that this self-appraisal, ego explanation for overconfidence is generally accurate. Then in order for it to explain the kinds of cross-cultural variations in overconfidence that have been documented, people's assumptions about cultural differences in self-appraisals must be diametrically opposed to the truth. That is, on average, Asians' self-appraisals must be more highly inflated than those of Americans, for instance. Actually, however, there is evidence within the cultural psychology literature that personal modesty really is more common in Asia than in the United States (e.g., Bond & Cheung, 1983; Yik, Bond, & Paulhus, 1998).

One way out of this apparent contradiction is to concede that, regardless of its other merits, the conventional view of self-esteem simply does not apply to tasks such as responding to general-knowledge questions. Indeed, the documented high degrees of both general-knowledge overconfidence and self-effacement among the Chinese, for example, could be taken as evidence in and of itself against the self-appraisal account for overconfidence generally. Actually, there have also been numerous other indications that self-appraisals have little to do with general-knowledge overconfidence. Ronis and Yates (1987) reasoned that, if self-appraisals do indeed play a critical role in general-knowledge overconfidence, such overconfidence should be stronger when the respondent personally chooses the focal alternative than when it is picked at random. In fact, the results of Ronis and Yates's study indicated exactly the opposite. Sniezak, Paese, and Switzer (1990) reported similar findings.

In Lee et al.'s (1995) study, participants from Taiwan, Japan, India, Singapore, and the United States performed two tasks. The first was a standard general-knowledge procedure. The other, however, entailed peer comparisons. For each of a variety of items, the respondent was asked to imagine that a random sample of 100 students at his or her university had been selected and that the sample just happened to include the respondent him- or herself. The respondent was then asked to imagine that the sample was rank ordered with respect to some focal skill or personal characteristic, such as writing effectiveness, influence on other people, or interest in sports. Next, the respondent was asked to estimate his or her position in the rank ordering (i.e., his or her percentile rank). Self-enhancement or overconfidence in this peer comparison task is indexed by the degree to which, on average, such percentile rank estimates exceed 50%. Some of the skills and characteristics participants considered were "ego-engaging" and career-significant (e.g., writing skills). For this category, as shown in Fig. 15.2, peer-comparison overconfidence was substantial in three of the five cultures studied. Moreover, the pattern of "ego-engagement overconfidence" observed conformed to what one might expect on the basis of prior cross-cultural work on self-enhancement. We see, for example, in Fig. 15.2 that such overconfidence was greater for the Americans than for the Chinese in Taiwan. Characteristics in another class of filler items were neutral as far as self-esteem was concerned

Figure 15.2. Mean bias statistics ([estimated percentile rank]/100 − .5) by culture (TWN, Taiwan; JPN, Japan; SGP, Singapore; IND, India; USA, United States) for ego-engaging, career-significant skills and characteristics and for filler skills and characteristics. Redrawn from Lee et al. (1995), Fig. 1, with permission.

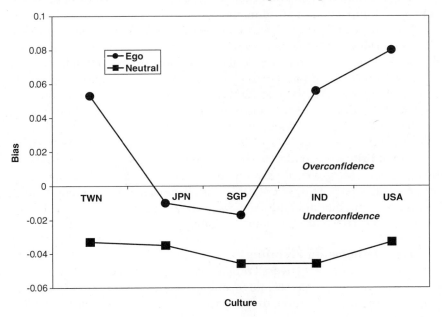

(e.g., interest in sports). Across the board, participants exhibited underconfidence for this category. Perhaps the most important result of the study, however, was that there was almost no correlation between general knowledge overconfidence and peer-comparison overconfidence for any category of skills and characteristics.

One conclusion indicated by these findings is that there are at least two different kinds of overconfidence that rest on quite different mechanisms. Another conclusion is that we should expect different patterns of cross-cultural variations in these distinct varieties of overconfidence. A third indication is that, although some forms of overconfidence probably do rest heavily on self-appraisals, others do not. Accounts for general knowledge overconfidence and its cross-cultural variations almost certainly fall into the latter category.

Set for Probabilistic Thinking

Wright and Phillips (1980) argued that their Asian respondents were especially susceptible to a *certainty illusion*, a tendency to hold beliefs with absolute certainty. They offered this proposal because of the high frequency with which their Asian respondents reported 100% probability judgments that their chosen answers to general-knowledge questions were correct. The incidence rates for such judgments were generally more than twice as high for their participants in Asia (e.g., Malaysian students, Hong Kong businessmen) as for those in Britain. Similar differences were observed in the general-knowledge study of Yates et al. (1989). The rates of 100% judgments for the American and Japanese participants in that study were 22.6% and 21.4%, respectively, whereas the corresponding rate for the mainland Chinese participants was an enormous 47.7%. Wright and Phillips did not attribute the certainty illusion to across-the-board assuredness; instead, they proposed that the illusion is merely one manifestation of a set to view the world in nonprobabilistic terms. Another manifestation of that set is quite different. In a task discussed more extensively later, Wright and Phillips (1980) asked participants to respond in an open-ended fashion to questions about various issues (e.g., "Will you catch a head cold in the next three months?"). Consistent with the notion of cross-cultural variations in a set for probabilistic thinking, Wright and Phillips's Asian respondents generally offered more than twice as many "Don't know" responses to such questions than did their British respondents. The probabilistic thinking set idea has some intuitive appeal. Moreover, it raises a variety of interesting additional questions: One concerns how different sets might have arisen in different parts of the world, and another asks how the decision strategies of people with nonprobabilistic sets cope with the actual probabilistic nature of the world.

Accuracy Dimension Premiums

We noted previously that overall probability judgment accuracy is not a unitary construct. Instead, it has several meaningfully distinguishable dimensions or contributors (i.e., calibration, discrimination, and noise). We also described instances in which, although two groups might share a common level of over-all accuracy, they arrive at that common level via different routes. One exam-ple occurred in the Yates et al. (1989) general knowledge study. The Chinese and American participants exhibited the same measure of overall accuracy. However, whereas the American participants' judgments displayed strong cal-ibration and weak discrimination, the opposite was true with the Chinese. It seemed conceivable to us that this might reflect differences in the relative em-phases that different cultures place on particular accuracy dimensions, with the Chinese putting more value on discrimination and less on calibration. This would seem consistent with Redding's (1978) contention that an especially dis-tinctive characteristic of Chinese business people is their acute sensitivity to any and all information in the business environment that might be significant for their enterprises. After all, such sensitivity would be highly supportive of good discrimination.

We tested this idea in a study with participants in Taiwan and the United States, using the methodology used by Yates, Price, Lee, and Ramirez (1996). In essence, that methodology requires the participant to review two collections of judgment-outcome pairs and express a preference for the forecasters (either meteorologists or stock brokers) who rendered the judgments. The collections of judgments were special in that they were identical in terms of overall ac-curacy but, whereas one was superior in terms of calibration, it was inferior to the other with respect to discrimination. Participants in both sites preferred better discrimination, and the preference was indeed stronger for the Chinese in Taiwan (84% versus 71%), but not significantly so, $\chi^2(1) = 1.74$, $p = .19$. Thus, there seems to be little reason to believe that differences in premiums on various accuracy dimensions are a major contributor to the kinds of cross-cultural variations that have been observed.

Experience and Customary Judgment Demands

When we are unfamiliar with a task, we tend to perform it inconsistently. Sup-pose, for instance, that expressing one's opinions about the chances of an event's occurrence in the form of probabilities is rarely demanded in Chinese cultures (e.g., people seldom ask one another, "What do you think is the probability of rain tomorrow?"). Then, when probability judgment studies such as those we have described are performed in those cultures, we should observe a high de-gree of inconsistency in respondents' assessments. As noted previously, Yates et al. (1998) observed greater inconsistency among the Chinese participants in their studies of probabilistic medical diagnoses in an artificial ecology. Similar inconsistency was likely to have been a major contributor to the noisiness of the judgments reported by the Chinese participants in Yates et al.'s (1989) general-knowledge study. There are two avenues by which unfamiliarity-induced in-consistency could degrade the quality of Chinese probability judgments. The first is direct, via the noise dimension of overall accuracy isolated in the covari-ance decomposition of $\overline{PS}$, as discussed before (Yates, 1982). The other route is more indirect, through overconfidence. Several investigators, including Erev, Wallsten, and Budescu (1994), have shown formally how, depending on particular assumptions about the underlying process, inconsistency can contribute to some measures of overconfidence.

Is there independent evidence that the expression of uncertainty in terms of probability is relatively uncommon in Chinese cultures? Unfortunately, there have been no direct investigations of the issue. However, there have been several studies using a methodology developed by the Wright and Phillips group that seem to imply this conclusion. That methodology relies on an instrument called the Views of Uncertainty Questionnaire (VUQ), which presents the respondent with a long list of questions such as whether one will catch a cold within the next 3 months and whether Baghdad is the capital of Iraq. It then asks the participant to write a "reasonable and appropriate response" to each question (Wright & Phillips, 1980, p. 241). The responses are sorted into several categories and key statistics noted, including the number of verbal probability expressions (e.g., "probably") the respondent reported and the number of different expressions of that type the respondent used. Repeatedly, the Wright and Phillips group found that their British participants used probability responses more often than their Asian participants and many more different probability responses. More recently, Lau and Ranyard (1999) performed a similar investigation and observed essentially the same pattern. They reported, for instance, that although their Chinese respondents on average used 1.8 different probability responses, their English respondents used 4.3. Verbal probability phrases are not the same as numeric probabilities, but if verbal probabilistic expression is relatively uncommon in Chinese discourse, it is hard to imagine that numeric likelihood expression would be common either.

Findings like these implicate the roles of customs and norms in cross-cultural variations. There is no reason to expect such differences to rest on immutable, biological foundations. That is, such variations must be learned. How easily and rapidly do culture-specific judgment routines change when people are exposed to other customs? Recall the experimental findings from the Yates et al. artificial medical ecology studies in which the Chinese participants spontaneously made especially great strides in reducing the overconfidence in their diagnoses over time. These results suggest that similar speed in custom changes might occur in more naturalistic settings. Indeed, it is not implausible that the same kinds of learning processes were responsible historically for the fact that overconfidence among Japanese and Singaporeans, as discussed previously, is more like that of Westerners than other Asians. Both Japan and Singapore are almost unique in Asia in their broad-based integration of international commerce into their cultures.

Attention Capture

Numerous studies have shown that the Chinese and at least some other East Asians are especially sensitive, in comparison to Westerners, to occurrences in their surroundings (see, for example, Hoosain, 1986; Nisbett, Peng, Choi, & Norenzayan, in press). This provides another mechanism by which cross-cultural variations in probability judgment might occur. The Yates et al. (1998) artificial medical ecology studies provided direct evidence on the judgment implications of the implied cultural differences in the ease with which attention is captured by physically salient information. Recall that there were two artificial ecology studies that were distinguished by the nature of the display of patient symptoms. In the first study, the current states of the same fixed set of six symptoms were automatically shown on the computer screen for every patient. In the second study, however, symptom display was at the discretion of the participant. That is, at the outset, none of the symptoms was displayed. The participant had to make an explicit request for every symptom that he or she wished to see in order to inform a diagnosis of Trebitis versus Philiosis. This distinction had little impact on the judgments of the Japanese and American participants, but the effect was substantial for the Chinese. Discretion markedly improved the overall accuracy of their diagnoses, and this improvement appeared to be localized in improved discrimination. When the symptoms were displayed automatically for every patient in the first experiment, this seemed to corrupt the discrimination in the Chinese participants' judgments. This plausibly could have occurred because, try as they might, the Chinese "physicians" simply could not ignore the weakly predictive symptoms that they realized, objectively, they ought to ignore. Alternatively, they might have tried to take so many symptoms into account that the processing demands required to handle them effectively exceeded the available cognitive capacity.

Argument Recruitment

When faced with the task of judging which of two possibilities is true, an "argument strategy" with the following elements seems eminently reasonable:

- Element 1: Accumulate as many arguments as possible that bear on the issue.
- Element 2: Examine each argument carefully and determine which of the two alternatives that argument supports and how strongly the argument supports it.
- Element 3: Weigh the cumulative import of all the arguments pointing toward each option and then pick the alternative that "wins" this competition.
- Element 4: If a degree of certainty that this winner really is correct must be rendered, make that judgment according to how convincing was the victory.

Several proposed accounts for overconfidence start with an assumption that people spontaneously (even if nonconsciously) do something like apply this strategy when confronted with general-knowledge questions of the usual form (e.g., "Potatoes grow better in: (a) warm climates or (b) cool climates"). Overconfidence is attributed to peculiarities in what happens in specific elements of the process. Variants within this class of explanation differ according to exactly what those peculiarities might be. The argument models of Koriat, Lichtenstein, and

Fischhoff (1980) and of Griffin and Tversky (1992) have been especially prominent and have enjoyed some measure of success in their ability to account for
actual judgment data. This then raises the question of whether there are differences in how people from various cultures tend to carry out the activities in the
argument process described previously that, in turn, might contribute to the
cultural variations in probability judgments at issue here.

There is reason to believe that this speculation could have some validity.
A review of psychological, historical, and philosophical literature conducted
by Yates, Lee, Shinotsuka, and Sieck (2000) indicated that traditional Chinese
learning has emphasized a kind of collective empiricism. This is embodied
in special reverence for (and emulation of) ways of doing things that have
proved their mettle over long periods of time. (Aphorisms such as "Why rein-
vent the wheel?" should seem especially compelling given this point of view.)
Furthermore, it appears that Chinese tradition has had little respect and use
for deliberation techniques such as debate, which pit competing ideas head
to head in open forum (see also Nisbett et al., 2001). This would suggest that,
when bringing to mind arguments pertinent to some issue, as in Element 1 of the
strategy sketched previously, Chinese argument recruitment customs should be
distinctive. Yates et al. (2000) reported data consistent with this possibility. In
one study, participants were asked to list arguments for and against each of the
alternative answers to general-knowledge questions posed to them. American
participants were almost twice as likely as Chinese participants to bring to mind
arguments that disagreed with the alternatives they ultimately indicated to be
the ones they thought were the correct ones, and the incidence of such choice-
inconsistent arguments cited by the Japanese participants was more than twice
that for the Chinese (and significantly higher than that for the Americans). The
idea certainly needs to be examined more carefully and extensively, but results
like these suggest that one plausible contributor to Chinese participants being
so distinctively highly confident in the correctness of their chosen answers to
general-knowledge questions is that they see little reason to doubt that those
answers are indeed correct.

IMPLICATIONS

Suppose that the cross-cultural variations we discussed are reliable and that
they generalize to real-life practical decision situations. Further suppose that
the same is true for the explanations for those effects indicated by the data
we reviewed. What are the implications of these "facts"? Almost all the cross-
cultural variations we discussed imply that, with respect to some particular
aspect of judgment quality, the judgments of one group are "better" than those of
another. Assuming that those two groups of people use judgment and decision
procedures that are identical in every other respect, this implies that the former
group will make better decisions than the latter. It is important to recognize
that that assumption could easily be invalid. It is not out of the question –

especially in view of the longevity and prosperity of most of the cultures we have considered – that there are, in fact, other substantial differences in the judgment and decision routines characteristic of those cultures, and in at least some instances, we can expect strengths in some procedures to compensate for weaknesses in others. The challenge is to determine what all the distinguishing features actually are.

Building from ideas introduced by Zhang (1992), Yates and Lee (1996) proposed that the distinctions might go considerably beyond minor "distinguishing features." Everyone, on different occasions, makes decisions according to several qualitatively distinct "decision modes" (see also Yates & Patalano, 1999). Therefore, whereas for one decision problem we might figure out what we should do from "first principles," for another problem we might follow the precedents established by other people (and even ourselves) in earlier, similar situations. The present idea, suggested by Zhang and elaborated by Yates and Lee, is that cultures differ in the priority they place on different modes (e.g., with the Chinese emphasizing precedent). The plausibility of such mode distinctions is consistent with Wright and Phillips' (1980) proposal regarding cultural differences in sets for probabilistic thinking, discussed previously. Depending on the mode by which one happens to decide, probabilistic thinking could be essentially irrelevant.

Regardless of how the present questions resolve themselves, the existence of the kinds of variations we have addressed poses significant practical problems for today's rapidly shrinking globe. Currently, we must increasingly engage in commerce with people from cultures other than our own. It is not implausible that the outcomes of those interactions – for example, in negotiations (Tauber, 1998) – are adversely affected when the parties involved are ignorant of one another's decision customs. Given the rapid globalization of activities of all sorts (e.g., the worldwide consolidation of the automobile industry), people more and more often find themselves having to work collaboratively with people who are used to decision-making customs different from those they normally encounter. We can easily imagine that these collaborations will be slowed down, if not sabotaged, when the participants observe that their opposites approach decision tasks in ways that differ from the ones they use themselves. Things are likely to be especially difficult when it is easy to construe the differences in a negative light. Awareness and understanding why such cross-cultural variations in judgment customs exist could help prevent such divisive inferences from arising.

16. Durability Bias in Affective Forecasting

Daniel T. Gilbert, Elizabeth C. Pinel, Timothy D. Wilson,
Stephen J. Blumberg, and Thalia P. Wheatley

> I am the happiest man alive. I have that in me that can convert poverty into riches,
> adversity into prosperity, and I am more invulnerable than Achilles; fortune hath
> not one place to hit me.
>
> Sir Thomas Browne, *Religio Medici* (1642)

Imagine that one morning your telephone rings and you find yourself speaking
with the King of Sweden, who informs you in surprisingly good English that
you have been selected as this year's recipient of a Nobel Prize. How would
you feel, and how long would you feel that way? Although some things are
better than instant celebrity and a significant bank deposit, most people would
be hard pressed to name three, and thus most people would probably expect
this news to create a sharp and lasting upturn in their emotional lives. Now
imagine that the telephone call is from your college president, who regrets
to inform you (in surprisingly good English) that the Board of Regents has
dissolved your department, revoked your appointment, and stored your books
in little cardboard boxes in the hallway. How would you feel, and how long
would you feel that way? Losing one's livelihood has all the hallmarks of a
major catastrophe, and most people would probably expect this news to have
an enduring negative impact on their emotional lives.

Such expectations are often important and often wrong. They are important
because people's actions are based in large measure on their implicit and explicit predictions of the emotional consequences of future events. A decision to
marry or divorce, to become a lawyer rather than a cornet player, or to pass up
the Twinkie at the convenience store in favor of a croissant from the inconve-
nient bakery is ordinarily predicated on the belief that one of these events will
bring greater emotional rewards than the other. Indeed, affective forecasts are
among the guiding stars by which people chart their lifecourses and steer themselves into the future (Baron, 1992; Herrnestein, 1990; Kahneman & Snell, 1990;
Loewenstein & Frederick, 1997; Totterdell, Parkinson, Briner, & Reynolds, 1997).
But are these forecasts correct? In some ways they undoubtedly are. For

Portions of this chapter are reprinted from: Gilbert, D. T., Pinel, E. C., Wilson, T. D., Blumberg,
S. J., & Wheatley, T. P. (1998). Immune neglect: A source of durability bias in affective forecast-
ing. *Journal of Personality and Social Psychology, 75*, 617–638. Copyright © 1998 by the American
Psychological Association. Adapted with permission.

example, most people recognize that a weekend in Paris would be more enjoyable than gall bladder surgery, and few people fear chocolate, or tingle in anticipation of next year's telephone directory. But even if people can estimate with some accuracy the valence and intensity of the affect that future events will evoke, they may be less adept at estimating the duration of that affect – and it is often the prediction of duration that shapes the individual's decisions. For instance, most people realize that divorce is anguishing and marriage is joyous, but the decision to commit oneself to either course is not predicated merely on one's beliefs about the valence and intensity of these emotional responses, but also on one's beliefs about how long each response is likely to last. People invest in monogamous relationships, stick to sensible diets, pay for vaccinations, raise children, invest in stocks, and eschew narcotics because they recognize that maximizing their happiness requires that they consider not only how an event will make them feel at first, but more importantly, how long those feelings can be expected to endure (see Ainslie, 1992; Mischel, Cantor, & Feldman, 1996).

THE DURABILITY BIAS

How long *can* feelings be expected to endure? Although the telephone calls from Sweden and the administration building would leave most professors respectively delirious or disconsolate, research suggests that regardless of which call they received, their general level of happiness would return to baseline in relatively short order. Common events typically influence people's subjective well-being for little more than a few months (Suh, Fujita, & Diener, 1996; Wortman & Silver, 1989), and even uncommon events – such as losing a child in a car accident, getting cancer, becoming paralyzed, or being sent to a concentration camp – seem to have less impact on long-term happiness than one might naively expect (e.g., Affleck & Tennen, 1996; Brickman, Coates, & Janoff-Bulman, 1978; Collins, Taylor, & Skokan, 1990; Diener, 1994; Helmreich, 1992; Kahana, Harel, & Kahana, 1988; Lehman et al., 1993; Suedfeld, 1997; Taylor, 1983; Taylor & Armor, 1996; Wortman & Silver, 1987). The causes of the remarkable stability of subjective well-being are not fully understood (McCrae & Costa, 1994), but the consequences seem clear: Most people are reasonably happy most of the time, and most events do little to change that for long.

If these findings are surprising, it is only because they violate the intuition that powerful events must have enduring emotional consequences. We believe that such intuitions are profoundly mistaken and that people often tend to overestimate the duration of their affective responses to future events. There are at least six distinct reasons why such a durability bias might arise in affective forecasting. We briefly describe five of them and then concentrate on the sixth.

Misconstrual
It is understandably difficult to forecast one's reactions to events that one has never experienced because it is difficult to know precisely what those events

will entail. Although most people feel certain that they would not enjoy going blind, phrases such as "going blind" actually describe a wide range of events (e.g., slowly losing one's eyesight due to a congenital defect, or suddenly losing one's eyesight during an heroic attempt to rescue a child from a burning house) and these events may have an equally wide range of emotional consequences. Research suggests that when people think about events, they often fail to consider the possibility that their particular, momentary conceptualization of the event is only one of many ways in which they might have conceptualized it, and that the event they are imagining may thus be quite different from the event that actually comes to pass (Dunning, Griffin, Milojkovic, & Ross, 1990; Griffin, Dunning, & Ross, 1990; Griffin & Ross, 1991). When forecasters misconstrue an event and imagine it as more powerful than it actually turns out to be, they naturally overestimate the duration of their affective responses.

Inaccurate Theories

It may be difficult to forecast one's affective reactions to events about which one knows little, but it can be just as difficult to forecast one's affective reactions to events about which one knows quite a bit. Both culture and experience provide people with detailed, domain-specific knowledge about how particular events are likely to make them feel ("A bris is a happy occasion as long as it isn't mine"), and some of that knowledge is bound to be wrong. For instance, Ross (1989) showed that North Americans vastly overestimate the strength and frequency of the emotional distress that women experience prior to menstruation. One might expect that experience with such ordinary events would cure misconceptions about them, but the ability to remember one's emotional experiences accurately is so prone to error and distortion that inaccurate theories about the affective consequences of ordinary events may persist indefinitely (Fredrickson & Kahneman 1993; Mitchell & Thompson, 1994). Because some of our acquired wisdom about the emotional consequences of common events is undoubtedly wrong ("Getting rich is the key to permanent happiness"), the affective forecasts that this wisdom generates ("If I win the lottery, I'll live happily ever after") are undoubtedly wrong as well.

Motivated Distortions

Affective forecasts do more than merely guide people into the future. They also comfort, inspire, and frighten people in the present. So, for example, people may overestimate the duration of their affective responses to the positive events they anticipate ("After Joel and I get married, life will be wonderful") because the mere act of making that forecast induces positive affect ("Just thinking about the wedding makes me smile!"). Similarly, people may overestimate the duration of their negative affective responses as a form of "defensive pessimism" that braces them against the consequences of a negative event, and thus leaves them pleasantly surprised when those consequences turn out to be less enduring than they had predicted (Norem & Cantor, 1986; Rachman, 1994).

People may even use dire affective forecasts to motivate themselves to expend effort in the pursuit of desirable ends (Mischel, Cantor, & Feldman, 1996). For example, just as parents often exaggerate the negative consequences of certain behaviors in order to control their children's actions ("If you let go of my hand in the store and get lost, why don't we just plan to meet over by the Child Eating Monster?"), people may exaggerate the negative affective consequences of certain outcomes to motivate themselves to pursue one course of action over another ("If I flunk the algebra test tomorrow, I will be doomed to a life of poverty, disease, and despair. So I'd better skip the party and hit the library"). In short, affective forecasts have immediate affective consequences, and thus it is only natural that they should sometimes be made in service of their immediate effects. The durability bias may be the result of that service.

Undercorrection
When people attempt to predict the duration of their affective responses ("How would I feel a week after getting fired?"), they may first imagine their initial affective response ("As soon as I saw the pink slip, I'd crawl under my desk and weep") and then correct for the passage of time ("But I guess eventually I'd get up, go home, and make popcorn"; Gilbert, Gill, & Wilson, in press). Experiments in a variety of domains indicate that when judgments are made in this fashion, they tend to suffer from undercorrection (Gilbert, 1991; Tversky & Kahneman, 1974), and people seem especially susceptible to this problem when correcting their predictions for the passage of time (Kahneman & Snell, 1992; Prelec & Loewenstein, 1997; Read & Loewenstein, 1995). Because affective reactions are generally most intense at the onset, the tendency to undercorrect a prediction of one's initial reaction typically produces a durability bias.

Focalism
When people attempt to predict their affective reactions to a particular event, they naturally focus on that event to the exclusion of others. So, for example, when a mother is asked to imagine how she would feel 7 years after the death of her youngest child, she is likely to focus exclusively on that tragedy and fail to consider the many other events that will inevitably unfold over that time period, capture her attention, require her participation, and hence influence her general affective state. Indeed, it would be truly perverse for a mother to pause and consider how much this sort of heartache might be assuaged by her other child's portrayal of the dancing banana in the school play, an important new project at work, or the taste of an especially gooey caramel on a cloudless summer day. But the fact of the matter is that trauma does not take place in a vacuum: Life goes on, and nonfocal events do happen and do have affective consequences. As such, perverse or not, accurate affective forecasts must somehow take those consequences into account. Because nonfocal events are likely to absorb attention and thus neutralize affective responses to focal events (Erber & Tesser, 1992), the failure to consider them should generally cause people to

overestimate the duration of their affective responses (Wilson, Wheatley, Meyers, Gilbert, & Axsom, 1998). (We should note that Schkade and Kahneman, 1997, and Loewenstein and Schkade, in press, independently developed a very similar analysis of a phenomenon they call the *focusing illusion*.)

All five of the foregoing mechanisms may cause the durability bias, all five are important, and all five require careful empirical analysis (see Gilbert & Wilson, 2000). Nonetheless, in this chapter, we concentrate on a sixth cause of the durability bias.

IMMUNE NEGLECT

In the quotation that opened this chapter, Sir Thomas Browne claimed to have something inside him that could convert adversity into prosperity, thus allowing him to claim the title of Happiest Man Alive. Whatever that thing was, most ordinary people seem to have it too. In science, literature, and folklore, people are famous for making the best of bad situations, remembering their successes and overlooking their excesses, trumpeting their triumphs and excusing their mistakes, milking their glories and rationalizing their failures – all of which allow them to remain relatively pleased with themselves despite all good evidence to the contrary. Psychologists from Freud to Festinger have described the artful methods by which the human mind ignores, augments, transforms, and rearranges information in its unending battle against the affective consequences of negative events (e.g., Festinger, 1957; Freud, 1936; Greenwald, 1980; Kunda, 1990; Steele, 1988; Taylor, 1983, 1991; Taylor & Armor, 1996; Taylor & Brown, 1988). Some of these methods are quite simple (e.g., dismissing as a rule all remarks that begin with "You drooling imbecile") and some are more complicated (e.g., finding four good reasons why we did not really want to win the lottery in the first place), but taken in sum, they seem to constitute a *psychological immune system* whose job it is to protect the individual from an overdose of gloom. As Vaillant (1993, p. 11) notes: "Defense mechanisms are for the mind what the immune system is for the body." *Ego defense, rationalization, dissonance reduction, motivated reasoning, positive illusions, self-serving attribution, self-deception, self-enhancement, self-affirmation,* and *self-justification* are just some of the terms that psychologists have used to describe the various strategies, mechanisms, tactics, and maneuvers of the psychological immune system.

One of the hallmarks of the psychological immune system is that it seems to work best when no one is watching, and when its operations are explicitly scrutinized it may cease functioning altogether. We may convince ourselves that we never really loved the ex-spouse who left us for another, but when a friend reminds us of the 47 love sonnets that we conveniently failed to remember writing, the jig is up, the fix is spoiled, and we shuffle off sheepishly to nurse old wounds (and find new friends). The mental machinery that transforms adversity into prosperity must work quietly if it is to work at all, and successful rationalization typically requires that rationalizers not regard themselves as such (Gur & Sackheim, 1979). People, then, may be generally unaware of the influence that their psychological immune system has on their emotional well-being (Loewenstein & Adler, 1995; Snell, Gibbs, & Varey, 1995), and it is easy to imagine how this tendency – which we call *immune neglect* – might give rise to the durability bias. If people fail to recognize that their negative affect will not merely subside, but will be actively antagonized by powerful psychological mechanisms that are specifically dedicated to its amelioration, then they will naturally tend to overestimate the longevity of those emotional reactions (see Loewenstein & Frederick, 1997).

Of the six mechanisms that can cause the durability bias, immune neglect is unique in an important way. Although five of these mechanisms – misconstrual, inaccurate theories, motivated distortion, and focalism – may lead people to overestimate the duration both of their positive and negative affective reactions, immune neglect should lead people to overestimate the duration of their negative affective reactions only. As Taylor (1991, p. 67) observed, "Once the threat of the negative event has subsided, counteracting processes are initiated that reverse, minimize, or undo the responses elicited at the initial stage of responding," and "this pattern seems to distinguish negative events from positive or neutral ones." Indeed, evidence suggests that although people do actively work to neutralize or transform their negative affect ("Phil was never really right for me, and I was able to see that much more clearly the moment he took back the engagement ring"), they generally do not actively work to augment their positive affect because active psychological work has the paradoxical consequence of neutralizing positive affect (Erber & Tesser, 1992; Erber, Wegner, & Therriault, 1996; Isen, 1987; Parrott, 1993; cf. Wegener & Petty, 1994). In short, the immune system works to repair us, not improve us, and this suggests that immune neglect should cause a negative – but not a positive – durability bias.

Do affective forecasts suffer from a durability bias, and if so, can this bias be caused by immune neglect? In the first three studies reprinted here, we sought to answer the first question by searching for the durability bias in two natural settings that we hoped would document its occurrence and highlight its ubiquity. In the fourth study reprinted here, we sought to answer the second question by returning to the laboratory for a more precise look at the mechanisms that might give rise to the durability bias.

THE BREAKUP STUDY

We asked a large group of college students to report their general happiness ("In general, how happy would you say you are these days?") on a 7-point scale that ranged from "not happy" to "very happy." The students were then asked whether they were currently involved in a close romantic relationship, which was defined for them as an exclusive, monogamous relationship that both partners expected would endure for a significant period. Participants who indicated that they were currently involved in such a relationship ("Lovers") then reported how long they had been in the relationship. Participants who indicated that they were not involved in a close romantic relationship ("Loners") predicted how happy in general they thought they would be 6 months after becoming involved in such a relationship. Students were also asked whether they had ever experienced the breakup of a close romantic relationship. Participants who indicated that they had experienced such a breakup ("Leftovers") then reported how long ago the breakup had occurred. Participants who indicated that they had not experienced such a breakup ("Luckies") predicted how happy in general they thought they would be 2 months after experiencing such a breakup.

Of the 532 participants, 334 (62.8%) reported that they were not currently in a close romantic relationship and were thus classified as Loners; 141 participants (26.5%) reported that they had been in such a relationship for more than 6 months and were thus classified as Old Lovers, and 57 participants (10.7%) reported that they had been in such a relationship for 6 months or less and were thus classified as Young Lovers; 194 (36.5%) reported that they had not experienced a breakup and were thus classified as Luckies; 302 participants (56.8%) reported that they experienced a breakup more than 2 months ago and were thus classified as Old Leftovers; and 36 participants (6.8%) reported that they had experienced a breakup 2 months ago or even more recently and were thus classified as Young Leftovers.

Consider first the experience of falling in love. As the top portion of Table 16.1 shows, Loners were less happy than either Young Lovers or Old Lovers, which suggests that being involved in a close romantic relationship may indeed increase one's happiness. Loners seemed to know this inasmuch as they predicted that 6 months after falling in love they would be significantly happier than they currently were. Finally, Loners' forecasts of how much happier they would be 6 months after becoming Lovers were reasonably accurate inasmuch as their forecasts did not differ from the experiences of Young Lovers or from the experiences of Old Lovers. In short, (a) Lovers were happier than Loners; (b) Loners

Table 16.1. Affective Forecasts and Experiences of Participants in the Breakup Study

Measure: Group:	Experiences Young Lovers	Experiences Old Lovers	Experiences Loners	Forecasts Loners
M	5.91	5.71	5.17	5.79
sd	1.12	1.02	1.31	1.19
N	57	141	334	334
Measure: Group:	Experiences Young Leftovers	Experiences Old Leftovers	Experiences Luckies	Forecasts Luckies
M	5.42	5.46	5.27	3.89
sd	1.16	1.26	1.25	1.56
N	36	302	194	194

Note: Greater values indicate greater actual or predicted happiness.

expected that becoming involved in a close romantic relationship would increase their happiness; and (c) Loners correctly predicted that if they were to become Lovers they would be just about as happy as Old Lovers and Young Lovers actually turned out to be. It is worth noting that there were no differences between the forecasts of Loners who had never experienced a romantic breakup and Loners who had.

Consider now the experience of breaking up. As the bottom portion of Table 16.1 shows, Luckies were not happier than Young Leftovers or Old Leftovers, which suggests that experiencing a breakup does not necessarily decrease one's happiness. Nonetheless, Luckies estimated that 2 months after breaking up, they would be significantly less happy than they currently were. Indeed, Luckies' estimates of how much less happy they would be 2 months after becoming Leftovers were inaccurate inasmuch as Luckies' forecasts differed significantly and substantially from the experiences of both Old Leftovers and Young Leftovers. In short, (a) Luckies were not happier than Leftovers; (b) Luckies expected that the dissolution of a romantic relationship would decrease their happiness; and (c) Luckies estimated that if they were to become Leftovers, they would be much less happy than Old Leftovers and Young Leftovers actually turned out to be. It is worth noting that there were no differences between the forecasts of Luckies who were currently in a romantic relationship and Luckies who were not currently in a romantic relationship.

THE TENURE STUDY

We studied the actual and predicted happiness of 97 current assistant professors ("Forecasters") and 123 former assistant professors at the University of Texas at Austin, 92 of whom had ultimately been promoted to associate professor with tenure ("Positive Experiencers") and 31 of whom had ultimately been denied that promotion ("Negative Experiencers"). Each of the Forecasters, Positive Experiencers, and Negative Experiencers in our pool received a questionnaire from a professor at the University of Virginia whose letter indicated that he was studying "the lives of people who are or have been faculty members at colleges or universities" and explaining that "public records indicate that you are or have in the last 10 years been a faculty member." Recipients were asked to complete a short questionnaire and return it in a postpaid envelope. All Experiencers and all Forecasters reported how happy they were in general on a 7-point scale anchored at the endpoints with the phrases "not happy" and "very happy," as well as completing other measures. In addition, Forecasters estimated how happy they would be in general at various points in time after being awarded or denied tenure.

We received complete responses from 33 (34.02%) of the Forecasters, 47 (51.1%) of the Positive Experiencers, and 20 (64.5%) of the Negative Experiencers. We took Forecasters' estimates of their happiness in the 1st through 5th years as their "short-term forecasts," and took their estimates of their happiness

Table 16.2. Affective Forecasts and Experiences of Participants in the Tenure Study

Measure	Forecast		Experience	
Outcome	Positive	Negative	Positive	Negative
Happiness				
Short-term				
M	5.90	3.42	5.24	4.71
sd	1.09	1.37	1.39	1.98
N	33	33	25	7
Long-term				
M	5.65	4.97	5.82	5.23
sd	1.35	1.81	.91	1.74
N	33	33	22	13

Note: Greater values indicate greater actual or predicted happiness.

in the 6th through 10th years as their "long-term forecasts." Analysis of the results shown in Table 16.2 were clear: Forecasters' estimates of their long-term reactions to either a positive or a negative tenure decision were accurate, but their forecasts of their short-term reactions showed evidence of the durability bias. In other words, successful and unsuccessful academics were not as happy or unhappy as they expected to be in the first few years after their tenure decisions.

THE ELECTION STUDY

In 1994, we studied the Texas gubernatorial election in which the Democratic incumbent, Ann Richards, faced a Republican challenger, George W. Bush. On election day, a female experimenter approached each of 57 voters as they exited a voting station and asked each to (1) report how happy they were "in general these days" (on a 7-point scale that ran from "not happy" to "very happy"); (2) circle the name of the gubernatorial candidate (Ann Richards or George W. Bush) whom they hoped would win the election; (3) evaluate each candidate by predicting how good a governor each would be (from "awful governor" to "fantastic governor"); (4) predict how happy they would be in general 1 month after the election if their candidate won or lost; and (5) estimate how they would evaluate the two candidates 1 month after the election if each won.

The results showed that of the 57 voters, 39 (68%) hoped Ann Richards would win the election and 18 (32%) hoped that George W. Bush would win. In fact, Bush won the election, and thus Bush supporters were classified as "Winners" and Richards supporters were classified as "Losers." Approximately 1 month after the election, a female experimenter telephoned each of the voters (ultimately reaching 10 Losers and 15 Winners) and identified herself as a psychology graduate student who was administering a survey. She made no reference to the first phase of the study and none of the voters inquired about it. Voters were asked to

Table 16.3. Affective Forecasts and Experiences of Participants
in the Election Study

Dependent Variable	Type of Measure		
	Preelection	Forecast	Postelection
Happiness			
Losers			
M	5.00	4.07	5.33
sd	1.20	1.58	.98
N	15	15	15
Winners			
M	4.10	4.90	4.40
sd	1.45	.57	1.58
N	10	10	10
Evaluation of Bush			
Losers			
M	2.93	2.93	3.60
sd	1.03	.96	.74
N	15	15	15
Winners			
M	5.20	5.40	5.00
sd	.63	.70	.47
N	10	10	10

Note: Greater values indicate greater actual or predicted happiness, or more
positive actual or predicted evaluation.

report how happy they were in general, the extent to which they now thought
about the election, and their current evaluations of the gubernatorial candidates.

The data in Table 16.3 revealed three things. First, they revealed that the election had no effect on the voters' general happiness: Richards supporters (the
ultimate Losers) were happier than Bush supporters (the ultimate Winners)
both before and after the election. Second, they revealed that Winners did not
predict that a win would influence their happiness, but Losers predicted that
a loss would decrease their happiness. Finally and most importantly, they revealed that 1 month after the election, Winners were about as happy as they had
expected to be, but Losers were significantly happier than they had expected
to be. In short, Losers showed a durability bias.

Why did Losers overestimate the duration of their affective reactions? Our
hypothesis suggests that Losers' psychological immune systems transformed
their negative affect in ways they could not foresee, and the data provide some
preliminary support for that suggestion. The data in Table 16.3 show that neither
Winners nor Losers expected their evaluations of Bush to change after he won
the election. In fact, Winners did evaluate Bush after the election precisely as
they had evaluated him before the election. However, Losers changed their
minds! That is, Losers evaluated Bush more positively after the election than
they had before. In short, Losers underestimated their ability to grow quite

quickly fond of a governor with whom they were, quite frankly, stuck. It is worth noting that new governors do not take office 1 month after an election, and thus the governor-elect's official actions could not have been responsible for any changes in citizens' evaluations of him.

THE JOB INTERVIEW STUDY

In the foregoing studies (and studies described in Gilbert et al., 1998, but not reprinted here), participants overestimated the duration of their negative affect, and they seemed to do so more dramatically and consistently than they overestimated the duration of their positive affect. What might have caused this asymmetry? One possibility is that immune neglect played an important role in the production of the durability bias in these studies. As noted earlier, an asymmetry of this sort is a signature of immune neglect because the immune system is specifically designed to ameliorate negative affect. But there are other possibilities as well. For instance, participants may have felt that the negative events were further from the psychological neutral point than were the positive events (i.e., the bad events were "badder" than the good events were good). Although winning and losing an election, for example, might seem to be a perfectly balanced pair of outcomes, research suggests that losses are generally experienced as larger than gains when the two are equated on an objective scale (Kahneman & Tversky, 1979). If participants considered the loss of an election to be a more powerful emotional event than the corresponding win, then it would have made sense for them to predict that the loss would have a more enduring emotional impact. In short, although the positive–negative asymmetry is consistent with the notion that immune neglect was a source of the durability bias observed in the foregoing study, it is merely suggestive, and more direct evidence is clearly required.

Our theorizing suggests that the durability bias occurs when people fail to consider the palliative influence that their psychological immune systems have on their negative affective states. To test this notion, in the following study, we staged a negative event in the laboratory. We arranged the negative event so that in one experimental condition, the psychological immune system would easily ameliorate the experiencer's negative affect, and in the other experimental condition it would not. We reasoned that if Forecasters do indeed consider the operation of the psychological immune system when making affective forecasts, then they should correctly expect to experience more enduring negative affect in the latter than in the former experimental condition. However, if Forecasters suffer from immune neglect, they should incorrectly expect to have similar reactions in these two experimental conditions.

The following study served another purpose as well. It is in the nature of prediction that people are focused on the particular future event about which they are making estimates, and it is in the nature of experience that people often are *not* focused on the particular event long after it has transpired. Naturally, then, the questions we asked Forecasters in the foregoing study ("How happy will you be in general some time after the negative event?") required that they consider the negative event, whereas the questions we asked Experiencers ("How happy are you in general?") did not. Might the difference between these questions provide an artifactual explanation for the appearance of the durability bias in our studies? We do not believe so, because we do not consider this explanation to be either artifactual or necessary. Recall that we asked forecasters to predict how they would feel *in general* at some future time after an event had occurred, and *not* how they would feel when asked about the event at some future time. If Forecasters overestimated the duration of their affective reactions because they failed to realize that they might not be thinking about the event at the future time, then their failure can be thought of as an instance of focalism. In other words, a Forecaster's failure to consider how much less salient an event will be long after it has passed is most certainly *not* an artifact of the questions a psychologist asks, but is instead an interesting phenomenon that reflects a natural feature of prediction and that is accounted for quite nicely by our explanatory framework (Wilson, Wheatley, Meyers, Gilbert, & Axsom, 1998).

More importantly, however, this interesting phenomenon may be a sufficient cause of the durability bias, but we do not believe it is a necessary cause. Rather, we suspect that even when experiencers *are* thinking about a negative event that happened in the past, the work performed by the psychological immune system often ensures that they will not feel as unhappy as Forecasters expected them to feel. To verify this suspicion, we asked Forecasters in the following study to make predictions about how unhappy they would feel a very short time after a very salient negative event had happened. We assumed that college students in a laboratory situation could be relied on to remember a salient negative event just a few minutes after it happened, and that such an event might even be *more* salient for those who had actually experienced it than for those who had merely made predictions about it. If the durability bias was observed under these conditions, it would be difficult to explain it by claiming that our questions had artificially focused Forecasters on a negative event about which Experiencers had long since forgotten.

To study these issues, we invited female students to our laboratory. They completed a brief questionnaire that, among other things, asked them to report how happy they were at that moment on a 10-point scale anchored at the endpoints with the phrases "not very happy" and "very happy." The experimenter then explained that several local businesses had provided samples of their products and advertisements, and that the current study required that participants try these products or view these advertisements and then report their opinions about them. Participants were told that university regulations required that anyone who participated in research that could benefit an extramural corporation must be paid $25 in addition to receiving experimental credit, but that because research funds were in short supply, the participant would have to undergo a brief screening procedure to determine if she was suitable for the job.

Participants were told that the screening procedure involved answering a series of questions by speaking into a microphone that was ostensibly connected to a speaker in an adjoining room. Participants were told that the persons in the adjoining room were MBA students who would listen to the participant's answers and then decide whether to hire the participant. The experimenter explained that the MBA students were being kept in another room so that the participant's appearance, race, and mannerisms would not play a role in their decision. Participants were given a list of 15 questions that they would be required to answer during the screening procedure, and were given ample time to study this list and prepare their answers.

Half the participants were randomly assigned to the *unfair decision condition*. In this condition, participants were told that their answers would be heard by (and the hiring decision made by) a single MBA student who had sole authority to hire or reject them. In addition, the questions shown to participants in this condition appeared to be only modestly relevant to the hiring decision, for example, "Why did you pick your major?" The remaining participants were assigned to the *fair decision condition*. In this condition, participants were told that their answers would be heard by (and the hiring decision made by) a team of three MBA students who would reject an applicant only if they independently and unanimously concluded that she was unfit for the job. Furthermore, each of the questions shown to participants in this condition included a few sentences that explained the relevance of the question for the hiring decision. So, for example, participants in the fair condition read: "We are looking to hire people who will be able to explain their thoughts and feelings on the products. These people generally can articulate clear reasons for their feelings and actions. Why did you pick your major?"

When participants had finished preparing their answers to the 15 questions, they read those answers into the microphone. Next, some participants (Forecasters) were asked to predict their affective reactions to being chosen or not chosen for the job, and the remaining participants (Nonforecasters) were not asked to make those forecasts. Specifically, Forecasters predicted how happy they would feel (a) immediately after learning that they had been chosen for the job, (b) immediately after learning that they had not been chosen for the job, (c) 10 minutes after learning that they had been chosen for the job, and (d) 10 minutes after learning that they had not been chosen for the job.

Next, all participants were given a letter from the MBA student(s) informing them that they had not been selected for the job. All participants then completed a short questionnaire that, among other things, asked to report their current happiness. The experimenter then explained that he or she needed to make some photocopies of the next questionnaire and would return in a few minutes. Ten minutes later, the experimenter returned with another questionnaire that,

Table 16.4. Affective Forecasts and Experiences
of Participants in the Job Interview Study

Time	Measure	
	Experiencers	Forecasters
Immediate		
Fair decision		
M	−.68	−2.11
sd	1.34	1.94
N	19	19
Unfair decision		
M	−.40	−2.10
sd	1.19	1.68
N	20	20
Delayed		
Fair decision		
M	−1.26	−2.00
sd	1.97	1.45
N	19	19
Unfair decision		
M	0.00	−1.90
sd	1.12	2.02
N	20	20

Note: Measures are changes from baseline. Smaller values
indicate greater actual or predicted decreases in happiness.

among other things, asked participants to report their current happiness once
again.

Analyses of the data revealed that the act of making a forecast did not influence the participants' subsequent reports of their experiences, and thus we
describe only the results from those participants who both made forecasts and
reported their experiences. As Table 16.4 shows, participants in the fair and
unfair decision conditions made similar predictions about how they would feel
immediately after hearing the bad news, and they made similar predictions
about how they would feel 10 minutes later, and indeed, participants in the
fair and unfair decision conditions felt just about the same immediately after
hearing the bad news. However – and this is most important – they felt quite
different 10 minutes later. Specifically, after 10 minutes, participants in the unfair condition felt better than did dual-role participants in the fair condition.
Apparently, participants did not realize how the basis of the decision would,
over time, change their affective reaction to it.

GENERAL DISCUSSION

The foregoing studies offer evidence for the existence of a durability bias in
affective forecasting. In these studies and others that are described in Gilbert

et al. (1998), students, professors, voters, newspaper readers, test-takers, and job-seekers overestimated the duration of their affective reactions to romantic disappointments, career difficulties, political defeats, distressing news, clinical devaluations, and personal rejections. Furthermore, on some occasions, these overestimates seemed to occur because participants did not consider how readily they would "explain away" setbacks, tragedies, and failures once they happened. Although these studies demonstrate the existence of the durability bias and suggest one of its underlying causes, they raise many questions. We consider five of those questions particularly worthy of discussion.

What Mechanisms Cause the Durability Bias?

The four studies described here revealed a durability bias in affective forecasts for negative events. Although the asymmetry between the positive and negative durability bias suggests that immune neglect may have played a role in producing the durability bias in the first three studies, other factors were undoubtedly at work in these studies too. For example, numerous events transpire in the month that follows an election or a tenure decisions, and the failure to consider those events when making affective forecasts (focalism) may well have played a role in Forecasters' mispredictions (see Wilson et al., 1998). Because several mechanisms were operating at once and because we did not include design features that would uniquely implicate any one of them, the election and tenure studies established the durability bias as a phenomenon without isolating its causes.

However, the job interview study did isolate causal mechanisms, and it is worth considering just what kinds of conclusions its results support. It is worth noting that this study was carefully designed to preclude the operation of misconstrual and focalism. We precluded misconstrual by making sure that Forecasters could imagine every detail of the event correctly. If Forecasters failed to predict how they would feel some time after the event occurred, it was not because they failed to understand what the event entailed. Similarly, we precluded focalism by asking Forecasters to predict how they would feel a very short time after a focal event took place, and we made sure that no significant nonfocal events happened in the interim. If Forecasters failed to predict how they would feel a few minutes after the event occurred, it was not because Experiencers forgot about the focal event or because something unexpected happened in the interval between the focal event and the Experiencers' reports. These features of our experimental designs allow us to say with confidence that the durability bias does not require that people misunderstand the nature of the events about which they are making forecasts, nor that people fail to consider the nonfocal events that transpire after the focal event. Misconstrual and focalism may be sufficient, but they are not necessary, causes of the durability bias.

But what of the other mechanisms? We did not attempt to preclude undercorrection, inaccurate theories, and motivational distortion, and thus any or all of these mechanisms may have played a role in producing the durability bias in the first study described here. None, however, can account for the pattern of data that uniquely implicates immune neglect in the job interview study. People may fail to correct their inferences about their initial reactions by taking into account the effects of the passage of time (undercorrection), they may motivate themselves to work harder by making overly dire predictions about the emotional consequences of failure (motivated distortion), or they may simply have inappropriate ideas about how much certain things hurt (inaccurate theories). Any one of these facts might explain why participants overestimated the duration of their negative affect, but only immune neglect explains why forecasters failed to distinguish between events that, according to experiencers' reports, facilitated or inhibited the immune system. In short, several causal mechanisms may have been operating in the job interview study, but immune neglect certainly was operating. We do not wish to claim that the durability bias was caused solely by immune neglect in any of our studies; rather, we merely wish to claim that immune neglect was clearly a causal factor in the job interview study.

Are Experiencers Really Happy?

Participants reported being happier than they expected to be, and one may wonder whether they were telling the truth. It is possible, for example, that participants experienced and recognized their unhappiness ("I can't believe I didn't get the job!") but deliberately concealed it in order to save face ("I'll never let them see me cry"). For several reasons, we consider "false bravado" to be an unlikely explanation of our results. First, such a face-saving maneuver would have required participants to contradict their own predictions, and admitting that one could not foresee one's own emotional reactions to failure is surely no less embarrassing than admitting that one feels bad after failure. Second, if participants felt compelled to display false bravado, then why were Forecasters perfectly willing to predict that they would feel bad after failing to get a job? Such predictions hardly smack of *machismo*. Third, if Experiencers were reluctant to confess their negative affective states, then why did we not observe similar reluctance among participants who reported their affective states immediately after being rejected for a job in the second study? All of this suggests that participants in our studies were indeed telling the truth as they knew it.

But did they know it? One might argue that those participants who claimed to be happy after a negative event were not really happy, even if they believed they were. Arguments such as these bring us face to face with one of philosophy's enduring conundrums: Can people be wrong about their own internal experiences? On the one hand, psychologists have amassed considerable evidence to suggest that people can be mistaken about how they feel toward an object (e.g., Greenwald & Banaji, 1995; Nisbett & Wilson, 1977; Quattrone, 1985; Wilson, 1985), and as such, their overt behaviors often provide better evidence of their internal states than do their verbal reports. As Rorty (1970, p. 400) argues:

If I say that I believe that p, or desire X, or am afraid, or am intending to do A, what I go on to do may lead others to say that I couldn't *really* have believed p, or desired X, or been afraid, or intended to do A. Statements about beliefs, desires, emotions, and intentions are implicit predictions of future behavior, predictions which may be falsified.

On the other hand, some theorists have suggested that candid self-reports of subjective experience are, by definition, correct. As Dennett (1981, p. 218) explains:

> Suppose someone is given the post-hypnotic suggestion that upon awakening he will *have* a pain in his wrist. If the hypnosis works, is it a case of pain, hypnotically induced, or merely a case of a person who has been induced to *believe* he has a pain? If one answers that the hypnosis has induced real pain, suppose the post-hypnotic suggestion had been: "On awakening, you will *believe* you have a pain in the wrist." If this suggestion works, is the circumstance just like the previous one? Isn't believing you are in pain tantamount to being in pain?

Can people be wrong about how they feel? We think it depends on what one means by *feel*. When a person is asked how she feels about something in particular ("Do you like rutabaga farmers?"), the word *feel* is being used in a dispositional rather than an occurrent sense (Ryle, 1949), and thus the person's most candid reply may be inaccurate. For example, the person may have a variety of conflicting beliefs about a single object (e.g.,"I often think of myself as a friend to farmers" and "Rutabagas are the cause of our nation's growing malaise"), and unless all of these are recalled at once, her verbal report of her attitude toward the object may be biased in the direction of those beliefs that come most quickly to mind. However, when a person is asked how he feels, period – and not how he feels about something – then the word *feel* is being used in an occurrent rather than a dispositional sense, and the person is being asked to say what it is like to be him at that moment. If he is candid and articulate, then one can make the case that his verbal report is unimpeachable.

The take home point is this: Verbal reports of relatively enduring tendencies can be distinguished from verbal reports of subjective experience, and psychologists may question the validity of the former while accepting the integrity of the latter. We believe that our Experiencers believed that they were happier than our Forecasters predicted they would be. Whether the Experiencers' beliefs were right or wrong is a question to which no one – Experiencer, philosopher, or psychologist – can at present offer a definitive answer.

Why Do People Neglect the Immune System?

People are quick to notice the immune responses of their friends and neighbors ("Isn't it interesting that just moments after learning his GRE score, Herb suddenly remembered that standardized tests are biased?"), and most reluctantly confess that they too have a modest talent for reasoning after the fact. If people know in the abstract that they have such talents, then why do they fail to consider those talents when attempting to forecast their own affective reactions? Although our studies do not address these issues directly, we can think of at least three reasons why Forecasters might consider it unwise to become too wise about their psychological immunity.

First, most events that are potentially aversive are also potentially appetitive, and if one allows oneself to think about how easily an undesired outcome can be explained away ("This job is a dime a dozen, and if I don't get it, I can get one just like it"), one may find that one has inadvertently explained away the desired outcome as well ("Which means that if I do get it, there's really not much to celebrate"). Although some of the rationalizations that the immune system produces can abrogate failure and accentuate success ("The umpire hates me and my family"), others have the unfortunate consequence of neutralizing both outcomes ("The umpire is blind"). Because the attempt to minimize defeat may sometimes minimize victory as well, it may not behoove people to consider such matters too carefully before the fact. Second, Forecasters may not look ahead and consider how their psychological immune systems will respond to a negative event because acute awareness of one's immune system may have the paradoxical effect of suppressing it. When people catch themselves in the act of bending the truth or shading the facts, the act may fail. Third, and finally, if people were aware of how readily their affective reactions to failure, misfortune, or bad news could be mentally undone, they might not be motivated to take the actions required to preclude those outcomes. As noted earlier, the durability bias may be part of a self-regulatory scheme by which people use forecasts of the future to control their behavior in the present (Ainslie, 1992; Elster, 1977; Mischel, Cantor, & Feldman, 1996; Schelling, 1984), and such schemes would be undermined if people recognized in prospect how easily they could deal in retrospect with undesired outcomes. In somewhat more clinical language, if people realized how capable they were of emotion-focused coping (i.e., dealing psychologically with negative affect), they might not engage in problem-focused coping (i.e., dealing physically with the environmental sources of their negative affect; see Lazarus, 1985). An organism that was aware of its ability to construct its own satisfaction might well lose its preferences for one outcome over another and become happily extinct.

Do People Learn from Their Forecasting Errors?
Several theorists have noted that people tend to focus on different kinds of information when they are pondering a decision, making a decision, implementing a decision, and retrospecting about a decision (Gollwitzer, 1993; Gollwitzer, Heckhausen, & Steller, 1990; Jones & Gerard, 1967). Rachman and colleagues (Rachman, 1994; Rachman & Bichard, 1988; Taylor & Rachman, 1994) applied this insight to the prediction of fear. For example, claustrophobics tend to believe that they will be more frightened by a small enclosure than they actually are, and Rachman et al. have suggested that this happens because people focus on *fear cues* when anticipating an encounter ("Oh my, that closet looks so

dark and cramped!"), but that once the encounter begins, they shift their focus to *safety cues* that enable them to tolerate or terminate the encounter ("The door knob is here by my left hand and the light switch is here by my right hand"; see also Telch, Valentiner, & Bolte, 1994). The claustrophobic overpredicts her fear because she does not realize that her attentional focus will shift once the closet door is closed. Normally this leads claustrophobics to avoid coffins, closets, and laundry hampers, but if forced to predict and then experience their fear in the laboratory, they learn to make more accurate predictions in just a few trials (see Rachman, Levitt, & Lopatka, 1988).

Our studies similarly suggest that people focus on one kind of information when making affective forecasts about an event ("Oh my, rejection is so embarrassing and demoralizing") and on another kind of information when experiencing the event ("So on the one hand, the rejection was from an MBA student, and on the other hand, who cares?"). If people do not realize in the present how things will look in the future, then we might expect that when the future arrives they will recognize their forecasting errors and learn from them. Yet, in our studies, the durability bias appeared in several contexts that ought to have been generally familiar to our participants. Surely participants in the job interview study had not gotten everything they had ever striven for. So why did these participants mispredict the duration of their affective reactions to ordinary traumas that were at least similar to those they had probably experienced before?

One possibility is that people ordinarily learn less from their forecasting errors than laboratory research would suggest. For example, when people experience less enduring outcomes than they initially predicted, they may not always realize that they initially mispredicted them. It is the unusual situation that requires an individual to make an explicit affective forecast ("After much internal debate, I've decided that I'll be happier with a BMW than a Miata"), and even when people do make such explicit forecasts, these forecasts are rarely so precise ("I thought the BMW would give me 5.3 units of happiness") that they can be unequivocally disconfirmed by subsequent experience ("So how come I only got 5.1 units?"). Furthermore, even the most explicit and precise forecast must be accurately recalled in order to be disconfirmed explicitly and precisely, and research suggest that the ability to remember one's own beliefs, attitudes, and expectations is far from perfect (Loewenstein & Adler, 1995; Ross, 1989). For all of these reasons, then, it seems likely that when errors of affective forecasting are disconfirmed by experience, those disconfirmations may often go unnoticed. As such, the evidence that might alert people to the operation of the psychological immune system may be especially hard for them to come by.

Even when people do recognize that they have mispredicted their affective reactions ("Gee, the roller coaster ride wasn't as terrible as I thought it would be"), the lessons they take away from those mispredictions may be specific ("I guess I can deal with speed better than I realized") rather than general ("I guess I can deal with everything better than I realized"). People may find it easier to blame their mispredictions on misconstruals of the event ("Well, it looked a lot higher from the ground than it actually was") than on their failure to consider their ability to internally regulate their affective states ("I failed to recognize that once I was strapped in, I would suddenly see that it was fruitless to worry"). In short, many factors may prevent people from noticing that they have made affective forecasting errors, and many more factors may keep them from realizing that the errors they do notice were brought about by immune neglect.

What Are the Limits of the Durability Bias?

In our studies we found the durability bias wherever we looked; but, of course, we looked where we thought we would find it. The durability bias may well be a pervasive phenomenon, but surely it is just as important to know its limits as it is to know its reach. One possible limit has to do with the valence of the event about which the affective forecast is made. In half of our studies, we examined forecasts and experiences of positive affect, and across those studies we found no significant evidence of a positive durability bias. Yet we all know that people occasionally overestimate the duration of their positive experiences, and we have found reliable evidence for such a bias in some of our own studies (Wilson et al., 1998). Nonetheless, the relative ease and difficulty with which these two biases are produced suggests that one may be more robust than another. Why should that be the case?

One possibility was noted at the outset: The psychological immune system ameliorates negative affect but does not augment positive affect, and therefore immune neglect produces only a negative durability bias. Thus, in any complex situation in which numerous mechanisms are simultaneously at work, more mechanisms are conspiring to produce a negative than a positive durability bias. Another possible explanation for the weakness of the positive durability bias has to do with the way in which affective forecasts guide behavior. People naturally avoid those events that they believe will produce negative affective consequences ("No, I'd prefer not to eat snails, thank you"), and hence may fail to learn that such beliefs are sometimes mistaken (e.g., Herrnstein, 1969; Seligman, 1975). Conversely, people may seek those events that they believe will produce positive affective consequences ("But yes, a few more vodka tonics, please"), and thus they may have ample opportunity to learn that such beliefs are sometimes mistaken. If people consistently act on their forecasts, they will inevitably experience fewer disconfirmations of their overly pessimistic predictions than of their overly optimistic predictions, and thus experience may cure the positive durability bias more quickly than the negative durability bias. Indeed, old age may be characterized by a loss of idealism in part because people may learn that the things they once thought would make them permanently happy did not actually do so; but, because they avoided the things that they believed would make them permanently unhappy, they may have failed to learn that those beliefs were equally untrue.

If the valence of an affective forecast describes one limit on the durability bias, then the direction of misprediction describes another. Simply put, people may underpredict as well as overpredict the duration of their affective reactions. For example, people may be surprised to find that the death of a great uncle pains them for much longer than they would have thought possible, that a new sports car gives them greater daily pleasure than they could have imagined, or that a decision to forego a job offer or marriage proposal led to years of unanticipated regret (Gilovich & Medvec, 1995). Although instances such as these surely do occur, our analysis suggests two reasons why overprediction of affective duration is probably more common than underprediction. First, some of the mechanisms we have identified (such as miscontrual, incorrect theories, motivational distortion, and focalism) can produce both underestimation and overestimation, but others (such as undercorrection and immune neglect) can produce overestimation only. We know of no mechanism that would produce underestimation only. Second, underpredictions may be more likely to be remedied by experience than are overpredictions. For example, Rachman and colleagues showed that people frequently overpredict their fear and anxiety, and that these overpredictions are slowly reduced over many experimental trials in which the person makes explicit predictions and then, moments later, makes an explicit experiential report that contradicts that prediction (see Rachman, 1994). However, when people occasionally underpredict their fear or anxiety, this mistake is usually eliminated in just one trial, and it is not difficult to see why: One may touch a stove gingerly several times before coming to believe that it is indeed cooler than anticipated, but it requires just one good scorching to remedy the opposite misapprehension. If underpredictions of negative affect are met with unexpected punishment, whereas overpredictions yield pleasant surprises (when they are noted at all), then we might well expect that over time the overpredictions will become more common than underpredictions. Although we see little evidence of underestimation in either our lives or our laboratories, it is certainly possible that such evidence is simply waiting to be found. For now, we place a public bet on the predominance of the durability bias, fully confident that should our faith prove misplaced, we will not be embarrassed for long.

17. Resistance of Personal Risk Perceptions to Debiasing Interventions

Neil D. Weinstein and William M. Klein

Perceived susceptibility, one's belief about the likelihood of personal harm, is a key concept in many theories of health behavior (Cummings, Becker, & Maile, 1980; Weinstein, 1993). Such beliefs often turn out to be unrealistically optimistic: People show a consistent tendency to claim that they are less likely than their peers to suffer harm. This optimistic bias in relative risk has been demonstrated with several methods, various age groups, and a wide range of hazards (Weinstein, 1987). In some situations, of course, such optimism may be beneficial (Taylor & Brown, 1988). Positive illusions about the effectiveness of precautions, for example, can sustain attempts to change behavior, and underestimations of risk can protect people from anxiety when there is little they can do to reduce their vulnerability (e.g., Taylor et al., 1992). However, when health problems have not yet appeared and are controllable, a tendency to downplay one's own risk may interfere with appropriate self-protective action.

A few studies have demonstrated that informing people about their susceptibility can increase preventive action (e.g., Blalock, DeVellis, & Afifi, 1990; Wurtele, 1988), but others have been unable to alter risk perceptions (Griffeth & Rogers, 1976; Sutton & Eiser, 1990) or have produced changes too small to result in significant changes in action (Schoenbach, 1987; Siero, Kok, & Pruyn, 1984; Weinstein, Sandman, & Roberts, 1991; Wurtele & Maddux, 1987).

The studies reported here varied the way in which risk-factor information was presented in an attempt to reduce optimistic biases. Study 1 reflected an "educational" approach to health promotion. This approach assumes that people do not understand the risks they face, that their optimistic biases result from an unsystematic or incomplete attention to risk-factor information, and that providing such information can correct their misunderstandings. If people think their risk is below average simply because they are unaware of major risk factors or because they overlook relevant factors, a manipulation that points out the most important risk factors and asks people to consider their own standing on these factors might lead to more realistic judgments. . . .

Manipulation of the comparison targets might also be a way of altering risk perceptions. Several strands of evidence suggest that people may come

This is an edited version of a paper that first appeared in *Health Psychology, 14*, 132–140. Copyright © 1995 by the American Psychological Association. Adapted by permission.

to the conclusion that they are less at risk than others by using as a standard of comparison someone whose risk is actually worse than average. Not only are comparative risk judgments sensitive to the person selected as the comparison other (e.g., Perloff & Fetzer, 1986), but it is also well known that people tend to engage in downward comparison under threat (Hakmiller, 1966; Wills, 1981, 1987). . . . These studies suggest that encouraging participants to compare themselves with a person possessing many risk-reducing characteristics, rather than with someone possessing many risk-increasing characteristics, should reduce optimistic biases.

Finally, we explored the possibility that unrealistic optimism may exist because people fail to give as much attention to their own risk-increasing attributes as they give to their risk-decreasing attributes. If this idea is correct, then requiring participants to think carefully about the attributes that could lead to their own victimization should lead to more realistic risk perceptions.

Thus, we attempted an educational intervention in Study 1, two social comparison-based interventions in Studies 2 and 3, and an intervention requiring participants to generate personal risk factors in Study 4. To maximize external validity and meet the different requirements of each study, we used a variety of health hazards, including heart problems, drinking problems, excessive weight gain, high radon level in the home, and automobile injury, all of which have elicited optimistic biases in past research (e.g., Weinstein, 1987).

STUDY 1

Study 1 was designed to test whether alerting participants to relevant risk factors would reduce optimistic biases. Participants estimated their likelihood of experiencing several hazards either before or after they had read about the major risk factors for these hazards and reported their standing on these factors. We hypothesized that participants who had estimated their overall risk after responding to the list of risk factors would show less optimism than would participants who had not seen this list.

We recognized, however, that providing risk-factor information might have undesirable consequences. If processing of information about personal risks tends to be biased, then pointing out previously overlooked risk factors – without telling participants how they or their peers stand on these factors – would provide new opportunities for biased interpretation and could actually increase unrealistic optimism (Gerrard et al., 1991; Weinstein, 1983).

Method
Participants and Procedure. Single-family homes in three New Jersey communities were visited. At each house, the interviewer asked to speak with the oldest or youngest man or woman over 18 years old who was at home. This individual was asked to complete a questionnaire about health and safety risks while the interviewer waited. The completion rate was 85.7%, yielding data from 222 respondents.

Materials. The hazards – having a heart attack, finding a high home radon level, and being injured in an automobile accident – were selected because many well-established risk factors could be cited. Participants were asked to compare themselves with other men or women their age and indicate the relative likelihood that they would experience the problem in the future. (For radon problems, they were asked to compare their expected home radon level with that of other homes in the same community. Respondents who had already tested their homes for radon were asked to skip this question.) Responses were made on 7-point scales, with endpoints of much below average (-3) and much above average ($+3$).

Participants also indicated their standing on the risk factors for each hazard. Some risk factor questions used comparative scales (e.g., much less dietary fat than average to much more than average); other risk factor scales were absolute (e.g., number of family members having heart attacks).

In one condition, all three comparative-risk judgments came first (on the cover page of a four-page brochure). In the other condition, the comparative-risk judgment for each hazard appeared immediately after the risk-factor questions for that hazard.

Results and Discussion

All three comparative-risk judgments showed small but significant optimistic biases (i.e., mean ratings of less than zero): heart attacks, $M = -.29$, $t(221) = 3.20$, $p < .002$; auto injuries, $M = -.34$, $t(221) = 3.90$, $p < .0001$; and radon levels, $M = -.62$, $t(221) = 9.98$, $p < .0001$. In a multivariate analysis of variance (MANOVA), these judgments were unaffected by whether the comparative-risk questions came before or after the risk-factor questions, $F(3, 188) = 1.0$, $p > .3$, nor was there a condition effect on any of the separate hazards, all $ps > .2$. (All multivariate F tests in this article are based on Wilks's lambda.) Merely having people think about their standing on relevant risk factors without providing clear feedback about what constitutes favorable or unfavorable standing on these factors did not decrease or increase the tendency to claim that one's risk is less than that of other people.

For those risk factors assessed on comparative-rating scales, it was possible to determine whether respondents were optimistically biased in their risk-factor ratings as well. Risk-decreasing biases were observed in the following cases (all significant beyond the .0001 level by t test unless otherwise indicated); blood-cholesterol level ($p < .05$), fat and cholesterol in diet, weight of automobile ($p < .01$), driving skill; driving carefulness, soil density, basement openings, and home air tightness. An optimistic bias in blood pressure ratings was not significant ($p = .11$), whereas risk-increasing biases were observed for exercise ($p < .01$) and speed of driving ($p < .0001$).

It is interesting that 11 of the 14 correlations between risk-factor ratings and comparative-risk judgments were more positive when the comparative-risk judgment came after the risk-factor questions rather than before (binomial $p < .01$). Thus, it appears that participants altered their comparative-risk judgments when preceded by risk-factor judgments to increase the consistency between the two sets of ratings. However, the creation of greater consistency between risk factors and risk judgments was not accompanied by any change in the mean values of the risk judgments themselves because the perceived standing on most risk factors was itself optimistically biased.

STUDY 2

Health and safety information is often presented in terms of what not to do. As a result, it is probably easier for people to bring to mind these negative attributes and use them as a standard of comparison than to bring to mind a more appropriate standard of the average person. In fact, one hypothesized origin for optimistic biases is a tendency to compare oneself with a person who embodies nothing but unfavorable attributes – a worst-case stereotype (Perloff & Fetzer, 1986; Weinstein, 1987).

In Study 2, we tried to reduce optimistic biases by presenting risk factors in such a way that participants would see their own attributes as less than ideal. The effects of focusing attention on the positive end of each risk factor (e.g., "Have never gotten drunk") were contrasted with those of a treatment in which attention was focused on the negative end of each risk factor (e.g., "Get drunk several times a week"). Presumably, allowing participants to see how different they were from the worst-case list would increase their optimism. If a significant difference between these two approaches were found, it would suggest that providing information about what people should do is less likely to create optimistic biases than offering information about what not to do.

Method

Participants and Procedure. Research assistants approached individuals in public places on the Rutgers University campus and asked them to fill out a questionnaire. Of those approached, 86% agreed to participate, yielding a sample of 164 (57.2% female).

Materials. Study 2 used two health concerns, heart disease and alcoholism. We chose these because both reveal optimistic biases in college populations and have several behavioral risk factors. In the "risk-decreasing attributes" condition, participants read a list of characteristics (the favorable ends of a list of risk factors) that would decrease the risk of developing one of these problems. The wording of the attributes was rather extreme so that all participants would see a large number of instances in which their own attributes differed from the lowest-risk case. Then they rated the likelihoods that they and the average student at the same university would experience this problem in the future. Seven attributes were listed for heart disease (e.g., "Getting physical exercise four times a week"), and eight attributes were listed for drinking problems (e.g., "Have never gotten drunk"). Each list of attributes was introduced with wording such as the following: "Many people in our society develop drinking

Table 17.1. Study 2 – Risk Perceptions in Different Experimental Conditions

Condition	N	Heart Disease Risk (Average)		Drinking Problem Risk (Average)	
		Own	Student's	Own	Student's
Risk-increasing attributes	53	4.18	6.27	2.71	6.11
Risk-decreasing attributes	55	4.51	6.49	3.30	6.51
Control	56	5.26	6.61	3.30	6.45

Note: Scale ranged from "no chance" (1) "to certain to happen" (12).

(alcohol) problems. Some factors that indicate you have a lower risk of developing a drinking problem are [list followed]. Look carefully at each item in this list to see how you stand." The two absolute-risk questions (for oneself and for the average student) appeared immediately beneath this text. The risk-likelihood questions used 12-point scales ranging from "no chance" to "certain to happen."

In the "risk-increasing attributes" condition, the list was formed from the unfavorable end of each risk factor (e.g., "Don't get any physical exercise") and by changing "lower risk" to "higher risk" in the introduction. The control group gave risk judgments for each problem without seeing a list of risk-influencing attributes.

RESULTS AND DISCUSSION

The mean risk judgments in each condition are shown in Table 17.1. Data were examined by a repeated-measures MANOVA with hazard (heart disease versus drinking problem) and person rated (self vs. other) as within-subject variables and condition and order as between-subject variables. Significant effects emerged for hazard, $F(1, 158) = 35.7$, $p < .0001$; person rated, $F(1, 158) = 277.5$, $p < .0001$; and Hazard $\times$ Person Rated, $F(1, 158) = 49.4$, $p < .0001$; there was a consistent tendency to rate one's own risk lower than that of other students and a greater bias for drinking problems than for heart disease. The key effects are those associated with the condition variable, but none of these proved significant, all $ps > .1$.

Thus, there was no indication that either of the experimental groups was less optimistic in its judgments than the control group. In fact, the tendency was for biases to be somewhat strengthened, suggesting that an intervention like this could actually worsen the biases it is meant to diminish.

STUDY 3

It is possible that the pallid lists of risk factors provided in Study 2 were not sufficiently involving or salient to alter participants' standard of comparison. Health promotion messages, in contrast, by the repetition of messages containing real people and a mixture of visual and auditory information, may create a standard against which people compare themselves. Thus, Study 3 used a new manipulation built on visual mental images, which have been shown to enhance the processing and memory of various stimuli such as food names (Boneau, 1990) and faces (Ellis, 1986). . . .

In Study 3, participants formed a mental image (from five risk factors we provided) of someone at high or low risk for having a weight problem. In contrast to Study 2, participants pictured the risk factors and combined them into an image of a single individual like themselves. (Indeed, all participants spontaneously imagined someone their age.) Our aim was to make this image readily available when participants later judged their own risk. We predicted that participants imaging a low-risk target would become less optimistic (and those imaging a high-risk target more optimistic) in comparison with a no-image control group.

Method

Participants. Participants were undergraduates (73% female) at Colby College ($n = 90$) or Rutgers University ($n = 100$) participating for course credit.

Materials. The difficulty of the imagery task was rated on an 11-point scale ranging from "extremely easy" (0) to "extremely difficult" (10). Image vividness was rated on a 7-point scale ranging from "perfectly clear and as vivid as a real experience" (1) to "no image present at all, only 'knowing' that I was thinking of an experience" (7). In the experimental conditions, participants also described the age, height, and similarity to themselves of the person created in the mental image (the last on a 11-point scale ranging from "not at all like me" to "extremely similar to me").

In the postmanipulation questionnaire, all participants rated their and the average college student's absolute risk of becoming "seriously overweight" (30 lbs or more overweight) using 11-point scales ranging from "no chance" (0) to "certain to happen" (10). Participants also compared their risk with that of other students on the 7-point scale used in Study 1, and then reported their comparative standing on nine factors associated with weight (e.g., involvement in sports), using 7-point scales.

Procedure. The experimenter described the study's purpose as exploring the use of mental images to help people remember information about health risks.

Participants learned that one of the health risks being investigated was excessive weight. The control group ($n = 53$) was then given the postmanipulation questionnaire. The other participants were told that they would be forming a mental image of a target with low risk ($n = 56$) or high risk ($n = 53$) of being seriously overweight. The low-risk group learned that the target was physically active (e.g., jogged two or three times a week), had a good pattern of eating (e.g., liked vegetarian dishes), rarely snacked between meals, had a high

Table 17.2. Study 3 – Risk Perceptions in Different Experimental Conditions

	Condition		
Rated Risk of Serious Weight Problem	High-Risk Image (*n* = 53)	Low-Risk Image (*n* = 56)	Control (*n* = 53)
Own risk[a]	2.75	3.60	3.86
Average student's risk[a]	4.82	5.25	5.36
Comparative risk[b]	−1.36	−.89	−0.54

[a] Scale ranged from "no chance" (0) to "certain to happen" (10).
[b] Scale ranged from "much below average" (−3) to "much above average" (+3).

rate of metabolism, and came from a thin family. The high-risk group was told that the target was not physically active (e.g., studied a lot), had a poor pattern of eating (e.g., went back for seconds on entrees), snacked between meals frequently, had a low rate of metabolism, and came from a heavy family. Risk factors were provided to participants one at a time, separated by 5-second intervals. Participants were encouraged to fit each piece of information into their image as they heard it, with the ultimate goal of generating a vivid image of the target person.

The experimental groups then rated the difficulty of creating this image and the vividness of the image, before the postmanipulation questionnaire.

Results

Risk Judgments. Mean values are shown in Table 17.2. When the absolute-risk judgments were analyzed by MANOVA, there was a significant effect of person rated, indicating an optimistic bias, $F(1, 184) = 105.6$, $p < .0001$, and a significant condition effect, $F(2, 184) = 5.3$, $p < .01$, but no significant Person Rated × Condition interaction, $F(2, 184) = 1.1$, $p > .3$. Post-hoc tests showed that the high-risk group's ratings were significantly lower ($p < .05$) than the other two groups' ratings on own risk and also lower, but not significantly, on others' risk.

Comparative-risk ratings were also optimistic, $M = -0.94, t(189) = 8.1$, $p < .0001$. An ANOVA on comparative-risk judgments revealed a significant condition effect, $F(2, 186) = 4.0$, $p < .02$. Post-hoc tests showed that ratings of the high-risk image group were significantly more optimistic ($p < .05$) than those of the control group. The low-risk image group was also more optimistic than the control group, but not significantly. Thus, creating a high-risk image made participants more optimistic in their own absolute ratings and in their comparative-risk ratings, but people creating a low-risk image were not significantly different from the control group.

Image Creation. The mean ratings for the difficulty of forming an image and the vividness of this image were 3.2 (on a 0–10 scale) and 3.0, respectively (where 3 = "moderately clear"). There were no between-group differences in these ratings ($ps > .5$).

Discussion

As in Studies 1 and 2, optimistic beliefs about personal health risks proved resistant to manipulation. Participants who formed an image of a very high-risk individual became even more optimistic. However, participants appeared to resist using the low-risk image as a comparison target. That a mental image of a high-risk individual can increase unrealistic optimism indirectly supports the notion that people construct negative stereotypes (e.g., Weinstein, 1980) or prototypes (e.g., Wood, 1989) of the type of person who experiences a health problem. If we assume that the high-risk target was seen as more the norm than the exception, it follows that making this target salient should have a greater effect on risk estimates than the low-risk target. . . .

STUDY 4

Several studies have shown that generating reasons why some outcome might occur (Hoch, 1984; Levi & Pryor, 1987; Sherman, Skov, Hervitz, & Stock, 1981) or generating a series of events (a scenario) that might lead to this outcome (Anderson, 1983; Carroll, 1978; Gregory, Cialdini, & Carpenter, 1982) increases the perceived likelihood that the event will actually take place.

Study 4 attempted to alter risk judgments by having subjects generate their own list of factors that might lead themselves to develop (or that would keep them from developing) a weight or drinking problem. It was expected that participants listing risk-increasing factors would subsequently judge themselves more at risk (and those listing risk-decreasing factors judge themselves less at risk) than would control-group participants who estimated their risk without listing any risk factors. . . .

Method

Participants and Procedure. Participants were undergraduates (57.4% female) at Rutgers University ($n = 194$) or Colby College ($n = 180$). They were approached in public places and asked to complete an anonymous questionnaire dealing with health and safety issues. Of those approached, the completion rate was 93%.

Materials. Two health hazards were included: serious weight problem (30 lbs or more overweight) and drinking problem. In the two experimental conditions (risk-increasing and risk-decreasing reasons), the first side of the questionnaire asked participants to "list all the factors you can think of that tend to increase [decrease] your own chances of eventually developing" the problem indicated. Factors were defined as anything about "your own behavior, habits, personality, body, environment, family, etc., that you think increase [decrease] your risk." Six blanks were provided in which participants

Table 17.3. Study 4 – Risk Perceptions in Different Experimental Conditions

	Condition		
Problem and Rating	Risk-Increasing Reasons	Risk-Decreasing Reasons	Control
Serious weight problem			
n	66	58	61
Own risk[a]	3.50	2.42	3.50
Average student[a]	5.47	5.20	5.19
Comparative risk[b]	−0.79	−1.16	−0.84
Drinking problem			
N	59	62	64
Own risk[a]	2.54	2.22	1.75
Average student[a]	5.20	5.11	4.80
Comparative risk[b]	−1.18	−1.38	−1.48

[a] Scale ranged from "no chance" (0) to "certain to happen" (10).
[b] Scale ranged from "much below average" (−3) to "much above average" (+3).

could enter these risk factors. The second side asked participants to compare their own risk to that of same-sex college students and also asked for absolute risk judgments for themselves and for an average college student, using the same risk scales as those in Study 3. Control participants responded only to the risk questions and did not list risk factors. Each participant considered only one health problem.

Results and Discussion

Absolute risk ratings (Table 17.3) were examined by a repeated-measures MANOVA, with person rated as a within-subject variable and condition and hazard as between-subject variables. Significant effects were found for person rated, $F(1, 367) = 348.5$, $p < .0001$, evidencing optimistic bias; for hazard, $F(1, 367) = 19.2$, $p < .0001$, indicating higher risk ratings for weight problems than for drinking problems; and for the Problem × Person Rated interaction, $F(1, 357) = 7.7$, $p < .01$, indicating a greater optimistic bias for drinking problems. There were also significant effects for condition, $F(2, 367) = 3.9$, $p < .02$, and for the Problem × Condition interaction, $F(2, 367) = 3.5$, $p < .05$, but no significant effects for the Condition × Person Rated interaction or the Condition × Problem × Person Rated interaction, both $ps > .15$.

Each health problem was then examined separately. For drinking problems, there was a significant condition effect, $F(2, 182) = 3.1$, $p < .05$, but no significant Condition × Person Rated interaction, $p > .7$. The control group gave the lowest ratings for both own and others' risk, though none of the post-hoc tests (using Tukey's studentized range test) that compared condition pairs were significant. For weight problems, there were significant effects for condition, $F(2, 185) = 4.4$, $p < .02$, and for the Condition × Person Rated interaction, $F(2, 185) = 3.6$, $p < .03$. As seen in Table 17.3, these effects reflect lower ratings for own risk in the risk-decreasing reasons condition than in the other conditions ($ps < .05$ by Tukey's test); the own risk ratings for the control and risk-increasing reasons conditions did not differ.

An ANOVA for comparative-risk judgments found a main effect for problem, $F(1, 362) = 6.9$, $p < .01$, suggesting greater bias for drinking problems, but no significant condition effect or Problem × Condition interaction, $ps > .3$.

Thus, we were not able to decrease optimistic biases. However, as in Study 3, we were able to exacerbate these biases for absolute risk ratings of weight problems.

GENERAL DISCUSSION

Four studies testing a variety of approaches and using a variety of health hazards were unsuccessful in reducing optimistic biases about familiar health hazards. In Study 1, informing participants about relevant risk factors and requiring them to describe their standing on these factors had no overall effect on subsequent risk judgments. Studies 2 and 3 attempted to alter risk perceptions by encouraging participants to compare themselves with a low- rather than a high-risk standard. Most risk ratings were unaffected. Moreover, when effects did occur, they were stronger on ratings of personal risk than on ratings of others' risk, even though one might think it easier to change perceptions of others' risk. In Study 4, the well-documented technique of influencing likelihood perceptions by having participants generate factors that would make an event more or less likely (Hoch, 1984; Levi & Pryor, 1987; Sherman et al., 1981) produced weak and inconsistent effects.

One common limitation of these manipulations is that none offered participants information about their own standing on risk factors or information about peers' standing on these factors. When such an approach was taken in past work, optimistic biases were successfully reduced, perhaps because it was more obvious to participants that they should use this information in making their judgments (e.g., Weinstein, 1983). We chose not to use these methods in the present research, preferring manipulations – especially those in Studies 1–3 – that would be easier to use in media-based health-promotion campaigns. Our findings strongly suggest that, at least for familiar health problems, reminding people of risk factors or encouraging people to compare themselves with a low-risk target has little impact on personal risk perceptions and does not reduce people's tendency to claim that they are less at risk than their peers.

Ironically, evidence was gathered to show that focusing attention on risk-increasing factors can exaggerate optimistic biases. Three studies produced some increase in optimistic biases (although these effects were sometimes inconsistent across hazards and risk-rating scales): in Study 2 by a list of worst-case risk factors, in Study 3 by an image of a high-risk comparison target, and in Study 4 by a personal list of risk-decreasing risk factors. It appears that health campaigns emphasizing high-risk targets (such as smoking interventions that show unattractive pictures of smokers) and campaigns conveying information about undesirable actions (as with pamphlets listing factors that raise the risk for a particular health problem) may unwittingly worsen the very biases they are designed to reduce.

18. Ambiguity and Self-Evaluation: The Role of Idiosyncratic Trait Definitions in Self-Serving Assessments of Ability

David Dunning, Judith A. Meyerowitz, and Amy D. Holzberg

When people are asked to evaluate their own abilities, the assessments they provide tend to be self-serving. Indeed, often the appraisals that people endorse appear to be favorable to a logically impossible degree.

Perhaps the most direct demonstration of self-serving appraisal is the *above average effect*. When asked to judge their own capacities and performances in a specific domain against those of their peers, people predominantly respond, "I'm above average." The above average effect has been demonstrated in the realm of driving ability (Svenson, 1981), ethics (Baumhart, 1968), health (Larwood, 1978: Weinstein, 1980), and managerial skills (Larwood & Whittaker, 1977). The most extreme documentation of this phenomenon comes from a survey conducted by the College Board in 1976–1977 of 1 million high school students. When rating themselves vis-à-vis their peers, 70% rated themselves as above average in leadership ability, whereas only 2% judged themselves as below average. When considering athletic ability, 60% considered themselves above the median and only 6%, below. When asked to judge their ability to get along with others, all students rated themselves as at least average, 60% placed themselves in the top 10%, and 25% placed themselves in the top 1%. The extremity of the phenomenon in this particular survey might be chalked up to youthful exuberance, although the above average effect occurs even among older and more educated people. For example, 94% of all college professors say they do above average work (Cross, 1977)....

The research reported here expressly examines one specific source of this self-serving pattern in assessments of ability: the use of idiosyncratic definitions of traits and abilities when providing assessments of this sort. It is proposed that the definition of *competence* or *excellence* in many domains is unclear. As a result, people are free to use divergent criteria and to draw on disparate types of behavioral evidence when evaluating themselves in comparison to their peers. It is argued here that people tend to use criteria and evidence, whether deliberately or inadvertently, that place them in an unduly positive light.

This is an edited and condensed version of a paper that first appeared in the *Journal of Personality and Social Psychology, 57*, 1082–1090. Copyright © 1978 by the American Psychological Association. Adapted with permission.

What does it mean, for example, to be a good leader? Is the good leader "task oriented," placing a premium on organization, attention to detail and the articulation of explicit goals? Is the good leader able to prod and bully his or her subordinates regardless of their happiness, health, or ego? Or is the leader "people oriented," attuned to the needs and concerns of employees, able to resolve conflicts and to assure group cohesion? The contention here is that people select those criteria that place them in the best light. In the example above, when evaluating leadership potential, an aggressive individual may define the good leader as compulsive and task oriented. A more nuturant individual might use a definition emphasizing social skills.

Both motivational and cognitive mechanisms could underlie the use of self-serving trait definitions in self-evaluation.

The motivational concern that would prompt the use of idiosyncratic definitions is self-evident. In order to maintain self-esteem, people may actively select the definition that puts them in a favorable light. Many researchers have argued that people place great weight on evidence that is consistent with desired outcomes while heavily discounting contrary evidence (cf. Gilovich, 1983; Kunda, 1987; Lord, Lepper, & Ross, 1979). If people distort their assessments in order to achieve positive self-images, then there is no more convenient avenue than the selection of the criteria of comparison.

However, the *availability heuristic* (Tversky & Kahneman, 1974) might be the factor driving the use of idiosyncratic evidence. Simply put, when people judge themselves and others, the criteria that are most easily brought to mind might be the particular behaviors that they themselves perform, the unusual skills that they possess, and the chronic habits that they exhibit. . . .

The goal of the present research was to explore directly the role of idiosyncratic evidence and criteria in self-serving appraisals of ability. Toward that end, the first two studies explored whether self-assessments become more self-serving, and seemingly objectively impossible, as the opportunity to construct idiosyncratic trait definitions increased (i.e., as the specific behaviors and skills referred to by the traits became more ambiguous). The third study investigated whether the criteria people use in self-evaluation are truly idiosyncratic and whether this ultimately leads to the favorable evaluations of self that people predominantly make.

STUDY 1: TRAIT AMBIGUITY AND SELF-SERVING ASSESSMENTS

Study 1 explores one preliminary prediction growing from the notion of idiosyncratic evidence in self-assessment. Specifically, people were expected to provide more favorable self-appraisals to the extent that the characteristic in question was ambiguous. By ambiguous, we mean something close to what Hampson, John, and Goldberg (1986) refer to as *trait breadth*; that is, the trait can refer to any number of behaviors or characteristics (e.g., sophisticated) as opposed to just a few (e.g., tall). Toward that end, subjects were presented with a list of characteristics that were either ambiguous (e.g., sensitive, sophisticated, insecure, inconsistent) or rather unambiguous (e.g., punctual, studious, clumsy, wordy). Subjects were asked to rate themselves on these characteristics relative to their peers. It was predicted that subjects would self-enhance more on ambiguous traits (that is, rate themselves high on positive traits and low on negative ones) than on unambiguous characteristics. . . .

Method

We asked 27 Cornell University students to rate their abilities relative to their peers for ambiguous versus unambiguous characteristics. Toward that end, 28 traits were selected from the list provided by Anderson (1968). Traits were divided into four categories: ambiguous positive (i.e., sensitive, sophisticated, idealistic, disciplined, sensible, ingenious, and quick), ambiguous negative (i.e., neurotic, inconsistent, impractical, naive, submissive, compulsive, and insecure), unambiguous positive (i.e., neat, well-read, mathematical, thrifty, athletic, studious, and punctual), and unambiguous negative (i.e., sarcastic, wordy, sloppy, clumsy, gullible, gossipy, and bragging).

Twenty additional undergraduates provided ratings for the 28 traits along the dimensions of ambiguity and social desirability. These judges rated the ambiguity for each trait on a 9-point scale by indicating whether it referred to one and only one type of behavior (scored as 1) or to many different behaviors in many different domains of life (scored as 9). Judges similarly rated the traits for social desirability on a 9-point scale from 1 (trait is undesirable) to 9 (trail is highly desirable). Ambiguous positive traits were seen as more ambiguous than unambiguous ones ($Ms = 6.3$ and 3.7, respectively), $t(19) = 6.96$, $p < .0001$. Ambiguous negative traits, as well, were seen as more ambiguous than the unambiguous negative set ($Ms = 5.8$ and 3.9, respectively), $t(19) = 4.55$, $p < .01$. In addition, the 14 positive traits were seen as more socially desirable than were the 14 negative ones ($Ms = 6.5$ and 2.4, respectively), $t(19) = 16.13$, $p < .0001$. Importantly, in this collection of traits, ambiguity was not confounded with social desirability. Ambiguous positive traits were just as socially desirable as unambiguous characteristics ($Ms = 6.4$ and 6.6, respectively), $t = -1.35$. Ambiguous and unambiguous negative traits also did not differ in terms of social desirability ($Ms = 2.4$ and 2.5, respectively), $t < 1$.

Subjects were asked to estimate what percentile among Cornell students they fell in. Subjects were reminded that a percentile score indicates the percentage of Cornell students performing below the subject's level and were provided with several examples.

Results

Did subjects provide self-serving assessments to a greater degree when the characteristic was ambiguous? To answer that question, we subjected the percentile ratings that subjects provided to a 2 (trait ambiguity) × 2 (social desirability) repeated measures analysis of variance (ANOVA). This analysis supported our guiding prediction, interaction $F(1, 107) = 25.06$, $P < .0001$. As can be seen in Table 18.1, for positive traits, subjects rated themselves more highly on ambiguous characteristics ($M = 64.2$) than on unambiguous ones ($M = 54.6$), $t(26) = 4.24$, $p < .0005$. For negative traits, subjects rated themselves lower on ambiguous characteristics ($M = 37.7$) than on unambiguous ones ($M = 49.7$), $t(26) = -3.97$, $p < .0005$. The analysis also revealed the expected effect for social desirability. Subjects rated themselves higher on positive traits ($M = 59.4$) than on negative characteristics ($M = 43.7$), $F(1, 107) = 52.95$, $p < .0001$....

Table 18.1. Mean Percentile Rankings as a Function of Trait Desirability and Ambiguity

	Trait Ambiguity	
Trait Desirability	Low	High
Positive		
M	54.6*	64.2**
sd	12.3	50.1
Negative		
M	49.7	37.7**
sd	13.8	14.5

Note: $n = 27$. Different from 50th percentile: $^*p < .10$; $^{**}p < .001$.

A correlational analysis that focused on the individual trait terms themselves also confirmed the role of ambiguity and desirability in self-serving assessments. For each trait, we computed a self-enhancement score. For positive traits, this consisted of how far subjects' mean response on each trait deviated positively from a response of 50. For negative traits, we computed how far subjects' responses deviated from 50 in a negative direction. When these self-enhancement scores were correlated with the degree of rated ambiguity of the traits, we found a significant correlation, $r(26) = .47$, $p < .02$....

STUDY 2: MANIPULATIONS OF TRAIT AMBIGUITY

Study 2 was designed to investigate the role of trait ambiguity more directly by manipulating the freedom subjects had in choosing the criteria of evaluation. Specifically, in this study we asked subjects to evaluate themselves in several domains, given an explicit set of criteria to consider. Some subjects were given ample freedom to construct an idiosyncratic definition of the trait, that is, they were given a list of six potential criteria to consider; other subjects were allowed less latitude (i.e., being given only two or four criteria to consider before providing their second set of assessments). A final group of subjects, serving as controls, gave a second set of appraisals without an explicit list of criteria. It was predicted that as the number of criteria subjects considered decreased, so would the favorability of their self-evaluations.

Method

One hundred and fifty-two Cornell University undergraduates provided a percentile ranking of their abilities in several domains vis-à-vis Cornell students. Four specific domains concerned positive traits (talented, athletic, cultured/sophisticated, active in extracurriculars). Three additional questions asked subjects to rank their standing for undesirable characteristics (trouble handling money, disorganized in schoolwork, social anxiety).

Four different versions of the questionnaire were constructed in order to manipulate the number of criteria that subjects could consider in their evaluations. In the *unspecified-criteria condition* ($n = 39$), subjects were given no specific criteria to consider. In the *six-criteria condition* ($n = 35$), six criteria of evaluation were listed for each trait. For example, in the domain of talent, subjects were presented with this list of potential criteria: (1) paints; (2) good storyteller, comedian; (3) writes stories, poetry, plays; (4) acts, does theater; (5) sings; and (6) does a craft (e.g., pottery, woodwork). Subjects were told that "For each trait or characteristic below, we have listed the specific criteria we want you to consider when evaluating yourself. Use only these criteria when estimating your percentile score." Subjects in the *four-criteria condition* ($n = 39$) were given four of the criteria to consider in their evaluations. Subjects in the *two-criteria condition* ($n = 39$) were only given a menu of two. For these last two conditions, three different versions of the questionnaire were created so that each specific criterion (of the six total shown to subjects) was seen by an equal number of subjects. Thus, no specific criterion was ever over- or underrepresented.

Results and Discussion

Our prediction for Study 2 was straightforward: For positive traits, self-ratings were expected to rise as the number of the criteria that subjects could consider increased. For negative traits, self-ratings were expected to become lower as the number of criteria increased. We collapsed evaluations across the four positive domains into an overall evaluation. The same was done for evaluations along the three negative domains. These ratings were then subjected to a 4 (ambiguity condition: two, four, six, unspecified number of criteria) × 2 (positive versus negative trait) ANOVA, with the last factor serving as a within-subject variable. Two significant effects were observed. First, self-ratings for positive traits were higher than ratings on negative characteristics, $F(1, 148) = 26.06$, $p < .0001$. More central to our present concerns, there was a main effect for the number of criteria subjects were allowed to consider, $F(3, 148) = 4.11$, $p < .01$. No interaction between these two factors was observed, $F < 2$.

Table 18.2 displays responses of subjects under the various ambiguity conditions. As can be seen in the table, for positive traits, the effect of ambiguity was straightforward. As the number of criteria increased, self-evaluations rose, $F(3, 148) = 4.32$, $p < .01$. The progression is rather orderly from the two-criteria ($M = 48.0$) to the four-criteria ($M = 52.2$) to the six-criteria ($M = 57.6$) to the unspecified condition ($M = 58.9$).

Responses to negative characteristics were somewhat more complex. Self-ratings increased from the two- to the four- to the six-criteria conditions ($Ms = 39.4$, 42.3, and 49.8, respectively), but then fell in the unspecified criteria condition ($M = 38.8$). These group differences, however, were not significantly

Table 18.2. Percentile Rankings as a Function of Trait
Desirability and Number of Criteria Allowed to Consider

Trait Desirability	Number of Criteria			
	Two	Four	Six	Unspecified
Positive				
M	48.0	52.2	57.6*	58.9*
sd	15.4	14.2	14.0	16.5
Negative				
M	39.4*	42.3	49.8	38.8*
sd	22.5	21.4	22.5	21.2
n	39	39	35	39

* Significantly different from 50th percentile; $p < .05$.

different, $F(3, 148) = 1.94$, ns; and although each individual item displayed the same pattern of responses, the pattern was never observed to a statistically significant degree.

In sum, the results of Study 2 more directly implicated trait ambiguity in the favorability of self-assessments. Subjects provided positive appraisals of their abilities to the extent that they could pick and choose between criteria of evaluation. When the menu of potential criteria was constricted, self-assessments became lower.

Recall that in the first study, subjects were less likely to endorse negative traits as self-descriptive as those characteristics became ambiguous. In Study 2, however, as traits became more ambiguous, people endorsed them as more self-descriptive. How can this apparent contradiction be explained? One way to resolve these findings is to note that, in Study 2, people were constrained to consider criteria and evidence that would indicate that they, indeed, exhibited the negative trait in question. In the first study, however, people were free to consider criteria or evidence that indicated that they did not possess the relevant characteristic (i.e., they could consider "How am I not like this trait?"). For example, when considering the term *insecure*, they could consider situations or evidence that indicated that they were self-confident. In Study 2, however, we prevented people from considering that type of evidence, thus potentially producing this contradictory result.

STUDY 3: LINKING IDIOSYNCRATIC TRAIT DEFINITIONS WITH SELF-SERVING ASSESSMENTS

The previous studies demonstrated that people distort their self-assessments to the extent that the domain in question is ambiguous. However, it did not directly document that people are relying on idiosyncratic definitions in those appraisals; that is, that different individuals are considering divergent criteria and evidence when providing self-appraisals. That documentation was the aim of Study 3. In this study, we compared the self-appraisals of subjects who were allowed to generate freely their own criteria of evaluation against those forced to consider someone else's set of criteria. If people do generate idiosyncratic evidence, then the evaluations of the latter group should be lower than those of the first.

Specifically, in this study we asked subjects to provide self-evaluations under three different conditions. Initially, all subjects provided estimates of their percentile ranking among Cornell students in three different domains: athletics, artistic talent (including the performing arts), and activity in extracurricular activities. These three domains were chosen because pretests indicated that subjects tend to cite unambiguous evidence and criteria when considering these domains. In an *own-criteria condition*, subjects were asked to list the evidence and criteria they thought of when evaluating themselves before offering a second set of percentile estimates. In a *yoked-criteria group*, the subjects provided a second set of estimates after considering the criteria generated by an individual in the own-criteria group. The last condition was a control group, in which subjects merely offered a second set of estimates with no specific instructions. We expected that the second set of self-assessments offered by subjects in the control and own-criteria groups would not differ from their initial estimates, whereas those of the yoked group would be significantly lower.

Method

We asked 36 Cornell University students to rate themselves in athletics, artistic talent (including performing arts), and activity in extracurricular programs, using the percentile rating scale described earlier. In order not to draw undue attention to these three domains at this point, subjects provided these ratings among 29 other trait domains. After providing these initial estimates, subjects were instructed to give a second set of estimates for the three domains of interest.

In the control condition ($n = 12$), subjects were simply asked to estimate their percentile ranking among Cornell students again for the three domains. They were told that they could change their estimates if they saw fit, but they were not allowed to look back at their original estimates.

In the own-criteria group ($n = 12$), subjects were asked to

Assess your standing among Cornell students for the characteristic using a percentile ranking. But before doing that, we want you to tell us the specific evidence you are thinking of when you evaluate yourself. What specific abilities, habits, skills and behaviors are you considering when you arrive at a percentile score? What activities do you do or don't you do? What things have you done in the past? What was the evidence that prompts you to call yourself more or less X than the typical Cornell student.

Subjects were given an example of the task. They were presented with the characteristic "Health Conscious" and were told that an individual might list "Avoids red meat," "Goes to aerobics," "Doesn't smoke," and "Goes to doctor regularly." Subjects were asked to be as concrete as possible, but were given no limit on the number of criteria they could list. After listing their evidence, subjects provided a new estimate of their percentile rankings "considering *only* the evidence you provided – that is, give us your percentile score considering how much you and other Cornell students display the specific criteria or evidence you just cited above." They were instructed that they could change their estimates if they wished. They were not allowed to look back at their previous estimates.

Each subject in the yoked-criteria condition ($n = 12$) based his or her second set of estimates on the criteria generated by a particular subject in the own-criteria group. The language used by the own-criteria subjects underwent minimal changes for the purpose of removing specifics of place and time (e.g., "Has been a DJ at [name of radio station]" was changed to "Worked as a DJ": "Played tuba in band for 5 years" was changed to "Played instrument in band"). When an own-criteria subject generated negative evidence (e.g., "Have not played team sports"), it was changed to its positive form (e.g., "Played team sports"). In the yoked group, subjects were told that

For each characteristic, we have listed the specific criteria we want you to consider when evaluating yourself. We want you to evaluate yourself among Cornell students using only these criteria, no matter how well they fit your usual conception of the trait in question.

Results

We predicted that self-evaluations would remain the same between pretest and posttest for the control and own criteria groups, but would dramatically decrease in the yoked-criteria condition. In order to test this prediction, we collapsed self-evaluations across the three domains studied and subjected those evaluations to a 3 (criteria condition: own, yoked, control) × 2 (pretest vs. posttest) ANOVA, with the last factor serving as a repeated measure. This analysis revealed the expected Criteria Condition × Test interaction, $F(2, 33) = 7.39$, $p < .005$. Indeed, similar significant interactions were observed for two of the individual domains we examined: athletics, $F(2, 33) = 5.98$, $p < .01$, and talent, $F(2, 33) = 4.35$, $p < .03$.

As can be seen in Table 18.3, subjects did not reliably alter their self-assessments between pretest and posttest in the control and own-criteria

Table 18.3. **Mean Percentile Rankings as a Function of Using Own versus Someone Else's (Yoked) Criteria**

	Criteria Condition		
Measure	Control	Own Criteria	Yoked Criteria
Pretest			
M	52.8	50.3	53.3
sd	18.3	17.4	24.5
Posttest			
M	54.7	53.1	41.3
sd	16.6	14.6	21.6
Difference	1.9	2.8	−12.0*

Note: $n = 12$ per condition.
* Significantly different from 0.

conditions. Of eight possible pretest–posttest comparisons, only one revealed a statistically significant change, which was a small rise in ratings of athletic skill in the control condition (from $M = 50.1$ to 54.8), $t(11) = 2.45$, $p < .05$. Within the yoked-criteria group, however, subjects consistently lowered their self-evaluations from pretest to posttest. If we look at responses collapsed across domain, we find that percentile estimates went from M of 53.3 on the pretest to 41.3 on the posttest, $t(11) = 2.55$, $p < .05$. A significant decrease was also seen in the domain of athletics (from $M = 51.3$ to 34.3), $t(11) = 2.33$, $p < .05$, and artistic talent, $t(11) = 2.99$, $p < .05$. When considering activity in extracurricular programs, subjects did lower their assessments an average of 9.2 points, though that difference was not statistically significant. . . .

GENERAL DISCUSSION

These studies have immediate implications for recent treatments of the above average effect, specifically those that have treated this particular phenomenon as conclusive evidence that the judgments that people normally render in the social realm are fraught with unrealistic cognitive illusions and distortions (Taylor & Brown, 1988). The studies described here confirmed one assertion made by proponents of this viewpoint: In our studies, college students (who we take to be a nondepressed population) provided self-assessments that appear to be self-serving and biased.

However, the analysis of the above average effect presented here throws its status as conclusive evidence of unrealistic bias into doubt. It may be that the assessments our subjects provided were hopelessly distorted (for, indeed, how can almost everyone be above average), but it might also be the case that our subjects were largely accurate in the assessments they provided. More specifically, after considering and presumably defining ambiguous traits, subjects may have subsequently provided percentile rankings that were accurate given their own idiosyncratic definitions. Buttressing the notion that people may be accurate within their own peculiar definitions is the fact that when considering unambiguous traits, people exhibited hardly any self-serving pattern whatsoever. That is, once the criteria of judgment are clearly established, people have the ability to assess their own standing in relation to their peers accurately.

Under this analysis, the above average effect by itself fails to serve as clear evidence of bias and distortion in social judgment. In effect, when people consider their own definition, and perhaps the one most relevant to the daily tasks they face, they may be largely accurate. However, even if this is the case, we can still conjecture that the above average effect, and the self-serving use of trait ambiguity, may have alarming social costs. These costs occur when one individual considers his or her peculiar definition as the only one worthy of consideration and fails to recognize when other plausible definitions are relevant.

One cost may occur when an individual believes that his or her definition of ability is the only one relevant to achievement outcomes. Specifically, when people attempt to predict how well they will perform in comparison to their peers on some common achievement metric (e.g., grades, games won, salary, rate of promotion), they may reliably overestimate how much they will achieve because they consider only their own self-serving definition of the relevant ability domain. For example, consider a company that has three vice presidents – one from sales, one from accounting, and one from engineering – who are being considered for promotion to president. Each considers him- or herself to be an outstanding manager among his or her peers because he or she only considers a self-serving definition of "managerial skill." The vice president for sales, for example, can cite his well-developed ability to persuade. The vice president from accounting can cite her ability to keep track of all details of a project. The vice president from engineering can cite her ability to coordinate different individuals into an organized project. If each of these people only considers one peculiar definition of leadership ability when estimating the likelihood of receiving the promotion, there will clearly be some overconfidence and error.

From this example, it is also apparent that self-serving definitions of ability can also be a springboard for social disharmony. Consider the promotion once it is made. To two of the vice presidents, it will appear more mysterious than to the third. The choice may seem capricious, or even malicious, and may lead to some rancor. For another example, consider a group of professors awaiting word on a merit raise in their salary. Social conflict can occur when one receives an average or less than average pay increase when one's self-assessment is higher (and recall, 94% of professors believe they do above average work; Cross, 1977).

In sum, it is impossible to tell whether subjects in four studies were largely accurate or biased in their assessments of ability when their idiosyncratic trait definitions were taken into consideration. From the preceding analysis, however, one point does become clear. To the extent that people fail to recognize when other definitions of ability are relevant for success and achievement, estimates of their future well-being will be exaggerated. . . .

19. When Predictions Fail: The Dilemma of Unrealistic Optimism

David A. Armor and Shelley E. Taylor

One of the most robust findings in the psychology of prediction is that people's predictions tend to be optimistically biased. By a number of metrics and across a variety of domains, people have been found to assign higher probabilities to their attainment of desirable outcomes than either objective criteria or logical analysis warrants. Yet the very prevalence of optimistic biases presents an intriguing dilemma: Given that many of the decisions people make, most of their choices, and virtually all plans are based on expectations about the future, it would seem imperative that people's predictions and expectations be free from bias. If the majority of predictions, expectations and performance-relevant perceptions are optimistically biased, how can people make appropriate decisions, or choose effective courses of action?

We review research on optimistic biases in personal predictions and address the question of how people can maintain these biases when doing so would seem to be maladaptive. We begin by reviewing empirical evidence that has shown optimistic biases to be a common feature of people's predictions and expectations.

EVIDENCE OF OPTIMISTIC BIAS IN PERSONAL PREDICTIONS

Henrik Ibsen maintained "that man is in the right who is most clearly in league with the future" (in Sprinchorn, 1964). By similar logic, one might argue that the clearest demonstrations of optimistic biases are those that have revealed systematic discrepancies between people's predictions and the outcomes they ultimately attain. Empirical studies of the planning fallacy, for example, have shown that people expect to complete personal projects in less time than it actually takes to complete them (e.g., Buehler, Griffin, & Ross, 1994). Evidence that predictions often exceed outcomes has not been limited to estimates of task completion times, however. Documenting a tendency familiar to most students, if not their instructors, Shepperd, Ouellette, and Fernandez (1996) found that students expect to receive higher scores on exams, at least when those exams are still some time away, than they actually receive when they take those exams (see also Doleys & Renzaglia, 1963; Radhakrishnan, Arrow, & Sniezek, 1996). Second-year MBA students were found to overestimate the number of job offers they would receive, the magnitude of their starting salary, and how early they would receive their first offer (Hoch, 1985). Even the forecasts of professional financial analysts have been found to be optimistically biased: Although the studied analysts were reasonably able to anticipate periods of growth and decline in corporate earnings, their forecasts consistently overestimated earnings realized (Calderon, 1993; see also Barefield & Comiskey, 1975). Also, in a set of studies by Mitchell, Thompson, Peterson, and Cronk (1997), incipient vacationers were found to anticipate greater enjoyment during upcoming trips than they actually expressed during their trips, suggesting that people may be overly optimistic even when asked to anticipate their own evaluations of future experiences.

Despite the conceptual clarity of these results and the lack of ambiguity of the criterion against which predictions are regarded optimistic, researchers have largely resorted to other methods in their investigations of optimistic bias. These methods, although less direct, have yielded a number of important insights about the nature of optimistic predictions.

One alternate strategy has been to compare people's predictions to outcomes attained by similar others. For example, Sherman (1980) asked college students to predict how they would behave in one of a variety of specific situations, and then compared their predictions to the observed behavior of students who had actually been placed in one of the targeted situations. The results of Sherman's studies revealed that students' predictions were optimistically biased: Participants consistently reported that they would behave in more socially desirable ways – for example, that they would be more resistant to unwanted social influence, or more likely to donate time to a worthy charity – than did people who had not first been asked to make predictions about their behavior. By the same logic, many newlyweds – who almost uniformly expect that their marriages will endure a lifetime (Baker & Emery, 1993) – can be considered unrealistically optimistic when their expectations are viewed against the high rate of divorce in contemporary society.

Research comparing personal expectations to population base rates has not uniformly revealed evidence of optimistic bias, however. Several studies have shown that, for important and personally relevant events such as unwanted pregnancy, people's expectations can be quite accurate with respect to the base rates of relevant populations (Whitley & Hern, 1991; Gerrard & Luus, 1995). People also appear to consistently overestimate the prevalence of, and their own likelihood of experiencing, low-frequency events (including extremely negative, life-threatening events such as AIDS) and to underestimate high-frequency events (e.g., Lichtenstein, Slovic, Fischoff, Layman, & Combs, 1978; Rothman, Klein, & Weinstein, 1996). One might hesitate to label the overestimation of negative but statistically infrequent outcomes as evidence of genuine, psychologically meaningful pessimism, however, as these estimates may simply reflect difficulties interpreting and reporting extreme probabilities. Indeed, these apparent pessimistic responses may make the unwanted consequence seem likely enough to warrant preventative action, but still sufficiently unlikely to not be the cause for feelings of hopelessness, panic, or self-defeating behavior. Consistent with this interpretation, Rothman et al. (1996) found that even people who appeared pessimistic when their predictions were compared to population base rates appeared to be optimistic when assessed on an alternate measure of optimistic bias that relies on people's assessments of their relative likelihood of experiencing future events.

By far the most commonly used method of assessing excessive optimism relies on the comparison of what people expect for themselves and what they expect for others (e.g., Weinstein, 1980; Perloff & Fetzer, 1986). Results from hundreds of empirical investigations have shown that, on average, people tend to view themselves as more likely to experience positive outcomes, and less likely to experience negative ones, than the average members of the group from which they have been drawn (Weinstein, 1998b). For example, most people expect that they have a better-than-average chance of living long, healthy lives; being successfully employed and happily married; and avoiding a variety of unwanted experiences such as being robbed or assaulted, injured in an automobile accident, or experiencing health problems (Weinstein, 1980). Although such comparisons cannot be used to identify optimistic biases within any one individual – any one person may be (and up to half of any group will be) more likely to attain favorable outcomes relative to the average member of their group – the proportion of individuals expecting to be above the median in terms of future outcomes is commonly found to be impossibly large. Representative studies from our own lab, for example, have found that between 85% and 90% of respondents claim that their future will be better – more pleasant and less painful – than the future of an average peer (Armor, 2000, unpublished raw data). This suggests that at least some (and possibly many) are assessing their relative prospects too favorably.

THE DILEMMA

Although expressions of unrealistic optimism appear to be quite common, intuition dictates a number of compelling reasons why unrealistic optimism might be expected to be inhibited or even extinguished. First, and most obviously, for those who expect to attain positive outcomes, there is a very real possibility that those outcomes will not be attained, and for those who maintain optimistically biased expectations, the failure to attain these outcomes would, by definition, be guaranteed. The failure to attain desired outcomes can have obvious social and psychological costs (such as disappointment in one's efforts, mistrust in one's ability, or even hostile ridicule for promises unfulfilled) as well as costs associated with any investment of time, effort, or financial resources that had been expended in the failed effort. Moreover, the cumulative effects of continued failure to meet optimistically biased predictions might be expected to have disastrous consequences for people's abilities to effectively regulate their behavior, as repeated disappointment has been found to compromise people's ability to set and meet future goals and undermine motivation (e.g., Hiroto & Seligman, 1975).

Additional concerns arise if, as many researchers suggest, people use their optimistic expectations as a basis for action. People who have unrealistic expectations about how likely they will be to attain positive outcomes may feel it less necessary to complete actions that are necessary for them to attain these outcomes. Similarly, people who do not expect negative events to happen to them may behave in ways that put themselves in actual danger. Much of the research on unrealistic optimism has been conducted in the domain of health, and many researchers in this area have expressed concern that false belief about personal invulnerability to a variety of health threats may lead people to forgo necessary preventative actions (e.g., Weinstein, 1987). There is also some concern that overly positive expectations about the consequences of one's actions may lead people to persist in vain to complete actions for which they are ill-prepared, or to seek outcomes that are impossible to achieve or that are noncontingent on continued efforts (e.g., Janoff-Bulman & Brickman, 1982; but see Aspinwall & Richter, 1999). Finally, optimistic social comparisons – in which people believe their own chances of success are greater than the likelihood that other people will succeed – may be especially problematic when accurate understanding of one's relative chances of success is relevant for particular decisions, such as whether to enter into a competitive market (Camerer & Lovallo, 1999).

Although there are a number of intuitively plausible concerns about the negative consequences of optimistic biases, there has been surprisingly little research to justify them. It is possible that research relevant to the potentially punishing effects of optimistic biases has not been conducted because these effects seem so intuitively plausible that researchers may find them hardly worth testing. The overall lack of evidence documenting any of the punishing consequences of optimistic bias is nonetheless surprising given that the potential for these consequences is often cited as a reason for why the study of optimistic biases is so important. Moreover, what little evidence there is that speaks to these issues does not consistently reveal adverse effects of optimistic bias. For example, there have been a number of studies in which optimistic expectations were disconfirmed, and disappointment, although expected, had not been found. In one study, heart transplant patients who had initially expressed optimistic expectations were no more discouraged following medical complications than were patients who initially had been less optimistic (Leedham, Meyerwitz, Muirhead, & Frist, 1995; see also Wagener & Taylor, 1986). Prospective studies on the relationship between optimistic expectations of personal invulnerability and risk-related activity have consistently failed to confirm the common-sense fear that overly optimistic expectations predict risky behavior (Aspinwall, Kemeny, Taylor, Schneider, & Dudley, 1991; Joseph et al., 1987; Montgomery et al., 1989; Taylor et al., 1992). In fact, at least some evidence suggests that the opposite is true: A study by Taylor et al. (1992) found that unrealistic optimism about developing AIDS among HIV-seropositive men was associated with several positive health behaviors and was not associated with any health-compromising behaviors.

This lack of evidence of adverse effects does little to resolve the dilemma of unrealistic optimism. If predictions are unrealistically optimistic, how can they not have negative consequences? Why are people who make unrealistically optimistic predictions not especially vulnerable to disappointment, endangerment, and despair? The very prevalence of evidence showing that people are optimistically biased would seem to indicate that these biases have not been so punished that they have been stricken from our cognitive repertoire. How optimistic beliefs can be maintained and the dangers associated with these beliefs avoided are issues to which we now turn.

RESOLVING THE DILEMMA OF UNREALISTIC OPTIMISM

People Are Not Indiscriminately Optimistic

Although a considerable amount of evidence suggests that people's predictions tend to be optimistically biased, the predictions that people make do not appear to be entirely unreasonable. For example, although people's predictions about their future are often not accurate in an absolute sense, their predictions do tend to show a high degree of relative accuracy. In other words, even though people's predictions tend to be optimistically biased when their predictions are compared to the outcomes they attained, correlations between predictions and outcomes are positive and often substantial (e.g., in the studies of the planning fallacy conducted by Buehler et al., correlations between predicted and actual task completion times ranged from .4 to .7). People also appear to be sensitive to their skills and circumstances when making predictions. For example, whereas most people tend to believe that they are relatively invulnerable to a variety of unwanted outcomes, studies of people who are actually at risk reveal that these people are not oblivious to the fact that they are at risk. Most smokers do recognize that they are more at risk for developing any of a variety of smoking-related diseases than is the average nonsmoker (notably, however, most smokers maintain the belief that they are less at risk than are others who smoke; see, e.g., Weinstein, 1998a). Similarly, people's performance predictions appear to reflect an appreciation of their own capabilities, and not simply fanciful projections of what might be accomplished. In a study that assessed predictions and performance on a verbal skills task, people's predictions – including the predictions of those who were optimistically biased – were found to correlate strongly with their own past performance on similar tasks, implying that participants were sensitive to this information when formulating their predictions (Buehler, Griffin, & MacDonald, 1997).

People also appear to be more optimistically biased under conditions of greater uncertainty. Early research on optimistic bias (e.g., Irwin, 1953; Marks, 1951), for example, revealed that the tendency to expect success unreasonably on a task determined purely by chance was greatest when the objective odds for success or failure was closest to 50–50 (i.e., when uncertainty was at a maximum). When the objective odds for success over failure were more extreme (i.e., either very high or very low), optimistic biases were considerably reduced in magnitude (see also Buckley & Sniezek, 1992; McGregor, 1938; cf. Dunning, Meyerowitz, & Holzberg, 1989).

Finally, people appear to be sensitive to the context in which they make their predictions, and tend to exhibit greater optimism when it less likely that the accuracy of their predictions will be tested or challenged or when they expect that the consequences of being inaccurate will be less severe. Most studies of optimistic bias, however, have not taken such context-based variability into account. Indeed, studies of optimistic bias have almost uniformly been conducted in settings in which participants make predictions anonymously and without regard to the consequences of their predictions. Participants in these studies had thus been free to indulge in grandiose estimates of what could be done in the situations that were described to them without fear of adverse consequences if their predictions were found to be erroneous. Of course, many situations in which people make predictions will not provide such a psychological safe haven. In recognition of this, social psychologists have begun to examine how features of the prediction context influence the expression of optimistic biases.

Temporal Proximity. One set of studies has found that people's predictions tend to be more optimistic – and more optimistically biased – when the outcome of their predictions will not be revealed for some time. For example, Calderon's (1993) analysis of analysts' predictions of corporate earnings revealed a systematic decline in optimistic bias as a function of the proximity of the forecast date to the realization date (although optimistic bias was still evident even among the most proximal predictions). These results are sensible because analysts who made more proximal predictions undoubtedly had access to additional information that would allow them to make more accurate predictions. The availability of additional information may not be necessary for the reduction of optimistic bias, however. Gilovich, Kerr, and Medvec (1993) were able to obtain distal and proximal predictions from research participants who had been asked to estimate how well they would perform on a number of laboratory-based tasks (e.g., memory tests) for which additional information was not available between predictions. Predictions that were made well before the performance was to take place were considerably more optimistic than were predictions made immediately before the tasks were completed (notably, however, even the "proximal" predictions appeared to be optimistically biased, as the means of the estimated percentile rankings for all tasks were higher than .50). Additional data provided by Shepperd et al. (1996) revealed that people's expectations not only became less optimistic when the time to perform a task grew near, but became pessimistic (relative to actual performance) immediately prior to receiving feedback about that performance.

Several explanations for the effects of outcome proximity on prediction biases have been offered. One suggests that people are motivated to protect themselves from disappointment and thus express optimism and pessimism strategically (although not necessarily deliberately) by changing their expectations in situations in which feedback is more or less likely. According to this view, people may become preemptively pessimistic in anticipation of potentially negative feedback so that the feedback they actually receive will be experienced as less negative by comparison (cf. Norem & Cantor, 1986; see also Taylor & Shepperd, 1998). Another explanation suggests that the very awareness that one's predictions will be publicly tested motivates people to try to be more accurate when making predictions; people, in this view, feel accountable to their own performance and then respond to this accountability by critically evaluating the basis of their predictions (Gilovich et al., 1993; cf. Tetlock, 1992). Still another explanation suggests that people may feel greater anxiety when a performance situation is imminent, and that people may interpret this anxiety as reflecting lesser confidence and consequently make more modest, if not overtly pessimistic, predictions (Savitsky, Medvec, Charlton, & Gilovich, 1998; Shepperd et al., 1996). Although the anxiety interpretation hypothesis is the only one to be researched directly to date, the alternative accounts remain plausible and, at present, there is no basis for choosing among them.

Deliberative and Implemental Mind Sets. Another line of research suggests that optimistic biases may be minimized before decisions are made to implement plans that are based on potentially biased assessments, expectations, and predictions. Several studies suggest that temporal positioning with respect to decisions – that is, whether one is in a predecisional state of deliberation or in a postdecisional (but still preactional) state marked by thoughts of implementation – influences how people evaluate themselves, the tasks they are considering, and their expectancies for success (Armor & Taylor, 2000; Taylor & Gollwitzer, 1995). This research has found that optimistic biases are attenuated when people are choosing between goals or selecting among possible courses of action to attain those goals, but exaggerated once a particular goal is selected and the individual begins thinking about implementing particular plans for action. For example, Armor and Taylor (2000) found that people who had been asked to deliberate the pros and cons of participating in a particular task were less optimistic about how they might perform on that task as compared to people who were asked to imagine that they were about to complete the task. These effects appear to have been at least partially mediated by the manner in which the two groups thought about the task. Not surprisingly, participants who had been asked to imagine that they were about to complete the task generated specific plans about how they would go about it. The participants who had been asked to deliberate whether they would want to complete the task, however, did more than just consider pros and cons: These participants appeared to consider the task from a variety of perspectives and to think about how alterations in task parameters might influence their performance, or how other people might perform on the task at hand.

Taken together, these results suggest that at the moment when unrealistic optimism might be especially likely to be injurious or to lead to actions that ought be avoided, optimistic biases may be at their lowest ebb; in contrast, at times when optimistic biases may provide a motivational edge, as when an already chosen course of action is being initiated, these biases may be more prevalent.

Optimism May Lead to (Almost) Self-Fulfilling Prophecies

In circumstances in which the attainment of predicted outcomes is at least partially under the predictor's control, the potentially negative consequences associated with overly optimistic expectations may be avoided to the extent that the statement of optimistic expectations helps people attain the outcomes they desire. Studies that have manipulated people's expectations about how they would perform on particular tasks have found that the induction of positive expectations can lead to significant improvements in performance (Armor & Taylor, 2000; Buehler & Griffin, 1996; Campbell & Fairey, 1985; Peake & Cervone, 1989; Sherman, Skov, Hervitz, & Stock, 1981). This appears to be true even for predictions that can, at the time they are made, be considered to be overly optimistic. In an early and influential set of studies (Sherman, 1980), people were found to predict that they would behave in more socially desirable ways than base-rate data indicated (thereby demonstrating unrealistic optimism); however, people who had initially made these "unrealistic" predictions were subsequently more likely to behave in a socially desirable manner than were people who had not been first asked to make predictions about their behavior. In these studies, then, optimistic errors in prediction could be considered "self-erasing." Additional evidence of self-erasing errors has been obtained in studies of voting behavior, in which merely asking people if they intend to vote has been found to increase the likelihood that they will vote (Greenwald, Carnot, Beach, & Young, 1987) and of consumer decision making, in which a mere inquiry of purchasing intent increased the likelihood of purchasing even big-ticket items such as automobiles (Morwitz, Johnson, & Schmittlein, 1993).

An important caveat, however, is that optimistic predictions are rarely completely fulfilled: Although people who make optimistic predictions tend to attain more than they would have had they not made those predictions, they do not necessarily achieve the standards they initially set for themselves. A study by Buehler and Griffin (1996) illustrates this point. In this study, expectations about how long it would take to complete a particular assignment were manipulated by anchoring participants' predictions around relatively optimistic or pessimistic estimates (cf. Tversky & Kahneman, 1974). Although neither group completed their assignments within the time they said they would, the group that had been induced to predict relatively early completion times did complete the assignment significantly earlier than did the group induced to predict relatively late completion times. These results suggest that even overly optimistic expectations tend to get people further toward their goals than they would have otherwise.

At present, the mechanisms by which optimistic expectations enhance performance are not fully understood. One explanation is outcome based, and derives largely from social learning theories (e.g., Bandura, 1977, 1997), expectancy-value theories of motivation (e.g., Atkinson, 1964) and, more recently, from cybernetic models of self-regulation (e.g., Carver & Scheier, 1981, 1998; Scheier & Carver, 1988). According to these models, goal-directed behaviors are strongly influenced by people's expectations about what the outcomes of their behaviors might be. If people anticipate success, behavior is initiated (and ongoing behaviors maintained); if success appears to be less likely, people disengage from their pursuit (or refrain from initiating that pursuit) and abandon either the task or the currently selected means for completing that task. These models make a straightforward prediction: At least in situations where tenacity is rewarded (cf. Aspinwall & Richter, 1999), people who are optimistic – even people who are unrealistically optimistic – should achieve more than people with more modest expectations.

Another possible explanation for how even unrealistically optimistic expectations may influence behavior is more process-oriented, and draws on information about how these expectations are derived. According to one of the leading explanations for why people exhibit optimistic biases, people tend to infer the likelihood of different outcomes on the basis of case-specific plans or scenarios about how the future will unfold, and several lines of evidence suggest that the very processes of constructing and considering these scenarios tends to render people prone to bias (Buehler et al., 1994; Griffin & Buehler, 1999; Kahneman & Tversky, 1979, 1982; Newby-Clark, Ross, Buehler, Koehler, & Griffin, 1999). To the extent that the scenarios people generate in the context of making predictions provide a mental script for how to behave, however, these scenarios may facilitate effective performance (Anderson, 1983; Pham & Taylor, 1999). According to this model, optimistic forecasts may be associated with the attainment of desired outcomes (or the avoidance of undesired ones) only when the person making the forecast has a clear idea of how the considered outcome could reasonably be attained (or avoided). If the scenarios that people generate in an effort to divine the future provide a sort of mental road map for how that future might be attained, then it may be that one of the causes of optimistic bias will be a source for its cure.

Several other explanations for the prediction–performance link have been offered, although the unique aspects of these explanations have not yet been subjected to empirical test. One hypothesis is that the statement of prediction implies some amount of self-definition (e.g., "I am the type of person who can accomplish X"), and that people strive to meet their predictions in order to maintain consistency with the implied self-image (e.g., Sherman, 1980; cf. Aronson & Carlsmith, 1962). Another possibility is that the statement of optimistic expectations may be associated with an enhanced motivational state (here optimistic bias could be seen either as a cause of this motivational state or as a consequence of it), and it may be this state that either directly or indirectly facilitates the attainment of desired outcomes. At present, there are insufficient grounds for choosing among these explanations.

Optimistic Reinterpretation

Although people do not appear to be indiscriminately optimistic, and although stating optimistic expectations may help facilitate the attainment of desired outcomes, optimistic predictions will sometimes be disconfirmed. It may still be possible, however, for the disappointment associated with unmet expectations to be avoided if the evaluation of outcomes is biased in a manner that minimizes any discrepancies between what had been expected and what was ultimately attained. Evidence consistent with this notion reveals that, following failure, people may bias both their perceptions of what was achieved and their recall of what they had initially expected.

Reinterpreting Outcomes.   A series of studies conducted by Klaaren, Hodges, and Wilson (1994) provides what may be the most direct evidence that people with positive expectations put a favorable spin on outcomes they receive, even when these outcomes might reasonably be considered to be disappointing. In these studies, people who had expected a positive experience but actually experienced a negative one (i.e., those who had been overly optimistic) subsequently evaluated their experiences in a way that appeared to be more consistent with their initial expectations than with the experiences themselves. In their first study, students' expectations about how much they would enjoy their winter vacations were found to influence their subsequent evaluations of their vacations, independent of how favorably they had reported their actual vacation experiences to be (similar results were obtained by Mitchell et al. (1997), who found that vacationers' evaluations of their trips were lower during their trips than they either expected or recalled them to be). In Klaaren et al.'s second study, in which both expectations and the actual pleasantness of experience were manipulated, the induction of favorable expectations led people to evaluate the experience more favorably (regardless of whether the actual experience was pleasant), and to report greater willingness to repeat the experience by participating in the study again.

Similar results have been obtained in correlational analyses of the determinants of entrepreneurs' satisfaction with their business ventures (Cooper & Artz, 1995). In this study, and counter to the researcher's initial expectations, entrepreneurs' level of satisfaction after three years of business ownership were positively related to their initial expectations (measured at startup) even after the performance of their businesses had been controlled. Together with the results of Klaaren et al.'s (1994) experiments, these results suggest that those who are the most optimistic going into a situation may be the most likely to view their outcomes favorably, regardless of whether their predictions are ultimately fulfilled. These results are the opposite of what one would expect if excessive optimism provided a strong point of contrast against which any lesser outcome would be seen as disappointing.

Shifting Standards of Comparison. In addition to direct reinterpretations of outcomes, people may avoid the ramifications of disconfirmed expectations by shifting the standard against which outcomes are evaluated. There are at least three ways in which these shifts may occur. First, people may simply forget their initial standard, thereby removing it as a basis for evaluating the outcomes they receive. Even in situations in which people claim to remember their initial predictions, their recollections may be distorted so that the predictions they recall are more in-line with eventual outcomes than they actually had been (Fischhoff & Beyth, 1975). At least some evidence suggests that these distortions tend to be larger when initially positive expectations are disconfirmed by a negative outcome (Schkade & Kilbourne, 1991), as would occur if people's initial expectations had been excessively optimistic.

Second, people may reevaluate the standard that they had initially set for themselves. In other words, people may respond to an otherwise obvious failure by questioning how reasonable their initial prediction had been. Because people make predictions in states ranging from partial to complete uncertainty, they may be more likely to disregard their initial (potentially naive) predictions than to accept the conclusion that they had failed to meet an entirely reasonable and indisputable goal. This sort of response is at least partly justifiable because people will have new information about the objective likelihood of the outcome, the difficulties involved in bringing about that outcome, and their own motives, qualities, and resources that may have been difficult (if not impossible) to ascertain at the time of the initial prediction. To the extent that this new information may influence retrospective evaluations of initial expectations, potential disappointment may fade with the newfound clarity of hindsight (cf. Fischoff, 1982).

A third strategy for shifting standards involves the selection of a worse-off social comparison target that allows the individual to maintain a belief that his or her current status is not as bad as more objective standards might suggest it would be (Taylor & Lobel, 1989). Results of studies with cancer patients, for example, have shown that patients at all levels of physical outcomes see themselves as somewhat better off than other cancer patients (except, perhaps, at the very end-stages of the disease; e.g., Wood, Taylor, & Lichtman, 1985). This constant advantage across physical conditions can be achieved, of course, only by manipulating and continually shifting the person or group with whom one compares oneself. So robust is this tendency that if a worse-off social comparison target is not available, people often generate hypothetical others who are "doing worse" for the purposes of these comparisons (Taylor, Wood, & Lichtman, 1983).

Getting What You Want by Revising What You Had. Another means by which people may effectively reinterpret their outcomes to be more in line with their initial expectations is to exaggerate progress by reinventing the past (Conway & Ross, 1984; Ross, 1989). In a classic demonstration, Conway and Ross (1984) found that students who had participated in an (ineffective) study-skills program misremembered their initial skills as being worse than they had originally reported them to be. By changing their views of their initial skill, students subsequently perceived their current (and unchanged) skill level to have improved by comparison. These results have generally been interpreted as being mediated by people's naive theories of change in a situation of actual stability; the underestimation of past skills could thus be understood as a consequence of people assuming change when none occurred. To the extent that optimistic expectations imply an expectation of positive change, people may derogate their past out of a conviction that they have achieved something in the present.

Alternatives to Reinterpretation: Explaining Away Failure. One well-documented strategy for avoiding the disappointment associated with even the most clearly disconfirmed expectations involves the generation of excuses (e.g., Buehler et al., 1994; Gilovich, 1983; see also Snyder, 1989; Snyder & Higgins, 1988). Several lines of research suggest reasons why the generation of excuses may be especially common following the disconfirmation of optimistic expectations. First, research has shown that people are particularly likely to search for causal explanations for events that are negative or unexpected (Pyszczynki & Greenberg, 1981; Weiner, 1985; Wong & Weiner, 1981). Given that the disconfirmation of optimistic expectations will, by definition, be experienced as both negative and unexpected, the active search for causal explanations seems especially likely. Commonly observed attributional asymmetries – by which people take credit for positive outcomes and deny responsibility for negative ones (see Miller & Ross, 1975, for a review) – may then bias this search in favor of excuses. Second, to the extent that people recognize that their expectations have been disconfirmed, they often react with surprise, and surprise itself indicates that a mental representation of some more expected outcome has been activated and is being used as a point of contrast (e.g., Kahneman & Miller, 1986). The ready availability of initial expectations following the disconfirmation of these expectations may help maintain their plausibility and, as a consequence, provide rationale for explaining away the expectancy violation as having been the consequence of essentially random, unanticipatable factors. To the extent that past failures and the recognition of past failures at prediction are so promptly explained away, they are not likely to influence outcome evaluations, relevant self-evaluations (Snyder, 1989), or future predictions (Buehler et al., 1994; Gilovich, 1983).

CONCLUSIONS AND IMPLICATIONS

A common concern among many who study optimistic biases is that these biases will have a number of costly consequences. People who are prone to excessive optimism might reasonably be expected to make poor decisions – to pursue unreasonable ambitions recklessly, to persist at fruitless endeavors, and to value prospects without fully appreciating their risks – and to suffer the consequences when reality fails to live up to their own lofty expectations. Although these concerns are certainly plausible, and although the costs of excessive optimism may be quite high at times, several lines of research reviewed here suggest that these concerns may be overstated.

First, people do not appear to be blindly optimistic: even excessively optimistic predictions tend to be made within reasonable bounds and to be quite highly correlated with both past and future performance. Moreover, people appear to be less optimistic in situations in which excessive optimism would be expected to have the most worrisome consequences. Evidence was reviewed that suggests that optimistic biases are reduced when people make predictions about events that will take place in the near versus distant future, or when people are deliberating between different possible goals as opposed to developing plans for one of them. One might expect similar reductions in optimistic bias when people are asked to state predictions in specific as opposed to general terms, when the criteria for evaluating the accuracy of people's predictions are clearly specified as opposed to ambiguous, or when predictions are made publicly in front of an audience demanding accuracy as opposed to in private.

Just as optimistic biases appear to be minimized in some situations, they may be exaggerated in others. Not only might one expect greater bias when people state general, difficult to confirm, private predictions, but one might find the most extreme biases in competitive or self-defining situations in which pride or one-upmanship may prompt people to generate optimistic forecasts in order to boost morale or to instill enthusiasm. Thus, even in situations in which accuracy of predictions would seem paramount, additional social pressures may encourage optimism over accuracy. In some sense, it may be these situations and not optimism per se that people should be worried about.

Second, people may avoid at least some of the negative consequences of unmet expectations to the extent that the statement of optimistic expectations helps people to achieve more than they would have had they not been initially optimistic. The causal significance of optimistic predictions – even unrealistically optimistic ones – in determining people's outcomes may have some important implications for interventions designed to reduce or eliminate optimistic biases. Although these interventions have been designed to enhance the accuracy of people's predictions, the net result of these interventions may be to undermine motivation and performance without actually improving predictive accuracy. Evidence of this can be seen is Buehler et al.'s (1994) studies of the planning fallacy. In their investigations, manipulations that were designed to enhance the accuracy of people's predictions succeeded in reducing optimism, but these manipulations did not improve the overall accuracy of the predictions that were made (see also Griffin & Buehler, 1999). Even if efforts to reduce optimistic biases do make people's predictions more accurate, it is not clear that the effects of being cautious but correct would be beneficial in all situations. One would not want a struggling student to resign himself to poor grades at the outset of a new academic term, nor would one want a bride and groom to believe in their hearts that their odds for living happily ever after were less than even.

To the extent that even optimistically biased predictions enhance performance and that optimistic predictions are associated with emotional and motivational variables such as mood, self-esteem, confidence, and determination, these predictions may sometimes have more self-regulatory benefits than costs and more self-regulatory benefits than accurate predictions would have.

Finally, people may avoid at least some of the consequences of unmet expectations by refusing to see their predictions as having been disconfirmed (or at least by not acknowledging the extent to which their predictions have been disconfirmed) or by making excuses if they do recognize that their predictions have not been met. Although hindsight biases and excusing rationalizations are often studied as judgmental errors, it is important to recognize that these post-hoc reinterpretations are often at least partially justifiable (although perhaps not to the degree that people take them). The prospects for making accurate predictions in complex, uncertain, and ever-changing environments appears to be rather limited, and people may use newly obtained information to evaluate their outcomes and to challenge or question the validity of their initial and potentially naive predictions. People may recognize, then, that what was realistic at the time of prediction may not seem so realistic by the time outcomes are attained, and that what appears realistic after the fact may not have been so readily foreseeable at the time predictions were made.

All predictions are made under varying degrees of uncertainty, with no meaningful prediction ever being completely certain. People's predictions will therefore necessarily contain at least some component of error. Most analyses of optimistic bias have focused on the costs of being wrong and have made strong assumptions about the benefits of being right. In the context of prediction, however, being realistic offers no guarantee that one's predictions will turn out to be accurate. Moreover, the consequences of optimistic and pessimistic deviations from accuracy may not be symmetrically valued; this suggests that the statistical strategy of minimizing squared deviations from a criterion may not provide the greatest benefit psychologically. Overly pessimistic predictions may be demoralizing if these predictions are believed and, if these predictions are fulfilled, the outcomes that are obtained may not be very satisfying. Overly optimistic predictions, however, may confer benefits simply by symbolizing a desired image of success, or more concretely by aiding people's progress to higher achievements. Given that predictions are often inaccurate at least to some degree, it is possible that people may derive benefits from shifting the range of their predictions to the positive, even if this means introducing an overall higher rate of error into the prediction process. Countering optimistic biases in the name of accuracy may undermine performance without achieving the accuracy that was intended, whereas the maintenance of optimistic predictions may serve to align us, both in thought and in action, more closely with our goals.

20. Norm Theory: Comparing Reality to Its Alternatives

Daniel Kahneman and Dale T. Miller

Reasoning flows not only forward, from anticipation and hypothesis to confirmation or revision, but also backward, from the experience to what it reminds us of or makes us think about. This chapter is largely dedicated to the power of backward thinking. Its aim is not to deny the existence of anticipation and expectation, but to encourage the consideration of alternative accounts for some of the observations that are routinely explained in terms of forward processing.

This chapter is concerned with category norms that represent knowledge of concepts and with stimulus norms that govern comparative judgments and designate experiences as surprising. In the tradition of adaptation level theory (Appley, 1971; Helson, 1964), the concept of *norm* is applied to events that range in complexity from single visual displays to social interactions.

The central idea of the present treatment is that norms are computed after the event rather than in advance. We sketch a supplement to the generally accepted idea that events in the stream of experience are interpreted and evaluated by consulting precomputed schemas and frames of reference. The view developed here is that each stimulus selectively recruits its own alternatives (Garner, 1962, 1970) and is interpreted in a rich context of remembered and constructed representations of what it could have been, might have been, or should have been. Thus, each event brings its own frame of reference into being. We also explore the idea that knowledge of categories (e.g., "encounters with Jim") can be derived online by selectively evoking stored representations of discrete episodes and exemplars.

The present model assumes that a number of representations can be recruited in parallel, by either a stimulus event or an abstract probe such as a category name, and that a norm is produced by aggregating the set of recruited representations. The assumptions of distributed activation and rapid aggregation are not unique to this treatment. The present analysis relates most closely to exemplar models of concepts (Brooks, 1978, 1987; Hintzman, 1986; Hintzman & Ludlam, 1980; Jacoby & Brooks, 1984; Medin & Schaffer, 1978; Smith & Medin, 1981). We were drawn to exemplar models in large part because they provide the only satisfactory account of the norms evoked by questions about arbitrary

This is an edited and condensed version of a paper that first appeared in *Psychological Review, 93,* 237–251. Copyright © 1986 by American Psychological Association. Adapted with permission.

categories, such as, "Is this person friendlier than most other people on your block?"

Exemplar models assume that several representations are evoked at once and that activation varies in degree. They do not require the representations of exemplars to be accessible to conscious and explicit retrieval, and they allow representations to be fragmentary. The present model of norms adopts all of these assumptions. In addition, we propose that events are sometimes compared to counterfactual alternatives that are constructed ad hoc rather than retrieved from past experience. These ideas extend previous work on the availability and simulation heuristics (Kahneman & Tversky, 1982; Tversky & Kahneman, 1973). . . .

An abnormal event is one that has highly available alternatives, whether retrieved or constructed; a normal event mainly evokes representations that resemble it. The treatment of normality in this chapter is guided by the phenomenology of surprise rather than by formal or informal conceptions of probability. The main difference between the two notions is that probability is always construed as an aspect of anticipation, whereas surprise is the outcome of what we call *backward processing* – evaluation after the fact. Probability reflects expectations. Surprise (or its absence) reflects the failure or success of an attempt to make sense of an experience, rather than an evaluation of the validity of prior beliefs. In his critique of standard notions of probability, the statistician Shafer (1976) developed the related idea that events do not merely alter the strength of belief in existing possibilities, they also evoke and shape the set of relevant possibilities. . . .

MUTABILITY AND THE AVAILABILITY OF COUNTERFACTUALS

One theme of this chapter is that the experienced facts of reality evoke counterfactual alternatives and are compared to these alternatives. The development of this theme takes us to regions more often traveled by philosophers than by psychologists. Philosophical treatments of counterfactuals and possible worlds have explored the compelling intuition that some alternatives are closer to reality than others and that some changes of reality are smaller than others (see Lewis, 1973, for a particularly engaging treatment). As Hofstadter (1985) noted, the word *almost* provides a key to some of these intuitions. For example, the statement, "I almost caught the flight" is appropriate for an individual who reached the departure gate when the plane had just left, but not for a traveler who arrived half an hour late. The world in which the passenger arrives 5 minutes earlier than she did is closer to reality than a world in which she arrives half an hour earlier. The present analysis links these intuitions to mutability: A counterfactual possibility should appear "close" if it can be reached by altering some mutable features of reality.

Our notion of mutability is similar to the concept of *slippability* introduced by Hofstadter (1979, 1985). The shared ideas are that the mental representation of a state of affairs can always be modified in many ways, that some modifications are much more natural than others, and that some attributes are particularly resistant to change.

Another cognate of mutability is the distinction between the information presupposed and the information asserted in a verbal message (Clark & Haviland, 1977). The cleft sentence, "It was Tom who set fire to the hotel" designates an immutable aspect of the situation (the hotel was set on fire) and a mutable one (the identity of the arsonist). Note that either aspect of the sentence could be presupposed: "It was a hotel that Tom set on fire" has the same basic structure, with the two components interchanging their roles. The cleft sentence invites the listener to consider alternatives to the asserted content, even as it denies these alternatives. The presupposition is shared by all the alternatives.

As this example illustrates, presuppositions are highly flexible, and the relative mutability of attributes can be controlled almost at will. In the absence of deliberate intent or conversational guidance, however, differences in the mutability of attributes affect the spontaneous recruitment of norm elements.

In the following sections, we examine several hypotheses about factors that determine the relative mutability of different aspects of an event. We also illustrate some of the ways in which the elusive concept of *availability of counterfactual alternatives* can be operationalized.

Exception and Routine

A complex situation may combine some routine and some exceptional features. Kahneman and Tversky (1982) tested the hypothesis that exceptional features are more mutable than routine ones by eliciting alternatives to a stipulated reality. Subjects were given a story describing a fatal road accident, in which a truck driven by a drug-crazed teenager ran a red light and crashed into a passing car, killing Mr. Jones, its occupant. The following instructions were given:

As commonly happens in such situations, the Jones family and their friends often thought and often said, "If only . . ." during the days that followed the accident. How did they continue that thought? Please write one or more likely completions.

Two versions of the story were constructed, labeled *route* and *time*, which were identical except for one paragraph. In the route version, the critical paragraph read as follows:

On the day of the accident, Mr. Jones left his office at the regular time. He sometimes left early to take care of household chores at his wife's request, but this was not necessary on that day. Mr. Jones did not drive home by his regular route. The day was exceptionally clear and Mr. Jones told his friends at the office that he would drive along the shore to enjoy the view.

The time version of this paragraph was as follows:

On the day of the accident, Mr. Jones left the office earlier than usual to attend to some household chores at his wife's request. He drove home along his regular route. Mr. Jones occasionally chose to drive along the shore, to enjoy the view on exceptionally clear days, but that day was just average.

Both versions suggest route and time as possible attributes that might be changed to undo the accident, but the change introduces an exception in one case, and restores the routine in the other. As predicted, more than 80% of the responses that mentioned either time or route altered the exceptional value and made it normal. The results support two related propositions about the availability of counterfactual alternatives: (1) Exceptions tend to evoke contrasting normal alternatives, but not vice versa; and (2) an event is more likely to be undone by altering exceptional than routine aspects of the causal chain that led to it.

Ideals and Violations

Barsalou (1985) have and Lakoff (1987) have emphasized the role of distance from an ideal or paragon as a determinant of typicality. For example, zero-calorie foods are judged to be highly typical members of the category "Things to eat on a diet," although they are neither the most common nor the most similar to the prototypical diet food (Barsalou, 1985). In the terms of the present model, elements that have ideal values on significant attributes appear to be highly available. A hypothesis about differential mutability follows: When an alternative to an event could be produced either by introducing an improvement in some antecedent or by introducing a deterioration, the former will be more available.

Evidence for this proposition was obtained in unpublished research by Read (1985). Subjects were taught the rules of a simple two-person card game. They were then shown pictures of the players' hands and were asked to complete the blanks in the following statement by changing one card: "The outcome would have been different if the _____ had been a _____." The question of interest was whether the subjects would choose to weaken the winning hand or to strengthen the losing one. The rule discussed in the preceding section suggests that the winning hand might be more readily altered because the strongest combinations (e.g., four of a kind) are more exceptional than weaker ones (e.g., three of a kind). However, the tendency to eliminate exceptions was overcome in the data by a tendency to approach an ideal value. In a significant majority of cases, subjects chose to modify the outcome by strengthening the losing hand rather than by weakening the stronger one. Informal observations of spectators at sports events suggest that the outcome of a contest is more commonly undone by improving the losing performance (e.g., imagining the successful completion of a long pass in the last few seconds) than by imagining a poorer performance of the winning team.

Differential availability of changes that improve or degrade a performance could be one of the factors that explain the answers to the following question:

Tom and Jim were both eliminated from a tennis tournament, both on a tie-breaker. Tom lost when his opponent served an ace. Jim lost on his own unforced error. Who will spend more time thinking about the match that night?

Jim   85%   Tom   15% $(N = 92)$

Note that Tom and Jim could both imagine themselves winning the game, but the judgment of our subjects is that these thoughts are likely to be more available when they involve an imagined improvement of one's own performance than an imagined deterioration of the opponent's game.

Reliable and Unreliable Knowledge

Tversky and Kahneman (1982) noted an asymmetry in the confidence with which people made inferences and predictions from one attribute to another. Inferences from a reliable measure to an unreliable one are made with greater confidence than inferences in the opposite direction, although correlation is actually symmetric. For example, people were more confident in predicting the score on a short IQ test from a long form of the test than vice versa. They also believed, erroneously, that the statement, "The individual who won the decathlon won the first event" is more probable than, "The individual who won the first event won the decathlon."

Similar asymmetries are observed when subjects are presented with a statement that includes an apparent discrepancy and are asked to choose how to eliminate the discrepancy. Most subjects do so by altering the less-reliable item (e.g., the performance on the short test or in the first event of the decathlon) to fit the more reliable one. Thus, attributes about which little is known appear to be relatively mutable.

Causes and Effects

We propose the hypothesis that, when people consider a cause–effect pair, alternatives to the effect are more available than alternatives to the cause. The tendency to presuppose causes is reflected in everyday conversation. When an observation departs from the normal covariation of cause and effect, the discrepancy is usually attributed to the effect rather than to the cause. Thus, a child may be described as "big for her age" but not as "young for her size," and students may be described as overachievers, not as undertalented.

When a particular conjunction of effect and causal attribute is observed, the alternatives that are recruited should mainly consist of cases in which the same cause is followed by variable effects. A spectator at a weight-lifting event, for example, will find it easier to imagine the same athlete lifting a different weight than to keep the achievement constant and vary the athlete's physique. We turned this hunch into a small experiment. The participants were given information that was described as a form sheet for the members of a club of weightlifters. The data were presented in two columns, stating the body weight of each athlete and his best achievement (the order of columns was varied in alternate forms). The numbers in both columns were in strict ascending order. Data for 10 athletes were given, with the 10th observation deviating markedly from the trend established in the first 9 cases. Half of the participants received a form in which the 10th athlete was only heavier than the 9th by 3 kg but lifted 30 kg more. In the other forms, the 10th athlete was 30 kg heavier than the 9th and lifted only 3 kg more. All forms included the following question:

Do you find the relationship between body weight and lifted weight in the last entry surprising? (Yes/No) If you do, please change it to make it conform better to what you would expect. Mark your change on the sheet and return it.

Most subjects found the entry to be surprising and changed only one of the two items of information on the critical line. As predicted, a substantial majority (86%) of those who changed one item altered the weight lifted by the athlete rather than his body weight. The order of the two columns on the sheet did not matter.

The differential mutability of effects and causes suggests an apparently untested hypothesis concerning the social comparison process (Suls & Miller, 1977). People should prefer to compare themselves to others who resemble them on causal factors rather than to others who resemble them on outcome variables. For example, a student should be more interested in discovering how well a peer of comparable industry did on an exam than in discovering the industriousness of a student who achieved a comparable grade.

Focal and Background Actors

We propose that the mutability of any aspect of a situation increases when attention is directed to it and that unattended aspects tend to become part of the presupposed background. The hypothesis that the attributes of a focal object or agent are more mutable than those of nonfocal ones was explored by D. Read (1985). In the card-game study described earlier, he showed subjects the hands of two players, A and B, and asked them to "complete stems such as, "A would have won if . . ." or "A would have lost if. . . ." The large majority of completions involved changes in the hand held by A, although the same outcome could have been generated just as well by altering B's hand. Other tests of the hypothesis used vignettes such as the following:

Helen was driving to work along a three-lane road, where the middle lane is used for passing by traffic from both directions. She changed lanes to pass a slow-moving truck, and quickly realized that she was headed directly for another car coming in the opposite direction. For a moment, it looked as if a collision was inevitable. However, this did not occur. Please indicate in one sentence how you think the accident was avoided.

The situation of the two cars is symmetric, or perhaps biased against Helen's being able to do much to prevent the accident, given that the circumstances of the other car are not described. Nevertheless, a substantial majority of subjects completed the story by ascribing the critical action to Helen.

The idea that the actions of a focal individual are mutable may help explain the well-documented tendency for victims of violence to be assigned an unreasonable degree of responsibility for their fate (Lerner & Miller, 1978). Information about a harmful act often presents the actions of the perpetrator in a way that makes them part of the presupposed background of the story, and therefore relatively immutable Alternatives to the victim's actions are likely to be more mutable, and counterfactual scenarios in which the harm is avoided are therefore likely to be ones that change the victim's actions but keep the aggressor's behavior essentially constant. The high availability of such counterfactual scenarios can induce an impression that the victim is responsible for her fate – at least in the sense that she could easily have altered it. Any factor that increases the attention focused on the victim increases the availability of alternatives to the victim's reactions and the blame attached to the victim. The finding that emotional involvement with victims can increase the blame attributed to them (Lerner, 1980) is consistent with this speculation.

Our analysis is based on the idea that features of a situation that have highly available alternatives are attributed greater causal effectiveness than equally potent but less mutable factors. This analysis does not imply, of course, that causal responsibility is never assigned where it belongs. Probes that draw attention to the perpetrator, such as those concerning the punishment to be given, can be expected to evoke appropriate degrees of blame. The point made here is simply that the actions of the perpetrator, unless made salient, are likely to be presupposed, with the result that constructed scenarios of how the victimization might have been avoided will focus on the actions of the victim. Although seemingly paradoxical, it is not a new discovery that apparent immutability reduces attributions of responsibility. This fact has been known to bullies since time immemorial.

The hypotheses that we have discussed illustrate, but do not exhaust, the factors that control the differential mutability of attributes and the differential availability of alternatives to reality. In other exploratory work we have found suggestive support for several additional hypotheses. One of these hypotheses is that temporal order affects mutability. Consider the pair of consonants XF. Now quickly change it by replacing one of the letters by another consonant. Which letter did you change? A robust majority of respondents replace the second letter rather than the first. This example illustrates a general rule: The second member of an ordered pair of events is likely to be more mutable than the first. Another hypothesis is that a change that can be visualized (e.g., undoing an accident) is more available than a change that cannot be visualized (e.g., undoing a heart attack). . . .

AFFECTIVE ROLE OF COUNTERFACTUALS

This section develops some implications of the analysis of counterfactual thought for the domain of affect. We examine this question in conjunction with a hypothesis of emotional amplification that states that the affective response to an event is enhanced if its causes are abnormal. In each of the following examples, the same misfortune is produced by two sequences of events that differ in normality. The respondents assess the intensity of the affective responses that are likely to arise in the two situations. The first demonstration (Kahneman & Tversky, 1982) tested the prediction that outcomes that are easily undone by constructing an alternative scenario tend to elicit strong affective reactions.

Mr. C and Mr. D were scheduled to leave the airport on different flights at the same time. They traveled from town in the same limousine, were caught in a traffic jam, and arrived at the airport 30 minutes after the scheduled departure time of their flights. Mr. D is told that his flight left on time. Mr. C is told that his flight was delayed, and only left 5 minutes ago. Who is more upset?

Mr. D   4%   Mr. C   96%   ($N = 138$)

There is essentially unanimous agreement that Mr. C is more upset than Mr. D, although their objective situations are identical – both have missed their planes. Furthermore, their expectations were also identical because both had expected to miss their planes. The difference in the affective state of the two men appears to arise from the availability of a counterfactual construction. Mr. C and Mr. D differ in the ease with which they can imagine themselves – contrary to fact – catching up with their flights. This is easier for Mr. C, who needs only to imagine making up 5 minutes, than for Mr. D, who must construct a scenario in which he makes up half an hour. A preferred alternative is thus more available (normal) for Mr. C than for Mr. D, which makes his experience more upsetting.

The next demonstration tests the prediction that outcomes that follow exceptional actions – and therefore seem abnormal – will elicit stronger affective reactions than outcomes of routine actions.

Mr. Adams was involved in an accident when driving home after work on his regular route. Mr. White was involved in a similar accident when driving on a route that he only takes when he wants a change of scenery. Who is more upset over the accident?

Mr. Adams   18%   Mr. White   82%   ($N = 92$)

As predicted, the same undesirable outcome is judged to be more upsetting when the action that led to it was exceptional than when it was routine.

The next example tests the prediction that people are most apt to regret actions that are out of character:

Mr. Jones almost never takes hitchhikers in his car. Yesterday he gave a man a ride and was robbed. Mr. Smith frequently takes hitchhikers in his car. Yesterday he gave a man a ride and was robbed. Who do you expect to experience greater regret over the episode?

Mr. Jones   88%   Mr. Smith   12%

Who will be criticized most severely by others?

Mr. Jones   23%   Mr. Smith   77%   ($N = 138$)

The results confirm the hypothesis and, incidentally, indicate that regret cannot be identified with an internalization of others' blame.

The final example (Kahneman & Tversky, 1982) tests the hypothesis that consequences of actions evoke stronger emotional responses than consequences of failures to act. The intuition to which this example appeals is that it is usually easier to imagine oneself abstaining from actions that one has carried out than carrying out actions that were not in fact performed.

Mr. Paul owns shares in Company A. During the past year, he considered switching to stock in Company B, but decided against it. He now finds out that he would have been better off by $1,200 if he had switched to the stock of Company B. Mr. George owned shares in Company B. During the past year he switched to stock in Company A. He now finds that he would have been better off by S1,200 if he had kept his stock in Company B. Who feels greater regret?

Mr. Paul   8%   Mr. George   92%   (N = 138)

The finding that acts of commission produce greater regret than acts of omission was replicated by Landman (1987) and is in accord with formulations that distinguish omission from commission in attributions of causality and responsibility (Hart & Honore, 1959; Heider, 1958).

Miller and McFarland (1986) conducted a series of studies to test the hypothesis that the abnormality of a victim's fate affects the sympathy that the victim receives from others. Subjects were told that the purpose of the studies was to provide victim compensation boards with information about the public's view of various types of victims. Subjects were presented with a brief description of an incident and then were asked to indicate on an 11-point scale how much compensation they thought the victim should receive. Normality was manipulated in one study by varying the mutability of an action that led to a bad outcome. The victim was a man who had been severely injured during a robbery. In one condition, the robbery took place in the store at which the victim shopped most frequently. In a second condition, the robbery took place in a store to which the victim had decided to go only after finding his regular store closed for renovations. It was predicted that subjects would view the fate that befell the victim in the "unusual" store to be more abnormal, and hence more unjust, than the fate that befell the victim in the "usual" store. Consistent with this hypothesis, subjects recommended significantly more compensation (more than $100,000 more) for the same injury in the exceptional context than they did in the routine context.

This study demonstrates that even morally charged judgments such as those involving compensation can be influenced by the normality of the outcome. It is as though a negative fate for which a more positive contrast is highly available is worse or more unfair than one for which there is no highly available positive alternative. It is important to note that the different reaction to the two victims is not due to the perceived probability of their fate. The probabilities of being shot in the two stores were both judged very low and indistinguishable from one another. The subjects apparently presupposed both the robbery and the store at which it took place. Given this presupposition, it is relatively more normal for an individual to be shot where it is normal for that individual to be – in the store that is regularly frequented.

A second compensation study, paralleling the missed-flight script, varied the distance between the negative outcome and a more positive alternative. The victim in this study had died from exposure after surviving a plane crash in a remote area. He had made it to within 75 miles of safety in one condition and to within $\frac{1}{4}$ mile in the second condition. Assuming that it is easier to imagine an individual continuing another $\frac{1}{4}$ mile than another 75 miles, it was predicted that the fate of the "close" victim would be perceived to be more abnormal, and hence more unfair, than the fate of the "distant" victim. The results supported the prediction, inasmuch as subjects once again recommended significantly more compensation for the family of the victim whose fate was more easily undone.

These results confirm the correlation between the perception of abnormality of an event and the intensity of the affective reaction to it, whether the affective reaction be one of regret, horror, or outrage. This correlation can have consequences that violate other rules of justice. An example that attracted international attention a few years ago was the bombing of a synagog in Paris, in which some people who happened to be walking their dogs near the building were killed in the blast. Condemning the incident, a government official singled out the tragedy of the "innocent passers-by." The official's embarrassing comment, with its apparent (surely unintended) implication that the other victims were not innocent, merely reflects a general intuition: The death of a person who was not an intended target is more poignant than the death of a target. Unfortunately, there is only a small step from this intuition to the sense that the persons who are chosen as targets thereby lose some of their innocence.

CODES AND CATEGORY NORMS IN PERSON PERCEPTION

The present approach, like several others (Anderson, 1981; Hastie & Kumar, 1979; Higgins & Lurie, 1983; Wyer & Gordon, 1984; Wyer & Srull, 1981), assumes the possibility of dual memory representations – raw memories of episodes and stored codes. Many features of a person can be stored (1) as comparative trait labels, which assign the individual to a position in an interpersonal norm; (2) as a set of episodes that define an intrapersonal norm of behavior for that individual; or (3) in both forms at once. In this section, we pursue the implications of norm theory for two aspects of knowledge about persons: the ambiguity of codes and the formation and retrieval of intrapersonal norms. We discuss these issues in turn.

Norms and Ambiguous Codes

The interpretation of a comparative code is necessarily dependant on the norm to which the object of judgment is related. For example, hearing, "Jim has been given a long jail term" suggests different jail terms to listeners if they differ in the norm for jail terms that they attribute to the speaker. Communication fails if speakers and listeners do not share, or at least coordinate, their norms. Coordination of norms is also involved when an individual uses a remembered code to reconstruct the literal detail of an experience – for example, the length of a jail sentence that is only remembered as long. Accurate performance depends on the match between the norm that is applied when the code is interpreted and the norm that supported the initial judgment. As Higgins and Lurie (1983) demonstrated in an impressive experiment, the reconstruction of the initial episode is systematically biased if the norm changes in the interval. This effect, which Higgins and Lurie termed *change of standard*, can yield a range of cognitive and affective responses, including the disappointment that people often experience when they meet a former teacher whom they had always remembered as brilliant (Higgins & King, 1981).

Trait labels and expressions fall into two categories: (1) relative predicates, which specify the individual's position on an interpersonal norm; and (2) absolute predicates, which summarize an intrapersonal norm of actions or feelings on relevant occasions. The same trait name can sometimes serve in both functions. The statement that "Jane is assertive" can be understood as saying either that she is more assertive than most people or that her behavior is assertive on most occasions. In the latter interpretation, the word *assertive* is a category label that evokes exemplars of assertive behaviors.

Trait labels that have both an absolute and a relative sense are potentially ambiguous. This ambiguity appears to underlie the tendency of people to accept general descriptions as uniquely relevant to them, also known as the *Barnum effect* (Snyder, Shenkel, & Lowery, 1977). Barnum statements typically evoke both absolute and relative interpretations. For example, the statement, "You are shy in the presence of strangers" can be recognized by most people as a valid description of themselves – if shyness indicates that one is less comfortable with strangers than with familiar others. In its relative sense, of course, the description is applicable only to the minority of people who are sufficiently extreme to deserve special mention. It is the validity of the Barnum statement in its absolute sense that makes it believable to the individual, but it is the unwarranted extension to the interpersonal comparison that makes it interesting. A similar mixture of meanings was noted by Higgins and Winter (cited in Kraut & Higgins, 1984) in their analysis of trait ambiguity. They asked subjects what percentage of people possessed various personality traits (e.g., friendliness, aggressiveness) and found many traits that were assumed to apply to an absolute majority of people. It appears that the assignment of these traits involves a mixture of comparative and absolute criteria.

Trait descriptions vary in the degree to which they lend themselves to interpersonal and intrapersonal interpretation. For example, the expression, "He is not very intelligent" evokes an interpersonal norm, but the statement "I like Coke" has an intrapersonal reference (more than other beverages, not necessarily more than other people). The difference has a predictable effect on the impact that information about others has on self-description. Whether a person is more or less intelligent than her reference group influences how intelligent she judges herself to be (Davis, 1966), but whether a person consumes more or less of a drink than her reference group does not influence her expressed liking for the drink (Hansen & Donoghue, 1977; Nisbett, Borgida, Crandall, & Reed, 1976).

Norms from Single Elements

The present model of category norms assumes both that a single instance suffices to set up a norm and that a reference to the category label serves to restrict consideration to members of that category. These assumptions entail nonregressive predictions and a tendency to neglect relevant base rates.

To illustrate, imagine that you were shown a single exemplar of an unfamiliar species of insect, which was larger than any other insect you have ever seen. How large would you expect another exemplar of that species to be? Would it occur to you that the single insect you saw is likely to be larger than most of its conspecifics? The canons of inference prescribe that the single insect you saw is likely to be larger than most others in its species. Predictions of the size of the next member of the new species should accordingly regress toward the general norm for insects. Intuitive expectations, in contrast, are firmly centered on the single observed value, which constitutes the norm for that category. In the context of social judgment, the ease with which category norms are established leads to radical generalization from a single observation of behavior to an interpersonal norm for the behavior of other people in the same setting, or to a norm for a person's behavior on future occasions (Nisbett & Ross, 1980; Read, 1984). . . .

Radical generalization from observed behavior to an intrapersonal norm is manifest in the nonregressiveness of behavioral predictions (Kahneman & Tversky, 1973; Ross & Anderson, 1982). A single observed instance of unusually generous tipping appears sufficient to set up a norm that will be consulted in predictions of a person's future tips. The interpersonal base rate for the behavior of other people is effectively excluded from consideration when thinking about this person's tips, just like one's knowledge of the size of insects in the previous example.

Radical generalizations can be made with high and unwarranted confidence. Experimental results suggest that subjective confidence depends mainly on the consistency of available evidence rather than on its quality or quantity (Einhorn & Hogarth, 1982; Kahneman & Tversky, 1973; Tversky & Kahneman, 1971). Subjective confidence in a prediction is likely to reflect the *breadth*, or variability, of the category norm on which the judgment is based. Confidence will be high if all elements cluster around a single value of the attribute, independently of the number of these elements. However, it would be incorrect to conclude that judgments are entirely insensitive to the quantity of evidence. A category norm based on one or two elements can support confident judgments, but it can also be altered relatively easily under the impact of new evidence.

Many inferences bridge across situations and across attributes. In the absence of better evidence, people readily predict success in graduate school from an IQ test score, research productivity from performance in a colloquium, or the size of a mother's graduation gift to her daughter from the size of a tip that she gave to a waiter. Such generalizations are involved both in deliberate predictions of future behaviors and in spontaneous inferences about traits and about unobserved aspects of situations.

Inferences that bridge attributes are no more regressive than direct generalizations (Nisbett & Ross, 1980; Ross & Anderson, 1982). Nonregressive predictions can be generated in two ways. First, the predicted value may be chosen so that its position matches that of the known attribute in their respective interpersonal norms (Kahneman & Tversky, 1973). Thus, a predicted graduation gift can be chosen that is as extreme in the norm for gifts as the observed tip is in the interpersonal norm for tips. Second, nonregressive predictions can also be generated by matching descriptive labels (e.g., if a tip is remembered as very generous, what graduation gift would be considered equally generous?). The intention to predict a behavior elicits a search for relevant incidents or for pertinent descriptive labels. The search is guided by the similarity of potential elements to the target attribute, and it is probably concentric: The nearest incidents or labels that turn up in the search are used, nonregressively, to generate a prediction. In the absence of better data, people are willing to make extreme predictions from evidence that is both flimsy and remote. The process of concentric search yields radical (and overconfident) predictions from observations of dubious relevance. However, the same process also makes it likely that distant labels or incidents will be ignored when evidence that is closer to the target attribute is available. Thus, generous tipping habits will not be given much weight in predicting a mother's graduation gift to her daughter if pertinent incidents of their interaction can be retrieved.

Unwanted Elements of Norms

The elicitation of a norm has been described here as a process of parallel activation of multiple representations that are recruited by a stimulus or by a category. We assume that the process of recruitment is rapid, automatic, and essentially immune to voluntary control after its initiation. In particular, it is not possible for the individual to sift through activated elements and discard irrelevant or misleading ones. This limitation on the voluntary control of norms helps explain two well-documented phenomena of social judgment: the perseverance of discredited beliefs and the correspondence bias in person perception.

Imagine a discussion of a Canadian athlete, in which someone who is unfamiliar with metric measures reads from a sheet: "Brian weighs 102 kg. That's 280 lbs, I think. No, it's actually about 220 lbs." Does the speaker's initial error affect listeners' subsequent responses to questions about Brian's size and strength? The literature on perseverance of discredited beliefs (C. A. Anderson,

1983; Fleming & Arrowood, 1979; Ross & Anderson, 1982; Ross & Lepper, 1980; Schul & Bernstein, 1985) suggests that it does. The message of this literature is that traces of an induced belief persist even when its evidential basis has been discredited. The discarded message is not erased from memory, and the norm elicited by a subsequent question about Brian's weight could therefore contain the original message as well as its correction. Thus, a listener might "know" immediately after the message that Brian's true weight is 220 lbs, and this value would presumably retain an availability advantage, but the category norm associated with Brian's weight would still be biased toward the erroneous value of 280 lbs. Judgments that depend indirectly on the activation of the norm would be biased as well.

Some aspects of the phenomenon known as the *correspondence bias* (Jones, 1979) or the *fundamental attribution error* (Ross, 1977) could be explained in similar terms. Many studies have shown that people make unwarranted inferences concerning personal traits and attitudes from observations of behavior that are in fact entirely constrained by the situation. Subjects in one famous series of experiments in this tradition observed an individual who was explicitly instructed to write an essay or to read aloud a speech advocating an unpopular position (Jones, 1979; Jones & Harris, 1967; Jones & McGillis, 1976). In response to subsequent questions, observers commonly attributed to target persons an attitude consistent with the position that these persons had been constrained to advocate.

In these experiments, as in studies of discredited beliefs, a behavioral observation is accompanied by information that challenges its validity. As in a theatrical performance, the actor in the experiments conducted by Jones (1979; see also Jones & Harris, 1967; Jones & McGillis, 1976) engages in a behavior (e.g., advocating the regime of Fidel Castro) that does not have its usual significance because of the special demands of the situation. We propose that in both the theater and these experiments, two traces are laid down: (1) a literal memory of the person expressing pro-Castro sentiments, and (2) a memory of the behavior in the context of the situational constraints. Both memories are elements of the set that is evoked by further observations of the actor's political opinions or by a question concerning those opinions. As in the preceding example, this norm is biased even for an observer who "knows" that the actor's behavior is constrained, and therefore uninformative. Quite simply, pro-Castro behaviors are more normal for the actor than for a random stranger. Belief perseverance, generalizations from atypical examples, and failures of discounting all illustrate the same principle: Any observation of behavior – even if it is discounted or discredited – increases the normality of subsequent recurrences of compatible behaviors.

CAUSAL QUESTIONS AND ANSWERS

In this section, we consider the role of norms in causal judgments. This topic was chosen to illustrate the concepts of presupposition and norm coordination introduced earlier. We begin by examining a routine conversational exchange, which provides a conceptual model for much attribution research. A questioner, whom we call Quentin (Q), asks a Why question and receives an answer from Ann (A). An example might be:

Q: "Why did Joan pass this math exam?"
A: "She used the Brown textbook."

We focus on two issues: (1) the inferences that A must make about Q's norms to interpret a Why question, and (2) the constraints that this interpretation of the question places on appropriate answers.

Norms and Causal Questions

Causal questions about particular events are generally raised only when these events are abnormal. The close connection between causal reasoning and norms is evident in the rules that govern the homely Why question as it is used in conversations about particular events (Lehnert, 1978). The Why question implies that a norm has been violated. Thus, the question, "Why was John angry?" indicates Q's belief that it was normal for him not to be, and the question, "Why was John not angry?" indicates the contradictory belief. Even the question, "Why is John so normal?" implies that he is normal to an abnormal degree. A Why question, then, presupposes that some state X is the case, and also implies an assertion that not-X was normal. The strongest indication of the implicit assertion of a norm is that the Why question, unlike most others, can be denied. The denial can be expressed by a question, as in the familiar exchange:

Q: "Why do you so often answer a question with a question?"
A: "Why not?"

The Why not retort denies the assertion that not-X is normal. It is a legitimate answer that, if accepted, leaves nothing to be explained.

We suggest that Why questions (at least those of the deniable variety, for which "Why not?" is a sensible answer) are not requests for the explanation of the occurrence or nonoccurrence of an event. A Why question indicates that a particular event is surprising and requests the explanation of an *effect*, defined as a contrast between an observation and a more normal alternative. A successful explanation eliminates the state of surprise. This is commonly done in one of three ways. First, A may deny the implied assertion that X is abnormal in the light of what Q already knows. This is the Why not answer, which invites Q to change his opinion that X is abnormal. Second, A may inform Q of some fact of which Q was previously ignorant, which makes the occurrence of X normal. For example, Q may not have known that Joan used the Brown text, which he knows to be excellent. Third, A may indicate that there is a causal link, of which Q was presumably ignorant, between the effect X and some known aspect of the situation. For example, Q may know that Joan had used the Brown textbook, but he may need to be told that it is excellent.

The choice of causal feature is constrained in many ways that have been discussed extensively by philosophers (for particularly relevant treatments, see

Hart & Honore, 1959; Mackie, 1974) and by psychologists (Einhorn & Hogarth, 1986; Kelley, 1967; Schustack & Sternberg, 1981). We are not concerned with the factors that determine impressions of causal efficacy; instead we focus here on a constraint that relates directly to the notion of norm: A cause must be an event that could easily have been otherwise. In particular, a cause cannot be a default value among the elements that the event X has evoked. The rule that a default value cannot be presented as a cause was noted by Hart and Honore (1959), who observed that the statement, "It was the presence of oxygen that caused the fire" makes sense only if there were reasons to view the presence of oxygen as abnormal. It is important to note, however, that a property need not be statistically unusual to serve as an explanation; it is only precluded from being a default value. Peculiar behaviors of cars observed on the road are frequently "explained" by reference to the drivers being young, elderly, or female, although these are hardly unusual cases. The default value for an automobile driver appears to be middle-age male, and driving behavior is rarely explained by it.

Ambiguities in Causal Questions

Conversations in general, and answers to questions in particular, are governed by subtle rules that determine what is said and what is presupposed or implicated (Clark, 1979; Grice, 1975). The situation is especially complicated when the conversation is actually a test, as is frequently the case in psychological experiments. The unique feature of a test is that the questioner is not ignorant or puzzled, as questioners usually are. When the question is ambiguous, the respondent faces the bewildering task of choosing a state of ignorance for the questioner.

The Why question appears to be especially susceptible to ambiguities. Consider a perennial favorite of attribution research: "Why did Ralph trip on Joan's feet?" (McArthur, 1972). The event in question is clearly specified, but the *effect* – defined as a contrast between the event and its norm – is not. To answer this question, the respondent must first identify what it is that the experimenter considers surprising. In everyday conversations, intonation provides a potent cue to the intended meaning of a question and the violated presupposition that underlies it. It is instructive to read the question about Ralph and Joan aloud several times, each time stressing a different word. The location of the major stress substantially reduces the number of possible interpretations, although it does not suffice to disambiguate the question completely. For example, the reading, "Why did *Ralph* trip over Joan's feet?" suggests either that (1) it is unusual for Joan's partners to trip over her feet, or that (2) although Joan's partners usually trip over her feet, there was special reason to expect Ralph to be more fortunate.

An experimental demonstration of the ambiguity of why questions was described by Miller (1981). Several groups of student and graduate nurses were asked to explain their decision to enter the nursing profession. Different versions of the same basic question were used in the different groups. The basic question was, "Why did you go into nursing?" An analysis of the answers to this question indicated that student nurses cited significant aspects of nursing (e.g., "It is a respected profession") more often than did graduate nurses. However, the graduate nurses were more likely to cite personal qualities (e.g., "I like people"). The critical finding of Miller's study was that the differences between students and graduate nurses vanished when they were asked questions that explicitly specified the relevant norm: "Why did you decide to go into nursing rather than some other profession?" or "Why did you decide to go into nursing when most of your friends did not?" As expected, the former elaboration yielded a majority of answers for both groups that referred to nursing, whereas the answers to the second question referred predominantly to personal dispositions. In view of this result, the contrasting answers of the two groups to the unelaborated Why question appear to reflect different interpretations of an ambiguous question rather than different causal beliefs.

Questioners convey cues that broadly specify the content of the causal answers that they wish to receive (Lehnert, 1978). For example, the questions, "Why did Carter lose the 1980 election?" and "Why did Reagan win the 1980 election?" refer to the same event, but differ in the explanations that they request: some noteworthy fact about Carter in the first question and about Reagan in the second. In the absence of indications to the contrary, the subject of the sentence is supposed to be its focus (Pryor & Kriss, 1977), and the syntactic form of the question suggests an equivalent form for the answer.

Perspective Differences

The coordination of the norms that apply to an effect and to a proposed cause is illustrated in an example discussed by the legal philosophers Hart and Honore in their classic book, *Causation in the Law* (1959c, p. 33):

A woman married to a man who suffers from an ulcerated condition of the stomach might identify eating parsnips as the cause of his indigestion. The doctor might identify the ulcerated condition as the cause and the meal as a mere occasion.

The causes chosen by his wife and by the physician refer to the same event, but explain different effects. It is evident from her answer that the wife is concerned with an exception to an intrapersonal norm: "Why does he have indigestion today but not on other days?" The physician, however, is concerned with an interpersonal norm: "Why does this patient suffer from indigestion when others do not?" The difference could reflect the role of availability in the recruitment of norm elements: The wife is likely to retrieve many memories of recent days on which her husband, although known to have an ulcer, did not suffer indigestion. These memories, which resemble the present occasion in most respects, define a norm for it. The physician, of course, is unlikely to have had the same amount of exposure to the patient. According to the rule that coordinates causes to effects (and explanations to questions), the wife chooses as a cause a property that distinguishes this particular day from other days, and the physician selects a feature that distinguishes this patient from other patients.

The situational attribution made by the wife and the dispositional attribution made by the physician in Hart and Honore's example recall the actor–observer differences described by Jones and Nisbett (1971). Actors often explain their actions and attitudes by reference to eliciting properties of situations, whereas observers of the same actions and attitudes attribute them to the actor's distinctive characteristics. As in Hart and Honore's example, the situational attribution corresponds to an intrapersonal norm, whereas a dispositional attribution of the same behavior relates it to an interpersonal norm. The intuitions about differential availability that make the indigestion example so compelling apply as well to the case of actors and observers. The question, "Why do you like this particular girl?" appears to favor the recruitment of thoughts about the respondent's attitude toward other girls. The question, "Why does he like this particular girl?" is more likely to evoke in an observer thoughts of the attitudes of other people toward that girl (Nisbett, Caputo, Legant, & Maracek, 1973). The different elements that are evoked produce quite different questions: "Why do you like this girl more than most other girls?" and "Why does he like this girl more than most others do?" Each question, in turn, constrains appropriate answers to factors that vary among the elements of the evoked set – other girls for the actor, other individuals for the observer.

The intuitions about the wife–physician example cannot be reduced to the accounts commonly offered for actor–observer differences. The contrast could not be explained by difference of knowledge (Jones & Nisbett, 1971) or of perceptual salience (Arkin & Duval, 1975; Storms, 1973). It is not explained by the distinction between a state of self-consciousness and other states of consciousness (Duval & Wicklund, 1972). Nor is it compatible with the hypothesis that the focus of attention is assigned a dominant causal role (Fiske, Kenny, & Taylor, 1982; Ross, 1977; Taylor & Fiske, 1978), inasmuch as the husband surely plays a more focal emotional role for the wife than for the physician.

The hypothesis of the present treatment is that the same event evokes different norms in the wife and the physician of the example, and in actors and observers in other situations. Different descriptions of the same event can appear to provide conflicting answers to the same question, when in fact they are concerned with different questions. This proposal can be subjected to a simple test: Do the observers actually disagree? A negative answer is suggested by several studies. Nisbett et al. (1973) found that subjects easily adopt a typical observer perspective in reporting how their choice of a girlfriend would be described by a close friend. Other data confirm the ability of actors to mimic observers (Miller, Baer, & Schenberg, 1979). However, observers instructed to empathize with one of the participants in a dialogue tend to adopt an actor perspective in explaining that person's behavior (Regan & Totten, 1975).

In summary, we contend that there are a number of advantages to viewing the process of causal reasoning from the perspective of norms. First, our analysis provides an account of the antecedents of causal reasoning. A search for explanation may occur spontaneously when a significant event violates a norm it evokes (see also Hastie, 1984; Weiner, 1985). Causal search can also be prompted by a question that presupposes a violated norm (see Lalljee & Abelson, 1983). Second, the present approach draws attention to the difficulty of assessing the accuracy of attributers who differ in their perspectives (Funder, 1982; Monson & Snyder, 1977). It is important to distinguish real disagreements in causal attributions from specious disagreements that arise when people answer different questions. Finally, the present analysis identifies a necessary feature of any factor that is considered a possible cause of a surprising event: A cause cannot be a default value of the norm that the consequence has evoked.

CONCLUDING REMARKS

This essay has proposed a theory of norms. The two main functions of norms are the representation of knowledge of categories and the interpretation of experience. We challenged the conception of norms as precomputed structures and suggested that norms – and sometimes even their elements – are constructed on the fly in a backward process that is guided by the characteristics of the evoking stimulus and by the momentary context. In this regard, our treatment resembles other approaches that emphasize the role of specific episodes and exemplars in the representation of categories (Barsalou, 1987; Brooks, 1978; Hintzman, 1986; Jacoby & Brooks, 1984; McClelland & Rumelhart, 1985; Medin & Schaffer, 1978; Schank, 1982). A distinctive aspect of the present analysis is the separation of normality and post-hoc interpretation on the one hand from probability and anticipation on the other. Another distinctive aspect is our attempt to identify the rules that determine which attributes of experience are immutable and which are allowed to vary in the construction of counterfactual alternatives to reality. Our closest neighbor in this enterprise is Hofstadter (1979, 1985), with his highly evocative treatment of what he calls slippability. Like him, we believe that it is "very hard to make a counterfactual world in which counterfactuals were not a key ingredient of thought" (Hofstadter, 1985, p. 239). . . .

21. Counterfactual Thought, Regret, and Superstition: How to Avoid Kicking Yourself

Dale T. Miller and Brian R. Taylor

Some years ago, a charismatic 19-year-old Spanish matador nicknamed "Yiyo" was gored to death. Yiyo's death evoked considerable public anguish and debate (Schumacher, 1985). Making his fans' reaction especially intense was the circumstance of his death: He was killed while serving as a last-minute substitute for another matador. Students of counterfactual thinking can be forgiven sly smiles and knowing nods as they read this story, for it contains all the elements necessary to provide a dramatic test of the oft-cited hypothesis that events preceded by exceptional actions, such as substituting for another matador, are more easily imagined otherwise and generate more affect than events preceded by routine actions. A simple test of this hypothesis, first proposed by Kahneman and Tversky (1982b), would contrast the highly "mutable" fate of poor Yiyo with the less mutable fate of some other unfortunate "Yiyo" who had been killed by a bull he had long been scheduled to face. The two versions of the event could be presented to participants in scenario format and their reactions probed through a list of questions that might include the following: Did you have any "if only" thoughts when reading of Yiyo's death? How intense was your affective reaction to Yiyo's death? What degree of regret do you think Yiyo would have experienced if he had suffered only serious injuries rather than death? Presumably, those participants who had read the highly mutable version of Yiyo's death would report more "if only" thoughts, stronger affective reactions, and greater expectations of regret.

But it was not its potential as a scenario study that intrigued us most about the account of Yiyo's death. It was what the article itself claimed made Yiyo's death so tragic: His actions had violated the widely shared belief that it is bad luck to substitute for another matador. This struck us as a curious superstition. How, we wondered, might such a belief have arisen? One possibility, of course, is that the belief is empirically grounded. There might be some reason why matadors are more likely to get injured when substituting; for example, they might be less knowledgeable about the bull. But we were drawn to another possibility, one that focused on the greater availability of counterfactual thoughts following deaths or injuries that are preceded by substitutions. In the remainder of this chapter, we explore possible links between counterfactual thought and superstitions.

SUPERSTITIOUS BELIEFS AND COUNTERFACTUAL THOUGHT

We propose that there are two routes by which the counterfactual thoughts generated by a highly mutable event sequence can foster superstitious beliefs pertaining to that sequence. The first implicates memory distortion. The greater incidence of "if only" thoughts following ill-fated mutable actions might serve to make these events more available in memory and hence more subjectively probable. This hypothesis links the two processes that Tversky and Kahneman (1973) described in their original formulation of the availability heuristic: the process by which events become available in memory and the process by which events become available in imagination. We propose that event sequences that yield highly available alternative constructions tend also to be highly available in memory.

The second account for how counterfactual thoughts might affect people's decision strategies draws attention not to people's recollection of the past, but to their contemplation of the future. People's reluctance to engage in actions easily imagined otherwise need not reflect distorted estimates of the likelihood that misfortune will follow such actions (their subjective expectancies). Such reluctance could simply reflect the regret they anticipate experiencing should misfortune occur (their subjective utilities). The force of the omen against matador substitution, for instance, might stem not from the belief that bad things are more likely to happen when you do so, but from the belief that any bad thing that does happen will be psychologically more painful. Certainly, Yiyo's death seems to derive much of its poignancy from its circumstances. In effect, this hypothesis proposes that the *postcomputed* thoughts to which easily un-doable events give rise (Kahneman & Miller, 1986) are sometimes anticipated – *precomputed*, if you will.

Separating the respective roles played by anticipatory regret and memory distortion in the development of superstitious beliefs is difficult because the two processes so often operate in tandem. Thus, people facing the prospect of loss tend to refrain from taking highly mutable actions both because they anticipate the aversive counterfactual thoughts that such actions could yield *and* because they better remember sequences in which similar actions led to negative outcomes. Nevertheless, we contend it is important to distinguish empirically and conceptually between these two processes, and we endeavor to do so in the present chapter. We first consider the biased-memory hypothesis.

BIASED MEMORY FOR EVENTS THAT ALMOST DID NOT HAPPEN

The hypothesis that events that almost did not happen tend to be highly available in memory might help explain a wide variety of common intuitions that have the "feel" of superstitions. As an example, consider the sense – widely shared, if our informal survey is correct – that the act of switching lines in front of busy counters virtually ensures that one's old line will speed up and one's new line will slow down. It is possible that a factual basis underlies this belief, but our analysis suggests how this belief could emerge without any empirical basis. First, following Kahneman and Tversky's (1982b) and Landman's (1987) accounts, we propose that negative events preceded by acts of commission (e.g., being delayed after switching lines) are more likely to give rise to counterfactual, "if only" self-recriminations than either negative events preceded by acts of omission (e.g., being delayed after contemplating but deciding against switching lines) or positive outcomes preceded by acts of either commission or omission (e.g., being accelerated after either switching or not switching lines). Second, we propose that the greater self-recriminations that follow ill-fated acts of commission make those experiences more available in memory. Finally, we propose that the greater availability in memory of ill-fated acts of commission leads people to overestimate the commonness of these events.

The world of sports provides a rich source of beliefs that appear to derive from the tendency of some events to evoke counterfactual alternatives more strongly, and hence to be more available in memory, than others. Consider the account given by Juan Marichal, a Baseball Hall of Fame pitcher, as to why pitchers "hate" to walk batters intentionally: "It always seems that an intentionally walked batter ends up scoring." Now it is not obvious, at least to us, why intentionally walked batters would score more often than unintentionally walked batters. The holding of such a belief is understandable, however, if one assumes that the negative consequences of intentional actions (e.g., intentional walks), because they are so easily imagined otherwise, will be more available in memory. Consider another common observation from baseball authorities: The team that gets the most two-out hits generally wins the game. Why might hits that occur with two players out be any more crucial to success than hits that occur with no one out or with one player out? There may be some reason this pattern is so, but even if the belief has no factual basis, our findings suggest why students of baseball might subscribe to it. The key is this: Opponents' hits that come with two players out evoke frustrating counterfactual thoughts more readily than hits that come with no one or one player out. Because a team's at-bat ends with its third out, hits that occur with two players out seem closer to not having happened than those that come with no one or one player out (Miller & Gunasegaram, 1990; Miller & McFarland, 1986). Furthermore, two-out hits, by generating more "if only" self-recriminations and hindsight musings, tend to be more available in memory. Thus, the perception that permitting two-out hits is especially costly might rest not on fact, but on distorted memory. It is simply hard for people to forget what almost did not happen.

A similar process might underlie the widely held (and often ponderously repeated) belief of "experts" that third-down conversions play an especially critical role in the game of American football. Why might a team's success at gaining first downs (10-yard increments) on its (effectively) last try be any more predictive of its ultimate success than its success at gaining first downs on its first or second try? Again, regardless of whether an empirical relationship exists here, our account of the link between event mutability and memory availability indicates how such a belief might emerge. First, because the team in possession of the ball (i.e., offense) generally kicks the ball away if it does not gain a first down by its third try, the defense can be said to have come closer to having stopped an offense when it prevents the offense from gaining 10 yards until the offense's third down. Second, because events that almost did not happen generate more affect and counterfactual thought, third-down conversions (from the perspective of both the offense and defense) are more available in memory. Winners and losers alike remember those events that almost did not happen and, consequently, accord them undue causal significance in their respective fates. . . .

Kicking Oneself Under the Blackjack Table

We now shift the venue of our examination to the gambling casino. In a fascinating investigation of real-life decision making, Keren and Wagenaar (1985) studied experienced blackjack players in casinos throughout the Netherlands. Blackjack is a game played with an ordinary deck of playing cards, a dealer, and from one to seven players. To begin a round of blackjack, the dealer deals each player two cards facedown and deals him- or herself two cards, one facedown and one faceup. All face cards (kings, queens, jacks) are worth 10 points, other cards are worth the value of the number on the card, and an ace can be counted as either 1 or 11 points. A player may continue to ask for additional cards ("hits") until he or she wants to stop ("stand") or the total of points exceeds 21 ("bust"). The dealer must hit when his or her total hand is 16 or fewer points and stand when his or her total hand is 17 or more points. The player's object is to accumulate more points than the dealer without busting. After all hands have been played, the dealer pays the amount bet to those players whose totals do not exceed 21 but are higher than the dealer's hand and collects the amount bet from the players who have busted or whose total is lower than the dealer's. When a player's hand equals the dealer's, that bet is not paid, nor is it collected.

Keren and Wagenaar (1985) compared the playing strategies of the players they observed to an optimal strategy, called *Basic*, which dictates that a player's decision to respond hit or stand should be based on not only the total of his or her hand, but also on the value of the dealer's faceup card. Playing blackjack according to this strategy can reduce a player's losses to −0.4% of the expected values and is second only to card-counting in effectiveness. The players observed by Keren and Wagenaar generally played optimally, with one striking exception. When a player was holding cards totaling 16 points and the dealer's upturned card ranged from a 7 through an ace (1 or 11), Basic strategy dictates that the player take another card. (Players lose about 65% of the time whatever they do in this situation, but the odds of winning are increased by taking another card.) However, 84% of the players observed by Keren and Wagenaar chose *not* to take another card when their card total was 16 points, a strategy contrary to the Basic prescription.

Why might players choose to stand at 16 when doing so reduces their chances of winning? Our analysis suggests one possibility. As noted, when a blackjack player's cards total 16, the odds are that he or she will lose; but there are two ways of losing, and we propose that they will not be equally painful or equally memorable. The first type of loss involves an act of commission – the player's taking another card and busting; the second involves an act of omission – the player's standing and being outdrawn by the dealer. Losses following acts of commission, as discussed previously, can be expected both to produce greater counterfactual regret and to be more memorable. In brief, blackjack players might misjudge the odds of winning (or losing) at 16 by one strategy versus another because the differential counterfactual regret elicited by the two strategies biases players' memories. . . .

ANTICIPATORY REGRET: TRYING TO AVOID A MENTAL KICKING

Biased recall of past experience can lead people to misjudge the likelihood that a particular course of action will lead to a negative outcome. Biasing subjective expectancies, however, is only one of the ways that counterfactual regret can affect decision-making strategies. Counterfactual regret can also influence decision strategies through its impact on the decision maker's subjective utility function: how he or she evaluates the different possible outcomes. The more counterfactual regret an outcome is expected to generate, the more motivated the decision maker is to avoid the outcome. This account implies that one need not look to biased experiential memory to explain superstitious behavior. People might hesitate to engage in certain "irrational" actions, not because of an unrealistic estimate of the likelihood of a negative event ensuing, but because of a (quite possibly) realistic estimate of the psychological pain that a particular action–outcome sequence might cause them. That regret can be anticipated and can guide the decisions people make has been proposed by theorists from a wide range of theoretic orientations (Bell, 1982, 1983, 1985a; Fishburn, 1983; Janis & Mann, 1977; Kahneman & Tversky, 1982a; Loomes, 1988; Loomes & Sugden, 1982, 1987a, 1987b; Simonson, 1992; Sugden, 1985; Walster, Walster, Piliavin, & Schmidt, 1973; see also Gleicher, Boninger, Strathman, Armor, Hetts, & Ahn, 1995).

An illustration of how anticipatory regret can guide decisions is the Spanish prohibition against matadors switching bulls. One need not posit that matadors and their fans exaggerate the likelihood that switching bulls will lead to misfortune to account for why such behavior is proscribed. It is sufficient to propose that misfortunes following mutable actions are judged more aversive (see also Gilovich, Medvec, & Chen, 1995; Ritov & Baron, 1990, 1992; Spranca, Minsk, & Baron, 1991). Regardless of whether switching bulls is more or less likely to lead to misfortune, any misfortune that does follow a switch can be expected to generate more distress among fans and victims alike. A similar point can be made about the advice to a person to follow his or her first instinct on multiple-choice tests. Students need not think that changing answers increases the risk of a lowered score to avoid doing so. If a student anticipates being tormented by having changed a correct answer to a wrong one, he or she might reasonably ask, "Why risk it?"

Because circumstances that elicit anticipatory regret also tend to induce biased recall estimates, the assessment of the independent effects of anticipatory regret is difficult. Nevertheless, there do seem to be some instances of superstitious behavior for which a biased-memory account seems highly implausible. Consider the psychology captured by the following sportswriter's observation: "It is a cardinal rule in basketball that when the game is on the line, you don't put your opponent there. That's why coaches repeatedly impress their players that they should refrain from committing fouls under circumstances that could give game-winning free shots to the other team" (Goldaper, 1990, p. C46). Why exactly is this a cardinal rule? Might it be a cardinal rule simply because a loss that results from your opponent's free shot – a shot that you in some sense caused – provokes more haunting counterfactual thoughts than a loss that results from a shot that is less capable of being mentally undone? If so, how many basketball losses occur because players and coaches would rather lose by playing too conservatively (erring by omission) than by playing too aggressively (erring by commission)? . . .

When We Won't Part with a Lottery Ticket

Seeking support for the link between anticipatory regret and counterfactual thought, we conducted a scenario study. In the scenario, two individuals were provided with the opportunity to sell a lottery ticket each had purchased. The manipulated variable was the temporal proximity to the drawing (1 hour vs. 2 weeks). Based on our anticipatory regret analysis, we predicted that people would be less willing to part with a ticket the shorter the temporal distance to the drawing. Our logic went as follows: When confronted with the situation described in the scenario, people anticipate the regret that selling a once-held winning lottery ticket would induce in them and factor this anticipatory regret into their decision about whether to sell the ticket. Furthermore, as predicted by norm theory (Kahneman & Miller, 1986), people's anticipatory regret, along with their reluctance to sell the ticket, should increase with their ease of imagining themselves still owning the winning ticket. The more recently one sold the winning ticket, the closer will be the counterfactual world in which one was a winner and, therefore, the greater will be the experienced regret. The scenario presented to and the questions asked of them were as follows.

Mr. K. and Mr. T. each purchased a ticket for a lottery with a multimillion-dollar jackpot. Subsequently, each man was approached by a friend who offered to buy his ticket. The

friend approached Mr. K. 2 weeks before the draw and Mr. T. 1 hour before the draw. Each man had held his ticket for about 2 weeks when approached, and each had sufficient time to buy another ticket before the draw if he so wished.
Who do you think would want the highest price for his ticket?

Mr. K.	19%	
Mr. T.	81%	$N = 78$

Who do you think would be most reluctant to sell his ticket?

Mr. K.	17%	
Mr. T.	83%	$N = 78$

Who would have the strongest sense of having almost won the lottery if he were to sell his ticket and it won?

Mr. K.	22%	
Mr. T.	78%	$N = 78$

Who would experience the greatest amount of regret if he were to sell his ticket and it won?

Mr. K.	9%	
Mr. T.	91%	$N = 78$

Participants' responses conformed to predictions. They predicted that the anticipatory regret generated by the prospect of selling a winning ticket would be greatest when the time to the drawing was the shortest. Now, it is difficult to see how participants' predictions about Mr. K.'s and Mr. T.'s differential reluctance to sell their lottery tickets could derive from participants' biased memories of their own ticket-selling experience. This is not to say that such a belief would not develop if people were in the custom of selling tickets. The results do suggest, however, that holding such a belief is not necessary to explain the greater reluctance to do so; they also raise the possibility that the holding of similar beliefs may not be necessary to explain other behaviors that have the feel of superstitions, such as the reluctance to switch bulls. . . .

Implications for the Psychology of Counterfactual Thinking

With the present analysis, we have aspired to more than the development of an understanding of the role of regret in decision making. We have also sought to develop the implications of a phenomenon Kahneman and Miller (1986) termed the *emotional amplification effect*: the tendency for people's affective response to an event to be enhanced when the event's causes were abnormal or mutable. Findings from the present research show that the amplified affect generated by a mutable negative action–outcome sequence itself has important psychological sequelae. First, the amplified affect biases people's memories for the commonness of the sequence; second, it induces anticipatory regret in people when they contemplate taking an action that might initiate the sequence.

One question pertaining to anticipatory regret that we have not yet addressed concerns its prevalence. In particular, do people anticipate regret whenever they engage in an abnormal action (*for example, deviate from routine*)? The answer clearly seems to be No. Not all ill-fated actions that evoke regret will, in prospect, have elicited anticipatory regret. People might experience considerable regret when they have an accident after deciding to take a different route home from work (Kahneman & Tversky, 1982b), but they are unlikely when contemplating this decision to have thought to themselves, "If I take a different route home and have an accident, I will never forgive myself." Whether the magnitude of the anticipatory regret evoked by a prospective action–outcome sequence matches the regret the sequence actually produces depends on the salience of the negative outcome. On the one hand, people do not typically worry about having an accident on the way home from work, and thus do not typically experience anticipatory regret over the decision to take a different route home, however much regret that decision may subsequently evoke in them. On the other hand, if they did have such worries, they would likely experience anticipatory regret and would likely be hesitant to take the different route. We propose as a general principle that people's differential reluctance to engage in mutable as compared to immutable acts increases as a function of their fear of a negative outcome, with that fear being a joint product of people's subjective judgment of the probability of the outcome's occurrence and their evaluation of the outcome. The more painful the negative outcome, the more regret people anticipate and the more reluctant they are to engage in an abnormal course of action. This principle predicts that the hesitancy to deviate from the status quo increases with the perceived stakes. Thus, the hesitancy to change multiple-choice answers should increase with the importance of one's performance on the test.

Anticipatory regret also increases with individuals' subjective probability estimates. Consider people's willingness to switch commercial air flights at the last minute. Findings from previous research have shown that a survivor of a plane crash is expected to experience more regret if he or she engages in the highly mutable action of switching flights shortly before takeoff (Miller et al., 1990). Should one assume from this finding that people would be reluctant to switch flights at the last minute? We propose that the reluctance will depend on their fear of crashing. People with an intense fear of flying, who presumably think incessantly of crashing, can be expected to be very reluctant to switch flights, and possibly even to switch seats. However, people comfortable with flying might be no more hesitant to switch flights at the last minute than to take a different route home from work. In many cases, the differential hesitancy to engage in abnormal actions reflects both the subjective probability the decision maker attaches to the occurrence of negative fate and his or her perceptions of its severity. The greater willingness of professors to switch classes than of matadors to switch bulls would seem to reflect just such a confluence of subjective probabilities and subjective utilities.

Two Processes or One?

We have claimed that people's tendency to avoid abnormal actions could reflect the regret they anticipate feeling if misfortune results, and that it need not reflect their memory-distorted beliefs about the likelihood of the misfortune's occurring. Thus, we argued that the greater reluctance to sell a lottery ticket as the drawing approached did not derive from people's memories of their experiences with selling lottery tickets, but from their subjective utility function: They perceived that the closer the drawing was when they parted with a winning lottery ticket the more intense their regret would be. We confess, however, that it is very difficult to rule out the presence of memory bias even in the lottery example. The difficulty arises with specifying precisely what principle it is that experience teaches. It is true people might not have previous experience with selling lottery tickets, but this does not mean they have not had previous experience with similar situations; that is, situations in which they have experienced a misfortune after engaging in a highly mutable action. The lottery situation might fit the template of a more general situation, and therefore, evoke a more general principle; for example, "Don't tempt fate." Perhaps the experience of having unwisely changed a multiple-choice answer at the last minute would be sufficient for people to fear that selling a lottery ticket at the last minute might be similarly ill-fated. It is left to other researchers to pursue more vigorously the possibility that subjective utility functions alone can deter people from pursuing a highly mutable course of action.

Establishing the independent role of anticipatory regret is not easy. The most straightforward means of assessing the independent power of anticipatory regret is to show that people avoid an abnormal action even if they do not believe that the action is any more likely than another to lead to a negative outcome. This standard, however, may prove too strong a test for the anticipatory-regret hypothesis. The problem is this: One of the effects of anticipating that an event will make a person feel bad is that its occurrence seems more likely (cf. Johnson & Tversky, 1983). Subjective expectancies are influenced by subjective utilities, not just by recollected experiences. Thus, as the dread of a negative outcome occurring through a particular action increases so will its subjective probability. There are at least two reasons for this pattern. First, people consider their feelings to be information (Miller & Turnbull, 1990; Schwarz, 1990), and therefore are disposed to overestimate the likelihood of a negative outcome based on their fear of its happening. Second, people estimate the probability of an event at least partly by the vividness with which they can imagine it (Carroll, 1978; Sherman, Cialdini, Schwartzman, & Reynolds, 1985). Thus, anticipating the counterfactual thoughts that a negative event evoke, because it tends to make the event more vivid, tends to make it more subjectively likely.

Consider once again the lottery scenario involving Mr. K. and Mr. T. Might the fear these men have of experiencing self-recrimination in the event they sold a winning ticket affect their estimates of the chances that a sold ticket will win? To

examine this question, we provided a group of participants with the previously
described lottery scenario and asked them the following three questions:

Who would be most optimistic of winning if he resisted selling his ticket?

Mr. K.	12%	
Mr. T.	5%	
No difference	83%	$N = 92$

Who would have the strongest expectation that his ticket would win if he were to sell it?

Mr. K.	12%	
Mr. T.	58%	
No difference	30%	$N = 92$

Who would have the greatest sense that he was tempting fate if he were to sell his ticket?

Mr. K.	8%	
Mr. T.	62%	
No difference	30%	$N = 92$

The results indicated that participants believed there would be no difference in the two men's hopes of winning were they to refuse the friend's offer. However, participants predicted that the two men would have different
expectancies were they to accept the friend's offer. Mr. T. (the man who sold
his ticket closest to the drawing) was expected to be more optimistic that his
(former) ticket would win. This result suggests that the participants' prediction
that Mr. T. would show greater reluctance to sell his ticket was not guided by
their belief that his *retained* ticket is more likely to win. Rather, it seems guided
by their belief that his *sold* ticket would be more likely to win. The decision not
to sell, then, is just that – a decision not to part with the ticket, not a decision to
keep the ticket. The ticket's capacity to yield satisfaction is not assumed to be
enhanced by one's retaining it, even though its capacity to yield dissatisfaction
is assumed to be enhanced by one's selling it.

To undertake a risky action one easily imagined otherwise (such as selling a
lottery ticket close to the drawing) is to tempt fate. We contend that one tempts
fate not only when one opts for one action when there is an alternative action
that makes more sense or has a better chance of a positive outcome, but also any
time one takes an action that will be easy to undo mentally. To say, "It would be
just my luck if I switched from this line to the other, that this line will speed up
and the other will slow down" is not to commit oneself to the proposition that
not switching means one's line is likely to speed up. One is just "asking for it"
if one takes an action he or she knows, in retrospect, will be easy to imagine
otherwise. Similarly, to insist on wearing one's lucky shoes to the final exam
is not necessarily to commit oneself to the proposition that he or she will do
better than others who do not own lucky shoes. Wearing the lucky shoes might
not even commit the person to the proposition that he or she would do worse if

he or she did not wear the lucky shoes. It might commit the person only to the proposition that he or she is just asking for it by not wearing them. If things turn out badly after the person chooses not to wear his or her lucky shoes, he or she will be forced to endure intense self-recriminations. In essence, having lucky shoes means one also has one or more pairs of "unlucky" shoes, the wearing of which will leave him or her fearful of impending disaster and vulnerable to relentless self-recrimination.

Reflections on Superstitions

With our present analysis we probed the psychology of superstition at a number of levels. For one thing, the analysis offers an account for why people might be hesitant to do things that they fear will lead to a bad outcome even when they cannot provide a rational account for the fear. People's hesitancies to switch lines or throw out long-held possessions qualify as examples of this type. People often claim that although they do not know the reason that when they throw out some long-unused object they soon find themselves needing it, they know it is so and engage in the practice only against their better judgment (e.g., "You know, I have had this bat repellent for 10 years and have never used it, but – just you wait – now that I'm throwing it out, we'll be infested with bats"). The previously discussed Spanish superstition against matador substitution provides an even more dramatic example of this process.

Of course, many behaviors having the same psychological underpinnings as superstitions do not seem to be superstitions because they are assumed to be rational. The reason that blackjack players stand when they are holding 16 may have everything to do with nascent feelings of anticipatory regret, but the players appear to think the strategy merely reflects playing the odds. Indeed, Meyer Lansky, the legendary crime figure and reputed gambling genius, regularly instructed blackjack players that the odds dictated that one hold at 16. The mistaken belief that the odds dictate standing at 16 might even increase with experience. Keren and Wagenaar (1985) found that experienced blackjack players frequently claimed that amateurs could be distinguished from the professional gamblers because of their tendency to take too many cards.

The fact that psychologically painful sequences (regardless of whether the pain is produced by self-recriminations) tend to be memorable sequences may underlie a great many superstitions. We ask the reader to consider which of the following sequences is more common in his or her experience: (1) The data from the first few research participants look good and look even better when you have run 15 per cell; or (2) the data from the first few participants look good but turn to mush by the time you have run 15 per cell. Many researchers may share our intuition that the latter sequence is much more common than the former (even allowing for regression to the mean); in fact, many may even share our belief that one should not look at early data because doing so "jinxes" them. We suggest that this belief (superstition?) emerges because of the tendency for bad data following good data to be so painful. Sequences that raise and then dash hopes are more available in memory, and therefore lead to the formation of erroneous beliefs.

Is Fearing Regret Rational or Irrational?

We end with a consideration of the question of rationality. Is the behavior we have attributed to anticipatory regret more appropriately termed rational or irrational? The answer depends on what the person is trying to maximize through his or her behavior. If a person's goal is to maximize satisfaction rather than profit, then to be guided by anticipatory regret cannot be considered irrational. If changing a correct answer to a wrong answer causes a person much more pain than earning another point brings the person pleasure, then the person is hardly being irrational by refusing to change an answer that he or she thinks – but does not know for sure – is wrong. Similarly, if losing a point in tennis through double-faulting causes more pain than winning a point gives pleasure, then it is hardly irrational to have a weak second serve. Likewise, people can hardly be called irrational if their custom is to arrive at airports so early that they waste much more time than an occasional missed flight would cost them. The "if only" thoughts that arise when one arrives a few minutes late for a flight might be so aversive that people are happy to trade hours of boredom to ensure that they are never beset by the thought, "If only I had left a few minutes earlier, I would have made it." However, if people do wish to maximize profit exclusively, then the beliefs we have focused on can more appropriately be termed irrational. If a person's only goal in blackjack is to maximize profit (minimize loss), then it is irrational to refuse a card at 16.

FINAL THOUGHTS

We sought in this chapter to expand the dominion of norm theory to encompass psychological domains not previously considered to lie within its sphere of influence; in particular, people's memory for the past and their beliefs about the future. Two central claims guided our quest. The first is that the counterfactual thoughts evoked by an event sequence affect the availability of that sequence in memory. The more powerfully an event sequence evokes thoughts of what might have been, the more available in memory the sequence is, and as a result, the more common the sequence seems. The second central claim is that the postcomputed thoughts and images that a negative event sequence brings to mind can be precomputed. People can anticipate the self-recriminations that an ill-fated behavioral sequence will evoke in them. Moreover, it is often these feelings, the intensity of which follows from various rules of mutability, rather than people's estimates of the chances of a negative outcome that determine the actions they take. We hope that the steps taken here, as preliminary and tentative as they are, have made it at least a little easier to imagine the counterfactual world in which counterfactual thinking is well understood.

PART TWO

NEW THEORETICAL DIRECTIONS

22. Two Systems of Reasoning

Steven A. Sloman

THE EMPIRICAL CASE FOR TWO SYSTEMS OF REASONING

The stimulation from a classic paper in the heuristics and biases tradition does not come only from the insights provided into processes of judgment and decision making; it also comes from anxiety, from the tension introduced between immediate intuition and more measured rational belief. Clearly, there is a limit to how much one's interest is piqued by reading about other people's mistakes. It is our own mistakes, and the insights they bring, that are so arresting and compelling. The tension is revealing because it reflects a gap within our own heads between, on one hand, our intuitions and, on the other hand, those of our beliefs that we consider *rational*. The classic demonstrations often suggest two minds at work: one following the "natural assessment methods" like representativeness and availability; and the other working to form coherent, justifiable sets of beliefs and plans of action. As Tversky and Kahneman have repeatedly shown, the two minds do not always agree.

The distinction between these two minds can be construed in terms of one of the central puzzles in experimental psychology – whether people are best conceived as parallel processors of information who operate along diffuse associative links, or as analysts who operate by deliberate and sequential manipulation of internal representations. Do we draw inferences through a network of learned associative pathways or by applying some kind of psycho-logic that manipulates symbolic tokens in a rule-governed manner? The debate has raged (again) in cognitive psychology for well over a decade now. It pits those who prefer models of mental phenomena to be built out of networks of associative devices that pass activation around in parallel and distributed form (the way brains probably function) against those who prefer models built out of formal languages in which symbols are composed into sentences that are processed sequentially (the way computers function).

An obvious solution to the conundrum is to conceive of the mind both ways: to argue that the mind has dual aspects, one of which conforms to the associationistic view and one of which conforms to the analytic, sequential view. Such a dichotomy has its appeal: Associative thought *feels* as though it arises from a different cognitive mechanism than does deliberate, analytical reasoning. Sometimes conclusions simply appear at some level of awareness, as if our minds go off, do some work, and then come back with a result, and sometimes coming to a conclusion requires doing the work yourself, making an effort to construct a chain of reasoning. This distinction has not been missed by philosophers or psychologists; it can be traced back to Aristotle and has been discussed, for example, by James (1890), Piaget (1926), Vygotsky (1934/1987), Neisser (1963), and Johnson-Laird (1983) among others, as shown later.

This distinction is implicit in the notion of "transparency" (Tversky & Kahneman, 1983). A manipulation that reduces bias by making an extensional probabilistic or logical relation transparent is in essence providing a representation that affords rule-based inference, allowing people to go beyond associative reasoning. But the presence of two systems for judgment and choice can make life difficult. Cases of inconsistency between rules and associations are one of the primary sources of conflict both within and between individuals. Decisions that we make every day are made more difficult by opposing recommendations from the two systems. This sort of conflict dominates much of choice behavior. Consumer choices are often between products that conjure up strong associations due to effective advertising or market longevity and products whose value can be justified analytically. Choosing between brand names, with which we have had long experience, and generic products, which sometimes have identical ingredients and a lower price, has this character. This type of conflict is even more palpable when we consider political options. A politician may seem attractive when expressing our values or promising to solve our problems, but analysis may suggest that enacting the candidate's policies is impractical, immoral, or both. More generally, people can be torn between descriptions that they "resonate" to and descriptions that they find analytically more accurate.

TWO FORMS OF COMPUTATION

The most lucid expression of the distinction and its psychological reality is that of William James (1890/1950), who describes *associative thought* or *empirical thinking* as "trains of images suggested one by another." James believed that associative thought is "only reproductive" in that the objects of associative thought are all elements of or abstractions from our past experience, although the data reviewed here suggest otherwise. True reasoning is "productive" according to James because it can deal with novel data: "Reasoning helps us out of unprecedented situations" (p. 330).

Associative System

Today, we might describe James as distinguishing between two systems that implement different computational principles. Roughly, one system is associative and its computations reflect similarity and temporal structure; the other system is symbolic and its computations reflect a rule structure.

The associative system encodes and processes statistical regularities of its environment, frequencies and correlations amongst the various features of the world. Generally speaking, associative systems are able to divide perceptions into reasonable clusters on the basis of statistical (or at least quasi-statistical) regularities. They treat objects in similar ways to the extent the objects are perceived as similar (e.g., Rumelhart & Zipser, 1985). The primary reason for this is that the degree to which an association is operative is proportional to the similarity between the current stimulus and previously associated stimuli. On this view, associative thought uses temporal and similarity relations to draw inferences and make predictions that approximate those of a sophisticated statistician. Rather than trying to reason on the basis of an underlying causal or mechanical structure, it constructs estimates based on underlying statistical structure. (Lacking highly predictive causal models, this is the preferred mode of analysis for many forecasters.)

Rule-Based System

The computational principles underlying rule-based reasoning are more opaque and more controversial than those of associative reasoning. One such principle, mentioned by James (1890/1950) and reasserted by Fodor and Pylyshyn (1988), is *productivity*. Rule-based systems are productive in that they can encode an unbounded number of propositions (i.e., rules can be combined with each other to generate an ever-larger set of propositions). To understand this, consider arithmetic, in which we can always generate a new number by adding 1 to the largest number in our set. A second principle is that rules are systematic in the sense that their ability to encode certain facts implies an ability to encode others. For example, if one can reason about John loving Mary, one also has the capacity to reason about Mary loving John. Fodor and Pylyshyn (1988) argue that the productivity, systematicity, and, therefore, compositionality of mental representations necessitate that human reasoning is generated by a language of thought that has a combinatorial syntax and semantics.

My claim is that their argument is relevant only to one form of reasoning. I call this form of reasoning *rule-based* because rules are the form of representation that exhibit the properties of productivity and systematicity most transparently. Rules are abstractions that apply to any and all statements that have a certain well-specified symbolic structure. Most importantly, they have both a logical structure and a set of variables. The relation is purely formal or syntactic in the sense that correct application of the rule is determined by relations amongst symbols and not by any sort of meaning that we attribute to the symbols.

Variables *vary* (i.e., they can be instantiated in more than one way). Because they assume a class of possible values, they are necessarily abstract. My discussion concerns rules that contain variables, and therefore rules are abstract; they can be instantiated in more than one way. This does not imply that rules have to be content independent. For instance, Cheng and Holyoak (1985) discuss sets of rules for reasoning that they call *pragmatic reasoning schemas* associated with particular content domains. They suggest that certain rules are associated with reasoning about situations involving domains such as permission. An example of such a rule is, "If the action is to be taken, then the precondition must be satisfied." Such rules involve both variables (e.g., *precondition* and *action*, which must be specified on each occasion of use) and, they involve logical structure (the form *if – then*); therefore, I count them as rules.

Rules come in different kinds. Some rules are instructions, like statements in a computer program or a recipe; other rules are laws of nature or society or rules of logic. People are capable of following all of these rules (and of disobeying some). Rules can be normative, telling us how we should behave to reach some prespecified goal (such as the conjunction rule in order to maintain a coherent set of probabilities); or descriptive, telling us how we do behave in certain contexts. In contexts in which a normative rule obviously applies, it usually becomes descriptive as well. So, some rules are handed down to us by our culture, others we make up ourselves, and some are discovered in nature or logic. Humans can understand and apply all of these rules without external support as long as they have become internalized, as long as their analytic machinery has access to and mastery of them.

Johnson-Laird and his colleagues (e.g., 1983; Johnson-Laird & Byrne, 1991) have argued persuasively that much of everyday deduction is unlike theorem-proving. They have posited a procedure to arrive at a determination of the logical relation between the premises and conclusion of an argument that has a fundamentally different rationale and design than the sequential application of inference rules advocated by theorists such as Braine (1990) and Rips (1994). Nevertheless, their "mental models" theory shares key assumptions with rule-based theories. Both approaches depend heavily on symbols. Like rules, mental models consist entirely of symbols. Some symbols are tokens that refer to entities in the statements of an argument. Other symbols represent negation and still others represent superset–subset relations. Mental models enjoy the criterial properties that I have assigned to rules: They have both logical structure and variables. The criterial properties of the rule-based system are thus sufficiently general to encompass central aspects of the mental models theory.

Evans and Over (1996) come to a similar conclusion to mine about the dual process nature of thought. They draw their conclusion from a thorough survey of the deductive reasoning literature and related decision-making phenomena, and from the evidence supporting the distinction between implicit and explicit learning. They argue that the two systems of thought are driven by different types of rationality. The associative system is generally useful for achieving one's goals; the rule-based system is more adept at ensuring that one's conclusions are sanctioned by a normative theory.

Table 22.1 summarizes my characterization of the two systems. The point of this chapter is not that both systems are applied to every problem a person confronts, nor that each system has an exclusive problem domain; rather, the forms have overlapping domains that differ depending on the individual reasoner's knowledge, skill, and experience. Table 22.1 lists some functions that show off each system's capacities. However, the common mode of

Table 22.1. Characterization of Two Forms of Reasoning

	Associative System	Rule-Based System
Principles of operation	Similarity and contiguity	Symbol manipulation
Source of knowledge	Personal experience	Language, culture, and formal systems
Nature of representation		
Basic units	Concrete and generic concepts, images, stereotypes, and feature sets	Concrete concepts, generic, and abstract concepts, abstracted features, compositional symbols
Relations	(a) Associations (b) Soft constraints	(a) Causal, logical, and hierarchical (b) Hard constraints
Nature of processing	(a) Reproductive but capable of similarity-based generalization (b) Overall feature computation and constraint satisfaction (c) Automatic	(a) Productive and systematic (b) Abstraction of relevant features (c) Strategic
Illustrative cognitive functions	Intuition Fantasy Creativity Imagination Visual recognition Associative memory	Deliberation Explanation Formal analysis Verification Ascription of purpose Strategic memory

operation of the two systems is clearly interactive. Together they lend their different computational resources to the task at hand; they function as two experts who are working cooperatively to compute sensible answers. One system may be able to mimic the computation performed by the other, but only with effort and inefficiency, and even then not necessarily reliably. The systems have different goals and are specialists at different kinds of problems. However, when a person is given a problem, both systems may try to solve it, each may compute a response, and the responses may not agree. Cases can be found in every domain of reasoning that has been studied in detail in which they do not. Because the systems cannot be distinguished by the problem domains to which they apply, deciding which system is responsible for a given response is not always easy. It may not even be possible, because both systems may contribute to a particular response.

One rule of thumb to help identify the source of an inference has to do with the contents of awareness. When a response is produced solely by the associative system, we are conscious only of the result of the computation, not the process. In contrast, we are aware of both the result and the process in a rule-based computation.

Various sources of evidence support the associative/rule-based distinction. One source is the study of conceptual structure. On one hand, scholars have been aware since the time of Aristotle that our concepts reflect similarity structure (for recent evidence, see Brooks, Norman, & Allen, 1991). Similarity is one of the hallmarks of associative processing. On the other hand, concepts serve analytic ends: they are used by rules to construct explanations. Some theorists argue that psychological concepts have a status analogous to that of scientific concepts (Carey, 1985; Quine, 1977). In support of this claim, experimental evidence makes clear that explanatory principles can guide the way even young children make classifications (Keil, 1989). The strength of the evidence on both sides of this issue suggests that both types of principles are operative in categorization. Indeed, Ashby, Alfonso-Reese, Turken, and Waldron (1998) propose a dual process neuropsychological theory of category learning that parallels the associative/rule-based dichotomy.

The case for two systems of thought can be made on several grounds (see Sloman, 1996). For the purposes of this chapter, I focus on one – the existence of simultaneous, contradictory beliefs.

TWO FORMS OF REASONING

Simultaneous Contradictory Belief

Among the most compelling evidence for the hypothesis of two reasoning systems are data drawn from a diverse set of reasoning tasks that share a single crucial characteristic. They all satisfy what I call *Criterion S*. A reasoning problem satisfies Criterion S if it causes people to believe two contradictory responses simultaneously. By "believe," I mean a propensity, feeling, or conviction that a response is appropriate even if it is not strong enough to be acted on. A taste of this form of evidence, although one that may not entail rule application, can be found in statements like, "Technically, a whale is a mammal" (Lakoff, 1972). The statement makes sense, more sense than, "Technically, a horse is a mammal," because a common mode of conceiving of whales has them more similar to fish. A whale is simultaneously both a mammal (technically) and a fish (informally). Situations abound in which people first solve a problem in a manner consistent with one form of reasoning and then, either with or without external prompting, realize and admit that a different form of reasoning provides an alternative and more justifiable answer. Judges are often forced to ignore their sense of justice in order to mete out punishment according to the law. These instances provide evidence for two forms of reasoning if, and only if, the tendency to provide the first response continues to be compelling irrespective of belief in the second answer, irrespective even of certainty in the second answer.

The logic of this form of evidence is easily illustrated by considering how perceptual illusions provide evidence for a dichotomy in a domain other than reasoning. The Müller–Lyer illusion suggests that perception and knowledge derive from distinct systems. Perception provides one answer (the horizontal lines are of unequal size), although knowledge (or a ruler) provides quite a different one – they are equal. The *knowledge* that the two lines are of equal size does little to affect the *perception* that they are not. The conclusion that two independent systems are at work depends critically on the fact that the perception and the knowledge are maintained simultaneously. Even while I tell myself that the lines are of equal length, I see lines of different length. At each point in time, we hold two contradictory opinions: one provided by our perceptual system, another by a system of abstract comprehension. Of course, usually perception and knowledge do not contradict one another, but that does not mean that they constitute a single system. Similarly, the failure of a reasoning problem to satisfy Criterion S is not evidence against two reasoning systems. The associative and rule-based systems may converge to the same answer, in which case no contradictory beliefs would arise.

Judgment. A variety of phenomena in the field of judgment satisfy Criterion S (many of which are reviewed in this book). Perhaps the best-known and most compelling example of simultaneous contradictory belief is an example of the conjunction fallacy reported by Tversky and Kahneman (1983), the Linda-the-bank-teller problem. They gave their participants the following paragraph describing the hypothetical person Linda:

Linda is 31 years old, single, outspoken, and very bright. She majored in philosophy. As a student, she was deeply concerned with issues of discrimination and social justice, and also participated in anti-nuclear demonstrations.

Then they asked participants to rank order eight statements about Linda according to the statement's probability. The statements included the following two:

Linda is a bank teller. (T)
Linda is a bank teller and is active in the feminist movement. ($T\&F$)

More than 80% of groups of graduate and medical students with statistical training and a group of doctoral students in the decision science program of the Stanford Business School ranked statement $T\&F$ as more probable than statement T. A general principle participants used to make this judgment is similarity or representativeness. In the paragraph description, Linda is more similar to a feminist bank teller than she is to a stereotypical bank teller (as participants' ratings confirm). We can more easily imagine Linda as a feminist bank teller, which leads us to conclude that she is more likely to be one. Of course, statement $T\&F$ could not possibly be more probable than statement T because it presupposes T; the truth of $T\&F$ entails that T be true.

Apparently, we have two mechanisms that lead us to divergent conclusions. On one hand, an intuitive heuristic leads us to conclude that $T\&F$ is more probable; on the other hand, a logical argument leads us to conclude that T is more probable. Both mechanisms have psychological force. Most researchers are willing to assent to the logic of the conjunction rule of probability in this case, and therefore believe that T is more likely. Indeed, Tversky and Kahneman (1983) report that few participants attempted to defend their responses. Nevertheless, a compulsion remains to respond that $T\&F$ describes a possible world that seems more likely. (Gould, 1991, shares this intuition: "I know that the [conjunction] is least probable, yet a little homunculus in my head continues to jump up and down, shouting at me – 'but she can't just be a bank teller; read the description' " p. 469). I can trace through the probability argument and concede its validity while sensing that a state of affairs that I can imagine much more easily has a greater chance of obtaining. As one participant who acknowledged the validity of the conjunction rule said, "I thought you only asked for my opinion" (Tversky & Kahneman, 1983, p. 300). Fortunately, opinions and reasoned conclusions do not usually diverge.

To buttress my claim, I ran a small, informal experiment. The three-prisoners problem (formally equivalent to the "three doors" or "Monty Hall" problems), like the Linda problem, is a problem of uncertain reasoning that involves two different responses: one intuitively compelling and one probabilistically correct. However, unlike the Linda problem, it does not satisfy Criterion S; people do not simultaneously believe the two responses in this problem. Indeed, this is an extremely difficult problem for both laypersons and experts in uncertain reasoning, who often do not resolve on even one interpretation (Falk, 1992; Shimojo & Ichikawa, 1989). When they are able to resolve more than one interpretation, they do it sequentially (in analogy to the sequential resolution of the Necker cube), not simultaneously (in analogy to the Müller–Lyer illusion). They convince themselves of one response and then resolve to an interpretation that elicits a different response that undermines the first.

I described both the Müller–Lyer and Necker cube illusions to five colleagues (faculty and graduate students in the Department of Cognitive and Linguistic Sciences at Brown University) and pointed out the difference in the temporal relation between the conflicting responses in the two cases (simultaneous vs. serial). I then described the Linda-the-bank-teller problem and discussed the two responses (she is more likely to be a bank teller versus she is more likely to be a feminist bank teller). Next, I asked participants whether the relation between the points in time in which the responses seemed compelling was more analogous to the Müller–Lyer illusion or to the Necker cube. Every participant said the Müller–Lyer illusion. I also gave participants the three-prisoners problem, obtained their response, and discussed the Bayesian reasoning that leads to a different response. Finally, I asked them whether the temporal relation between the interpretations that led to the two responses was more analogous to the Müller–Lyer illusion or to the Necker cube. Every participant said the Necker cube. In summary, everyone I asked ($p = 1/32$) agreed that the Linda-the-bank-teller problem satisfied Criterion S and that the three-prisoners problem violated it. The credibility of the intuition that beliefs are simultaneous in some problems is increased by the observation that the intuition is not ubiquitous.

People tend to make judgments on the basis of representativeness that violate a rule, a rule that most of us are happy to grant. Even after granting the rule, we feel a compulsion to report an answer that violates it. We may not report such an answer, but the fact that we are able to inhibit the response suggested by similarity is evidence for two systems.

Argument Strength. Other demonstrations that satisfy Criterion S can be found by observing how people project unfamiliar properties amongst categories. Sloman (1998) found that people tended to project properties from a superordinate category to a subordinate only to the extent that the categories were similar. For example, consider the following argument:

> *Fact: Every individual piece of electronic equipment exhibits magnetic picofluctuation.*
> Conclusion: Every individual piece of audio equipment exhibits magnetic picofluctuation.

Participants were implored to assume that the fact (premise) was true and to rate the conditional probability of the conclusion given the fact. Set-theoretic logic dictates that if all audio equipment is electronic equipment, then audio equipment should inherit whatever properties electronic equipment has. In other words, someone who agrees that audio equipment is electronic should assign a conditional probability of 1 to the conclusion. I considered only the probability judgments of those participants who affirmed the category inclusion relation between audio and electronic equipment. Their mean conditionalized probability judgment was .89. Not only were a substantial proportion of judgments less than 1, but when the conclusion category was atypical of the premise category, judgments were even lower. For example, the argument

> *Fact: Every individual piece of electronic equipment exhibits magnetic picofluctuation.*
> Conclusion: Every individual kitchen appliance exhibits magnetic picofluctuation.

received a mean probability judgment (again, conditional on affirmation of the category inclusion relation) of only .76. Sloman (1993) provides evidence that a measure of feature overlap plays a dominant role in determining judgments. When told in debriefing interviews that a good reason was available to assign both arguments the maximal probability judgment – namely, the obvious category inclusion rule – participants consistently agreed. They were also adamant (some more so than others) that their responses were also sensible, although they inevitably failed to express why. I conclude that, after debriefing, participants had two answers in mind to the given problem: one associative and one rule-based. The associative or similarity-based answer was generated automatically on presentation of the question, but the rule- or inclusion-based answer, arrived at later, was able to inhibit the associative response.

A related demonstration, the inclusion fallacy, was reported by Osherson, Smith, Wilkie, Lopez, and Shafir (1990), who asked people to choose which of the following two arguments seemed stronger:

Robins have an ulnar artery.
Therefore, birds have an ulnar artery.

Robins have an ulnar artery.
Therefore, ostriches have an ulnar artery.

The majority of participants chose the first argument, because robins and birds are more similar than robins and ostriches. However, most people will also concede that the second argument is at least as strong because ostriches are birds, so any evidence that increases belief that all birds have some property necessarily increases belief to at least the same extent that all ostriches have the property. This is a striking example in which a compelling logical argument fails to erase an even more compelling intuition: How much evidence can a fact about robins provide for an animal as dissimilar as an ostrich?

Syllogistic Reasoning. A syllogism is a kind of deductive argument with two premises and a conclusion consisting of quantified categories assigned to predicates, such as the famous one

All men are mortal.
Socrates is a man.
Therefore, Socrates is mortal.

Demonstrations abound that our willingness to affirm the conclusion of a syllogism, even an invalid syllogism, varies with our prior beliefs. Our reasoning is not based on formal considerations alone; it is affected by content or "belief bias" effects. For example, Revlin, Leirer, Yopp, and Yopp (1980) asked participants to "decide which of five possible conclusions have to follow unambiguously from the given premises" of the following:

No members of the ad-hoc committee are women.
Some U.S. senators are members of the ad-hoc committee.
Therefore:
    a. All U.S. senators are women.
    b. No U.S. senators are women.
    c. Some U.S. senators are women.
    d. Some U.S. senators are not women.
    e. None of the above is proven.

No U.S. governors are members of the Harem Club.
Some Arabian sheiks are members of the Harem Club.
Therefore:
    a. All Arabian sheiks are U.S. governors.
    b. No Arabian sheiks are U.S. governors.
    c. Some Arabian sheiks are U.S. governors.
    d. Some Arabian sheiks are not U.S. governors.
    e. None of the above is proven.

In the first case, syllogistic logic agrees with our belief that some U.S. senators are not women. As a consequence, 83% of responses were correct. In the second case, logic conflicts with belief. Logic tells us, as it did in the first case, that again, d is correct. However, a more appealing conclusion is the one we know to be empirically true, conclusion b: No Arabian sheiks are U.S. governors. Only 67% of participants chose d in the second case. Participants do not ignore logical entailments; they accept more valid syllogisms than invalid ones (e.g., Evans, Barston, & Pollard, 1983). Nevertheless, belief bias effects do occur, as in the case at hand. The current example shows that empirical belief obtained fairly directly through associative memory can inhibit the response generated by psycho-logic.

RELATED EVIDENCE

Windschitl and Weber (1999) point out that expressions of certainty are differentially sensitive to context depending on whether they are expressed on precise numeric scales or imprecise nonnumeric ones. If given a precise numeric forecast (e.g., "Experts believe that the chance of rain is 70%") and asked to make a numeric probability judgment (e.g., "What's the probability of rain?"), people normally provide a judgment that matches the expert's forecast. Windschitl and Weber show that given the same forecast but asked to make their judgment using a nonnumeric scale (a verbal scale or one represented by line length), people's judgments are affected by the representativeness of the event. Representative events (e.g., rain in London) are judged more likely than unrepresentative events (e.g., rain in Madrid), despite identical expert forecasts. Their interpretation is that numeric judgments tend to elicit rule-based responding; nonnumeric judgments are more often products of associative reasoning.

Logan (1988) describes and tests a model of automatization consistent with my conclusion. His model applies to tasks, like arithmetic, for which an answer can be obtained in two ways, either by using an algorithm (by rule) or automatically, by retrieving an answer from memory (by similarity between the current problem and a previous one). Logan assumes that performance results from a race between these two processes. As participants gain experience with the task, their memory base of instances increases, which increases the probability that automatic memory retrieval will provide an answer prior to the completion of the algorithm. His statistical model of these competing processes successfully fit both lexical decision and alphabet arithmetic (e.g., $A = 1, B = 2, \ldots Z = 26$; $C + F = ?$) reaction time data. He also confirmed some qualitative predictions of the model. Logan's model makes the strong assumption that the effect of practice is to increase the associative knowledge base without affecting the processing of rules at all.

The evidence that alphabet arithmetic has an associative component helps to make sense of data showing that arithmetic has much the same character as other kinds of associative retrieval. For example, people give correct answers more quickly to arithmetic problems that they have practiced recently (Campbell, 1987; Stazyk, Ashcraft, & Hamman, 1982).

A host of evidence exists in the literature on social cognition that suggests that dual processes control impression formation and attitude change (cf. Chaiken & Trope, 1999). For example, a variety of "correction" phenomena have been observed wherein participants are presented with a stimulus that they believe biases their impressions. People tend to correct for the bias unless they are distracted, suggesting that correction involves an optional, controlled process that is independent of some more automatic impression formation process. For example, Martin, Seta, and Crelia (1990) primed participants with positive or negative concepts and then gave information about an individual that could be construed in positive or negative terms. When tested without distraction, participants' impressions contrasted with the priming stimuli; they overcorrected for the primes. But when tested with distraction, impressions showed an assimilation effect; participants failed to correct sufficiently for the primes. Wegener and Petty (1995) showed that the direction of a correction is flexible, and depends on how participants understand and explain the source of bias, suggesting that correction is governed by deliberate rule application. These differential effects of distraction amount to a dissociation between a controlled, analytic correction process and more automatic ones. However, the research does not imply a specific characterization of these automatic processes.

Two dual process models have emerged in the social cognition literature that contrast with the associative/rule-based distinction: Petty and Cacioppo's (1986) elaboration likelihood model and Chaiken, Liberman, and Eagly's (1989) heuristic/systematic model (both reviewed in Eagly and Chaiken, 1993, chapter 7). The elaboration likelihood model assumes dual routes for constructing attitudes: a central one based on analysis and elaboration of arguments and a peripheral one defined by all other variables that affect attitudes such as attractiveness, group identification, and conditioning. The heuristic/systematic model differs from elaboration likelihood mainly in the degree to which it constrains the nonelaborative route. It proposes that this mode of processing makes use of a set of heuristics – learned procedural knowledge – that must be accessed in order to affect judgment. A heuristic cue refers "to any variable whose judgmental impact is hypothesized to be mediated by a simple decision rule" (Eagly & Chaiken, 1993, p. 327). Thus, the model departs from the associative/rule-based distinction in assuming that nonanalytic processing makes use of rules as opposed to associations. Unlike the elaboration likelihood model, it shares with the current distinction the assumption that the dual processes occur in parallel, not sequentially.

EMPIRICAL CONCLUSIONS

I reviewed evidence from multiple domains in which people were simultaneously compelled to believe two contradictory answers to a reasoning problem, in some cases with more than one demonstration from the same domain. Notice that the reader need only accept my conclusion in a single demonstration for the thesis of this paper to hold. These data are complemented by Windschitl and Weber's (1999) demonstration of the effect of associative inference on nonnumeric forecasting, the evidence for Logan's (1988) instance theory, which assumes that certain cognitive tasks can be performed either algorithmically or through associations to an instance memory, and the evidence that correction processes in social judgment can be dissociated from other, less theory-bound, processes.

Associative Intrusion and Rule-Based Suppression

These data help us to characterize the interaction between the two systems. In all the demonstrations of simultaneous contradictory belief, associative responses were shown to be automatic in that they persisted in the face of participants' attempts to ignore them. Despite recognition of the decisiveness of the rule-based argument, associative responses remained compelling (see Allen & Brooks, 1991, for analogous effects in categorization). Both systems seem to try, at least some of the time, to generate a response. The rule-based system can suppress the response of the associative system in the sense that it can overrule it. However, the associative system always has its opinion heard and, because of its speed and efficiency, often precedes and thus neutralizes the rule-based response. Epstein, Lipson, Holstein, and Huh (1992) come to a closely related conclusion. In research directed at a distinction alike in many respects to the current one, they asked participants to consider vignettes describing people's reactions to negative outcomes. The vignettes described different actors suffering identical consequences for which they were equally responsible. Participants assumed both a self-orientation (e.g., "How foolish would you feel if you had reacted that way?") and a "rational" orientation (e.g., "How foolishly did the person in the vignette actually behave?"). The rational orientation asked participants to make a more objective response than the self-orientation that asked them to guess only at a subjective feeling. By demanding objectivity, the rational orientation demanded responses that participants could justify; the self-orientation asked only that participants report their impressions. Rules provide a firmer basis for justification than do impressions, and therefore participants were more likely to respond on the basis of rules in the rational than in the self-orientation condition. Epstein et al. found that self-orientation judgments differed for different vignettes, depending on such causally irrelevant factors as whether actors had behaved as usual or unusually. Most pertinent here, judgments made with a rational orientation reduced but failed to eliminate this effect. In conformity with Epstein et al., I conclude that even when one is attempting to be rule-governed, associative responses encroach on judgment. The force of the evidence is to support not only the conclusion that human beings have and use two computationally distinct systems of reasoning, but also that the associative system intrudes on the rule-based one.

Representation in the Associative System

All the associative responses discussed previously were based on fairly global correspondences between concepts represented as (more or less structured) sets of features. Concepts were not first distilled into one or two relevant features. For example, participants had to use features to compute the similarity between Linda and feminists because they had no information about Linda other than a feature list. Little task-specific selection or differential weighting of features took place because performance was predictable from similarity judgments taken out of the problem context.

The conspicuous feature of the data I have reviewed is the extent to which people's modal inferences involved computations that considered only similarity structure and associative relations. This claim might appear contrary to work showing that associative judgments of similarity and probability can depend on hierarchical and causal structure. Markman and Gentner (1993) and Medin, Goldstone, and Gentner (1993) have shown that similarity judgments can be strongly influenced by structured relations. The point is buttressed by Tversky and Kahneman (1983), who showed that the presence of a causal relation can increase a statement's representativeness. Their participants judged that John P. was less likely to kill one of his employees than he was to kill one of his employees to prevent him from talking to the police (a conjunction fallacy). The added motivation produced by the causal relation made the proposition seem more likely. The causal statement is more representative than the noncausal one of the standard model of murderers; we tend to think of murderers as motivated. In short, people seem to be sensitive to both hierarchical and causal structure when performing associative operations.

On one hand, I argue that certain judgments are associative and yet they are sensitive to hierarchical and causal structure. On the other hand, I argue that only rules, and not associations, can represent such structure. These arguments are not contradictory because mere sensitivity does not imply representational capacity. Similarity and probability judgments could be sensitive to hierarchical and causal relations because they depend on representations constructed by rules and those rules could construct different representations depending on hierarchical and causal knowledge. To illustrate, we can conclude from the example of our suspected murderer John P. that the similarity of an action to the actions we expect of a murderer is increased by providing a cause for the action, in particular a motivation for a murder. Such a conclusion has two conditions. First, we must be able to comprehend that killing an employee to prevent him from talking to the police is a causal relation from the motive of preventing to the action of killing. Because it involves a causal relation, I claim that such comprehension involves at least one rule. Second, we must decide that a description that includes a motivation is more similar to our model of a murderer than a description that does not. I claim that this operation is associative. In this fashion, we can take the causal analysis out of the associative part of the computation.

Two further properties of associative thought are noteworthy. The first is attributable to James (1890), who pointed out that although associative thought often deals in concrete images, it can also deal in abstract concepts. For instance, we can easily think about water or sheep as general categories, not only as particular instances. When thinking about wool, we might make use of an association to sheep, but not to any sheep in particular, rather to sheep as a category. Second, and contrary to James, the associative system is not simply reproductive, but can deal with novel stimuli. The similarity judgments underlying the conjunction fallacy and the inductive argument strength phenomena were not retrieved from memory. The comparison process took place on-line.

Automatic/Controlled Processing and Development

I have characterized *associative inference* as a reflexive and *rule-based inference* as a deliberate form of symbol manipulation. The deliberate quality of rule-based reasoning suggests that it is accomplished through goal-oriented, "optional" strategies (Posner & Snyder, 1975). These characterizations suggest a parallel, on one hand, between associative and rule-based reasoning and, on the other hand, between automatic and controlled processing (Schneider & Shiffrin, 1977; Shiffrin & Schneider, 1977). Historically, the automatic/controlled distinction has been applied to perceptual–motor tasks, like visual search, and not to reasoning, but it may turn out to subsume the associative/rule distinction.

Associative processes may be shown to satisfy the two criteria laid out for automatic processes (Shiffrin, Dumais, & Schneider, 1981): "1: Any process that does not use general, nonspecific processing resources and does not decrease the general, nonspecific processing capacity available for other processes. . . . 2: Any process that demands resources in response to external stimulus inputs, regardless of participants' attempts to ignore the distraction" (pp. 227–228). I argued earlier that associative processes satisfy the second criterion. No evidence I know of speaks directly to the first, although the correction phenomena in social judgment described earlier are suggestive. The prediction is that cognitive load should place a greater burden on rule-based than associative processes. Tasks that have a large rule-based component, like theorem-proving, should be more adversely affected by a secondary conceptual task than tasks that are mostly associative, like similarity judgment.

Theoretical discussions of the automatic/controlled distinction have focused on learning, in particular the nature of the transformation of controlled processes into automatic ones, analogous to the transformation of rule-based processes into associative ones. The existence of such transformations follows from a modification of an argument made by Vygotsky's (1934/1987): The rule-based system must developmentally precede the associative system because an organism with only an associative system would not have the resources to develop analytic thinking skills. Unstructured associative devices are unlikely to find descriptions of their environment that obey rule-based principles like productivity and systematicity. But an organism that can analyze its environment by generating useful and descriptive rules can internalize those rules by using them to nominate features to be associated.

Most associationists take this position. Hinton (1990) states that rational inferences become intuitive over time: "people seem to be capable of taking frequently repeated sequences and eliminating the sequential steps so that an inference that was once rational becomes intuitive" (p. 51). Rumelhart (1989) claims that we develop formal skills like mathematics by internalizing the symbolic manipulations that we learn to do externally. We start doing algebra by manipulating marks that we put on blackboards and paper, but eventually we can do simple manipulations in our heads. The claim is that people first figure the world out deliberately and sequentially and only with time and practice does the knowledge become integrated into our associative network. The idea is not that we are born with a fully functioning system of abstract comprehension, only that we try to analyze the world from the beginning (Carey, 1985).

However, the developmental story is not that simple; effects between reasoning systems are not unidirectional. Evidence also suggests that people rely on associative processes when they do not have knowledge of or access to rule-based ones (Quine, 1977, said that we fall back on our "animal sense of similarity" when a lay theory is not available). In summary, associative and rule-based reasoning are interwoven in development just as they are in task performance. Some rule-based reasoning is needed to know what features to begin with in domains that humans are neither phylogenetically nor ontogenetically adapted to, but associative reasoning predominates when rules that might prove more definitive or certain are inaccessible.

GENERAL DISCUSSION

What the Distinction Is Not

The distinction between associative and rule-based reasoning is not the same as one that is often assumed to be key psychologically, that between induction and deduction. Induction and deduction are not well-defined psychological processes; they are only well defined as argument types (Skyrms, 1986). Very roughly, inductive arguments are those in which the premises make the conclusion more probable; deductive ones are those in which the conclusion is necessarily true if the premises are. Rips (1990) points out that even the set of arguments cannot be partitioned independently into deductive and inductive ones. Our definition only distinguishes methods of assessing the strength of an undifferentiated set of arguments. The distinction is orthogonal to the current one because both reasoning systems influence people's judgments of the validity of both kinds of arguments. I have described examples of both inductive arguments (e.g., the inclusion fallacy) and deductive arguments (e.g., belief-bias effects) that are assessed, and assessed in contradictory ways, by the two reasoning systems. Both kinds of arguments are influenced by at least one common process – namely, a matching process that reflects similarity structure.

The distinction is also not the same as the one between analytic and non-analytic cognition (e.g., Allen & Brooks, 1991). That distinction focuses on the dual influences of abstractions and more concrete exemplars in perception, categorization, and reasoning. According to it, processing is analytic if responses are made on the basis of a stored abstraction, whether that abstraction is in the form of a prototype or a rule. I am distinguishing prototypes from rules. Prototypes are indeed abstract, but reasoning from them is essentially similarity based in that, according to prototype models, decisions are based on similarity to a prototype. Exemplar processes are also similarity based. Therefore, I am grouping exemplar and prototype-based processes together and contrasting them to rule-based processes. My distinction happens to fit more comfortably with the connectionist paradigm, in which exemplars, prototypes, and combinations of the two are all stored together (McClelland & Rumelhart, 1985).

The Systems' Functions

Why should human beings need two systems of thought? One answer is that the systems serve complementary functions. The associative system is able to draw on statistical structure, whereas a system that specializes in analysis and abstraction is able to focus on relevant features. A different sort of complementarity is that associative paths that are followed without prejudice can be a source of creativity, whereas more careful and deliberative analyses can provide a logical filter guiding thought to productive ends. Mathematics, law, and (probably) all disciplines demand this combination of creativity and rigorous rule application.

Freud (1913) supplied an answer of a completely different sort. He suggested that our two forms of thought, or *psychic processes*, have their source in two aspects of human experience. On one hand, we desire gratification and avoidance of pain. On the other hand, we must try to satisfy these urges in a world full of obstacles and boundaries; gratification must sometimes be delayed. Inhibiting this primary process, and thus making both gratification more likely in the long run and behavior more socially acceptable, is secondary process thought, governed by the reality principle. Primary process thought sets the stage for fantasy and imagination; secondary process, for purposive activity.

Freud – indeed, every theorist who discusses the issue – believes the source of most rule-based knowledge is cultural. Consistent with this claim, all the rule-based reasoning detailed previously reflects cultural knowledge (e.g., probability theory, class-inclusion logic) imparted by the experimenter to the participant. This notion of internalizing rules was axiomatic to Vygotsky, who emphasized the role of language in the cultural diffusion of rules. He believed that learning to think analytically is mostly a process of internalizing speech. He argued that a child's thinking begins with social speech, passes through a stage of egocentric speech, and crystallizes in the form of inner speech and logical thought.

Implications for Conceptual Structure

Associationists and rule-based theorists tend to have different views concerning the determinants and extent of conceptual coherence. Associationists tend to believe that our beliefs are usually consistent with each other because they reflect the world and the world is necessarily coherent, for it must obey the laws of nature. People may have contradictory beliefs because different aspects of our experience may provide evidence for opposing views. Our experience in the home may suggest that people tend to be generous but our experience on the highway may suggest that people tend to be selfish. On this view, coherence is a property of concepts by virtue and to the extent that experience in the world is coherent.

Rule-based theorists tend to believe that we possess a more potent urge for coherence. Rules can reflect structure in the world as well as conform to their own syntax and semantics, which may impose further structure. Any formal calculus of belief embodies assumptions about which beliefs are consistent with each other. Thus, rules enforce their own principles of coherence and, accordingly, rule-based theorists tend to believe that people try to conform. Some of them (e.g., Keil, 1989; Murphy, 1993) imply that people try to construct a global rule-based theory that causes them to try to be globally coherent in their everyday lives (and not just when doing philosophy or science).

Allowing humans to be both associationists and rule-governed suggests a way to reconcile these views. People may have an urge for coherence, but that urge is for *local* coherence. Rules are applied in such a way that current explanations, the temporary contents of working memory, are internally consistent and consistent with the long-term knowledge deemed relevant. For the most part, people can rely on the world to maintain coherence across situations (unless our perceptions are terribly distorted). Because they reflect objects and events in the world fairly directly, the associative system can do some of that work.

CONCLUSIONS

People are renowned for their willingness to behave in ways that they cannot justify, let alone explain. Instead of performing a complete analysis of their interests, people vote for a politician because they have always for voted for that person or buy an item because it is associated with an image that they would like to project. However, most people only go so far. They would not do something that they consider irrational if it entailed a real penalty or cost. Fewer people buy an item after it has been linked to cancer. So, on one hand, people "follow their noses" by allowing associations to guide them; on the other hand, they are compelled to behave in a manner more justifiable. The fact that people are pulled in two directions at once suggests two forces pulling.

23. The Affect Heuristic

Paul Slovic, Melissa Finucane, Ellen Peters,
and Donald G. MacGregor

This chapter introduces a theoretical framework that describes the importance of affect in guiding judgments and decisions. As used here, *affect* means the specific quality of "goodness" or "badness" (1) experienced as a feeling state (with or without consciousness) and (2) demarcating a positive or negative quality of a stimulus. *Affective responses* occur rapidly and automatically – note how quickly you sense the feelings associated with the stimulus words *treasure* or *hate*. We argue that reliance on such feelings can be characterized as the *affect heuristic*. In this chapter, we trace the development of the affect heuristic across a variety of research paths followed by ourselves and many others. We also discuss some of the important practical implications resulting from ways that this heuristic impacts our daily lives.

BACKGROUND

Although affect has long played a key role in many behavioral theories, it has rarely been recognized as an important component of human judgment and decision making. Perhaps befitting its rationalistic origins, the main focus of descriptive decision research has been cognitive, rather than affective. When principles of utility maximization appeared to be descriptively inadequate, Simon (1956) oriented the field toward problem-solving and information-processing models based on bounded rationality. The work of Tversky and Kahneman (1974) and Kahneman, Slovic, and Tversky (1982) demonstrated how boundedly rational individuals use such heuristics as availability, representativeness, and anchoring and adjustment to make judgments, and how they use simplified strategies such as "elimination by aspects" to make choices (Tversky, 1972). Other investigators elaborated the cognitive strategies underlying judgment and choice through models of constructed preferences (Slovic, 1995; Payne, Bettman, & Johnson, 1993), dominance structuring (Montgomery, 1983), and comparative advantages (Shafir, Osherson, & Smith, 1989). In 1993, the entire volume of the journal *Cognition* was dedicated to the topic Reason-Based Choice, in which it was argued that "Decisions . . . are often reached by focusing

Financial support for the writing of this chapter was provided by the National Science Foundation under grant SES 9876587.

on reasons that justify the selection of one option over another" (Shafir, Simonson, & Tversky, 1993, p. 34). Similarly, a state-of-the-art review by Busemeyer, Hastie, and Medin (1995) was titled "Decision Making from a Cognitive Perspective." In keeping with its title, it contained almost no references to the influence of affect on decisions.

Despite this cognitive emphasis, the importance of affect is being recognized increasingly by decision researchers. A limited role for affect was acknowledged by Shafir et al. (1993), who conceded, "People's choices may *occasionally* stem from affective judgments that preclude a thorough evaluation of the options" (p. 32, emphasis added).

A strong early proponent of the importance of affect in decision making was Zajonc (1980), who argued that affective reactions to stimuli are often the very first reactions, occurring automatically and subsequently guiding information processing and judgment. According to Zajonc, all perceptions contain some affect. "We do not just see 'a house': We see a *handsome* house, an *ugly* house, or a *pretentious* house" (p. 154). He later adds,

We sometimes delude ourselves that we proceed in a rational manner and weight all the pros and cons of the various alternatives. But this is probably seldom the actual case. Quite often "I decided in favor of X" is no more than "I liked X".... We buy the cars we "like," choose the jobs and houses we find "attractive," and then justify these choices by various reasons. (p. 155)

Affect also plays a central role in what have come to be known as *dual-process theories* of thinking, knowing, and information processing (Chaiken and Trope, 1999; Sloman, 1996). As Epstein (1994) observed,

There is no dearth of evidence in every day life that people apprehend reality in two fundamentally different ways, one variously labeled intuitive, automatic, natural, nonverbal, narrative, and experiential, and the other analytical, deliberative, verbal, and rational. (p. 710)

One of the characteristics of the experiential system is its affective basis. Although analysis is certainly important in some decision-making circumstances, reliance on affect and emotion is a quicker, easier, and more efficient way to navigate in a complex, uncertain, and sometimes dangerous world. Many theorists have given affect a direct and primary role in motivating behavior. Epstein's (1994) view on this is as follows:

The experiential system is assumed to be intimately associated with the experience of affect,... which refer[s] to subtle feelings of which people are often unaware. When a person responds to an emotionally significant event,... the experiential system automatically searches its memory banks for related events, including their emotional accompaniments.... If the activated feelings are pleasant, they motivate actions and thoughts anticipated to reproduce the feelings. If the feelings are unpleasant, they motivate actions and thoughts anticipated to avoid the feelings. (p. 716)

Also emphasizing the motivational role of affect, Mowrer (1960a, 1960b) conceptualized conditioned emotional responses to images as prospective gains and losses that directly "guide and control performance in a generally sensible adaptive manner" (1960a, p. 30). He criticized theorists who postulate purely cognitive variables such as expectancies (probabilities) intervening between stimulus and response, cautioning that we must be careful not to leave the organism at the choice point "lost in thought." Mowrer's solution was to view expectancies more dynamically (as conditioned emotions such as hopes and fears) serving as motivating states leading to action.

One of the most comprehensive and dramatic theoretical accounts of the role of affect in decision making is presented by neurologist Antonio Damasio (1994), in his book *Descartes' Error: Emotion, Reason, and the Human Brain*. Damasio's theory is derived from observations of patients with damage to the ventromedial frontal cortices of the brain that has left their basic intelligence, memory, and capacity for logical thought intact but has impaired their ability to feel – that is, to associate affective feelings and emotions with the anticipated consequences of their actions. Close observation of these patients combined with a number of experimental studies led Damasio to argue that this type of brain damage induces a form of sociopathy (Damasio, Tranel, & Damasio, 1990) that destroys the individual's ability to make rational decisions; that is, decisions that are in his or her best interests. Persons suffering this damage became socially dysfunctional even though they remain intellectually capable of analytical reasoning. Commenting on one particularly significant case, Damasio observes:

The instruments usually considered necessary and sufficient for rational behavior were intact in him. He had the requisite knowledge, attention, and memory; his language was flawless; he could perform calculations; he could tackle the logic of an abstract problem. There was only one significant accompaniment to his decision-making failure: a marked alteration of the ability to experience feelings. Flawed reason and impaired feelings stood out together as the consequences of a specific brain lesion, and this correlation suggested to me that feeling was an integral component of the machinery of reason. (p. XII)

In seeking to determine "what in the brain allows humans to behave rationally," Damasio argues that thought is made largely from images, broadly construed to include sounds, smells, real or imagined visual impressions, ideas, and words. A lifetime of learning leads these images to become "marked" by positive and negative feelings linked directly or indirectly to somatic or bodily states (Mowrer and other learning theorists would call this *conditioning*): "In short, *somatic markers are . . . feelings generated from secondary emotions*. These emotions and feelings *have been connected, by learning, to predicted future outcomes of certain scenarios*" (Damasio, 1994, p. 174). When a negative somatic marker is linked to an image of a future outcome, it sounds an alarm. When a positive marker is associated with the outcome image, it becomes a beacon of incentive. Damasio concludes that somatic markers increase the accuracy and efficiency of the decision process, and their absence degrades decision performance.

Damasio tested the somatic marker hypothesis in a decision-making experiment in which subjects gambled by selecting cards from any of four decks. Turning each card resulted in the gain or loss of a sum of money, as revealed on the back of the card when it was turned. Whereas normal subjects and patients with brain lesions outside the prefrontal sectors learned to avoid decks with attractive large payoffs but occasional catastrophic losses, patients with frontal lobe damage did not, thus losing a great deal of money. Although these patients responded normally to gains and losses when they occurred (as indicated by skin conductance responses immediately after an outcome was experienced), they did not seem to learn to anticipate future outcomes (e.g., they did not produce normal skin conductance responses when contemplating a future choice from a dangerous deck). In other words, they failed to show any proper anticipatory responses, even after numerous opportunities to learn them.

Despite the increasing popularity of affect in research programs and recent attempts to acknowledge the importance of the interplay between affect and cognition, further work is needed to specify the role of affect in judgment and decision making. The ideas articulated here are intended as a step toward encouraging the development of theory about affect and decision making and demonstrating how such a theory can be tested.

The basic tenet of this chapter is that images, marked by positive and negative affective feelings, guide judgment and decision making. Specifically, it is proposed that people use an *affect heuristic* to make judgments; that is, representations of objects and events in people's minds are tagged to varying degrees with affect. In the process of making a judgment or decision, people consult or refer to an "affect pool" containing all the positive and negative tags consciously or unconsciously associated with the representations. Just as imaginability, memorability, and similarity serve as cues for probability judgments (e.g., the availability and representativeness heuristics), affect may serve as a cue for many important judgments. Using an overall, readily available affective impression can be far easier – more efficient – than weighing the pros and cons or retrieving from memory many relevant examples, especially when the required judgment or decision is complex or mental resources are limited. This characterization of a mental short-cut leads to labeling the use of affect a "heuristic."

EMPIRICAL EVIDENCE: MANIPULATING PREFERENCES THROUGH CONTROLLED EXPOSURES

The fundamental nature and importance of affect has been demonstrated repeatedly in a remarkable series of studies by Zajonc and his colleagues (see, e.g., Zajonc, 1968; Zajonc & Markus, 1982). The concept of stimulus exposure is central to all of these studies. The central finding is that, when objects are presented to an individual repeatedly, the "mere exposure" is capable of creating a positive attitude or preference for these objects.

In the typical study, stimuli such as nonsense phrases, or faces, or Chinese ideographs are presented to an individual with varying frequencies. In a later session, the individual judges these stimuli on liking, or familiarity, or both. The more frequent the prior exposure to a stimulus, the more positive the response. A meta-analysis by Bornstein (1989) of mere exposure research published between 1968 and 1987 included more than 200 experiments examining the exposure–affect relationship. Unreinforced exposures were found to reliably enhance affect toward visual, auditory, gustatory, abstract, and social stimuli.

Winkielman, Zajonc, and Schwarz (1997) demonstrated the speed with which affect can influence judgments in studies using a subliminal priming paradigm. Participants were "primed" through exposure to a smiling face, a frowning face, or a neutral polygon presented for 1/250th second, an interval so brief that there is no recognition or recall of the stimulus. Immediately following this exposure, an ideograph was presented for 2 seconds, following which the participant rated the ideograph on a scale of liking. Mean liking ratings were significantly higher for ideographs preceded by smiling faces. This effect was lasting. In a second session, ideographs were primed by the other face: the face not associated with the stimulus in the first session. This second priming was ineffective because the effect of the first priming remained.

It is not just subliminal smiles that affect our judgment. La France and Hect (1995) found that students accused of academic misconduct who were pictured as smiling received less punishment than nonsmiling transgressors. Smiling persons were judged as more trustworthy, good, honest, genuine, obedient, blameless, sincere, and admirable than nonsmiling targets.

The perseverance of induced preferences was tested by Sherman, Kim, and Zajonc (1998), who asked participants to study Chinese characters and their English meanings. Half of the meanings were positive (e.g., beauty), half were negative (e.g., disease). Then participants were given a test of these meanings followed by a task in which they were given pairs of characters and were asked to choose the one they preferred. Participants preferred characters with positive meaning 70% of the time. Next, the characters were presented with neutral meanings (desk, linen) and subjects were told that these were the "true" meanings. The testing procedure was repeated and, despite learning the new meanings, the preferences remained the same. Characters that had been paired initially with positive meanings still tended to be preferred.

These various studies demonstrate that affect is a strong conditioner of preference, regardless of whether the cause of that affect is consciously perceived. They also demonstrate the independence of affect from cognition, indicating that there may be conditions of affective or emotional arousal that do not necessarily require cognitive appraisal. This affective mode of response, unburdened by cognition and therefore much faster, has considerable adaptive value.

EVALUATING GAMBLES

The affect heuristic can explain a finding that has intrigued and perplexed the first author since he first observed it in 1984. Slovic and Amos Tversky were re-examining the early studies by Slovic and Lichtenstein (1968) and Lichtenstein and Slovic (1971, 1973) that pointed to compatibility between stimulus attributes and response scales as an explanation for preference reversals. Such reversals were exhibited when an individual chose Gamble A (with a high probability of winning a modest amount of money) over Gamble B (with a smaller probability of a larger payoff) but assigned a larger monetary value (buying price or selling price) to Gamble B. Presumably, the reversal occurred because the gamble payoffs were given more weight in the pricing response mode than in choice, due to the compatibility between prices and payoffs, both of which were measured in dollars.

Tversky and Slovic decided to replicate the earlier reversal studies with three changes:

1. The complexity of the gamble was minimized by eliminating losses. Each gamble consisted merely of a stated probability of winning a given amount. There was no possible loss of money.
2. Following Goldstein (1984) and Goldstein and Einhorn (1987), who observed reversals with ratings and prices, we included ratings of a gamble's attractiveness along with choices and pricing as methods of eliciting preferences. The attractiveness scale ranged between 0 (not at all attractive) and 20 (very attractive).
3. To ensure the strategic equivalence of our three elicitation procedures, we devised a method for linking preferences to outcomes that was identical across all conditions. Subjects were told that a pair of bets would be selected and the bet that received the higher attractiveness rating (or the higher price, or that was preferred in the choice task) would be the bet they would play. Consequently, the preferences elicited by prices and ratings should not differ from each other or from the preferences elicited by direct choices. Some of the gambles were, in fact, actually played.

Using this design, we observed strong differences between response modes, leading to many preference reversals. Particularly striking was the difference between ratings and prices. Ratings produced an overwhelming dominance of high probability bets over high payoff bets (the bet with higher probability of winning had the higher attractiveness rating 80% to 90% of the time, but was assigned a higher price only 10% to 15% of the time). The mean evaluations of the two bets shown in Table 23.1 were typical.

Seeking to explain the results shown in Table 23.1 in terms of compatibility, we linked the compatibility effect to the ease of mapping the stimulus component of a gamble onto the response scale. The easier it is to execute such a mapping, the greater the weight given the component. In principle, a gamble's payoff is more compatible with a price response than with a rating because prices and payoffs are both expressed in dollars. Therefore, payoffs should get greater weight in pricing

Table 23.1. Mean Evaluations of Two Bets

Bet	Mean Price	Mean Rating (0–20 Scale)
29/36 to win $2	$1.25	13.2
7/36 to win $9	$2.11	7.5

than in rating. The extremely high weight given probabilities when rating attractiveness may be explained by the fact that the probabilities are more readily coded as attractive or unattractive than are the payoffs. For example, 29 out of 36 chances to win are very attractive odds. However, a $9 payoff may be harder to map on a rating scale because its attractiveness depends on what other payoffs are available.

According to this explanation, if we could make a gamble's payoff more compatible with the attractiveness rating, we would presumably enhance the weight given to payoff in the rating response mode. We attempted to do this in a new experiment, focusing on the gamble 7/36 to win $9. To make the payoff more compatible with regard to the scale of attractiveness, we added a very small loss (5¢) to the gamble:

7/36 win $9
29/36 lose 5¢

Whereas the attractiveness of $9 might not be readily apparent, we reasoned that a bet offering $9 to win and only 5¢ to lose should appear to have a very attractive payoff ratio. This led us to predict that one might increase the attractiveness of a gamble (p to win X) by adding a loss component to it.

The results exceeded our expectations. The gamble with no loss had the lower attractiveness rating (mean = 9.4 on the 0–20 scale). Adding a 5¢ loss led to a much higher attractiveness rating (mean = 14.9). Even the bet

7/36 win $9
29/36 lose 25¢

was judged more attractive (mean = 11.7) than the bet with no loss.

Would adding a small loss to the gamble enhance its attractiveness in choice as it did in rating? We addressed this question by asking 96 University of Oregon students to choose between playing a gamble and receiving a gain of $2. For half of the students, the gamble was 7/36 win $9; for the others, the gamble had the 5¢ loss. Whereas only 33.3% chose the $9 gamble over the $2, 60.8% chose the ($9, −5¢) gamble over the $2. A replication study with $4 as the alternative to the gamble produced similar results. The enhancement produced by adding a small loss thus holds for choices as well as for rating responses.

The enhanced attractiveness produced by small losses was originally predicted and explained in terms of compatibility, and we now see it also as an example of the affect heuristic. This broader perspective was induced, in part, by results obtained later by Mellers, Richards, and Birnbaum (1992), Hsee (1995, 1996a, 1996b, 1998), and our own subsequent studies of imagery, affect, and decision making. These convergent streams of research are described in the following sections.

IMAGE, AFFECT, AND DECISION MAKING

The early anomalous findings with gambles were laid aside while other means of explaining the differences between ratings, choices, and pricing responses were developed (see Tversky, Slovic, & Kahneman, 1990). At the same time, Slovic and colleagues at Decision Research embarked on a research program designed to test whether introducing a hazardous facility into a region might stigmatize that region and cause people to avoid going there to recreate, retire, or do business (Slovic et al., 1991). Believing self-report to be unreliable ("If they build it, will you not come?"), research on stigmatization was conducted through a number of empirical studies designed to examine the relationship between imagery, affect, and decision making. After conducting these studies, we learned that they fit closely with a large body of existing theory and research, such as the work of Damasio, Mowrer, and Epstein, described earlier.

Several empirical studies have demonstrated a strong relationship between imagery, affect, and decision making. Many of these studies used a word-association technique, which involves presenting subjects with a target stimulus, usually a word or very brief phrase and asking them to provide the first thought or image that comes to mind. The process is then repeated a number of times (e.g., three to six), or until no further associations are generated. Following the elicitation of images, subjects are asked to rate each image they give on a scale ranging from very positive (e.g., +2) to very negative (e.g., −2), with a neutral point in the center. Scoring is done by summing or averaging the ratings to obtain an overall index.

This imagery method has been used successfully to measure the affective meanings that influence people's preferences for different cities and states (Slovic et al., 1991) as well as their support or opposition to technologies such as nuclear power (Peters & Slovic, 1996).

Table 23.2 illustrates the method in a task where one respondent was asked to give associations to each of two cities and, later, to rate each image affectively. The cities in this example show a clear affective preference for San Diego over Denver. Slovic et al. (1991) showed that summed image scores such as these were highly predictive of expressed preferences for living in or visiting cities. In one study, they found that the image score predicted the location of *actual* vacations during the next 18 months.

Subsequent studies have found affect-laden imagery elicited by word associations to be predictive of preferences for investing in new companies on the stock market (MacGregor, Slovic, Dreman, & Berry, 2000) and predictive of adolescents' decisions to take part in health-threatening and health-enhancing behaviors such as smoking and exercise, respectively (Benthin et al., 1995).

EVALUABILITY

The research with images points to the importance of affective impressions in judgments and decisions. However, the impressions themselves may vary

Table 23.2. Images, Ratings, and Summation Scores
for One Respondent

Stimulus	Image Number	Image	Image Rating
San Diego	1	Very nice	2
San Diego	2	Good beaches	2
San Diego	3	Zoo	2
San Diego	4	Busy freeway	1
San Diego	5	Easy to find way	1
San Diego	6	Pretty town	2
			10
Denver	1	High	2
Denver	2	Crowded	0
Denver	3	Cool	2
Denver	4	Pretty	1
Denver	5	Busy airport	−2
Denver	6	Busy streets	−2
			1

Note: Based on these summation scores, this person's predicted preference for a
vacation site would be San Diego.
Source: Slovic et al. (1991).

not only in their valence, but also in the precision with which they are held.
It turns out that the precision of an affective impression substantially impacts
judgments.

We refer to the distributional qualities of affective impressions and responses
as *affective mappings*. Consider, for example, some questions posed by Mellers
et al. (1992): "How much would you like a potential roommate if all you knew
about her was that she was said to be intelligent?" Or, "Suppose, instead, all
you knew about her was that she was said to be obnoxious?" Intelligence is a
favorable trait but it is not very diagnostic (e.g., meaningful) for likeableness,
hence its affective map is rather diffuse. In contrast, obnoxiousness will likely
produce a more precise and more negative impression.

How much would you like a roommate said to be both intelligent *and* obnoxious? Anderson (1981) has shown that the integration of multiple pieces of
information into an impression of this sort can be described well by a weighted
average model where separate weights are given to intelligence and obnoxiousness, respectively. Mellers et al. (1992) further showed that the weights in
such integrative tasks are inversely proportional to the variance of the impressions. Thus we would expect the impression produced by the combination of
these two traits to be closer to the impression formed by obnoxiousness alone,
reflecting greater weight given to obnoxiousness due to its smaller variance
(more precise affective mapping). The meaning of a stimulus image appears
to be reflected in the precision of the affective feelings associated with that image. More precise affective impressions reflect more precise meanings and carry
more weight in impression formation, judgment, and decision making.

406   Paul Slovic et al.

Table 23.3. Attributes of Two Dictionaries

	Year of Publication	Number of Entries	Defects
Dictionary A	1993	10,000	No, it's like new
Dictionary B	1993	20,000	Yes, the cover is torn; otherwise it's like new

Source: Adapted from Hsee (1998).

Hsee (1996a, 1996b, 1998) developed the notion of *evaluability* to describe the interplay between the precision of an affective impression and its meaning or importance for judgment and decision making. Evaluability is illustrated by an experiment in which Hsee asked people to assume they were music majors looking for a used music dictionary. In a joint-evaluation condition, participants were shown two dictionaries, A and B (Table 23.3), and asked how much they would be willing to pay for each. Willingness-to-pay was far higher for Dictionary B, presumably because of its greater number of entries. However, when one group of participants evaluated only A and another group evaluated only B, the mean willingness to pay was much higher for Dictionary A. Hsee explains this reversal by means of the *evaluability principle*. He argues that, without a direct comparison, the number of entries is hard to evaluate, because the evaluator does not have a precise notion of how good or how bad 10,000 (or 20,000) entries is. However, the defects attribute is evaluable in the sense that it translates easily into a precise good/bad response and thus it carries more weight in the independent evaluation. Most people find a defective dictionary unattractive and a like-new one attractive. Under joint evaluation, the buyer can see that B is far superior on the more important attribute, number of entries. Thus number of entries becomes *evaluable* through the comparison process.

According to the evaluability principle, the weight of a stimulus attribute in an evaluative judgment or choice is proportional to the ease or precision with which the value of that attribute (or a comparison on the attribute across alternatives) can be mapped into an affective impression. In other words, affect bestows meaning on information (cf., Osgood, Suci, & Tannenbaum, 1957; Mowrer, 1960a, 1960b) and the precision of the affective meaning influences our ability to use information in judgment and decision making. *Evaluability* can thus be seen as an extension of the general relationship between the variance of an impression and its weight in an impression-formation task (Mellers et al., 1992).

Hsee's work in evaluability is noteworthy because it shows that even very important attributes may not be used by a judge or decision maker unless they can be translated precisely into an affective frame of reference. As described in the next section, Hsee finds evaluability effects even with familiar attributes such as the amount of ice cream in a cup (Hsee, 1998). We also demonstrate similar effects with other familiar concepts such as amounts of money or human lives.

PROPORTION DOMINANCE

In situations that involve uncertainty about whether we will win or lose or that involve ambiguity about some quantity of something (i.e., how much is enough), there appears to be one information format that is highly evaluable, leading it to carry great weight in many judgment tasks. This is a representation characterizing an attribute as a proportion or percentage of something, or as a probability. At the suggestion of Chris Hsee (personal communication), we refer to the strong effects of this type of representation as *proportion dominance*.

Proportion (or probability) dominance was evident in the studies of gambles described at the beginning of this chapter. Ratings of a gamble's attractiveness tend to be determined far more strongly by the probabilities of winning and losing than by the monetary payoffs. The curious finding that adding a small loss to a gamble increases its rated attractiveness, explained originally as a compatibility effect, can now be seen to fit well with the notions of affective mapping and evaluability.

According to this view, a probability maps relatively precisely onto the attractiveness scale because probability has a lower and upper bound (0 and 1) and a midpoint below which a probability is "poor" or "bad" (i.e., has worse than an even chance) and above which it is "good" (i.e., has a better than even chance). People know where a given value, such as 7/36, falls within the bounds, and exactly what it means – "I'm probably not going to win." In contrast, the mapping of a dollar outcome (e.g., $9) onto the attractiveness scale is diffuse, reflecting a failure to know how good or bad or how attractive or unattractive $9 is. Thus, the impression formed by the gamble offering $9 to win with no losing payoff is dominated by the relatively precise and unattractive impression produced by the 7/36 probability of winning. However, adding a very small loss to the payoff dimension brings the $9 payoff into focus and thus gives it meaning. The combination of a possible $9 gain and a 5¢ loss is a *very attractive* win/loss ratio, leading to a relatively precise mapping onto the upper end of the scale. Whereas the imprecise mapping of the $9 carries little weight in the averaging process, the more precise and now favorable impression of ($9, −5¢) carries more weight, thus leading to an increase in the overall favorability of the gamble.

The effect of adding a small loss to the gamble can also be explained by norm theory (Kahneman & Miller, 1986; Kahneman & Miller, Chapter 20, this volume). However, a norm-theoretical explanation is consistent with an affective account. It asserts that the gamble with no loss is a relatively mediocre representative of the set of all positive gambles, whereas the gamble with a small loss is a relatively attractive member of the class of mixed (win/loss) gambles.

Proportion dominance surfaces in a powerful way in a very different context, the life-saving interventions studied by Fetherstonhaugh, Slovic, Johnson, and Friedrich (1997), Baron (1997), Jenni and Loewenstein (1997), and Friedrich et al.

(1999). For example, Fetherstonhaugh et al. found that people's willingness to intervene to save a stated number of lives was determined more by the proportion of lives saved than by the actual number of lives that would be saved. However, when two or more interventions were directly compared, number of lives saved become more important than proportion saved. Thus, number of lives saved, standing alone, appears to be poorly evaluable, as was the case for number of entries in Hsee's music dictionaries. With a side-by-side comparison, the number of lives became clearly evaluable and important, as also happened with the number of dictionary entries.

Slovic (unpublished), drawing on proportion dominance and the limited evaluability of numbers of lives, predicted (and found) that people, in a between-groups design, would more strongly support an airport-safety measure expected to save 98% of 150 lives at risk than a measure expected to save 150 lives. Saving 150 lives is diffusely good, and therefore only weakly evaluable, whereas saving 98% of something is clearly very good because it is so close to the upper bound on the percentage scale, and hence is readily evaluable and highly weighted in the support judgment. Subsequent reduction of the percentage of 150 lives that would be saved to 95%, 90%, and 85% led to reduced support for the safety measure but each of these percentage conditions still garnered a higher mean level of support than did the Save 150 Lives Condition (Table 23.4).

Turning to a more mundane form of proportion dominance, Hsee (1998) found that an overfilled ice cream container with 7 oz of ice cream was valued more highly (measured by willingness to pay) than an underfilled container with 8 oz of ice cream (Fig. 23.1). This "less is better effect" reversed itself when the options were juxtaposed and evaluated together. Thus, the proportion of the serving cup that was filled appeared to be more evaluable (in separate judgments) than the absolute amount of ice cream.

Table 23.4. Proportion Dominance and Airport Safety: Saving a Percentage of 150 Lives Receives Higher Support Ratings Than Does Saving 150 Lives.

	Potential Benefit				
	Save 150 Lives	Save 98%	Save 95%	Save 90%	Save 85%
Mean support[a]	10.4	13.6	12.9	11.7	10.9
Median[a]	9.8	14.3	14.1	11.3	10.8
Percentage of ratings ≥ 13	37	75	69	35	31

[a] Cell entries in these rows describe mean and median responses to the question, "How much would you support this proposed measure to purchase the new equipment?" (Critics argue that the money spent on this system could be better spent enhancing other aspects of airport safety.) The response scale ranged from 0 (*would not support at all*) to 20 (*very strong support*). An overall ANOVA resulted in $F_{4,200} = 3.36$, $p = .01$. The Save 98% and Save 95% conditions were both significantly different from the Save 150 Lives condition at $p < .05$, Tukey HSD test.

Figure 23.1. Stimuli in ice cream study by Hsee (1998). Participants were given the sizes of the cups and the amounts of ice cream.

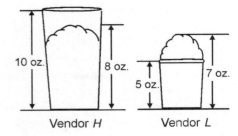

Vendor *H*   Vendor *L*

INSENSITIVITY TO PROBABILITY

Outcomes are not always affectively as vague as the quantities of money, ice cream, and lives that were dominated by proportion in the above experiments. When consequences carry sharp and strong affective meaning, as is the case with a lottery jackpot or a cancer, the opposite phenomenon occurs – variation in probability often carries too little weight. As Loewenstein, Weber, Hsee, and Welch (2001) observe, one's images and feelings toward winning the lottery are likely to be similar whether the probability of winning is 1 in 10 million or 1 in 10,000. They further note that responses to uncertain situations appear to have an all or none characteristic that is sensitive to the *possibility* rather than the *probability* of strong positive or negative consequences, causing very small probabilities to carry great weight. This they argue, helps explain many paradoxical findings such as the simultaneous prevalence of gambling and the purchasing of insurance. It also explains why societal concerns about hazards such as nuclear power and exposure to extremely small amounts of toxic chemicals fail to recede in response to information about the very small probabilities of the feared consequences from such hazards. Support for these arguments comes from Rottenstreich and Hsee (2001), who show that, if the potential outcome of a gamble is emotionally powerful, its attractiveness or unattractiveness is relatively insensitive to changes in probability as great as from .99 to .01.

MIDCOURSE SUMMARY

We now see that the puzzling finding of increased attractiveness for the gambles to which a loss was appended is part of a larger story that can be summarized as follows:

1. Affect attached to images influences judgments and decisions.
2. The evaluability of a stimulus image is reflected in the precision of the affective feelings associated with that image. More precise affective impressions reflect more precise meanings (i.e., greater evaluability) and carry more weight in impression formation, judgment, and decision making.

3. The anomalous findings from the experiments with gambles, ice-cream preferences, and life-saving interventions, suggest that, without a context to give affective perspective to quantities of dollars, ice cream, and lives, these quantities may convey little meaning. Amounts of anything, no matter how common or familiar or intrinsically important, may in some circumstances not be evaluable.

4. Probabilities or proportions, however, are often highly evaluable, reflecting the ease with which people recognize that a high probability of a desirable outcome is good and a low probability is bad. When the quantities or outcomes to which these probabilities apply are affectively pallid, probabilities carry much more weight in judgments and decisions. Just the opposite occurs when the outcomes have precise and strong affective meanings – variations in probability carry too little weight.

THE AFFECT HEURISTIC IN JUDGMENTS OF RISK AND BENEFIT

Another stream of research that, in conjunction with many of the findings reported previously, led us to propose the affect heuristic had its origin in the early study of risk perception reported by Fischhoff, Slovic, Lichtenstein, Reid, and Coombs (1978). One of the findings in this study and numerous subsequent studies was that perceptions of risk and society's responses to risk were strongly linked to the degree to which a hazard evoked feelings of dread (see also Slovic, 1987). Thus, activities associated with cancer are seen as riskier and more in need of regulation than activities associated with less dreaded forms of illness, injury, and death (e.g., accidents).

A second finding in the study by Fischhoff et al. (1978) was even more instrumental in the study of the affect heuristic: The finding that judgments of risk and benefit are negatively correlated. For many hazards, the greater the perceived benefit, the lower the perceived risk and vice versa. Smoking, alcoholic beverages, and food additives, for example, tend to be seen as very high in risk and relatively low in benefit, whereas vaccines, antibiotics, and X-rays tend to be seen as high in benefit and relatively low in risk. This negative relationship is noteworthy because it occurs even when the nature of the gains or benefits from an activity is distinct, and qualitatively different from the nature of the risks. That the inverse relationship is generated in people's minds is suggested by the fact that risk and benefits generally tend to be positively (if at all) correlated in the world. Activities that bring great benefits may be high or low in risk, but activities that are low in benefit are unlikely to be high in risk (if they were, they would be proscribed).

A study by Alhakami and Slovic (1994) found that the inverse relationship between perceived risk and perceived benefit of an activity (e.g., using pesticides) was linked to the strength of positive or negative affect associated with that activity. This result implies that people base their judgments of an activity or a technology not only on what they *think* about it but also on what they *feel*

Figure 23.2. A model of the affect heuristic explaining the risk/benefit confounding observed by Alhakami and Slovic (1994). Judgments of risk and benefit are assumed to be derived by reference to an overall affective evaluation of the stimulus item.
Source: Finucane et al. (2000).

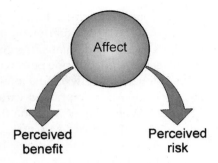

about it. If they like an activity, they are moved to judge the risks as low and the benefits as high; if they dislike it, they tend to judge the opposite – high risk and low benefit.

Alhakami and Slovic's (1994) findings suggested that use of the affect heuristic guides perceptions of risk and benefit as depicted in Fig. 23.2. If so, providing information about risk should change the perception of benefit and vice-versa (Fig. 23.3). For example, information stating that risk was low for some technology should lead to more positive overall affect that would, in turn,

Figure 23.3. Model showing how information about benefit (A) or information about risk (B) could increase the overall affective evaluation of nuclear power and lead to inferences about risk and benefit that coincide affectively with the information given. Similarly, information could decrease the overall affective evaluation of nuclear power as in C and D. *Source:* Finucane et al. (2000).

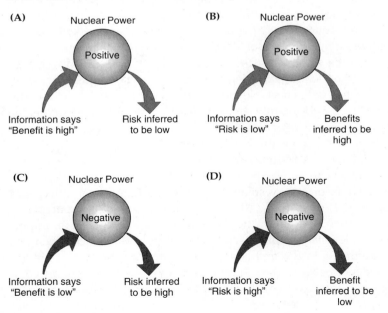

increase perceived benefit. Indeed, Finucane, Alhakami, Slovic, and Johnson (2000) conducted this experiment, providing four different kinds of information designed to manipulate affect by increasing or decreasing perceived risk and increasing or decreasing perceived benefit. In each case there was no apparent logical relation between the information provided (e.g., information about risks) and the nonmanipulated variable (e.g., benefits). The predictions were confirmed. When the information that was provided changed either the perceived risk or the perceived benefit, an affectively congruent but inverse effect was observed on the nonmanipulated attribute as depicted in Fig. 23.3. These data support the theory that risk and benefit judgments are causally determined, at least in part, by the overall affective evaluation.

The affect heuristic also predicts that using time pressure to reduce the opportunity for analytic deliberation (and thereby allowing affective considerations freer rein) should enhance the inverse relationship between perceived benefits and risks. In a second study, Finucane et al. (2000) showed that the inverse relationship between perceived risks and benefits increased greatly under time pressure, as predicted. These two experiments with judgments of benefits and risks are important because they support the contention by Zajonc (1980) that affect influences judgment directly and is not simply a response to a prior analytic evaluation.

Further support for the model in Fig. 23.2 has come from two very different domains – toxicology and finance. Slovic, MacGregor, Malmfors, and Purchase (1999) surveyed members of the British Toxicological Society and found that these experts, too, produced the same inverse relation between their risk and benefit judgments. As expected, the strength of the inverse relation was found to be mediated by these experts' affective reactions toward the hazard items being judged. In a second study, these same toxicologists were asked to make a "quick intuitive rating" for each of 30 chemical items (e.g., benzene, aspirin, second-hand cigarette smoke, dioxin in food) on an affect scale (bad–good). Next, they were asked to judge the degree of risk associated with a *very small exposure to the chemical*, defined as an exposure that is less than 1/100th the exposure level that would begin to cause concern for a regulatory agency. Rationally, because exposure was so low, one might expect these risk judgments to be uniformly low and unvarying, resulting in little or no correlation with the ratings of affect. Instead, there was a strong correlation across chemicals between affect and judged risk of a very small exposure. When the affect rating was strongly negative, judged risk of a very small exposure was high; when affect was positive, judged risk was small. Almost every respondent (95 out of 97) showed this negative correlation (the median correlation was −.50). Importantly, those toxicologists who produced strong inverse relations between risk and benefit judgments in the first study also were more likely to exhibit a high correspondence between their judgments of affect and risk in the second study. In other words, across two different tasks, reliable individual differences emerged in toxicologists' reliance on affective processes in judgments of chemical risks.

In the realm of finance, Ganzach (2000) found support for a model in which analysts base their judgments of risk and return for unfamiliar stocks upon a global attitude. If stocks were perceived as good, they were judged to have high return and low risk; if they were perceived as bad, they were judged to be low in return and high in risk. However, for familiar stocks, perceived risk and return were positively correlated, rather than being driven by a global attitude.

JUDGMENTS OF PROBABILITY, RELATIVE FREQUENCY, AND RISK

The affect heuristic has much in common with the model of "risk as feelings" proposed by Loewenstein et al. (2001) and with dual process theories put forth by Epstein (1994), Sloman (1996), and others. Recall that Epstein argues that individuals apprehend reality by two interactive, parallel processing systems. The *rational* system is a deliberative, analytical system that functions by way of established rules of logic and evidence (e.g., probability theory). The *experiential* system encodes reality in images, metaphors, and narratives to which affective feelings have become attached.

To demonstrate the influence of the experiential system, Denes-Raj and Epstein (1994) showed that, when offered a chance to win a prize by drawing a red jelly bean from an urn, subjects often elected to draw from a bowl containing a greater absolute number, but a smaller proportion, of red beans (e.g., 7 in 100) than from a bowl with fewer red beans but a better probability of winning (e.g., 1 in 10). For these individuals, images of 7 winning beans in the large bowl appeared to dominate the image of 1 winning bean in the small bowl.

We can characterize Epstein's subjects as following a mental strategy of "imaging the numerator" (i.e., the number of red beans) and neglecting the denominator (the number of beans in the bowl). Consistent with the affect heuristic, images of winning beans convey positive affect that motivates choice.

Although the jelly bean experiment may seem frivolous, imaging the numerator brings affect to bear on judgments in ways that can be both nonintuitive and consequential. Slovic, Monahan, and MacGregor (2000) demonstrated this in a series of studies in which experienced forensic psychologists and psychiatrists were asked to judge the likelihood that a mental patient would commit an act of violence within 6 months after being discharged from the hospital. An important finding was that clinicians who were given another expert's assessment of a patient's risk of violence framed in terms of relative frequency (e.g., "Of every 100 patients similar to Mr. Jones, 10 are estimated to commit an act of violence to others") subsequently labeled Mr. Jones as more dangerous than did clinicians who were shown a statistically "equivalent" risk expressed as a probability (e.g., "Patients similar to Mr. Jones are estimated to have a 10% chance of committing an act of violence to others").

Not surprisingly, when clinicians were told that "20 out of every 100 patients similar to Mr. Jones are estimated to commit an act of violence," 41% would refuse to discharge the patient. But when another group of clinicians was given the risk as "patients similar to Mr. Jones are estimated to have a 20% chance of committing an act of violence," only 21% would refuse to discharge the patient. Similar results have been found by Yamagishi (1997), whose judges rated a disease that kills 1,286 people out of every 10,000 as more dangerous than one that kills 24.14% of the population.

Unpublished follow-up studies showed that representations of risk in the form of individual probabilities of 10% or 20% led to relatively benign images of one person, unlikely to harm anyone, whereas the "equivalent" frequentistic representations created frightening images of violent patients (example: "Some guy going crazy and killing someone"). These affect-laden images likely induced greater perceptions of risk in response to the relative-frequency frames.

Although frequency formats produce affect-laden imagery, story and narrative formats appear to do even better in that regard. Hendrickx, Vlek, and Oppewal (1989) found that warnings were more effective when, rather than being presented in terms of relative frequencies of harm, they were presented in the form of vivid, affect-laden scenarios and anecdotes. Sanfey and Hastie (1998) found that compared with respondents given information in bar graphs or data tables, respondents given narrative information more accurately estimated the performance of a set of marathon runners. Furthermore, Pennington and Hastie (1993) found that jurors construct narrative-like summations of trial evidence to help them process their judgments of guilt or innocence.

Perhaps the biases in probability and frequency judgment that have been attributed to the availability heuristic may be due, at least in part, to affect. Availability may work not only through *ease* of recall or imaginability, but because remembered and imagined images come tagged with affect. For example, Lichtenstein, Slovic, Fischhoff, Layman, and Combs (1978) invoked availability to explain why judged frequencies of highly publicized causes of death (e.g., accidents, homicides, fires, tornadoes, cancer) were relatively overestimated and underpublicized causes (e.g., diabetes, stroke, asthma, tuberculosis) were underestimated. The highly publicized causes appear to be more affectively charged, that is, more sensational, and this may account both for their prominence in the media and their relatively overestimated frequencies.

FURTHER EVIDENCE

The studies described above represent only a small fraction of the evidence that can be marshaled in support of the affect heuristic. Although we have developed the affect heuristic to explain findings from studies of judgment and decision making (e.g., the inverse relationship between perceived risks and benefits), one can find related proposals in the literature of marketing and social cognition. For example, Wright (1975) proposed the "affect-referral heuristic" as a mechanism by which the remembered affect associated with a product influences subsequent choice of that product (see also Pham, 1998).

Attitudes have long been recognized as having a strong evaluative component (see, e.g., Thurstone, 1928; Edwards, 1957). Pratkanis (1989) defined *attitude* as "a person's evaluation of an object of thought" (p. 72). He went on to propose that attitudes serve as heuristics, with positive attitudes invoking a favoring strategy toward an object and negative attitudes creating disfavoring response. More specifically, he defined the *attitude heuristic* as the use of the evaluative relationship as a cue for assigning objects to a favorable class or an unfavorable class, thus leading to approach or avoidance strategies appropriate to the class. Pratkanis described numerous phenomena that could be explained by the attitude heuristic, including halo effects not unlike the consistency described earlier between risk and benefit judgments (Finucane et al., 2000).

Other important work within the field of social cognition includes studies by Fazio (1995) on the accessibility of affect associated with attitudes, and by Schwarz and Clore (1988) on the role of affect as information.

Returning to the recent literature on judgment and decision making, Kahneman and Ritov (1994) and Kahneman, Schkade, and Sunstein (1998) demonstrated that responses as diverse as willingness to pay for the provision of a public good (e.g., protection of an endangered species) or a punitive damage award in a personal injury lawsuit seem to be derived from attitudes based on emotion rather than on indicators of economic value.

Hsee and Kunreuther (2000) demonstrated that affect influences decisions about whether to purchase insurance. In one study, they found that people were willing to pay twice as much to insure a beloved antique clock (that no longer works and cannot be repaired) against loss in shipment to a new city than to insure a similar clock for which "one does not have any special feeling." In the event of loss, the insurance paid $100 in both cases. Similarly, Hsee and Menon (1999) found that students were more willing to buy a warranty on a newly purchased used car if it was a beautiful convertible than if it was an ordinary looking station wagon, even if the expected repair expenses and cost of the warranty were held constant.

Loewenstein et al. (2001) provide a particularly thorough review and analysis of research that supports their *risk-as-feelings hypothesis*, a concept that has much in common with the affect heuristic. They present evidence showing that emotional responses to risky situations, including feelings such as worry, fear, dread, or anxiety, often diverge from cognitive evaluations and have a different and sometimes greater impact on risk-taking behavior than do cognitive evaluations. Among the factors that appear to influence risk behaviors by acting on feelings rather than cognitions are background mood (e.g., Johnson & Tversky, 1983; Isen, 1993), the time interval between decisions and their outcomes (Loewenstein, 1987), vividness (Hendrickx et al., 1989), and evolutionary preparedness. Loewenstein et al. (2001) invoke the evolutionary perspective to explain why people tend to react with little fear to certain types of objectively dangerous stimuli that evolution has not prepared them for, such as guns, hamburgers, automobiles, smoking, and unsafe sex, even when they recognize the threat at a cognitive level. Other types of stimuli, such as caged spiders, snakes, or heights, which evolution may have prepared us to fear, evoke strong visceral responses even when we recognize them, cognitively, to be harmless.

Individual differences in affective reactivity also are informative. Damasio relied upon brain-damaged individuals, apparently lacking in the ability to associate emotion with anticipated outcomes, to test his somatic-marker hypothesis. Similar insensitivity to the emotional meaning of future outcomes has been attributed to psychopathic individuals and used to explain their aberrant behaviors (Hare, 1965; Patrick, 1994). Using the Damasio card-selection task, Peters and Slovic (2000) found that normal subjects who reported themselves to be highly reactive to negative events made fewer selections from decks with large losing payoffs. Conversely, greater self-reported reactivity to positive events was associated with a greater number of selections from high-gain decks. Thus individual differences in affective reactivity appear to play a role in the learning and expression of risk-taking preferences.

THE DOWNSIDE OF AFFECT

Throughout this chapter, we make many claims for the affect heuristic, portraying it as the centerpiece of the experiential mode of thinking, the dominant mode of survival during the evolution of the human species. However, like other heuristics that provide efficient and generally adaptive responses but occasionally lead us astray, reliance on affect can also deceive us. Indeed, if it was always optimal to follow our affective and experiential instincts, there would have been no need for the rational/analytic system of thinking to have evolved and become so prominent in human affairs.

There are two important ways that experiential thinking misguides us. One results from the deliberate manipulation of our affective reactions by those who wish to control our behaviors. The other results from the natural limitations of the experiential system and the existence of stimuli in our environment that are simply not amenable to valid affective representation. Both types of problems are discussed below.

MANIPULATION OF AFFECT IN OUR DAILY LIVES

Given the importance of experiential thinking, it is not surprising to see many forms of deliberate efforts being made to manipulate affect in order to influence our judgments and decisions. Consider, for example, some everyday questions about the world of entertainment and the world of consumer marketing:

1. Question: Why do entertainers often change their names?
   Answer: To make them affectively more pleasing. One wonders whether the careers of John Denver, Sandra Dee, and Judy Garland would have

been as successful had they performed under their real names – Henry Deutschendorf, Alexandra Zuck, and Frances Gumm. Students of *onomastics*, the science of names, have found that the intellectual products of persons with less attractive names are judged to be of lower quality (Harari & McDavid, 1973; Erwin & Calev, 1984) and some have even asserted that the affective quality of a presidential candidate's name influences the candidate's chances of being elected (Smith, 1997).

2. Question: Why do movies have background music? After all, can't we understand the events we are watching and the dialog we are hearing without music?
   Answer: Music conveys affect and thus enhances meaning even for common human interactions and events.

3. Question: Why are all the models in the mail-order catalog smiling?
   Answer: To link positive affect to the clothing they are selling.

4. Question: Why do packages of food products carry all those little blurbs such as "New," "Natural," "Improved," or "98% fat-free"?
   Answer: These are "affective tags" that enhance the attractiveness of the product and increase the likelihood it will be purchased, much as adding "Save 98%" increased the attractiveness of saving 150 lives.

Clearly, entertainers and marketers of consumer products have long been aware of the powerful influence of affect. Perhaps no corporate entities have more zealously exploited consumers' affective sensitivities than the tobacco companies. An ad for Kool Natural Lights, for example, repeats the word *natural* 13 times in a single half-page advertisement (Brown & Williamson Tobacco Company, 1999). The attractive images of rugged cowboys and lush waterfalls associated with cigarette ads are known to all of us. Indeed, affective associations between cigarettes and positive images may begin forming in children as young as 3 years old (Fischer, 1991). As Epstein (1994) observes, "Cigarette advertising agencies and their clients are willing to bet millions of dollars in advertising costs that the ... appeal of their messages to the experiential system will prevail over the verbal message of the Surgeon General that smoking can endanger one's life, an appeal directed at the rational system" (p. 712). Through the workings of the affect heuristic, as explicated by Finucane et al. (2000), we now have evidence suggesting that cigarette advertising designed to increase the positive affect associated with smoking will quite likely depress perceptions of risk. The factual (impassionate) appeal by the surgeon general will likely have little effect.

Attempts at affective manipulation often work directly on language. Communicators desiring to change attitudes toward stigmatized technologies, for example, created "nukespeak" to extol the virtues of *clean bombs* and *peacekeeper missiles*, whereas promoters of nuclear power coined a new term for reactor accidents: *excursions*. Genetically modified food has been promoted as "enhanced" by proponents and "Frankenfood" by opponents.

Manipulation of attitudes and behavior by persuasive argumentation is often quite effective, but at least it tends to be recognized as an attempt to persuade. Manipulation of affect is no less powerful but is made more insidious by often taking place without our awareness. It is unlikely that Hsee's subjects recognized that what they were willing to pay for the used music dictionary was determined far more by the torn cover than by the more important dimension, number of entries.

Legal scholars such as Hanson and Kysar (1999a, 1999b), paying close attention to research on affect and other judgment heuristics, have begun to speak out on the massive manipulation of consumers by the packaging, marketing, and public relations practices of manufacturers. Such manipulation, they argue, renders ineffective three primary forms of legal control over dangerous products – warning requirements, product liability suits, and regulation of advertising. Hanson and Kysar (2001) point to the need for new regulatory strategies that would take into account the full liability of manufacturers who manipulate consumers into purchasing and using hazardous products.

FAILURE OF THE EXPERIENTIAL SYSTEM: THE CASE OF SMOKING

Judgments and decisions can be faulty not only because their affective components are manipulable, but also because they are subject to inherent biases of the experiential system. For example, the affective system seems designed to sensitize us to small changes in our environment (e.g., the difference between 0 and 1 deaths) at the cost of making us less able to appreciate and respond appropriately to larger changes (e.g., the difference between 570 deaths and 670 deaths). Fetherstonhaugh et al. (1997) referred to this insensitivity as *psychophysical numbing*.

Similar problems arise when the outcomes that we must evaluate change very slowly over time, are remote in time, or are visceral in nature. The irrationality of decisions to smoke cigarettes provides dramatic examples of these types of failure (Slovic, 2000, 2001). Despite the portrayal of beginning smokers as "young economists" rationally weighing the risks of smoking against the benefits when deciding whether to initiate that activity (e.g., Viscusi, 1992), research paints a different picture. This account (Slovic, 2001) shows young smokers acting experientially in the sense of giving little or no thought to risks or to the amount of smoking they will be doing. Instead, they go with the affective impulses of the moment, enjoying smoking as something new and exciting, a way to have fun with their friends. Even after becoming "regulars," the great majority of smokers expect to stop soon, regardless of how long they have been smoking, how many cigarettes they currently smoke per day, or how many previous unsuccessful attempts they have experienced. Only a fraction actually quit, despite many attempts. The problem is nicotine addiction, a condition that young smokers recognize by name as a consequence of smoking but do not understand experientially until they are caught up in it.

The process of becoming addicted appears to begin surprisingly soon after one begins to smoke. Research indicates that adolescents begin to show signs of nicotine dependence within days to weeks of the onset of occasional tobacco use (DiFranza et al., 2000). Loewenstein (1999) explains the process of addiction as being governed by immensely powerful visceral factors or cravings that, from an experiential perspective, are very hard to anticipate and appreciate:

> Unlike currently experienced visceral factors, which have a disproportionate impact on behavior, delayed visceral factors tend to be ignored or severely underweighted in decision making. Today's pain, hunger, anger, etc. are palpable, but the same sensations anticipated in the future receive little weight. (p. 240)

The failure of the experiential system to protect many young people from the lure of smoking is nowhere more evident than in the responses to a survey question that asks smokers: "If you had it to do all over again, would you start smoking?" More than 85% of adult smokers and about 80% of young smokers (ages 14 to 22) answer "No" (Slovic, 2001). Moreover, the more individuals perceive themselves to be addicted, the more often they have tried to quit, the longer they have been smoking, and the more cigarettes they are smoking per day, the more likely they are to answer "No."

We can now address a central question posed by Viscusi (1992): "at the time when individuals initiate their smoking activity, do they understand the consequences of their actions and make rational decisions?" Visusi went on to define the appropriate test of rationality in terms of "whether individuals are incorporating the available information about smoking risks and are making sound decisions, given their own preferences" (p. 11).

The data indicate that the answer to Viscusi's question is "No." Most beginning smokers lack the experience to appreciate how their future selves will perceive the risks from smoking or how they will value the tradeoff between health and the need to smoke. This is a strong repudiation of the model of informed rational choice. It fits well with the findings indicating that smokers give little conscious thought to risk when they begin to smoke. They appear to be lured into the behavior by the prospects of fun and excitement. Most begin to think of risk only after starting to smoke and gaining what to them is new information about health risks.

These disturbing findings underscore the distinction that behavioral decision theorists now make between decision utility and experience utility (Kahneman, 1997; Kahneman & Snell, 1992; Loewenstein & Schkade, 1999). Utility predicted or expected at the time of decision often differs greatly from the quality and intensity of the hedonic experience that actually occurs.

CONCLUSION

We hope that this rather selective and idiosyncratic tour through a mélange of experiments and conjectures has conveyed the sense of excitement we feel toward the affect heuristic. This heuristic appears at once both wondrous and frightening: wondrous in its speed, and subtlety, and sophistication, and its ability to "lubricate reason"; frightening in its dependency upon context and experience, allowing us to be led astray or manipulated – inadvertently or intentionally – silently and invisibly.

It is sobering to contemplate how elusive meaning is, due to its dependence upon affect. Thus the forms of meaning that we take for granted and use to justify immense effort and expense toward gathering and disseminating "meaningful" information, may be illusory. We cannot assume that an intelligent person can understand the meaning of and properly act upon even the simplest of numbers such as amounts of money, not to mention more esoteric measures or statistics, unless these numbers are infused with affect.

Contemplating the workings of the affect heuristic helps us appreciate Damasio's (1994) contention that rationality is not only a product of the analytical mind, but of the experiential mind as well:

> The strategies of human reason probably did not develop, in either evolution or any single individual, without the guiding force of the mechanisms of biological regulation, of which emotion and feeling are notable expressions. Moreover, even after reasoning strategies become established . . . their effective deployment probably depends, to a considerable extent, on a continued ability to experience feelings. (p. xii)

Ironically, the perception and integration of affective feelings, within the experiential system, appears to be the kind of high-level maximization process postulated by economic theories since the days of Jeremy Bentham. These feelings form the neural and psychological substrate of utility. In this sense, the affect heuristic enables us to be rational actors in many important situations. But not in all situations. It works beautifully when our experience enables us to anticipate accurately how we will like the consequences of our decisions. It fails miserably when the consequences turn out to be much different in character than we anticipated.

The scientific study of affective rationality is in its infancy. It is exciting to contemplate what might be accomplished by future research designed to help humans understand the affect heuristic and use it beneficially.

24. Individual Differences in Reasoning: Implications for the Rationality Debate?

Keith E. Stanovich and Richard F. West

The interpretation of the gap between descriptive and normative models in the human reasoning and decision making literature has been the subject of contentious debate since the early 1980s (Baron, 1994; Cohen, 1981, 1983; Evans & Over, 1996; Gigerenzer, 1996; Kahneman, 1981; Kahneman, Slovic, & Tversky, 1982; Kahneman & Tversky, 1983, 1996; Koehler, 1996; Nisbett & Ross, 1980; Stein, 1996), a debate that has arisen because some investigators wish to interpret the gap between the descriptive and the normative as indicating that human cognition is characterized by systematic irrationalities. Due to the emphasis that these theorists placed on reforming human cognition, they have been labelled the *Meliorists* by Stanovich (1999). Disputing this contention are numerous investigators (termed the *Panglossians*; see Stanovich, 1999) who argue that there are other reasons why reasoning might not accord with normative theory – reasons that prevent the ascription of irrationality to subjects (Cohen, 1981; Stein, 1996). First, instances of reasoning might depart from normative standards due to performance errors – temporary lapses of attention, memory deactivation, and other sporadic information processing mishaps. Second, there may be stable and inherent computational limitations that prevent the normative response (Cherniak, 1986; Goldman, 1978; Harman, 1995; Oaksford & Chater, 1993, 1995, 1998; Stich, 1990). Third, in interpreting performance, we might be applying the wrong normative model to the task (Koehler, 1996). Alternatively, we may be applying the correct normative model to the problem as set, but the subject might have construed the problem differently and be providing the normatively appropriate answer to a different problem (Adler, 1984, 1991; Berkeley & Humphreys, 1982; Broome, 1990; Hilton, 1995; Schwarz, 1996).

However, in referring to the various alternative explanations (other than systematic irrationality) for the normative/descriptive gap, Rips (1994) warns that "a determined skeptic can usually explain away any instance of what seems at first to be a logical mistake" (p. 393). The most humorous version of this argument was made by Kahneman (1981) in his dig at the Panglossians, who seem to have only two categories of errors, "pardonable errors by subjects and unpardonable ones by psychologists" (p. 340).

These comments by Rips (1994) and Kahneman (1981) highlight the need for principled constraints on the alternative explanations of normative/descriptive discrepancies. In this chapter, we describe a research logic aimed at inferring such constraints from patterns of individual differences revealed across a wide range of tasks in the heuristics and biases literature. We argue that these individual differences and their patterns of covariance have implications for explanations of why human behavior often departs from normative models.

PERFORMANCE ERRORS AND COMPUTATIONAL LIMITATIONS

We view the magnitude of the correlation between performance on a reasoning task and cognitive ability as an empirical clue about the importance of algorithmic limitations in creating discrepancies between descriptive and normative models. A strong correlation suggests important algorithmic-level limitations that might make the normative response not prescriptive for those of lower cognitive capacity (Panglossian theorists drawn to this alternative explanation of normative/descriptive gaps were termed *Apologists* by Stanovich, 1999). In contrast, the absence of a correlation between the normative response and cognitive ability suggests no computational limitation and thus no reason why the normative response should not be considered prescriptive (see Baron, 1985).

In a series of investigations (Sá, West, & Stanovich, 1999; Stanovich, 1999; Stanovich & West, 1997, 1998c, 1999) we have found moderate correlations between measures of cognitive ability and several tasks well-known in the heuristics and biases literature (e.g., informal argument evaluation tasks, belief bias in syllogistic reasoning, covariation detection, causal base-rate use, selection task performance). In addition, much smaller but still significant correlations were observed between cognitive ability and a host of other tasks in this literature (e.g., assessing the likelihood ratio, sunk cost effects, outcome bias, "if only" thinking, searching for unconfounded variables). Finally, there are some tasks in the heuristics and biases literature which lack any association at all with cognitive ability – the so-called false consensus effect in the opinion prediction paradigm (Krueger & Clement, 1994; Krueger & Zeiger, 1993) and the overconfidence effect in the knowledge calibration paradigm (e.g., Lichtenstein, Fischhoff, & Phillips, 1982).

These results indicate that although computational limitations appear implicated to some extent in many of the tasks, the normative responses for all of them were nonetheless arrived at by some university students who had modest cognitive abilities (e.g., below the mean in a university sample). For most of these tasks, only a small number of the students with the very lowest cognitive ability in these samples would have prescriptive models that deviate substantially from the normative model for computational reasons. Such findings might be taken to suggest that perhaps *other* factors might account for variation in the magnitude of the normative/descriptive gap – a prediction confirmed in our work on styles of epistemic regulation (Sá et al., 1999; Stanovich & West, 1997). Thus, the failure of performance errors and computational limitations to completely explain the normative/descriptive gap (on the former, see chapters 2 and 6 of Stanovich, 1999) implies that there may well be true individual differences in intentional-level psychologies – that is, true individual differences in rational thought.

All of the camps in the dispute about human rationality recognize that positing computational limitations as an explanation for differences between normative and descriptive models is a legitimate strategy. Meliorists and Panglossians alike agree on the importance of assessing such limitations. In the next section, however, we examine an alternative explanation of the normative/descriptive gap that is much more controversial – the notion that inappropriate normative models have been applied to certain tasks in the heuristics and biases literature.

APPLYING THE WRONG NORMATIVE MODEL

The possibility of incorrect norm application arises because psychologists must appeal to the normative models of other disciplines (e.g., statistics, logic) in order to interpret the responses on various tasks, and these models must be applied to a particular problem or situation. Matching a problem to a normative model is rarely an automatic or clear cut procedure. Indeed, it has been claimed that psychologists have invoked inappropriate normative standards in the random number generation literature (Lopes, 1982), in the work on base rate use in Bayesian reasoning (Birnbaum, 1983), in the overconfidence literature (Gigerenzer (1991a, 1991b, 1993)), with respect to the conjunction effect in probability judgment (Tversky & Kahneman, 1983), and in labeling performance in opinion prediction experiments a so-called false consensus effect (Dawes, 1989, 1990).

The complexities involved in matching problems to norms make possible the argument that the gap between the descriptive and normative occurs because psychologists are applying the wrong normative model to the situation. It is a potent strategy for the Panglossian theorist to use against the advocate of Meliorism and such claims have become quite common in critiques of the heuristics and biases literature: "many critics have insisted that in fact it is Kahneman and Tversky, not their subjects, who have failed to grasp the logic of the problem" (Margolis, 1987, p. 158); "if a 'fallacy' is involved, it is probably more attributable to the researchers than to the subjects" (Messer & Griggs, 1993, p. 195); "in the examples of alleged base rate fallacy considered by Kahneman and Tversky, they, and not their experimental subjects, commit the fallacies" (Levi, 1983, p. 502); "Perhaps the only people who suffer any illusion in relation to cognitive illusions are cognitive psychologists" (Ayton & Hardman, 1997, p. 45).

FROM THE DESCRIPTIVE TO THE NORMATIVE IN REASONING AND DECISION MAKING

The cases mentioned previously provide examples of how the existence of deviations between normative models and actual human reasoning has been called into question by casting doubt on the appropriateness of the normative models used to evaluate performance. Stein (1996, p. 239) terms this the *reject-the-norm strategy*. It is noteworthy that this strategy is frequently used by the Panglossian camp in the rationality debate. Specifically, Panglossians exclusively use the reject-the-norm strategy to *eliminate* gaps between descriptive models of performance and normative models, although this connection is not a necessary one. When this type of critique is used, the normative model that is suggested as a substitute for the one traditionally used in the heuristics and biases literature is one that coincides perfectly with the descriptive model of the subjects' performance – thus preserving a view of human rationality as ideal. It is rarely noted that the strategy could be used in just the opposite way – to *create* gaps between the normative and descriptive. Situations in which the modal response coincides with the standard normative model could be critiqued, and alternative models could be suggested that would result in a new normative/descriptive gap; but this is never done. The Panglossian camp, often highly critical of empirical psychologists, is never critical of psychologists who design reasoning tasks in instances in which the modal subject gives the response the experimenters deem correct. Puzzlingly, in these cases, according to the Panglossians, the same psychologists seem never to err in their task designs and interpretations.

The fact that, for the Panglossian, the use of the reject-the-norm application strategy is entirely contingent on the existence or nonexistence of a normative/descriptive gap suggests that in an important sense the applications of norms being endorsed by the Panglossian camp are conditioned (if not indexed entirely) by descriptive facts about human behavior. The rationality debate itself is, reflexively, evidence that the descriptive models of actual behavior guide expert notions of the proper norm for a situation. That is, there would have been no rationality debate (or at least much less of one) had people behaved in accord with the then-accepted norms.

Thus, the Panglossian reject-the-norm strategy can be seen as a conscious application of the naturalistic fallacy (deriving "ought" from "is"). For example, Cohen (1981), like Gigerenzer (1991b), feels that the normative is indexed to the descriptive in the sense that a competence model of actual behavior can simply be interpreted as the normative model. Although both endorse this linking of the normative to the descriptive, they do so for somewhat different reasons. For Cohen (1981), it follows from his endorsement of narrow reflective equilibrium as the *sine qua non* of normative justification. Gigerenzer's (1991b) endorsement is related to his position in the *cognitive ecologist* camp (to use the term coined by Piattelli-Palmarini, 1994, p. 183) with its emphasis on the ability of evolutionary mechanisms to achieve an optimal Brunswikian tuning of the organism to the local environment (Brase, Cosmides, & Tooby, 1998; Cosmides & Tooby, 1994, 1996; Oaksford & Chater, 1994, 1998; Pinker, 1997).

That Gigerenzer and Cohen concur here – even though they have somewhat different positions on normative justification – simply shows how widespread is the acceptance of the principle that descriptive facts about human behavior should guide our notions about the appropriateness of the normative models used to evaluate behavior. In fact, stated in such broad form, this principle is not restricted to the Panglossian position. For example, in decision science, there is a long tradition of acknowledging descriptive influences when deciding which normative model to apply to a particular situation. Slovic (1995) refers to this "deep interplay between descriptive phenomena and normative principles" (p. 370). Larrick, Nisbett, and Morgan (1993) remind us that "there is also a tradition of justifying, and amending, normative models in response to empirical considerations" (p. 332). March (1988) refers to this tradition when he discusses how actual human behavior has conditioned models of efficient problem solving in artificial intelligence and in the area of organizational decision making.

One thing that all of the various camps in the rationality dispute have in common is that each conditions their beliefs about the appropriate norm to apply based on the *central tendency* of the responses to a problem. They all seem to see that single aspect of performance as the only descriptive fact that is relevant to their views about the appropriate normative model to apply. One goal of our own research program is to expand the scope of the descriptive information used to condition our views about the which norms are appropriate to apply to a particular situation.

PUTTING DESCRIPTIVE FACTS TO WORK:
THE UNDERSTANDING/ACCEPTANCE ASSUMPTION

How should we interpret situations in which the majority of individuals respond in ways that depart from the normative model applied to the problem by reasoning experts? Thagard (1982) calls the two different interpretations the populist strategy and the elitist strategy: "The populist strategy, favored by Cohen (1981), is to emphasize the reflective equilibrium of the average person.... The elitist strategy, favored by Stich and Nisbett (1980), is to emphasize the reflective equilibrium of experts" (p. 39). Thus, Thagard (1982) identifies the populist strategy with the Panglossian position and the elitist strategy with the Meliorist position.

Yet there are few controversial tasks in the heuristics and biases literature in which all untutored laypersons disagree with the experts. There are always some who agree. Thus, the issue is not the untutored average person versus experts (as suggested by Thagard's formulation), but experts plus some laypersons versus other untutored individuals. Might the cognitive characteristics of those departing from expert opinion have implications for which normative model we deem appropriate?

Slovic and Tversky (1974) made essentially this argument years ago, when they maintained that descriptive facts about argument endorsement should condition the inductive inferences of experts regarding appropriate normative principles. In response to the argument that there is "no valid way to distinguish between outright rejection of the axiom and failure to understand it" (p. 372), Slovic and Tversky (1974) observed that "the deeper the understanding of the axiom, the greater the readiness to accept it" (pp. 372–373). Thus, a correlation between understanding and acceptance would suggest that the gap between the descriptive and normative was due to an initial failure to fully process or understand the task.

We might call Slovic and Tversky's argument the *understanding/acceptance assumption* – that more reflective and engaged reasoners are more likely to affirm the appropriate normative model for a particular situation. From their understanding/acceptance principle, it follows that if greater understanding resulted in more acceptance of the axiom, then the initial gap between the normative and descriptive would be attributed to factors that prevented problem understanding (e.g., lack of ability or reflectiveness on the part of the subject). Such a finding would increase confidence in the normative appropriateness of the axioms or in their application to a particular problem. In contrast, if better understanding failed to result in greater acceptance of the axiom, then its normative status for that particular problem might be considered to be undermined. The central idea behind Slovic and Tversky's (1974) development of the understanding/acceptance assumption is that increased understanding should drive performance in the direction of the truly normative principle for the particular situation – so that the direction that performance moves in response to increased understanding provides an empirical clue as to what is the proper normative model to be applied.

One might conceive of two generic strategies for applying the understanding/acceptance principle: variation in understanding can be created, and naturally occurring individual differences can be examined. Slovic and Tversky used the former strategy by providing subjects with explicated arguments supporting the Allais or Savage normative interpretation (see also, Sieck & Yates, 1997; Stanovich & West, 1999). Alternatively, from an individual differences perspective, the understanding/acceptance principle can be interpreted as dictating that more reflective, engaged, and intelligent reasoners should be more likely to respond in accord with normative principles. Thus, it might be expected that those individuals with cognitive/personality characteristics more conducive to deeper understanding would be more accepting of the appropriate normative principles for a particular problem. This application of the understanding/acceptance principle derives from the assumption that a normative/descriptive gap that is disproportionately created by subjects with a superficial understanding of the problem provides no warrant for amending the application of standard normative models.

TACIT ACCEPTANCE OF THE UNDERSTANDING/ACCEPTANCE PRINCIPLE AS A MECHANISM FOR ADJUDICATING DISPUTES ABOUT THE APPROPRIATE NORMATIVE MODELS TO APPLY

It is important to point out that theorists on all sides of the rationality debate have acknowledged the force of the understanding/acceptance argument (without always labeling the argument as such). For example, critics of the heuristics and biases literature have repeatedly drawn on an individual differences version of the understanding/acceptance principle to bolster their critiques. Cohen (1982) critiques the older "bookbag and poker chip" literature on Bayesian conservatism (Phillips & Edwards, 1966; Slovic, Fischhoff, Lichtenstein, 1977) by noting that

if so-called "conservatism" resulted from some inherent inadequacy in people's information-processing systems one might expect that, when individual differences in information-processing are measured on independently attested scales, some of them would correlate with degrees of "conservatism." In fact, no such correlation was found by Alker and Hermann (1971). And this is just what one would expect if "conservatism" is not a defect, but a rather deeply rooted virtue of the system. (pp. 259–260)

This is precisely how Alker and Hermann (1971) themselves argued in their paper:

Phillips, Hays, and Edwards (1966) have proposed that conservatism is the result of intellectual deficiencies. If this is the case, variables such as rationality, verbal intelligence, and integrative complexity should have related to deviation from optimality – more rational, intelligent, and complex individuals should have shown less conservatism. (p. 40)

Stanovich (1999) discusses several examples of the tacit endorsement of the understanding/acceptance principle in the work of Gigerenzer and Goldstein (1996), Funder (1987), Lopes and Oden (1991), Wetherick (1971, 1995), and others. Many Panglossian theorists make recourse to patterns of individual differences (or the lack of such patterns) to undermine the standard interpretations of the tasks under consideration. In other cases, however, examining individual differences may actually reinforce confidence in the appropriateness of the normative models applied to problems in the heuristics and biases literature.

THE UNDERSTANDING/ACCEPTANCE PRINCIPLE AND SPEARMAN'S POSITIVE MANIFOLD

The understanding/acceptance principle simply formalizes the judgment of most theorists that we should resist the conclusion that individuals with more computational power are systematically computing the *non*normative response. Such an outcome would be an absolute first in a psychometric field that is 100 years and thousands of studies old (Brody, 1997; Carroll, 1993, 1997; Lubinski & Humphreys, 1997; Neisser et al., 1996; Sternberg & Kaufman, 1998). It would mean that Spearman's (1904, 1927) positive manifold for cognitive tasks – virtually unchallenged for 100 years – had finally broken down.

In fact, it is probably helpful to articulate the understanding/acceptance principle somewhat more formally in terms of positive manifold – the fact that different measures of cognitive ability almost always correlate with each other (see Carroll, 1993, 1997). The individual differences version of the understanding/acceptance principle puts positive manifold to use in areas of cognitive psychology in which the nature of the appropriate normative model to apply is in dispute. The point is that scoring a vocabulary item on a cognitive ability test and scoring a probabilistic reasoning response on a task from the heuristics and biases literature are not the same. The correct response in the former task has a canonical interpretation agreed on by all investigators; whereas the normative appropriateness of responses on tasks from the latter domain has been the subject of extremely contentious dispute (Cohen, 1981, 1982, 1986; Cosmides & Tooby, 1996; Einhorn & Hogarth, 1981; Gigerenzer, 1991a, 1993, 1996; Kahneman & Tversky, 1996; Koehler, 1996; Stein, 1996). Positive manifold between the two classes of tasks would only be expected if the normative model being used for directional scoring of the tasks in the latter domain is correct. Positive correlations with developmental maturity (e.g., Byrnes & Overton, 1986; Klahr, Fay, & Dunbar, 1993; Markovits & Vachon, 1989; Moshman & Franks, 1986) would seem to have the same implication.

Likewise, given that positive manifold is the norm among cognitive tasks, a negative correlation (or, to a lesser extent, the lack of a correlation) between a probabilistic reasoning task and more standard cognitive ability measures might be taken as a signal that the wrong normative model is being applied to the former task or that there are alternative models that are equally appropriate. The latter point is relevant because the pattern of results in our studies has not always displayed positive manifold. Although, as previously mentioned, for a wide variety of tasks in the heuristics and biases literature we have found positive correlations (belief bias in syllogistic reasoning, covariation detection, causal base-rate use, selection task performance, assessing the likelihood ratio, sunk cost effects, outcome bias, if/only thinking, searching for unconfounded variables), in some cases we have found no correlations (overconfidence effect and false consensus effect). In the next section, we discuss some problems in which the correlation is sometimes negative.

NONCAUSAL BASE RATES

The statistical reasoning problems used in the experiments in which we obtained positive correlations with cognitive ability (Stanovich & West, 1998c) have involved causal aggregate information, analogous to the causal base rates discussed by Ajzen (1977) and Bar-Hillel (1980, 1990) – that is, base rates that had a causal relationship to the criterion behavior. Noncausal base-rate problems – those involving base rates with no obvious causal relationship to the criterion behavior – have had a much more controversial history in the research literature (Bar-Hillel, 1990; Birnbaum, 1983; Cohen, 1981, 1982, 1986; Cosmides & Tooby, 1996; Gigerenzer, 1991b, 1993, 1996; Gigerenzer & Hoffrage, 1995; Kahneman & Tversky, 1996; Koehler, 1996; Kyburg, 1983; Levi, 1983; Macchi, 1995).

In several experiments, we examined some of the noncausal base-rate problems that are notorious for provoking philosophical dispute. One was an AIDS testing problem modeled on Casscells, Schoenberger, and Grayboys (1978):

Imagine that AIDS occurs in 1 in every 1000 people. Imagine also there is a test to diagnose the disease that always gives a positive result when a person has AIDS. Finally, imagine that the test has a false-positive rate of 5%. This means that the test wrongly indicates that AIDS is present in 5% of the cases where the person does not have AIDS. Imagine that we choose a person randomly, administer the test, and that it yields a positive result (indicates that the person has AIDS). What is the probability that the individual actually has AIDS, assuming that we know nothing else about the individual's personal or medical history?

The Bayesian posterior probability for this problem is slightly less than .02. In several analyses and replications (see Stanovich, 1999; Stanovich & West, 1998c) in which we classified responses of less than 10% as Bayesian, responses of more than 90% as indicating strong reliance on indicant information, and responses between 10% and 90% as intermediate, we have found that subjects giving the indicant response were higher in cognitive ability than those giving the Bayesian response. In addition, when tested on causal base-rate problems (e.g., Fong et al., 1986), the greatest base-rate usage was displayed by the group highly reliant on the indicant information in the AIDS problem. The subjects giving the Bayesian answer on the AIDS problem were least reliant on the aggregate information in the causal statistical reasoning problems.

A similar violation of the expectation of positive manifold was observed on the notorious cab problem (see Bar-Hillel, 1980; Lyon & Slovic, 1976; Tversky & Kahneman, 1982):

A cab was involved in a hit-and-run accident at night. Two cab companies, the Green and the Blue, operate in the city in which the accident occurred. You are given the following facts: 85% of the cabs in the city are Green and 15% are Blue. A witness identified the cab as Blue. The court tested the reliability of the witness under the same circumstances that existed on the night of the accident and concluded that the witness correctly identified each of the two colors 80% of the time. What is the probability that the cab involved in the accident was Blue?

Bayes' rule yields .41 as the posterior probability of the cab being Blue. Thus, responses over 70% were classified as reliant on indicant information, responses between 30% and 70% as Bayesian, and responses less than 30% as reliant on base-rate information (these labels are to be taken only as pointers to response classes – we do not mean to imply that responses labelled as Bayesian necessarily imply Bayesian reasoning). Again, it was found that subjects giving the indicant response were higher in cognitive ability and need for cognition than those giving the Bayesian or base-rate response (Stanovich & West, 1998c, 1999). Finally, both the cab problem and the AIDS problem were subjected to the second of Slovic and Tversky's (1974) methods of operationalizing the understanding/acceptance principle – presenting respondents with arguments explicating the traditional normative interpretation (Stanovich & West, 1999). On neither problem was there a strong tendency for responses to move in the Bayesian direction subsequent to explication.

The results from both of these problems indicate that the noncausal base-rate problems display patterns of individual differences quite unlike those shown on the causal aggregate problems (Stanovich & West, 1998c). This is particularly interesting considering that it is precisely such noncausal base-rate problems like the AIDS and cab problem that have been the focus of the most intense debate in the literature (Cohen, 1979, 1981, 1982, 1986; Koehler, 1996; Kyburg, 1983; Levi, 1983). Several authors argue that a rote application of the Bayesian formula to these problems is unwarranted because noncausal base rates of the AIDS-problem type lack relevance and reference-class specificity. Finally, our results might also suggest that the "Bayesian" participants on the AIDS problem might not actually be arriving at their response through anything resembling Bayesian processing, because on causal reasoning problems these respondents were less likely to rely on the aggregate information.

ALTERNATIVE TASK CONSTRUALS

Theorists who resist interpreting the gap between normative and descriptive models as an indication of human irrationality have one more strategy available in addition to those described previously. It is a commonplace argument in cognitive psychology, but it is one that continues to create enormous controversy and to bedevil efforts to compare human performance to normative standards. It is the argument that although the experimenter may well be applying the correct normative model to the problem as set, the subject might be construing the problem differently and be providing the normatively appropriate answer to a different problem – in short, that subjects have a different interpretation of the task (Adler, 1984, 1991; Broome, 1990; Henle, 1962; Hilton, 1995; Levinson, 1995; Margolis, 1987; Schick, 1987, 1997; Schwarz, 1996).

Such an argument is somewhat different from any of the critiques examined thus far. It is not the equivalent of positing that a performance error has been made, because performance errors (e.g., attention lapses) – being transitory and random – would not be expected to recur in exactly the same way in a readministration of the same task. Yet if participants have truly misunderstood the task, they would be expected to do so again on an identical readministration of the task.

This criticism also differs from the argument that the task exceeds the computational capacity of the subject. The latter explanation locates the cause of the suboptimal performance within the subject. In contrast, the alternative task construal argument places the blame at least somewhat on the shoulders of the experimenter for failing to realize that there are task features that might lead subjects to frame the problem in a manner different from that intended.

As with incorrect norm application, the alternative construal argument locates the problem with the experimenter. However, it is different in that in the wrong norm explanation it is assumed that the subject is interpreting the task as the experimenter intended – but the experimenter is not using the right criteria to evaluate performance. In contrast, the alternative task construal argument allows that the experimenter may be applying the correct normative model to the problem the experimenter intends the subject to solve – but posits that the subject has construed the problem in some other way and is providing a normatively appropriate answer to a *different* problem. It seems that in order to comprehensively evaluate the rationality of human cognition it is necessary to evaluate the appropriateness of various task construals. This is because – contrary to thin theories of means/ends rationality that avoid evaluating the subject's task construal (Elster, 1983; Nathanson, 1994) – it will be argued here that if we are going to have any normative standards at all, then we must also have standards for what are appropriate and inappropriate task construals.

EVALUATING PRINCIPLES OF RATIONAL CONSTRUAL: THE UNDERSTANDING/ACCEPTANCE ASSUMPTION REVISITED

Given that principles of rational construal are necessary for a full normative theory of human rationality (Broome, 1990; Einhorn & Hogarth, 1981; Jungermann, 1986; Schick, 1987, 1997; Shweder, 1987; Tversky, 1975), how are such principles to be derived? When searching for principles of rational task construal, the same mechanisms of justification used to assess principles of instrumental rationality are available. Perhaps in some cases – instances where the problem structure maps the world in an unusually close and canonical way – problem construals could be directly evaluated by how well they serve the decision maker in achieving his or her goals (Baron, 1993, 1994). In such cases, it might be possible to prove the superiority or inferiority of certain construals by appeals to Dutch Book or money pump arguments (de Finetti, 1970/1990; Maher, 1993; Skyrms, 1986; Osherson, 1995; Resnik, 1987).

Also available is the expert wide reflective equilibrium view discussed by Stich and Nisbett (1980; see Stanovich, 1999; Stein, 1996). However, note that there are few controversial tasks in the heuristics and biases literature in which *all* untutored laypersons interpret tasks differently from those of the experts who designed them. The issue is not the untutored average person versus experts, but experts plus some laypersons versus other untutored individuals. The cognitive characteristics of those departing from the expert construal might – for reasons parallel to those argued previously – have implications for how we evaluate particular task interpretations. We contend that Slovic and Tversky's (1974) assumption ("the deeper the understanding of the axiom, the greater the readiness to accept it"; pp. 372–373) can again be used as a tool to condition the expert reflective equilibrium regarding principles of rational task construal (see Stanovich, 1999; Stein, 1996; Stich & Nisbett, 1980).

Framing effects are ideal vehicles for demonstrating how the understanding/acceptance principle might be utilized. First, it has already been shown that there are consistent individual differences across a variety of framing problems (Frisch, 1993). Second, framing problems have engendered much dispute regarding issues of appropriate task construal. Consider the Disease Problem introduced by Tversky and Kahneman (1981):

Problem 1: Imagine that the United States is preparing for the outbreak of an unusual disease that is expected to kill 600 people. Two alternative programs to combat the disease have been proposed. Assume that the exact scientific estimates of the consequences of the programs are as follows: If Program A is adopted, 200 people will be saved. If Program B is adopted, there is a one-third probability that 600 people will be saved and a two-thirds probability that no people will be saved. Which of the two programs would you favor, Program A or Program B?

Problem 2: Imagine that the United States is preparing for the outbreak of an unusual disease that is expected to kill 600 people. Two alternative programs to combat the disease have been proposed. Assume that the exact scientific estimates of the consequences of the programs are as follows: If Program C is adopted, 400 people will die. If Program D is adopted, there is a one-third probability that nobody will die and a two-thirds probability that 600 people will die. Which of the two programs would you favor, Program C or Program D?

Many subjects select alternatives A and D in these two problems despite the fact that the two problems are redescriptions of each other and that Program A maps to Program C rather than D. This response pattern violates utility theory's assumption of descriptive invariance. However, Berkeley and Humphreys (1982) argue that Programs A and C might not be descriptively invariant in subjects' interpretations. They argue that the wording of the outcome of Program A ("will be saved") suggests the possibility of saving more lives (see also, Kuhberger, 1995). The wording of the outcome of Program C ("will die") does not suggest the possibility of saving more lives (indeed, the possibility of losing a few more might be inferred by some people). Under such a construal of the problem, it is no longer nonnormative to choose Programs A and D.

However, consistent with the finding that being forced to provide a rationale or to take more time reduces framing effects (e.g., Larrick et al., 1992; Sieck & Yates, 1997; Takemura, 1994) and that people higher in need for cognition displayed reduced framing effects (Smith & Levin, 1996), in our within-subjects study of framing effects (Stanovich & West, 1998b), we found that individuals giving a consistent response to both descriptions of the disease problem – who were actually the majority in our within-subjects experiment – were significantly higher in cognitive ability than those displaying a framing effect. Taken together, then, findings from the pertinent studies suggest that the response dictated by the construal of the problem originally favored by Tversky and Kahneman (1981) should be considered the correct response because it is endorsed even by untutored subjects as long as they are cognitively engaged with the problem, have enough time to process the information, and have the cognitive ability to fully process the information.

Perhaps no finding in the heuristics and biases literature has been the subject of as much criticism as Tversky and Kahneman's (1983) claim to have demonstrated a conjunction fallacy in probabilistic reasoning. Most of the criticisms have focused on the issue of differential task construal, and several critics have argued that there are alternative construals of the tasks that are, if anything, more rational than that which Tversky and Kahneman (1983) regard as normative for examples such as the well-known Linda problem:

> Linda is 31 years old, single, outspoken, and very bright. She majored in philosophy. As a student, she was deeply concerned with issues of discrimination and social justice, and also participated in anti-nuclear demonstrations. Please rank the following statements by their probability, using 1 for the most probable and 8 for the least probable.
> a. Linda is a teacher in an elementary school
> b. Linda works in a bookstore and takes Yoga classes
> c. Linda is active in the feminist movement
> d. Linda is a psychiatric social worker
> e. Linda is a member of the League of Women Voters
> f. Linda is a bank teller
> g. Linda is an insurance salesperson
> h. Linda is a bank teller and is active in the feminist movement

Because alternative h is the conjunction of alternatives c and f, the probability of h cannot be higher than that of either c or f, yet 85% of the respondents in Tversky and Kahneman's (1983) study rated alternative h as more probable than f. What concerns us here is the argument that there are subtle linguistic and pragmatic features of the problem that lead participants to evaluate the alternatives other than as intended. For example, Hilton (1995) argues that the detailed information given about the target implies that the experimenter knows a considerable amount about Linda, and so it is reasonable to assume that the phrase "Linda is a bank teller" does not contain the phrase "and is not active in the feminist movement" because the experimenter already knows this to be the case. If "Linda is a bank teller" is interpreted in this way, then rating h as more probable than f no longer represents a conjunction fallacy. Actually, Tversky and Kahneman (1983) themselves had concerns about such an interpretation of the "Linda is a bank teller" alternative and ran a condition in which this alternative was rephrased as "Linda is a bank teller, whether or not she is active in the feminist movement." They found that the conjunction fallacy was reduced from 85% of their sample to 57% when this alternative was used. Several other investigators have suggested that pragmatic inferences lead to seeming violations of the logic of probability theory in the Linda Problem (see Adler, 1991; Dulany & Hilton, 1991; Levinson, 1995; Macdonald &

Gilhooly, 1990; Politzer & Noveck, 1991; Slugoski & Wilson, 1998). These criticisms all share the implication that actually committing the conjunction fallacy is a rational response to an alternative construal of the different statements about Linda.

Assuming that those committing the so-called conjunction fallacy are making the pragmatic interpretation and that those avoiding the fallacy are making the interpretation that the investigators intended, we examined whether the those making the pragmatic interpretation were individuals who were disproportionately of higher cognitive ability. Because the conjunction error is the modal response in most studies – and because the use of such pragmatic cues and background knowledge is often interpreted as reflecting adaptive information processing (e.g., Hilton, 1995) – it might be expected that individuals who fall victim to the conjunction fallacy would be the subjects of higher cognitive ability.

In our study (Stanovich & West, 1998b), we examined the performance of 150 subjects on the Linda Problem presented above. Consistent with the results of previous experiments on this problem (Tversky & Kahneman, 1983), 80.7% of our sample committed the conjunction effect – they rated the feminist bank teller alternative as more probable than the bank teller alternative. Tellingly, the mean SAT score of the 121 subjects who committed the conjunction fallacy was 82 points lower than the mean score of the 29 who avoided the fallacy.

Tversky and Kahneman (1983) and Reeves and Lockhart (1993) have demonstrated that the incidence of the conjunction fallacy can be decreased if the problem describes the event categories in some finite population or if the problem is presented in a frequentist manner (see also Fiedler, 1988; Gigerenzer, 1991b, 1993). We have replicated this well-known finding, but we have also found that frequentist representations of these problems markedly reduce – if not eliminate – cognitive ability differences (Stanovich & West, 1998b).

Another problem that has spawned many arguments about alternative construals is Wason's (1966) selection task. Performance on abstract versions of the selection task is poor (see Evans, Newstead, & Byrne, 1993). The preponderance of P and Q responses has most often been attributed to a so-called matching bias that is automatically triggered by surface-level relevance cues (Evans, 1996; Evans & Lynch, 1973), but some investigators have championed an explanation based on an alternative task construal. For example, Oaksford and Chater (1994, 1996) argue that rather than interpreting the task as one of deductive reasoning (as the experimenter intends), many subjects interpret it as an inductive problem of probabilistic hypothesis testing. They show that the P and Q response is expected under a formal Bayesian analysis which assumes such an interpretation and optimal data selection.

We examined individual differences in responses to a variety of abstract and deontic selection task problems (Stanovich & West, 1998a, 1998c). Typical results are displayed in Table 24.1. The table presents the mean SAT scores of subjects responding correctly (as traditionally interpreted – with the responses

Table 24.1. Mean SAT Total Scores of Subjects Who Gave the Correct and Incorrect Responses to Three Different Selection Task Problems

	Incorrect[a]	P & not Q (Correct)	t Value	Effect Size[b]
Nondeontic problem				
Destination problem	1187 (197)	1270 (17)	3.21***	.815
Deontic problems				
Drinking-age problem	1170 (72)	1206 (143)	2.39**	.347
Sears problem	1189 (87)	1198 (127)	0.63	.088
	P&Q	**P & not Q**	**t Value**	**Effect Size[b]**
Nondeontic problem				
Destination problem	1195 (97)	1270 (17)	3.06***	.812

Note: $df = 212$ for the Destination and Sears problems and 213 for the Drinking-Age Problem; $df = 112$ for the P&Q comparison on the Destination Problem.
* $= p < .05$; ** $= p < .025$; *** $= p < .01$; all two-tailed.
[a] Numbers in parentheses are the number of subjects.
[b] Cohen's d.

"P & not Q") on various versions of selection task problems. One was a commonly used nondeontic problem with content, the so-called Destination Problem (e.g., Manktelow & Evans, 1979). Replicating previous research, few subjects responded correctly on this problem. However, those who did had significantly higher SAT scores than those who did not and the difference was quite large in magnitude (effect size of .815). Also presented in the table are two well-known problems with deontic rules (reasoning about rules used to guide human behavior – about what "ought to" or "must" be done; see Manktelow & Over, 1991) – the Drinking-Age Problem (If a person is drinking beer, then the person must be over 21 years of age) and the Sears Problem (Any sale over $30 must be approved by the section manager, Mr. Jones). Both are known to facilitate performance (see Dominowski, 1995; Griggs & Cox, 1982, 1983), and this effect is clearly replicated in the data presented in Table 24.1. However, it is also clear that the differences in cognitive ability are much less in these two problems. The effect size is reduced from .815 to .347 in the case of the Drinking-Age Problem and it fails to reach statistical significance in the case of the Sears Problem (effect size of .088). The bottom half of the table indicates that the same pattern was apparent when the "P & not Q" responders were compared only with the P and Q responders on the Destination Problem – the latter being the response that is most consistent with an inductive construal of the problem (see Nickerson, 1996; Oaksford & Chater, 1994, 1996).

Thus, on the selection task, it appears that cognitive ability differences are strong in cases where there is a dispute about the proper construal of the task and attenuated in cases where there is little controversy about alternative construals. This pattern – cognitive ability differences large on problems where there is contentious dispute regarding the appropriate construal and cognitive ability differences small when there is no dispute about task construal – is mirrored in our results on the conjunction effect and framing effect (Stanovich & West, 1998b).

DUAL PROCESS THEORIES AND THE FUNDAMENTAL COMPUTATIONAL BIAS

How might we interpret this consistent pattern of individual differences on several tasks from the heuristics and biases literature where alternative task construals have been championed? One possible interpretation is in terms of two-process theories of reasoning (Epstein, 1994; Evans, 1984, 1996; Evans & Over, 1996; Sloman, 1996). Although there are several two-process theories of reasoning that differ somewhat in their details, all agree on the general features of the two systems which, for simplicity, we label System 1 and System 2 (see Sloman, Chapter 22, this volume; Stanovich, 1999). System 1 is characterized as automatic, heuristic-based, and relatively undemanding of computational capacity. System 2 conjoins the various characteristics associated with controlled processing. System 2 encompasses the processes of analytic intelligence that have traditionally been studied by information processing theorists trying to uncover the computational components underlying intelligence.

For the purposes of the present discussion, the most important difference between the two systems is that they tend to lead to different types of task construals. Construals triggered by System 1 are highly contextualized, personalized, and socialized. They are driven by considerations of relevance and are aimed at inferring intentionality by the use of conversational implicature even in situations that are devoid of conversational features (see Margolis, 1987). The primacy of these mechanisms leads to what has been termed the fundamental computational bias in human cognition (Stanovich, 1999) – the tendency toward automatic contextualization of problems. In contrast, System 2's more controlled processes serve to decontextualize and depersonalize problems. This system is more adept at representing in terms of rules and underlying principles. It can deal with problems without social content and is not dominated by the goal of attributing intentionality nor by the search for conversational relevance.

In summary, the biases introduced by System 1 heuristic processing may well be universal – because the computational biases inherent in this system are ubiquitous and shared by everyone. However, it does not necessarily follow that *errors* on tasks from the heuristics and biases literature will be universal (indeed, we have known for some time that they are not). This is because, for some individuals, System 2 processes operating in parallel will have the requisite computational power (or a low enough threshold) to override the response primed by System 1.

Using the distinction between System 1 and System 2 processing, we conjecture that in order to observe large cognitive ability differences in a problem situation, the two systems must lead to *different* responses. One reason for this prediction is that we assume that individual differences in System 1 processes (interactional intelligence) bear little relation to individual differences in System 2 processes (analytic intelligence). This is a conjecture for which there is a modest amount of evidence (see McGeorge, Crawford, & Kelly, 1997; Reber, 1993).

If nature of the problem is such that the two systems generate opposite responses, rule-based System 2 – used disproportionally by those of high analytic intelligence – will not be diluted by System 1 nondifferentially drawing other subjects, lower in analytic intelligence, to the same response. For example, in nondeontic selection tasks the two systems lead to different responses. A deductive interpretation conjoined with an exhaustive search for falsifying instances yields the response P & not Q. This interpretation and processing style is likely associated with the rule-based System 2 – individual differences in which underlie the psychometric concept of analytic intelligence. In contrast, within the heuristic – analytic framework of Evans (1984, 1989, 1996), the matching response of P&Q reflects the heuristic processing of System 1 (in Evans' theory, a linguistically cued relevance response). In deontic tasks, both System 2 and System 1 processes (the latter in the form of preconscious relevance judgments, pragmatic schemas, or Darwinian algorithms; see Cheng & Holyoak, 1989; Cosmides, 1989; Cummins, 1996; Evans, 1996) operate to draw people to the correct response, thus diluting cognitive ability differences between correct and incorrect responders (see Stanovich & West, 1998a, for a data simulation).

The experimental results reviewed here (see Stanovich, 1999, for further examples) reveal that the response dictated by the construal of the inventors of the Linda Problem (Tversky & Kahneman, 1983), Disease Problem (Tversky & Kahneman, 1981), and selection task (Wason, 1966) is the response favored by subjects of high analytic intelligence. The alternative responses dictated by the construals favored by the critics of the heuristics and biases literature were the choices of the subjects of lower analytic intelligence. These latter alternative construals may have been triggered by heuristics that make evolutionary sense (Cosmides & Tooby, 1994, 1996), but individuals higher in a more flexible type of analytic intelligence (and those more cognitively engaged, see Smith & Levin, 1996) are more prone to follow normative rules that maximize personal utility for the so-called vehicle, which houses the genes. Cognitive mechanisms that were fitness enhancing might well thwart our goals as personal agents in an industrial society (see Baron, 1998) because the assumption that our cognitive mechanisms are adapted in the evolutionary sense (Pinker, 1997) does not entail normative rationality. Thus, situations where evolutionary and normative rationality dissociate might well put the two processing Systems in conflict. These conflicts may be rare, but the few occasions on which they occur might be important ones. This is because knowledge-based, technological societies often put a premium on abstraction and decontextualization, and they sometimes require that the fundamental computational bias of human cognition be overridden by System 2 processes.

THE FUNDAMENTAL COMPUTATIONAL BIAS AND THE ECOLOGY OF THE MODERN WORLD

The fundamental computational bias, that "specific features of problem content, and their semantic associations, constitute the dominant influence on thought" (Evans et al., 1983, p. 295; Stanovich, 1999), is no doubt rational in the evolutionary sense. Selection pressure was probably in the direction of radical contextualization. An organism that could bring more relevant information to bear (not forgetting the frame problem) on the puzzles of life probably dealt with the world better than competitors and thus reproduced with greater frequency and contributed more of its genes to future generations.

Evans and Over (1996) argue that an overemphasis on normative rationality has led us to overlook the adaptiveness of contextualization and the nonoptimality of always decoupling prior beliefs from problem situations. They note the mundane but telling fact that when scanning a room for a particular shape, our visual systems register color as well. They argue that we do not impute irrationality to our visual systems because they fail to screen out the information that is not focal. Our systems of recruiting prior knowledge and contextual information to solve problems with formal solutions are probably likewise adaptive in the evolutionary sense. However, Evans and Over (1996) note, there is an important disanalogy here as well, because studies of belief bias in syllogistic reasoning have shown that "subjects can to some extent ignore belief and reason from a limited number of assumptions when instructed to do so" (p. 117). That is, in the case of reasoning – as opposed to the visual domain – some people do have the cognitive flexibility to decouple unneeded systems of knowledge and some do not. The studies reviewed here indicate that those who do have the requisite flexibility are somewhat higher in cognitive ability and in actively open-minded thinking (see Stanovich & West, 1997).

A conflict between the decontextualizing requirements of normative rationality and the fundamental computational bias may perhaps be one of the main reasons that normative and evolutionary rationality dissociate. The fundamental computational bias is meant to be a global term that captures the pervasive bias toward the contextualization of all informational encounters. It conjoins the following processing tendencies: (a) the tendency to adhere to Gricean conversational principles even in situations that lack many conversational features (Adler, 1984; Hilton, 1995); (b) the tendency to contextualize a problem with as much prior knowledge as is easily accessible, even when the problem is formal and the only solution is a content-free rule (Evans, 1982, 1989; Evans, Barston, & Pollard, 1983); (c) the tendency to see *design* and pattern in situations that are either undesigned, unpatterned, or random (Levinson, 1995); (d) the tendency to reason enthymematically – to make assumptions not stated in a problem and then reason from those assumptions (Henle, 1962; Rescher, 1988); (e) the tendency toward a narrative mode of thought (Bruner, 1986, 1990). All of these properties conjoined together represent a cognitive tendency toward radical contextualization. The bias is termed *fundamental* because it is thought to stem largely from System 1 and that system is assumed to be primary in that it permeates virtually all of our thinking (e.g., Evans & Over, 1996). If the properties of this system are not to be the dominant factors in our thinking, then they must be overridden by System 2 processes so that the particulars of a given problem are abstracted into canonical representations that are stripped of context.

In short, one of the functions of System 2 is to override some of the automatic contextualization provided by System 1. This override function might only be needed in a tiny minority of information processing situations (in most cases, the two systems interact in concert), but they may be unusually important ones. For example, numerous theorists have warned about a possible mismatch between the fundamental computational bias and the processing requirements of many tasks in a technological society containing many symbolic artifacts and often requiring skills of abstraction (Adler, 1984, 1991; Donaldson, 1978, 1993; Hilton, 1995).

Einhorn and Hogarth (1981) highlighted the importance of decontextualized environments in their discussion of the optimistic (Panglossian/Apologist) and pessimistic (Meliorist) views of the cognitive biases revealed in laboratory experimentation. They noted that "the most optimistic asserts that biases are limited to laboratory situations which are unrepresentative of the natural ecology" (p. 82), but go on to caution that "in a rapidly changing world it is unclear what the relevant natural ecology will be. Thus, although the laboratory may be an unfamiliar environment, lack of ability to perform well in unfamiliar situations takes on added importance" (p. 82). There is a caution in this comment for critics of the abstract content of most laboratory tasks and standardized tests. The argument that the laboratory tasks and tests are not like "real life" is becoming less and less true. "Life," in fact, is becoming more like the tests!

Evolutionary psychologists in the Apologist camp have concentrated on shaping the environment (changing the stimuli presented to subjects) so that the same evolutionarily adapted mechanisms that fail the standard of normative rationality under one framing of the problem give the normative response under an alternative (e.g., frequentistic) version. Their emphasis on environmental alteration provides a much-needed counterpoint to the Meliorist emphasis on *cognitive* change. The latter, with their emphasis on reforming human thinking, no doubt miss opportunities to shape the environment so that it fits the representations that our brains are best evolved to deal with. Investigators framing cognition within a Meliorist perspective are often blind to the fact that there may be remarkably efficient mechanisms available in the brain – if only it was provided with the right type of representation. However, it is not always the case that the world will *let* us deal with representations that are optimally suited to our evolutionarily designed cognitive mechanisms.

INDIVIDUAL DIFFERENCES AND THE
NORMATIVE/DESCRIPTIVE GAP

We attempted to demonstrate that a consideration of individual differences in the heuristics and biases literature may have implications for debates about the cause of the gap between normative models and descriptive models of actual performance. Patterns of individual differences may alter our reflective equilibrium regarding the plausibility of the four alternative explanations for the normative/descriptive gap (performance errors, algorithmic limitations, wrong norm, and alternative construal).

Different outcomes were obtained across the wide range of tasks we have examined in our research program. Of course, all the tasks had some unreliable variance and thus some responses that deviated from the response considered normative could easily be considered as performance errors. However, not all deviations could be so explained. Several tasks (e.g., syllogistic reasoning with interfering content, four-card selection task) were characterized by heavy computational loads that made the normative response not prescriptive for some subjects – but these were usually few in number. Finally, a few tasks yielded patterns of covariance that served to raise doubts about the appropriateness of the normative models applied to them or the task construals assumed by the problem inventors (e.g., several noncausal baserate items, false consensus effect).

Although many normative/descriptive gaps could be reduced by these mechanisms, not all of the discrepancies could be explained by factors that do not bring human rationality into question. Algorithmic-level limitations were far from absolute. The magnitude of the associations with cognitive ability left much room for the possibility that the remaining reliable variance indicates that there are systematic irrationalities in intentional-level psychology. A component of our research program mentioned only briefly has produced data consistent with this possibility. Specifically, once capacity limitations are controlled, the remaining variation from normative responding is not random (which would have indicated that the residual variance consisted largely of performance errors). In several studies, we have shown that there is significant covariance among the scores from a variety of tasks in the heuristics and biases literature after they are residualized on measures of cognitive ability (Stanovich, 1999). The residual variance (after partialling cognitive ability) is also systematically associated with questionnaire responses that can be conceptualized as intentional-level styles relating to epistemic regulation (Sá et al., 1999; Stanovich & West, 1997, 1998c). These findings falsify models that attempt to explain the normative/descriptive gap entirely in terms of computational limitations and random performance errors. Instead, the findings support the notion that the normative/descriptive discrepancies that remain after computational limitations have been accounted for reflect a systematically suboptimal intentional-level psychology.

25. Support Theory: A Nonextensional Representation of Subjective Probability

Amos Tversky and Derek J. Koehler

Both laypeople and experts are often called upon to evaluate the probability of uncertain events such as the outcome of a trial, the result of a medical operation, the success of a business venture, or the winner of a football game. Such assessments play an important role in deciding, respectively, whether to go to court, undergo surgery, invest in the venture, or bet on the home team. Uncertainty is usually expressed in verbal terms (e.g., unlikely or probable), but numeric estimates are also common. Weather forecasters, for example, often report the probability of rain (Murphy, 1985), and economists are sometimes required to estimate the chances of recession (Zarnowitz, 1985). The theoretical and practical significance of subjective probability has inspired psychologists, philosophers, and statisticians to investigate this notion from both descriptive and prescriptive standpoints.

Indeed, the question of whether degree of belief can, or should be, represented by the calculus of chance has been the focus of a long and lively debate. In contrast to the Bayesian school, which represents degree of belief by an additive probability measure, there are many skeptics who question the possibility and the wisdom of quantifying subjective uncertainty and are reluctant to apply the laws of chance to the analysis of belief. Besides the Bayesians and the skeptics, there is a growing literature on what might be called *revisionist models of subjective probability*. These include the Dempster–Shafer theory of belief (Dempster, 1967; Shafer, 1976), Zadeh's (1978) possibility theory, and the various types of upper and lower probabilities (e.g., see Suppes, 1974; Walley, 1991). Recent developments have been reviewed by Dubois and Prade (1988), Gilboa and Schmeidler (1994), and Mongin (1994). Like the Bayesians, the revisionists endorse the quantification of belief, using either direct judgments or preferences between bets, but they find the calculus of chance too restrictive for this purpose. Consequently, they replace the additive measure, used in the classical theory, with a nonadditive set function satisfying weaker requirements.

A fundamental assumption that underlies both the Bayesian and the revisionist models of belief is the extensionality principle: Events with the

This is an edited version of a paper that first appeared in *Psychological Review, 101,* 547–567. See original for appended proof. Copyright © 1994 by the American Psychological Association. Adapted by permission.

same extension are assigned the same probability. However, the extensionality assumption is descriptively invalid because alternative descriptions of the same event often produce systematically different judgments. The following three examples illustrate this phenomenon and motivate the development of a descriptive theory of belief that is free from the extensionality assumption.

1. Fischhoff, Slovic, and Lichtenstein (1978) asked car mechanics, as well as laypeople, to assess the probabilities of different causes of a car's failure to start. They found that the mean probability assigned to the residual hypothesis ("The cause of failure is something other than the battery, the fuel system, or the engine") increased from .22 to .44 when the hypothesis was broken up into more specific causes (e.g., the starting system, the ignition system). Although the car mechanics, who had an average of 15 years of experience, were surely aware of these possibilities, they discounted hypotheses that were not explicitly mentioned.

2. Tversky and Kahneman (1983) constructed many problems in which both probability and frequency judgments were not consistent with set inclusion. For example, one group of subjects was asked to estimate the number of seven-letter words in four pages of a novel that end with *ing*. A second group was asked to estimate the number of seven-letter words that end with __ *n* __. The median estimate for the first question (13.4) was nearly three times higher than that for the second (4.7), presumably because it is easier to think of seven-letter words ending with *ing* than to think of seven-letter words with *n* in the sixth position. It appears that most people who evaluated the second category were not aware of the fact that it includes the first.

3. Violations of extensionality are not confined to probability judgments; they are also observed in the evaluation of uncertain prospects. For example, Johnson, Hershey, Meszaros, and Kunreuther (1993) found that subjects who were offered (hypothetical) health insurance that covers hospitalization for any disease or accident were willing to pay a higher premium than subjects who were offered health insurance that covers hospitalization for any reason. Evidently, the explicit mention of disease and accident increases the perceived chances of hospitalization and, hence, the attractiveness of insurance.

These observations, like many others described later in this article, are inconsistent with the extensionality principle. We distinguish two sources of nonextensionality: First, extensionality may fail because of memory limitation. As illustrated in Example 2, a judge cannot be expected to recall all of the instances of a category, even when he or she can recognize them without error. An explicit description could remind people of relevant cases that might otherwise slip their minds. Second, extensionality may fail because different descriptions of the same event may call attention to different aspects of the outcome and thereby affect their relative salience. Such effects can influence probability judgments even when they do not bring to mind new instances or new evidence.

The common failures of extensionality, we suggest, represent an essential feature of human judgment, not a collection of isolated examples. They indicate that probability judgments are attached not to events but to descriptions of events. In this article, we present a theory in which the judged probability of an event depends on the explicitness of its description. This treatment, called *support theory*, focuses on direct judgments of probability, but it is also applicable to decision under uncertainty. . . .

Support Theory

Let T be a finite set including at least two elements, interpreted as states of the world. We assume that exactly one state obtains but it is generally not known to the judge. Subsets of T are called *events*. We distinguish between events and descriptions of events, called *hypotheses*. Let H be a set of hypotheses that describe the events in T. Thus, we assume that each hypothesis $A \in H$ corresponds to a unique event $A' \subset T$. This is a many-to-one mapping because different hypotheses, say A and B, may have the same extension (i.e., $A' = B'$). For example, suppose one rolls a pair of dice. The hypotheses, "The sum is 3" and "The product is 2" are different descriptions of the same event; namely, one die shows 1 and the other shows 2. We assume that H is finite and includes at least one hypothesis for each event. The following relations on H are induced by the corresponding relations on T: A is *elementary* if $A' \in T$. A is *null* if $A' = \varnothing$. A and B are *exclusive* if $A' \cap B' = \varnothing$. If A and B are in H, and they are exclusive, then their explicit disjunction, denoted $A \vee B$ is also in H. Thus, H is closed under exclusive disjunction. We assume that $\vee$ is associative and commutative and that $(A \vee B)' = A' \cup B'$.

A key feature of the present formulation is the distinction between explicit and implicit disjunctions. A is an *implicit disjunction*, or simply an implicit hypothesis, if it is neither elementary nor null, and it is not an explicit disjunction (i.e., there are no exclusive nonnull B, C in H such that $A = B \vee C$). For example, suppose A is "Ann majors in a natural science," B is "Ann majors in a biological science," and C is "Ann majors in a physical science." The explicit disjunction, $B \vee C$ ("Ann majors in either a biological or a physical science"), has the same extension as A (i.e., $A' = (B \vee C)' = B' \cup C'$), but A is an implicit hypothesis because it is not an explicit disjunction. Note that the explicit disjunction $B \vee C$ is defined for any exclusive $B, C \in H$, whereas a coextensional implicit disjunction may not exist because some events cannot be naturally described without listing their components.

An *evaluation frame* (A, B) consists of a pair of exclusive hypotheses: The first element A is the *focal* hypothesis that the judge evaluates and the second element B is the *alternative* hypothesis. To simplify matters, we assume that when A and B are exclusive, the judge perceives them as such, but we do not assume that the judge can list all of the constituents of an implicit disjunction.

In terms of the above example, we assume that the judge knows, for instance, that genetics is a biological science, that astronomy is a physical science, and that the biological and the physical sciences are exclusive. However, we do not assume that the judge can list all of the biological or the physical sciences. Thus, we assume recognition of inclusion but not perfect recall.

We interpret a person's probability judgment as a mapping P from an evaluation frame to the unit interval. To simplify matters we assume that $P(A, B)$ equals zero if and only if A is null and that it equals one if and only if B is null; we assume that A and B are not both null. Thus, $P(A, B)$ is the judged probability that A rather than B holds, assuming that one and only one of them is valid. Obviously, A and B may each represent an explicit or an implicit disjunction. The extensional counterpart of $P(A, B)$ in the standard theory is the conditional probability $P(A'|A' \cup B')$. The present treatment is nonextensional because it assumes that probability judgment depends on the descriptions A and B, not just on the events A' and B'. We wish to emphasize that the present theory applies to the hypotheses entertained by the judge, which do not always coincide with the given verbal descriptions. A judge presented with an implicit disjunction may, nevertheless, think about it as an explicit disjunction, and vice versa.

Support theory assumes that there is a ratio scale s (interpreted as degree of support) that assigns to each hypothesis in H a nonnegative real number such that, for any pair of exclusive hypotheses $A, B \in$ H,

$$P(A, B) = \frac{s(A)}{s(A) + s(B)} \tag{1}$$

If B and C are exclusive, A is implicit, and $A' = (B \vee C)'$, then

$$s(A) \leq s(B \vee C) = s(B) + s(C). \tag{2}$$

Equation 1 provides a representation of subjective probability in terms of the support of the focal and the alternative hypotheses. Equation 2 states that the support of an implicit disjunction A is less than or equal to that of a coextensional explicit disjunction $B \vee C$ that equals the sum of the support of its components. Thus, support is additive for explicit disjunctions and subadditive for implicit ones.

The subadditivity assumption, we suggest, represents a basic principle of human judgment. When people assess their degree of belief in an implicit disjunction, they do not normally unpack the hypothesis into its exclusive components and add their support, as required by extensionality. Instead, they tend to form a global impression that is based primarily on the most representative or available cases. Because this mode of judgment is selective rather than exhaustive, unpacking tends to increase support. In other words, we propose that the support of a summary representation of an implicit hypothesis is generally less than the sum of the support of its exclusive components. Both memory and attention may contribute to this effect. Unpacking a category (e.g., death from an unnatural cause) into its components (e.g., homicide, fatal car accidents, drowning) might remind people of possibilities that would not have been considered otherwise. Moreover, the explicit mention of an outcome tends to enhance its salience and hence its support. Although this assumption may fail in some circumstances, the overwhelming evidence for subadditivity (described in the next section) indicates that these failures represent the exception rather than the rule.

The support associated with a given hypothesis is interpreted as a measure of the strength of evidence in favor of this hypothesis that is available to the judge. The support may be based on objective data (e.g., the frequency of homicide in the relevant population) or on a subjective impression mediated by judgmental heuristics, such as representativeness, availability, or anchoring and adjustment (Kahneman, Slovic, & Tversky, 1982). For example, the hypothesis "Bill is an accountant" may be evaluated by the degree to which Bill's personality matches the stereotype of an accountant; the prediction "An oil spill along the eastern coast before the end of next year" may be assessed by the ease with which similar accidents come to mind. Support may also reflect reasons or arguments recruited by the judge in favor of the hypothesis in question (e.g., If the defendant were guilty, he would not have reported the crime). Because judgments based on impressions and reasons are often nonextensional, the support function is nonmonotonic with respect to set inclusion. Thus, $s(B)$ may exceed $s(A)$ even though $A' \supset B'$. Note, however, that $s(B)$ cannot exceed $s(B \vee C)$. For example, if the support of a category is determined by the availability of its instances, then the support of the hypothesis that a randomly selected word ends with *ing* can exceed the support of the hypothesis that the word ends with __ *n* __ . Once the inclusion relation between the categories is made transparent, the __ *n* __ hypothesis is replaced by "*ing* or any other __ *n* __," whose support exceeds that of the *ing* hypothesis.

The present theory provides an interpretation of subjective probability in terms of relative support. This interpretation suggests that, in some cases, probability judgment may be predicted from independent assessments of support. This possibility is explored later. The following discussion shows that, under the present theory, support can be derived from probability judgments, much as utility is derived from preferences between options.

Consequences

Support theory has been formulated in terms of the support function s, which is not directly observable. We next characterize the theory in terms of the observed index P. We first exhibit four consequences of the theory and then show that they imply Eqs. 1 and 2. An immediate consequence of the theory is *binary complementarity*:

$$P(A, B) + P(B, A) = 1. \tag{3}$$

A second consequence is *proportionality*:

$$\frac{P(A, B)}{P(B, A)} = \frac{P(A, B \vee C)}{P(B, A \vee C)} \tag{4}$$

provided that A, B, and C are mutually exclusive and B is not null. Thus, the "odds" for A against B are independent of the additional hypothesis C.

To formulate the next condition, it is convenient to introduce the probability ratio $R(A, B) = P(A, B)/P(B, A)$, which is the odds for A against B. Equation 1 implies the following *product rule*:

$$R(A, B)R(C, D) = R(A, D)R(C, B), \tag{5}$$

provided that A, B, C, and D are not null and the four pairs of hypotheses in Eq. 5 are pairwise exclusive. Thus, the product of the odds for A against B and for C against D equals the product of the odds for A against D and for C against B. To see the necessity of the product rule, note that, according to Eq. 1, both sides of Eq. 5 equal $s(A)s(C)/s(B)s(D)$. Essentially the same condition has been used in the theory of preference trees (Tversky & Sattath, 1979).

Equations 1 and 2 together imply the *unpacking principle*. Suppose B, C, and D are mutually exclusive, A is implicit, and $A' = (B \vee C)'$. Then

$$P(A, D) \leq P(B \vee C, D) = P(B, C \vee D) + P(C, B \vee D). \tag{6}$$

The properties of s entail the corresponding properties of P: Judged probability is additive for explicit disjunctions and subadditive for implicit disjunctions. In other words, unpacking an implicit disjunction may increase, but not decrease, its judged probability. Unlike Eqs. 3–5, which hold in the standard theory of probability, the unpacking principle (Eq. 6) generalizes the classical model. Note that this assumption is at variance with lower probability models, including Shafer's (1976), which assume extensionality and superadditivity [i.e., $P(A' \cup B') \geq P(A') + P(B')$ if $A' \cap B' = \emptyset$].

There are two conflicting intuitions that yield nonadditive probability. The first intuition, captured by support theory, suggests that unpacking an implicit disjunction enhances the salience of its components and consequently increases support. The second intuition, captured by Shafer's (1976) theory, among others, suggests that in the face of partial ignorance the judge holds some measure of belief "in reserve" and does not distribute it among all elementary hypotheses, as required by the Bayesian model. Although Shafer's theory is based on a logical rather than a psychological analysis of belief, it has also been interpreted by several authors as a descriptive model. Thus, it provides a natural alternative to be compared with the present theory.

Whereas proportionality (Eq. 4) and the product rule (Eq. 5) have not been systematically tested before, a number of investigators have observed binary complementarity (Eq. 3) and some aspects of the unpacking principle (Eq. 6). These data, as well as several new studies, are reviewed in the next section. The following theorem shows that the above conditions are not only necessary but also sufficient for support theory. The proof is given in the Appendix of Tversky and Koehler (1994).

Theorem 1: Suppose $P(A, B)$ is defined for all exclusive $A, B \in H$ and that it vanishes if and only if A is null. Equations 3–6 hold if and only if there exists a nonnegative ratio scale s on H that satisfies Eqs. 1 and 2.

The theorem shows that if probability judgments satisfy the required conditions, it is possible to scale the support or strength of evidence associated with each hypothesis without assuming that hypotheses with the same extension have equal support. An ordinal generalization of the theory, in which P is treated as an ordinal rather than cardinal scale, is presented in Tversky and Koehler (1994). In the remainder of this section, we introduce a representation of subadditivity and a treatment of conditioning.

Subadditivity

We extend the theory by providing a more detailed representation of subadditivity. Let A be an implicit hypothesis with the same extension as the explicit disjunction of the elementary hypotheses $A_1, \ldots, A_n$; that is, $A' = (A_1 \vee \ldots \vee A_n)'$. Assume that any two elementary hypotheses, B and C, with the same extension have the same support; that is, $B', C' \in T$ and $B' = C'$ implies $s(B) = s(C)$. It follows that, under this assumption we can write

$$s(A) = w_{1A}s(A_1) + \cdots + w_{nA}s(A_n), \ 0 \leq w_{iA} \leq 1, \quad i = 1, \ldots, n. \tag{7}$$

In this representation, the support of each elementary hypothesis is "discounted" by its respective weight, which reflects the degree to which the judge attends to the hypothesis in question. If $w_{iA} = 1$ for all i, then $s(A)$ is the sum of the support of its elementary hypotheses, as in an explicit disjunction. However, $w_{jA} = 0$ for some j indicates that A_j is effectively ignored. Finally, if the weights add to one, then i is a weighted average of the $s(A_i)$, $1 \leq i \leq n$. Equation 7 should not be interpreted as a process of deliberate discounting in which the judge assesses the support of an implicit disjunction by discounting the assessed support of the corresponding explicit disjunction. Instead, the weights are meant to represent the result of an assessment process in which the judge evaluates A without explicitly unpacking it into its elementary components. It should also be kept in mind that elementary hypotheses are defined relative to a given sample space. Such hypotheses may be broken down further by refining the level of description.

Note that whereas the support function is unique, except for a unit of measurement, the "local" weights w_{iA} are not uniquely determined by the observed probability judgments. These data, however, determine the "global" weights

w_A defined by

$$s(A) = w_A[s(A_1) + \cdots + s(A_n)], \quad 0 \leq w_A \leq 1. \tag{8}$$

The global weight w_A, which is the ratio of the support of the corresponding implicit (A) and explicit ($A_1 \vee \ldots \vee A_n$) disjunctions, provides a convenient measure of the degree of subadditivity induced by A. The degree of subadditivity, we propose, is influenced by several factors, one of which is the interpretation of the probability scale. Specifically, subadditivity is expected to be more pronounced when probability is interpreted as a propensity of an individual case than when it is equated with, or estimated by, relative frequency. Kahneman and Tversky (1979, 1982) referred to these modes of judgment as singular and distributional, respectively, and argued that the latter is usually more accurate than the former (see also Reeves & Lockhart, 1993). Although many events of interest cannot be interpreted in frequentistic terms, there are questions that can be framed in either a distributional or a singular mode. For example, people may be asked to assess the probability that an individual, selected at random from the general population, will die as a result of an accident. Alternatively, people may be asked to assess the percentage (or relative frequency) of the population that will die as a result of an accident. We propose that the implicit disjunction "accident" is more readily unpacked into its components (e.g., car accidents, plane crashes, fire, drowning, poisoning) when the judge considers the entire population rather than a single person. The various causes of death are all represented in the population's mortality statistics, but not in the death of a single person. More generally, we propose that the tendency to unpack an implicit disjunction is stronger in the distributional than in the singular mode. Hence, a frequentistic formulation is expected to produce less discounting (i.e., higher ws) than a formulation that refers to an individual case.

Conditioning
Recall that $P(A, B)$ is interpreted as the conditional probability of A, given A or B. To obtain a general treatment of conditioning, we enrich the hypothesis set H by assuming that if A and B are distinct elements of H, then their conjunction, denoted AB, is also in H. Naturally, we assume that conjunction is associative and commutative and that $(AB)' = A' \cap B'$. We also assume distributivity; that is, $A(B \vee C) = AB \vee AC$. Let $P(A, B|D)$ be the judged probability that A rather than B holds, given some data D. In general, new evidence (i.e., a different state of information) gives rise to a new support function s_D that describes the revision of s in light of D. In the special case in which the data can be described as an element of H, which merely restricts the hypotheses under consideration, we can represent conditional probability by

$$P(A, B \mid D) = \frac{s(AD)}{s(AD) + s(BD)} \tag{9}$$

provided that A and B are exclusive but $A \vee B$ and D are not.

Several comments on this form are in order. First, note that if s is additive, then Eq. 9 reduces to the standard definition of conditional probability. If s is subadditive, as we have assumed throughout, then judged probability depends not only on the description of the focal and the alternative hypotheses but also on the description of the evidence D. Suppose $D' = (D_1 \vee D_2)'$, D_1 and D_2 are exclusive, and D is implicit. Then

$$P(A, B|D_1 \vee D_2) = \frac{s(AD_1 \vee AD_2)}{s(AD_1 \vee AD_2) + s(BD_1 \vee BD_2)}.$$

But because $s(AD) \leq s(AD_1 \vee AD_2)$ and $s(BD) \leq s(BD_1 \vee BD_2)$ by subadditivity, the unpacking of D may favor one hypothesis over another. For example, the judged probability that a woman earns a very high salary given that she is a university professor is likely to increase when "university" is unpacked into "law school, business school, medical school, or any other school" because of the explicit mention of high-paying positions. Thus, Eq. 9 extends the application of subadditivity to the representation of evidence. As shown later, it also allows us to compare the impact of different bodies of evidence, provided they can be described as elements of H.

Consider a collection of $n \geq 3$ mutually exclusive and exhaustive (nonnull) hypotheses, $A_1 \ldots A_n$, and let $\bar{A}_i$ denote the negation of A_i that corresponds to an implicit disjunction of the remaining hypotheses. Consider two items of evidence, $B, C \in H$, and suppose that each A_i is more compatible with B than with C in the sense that $s(BA_i) \geq s(CA_i)$, $1 \leq i \leq n$. We propose that B induces more subadditivity than C so that $s(B\bar{A}_i)$ is discounted more heavily than $s(C\bar{A}_i)$ (i.e., $w_{B\bar{A}_i} \leq w_{C\bar{A}_i}$; see Eq. 7). This assumption, called *enhancement*, suggests that the assessments of $P(A_i, \bar{A}_i|B)$ will be generally higher than those of $P(A_i, \bar{A}_i|C)$. More specifically, we propose that the sum of the probabilities of $A_1 \ldots A_n$, each evaluated by different judges, is no smaller under B than under C. That is,

$$\sum_{i=1}^{n} P(A_i, \bar{A}_i|B) \geq \sum_{i=1}^{n} P(A_i, \bar{A}_i|C) \tag{10}$$

Subadditivity implies that both sums are greater than or equal to one. The preceding inequality states that the sum is increased by evidence that is more compatible with the hypotheses under study. It is noteworthy that enhancement suggests that people are inappropriately responsive to the prior probability of the data, whereas base-rate neglect indicates that people are not sufficiently responsive to the prior probability of the hypotheses. The following schematic example illustrates an implication of enhancement and compares it with other models.

Suppose that a murder was committed by one (and only one) of several suspects. In the absence of any specific evidence, assume that all suspects are considered about equally likely to have committed the crime. Suppose further that a preliminary investigation has uncovered a body of evidence (e.g., motives and opportunities) that implicates each of the suspects to roughly the same degree. According to the Bayesian model, the probabilities of all of the suspects remain unchanged because the new evidence is nondiagnostic. In Shafer's theory of belief functions, the judged probability that the murder was committed by one suspect rather than by another generally increases with the amount of evidence; thus, it should be higher after the investigation than before. Enhancement yields a different pattern: The binary probabilities (i.e., of one suspect against another) are expected to be approximately one half, both before and after the investigation, as in the Bayesian model. However, the probability that the murder was committed by a particular suspect (rather than by any of the others) is expected to increase with the amount of evidence. Experimental tests of enhancement are described in the next section.

DATA

Studies of Unpacking

Recall that the unpacking principle (Eq. 6) consists of two parts: additivity for explicit disjunctions and subadditivity for implicit disjunctions, which jointly entail nonextensionality. [Binary complementarity (Eq. 3) is a special case of additivity.] Because each part alone is subject to alternative interpretations, it is important to test additivity and subadditivity simultaneously. For this reason, we first describe several new studies that have tested both parts of the unpacking principle within the same experiment, and then we review previous research that provided the impetus for the present theory.

Study 1: Causes of Death. Our first study followed the seminal work of Fischhoff et al. (1978) on fault trees, using a task similar to that studied by Russo and Kolzow (1992). We asked Stanford undergraduates ($N = 120$) to assess the likelihood of various possible causes of death. The subjects were informed that each year approximately 2 million people in the United States (nearly 1% of the population) die from different causes, and they were asked to estimate the probability of death from a variety of causes. Half of the subjects considered a single person who had died recently and assessed the probability that he or she had died from each in a list of specified causes. They were asked to assume that the person in question had been randomly selected from the set of people who had died the previous year. The other half, given a frequency judgment task, assessed the percentage of the 2 million deaths in the previous year attributable to each cause. In each group, half of the subjects were promised that the five most accurate subjects would receive $20 each.

Each subject evaluated one of two different lists of causes, constructed such that he or she evaluated either an implicit hypothesis (e.g., death resulting from natural causes) or a coextensional explicit disjunction (e.g., death resulting from heart disease, cancer, or some other natural cause), but not both. The full set

Table 25.1. Mean Probability and Frequency Estimates for Causes of Death in Study 1: Comparing Evaluations of Explicit Disjunctions with Coextensional Implicit Disjunctions

Hypothesis	Mean Estimate (%)		Actual %
	Probability	Frequency	
Three component			
P (heart disease)	22	18	34.1
P (cancer)	18	20	23.1
P (other natural cause)	33	29	35.2
Σ (natural cause)	73	67	92.4
P (natural cause)	58	56	
Σ/P	1.26	1.20	
P (accident)	32	30	4.4
P (homicide)	10	11	1.1
P (other unnatural cause)	11	12	2.1
Σ (unnatural cause)	53	53	7.6
P (unnatural cause)	32	39	
Σ/P	1.66	1.36	
Seven component			
P (respiratory cancer|natural)	12	11	7.1
P (digestive cancer|natural)	8	7	5.9
P (genitourinary cancer|natural)	5	3	2.7
P (breast cancer|natural)	13	9	2.2
P (urinary cancer|natural)	7	3	1.0
P (leukemia|natural)	8	6	1.0
P (other cancer|natural)	17	10	5.1
Σ (cancer|natural)	70	49	25.0
P (cancer|natural)	32	24	
Σ/P	2.19	2.04	
P (auto accident|unnatural)	33	33	30.3
P (firearm accident|unnatural)	7	12	1.3
P (accidental fall|unnatural)	6	4	7.9
P (death in fire|unnatural)	4	5	2.6
P (drowning|unnatural)	5	4	2.6
P (accidental poisoning|unnatural)	4	3	3.9
P (other accident|unnatural)	24	17	9.2
Σ (accident|unnatural)	83	78	57.9
P (accident|unnatural)	45	48	
Σ/P	1.84	1.62	

Note: Actual percentages were taken from the 1990 *U.S. Statistical Abstract.* Σ = sum of mean estimates.

of causes considered is listed in Table 25.1. Causes of death were divided into natural and unnatural types. Each type had three components, one of which was further divided into seven subcomponents. To avoid very small probabilities, we conditioned these seven subcomponents on the corresponding type of death (i.e., natural or unnatural). To provide subjects with some anchors, we informed them that the probability or frequency of death resulting from respiratory illness is about 7.5% and the probability or frequency of death resulting from suicide is about 1.5%.

Table 25.1 shows that, for both probability and frequency judgments, the mean estimate of an implicit disjunction (e.g., death from a natural cause) is smaller than the sum of the mean estimates of its components (heart disease, cancer, or other natural causes), denoted Σ (natural causes). Specifically, the former equals 58%, whereas the latter equals 22% + 18% + 33% = 73%. All eight comparisons in Table 25.1 are statistically significant ($p < .05$) by Mann–Whitney U test. (We used a nonparametric test because of the unequal variances involved when comparing a single measured variable with a sum of measured variables.)

Throughout this article, we use the ratio of the probabilities assigned to coextensional explicit and implicit hypotheses as a measure of subadditivity. The ratio in the preceding example is 1.26. This index, called the *unpacking factor*, can be computed directly from probability judgments, unlike w, which is defined in terms of the support function. Subadditivity is indicated by an unpacking factor greater than 1 and a value of w less than 1. It is noteworthy that subadditivity, by itself, does not imply that explicit hypotheses are overestimated or that implicit hypotheses are underestimated relative to an appropriate objective criterion. It merely indicates that the former are judged as more probable than the latter.

In this study, the mean unpacking factors were 1.37 for the three-component hypotheses and 1.92 for the seven-component hypotheses, indicating that the degree of subadditivity increased with the number of components in the explicit disjunction. An analysis of medians rather than means revealed a similar pattern, with somewhat smaller differences between packed and unpacked versions. Comparison of probability and frequency tasks showed, as expected, that subjects gave higher and thus more subadditive estimates when judging probabilities than when judging frequencies, $F(12, 101) = 2.03$, $p < .05$. The average unpacking factors were 1.74 for probability and 1.56 for frequency.

The judgments generally overestimated the actual values, obtained from the 1990 *U.S. Statistical Abstract*. The only clear exception was heart disease, which had an actual probability of 34% but received a mean judgment of 20%. Because subjects produced higher judgments of probability than of frequency, the former exhibited greater overestimation of the actual values, but the correlation between the estimated and actual values (computed separately for each subject) revealed no difference between the two tasks. Monetary incentives did not improve the accuracy of people's judgments.

The following design provides a more stringent test of support theory and compares it with alternative models of belief. Suppose A_1, A_2, and B are mutually exclusive and exhaustive; $A' = (A_1 \vee A_2)'$; A is implicit; and $\bar{A}$ is the negation of A. Consider the following observable values:

$$\alpha = P(A, B)$$
$$\beta = P(A_1 \lor A_2, B)$$
$$\gamma_1 = P(A_1, A_2 \lor B), \quad \gamma_2 = P(A_2, A_1 \lor B), \quad \gamma = \gamma_1 + \gamma_2$$
$$\delta_1 = P(A_1, \bar{A}_1), \quad \delta_2 = P(A_2, \bar{A}_2), \quad \delta = \delta_1 + \delta_2.$$

Different models of belief imply different orderings of these values:

support theory, $\alpha \leq \beta = \gamma \leq \delta$
Bayesian model, $\alpha = \beta = \gamma = \delta$
belief function, $\alpha = \beta \geq \gamma = \delta$
regressive model, $\alpha = \beta \leq \gamma = \delta$.

Support theory predicts $\alpha \leq \beta$ and $\gamma \leq \delta$ due to the unpacking of the focal and residual hypotheses, respectively; it also predicts $\beta = \gamma$ due to the additivity of explicit disjunctions. The Bayesian model implies $\alpha = \beta$ and $\gamma = \delta$, by extensionality, and $\beta = \gamma$, by additivity. Shafer's theory of belief functions also assumes extensionality, but it predicts $\beta \geq \gamma$ because of superadditivity. The above data, as well as numerous studies reviewed later, demonstrate that $\alpha < \delta$, which is consistent with support theory but inconsistent with both the Bayesian model and Shafer's theory.

The observation that $\alpha < \delta$ could also be explained by a *regressive model* that assumes that probability judgments satisfy extensionality but are biased toward .5 (e.g., see Erev, Wallsten, & Budescu, 1994). For example, the judge might start with a "prior" probability of .5 that is not revised sufficiently in light of the evidence. Random error could also produce regressive estimates. If each individual judgment is biased toward .5, then β, which consists of a single judgment, would be less than γ, which is the sum of two judgments. However, this model predicts no difference between α and β, each of which consists of a single judgment, or between γ and δ, each of which consists of two. Thus, support theory and the regressive model make different predictions about the source of the difference between α and δ. Support theory predicts subadditivity for implicit disjunctions (i.e., $\alpha \leq \beta$ and $\gamma \leq \delta$) and additivity for explicit disjunctions (i.e., $\beta = \gamma$), whereas the regressive model assumes extensionality (i.e., $\alpha = \beta$ and $\gamma = \delta$) and subadditivity for explicit disjunctions (i.e., $\beta \leq \gamma$).

To contrast these predictions, we asked different groups (of 25 to 30 subjects each) to assess the probability of various unnatural causes of death. All subjects were told that a person had been randomly selected from the set of people who had died the previous year from an unnatural cause. The hypotheses under study and the corresponding probability judgments are summarized in Table 25.2. The first row, for example, presents the judged probability β that death was caused by an accident or a homicide rather than by some other unnatural cause. In accord with support theory, $\delta = \delta_1 + \delta_2$ was significantly greater

Table 25.2. **Mean and Median Probability Estimates for Various Causes of Death**

Probability Judgments	Mean	Median
$\beta = P$ (accident or homicide, OUC)	64	70
$\gamma_1 = P$ (accident, homicide or OUC)	53	60
$\gamma_2 = P$ (homicide, accident or OUC)	16	10
$\gamma = \gamma_1 + \gamma_2$	69	70
$\delta_1 = P$ (accident, OUC)	56	65
$\delta_2 = P$ (homicide, OUC)	24	18
$\delta = \delta_1 + \delta_2$	80	83

Note: OUC = other unnatural causes.

than $\gamma = \gamma_1 + \gamma_2$, $p < .05$ (by Mann–Whitney U test), but γ was not significantly greater than β, contrary to the prediction of the regressive model. Nevertheless, we do not rule out the possibility that regression toward .5 could yield $\beta < \gamma$, which would contribute to the discrepancy between α and δ.

Study 2: Suggestibility and Subadditivity. Before turning to additional demonstrations of unpacking, we discuss some methodological questions regarding the elicitation of probability judgments. It could be argued that asking a subject to evaluate a specific hypothesis conveys a subtle (or not so subtle) suggestion that the hypothesis is quite probable. Subjects, therefore, might treat the fact that the hypothesis has been brought to their attention as information about its probability. To address this objection, we devised a task in which the assigned hypotheses carried no information so that any observed subadditivity could not be attributed to experimental suggestion.

Stanford undergraduates ($N = 196$) estimated the percentage of U.S. married couples with a given number of children. Subjects were asked to write down the last digit of their telephone numbers and then to evaluate the percentage of couples having exactly that many children. They were promised that the three most accurate respondents would be awarded $10 each. As predicted, the total percentage attributed to the numbers 0 through 9 (when added across different groups of subjects) greatly exceeded 1. The total of the means assigned by each group was 1.99, and the total of the medians was 1.80. Thus, subadditivity was very much in evidence, even when the selection of focal hypothesis was hardly informative. Subjects overestimated the percentage of couples in all categories, except for childless couples, and the discrepancy between the estimated and the actual percentages was greatest for the modal couple with 2 children. Furthermore, the sum of the probabilities for 0, 1, 2, and 3 children, each of which exceeded .25, was 1.45. The observed subadditivity, therefore, cannot be explained merely by a tendency to overestimate very small probabilities.

Other subjects ($N = 139$) were asked to estimate the percentage of U.S. married couples with "less than 3," "3 or more," "less than 5," or "5 or more" children. Each subject considered exactly one of the four hypotheses. The estimates added to 97.5% for the first pair of hypotheses and to 96.3% for the second pair. In sharp contrast to the subadditivity observed earlier, the estimates for complementary pairs of events were roughly additive, as implied by support theory. The finding of binary complementarity is of special interest because it excludes an alternative explanation of subadditivity according to which the evaluation of evidence is biased in favor of the focal hypothesis.

Subadditivity in Expert Judgments

Is subadditivity confined to novices, or does it also hold for experts? Redelmeier, Koehler, Liberman, and Tversky (1995) explored this question in the context of medical judgments. They presented physicians at Stanford University ($N = 59$) with a detailed scenario concerning a woman who reported to the emergency room with abdominal pain. Half of the respondents were asked to assign probabilities to two specified diagnoses (gastroenteritis and ectopic pregnancy) and a residual category (none of the above); the other half assigned probabilities to five specified diagnoses (including the two presented in the other condition) and a residual category (none of the above). Subjects were instructed to give probabilities that summed to one because the possibilities under consideration were mutually exclusive and exhaustive. If the physicians' judgments conform to the classical theory, then the probability assigned to the residual category in the two-diagnosis condition should equal the sum of the probabilities assigned to its unpacked components in the five-diagnosis condition. Consistent with the predictions of support theory, however, the judged probability of the residual in the two-diagnosis condition (mean $= .50$) was significantly lower than that of the unpacked components in the five-diagnosis condition (mean $= .69$), $p < .005$ (Mann–Whitney U test).

In a second study, physicians from Tel Aviv University ($N = 52$) were asked to consider several medical scenarios consisting of a one-paragraph statement including the patient's age, gender, medical history, presenting symptoms, and the results of any tests that had been conducted. One scenario, for example, concerned a 67-year-old man who arrived in the emergency room suffering a heart attack that had begun several hours earlier. Each physician was asked to assess the probability of one of the following four hypotheses: patient dies during this hospital admission (A); patient is discharged alive but dies within 1 year (B); patient lives more than 1 but less than 10 years (C); or patient lives more than 10 years (D). Throughout this chapter, we refer to these as *elementary judgments* because they pit an elementary hypothesis against its complement, which is an implicit disjunction of all of the remaining elementary hypotheses. After assessing one of these four hypotheses, all respondents assessed $P(A, B)$, $P(B, C)$, and $P(C, D)$ or the complementary set. We refer to these as *binary judgments* because they involve a comparison of two elementary hypotheses.

As predicted, the elementary judgments were substantially subadditive. The means of the four groups in the preceding example were 14% for A, 26% for B,

55% for C, and 69% for D, all of which overestimated the actual values reported in the medical literature. In problems like this, when individual components of a partition are evaluated against the residual, the denominator of the unpacking factor is taken to be 1; thus, the unpacking factor is simply the total probability assigned to the components (summed over different groups of subjects). In this example, the unpacking factor was 1.64. In sharp contrast, the binary judgments (produced by two different groups of physicians) exhibited near-perfect additivity, with a mean total of 100.5% assigned to complementary pairs.

Further evidence for subadditivity in expert judgment has been provided by Fox, Rogers, and Tversky (1996), who investigated 32 professional options traders at the Pacific Stock Exchange. These traders made probability judgments regarding the closing price of Microsoft stock on a given future date (e.g., it will be less than $88 per share). Microsoft stock is traded at the Pacific Stock Exchange, and the traders are commonly concerned with the prediction of its future value. Nevertheless, their judgments exhibited the predicted pattern of subadditivity and binary complementarity. The average unpacking factor for a fourfold partition was 1.47, and the average sum of complementary binary events was 0.98. Subadditivity in expert judgments has been documented in other domains by Fischhoff et al. (1978), who studied auto mechanics, and by Dube-Rioux and Russo (1988), who studied restaurant managers.

Review of Previous Research

We next review other studies that have provided tests of support theory. Tversky and Fox (1994) asked subjects to assign probabilities to various intervals in which an uncertain quantity might fall, such as the margin of victory in the upcoming Super Bowl or the change in the Dow Jones Industrial Average over the next week. When a given event (e.g., "Buffalo beats Washington") was unpacked into individually evaluated components (e.g., "Buffalo beats Washington by less than 7 points"; "Buffalo beats Washington by at least 7 points"), subjects' judgments were substantially subadditive. Figure 25.1 plots the unpacking factor obtained in this study as a function of the number of component hypotheses in the explicit disjunction. Judgments for five different types of event are shown: future San Francisco temperature (SFO), future Beijing temperature (BJG), the outcome of the Super Bowl of the National Football League (NFL), the outcome of a playoff game of the National Basketball Association (NBA), and weekly change in the Dow Jones index (DOW). Recall that an unpacking factor greater than 1 (i.e., falling above the dashed line in the plot) indicates subadditivity. The results displayed in Fig. 25.1 reveal consistent subadditivity for all sources that increases with the number of components in the explicit disjunction.

Figure 25.2 plots the median probabilities assigned to complementary hypotheses. (Each hypothesis is represented twice in the plot: once as the focal hypothesis and once as the complement.) As predicted by support theory, judgments of intervals representing complementary pairs of hypotheses were

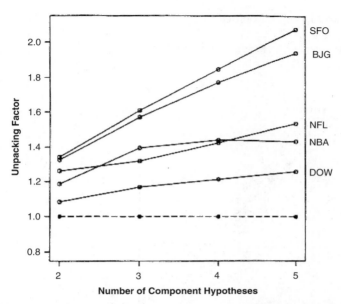

Figure 25.1. Unpacking factors from Tversky and Fox's (1994) data. SFO, San Francisco temperature; BJG, Beijing temperature; NFL, 1991 National Football League Super Bowl; NBA, National Basketball Association playoff; DOW, weekly change in Dow–Jones index.

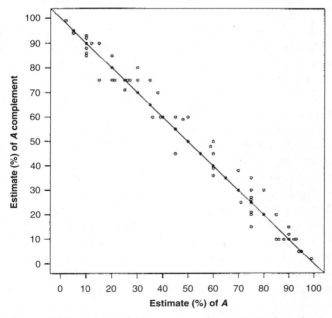

Figure 25.2. A test of binary complementarity based on Tversky and Fox (1994).

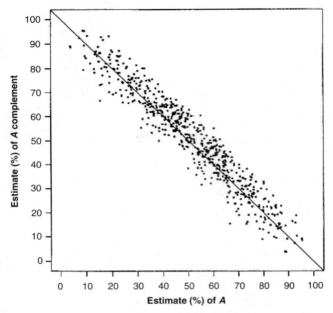

Figure 25.3. A test of binary complementarity based on Wallsten, Budescu, and Zwick (1992).

essentially additive, with no apparent tendency toward either subadditivity or superadditivity.

Further evidence for binary complementarity comes from an extensive study conducted by Wallsten, Budescu, and Zwick (1992), who presented subjects with 300 propositions concerning world history and geography (e.g., "The Monroe Doctrine was proclaimed before the Republican Party was founded") and asked them to estimate the probability that each was true. True and false (complementary) versions of each proposition were presented on different days. Figure 25.3 plots the mean probabilities assigned to each of the propositions in both their true and false versions using the format of Fig. 25.2. Again, the judgments are additive (mean = 1.02) through the entire range.

We next present a brief summary of the major findings and list both current and previous studies supporting each conclusion.

Subadditivity. Unpacking an implicit hypothesis into its component hypotheses increases its total judged probability, yielding subadditive judgments. Tables 25.3 and 25.4 list studies that provide tests of the unpacking condition. For each experiment, the probability assigned to the implicit hypothesis and the total probability assigned to its components in the explicit disjunction are listed along with the resulting unpacking factor. All of the listed studies used an experimental design in which the implicit disjunction and the components of the explicit disjunction were evaluated independently, either by separate

Table 25.3. Results of Experiments Using Qualitative Hypotheses: Average Probability Assigned to Coextensional Implicit and Explicit Disjunctions and the Unpacking Factor Measuring the Degree of Subadditivity

Study and Topic	n	Explicit P	Implicit P	Unpacking Factor
Fischhoff, Slovic, & Lichtenstein (1978)				
Car failure, Experiment 1	4	0.54	.18	3.00
Car failure, Experiment 5	2	0.27	.20	1.35
Car failure, Experiment 6 (experts)	4	0.44	.22	2.00
Mehle, Gettys, Manning, Baca, & Fisher (1981): College majors	6	0.27	.18	1.50
Russo & Kolzow (1992)				
Causes of death	4	0.55	.45	1.22
Car failure	4	0.55	.27	2.04
Koehler & Tversky (1993)				
College majors	4	1.54	1.00[a]	1.54
College majors	5	2.51	1.00[a]	2.51
Study 1: Causes of death	3	0.61	.46	1.33
	7	0.70	.37	1.86
Study 4: Crime stories	4	1.71	1.00[a]	1.71
Study 5: College majors	4	1.76	1.00[a]	1.76

Note: The number of components in the explicit disjunction is denoted by *n*. Numbered studies with no citation refer to Tversky & Koehler, 1994.
[a] Because the components partition the space, it is assumed that a probability of 1.00 would have been assigned to the implicit disjunction.

groups of subjects or by the same subjects but with a substantial number of intervening judgments. The probabilities are listed as a function of the number of components in the explicit disjunction and are collapsed over all other independent variables. Table 25.3 lists studies in which subjects evaluated the probability of qualitative hypotheses (e.g., the probability that Bill W. majors in psychology); Table 25.4 lists studies in which subjects evaluated quantitative hypotheses (e.g., the probability that a randomly selected adult man is between 6 ft and 6 ft 2 in. tall).

Tables 25.3 and 25.4 show that the observed unpacking factors are, without exception, greater than one, indicating consistent subadditivity. The fact that subadditivity is observed both for qualitative and for quantitative hypotheses is instructive. Subadditivity in assessments of qualitative hypotheses can be explained, in part at least, by the failure to consider one or more component hypotheses when the event in question is described in an implicit form. The subadditivity observed in judgments of quantitative hypotheses, however, cannot be explained as a retrieval failure. For example, Teigen (1974b, Experiment 2) found that the judged proportion of college students whose

Table 25.4. Results of Experiments Using Quantitative Hypotheses: Average
Probability Assigned to Coextensional Implicit and Explicit Disjunctions
and the Unpacking Factor Measuring the Degree of Subadditivity

Study and Topic	n	Explicit P	Implicit P	Unpacking Factor
Teigen (1974b), Experiment 1:				
Binomial outcomes	2	0.66	.38	1.73
	3	0.84	.38	2.21
	5	1.62	1.00^a	1.62
	9	2.25	1.00^a	2.25
Teigen (1974b), Experiment 2:				
Heights of students	2	0.58	.36	1.61
	4	1.99	.76	2.62
	5	2.31	.75	3.07
	6	2.55	1.00^a	2.55
Teigen (1974a), Experiment 2:				
Binomial outcomes	11	4.25	1.00^a	4.25
Olson (1976), Experiment 1:				
Gender distribution	2	0.13	.10	1.30
	3	0.36	.21	1.71
	5	0.68	.40	1.70
	9	0.97	.38	2.55
Peterson and Pitz (1988),				
Experiment 3: Baseball victories	3	1.58	1.00^a	1.58
Tversky and Fox (1994):				
Uncertain quantities	2	0.77	.62	1.27
	3	1.02	.72	1.46
	4	1.21	.79	1.58
	5	1.40	.84	1.27
Study 2: Number of children	10	1.99	1.00^a	1.99

Note: The number of components in the explicit disjunction is denoted by n. Numbered study
with no citation refers to Tversky & Koehler, 1994.
[a] Because the components partition the space, it is assumed that a probability of 1.00 would
have been assigned to the implicit disjunction.

heights fell in a given interval increased when that interval was broken into
several smaller intervals that were assessed separately. Subjects evaluating the
implicit disjunction (i.e., the large interval), we suggest, did not overlook the
fact that the interval included several smaller intervals; rather, the unpacking
manipulation enhanced the salience of these intervals and, hence, their judged
probability. Subadditivity, therefore, is observed even in the absence of memory
limitations.

   Number of Components. The degree of subadditivity increases with the number of components in the explicit disjunction. This follows readily from support
theory: Unpacking an implicit hypothesis into exclusive components increases

Table 25.5. Results of Experiments Testing Binary
Complementarity: Average Total Probability Assigned to
Complementary Pairs of Hypotheses, Between-Subjects Standard
Deviations, and the Number of Subjects in the Experiment

Study and Topic	Mean Total P	SD	N
Wallsten, Budescu, & Zwick			
(1992): General knowledge	1.02	0.06	23
Tversky & Fox (1994)			
NBA playoff	1.00	0.07	27
Super Bowl	1.02	0.07	40
Dow Jones	1.00	0.10	40
San Francisco temperature	1.02	0.13	72
Beijing temperature	0.99	0.14	45
Koehler & Tversky (1993):			
College majors[a]	1.00		170
Study 2: Number of children[a]	0.97		139
Study 4: Crime stories[a]	1.03		60
Study 5: College majors[a]	1.05		115

Note: Numbered studies with no citation refer to Tversky & Koehler, 1994.
NBA = National Basketball Association.
[a] A given subject evaluated either the event or its complement, but not both.

its total judged probability, and additional unpacking of each component should further increase the total probability assigned to the initial hypothesis. Tables 25.3 and 25.4 show, as expected, that the unpacking factor generally increases with the number of components (see also Fig. 25.1).

Binary Complementarity. The judged probabilities of complementary pairs of hypotheses add to one. Table 25.5 lists studies that have tested this prediction. We considered only studies in which the hypothesis and its complement were evaluated independently, either by different subjects or by the same subjects but with a substantial number of intervening judgments. (We provide the standard deviations for the experiments that used the latter design.) Table 25.5 shows that such judgments generally add to one. Binary complementarity indicates that people evaluate a given hypothesis relative to its complement. Moreover, it rules out alternative interpretations of subadditivity in terms of a suggestion effect or a confirmation bias. These accounts imply a bias in favor of the focal hypothesis yielding $P(A, B) + P(B, A) > 1$, contrary to the experimental evidence. Alternatively, one might be tempted to attribute the subadditivity observed in probability judgments to subjects' lack of knowledge of the additivity principle of probability theory. This explanation, however, fails to account for the observed subadditivity in frequency judgments (in which additivity is obvious) and for the finding of binary complementarity (in which additivity is consistently satisfied).

The combination of binary complementarity and subadditive elementary judgments, implied by support theory, is inconsistent with both Bayesian and revisionist models. The Bayesian model implies that the unpacking factor should equal one because the unpacked and packed hypotheses have the same extension. Shafer's theory of belief functions and other models of lower probability require an unpacking factor of less than one, because they assume that the subjective probability (or belief) of the union of disjoint events is generally greater than the sum of the probabilities of its exclusive constituents. Furthermore, the data cannot be explained by the dual of the belief function (called the plausibility function) or, more generally, by an upper probability (e.g., see Dempster, 1967) because this model requires that the sum of the assessments of complementary events exceed unity, contrary to the evidence. Indeed, if $P(A, B) + P(B, A) = 1$ (see Table 25.5), then both upper and lower probability reduce to the standard additive model. The experimental findings, of course, do not invalidate the use of upper and lower probability, or belief functions, as formal systems for representing uncertainty. However, the evidence reviewed in this section indicates that these models are inconsistent with the principles that govern intuitive probability judgments.

Probability versus Frequency. Of the studies discussed earlier and listed in Tables 25.3 and 25.4, some (e.g., Fischhoff et al., 1978) used frequency judgments and others (e.g., Teigen, 1974a, 1974b) used probability judgments. The comparison of the two tasks, summarized in Table 25.6, confirms the predicted pattern: Subadditivity holds for both probability and frequency judgments, and the former are more subadditive than the latter.

Table 25.6. Results of Experiments Comparing Probability and Frequency Judgments: Unpacking Factor Computed From Mean Probability Assigned to Coextensional Explicit and Implicit Disjunctions

Study and Topic	n	Unpacking Factor	
		Probability	Frequency
Teigen (1974b)			
Experiment 1: Binomial outcomes	2	1.73	1.26
	5	2.21	1.09
	9	2.25	1.24
Teigen (1974b)			
Experiment 2: Heights of students	6	2.55	1.68
Koehler & Tversky (1993)			
College majors	4	1.72	1.37
Study 1: Causes of death	3	1.44	1.28
	7	2.00	1.84

Note: The number of components in the explicit disjunction is denoted by n. Numbered studies with no citation refer to Tversky & Koehler, 1994.

SCALING SUPPORT

In the formal theory developed in the preceding section, the support function is derived from probability judgments. Is it possible to reverse the process and predict probability judgments from direct assessments of evidence strength? Let $\hat{s}(A)$ be the rating of the strength of evidence for hypothesis A. What is the relation between such ratings and the support estimated from probability judgments? Perhaps the most natural assumption is that the two scales are monotonically related; that is, $\hat{s}(A) \geq \hat{s}(B)$ if and only if (iff) $s(A) \geq s(B)$. This assumption implies, for example, that $P(A, B) \geq \frac{1}{2}$ iff $\hat{s}(A) \geq \hat{s}(B)$, but it does not determine the functional form relating $\hat{s}$ and s. To further specify the relation between the scales, it may be reasonable to assume, in addition, that support ratios are also monotonically related. That is, $\hat{s}(A)/\hat{s}(B) \geq \hat{s}(C)/\hat{s}(D)$ iff $s(A)/s(B) \geq s(C)/s(D)$.

It can be shown that if the two monotonicity conditions are satisfied, and both scales are defined, say, on the unit interval, then there exists a constant $k > 0$ such that the support function derived from probability judgments and the support function assessed directly are related by a power transformation of the form $s = \hat{s}^k$. This gives rise to the *power model*

$$R(A, B) = P(A, B)/P(B, A) = [\hat{s}(A)/\hat{s}(B)]^k,$$

yielding

$$\log R(A, B) = k \log[\hat{s}(A)/\hat{s}(B)].$$

We next use this model to predict judged probability from independent assessments of evidence strength obtained in two studies.

Study 3: Basketball Games

Subjects ($N = 88$) were NBA fans who subscribe to a computer news group. We posted a questionnaire to this news group and asked readers to complete and return it by electronic mail within 1 week. In the questionnaire, subjects assessed the probability that the home team would win in each of 20 upcoming games. These 20 outcomes constituted all possible matches among five teams (Phoenix, Portland, Los Angeles Lakers, Golden State, and Sacramento) from the Pacific Division of the NBA, constructed such that, for each pair of teams, two games were evaluated (one for each possible game location). Use of this "expert" population yielded highly reliable judgments, as shown, among other things, by the fact that the median value of the correlation between an individual subject's ratings and the set of mean judgments was .93.

After making their probability judgments, subjects rated the strength of each of the five teams. The participants were instructed:

First, choose the team you believe is the strongest of the five, and set that team's strength to 100. Assign the remaining teams ratings in proportion to the strength of the

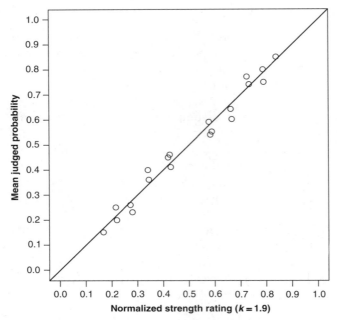

Figure 25.4. Judged probability for basketball games as a function of normalized strength ratings.

strongest team. For example, if you believe that a given team is half as strong as the strongest team (the team you gave a 100), give that team a strength rating of 50.

We interpreted these ratings as a direct assessment of support.

Because the strength ratings did not take into account the home court effect, we collapsed the probability judgments across the two possible locations of the match. The slope of the regression line predicting $\log R(A, B)$ from $\log [\hat{s}(A)/\hat{s}(B)]$ provided an estimate of k for each subject. The median estimate of k was 1.8, and the mean was 2.2; the median R^2 for this analysis was .87. For the aggregate data, k was 1.9 and the resulting R^2 was .97. The scatterplot in Fig. 25.4 exhibits excellent correspondence between mean prediction based on team strength and mean judged probability. This result suggests that the power model can be used to predict judged probability from assessments of strength that make no reference to chance or uncertainty. It also reinforces the psychological interpretation of s as a measure of evidence strength.

Study 4: Crime Stories

This study was designed to investigate the relation between judged probability and assessed support in a very different context and to explore the enhancement effect, described in the next subsection. To this end, we adapted a task introduced by Teigen (1983) and Robinson and Hastie (1985) and presented subjects with two criminal cases. The first was an embezzlement at a computer-parts manufacturing company involving four suspects (a manager, a buyer, an accountant, and a seller). The second case was a murder that also involved four suspects (an activist, an artist, a scientist, and a writer). In both cases, subjects were informed that exactly one suspect was guilty. In the low-information condition, the four suspects in each case were introduced with a short description of their role and possible motive. In the high-information condition, the motive of each suspect was strengthened. In a manner resembling the typical mystery novel, we constructed each case so that all the suspects seemed generally more suspicious as more evidence was revealed.

Subjects evaluated the suspects after reading the low-information material and again after reading the high-information material. Some subjects ($N = 60$) judged the probability that a given suspect was guilty. Each of these subjects made two elementary judgments (that a particular suspect was guilty) and three binary judgments (that Suspect A rather than Suspect B was guilty) in each case. Other subjects ($N = 55$) rated the suspiciousness of a given suspect, which we took as a direct assessment of support. These subjects rated two suspects per case by providing a number between 0 (indicating that the suspect was "not at all suspicious") and 100 (indicating that the suspect was "maximally suspicious") in proportion to the suspiciousness of the suspect.

As in the previous study, we assumed binary complementarity and estimated k by a logarithmic regression of $R(A, B)$ against the suspiciousness ratio. For these data, k was estimated to be .84, and R^2 was .65. Rated suspiciousness, therefore, provides a reasonable predictor of the judged probability of guilt. However, the relation between judged probability and assessed support was stronger in the basketball study than in the crime study. Furthermore, the estimate of k was much smaller in the latter than in the former. In the basketball study, a team that was rated twice as strong as another was judged more than twice as likely to win; in the crime stories, however, a character who was twice as suspicious as another was judged less than twice as likely to be guilty. This difference may be due to the fact that the judgments of team strength were based on more solid data than the ratings of suspiciousness. . . .

The Enhancement Effect

Recall that assessed support is noncompensatory in the sense that evidence that increases the support of one hypothesis does not necessarily decrease the support of competing hypotheses. In fact, it is possible for new evidence to increase the support of all elementary hypotheses. We have proposed that such evidence will enhance subadditivity. In this section, we describe several tests of enhancement and compare support theory with the Bayesian model and with Shafer's theory.

We start with an example discussed earlier, in which one of several suspects has committed a murder. To simplify matters, assume that there are four suspects who, in the absence of specific evidence (low information), are considered equally likely to be guilty. Suppose further evidence is then introduced (high information) that implicates each of the suspects to roughly the same degree, so that they remain equally probable. Let L and H denote the evidence available under low and high information conditions, respectively. Let $\bar{A}$ denote the negation of A; that is, "Suspect A is not guilty." According to the Bayesian model, then, $P(A, B \mid H) = P(A, B \mid L) = \frac{1}{2}$, $P(A, \bar{A} \mid H) = P(A, \bar{A} \mid L) = \frac{1}{4}$, and so forth.

In contrast, Shafer's (1976) belief-function approach requires that the probabilities assigned to each of the suspects add to less than one and suggests that the total will be higher in the presence of direct evidence (i.e., in the high-information condition) than in its absence. As a consequence, $\frac{1}{2} \geq P(A, B \mid H) \geq P(A, B \mid L)$, $\frac{1}{4} \geq P(A, \bar{A} \mid H) \geq P(A, \bar{A} \mid L)$, and so forth. In other words, both the binary and the elementary judgments are expected to increase as more evidence is encountered. In the limit, when no belief is held in reserve, the binary judgments approach one-half and the elementary judgments approach one-fourth.

The enhancement assumption yields a different pattern; namely, $P(A, B \mid H) = P(A, B \mid L) = \frac{1}{2}$, $P(A, \bar{A} \mid H) \geq P(A, \bar{A} \mid L) \geq \frac{1}{4}$, and so forth. As in the Bayesian model, the binary judgments are one-half; in contrast to that model, however, the elementary judgments are expected to exceed one-fourth and to be greater under high- than under low-information conditions. Although both support theory and the belief-function approach yield greater elementary judgments under high- than under low-information conditions, support theory predicts that they will exceed one-fourth in both conditions, whereas Shafer's theory requires that these probabilities be less than or equal to one-fourth.

The assumption of equally probable suspects is not essential for the analysis. Suppose that initially the suspects are not equally probable, but the new evidence does not change the binary probabilities. Here, too, the Bayesian model requires additive judgments that do not differ between low- and high-information conditions; the belief-function approach requires superadditive judgments that become less superadditive as more information is encountered; and the enhancement assumption predicts subadditive judgments that become more subadditive with the addition of (compatible) evidence.

Evaluating Suspects

With these predictions in mind, we turn to the crime stories of Study 4. Table 25.7 displays the mean suspiciousness ratings and elementary probability judgments of each suspect in the two cases under low- and high-information conditions. The table shows that, in all cases, the sums of both probability judgments and suspiciousness ratings exceed one. Evidently, subadditivity holds not only in probability judgment, but also in ratings of evidence strength or degree of belief (e.g., that a given subject is guilty). Further examination of the suspiciousness ratings shows that all but one of the suspects increased in suspiciousness as more information was provided. In accord with our prediction, the judged probability of each of these suspects also increased with the added

Table 25.7. Mean Suspiciousness Rating and Judged Probability of Each Suspect Under Low- and High-Information Conditions

	Suspiciousness		Probability	
Case and Suspect	Low Information	High Information	Low Information	High Information
Case 1: Embezzlement				
Accountant	41	53	40	45
Buyer	50	58	42	48
Manager	47	51	48	59
Seller	32	48	37	42
Total	170	210	167	194
Case 2: Murder				
Activist	32	57	39	57
Artist	27	23	37	30
Scientist	24	43	34	40
Writer	38	60	33	54
Total	122	184	143	181

information, indicating enhanced subadditivity (see Eq. 10). The one exception was the artist in the murder case, who was given an alibi in the high-information condition and, as one would expect, subsequently decreased both in suspiciousness and in probability. Overall, both the suspiciousness ratings and the probability judgments were significantly greater under high- than under low-information conditions ($p < .001$ for both cases by t test).

From a normative standpoint, the support (i.e., suspiciousness) of all the suspects could increase with new information, but an increase in the probability of one suspect should be compensated for by a decrease in the probability of the others. The observation that new evidence can increase the judged probability of all suspects was made earlier by Robinson and Hastie (1985; Van Wallendael & Hastie, 1990). Their method differed from ours in that each subject assessed the probability of all suspects, but this method also produced substantial subadditivity, with a typical unpacking factor of about two. These authors rejected the Bayesian model as a descriptive account and proposed Shafer's theory as one viable alternative. As was noted earlier, however, the observed subadditivity is inconsistent with Shafer's theory, as well as the Bayesian model, but it is consistent with the present account.

In the crime stories, the added evidence was generally compatible with all of the hypotheses under consideration. Peterson and Pitz (1988, Experiment 3), however, observed a similar effect with mixed evidence, which favored some hypotheses but not others. Their subjects were asked to assess the probability that the number of games won by a baseball team in a season fell in a given interval on the basis of one, two, or three cues (team batting average, earned run average, and total home runs during that season). Unbeknownst to subjects, they were asked, over a large number of problems, to assign probabilities to all three components in a partition (e.g., less than 80 wins, between 80 and 88 wins, and more than 88 wins). As the number of cues increased, subjects assigned a greater probability, on average, to all three intervals in the partition, thus exhibiting enhanced subadditivity. The unpacking factors for these data were 1.26, 1.61, and 1.86 for one, two, and three cues, respectively. These results attest to the robustness of the enhancement effect, which is observed even when the added evidence favors some, but not all, of the hypotheses under study. . . .

Implications

To this point, we have focused on the direct consequences of support theory. We conclude this section by discussing the conjunction effect, hypothesis generation, and decision under uncertainty from the perspective of support theory.

The Conjunction Effect

Considerable research has documented the *conjunction effect*, in which a conjunction AB is judged more probable than one of its constituents A. The effect is strongest when an event that initially seems unlikely (e.g., a massive flood in North America in which more than 1,000 people drown) is supplemented by a plausible cause or qualification (e.g., an earthquake in California causing a flood in which more than 1,000 people drown), yielding a conjunction that is perceived as more probable than the initially implausible event of which it is a proper subset (Tversky & Kahneman, 1983). Support theory suggests that the implicit hypothesis A is not unpacked into the coextensional disjunction $AB \vee A\bar{B}$ of which the conjunction is one component. As a result, evidence supporting AB is not taken to support A. In the flood problem, for instance, the possibility of a flood caused by an earthquake may not come readily to mind; thus, unless it is mentioned explicitly, it does not contribute any support to the (implicit) flood hypothesis. Support theory implies that the conjunction effect would be eliminated in these problems if the implicit disjunction were unpacked before its evaluation (e.g., if subjects were reminded that a flood might be caused by excessive rainfall or by structural damage to a reservoir caused by an earthquake, an engineering error, sabotage, etc.).

The greater tendency to unpack either the focal or the residual hypothesis in a frequentistic formulation may help explain the finding that conjunction effects are attenuated, although not eliminated, when subjects estimate frequency rather than probability. For example, the proportion of subjects who judged the conjunction "X is over 55 years old and has had at least one heart attack" as more probable than the constituent event "X has had at least one heart attack" was significantly greater in a probabilistic formulation than in a frequentistic formulation (Tversky & Kahneman, 1983).

It might be instructive to distinguish two different unpacking operations. In *conjunctive unpacking*, an (implicit) hypothesis (e.g., nurse) is broken down into exclusive conjunctions (e.g., male nurse and female nurse). Most, but not all initial demonstrations of the conjunction effect were based on conjunctive unpacking. In *categorical unpacking*, a superordinate category (e.g., unnatural death) is broken down into its "natural" components (e.g., car accident, drowning, homicide). Most of the demonstrations reported in this chapter are based on categorical unpacking. A conjunction effect using categorical unpacking has been described by Bar-Hillel and Neter (1993; Chapter 3, this volume).

Hypothesis Generation

All of the studies reviewed thus far asked subjects to assess the probability of hypotheses presented to them for judgment. There are many situations, however, in which a judge must generate hypotheses as well as assess their likelihood. In the current treatment, the generation of alternative hypotheses entails some unpacking of the residual hypothesis and, thus, is expected to increase its support relative to the focal hypothesis. In the absence of explicit instructions to generate alternative hypotheses, people are less likely to unpack the residual hypothesis and thus tend to overestimate specified hypotheses relative to those left unspecified.

This implication has been confirmed by Gettys and his colleagues (Gettys, Mehle, & Fisher, 1986; Mehle et al., 1981), who have found that, in comparison with veridical values, people generally tend to overestimate the probability of specified hypotheses presented to them for evaluation. Indeed, overconfidence that one's judgment is correct (e.g., Lichtenstein, Fischhoff, & Phillips, 1982) may sometimes arise because the focal hypothesis is specified, whereas its alternatives often are not. Mehle et al. (1981) used two manipulations to encourage unpacking of the residual hypothesis: One group of subjects was provided with exemplar members of the residual, and another was asked to generate its own examples. Both manipulations improved performance by decreasing the probability assigned to specified alternatives and increasing that assigned to the residual. These results suggest that the effects of hypothesis generation are due to the additional hypotheses it brings to mind, because simply providing hypotheses to the subject has the same effect. Using a similar manipulation, Dube-Rioux and Russo (1988) found that generation of alternative hypotheses increased the judged probability of the residual relative to that of specified categories and attenuated the effect of omitting a category. Examination of the number of instances generated by the subjects showed that, when enough instances were produced, the effect of category omission was eliminated altogether.

Now consider a task in which subjects are asked to generate a hypothesis (e.g., to guess which film will win the best picture Oscar at the next Academy Awards ceremony) before assessing its probability. Asking subjects to generate the most likely hypothesis might actually lead them to consider several candidates in the process of settling on the one they prefer. This process amounts to a partial unpacking of the residual hypothesis, which should decrease the judged probability of the focal hypothesis. Consistent with this prediction, one study (Koehler, 1994) found that subjects asked to generate their own hypotheses assigned them a lower probability of being true than did other subjects presented with the same hypotheses for evaluation. The interpretation of these results – that hypothesis generation makes alternative hypotheses more salient – was tested by two further manipulations. First, providing a closed set of specified alternatives eliminated the difference between the generation and evaluation conditions. In these circumstances, the residual should be represented in the same way in both conditions. Second, inserting a distracter task between hypothesis generation and probability assessment was sufficient to reduce the salience of alternatives brought to mind by the generation task, increasing the judged probability of the focal hypothesis.

Decision under Uncertainty

This article has focused primarily on numeric judgments of probability. In decision theory, however, subjective probabilities are generally inferred from preferences between uncertain prospects rather than assessed directly. It is natural to inquire, then, whether unpacking affects people's decisions as well as their numeric judgments. There is considerable evidence that it does. For example, Johnson et al. (1993) observed that subjects were willing to pay more for flight insurance that explicitly listed certain events covered by the policy (e.g., death resulting from an act of terrorism or mechanical failure) than for a more inclusive policy that did not list specific events (e.g., death from any cause).

Unpacking can affect decisions in two ways: First, as has been shown, unpacking tends to increase the judged probability of an uncertain event. Second, unpacking can increase an event's impact on the decision, even when its probability is known. For example, Tversky and Kahneman (1986) asked subjects to choose between two lotteries that paid different amounts depending on the color of a marble drawn from a box. (As an inducement to consider the options with care, subjects were informed that one-tenth of the participants, selected at random, would actually play the gambles they chose.) Two different versions of the problem were used, which differed only in the description of the outcomes. The fully unpacked Version 1 was as follows:

Box A:	90% White	6% Red	1% Green	1% Blue	2% Yellow
	$0	Win $45	Win $30	Lose $15	Lose $15

Box B:	90% White	6% Red	1% Green	1% Blue	2% Yellow
	$0	Win $45	Win $45	Lose $10	Lose $15

It is not difficult to see that Box B dominates Box A; indeed, all subjects chose Box B in this version. Version 2 combined the two outcomes resulting in a loss of $15 in Box A (i.e., Blue and Yellow) and the two outcomes resulting in a gain of $45 in Box B (i.e., Red and Green):

Box A:	90% White	6% Red	1% Green	3% Yellow/Blue
	$0	Win $45	Win $30	Lose $15

Box B:	90% White	7% Red/Green	1% Blue	2% Yellow
	$0	Win $45	Lose $10	Lose $15

In accord with subadditivity, the combination of events yielding the same outcome makes Box A more attractive because it packs two losses into one and makes Box B less attractive because it packs two gains into one. Indeed, 58% of subjects chose Box A in Version 2, even though it was dominated by Box B. Starmer and Sugden (1993) further investigated the effect of unpacking events with known probabilities (which they called an event-splitting effect) and found that a prospect generally becomes more attractive when an event that yields a positive outcome is unpacked into two components. Such results demonstrate that unpacking affects decisions even when the probabilities are explicitly stated.

The role of unpacking in choice was further illustrated by Redelmeier et al. (1995). Graduating medical students at the University of Toronto ($N = 149$) were presented with a medical scenario concerning a middle-age man suffering acute shortness of breath. Half of the respondents were given a packed description that noted that, "obviously, many diagnoses are possible ... including pneumonia." The other half were given an unpacked description that mentioned other potential diagnoses (pulmonary embolus, heart failure, asthma, and lung cancer) in addition to pneumonia. The respondents were asked whether they would prescribe antibiotics in such a case, a treatment that is effective against pneumonia but not against the other potential diagnoses mentioned in the unpacked version. The unpacking manipulation was expected to reduce the perceived probability of pneumonia and, hence, the respondents' inclination to prescribe antibiotics. Indeed, a significant majority (64%) of respondents given the unpacked description chose not to prescribe antibiotics, whereas respondents given the packed description were almost evenly divided between prescribing (47%) and not prescribing them. Singling out pneumonia increased the tendency to select a treatment that is effective for pneumonia, even though the presenting symptoms were clearly consistent with a number of well-known alternative diagnoses. Evidently, unpacking can affect decisions, not only probability assessments.

Although unpacking plays an important role in probability judgment, the cognitive mechanism underlying this effect is considerably more general. Thus, one would expect unpacking effects even in tasks that do not involve uncertain events. For example, van der Pligt, Eiser, and Spears (1987, Experiment 1) asked subjects to assess the current and ideal distribution of five power sources (nuclear, coal, oil, hydro, solar/wind/wave) and found that a given power source was assigned a higher estimate when it was evaluated on its own than when its four alternatives were unpacked (see also Fiedler & Armbruster, 1994; Pelham, Sumarta, & Myaskovsky, 1994). Such results indicate that the effects of unpacking reflect a general characteristic of human judgment.

EXTENSIONS

We have presented a nonextensional theory of belief in which judged probability is given by the relative support, or strength of evidence, of the respective focal and alternative hypotheses. In this theory, support is additive for explicit disjunctions of exclusive hypotheses and subadditive for implicit disjunctions. The empirical evidence confirms the major predictions of support theory: (1) Probability judgments increase by unpacking the focal hypothesis and decrease by unpacking the alternative hypothesis; (2) subjective probabilities are complementary in the binary case and subadditive in the general case; and (3) subadditivity is more pronounced for probability than for frequency judgments, and it is enhanced by compatible evidence. Support theory also provides a method for predicting judged probability from independent assessments of evidence strength. Thus, it accounts for a wide range of empirical findings in terms of a single explanatory construct. . . .

Prescriptive Implications

Models of subjective probability or degree of belief serve two functions: descriptive and prescriptive. The literature on nonstandard probability models is primarily prescriptive. These models are offered as formal languages for the evaluation of evidence and the representation of belief. In contrast, support theory attempts to describe the manner in which people make probability judgments, not to prescribe how people should make these judgments. For example, the proposition that judged probability increases by unpacking the focal hypothesis and decreases by unpacking the alternative hypothesis represents a general descriptive principle that is not endorsed by normative theories, additive or nonadditive.

Despite its descriptive nature, support theory has prescriptive implications. It could aid the design of elicitation procedures and the reconciliation of inconsistent assessments (Lindley, Tversky, & Brown, 1979). This role may be illuminated by a perceptual analogy. Suppose a surveyor has to construct a map of a park on the basis of judgments of distance between landmarks made by a fallible observer. A knowledge of the likely biases of the observer could help the surveyor construct a better map. Because observers generally underestimate distances involving hidden areas, for example, the surveyor may discard these assessments and compute the respective distances from other assessments using the laws of plane geometry. Alternatively, the surveyor may wish to reduce the bias by applying a suitable correction factor to the estimates involving hidden areas. The same logic applies to the elicitation of probability. The evidence shows that people tend to underestimate the probability of an implicit disjunction, especially the negation of an elementary hypothesis. This bias may be reduced by asking the judge to contrast hypotheses of comparable level of specificity instead of assessing the probability of a specific hypothesis against its complement.

The major conclusion of the present research is that subjective probability, or degree of belief, is nonextensional and hence nonmeasurable in the sense that alternative partitions of the space can yield different judgments. Like the measured length of a coastline, which increases as a map becomes more detailed, the perceived likelihood of an event increases as its description becomes more specific. This does not imply that judged probability is of no value, but it indicates that this concept is more fragile than suggested by existing formal theories. The failures of extensionality demonstrated in this article highlight what is perhaps the fundamental problem of probability assessment – namely, the need to consider unavailable possibilities. The problem is especially severe in tasks that require the generation of new hypotheses or the construction of novel scenarios. The extensionality principle, we argue, is normatively unassailable but practically unachievable because the judge cannot be expected to fully unpack any implicit disjunction. People can be encouraged to unpack a category into its components, but they cannot be expected to think of all relevant conjunctive unpackings or to generate all relevant future scenarios. In this respect, the assessment of an additive probability distribution may be an impossible task. The judge could, of course, ensure the additivity of any given set of judgments, but this does not ensure that additivity will be preserved by further refinement.

The evidence reported here and elsewhere indicates that both qualitative and quantitative assessments of uncertainty are not carried out in a logically coherent fashion, and one might be tempted to conclude that they should not be carried out at all. However, this is not a viable option because, in general, there are no alternative procedures for assessing uncertainty. Unlike the measurement of distance, in which fallible human judgment can be replaced by proper physical measurement, there are no objective procedures for assessing the probability of events such as the guilt of a defendant, the success of a business venture, or the outbreak of war. Intuitive judgments of uncertainty, therefore, are bound to play an essential role in people's deliberations and decisions. The question of how to improve their quality through the design of effective elicitation methods and corrective procedures poses a major challenge to theorists and practitioners alike.

26. Unpacking, Repacking, and Anchoring: Advances in Support Theory

Yuval Rottenstreich and Amos Tversky

The study of intuitive probability judgment has shown that people often do not follow the extensional logic of probability theory (see, e.g., Kahneman, Slovic, & Tversky, 1982). In particular, alternative descriptions of the same event can give rise to different probability judgments, and a specific event (e.g., that 1,000 people will die in an earthquake) may appear more likely than a more inclusive event (e.g., that 1,000 people will die in a natural disaster). To accommodate such findings, Tversky and Koehler (1994) have developed a nonextensional theory of belief in which subjective probability is not attached to events, as in other models, but to descriptions of events, called *hypotheses*. According to this account, called *support theory*, each hypothesis A has a support value, $s(A)$, corresponding to the strength of the evidence for this hypothesis. The judged probability, $P(A, B)$, that hypothesis A rather than B holds, assuming that one and only one of them obtains, is given by

$$P(A, B) = \frac{s(A)}{s(A) + s(B)}$$

Thus, judged probability is interpreted in terms of the support of the focal hypothesis A relative to the alternative hypothesis B. The key assumption of support theory is that unpacking a description of an event (e.g., a plane crash, C) into disjoint components (e.g., an accidental plane crash, C_a, caused by human error or mechanical failure; or a nonaccidental plane crash, C_n, caused by terrorism or sabotage) generally increases its support. Thus, the support of the explicit disjunction $C_a \vee C_n$ is equal to or greater than the support of the implicit disjunction C that does not mention any cause; that is, $s(C) \le s(C_a \vee C_n)$. The rationale for this assumption is twofold. First, unpacking an implicit hypothesis may remind people of possibilities they might have overlooked. Second, the explicit mention of a possibility tends to increase its salience and hence its perceived support.

Support theory provides a unified framework for the analysis and the interpretation of a wide range of findings. It predicts that the judged probability of an event increases by unpacking the focal hypothesis and decreases by

This is an edited version of a paper that first appeared in *Psychological Review, 104,* 406–415. Copyright © 1997 by the American Psychological Association. Adapted with permission.

unpacking the alternative hypothesis. For instance, the judged probability that a given person will die a natural rather than an unnatural death increases by listing various causes of natural death (e.g., heart attack, stroke, cancer) and decreases by listing various causes of unnatural death (e.g., car accident, homicide, fire). Furthermore, support theory implies that the judged probability of a hypothesis plus the judged probability of its complement, evaluated by different groups of participants, adds up to one. For finer partitions, however, the sum of the judged probabilities of a set of mutually exclusive and exhaustive hypotheses generally is greater than one. These predictions have been confirmed in numerous studies; earlier experiments are reviewed by Tversky and Koehler (1994), some later experiments are discussed by Fox and Tversky (1998).

This article presents a significant generalization of support theory that allows subadditivity for explicit disjunctions. To illustrate this extension, consider the possibilities that the winner of the next presidential election in the United States will be a Democrat (*Dem*), a Republican (*Rep*), or an Independent (*Ind*). The original version of support theory assumes that support is additive for explicit disjunctions, such that $s(Rep \vee Ind) = s(Rep) + s(Ind)$, and consequently, judged probability (P) is also additive for explicit disjunctions, as in the standard theory of probability. As shown next, however, several observations suggest that support is subadditive for explicit disjunctions, such that $s(Rep \vee Ind) \leq s(Rep) + s(Ind)$, and hence

$$P(Rep \vee Ind, Dem) \leq P(Rep, Dem \vee Ind) + P(Ind, Rep \vee Dem).$$

That is, the judged probability that the winner of the upcoming election will be a Republican or an Independent rather than a Democrat is less than or equal to the judged probability that the winner will be a Republican rather than a Democrat or an Independent plus the judged probability that the winner will be an Independent rather than a Republican or a Democrat. More generally, we assume that if A and B are mutually exclusive hypotheses, and (A_1, A_2) is recognized as a partition of A, then $s(A) \leq s(A_1 \vee A_2) \leq s(A_1) + s(A_2)$. This assumption regarding the support function s imposes the following constraints on the observed measure P. In particular, the left inequality implies a testable condition, called *implicit subadditivity*,

$$
\begin{aligned}
P(A, B) &= \frac{s(A)}{s(A) + s(B)} \\
&\leq \frac{s(A_1 \vee A_2)}{s(A_1 \vee A_2) + s(B)} \quad \text{because } s(A) \leq s(A_1 \vee A_2) \\
&= P(A_1 \vee A_2, B)
\end{aligned}
$$

and the right inequality implies a second testable condition, called *explicit subadditivity,*

$$P(A_1 \lor A_2, B) = \frac{s(A_1 \lor A_2)}{s(A_1 \lor A_2) + s(B)}$$

$$\leq \frac{s(A_1) + s(A_2)}{s(A_1) + s(A_2) + s(B)} \text{ because } s(A_1 \lor A_2) \leq s(A_1) + s(A_2)$$

$$\leq \frac{s(A_1)}{s(A_1) + s(B \lor A_2)} + \frac{s(A_2)}{s(A_2) + s(B \lor A_1)}$$

by the same logic

$$= P(A_1, B \lor A_2) + P(A_2, B \lor A_1).$$

Note that probability theory requires additivity throughout, whereas the theory of belief functions (Shafer, 1976) assumes superadditivity. Thus, support theory and Shafer's theory depart from the probability calculus in opposite directions. The contrast between the two theories is discussed in the last section.

Before addressing the cognitive processes that give rise to explicit subadditivity, we discuss three issues regarding the interpretation of support theory. First, we wish to emphasize that the predictions of the theory, notably binary complementarity – that is, $P(A, B) + P(B, A) = 1$ – concern hypotheses, not events. This distinction is particularly important in tasks where the alternative to the focal hypothesis is not explicitly stated. Consider, for example, the outcome of a race between an incumbent and a challenger, and let *In* denote the hypothesis that the incumbent will win the race and *Ch* denote the hypothesis that the challenger will win the race. Support theory implies that the judged probability of *In* plus the judged probability of not-*In* (i.e., the incumbent will not win the race) equals one, but the theory is not committed to the prediction that the judged probability of *In* plus the judged probability of *Ch* will equal one. In this simple example it is immediately obvious that *Ch* is the same as not-*In*; therefore, additivity is likely to hold, assuming it is clear that there are no other candidates and that ties are excluded. However, when the hypotheses under discussion are more complicated and the setting is less familiar, additivity need not hold (see Gonzales & Bonini, 1995; Macchi, Osherson, & Legrenzi, 1995).

Second, the unpacking inequality $s(A) \leq s(A_1 \lor A_2)$ is assumed to hold only when the judge knows, or believes, that $A_1 \lor A_2$ has the same extension as A. Thus, the theory predicts that the judged probability that a patient has meningitis (M), for example, is less than or equal to the judged probability that the patient has either viral meningitis or nonviral meningitis because their disjunction is clearly coextensional with M. However, the theory does not require that the judged probability of meningitis will be less than or equal to the judged probability of either viral meningitis (M_v) or bacterial meningitis (M_b), unless the judge happens to know $M_v \lor M_b$ is coexten-sional with M. Note that a judge presented with the explicit disjunction $M_v \lor M_b$ may recognize that it has the same extension as the implicit dis-junction M even though, presented with M alone, the judge may not be able to unpack it into M_u and M_b. Thus, the theory permits recognition without recall.

Third, the present theory expresses an observed probability judgment, $P(A, B)$, in terms of the underlying support, $s(A)$ and $s(B)$, of the individual hypotheses. Although it is possible, in some cases, to predict judged probability from independent assessments of support (see Tversky & Koehler, 1994), the present theory treats support as a psychological construct derived from proba-bility judgment. A formal statement of the theory is presented in the Appendix in Rottenstreich and Tversky (1997). It provides necessary and sufficient con-ditions for the representation of probability judgments in terms of subadditive support; it also provides a simple method for constructing an essentially unique support function from observed judgments of probability.

Let us turn now from the interpretation of support theory to the main topic of this article, namely the psychological processes that can produce explicit sub-additivity. More specifically, we investigate two such mechanisms, repacking and anchoring, that are discussed in turn.

As noted in the original version of the theory, a judge presented with an explicit disjunction may, nevertheless, think about it as an implicit disjunction, and vice versa. Consider, for example, the probability that a particular student majors in industrial, mechanical, or electrical engineering. A judge presented with such an explicit disjunction may repack the various disciplines and eval-uate the implicit disjunction *engineering*. Because unpacking increases support, repacking reduces support giving rise to explicit subadditivity. Furthermore, we expect more explicit subadditivity for disjunctions of similar components than for disjunctions of dissimilar components because similar components are more easily repacked.

A second source of explicit subadditivity is the use of anchoring and adjust-ment. Instead of assessing independently the support of each component of an explicit disjunction and then adding the separate assessments, the judge may assess one of the components (perhaps the larger or the more familiar) and then adjust this value upward to accommodate the other components. Because such adjustments are generally insufficient (Poulton, 1994; Slovic & Lichtenstein, 1968; Tversky & Kahneman, 1974), the use of this heuristic is likely to produce explicit subadditivity. An individual who is asked to assess the combined pop-ulation of the United States and Canada, for example, may anchor on the U.S. population and then adjust it upward, without making an explicit assessment of the population of Canada. If frequency, probability, or support are evaluated in this manner, we expect subadditivity for explicit disjunctions, even if their components are not repacked.

STUDY 1: IMPLICIT AND EXPLICIT SUBADDITIVITY

Study 1 uses two problems that have the same formal structure. Let A_1, A_2, and B denote three mutually exclusive and exhaustive hypotheses, and let A be an implicit disjunction of A_1 and A_2. In each problem, different groups of participants evaluated the implicit disjunction $P(A, B)$, the explicit disjunction $P(A_1 \vee A_2, B)$, the component, $P(A_1, A_2 \vee B)$, and the component $P(A_2, A_1 \vee B)$.

A total of 178 Stanford students participated in the study to fulfill course requirements. They were divided into four groups of roughly equal size. Every group evaluated both problems, each in a different condition. The first problem concerns the outcome of the next presidential election in the United States. Participants in the implicit group evaluated "the probability that the winner of the next presidential election will not be a Democrat." Participants in the explicit group evaluated the probability that "the winner of the next presidential election will be a Republican or an Independent rather than a Democrat." Participants in the two remaining groups evaluated either "the probability that the winner of the next presidential election will be a Republican rather than a Democrat or an Independent" or "the probability that the winner of the next presidential election will be an Independent rather than a Democrat or a Republican."

The second problem concerns the outcome of a criminal trial. All participants read the following scenario:

Susan L. has accused her boss, Frank G., of unwelcome sexual advances and the promise of promotion in exchange for sexual favors. Frank G. denies any wrongdoing. The case has been brought before a jury consisting of seven men and five women. There were no eyewitnesses, but Susan's boyfriend has testified that she told him about the incidents in question. The jury is now deliberating.

Participants in the implicit group evaluated "the probability that this trial will not result in a guilty verdict." Participants in the explicit group evaluated "the probability of either a not guilty verdict or a hung jury rather than a guilty verdict." Participants in the two remaining groups evaluated either "the probability of a not guilty verdict rather than a guilty verdict or a hung jury" or "the probability of a hung jury rather than a not guilty verdict or a guilty verdict."

Table 26.1 presents median probability judgments for each of the two problems. Although support theory does not require strict inequalities for implicit and explicit subadditivity, the statistical tests reported in this article test the strict version of these inequalities against the null hypothesis of equality. In particular, we used the Mann–Whitney statistic to test the hypothesis that the judged probability of the implicit disjunction, $P(A, B)$, is strictly smaller than the judged probability of the explicit disjunction, $P(A_1 \vee A_2, B)$. This analysis provides some evidence for implicit subadditivity in Problem 2($p < .05$, one-sided) but not in Problem 1. We used the same statistic to test the hypothesis that the judged probability of the explicit disjunction, $P(A_1 \vee A_2, B)$, is strictly smaller than the sum of the judged probabilities of the single components, $P(A_1, A_2 \vee B) +$

Table 26.1. Median Probability Judgments Used to Test Implicit and Explicit Subadditivity in Study 1

Probability Judgments	Problem 1: Presidential Election	Problem 2: Criminal Trial
$\alpha = P(A, B)$	60	50
$\beta = P(A_1 \vee A_2, B)$	60	60
$\gamma = P(A_1, A_2 \vee B)$	59	58
$\delta = P(A_2, A_1, \vee B)$	5	40

Note: In Problem 1, $A_1 = $ Republican, $A_2 = $ Independent, $A = $ not Democrat, and $B = $ Democrat. In Problem 2, $A_1 = $ not guilty, $A_2 = $ hung jury, $A = $ result other than guilty, and $B = $ guilty.

$P(A_2, A_1 \vee B)$. Because the latter were assessed by different groups of participants, we generated 100 "synthetic" distributions of such sums by pairing at random participants from the two groups. The median of the Mann–Whitney statistics across these distributions was significant in both Problem 1 (median $p < .05$) and Problem 2 (median $p < .0001$). Thus, strict explicit subadditivity was confirmed for both problems, and strict implicit subadditivity was observed in the trial problem but not in the election problem. The latter observation is not too surprising because here the implicit disjunction, non-Democrat, is naturally unpacked into the explicit disjunction, Republican or Independent.

STUDY 2: CAUSAL VERSUS TEMPORAL UNPACKING

If implicit and explicit subadditivity are generated by different mechanisms, as suggested above, their relative contributions should vary depending on the nature of the partition. Some partitions are expected to induce primarily implicit subadditivity, whereas others are expected to produce primarily explicit subadditivity. The following study explores these effects and estimates their relative contributions.

Participants in the study were 165 Stanford students attending an introductory economics class. They answered, in a classroom setting, a few questions concerning the probability of various causes of death. Participants were informed that

Each year in the United States, approximately 2 million people (or 1% of the population) die from a variety of causes. In this questionnaire, you will be asked to estimate the probability that a randomly selected death is due to one cause rather than another. Obviously, you are not expected to know the exact figures, but everyone has some idea about the prevalence of various causes of death. To give you a feel for the numbers involved, note that 1.5% of deaths each year are attributable to suicide.

This study consists of two cases. In Case 1, the focal hypothesis, homicide (H), is unpacked according to the causal agent: homicide by an acquaintance (H_a) and homicide by a stranger (H_s). In Case 2, the same focal hypothesis, H, is unpacked according to the time of occurrence: daytime homicide (H_d)

and nighttime homicide (H_n). The alternative hypothesis in all judgments is accidental death (X).

In this study, unlike the previous one, the focal and the alternative hypotheses are not exhaustive; the cause of death may be other than homicide or accident. Thus, participants here are asked to evaluate the conditional probability of the focal against the alternative hypothesis, assuming that one and only one of them holds. It is essential, of course, that participants understand and respect this assumption. Because the alternative hypothesis (X) in this design is held constant, probability theory requires additivity of odds, not of conditional probability. In particular, it implies $R(H_a \vee H_s, X) = R(H_a, X) + R(H_s, X)$, where $R(A, B)$ denotes the probability ratio $P(A, B)/P(B, A)$, provided $P(B, A) \neq 0$.

We conjectured that the causal partition is more likely to bring to mind additional possibilities than the temporal partition. Homicide by an acquaintance suggests domestic violence or a partners' quarrel, whereas homicide by a stranger suggests armed robbery or drive-by shooting. In contrast, daytime homicide and nighttime homicide are less likely to bring to mind disparate acts and hence are more readily repacked as an implicit disjunction. Consequently, we expect more implicit subadditivity in Case 1, due to enhanced availability, and more explicit subadditivity in Case 2, due to repacking of the explicit disjunction.

The study was designed as follows. In Case 1, the participants were randomly divided into three groups. One group $(N = 55)$ evaluated the probability of the implicit disjunction that a randomly selected death is a homicide rather than an accidental death, $P(H, X)$. A second group $(N = 54)$ evaluated the probability of the explicit disjunction that a randomly selected death is a homicide committed by an acquaintance or a homicide committed by a stranger rather than an accidental death, $P(H_a \vee H_s, X)$. A third group $(N = 56)$ evaluated the probability of the two individual components, $P(H_a, X)$ and $P(H_s, X)$.

Case 2 was presented to the same participants a few weeks later. The design and the procedures were the same, except for the use of the temporal partition instead of the causal partition. As previously, the participants were randomly divided into three groups. One group $(N = 53)$ evaluated the implicit disjunction $P(H, X)$; a second group $(N = 53)$ evaluated the explicit disjunction $P(H_a \vee H_n, X)$; and a third group $(N = 56)$ evaluated the two individual components, $P(H_d, X)$ and $P(H_n, X)$. The median estimates for both cases are presented in the upper part of Table 26.2.

The lower part of Table 26.2 presents the supports and the weights derived from the median judgments, as shown later. Note that according to support theory, the odds $P(A, B)/[1 - P(A, B)] = s(A)/s(B)$. Letting $s(X) = 1$, the support of each focal hypothesis in this study equals the odds of this hypothesis against the alternative X. For example,

$$s(H) = \frac{s(H)}{s(X)} = \frac{P(H, X)}{1 - P(H, X)} = \frac{.20}{.80} = .25$$

Other support values were obtained similarly.

Table 26.2. Median Probability Judgments (*P*) and Estimated Supports (*s*) and Weights (*w*) for the Two Partitions in Study 2

	Homicide Unpacked	
Hypothesis	Case 1 (Casual Agent): Acquaintance versus Stranger	Case 2 (by Time): Day versus Night
Implicit	$P(H, X) = .20$	$P(H, X) = .20$
Explicit	$P(H_a \vee H_s, X) = .25$	$P(H_d \vee H_n, X) = .20$
	$P(H_a, X) = .15$	$P(H_d, X) = .10$
	$P(H_s, X) = .15$	$P(H_n, X) = .21$
Implicit	$s(H) = .25$	$s(H) = .25$
Explicit	$s(H_a \vee H_s) = .33$	$s(H_d \vee H_n) = .25$
	$s(H_a) + s(H_s) = .18 + .18 = .36$	$s(H_d) + s(H_n) = .11 + .29 = .40$
Implicit (*I*)	$w_{HI} = .25/.33 = .76$	$w_{HI} = .25/.25 = 1.00$
Explicit (*E*)	$w_{HE} = .33/.36 = .92$	$w_{HE} = .25/.40 = .63$
Global	$w_H = .25/.36 = .69$	$w_H = .25/.40 = .63$

Note: *H* denotes homicide, *X* denotes accidental death, and H_a, H_s, H_d, H_n denote, respectively, homicide by an acquaintance, homicide by a stranger, homicide during daytime, and homicide during nighttime.

Support theory offers simple measures of implicit and explicit subadditivity. Let $(A_1, \ldots, A_n)$ be a partition of the implicit hypothesis *A*. The ratio

$$w_A = \frac{s(A)}{s(A_1) + \cdots + s(A_n)}$$

provides a global measure of the degree of subadditivity induced by the above partition. Note that $w_A = 1$ if probability judgments are additive, and $w_A < 1$ if they exhibit either implicit or explicit subadditivity. Thus, lower *w* implies greater subadditivity. To assess the separate contributions of implicit and explicit subadditivity, define

$$w_{AI} = \frac{s(A)}{s(A_1 \vee \cdots \vee A_n)}$$

$$w_{AE} = \frac{s(A_1 \vee \cdots \vee A_n)}{s(A_1) + \cdots + s(A_n)}$$

so that $w_A = w_{AI} w_{AE}$. Therefore, the global measure of subadditivity, w_A, is decomposed into its implicit (w_{AI}) and explicit (w_{AE}) components that can be estimated from the data.

Applying the preceding analysis to the data of Table 26.2 reveals more implicit subadditivity in Case 1 ($w_{HI} = .76$) than in Case 2 ($w_{HI} = 1.00$), and more explicit subadditivity in Case 2 ($W_{HE} = .63$) than in Case 1 ($W_{HE} = .92$). Strict implicit subadditivity was tested by comparing the supports of the implicit and explicit disjunctions in each case; that is, $s(H)$ versus $s(H_a \vee H_s)$ and $s(H)$ versus $s(H_d \vee H_n)$, using the Mann–Whitney statistic. Strict explicit subadditivity was tested by comparing the sum of the supports of the component hypotheses, within the data of a participant, to the support of the corresponding explicit disjunction; that is, $s(H_a) + s(H_s)$ versus $s(H_a \vee H_s)$ and $s(H_d) + s(H_n)$ versus $s(H_d \vee H_n)$. The analysis yielded significant strict implicit subadditivity in Case 1 ($p < .01$) but not in Case 2, and significant strict explicit subadditivity in Case 2 ($p < .005$), but not in Case 1. These findings support our conjecture that the causal partition induces more implicit subadditivity, whereas the temporal partition induces more explicit subadditivity.

STUDY 3: SIMILAR VERSUS DISSIMILAR COMPONENTS

Although support theory has been conceived as a model of probability judgment, it can be readily applied to assessments of percentage or relative frequency (Tversky & Koehler, 1994). Moreover, judgments of absolute frequency can serve as support for certain hypotheses. For example, the probability that it will snow in Chicago next November may be based on an estimate of the frequency of snowy and nonsnowy Novembers in the previous decade. It is instructive, therefore, to test whether assessed frequency satisfies implicit and explicit subadditivity. One might expect that judgments of absolute frequency are less vulnerable to these biases because the additivity of frequency is simpler and more intuitive than the additivity of probability.

The study of frequency judgment also provides an opportunity for testing another potential source of explicit subadditivity, namely a regressive bias towards the midpoint of the scale (e.g., .5), reflecting either response bias or random error (see, e.g., Erev, Wallsten, & Budescu, 1994). This account implies explicit subadditivity when the two components are below the midpoint and explicit superadditivity when the two components are above the midpoint. Because the probability scale is bounded by one, the above prediction cannot be tested using judgments of probability or relative frequency, but it can be readily tested in judgments of absolute frequency.

The participants, 152 Stanford students, were asked to estimate the number of fellow undergraduates majoring in particular fields. Participants were given the following instructions:

Consider all Stanford students who have declared *one* major. We would like you to estimate the number of students majoring in particular fields. Obviously, you are not expected to know the exact figures. We are interested in your impressions regarding the popularity of different majors.

For your information, 120 students major in History. Using this number as a standard of comparison, please give your best estimates of the following. The three most accurate respondents will receive a prize of $20.

Twenty-four majors, listed in Table 26.3, were divided into three sets of 8. From each set of 8 majors, we constructed four pairs of similar majors (e.g., Mathematics and Computer Science), and four pairs of dissimilar majors

Table 26.3. Median Frequency Estimates and the Actual Number of Students in Each Major (Study 3)

Major	Median Estimate	Actual Number
Biology	250	265
Chemistry	100	51
Chemical engineering	70	56
Civil engineering	95	64
Communication	65	66
Comparative literature	40	6
Computer science	100	104
Electrical engineering	100	102
Earth systems	50	66
Economics	200	261
English	120	200
French	25	7
Geology	36	3
Industrial engineering	70	64
International relations	100	96
Italian	20	1
Mathematics	50	9
Mechanical engineering	100	97
Petroleum engineering	30	1
Philosophy	50	18
Political science	150	135
Public policy	80	72
Sociology	80	35
Symbolic systems	30	44

(e.g., Mathematics and Italian). Participants were randomly divided into three groups. The participants in each group evaluated each of the 8 individual majors from one set (e.g., "The number of students majoring in Mathematics"), the four similar pairs of majors from another set (e.g., "The total number of students majoring either in Political Science or International Relations"), and the four dissimilar pairs from a third set (e.g., "The total number of students majoring either in Chemistry or English"). Thus, each participant encountered each major exactly once.

Explicit subadditivity implies that the estimated number of students in a given pair of majors is less than or equal to the sum of the estimates of the individual majors. If this phenomenon is driven, at least in part, by participants' tendency to repack the individual components, then we should expect greater subadditivity for similar than for dissimilar pairs because it is easier and more natural to pack related majors (e.g., Mathematics and Computer Science) than unrelated majors (e.g., Mathematics and Italian). Finally, if participants estimate the total number of students who major in one of two fields by anchoring on the larger major and making an insufficient upward adjustment, then we expect

Table 26.4. *Median Frequency Estimates for Each Similar Pair (F_{AB}), Median Sum of Estimated Components ($F_A + F_B$) and Their Ratio (Study 3)*

Similar Pair	Median Estimate (F_{AB})	Median Sum ($F_A + F_B$)	$\left(\frac{F_{AB}}{F_A + F_B}\right)$
Chemical engineering and petroleum engineering	50	110	.45
Geology and earth systems	50	110	.45
Mechanical engineering and civil engineering	100	200	.50
Biology and chemistry	200	360	.56
Philosophy and symbolic systems	50	90	.56
Political science and international relations	150	260	.58
English and comparative literature	105	160	.66
Economics and public policy	190	275	.69
Math and computer science	130	173	.75
Communication and sociology	115	150	.77
French and Italian	40	50	.80
Electrical engineering and industrial engineering	180	160	1.13
Median			.62

the judgments to be more sensitive to the larger than to the smaller component of each pair.

Table 26.3 presents median estimates for each of the 24 majors, along with the official numbers. The correlation between the estimated and correct values is .93, and the average absolute deviation of prediction is 24, indicating that our respondents had a reasonably good idea of the relative popularity of the various majors at their university.

Tables 26.4 and 26.5 present, separately for similar and dissimilar pairs, the median frequency estimates for the pairs, denoted F_{AB}, the median sums of frequency estimates of the individual majors, computed within the data of each participant and denoted $F_A + F_B$, and the ratio of these values. The results provide strong evidence for subadditivity: The estimate of the pair is less than the sum of the individual estimates in 23 of 24 cases, and the mean value of $F_{AB}/(F_A + F_B)$ across all pairs is only .69. This effect cannot be explained by a regression towards a central value (e.g., 120, which was given as a standard of comparison) because subadditivity is very much in evidence for both large and small pairs of majors. Recall that a symmetric error model predicts subadditivity for pairs of small majors and superadditivity for pairs of large majors, contrary to the data in Tables 26.4 and 26.5.

In accord with repacking, the similar pairs tend to be more subadditive than the dissimilar pairs: The values of $F_{AB}/(F_A + F_B)$ are generally lower in Table 26.4 than in Table 26.5 ($p < .05$ by a one-sided Mann–Whitney test). However, the presence of strict explicit subadditivity in both cases suggests an anchoring and adjustment process.

Table 26.5. Median Frequency Estimates for Each Dissimilar Pair (F_{AB}), Median Sum of Estimated Components ($E_A + F_B$), and Their Ratio (Study 3)

Dissimilar Pair	Median Estimate (F_{AB})	Median Sum ($F_A + F_B$)	$\left(\frac{F_{AB}}{F_A+F_B}\right)$
Industrial engineering and political science	145	238	.61
Philosophy and earth systems	70	114	.61
Chemistry and English	150	230	.65
Chemical engineering and public policy	80	120	.67
Mechanical engineering and sociology	150	220	.68
Computer science and French	100	135	.74
Electrical engineering and international relations	150	195	.77
Geology and symbolic systems	50	65	.77
Communication and civil engineering	120	155	.77
Economics and petroleum engineering	200	250	.80
Biology and comparative literature	220	270	.81
Mathematics and Italian	58	70	.83
Median			.76

To test this account, we compared, separately for similar and dissimilar pairs, the median estimate of each pair, F_{AB}, with the higher of the two medians of estimates for individual majors forming the pair, denoted F_H. For similar pairs, the mean value of F_H was 108, whereas the mean value of F_{AB} was 113 ($t = .22$, ns). For dissimilar pairs, the mean value of F_H was 111, whereas the mean value of F_{AB} was 124 ($t = .56$, ns). Thus, the estimates for the pairs (overall mean $= 119$) are much closer to the higher of the two majors (overall mean $= 109$) than to the sum of the individual estimates (overall mean $= 165$). These data are consistent with the notion that participants estimated the pairs by focusing on the larger component.

STUDY 4: ANCHORING AND ADJUSTMENT

If, instead of evaluating each major separately and then adding these individual estimates, participants evaluate pairs of majors by adjusting one of the estimates, then participants who had already evaluated one of the majors are likely to use this estimate as an anchor. In this case, the frequency estimate of a pair should be higher when the participants had estimated beforehand the higher rather than the lower component of that pair. To test this prediction, we selected 12 pairs of majors and identified each of their components as high or low according to the median estimates in Table 26.3. The participants ($N = 81$) were recruited and run as in the preceding study. They were divided randomly into three groups. All participants evaluated all 12 pairs. Prior to this task, however, each group evaluated a different set of 8 single majors. The single majors were selected so that for each pair of majors one group evaluated beforehand the high or more popular major, a second group evaluated the low or less popular major, and a third group did not evaluate either of the individual components prior to the evaluation of the pair. The order of presentation of both individual majors and pairs of majors was randomized.

If people focus on their prior estimate, we expect participants who first evaluated the high component of a pair to give higher estimates than participants who first evaluated the low component of that pair. And if, in the absence of a prior estimate, people tend to choose the larger of the two majors as an anchor because it is closer to the required estimate, we expect participants who made no prior estimate for a given pair to be closer to those who evaluated the high component than to those who evaluated the low component.

The results confirmed both predictions. The mean estimate for a pair of majors in the high condition was 251 students, whereas the mean estimate for a pair of majors in the low condition was 202 students ($t = 3.50$, $p < .001$). The mean estimate in the neutral condition was 237, significantly higher than the median estimate in the low condition ($t = 1.96$, $p = .05$) but not significantly lower than the mean estimate in the high condition ($t = .70$, ns).

SUMMARY AND DISCUSSION

The present extension of support theory distinguishes between implicit subadditivity, induced by unpacking, and explicit subadditivity, resulting from the difference between the assessment of an explicit disjunction and separate assessments of its disjoint components. We propose that implicit subadditivity is caused by enhanced availability, whereas explicit subadditivity is produced, in part at least, by repacking or anchoring. Consequently, different partitions are likely to give rise to different patterns of subadditivity. Study 1 establishes strict implicit and explicit subadditivity in judgments of unconditional probability. Study 2 shows that a causal partition produced more implicit subadditivity, whereas a temporal partition produced more explicit subadditivity, in judgments of conditional probability. Study 3 demonstrates greater explicit subadditivity for similar than for dissimilar components in judgments of frequency. Study 4 suggests that people follow an anchoring and adjustment heuristic that focuses on the larger, or the more familiar, component and increases the assessment of that component slightly to accommodate the larger extension.

The use of an anchoring and adjustment heuristic in this context is somewhat surprising because it seems easy to estimate the components separately and then add the estimates. Evidently, people are reluctant to add uncertain quantities. If they do not know the population of Spain and also do not know the population of Portugal, they are reluctant to estimate each of these numbers separately and add their guesses. Instead, they apparently form an overall impression of the combined population of the two countries that is determined primarily by the larger of the two. Taken together, the present results imply that an adequate model of probability or frequency judgment should be able to accommodate both implicit and explicit subadditivity. The current version of support theory provides such a model.

We conclude with a discussion of the relation between support theory and Shafer's (1976) theory of belief functions. Although the theory of belief functions is based on logical rather than psychological considerations, it has been interpreted by several authors as a descriptive model of belief. In this theory, as in many other models, the belief in the disjunction of disjoint events is greater than or equal to the sum of the beliefs in each of the components. Thus, support theory and the theory of belief functions depart from the Bayesian model in opposite directions: Support theory predicts subadditivity, whereas the theory of belief functions assumes superadditivity. Using the notation of Table 26.1, probability theory requires $\alpha = \beta = \gamma + \delta$, Shafer's theory assumes $\alpha = \beta \geq \gamma + \delta$, and support theory implies $\alpha \leq \beta \leq \gamma + \delta$.

The experimental literature provides strong evidence that judged probability of both lay people and experts is subadditive rather than superadditive (see, e.g., Tversky & Koehler, 1994; Fox & Tversky, 1998). For example, options traders who evaluated a set of four mutually exclusive and exhaustive hypotheses regarding the closing price of Microsoft stock did not hold any belief in reserve, as required by the theory of belief functions. On the contrary, the sum of the probabilities assigned to these hypotheses was substantially greater than 1, and options traders were actually willing to bet on these values (Fox, Rogers, & Tversky, 1996). Although we do not wish to claim that superadditivity cannot arise in certain circumstances, the experimental evidence suggests that such instances represent the exception rather than the rule.

What then is the psychological basis for the superadditivity assumption that underlies post-Bayesian models of degree of belief? The answer to this question goes back to Keynes' (1921) distinction between the balance of evidence in favor of a given proposition and the weight (or strength) of evidence for this proposition. Keynes argued that the standard notion of probability can represent the balance of evidence but not the weight of evidence because a probability of one half, for example, may result either from strong evidence for and strong evidence against the proposition in question or from weak evidence for and weak evidence against that proposition. Following Keynes, we suggest that superadditivity often holds for judgments of evidence strength; that is, of the degree to which a designated body of evidence supports a particular hypothesis (see Briggs & Krantz, 1992), but it does not hold for probability judgments that reflect the global balance of evidence.

The contrast between these notions is most pronounced in situations where there is good evidence for some general hypothesis but there is no specific evidence for any of its components. Suppose, for example, that there is very strong evidence that a particular person was murdered, but there is no evidence regarding the identity of the killer. Let H, H_a, and H_s denote homicide, homicide by an acquaintance, and homicide by a stranger, respectively. If people can make sensible assessments of the degree to which the evidence confirms each of these hypotheses (e.g., on a scale from 0 to 1), we expect these assessments to be close to 1 for H, and close to 0 for H_a and for H_s in accord with Shafer's (1976) model. However, the judged probabilities of H_a and H_s are expected to be substantially greater than 0, and their sum may even exceed the judged probability of H. Judgments of strength of evidence, we suggest, reflect the degree to which a specific body of evidence confirms a particular hypothesis, whereas judgments of probability express the relative support for the competing hypotheses based on the judge's general knowledge and prior belief. The two types of judgments, therefore, are expected to follow different rules. Indeed, Krantz (1991) has argued that Shafer's model is more suitable for judgments of evidence strength than for judgments of probability.

Because there is very little data on judgments of evidence strength, we can only speculate about the rules they follow. It appears that in the absence of specific evidence, as in the homicide example earlier, such judgments are likely to be superadditive. However, judgments of evidence strength are unlikely to be superadditive in general. To illustrate, consider a body of evidence, for example, a fragment of Linda's diary expressing moral objection to sexist language. Such evidence, we suggest, can provide stronger support for the hypothesis that Linda is a feminist bank teller than for the more inclusive hypothesis that Linda is a bank teller. This pattern, of course, is not only subadditive; it is actually nonmonotonic. Similarly, a postcard with an Alpine scene appears to provide stronger evidence for the hypothesis that it came from Switzerland than for the hypothesis that it came from Europe (see e.g., Bar-Hillel & Neter, 1993). In these cases, the evidence matches the narrower hypothesis better than it matches the broader hypothesis; hence an assessment based on matching (or representativeness) can give rise to nonmonotonicity in judgment of evidence strength, as well as in judgment of probability (Tversky & Kahneman, 1983).

To summarize, the experimental evidence described here and elsewhere indicates that probability judgments, which are based on the balance of evidence, are generally subadditive. The preceding discussion, however, suggests that judgments of the strength of a designated body of evidence may exhibit a different pattern. Such judgments are likely to be superadditive when there is little evidence for each of the component hypotheses, and they are likely to be subadditive (or even nonmonotonic) when the evidence strongly favors one of the components. Whether or not these conjectures are valid, we suggest that the discussion of alternative representations of belief can be illuminated by the distinction between probability judgments based on the balance of evidence and judgments of the strength of a specific body of evidence.

27. Remarks on Support Theory: Recent Advances and Future Directions

Lyle A. Brenner, Derek J. Koehler, and Yuval Rottenstreich

SUPPORT THEORY

A great deal of psychological research has addressed the nature and quality of people's intuitive judgments of likelihood. Much of this work has sought to characterize the simple mental operations, often termed *heuristics*, that govern people's assessments of probabilities and frequencies. The heuristics initially identified by Daniel Kahneman and Amos Tversky – availability, representativeness, and anchoring, among others – describe and explain many phenomena in judgment under uncertainty. These heuristics have been particularly helpful in identifying conditions under which people closely conform to, or radically deviate from, the requirements of probability theory.

Support theory, a formal descriptive account of subjective probability introduced by Tversky and Koehler (1994), offers the opportunity to weave together the different heuristics into a unified account. The theory can accommodate many mechanisms (such as the various heuristics) that influence subjective probability, but integrates them via the construct of support. Consequently, support theory can account for numerous existing empirical patterns in the literature on judgment under uncertainty.

The original works describing the major heuristics underlying likelihood judgments are presented in Kahneman, Slovic, and Tversky (1982). Previous chapters of this book contain selections from the initial statements of support theory that invoke several heuristics to account for various properties of support. Our goal in this chapter is twofold: to summarize recent developments in support theory, and to suggest some possible directions for future research. Our discussion draws on what we see as three key aspects of the theory.

1. *Description-dependence*: In most theories of subjective probability (both normative & descriptive), probabilities are assigned directly to events and thus are invariant across different descriptions of the same event. Intuitive judgments, however, are influenced by the way events are described. For example, the judged probability that "your home will be damaged by a *natural disaster*" will not necessarily coincide with the judged probability that "your home will be damaged by *fire, flood, hurricane, tornado, lightning strike, severe thunderstorm, or any other natural disaster.*"

489

To accommodate the observation that different descriptions of the same event can yield different probability judgments, support theory makes event descriptions, rather than the events themselves, the fundamental primitives of judgment. Rather than attaching probabilities to events, support theory attaches subjective probabilities to descriptions of events, which are termed *hypotheses*. The principle of description-dependence is consistent with the heuristics tradition because different descriptions of events will influence the operation and output of the various heuristics. For example, use of the availability heuristic is affected by the form of a hypothesis: a more detailed hypothesis may call to mind exemplars more easily than a less detailed hypothesis.

2. *Probability judgment as an assessment of the balance of evidence*: Support theory posits the construct of support as an intermediate component of judgment (hypotheses → support → probability). Each hypothesis A is assigned a support value $s(A)$, which is interpreted as the strength of evidence for that hypothesis. The probability that hypothesis A rather than hypothesis B holds, assuming one and only one of them obtains, is given by

$$P(A, B) = \frac{s(A)}{s(A) + s(B)}.$$

In this representation, likelihood judgment reflects an assessment of the balance of evidence favoring the focal hypothesis rather than the alternative hypothesis.

3. *Properties of support*: A third aspect of support theory concerns the properties of the support scale. In particular, given two hypotheses referring to the same event (a "composite" hypothesis A and an "unpacked" hypothesis $A_1 \vee A_2$), support theory proposes that $s(A) \leq s(A_1 \vee A_2) \leq s(A_1) + s(A_2)$. The pattern summarized by the left inequality is referred to as *implicit subadditivity*. The composite hypothesis A is assumed to evoke less support than the corresponding unpacked hypothesis $A_1 \vee A_2$. For example, the support for the implicit disjunction "your home will be damaged by a *natural disaster*" is likely to be less than the support for the equivalent explicit disjunction "your home will be damaged by *fire, flood, hurricane, tornado, lightning strike, severe thunderstorm, or any other natural disaster*." The pattern summarized by the right inequality is referred to as *explicit subadditivitiy*; the support of an unpacked hypothesis is assumed to be less than or equal to the sum of supports of its individual components, because the unpacked hypothesis may be "repacked" by the judge into a composite hypothesis (Rottenstreich & Tversky, 1997).

To summarize, the first aspect of support theory is the general observation of description-dependence: Judgments are tied to hypotheses rather than events, with support invoked as an intermediary construct between hypotheses and judged probability. The second aspect of the theory specifies a particular relationship between probability and support: Probability corresponds to the balance of support for competing hypotheses. The third aspect concerns systematic properties of the support scale: among other properties, the scale exhibits various forms of subadditivity. Different properties of support may reflect the operation of different judgment processes or heuristics. For example, *implicit subadditivity* can be explained naturally by the availability heuristic: an unpacked hypothesis calls instances to mind more easily than a packed hypothesis, leading to an increase in perceived support. Motivating or explaining properties of support in terms of various psychological processes allows support theory to integrate the heuristics, as well as other hypothesized mechanisms, into one framework.

The remainder of the chapter is organized into two main sections. We first review developments in support theory since the initial statements by Tversky and Koehler (1994) and Rottenstreich and Tversky (1997). We then provide some speculations regarding future applications of support theory. Both sections touch on each of the three aspects of support theory outlined previously, but to different degrees. The recent developments we review tend to focus on specific properties of the support scale, whereas our discussion of future directions emphasizes potential applications of description dependence and the notion of likelihood judgment as a balance of evidence.

RECENT ADVANCES

Recent research in support theory can be broadly characterized as investigating four distinct topics: (1) direct assessments of support, (2) tests of the axioms of support theory, (3) determinants of subadditivity of support, and (4) extensions of support theory to decision making and subjective probability calibration.

Direct Assessments of Support

Support – unlike probability – is a function of a single hypothesis. In principle, then, it should be possible to elicit direct assessments of the support for a particular hypothesis without mentioning alternative hypotheses, and without making reference to chance or uncertainty. One test of the value of support theory is whether such *direct support ratings* can predict probability judgments (see Tversky & Koehler, 1994; Koehler, 1996).

Several studies have investigated this possibility, and have been successful in reproducing judgments of probability from direct ratings of support. For example, Koehler, Brenner, and Tversky (1997, Experiment 1) used judgments of the "relatedness" between academic fields (e.g., Economics & Statistics) to accurately predict the judged probability that a student who previously took a designated course (e.g., Statistics) had a designated academic major (e.g., Economics). Here, the support for the hypothesis *majors in Economics*, contingent on the evidence *took a course in Statistics*, is approximated by a rating of the conceptual relatedness between the two fields. In another application, Koehler et al. (1997, Experiment 5) presented participants with fictional crime stories and asked participants either to rate the "suspiciousness" of a designated suspect or to estimate the suspect's probability of guilt. Although the suspiciousness ratings did not require any assessment of the other suspects who might have committed the crime, when used as a proxy for support these ratings accurately predicted each suspect's judged probability of guilt. Koehler (2000, Experiment 5) found that probability judgments that a patient in a medical diagnosis task had a designated flu strain could be reproduced using judgments of the patient's resemblance to the prototypical patient with that flu strain. Finally, several studies of sports predictions have shown that direct ratings of "team strength" can predict the judged probability that one team will beat another in an upcoming game (e.g., Fox, 1999; Fox & Tversky, 1998, Study 1; Koehler, 1996; Tversky & Koehler, 1994).

The success with which direct ratings of support have been used to predict judged probability suggests that subjective probability can indeed be decomposed into separate assessments of the focal and alternative hypotheses. Furthermore, the close relationship between ratings of support and judgments of likelihood suggests that the study of probability judgment may benefit from advances in the study of the evaluation of evidence (e.g., Briggs & Krantz, 1992; Macchi, Osherson, & Krantz, 1999).

Support theory specifies how support is translated into subjective probability, but is largely agnostic about the source of support for a hypothesis. The determinants of support will depend on many factors, including the domain of judgment, the expertise of the judge, and the accessibility of different kinds of evidence. In assessing the likelihood that Joe will drop out of college, for example, an administrator may rely on relevant university statistics, Joe's residence hall advisor may consider how easily dropouts come to mind, and Joe's roommate may evaluate Joe's resemblance to the prototypical dropout. Assessments of support can vary both in the type of evidence on which they are based and in the kinds of cognitive processes that they evoke (Griffin, Gonzalez, & Varey 2000; Tversky & Koehler, 1994).

Although direct ratings of support may invoke considerations of both the strength and the weight of evidence (Griffin & Tversky, 1992), we suspect that most direct support ratings primarily reflect the strength component. For example, judgments of a suspect's suspiciousness are likely based on how strongly the evidence implicates that suspect, with less emphasis on the reliability or validity (i.e., weight considerations) of that evidence. The fact that a suspect fails a lie detector test, for instance, may contribute substantially to her perceived suspiciousness even if it is known that such evidence is unreliable. Precisely to guard against the overemphasis on evidence of high strength but low weight, the courts prohibit the introduction of evidence in which the "prejudicial value outweighs the probative value." Applying Griffin and Tversky's (1992) framework to support theory, evidence of high strength should lead to substantial support and evidence of low strength should lead to minimal support, with the weight of the evidence having little effect.

Axiom Tests: Focus-Dependence and Context Independence

Another set of investigations has concerned the behavioral axioms that are implied by the representation relating probability to support. One requirement of support theory is that the position of a given hypothesis – whether in the focal position or the alternative position – does not affect its support. This assumption of position-independence is best seen in the equation relating judged probability to support, in which there is a single support scale $s(\cdot)$ that applies to both the focal and alternative hypotheses. Position-independence implies binary complementarity: $P(A, B) + P(B, A) = 1$. Some recent studies document systematic violations of binary complementarity, suggesting potential position-dependent generalizations of support theory.

Macchi, Osherson, and Krantz (1999) asked participants to judge probabilities of hypotheses about which they had virtually no knowledge. For example, participants assessed the probability either that "the freezing point of gasoline is greater than that of alcohol" or that "the freezing point of alcohol is greater than that of gasoline." It was assumed that most participants would be able to recruit very little support for either hypothesis. The average sum of judgments for such pairs of questions was roughly .90, indicating a violation of binary complementarity. Macchi et al. (1999) explain this result by suggesting that participants recognize that the focal hypothesis has little support, but fail to recognize that the alternative hypothesis has little support as well. This explanation was corroborated by subsequent experiments in which binary complementarity was restored for responses to modified questions that made both hypotheses salient. When reminded of the alternative hypothesis, people appear to symmetrically consider both the focal and alternative hypothesis. However, when not reminded of the alternative hypothesis, people may directly map weak support for the focal hypothesis into a low probability judgment, with little regard for the comparably weak support of the alternative hypothesis.

Brenner and Rottenstreich (1999) found a different pattern of position-dependence. Recall that many studies have shown that unpacking a hypothesis into its components generally increases support. However, a judge presented with an unpacked hypothesis (e.g., *Bob is a chemical, industrial, mechanical, civil, or electrical engineer*) may *repack* the disjunction and consider it as if it were a single hypothesis (e.g., *Bob is an engineer*). Brenner and Rottenstreich (1999) proposed that the position of a hypothesis affects the degree of repacking. In particular, they predicted a greater tendency to repack a disjunction when it is in the focal rather than the alternative position, based on the intuition that it is more natural to compare a single possibility to a set of alternatives than to compare a set of possibilities to a single alternative. This prediction of *differential repacking* implies that for judgments involving an explicit disjunction $D_1 \vee D_2$ and some other singleton hypothesis S, the sum of $P(D_1 \vee D_2, S)$ and

$P(S, D_1 \vee D_2)$ should be less than 1, contrary to binary complementarity. The results of several experiments, involving both probability and frequency judgments, supported this prediction.

The results of Macchi et al. (1999) and Brenner and Rottenstreich (1999) suggest certain circumstances in which binary complementarity may fail (see also McKenzie, 1998, 1999). It should be noted, however, that a number of studies have found binary complementarity to hold quite well across large sets of judgment items (Wallsten, Budescu, & Zwick, 1992; Tversky & Koehler, 1994; Fox, 1999), suggesting that binary complementarity is a good first approximation in many cases. Additional research is needed to map out the conditions under which binary complementarity does and does not hold.

Support theory can be generalized to accommodate violations of binary complementarity by allowing separate support scales for focal and alternative hypotheses:

$$P(A, B) = \frac{s_f(A)}{s_f(A) + s_a(B)}.$$

This model – termed *asymmetric support theory* by Brenner and Rottenstreich (2000) – maintains the other central axiom of support theory, known as the *product rule*. Defining $Q(A, B) = P(A, B)/[1 - P(A, B)]$ to be the "odds" of hypothesis A relative to hypothesis B, the product rule states that, for disjoint hypotheses $A, B, C,$ and D:

$$Q(A, B)Q(C, D) = Q(A, D)Q(C, B).$$

The product rule requires that the support for a hypothesis does not depend on the hypothesis with which it is paired. This assumption greatly constrains the relationship between judged probability and evidential support. Empirical tests by Brenner and Rottenstreich (2000) supported the descriptive validity of the product rule, even when binary complementarity is violated, consistent with the asymmetric support theory model. Fox (1999) also reports empirical tests that support the product rule when binary complementarity holds. The success of direct support ratings in reproducing probability judgments is also an indirect validation of the separability of support that underlies the product rule.

Determinants of Subadditivity of Support

Tversky and Koehler (1994) introduced *subadditivity* as a general feature of the support scale: the total support for a disjunctive hypothesis was assumed to be less than or equal to the sum of the support values for its components. The amount of subadditivity, however, was essentially treated as a free parameter, likely to be influenced by various characteristics of the judgment context. Subsequent research has examined the relationship between various features of judgment tasks and the degree of subadditivity of support.

Original Demonstrations of Variations in Subadditivity. Tversky and Koehler (1994) initially proposed two influences on the degree of subadditivity.

The first is the number of components in an unpacked hypothesis. They predicted greater subadditivity would be found for unpacked hypotheses involving more components, and indeed found that hypotheses unpacked into seven components yielded more subadditivity than hypotheses unpacked into three components.

A second influence on subadditivity proposed by Tversky and Koehler concerned whether the judged probability is interpreted as a propensity of an individual case or interpreted in terms of a relative frequency applied to a collection of cases. As an illustration of this distinction, consider a physician evaluating either the *probability* that an individual patient will survive or evaluating the *percentage* of patients sharing common symptoms who will survive. Tversky and Koehler (1994) predicted more subadditivity for judged probabilities than for judged percentages because evaluating collections of instances is more likely to invoke considerations of inclusion and exclusion relations among hypotheses. They indeed found greater subadditivity for judgments of probability than for judgments of relative frequency.

Rottenstreich and Tversky (1997) considered two separate sources of subadditivity. Support for an implicit disjunction was assumed to be less than or equal to support for a corresponding explicit disjunction, and the latter was assumed to be less than or equal to the sum of supports for the disjunction's components. The former is labeled *implicit subadditivity*; the latter *explicit subadditivity*. In several experiments, Rottenstreich and Tversky (1997) examined how the similarity between the components of a disjunction influences the degree of explicit subadditivity. They found that explicit disjunctions involving similar components, which are more easily "repacked" into a composite hypothesis, yielded greater explicit subadditivity than disjunctions involving dissimilar components.

Similarity between Hypotheses and Evidence. Rottenstreich, Brenner, and Sood (1999) examined another aspect of similarity as a determinant of subadditivity. Support for a hypothesis may often be closely related to the similarity or conceptual match between a hypothesis and the background evidence (as when the representativeness heuristic is used to assess likelihood). For example, in a criminal trial, the likelihood of a defendant's guilt may be judged by the extent to which the evidence introduced at trial matches aspects of the scenario of guilt proposed by the prosecution. How the target hypothesis is described may influence the perceived degree of similarity or match with the evidence. The hypothesis "The defendant murdered Mr. Smith" may match the evidence less well than an elaborated and detailed hypothesis, such as, "The defendant used his key to enter the locked office and murdered Mr. Smith using the decorative bust on the mantle." Such elaborated (and more restrictive) hypotheses, may, due to their greater similarity to the evidence, be seen as more likely than more inclusive hypotheses, a pattern termed the *conjunction fallacy* (Tversky & Kahneman, 1983).

To address the role of similarity in subadditivity of support, Rottenstreich et al. (1999) contrasted judgments of disjunctive hypotheses in the presence of specific evidence (case judgments) with those made in the absence of specific evidence (class judgments). In case judgments, the perceived similarity between hypotheses and evidence is likely to dominate evaluation of support, but in class judgments the similarity between hypotheses and evidence is less readily evaluated, and other mechanisms (such as availability) presumably drive the assessment of support.

In one study, subjects read a description of a character Linda, whose background evidence closely matched the hypothesis *journalist*. Subjects then estimated the probability that Linda works as either a *journalist or realtor*. Whereas the description of Linda may appear highly similar to *journalist*, it may in fact appear less similar to the disjunction *journalist or realtor*, because the nonmatching component *realtor* dilutes the strong similarity with *journalist*. Such dilution is unlikely to occur in class judgments, where similarity does not form the basis of the judgments. As a result, Rottenstreich et al. (1999) predicted more subadditivity when judgments of likelihood were based on similarity, rather than other factors such as availability. Consistent with their predictions, judgment based on similarity yielded extreme forms of subadditivity. Judgments based on similarity often showed nonmonotonicity of support, in which support for a disjunction is less than the support for one of its components – a pattern analogous to the conjunction fallacy, but evaluated at the level of support rather than probability (cf. Tversky & Kahneman, 1983).

Subadditivity for Residual Hypotheses. Another stream of research has examined the determinants of subadditivity for *residual hypotheses*, defined as the complement of a particular hypothesis (e.g., "A team other than the New York Yankees will win the World Series"; "The patient suffers from something other than pneumonia").

Koehler et al. (1997) proposed that subadditivity would be greater for residual hypotheses defined by strong focal hypotheses. Specifically, they tested a *linear discounting model* in which the subadditivity weight $w_{\bar{A}}$ for a residual hypothesis decreases with the support for the focal hypothesis that defines the residual:

$$w_{\bar{A}} = 1 - \beta s(A).$$

The subadditivity weight $w_{\bar{A}}$ represents the degree of subadditivity for the residual hypothesis $\bar{A}$ (read as "not A" or "the complement of A"). For example, if there are four mutually exclusive and exhaustive hypotheses A, B, C, and D, then $w_{\bar{A}} = s(\bar{A})/[s(B) + s(C) + s(D)]$. Smaller values of w represent more subadditivity. The linear discounting model was intended to capture the intuition that when evidence for the focal possibility is strong, the residual hypothesis (i.e., the set of all other possibilities) is less likely to be spontaneously unpacked into its components, compared to when the focal hypothesis is weak (which might yield more careful scrutiny of alternative possibilities). Koehler et al. (1997) found consistent support for both the qualitative and quantitative predictions of the linear discounting model.

Brenner and Koehler (1999) examined subadditivity of residual hypotheses in greater detail. Rather than measuring subadditivity for a residual hypothesis with the *global weight* $w_{\bar{A}}$, Brenner and Koehler examined *local weights* that measure the specific contribution of each component included within the residual. Using local weights, the total support for a residual hypothesis can be expressed as a weighted sum of its components' support values:

$$s(\bar{A}) = w(B, \bar{A})s(B) + w(C, \bar{A})s(C) + w(D, \bar{A})s(D).$$

In this formulation, the local weight $w(B, \bar{A})$ is interpreted as, "the weight of component B within the residual hypothesis $\bar{A}$."

Brenner and Koehler (1999) proposed and tested several ordinal properties of local weights. Properties analogous to subadditivity and enhancement were found to hold for local weights as well as global weights. A generalization of the linear discounting model was able to successfully account for most of the variability in these local weights, yielding a parsimonious model of the "microstructure" of support for residual hypotheses.

Evidential Influences on Subadditivity. Koehler (2000) examined the effects of several evidential features on the degree of subadditivity. In a simulated medical diagnosis task, participants judged the likelihood of a designated diagnosis (flu strain 1, 2, or 3) on the basis of a pattern of symptoms (e.g., cough, sore throat, chills). Over many trials, participants judged the likelihood of each of the three possible flu strains for a given pattern of symptoms; the total of these judged probabilities reflects the degree of subadditivity of the residual hypothesis. Subadditivity was greater when symptoms were in conflict with each other – for example when a pattern of symptoms included both cough (implicating flu strain 1) and sore throat (implicating flu strain 2). The effect of cue conflict was largely accounted for by the linear discounting model of Koehler et al. (1997). According to this interpretation, cue conflict leads to greater perceived support for the focal hypothesis, which in turn produces greater discounting of the residual hypothesis.

Summary of Factors Influencing Subadditivity. Previous studies have found that the degree of subadditivity reliably depends on several factors, including the number of components in a hypothesis, the similarity of those components to each other and to the evidence, the strength of the focal hypothesis, the conflict among evidential cues, and whether the judgment is elicited in terms of probability or relative frequency. These seemingly unrelated factors all influence either (1) the ease with which a hypothesis is naturally or spontaneously broken into pieces, or (2) the extent to which compelling evidence is seen to support the components of a disjunctive hypothesis. The more easily evidence is seen to support individual components of a "packed" hypothesis, the less subadditivity is expected. Put another way: When a hypothesis is unpacked into components, the unpacking effect should be greatest when the act of unpacking recruits evidence for the unpacked components that would *not* be brought to mind by the packed hypothesis. Thus, evidence that encourages spontaneous unpacking of a hypothesis and supports individual components should yield little or no subadditivity.

Extensions of Support Theory

We now consider two recent attempts to expand the scope of support theory. The first extends support theory to predict the accuracy or calibration of subjective probabilities; the second incorporates support theory into a belief-based model of choice under uncertainty.

Support and Calibration. Support theory, as discussed thus far, addresses the *coherence* of a set of probability judgments rather than their *correspondence* to the actual likelihood of outcomes. The theory makes no commitment, for example, to whether unpacking a hypothesis will yield more or less accurate judgments of its actual probability. As formulated, support theory cannot be used to investigate the *calibration* of subjective probabilities, a topic of considerable interest in the field of judgment under uncertainty (for reviews, see Harvey, 1997; McClelland & Bolger, 1994, Lichtenstein, Fischhoff, & Phillips, 1982; Wallsten & Budescu, 1983). *Calibration* is defined as the match between the subjective probability of an event and the corresponding objective probability of that event, as measured either by empirical relative frequencies or via a normative model such as Bayes theorem.

To apply support theory to the study of calibration, Brenner (1995) developed a *random support model* that allows prediction of the accuracy of subjective probabilities. The random support model assumes that the support for a particular hypothesis is likely to vary from judgment occasion to judgment occasion; consequently, support is represented as a random variable to reflect variability in evidence strength. Similar to the approach of Ferrell and McGoey (1980), the random support model uses a signal-detection framework, in which different distributions of support represent the strength of evidence for correct and incorrect hypotheses (e.g., support for the hypothesis "rain" on days when rain does & does not occur). The separation between these distributions reflects the judge's ability to discriminate correct from incorrect hypotheses.

Unlike signal detection theory and the Ferrell and McGoey (1980) approach, however, the random support model does not invoke thresholds for converting the underlying random variable into a judgment; rather, support is mapped directly into a probability judgment based on the support theory representation $P(A, B) = s(A)/[s(A) + s(B)]$. This yields a parsimonious model in which the parameters describing the underlying distributions of support can be used to characterize the judgment domain. Furthermore, because direct assessments of support can be elicited (as described previously), the distributions of support derived from probability judgments may be validated against these direct support assessments.

Brenner (1995) applied the random support model to predicting calibration performance in a number of different judgment domains and contexts. A two-parameter version of the model closely reproduces calibration curves observed in the standard two-alternative judgment task, in which the judge selects which of two alternatives is correct and then assesses the probability of that alternative on a "half-range" (50 to 100%) probability scale. An extension with additional parameters likewise produces a close fit to data for zero-alternative (i.e., "fill in the blank") and one-alternative tasks in which the probability of a designated hypothesis is evaluated using a "full-range" (0 to 100%) probability scale. Koehler, Brenner, and Griffin (Chapter 39, this volume) use the random support model to estimate patterns of miscalibration by experts making probability judgments in their domains of expertise.

One attractive feature of the random support model is that its parameters have meaningful psychological interpretations. In the case of judging a designated hypothesis (such as the likelihood of rain), for instance, the parameters represent the judge's discrimination ability (i.e., how much more support accrues to the hypothesis "rain" when it rains, and to the hypothesis "no rain" when it does not rain), bias towards the focal hypothesis (i.e., how much more support accrues to the hypothesis "rain" rather than "no rain," regardless of the actual outcome), and extremity of judgment (i.e., the tendency to produce judgments near 0% and 100%). These parameters provide a convenient language for evaluating sources of observed miscalibration, and could also guide attempts to develop corrective procedures.

Support and Decision Making. One of the primary motivations for the study of subjective probability is the presumption that people's likelihood judgments of uncertain events influence the decisions that depend on those events. Accordingly, support theory has recently been used as the basis for a belief-based account of decision making under uncertainty (Fox & Tversky, 1998; Tversky & Fox, 1995; Wu & Gonzalez, 1999). This work focuses on people's choices among uncertain prospects in which the probabilities of different outcomes are not known but instead must be assessed by the decision maker. For example, a participant might be asked to choose between a certain gain of $40 and an uncertain prospect offering $160 if the Los Angeles Lakers win the NBA championship next year. By varying the value of the certain gain and examining its effect on people's choices, a *certainty equivalent* can be determined such that the decision maker is indifferent between the sure gain and the uncertain prospect.

A number of studies (Fox, 1999; Fox, Rogers, & Tversky, 1996; Fox & Tversky, 1998; Tversky & Fox, 1995; Wu & Gonzalez, 1999) using this method have revealed what Tversky and Wakker (1995) call *bounded subadditivity*: An event has greater impact on choices when it turns impossibility into possibility, or possibility into certainty than when it merely makes a possibility more likely in the intermediate range of the probability scale. Bounded subadditivity implies that decomposing an uncertain prospect into subprospects by unpacking the event on which the payoffs are contingent increases the attractiveness of the set of prospects. For example, in a study by Fox et al. (1996) involving judgments of professional options traders, the certainty equivalent placed on an uncertain prospect *paying $150 if Microsoft's stock price closes below $94* was less than the sum of the certainty equivalents associated with the prospect *paying $150 if Microsoft's stock price closes below $88* and the prospect *paying $150 if Microsoft's stock price closes between $88 and $94*.

This pattern for certainty equivalents is directly analogous to the effect of unpacking on probability judgments. Indeed, in the Fox et al. (1996) study, probability judgments for the relevant events were also elicited and exhibited precisely the pattern of subadditivity predicted by support theory. For example, unpacking the hypothesis "Microsoft's stock price will close below $94" into two component hypotheses, "Microsoft's stock price will close below $88" and "Microsoft's stock price will close between $88 and $94," produced a greater total judged probability. Fox et al.'s results suggest that the bounded subadditivity observed in choices may be attributable in large part to subadditivity in probability judgment.

Fox and Tversky (1998) and Wu and Gonzalez (1999) offer a two-stage belief-based model of decision making under uncertainty that combines insights from both support theory and prospect theory (Kahneman & Tversky, 1979; Tversky & Kahneman, 1992). The model assumes that the judged probabilities of the events involved in uncertain prospects are assessed in a manner consistent with support theory, and that the resulting subjective probabilities are then incorporated into choices according to the decision weighting function of prospect theory. Several studies (Fox et al., 1996; Fox & Tversky, 1998; Tversky & Fox, 1995; Wu & Gonzalez, 1999) used this approach to predict, with impressive accuracy, people's choices among uncertain prospects. Furthermore, Fox (1999) showed that such choices can even be reconstructed from direct support ratings of the kind discussed previously.

Several applied studies have also shown that unpacking uncertain events can influence decisions in domains such as sports prediction (Ayton, 1997), insurance (Johnson, Hershey, Meszaros, & Kunreuther, 1993), and medical diagnosis (Redelmeier, Koehler, Liberman, & Tversky, 1995). For example, in an analysis of bookmakers' published odds on soccer matches, Ayton (1997) found that the implied probability associated with an outcome such as England beating Switzerland in their upcoming match increased when the outcome was unpacked (based on half-time leader or on specific final scores). To the extent that published odds are driven by the market for various gambles, this observation implies that unpacking a hypothesis makes it appear more attractive as a wager. These studies suggest that the effect of unpacking captured by support theory has predictable consequences for decisions under uncertainty as well as for judgments of probability. The belief-based model of Fox and Tversky (1998) provides a detailed quantitative framework for applying support theory to predicting choices.

FUTURE DIRECTIONS

We now turn to some thoughts about avenues for future research. We focus on two aspects of support theory discussed in the introduction: (1) description-dependence and (2) probability judgment as a balance of evidence.

Description-Dependence

Many examples of description-dependence arise throughout the behavioral sciences. For instance, failures in Piagetian conservation tasks (Flavell, 1963) can be seen as illustrations of description-dependence (e.g., the same amount of liquid appears greater when in a tall narrow container than a short wide container). As another example, the influence on memory of variations in the wording of seemingly equivalent questions (e.g., Loftus, 1975) can be viewed as a form of description-dependence.

Decision framing effects offer what is perhaps the closest parallel to description dependence in probability judgment. The same medical procedure can be described in terms of either its survival or its mortality rates, leading to systematic changes in decisions made by experienced physicians (McNeil, Pauker, Sox, & Tversky, 1982). The same object can be valued differently by those who possess it versus those who do not, even when the object is distributed arbitrarily (Kahneman, Knetsch, & Thaler, 1990). In general, the way a choice option is described or the perspective from which it is viewed influences the attractiveness of that option.

A key element of description-dependence is the notion that people typically accept and treat problems as they are given without actively transforming those problems to some standard canonical representation (cf. Tversky & Kahneman, 1986). In the case of risky choice, people do not typically transform an offered gamble into a distribution of final wealth states. Analogously, in the case of judgment under uncertainty, people do not typically map a hypothesis onto some invariant sample space.

According to this view, probability judgment operates directly on the hypotheses and is not mediated through some representation of "event" (in the set-theoretic sense of the word). Descriptive models that invoke a canonical representation, such as event, may be inappropriately generalizing an important aspect of a normative model to the prediction and explanation of behavior (cf. Gigerenzer, 1991). Indeed, the notion of an event in probability theory is a subtle and nonintuitive concept. Instructors of probability and statistics classes often find that the fundamentals of probability theory are among the most difficult topics for their students. For example, recognizing that the hypothesis "A baseball batter will get at least one hit in four at-bats" is equivalent to "A baseball batter will not go hitless in each of four at-bats" is a difficult skill to acquire. Although a person may recognize the equivalence of two descriptions when presented with both and prompted to compare them, it is unlikely that when presented with one description the person will spontaneously recognize its equivalence to the many other possible descriptions and maintain consistency of judgment across those descriptions. The abstraction of events in probability theory is valuable precisely because people do not naturally engage in such abstraction themselves.

Demonstrations of description-dependence do not merely imply that people can be misled from their "true" beliefs, attitudes, or preferences. When there is not a single canonical description of some object, we cannot assume a single corresponding true belief, attitude, or preference toward that object. Descriptive theories of belief, attitude, or preference thus need to address the variability in responses due to changes in description, without simply appealing to the attractive but perhaps simplistic notion of an underlying canonical representation or "true score" (cf. Brenner, 2000).

We can distinguish between negative and positive analyses of description-dependence (Kahneman & Tversky, 1982). A negative analysis focuses on the failure to maintain invariant judgments across differences in description that (in a normative sense) should not matter. In contrast, a positive analysis provides some account (e.g., a causal explanation, processing model, or mathematical representation) that can be used to predict the occurrence, direction, and magnitude of description dependence. A positive analysis of conservation failures, for example, might posit that children focus primarily on the height of a container in judging its volume.

Support theory offers a partial positive analysis of description dependence in probability judgment: unpacking a hypothesis into components yields larger probability judgments, as does separate evaluation of the component hypotheses. However, the unpacking principle emphasized in the original formulation of support theory is just one of many possible forms of description-dependence. Clearly, other features of hypotheses besides their level of detail also influence support. Identification of the various determinants of description-dependence constitutes an important agenda for future research.

Two general points are worth stressing. First, the emphasis on subadditivity in previous research led researchers to focus almost exclusively on coextensional hypotheses. It may be liberating to abandon this constraint and investigate variations in description even if they entail changes in the referent event. Doing so would expand the scope of the theory by modeling judgment as a function of any identifiable features of hypotheses – not necessarily holding constant the referent event, as in studies of unpacking and repacking effects.

Second, it is worth noting that the evidence on which judgments are made, as well as the hypotheses under evaluation, is subject to description-dependence. Just as two hypotheses that refer to the same event can produce different judgments, so too can different descriptions of equivalent evidence.

Two broad research questions arise from this discussion. First: What features of hypotheses influence support, and how? Second: What features of evidence influence support, and how? In the remainder of this section, we offer some examples of features of hypotheses and evidence that may systematically influence support.

Features of Hypotheses

The Evaluative Quality of the Hypothesis. One feature that may have a systematic effect on support is the valence of a hypothesis – whether it is framed in positive or negative terms. Experimental variations of valence could be implemented via framing manipulations where the event stays constant (e.g., contrasting the judged likelihood that 9 of 10 patients survive their hospitalization to the judged likelihood that 1 of 10 patients does not). Alternatively, the valence of the event could be manipulated while changing the event itself. For example, consistent with past research on optimistic biases in judgment (e.g., Weinstein, 1980), people may be more willing (or more able) to recruit evidence supporting a positive hypothesis ("You will receive a very favorable evaluation from your boss") than a corresponding negative hypothesis ("You will receive a very unfavorable evaluation from your boss"). Furthermore, the effect of the valence of a hypothesis may interact with other features of the hypothesis. For example, the size of unpacking effects may be greater for negatively framed hypotheses than for similar positively framed hypotheses, perhaps because people are more likely to spontaneously unpack the latter.

Self-Relevance of the Hypothesis. A second notable feature of a hypothesis that may have a systematic effect on support is the relevance of the hypothesis to oneself. For example, contrast the "(un)favorable evaluation from boss" hypotheses described previously with equivalent hypotheses framed in terms of a coworker rather than oneself. Because self-relevant information is typically more abundant than information about others, self-relevant hypotheses generally draw on larger bodies of evidence and consequently may lead to greater variability in support (e.g., hypotheses that match the evidence may yield very high support values, and hypotheses that do not match the evidence may yield very low support values). This conjecture about self-relevant hypotheses suggests that in general, support may tend to be more sensitive to other hypothesis features (e.g., valence) for self- than for other-framed hypotheses.

Both the evaluative quality and self-relevance of a hypothesis will generally contribute to the extent to which the judge wants to believe that the hypothesis is true. Kunda (1990) discusses how people who are motivated to reach certain conclusions attempt to construct (in a biased fashion) a compelling case for their favored hypothesis that would convince an impartial audience. Gilovich (2000) suggests that conclusions a person does not want to believe are held to a higher standard than conclusions a person wants to believe. In the former case, the person asks if the evidence *compels* one to accept the conclusion, whereas in the latter case, the person asks instead if the evidence *allows* one to accept the conclusion. Clearly, in many circumstances, the desirability of believing a hypothesis may markedly influence its perceived support.

Features of Evidence

Evidence Ambiguity and Conflict. Evidence with ambiguous or conflicting implications may be likely to amplify the impact of other features on perceived support. For example, as mentioned earlier in the discussion of influences on subadditivity, Koehler (2000) found that the advantage afforded a focal hypothesis that is pitted against all its alternatives taken together is more pronounced in the face of conflicting evidence than in the face of consistent evidence. In short, unpacking effects may be enhanced by ambiguity or conflict in the evidence.

One possible explanation for this pattern is that evidential ambiguity or conflict allows the judge latitude in evaluating support, making it possible to interpret the evidence in a manner that fits the judge's desires or expectations. Numerous findings from the social psychological literature are consistent with this view. Lord, Ross, and Lepper (1979), for example, presented mixed evidence regarding the deterrent effectiveness of capital punishment to proponents and opponents of capital punishment. Both groups tended to discount whichever aspect of the evidence did not support their preferred hypothesis. Exposure to the same body of conflicting evidence led each group to believe more strongly in its own position. The conflict in the evidence presumably allowed both groups to be selective about the conclusions they drew from it.

Amount and Completeness of Evidence. The perceived amount of evidence available may also influence judgment, in a manner independent of its diagnostic value. Provision of highly detailed information may convey a sense of confidence, even if the additional detail is not particularly relevant or useful (e.g., Oskamp, 1965). By contrast, knowing that certain pieces of information exist but are not available may inappropriately reduce the support for hypotheses under consideration (Fox & Tversky, 1995). Finally, the amount of information available may also typically be correlated with the level of conflict in the evidence: With enough information, some of it is bound to support each hypothesis under consideration (e.g., Downs & Shafir, 1999).

Summary

Our discussion of features of hypotheses and evidence is, obviously, suggestive rather than exhaustive. Consideration of these and other features of hypotheses and evidence could serve both to broaden the scope of support theory research and to allow applications of support theory to related topics in social and cognitive psychology. In the next section, we sketch one such application.

ASSESSING THE BALANCE OF EVIDENCE: SUPPORT THEORY AND THE "ABOVE-AVERAGE EFFECT"

The intuition guiding support theory's representation of subjective probability in terms of the balance of evidence between two hypotheses may be applied to issues beyond likelihood judgment. To illustrate, we consider as a case study the well-documented *above-average effect*, in which people tend to rate themselves more positively than others with respect to personality traits, skills, or susceptibility to risks. Most people, for example, consider themselves to be happier with life (Klar & Giladi, 1999), better drivers (Svenson, 1981), and less likely to suffer a heart attack (Weinstein, 1980) than the average person.

Support theory is well suited for representing comparative judgments in which the judge evaluates his or her own standing relative to a group. One natural way to represent such judgments using support theory is to treat the focal hypothesis as concerning the self, and the alternative hypothesis as concerning others in the group. Increasing the support for the focal hypothesis produces judgments favoring the self over others, and increasing the support for the alternative hypothesis produces judgments favoring others over the self.

Support theory's emphasis on description-dependence suggests a consideration of how the focal and alternative hypotheses are represented by the judge. Based on the circumstances of the task or the framing of the query, there is substantial room for variability in how the hypotheses are represented. When asked, for example, to rate your driving skills relative to other people of your age, the focal hypothesis may take the form of something like, "I am a good driver." The alternative hypothesis may assume a number of forms – perhaps "The average person of my age is a good driver," "All people of my age are good drivers," or "My spouse (or some other salient person) is a good driver." Different representations of the alternative hypothesis call to mind different evidence, accrue different amounts of support, and yield different judgments.

Indeed, the selection of the alternative hypothesis has been shown to influence the magnitude of the above-average effect. The effect is larger when people evaluate themselves relative to a generic "average peer" than when they evaluate themselves relative to a specific peer (Klar et al., 1996; Perloff & Fetzer, 1986), even when they have little or no additional information about the specific peer (Alicke et al., 1995). A natural interpretation from the support theory perspective is that the alternative hypothesis recruits greater evidential support when it is represented as a concrete, specific individual than when it is represented as an abstract, conceptual entity.

Based on this view, *any* specific individual ought to be at an advantage when pitted against the generic average peer in terms of recruiting support. Consistent with this, specific others from one's group (and not just oneself) are systematically rated above the group average on positive traits (Klar & Giladi, 1997). This presupposes a positive attitude toward the group as a whole, which is then conveyed to any individual belonging to the group. Systematic "below average" effects are also observed – in which an individual belonging to a disliked group is rated below the group average on positive traits (Klar & Giladi, 1997). According to the support theory account, given a generally positive impression of the group and its members, one can more readily recruit support favoring individual group members than the group as a whole. Likewise, given a negative impression, support favoring a negative evaluation is more readily recruited regarding an individual than regarding the group as a whole.

Klar and Giladi (1997, 1999) offer a similar interpretation using somewhat different terms. They posit a tendency to base judgments pitting a "singular" target against a "distributional" comparison group almost exclusively on the features of the singular target. Consistent with this interpretation, Klar, and Giladi (1997) found that providing individuating information about the comparison group or generic average peer reduced the magnitude of the above-average effect.

Klar and Giladi (1997) argue that these findings reflect the "noncomparative nature of comparative judgments." Thus, people claim to be happier than others because, in absolute terms, they are happy with their lives in general (Klar & Giladi, 1999; cf. Fox & Kahneman, 1992). Along these lines, Kruger (1999) offered an anchoring-and-adjustment account of the above-average effect in which the absolute judgment serves as an anchor subject to subsequent (typically insufficient) adjustment, with the result that people tend to rate themselves above average on traits or skills for which their absolute standing is high. Most drivers, for example, are highly skilled in an absolute sense due to years of experience behind the wheel. An assessment of absolute level of skill may be a natural starting point for a comparative judgment, with insufficient adjustment for the skills of others producing an above-average effect. One straightforward prediction from this account is that the opposite pattern should be found when absolute standing is low – for example, in the case of playing chess or juggling. Indeed, participants in Kruger's (1999) studies gave themselves low absolute ratings with respect to these skills, and also rated themselves as systematically below average in a comparative judgment.

From the perspective of support theory, the findings of Kruger (1999) and Klar and Giladi (1999) imply that greater weight is placed on the focal, self-based hypothesis than on the alternative, other-based hypothesis in comparative judgments. One observation highlighted by a support theory analysis is that the self-based hypothesis typically occupies the focal position in the comparative judgment, making it difficult to determine if the resulting above-average effect reflects a tendency to overweight the self-based hypothesis specifically, or whichever hypothesis happens to be in the focal position more generally. The literature provides some evidence for both accounts. Klar and Giladi (1997) report that the tendency to rate a specific peer as above the group average on positive traits persists even when the direction of the comparison is reversed, such that the participant is asked to evaluate whether the generic "average peer" falls above or below the specific peer group member. The researchers, however, did not directly compare the magnitude of the effect with that found using the usual direction of comparison, which leaves the possibility that hypothesis position also plays a role. Consistent with this possibility, Hoorens (1995) reports that a larger above-average effect is found for positive attributes when people rate themselves relative to the average peer than when they rate the average peer relative to themselves. The evidence to date, then, suggests that the above-average effect reflects both position dependence and a tendency to place greater weight on an individuated target (typically the self) than on the comparison group.

These two influences require different explanations. Position dependence can be seen as an attentional effect; the focal hypothesis is considered more extensively, giving it greater weight in the final judgment. Indeed, the accounts of the above-average effect offered by Kruger (1999) and by Klar and Giladi

(1999) are quite similar to Macchi et al.'s (1999) account of position dependence in probability judgment. The notion of position dependence in the support theory framework may help to clarify questions about an unresolved issue in the study of the above-average effect, which concerns the role of the alternative hypothesis. Do people give judgments that merely underweight the alternative hypothesis, or do they entirely fail to treat the judgment as comparative at all, instead reporting an absolute judgment based exclusively on an evaluation of the focal hypothesis? In the terminology of support theory, this is analogous to asking whether participants are reporting a probability judgment (pitting focal against alternative hypothesis) or an assessment of the support for the focal hypothesis alone.

One method of addressing this question is to separately elicit absolute assessments of the self and of the comparison group, then predict the comparative judgment from the two separate assessments (e.g., Klar & Giladi, 1997, 1999; Kruger, 1999). Such studies have consistently found greater weight is placed on the self-based hypothesis (in the focal position) than on the other-based hypothesis (in the alternative position). Results have been mixed with respect to the precise role of the alternative hypothesis, with some studies (Kruger, 1999) reporting a negative regression coefficient (indicating that the greater the support for the alternative hypothesis, the lower the comparative judgment) and others (Klar & Giladi, 1997, 1999) reporting coefficients near zero. It is worth noting that regression coefficients of zero do not necessarily imply a completely non-comparative process, but are also consistent with the possibility that support for the alternative hypothesis has little variance.

If the judgment is truly comparative, then manipulations that facilitate recruitment of support for the alternative hypothesis ought to have some influence. Several findings are consistent with this claim, including Alicke et al.'s (1995) observation that providing information about the comparison individual decreases the size of the above-average effect. Weinstein (1980), Weinstein and Lachendro (1982), and Rothman, Klein, and Weinstein (1996) attribute people's tendency to underestimate their vulnerability to negative events in part to overestimation of the risks faced by others. They show, for example, that provision of accurate information regarding others' risks can reduce people's biased sense of invulnerability (Rothman et al., 1996). Even when no new information is provided, manipulations that prompt greater consideration of others' circumstances were sufficient to reduce the bias (Weinstein & Lachendro, 1982). These observations suggest that judgments in studies of the above-average effect may be comparative in a manner that could be captured by support theory, even if the alternative hypothesis is frequently underweighted.

The other apparent source of the above-average effect is a tendency to exaggerate the evidential support for the singular target (the self) in the comparative judgment. This may reflect both informational and motivational influences, which support theory might be useful in separating more clearly. The informational influence can arise because more is generally known about oneself than about specific others, about which in turn more is known than about the group as a whole or a generic average peer. A specific other may also serve as a better retrieval cue than a group, such that evidence known to characterize the entire group may nonetheless come more readily to mind when thinking about a specific group member. In terms of support theory, such influences generally yield greater support for the self or a specific other than for the group as a whole, regardless of whether the trait being evaluated is negative or positive; in either case, the judge should more readily recruit evidence supporting the hypothesis regarding oneself than the hypothesis regarding the average peer. This claim is consistent with research demonstrating that people asked whether they are characterized by a given attribute tend to rate themselves as higher on that attribute than when they are asked whether they are characterized by an opposite attribute (Kunda, Fong, Sanitioso, & Reber, 1993), presumably because they have so much self-relevant knowledge that some evidence supporting either attribute can be retrieved. Along these lines, Downs and Shafir (1999) showed that pairs of opposing traits are not only ascribed more frequently to oneself than to others, but also are more frequently ascribed to well-known celebrities than to less well-known individuals.

Motivational influences, by contrast, should be directed such that support for positive hypotheses regarding well-liked targets (e.g., self or close friend) should be more readily recruited and support for negative hypotheses regarding those targets should be less readily recruited. There is some evidence consistent with this possibility. Perloff and Fetzer (1986) reported that college students' self-ratings of susceptibility to risk exhibited a less pronounced illusion of invulnerability when the students compared themselves to a close friend than when they compared themselves to a less close friend or the average college student, suggesting a motivated tendency to underestimate the risks faced by friends. From the support theory perspective, such influences could arise from a tendency to exaggerate support for hypotheses one wishes to believe.

Such motivational influences ought to be limited under conditions that make it difficult to exaggerate support for the desired hypothesis. Consistent with this perspective, Dunning, Meyerowitz, and Holzberg (1989) showed that the tendency to rate oneself above average on positive attributes is substantially reduced or even eliminated when the attributes are clearly defined. Only when the attributes are relatively ambiguous do pronounced above-average effects emerge, which these researchers attribute to a tendency to interpret ambiguous traits in a manner that best fits one's own description; thus, the analytic individual considers herself a good leader due to her planning skills, and the friendly individual considers himself a good leader due to his communication skills.

The support theory framework can accommodate this finding: Motivational factors influence comparative judgments by maximizing support for desirable hypotheses and minimizing support for undesirable hypotheses. Circumstances that constrain the kind of evidence that can be recruited and the manner in which it can be interpreted necessarily limit the extent to which one can construct a judgment favoring the desirable hypothesis. One additional finding (e.g., Klar et al., 1996; Weinstein, 1980) consistent with this approach is that above-average effects in judgments of risks are more pronounced for controllable future outcomes (e.g., heart attack, for which exercise and diet play a large role) than for uncontrollable future outcomes (e.g., leukemia). In the case of uncontrollable future outcomes, it is presumably more difficult to recruit evidence supporting one's own relative invulnerability.

CONCLUSION

Our review of previous work in support theory reveals that there is far more to the theory than just the phenomenon of unpacking. Although a good deal of past work in support theory has investigated the determinants of unpacking, other research has made substantial progress in exploring ratings of support, testing the axioms implied by the support theory representation, and applying support theory to calibration and decision making.

Our discussion of possible future directions suggests additional questions to explore. The general phenomenon of description-dependence points to a research strategy in which researchers identify the features of hypotheses and evidence that influence support. In this spirit, support theory is a framework that can accommodate many empirical patterns as well as the psychological processes that produce those patterns. Finally, as illustrated by our case study of the above-average effect, support theory can be applied to phenomena outside the domain of probability judgment. Description-dependence and the notion of judgment as represented by a balance of evidence strength are principles that are broadly applicable to other topics within the many fields concerned with the principles and processes of human judgment.

28. The Use of Statistical Heuristics in Everyday Inductive Reasoning

Richard E. Nisbett, David H. Krantz, Christopher Jepson, and Ziva Kunda

Research on *nonstatistical heuristics* has been criticized on several grounds. Some critics have maintained that evolution should be expected to produce highly efficacious and generally correct principles of reasoning and that the research may therefore be misleading in some way (Cohen, 1979; Dennett, 1978, 1981, 1983; Lycan, 1981). Others have maintained that the research does not demonstrate that people fail to apply correct inferential rules but rather that (1) it is the researchers themselves who are mistaken about the correct inferential rules (Cohen, 1981), (2) subjects have been misled by illusionary circumstances of little general significance beyond the laboratory (Cohen, 1981; Lopes, 1982; Dennett, 1983), or (3) people's general inferential goals are such that at least some violations of statistical principles should be regarded as a form of *satisficing* or cost-effective inferential shortcuts (Einhorn & Hogarth, 1981; Miller & Cantor, 1982; Nisbett & Ross, 1980). . . .

In this chapter, we first summarize the work establishing failures to reason statistically. We then review anecdotal and experimental evidence indicating that people do sometimes reason statistically. Next we present original experimental work indicating some of the factors that influence statistical reasoning. Then we summarize research suggesting that people's ability to reason statistically about everyday life problems is affected by training in formal statistics. Finally, we speculate on the normative implications of people's ability and trainability for statistical reasoning.

STATISTICAL PROBLEMS AND NONSTATISTICAL HEURISTICS

In a succession of studies, Kahneman and Tversky have shown that much inductive reasoning is nonstatistical. People often solve inductive problems by use of a variety of intuitive heuristics – rapid and more or less automatic judgmental rules of thumb. These include the *representativeness heuristic* (Kahneman & Tversky, 1972, 1973), the *availability heuristic* (Tversky & Kahneman, 1973), the *anchoring heuristic* (Tversky & Kahneman, 1974), and the *simulation heuristic*

This is an edited and condensed version of a paper that first appeared in *Psychological Review, 90*, 339–363. Copyright © 1983 by the American Psychological Association. Adapted with permission.

(Kahneman & Tversky, 1982). In problems in which these heuristics diverge from the correct statistical approach, people commit serious errors of inference.

The representativeness heuristic is the best studied and probably the most important of the heuristics. People often rely on this heuristic when making likelihood judgments, for example, the likelihood that Object A belongs to Class B or the likelihood that Event A originates from Process B. Use of the heuristic entails basing such judgments on "the degree to which A is representative of B, that is, by the degree to which A resembles B" (Tversky & Kahneman, 1974, p. 1124). In one problem, for example, Kahneman and Tversky (1972) asked subjects whether days with 60% or more male births would be more common at a hospital with 15 births per day, or at a hospital with 45 births per day, or equally common at the two hospitals. Most subjects chose the latter alternative, and the remainder divided about evenly between 15 and 45. The law of large numbers requires that, with a random variable such as sex of infant, deviant sample percentages should be less common as sample size increases. The representativeness heuristic, however, leads subjects to compare the similarities of the two sample proportions to the presumed population proportion (50%); because the two sample proportions equally resemble the population proportion, they are deemed equally likely. The data indicate that, for this problem at least, most subjects used the representativeness heuristic and very few subjects used the law of large numbers.

In another demonstration, Kahneman and Tversky (1973) studied the prediction of an outcome for a target person based on various characteristics of that person or based on scores from various predictor tests. Subjects used the representativeness heuristic: In general, they predicted whichever outcome was most similar to the target person's characteristics or scores. For instance, in predicting the grade point average (GPA) for a target person who is in the 90th percentile on a predictor test, about the same results are obtained – that is, prediction of a GPA well above average – whether the predictor is the score on a test of sense of humor (which subjects do not regard as very diagnostic of GPA), the score on a test of mental concentration, or the GPA itself (!). Such predictions diverge from those that would be obtained from statistical considerations in which the average accuracy of prediction would be taken into account. Subjects do not seem to realize that if accuracy is very limited, then it is far more probable that the target person's outcome will be equal to the modal outcome (or near the mean of the unimodal symmetric distribution) than that it will take some relatively unusual value that happens to match the characteristics on the predictor. This is the statistical principle of regression to the mean, or base rate. . . .

STATISTICAL HEURISTICS

Selective Application of Statistical Reasoning

The foregoing work indicates that nonstatistical heuristics play an important role in inductive reasoning. But it does not establish that other heuristics, based on statistical concepts, are absent from people's judgmental repertoire. Indeed, if one begins to look for cases of good statistical intuitions in everyday problems, it is not hard to find some plausible candidates.

Even when judgments are based on the representativeness heuristic, there may be an underlying stratum of probabilistic thinking. In many of the problems studied by Kahneman and Tversky, people probably conceive of the underlying process as random, but they lack a means of making use of their intuitions about randomness and they fall back on representativeness. In the maternity ward problem, for example, people surely believe that the number of boys born on any particular day is a matter of chance, even though they rely on representativeness to generate their subjective sampling distributions. But consider the following thought experiment: If someone says, "I can't understand it; I have nine grandchildren and all of them are boys," the statement sounds quite sensible. The hearer is likely to agree that a causal explanation seems to be called for. However, imagine that the speaker says, "I can't understand it; I have three grandchildren and all of them are boys." Such a statement sounds peculiar, to say the least, because it seems transparent that such a result could be due just to chance – that is, there is nothing to understand. Such an intuition is properly regarded as statistical in our view.

The contrast between the statistical intuition in our anecdote and subjects' use of the representativeness heuristic in the maternity ward problem illustrates the selectivity with which people apply statistical concepts. The failure to do so in the maternity ward problem may be due to the use of "60%" in the problem, which evokes comparison between 60% and 50% and thence the dependence on the similarity judgment in choosing an answer. It may also be due to lack of concrete experience in thinking about samples in the range 15–45. As Piaget and Inhelder (1951/1975) put it, people seem to have an intuitive grasp of the "law of *small* large numbers," even though they may not generalize the intuition to large numbers.

People also seem to have an ability to use base rates for selected kinds of problems. Consider the concepts of *easy* and *difficult* examinations. People do not infer that a student is brilliant who received an A+ on an exam in which no one scored below A−, nor that the student is in trouble who flunked a test that was also failed by 75% of the class. Rather, they convert the base-rate information (performance of the class as a whole) into a location parameter for the examination (easy, . . . difficult) and make their inference about the particular student in terms of the student's relative position compared to the difficulty of the exam. Indeed, laboratory evidence has been available for some time that base rates are readily used for causal attributions for many kinds of abilities and achievements (Weiner et al., 1972).

As Nisbett and Ross (1980) suggested, one suspects that many lay concepts and maxims reflect an appreciation of statistical principles. It seems possible, for example, that people sometimes overcome sample bias by applying proverbs such as, "Don't judge a book by its cover" or, "All that glitters is not gold." Perhaps people sometimes even manage to be regressive in everyday predictions by using concepts such as "beginner's luck" or "nowhere to go but up/down."

There is one inductive reasoning task in particular for which there is good reason to suspect that statistical intuitions are very frequently applied. This is *generalization from instances* – perhaps the simplest and most pervasive of everyday inductive tasks. People surely recognize, in many contexts at least that when moving from particular observations to general propositions, more evidence is better than less. The preference for more evidence seems well understood as being due to an intuitive appreciation of the law of large numbers. For example, we think that most people would prefer to hold a 20-minute interview rather than a 5-minute interview with a prospective employee, and that if questioned, they would justify this preference by saying that 5 minutes is too short a period to get an accurate idea of what the job candidate is like. That is they believe that there is a greater chance of substantial error with the smaller sample. Similarly, most people would believe the result of a survey of 100 people more than they would believe that of a survey of 10 people; again, their reason would be based on the law of large numbers.

As we shall see, there is reason to believe that people's statistical understanding of the generalization task is deeper still. People understand, at least in some contexts, that the law of large numbers must be taken into account to the degree that the events in question arc uncertain and variable in a statistical sense. Thus they realize that some classes of events are very heterogeneous; that is, the events differ from one another, or from one occasion to another, in ways that are unpredictable, and it is these classes of events for which a large sample is particularly essential. . . .

FACTORS THAT AFFECT STATISTICAL REASONING

What factors make it difficult to apply statistical heuristics when these are required, and what factors can make it easier?

Clarity of the Sample Space and the Sampling Process

Randomizing devices are usually designed so that the sample space for a single trial is obvious and so that the repeatability of trials is salient. The die has six faces and can be tossed again and again; the pointer can stop on any of eight sectors and can be spun over and over. Clarity of sample space makes it easier to see what knowledge is relevant. For randomizing devices, the most relevant knowledge is often just the observation of symmetry of the different die faces, spinner sectors, and so forth. The salience of repeatability makes it easier to conceptualize one's observations as a sample.

In the social domain, sample spaces are often obscure, and repeatability is hard to imagine. For example, the sample space consisting, of different degrees of helpfulness that might be displayed by a particular person in a particular situation is quite obscure, and the notion of repetition is strained. What is it that could be repeated? Placing the same person in *different* situations? Or *other* people in the same situation? The probability that Person P will exhibit Behavior B in Situation S is abstract and not part of the inductive repertoire of most people most of the time. Even though people recognize the possibility of errors in their judgments of social situations, they do not try to construct probability models; rather, they rely on the representativeness heuristic.

Recognition of the Operation of Chance Factors

A second major factor encouraging the use of statistical heuristics is the recognition of the role of chance in producing events in a given domain or in a particular situation. For example, statistical understanding of some types of sports is undoubtedly facilitated by the manifestly random component in the movement of the objects used: "A football can take funny bounces." The random component probably does not have to be physical in order for people to recognize it. It is possible to recognize the unpredictability of academic test performance by repeated observations of one's own outcomes. Even with one's own efforts and the group against which one is competing held constant, outcomes can vary. One may even recognize that one's performance on particular occasions was particularly good or poor because of accidents: "I just happened to reread that section because Jill never called me back"; "It was very noisy in the study area that night so I didn't get a chance to review my notes."

In contrast, cues as to randomness in the production of events are much subtler for other kinds of events, especially for many social ones. When we interview someone, what signs would let us know that a particular topic got explored just by chance or that the person seems dour and lackluster because of an uncharacteristic attempt to appear dignified rather than because of a phlegmatic disposition? In addition, as Einhorn and Hogarth (1978) pointed out, the gatekeeping function of the interview may serve to prevent us from recognizing the error variance in our judgments: The great talent of some people not hired or admitted may never be observed. In most situations, cues as to the fact that an interview ought to be regarded as a sample from a population, rather than a portrait in miniature, are missing. The same may be true for visits to a city, country, or university. One of us long believed that reports of raininess in England were greatly exaggerated because he once stayed in London for 10 days and it only drizzled twice!

Cultural Prescriptions

A third factor that may contribute to the use of statistical heuristics is a cultural or subcultural prescription to reason statistically about events of a given kind. Statistical reasoning is the culturally prescribed way to think about randomizing devices in our culture, and this general approach undoubtedly trickles down to children. Similarly, statistical reasoning has become (or is becoming) the norm for experts in many fields – from insurance to medical diagnosis – and is rapidly becoming normative for the lay novice as well in such domains as sports and the weather. Models of statistical reasoning abound for sports in particular, as the following two examples indicate.

> Baseball's law of averages is nothing more than an acknowledgement that players level off from season to season to their true ability-reflected by their lifetime averages. A .250-hitter may hit .200 or .300 over a given period of time, but baseball history shows he will eventually level off at his own ability ("Law of Averages," 1981).
> The musky tends to be a deep-water fish. Most fishing success is in shallow water, but . . . this misleading statistic [is probably accounted for in part by the fact that] sheer statistical chance dictates that fish will come from the waters receiving the most man hours of fishing pressure. Shallow water fishing for muskies is very popular, and very few fishermen work them deep (Hamer, 1981).

The statistical spirit embodied in these quotations reaches many fans. Thus, it is commonplace to hear lay people endorse the proposition that, "On a given Sunday, any team in the NFL can beat any other team." (Compare with "On a given Sunday, any parishioner's altruism can exceed that of any other parishioner"!)

In our view, these three factors – clarity of the sample space and the sampling process, recognition of the role of chance in producing events, and cultural prescriptions to think statistically – operate individually, and perhaps more often, together to increase people's tendencies to apply statistical heuristics to problems that require a statistical approach. If these factors are genuinely important determinants of people's ability to reason statistically, then it should be possible to find support for the following predictions.

In cases in which the sample space is clear and the possibility of repetition is salient, people respond appropriately to statistical variables. In particular, in the task of generalizing from instances, in which the sample space is a clear dichotomy and the sampling process is just the observation of more members of a clearly defined population, (1) people generalize more cautiously when the sample size is small and when they have no strong prior belief that the sampled population is homogeneous, and (2) people can be influenced to generalize more or less readily by manipulations that emphasize the homogeneity or heterogeneity of the sampled population.

The following predictions should hold both for generalization and for other, more complex, inferential tasks:

1. Manipulations designed to encourage recognition of the chance factors influencing events should serve to increase statistical reasoning.

2. People who are highly knowledgeable about events of a given kind should be more inclined than less knowledgeable people to apply statistical reasoning to the events – because both the distributions of the events and the chance factors influencing the events should be clearer to such people.
3. People should be disinclined to reason statistically about certain kinds of events that they recognize to be highly variable and uncertain – notably social events – because the sample spaces for the events and the chance factors influencing the events are opaque.
4. Training in statistics should promote statistical reasoning even about mundane events of everyday life because such training should help people to construct distributional models for events and help them to recognize "error," or the chance factors influencing events.

GENERALIZING FROM INSTANCES

Generalization from observed cases is the classic concern of philosophers and other thinkers who are interested in induction. A number of instances of Class A are observed, and each of them turns out to have Property B. Possible inferences include the universal generalization *all As have B*, or the near universal *most As have B*, or at least the relinquishing of the contrary generalization; namely, *most As do not have B*.

The untrammeled employment of the representativeness heuristic would lead people to make the above inferences from quite small numbers of instances, and, indeed, this is often found, both anecdotally and in laboratory studies (Nisbett & Ross, 1980, pp. 77–82). However, philosophers since Hume have puzzled about how these generalizations can be logically justified, even when very large numbers of instances are observed. The puzzle has been compounded by the fact that sometimes it seems correct to generalize confidently from a few instances. Hume (1748/1955) wrote, "[Often, when] I have found that . . . an object has always been attended with . . . an effect . . . I foresee that other objects which are in appearance similar will be attended with similar effects" (p. 48). The problem is that only sometimes do we draw such a conclusion with confidence. "Nothing so like as eggs, yet no one, on account of this appearing similarity, expects the same taste and relish in all of them" (Hume, 1748/1955, p. 50). Mill (1843/1974), a century later, phrased the problem as: "Why is a single instance, in some cases, sufficient for a complete induction, while in others myriads of concurring instances, without a single exception known or presumed, go such a very little way towards establishing a universal proposition?" (p. 314).

The statistical advances since Mill's time make it clear that a large part of the answer to his question has to do with beliefs about the variability or *homogeneity* of certain kinds or classes of events (cf. Thagard & Nisbett, 1982). Generalization from a large sample is justified in terms of one's beliefs that the sampling itself is homogeneous (i.e., that the distribution of possible sample statistics is the same as would be predicted by random sampling). Generalization from a small sample or resistance to generalization, even from a large sample, are justified in terms of prior beliefs about the homogeneity or heterogeneity of objects or events of a certain kind with respect to a property of a certain kind. . . .

Homogeneity Study: Beliefs About Homogeneity and Reliance on the Law of Large Numbers

In this study, we simply guessed at the prevailing beliefs about homogeneity. We tried to obtain different degrees of heterogeneity by using conductivity of metals, colors of animals, and so on. Subjects were told of one instance or of several instances of a sampled object having a particular property and were asked to guess what percentage of the population of all such objects would have the property. The sample sizes used were 1, 3, or 20; in the latter cases, all 3 or all 20 of the objects had the property in question. We anticipated that subjects would generalize more readily from a given number of instances when the kind of object was perceived as homogeneous with respect to the kind of property than when the kind of object was perceived as heterogeneous with respect to the kind of property.

Method. Subjects were 46 University of Michigan students of both sexes who were enrolled in introductory psychology. (As sex did not affect any of the dependent variables in this or any of the other studies, it is not discussed further.) Eighty-five percent of the subjects had taken no statistics courses in college. The questionnaire was presented as one of several in a study on judgment. It read as follows for the $N = 1$ condition:

Imagine that you are an explorer who has landed on a little known island in the Southeastern Pacific. You encounter several new animals, people, and objects. You observe the properties of your "samples" and you need to make guesses about how common these properties would be in other animals, people or objects of the same type.

Suppose you encounter a new bird, the shreeble. It is blue in color. What percent of all shreebles on the island do you expect to be blue?

(This and the subsequent questions were followed by "_____ percent. Why did you guess this percent?")

Suppose the shreeble you encounter is found to nest in a eucalyptus tree, a type of tree which is fairly common on the island. What percent of all shreebles on the island do you expect to nest in eucalyptus trees?

Suppose you encounter a native, who is a member of a tribe he calls the Barratos. He is obese. What percent of the male Barratos do you expect to be obese?

Suppose the Barratos man is brown in color. What percent of male Barratos do you expect to be brown (as opposed to red, yellow, black, or white)?

Suppose you encounter what the physicist on your expedition describes as an extremely rare element called *floridium*. Upon being heated to a very high temperature, it burns with a green flame. What percent of all samples of floridium found on the island do you expect to burn with a green flame?

Suppose the sample of floridium, when drawn into a filament, is found to conduct electricity. What percent of all samples of floridium found on the island do you expect to conduct electricity?

The questionnaires for the $N = 3$ condition and the $N = 20$ condition were identical except that they specified larger samples of each object. For example, the first shreeble item for the $N = 3$ condition read as follows:

Suppose you encounter a new bird, the shreeble. You see three such birds. They are all blue in color. What percent of all shreebles on the island do you expect to be blue?

The reasons subjects gave for guessing as they did were coded as to their content. There were three basic sorts of answers: (1) references to the homogeneity of the kind of object with respect to the kind of property; (2) references to the heterogeneity of the kind of object with respect to the kind of property – due to the different properties of subkinds (e.g., male versus female), to some causal mechanism producing different properties (e.g., genetic mistakes), or to purely statistical variability (e.g., "Where birds nest is sometimes just a matter of chance"); and (3) other sorts of answers that were mostly based on representativeness or that were mere tautologies. Two independent coders achieved 89% exact agreement on coding category.

Results. Any one element is presumed by scientists to be homogeneous with respect to most properties. At the other extreme, most human groups are highly heterogeneous among themselves in many attributes, including body weight. If educated laypeople share these beliefs and if they reason statistically, then (1) they should exercise more caution in generalizing from single cases when heterogeneity is expected than when homogeneity is expected and (2) large N should be important primarily in the case of populations whom subjects believe to be heterogeneous with respect to the property in question.

Figure 28.1 presents subjects' estimates of the percentage of each population having the property associated with the sample as a function of sample size presented. It may be seen that subjects are quite willing to generalize from even a single instance of green-burning or electricity-conducting floridium and also from a single, brown, Barratos tribesman. The modal estimate for $N = 1$ (as well as for $N = 3$ and $N = 20$) in all of these cases is 100%. In contrast, generalizations are less extreme for even 20 instances of blue shreebles or eucalyptus-nesting shreebles or 20 obese Barratos. The t (31) contrasting $N = 1$ for floridium attributes and Barratos color with $N = 20$ for shreeble attributes and Barratos obesity is 3.00; $p < .01$.

Subjects' explanations for their estimates fully justify this pattern of inferences. It may be seen in Table 28.1 that subjects reported believing that elements are homogeneous with respect to color and conductivity and that tribes are homogeneous with respect to color. In contrast, subjects rarely expressed the belief that there is homogeneity for the other kinds of populations and properties and instead expressed belief in heterogeneity of one sort or another for these

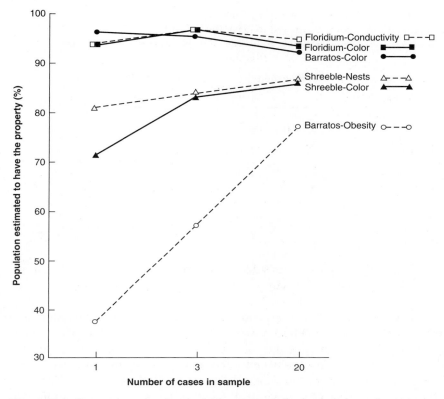

Figure 28.1. Percentage of each population estimated to have the sample property as a function of number of cases in the sample.

objects and properties. Figure 28.1 shows that it is only for these latter cases that subjects reasoned statistically in the sense that they were more willing to assume that the population resembles the sample when N is larger. N affects the estimates of the obesity of Barratos and the color of shreebles ($p < .001$ and $p = .11$, respectively). . . .

Finally, an internal analysis of the Table 28.1 data for each question showed that those subjects who believed the population to be homogeneous with respect to the property estimated that a higher percentage of the population was like the sample than did those subjects who believed the population was heterogeneous with respect to the property. The lowest t resulting from the six comparisons yielded $p < .05$. . . .

Manipulating the Salience of Chance Factors

It should also be possible to influence generalizations by manipulating the salience of chance factors. One potentially interesting way of doing this would be to highlight for subjects the degree to which evidence about an object should properly be regarded as a sample from the population of the object's attributes.

Table 28.1. Number of Subjects Giving Each Type of Reason and Percentage of Population Estimated to Have the Property

Object and Property	Homogeneity		Tautology		Heterogeneity	
	n	%	n	%	n	%
Shreeble						
Color	6	95	17	83	22	75
Nests	8	96	19	84	19	78
Barratos						
Obesity	5	79	10	62	31	53
Color	31	98	7	94	8	80
Floridium						
Color	31	97	9	91	6	82
Conductivity	31	98	7	92	8	82

Such a reminder ought to prompt subjects to reason more statistically, deemphasizing evidence from smaller samples and placing greater weight on evidence from larger samples.

Borgida and Nisbett (1977) argued that people often ignore the judgments of others when choosing between two objects and substitute their own initial impressions of the objects as the sole basis of choice. People do this in part because they do not recognize the relevance of the law of large numbers when reasoning about events of the personal preference kind. When the objects are multifaceted and complex, however, the law of large numbers is applicable in two ways: (1) The reactions of other people to the object, especially if they are based on more extensive contact with the object than one has had oneself, generally should be a useful guide to choice (although, of course, it is possible to construct cases in which other people's reactions would not be useful); and (2) One's own experience with the object, especially if it is brief or superficial, may be a poor guide to choice because of the error that plagues any small samples, even those that happen to be our own.

It seemed likely that if people were made explicitly aware of the role of chance in determining the impression one may get from a small sample, they might place less faith in a small personal sample and more faith in a large sample based on other people's reactions.

Method. Subjects were 157 University of Michigan students of both sexes who were enrolled in introductory psychology classes. Eighty-seven percent had taken no statistics courses in college. Subjects participated in small groups. They were presented with two versions of the following problem.

David L. was a senior in high school on the East Coast who was planning to go to college. He had compiled an excellent record in high school and had been admitted to his two top choices: a small liberal arts college and an Ivy League university. David had several older friends who were attending the liberal arts college and several who were attending the Ivy League university. They were all excellent students like himself and had interests similar to his. The friends at the liberal arts college all reported that they liked the place very much and that they found it very stimulating. The friends at the Ivy League university reported that they had many complaints on both personal and social grounds and on educational grounds.

David initially thought that he would go to the smaller college. However, he decided to visit both schools himself for a day.

He did not like what he saw at the private liberal arts college: Several people whom he met seemed cold and unpleasant, a professor he met with briefly seemed abrupt and uninterested in him, and he did not like the "feel" of the campus. He did like what he saw at the Ivy League university: Several of the people he met seemed like vital, enthusiastic, pleasant people; he met with two different professors, who took a personal interest in him; and he came away with a very pleasant feeling about the campus. Please say which school you think David should go to.

1. He should definitely go to the liberal arts college.
2. He should probably go to the liberal arts college.
3. It's a toss-up.
4. He should probably go to the Ivy League university.
5. He should definitely go to the Ivy League university.

Please indicate why you made the recommendation you did.

The remaining subjects were presented with am identical problem except that the possibilities for error in David L.'s sample were highlighted by having him draw up a list of all the things that might be seen on the two campuses and then selecting randomly from among them for his actual schedule. The following was added to the second paragraph of the no-cue version.

He proceeded systematically to draw up a long list for both colleges of all the classes which might interest him and all the places and activities on campus that he wanted to see. From each list, he randomly selected several classes and activities to visit, and several spots to look at (by blindly dropping a pencil on each list of alternatives and seeing where the point landed).

Open-ended responses to the probe question were coded (by a blind coder) as to whether subjects justified their choice by showing any recognition of the statistical questions involved – either the dubiousness of David L.'s impressions because of the quantity of his evidence or the superiority of his friends' testimony because of their greater experience. There was 90% agreement among coders as to the assignment of an answer to the statistical versus nonstatistical categories.

Results. When there was no sampling cue pointing to the probabilistic nature of David L.'s personal evidence base, 74% of the subjects recommended that David L. should go to the Ivy League university, which his friends did not much like but where he enjoyed his day. When the sampling cue was present, this dropped to 56% ($\chi^2 = 5.38$, $p < .025$). Moreover, subjects in the probabilistic-cue condition were much more likely to refer to statistical considerations having to do with the adequacy of the sample. Fifty-six percent of probabilistic-cue subjects raised statistical questions in their open-ended answers, whereas only 35% of subjects in the no-cue condition did so ($p < .01$). Thus, when subjects are prompted to consider the possibilities for error that are inherent in a small sample of events, they are likely to shift to a preference for large indirect samples over small personal ones, and their open-ended answers make it clear that it is statistical considerations that prompt this shift.

The findings of Study 3 are extremely ironic in that subjects are more likely to reject the superior personal evidence in the probabilistic-cue condition than to reject the inferior personal evidence in the control condition. This is because the same circumstances that serve to make the evidence superior in the probabilistic-cue condition also serve to make salient the extreme heterogeneity of the event population to be estimated and the small size of the personal sample of those events. It is important to note that when Study 3 is run with a "within" design, subjects assess the relative value of the personal evidence correctly; that is, they generally rate the quality of evidence in the probabilistic-cue condition as superior to that in the control condition. In two slightly different within-design follow-ups to Study 3, subjects rated the probabilistic-cue sample as being superior to the sample in the control version. In one of the follow-ups (where subjects read the control problem and rated the quality of the personal evidence, then read the cue paragraph and compared the quality of the evidence there with the control version) four times as many subjects preferred the probabilistic-cue evidence as preferred the control evidence. In the other follow-up (where subjects actually acted as subjects in the control condition and then were shown the cue version), 40% more subjects preferred the probabilistic-cue evidence than preferred the control evidence.

EXPERTISE AND STATISTICAL REASONING

Recognition of a Regression Effect in Sports and Acting

The studies we have just described indicate that subjects reason statistically when they recognize the heterogeneity of the events in question and the sample-like nature of their evidence about the events. If people are capable of learning from experience that events of a given kind are heterogeneous and are produced in part by chance, then it should be possible to show that greater expertise in a domain is associated with a greater tendency to reason statistically in that domain. The two domains we selected to test this proposition were sports and acting. We anticipated that experience with sports would facilitate recognition of a regression effect in sports and that experience with acting would facilitate recognition of a regression effect in acting. Subjects were told about a small sample of extreme behavior followed by a larger sample of less extreme behavior. It was anticipated that inexpert subjects would generalize from the small sample and then would be obligated to give a causal explanation for the discrepancy between the small sample and the large sample. Expert subjects were expected to generalize less and to recognize that the discrepancy could be due to chance factors making the small sample appear extreme.

Method. Subjects were the same as those in Study 3. The problem presented to them was one of several in a study described as being aimed at finding out "how people go about explaining and predicting events under conditions of very limited information about the events." Subjects were given one of two nearly identically worded problems. One concerned a football coach who usually found that the most brilliant performers at tryout were not necessarily the best players during the football season, and the other concerned a repertory company director who usually found that the most brilliant performers at audition were not necessarily the best actors during the drama season. The full text of the football version was as follows:

Football. Harold is the coach for a high school football team. One of his jobs is selecting new members of the varsity team. He says the following of his experience: "Every year, we add 10 to 20 younger boys to the team on the basis of their performance at the try-out practice. Usually, the staff and I are extremely excited about the potential of two or three of these kids – one who throws several brilliant passes or another who kicks several field goals from a remarkable distance. Unfortunately, most of these kids turn out to be only somewhat better than the rest." Why do you suppose that the coach usually has to revise downward his opinion of players that he originally thought were brilliant?

The acting version of the problem was almost identical except that it was about Susan, the director of a student repertory company, who gets excited about "a young woman with great stage presence or a young man who gives a brilliant reading."

Subjects were asked which of the following explanations they preferred for the fact that the coach/director usually had to revise downward his or her opinion of the brilliant performers. The second alternative is the statistical one, suggesting that the explanation is simply that the tryout performances were uncharacteristically good for the "brilliant" performers.

1. Harold was probably mistaken in his initial opinion. In his eagerness to find new talent, he exaggerates the brilliance of the performances he sees at the try-out.
2. The brilliant performances at try-out are not typical of those boys' general abilities. They probably just made some plays at the try-out that were much better than usual for them.
3. The boys who did so well at try-out probably could coast through the season on their talent alone and don't put out the effort necessary to transform talent into consistently excellent performance.
4. The boys who did so well at try-out may find that their teammates are jealous. They may slack off so as not to arouse envy.
5. The boys who did so well at try-out are likely to be students with other interests. These interests would deflect them from putting all their energies into football.

Table 28.2. Percentage of Experienced and Inexperienced Subjects Who Preferred the Statistical Explanation for the Football and the Acting Problems

Problem	Subjects		χ^2	p
	Experienced	Inexperienced		
Football			3.10	.10
%	56	35		
N	52	26		
Acting			5.18	.025
%	59	29		
N	17	62		
Both versions			10.60	.001
%	57	31		
N	69	88		

Wording was altered very slightly for the acting version: "Boys" became "actors" and "try-out" became "audition."

Experience in sports was assessed by asking subjects whether they had played any organized team sports in high school or college. Those who had were defined as *experienced*. Experience in acting was defined as having had "more than a bit part" in a play in high school or college.

Results. It may be seen in Table 28.2 that experience affects the likelihood of preferring a statistical explanation for both the football version of the problem and the acting version. Most of the subjects with athletic team experience (a majority) preferred the statistical explanation for the football problem, whereas most of the subjects without team experience preferred one of the other, deterministic explanations. Most of the subjects with acting experience (a small minority) preferred the statistical explanation for the acting problem, whereas most of the subjects without acting experience preferred one of the deterministic explanations.

We do not wish to infer from these results that experience in a domain will make statistical explanations more salient for *every* kind of problem. Expertise brings a recognition of the causal factors at work in a domain as well as a recognition of the remaining uncertainty. When the problem can be approached with this expert causal knowledge, the expert may give answers that are less statistical, at least in form, than those of the novice. We may speculate that expertise reduces reliance on the representativeness heuristic, which encourages unreflective assumptions that the future will resemble the past and that populations will resemble samples, and substitutes either statistical reasoning or reasoning in accordance with well-justified causal rules.

We should note also that it is possible that the tendency of experts to reason statistically may have less to do with knowledge of variability and uncertainty than with a subcultural norm for them to do so. The statistical answer may simply look more like a familiar, standard answer to the experts than to the nonexperts. For a correlational study such as Study 4, it is not easy to disentangle the undoubtedly related factors influencing statistical reasoning.

DOMAIN SPECIFICITY OF INDUCTIVE RULES

One of the major implications of the present viewpoint is that there should be a substantial degree of domain specificity of statistical reasoning. Its use should be rare for domains in which (1) it is hard to discern the sample space and the sampling process, (2) the role of chance in producing events is unclear, and (3) no cultural prescription for statistical reasoning exists. We have noted that many of the studies showing people's failures in statistical reasoning examined judgments about events characterized by one or more of these factors. We have also noted that some of people's few demonstrated successes in statistical reasoning have been observed for people's reasoning about sports and academic achievements that seem to be characterized by clearer distributions for events, a more obvious role of chance, and, probably, cultural prescriptions as well. These observations were made across studies, across tasks, and across subject populations, however.

To demonstrate that the same subjects dealing with the same tasks in the same experiment are more likely to reason statistically for some events characterized by uncertainty than for others, Jepson, Krantz, and Nisbett (1983) presented subjects with two broad classes of problems. The first class of problems dealt with events that are assessable by objective means, such as abilities, achievements, and physical illness. The second class dealt with events that are assessable only by subjective means, for example, personal preferences among objects, assessments of leadership potential, and judgments about the need for sexual fidelity in relationships. It was reasoned that, in general, it is relatively easy to apply statistical reasoning to objective events because one is likely to have some idea of their distributions (or to be able to guess what the distributions might look like because the units of measurement and the sample space are likely to be relatively clear). In general, also, the role of chance is likely to be relatively transparent for those objectively assessable events that in fact have been observed under repeated, relatively fixed conditions. Finally, cultural prescriptions to reason statistically probably exist for many such events. In contrast, none of these things is true for most events that can be assessed only by subjective means. The first problem below is an example of the Jepson et al., *objective* problems; the second is an example of the *subjective* problems.

Championship Selection Problem
Two sports fans are arguing over which sport – baseball or football – has the best (most accurate) playoff system. Charlie says that the Super Bowl is the best way of determining the world champion because, according to him, "The seven games of the World Series

are all played in the home cities of the two teams, whereas the Super Bowl is usually played in a neutral city. Since you want all factors not related to the game to be equal for a championship, then the Super Bowl is the better way to determine the world championship." Which procedure do you think is a better way to determine the world champion – World Series or Super Bowl? Why?

Class Selection Problem

It is the first week of the winter term. Henry has signed up for five classes, but plans to take only four. Three of these classes he knows he wants, so he must decide between the other two. Both are on subjects interesting to him. The student course evaluations indicate that Course A is better taught. However, he attended the first meeting of both classes this week, and found Course B's session more enjoyable. Which class should he take and why?

Subjects wrote open-ended answers to problems of each type. These were coded as to whether they reflected the use of statistical principles – chiefly, the law of large numbers or the regression principle – or not. An example of a nonstatistical answer for the championship problem is the following: "Super Bowl, because of neutral ground and also a one shot deal. Either you make it or break it – one chance. The pressure is on to perform the team's best." An example of a statistical answer is the following: "World Series is better. Anyone can get lucky for one game, but it is harder to be lucky for four. Besides, being home or away is part of the game, you don't play on neutral ground during the season." An example of a nonstatistical answer for the class-choice problem is the following: "He's got to choose for himself." An example of a statistical answer is: "You can't tell from one time – thus a survey that is over a longer range is better. Although Henry's idea of a good class could be different from most students."

Statistical answers were much more common for problems about objective events than for problems about subjective events. Forty-one percent of the answers for the former were statistical; the range of mean percentage statistical answers across problems was 30% to 93%. Only 12% of the answers to subjective problems were statistical; the range was 5% to 16%.

The results also showed that subjects were consistent in their tendency to give statistical answers. Those who gave statistical answers for any given problem were more likely to give them for any other. This tendency was correlated with both verbal and mathematical scores on the Scholastic Aptitude Test. . . .

THE EFFECTS OF TRAINING IN STATISTICS ON REASONING ABOUT EVERYDAY EVENTS

Perhaps the most important implication of the present view is that statistical reasoning about everyday events should be highly trainable. A major reason for optimism is that, as we demonstrated, people's intuitive reasoning skills include strategies that may be called statistical heuristics. Formal training in statistics, therefore, should represent less a grafting on of procedures than a refinement of preexisting ones. Formal training seems likely to improve reasoning for three distinct, but mutually supportive, reasons.

1. *Training in statistics is apt to facilitate the recognition of event distributions and their statistical parameters.* It can be difficult to apply rules such as the law of large numbers unless the units of evidence can be identified and, hence, the sample space and distribution of the event units. It seems likely that training in statistics could provide quite general skills in construing evidence in such a way that it can be properly unitized, the sample space identified, and parameters recognized. Training in probability theory, especially in permutations and combinations, should be particularly likely to be helpful in this regard as should test theory, which requires the student to recognize, for example, the different reliability of tests composed of different numbers of units – items, trials, occasions, and so on. But ordinary inferential statistics also introduces a fair amount of instruction in unitizing evidence: In order to measure the corn yield of a type of seed, for example, it is necessary to measure the yield for some unit of sampling (e.g., individual plot, individual farm). Statistics courses should also make it easier for people to think usefully about parameters of distributions – about central tendencies and about dispersion.

2. *Training in statistics in apt to facilitate the recognition of the role of chance in producing events.* A major concept of parametric statistics is that of error. Every inferential test features an estimate of error, and much of statistical training centers on questions of allocation of effects to the systematic category versus the random category. It seems possible that the focus on the concept of error in statistics might heighten the salience of uncertainty in daily life. A second major concept that might be helpful in recognizing uncertainty is the formal notion of sampling. This might be of general use in construing evidence as a (possibly small and inaccurate) sample from a (possibly heterogeneous) population.

3. *Training in statistics is apt to improve the clarity and accessibility of statistical rules and should expand the repertoire of statistical rules.* In effect, statistics training should hone intuitive heuristics into more precise tools. It seems clear that without training some statistical rules are poorly understood at any level of abstraction and in any context. Rules of covariation assessment and some versions of the regression principle are particularly difficult and may not even be represented in most people's intuitive repertoire. But even relatively intuitive rules such as the law of large numbers have nearly limitless corollaries and implications, some of which may be much easier to discern with formal training. Although people understand the "law of small large numbers," they may not be able to extend the principle to numbers of nonexperiential magnitudes without formal training. It may be the lack of a fully formal understanding of the law of large numbers that prevents people from applying it in the maternity ward

problem, for example, where the sample sizes involved (15 and 45) are not often represented in people's everyday experience of sampling and variability.

The evidence indicates that statistical training does indeed have profound effects on people's reasoning about everyday life events. In one series of studies, Krantz, Fong, and Nisbett (1983) examined four groups of subjects differing widely in educational level. Subjects, who were college students with or without statistical training, graduate students with a fair amount of statistical training, or PhD level scientists with several years of training, were presented with one of a pair of restaurant problems. In each problem, a protagonist experienced a truly outstanding meal on the first visit to a restaurant but was disappointed on a repeat visit. The subjects were asked to explain, in writing, why this might have happened. A subject's explanation was classified as nonstatistical if it assumed that the initial good experience was a reliable indicator that the restaurant was truly outstanding and attributed the later disappointment to a definite cause, such as a permanent or temporary change in the restaurant (e.g., "Maybe the chef quit") or a change in the protagonist's expectation or mood. The explanation was classified as statistical if it suggested that meal quality on any single visit might not be a reliable indicator of the restaurant's overall quality (e.g., "Very few restaurants have only excellent meals; odds are she was just lucky the first time"). Statistical explanations were coded as to how articulate they were in indicating that a single visit may be regarded as a small sample and, hence, as unreliable. Explanations were thus coded as falling into one of three categories: (1) nonstatistical, (2) poor statistical, and (3) good statistical. The frequencies in each of these categories were used to define two dependent variables: *frequency* of statistical answers, defined as the proportion of responses in categories 2 and 3, and *quality* of statistical answers, defined as the proportion of categories 2 and 3 answers that were Category 3.

The two versions of the restaurant problem differed. The probabilistic-cue version included a random mechanism for selection from the menu: The protagonist did not know how to read a Japanese menu and selected a meal by blindly dropping a pencil on the menu and observing where the point lay. The other version had no such cue. Within each group tested, half of the subjects received the cue and half did not.

The effects of training on both dependent measures were dramatic. College students without statistical training almost never gave an answer that was at all statistical unless the problem contained the probabilistic cue, in which case about half of the answers were statistical. In contrast, more than 80% of the answers of PhD-level scientists were statistical, whether or not there was a cue. Quality of statistical answers also depended on level of training. Only 10% of the statistical answers by untrained college students were rated as good, whereas almost 80% of the statistical answers by PhD-level scientists were rated as good. It is interesting that although the presence of the probabilistic cue was very important in determining whether less trained subjects would give a statistical answer, it did not affect the quality of statistical answers for subjects at any level of training. Apparently probabilistic cues can trigger the use of statistical heuristics, but they do not necessarily improve the quality of answers: the appropriate skills must be in the individual's repertoire to insure good quality.

The preceding study confounds training and native mathematical ability, but subsequent studies both avoid the confounding with ability and show that statistical training influences inductive reasoning outside the classroom and laboratory. Krantz et al. (1983) conducted a telephone "survey of opinions about sports." Subjects were males who were enrolled in an introductory statistics course and who admitted to being at least somewhat knowledgeable about sports. One hundred subjects were randomly selected and surveyed during the first 2 weeks of the term they were enrolled in statistics. Another 93 students were surveyed at or near the end of the term. In addition to filler questions on NCAA rules and NBA salaries, subjects were asked questions for which a statistical approach was relevant, as in the example below.

In general, the major league baseball player who wins Rookie of the Year does not perform as well in his second year. This is clear in major league baseball in the past 10 years. In the American League, 8 rookies of the year have done worse in their second year; only 2 have done better. In the National League, the rookie of the year has done worse the second year 9 times out of 10.

Why do you suppose the rookie of the year tends not to do as well his second year?

Most subjects answered this question in a nonstatistical way, invoking notions like "too much press attention" and "slacking off." Some subjects answered the question statistically (e.g., "There are bound to be some rookies who have an exceptional season; it may not be due to any great talent advantage that one guy has over the others – he just got a good year").

The statistics course increased the percentage of statistical answers and also increased the quality of statistical answers. The course also markedly influenced both the frequency and the quality of statistical answers to another question asking subjects to explain why .450 batting averages are common the first 2 weeks of the baseball season but are unheard of as a season average. In all, the course had a significant effect on three of the five questions asked.

Finally, Fong, Krantz, and Nisbett (1983) showed that even a very brief training procedure can suffice to affect markedly subjects' answers to problems about everyday events. There were two major elements in their training package: One covered formal aspects of sampling and the law of large numbers and the other showed how to use sampling notions as a heuristic device in modeling problems. In the sampling instruction, subjects received definitions of population and sample distributions, a statement of the law of large numbers, and a demonstration (by drawing colored gumballs from a glass vase) that a population distribution is estimated more accurately, on the average, from larger samples. The

530   Richard E. Nisbett et al.

modeling, or mapping, instruction consisted of three problems (in the general style of the restaurant problem and similar to the subsequent test problems), each followed by a written solution that used the law of large numbers and emphasized the analogy between amount of evidence and size of sample.

There were four major conditions: a control group given no instruction and three experimental groups – one given sampling training only, one given mapping training only, and one given both types of training. The subjects were adults and high school students. The test consisted of 15 problems: 5 had clear probabilistic cues, 5 dealt with objective attributes such as abilities or achievements, and 5 dealt with subjective judgments. Training effects were marked for all three problem types and for both the frequency of statistical answers and the quality of statistical answers. Sampling training and mapping training were about equally effective, and in combination they were substantially more effective than either was alone. A particularly encouraging finding is that training showed no domain specificity effects. In a companion study, Fong et al. (1983) showed that it made no difference to performance whether mapping training had been on probabilistic-cue problems, objective attribute problems, or subjective judgment problems. The latter finding suggests that training on specific problem types can be readily abstracted to a degree sufficient for use on widely different problem types.

The work on training should not be taken to indicate that a statistical education is sufficient to guarantee that people will avoid errors in inductive reasoning. Kahneman and Tversky (1982; Tversky & Kahneman, 1971, 1983) have shown repeatedly that statistical expertise provides no such guarantee against errors. However, it should also be noted that courses in statistics do not emphasize ways to use statistical principles in everyday life. Were they to do so, one might see much larger differences between the educated and the uneducated than we have found. . . .

NORMATIVE CONSIDERATIONS

Ecological Representativeness of Problems Showing Errors

One criticism of the literature showing errors in inductive reasoning has been to argue that they are the result simply of examining people's judgment about particular kinds of problems, and in a particular kind of context, where judgments are particularly likely to be fallible (e.g., Cohen, 1981; Dennett, 1981; Lopes, 1982). The tenor of this criticism is that the studies show more about the cleverness of experimenters than they do about the real world failures of lay people.

The accusation that psychologists have been devising parlor tricks, which people are susceptible to in the laboratory context but either do not encounter or could solve in real world contexts, seems less plausible in view of the research reported here. First, for each problem we have reported, some of the subjects showed by their answers (and often by the rationales for their answers, subsequently elicited) an appreciation of the statistical principles that in previous work other subjects failed to appreciate. It seems more reasonable to explain the success of some of our subjects by saying that they are more skilled at statistical reasoning than the other subjects rather than to explain it by saying that they saw through the experimenters' tricks. Second, the factors that make statistical reasoning more or less likely, for example, recognition of heterogeneity and of the role played by chance, do not sound like factors that make people more or less dupable by experimenters but rather like factors that make the appropriateness of statistical reasoning more or less obvious. Third, statistical training markedly influences answers to the sort of problems we studied. This suggests that it is not problem- or context-produced illusions that make people unable to solve statistical problems but simply lack of statistical knowledge.

"Satisficing" in Decision Making and Inductive Reasoning

Since Simon's (1957) important work on decision making, it has been a standard part of normative analysis to point out that because of time pressures and other constraints, it may be quite sensible for people to depart from formal decision models. This corner-cutting practice is called *satisficing* (in distinction to the presumed *optimizing* that would result from the formal procedures). This same defense is often applied to people's failures to reason statistically (Einhorn & Hogarth,1981; Miller & Cantor, 1982; Nisbett & Ross, 1980). People who study inductive reasoning seem to have presumed that normatively correct inductive reasoning is usually more laborious and time-consuming than is purely intuitive inductive reasoning, just as formal decision making is usually more time consuming than is intuitive decision making. The present work makes it clear that this presumption cannot be imported uncritically into the realm of inductive reasoning. Exclusively causal reasoning and the search for values on putatively relevant causal factors can be extraordinarily laborious. Statistical reasoning, once it is mastered, can be very rapid, even automatic. We found it striking, for example, to contrast the answers given over the telephone by subjects in the sports survey by Krantz et al. (1983). Some subjects doggedly persisted in causal explanations for problems such as the rookie of the year, sophomore slump ("Well, the success goes to their heads . . . and there's pressure to keep up the performance after the great first year . . . and . . . "), which did not seem to satisfy even the subjects who were generating them. Other subjects generated quick, crisp statistical explanations ("They just happened to have a first year that was better than their lifetime average") that still left them free to explore possible causal explanations.

It is also important to note that one has very little sense of subjects' *choosing* inferential strategies when one reads such protocols, in the sense that people may choose a formal decision-making strategy over an intuitive one. Rather, subjects either seem to spontaneously pursue a statistical approach or they do not.

Formal decision-making procedures involve novel and counterintuitive practices such as drawing tree diagrams and multiplying probability and utility assessments. However, many statistical procedures, as we have shown, have their simpler intuitive counterparts in the equipment of everyday thought. There is no reason to presume that these are any more cumbersome to use or require any more conscious deliberation to access than other intuitive approaches. Similarly, training in formal statistics may produce automatic, nonreflective transfer to everyday problems in a way that formal decision training would not.

Evolution and Inductive Reasoning

Many people have responded to the work demonstrating inferential errors by assuming that the errors are either exaggerated or that they are the incidental by-product of some overwhelmingly useful inferential procedure that happens to go astray under ecologically rare circumstances. This is essentially the argument from design, and several philosophers have endorsed it. (See, e.g., Cohen, 1979; Dennett, 1978, 1981, 1983; Lycan, 1981; Einhorn & Hogarth, 1981, have presented several very compelling arguments against the design view, and we do not repeat them here.)

Endorsement of the evolutionary, or design, view requires a rather static, wired-in assumption about the nature of inferential procedures. Philosophers are not alone in making this assumption, it should be noted. Psychologists who are wont to presume unlimited plasticity in social behavior often seem to presume complete rigidity in inferential rules, as if these could be influenced at most by maturation. In our view, there are few grounds for such a presumption. Whatever may be true for deduction, there are good grounds for assuming that inductive procedures can be changed. Renaissance physicians adhered to the doctrine of signatures, an inductive system with both descriptive and procedural components. Modern physicians have curtailed the scope of the representativeness heuristic in their daily inferential lives. (Although it is still relied on in interviews of applicants to medical schools. See Dawes, 1980, for a description of the doctrine of signatures at work in the admissions process for American universities.) Sophisticated causal analysis and statistical reasoning will eventually result in the further curtailment of simple intuitive heuristics, for physicians and for everyone else.

Although we see no merit in an evolutionary defense of the inferential behaviors that happen to characterize American college students in the latter part of the 20th century, we see a powerful argument in the work we have reviewed for the role of cultural evolution. It does not require unusual optimism to speculate that we are on the threshold of a profound change in the way that people reason inductively. The range of events that scientists can think about statistically has been increasing slowly but in a decided, positively accelerated fashion at least since the 17th century. The work of Kahneman and Tversky may be regarded as the most recent and one of the most dramatic inflection points on that curve.

We believe that, with a lag in time, lay people have been following a similar curve of ever widening application of statistical reasoning. Most people today appreciate entirely statistical accounts of sports events, accident rates, and the weather; also, we found many subjects who gave statistical explanations even for subjective events such as disappointment about meals served by a restaurant. Will our own descendants differ as much from us as we do from Bernoulli's contemporaries?

29. Feelings as Information: Moods Influence Judgments and Processing Strategies

Norbert Schwarz

Everyday experience and lay intuition suggest that we see the world as a better place when we feel happy rather than sad. Numerous experimental studies confirm this intuition. In fact, finding a dime is sufficient to increase an individual's general life-satisfaction for a limited time (Schwarz, 1987). The first section of this chapter reviews relevant findings and discusses different process assumptions. Less intuitively obvious is that our moods may also influence which strategy of information processing we use. Yet a growing body of research indicates that happy moods foster reliance on a top-down, heuristic processing strategy, whereas sad moods foster reliance on a detail-oriented, bottom-up processing strategy. The second section of this chapter reviews this research. Theoretically, the impact of moods on evaluative judgment and processing style can be traced to the informative functions of affective states, although other processes are likely to contribute as well under specific conditions, as developed in more detail later.

MOOD AND EVALUATIVE JUDGMENT

As many researchers have observed, almost any target is likely to be evaluated more favorably when the judge is in a positive rather than negative mood (for reviews see Clore, Schwarz, & Conway, 1994; Forgas, 1995; Morris, 1989; Schwarz & Clore, 1996). Experimental demonstrations of this basic finding range from satisfaction with consumer goods (e.g., Isen, Shalker, Clark, & Karp, 1978) and the evaluation of other persons (e.g., Forgas & Bower, 1987), activities (e.g., Carson & Adams, 1980), and past life events (e.g., Clark & Teasdale, 1982) to reports of happiness and satisfaction with one's life as a whole (e.g., Schwarz & Clore, 1983). Moreover, these influences translate into overt behavior (see Isen, 1984, for a review). For example, Saunders (1993) observed that "the weather in New York City has a long history of significant correlation with major stock market indexes" (p. 1344): The market is more likely to go up on sunny than on cloudy days, and this relationship is reliable when nonweather

Completion of this chapter was supported through a fellowship from the Center for Advanced Study in the Behavioral Sciences.

variables are controlled for. Hirshleifer and Shumway (2001) confirmed this observation for 26 stock exchanges in different countries. Apparently, "investor psychology influences asset prices" (Saunders, 1993, p. 1345) and investors are more optimistic about their likely returns on sunny than on gloomy days.

In most studies, moods have been experimentally induced, either by minor events (e.g., finding a dime, receiving a cookie), exposure to valenced material (e.g., watching a sad video, recalling a happy event from one's past), or natural circumstances (e.g., sunny or rainy weather), with similar results across different manipulations. The impact of moods on evaluative judgment has been traced to two different processes, namely mood-congruent recall of valenced material from memory and the use of one's feelings as a source of information.

Mood-Congruent Memory

According to models of mood-congruent memory, individuals are more likely to recall positive material from memory when they are in a happy rather than sad mood. Following initial suggestions by Isen and colleagues (1978), Bower (1981) conceptualized these effects in an associative network model of memory. Moods, thought to function as central nodes in an associative network, are linked to related ideas, events of corresponding valence, autonomic activity, and muscular and expressive patterns. When new material is learned, it is associated with the nodes that are active at learning. Accordingly, material acquired while in a particular mood is linked to the respective mood node. When the person is in the same mood later, activation spreads from the mood node along the pathways, increasing the activation of other nodes, which represent the related material. When the activation exceeds a certain threshold, the represented material comes into consciousness.

This model makes two key predictions: First, memory is enhanced when the affective state at the time of encoding matches the affective state at the time of retrieval (*state-dependent learning*). Thus, we are more likely to recall material acquired in a particular mood when we are in the same, rather than a different, mood at the time of recall. Second, any given material is more likely to be retrieved when its affective tone matches the individual's mood at the time of recall (*mood-congruent memory*). Thus, information of a positive valence is more likely to come to mind when we are in a happy rather than sad mood. Although both predictions received considerable empirical support in experimental and clinical research, this research also revealed a number of complications that are beyond the scope of this chapter (see Blaney, 1986; Bower & Mayer, 1985; Clore et al., 1994; Morris, 1989; Singer & Salovey, 1988). In general, mood-congruent recall is a relatively fragile phenomenon that is most likely to be obtained for self-referenced material, such as autobiographic events, that meets the conditions of both of the previously mentioned hypotheses: When something good (bad) happens to us, it puts us in a positive (negative) affective state, and its subsequent recall is facilitated when we are again in a similar affective state.

Note that this situation simultaneously provides for matching mood states at learning and recall, thus satisfying the conditions of state-dependent learning as well as for matches between the valence of the material and the mood at recall, thus satisfying the conditions of mood-congruent memory.

From this perspective, mood effects on judgment are mediated by mood-congruent recall from memory: When asked how satisfied we are with our life, for example, we recall relevant information from memory. However, positive (negative) material is more likely to come to mind when we are in a happy (sad) mood, resulting in a mood-congruent sample of relevant information, and therefore a mood-congruent judgment.

Feelings as Information: The "How-Do-I-Feel-About-It?" Heuristic

As an alternative approach, Schwarz and Clore (1983), drawing on earlier suggestions by Wyer and Carlston (1979), proposed that individuals may use their apparent affective reactions to the target as a basis of judgment. In fact, some evaluative judgments refer, by definition, to our feelings about the stimulus. For example, when asked how "likeable" a person is, we may base this judgment on our own feelings toward the person rather than on a review of the person's features. Other judgment tasks may not pertain directly to our feelings but may pose a task that is complex and demanding. In this case, we may simplify the task by assessing our apparent affective reactions to the target, essentially asking ourselves, "How do I feel about this?" Because we have only one window on our immediate experiences, however, we may mistake feelings due to a preexisting mood state as a reaction to the target, resulting in more positive evaluations under happy than under sad moods. This feelings-as-information assumption generates a number of predictions that cannot be derived from the assumption that mood effects on evaluative judgments are mediated by mood-congruent recall or encoding, of which I address only two (see Schwarz, 1990; Schwarz & Clore, 1988, 1996, for more detailed discussions).

Perceived Informational Value. The most crucial prediction is that the impact of feelings on evaluative judgments is a function of the feelings' perceived informational value. If individuals attribute their current feelings to a source that is irrelevant to the evaluation of the target, the informational value of their feelings should be discredited and their feelings should not influence the evaluative judgment. According to models of mood-congruent recall, however, the impact of affective states should depend only on the evaluative implications of the information retrieved from memory, rather than on information provided by the affective state itself. Therefore, models of mood-congruent recall predict that manipulations of the informational value of one's current mood will not influence its impact on evaluative judgments.

In line with the feelings-as-information hypothesis, Schwarz and Clore (1983) observed that the impact of moods on judgments of life-satisfaction was eliminated when subjects attributed their current feelings either correctly (Experiment 2) or incorrectly (Experiment 1) to a transient source. For example, subjects reported higher life satisfaction and a more elated current mood in telephone interviews when called on sunny rather than rainy days. In some conditions, however, the interviewer, who pretended to call from out of town, asked, "By the way, how's the weather down there, where you live?" This question, presented as part of a private aside, was introduced to draw subjects attention to the weather as a plausible transient cause of their current mood. As expected, this manipulation eliminated the otherwise observed difference in life-satisfaction: Once subjects realized that they may feel bad because of the rainy weather, they did not draw on their feelings in evaluating their life satisfaction. Subjects' reports of their current mood, on the other hand, were not influenced by the weather question, indicating that this question did not change their current feelings but only the perceived informational value of these feelings. Similarly, recalling a sad life event did not influence subjects' judgments of life satisfaction when they could misattribute the resulting sad feelings to the alleged impact of the experimental room (Experiment 1). In addition, current mood, as assessed at the end of the experiment, was more strongly correlated with judgments of life satisfaction when subjects' attention was not directed to a transient source of their feelings than when it was. Conceptual replications of these findings have been reported by Keltner, Locke, and Audrain (1993); Schwarz, Servay, and Kumpf (1985); Savitsky, Medvec, Charlton, and Gilovich (1998); and Siemer and Reisenzein (1998), among others.

In combination, these findings indicate that individuals may use their current feelings as a basis of judgment unless the diagnostic value of their feelings for the judgment at hand is called into question. This discounting effect (Kelley, 1972) is incompatible with predictions based on mood-congruent recall because the attributional manipulations only discredit the implications of one's current feelings but not the implications of valenced information about one's life, recalled from memory: Attributing one's bad mood to the weather, for example, only undermines the informational value of one's mood, but does not affect the implications of a recalled negative event, such as failing an exam. Given these findings, it is not surprising that mood effects on evaluative judgments have been observed in the absence of any evidence for mood effects on the recall of relevant information from memory (e.g., Fiedler, Pampe, & Scharf, 1986).

Relative Contributions of Mood and Thought Content. In addition, the predictions of both models differ with regard to the contributions of mood at the time of judgment and the specific content by which the mood is induced. From the perspective of an associative network model of memory, judgments should be most consistent with a person's current mood when the mood is induced by a technique that itself increases the accessibility of mood-congruent material that is relevant to the judgment at hand. For example, a depressed mood that is induced through thoughts about a serious disease should affect judgments about diseases more strongly than a depressed mood that is induced by other thoughts, because information about diseases would be activated by both the content of one's thoughts and one's depressed mood. According to the feelings-as-information hypothesis, however, the nonemotional content of the mood-inducing stimulus should be irrelevant, unless it influences the apparent informational value of the accompanying feelings.

In line with the latter hypothesis, several studies indicate that mood effects on evaluative judgments are largely independent of the specific content by which the mood was induced (e.g., Johnson & Tversky, 1983; Mayer, Gaschke, Braverman, & Evans, 1992). For example, Johnson and Tversky (1983) observed that reading descriptions of negative events, which presumably induced a depressed and slightly anxious mood, increased judgments of risk across a wide set of targets. Most important, the impact of mood was independent of the object of judgment or the content by which the mood was induced. Reading about cancer, for example, affected judgments of the risk of cancer, but had equally strong effects on judgments of the risk of accidents and divorce. Such thoroughly generalized effects, undiminished over dissimilar content domains, are incompatible with models of mood congruent recall. However, they are consistent with the feelings-as-information hypothesis. From this perspective, participants presumably simplified the difficult task of evaluating unknown risks by consulting their depressed and anxious feelings, resulting in judgments of higher risk.

When Positive Feelings Result in Negative Evaluations

Although feeling good typically results in positive evaluations, there are conditions under which individuals arrive at more negative judgments when they are in a positive mood. To use an example from an ingenious series of experiments by Martin, Abend, Sedikides, and Green (1997), suppose that a person is put in a happy mood and asked to read a sad story. Feeling happy due to the preceding mood induction, the person infers that the story is not a good exemplar of the category "sad stories," or else she would now feel sad rather than happy. Note that such mood-incongruent judgments are due to shifts in the judgmental criterion used, rather than to changes in the informational value of one's mood itself: Much as a sweet cookie makes for a poor salty snack, a story that apparently leaves us in a happy mood is a poor sad story. Therefore, a positive affective response may result in a negative evaluation under these specific conditions.

When Are Feelings Used in Forming a Judgment?

The reviewed findings indicate that mood effects on evaluative judgments often reflect the use of one's affective state as a source of information, rather than any impact of mood-congruent recall of information from memory. However, these findings do not preclude that mood-congruent recall may produce evaluative biases as well. Consistent with what one would expect on theoretical grounds, the available evidence suggests that reliance on one's feelings is particularly likely (1) under conditions in which one's feelings are a highly relevant source of information, and (2) under conditions in which one's feelings allow for the simplification of an otherwise demanding task.

First, individuals are likely to rely on their feelings as a basis of judgment when these feelings seem highly relevant to the judgment at hand. Not surprisingly, this is the case when the judgment explicitly pertains to one's feelings (e.g., liking for another person; Clore & Byrne, 1974), in which case one's feelings are the most diagnostic input available.

Second, reliance on one's feelings is also likely when little other information is available, for example, because the target is unfamiliar (e.g., Srull, 1983, 1984).

Third, reliance on one's feelings increases with increasing task demands and decreasing cognitive resources. For example, when the judgment is overly complex and cumbersome to make on the basis of a piecemeal information processing strategy, individuals are likely to resort to the "How-do-I-feel-about-it?" heuristic. Accordingly, judgments of general life satisfaction, which would require the integration of many different aspects of one's life, have been found to show stronger mood effects than judgments of specific life domains, such as income satisfaction or housing satisfaction, for which relevant comparison information is easily available (e.g., Borg, 1987; Schwarz, Strack, Kommer, & Wagner, 1987). Similarly, mood effects increase when time constraints or competing task demands limit the attentional resources that may be devoted to forming a judgment (e.g., Siemer & Reisenzein, 1998).

Finally, several studies observed that misattribution manipulations are more effective when individuals are in a sad rather than happy mood (e.g., Schwarz & Clore, 1983), suggesting that happy individuals are more likely to rely on their feelings than sad individuals, even under conditions designed to undermine their informational value. This observation is consistent with the general finding that happy moods foster heuristic processing, whereas sad moods foster systematic processing, as reviewed later. From this perspective, sad individuals are more likely to engage in the causal analysis of their feelings that is required for a successful misattribution manipulation.

The conditions under which mood effects on evaluative judgments are likely to be mediated by mood congruent recall are markedly different (see Forgas, 1995). Specifically, recall mediated mood effects are particularly likely when individuals engage in an effortful piecemeal strategy, have sufficient time and attentional resources to do so, and when the somewhat tricky prerequisites for mood-congruent recall (discussed previously) are met. As a result, moods may influence evaluative judgments under heuristic as well as systematic processing conditions, either by serving as input into a heuristic strategy or by influencing which features of the target are likely to come to mind.

Note, however, that it is difficult to determine whether an observed mood effect is due to the use of feelings as information or to mood-congruent recall, unless the study includes a (mis)attribution manipulation that varies the perceived informational value of participants' mood. Unfortunately, such manipulations are often missing, rendering many studies thoroughly nondi-agnostic with regard to the underlying processes (see Schwarz, in press, for a discussion).

Beyond Moods: Specific Emotions and Other Subjective Experiences

It is also worth noting that the use of one's feelings as a source of information is not limited to global positive and negative moods. Instead, the basic feelings-as-information logic applies to a wide range of subjective experiences, including specific emotions, arousal, bodily sensations, and cognitive experiences (see Schwarz & Clore, 1996 for a review).

With regard to specific emotions, Schwarz et al. (1985) observed that the impact of a fear-arousing communication on subjects' attitudes was eliminated when subjects attributed their subjective experience to the arousing side effects of a pill, but was enhanced when subjects assumed the pill would have tranquilizing effects. Note, however, that the informational value of specific emotions is more restricted than the informational value of global moods. Emotions are specific reactions to specific events (see Clore et al., 1994, for a review of emotion theories), whereas moods are of a diffuse and unfocused nature (Morris, 1989). As a result of their undifferentiated and unfocused nature, mood states may be used as information in making a wide variety of different judgments. In fact, when subjects are induced to attribute their mood to specific causes – as in the Schwarz and Clore (1983) experiments reviewed previously – its impact on judgments that are unrelated to that source vanishes. The source of a specific emotion, however, is more likely to be in the focus of attention, thus rendering the emotion uninformative for judgments that are unrelated to the emotion-inducing event. Support for this prediction comes from research by Keltner, Locke, and Audrain (1993b), who induced a sad mood by having subjects imagine vividly a negative life event. Subsequently, some subjects were asked to describe what emotions they felt, whereas others indicated where and when the negative event took place. As expected, having to label their current feelings with specific emotion terms induced subjects to identify specific causes for their current feelings, thus undermining their informational value for unrelated targets. Accordingly, these subjects reported higher life satisfaction than subjects who merely identified the time and location of the event, despite being in a similarly depressed mood. In fact, describing one's current specific emotions was as effective in reducing the impact of a sad mood as misattributing one's sad feelings to the experimental room.

If specific emotions imply the identification of a specific cause, they may be unlikely to affect unrelated judgments shortly after their onset, when the event that elicited them is still salient. Once the emotion dissipates, however, it may leave the individual in a diffuse mood state (Bollnow, 1956), which would be likely to affect a wide range of judgments. If so, the impact of an emotion-eliciting event may be quite limited shortly after the onset of the emotional reaction, but may generalize to unrelated targets after a sufficient delay.

In addition to being more restricted with regard to the range of applicable targets, the informational value of specific emotions is also more specific than that of diffuse moods. On theoretical grounds, we may expect that the information conveyed by specific emotions reflects the implications of the appraisal pattern that underlies the respective emotion. In line with this hypothesis, Gallagher and Clore (1985) observed that feelings of fear affected judgments of risk but not of blame, whereas feelings of anger affected judgments of blame but not of risk. Similarly, Keltner, Ellsworth, and Edwards (1993) observed in several experiments that angry subjects assigned more responsibility to human agents than to impersonal circumstances, whereas sad subjects assigned more responsibility to impersonal circumstances than to human agents, reflecting the differential appraisal patterns of anger and sadness.

In combination, these findings illustrate that unlike global mood states, specific emotions have very localized effects on judgment. Much as in the case of moods, however, these effects are eliminated when the informational value of the emotion for the judgment at hand is called into question (e.g., Keltner et al., 1993b; Schwarz et al., 1985). Research into the informative functions of physical arousal and cognitive experiences reiterates this theme. For example, Zillman and colleagues (for a review, see Zillman, 1978) had subjects engage in various forms of exercise. Shortly after the exercise, subjects' heightened excitation level did not affect evaluative judgments, presumably reflecting that subjects were still aware of the source of their arousal. After some delay, however, judgments were affected by the residual arousal, suggesting that subjects misinterpreted their arousal as a reaction to the target, once the temporal distance of the exercise rendered this alternative source less accessible and plausible. Finally, the informational value of cognitive experiences, like ease or difficulty of recall, has also been found to depend on individuals' assumptions about their source, as reviewed by Schwarz and Vaughn (Chapter 5, this volume). Throughout, the accumulating findings indicate that feelings and phenomenal experiences are an important source of information that individuals draw on in forming evaluative judgments, unless their informational value is called into question.

MOODS AND PROCESSING STRATEGIES

In addition to influencing memory and judgment, individuals' moods have also been found to influence performance on a wide variety of cognitive tasks (for reviews and different theoretical perspectives, see Bless, 2001; Forgas, 1995; Isen, 1987; Schwarz & Clore, 1996; and the contributions in Martin & Clore, 2001). Although the findings bearing on well-defined formal reasoning tasks (such as syllogistic reasoning, puzzles, or anagrams) are complex and inconsistent (see Clore et al., 1994), the findings bearing on less-structured social reasoning tasks (most notably, impression formation, stereotyping, and persuasion) show a more coherent pattern. In general, individuals in a sad mood are more likely to use a systematic, data-driven strategy of information processing, with considerable attention to detail. In contrast, individuals in a happy mood are more likely to rely on preexisting general knowledge structures, using a top-down, heuristic strategy of information processing, with less attention to detail.

These differences can again be traced to the informative functions of affective states (Bless, 1997; Schwarz, 1990, 2001). We usually feel bad when we encounter a threat of negative or a lack of positive outcomes, and feel good when we obtain positive outcomes and are not threatened by negative ones. As a result, our moods reflect the state of our environment and being in a bad mood signals a problematic situation, whereas being in a good mood signals a benign situation. A growing body of research suggests that individuals' thought processes are tuned to meet the situational requirements signalled by their feelings. When negative feelings signal a problematic situation, the individual is likely to attend to the details at hand, investing the effort necessary for a careful analysis. In contrast, when positive feelings signal a benign situation, the individual may see little need to engage in cognitive effort, unless this is required by other current goals. Therefore, the individual may rely on preexisting knowledge structures that worked well in the past, and may prefer simple heuristics over more effortful, detail-oriented judgmental strategies.

Numerous studies are compatible with this general perspective, as illustrated later. Importantly, mood effects on processing style are eliminated when the informational value of the mood is undermined (Sinclair, Mark, & Clore 1994), paralleling the findings in the judgment domain discussed previously. This finding supports the informative functions logic and is difficult to reconcile with competing approaches that trace mood effects on processing style to differential influences of happy and sad moods on individuals' cognitive capacity (e.g., Mackie & Worth, 1989; for a review, see Schwarz & Clore, 1996) or to differential brain dopamine levels (Ashby, Isen, & Turken, 1999). Both approaches would predict main effects of mood, rather than effects that are contingent on the mood's perceived informational value.

Impression Formation and Stereotyping

In forming an impression of others, we may either rely on detailed information about the target person or simplify the task by drawing on preexisting knowledge structures, such as stereotypes pertaining to the target's social category (e.g., Brewer, 1988; Fiske & Neuberg, 1990; Macrae, Milne, & Bodenhausen, 1994). Consistent with the mentioned perspective, being in a good mood has been found to increase stereotyping consistently (e.g., Bodenhausen, Kramer, & Süsser, 1994), unless the target person is clearly inconsistent with the stereotype, thus undermining the applicability of the general knowledge structure (e.g. Bless, Schwarz, & Wieland, 1996). In contrast, being in a sad mood reliably decreases stereotyping and increases the use of individuating information (for a review, see Bless, Schwarz, & Kemmelmeier, 1996). Across many person-perception tasks, individuals in a chronic or temporary sad mood have been found to make more use of detailed individuating information, show less halo effects, and are less influenced by the order of information presentation and more accurate in performance appraisals than individuals in a happy mood, with individuals in a neutral mood falling in between (see Sinclair & Mark, 1992 for a review). Similar findings have been obtained for individuals' reliance on scripts pertaining to typical situations (such as having dinner in a restaurant) versus their reliance on what actually transpired in the situation (Bless et al., 1996a). Throughout, individuals in a good mood are more likely to rely on preexisting general knowledge structures, proceeding on a "business-as-usual" routine; conversely, individuals in a sad mood are more likely to pay close attention to the specifics at hand, much as one would expect when negative feelings provide a problem signal.

Persuasion

Research into mood and persuasion parallels these findings. In general, a message that presents strong arguments is more persuasive than a message that presents weak arguments, provided that recipients are motivated to process the content of the message and to elaborate on the arguments. If recipients do not engage in message elaboration, the advantage of strong over weak arguments is eliminated (for reviews, see Eagly & Chaiken, 1993; Petty & Cacioppo, 1986). Numerous studies demonstrate that sad individuals are more likely to engage in spontaneous message elaboration than happy individuals, with individuals in a neutral mood falling in between (for a review see Schwarz, Bless, & Bohner, 1991). As a result, sad individuals are strongly influenced by compelling arguments and not influenced by weak arguments, whereas happy individuals are moderately, but equally, influenced by both. Therefore, a strong message fares better with a sad than with a happy audience, but if communicators have nothing compelling to say they better put recipients into a good mood.

More important, happy individuals' spontaneous tendency not to think about the arguments in much detail can be overridden by other goals (e.g., Wegener, Petty, & Smith, 1995) or explicit task instructions (e.g., Bless, Bohner, Schwarz, & Strack, 1990; Martin, Ward, Achee, & Wyer 1993). What characterizes the information processing of happy individuals is not a general cognitive or motivational impairment, but a tendency to spontaneously rely on simplifying heuristics and general knowledge structures in the absence of goals that require otherwise (Bless & Schwarz, 1999).

Other Judgment and Decision Tasks

These mood-induced differences in spontaneous processing style are likely to affect individuals' performance on many judgment and decision tasks. For example, Luce, Bettman, and Payne (1997) observed that "decision processing under increasing negative emotion both becomes more extensive and proceeds more by focusing on one attribute at a time" (p. 384), consistent with the assumption that negative feelings foster a more detail-oriented processing style. Moreover, Hertel, Neuhof, Theuer, and Kerr (2000) observed pronounced mood effects on individuals' decision behavior in a chicken game. Consistent with the present theorizing, their findings suggest that individuals in a happy mood are likely to heuristically imitate the behavior of other players, whereas individuals in a sad mood base their moves on a rational analysis of the structure of the game.

Note, however, that more extensive reasoning about a task does not always result in better solutions. As an example, consider the well-known phenomenon of anchoring effects in quantitative judgments (Tversky & Kahneman, 1974). In a typical study, participants are provided with an arbitrary number (e.g., 50, 5,000) and are asked to make a binary comparative judgment (e.g., "Is the Mississippi River longer or shorter than 5,000 miles?"). Next, they must provide an absolute estimate (e.g., "How long is the Mississippi River?"). The latter estimate is typically biased toward the anchor value. As Strack and Mussweiler (1997; Mussweiler & Strack, 1999) demonstrated, this bias is due to a process of positive hypothesis testing (e.g., "Can the Mississippi River really be that long/short?") that renders hypothesis-consistent information selectively accessible. If so, this bias may be exaggerated the more individuals engage in elaborative hypothesis testing. Confirming this prediction, Bodenhausen, Gabriel, and Lineberger (1999) observed that sad individuals showed more pronounced anchoring effects than individuals in a neutral mood, presumably because their sad mood fostered more elaborative hypothesis testing, thus rendering more hypothesis-consistent information accessible.

As these examples illustrate, the differential processing styles elicited by being in a happy or sad mood can increase as well as decrease judgmental biases, depending on the nature of the task. Future research will benefit from testing the impact of affective states across a wider variety of tasks.

Beyond Moods

As in the case of evaluative judgment, the conceptual logic can be extended from global moods to other feelings, including specific emotions and bodily sensations.

Specific Emotions. Theoretically, experiencing a specific emotion can be expected to inform the individual that the appraisal pattern underlying this emotion has been met (Schwarz, 1990): Feeling angry, for example, informs us that somebody has faulted us and angry individuals have been found to assign more responsibility to human actors than to situational circumstances, as noted earlier (Keltner et al., 1993a). We may therefore expect that specific emotions elicit processing strategies that are tuned to meet the requirements entailed by the appraisal pattern that underlies the respective emotion. To date, experimental research bearing on this possibility is limited, although the available data are generally consistent with this proposal.

Recall that earlier research into mood and persuasion documented more systematic message processing under sad rather than happy moods. Extending this work, Tiedens and Linton (in press) noted that the appraisal pattern underlying sadness entails a sense of uncertainty, whereas other negative emotions, like anger or disgust, do not. Consistent with this proposal, they found that uncertainty-related emotions elicited more systematic message processing, whereas other negative emotions did not. Presumably, when we are angry or disgusted, we know what our feeling is about and see no need to engage in detailed processing of unrelated information. Sadness or anxiety, however, entail a sense of uncertainty and hence motivate the kind of detail-oriented systematic processing observed in earlier research.

Although sadness and anxiety share an uncertainty appraisal, they differ in other respects. In general, sadness is a response to the loss or absence of a reward, whereas anxiety is a response to threats (e.g., Ortony, Clore, & Collins, 1988). As a result, sadness may prompt a goal of reward acquisition, whereas anxiety may prompt a goal of uncertainty reduction. Raghunathan and Pham (1999) tested these predictions in a choice paradigm. They provided sad or anxious participants with a choice task that required a trade-off between risk and rewards. As expected, they observed that sad individuals pursued a goal of reward acquisition and preferred high risk/high reward options over any other combination. Conversely, anxious individuals pursued a goal of uncertainty reduction and preferred low-risk/low-reward options over any other combination. These findings demonstrate that incidental feelings, induced by an unrelated task, can influence which goal an individual pursues. Whether individuals' processing strategies were also influenced by these affect-elicited goals was not assessed in this study, but seems likely in light of a wide range of findings that suggest that processing strategies are tuned to meet individuals' current goals (for a review, see Kunda, 1999).

As these examples illustrate, systematic explorations of the role of specific emotions in reasoning and decision making provide a promising avenue for future research.

Bodily Feedback. Further extending the logic of the feelings-as-information approach, Friedman and Förster (2000) suggested that bodily sensations may also signal benign or problematic situations. In general, people try to approach situations that are characterized by a promise of positive, or a lack of negative, outcomes. Conversely, they try to avoid situations that entail a threat of negative outcomes or lack positive ones. If so, bodily responses that are typically associated with approach situations may elicit the heuristic, top-down processing style spontaneously preferred in benign situations, whereas bodily responses that are typically associated with avoidance situation may elicit the systematic, bottom-up processing style spontaneously preferred in problematic situations. One bodily response closely associated with approach is the contraction of the arm flexor, which is involved in pulling an object closer to the self. Conversely, contraction of the arm extensor is involved in pushing an object away from the self and is closely associated with avoidance. Therefore, arm flexion provides bodily feedback that is usually associated with approaching positive stimuli, whereas arm extension provides bodily feedback that is usually associated with avoiding negative stimuli (see Cacioppo, Priester, & Berntson, 1993). In fact, affectively neutral stimuli encoded during arm flexion are later preferred over neutral stimuli encoded during arm extension, presumably reflecting the approach/avoidance information provided by the bodily feedback (Cacioppo et al., 1993).

Taking advantage of this association, Friedman and Förster (2000) asked seated participants to press the right palm upward against the bottom of the table (arm flexion), or downward against the top of the table (arm extension). Although these movements engage the same muscles, they have no surface similarity to pulling an object closer or pushing it away, thus avoiding the introduction of demand characteristics. As theoretically predicted, arm flexion fostered a heuristic processing style, whereas arm extension fostered a systematic processing style, across a variety of problem solving tasks.

Situational Cues. Theoretically, the observed effects of moods, emotions, and bodily sensations reflect that our thought processes are tuned to meet the processing requirement signaled by our feelings. If so, affective cues in the environment may serve similar functions. To test this conjecture, some researchers have presented reasoning tasks from the Graduate Record Examination (GRE; e.g., Soldat, Sinclair, & Mark, 1997) or persuasive messages (Soldat & Sinclair, 2001) on colored paper – namely, an "upbeat" red or a "depressed" blue. Paralleling the effects of happy and sad moods, they observed that upbeat colors fostered heuristic processing, whereas more depressing colors fostered systematic processing, resulting in differential performance on the GRE tasks and differential persuasion effects.

In combination, the available findings suggest that internal (moods, emotions, bodily sensations) as well as external (e.g., colored paper) affective cues can elicit different processing styles, presumably by providing a "benign" or "problematic" signal.

SUMMARY

As this selective review indicates, our feelings can have a pronounced impact on judgment and decision making. Depending on conditions, they may influence which information comes to mind and is considered in forming a judgment, or serve as a source of information in their own right. The use of one's feeling as a source of information is particularly likely when the feelings are relevant to the judgment at hand or allow the judge to simplify the task by relying on a "How-do-I-feel-about-it?" heuristic. When our feelings do, in fact, reflect our actual affective reaction to the target, this heuristic does not result in undue biases. Yet, it is often difficult to distinguish between one's reactions to the target and one's preexisting mood state. In this case, reliance on the "How-do-I-feel-about-it?" heuristic results in systematic biases, as reviewed previously. However, individuals do not rely on this heuristic when the informational value of their feelings is called into question.

In addition, our feelings may inform us about the nature of the current situation, with good moods signaling a benign situation and bad moods signaling a problematic one. Individuals' thought processes are tuned to meet these situational requirements, resulting in mood-induced differences in spontaneously adopted processing style. Individuals in a happy mood are likely to spontaneously adopt a top-down, heuristic processing style, whereas individuals in a sad mood are likely to spontaneously adopt a bottom-up, systematic processing style. This influence of moods is not observed when the informational value of the mood is called into question, and it can be overridden by other goals or task instructions. Specific emotions, bodily approach and avoidance signals, as well as environmental cues serve similar informative functions and elicit corresponding differences in the spontaneously adopted processing style. Not surprisingly, which processing style results in better performance depends on the match between the adopted processing style and the characteristics of the task (see Schwarz & Skurnik, in press).

Given these pervasive influences of moods and emotions, what are we to conclude about the rationality of human judgment? Would we be better off if we did not attend to our feelings? A growing body of neuropsychological research suggests otherwise and illustrates how not attending to affective information can dramatically impair judgment and decision making (for a review, see Damasio, 1994). As an example, consider a study that compared the decision behavior of healthy individuals and patients with damage to the prefrontal cortex, which controls emotional reactions (Bechera, Damasio, Tramel, & Damasio, 1997). Consistent with the assumption that feelings provide useful information, healthy individuals displayed negative affective reactions to disadvantageous moves in an experimental card game. Drawing on these reactions, they began to avoid these moves long before they could consciously identify them as disadvantageous, supporting Zajonc's (1980) controversial proposition that "preferences need no inferences." In contrast, patients with impaired emotional reactions lacked the danger signal provided by a negative affective response and continued to make disadvantageous moves even after they had conscious insight into their disadvantageous nature. The "problem" is not that attending to the information provided by our feelings interferes with what would otherwise be a rational judgment process, but that we may misread feelings that are due to an unrelated source as our response to the current situation or the target at hand. Therefore, we may scrutinize a persuasive message less than might be useful when we happen to be in a good mood, or may be unduly optimistic about likely asset returns when we make our investment decisions on a sunny day. As with any other piece of information, our feelings are of variable diagnosticity and much as reliance on nondiagnostic propositional information can lead us astray, so can reliance on nondiagnostic affective information. Unfortunately, we are not very good at assessing the diagnosticity of either type of information, as the diverse contributions to this volume illustrate.

30. Automated Choice Heuristics

Shane Frederick

In his Nobel Prize address, Herbert Simon urged choice theorists to stop pretending that actual choices can be predicted from theoretical models of optimal choice. He argued that any descriptively adequate account of human decision making must make contact with the actual psychological processes that are involved and that "the neoclassical ambition of avoiding [this] necessity is unrealizable" (1978, p. 507).

Many choice theorists have taken up Simon's challenge. They have sought to identify the various "heuristics" people use to simplify choice – the procedures they use to limit the amount of information that is processed or the complexity of the ways it is combined. In a prototypical study, a respondent might be asked to make several hypothetical choices among apartments, whose attributes (e.g. monthly rent, miles from work, square footage) are listed as rows of numeric values (e.g. $560, 12, 900, respectively). The respondent's choice processes are then either inferred from the choices she makes or are more directly observed through "process tracing" methods that use computerized displays to track the attributes and options that the respondent considers, the order in which they are considered, and, sometimes, the time spent pondering each piece of information.

On the basis of process tracing methods, verbal protocols, introspection, and theory, many different choice heuristics have been postulated (for reviews, see Payne, Bettman, & Johnson, 1993; Gigerenzer, Todd, & the ABC Group, 1999; Gigerenzer, Czerlinski, & Martignon, Chapter 31, this volume; Gigerenzer & Goldstein, 1996). These choice heuristics, such as "elimination by aspects" (Tversky, 1972), are conscious strategies that are intentionally designed to simplify choice. When a decision maker is presented with a matrix of numbers summarizing the attributes of six different apartments, nothing spontaneously "happens"; no intuitive computation generates an impression of which option is best. The decision maker must consciously decide how to process that information. These deliberate choice heuristics are viewed as heuristics by the

The idea for this paper and its central emphases were developed jointly with Daniel Kahneman; I am indebted to him for his guidance and help – so much so, in fact, that he should be exempted from the customary disclaimer. I also thank Tom Gilovich, Dale Griffin, George Loewenstein, Greg Pogarsky, and Eldar Shafir for comments received on prior drafts.

548

people who use them – they would describe what they are doing as a sim-plifying strategy. Indeed, the "adaptive decision maker" envisioned by some choice theorists (Payne, Bettman, & Johnson, 1993) is not only aware that he is using heuristics, but modifies them strategically as choice conditions change. The deficiencies of these heuristics are not lost on decision makers – they often recognize when they are ignoring potentially relevant information, but may regard their strategies as appropriate given their computational limitations or their desire to conserve effort.

These deliberate choice heuristics differ substantially from the judgmental heuristics of the "heuristics and biases" research program, which are largely based on impressions that occur automatically and independently of any ex-plicit judgmental goal (Tversky & Kahneman, 1983, Chapter 1, this volume). For example, when presented with a description of a political activist and the category bank teller, people notice the dissimilarity spontaneously. This rapid and intuitive judgment may, in turn, be used to conclude that the per-son is unlikely to be a bank teller by a process that Kahneman & Frederick (Chapter 2 this volume) term *attribute substitution*. Importantly, however, the people making the judgment do not typically view this process as a heuristic. They are not deciding to use resemblance in favor of some other procedure for judging probability. They do not see it as an effort conserving procedure, or a simpler version of another procedure they might instead perform. Using resemblance to judge probability is called a *heuristic* (the "representativeness heuristic") only by reference to an "outside" normative standard of judgment, which requires that these probability judgments reflect considerations other than resemblance alone.

The distinctions between the "deliberate" choice heuristics (e.g. elimination by aspects) and the "automatic" judgmental heuristics (e.g. representativeness) largely reflect the different types of stimuli used in choice tasks and judgment tasks. Research on choice heuristics was conducted with an eye toward the computational and memory limitations that Simon repeatedly emphasized, and focused on how people cope with complexity; how they make reason-able decisions when the amount of information confronting them exceeds the amount they can comfortably process. The experimental stimuli used by these researchers are often abstract and do not evoke any type of intuitive impres-sion. Consequently, respondents must rely on some type of analytic solution (though the "analysis" may be rather crude). In contrast, much of the research on judgment heuristics was guided by the analogy with perception, and pre-sented respondents with more concrete stimuli (e.g. personality descriptions) that evoke an immediate impression upon which the requested judgment can be based. In the shorthand used by Kahneman and Frederick (Chapter 2, this volume), traditional judgment heuristics are *System 1 heuristics* – they result from cognitive processes that are rapid and not entirely controllable – whereas traditional choice heuristics are *System 2 heuristics* – they result from slower and more deliberate mental processes.

Although the prototypical choice heuristic is considerably more deliberate than the prototypical judgmental heuristic, there are situations in which choices are governed by (and simplified by) intuitive impressions. This chapter discusses two such automated choice heuristics: "choosing by liking" – basing choice on an immediate affective evaluation; and "choosing by default" – choosing the option that first comes to mind. These two automated choice heuristics are akin to the judgment heuristics of the heuristics and biases literature – they are governed by rapid and intuitive processes, they are relatively immune to introspection, and their associated biases may not be recognized by the people who use them.

CHOOSING BY LIKING

Choice is typically modeled as a cognitive procedure involving an analysis of an option's constituent features. However, some have proposed an alternate view, arguing that choices might also be made intuitively; by the spontaneous affective evaluation of liking or disliking that options may elicit – a procedure that Wright (1975) calls *affect referral*, Schwarz and Clore (1988) term the *"How-do-I-feel-about-it" heuristic*, and Slovic, Finucane, Peters, and MacGregor (Chapter 23, this volume) call the *affect heuristic*. Image theory (Beach & Mitchell, 1987; Beach, 1990) advanced a similar view, proposing that affective evaluation may work in conjunction with cognitive evaluation – that affective valuation is used as a quick initial screen for alternatives, whereas cognitive evaluation is reserved for those alternatives that surpass some affective threshold.

Relying on intuitive affective impressions (what Kahneman terms *choosing by liking*) may be a successful heuristic if the features that mediate our initial affective response correspond closely with the features that determine our subsequent enjoyment. If the spaciousness of apartments determines how much we like them while apartment hunting and determines how much we actually enjoy living in them, choosing by liking may be a perfectly adequate heuristic. However, if affective evaluation is unconsciously governed by something not closely correlated with subsequent satisfaction (e.g. similarity to our previous apartment, the song that is playing when we enter), choosing by liking could lead one astray.

In general, the reliance on spontaneous affective response may be an effective decision heuristic. Indeed, Wilson and colleagues have suggested that affective impressions may be more accurate than analytic assessments of an option's constituent features – that a more thorough cognitive analysis can degrade rather than enhance evaluative validity. To this effect, Wilson et al. (1989) quote a judge at the Berlin Film Festival who noted:

I went to every screening with a fresh pack of note cards that I would dutifully cover with my impressions of each and every film. The result, of course, was that the movies ceased to be fun and turned into problems, a struggle against time, darkness and my own esthetic emotions which these autopsies confused. I was so worried about evaluating every aspect of every film that my entire system of values went into shock, and I quickly realized that I could no longer easily tell what I liked or didn't or why (p. 288; originally published in Vargas Llosa, 1986, p. 23).

Some experimental results seem to confirm this observation. For example, Wilson and Schooler (1991) found that subjects who simply rated how much they liked various brands of strawberry jam produced ratings that corresponded better with gustatory experts than subjects who first listed the reasons they liked or disliked a jam before rendering their global ratings. Similarly, Wilson et al. (1993) found that subjects who were instructed simply to choose the poster they liked most ended up liking their poster more (and were more likely to still be sporting it on their dormitory wall) than subjects who first analyzed each poster along several dimensions before making their final decision. When people reflect about the reasons they like or dislike something they may focus on features that seem to be plausible determinants of liking rather than the features that actually mediate liking.

Although affective impressions may be often an accurate proxy for the overall quality of an option, and superior to clumsy attempts at multiattribute utility analysis, several properties of affect render it an imperfect and, sometimes, markedly deficient basis for choice: (1) it is insufficiently sensitive to quantitative detail; (2) it is unduly influenced by transient contextual cues; (3) it is excessively affected by familiarity. The following sections discuss these properties of affect, and the biases that may be introduced by using affective response as a choice heuristic.

Insensitivity to Features that Affect Enjoyment/Aversiveness

Hedonic efficiency is served when the intensity of our desires and aversions corresponds closely with the intensity of our pleasures and pains. The link is strong most of the time (e.g., people take greater steps to avoid a bee's stinger than a mosquito's proboscis). However, affect is not an infallible guide, and may be insensitive to certain features of an outcome that matter. For example, the fear generated by the prospect of an electric shock is insensitive to its probability of occurrence (see, e.g., Bankhart & Elliott, 1974; Elliott, 1975; Monat, Averill, & Lazarus, 1972; Snortum & Wilding, 1971). Loewenstein, Weber, Hsee, and Welch (2001) argue that this may explain why judgments and choices are often insensitive to variations in probability except for those involving a transition from impossibility to possibility or from likelihood to certainty.

Consistent with such an account, Rottenstreich and Hsee (2001) found that people would pay nearly as much to avoid a 1% chance of an electric shock as they would pay to avoid a 99% chance of it ($7 and $10, respectively). Similarly, Kahneman, Ritov, and Schkade (2000) argue that the dramatic scope insensitivity displayed in contingent valuation studies (see Frederick & Fischhoff, 1998, for a review) occurs because willingness to pay is an expression of affective response and affective response is insensitive to quantitative detail (e.g. whether the proposed intervention saves 2,000 birds or 200,000).

The link between liking and enjoyment may also be weakened or broken when decisions are made by consulting one's memories, because important aspects of an experience, such as its duration, may be lost in its transcription to memory (see Kahneman, 2000 for a discussion). A simple and memorable experiment reported in Kahneman, Fredrickson, Schreiber, and Redelmeier (1993) illustrates this. In that study, subjects were sequentially (the order was randomized) exposed to two mildly painful experiences: a "short" episode, in which they immersed one hand in cold water (57° F) for 60 seconds; and a "long" episode, in which they immersed their other hand in cold water for 90 seconds: 60 seconds in 57° water plus an additional 30 seconds during which the water was warmed to 59 degrees (which made the water less uncomfortable, but not pleasant). When the participants were later asked which of the two experiences they preferred to repeat, most chose the "long" trial. For someone who wants to minimize pain, this choice is obviously not correct, because the 30 seconds of diminishing pain is still additional pain. However, although these choices are wrong, they are not crazy or silly. As Kahneman and colleagues note, choosing by liking is certainly a sensible strategy – what could be more reasonable than preferring the experience that is remembered as being better?

Excessive Responsiveness to Co-occurring Yet Irrelevant Features

Affective responses to a particular object or event may be strongly influenced by contextual features that do not influence the actual enjoyment it provides. As marketers well know, pairing beer with images of camp fires or trout streams or attractive women may enhance consumers' affective response to it. However, to the extent that these contextual features either do not actually enhance the enjoyment of beer or are not present when the beer is consumed, affective response (liking) is divorced from subsequent hedonic response (enjoyment).

Evaluations made by other animals may also be susceptible to idiosyncratic features that do not correspond to the quality of outcomes. For example, female zebra finches strongly prefer to mate with male finches whose heads are artificially adorned with crests of white feathers (Burley, cited in Angier, 1999). In fact, the preference is so strong that these curious crested males are permitted liberties not normally enjoyed (e.g., shirking on nest-building responsibilities, mating with other females who are eager for their services). Because these artificial crests resemble nothing that finches ordinarily possess, the usual evolutionary story breaks down, as it is unclear why the crested finches should be thought to bear superior finch genes when they are not supposed to have a crest in the first place. Similar results were found with red leg bands (but not white ones). The source of such aesthetic preferences remains a mystery, and the only "explanation" is the speculation that the white hats or red socks co-opt and arouse some neurophysiological pathway that exists for some other unknown purpose.

When the relevant currency is experienced utility rather than reproductive success, the standards for "rational" choice may be more permissive. If we prefer mates with large breasts or sideburns or flat stomachs, we may regard our preferences as their own justification. Or not. Mismatches might still exist between the degree to which a feature excites our affective response at the moment of decision and its eventual importance to our overall satisfaction. Some features (e.g. a sexy voice) may be more durable and important sources of enjoyment than others that are initially more affect-inducing. The extent to which reliance on our affective responses serves our interests is an open question. It may be a better guide for jams than for cars, and better for posters than for books. Often, the validity of our affective response depends on a normative judgment about the types of utility that ought to count. The answer is not always straightforward: Do charismatic students deserve higher class participation grades (or not)? Is it wrong to be especially concerned about animals that are cute (or not)? Is it irrational to pay more for water that comes in a snazzy bottle (or not)?

The correspondence between affective evaluation and subsequent enjoyment may also be degraded by the influence of transient physiological states. Read and van Leeuwen (1998) found that hungry people were more likely to select a caloric snack for consumption the following week, although current hunger level is irrelevant with respect to the type of snack that will taste best then. Correspondingly, affective responses may provide an insufficient motivation if the contextual features that excite both affective and hedonic responses are not present now, but will be present later. Loewenstein (1996, p. 287) speculates that declining sexual activity in married couples may occur despite constant enjoyment of the sex itself, because the pleasures of sex cannot be appreciated from a "cold" state that begins to prevail once proximity alone ceases to be sufficiently arousing. He suggests that having sex only when we feel like it (choosing by liking) may be a less adequate guideline than an equally simple rule like: "Have sex nightly, regardless of immediate desire." For further discussion of failures to predict changes in preference brought about by changes in arousal or circumstance, see Loewenstein and Adler (1995), Loewenstein, Nagin, and Paternoster (1997), Loewenstein, Prelec, and Shatto (1998).

It is unclear whether prevailing affective states bias choices because people overestimate the durability of this state (e.g., currently hungry people erroneously believe they will be equally hungry in the future) or because people are unable to disregard feelings they "know" to be irrelevant – much as they are unable to ignore obviously irrelevant anchors in quantity judgments. Perhaps, hedonic predictions are first anchored on the emotion one feels while contemplating the future outcome and then adjusted to reflect the recognition that intervening events will alter future enjoyment.

Familiarity Effects
Extensive and diverse evidence shows that familiarity to a stimulus increases affective response to it. Rats raised to Mozart prefer Mozart to Schoenberg (Cross, Holcomb, & Matter, 1967). Chicks raised with matchboxes prefer the company of matchboxes to the company of other chicks (Taylor & Sluckin, 1964). People prefer the number 4 to the number 19 (Zajonc, 1968), prefer the

letters in their name to other letters (Nuttin, 1985, 1987), and prefer their mirror image, which they see every day, to their actual image, which they see only in photographs (Mita, Dermer, & Knight, 1997). These "mere exposure" effects have also been found with geometric figures, Chinese and Japanese ideographs, Turkish words, foods, odors, flavors, colors, people, and random sequences of tones (see Zajonc, 1998, for a review).

Many of these examples admit little room for a divergence between liking and enjoyment – it is not clear whether any distinction can be made between how much one "likes" a particular trapezoid and how much one "enjoys" it. In other cases in which there is a temporal separation between choice and consumption, the distinction becomes sharper. For example, although a familiarity-based affective response might cause chicks to prefer a nearby matchbox to another nearby chick, they might actually enjoy the companionship of other chicks more than they enjoy the proximity of matchboxes. Similarly, familiarity could increase the tendency to choose a particular brand of spaghetti sauce without actually improving its taste. Indeed, strong familiarity effects could sustain the selection of the status quo brand in the face of steadily decreasing enjoyment.

Discussion

Choosing by liking qualifies as an automated decision heuristic because affective impressions are readily available and provide an easier basis for decisions than a deliberate cognitive assessment of each option (see Slovic et al., Chapter 23, this volume). Bargh (1997, p. 23) proposes that "all stimuli are evaluated immediately as good or bad, without the participant intending to evaluate ... everything that one encounters is preconsciously screened and classified as either good or bad, within a fraction of a second after encountering it." The success of using one's immediate affective response as a choice heuristic depends on how closely it corresponds to the actual value or subsequent utility. Several characteristics may attenuate this correspondence and render affective response an imperfect basis for choice. First, affect can be insufficiently responsive to relevant aspects of options, such as their probability or duration. Second, affect may be overly responsive to irrelevant features, such as cooccurring, but logically irrelevant stimuli. Third, affect may be heightened by familiarity, though familiarity may not increase enjoyment.

Regardless of whether we intend to rely on it, our spontaneous affective evaluations likely play an important role in our decision making, and often intrude even when we want to make decisions on a cognitive basis. First, because affective responses precede more cognitive evaluations, they may dominate judgments and choices when respondents have too little time for deliberative reflection (see, e.g., Finucane, Alhakami, Slovic, & Johnson, 2000). Second, by providing *some* basis for choice, our initial affective response may discourage further effortful analytic assessment. Third, judgments may be anchored on one's initial affective evaluation even when attempts are made to supplement this with more analytic evaluations. Furthermore, because affective evaluation comes first, the option that elicits the most favorable affective response may enjoy the special status of being a default option – of being the thing we choose unless we can marshal a decisive case in favor of something else. The following section discusses the role of defaults in choice, and argues that "choosing by default" has aspects of an automated decision heuristic because defaults may be established by intuitive psychological processes.

CHOOSING BY DEFAULT

Choices are ordinarily thought to be based on some type of assessment of options (if only an intuitive affective impression). However, some choice procedures may bypass the evaluation stage altogether, deferring instead to a default option. Defaults may be established via historical precedent, perceptual salience, conspicuousness, or some other feature that qualitatively distinguishes one option from the rest. The following sections discuss two sources of defaults and the biases associated with choosing by default.

The Status Quo

Considerable anecdotal and experimental evidence suggests that the option one currently possesses or customarily chooses is preferred over other options to a degree that is difficult to justify. Hartman, Doane, and Woo (1991) provide a prototypical example: Customers who currently enjoyed reliable electrical service were unwilling to accept less reliable service for a discount on their electric bill, yet few of those who currently suffered from unreliable service were willing to pay an equivalent premium to obtain reliable service. Johnson, Meszaros, Hershey, and Kunreuther (1993) found a similar result. In New Jersey, the "standard" (or default) auto insurance policy does not entail the right to sue for pain and suffering from minor injuries, although that right may be obtained by choosing a higher-priced policy. Only 20% of New Jersey residents chose to acquire that right. However, in Pennsylvania, where the "standard" (or default) policy does entail a full right to sue, 75% chose to retain that option, in preference to the cheaper limited-rights option. Johnson and colleagues calculated that Pennsylvanians spent $200 million more on insurance than they would have if limited rights had been designated as the default option.

The status quo is given favored treatment in the NFL's instant replay system as well. When the "on-field" call is challenged, it is reviewed by the replay official, who has access to multiple angles and slow motion photography. However, despite these advantages, the on-field call is given preference in any "close calls"; the replay official is instructed to defer to the on-field call unless he has "indisputable visual evidence." Although there are reasons to minimize challenges of on-field calls (such as maintaining the flow of the game), once a ruling has been challenged and is going to be reviewed anyway, it makes little sense to give more weight to the first call when the second can be made with better information.

Focal Points

Historical precedent is not the only way a default option might be established. Sometimes, an option may become a default by virtue of its conspicuousness or psychological prominence. For example, Schelling (1960) has argued that equal division is often chosen merely by virtue of its mathematical simplicity – not because equality is compelling in a logical, moral, or legal sense. He notes that the results of long negotiations involving many complicated issues and parties with greatly differing bargaining power often converge on some crudely simple, but psychologically conspicuous benchmark like "splitting the difference" or "the 38th parallel," because those focal points possess prominence, uniqueness, simplicity, or something else that makes them qualitatively differentiable from the continuum of alternatives that one could consider.

Schelling's speculation is supported by experimental evidence. Harris and Joyce (1980) found that when people allocated profits among members of a group venture, they chose to distribute profits equally, even when members generated different amounts of revenue. However, when asked to allocate expenses, equal division was again favored, even though this left profits unequally distributed. The authors commented that respondents' choices seemed to be motivated by the simple heuristic of dividing equally rather than a true preference for equality of outcome per se; that responses reflected an overlearned share-and-share-alike rule "without regard to *what* is being shared or what each participant's ultimate fate is" (p. 177). Similarly, Rabin (1997) observed that people generally have a "one-pie-at-a-time" conception of allocation problems, favoring equal distribution of the focal pie, without considering the initial or final wealth levels of the parties involved.

Allison and Messick (1990) and Messick (1993) argue that "divide equally" is a social decision heuristic that is often applied with little deliberation. Results by Roch, Lane, Samuelson, Allison, and Dent (2000) support this view. In that study, respondents participated in a confidential, 8-person, resource-sharing task, and were told that they could stake the first claim to some amount of $60. Half of the respondents were put under cognitive load (by being required to remember the number 91704305) and half were not. The mean request of the cognitive load group was $8.18, which was not significantly different from their "fair" share of $7.50 ($60 ÷ 8 people). However, the control group, who was not impaired by the additional memory task, requested $17.00 – more than twice their fair share. The authors concluded that individuals first anchor on equal division, and adjust from that when they possess sufficient cognitive resources to do so. In the language used by Kahneman and Frederick (Chapter 2, this volume), being fair required only System 1, because equal division is an "obvious" solution, whereas being greedy required the help of System 2 to override the "obvious" solution proposed by System 1.

Much evidence suggests that the pull of equal allocation is strong for intra-personal allocation as well. Samuelson and Zeckhauser (1988, pp. 31–33) reported that about half of all Harvard employees divided their retirement funds equally between TIAA (a portfolio of bonds, commercial loans, mortgages, and real estate) and CREF (a broadly diversified common stock fund), and that most retained that equal division regardless of stock market performance. Benartzi and Thaler (2001) proposed, more generally, that investors often apply a "$1/n$ heuristic" dividing their resources equally between whatever set of funds they happen to consider. Equal division may apply across time as well. Frederick and Loewenstein (2001) found that when intertemporal choices were framed as allocating goods among time periods, the modal response was equal division. The popularity of equal division contrasts with the typical findings of positive time preference (preference in favor of early periods) found when people are asked to choose between a smaller proximate reward and a larger distal reward and also contrasts with the preference for improvement when people are asked to choose between declining, flat, or improving sequences.

Is Choosing the Default a Sensible Heuristic?

In some cases, the preference for defaults and the asymmetric treatment of choice options may be justified. For example, there are often good reasons for retaining the status quo. First, other alternatives may be more uncertain, and the downside risk might be considered larger than the upside benefit. Second, the transaction costs associated with switching must be weighed against the potential benefits of finding a better alternative. Third, one might legitimately infer that previous choices were based on good reasons – even if those reasons can no longer be recalled. We can probably all recall an instance of trying something "new" only to discover that we have tried that option before, and to be reminded of why it became dispreferred in the first place.

However, the reliance on psychologically conspicuous defaults can bias choice because the factors that determine psychological prominence may diverge from those that determine outcome quality. For example, as Schelling (1960) noted, the attractiveness of equal division may extend well beyond its actual merits in a particular choice. Individuals may allocate retirement funds equally between bonds and stocks because equal division immediately suggests itself as a basis for choice, not because that allocation necessarily serves fundamental interests (such as growth potential and security) any better than a 40–60 or 65–35 split.

CONCLUSION

The heuristics most commonly discussed in the literature on judgment (e.g., representativeness, availability) are based on mental computations (e.g., of similarity) that may be spontaneously generated (see Kahneman & Frederick, Chapter 2, this volume). In contrast, most of the heuristics discussed in the decision-making literature (e.g., elimination by aspects) are deliberate analytic procedures intentionally designed to simplify choice. Some have even endorsed the view of "adaptive decision makers" (Payne, Bettman, & Johnson, 1993), who balance effort and accuracy by tailoring the sophistication of heuristics to the importance of the decision.

In some cases, however, choices are mediated by the type of spontaneous assessments that underlie many intuitive judgments. This chapter discussed two automated choice heuristics – *choosing by liking* (choosing the option that generates the most favorable affective response) and *choosing by default* (choosing the option that first comes to mind). These may be considered "automated" choice heuristics because affective response and psychological conspicuousness may be rapidly and unconsciously generated, rather than deliberately selected. Also, like many judgmental heuristics, they are qualitatively distinct strategies, rather than stripped down versions of theoretically optimal procedures.

Not all choices permit the operation of these automated heuristics. Some choices may be too "dry" to evoke any affective response. It seems unlikely that affective response could be used to distinguish between different health insurance plans or retirement packages or staplers or motor oils or abstract representations of multiattribute options. Similarly, situations in which one option enjoys much greater psychological salience may be the exception rather than the rule. When the intuitive impressions that could support these automated choice heuristics are absent, more deliberate choice heuristics may prevail.

31. How Good Are Fast and Frugal Heuristics?

Gerd Gigerenzer, Jean Czerlinski, and Laura Martignon

Rationality and optimality are the guiding concepts of the probabilistic approach to cognition, but they are not the only reasonable guiding concepts. Two concepts from the other end of the spectrum, simplicity and frugality, have also inspired models of cognition. These fast and frugal models are justified by their psychological plausibility and adaptedness to natural environments. For example, the real world provides only scarce information, the real world forces us to rush when gathering and processing information, and the real world does not cut itself up into variables whose errors are conveniently independently normally distributed, as many optimal models assume.

However, optimal models already address these constraints. There are many methods for dealing with missing information. Optimal models can also be extended to take into account the cost of acquiring information. Finally, variables with unusual distributions can be transformed into nearly normal distributions, and outliers can be excluded. So what's the big deal? Optimal models seem to have met the challenge of adapting to natural environments. If people do not already use these models, then they would want to learn how to use them because they are, after all, optimal.

Thus it would seem that there is no need to turn to fast and frugal heuristics, which appear doomed to be both simplistic and inaccurate. Besides, there is an even stronger reason to shun simplicity and frugality as the basis for human cognition. They deny some of the most striking self-images Homo sapiens has constructed of itself, from "l'homme éclairé" of the Enlightenment to Homo economicus of modem business schools (Gigerenzer et al., 1989).

These are the typical intuitive arguments in the debate between optimality and rationality on the one hand and simplicity and frugality on the other. But before you pass judgment on which side you stand, move beyond these mere intuitions to consider the real substance of the two approaches and the actual relationship between them. This chapter provides some food for thought on these issues in the form of a review of our recent findings on fast and frugal heuristics (Gigerenzer, Todd, & the ABC group, 1999). How great is the advantage in terms of speed and simplicity? How large is the loss of accuracy?

How robust are fast and frugal heuristics under a variety of conditions – and under which conditions should we avoid using them? We answer these questions by comparing fast and frugal heuristics with benchmark models from the optimality and rationality tradition. Our intention is not to rule out one set of guiding concepts or the other, forcing us to choose rationality and optimality or simplicity and frugality. Rather, we wish to explore how far we can get with simple heuristics that may be more realistic models of how humans make inferences under constraints of limited time and knowledge.

First, however, we must understand the guiding concepts. The fundamental distinction in approaches to reasonableness is between unbounded rationality and bounded rationality (e.g., Simon, 1982, 1992). Unbounded rationality suggests building models that perform as well as possible with little or no regard for how time-consuming or informationally greedy these models may be. This approach includes Bayesian models and expected utility maximization models (e.g., Edwards, 1954, 1961). In contrast, bounded rationality suggests designing models specifically to reflect the peculiar properties and limits of the mind and the environment. The decision maker is bounded in time, knowledge, and computational power. In addition, each environment has a variety of irregular informational structures, such as departures from normality.

There are, however, two approaches which compete for the title of bounded rationality: *constrained maximization* and *satisficing* (Fig. 31.1). Constrained maximization means maximization under deliberation cost constraints. This demands even more knowledge and computation than unbounded rationality because the decision maker must compute the optimal trade-off between accuracy and various costs, such as information search costs and opportunity costs. The paradoxical result is that "limited" minds are assumed to have the knowledge and computational ability of mathematically sophisticated econometricians and their statistical software packages (e.g., Sargent, 1993). The "father" of bounded

Figure 31.1. Visions of reasonableness

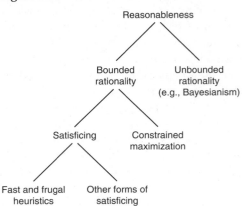

rationality, Herbert Simon, has vehemently rejected this approach. In personal conversation, he once remarked in a mixture of anger and humor that he had thought of suing authors who misuse his concept of bounded rationality to construct ever more complicated models of human decision making.

Simon's view of bounded rationality is that of satisficing, which he contrasts to constrained maximization. In the satisficing interpretation, the two sides of bounded rationality, limited minds and structured environments, are not merely two additional complications to the optimality story. Rather, they form a happy and beneficial marriage: subtle environmental structures that were neglected by standard rational models are potentially exploitable by simple heuristics. (Egon Brunswik, in particular, has emphasized the interrelationship of cognition and environment; e.g., Brunswik, 1964). Satisficing asserts that our minds have evolved all sorts of nimble tricks to perform well in the quirky structures of the real world.

The types of models developed by the satisficing view are thus fairly simple, in stark contrast to those of the constrained maximization view. For instance, one of the best known examples of Simon's satisficing is to start with an aspiration level and then choose the first object encountered that satisfies this level (e.g., buy the first acceptable house). Still, satisficing can use rather computationally expensive procedures (e.g., Simon, 1956). We use the term fast and frugal heuristics for a subset of satisficing strategies that work with a minimum of knowledge, time, and computations. We call these heuristics "fast" because they process information in a relatively simple way, and we call them "frugal" because they use little information. The next section presents several examples of such heuristics.

SATISFICING BY FAST AND FRUGAL HEURISTICS

There are infinitely many kinds of tasks that heuristics can be designed to perform. This chapter focuses on the task of predicting or inferring which of two objects scores higher on a criterion. Which soccer team will win? Which of two cities has a higher homelessness rate? Which applicant will do a better job? To make such predictions, the heuristics use uncertain cues that indicate, with some probability, higher values on the criterion.

Consider, for example, the task of inferring which of two cities has a higher homelessness rate, using the data on 50 U.S. cities from Tucker (1987). An excerpt from this data including the values for Los Angeles, Chicago, New York, and New Orleans on six cues and the criterion is shown in Table 31.1. One cue (rent control) is binary, and the other five have been dichotomized at the median. Unitary cue values (1) indicate higher values on the criterion and zero cue values (0) indicate lower values. For example, because cities with rent control more often have a higher homelessness rate than cities without rent control,

Table 31.1. Cues for Predicting Homelessness in U.S. Cities[a]

	Los Angeles	Chicago	New York	New Orleans
Homeless per million	10,526	6,618	5,024	2,671
Rent control (1 is yes)	1	0	1	0
Vacancy rate (1 is below median)	1	1	1	0
Temperature (1 is above median)	1	0	1	1
Unemployment (1 is above median)	1	1	1	1
Poverty (1 is above median)	1	1	1	1
Public housing (1 is below median)	1	1	0	0

[a] Cues are ordered by validity, with rent control having the highest validity (.90). Further explanation in text.
Source: Tucker (1987).

cities that have rent control are marked with a cue value of 1 for this cue. (In contrast, if cities without rent control more often had the higher homelessness rate, then having rent control would be marked by a 0.)

Of course, people generally do not have such tables of information handy; they have to search for information, in their memories or in libraries. But how could one construct a heuristic that cheaply (rather than optimally) limits search and computations? Two examples of such heuristics are Minimalist and Take the Best, which are drawn from a family of fast and frugal heuristics (Gigerenzer & Goldstein, 1996; Gigerenzer, Hoffrage, & Kleinbolting, 1991; Gigerenzer, Todd, & the ABC group, 1999).

Minimalist

The minimal knowledge needed for cue-based inference is in which direction a cue "points." For instance, the heuristic needs to know whether warmer or cooler weather indicates a city with a higher rate of homelessness. In the 50 U.S. cities, warmer weather is indeed associated more often with higher homelessness rates than with lower rates, so a cue value of 1 is assigned to cities with warmer weather. Minimalist has only this minimal knowledge. Nothing is known about which cues have higher validity than others. The ignorant strategy of Minimalist is to look up cues in random order, choosing the city that has a cue value of 1 when the other city does not. Minimalist can be expressed in the following steps:

1. Random search: Randomly select a cue and look up the cue values of the two objects.

2. Stopping rule: If one object has a cue value of one (1) and the other does not, then stop search. Otherwise, go back to Step 1 and search for another cue. If no further cue is found, guess.

3. Decision rule: Predict that the object with the cue value of one (1) has the higher value in the criterion.

For instance, when inferring whether Chicago or New Orleans has a higher homelessness rate, the unemployment cue might be the first cue randomly selected, and the cue values are found to be one and one (Table 31.1). Search is continued, the public housing cue is randomly selected, and the cue values are 1 and 0. Search is stopped, and the inference is made that Chicago has a higher homelessness rate, as it indeed does. So far, the only thing a person needs to estimate is which direction a cue points; that is, whether it indicates a higher or a lower value on the criterion. But there are environments for which humans know not just the signs of cues, but roughly how predictive they are. If people can order cues according to their validities (regardless of whether this subjective order corresponds to the ecological order), then the search can follow this order of cues. One of the heuristics that differs from the Minimalist in only this respect is called Take the Best; its motto is "Take the Best, Ignore the Rest."

Take the Best

This heuristic is exactly like Minimalist except that the cue with the highest validity, rather than a random cue, is tried first. If this cue does not discriminate, the next best cue is tried, and so forth. Thus, Take the Best differs from Minimalist only in Step 1.

Step 1. Ordered search: Select the cue with the highest validity and look up the cue values of the two objects.

The validity v_i of cue i is the number of right (correct) inferences R_i divided by the number of right and wrong inferences $R_i + W_i$ based on cue i alone, independent of the other cues. We count which inferences are right and wrong across all possible inferences in a reference class of objects. That is,

$$v_i = \frac{\text{right inferences}}{\text{right inferences} + \text{wrong inferences}} = \frac{R_i}{R_i + W_i}.$$

For example, because Los Angeles has a cue value of 1 for rent control whereas Chicago has a cue value of 0, the rent control cue suggests that Los Angeles has a higher homelessness rate; because Los Angeles does have a higher homelessness rate; this counts as a right inference. Between Chicago and New York, the rent control cue makes a wrong inference. And between Chicago and New Orleans, it does not discriminate – and cannot make an inference – because both cities have 0 cue values for rent control. If we count the number of right and wrong inferences for all possible pairings of the 50 U.S. cities, we find that 90% of the inferences based on rent control are right; thus the cue validity of rent control is .90. Note that we only count as inferences the cases that are discriminated; that is, in which one object has a positive cue value and the other does not. Thus the sum of all right and wrong inferences in the denominator is equal to the number of pairs of cities on which the cue discriminates. In the simulations that follow, we compute the validity from the actual ecological cue values. However, when Take the Best is used as a model of human inference, the validities are computed only from the cue values the person actually knows (or believes).

For instance, when inferring whether Chicago or New Orleans has a higher homelessness rate, Take the Best looks up first the cue values of the two cities for rent control because it is the cue with the highest validity (.90). Unfortunately, this cue does not discriminate – both cities have cue values of zero (Table 31.1). So, Take the Best looks up the second-best cue, the vacancy rate cue (validity .73). This cue does discriminate, so search is stopped. Take the Best infers that Chicago, the city with the unitary cue value in contrast to New Orleans' 0, has the higher homelessness rate.

Take the Best and Minimalist are constructed from several building blocks of fast and frugal heuristics (Gigerenzer & Goldstein, 1996). These building blocks help us both in understanding the heuristics and in generating new heuristics.

The first building block is *step-by-step procedures*; that is, a cognitive strategy that searches for some information and checks whether this is sufficient to make a decision; if not, it searches for more information, checks whether this new information is sufficient, and so on (e.g., Miller, Galanter, & Pribram, 1960).

The second building block is *simple stopping rules*, which specify computationally simple conditions for halting the gathering of more cue information. There are a number of heuristics that use stopping rules, especially those that already use "attribute-based" rather than "alternative-based" information gathering (to use the terminology of Payne, Bettman, & Johnson, 1988). In the constrained maximization paradigm, for example, information search is halted when the marginal cost of another piece of information outweighs the marginal gain in accuracy expected. But calculating these marginals is a difficult game. In contrast, we propose stopping rules that do not need such cost–benefit computations. Take the Best and Minimalist stop gathering further cue information if one object has a unitary (1) value for a cue and the other does not (i.e., has a zero, 0, or unknown value for that cue).

This simple stopping rule is in harmony with our third building block, *one-reason decision making*. Once the search is stopped, a variety of computations could be performed on the information collected thus far. For example, multiple regression integrates all the cue values in a linear sum, and Bayesian models usually condition their probabilities on the values of several cues. However, because Minimalist and Take the Best stop after the first piece of information that discriminates between the two objects, they base their decision on this recent information only, the last cue considered. Trade-offs between cues never surface. The vision behind such one-reason decision making is to avoid conflicts and avoid integrating information. Thus, the process underlying decisions is non-compensatory. Note that one-reason decision making could be used with less simple stopping rules, such as gathering a larger number of cues (e.g., in a situation in which one must justify one's decision); the decision, however, is based on only one cue.

To summarize, Minimalist and Take the Best use the following building blocks:

- Step-by-step procedures
- Search limited by simple stopping rules
- One-reason decision making

In the following sections, we see how these building blocks exploit certain structures of environments. We do not deal here with how they exploit a lack of knowledge (see Gigerenzer & Goldstein, 1996).

Some of these building blocks appear in other heuristics that are related to Take the Best. Lexicographic strategies (e.g., Keeney & Raiffa, 1993; Payne, Bettman, & Johnson, 1993) are very close to Take the Best, but not Minimalist. The term *lexicographic* signifies that cues are looked up in a fixed order and the first discriminating cue makes the decision, like in the alphabetic ordering used to decide which of two words comes first in a dictionary. Take the Best can exploit a lack of knowledge by means of the recognition heuristic (when there is only limited knowledge; a case dealt with in Gigerenzer & Goldstein, 1996). A more distantly related strategy is Elimination by Aspects (Tversky, 1972), which is also an attribute-based information processor and also has a stopping rule. Elimination by Aspects (EBA) differs from Take the Best in several respects; for instance, EBA chooses cues not according to the order of their validities, but by another probabilistic criterion, and it deals with preference rather than inference. Another related strategy is classification and regression trees (CART), which deals with classification and estimation rather than two-alternative prediction tasks. The key difference is that in CARTs, heavy computation and optimizing are used to determine the trees and the stopping rules.

In Section 1 we have defined two fast and frugal heuristics. These heuristics violate two maxims of rational reasoning: They do not search for all available information and do not integrate information. Thus, Minimalist and Take the Best are fast and frugal, but at what price? How much more accurate are benchmark models that use and integrate all information when predicting unknown aspects of real environments?

This question was posed by Gigerenzer and Goldstein (1996), who studied the price of frugality in inferring city populations. The surprising result was that Take the Best made as many accurate inferences as standard linear models, including multiple regression, which uses both more computational power and more information. Minimalist generated only slightly fewer accurate inferences.

In Section 2 we test whether these results generalize to other real-world environments and to situations in which the training set and the test set are different. For simplicity, we only study the performance of the heuristics under complete knowledge of cue values, whereas Gigerenzer and Goldstein (1996) varied the degree of limited knowledge. In Section 3, we analyze the structure of information in real-world environments that fast and frugal heuristics can exploit, that is, their ecological rationality. Finally, in Section 4, we take up Ward Edwards' challenge to compare the performance of fast and frugal heuristics with more powerful strategies than multiple regression, in particular with Bayesian models.

FAST AND FRUGAL AT WHAT PRICE?

Some psychologists propose multiple linear regression as a description of human judgment; others argue that it is too complex a model for humans to instinctively perform. Nevertheless, both camps often regard it as an approximation of the optimal strategy people should use, Bayesian models aside. A more psychologically plausible version of a linear strategy employs unit weights (rather than beta weights), as suggested by Robyn Dawes (e.g., 1979). This heuristic adds up the number of unitary (1) cue values and subtracts the number of zero (0) cue values. Thus, it is fast (it does not involve much computation), but not frugal (it looks up all cues). For simplicity, we call this heuristic *Dawes' Rule*.

In this section, we compare the performance of fast and frugal heuristics against these standard linear models. We begin by describing a single task in detail: to predict which U.S. cities have higher homelessness rates. Thereafter, we present the full data – the average results of the contests in 20 empirical data sets. But performance is not everything – we also want to know what price we must pay for our accuracy. For example, heuristic A might need twice as many cue values as heuristic B in order to make its inferences, but might be only a few percentage points more accurate. We determine these accuracy–effort trade-offs for our heuristics using measures of computational simplicity and frugality of cue use.

Predicting Homelessness

The first contest deals with a problem prevalent in many cities, homelessness, and we challenge our heuristics to predict which cities have higher homelessness rates. As mentioned above, the data stem from an article by William Tucker (1987) exploring the causes of homelessness. He presents data for six possible factors for homelessness in 50 U.S. cities. Some possible factors have an obvious relationship to homelessness because they affect the ability of citizens to pay for housing, such as the unemployment rate and the percentage of inhabitants below the poverty line. Other possible causes affect the ability to find housing, such as high vacancy rates. When many apartments are vacant, tenants have more options of what to rent and landlords are forced to lower rents in order to get any tenants at all. Rent control is also believed to affect ability to find housing. It is usually instituted to make housing more affordable, but many economists believe landlords would rather have no rent than low rent. Thus less housing is available for rent and more people must live on the streets. The percentage of public housing also affects the ability to find housing because more public housing means that more cheap housing options are available. Finally, one possible cause does not relate directly to the landlord–tenant relationship. Average temperature in a city can effect how tolerable it is to sleep outside, leading to a number of possible effects, all of which suggest that warmer cities have higher homelessness rates; warmer cities might attract the homeless from cooler cities, landlords might feel less guilty about throwing people out in warmer cities, and tenants might fight less adamantly against being thrown out in more tolerable climates.

We ask our heuristics to use these six (dichotomized) cues to predict homelessness rates in the 50 cities. The heuristics are required to choose the city with more homelessness for all $50 \times 49/2 = 1225$ pairs of cities. Regression uses the matrix of cue values to derive optimal weightings of the cues (possible causes). There are two types of competitions. In the first competition, the test set is the same as the training set (from which a strategy learns the information it needs, such as the weights of the cues). In the second, more realistic competition, the test set is different from the training set (also known as cross-validation). The second competition can reveal how much a heuristic overfits the data. Only the first type of competition was studied in Gigerenzer and Goldstein (1996).

Performance: Test Set = Training Set
We begin with the case of learning the entire data set and trying to fit it as well as possible. Performance is measured by the percentage of the 1225 inferences that are correct (e.g., Which city has higher homelessness?). Sometimes the heuristics must guess, for example between New Orleans and Miami, which have the same characteristics on the six cues (both are 1 on temperature, both are 0 on rent control, both are 1 on poverty, etc.). When a heuristic guesses, it earns a score of 0.5 correct, on the grounds that half the time the heuristic will be correct in its guess.

How well do the heuristics predict homelessness? Table 31.2 shows the results for the situation when the test set coincides with the training set. There are two surprises in these numbers. The first is that Take the Best, which uses only 2.4 cues on average, scores higher than Dawes' Rule, which uses all 6 cues. The second surprise is that Take the Best is almost as good as linear regression, which not only looks up all the cues but also performs complicated calculations on them. So it seems that fast and frugal heuristics can be about as accurate as the more computationally expensive multiple regression! This confirms the findings of Gigerenzer and Goldstein (1996) in a task of predicting city populations.

Table 31.2. Trade-off between Accuracy and Cues Looked Up in Predicting Homelessness[a]

Strategy	Average Number of Cues Looked Up	Percent Correct When Test Set Same as Training Set	Percent Correct When Test Set Differs from Training Set
Minimalist	2.1	61	56
Take the Best	2.4	69	63
Dawes' Rule	6	66	58
Multiple regression	6	70	61

[a] For two kinds of competition (test set = training set, and test set ≠ training set). The average number of cues looked up was about the same for both kinds of competition.

Although Take the Best's accuracy is very close to that of regression, its absolute value does not seem to be very high. What is the upper limit on performance? The upper limit is not 100%, but 82%. This would be obtained by an individual who could memorize the whole table of cue values and, for each pair of cue profiles, memorize which one has the higher homelessness rate (but for the purpose of the test forgets the city names). If a pair of cue profiles appears more than once, this Profile Memorization Method goes for the profile that leads to the right answer more often. The Profile Memorization Method results in 82% correct inferences for the homelessness data (see Section 4).

Performance: Test Set ≠ Training Set

The prediction task we have considered thus far is limited to static situations in which we are merely trying to "fit" a phenomenon about which we already have all information. How well do the heuristics perform if the test set is different from the training set? This situation is a version of one-step learning and prediction. The data set is broken into two halves, with random assignment of cities to either one half or the other. The heuristics are allowed to use one half to build their models (calculate regression weights, get cue orders, determine cue direction); then they must make predictions on the other half, using the parameters estimated on the first half, and their accuracy is scored. This process is repeated 1,000 times, with 1,000 random ways of breaking the data into two halves in order to average out any particularly helpful or hurtful ways of halving the data.

Training might not seem to affect Dawes' Rule and Minimalist, but, in fact, it does. Both strategies use the first half of the data set to estimate the direction of the cue (whether a higher or a lower cue value signals a higher criterion value). When the test set was different from the training set, the performance of Minimalist dropped from 61% to 56% correct, and that of Dawes' Rule from 66% to 58% (Table 31.2). Take the Best must learn more than merely the direction of the cues; it must also learn the order of the cue validities. With this slight additional knowledge, Take the Best scores 63% correct, down from 69%. Regression must learn not only the direction of the cues, but also their interrelationship in order to determine the best linear weighting scheme. Despite all this knowledge, regression's performance falls more than that of Take the Best: Whereas regression scored 70% correct when it had to merely fit the data, it scores only 61% correct in the cross-validated case, falling to second place.

In summary, when heuristics built their models on half of the data and inferred on the other half, Take the Best was the most accurate strategy for predicting homelessness, followed closely by regression. This seems counterintuitive because Take the Best looks up only 2.4 of the 6 cues and (as we show later) is simpler computationally.

Note that we no longer determine the upper limit by the Profile Memorization method, which cannot be used if cue profiles that were not present in the first half are present in the second half.

Generalization

How well do these results generalize to making predictions about other environments? We now consider results across 20 data sets that have real-world structure in them rather than artificial, multivariate normal structures. In order to make our conclusions as robust as possible, we also tried to choose as wide a range of empirical environments as possible. So they range from having 17 objects to 395 objects, and from 3 cues (the minimum to distinguish between the heuristics) to 19 cues. Their content ranges from social topics, like high school dropout rates, to chemical topics, such as the amount of oxidant produced from a reaction, to biological topics, like the number of eggs found in individual fish.

Table 31.3 shows the performance of the heuristics averaged across the 20 data sets. When the task is merely fitting the given data (test set = training set), multiple linear regression is the most accurate strategy by two percentage points, followed by Take the Best. However, when the task is to generalize from a training set to a test set, Take the Best is the most accurate, outperforming multiple regression by four percentage points. Note that multiple regression has all the information Take the Best uses plus more. Dawes' Rule lives up to its

Table 31.3. Trade-off between Accuracy and Cues Looked Up, Averaged Across 20 Data Sets[a]

Strategy	Average Number of Cues Looked Up	Percent Correct When Test Set Same as Training Set	Percent Correct When Test Set Differs from Training Set
Minimalist	2.2	70	65
Take the Best	2.4	76	71
Dawes' Rule	7.4	73	70
Multiple regression	7.4	78	67

[a] For two kinds of competitions (test set = training set, and test set ≠ training set). The average number of cues looked up was about the same for both kinds of competition.

reputation for robustness in the literature (Dawes, 1979) by taking second place and beating regression by three percentage points. Finally, Minimalist performs surprisingly well, only two percentage points behind regression. In short, Dawes' Rule is not the only robust yet simple model; Take the Best and Minimalist are also fairly accurate and robust under a broad variety of conditions. In Section 3, we explore how this is possible – how fast and frugal heuristics can also be accurate.

How Much Information Processing Is Performed?

We established empirically that Take The Best and Minimalist are frugal – on average, they stopped searching and made a prediction after having looked up fewer than one-third of the cues. But are the heuristics also fast – that is simple – in their computations? Given that Take the Best performs so well, it must be doing some work, perhaps hidden in the training phase of the cross-validation if not in the test phase. Thus, we now wish to be more precise about measuring how fast (computationally simple) our heuristics are, both in the training and in the test phase.

Let us begin by measuring the amount of learning required by the heuristics to build their models in order to perform their predictions later. We can use the suggestion of Newell and Simon (1972) and Payne, Bettman, and Johnson (1990) – count the number of elementary information processing (EIP) units necessary for the training phase. These EIPs include addition, subtraction, multiplication, division, comparison of two numbers, reading a number, writing a number, and so on. For each such operation, we count 1 unit. These EIP units are easy to count, and Payne, Bettman, and Johnson (1990) present experimental evidence that they are a reasonable estimate of the cognitive effort involved in executing a particular choice strategy in a specific task environment. For our tasks, the number of EIPs required depends on N, the number of objects, and M, the number of cues in the data set. Table 31.4 specifies both the approximate number of EIPs used for any values of N and M that a data set has, and the

Table 31.4. Approximate Number of EIPs Needed for the Training Phase of Each Strategy[a]

Strategy	Knowledge About Cues Obtained in Training Phase	Approximate Number of EIPs Used in Training Phase for Any N, M	Number of EIPs in Training for Homelessness ($N = 50$, $M = 6$)
Minimalist	Direction	$\approx 10NM$	3,398
Take the Best	Direction + order	$\approx 10NM$	3,448
Dawes' Rule	Direction	$\approx 10NM$	3,398
Multiple regression	Beta weights	$\approx 10NM^2$	20,020

[a] EIPs = Elementary Information Processing Units; N = number of objects; M = number of cues. The task is predicting homelessness (for details, see Czerlinski, 1997).

Table 31.5. Number of EIPs Needed for the Test Phase of Each Strategy [a]

Strategy	Process of Inference	Number of EIPs Used in Test Phase for Any N, M, M_a	Number of EIPs in Inferring Homelessness ($N = 50$, $M = 6$)
Minimalist	Search through cues randomly until decision possible	$3\,M_a$	6.2 ($M_a = 2.1$)
Take the Best	Search through ordered cues until decision possible	$3\,M_a$	7.2 ($M_a = 2.4$)
Dawes' Rule	Count number of unitary and zero cue values; compare	$8\,M$–7	41
Multiple regression	Linearly use beta weights to estimate criterion; compare	$16\,M$–7	89

[a] EIPs = Elementary Information Processing Units; N = number of objects; M = number of cues; M_a = average number of cues used. The task is predicting homelessness (for details, see Czerlinski, 1997).

number of EIPs for the specific case of predicting homelessness, with $N = 50$ and $M = 6$.

Fast and frugal heuristics require significantly less calculation in the training phase than multiple regression. This is the case, even though in calculating the number of EIPs in regression, we neglected the usual invertibility and computer overflow checks, so 20,000 EIPs is really a lower bound. In practical applications, fast and frugal heuristics might be as much as 1/100 simpler. Note that we differ from earlier theorists such as Dawes (1979) in including learning the direction of cues as a real problem; other theorists have assumed this is known already, making fast and frugal heuristics even simpler.

Of course, learning a model of the data is only the first step. Implementing the heuristic has a cost, too. Table 31.5 specifies the number of EIPs in the test phase. Fast and frugal heuristics are always at least as efficient as the others because they look up fewer cues and perform fewer calculations on those cues. Because fast and frugal heuristics generally do not use all of the available cues, we also need to consider the actual number of cues looked up, M_a. For example, Take the Best uses, on average, only 2.4 cues for predicting homelessness.

Table 31.5 clearly shows that the cue-based predictions of Minimalist and Take the Best are highly efficient, about 5 times simpler than the simplest linear model, Dawes' Rule, and about 10 times simpler than Multiple Regression. We now have a measure of how fast (computationally simple) the heuristics are, and we have shown that theoretically, fast and frugal heuristics can be from 5 to 10 times faster than regression (and practically even more). The calculation of

EIPs does not have to assume serial processing; if the brain implements certain aspects of the calculation in parallel, then the total number of calculations would be the same, but they would be completed more quickly. For example, if we could compute the validity of all cues in parallel, we would effectively have $M = 1$, and this could be plugged in to the formulae presented earlier. However, even under such conditions, fast heuristics could not be slower than regression and could still be faster, just not as much faster as they are under the assumption of serial processing. And, of course, they would still be more frugal.

In summary, our fast and frugal heuristics learn with less information, perform fewer computations while learning, look up less information in the test phase, and perform fewer computations when predicting. Nevertheless, fast and frugal heuristics can be almost as accurate as multiple regression when fitting data. Even more counterintuitively, one of these fast and frugal heuristics, Take the Best, was, on average, more accurate than Regression in the more realistic situation in which the training set and test set were not the same (cross-validation). How is this possible?

ECOLOGICAL RATIONALITY: WHY AND WHEN ARE FAST AND FRUGAL HEURISTICS GOOD?

Note first that these data sets have been collected from "real-world" situations. What are the characteristics of information in real-world environments that make Take the Best a better predictor than other strategies, and where will it fail? When we talk of properties of information, we mean the information about an environment known to a decision maker. We discuss three properties, the first of which is one that characterizes many real-world situations: the available information is scarce. Take the Best is smarter than its competitors when information is scarce.

Scarce Information

In order to illustrate the concept of scarce information, let us recall an important fact from information theory: a class of N objects contains $\log N$ bits of information. This means that if we were to encode each object in the class by means of binary cue profiles of the same length, this length should be at least $\log N$ if each object is to have a unique profile. The example in Table 31.6 illustrates this relation for $N = 8$ objects. The eight objects are perfectly predictable by the three ($\log 8 = 3$) binary cues. If there were only two cues, perfect predictability simply could not be achieved.

> **THEOREM** *If the number of cues is less than $\log N$, the Profile Memorization Method will never achieve 100% correct inferences. Thus, no other strategy will either.*

This theorem motivates the following definition:

> **DEFINITION** *A set of M cues provides scarce information for a reference class of N objects if $M < \log N$.*

Table 31.6. Illustration of the Fact That 8 Objects Can Be Predicted Perfectly by log8 = 3 Binary Cues

Objects	First Cue	Second Cue	Third Cue
A	1	1	1
B	1	1	0
C	1	0	1
D	1	0	0
E	0	1	1
F	0	1	0
G	0	0	1
H	0	0	0

We can now formulate a theorem that relates the performance of Take the Best to that of Dawes' Rule.

> **THEOREM** *In the case of scarce information, Take the Best is on average more accurate than Dawes' Rule.*

The proof is in Martignon, Hoffrage, and Kriegeskorte (1997). The phrase "on average" means across all possible environments; that is, all combinations of binary entries for $N \times M$ matrices. The intuition underlying the theorem is the following: In scarce environments, Dawes' Rule can take little advantage of its strongest property – namely, compensation. If, in a scarce environment, cues are redundant – that is, if a subset of these cues does not add new information – things will be even worse for Dawes' Rule. Take the Best suffers less from redundancy because decisions are taken at a very early stage.

Abundant Information

Adding cues to a scarce environment will do little for Take the Best if the best cues in the original environment are already highly valid, but it may compensate for various mistakes Dawes' Rule would have made based on the first cues. In fact, by adding and adding cues we can make Dawes' Rule achieve perfection. This is true even if all cues are favorable (i.e., their validity is > 0.5) but uncertain (i.e., their validity is < 1).

> **THEOREM** *Assume that the environment consists of $N \geq 5$ objects. If an environment consists of all possible uncertain but favorable cues, Dawes' Rule will discriminate among all objects and make only correct inferences.*

The proof is given in Martignon et al. (1997). Note that we are using the term cue to denote a binary-valued function on the reference class. Therefore, the number of different cues on a finite reference class is finite. The theorem can be generalized to linear models that use cue validities as weights rather than unit weights. As a consequence, Take the Best will be outperformed on average by linear models in abundant environments.

Noncompensatory Information

Environments may be compensatory or noncompensatory. Among the 20 environments studied in Section 2, we found 4 in which the weights for the linear models were noncompensatory (i.e., each weight is larger than the sum of all other weights to come, such as $1/2, 1/4, 1/8, \ldots$). The following theorem states an important property of noncompensatory models and is easily proved (Martignon et al., 1997).

> **THEOREM** *Take the Best is equivalent in performance to a weighted linear model whose weights form a noncompensatory set.*

If multiple regression happens to have a noncompensatory set of weights (where the order of this set corresponds to the order of cue validities), then its accuracy is equivalent to Take the Best.

Why Is Take the Best So Robust?

The reason that Take the Best is so robust is simple: Take the Best uses few cues (only 2.4 cues on average in the data sets presented here); thus, its performance depends on very few parameters. The top cues usually have high validity. In general, highly valid cues remain highly valid across different subsets of the same class of objects. Even the order of their cue validities tends to be fairly stable. The stability of highly valid cues is a main factor for the robustness of Take the Best, in cross-validation as well as in other forms of incremental learning.

Strategies that use all cues must estimate a number of parameters larger than or equal to the number of cues. Some, like multiple regression, use a huge number of parameters. Thus they suffer from overfitting, in particular with small data sets.

To conclude, scarceness and redundancy of information are characteristics of information gathered by humans. Humans are not always good at finding large numbers of cues for making predictions. The magic number 7 ± 2 seems to represent the basic information capacity human minds work with in a short time interval. Furthermore, humans are not always good at detecting redundancies between cues, and quantitatively estimating the degree of these redundancies. Fast and frugal Take the Best is a heuristic that works well with scarce information and does not even try to estimate redundancies and cue intercorrelations. In this way, it compensates for the limits in human information processing. If the structure of the information available to an organism is scarce or noncompensatory, then Take the Best will be not only fast and frugal, but also fairly accurate, even relative to more computationally expensive strategies.

HOW DOES TAKE THE BEST COMPARE WITH GOOD BAYESIAN MODELS?

It happened that Ward Edwards was a reviewer of one of our group's first papers on fast and frugal heuristics (Goldstein & Gigerenzer, 1996). Ward sent us a personal copy of his review, as he always does. No surprise, his first point was, "Specify how a truly optimal Bayesian model would operate." But Ward did not tell us which Bayesian model of the task (to predict the populations of cities) he would consider truly optimal.

In this section, we present a possible Bayesian approach to the type of task discussed in the previous sections. We do not see Bayesian models and fast and frugal heuristics as incompatible, or even opposed. On the contrary, considering the computational complexity Bayesian models require, and the fact (as we show later) that fast and frugal heuristics do not fall too far behind in accuracy, one can be a satisficer when one has limited time and knowledge, and a Bayesian when one is in no hurry and has a computer at hand. A Bayesian can decide when it is safe and profitable to be a satisficer.

Bayesian Networks

If training set and test set coincide, the Bayesian knows what she will do: use the Profile Memorization Method if she has perfect memory. If training set and test set are different, the Bayesian has to construct a good model. Regression is not necessarily the first model that would come to her mind. Given the kind of task, she may tend to choose from the flexible family of Bayesian networks. Another possibility is a Bayesian CART, and a third is a mixture of these two.

The task is to infer which of two objects A or B scores higher on a criterion, based on the values of a set of binary cues. Assume, furthermore, that the decision maker has nine cues at her disposal and she has full knowledge of the values these cues take on A and B. To work out a concrete example, let A and B have the cue profiles (100101010) and (011000011) respectively. The Bayesian asks herself: What is the probability that an object with cue profile (100101010) scores higher than an object with cue profile (011000011) on the established criterion? In symbols:

$$\text{Prob}(A > B \mid A \cong (100101010),\ B \cong (011000011)) = ? \qquad (*).$$

Here, the symbol $\cong$ is used to signify "has the cue profile." As a concrete example, let us discuss the task investigated in Gigerenzer and Goldstein (1996), in which pairs of German cities were compared as to which had a larger population. There were nine cues: "Is the city the national capital?" (NC); "Is the city a state capital?" (SC); "Does the city have a soccer team in the major national league?" (SO); "Was the city once an exposition site?" (EX); "Is the city on the Intercity train line?" (IT); "Is the abbreviation of the city on the license plate only one letter long?" (LP); "Is the city home to a university?" (UN); "Is the city in the industrial belt?" (IB); "Is the city in former West Germany?" (WG).

A network for our type of task considers pairs of objects (A, B) and the possible states of the cues, which are the four pairs of binary values (0,0), (0,1), (1,0), (1,1) on pairs of objects. A very simple Bayesian network would neglect all interdependencies between cues. This is known as *Idiot Bayes*. It computes $(*)$ from the product of the different probabilities of success of all cues. Forced to a deterministic answer, Idiot Bayes will predict that A scores higher than B on the criterion if the probability of $A > B$ computed in terms of this product is larger than the probability of $B > A$. Due to its simplicity, Idiot Bayes is sometimes used as a crude estimate of probability distributions. This is not the procedure the Bayesian uses if she wants accuracy.

The other extreme in the family of Bayesian networks is the fully connected network, where each pair of nodes is connected both ways. Computing ($*$) in terms of this network when training and test set coincide amounts to using the Profile Memorization Method. Both these extremes, namely Idiot Bayes and the fully connected network, are far from being optimal when training set and test set differ. A more accurate Bayesian network must concentrate on the important conditional dependencies between cues, as some dependencies are more relevant than others. Some may be so weak that it is convenient to neglect them in order to avoid overfitting. The Bayesian needs a Bayesian strategy to decide which are the relevant links that should remain and also to prune all the irrelevant ones. She needs a strategy to search through the possible networks and evaluate each network in terms of its performance. Bayesian techniques for performing this type of search in a smart and efficient way have been developed both in statistics and artificial intelligence. These methods are efficient in learning both structure and parameters. Nir Friedman and Leo Goldszmit (1996), for instance, have devised software for searching over networks and finding a good fit for a given set of data in a classification task. Because our task is basically a classification task (we are determining whether a pair of objects is rightly ordered), we are able to make use of Friedman and Goldszmit's network. However, a smart Bayesian network is often too complex to be computed. The following theorem offers a way to reduce the huge number of computations that would be, at first glance, necessary for computing ($*$) based on a Bayesian network. In a Bayesian network, the nodes with arrows pointing to a fixed node are called the *parents* of that node. The node itself is called a *child* of its parents. What follows is a fundamental rule for operating with Bayesian networks.

THEOREM *The conditional probability of a node j being in a certain state given knowledge on the state of all other nodes in the network is proportional to the product of the conditional probability of the node given its parents times the conditional probability of each of its children given its parents.*

In symbols:

Prob(node j | other nodes) =

$K \times$ Prob(node j | parents of j) $\times$ Π Prob(child k of j | parents of k).

Here, K is a normalizing constant. The set, consisting of a node, its parents, its children, and the other parents of its children, is called the *Markov Blanket* of that node. What the theorem states is that the Markov Blanket of a node determines the state of the node regardless of the state of all other nodes not in the Blanket.

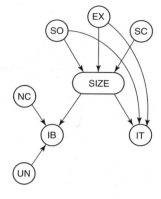

Figure 31.2. A Bayesian network for predicting population size (which of two German cities A or B is larger). The cues are: SO, soccer team; EX, exposition site; SC, state capital; IB, industrial belt; NC, national capital; UN, university; IT, intercity train.

The theorem just stated, based essentially on Bayes' rule, represents an enormous computational reduction in the calculation of probability distributions. It is precisely due to this type of reduction of computational complexity that Bayesian networks have become a popular tool both in statistics and in artificial intelligence since the 1980s.

Figure 31.2 shows the Bayesian network obtained with Friedman's search method for the task of comparing German cities according to their population, as in Gigerenzer and Goldstein (1996). In that paper, the reference class of the 83 German cities with more than 100,000 inhabitants was analyzed. The Bayesian network reveals that two of the nine cues, LP and WG, are irrelevant when the other seven cues are known. Figure 31.2 illustrates the Markov Blanket of the node size, which represents the hypothesis, "City A has more inhabitants than city B" and obviously can be in two states (the other state is "City B has more inhabitants than city A"). According to the theorem specified above:

$$\text{Prob(size | UN, NC, IB, SO, EX, SC, IT)} = K \times \text{Prob(size | SO, EX, SC)}$$
$$\times \text{Prob(IB | size, UN, NC)} \times \text{Prob (IT | size)},$$

where K is a constant. In order to determine each of the probabilities on the right side of the equation, the program produces simple decision trees (actually CARTs), as illustrated in Fig. 31.3 for Prob(size | SO, EX, SC). The program searches among all possible trees for the one that best fits the data, pruning all irrelevant branches. That is, this approach combines a Bayesian network with a CART step at the end. CART models were popularized in the statistical community by the seminal book by Breiman, Friedman, Olshen, and Stone (1984).

This method, a mixture of a Bayesian network and CART, is much more computationally intensive than multiple regression, not to mention Take the Best. In fact, if we were to compute its EIPs as we did in the previous section, we would clearly reach a function of M and N containing an exponential term in M.

How much more accurate is such a computationally complex Bayesian network than the simple Take the Best? Table 31.7 shows the performance of the

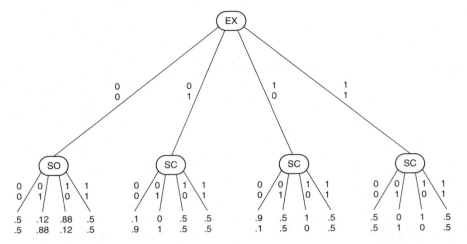

Figure 31.3. Classification and regression tree (CART) for quick computation of Prob(size | SO,EX, SC). For instance, if neither of the two cities A and B is an exposition site (symbolized by the two zeros in the left branch), then the only relevant cue is SO; that is, whether a city has a soccer team in the major league (SC is irrelevant). If A has a soccer team but B does not (1 and 0), then Prob($A > B$ | SO, EX, SC) = .88, and Prob($A < B$ | SO, EX, SC) = .12. "$A > B$" stands for "A has a larger population than B."

Bayesian network and the Profile Memorization Method (the upper limit) when training and test set coincide. Performance was tested in four environments:

1. Which of two German cities has the higher population?
2. Which of two U.S. cities has a higher homelessness rate?
3. Which of two individual Arctic female charr fish produces more eggs?
4. Which of two professors at a Midwestern college has a higher salary?

For predicting city populations, the Bayesian network gets 2 percentage points more correct answers than Take the Best. The upper limit of correct predictions can be computed by the Profile Memorization Method as 80%, which is 4 percentage points higher than the performance of the Bayesian network. When the test set is different from the training set (Table 31.8), then multiple regression

Table 31.7. Percentage of Correct Inferences When Test Set = Training Set

Environment	Take the Best	Multiple Regression	Bayesian Network	Profile Memorization Method
City population	74	74	76	80
Homelessness	69	70	77	82
Fish fertility	73	75	75	75
Professors' salaries	80	83	84	87

Table 31.8. Percentage of Correct Inferences When Test Set Is Different from Training Set (Cross-Validation)

Environment	Take the Best	Multiple Regression	Bayesian Network
City population	72	71	74
Homelessness	63	61	65
Fish fertility	73	75	75
Professors' salaries	80	80	81

takes a slightly larger loss than Take the Best and the Bayesian network. Recall that the upper limit cannot be calculated by the Profile Memorization Method when the test set is different from the training set.

When predicting homelessness, the Bayesian network performs 8 percentage points better than Take the Best (Table 31.7). This difference is reduced to 2 percentage points when the test set is different from the training set (Table 31.8). Here, Take the Best is the most robust heuristic under cross-validation.

The fish fertility data set is of particular interest because it contains a large set of objects (395 individual fish). The cues for the criterion (number of eggs found in a given fish) were weight of fish, age of fish, and average weight of her eggs. Here, as one would expect for a reasonably large data set, all results are quite stable when one cross-validates.

The next problem is to predict which of two professors at a Midwestern college has a higher salary. The cues are gender, his or her current rank, the number of years in current rank, the highest degree earned, and the number of years since highest degree earned. When the test set is the same as the training set, Take the Best makes 4 percentage points fewer accurate inferences than the Bayesian network. However, when the test set is different from the training set, then Take the Best almost matches the Bayesian network.

Across these four environments, the following generalizations emerge:

1. When the test set is the same as the training set, the Bayesian network is considerably more accurate than Take the Best. On average, it was only 3 percentage points behind the Profile Memorization Method, which attains maximal accuracy. However, when the test set is different from the training set, the accuracy of Take the Best is, on average, only 1 to 2 percentage points less than that of the Bayesian network. This result is noteworthy given the simplicity and frugality of Take the Best compared with the computational complexity of the Bayesian network.
2. Take the Best is more robust – measured in loss of accuracy from Table 31.7 to Table 31.8 – than both multiple regression and the Bayesian network.

What is extraordinary about fast and frugal Take the Best is that it does not fall too far behind the complex Bayesian network, and it can easily compete in 20 different environments (Section 2) with Dawes' Rule and multiple regression.

CONCLUSIONS

L. J. Savage wrote that the only decision we must make in our lives is how to live our lives (1954, p. 83). But "How to live our lives" means basically "How to make decisions." Do we adopt Bayesian decision making, or do we use some simple heuristics, like the satisficing ones presented in this chapter? This might not be an exclusive "or": Fast and frugal heuristics can have their place in everyday affairs in which time is limited and knowledge is scarce, and Bayesian tools can be the choice for someone who is in no hurry and has a computer in her bag (von Winterfeldt & Edwards, 1986). A Bayesian who tries to maximize under deliberation constraints must choose a strategy under a combination of criteria, such as computational cost, frugality, accuracy, and perhaps even transparency. Thus, it may happen that a Bayesian herself may choose Take the Best or another fast and frugal heuristic over expensive but less robust Bayesian networks in some situations. Bayesian reasoning itself may tell us when to satisfice.

The major results summarized in this chapter are as follows: First, across 20 real-world environments, the fast and frugal Take the Best outperformed multiple regression in situations with learning (test set ≠ training set), and even the simpler Minimalist came within 2 percentage points. Second, we specified which characteristics of information in real-world environments enable Take the Best to match or outperform linear models. Third, we showed that sophisticated Bayesian networks were only slightly more accurate than Take the Best.

The results reported in this chapter were obtained with real-world data but must be evaluated with respect to the conditions used, which include the following: First, we studied inferences only under complete knowledge, unlike Gigerenzer and Goldstein (1996), who studied the performance of heuristics under limited knowledge. Limited knowledge (e.g., knowing only a fraction of all cue values) is a realistic condition that applies to many situations in which predictions must be made. In the simulations reported by Gigerenzer and Goldstein, the major result was that the more limited the knowledge, the smaller the discrepancy between Minimalist and other heuristics becomes. Thus Minimalist, whose respectable scores were nevertheless always the lowest, really flourishes when there is only limited knowledge. Gigerenzer and Goldstein (1996) also develop circumstances under which the counterintuitive less-is-more effect is possible: when knowing less information can lead to better performance than knowing more information.

Other conditions of the studies reported here include the use of binary and dichotomized data, which can be a disadvantage to multiple regression and Bayesian networks. Finally, we have used only correct data, and not studied predictions under the realistic assumption that some of the information is wrong.

Some of the results obtained are reminiscent of the phenomenon of flat maxima. If many sets of weights, even unit weights, can perform about as well as the optimal set of weights in a linear model, this is called a flat maximum. The work by Dawes and others (e.g., Dawes & Corrigan, 1974) made this phenomenon known to decision researchers, but it is actually much older (see John, Edwards, & von Winterfeldt, n.d.). The performance of fast and frugal heuristics in some of the environments indicates that a flat maximum can extend beyond the issue of weights: inferences based solely on the best cue can be as accurate as those based on any weighted linear combination of all cues. The results in Section 3, in particular, the theorem on noncompensatory information, explain conditions under which we can predict flat maxima.

The success of fast and frugal heuristics emphasizes the importance of studying the structure of the information in the environment. Such a program is Brunswikian, but it is one that dispenses with multiple regression as the tool for describing both the processes of the mind and the structure of the environment. Fast and frugal heuristics can be ecologically rational in the sense that they exploit specific and possibly recurrent characteristics of the environment's structure (Tooby & Cosmides, in press). Models of reasonable judgment should look outside of the mind to its environment. And models of reasonableness do not have to forsake accuracy for simplicity – the mind can have it both ways.

32. Intuitive Politicians, Theologians, and Prosecutors: Exploring the Empirical Implications of Deviant Functionalist Metaphors

Philip E. Tetlock

In 1890, one of psychology's patron saints, William James (1890/1983), voiced the suspicion that all psychological explanations ultimately rest on functionalist premises. He felt that, whenever you scratch the surface of even the most forbiddingly formal psychological explanation, you discover informal assumptions about the goals that people are consciously or unconsciously trying to accomplish by thinking, feeling, and acting as they do.

Research on judgment and choice is no exception. The starting points for the dominant research programs have been functionalist postulates of one form or another: In the domain of judgment, people are assumed to be intuitive scientists, psychologists, and statisticians who seek causal understanding and predictive leverage and, in the domain of choice, they are assumed to be intuitive economists who seek to maximize subjective expected utility – in each case, of course, within the constraints of bounded rationality. These assumptions profoundly shape empirical work. Key questions become: How well do people size up against professional standards of competence? Do they draw causal inferences in the rigorous fashion that we might expect of real scientists and do they make choices in the analytical manner that we might expect of real economists?

Both research programs have been phenomenally successful, triggering an avalanche of discoveries of when judgment and choice deviate from conventional standards of scientific or economic rationality. It would be curmudgeonly – and, even worse, wrong – to deny that both research programs pass classic philosophy-of-science tests of knowledge advancement, an all-too-rare achievement in the behavioral and social sciences (Meehl, 1990). A small set of explanatory constructs – judgmental heuristics, the framing of outcomes, the psychophysics of gain and loss functions – organizes a vast array of findings and stimulates falsifiable hypotheses that hold up in an impressive array of settings. However, there is no compelling reason to suppose that, just because these dominant research programs have yet to run out of steam, we should be barred from exploring the empirical implications of alternative functionalist metaphors. As I show in this chapter, in certain well-defined contexts it proves illuminating to posit that people function like intuitive politicians striving to create desired impressions on target audiences, intuitive prosecutors communicating their resolve to make harsh dispositional attributions designed to punish violators of social rules (even if the suspected miscreants can invoke plausible denials, justifications, or excuses in their defense), and intuitive theologians rising to the defense of sacred values against secular, especially monetary, encroachments.

This chapter focuses on the most extensively examined of these metaphoric alternatives: the notion that people can be modeled usefully as intuitive politicians whose primary goal is to protect and enhance their social identities in the eyes of the constituencies to whom they feel accountable.

EMPIRICAL BOUNDARY CONDITIONS ON THE ERROR-AND-BIAS PORTRAIT

Accountability refers to the expectation that one will be called on to justify one's opinions or conduct to others. Following Weber (1910/1978) and Coleman (1990), Tetlock (1992) argues that accountability is a pervasive presence in our lives because it represents a fundamental sociocultural adaptation to the problem of coordinating relationships among agents who are capable of observing, commenting on, and controlling their own actions. In effect, accountability is part of the solution to the Hobbesian riddle of how society is possible. Organized social life cannot exist without regularities, which are provided by shared rules, norms, and social practices. Accountability is a critical norm-enforcement mechanism – the social psychological link between individual decision makers on the one hand and social systems on the other. Expectations of accountability constrain virtually everything people do (in the Mead–Vygotsky symbolic–interactionist tradition, people are constantly asking themselves, "If I did this, how would others react?" and "What could I say in response?"). Failure to act in ways for which one can construct acceptable accounts leads to varying degrees of censure, depending on the gravity of the offense and the norms of the society.

It is, however, a common mistake to depict accountability as a unitary phenomenon. Even the simplest accountability manipulations implicate several distinct components, each a potential independent variable in its own right: the mere presence of an observer, the belief among decision makers that their individual inputs can be identified and will be monitored, the expectation of some form of evaluation, and the expectation of the need to generate reasons for one's views that will be scrutinized (Lerner & Tetlock, 1999). This chapter does not, however, try to decompose accountability into its elementary components. Rather, it treats accountability as a natural bridging construct between the individual and institutional levels of analysis in the study of judgment and choice. The accountability relationships that govern our lives are not only complex (because we must answer to a variety of others under a variety of ground rules), but also fluid and dynamic (as each party in the relationship learns to anticipate the reactions of the other, we observe subtle patterns of mutual adaptation). To paraphrase William James' famous observation about the social self: There are as many distinct types of accountability as there are distinct relationships among people.

OPTIMAL CONDITIONS FOR ACTIVATING STRATEGIES OF COPING WITH ACCOUNTABILITY

Accountability is a vast topic that can be not only studied experimentally, but also in a wide range of institutional settings in which debates over who should be answerable to whom, and under what ground rules, are central to political contests for power (March & Olson, 1995). It is easy to get lost without a conceptual roadmap. To this end, Tetlock (1992) proposed a middle-range theory of how people function as intuitive politicians: the *social contingency model* (SCM) *of accountability*. This framework is best viewed as but one explanatory option in a spectrum of options consistent with the politician metaphor (in much the same way that there is a broad spectrum of testable middle-range theories consistent with the economist and scientist metaphors). The key postulates of the model are as follows:

1) *The universality of accountability.* People do some things alone, but it is difficult to escape the evaluative scrutiny of others in a complex, interdependent society. Escape arguably becomes impossible when we count *self-accountability* – the obligation that most human beings feel to internalized representations of significant others who keep watch over them when no one else is looking (Mead, 1934; Schlenker, 1985).

2) *The approval motive.* Most people are pragmatic intuitive politicians who seek the approval of the constituencies pressing on them at the moment for combinations of intrinsic and extrinsic reasons. Evidence for an *intrinsic-approval motive* comes from developmental studies that point to the remarkably early emergence in human life of automatic and visceral responses to signs of censure, such as angry words and contemptuous facial expressions (Baumeister & Leary, 1995). Evidence for an *extrinsic motive* comes from the exchange-theory tradition that, in its crassest version, maintains that we care about what others think of us only insofar as others control resources that we value to a greater degree than we control resources that they value (asymmetric resource dependency).

3) *Competition among motives.* Although social approval is a major driving force for intuitive politicians, the SCM does not reify it as the sovereign motive for human conduct. A realistic composite portrait requires identifying at least four potentially conflicting motives: the goals of (1) achieving cognitive mastery of causal structure, (2) minimizing mental effort and achieving reasonably rapid cognitive closure, (3) maximizing benefits and minimizing the costs of relationships, and (4) asserting one's autonomy and personal identity by remaining true to one's innermost convictions.

4) *Linking motives to coping strategies.* A testable model must connect broad motivational assumptions to specific coping strategies by indicating how each motive can be amplified or attenuated by the prevailing accountability norms. The SCM identifies a host of situational and dispositional variables that either increase or decrease the perceived importance of a given motive or the perceived feasibility of achieving a given objective in a given context.

The next sections of the chapter deploy this schematic formula to identify the optimal preconditions for activating the four strategies for coping with accountability that have received the most attention: strategic attitude shifting; preemptive self-criticism; defensive bolstering; and the decision evasion tactics of buck-passing, procrastination, and obfuscation.

Strategic Attitude Shifting

Decision makers are predicted to adjust their public attitudes toward the views of the anticipated audience when the approval motive is strong. Ideally, the evaluative audience should be perceived to be powerful, firmly committed to its position, and intolerant of other positions. Strategic attitude shifting is viable, however, only to the degree that decision makers think they know the views of the anticipated audience. Attitude shifting becomes psychologically costly to the degree that it requires compromising basic convictions and principles (stimulating dissonance) or back-tracking on past commitments (making decision makers look duplicitous, hypocritical, or sycophantic). Lerner and Tetlock (1999) reviewed evidence that indicates that when these obstacles have been removed and the facilitative conditions are present, attitude shifting serves as a cognitively efficient and politically expedient means of gaining approval that does not undermine the decision maker's self-concept as a moral and principled being, or his or her reputation for integrity in the wider social arena. Moreover, people are sometimes "taken in" by their own self-presentational maneuvering, internalizing positions they publicly endorse. Strange as it sounds, strategic shifting can occasionally be sincere.

Preemptive Self-Criticism

Cognitively economic and socially adaptive although the attitude shifting can be, its usefulness is limited to settings in which decision makers can discern easily what others want or expect. The SCM predicts that decision makers will engage in flexible perspective taking, in which they try to anticipate plausible objections of reasonable critics, when they are accountable either to an audience with unknown views or to multiple audiences with conflicting views. To maximize the likelihood of preemptive self-criticism, the evaluative audience should be perceived to be well informed (so that it cannot be tricked easily) and powerful (so that decision makers want its approval), and the decision makers should not feel constrained by prior commitments that it would now be embarrassing to reverse. In the case of accountability to conflicting audiences, the audiences should be approximately equally powerful (otherwise a low-effort expedient is to align oneself with the more powerful audience), the two audiences should recognize each other's legitimacy (otherwise searching for complex integrative solutions is seen as futile), and there should be no institutional precedents for escaping responsibility (otherwise the evasion tactics of buck-passing, procrastination, or obfuscation become tempting).

Several experiments demonstrate that the hypothesized forms of accountability do activate more complex and self-critical patterns of thinking (Ashton, 1992; Weldon & Gargano, 1988; Hagafors & Brehmer, 1983). For instance, Tetlock et al. (1989) reported a set of experiments in which subjects took positions on controversial policy issues under one of four conditions: expecting the positions they took to be confidential (low accountability) or expecting to justify their positions to a liberal, conservative, or unknown audience. In addition, subjects reported their thoughts (confidentiality always guaranteed) on each issue prior to committing themselves to positions. These thought protocols were subjected to detailed content analysis designed to assess the integrative complexity of subjects' thinking on the issues: How many facets of each issue did they distinguish? Did they interpret issues in dichotomous, good–bad terms, or did they recognize positive and negative features of both sides of the issues?

Subjects coped in two qualitatively distinct ways: shifting their public positions (thus making the task of justification easier) and thinking about issues in more flexible multidimensional ways (thus preparing themselves for possible counterarguments). They relied on attitude shifting when they felt accountable to an audience with known liberal or conservative views. Accountability to known audiences had minimal impact, however, on the complexity of private thoughts. The reverse pattern emerged among subjects accountable to an unknown audience. Accountability now had virtually no effect on public attitudes, but a substantial effect on the complexity of private thoughts. Subjects were markedly more tolerant of evaluative inconsistency (recognizing good features of rejected policies and bad features of accepted ones) and more aware of difficult value trade-offs. Subjects accountable to unknown audiences appeared to engage in preemptive self-criticism in which they tried to anticipate arguments of potential critics. This can be viewed as an adaptive strategy to protect both one's self-image and social image. Expecting to justify one's views to an unknown audience raised the prospect of failure: the other person might find serious flaws in one's position. To minimize potential embarrassment, subjects demonstrated their awareness of alternative perspectives: "You can see that I am no fool. I may believe X, but I understand the arguments for Y."

Defensive Bolstering

There is a fine line between types of accountability that trigger self-critical thought and types of accountability that trigger self-justifying trains of thought. The SCM predicts self-justifying thinking when decision makers are accountable to a skeptical or even hostile audience for actions that it is now impossible to reverse and implausible to deny.

Tetlock et al. (1989) demonstrated how a seemingly minor variation in the timing of an accountability manipulation can determine whether we observe preemptive self-criticism or the mirror-image coping strategy of defensive bolstering. Participants in this study reported their thoughts on four controversial issues either before or after they had committed themselves to stands. Some subjects believed that their stands were private; others believed that they would later justify their views to an audience with unknown, liberal, or conservative views. Accountable participants who reported their thoughts after making commitments became markedly less tolerant of dissonant arguments than were three other groups: unaccountable participants who reported their thoughts after making commitments and both unaccountable and accountable participants who reported their thoughts prior to taking a stand. Once people had publicly committed themselves to a position, a major function of thought became generating justifications for those positions. As a result, the integrative complexity of thoughts plunged (subjects were less likely to concede legitimacy to other points of view) and the number of pro-attitudinal thoughts increased (subjects generated more reasons why they were right and would-be critics were wrong).

Decision Evasion

The SCM predicts that decision makers will resort to one of the trio of decision-evasion tactics – buck-passing, procrastination, and obfuscation – when they are accountable to audiences that not only hold conflicting views but also hold each other in contempt. Ideally, each audience should deny the legitimacy of the accountability demands of the other, thereby rendering the prospects of either a log rolling or an integratively complex solution hopeless. The audiences should also be approximately equal in power, thereby reducing the attractiveness for decision makers of aligning themselves with one or the other camp. There should also be widely accepted institutional precedents for engaging in decision evasion (that is, no Trumanesque "the-buck-stops-here" norm). Finally, decision makers should have weak personal convictions and be strongly motivated to maintain good relations with both of the affected parties.

Several experimental and field studies provide supportive evidence (Janis & Mann, 1977; Wilson, 1989). Consider the predicament that Tetlock and Boettger (1994) created in a laboratory simulation of Food and Drug Administration decision making on the acceptability of a controversial anti-clotting drug into the U.S. pharmaceuticals market – a drug that would benefit more patients than it would harm, sometimes by a massive margin, but would always harm a substantial number of people. The experimental manipulations included: (1) whether the drug was already on the market (so decision makers would have to take responsibility for removing it) or was not yet on the market (so decision makers would have to take responsibility for introducing it); (2) whether decision makers expected their recommendations to be anonymous or scrutinized by the affected constituencies; and (3) the benefit–cost ratio of the drug which ranged from 3:1 to 9:1 in favor of the drug. Confronted by pressures to take a stand one way or the other that was guaranteed to earn the enmity of an influential constituency, subjects, especially those in the off-the-market/accountability condition, sought options that allowed them to avoid taking any stand. This was true, moreover, even when the buck-passing and procrastination options had been rendered unattractive. Subjects still performed buck-passing when they thought that the agency to which they could refer the decision had no more information than they possessed, and they still procrastinated when there was virtually no prospect that additional useful evidence would materialize in the permissible delayed-action period. These decision-avoidant respondents also had remarkably loss-averse policy preferences even by the standards of prospect theory (requiring that the new drug have a much higher benefit–cost ratio, up to 9:1, to enter the market than the old drug had to have to remain in the market).

IMPLICATIONS OF COPING STRATEGIES
FOR JUDGMENTAL SHORTCOMINGS

Skeptics might concede all of the claims concerning how people cope with diverse sorts of accountability outlined in the previous section, but still insist that none of the claims bears on the foveal concern of the intuitive-scientist and economist research programs – namely, how do people think, and when do these thought processes deviate from well-defined normative benchmarks? The skeptics might even dust off a slightly modified version of the disciplinary division of labor between psychology and the social sciences initially proposed by Miller and Dollard (1946): The mission of the cognitive research program is to shed light on how people think, whereas the mission of the intuitive-politician research program (and other deviant metaphoric traditions) is to shed light on what people think about and when they are willing to say what is on their minds (raising or lowering response thresholds for expressing certain views).

There is some merit in this traditional stance. Certain coping strategies have socially significant but cognitively uninteresting implications for the conditions under which biases and errors manifest themselves. It is easy to imagine the types of heavy-handed social pressures that trigger strategic attitude shifting also suppressing evidence of cognitive bias. People can readily learn that their boss expects them to use certain cues or to disregard others, and it is easy to see why cognitive theorists would find evidence of such bias suppression less than intriguing. There is no great surprise in learning that conformity pressures can alter response thresholds. The *acceptability heuristic* (as Tetlock, 1992, semi-facetiously labeled it) represents a minor content embellishment on the heuristics-and-biases portrait of the decision maker. The most salient consideration in many decisions is the justifiability of policy options to others. The cognitive research programs tell us that people often use a small number of cues in making up their minds; the intuitive-politician research program tells us that decision makers' estimates of the probable reactions of those to whom they are accountable will be prominent among the few items considered. The traditional disciplinary division of labor still stands.

In other cases, however, the division begins to crumble. The self-presentational processes triggered by accountability can interact in complex ways with putatively basic cognitive processes. Within the intuitive-politician framework, a key function of private thought is preparation for public performances. Thought frequently takes the form of internalized dialogs in which people gauge the relative justifiability of alternative courses of action by imagining conversations with others in which accounts are exchanged, debated, revised, and evaluated. Indeed, converging lines of evidence demonstrate that certain forms of accountability do change how people think, not just what they are willing to say they think:

1. Predecisional forms of accountability to unknown audiences increase the complexity of argumentation, as revealed by content analysis of confidential thought protocols and the complexity of cue use as revealed by statistical modelling of judgment policies (Hagafors & Brehmer, 1983; Tetlock et al., 1989).
2. Accountability manipulations are much more effective in attenuating certain cognitive biases – primacy, overattribution, overconfidence – when participants learn of being accountable prior to (as opposed to after) exposure to the evidence on which they are basing their judgments (Tetlock, 1983b, 1985; Tetlock & Kim, 1987). There is also evidence that increased complexity of thought at least partly mediates these debiasing demonstrations.
3. The power of certain accountability manipulations to attenuate bias is attenuated by impositions of cognitive load that disrupt more effort and attention-demanding forms of information processing (Kruglanski & Freund, 1983; Tetlock, 1992) – disruption that should not occur if people coped with accountability by relying exclusively on low-effort attitude shifting.
4. When accountability manipulations do improve the quality of judgment and choice, the effects are often too differentiated to reproduce via simple response-threshold adjustment models; for example, enhanced "differential accuracy" from a Cronbach decomposition of person-perception accuracy scores (Tetlock & Kim, 1987) or improved calibration without degradation in resolution from analytical decomposition of Brier scores (Siegel-Jacobs & Yates, 1996; Tetlock & Kim, 1987) or closer correspondence between subjective importance rankings of cues in judgment tasks and "objectively" derived weightings from multiple regression equations (Hagafors & Brehmer, 1983).
5. The effects of accountability manipulations on "thoughts" sometimes persist even after the cancellation of the anticipated interview (Lerner & Tetlock, 1999).

Putting to the side the exact locus of accountability effects, the research of greatest interest to the judgment and decision-making community focused on variants of the hypothesis that accountability, which encourages preemptive self-criticism, also confers protection from cognitive biases rooted in reliance on simple, easy-to-execute heuristics. There is indeed a substantial list of biases that are attenuated, if not eliminated, by these forms of accountability. This list must, however, be followed by a compilation of biases that are either unaffected or even amplified by approximately the same forms of accountability.

On the debiasing side of the ledger, predecisional accountability to audiences with difficult-to-decipher views has been found to

1. Reduce, and occasionally eliminate, the fundamental attribution error (Cornielle, Leyens, Yzerbt, & Walter, 1999; Tetlock, 1985). Preemptively self-critical information processors are more reticent about drawing confident dispositional attributions from conduct that is clearly constrained by the situation (the so-called low-choice conditions of essay-attribution experiments), but no more reticent about drawing such conclusions from conduct that is unconstrained by the situation (the high-choice conditions of such experiments).

2. Reduce primacy and recency effects (Lerner & Tetlock, 1999). Preemptively self-critical thinkers are apparently more cautious about drawing conclusions from incomplete or fragmentary evidence, more willing to revise their preliminary conclusions in response to unexpected feedback, and less likely to be swayed by the last most memorable items of evidence presented.

3. Improve the calibration of the subjective probabilities that people attach to their predictions (Siegel-Jacobs & Yates, 1996; Tetlock & Kim, 1987). Preemptively self-critical thinkers are more likely (according to thought-protocol evidence) to take seriously the possibility that they might be wrong. Accountability that encourages this pattern of thinking has been found to improve the covariation between subjective confidence and predictive accuracy. Moreover, these improvements in "calibration" can be achieved at minimal cost in "resolution" – evidence that subjects are not simply scaling down all confidence estimates indiscriminantly, but rather are carefully weighing the balance of evidence for each judgment.

4. Reduce the incompatibility bias – the tendency for negotiators to assume incorrectly that relationships are zero-sum and that the other party's interests are opposed to their own (Thompson, 1995).

5. Reduce the influence of an initial and arbitrary reference point on subsequent judgments (the numeric–anchoring effect) by encouraging subjects to consider further relevant evidence and to revise estimates in light of that evidence – a beneficial effect of accountability that holds up as long as subjects are not under time pressure or other cognitive loads (Kruglanski & Freund, 1983).

6. Decrease reliance on simple, noncompensatory decision rules in favor of more complex compensatory ones that explicitly acknowledge trade-offs (McAllister, Mitchell, & Beach, 1979; Tetlock, 1983a).

7. Decrease the influence of incidental affect evoked in one situation on judgments made in a completely unrelated situation (Lerner, Goldberg, & Tetlock, 1998).

8. Decrease the influence of sunk costs on future investment decisions, in part by increasing willingness to adhere to self-imposed earlier limits on the amount planned to invest, and in part by increasing the salience of decision-making procedures (as opposed to outcomes) in evaluation (Brockner et al., 1981; Simonson & Staw, 1992).

9. Reduce illusory correlations and improve accuracy of covariation assessment in part by motivating more complex inferential strategies (Murphy, 1994).

10. Increase correspondence between the judgment strategies that people claim to be using and the strategies that statistical models impute to them (Cvetkovich, 1978; Hagafors & Brehmer, 1983).

On the bias-amplification side of the ledger, preemptively self-critical thinkers seem more, not less, susceptible to the following effects:

1. Ambiguity aversion – the tendency to prefer less ambiguous alternatives when given a choice between options that differ only in uncertainty about the probabilities with which outcomes may occur (Curley, Yates, & Abrahms, 1986). Postexperimental interviews reveal that a preoccupation with how to justify the choice increased preferences for options with well-defined probabilities over those with ambiguous probabilities, holding expected value constant.

2. The compromise effect – the tendency for a product to gain attractiveness simply by virtue of becoming a middle option in a choice set (Simonson & Nye, 1992). Accountable participants are more likely to select the compromise product because they apparently believed that it was more defensible than options that were superior on one dimension but inferior on another.

3. The attraction effect – the power of a relatively inferior alternative (Brand X) when added to a set of closely competing options (Brands A and B) to increase the attractiveness of the preexisting option that happens to be superior to X on all evaluative dimensions (Simonson, 1989). Again, accountable subjects are especially likely to select dominating options, apparently because they thought that the dominating options were less vulnerable to criticism.

4. The dilution effect – the tendency for nondiagnostic evidence to dilute the predictive power of diagnostic evidence (Tetlock & Boettger, 1989). Motivating self-critical thought can sometimes induce people to try too hard to discern relevance amidst irrelevance. Rather than zeroing in on the one relevant cue, accountable subjects often struggle to integrate irrelevant cues into their schematic representations of the target individuals. In environments with unfavorable signal-to-noise ratios, accountability can send people off on inferential wild goose chases.

5. The status quo effect – the tendency for the status quo to occupy a privileged position in decision making that makes it possible to reverse preferences for decision alternatives by holding expected value constant and arbitrarily designating one option as the status quo and the other as the option that requires change (Samuelson & Zeckhauser, 1988). The "change" option is typically held to a higher standard of proof – and accountable subjects are particularly prone to do so when there are identifiable losers as a result of modifying the status quo (Tetlock & Boettger, 1994).

Finally, turning to the null-hypothesis column of the ledger, it is worth contemplating a subset (from the proverbial file drawer) of studies in which accountability has no effect on established judgmental biases. These noneffects have included insensitivity to base-rate information, giving more predictive weight to causal as opposed to merely statistical relationships between variables, preference reversals as a function of choice-versus-matching elicitation procedures, insensitivity to sample size, and the conjunction fallacy.

It is hardly helpful, however, to abandon readers with a list – or, still less helpful, a list of lists. The key theoretical question concerns the nature of the underlying moderators of when one or another class of effect or noneffect emerges. My best guess is that much hinges on the correspondence or lack thereof between the intuitive theories that ordinary people hold about what constitutes good decision making and the more formal theories that academic observers hold about what constitutes rationality (cf. Wegener & Petty, 1995). In cases in which accountability attenuates bias, scholars have made good *prima facie* cases that the biases result, in part, from lack of mental effort and self-critical attention to one's judgment processes. Subjects intuit that the social expectation in the accountability relationship is that they are supposed to process task-relevant information in more self-critical and thoughtful ways. Accordingly, they do so and thereby bring their judgments into closer correspondence with those that the expert community, the ultimate arbiters of normative standards, deems defensible. Accountability should be an effective debiasing manipulation to the degree it induces research participants to (1) consider a wider range of relevant cues or arguments; (2) pay more attention to the cues that they do use; (3) anticipate plausible counterarguments, evaluate their strengths relatively impartially, and factor those that pass some threshold of plausibility into their overall assessment.

In cases in which accountability amplifies bias, scholars have made a good *prima facie* case that the biases result from trying too hard to integrate irrelevant considerations into one's mental representation of the problem. Here, efforts by subjects to put on the cognitive equivalent of their "Sunday's best" – to become more thoughtful and to have a "neat justification package" readily available – lead to judgments that depart ever more markedly from those that expert observers deem rational. In effect, there is a negative correlation between lay observers', and acadmic observers', conceptions of good judgment. Finally, in cases in which accountability has virtually no effect, there is a good case either that subjects are completely unaware that they are thinking incorrectly (failing to use relevant cues or using irrelevant ones) or that subjects have conflicting normative intuitions (some of which coincide with the expert community's conception of procedural rationality and some of which sharply diverge).

NORMATIVE BOUNDARY CONDITIONS ON THE ERROR-AND-BIAS PORTRAIT

Up to this point, the spotlight has been on the social and cognitive strategies that people (intuitive politicians) use to cope with accountability demands and on the implications of these strategies for the empirical robustness of judgmental tendencies widely hypothesized to constitute deviations from rationality. It is worth noting, however, that many effects examined here are open to challenge on pragmatic, philosophical, and political grounds. The intuitive-politician metaphor is one of the number of deviant functionalist metaphors that can be invoked in defense of particular judgmental tendencies. Evidence of irrationality within one functionalist framework may be judged fully rational within another – an example of what Tetlock (1998) calls a *normative boundary condition*.

These normatively contested effects take diverse forms. When does nonutilization of base rates count as evidence that people are lousy intuitive statisticians and when as evidence that people are rightly rising to the defense of a core egalitarian value, such as "Do not discriminate against groups that have already suffered much" – no matter how compelling an actuarial justification the evidence might provide for charging differential premiums or for subjecting group members to differential police scrutiny (cf. Tetlock, Kristel, Elson, Green, & Lerner, 2000)? When do efforts to recoup sunk costs reveal our failings as intuitive economists or our skills as wily impression managers who capitalize on a widely held stereotype that strong leaders stay the course (cf. Staw, 1980)? When should effects such as ambiguity aversion, the status quo effect, or the compromise effect count as evidence of our shortcomings as intuitive economists, and when as prudent strategies for protecting self from intrapsychic recriminations or from interpersonal criticism? I focus next on three of these contested effects.

The Dilution Effect: Defective Intuitive Statistician or Attentive Conversationalist ?

Nisbett et al. (1981) demonstrated that coupling diagnostic with non-diagnostic evidence produced more regressive predictions than people would otherwise have made. They also established the replicability of this *dilution effect* and explained it by invoking the representativeness heuristic discussed in Tversky and Kahneman (1974). In this account, people judge possible futures for a target person by comparing key features of the individual with key features of the possible outcomes and predicting the outcome most similar to, or representative of, the individual. In Tversky's (1977) framework, similarity is a positive function of the number of common features and a negative function of the number of unique features. Common features are attributes of the target person that people associate with the outcome. For instance, the image of a student who studies only 3 hours a week is strongly associated with the image of the prototypical student with a low-grade point average. Unique features are attributes of the target individual that people rarely associate with the outcome. Thus, one reduces the similarity – and, therefore, the perceived predictive link – between the indolent student and poor grades by incorporating irrelevant details into the description of the student (e.g., tennis player, dating habits, number of plants in his apartment).

Assessed against the logical standards of multiple regression, it is unreasonable to reduce one's confidence in the potency of a valid predictor merely because that predictor is embedded in an array of irrelevant information. It is useful, however, to look at the dilution effect from a social–functionalist vantage point. Far from representing an error, dilution may constitute a rational response to the interpersonal and institutional context. The presentation of information in dilution experiments can be likened to a conversation in which subjects assume that the experimenter, their conversational partner, is following widely accepted norms of social discourse such as truthfulness and relevance (Grice, 1975). In most conversations, people refrain from making statements that are utterly irrelevant or grossly deceptive. Given that the experimenters deemed it appropriate to include an assortment of evidence in their communications, one would expect a good Bayesian to attach a high prior probability to the relevance of the evidence. The intuitive statistician and politician are thus reconciled.

This normative reinterpretation is not entirely speculative. Several studies show that manipulations of conversational norms moderate a number of experimental effects, including the underuse of base-rate information, the overuse of recently presented information, and the overestimation of the likelihood of conjunctions of events. Schwarz (1994) stated this position forcefully: Many purported demonstrations of cognitive shortcomings occur because basic assumptions that underlie all social discourse in everyday settings are "routinely violated" in studies on judgmental biases.

Amplification of dilution by accountability could be consistent with either a judgmental-heuristics or conversational-norm interpretation. To disentangle the two explanations, Tetlock et al. (1996) manipulated whether subjects believed that conversational norms held in the experimental setting. Following a procedure developed by Schwarz (1994), some subjects were told that the axioms of conversation applied: the experimenter had screened the information to ensure its relevance for the prediction task. Other subjects were told that the research team could not vouch for the usefulness of the information as it had been randomly selected from a computer database.

If dilution is a rational response to conversational norms, the effect should disappear when conversational norms have been deactivated explicitly.

Moreover, accountability should cease to magnify the dilution effect when conversational norms have been deactivated. By contrast, if dilution is the product of a judgmental heuristic that involves automatic similarity-matching of causes and effects, there is less reason to expect explicit deactivatation of conversational norms to moderate either the magnitude of the dilution effect or the tendency for accountability to amplify it. Consistent with a conversational-norms interpretation, dilution disappeared among accountable subjects who thought that conversational norms did not apply. Accountability also ceased to motivate more complex patterns of thinking when conversational norms had been deactivated. By contrast, dilution persisted among subjects who had been told that conversational norms do apply, as well as among subjects in a no-norm-primed control condition, who were told nothing about the relevance of the information. Contrary to the conversational-norm hypothesis, however, and consistent work with a judgmental-heuristics interpretation, deactivating conversational norms was not sufficient to eliminate dilution among unaccountable subjects.

The judgmental-heuristic and social-functionalist explanations need not, of course, be mutually exclusive. Indeed, whenever accountability amplifies a given error or bias, the two classes of processes may well be mutually reinforcing. Plausible-candidate effects include not only dilution, but also the compromise, attraction, and reason-augmentation effects (Shafir et al., 1993). Consider the reason-augmentation effect, in which "enriched options," which possess both more positive and more negative features, are more likely to be selected when decision makers are asked to choose their preferred option, but less likely to be selected when decision makers are asked to reject their less-preferred option. This phenomenon is consistent with a view of decision makers as intuitive politicians who, prior to deciding, weigh the relative justifiability of response options, but do so in a superficial manner such that when they are asked to choose an option, they count the number of good reasons for doing so, and when they are asked to reject an option, they count the number of reasons for doing that (thereby short-circuiting the need for complex compensatory comparisons).

Taboo Trade-offs: Defective Intuitive Economist or Principled Defender of Sacred Values ?

Since the times of Adam Smith, scholars have commented on people's reluctance to acknowledge certain value trade-offs and their occasionally fierce opposition to the very notion of a unified utility metric on which people weigh certain values against others. Traditional cognitive explanations emphasized the difficulty of working through apple–orange comparisons that cut across qualitatively different dimensions of value. This explanation is, however, inadequate from a social-functionalist perspective. Interdimensional comparisons can be difficult, but they are not typically cause for moral outrage. We do not usually find it shameful to admit that we make trade-offs between money and the wine or meat or leisure time that we consume. Indeed, it is not only acceptable to think in complex compensatory terms about one's household budget; we expect, even require, such trade-offs of all competent, self-supporting adults in competitive-market economies (Becker, 1996).

Tetlock et al. (1996) argue that opposition to reducing all values to a single utility or monetary metric runs deeper than mere incommensurability; it is rooted in constitutive incommensurability – a concept that plays an important role in both modern moral philosophy (Raz, 1982) as well as in classic sociological theory (Durkheim, 1925/1973). The guiding idea is that our commitments to other people require us to deny that we can compare certain things quantitatively. To transgress this normative boundary, to attach a monetary value to one's friendships or to one's children or to loyalty to one's country, is to disqualify oneself from certain social roles, to demonstrate that one does not have the faintest idea of what it means to be a true friend or parent or scholar ("You just don't get it"). We experience constitutive incommensurability whenever treating values as commensurable subverts one of the values in the trade-off calculus; to compare is to destroy. Merely thinking about certain trade-offs degrades one's standing as a moral being. Durkheim expressed the same sentiment in more sociological language when he observed that in both "primitive religious" and "advanced secular" societies, people ascribe a transcendental quality to the fundamental values of their social order. It is as though they need to believe that these values are infinitely important and cannot be compromised. Durkheim warned us not to be surprised, therefore, when even sophisticated citizens of secular societies tenaciously resist treating sacred values as objects of utilitarian calculation. Their attitude is less one of market calculation than it is one of believers to their God, a stance of absolute faith that imposes an "aura" or "mysterious barrier" around social morality. This Durkheimian perspective leads us to expect that violations of sacred values reliably provoke both outrage and cries for punishment. Secular–sacred trade-offs are not just cognitively perplexing; they are morally disturbing.

Empirical support exists for several testable predictions that flow from this intuitive-theologian (or, if one prefers, principled-politician) analysis:

1. Secular–sacred trade-offs – such as proposals to attach dollar values to lives or to auction babies for adoption – trigger moral outrage, which is a composite reaction that includes anger, contempt, and punitiveness toward those willing even to consider such proposals. By contrast, secular–secular trade-offs – such as proposals to exchange money for goods and services that are widely regarded as permissible commodities in our society – are judged routine, and sacred–sacred trade-offs (e.g., the lives of one group against another; one promise in conflict with another) are judged to be tragic (Fiske & Tetlock, 1997; Tetlock, Kristel, Elson, Green & Lerner, 2000).
2. Secular–sacred trade-offs are taboo in the primal Polynesian sense that they possess the power to contaminate previously respected decision

makers and acceptable proposals as soon as it is discovered that the secular–sacred boundary has been breached. It is politically better to mask such proposals with vague deontic or utilitarian rationales – "In principle or on balance, X is the right thing to do" – than it is to acknowledge candidly the real calculations underlying the proposals when those real calculations involve affixing monetary values to human life or national honor or other sacred entities (Tetlock et al., 2000).

3. The longer observers believe a decision maker contemplated a taboo trade-off (which pits a sacred value, such as the lives of children, against a secular one, such as medical costs), the more punitive the dispositional attributions to the decision maker, even if the decision maker winds up doing the "right thing" and affirming the sacred value. "Mere contemplation" contaminates, even controlling for decision outcome. By contrast, the longer observers believe a decision maker contemplated a tragic trade-off (which pits one sacred value against another – for instance, the lives of one group of children against another group), the fairer and wiser the decision maker is thought to be, no matter which outcome is chosen (Tetlock et al., 2000).

4. When subjects are led to believe that they have committed a taboo trade-off, they often engage in acts of moral cleansing to reaffirm their social identities as virtuous beings (Tetlock et al., 2000).

Taboo trade-offs are but one subset of a large class of proscribed forms of social cognition. Tetlock et al. (2000) documented two other forms:

1) *Forbidden base rates* – which could provide actuarial justifications for differential insurance premiums or police scrutiny as a function of race or ethnicity – threaten the images that Americans – especially liberal Americans – have of themselves as racially egalitarian. Decision makers who use such base-rate information stand condemned (in much the same way as those "guilty" of taboo trade-offs); decision makers who discover that they have inadvertently used such information quickly seize opportunities to engage in symbolic acts of moral cleansing that reaffirm their social identities as racially fair minded.

2) *Heretical counterfactuals* – which imply that the lives of founders of religious movements were the product of chance and contingency, just like the lives of ordinary mortals – provoke sharp condemnation from the faithful. Not surprisingly, this is the modal reaction of Christian fundamentalists to counterfactuals that imply the mutability of key events in the Biblical narrative of the life of Christ, for example: "If Joseph had not believed Mary's account of how she became pregnant, he would have left her, and Jesus would have grown up in a single-parent household and formed a very different personality." Perhaps more surprisingly, fundamentalists who are not given a social opportunity to distance themselves from heretical counterfactuals by condemning the source of the propositions are especially likely to engage in moral cleansing – in this case, via reaffirmations of commitment to their churches.

The Overattribution Effect: Defective Intuitive Psychologist or Relentless Intuitive Prosecutor ?

One central implication of the intuitive-politician metaphor has thus far been slighted. In the political arena, what constitutes an error or bias is often sharply ideologically contested (Sniderman, Brody, & Tetlock, 1991). In a series of studies of managerial and political elites, Tetlock (2000) showed that liberals and conservatives frequently disagree over the defensibility or rationality of decision-making strategies at the individual, small group, institutional, and societal levels of analysis. Consider the clashing perspectives on the fundamental attribution error, more appropriately and modestly known as the *overattribution effect*. Traditional conservatives and, to a lesser extent, modern libertarians, believe that "most people" are likely to look for and exploit loopholes in social-control systems, whereas traditional liberals and social democrats believe that most people will refrain from exploiting loopholes as long as they feel fairly treated. These diverging views lead to diverging assessments of the fundamental attribution error. Many conservatives think it only prudent managerial practice to communicate to subordinates a low tolerance for justifications and excuses for conduct that falls short of organizational expectations. People are more motivated to behave themselves if they believe that improper conduct automatically tarnishes their reputations – a social variant of the legal doctrine of strict liability. From a conservative perspective, failing to hold people responsible for outcomes that they could have controlled is every bit as serious, and sometimes more serious, an error than holding people responsible for outcomes that they could not control. By contrast, people on the liberal left often see the fundamental attribution error as punitive, not prudent. They disagree with conservatives about both (1) the frequency with which subordinates invent specious justifications and excuses for substandard performance and (2) the relative importance of avoiding type-I errors (condemning the innocent) versus type-II errors (acquitting the guilty).

Beyond documenting chronic individual differences and ideological variation in the prosecutorial mindset, it is possible to activate or deactivate this mindset. Manipulations that convince people that the social order is under siege and that serious misconduct is going unpunished are sufficient to de-sensitize people to extenuating situational circumstances that they would otherwise have taken into consideration (Goldberg, Lerner, & Tetlock, 1998; Tetlock, in press). Moreover, it is possible to identify circumstances under which conservatives become liberals and liberals become conservatives in their openness to mitigating circumstances. The underlying moderator is apparently whose ox is being gored or whose core values are under assault. Of course, this does not negate the voluminous evidence for a perceptual bias toward overattribution, but it does raise the useful qualification that at least some of the time our flaws as intuitive psychologists may be in the service of our goals as intuitive prosecutors. The fundamental attribution error may be neither as fundamental nor as erroneous as sometimes supposed.

CONCLUDING REMARKS

Mixed metaphors can be ugly, but they are the crucial next step in theory building in judgment and choice. On the one hand, basic laws of human information
processing – revealed by work within the intuitive-scientist and economist research programs – permeate how intuitive politicians go about assessing the
justifiability of response options; on the other hand, the social necessity of constructing compelling accounts for one's views inevitably shapes how participants in basic research on judgement and choice react to the problems that
experimenters give them. Skeptics might argue that mixed-metaphor theories –
which begin to take on the promethean aspirations of traditional theories of personality – are premature. We just do not know enough about how people go
about their business as intuitive economists or scientists or politicians to begin
merging these distinct functionalist facets of human nature. However, the coun-
terargument of this chapter is that these functionalist facets are not so distinct,
often blurring into each other, and that willfully unifunctionalist tunnel vision
leads us to overlook basic empirical and normative boundary conditions on
the response tendencies we do study. Like it or not, we study multifunctional
entities that sometimes require cumbersome complex explanations.

PART THREE
REAL-WORLD APPLICATIONS

33. The Hot Hand in Basketball: On the Misperception of Random Sequences

Thomas Gilovich, Robert Vallone, and Amos Tversky

In describing an outstanding performance by a basketball player, reporters and spectators commonly use expressions such as "Larry Bird has the hot hand" or "Andrew Toney is a streak shooter." These phrases express a belief that the performance of a player during a particular period is significantly better than expected on the basis of the player's overall record. The belief in "the hot hand" and in "streak shooting" is shared by basketball players, coaches, and fans, and it appears to affect the selection of plays and the choice of players. In this chapter, we investigate the origin and the validity of these beliefs.

People's intuitive conceptions of randomness depart systematically from the laws of chance. It appears that people expect the essential characteristics of a chance process to be represented not only globally in the entire sequence, but also locally, in each of its parts. For instance, people expect even short sequences of heads and tails to reflect the fairness of a coin and contain roughly 50% heads and 50% tails. This conception of chance has been described as a "belief in the law of small numbers" according to which the law of large numbers applies to small samples as well (Tversky & Kahneman, 1971). A locally representative sequence, however, deviates systematically from chance expectation: It contains too many alternations and not enough long runs.

A conception of chance based on representativeness, therefore, produces two related biases. First, it induces a belief that the probability of heads is greater after a long sequence of tails than after a long sequence of heads – this is the notorious *gambler's fallacy* (see, e.g., Tversky & Kahneman, 1974). Second, it leads people to reject the randomness of sequences that contain the expected number of runs because even the occurrence of, say, four heads in a row – which is quite likely in a sequence of 20 tosses – makes the sequence appear nonrepresentative (Falk, 1981; Wagenaar, 1972).

Sequences of hits and misses in a basketball game offer an interesting context for investigating the perception of randomness outside the psychological laboratory. Consider a professional basketball player who makes 50% of his shots. This player occasionally hits four or more shots in a row. Such runs can be properly called streak shooting, however, only if their length or frequency

Originally published in *Cognitive Psychology*, 17, 295–314, copyright © 1985 by Academic Press. Reprinted by permission of the publisher.

exceeds what is expected on the basis of chance alone. The player's performance, then, can be compared to a sequence of hits and misses generated by tossing a coin. A player who produces longer sequences of hits than those produced by tossing a coin can be said to have a *hot hand* or be described as a *streak shooter*. Similarly, these terms can be applied to a player who has a better chance of hitting a basket after one or more successful shots than after one or more misses.

This analysis does not attempt to capture all that people might mean by the hot hand or streak shooting. Nevertheless, we argue that the common use of these notions – however vague or complex – implies that players' performance records should differ from sequences of heads and tails produced by coin tossing in two essential respects. First, these terms imply that the probability of a hit should be greater following a hit than following a miss (i.e., positive association). Second, they imply that the number of streaks of successive hits or misses should exceed the number produced by a chance process with a constant hit rate (i.e., nonstationarity).

It may seem unreasonable to compare basketball shooting to coin tossing because a player's chances of hitting a basket are not the same on every shot. Lay-ups are easier than 3-point field goals and slam dunks have a higher hit rate than turnaround jumpers. Nevertheless, the simple binomial model is equivalent to a more complicated process with the following characteristics: Each player has an ensemble of shots that vary in difficulty (depending, for example, on the distance from the basket and on defensive pressure), and each shot is randomly selected from this ensemble. This process provides a more compelling account of the performance of a basketball player, although it produces a shooting record that is indistinguishable from that produced by a simple binomial model in which the probability of a hit is the same on every trial.

We begin with a survey that explores the beliefs of basketball fans regarding streak shooting and related phenomena. We then turn to an analysis of field goal and free-throw data from the NBA. Finally, we report a controlled experiment performed by the men and women of Cornell's varsity teams that investigates players' ability to predict their performance.

STUDY 1: SURVEY OF BASKETBALL FANS

One hundred basketball fans were recruited from the student bodies of Cornell and Stanford University. All participants play basketball at least "occasionally" (65% play "regularly"). They all watch at least five games per year (73% watch more than 15 games per year). The sample included 50 captains of intramural basketball teams.

The questionnaire examined basketball fans' beliefs regarding sequential dependence among shots. Their responses revealed considerable agreement: 91% of the fans believed that a player has "a better chance of making a shot after having just *made* his last two or three shots than he does after having just *missed* his last two or three shots"; 68% of the fans expressed essentially the same belief for free throws, claiming that a player has "a better chance of making his second shot after *making* his first shot than after *missing* his first shot"; 96% of the fans thought that "after having made a series of shots in a row ... players tend to take more shots than they normally would"; 84% of the fans believed that "it is important to pass the ball to someone who has just made several (two, three, or four) shots in a row."

The belief in a positive dependence between successive shots was reflected in numerical estimates as well. The fans were asked to consider a hypothetical player who shoots 50% from the field. Their average estimate of his field goal percentage was 61% "after having just made a shot," and 42% "after having just missed a shot." When asked to consider a hypothetical player who shoots 70% from the free-throw line, the average estimate of his free-throw percentage was 74% "for second free throws after having made the first," and 66% "for second free throws after having missed the first."

STUDY 2: PROFESSIONAL BASKETBALL FIELD GOAL DATA

Field goal records of individual players were obtained for 48 home games of the Philadelphia 76ers and their opponents during the 1980–1981 season. These data were recorded by the team's statistician. Records of consecutive shots for individual players were not available for other teams in the NBA. Our analysis of these data divides into three parts. First we examine the probability of a hit conditioned on players' recent histories of hits and misses, second we investigate the frequency of different sequences of hits and misses in players' shooting records, and third we analyze the stability of players' performance records across games.

Analysis of Conditional Probabilities

Do players hit a higher percentage of their shots after having just *made* their last shot (or last several shots), than after having just *missed* their last shot (or last several shots)? Table 33.1 displays these conditional probabilities for the nine major players of the Philadelphia 76ers during the 1980–1981 season. Column 5 presents the overall shooting percentage for each player ranging from 46% for Hollins and Toney to 62% for Dawkins. Columns 6 through 8 present the players' shooting percentages conditioned on having *hit* their last shot, their last two shots, and their last three shots, respectively. Columns 2 through 4 present the players' shooting percentages conditioned on having *missed* their last shot, their last two shots, and their last three shots, respectively. Column 9 presents the (serial) correlation between the outcomes of successive shots.

A comparison of columns 4 and 6 indicates that for eight of the nine players the probability of a hit is actually lower following a hit (weighted mean: 51%) than following a miss (weighted mean: 54%), contrary to the hot-hand hypothesis. Consequently, the serial correlations in column 9 are negative for

Table 33.1. Probability of Making a Shot Conditioned on the Outcome of Previous Shots for Nine Members of the Philadelphia 76ers

Player	P(hit/3 misses)	P(hit/2 misses)	P(hit/1 misses)	P(hit)	P(hit/1 hit)	P(hit/2 hits)	P(hit/3 hits)	Serial Correlation r
Clint Richardson	.50 (12)	.47 (32)	.56 (101)	.50 (248)	.49 (105)	.50 (46)	.48 (21)	−.020
Julius Erving	.52 (90)	.51 (191)	.51 (408)	.52 (884)	.53 (428)	.52 (211)	.48 (97)	.016
Lionel Hollins	.50 (40)	.49 (92)	.46 (200)	.46 (419)	.46 (171)	.46 (65)	.32 (25)	−.004
Maurice Cheeks	.77 (13)	.60 (38)	.60 (126)	.56 (339)	.55 (166)	.54 (76)	.59 (32)	−.038
Caldwell Jones	.50 (20)	.48 (48)	.47 (117)	.47 (272)	.45 (108)	.43 (37)	.27 (11)	−.016
Andrew Toney	.52 (33)	.53 (90)	.51 (216)	.46 (451)	.43 (190)	.40 (77)	.34 (29)	−.083
Bobby Jones	.61 (23)	.58 (66)	.58 (179)	.54 (433)	.53 (207)	.47 (96)	.53 (36)	−.049
Steve Mix	.70 (20)	.56 (54)	.52 (147)	.52 (351)	.51 (163)	.48 (77)	.36 (33)	−.015
Daryl Dawkins	.88 (8)	.73 (33)	.71 (136)	.62 (403)	.57 (222)	.58 (111)	.51 (55)	−.142**
Weighted means	.56	.53	.54	.52	.51	.50	.46	−.039

Note: Since the first shot of each game cannot be conditioned, the parenthetical values in columns 4 and 6 do not sum to the parenthetical value in column 5. The number of shots upon which each probability is based is given in parentheses.

$*\ p < .05.$
$**\ p < .01.$

eight of the nine players, but the coefficients are not significantly different from zero except for one player (Dawkins). Comparisons of column 7, $P(\text{hit}/2 \text{ hits})$, with column 3, $P(\text{hit}/2 \text{ misses})$, and of column 8, $P(\text{hit}/3 \text{ hits})$, with column 2, $P(\text{hit}/3 \text{ misses})$, provide additional evidence against streak-shooting; the only trend in these data runs counter to the hot-hand hypothesis (paired $t = -2.79$, $p < .05$ for columns 6 and 4; $t = -3.14$, $p < .05$ for columns 7 and 3; $t = -4.42$, $p < .01$ for columns 8 and 2). Additional analyses show that the probability of a hit following a "hot" period (three or four hits in the last four shots) was lower (weighted mean: 50%) than the probability of a hit (weighted mean: 57%) following a "cold" period (zero or one hit in the last four shots).

Analysis of Runs

Table 33.2 displays the results of the Wald–Wolfowitz run test for each player (Siegel, 1956). For this test, each sequence of consecutive hits or misses is counted as a "run." Thus, a series of hits and misses such as XOOOXXO contains four runs. The more a player's hits (and misses) cluster together, the fewer runs there are in his record. Column 4 presents the observed number of runs in each player's record (across all 48 games), and column 5 presents the expected number of runs if the outcomes of all shots were independent of one another. A comparison of columns 4 and 5 indicates that for five of the nine players the observed number of runs is actually greater than the expected number of runs, contrary to the streak-shooting hypothesis. The Z statistic reported in column 6 tests the significance of the difference between the observed and the expected number of runs. A significant difference between these values exists for only one player (Dawkins), whose record includes significantly more runs than expected under independence, again, contrary to streak shooting.

Run tests were also performed on each player's records within individual games. Considering both the 76ers and their opponents together, we obtained

Table 33.2. Runs Test – Philadelphia 76ers

Players	Hits	Misses	Number of Runs	Expected Number of Runs	z
Clint Richardson	124	124	128	125.0	−0.38
Julius Erving	459	425	431	442.4	0.76
Lionel Hollins	194	225	203	209.4	0.62
Maurice Cheeks	189	150	172	168.3	−0.41
Caldwell Jones	129	143	134	136.6	0.32
Andrew Toney	208	243	245	225.1	−1.88
Bobby Jones	233	200	227	216.2	−1.04
Steve Mix	181	170	176	176.3	0.04
Daryl Dawkins	250	153	220	190.8	−3.09**
$M =$	218.6	203.7	215.1	210.0	−0.56

* $p < .05$.
** $p < .01$.

727 individual player game records that included more than two runs. A comparison of the observed and expected number of runs did not provide any basis for rejecting the null hypothesis [$t(726) < 1$].

Test of Stationarity

The notions of "the hot hand" and "streak shooting" entail temporary elevations of performance – i.e., periods during which the player's hit rate is substantially higher than his overall average. Although such changes in performance would produce a positive dependence between the outcomes of successive shots, it could be argued that neither the runs test nor the test of the serial correlation are sufficiently powerful to detect occasional "hot" stretches embedded in longer stretches of "normal" performance. To obtain a more sensitive test of stationarity, or a constant hit rate, we partitioned the entire record of each player into nonoverlapping sets of four consecutive shots. We then counted the number of sets in which the player's performance was high (three or four hits), moderate (two hits), or low (zero or one hit). If a player is occasionally hot, then his record must include more high-performance sets than expected by chance.

The number of high, moderate, and low sets for each of the nine players were compared to the values expected by chance, assuming independent shots with a constant hit rate (derived from column 5 of Table 33.1). For example, the expected proportions of high-, moderate-, and low-performance sets for a player with a hit rate of 0.5 are 5/16, 6/16, and 5/16, respectively. The results provided no evidence for nonstationarity, or streak shooting, as none of the nine X^2 values approached statistical significance. This analysis was repeated four times, starting the partition into consecutive quadruples at the first, second, third, and fourth shot of each player's shooting record. All of these analyses failed to support the nonstationarity hypothesis.

Analysis of Stability across Games – Hot and Cold Nights

To determine whether players have more "hot" and "cold" nights than expected by chance, we compared the observed variability in their per game shooting percentages with the variability expected on the basis of their overall record. Specifically, we compared two estimates of the standard error of each players' per game shooting percentages: one based on the standard deviation of the player's shooting percentages for each game, and one derived from the player's overall shooting percentage across all games. If players' shooting percentages in individual games fluctuate more than would be expected under the hypothesis of independence, then the (Lexis) ratio of these standard errors (SE observed/SE expected) should be significantly greater than 1 (David, 1949). Seven 76ers played at least 10 games in which they took at least 10 shots per game, and thus could be included in this analysis (Richardson and C. Jones did not meet this criterion). The Lexis ratios for these seven players ranged from 0.56 (Dawkins) to 1.03 (Erving), with a mean of 0.84. No player's Lexis ratio was significantly greater than 1, indicating that variations in shooting percentages across games do not deviate from their overall shooting percentage enough to produce significantly more hot (or cold) nights than expected by chance.

Discussion

It could be argued that streak shooting exists but it is not common and we failed to include a "real" streak shooter in our sample of players. However, there is a general consensus among basketball fans that Andrew Toney is a streak shooter. In an informal poll of 18 recreational basketball players who were asked to name five streak shooters in the NBA, only two respondents failed to include Andrew Toney, and he was the first player mentioned by half the respondents. Despite this widespread belief that Toney runs hot and cold, his runs of hits and misses did not depart from chance expectations. We have also analyzed the field goal records of two other NBA teams: the New Jersey Nets (13 games) and the New York Knicks (22 games). These data were recorded from live television broadcasts. A parallel analysis of these records provides evidence consistent with the findings reported above. Of seven New York Knicks and seven New Jersey Nets, only one player exhibited a significant positive correlation between successive shots (Bill Cartwright of the Knicks). Thus, only two of the 23 major players on three NBA teams produced significant serial correlations, one of which was positive, and the other negative.

The failure to detect evidence of streak shooting might also be attributed to the selection of shots by individual players and the defensive strategy of opposing teams. After making one or two shots, a player may become more confident and attempt more difficult shots; after missing a shot, a player may get conservative and take only high-percentage shots. This would obscure any evidence of streak shooting in players' performance records. The same effect may be produced by the opposing team's defense. Once a player has made one or two shots, the opposing team may intensify their defensive pressure on that player and "take away" his good shots. Both of these factors may operate in the game and they are probably responsible for the (small) negative correlation between successive shots. However, it remains to be seen whether the elimination of these factors would yield data that are more compatible with people's expectations. The next two studies examine two different types of shooting data that are uncontaminated by shot selection or defensive pressure.

STUDY 3: PROFESSIONAL BASKETBALL FREE-THROW DATA

Free-throw data permit a test of the dependence between successive shots that is free from the contaminating effects of shot selection and opposing defense. Free throws, or foul shots, are commonly shot in pairs, and they are always shot from the same location without defensive pressure. If there is a positive correlation between successive shots, we would expect players to hit a higher percentage of their second free throws after having made their first free throw than after having missed their first free throw. Recall that our survey of basketball fans

Table 33.3. Probability of Making a Second Free Throw Conditioned on the Outcome of the First Free Throw for Nine Members of the Boston Celtics during the 1980–1981 and 1981–1982 Seasons

Player	$P(H_2/M_1)$	$P(H_2/H_1)$	Serial Correlation r
Larry Bird	.91 (53)	.88 (285)	−.032
Cedric Maxwell	.76 (128)	.81 (302)	.061
Robert Parish	.72 (105)	.77 (213)	.056
Nate Archibald	.82 (76)	.83 (245)	.014
Chris Ford	.77 (22)	.71 (51)	−.069
Kevin McHale	.59 (49)	.73 (128)	.130
M. L. Carr	.81 (26)	.68 (57)	−.128
Rick Robey	.61 (80)	.59 (91)	−.019
Gerald Henderson	.78 (37)	.76 (101)	−.022

Note: The number of shots upon which each probability is based is given in parentheses.

found that most fans believe there is positive dependency between successive free throws, though this belief was not as strong as the corresponding belief about field goals. The average estimate of the chances that a 70% free-throw shooter would make his second free throw was 74% after making the first shot and 66% after missing the first shot.

Do players actually hit a higher percentage of their second free throws after having just made their first free throw than after having just missed their first free throw? Table 33.3 presents these data for all pairs of free throws by Boston Celtics players during the 1980–1981 and the 1981–1982 seasons. These data were obtained from the Celtics' statistician. Column 2 presents the probability of a hit on the second free throw given a *miss* on the first free throw, and column 3 presents the probability of a hit on the second free throw given a *hit* on the first free throw. The correlations between the first and the second shot are presented in column 4. These data provide no evidence that the outcome of the second free throw is influenced by the outcome of the first free throw. The correlations are positive for four players, negative for the other five, and none of them are significantly different from zero. (Aggregating data across players is inappropriate in this case because good shooters are more likely to make their first shot than poor shooters. Consequently, the good shooters contribute more observations to P(hit/hit) than to P(hit/miss) while the poor shooters do the opposite, thereby biasing the pooled estimates.)

STUDY 4: CONTROLLED SHOOTING EXPERIMENT

As an alternative method for eliminating the effects of shot selection and defensive pressure, we recruited members of Cornell's intercollegiate basketball teams to participate in a controlled shooting study. This experiment also allowed us to investigate the ability of players to predict their performance.

The players were 14 members of the men's varsity and junior varsity basketball teams at Cornell and 12 members of the women's varsity team. For each player we determined a distance from which his or her shooting percentage was roughly 50%. At this distance we then drew two 15-ft arcs on the floor from which each player took all of his or her shots. The centers of the arcs were located 60° out from the left and right sides of the basket. When shooting baskets, the players were required to move along the arc between shots so that consecutive shots were never taken from exactly the same spot. Each player was to take 100 shots, 50 from each arc. The players were paid for their participation. The amount of money they received was determined by how accurately they shot and how accurately they predicted their hits and misses. This payoff procedure is described below. The initial analyses of the Cornell data parallel those of the 76ers.

Analysis of Conditional Probabilities

Do Cornell players hit a higher percentage of their shots after having just *made* their last shot (or last several shots), than after having just *missed* their last shot (or last several shots)? Table 33.4 displays these conditional probabilities for all players in the study. Column 5 presents the overall shooting percentage for each player ranging from 25 to 61% (mean: 47%). Columns 6 through 8 present the players' shooting percentages conditioned on having *hit* their last shot, their last two shots, and their last three shots, respectively. Columns 2 through 4 present the players' shooting percentages conditioned on having *missed* their last shot, their last two shots, and their last three shots, respectively. Column 9 presents the serial correlation for each player.

A comparison of players' shooting percentages after hitting the previous shot (column 6, mean: 48%) with their shooting percentages after missing the previous shot (column 4, mean: 47%) indicates that for most players $P(\text{Hit}/\text{Hit})$ is less than $P(\text{Hit}/\text{Miss})$, contrary to the hot-hand hypothesis. Indeed, the serial correlations were negative for 14 out of the 26 players, and only one player (9) exhibited a significant positive correlation. Comparisons of column 7, $P(\text{hit}/2$ hits), with column 3, $P(\text{hit}/2$ misses), and column 8, $P(\text{hit}/3$ hits), with column 2, $P(\text{hit}/3$ misses), lead to the same conclusion (paired t's < 1 for all three comparisons). Additional analyses show that the probability of a hit following a "hot" period (three or four hits in the last four shots) was not higher (mean: 46%) than the probability of a hit (mean: 47%) following a "cold" period (zero or one hit in the last four shots).

Analysis of Runs

Table 33.5 displays the results of the Wald–Wolfowitz run test for each player (Siegel, 1956). Recall that for this test, each streak of consecutive hits or misses is counted as a run. Column 4 presents the observed number of runs in each player's performance record, and column 5 presents the number of runs expected by chance. A comparison of these two columns reveals 14 players with

Table 33.4. Probability of Making a Shot Conditioned on the Outcome of Previous Shots for All Cornell Players

Player	P(hit/3 misses)	P(hit/2 misses)	P(hit/1 miss)	P(hit)	P(hit/1 hit)	P(hit/2 hits)	P(hit/3 hits)	Serial Correlation r
Males								
1	.44 (9)	.50 (18)	.61 (46)	.54 (100)	.49 (53)	.48 (25)	.50 (12)	−.118
2	.43 (28)	.33 (42)	.35 (65)	.35 (100)	.35 (34)	.25 (12)	.00 (3)	−.001
3	.67 (6)	.68 (19)	.49 (39)	.60 (100)	.67 (60)	.62 (40)	.60 (25)	.179
4	.47 (15)	.45 (29)	.43 (53)	.40 (90)	.36 (36)	.23 (13)	.33 (3)	−.073
5	.75 (12)	.60 (30)	.47 (57)	.42 (100)	.36 (42)	.40 (15)	.33 (6)	−.117
6	.25 (12)	.38 (21)	.48 (42)	.57 (100)	.65 (57)	.62 (37)	.65 (23)	.173
7	.29 (7)	.50 (16)	.47 (32)	.56 (75)	.64 (42)	.63 (27)	.65 (17)	.174
8	.50 (6)	.50 (12)	.52 (25)	.50 (50)	.46 (24)	.64 (11)	.57 (7)	−.062
9	.35 (20)	.33 (30)	.35 (46)	.54 (100)	.72 (53)	.79 (38)	.83 (30)	.370**
10	.57 (7)	.50 (14)	.64 (39)	.59 (100)	.79 (38)	.60 (35)	.57 (21)	−.058
11	.57 (7)	.61 (18)	.56 (41)	.58 (100)	.59 (58)	.62 (34)	.62 (21)	.025
12	.41 (17)	.43 (30)	.46 (56)	.44 (100)	.42 (43)	.39 (18)	.43 (7)	−.046
13	.40 (5)	.62 (13)	.67 (39)	.61 (100)	.58 (60)	.56 (34)	.50 (18)	−.084
14	.50 (6)	.62 (16)	.60 (40)	.59 (100)	.58 (59)	.59 (34)	.60 (20)	−.031
Females								
1	.67 (9)	.61 (23)	.55 (51)	.48 (100)	.42 (48)	.45 (20)	.33 (9)	−.132
2	.43 (28)	.36 (44)	.31 (65)	.34 (100)	.41 (34)	.36 (14)	.40 (5)	.104
3	.36 (25)	.38 (40)	.33 (60)	.39 (100)	.49 (39)	.42 (19)	.50 (8)	.154
4	.27 (30)	.33 (45)	.34 (68)	.33 (100)	.29 (31)	.33 (9)	.33 (3)	−.048
5	.22 (27)	.36 (42)	.34 (64)	.35 (100)	.37 (35)	.50 (12)	.20 (5)	.028
6	.54 (11)	.58 (26)	.52 (54)	.46 (100)	.38 (45)	.41 (17)	.29 (7)	−.141
7	.32 (25)	.28 (36)	.36 (58)	.41 (100)	.49 (41)	.65 (20)	.62 (13)	.126
8	.67 (9)	.55 (20)	.57 (43)	.53 (100)	.50 (52)	.58 (26)	.73 (15)	−.075
9	.46 (13)	.55 (29)	.47 (55)	.45 (100)	.41 (44)	.47 (17)	.50 (8)	−.064
10	.32 (19)	.34 (29)	.46 (54)	.47 (100)	.47 (45)	.67 (21)	.71 (14)	.004
11	.50 (10)	.56 (23)	.51 (43)	.53 (100)	.56 (52)	.50 (28)	.39 (13)	.047
12	.32 (37)	.32 (54)	.27 (74)	.25 (100)	.20 (25)	.00 (5)	−(0)	.036
M =	.45	.47	.47	.47	.48	.49	.49	.015

Note: Since the first shot cannot be conditioned, the parenthetical values in columns 4 and 6 sum to one less than the parenthetical value in column 5. The number of shots upon which each probability is based is given in parentheses.

** p < .01

Table 33.5. Runs Test – Cornell Players

Player	Hits	Misses	Number of Runs	Expected Number of Runs	z
Males					
1	54	46	56	50.7	−1.08
2	35	65	46	46.5	0.11
3	60	40	40	49.0	1.89
4	36	54	47	44.2	−0.62
5	42	58	55	49.7	−1.09
6	57	43	41	50.0	1.85
7	42	33	31	38.0	1.64
8	25	25	27	26.0	−0.29
9	54	46	32	50.7	3.78**
10	60	40	51	49.0	−0.42
11	58	42	48	49.7	0.35
12	44	56	52	50.3	−0.35
13	61	39	52	48.6	−0.72
14	59	41	50	49.4	−0.13
Females					
1	48	52	57	50.9	−1.22
2	34	66	41	45.9	1.09
3	39	61	41	48.6	1.60
4	32	68	46	44.5	−0.34
5	36	64	45	47.1	0.45
6	46	54	57	50.7	−1.28
7	41	59	43	49.4	1.33
8	53	47	54	50.8	−0.64
9	45	55	53	50.5	−0.51
10	46	54	50	50.7	0.14
11	53	47	48	50.8	0.57
12	25	75	41	38.5	−0.67
$M =$	45.6	51.2	46.3	47.3	.21

** $p < .01$.

slightly more runs than expected and 12 players with slightly fewer than expected. The Z statistic reported in column 6 shows that only the record of player 9 contained significantly more clustering (fewer runs) of hits and misses than expected by chance.

Test of Stationarity

As in Study 2, we divided the 100 shots taken by each player into nonoverlapping sets of four consecutive shots and counted the number of sets in which the player's performance was high (three or four hits), moderate (two hits), or low (zero or one hit). If a player is sometimes hot, the number of sets of high performance must exceed the number expected by chance, assuming a constant hit rate and independent shots. A χ^2 test for goodness of fit was used to compare the observed and the expected number of high, moderate, and low sets for each player. As before, we repeated this analysis four times for each player, starting at the first, second, third, and fourth shots in each player's record. The results provided no evidence for departures from stationarity for any player but 9.

Test of Predictability

There is another cluster of intuitions about "being hot" that involves predictability rather than sequential dependency. If, on certain occasions, a player can predict a "hit" before taking a shot, he or she may have a justified sense of being "hot" even when the pattern of hits and misses does not stray from chance expectation. We tested players' ability to predict hits and misses by having them bet on the outcome of each upcoming shot. Before every shot, each player chose whether to bet *high* in which case he or she would win 5 cents for a hit and lose 4 cents for a miss; or bet low, in which case he or she would win 2 cents for a hit and lose 1 cent for a miss. The players were advised to bet high when they felt confident in their shooting ability, and to bet low when they did not.

We also obtained betting data from another player who observed the shooter. The players were run in pairs, alternating between the roles of "shooter" and "observer." On each trial, the observer also bet high or low on the outcome of the upcoming shot. The shooter and observer did not know each other's bets. Each player was paid $2, plus or minus the amount of money won or lost on the bets made as a shooter and observer.

If players can predict their hits and misses, their bets should correlate with their performance. The correlations between the shooters' performance and the bets made by the shooters and observers reveal that the players were generally unsuccessful in predicting hits and misses. The average correlation between the shooters' bets and their performance was .02. Only 5 of the 26 individual correlations were statistically significant, of which 4 were quite low (.20 to .22), and the 5th was negative ($-.51$). The four small but significant positive correlations may reflect either a limited ability to predict the outcome of an upcoming shot, or a tendency to try harder following a high bet.

As one might expect, the observers were also unsuccessful in predicting the shooters' performance. The average correlation between the observers' bets and the shooters' performance was .04. On the other hand, the bets of both shooters and observers *were* correlated with the outcome of the shooter's *previous* shot (mean $r = .40$ for the shooters and .42 for the observers). It appears that both the shooter and observer anticipated a hit if the shooter had made the last shot. This betting strategy, which reflects a belief in the hot hand, produced chance performance because of the absence of a positive serial correlation. It also produced agreement between shooters' and observers' bets (mean $r = .22$) that vanishes when the effect of the previous shot is partialed out (mean $r = .05$).

DISCUSSION

This article investigated beliefs and facts concerning the sequential characteristics of hits and misses in basketball. Our survey shows that basketball fans believe that a player's chances of hitting a basket are greater following a hit than following a miss. However, the outcomes of both field goal and free throw attempts were largely independent of the outcome of the previous attempt. Moreover, the frequency of streaks in players' records did not exceed the frequency predicted by a binomial model that assumes a constant hit rate. A controlled experiment, with the varsity players of Cornell University, led to the same conclusions. With the exception of one player, no significant correlation between shots was found. Players' predictions of their own performance, expressed in the form of a betting game, revealed a consistent belief in the hot hand, although their actual performance did not support this belief. Evidently, the sense of being "hot" does not predict hits or misses.

How can we account for the prevalent belief in streak shooting despite the absence of sequential dependencies? This phenomenon could be due to a memory bias. If long sequences of hits (or misses) are more memorable than alternating sequences, the observer is likely to overestimate the correlation between successive shots. Alternatively, the belief in the hot hand may be caused by a misperception of chance that operates even when the data are in front of the subject rather than retrieved from memory.

The misperception hypothesis received support from our study of 100 basketball fans (Experiment 1). Following the survey, we presented each fan with six different sequences of hits (indicated by Xs) and misses (indicated by Os). Subjects were asked to classify each sequence as "chance shooting," "streak shooting," or "alternate shooting." Chance shooting was defined as sequences of hits and misses that are just like the sequences of heads and tails usually found when flipping coins. Streak shooting and alternate shooting were defined as clusters of hits and misses that are longer or shorter, respectively, than the clusters of heads and tails usually found in coin tossing.

All six sequences included 11 hits and 10 misses. They differed in the number of runs $(9, 11, \ldots, 19)$, and thus the probability of alternation $(0.4, 0.5, \ldots, 0.9,$ respectively), or the probability that the outcome of a given shot will be different from the outcome of the previous shot. In coin tossing, the probability of alternation is 0.5 – the outcome of a given trial is independent of the outcome of the previous trial. Streaks are produced when the probability of alternation is less than 0.5, and alternating sequences are produced when the probability of alternation is greater than 0.5. For example, the sequence

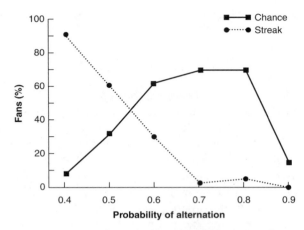

Figure 33.1. Percentage of basketball fans classifying sequences of hits and misses as examples of streak shooting or chance shooting, as a function of the probability of alternation within the sequences.

XOXOXOOOXXOXOXOOXXXOX, and its mirror image, which consist of 15 runs, were used for the probability of alternation of 0.7.

The percentage of "streak" and "chance" responses for each sequence is presented in Fig. 33.1. The percentage of "alternate" responses is the complement of these values. As expected, the tendency to perceive a sequence as streak shooting decreases with the probability of alternation. The most significant feature of Fig. 33.1, however, is the respondents' perception of chance shooting. The sequences selected as best examples of chance shooting had probabilities of alternation of 0.7 and 0.8 rather than 0.5. Furthermore, the sequence with the probability of alternation of 0.5 (the proper example of chance shooting) was classified as chance shooting only by 32% of subjects, whereas 62% identified it as an example of streak shooting.

Evidently, people tend to perceive chance shooting as streak shooting, and they expect sequences exemplifying chance shooting to contain many more alternations than would actually be produced by a random (chance) process. Thus, people "see" a positive serial correlation in independent sequences, and they fail to detect a negative serial correlation in alternating sequences. Hence, people not only perceive random sequences as positively correlated, they also perceive negatively correlated sequences as random. These phenomena are very much in evidence even when the sequences are displayed to the subject rather than retrieved from memory. Selective coding or biased retrieval, therefore, are not necessary for generating an erroneous belief in streak shooting, although they may enhance the effect. We attribute this phenomenon to a general misconception of the laws of chance associated with the belief that small as well as large sequences are representative of their generating process (Tversky & Kahneman, 1974). This belief induces the expectation that random sequences should be far more balanced than they are, and the erroneous perception of a positive correlation between successive shots.

This account explains both the formation and maintenance of the erroneous belief in the hot hand: If random sequences are perceived as streak shooting, then no amount of exposure to such sequences will convince the player, the coach, or the fan that the sequences are in fact random. The more basketball one watches and plays, the more opportunities one has to observe what appears to be streak shooting. In order to appreciate the sequential properties of basketball data, one has to realize that coin tossing produces just as many runs. If people's perceptions of coin tossing are biased, it should not be surprising that they perceive sequential dependencies in basketball when none exist.

The independence between successive shots, of course, does not mean that basketball is a game of chance rather than of skill, nor should it render the game less exciting to play, watch, or analyze. It merely indicates that the probability of a hit is largely independent of the outcome of previous shots, although it surely depends on other parameters such as skill, distance to the basket, and defensive pressure. This situation is analogous to coin tossing where the outcomes of successive tosses are independent but the probability of heads depends on measurable factors such as the initial position of the coin, and its angular and vertical momentum (see Keller, 1985). Neither coin tossing nor basketball are inherently random, once all the relevant parameters are specified. In the absence of this information, however, both processes may be adequately described by a simple binomial model. A major difference between the two processes is that it is hard to think of a credible mechanism that would create a correlation between successive coin tosses, but there are many factors (e.g., confidence, fatigue) that could produce positive dependence in basketball. The availability of plausible explanations may contribute to the erroneous belief that the probability of a hit is greater following a hit than following a miss.

The preceding discussion applies to the perception of randomness in general with no special reference to sports events or basketball. However, there are several specific factors linked to basketball that might enhance the effect. First, the intuition that a player is "hot" may stem from observations of his defense, hustling, and passing, which may be overgeneralized to shooting as well. Second, the coding of events may also help support the belief in sequential dependency. The common occurrence of a shot that pops out of the rim of the basket after having seemingly been made may be interpreted as continued evidence of being "hot" if the player had made the previous shot and as evidence of being "cold" if the player missed the previous shot (cf. Gilovich, 1983).

The present data demonstrate the operation of a powerful and widely shared cognitive illusion. Such illusions or biases have been observed in the judgments of both laypeople and experts in several fields (see, e.g., Fischhoff, Slovic, & Lichtenstein, 1981; Kahneman, Slovic, & Tversky, 1982; Nisbett & Ross, 1980; Tversky & Kahneman, 1983). If the present results are surprising, it is because of the robustness with which the erroneous belief in the "hot hand" is held by experienced and knowledgeable observers. This belief is particularly intriguing because it has consequences for the conduct of the game. Passing the ball to the player who is "hot" is a common strategy endorsed by basketball players. It is also anticipated by the opposing team who can concentrate on guarding the "hot" player. If another player, who is less "hot" on that particular day, is equally skilled, then the less guarded player would have a better chance of scoring. Thus the belief in the "hot hand" is not just erroneous, it could also be costly.

34. Like Goes with Like: The Role of Representativeness in Erroneous and Pseudo-Scientific Beliefs

Thomas Gilovich and Kenneth Savitsky

As its name implies, the *heuristics and biases* approach to human judgment has both positive and negative agendas (Griffin, Gonzalez, & Varey, 2001). The positive agenda is to identify the mental operations that yield rapid and compelling solutions to a host of everyday judgmental problems. Most notably, Kahneman and Tversky identified a small number of *automatic assessments* – similarity, generation of examples, causal judgments – that are made rapidly in response to particular problems and thus exert considerable influence on the judgments that are ultimately rendered (Kahneman & Tversky, 1972; Tversky & Kahneman, 1974). When ascertaining the likelihood that someone is an engineer, for example, one cannot help but assess the similarity between the person in question and the prototypical engineer, and the resultant assessment is, at the very least, the starting point for the judgment of likelihood. Thus, the positive agenda is to understand what the processes of judgment are like.

The negative agenda is to understand what the processes of judgment are *not* like. Because assessments of similarity, the generation of examples, and causal judgments obey their own logic, everyday judgment will not always be fully "rational" and will not always conform to the laws of probability. Thus, Kahneman and Tversky demonstrated that people's judgments are insufficiently sensitive to sample size, regression effects, prior odds, or, more generally, the reliability and diagnosticity of evidence. Their experiments were carefully crafted to reveal discrepancies between intuitive judgment and what is called for by the appropriate normative analysis.

Not surprisingly, the negative agenda appears to have garnered more attention and motivated more subsequent research – both hostile and congenial to Kahneman and Tversky's original ideas – than the positive. This may be because accusations of irrationality raise the ire of some scholars and challenge the theoretical foundation of much work in the social sciences. In addition, a demonstration of what is wrong points the way to improvement – a prospect that may have particular appeal to psychologists, many of whom entered the discipline with some interest in improving the human condition. The focus

This is an edited version of a paper that first appeared in *Skeptical Inquirer, 20*, 1996:34–40. In addition to the deletions indicated in the standard fashion, the introduction has been altered to create a better fit to this book. Used by permission of the *Skeptical Inquirer* magazine.

on errors is also a natural outgrowth of the logic of hypothesis testing that constitutes the evidential core of the behavioral sciences (Kahneman, 1991). The laws of probability provide crisp null hypotheses to which actual judgment can be tellingly compared.

The logic of hypothesis testing and the negative agenda of the heuristics and biases approach have thus shaped much of the work on everyday judgment since the 1960s. Note, however, that this implies that judgments not so clearly at variance with a precise normative standard have received less attention, even if they are every bit as influenced by the same heuristic processes. In this article we wish to explore an important class of judgments that we believe have been relatively neglected for just this reason. In particular, we wish to explore the influence of representativeness on people's assessment of causal relations – of what causes what.

THE REPRESENTATIVENESS HEURISTIC

The representativeness heuristic consists of the reflexive tendency to assess the "fit" or similarity of objects and events along salient dimensions and to organize them on the basis of one overarching rule: "Like goes with like." The heuristic reflects the belief that a member of a given category ought to resemble the category prototype, and that an effect ought to resemble the cause that produced it. Thus, the representativeness heuristic is often used to assess whether a given instance belongs to a particular category, such as whether an individual is likely to be an accountant or a comedian. It is also used in assigning causes to effects, as when deciding whether a case of heartburn was caused by a plate of enchiladas or a bowl of rice.

In such contexts, assessments of similarity are often a big help. Instances often resemble their category prototypes and causes frequently resemble their effects. Members of various occupational groups, for example, frequently do resemble the group prototype. Likewise, "big" effects (such as the development of the atomic bomb) are often brought about by "big" causes (such as the Manhattan Project).

Still, the representativeness heuristic is only that – a heuristic. Judgments based on representativeness should therefore be viewed with caution. Although representativeness can help us make some judgments with accuracy and dispatch, it can also lead us astray. Not all members fit the category prototype. Some comedians are shy or taciturn, and some accountants are wild and crazy. Although causes are frequently representative of their effects, this relationship does not always hold: Tiny viruses give rise to devastating diseases like malaria or AIDS, and splitting the nucleus of an atom releases an awesome amount of energy. In some cases, then, representativeness yields inaccuracy and error – or even superstition. A charming example is provided by craps shooters, who roll the dice gently to coax a low number, and more vigorously to encourage a high one (Hanslin, 1967). A small effect (low number) requires a small cause (gentle roll), and a big effect (high number) requires a big cause (vigorous roll)....

Representativeness and Causal Judgments

In many cases, it can be difficult to establish with certainty that a judgmental error has been made. It is partly for this reason, we believe, that there has been less empirical research on representativeness and causal judgments than, say, representativeness and base-rate neglect. Furthermore, the research that has been conducted on representativeness-based causal judgments is more suggestive than definitive. Nonetheless, the suggestive evidence is rather striking, and it points to the possibility that representativeness may exert at least as much influence over causal judgments as it does over other, more exhaustively researched types of judgments. To see how much, we discuss some examples of representativeness thinking in medicine, in pseudoscientific systems, and in psychoanalysis.

Representativeness and Medical Beliefs. One area in which the impact of representativeness on causal judgments is particularly striking is the domain of health and medicine (see Gilovich, 1991). Historically, people have often assumed that the symptoms of a disease should resemble either its cause or its cure (or both). In ancient Chinese medicine, for example, people with vision problems were fed ground bat in the (typically) mistaken belief that bats have particularly keen vision and that some of this ability might be transferred to the recipient (Deutsch, 1977). Evans-Pritchard (1937) noted many examples of the influence of representativeness among the African Azande (although he discussed them in the context of magical thinking, not representativeness). For instance, the Azande used the ground-up skull of the red bush monkey to cure epilepsy. Why? The cure should resemble the disease, so the herky-jerky movements of the monkey make the essence of monkey stand out as a promising candidate to settle the violent movements of an epileptic seizure. As Evans-Pritchard put it:

Generally the logic of therapeutic treatment consists in the selection of the most prominent external symptoms, the naming of the disease after some object in nature it resembles, and the utilization of the object as the principal ingredient in the drug administered to cure the disease. The circle may even be completed by belief that the external symptoms not only yield to treatment by the object which resembles them but are caused by it as well. (quoted in Nisbett & Ross, 1980, p. 116)

Western medical practice has likewise been guided by the representativeness heuristic. For instance, early Western medicine was strongly influenced by what was known as the "doctrine of signatures," or the belief that "every natural substance which possesses any medicinal virtue indicates by an obvious and well-marked external character the disease for which it is a remedy, or the object for which it should be employed" (quoted in Nisbett & Ross, 1980, p. 116). Thus, physicians prescribed the lungs of the fox (known for its endurance) for asthmatics, and the yellow spice turmeric for jaundice. Again, disease and cure are linked because they resemble one another.

Or consider the popularity of homeopathy, which derives from the 18th century work of German physician Samuel Hahnemann (Barrett, 1987). One of the bedrock principles of homeopathy is Hahnemann's "law of similars," according to which the key to discovering what substance cures a particular disorder lies in noting the effect that different substances have on healthy people. If a substance causes a particular reaction in an unafflicted person, that substance is seen as a likely cure for a disease characterized by those same symptoms. As before, the external symptoms of a disease are used to identify a cure for the disease – a cure that manifests the same external characteristics.

Of course, there are instances in which substances that cause particular symptoms are used effectively as part of a therapeutic regimen to cure, alleviate, or prevent those very symptoms. Vaccines deliver small, inert quantities of disease-causing viruses to help individuals develop immunities. Likewise, allergy sufferers sometimes receive periodic doses of the exact substance to which they are allergic so that they will develop a tolerance over time. The problem with the discredited medical practices described above is the *general* assumption that the symptoms of a disease should resemble its cause, its cure, or both. Limiting the scope of possible cures to those that are representative of the disease can seriously impede scientific discovery. Such a narrow focus, for example, would have inhibited the discovery of the two most significant developments of modern medicine – sanitation and antibiotics.

Representativeness thinking continues to abound in modern "alternative" medicine, a pursuit that appears to be gaining in perceived legitimacy (Cowley, King, Hager, & Rosenberg, 1995). An investigation by the United States Congress into health fraud and quackery noted several examples of what appear to be interventions inspired by the superficial appeal of representativeness (House Subcommittee on Health and Long-Term Care, 1984). In one set of suggested treatments, patients are encouraged to eat raw organ concentrates corresponding to the dysfunctional body part (e.g., brain concentrates for mental disorders, heart concentrates for cardiac conditions, raw stomach lining for ulcers). Similarly, the fingerprints of representativeness are all over the practice of "rebirthing," a New Age therapeutic technique in which individuals reenact their own births in an effort to correct personality defects caused by having been born in an "unnatural" fashion (Ward, 1994). One person who was born breech (i.e., feet first) underwent the rebirthing procedure to cure his sense that his life was always going in the wrong direction and that he could never seem to get things "the right way round." Another, born Caesarean, sought the treatment because of a lifelong difficulty of seeing things to completion and always relying on others to finish tasks for her. As one author quipped, "God knows what damage forceps might inflict . . . a lifelong neurosis that you're being dragged where you don't want to go?" (p. 90).

A more rigorous examination of the kind of erroneous beliefs about health and the human body that can arise from the appeal of representativeness dealt with the adage, "You are what you eat." Just how far do people take this idea? In certain respects, the saying is undeniably true: Bodies are composed to a large extent of the molecules that were once ingested as food. Quite literally, we are what we have eaten. Indeed, there are times when we even take on the character of what we ingest: People gain weight by eating fatty foods, and a person's skin can acquire an orange tint from the carotene found in carrots and tomatoes. But the notion that we develop the characteristics of the food we eat sometimes goes beyond such examples to almost magical extremes. The Hua of Papua New Guinea, for example, believe that individuals will grow quickly if they eat rapidly growing food (Meigs, 1984, cited by Nemeroff & Rozin, 1989).

But what about a more "scientifically minded" population? Carol Nemeroff and Paul Rozin (1989) asked college students to consider a hypothetical culture known as the "Chandorans," who hunt wild boar and marine turtles. Some of the students learned that the Chandorans hunt turtles for their shells and wild boar for their meat. The others heard the opposite: The tribe hunts turtles for their meat, and boar for their tusks.

After reading one of the two descriptions of the Chandorans, the students were asked to rate the tribe members on numerous characteristics. Their responses reflected a belief that the characteristics of the food would "rub off" onto the tribe members. Boar-eaters were thought to be more aggressive and irritable than their counterparts – and more likely to have beards! The turtle-eaters were thought to live longer and be better swimmers.

However educated a person may be (the participants in Nemeroff and Rozin's experiment were University of Pennsylvania undergraduates), it can be difficult to get beyond the assumption that like goes with like. In this case, it leads to the belief that individuals tend to acquire the attributes of the food they ingest. Thus, a wide swath of the educated public avoids milk when suffering from a cold to avoid the build up of additional phlegm, tells their oily-faced teenagers to avoid oily potato chips, and swears that spicy foods are what give a person heartburn.

Representativeness and Pseudoscientific Beliefs. A core tenet of the field of astrology is that an individual's personality is influenced by the astrological sign under which he or she was born (Huntley, 1990). A glance at the personality types associated with the various astrological signs reveals an uncanny concordance between the supposed personality of someone with a particular sign and the characteristics associated with the sign's namesake (Huntley, 1990; Howe, 1970; Zusne & Jones, 1982). Those born under the sign of the goat (Capricorn) are said to be tenacious, hard-working, and stubborn, whereas those born under the lion (Leo) are proud, forceful leaders. Likewise, those born under the sign of Cancer (the crab) share with their namesake a tendency to appear hard on the outside, while inside their "shells" they are soft and vulnerable. One account of astrology even goes so far as to suggest that, like the crab, those born under the sign of Cancer tend to be "deeply attached to their homes" (Read et al., 1978).

What is the origin of these associations? They are not empirically derived, as they have been shown time and time again to lack validity (e.g., Carlson,

1985; Dean, 1987; for reviews, see Abell, 1981; Schick & Vaughn, 1995; Zusne & Jones, 1982). They are thus conceptually driven by simple, representativeness-based assessments of the personalities that *should* be associated with various astrological signs. After all, who is more likely to be retiring and modest than a Virgo (the virgin)? Who better to be well balanced, harmonious, and fair than a Libra (the scales)? By taking advantage of people's reflexive associations, the system gains some surface plausibility.

It doesn't stop there. Consider another elaborate "scientific" system designed to assess the "secrets" of an individual's personality – graphology, or handwriting analysis. Corporations pay graphologists sizable fees to screen job applicants by developing personality profiles of those who apply for jobs. Graphologists are also called on to provide "expert" testimony in trial proceedings and help the Secret Service determine if any real danger is posed by threatening letters to government officials. How much stock can we put in the work of handwriting analysts?

Unlike astrology, graphology is not worthless. It has been, and continues to be, the subject of careful empirical investigation (Nevo, 1986), and it has been shown that people's handwriting can reveal certain things about them. Particularly shaky writing can be a clue that an individual suffers from some neurologic disorder that causes hand tremors; whether a person is male or female is often apparent from his or her writing. In general, however, what handwriting analysis can determine most reliably tends to be things that can be even more reliably ascertained through other means. As for the "secrets" of an individual's personality, graphology has yet to show that it is any better than astrology.

This has not done much to diminish the popularity of handwriting analysis, however. One reason for this is that graphologists, like astrologers, gain some surface plausibility or "face validity" for their claims by exploiting the tendency for people to use the representativeness heuristic. Many of their claims have a superficial sensible quality, rarely violating the principal that like goes with like. Consider, for instance, the "zonal theory" of graphology, which divides a person's handwriting into the upper, middle, and lower regions. A person's "intellectual," "practical," and "instinctual" qualities supposedly correspond to these different regions (Basil, 1989). Can you guess which is which? Could our "lower" instincts be reflected anywhere other than the lower region, or our "higher" intellect anywhere other than the top?

The list of such representativeness-based connections goes on and on. Handwriting slants to the left? The person must be holding something back, repressing his or her true emotions. Slants to the right? The person gets carried away by his or her feelings. A signature placed far below a paragraph suggests that the individual wishes to distance him- or herself from what was written (Scanlon & Mauro, 1992). Handwriting that stays close to the left margin belongs to individuals attached to the past, whereas writing that hugs the right margin comes from those oriented toward the future.

What is ironic is that the very mechanism that many graphologists rely on to argue for the persuasive value of their endeavor – that the character of the handwriting resembles the character of the person – is what ultimately betrays them: They call it "common sense"; we call it judgment by representativeness.

Representativeness and Psychoanalysis. Nisbett and Ross (1980) contend that "the enormous popularity of Freudian theory probably lies in the fact that, unlike all its competitors among contemporary views, it encourages the layperson to do what comes naturally in causal explanation, that is, to use the representativeness heuristic"(p. 244). Although their claim may be difficult to put to empirical test, there can be little doubt that much of the interpretation of symbols that lies at the core of psychoanalytic theory is driven by representativeness. Consider the interpretation of dreams, in which the images a client reports from his or her dreams are considered indicative of underlying motives. There are, of course, an almost infinite set of potential relationships between dream content and underlying psychodynamics, and it is interesting that virtually all of the "meaningful" ones identified by psychodynamically oriented clinicians are ones in which there is an obvious fit or resemblance between the reported image and inner dynamics. A man who dreams of a snake or a cigar is thought to be troubled by his penis or his sexuality. People who dream of policemen are thought to be concerned about their fathers or authority figures. Knowledge of the representativeness heuristic compels one to wonder whether such connections reflect something important about the psyche of the client, or whether they exist primarily in the mind of the therapist.

One area of psychodynamic theorizing in which the validity of such superficially plausible relationships has been tested and found wanting is the use of projective tests. The most widely known projective test is the Rorschach, in which clients report what they "see" in ambiguous patches of ink appearing on various cards. As in all projective tests, the idea is that in responding to such an unstructured stimulus, a person must "project," and thus reveal, some of his or her inner dynamics. Countless studies, however, have failed to produce evidence that the test is valid – that is, that the assessments made about people on the basis of the test correspond to the psychopathological conditions from which they suffer (Burros, 1978).

The research findings notwithstanding, clinicians frequently report the Rorschach to be extremely helpful in clinical practice. Might representativeness contribute to this paradox of strongly held beliefs coexisting with the absence of any real relationship? You be the judge. A person who interprets the whole Rorschach card, and not its specific details, is considered by clinicians to suffer from a need to form a "big picture,"and a tendency toward grandiosity, even paranoia. In contrast, a person who refers only to small details of the ink blots is considered to have an obsessive personality – someone who attends to detail at the expense of the more important holistic aspects (Dawes, 1994). Once again, systematic research has failed to find evidence for these relationships, but the sense of representativeness gives them some superficial plausibility.

Conclusion

We have described numerous erroneous beliefs that appear to derive from the over-use of the representativeness heuristic. Many of them arise in domains in which the reach for solutions to important problems exceeds our grasp – such as the attempt to uncover (via astrology or handwriting analysis) simple cues to the complexities of human motivation and personality. In such domains, in which no simple solutions exist and yet the need or desire for such solutions remains strong, dubious cause–effect links are uncritically accepted because they satisfy the principle of "Like goes with like."

Representativeness can also have the opposite effect, inhibiting belief in valid claims that violate the expectation of resemblance. As Nisbett and Ross (1980) note, people initially scoffed at Walter Reed's suggestion that malaria was carried by the mosquito. From a representativeness standpoint, it is easy to see why: The cause (a tiny mosquito) is not at all representative of the result (a devastating disease). Reed's claim violated the notion that big effects should have big causes, and thus was difficult to accept.

Our final bit of evidence for the importance of representativeness in everyday causal assessments comes not from further examples we could generate, but from the further examples you can generate. That is, we have been struck by the ways in which individuals steeped in the research literature on heuristics and biases use the word *representativeness* in everyday discourse. It is rarely used – in nonprofessional contexts, at least – to account for the gambler's fallacy, the failure to anticipate regression effects, the disregard of base rates, and so on. Instead, the term is typically invoked to refer to some instance in which an assessment of similarity has guided – or misguided – a person's inference of the cause responsible for a given effect. *Representativeness* thus fills a commonly encountered lexical void, something it could not do if everyday assessments of causality were not noticeably influenced by the principle of "Like goes with like."

35. When Less Is More: Counterfactual Thinking and Satisfaction among Olympic Medalists

Victoria Husted Medvec, Scott F. Madey, and Thomas Gilovich

> So, we have the paradox of a man shamed to death because he is only the second pugilist or the second oarsman in the world. That he is able to beat the whole population of the globe minus one is nothing; he has "pitted" himself to beat that one; and as long as he doesn't do that nothing else counts.
>
> William James, 1892, p. 186

James's observation represents an early statement of a fundamental principle of psychology: A person's objective achievements often matter less than how those accomplishments are subjectively construed. Being one of the best in the world can mean little if it is coded not as a triumph over many, but as a loss to one. Being second best may not be as gratifying as perhaps it should.

Since James's time, of course, this idea has been both theoretically enriched and extensively documented. Social psychologists have shown that people's satisfaction with their objective circumstances is greatly affected by how their own circumstances compare with those of relevant others (Festinger, 1954; Suls & Miller, 1977; Taylor & Lobel, 1989). A 5% merit raise can be quite exhilarating until one learns that the person down the hall received an 8% increase. Psychologists have also demonstrated that satisfaction with an outcome likewise depends on how it compares with a person's original expectations (Atkinson, 1964; Feather, 1967, 1969). Someone who receives a 5% raise might be happier than someone who receives an 8% increase if the former expected less than the latter. Often it is the *difference* between the actual outcome and the expected outcome, or the actual outcome and the outcomes of others that is decisive (Crosby, 1976; Olson, Herman, & Zanna, 1986).

More recently, psychologists have discovered a third way in which the determinants of satisfaction are relative. In particular, people seem to be greatly affected by how their objective outcomes compare to imagined outcomes that "might have been" (Kahneman & Miller, 1986; Kahneman & Tversky, 1982b; Markman, Gavanski, Sherman, & McMullen, 1993; Miller, Turnbull, & McFarland, 1990; Roese, 1994; Roese & Olson, 1995). The intensity of people's

This is an edited and condensed version of a paper that first appeared in the *Journal of Personality and Social Psychology, 69*, 603–610. Copyright © 1995 by the American Psychological Association. Adapted with permission.

reactions to events appears to be proportional to how easy it is to conjure up greater or lesser outcomes that "almost happened." An 8% return on one's investment might exceed expectations and yet be disappointing if one is reminded of an alternative investment one "almost" made that yielded a substantially higher return. The critical comparison in this case is a postcomputed response to what has occurred, rather than a precomputed representation of what seems likely, *ex ante*, to occur (Kahnernan & Miller, 1986).

Most of the research on counterfactual thinking has held outcome constant and examined the reactions of people contemplating different counterfactual alternatives. For example, Kahneman and Tversky (1982b) asked their participants to imagine the reactions of two travelers who both missed their scheduled flights, one by 5 minutes and the other by 30 minutes. The outcome is the same – both must wait for the next flight – but it is easier to imagine a counterfactual world in which the first traveler arrives on time. Studies such as this have repeatedly shown that the same outcome can produce strikingly different reactions as a function of the ease of generating various counterfactual alternatives (Johnson, 1986; Kahneman & Miller, 1986; Kahneman & Tversky, 1982a, 1982b; Miller & McFarland, 1986; Miller et al., 1990; Turnbull, 1981; Wells & Gavanski, 1989).

We wished to take this a step further. We were interested in whether the effects of different counterfactual comparisons are sufficiently strong to cause people who are objectively *worse* off to sometimes feel better than those in a superior state. Moreover, we were interested not just in documenting isolated episodes in which this might happen, but in identifying a specific situation in which it occurs with regularity and predictability. The domain we chose to investigate was athletic competition.

We chose this domain of investigation because in athletic competition outcomes are typically defined with unusual precision. Someone finishes first, second, or third, for example, thereby earning a gold, silver, or bronze medal. With all else equal, one would expect the athletes' levels of satisfaction to mirror this objective order. We suspected, however, that all else is not equal – that the nature of athletes' counterfactual thoughts might cause their levels of satisfaction to depart from this simple, linear order.

Consider the counterfactual thoughts of bronze and silver medalists. What might their most compelling counterfactual thoughts be? One would certainly expect the silver medalist to focus on almost winning the gold because there is a qualitative difference between coming in first and any other outcome. Each event has only one winner, and to that victor belongs the considerable spoils that the modern commercial-athletic world bestows (Frank & Cook, 1995). Moreover, for the silver medalist, this exalted status was only one step away. To be sure, the silver medalist also finished only one step from winning a bronze, but such a downward social comparison does not involve much of a change in status (i.e., neither the bronze nor silver medalist won the event, but both won medals), and thus does not constitute as much of a counterfactual temptation.

In contrast, bronze medalists are likely to focus their counterfactual thoughts downward. Like the qualitative jump between silver and gold, there is a categorical difference between finishing third and finishing fourth. Third place merits a medal whereas the fourth-place finisher is just one of the field. This type of categorical difference does not exist in the upward comparison between second and third place.

Because of this asymmetry in the direction of counterfactual comparison, the person who is objectively worse off (the bronze medalist) might nonetheless feel more gratified than the person who is objectively better off (the silver medalist). Like William James's (1892) pugilist, silver medalists may torment themselves with counterfactual thoughts of "If only . . ." or "Why didn't I just . . ." Bronze medalists, in contrast, may be soothed by the thought that "At least I won a medal." The net result is that with respect to athletic competition, there may be times when less is more.

We conducted three studies to examine this question. First, we analyzed the affective reactions of bronze and silver medalists as they won their medals in the 1992 Olympic Games in Barcelona, Spain. Second, we had participants evaluate the Olympians' postcompetition interviews to see whether silver medalists seemed to be focused on the medal they almost won, whereas third-place finishers appeared to relish the pleasure simply of being medalists. In the third study, we asked athletes themselves about the nature of their counterfactual thoughts.

STUDY 1

We videotaped all of the National Broadcasting Company (NBC) coverage of the 1992 Summer Olympic Games in Barcelona, Spain. From this footage, two master tapes were constructed. The first showed the immediate reactions of all bronze and silver medalists that NBC chose to televise at the time the athletes learned how they had finished. Thus, the tape shows Janet Evans as she touched the wall of the pool and discovered she had come in second, and Jackie Joyner-Kersey after she completed her last long jump and earned a bronze medal. The second tape consisted of all bronze and silver medalists whom NBC showed on the medal stand during the award ceremony. For example, this tape shows Matt Biondi receiving a silver medal for his performance in the 50-m freestyle, and the Lithuanian men's basketball team (in uniforms designed by *The Grateful Dead*) after they received their bronze medals. Each tape was shown to a separate group of participants who were asked to rate the expressed emotion of each athlete. . . .

Method
Stimulus Materials. The tape of the athletes' immediate reactions included shots of 23 silver and 18 bronze medalists. Not surprisingly, given NBC's main audience, most of these shots (25) were of Americans. To create the master tape,

we simply copied all footage of the finish and immediate aftermath of all silver and bronze medal winners. These shots tended to be rather brief ($M = 14.4$ s; $SD = 8.3$ s), and we stayed with the scene for as long as NBC did. Because the issue of what footage to include involved minimal judgment, we did the editing ourselves.

This was not the case for the medal stand videotape. Here there were too many editing decisions to be made. Should a shot of the athlete leaving the medal stand be included? Should a certain head-and-shoulder shot on the medal stand be included? To eliminate the possibility of our expectations guiding these editorial decisions, we turned the job over to someone unaware of our hypothesis. We identified all medal stand shots of second- and third-place finishers in NBC's coverage, and asked our editor to copy those moments that best captured the emotion that the athletes appeared to be feeling. This resulted in a master tape of 20 silver and 15 bronze medal winners. The average length of each shot was 14.7 s, with an SD of 13.8 s. In this case fewer than half of the shots (15) were of American athletes.

Two versions of each tape were created, with the order of presentation of the athletes varied across versions. . . .

Procedure. Participants arrived at the laboratory in groups and were told that they would be watching a videotape of athletes from the 1992 Olympic Games. They were informed that they were to rate the expressed emotions of each athlete on a 10-point "agony to ecstasy" scale. To ensure that participants' ratings would not be affected by preexisting knowledge about the athletes or their performance in the Olympic games, only people who indicated they were uninterested in and uninformed about sports were recruited. . . .

Five participants rated each version of each of the two videotapes. The tapes were shown without sound to eliminate the chance that commentators' remarks might affect participants' evaluations of the athletes' expressed emotions. A 1.5-in. (3.8-cm) strip of paper was affixed to the bottom of the video screen to occlude various graphics used by NBC to indicate the athlete's order of finish.

Results

Participants' ratings were highly reliable, for both the immediate-reactions videotape (Spearman–Brown index = .97) and the medal stand tape (Spearman–Brown index = .96). Thus, the ratings of all participants viewing the same tape were averaged to create an index of the happiness of each of the athletes. Preliminary analyses revealed no effect of order of presentation, so the data were collapsed across the two versions of each tape.

As predicted, bronze medalists appeared happier on average than their counterparts who won silver medals. When assessing the athletes' immediate reactions, participants assigned the bronze medalists a mean happiness rating of 7.1 (SD 2.0), but the silver medalists a mean rating of only 4.8 (SD 1.9). When examining the athletes on the medal stand, participants assigned the bronze medalists a mean rating of 5.7 ($SD = 1.7$) and silver medalists a mean rating of only 4.3 ($SD = 1.8$). These data were analyzed with a 2 (type of medal: bronze vs. silver) × 2 (tape: immediate vs. medal stand) analysis of variance (ANOVA). This analysis revealed two significant main effects, but no interaction. The main effect of tape, $F(1, 72) = 4.78$, $p < .05$, indicates that the athletes on the whole looked happier immediately after their performances than when they were on the medal stand. More important, the main effect of type of medal, $F(1, 72) = 18.98$, $p < .001$, indicates that the athletes who finished third looked significantly happier than those who finished second.

There is a potential artifactual explanation of these results, however. In certain Olympic events, the competition is structured such that bronze medalists have just won a match or a game, whereas silver medalists have just lost. A bronze medalist in wrestling, for example, would have just defeated the fourth place finisher, and the silver medalist would have just lost to the gold medal winner. We were concerned that being in the immediate aftermath of victory or defeat might have contaminated our comparison of bronze and silver medalists. Fortunately, most Olympic events (such as those in track, swimming, and gymnastics) are not structured in this way. In these events the athletes simply finish first, second, and third depending on how well they do.

To eliminate this just–won/just–lost artifact, we reanalyzed the data excluding all athletes involved in sports with this structure. This reduced our pool of 23 silver and 18 bronze medalists in the immediate-reactions videotape to 20 and 15, respectively. Similarly, it reduced our pool of 20 silver and 15 bronze medalists in the medal-stand tape to 14 and 13, respectively. A 2 × 2 ANOVA of these data yielded the same significant main effect of type of medal as before, $F(1, 58) = 6.70$, $p < .02$. Bronze medalists appeared happier both immediately after their events ($M = 6.7$) and on the medal stand ($M = 5.6$) than their counterparts who had won silver medals ($Ms = 5.0$ and 4.7, respectively). Consistent with our thesis, impartial judges viewed bronze medalists as being happier than silver medalists, and this effect was not limited to those few events in which bronze and silver medalists were in the immediate aftermath of a victory or a defeat, respectively.

Is there any other alternative interpretation of these data? Might these results be due to differences in the *ex ante* expectations of bronze and silver medalists rather than – as we propose – their *ex post* thoughts about what might have been? We think not. First of all, there is no reason to believe that bronze medalists as a whole tended to exceed their expectations or that silver medalists on average tended to fall short of theirs. To be sure, our sample of silver medalists probably entered the Olympics with higher expectations on average than our sample of bronze medalists, but they also *performed* better as well. There is certainly no compelling reason to believe that one group over or underperformed relative to their initial expectations.

This alternative interpretation can also be dismissed on empirical grounds. We obtained an unbiased measure of the athletes' likely expectations prior to the Olympics and then used a regression analysis to examine the effect of medal won (bronze or silver) after initial expectations were controlled statistically. The athletes' likely expectations were derived from *Sports Illustrated*'s Olympic preview (Verschoth, 1992). *Sports Illustrated* predicted the likely bronze, silver, and gold medal winners of every Olympic event the week before the games began. Athletes who were expected to win gold, silver, or bronze medals were assigned expectation scores of 1, 2, and 3, respectively. Those not predicted to win a medal were assigned an expectation score of 4. As anticipated, the athletes in our samples who won silver medals were originally expected to do better ($M = 2.8$) than those who won bronze medals ($M = 3.0$), although not significantly so, $t < 1.0$. More important, however, is that a comparison of actual and anticipated performance argues against the claim that our results are due to differences in initial expectations of bronze and silver medalists. Silver medalists as a whole did better than anticipated (actual = 2.0; anticipated = 2.8), and therefore should have been relatively happy. Bronze medalists, however, performed on average exactly as expected (actual and anticipated = 3.0).

More formally, we entered the expected finish of each athlete into a regression equation that predicted the agony–ecstasy ratings from the medal won (silver or bronze), the medal predicted (gold, silver, bronze, or none), and the type of videotape segment (immediate reactions or medal stand). This analysis revealed that the effect of medal won remained significant when expectations were statistically controlled, $t(72) = 4.3$, $p < .0001$. Silver medalists looked less satisfied with their performances than did bronze medalists, and they did so for reasons unrelated to how well they were expected to perform.

Discussion

Can we confidently attribute these results to the athletes' counterfactual thoughts? Although the data from Study 1 are consistent with this claim, it is important to examine directly the proposed asymmetry in the athletes' counterfactual comparisons. The following two studies were designed to do exactly that. Do silver medalists tend to think about how they almost won the gold? Do bronze medalists focus on how close they came to missing out on a medal altogether? What exactly do athletes think about after they learn their medal standing?

STUDY 2

To examine the nature of Olympic medalists' counterfactual thoughts, we turned once again to NBC's coverage of the 1992 Summer Olympic Games. NBC's sportscasters interviewed numerous medal winners immediately following their events, and from this footage we developed a master tape of all of NBC's interviews of bronze and silver medalists. Participants were shown the tape and asked to assess the extent to which the athletes seemed preoccupied with thoughts of how they did perform versus how they almost performed.

Method
Stimulus Materials. NBC interviewed 13 silver medalists and 9 bronze medalists immediately after their events, and these 22 interviews comprised

the stimulus tape for this study. Two versions of the tape were created, with the order of presentation of the athletes varied across the versions. The average length of each interview clip was 27 s ($SD = 14$ s).

Procedure. Participants arrived at the laboratory in groups and were told that they would be watching a videotape of athletes from the 1992 Olympic Games. They were asked to watch and listen to each interview carefully and to rate each athlete's comments on a 10-point scale, ranging from "at least I ..." (1) to "I almost ..." (10). To clarify the meaning of this scale, participants were given an example of how a student who receives a B in a course could have various thoughts ranging from "at least I didn't get a C" to "I almost got an A." ...

Five participants rated each of the two versions of the videotape. As in the first study, a 1.5-in. (3.8-cm) strip of paper was affixed to the bottom of the video screen to occlude various graphics depicting the athlete's order of finish.

Results

The interrater reliability of participants' ratings was acceptably high (Spearman–Brown index $= .74$), so the ratings were averaged to create indices of the apparent thoughts of each athlete. Preliminary analyses of these data revealed no effect of order of presentation, so the data were collapsed across the two versions of the tape.

As predicted, silver medalists' thoughts were rated as being more focused on "I almost ..." than were those of bronze medalists. On the 10-point "At least I ..." to "I almost ..." scale, participants assigned silver medalists' thoughts an average rating of 5.7 ($SD = 1.5$) and bronze medalists' thoughts an average rating of only 4.4 ($SD = 0.7$), $t(20) = 2.37$, $p < .03$. . . .

Discussion

The results of the second study provide support for the hypothesized difference in the counterfactual thoughts of the bronze and silver medalists. Silver medalists seem to be focused on the gold medal they almost won, whereas bronze medalists seem content with the thought that "At least I did this well." This asymmetry can thus explain the observed differences in the athletes' expressed emotions in Study 1. This can be seen most clearly through an analysis that combines the data from studies 1 and 2. Fifteen of the 22 athletes whose counterfactual thoughts were assessed in Study 2 were on the immediate-reactions videotape in Study 1, and thus were also rated on the agony–ecstasy scale. As we predicted, the two ratings correlated significantly: The more focused the athletes were on almost finishing higher, the less happy they seemed ($r = -.56$, $p < .05$). This relationship was also observed when the data for silver ($r = -.51$; $n = 10$) and bronze ($r = -.34$; $n = 5$) medalists were considered separately, although the sample sizes were then too small to yield statistical significance. Thus, by focusing on what they achieved, bronze medalists are rather happy; in contrast, a concern with what they failed to achieve makes the silver medalists seem less so.

In this study we did not have direct access to the athletes' thoughts; we had participants infer them on the basis of the athletes' comments. It is certainly possible, of course, that the athletes had various thoughts they did not verbalize. To overcome this limitation, we conducted a third study that examined bronze and silver medalists' own reports of their thoughts following an athletic competition.

STUDY 3

In designing Study 3, we sought an athletic forum with significant stakes where we could gain access to bronze and silver medalists immediately after their events. The 1994 Empire State Games provided such a forum. The Empire State Games have been a prominent amateur athletic event in New York State since 1978. Athletes from across the state compete on a regional basis to qualify for the Empire State Games. Notable participants have included such athletes as Olympic gold medalists Dianne Roffe-Steinrotter and Jeff Blatnick, and NBA basketball stars (and "Dream Team" members) Christian Laettner and Chris Mullin. In 1994, more than 5,000 athletes from across New York State competed in the 4-day event.

Method

Participants. One hundred fifteen Empire State Game medalists participated in this study. All of the participants won bronze ($n = 55$) or silver ($n = 60$) medals in swimming or track events. The athletes competed in either the Scholastic Division (composed exclusively of students up to 12th grade; $n = 31$ males, 34 females) or the Open Division (consisting mainly of college students; $n = 25$ males, 25 females).

Procedure. The athletes were approached individually following their events and asked to rate their thoughts about their performance on the same 10-point scale used in Study 2. Specifically, they were asked to rate the extent to which they were concerned with thoughts of "At least I . . ." (1) versus "I almost . . ." (10). Special effort was made to ensure that the athletes understood the scale before making their ratings. This was accomplished by mentioning how athletes might have different thoughts following an athletic competition, ranging from "I almost did better" to "At least I did this well."

Results

As predicted, silver medalists' thoughts following the competition were more focused on "I almost" than were bronze medalists'. Silver medalists described their thoughts with a mean rating of 6.8 ($SD = 2.2$), whereas bronze medalists assigned their thoughts an average rating of 5.7 ($SD = 2.7$), $t(113) = 2.4$, $p < .02. . . .$

GENERAL DISCUSSION

The purpose of this research was to examine whether there are reliable situations in which those who are objectively better off nonetheless feel worse than those in an inferior position. Athletics offered an ideal context in which to test this question for the same reason that it offers a useful context for investigating many psychological hypotheses – the availability of data of unusual objectivity and precision (Baumeister & Steinhilber, 1984; Frank & Gilovich, 1988; Gilovich, Vallone, & Tversky, 1985; Lau & Russell, 1980). In addition, athletics was chosen as the domain of investigation in this case because performance in athletics often yields a clearly defined rank order. Someone enters the record books as the first-, second-, or third-place finisher.

It should be clear, however, that the significance of the present results extends far beyond the playing field or the medal stand. There are many other situations in which the same processes documented here can likewise cause those who are better off to feel worse. A student who misses out on an A— by one point and earns a B+ could easily feel less satisfied with the grade than someone who is in the middle of the pack of Bs. Or consider a person who correctly guesses all but one number in a lottery. Such an individual misses out on the jackpot, but usually wins a modest sum for coming close. The prize no doubt provides some enjoyment, but the knowledge of having just missed the jackpot is bound to come up from time to time and ruin otherwise blissful moments. More generally, as our opening quote from William James suggests, being one of the best may not be as satisfying as it might seem. The existence of a rival "best" can turn a gratifying appreciation of what one *is* into a disquieting focus on what one is *not*. . . .

Our results extend previous findings in this area by emphasizing the "automatic" or "imposed" nature of many counterfactual thoughts. Much of the recent work on counterfactual thinking has emphasized a person's ability to choose the most strategic counterfactual comparisons (Markman et al., 1993; Roese, 1994). "Counterfactual generation has functional value, and people tend to generate those counterfactuals that hold the greatest psychological value for them in a given situation" (Markman et al., 1993, p. 103). Downward comparisons (i.e., thinking about a worse outcome) are thought to provide comfort, whereas upward comparisons (i.e., thinking about a better outcome) are thought to improve future performance. Indeed, it has been shown that people who expect to perform again in the future are more likely to generate upward counterfactuals than those who expect to move on (Markman et al., 1993).

Although many counterfactual thoughts are doubtless strategically chosen in this way, such motivational considerations cannot account for the present findings. On the whole, the silver and bronze medalists at the Barcelona Olympics were at the peak of their athletic careers and therefore likely to continue to engage in similar high-level competitions in the future. From a motivational perspective, then, both groups should have made upward counterfactual comparisons in order to prepare for future contests. The asymmetry in counterfactual comparisons that we observed implies that many counterfactuals are imposed by the nature of the events experienced.

Indeed, Kahneman (1995) outlined a continuum of counterfactual thinking that ranges from "automatic" to "elaborative." Elaborative counterfactual processing is partly brought on through the exercise of choice, and its direction and intensity is influenced by the individual's motives and intentions. Automatic counterfactual thinking, in contrast, is "explainable largely in cognitive terms" (Kahneman, 1995, p. 376). The counterfactual thoughts that distinguish silver and bronze medalists shade toward the latter end of this continuum. Coming close to winning the gold, for example, appears to automatically activate frustrating images of having almost won it all.

We are not suggesting, of course, that finishing second or coming close to a cherished outcome always leads to less satisfaction than a slightly more modest performance. Finishing second is truly a *mixed* blessing. Performing that well provides a number of direct benefits that increase our well being – recognition from others, boosts to self-esteem, and so on. At the same time, it can indirectly lower satisfaction by the unfortunate contrast with what might have been. Thus, the inconsistent effect of finishing second is analogous to the "endowment" and "contrast" polarity that Tversky and Griffin (1991) claimed affects the hedonic significance of *all* experienced events. According to their analysis, any experience has a direct effect on well-being by what it brings to one's endowment – that is, the pleasure or pain derived from the event itself. But a person's experiences also have an indirect effect on well being by altering the adaptation level against which future experiences are contrasted. Their contrast (in which the event itself establishes a new standard against which future events are compared) is different than the one at work here (in which the events' proximity to a better outcome causes one to lose sight of what is and focus on what might have been). The core idea is the same, however. In both cases, the direct effect of the event itself is offset by a comparison process with the opposite effect, be it a comparison of future outcomes to the present, or the present outcome to a counterfactual alternative that was almost attained. . . .

An unresolved issue concerns the duration of the effects we have documented here. We have established that bronze medalists are happier than silver medalists in the short run, but does this effect hold up over time? As yet there are no data to answer this question. Nevertheless, one of the most noteworthy features of life's near misses seems to be their durability. Consider the account of finishing second that Nicholson Baker (1991) provides his wife:

[I] told her my terrible story of coming in second in the spelling bee in second grade by spelling *keep* "c-e-e-p" after successfully tossing off *microphone*, and how for two or three years afterward I was pained every time a yellow garbage truck drove by on Highland Avenue and I saw the capitals printed on it, "Help Keep Our City Clean," with that impossible irrational "K" that had made me lose so humiliatingly. (p. 70)

Or consider the case of Abel Kiviat, the 1,500-m silver medalist in the 1912 Olympics in Stockholm. Kiviat had the race won until Britain's Arnold Jackson "came from nowhere" to beat him by one-tenth of a second. "I wake up sometimes and say, 'What the heck happened to me? It's like a nightmare." Kiviat was 91 years old when he said this in an interview with the *Los Angeles Times* (cited in Tait & Silver, 1989, p. 351). It appears that thoughts about "What might have been" may plague us for a very long time.

36. Understanding Misunderstanding: Social Psychological Perspectives

Emily Pronin, Carolyn Puccio, and Lee Ross

Researchers in many subdisciplines of psychology have made their reputations cleverly documenting the various cognitive, perceptual, and motivational biases that systematically distort human judgment and inference. In this chapter, we explore some of the interpersonal and intergroup *consequences* of such biases. In particular, we consider the role these biases can play in creating, exacerbating, and perpetuating conflict between individuals and between groups.

One way in which biases contribute to conflict is obvious. When different people are subject to the influence of different biases, they are bound to think and feel differently about issues. And people who disagree with each other – indeed, even people who are reasonably like minded but attach different priorities to the problems they feel should be addressed or the actions they feel should be taken – are apt to frustrate each other's efforts and ambitions. There is, however, a second way in which biases fuel enmity that is less direct, but not less important. People and groups who disagree about matters of mutual concern not only interact in conflictual ways; they also *interpret*, and frequently *misinterpret*, each other's words and deeds. The nature of such misattributions, and their consequences, occupies most of our attention in this chapter. First, however, we begin by simply noting some well-studied cognitive and motivational biases and illustrating how they might foster interpersonal and intergroup enmity.

FROM INTRAPERSONAL BIASES TO INTERPERSONAL CONFLICT

Attention, Perception, and Assimilation Biases

Following Bruner (1957), legions of researchers have demonstrated that, in disambiguating stimuli, people "go beyond the information given." They perceive things as they have been led by experience or suggestion to expect them to be, and their perceptions are further biased by their hopes, fears, needs, and immediate emotional state. Investigators concerned with attitude change similarly challenged simple learning theory formulations by arguing that the recipients of persuasive arguments often prove to be *rationalizing* rather than *rational* animals, and as such are influenced less by logical rigor or objective evidence than by the interests and preconceptions that they bring to their task (see Katz, 1960).

Disagreements and misunderstandings about capital punishment, abortion policy, how to achieve peace in the Middle East, or the wisdom of trying a deposed political leader for war crimes, thus become inevitable. Even when (indeed, *especially* when) people earnestly attend to the facts and arguments offered by those on the "other side," their opinions become even more polarized. This "polarization" reflects the tendency for partisans to accept at face value arguments and evidence congruent with their interests and beliefs, while critically scrutinizing arguments and evidence that threaten those interests and beliefs (see Edwards & Smith, 1996; Ross & Lepper, 1980). Moreover, we suggest, such biased processing of information fosters harsh evaluations of individuals on the other side whose perceptions and arguments, in the eyes of the opposing partisan, appear biased and self-serving.

Intergroup enmity can also arise from simple availability and representativeness biases (Kahneman & Tversky, 1973; Tversky & Kahneman, 1974) – biases with which readers of this book are likely to be quite familiar. Once again, illustrative examples are commonplace. Estimates of the severity of social ills like poverty, unemployment, or discrimination are bound to be influenced by availability biases reflecting where one lives, whom one talks to, and what one reads. Our media-based notions of what a "representative" INS agent, follower of Islam, Texan, lesbian, or homophobe *looks* and *acts* like influence our expectations, and thus help determine which claims about particular group members we find credible or noncredible. They also determine whether accounts about individual deeds by group members are treated as stereotypical or dismissed as unrevealing aberrations. The present thesis is that blindness about the role that such biases play in shaping our own political views, and a penchant for seeing self-serving or ideologically determined biases in other's views, exacerbates group conflict.

Dissonance Reduction and Reactance

The dissonance researchers (Festinger, 1957; see also Aronson, 1969; Brehm & Cohen, 1962) showed unparalleled ingenuity in demonstrating the ways in which people rationalize their actions and reduce discrepancies in their belief systems. These social psychologists were not the first, of course, to appreciate the human capacity for rationalization. Students of the psychoanalytic tradition, and other canny observers who have noted correlations between political beliefs and individual or group interests, long ago recognized that capacity. What dissonance research highlighted that is relevant to the concerns of this chapter is the barriers to rational judgment and dispute resolution that are created by prior commitment, personal sacrifice, and perseverance in the face of earlier temptations to abandon a cause. Thus, Vietnam War veterans who were injured or held in POW camps and draft resisters who left the country or went to jail for their actions must either continue to disagree about the events of 30 years ago, and about the nature of patriotism and the appropriate limits of political dissent, or else pay a heavy psychic price. Our further contention is that such practitioners of dissonance reduction and rationalization are apt to make unwarranted inferences about each other's objectivity and honesty in facing the past and drawing lessons for the future – and to feel wronged and misunderstood by the rest of us who seem content to "move on" and adopt a more conciliatory view.

The veterans, moreover, are apt to think draft evaders were cowards and traitors who even today are unwilling or unable to face that "truth" about themselves. The draft evaders, conversely, are apt to believe that it is the veterans who persist in their delusions because they cannot bear the pain of "facing reality" by recognizing that their personal sacrifices, and the even greater sacrifices of their fallen comrades, were pointless. Both groups agree only that the rest of us have too readily forgotten that unhappy chapter in American history. This characterization of Vietnam veterans and draft resisters, like our previous characterizations of opposing partisans, anticipates another of the main points that we explicate and begin to document in this chapter. We argue that people readily recognize biases in others that they do not recognize in themselves, and as a result, they make overly negative attributions about others whose views and self-interested motives seem "conveniently" congruent.

Although less well known, and perhaps less intuitive, than dissonance reduction, the process of *psychological reactance* (Brehm, 1966; Brehm & Brehm, 1981; Wicklund, 1974) also belongs on our list of biases that create barriers to dispute resolution. Of particular relevance is the phenomenon we call *reactive devaluation*, whereby potential compromise offers or concessions become less attractive to the recipient as a consequence of the fact that they have been offered. In one study (Maoz, Ward, Katz, & Ross, 2000), Arab and Israeli university students evaluated peace proposals actually offered by the two sides in the latest round of Middle East negotiations. The participants all read exactly the same proposals, which were necessarily vague about exactly what kind of Palestinian state would emerge after the negotiation process was complete. What varied was purported *authorship*; that is, some respondents were told that the proposal under examination had been offered by the Israelis whereas others were told that it had been offered by the Palestinians. The results were dramatic. Purported authorship mattered more than the actual authorship and content of the proposal, so that when the proposals' purported authorships were reversed, partisans preferred the other side's proposal to their own.

In earlier studies of the relevant phenomenon (see Ross, 1995; Ross & Stillinger, 1991; Ross & Ward, 1995, 1996), the investigators manipulated not the authorship but the status (i.e., "on the table" versus "merely hypothetical" or "not yet offered") of proposals to end a conflict or disagreement. The result was a consistent one. Proposed concessions that seemed relatively attractive before they had been offered became significantly less attractive once put on the table. The attributional consequences that ensue from such devaluation are familiar, and unfortunate. The party receiving the proposal responds coolly, complaining that the proposed terms offer too little or came too late – a response that induces distrust and denunciation from the party offering it, thus further heightening the cycle of ill-will and intransigence.

Lessons from Prospect Theory

Prospect theory (Kahneman & Tversky, 1979, 1984) deals with normatively suspect decisions and preference orderings that arise from the way people deal with potential gains versus losses. Its predictions are highly relevant to interpersonal and intergroup negotiation because changes in the status quo that represent a prospective gain to one side may represent a prospective loss to the other side. Furthermore, because "losses loom larger than gains," parties should be reluctant to make agreements that require them to accept losses in order to achieve gains – especially under circumstances where the relevant losses are perceived as certain while the relevant gains are subject to uncertainty.

To our knowledge, no empirical research has examined *loss aversion* and *unwillingness to trade* (Kahneman, Knetsch, & Thaler, 1991) in the context of conflict and negotiation, but the unhappy scenario suggested by prospect theory is a familiar one to observers of interethnic or international conflict. In the Middle East, Northern Ireland, and other troubled parts of the world, longstanding adversaries remain deadlocked in a "hurting stalemate" (Pruitt, Rubin, & Kim, 1994), unwilling to risk a change in the status quo that seemingly would be mutually beneficial. In so doing, they fail to recognize that inaction, far from being a neutral or safe option, incurs not only the costs of deadlock, but also the risk of future deterioration in the situation. Perhaps even more importantly, the parties forfeit potential joint gains that could result from real peace and a truly cooperative relationship.

Although this scenario has not been explored in the laboratory, a study of actual tort case outcomes (Rachlinski, 1994) demonstrates that prospect theory axioms and utility functions can indeed be applied to consequential decisions made by sophisticated individuals engaged in conflict. The study revealed that plaintiffs, who face the prospect of gain – and thus should prefer certain outcomes that guarantee gain – proved to be "risk averse" (i.e., "settled" in cases in which their expected financial outcome would have been better if they had accepted the risks of trial). By contrast, defendants proved to be "loss averse" in that they opted to accept the risks of trial rather than accept a certain loss even when their expected outcome would have been better if they had agreed to the other side's pretrial settlement offer.

Our contention again is twofold. First, we argue that reluctance to trade concessions, coupled with a willingness to take foolish risks in order to avoid certain losses and refusal to take sensible risks in order to achieve prospective gains, operate not only in the courtroom, but also in labor negotiations, trade disputes, and territorial and self-determination conflicts that rage throughout the world. Second, we argue that the adversaries in question are inclined to defend their own "prudence" even while making harsh attributions about their adversaries' "intransigence."

Biases in Attributions Made about Self and Others

Two much-researched attributional biases directly affect interpersonal misunderstanding and enmity. The first bias involves people's tendency to underestimate the impact of situational or contextual factors on overt action, and as a result to make overly broad and overly "dispositional" attributions about other actors (see Ross, 1977; Ross & Nisbett, 1991; also Jones, 1979, 1990). The second bias involves the tendency for people to give greater weight to situational factors in assessing their own actions and outcomes than those of their peers (Jones & Nisbett, 1971; see also Gilbert & Malone, 1995). These attributional biases, we argue, leave the "losers" in the various struggles of our contemporary world (e.g., the homeless, workers victimized by the global economy, members of stigmatized minorities, and parties to ethnic strife) feeling doubly victimized. They feel victimized not only by the objective privations of their situations, but also by the assessments and suggested remedies offered by their victimizers and others who "do not understand the real situation." Furthermore, their own accounts of their travails and their proposals for redress are apt to provoke highly negative responses from those whose assistance they seek. These observers are apt to complain about the victims' "refusal to accept any responsibility for their circumstances" and "unwillingness to do anything to help themselves," and a downward cycle of misattribution and mistrust is likely to ensue that further compromises opportunities for collaborative problem solving.

Conflict can be exacerbated not only by misattributions about others, but also by biased assessments about the self. Consider the "better-than-average" effect (Alicke, Klotz, Breitenbacker, Yurak, & Vredenberg, 1995; Dunning, Meyerowitz, & Holzberg, 1989; Kruger & Dunning, 1999), whereby the majority of people believe that their abilities, performances, or attributes exceed those of the "typical" individual. Similarly, consider the tendency for actors to overestimate their own contributions to joint products (Ross & Sicoly, 1979). Such biases may be adaptive in fostering increased effort, enhancing self-efficacy, creating self-fulfilling prophesies of success (see Bandura, 1977; Dweck, 1986), and perhaps even in fostering mental and physical health (Taylor & Brown, 1988). Yet the same biases are apt to leave people feeling overworked, underappreciated, and undercompensated relative to the other parties with whom they transact their affairs. In any negotiations involving allocation of rewards, resources, and opportunities, individuals or groups showing such self-enhancement biases are likely to feel they have been denied outcomes commensurate with their entitlements and further denied the gratitude and recognition they deserve for their past forbearance.

In the two sections that follow, we pursue the discussion of attributional biases and perceptions of bias in self versus others in more detail. In so doing, we attempt to present a general conceptual framework that hinges on an account of "naive realism," and to offer some speculations and research results that build upon on this framework.

NAIVE REALISM: BIASED PERCEPTIONS AND PERCEPTIONS OF BIAS

We tend to resolve our perplexity arising out of the experience that other people see the world differently than we see it ourselves by declaring that these others, in consequence of some basic intellectual and moral defect, are unable to see things "as they really are" and to react to them "in a normal way." We thus imply, of course, that things are in fact as we see them, and that our ways are the normal ways. (Ichheiser, 1949, p. 39)

As Ichheiser suggested more than half a century ago, people are often aware that others do not share their view of the world and they are willing to account for the relevant disparity in viewpoints by citing particular biases. Indeed, in interpreting and predicting the behavior of their peers, people may be inclined to *overestimate* the impact of many of the shortcomings and biases that we reviewed in the opening section. The real source of misunderstanding and enmity arises from people's failure to recognize the operation of such biases in their *own* judgments and decisions. People, we argue, are inclined to hold the misguided conviction that they somehow see the world, and evaluate divisive issues, in a uniquely clear, unbiased, and "unmediated" fashion.

In this section, we introduce the more general issue of egocentrism and related failures in perspective taking. We begin by describing the well-documented "false consensus" effect, and reporting three simple demonstration experiments that highlight the particular difficulty that individuals face in separating their own experience of stimulus events from the nature of the events themselves. We then offer a more general account of "lay epistemology" that can lead people to make invidious distinctions in assessing their own objectivity relative to that of their adversaries or even their peers. We conclude by exploring implications of the layperson's epistemological bias for interpersonal and intergroup conflict.

Egocentrism and Other Failures in Perspective Taking

Piaget described the stages by which the child conquers his or her egocentrism and comes to recognize that different actors can have different perspectives on the same object or event (Inhelder & Piaget, 1958; Piaget, 1926, 1928; see also Flavell, 1963, 1985). As Piaget noted, all people of normal intelligence not only learn to recognize the existence of differences in perspectives, they even gain some skill at anticipating specific sources of perceptual, cognitive, or motivational bias. What most psychologists fail to emphasize in discussing Piaget's account of social development, however, is that this process never reaches fruition. Although some aspects of children's egocentrism disappear through maturation and experience, adults continue to show important limitations in perspective taking. Let us begin by exploring some of these limitations.

The False Consensus Effect

One manifestation of adult egocentrism has been termed the *false consensus effect* (Ross, Greene, & House, 1977). This effect involves an overestimation of the commonness of one's own responses and reactions. More specifically, it involves the tendency for people who make a given choice or hold a given conviction to see that response as more common and less revealing of personal attributes than do people who make the opposite response. In a particularly memorable false consensus demonstration by Ross, Greene, and House, students (participating in a study ostensibly concerned with the impact of "unusual media") were asked if they would be willing to walk around campus wearing a sandwich-board sign bearing a simple message (e.g., "Eat at Joe's"). The participants were also told that, if they preferred, they could simply opt to return on another day for a different study.

As anticipated, both those who agreed to wear the sign and those who declined thought that their response would be the more common, and less revealing, choice. In interpreting this result, Ross et al. anticipated a central thesis of the present chapter by suggesting that the participants' divergent estimates and inferences resulted from their differing *construals* of the situation they faced. Thus, to the extent that participants imagined that they and other potential sign-wearers would meet expressions of interest from peers and (when they explained their costume) admiration for their willingness to be a good sport, they agreed to don the sign and expected that only "uptight people with no sense of humor" would decline. Conversely, to the extent that they imagined that sign-wearers would face contemptuous snickers (and be given no opportunity to explain their task), they expected that only fools, showoffs, or patsies would comply.

A set of studies by Gilovich (1990) provided evidence for this "construal interpretation" of false consensus. First, he demonstrated that the items providing the strongest evidence for false consensus in an extensive questionnaire used by Ross et al. were precisely those items that allowed the most room for personal interpretation regarding the relevant choices. Gilovich then offered more direct evidence for the proposed mechanism. In one study, for example, he asked participants first whether they preferred music from the 1960s or the 1980s, and then what percentage of their peers would share that preference. The predicted false consensus effect was obtained. More importantly, further analysis revealed that the group preferring 1960s music and the group preferring 1980s music had generated different exemplars of the two musical eras – exemplars whose differing merits were recognized readily by subsequent raters. Participants expressing a preference for 1960s music generated a more agreeable sample of 1960 performers and tunes, and those expressing a preference for 1980s music generated a more agreeable sample of 1980s performers and tunes. In other words, the two groups construed the respective objects of judgment quite differently, and then failed to recognize or make adequate allowance for this construal difference in estimating the preferences of their peers.

"Childish" Games

A special and extreme case of false consensus occurs when we try to communicate information that is familiar and meaningful to us, but not to the individual whom we are trying to enlighten. A famous *New Yorker* cartoon on the subject presents an initial "bubble" in which we see the clear and orderly cognitive map of a man giving well-rehearsed directions to a fellow motorist, followed by a second bubble in which we see the vague and confused map of the man who is hearing those directions. Although the cartoon does not complicate matters by offering a third bubble showing us how the direction-giver imagines that his map has been received, the implication is clear; that is, the direction-giver fails to appreciate the difficulty of the relevant decoding task and the resulting difference between the two maps. As a result, he leaves the encounter overly optimistic about the fate of the motorist whom he has tried to enlighten. Three studies conducted in our laboratory illustrate how difficult it can be to appreciate the perspective of a peer who is facing a task or problem, especially when our own "privileged" vantage point dominates our experience of the interchange.

Encoding and Decoding "Musical" Tapping. Dissertation research by Elizabeth Newton (1990) in our laboratory showed how difficult it can be to separate one's own "privileged" experience of a stimulus from the features of that stimulus that are available to other perceivers. Participants in the study were assigned to one of two roles: "tappers" or "listeners." Each tapper was given a list of 25 well-known songs ranging from "America the Beautiful" to "Rock Around the Clock," and asked to choose a song whose rhythm they then tapped out to a listener. The tapper was then asked to assess the likelihood that his or her particular listener would successfully identify the title of the song, and also to estimate the proportion of students who would be able to do so when given the same listening opportunity. Listeners tried first to identify the tune, and then to estimate the proportion of their peers who would succeed or fail at the same task.

Before considering Newton's results, let us contrast the subjective experiences of the two types of participants. Imagine yourself first as the tapper. As you rhythmically tap out the tune you have chosen, you inevitably "hear" the melody and even the words of the song. Indeed, many of Newton's tappers reported hearing the full orchestration, complete with rich harmonies between strings, winds, brass, and human voice. Now imagine yourself as the listener. For you, there are no notes, words, chords, or instruments – only a series of monotone taps. You cannot even tell whether the brief, irregular periods of silence between taps should be construed as sustained notes or musical rests between notes. This difference in perspectives and in experiences is easy to stipulate. The question posed by the study involves the capacity of the tappers to distinguish their private embellishments from the impoverished stimuli they were presenting to their listeners – or their ability to make adequate allowances for the relevant differences in perspective and experience when called upon to estimate their listeners' success.

Newton's results provided clear evidence for the "inadequate allowance" thesis. Tappers' predictions of listener success ranged from 10 to 95%, with an average of 50%. Listeners, by contrast, correctly identified only three tunes in the entire study – a success rate of less than 3%! In a separate study, Morris, Heath, and Jost (1999) replicated the Newton result and explored the interpersonal attributions made by the tappers. In particular, the investigators showed that tappers attributed the listeners' failures to inattentiveness or lack of effort rather than to the objective difficulty of their task.

Such results prompt us to begin considering other instances in everyday life in which analogous failures in perspective taking occur and contribute to misattributions and inappropriately harsh interpersonal inferences. Consider, for example, a teacher's attempt to set aside her own knowledge and mastery of the material she is teaching in order to appreciate the perspective of a student being exposed to the information and ideas for the first time. All too often, we suspect, the result is a student who sees the teacher as unclear and impatient and perhaps also a teacher who sees the student as inattentive, unmotivated, or even stupid (see Hinds, 1999; also related research by Keysar, 1994; Keysar, Ginzel, & Bazerman, 1995.)

Figuring Out "My World." A second demonstration (Puccio & Ross, 1999), designed with the results of Newton's musical tapping study very much in mind, dealt again with a situation in which people who know the message or intent behind a series of "clues" make guesses about the insights gleaned by the recipients of those clues. In this study, the experimenter introduced participants to the following problem:

I'm going to tell you about "My World," and about some of the things that are and are not a part of my world, some of the things that people in my world do and do not do, and some of the things that they like and dislike. There is one characteristic or principle that unifies all of the things that are part of, or that are done and liked, in my world – a principle that distinguishes them from the things that are not part of it or are not done or liked there.

The experimenter then proceeded to offer verbally a series of 25 clues, each consisting of a statement such as, " In my world, there are *trees* and *grass*, but not *flowers*," or "In my world, people like *swimming* and *racquetball*, but not *snowboarding* and *skating*." After each set of five clues, the participants were asked if they had figured out the operative rule and also to estimate what percentage of the people in the room facing the same task had figured it out.

Prior to administering the instructions and clues, the experimenter assigned participants either to the role of "solvers," who undertook the task described,

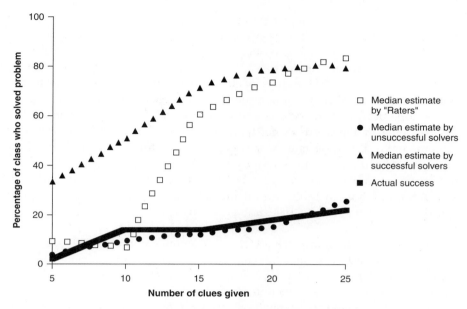

Figure 36.1. Actual versus estimated success in the "My World" problem.

or to that of "raters." In contrast to solvers, raters were preinformed of the solution, which was that only objects or activities that contained *double letters* belonged in "My World." Like the solvers, the raters were asked after each set of five clues to estimate the proportion of the class who had solved the problem at that point in the proceedings. Raters were also asked to indicate the point at which they thought they personally would have solved it, had they not been preinformed. The question of concern to us, of course, was whether in making these estimates the raters would be able to separate their own knowledge and subjective experience as they offered the clues from the information they actually were providing to the aspiring problem solvers.

Our results provided clear support for the inadequate allowance thesis (see Fig. 36.1). Although only 21% of the class solved the problem on the basis of the 25 clues provided, the raters' median estimate was close to 83%. Moreover, every single rater said that there was at least a 50% chance or better that they personally would have solved it, and 42% said that they were *certain* that they would have done so. It is further interesting to note that successful solvers estimated a success rate of 78% for their peers – that is, a percentage almost as high as the 83% figure estimated by raters who had been told the solution in advance. By contrast, participants who failed to find the solution were quite accurate in their predictions; they estimated that only 25% of their peers would succeed where they personally had failed.

As in the musical tapping study, what we observe is a particularly strong version of the false consensus effect. Once one knows the message being conveyed by the clue giver, that message (regardless of whether one initially discerned it for oneself) appears very obvious. Moreover, one loses the ability to appreciate the perspective of someone who does not know it. The double letters in each clue seem to "jump out," and it is nearly impossible to imagine them not doing so. The "obviousness" of the clues, of course, is far from apparent to the naive problem solver, who is entertaining countless possible theories (many of which prove to be dead-end conjectures about the nature of the objects and activities connoted by the words rather than the nature of the words themselves). Reminiscent of the subjects in Morris et al.'s (1999) follow-up to the musical tapping study, the raters in our study typically thought that peers who did not solve the problem were likely to be "bad at word games, puzzles, riddles, etc." Again, a failure to appreciate the impact of the relevant difference in perspectives led participants to make unwarranted negative inferences about their peers.

Two Views of Romantic "Break-Ups." Asymmetry in assessing the obviousness of a message can make its influence felt with particular poignancy in the context of intimate relationships – especially ones that have deteriorated. In a simple study of this phenomenon, Pronin and Ross (1999) explored the perceptions of young men and women reflecting on the most recent case in which they had ended a relationship with someone else, and the most recent case in which it was the other person who had ended the relationship. What participants rated, in a suitably counterbalanced research design, was the clarity of the communications that occurred in both instances. As predicted, our participants perceived their own efforts in initiating the break-up as significantly clearer, and less characterized by "mixed signals," than the efforts of the person who initiated the break-up with them. Furthermore, the specific words participants recalled having spoken when they initiated the break-up were less ambiguous (according to neutral raters) than the words they recalled their partner having spoken in breaking-up with them.

The participants in our break-up study thus appeared to have some difficulty in separating what that they thought they had said, or perhaps what they felt and had intended to convey, from that which they had actually communicated to the other party. Borrowing a metaphor from the tapping study, we might say that in initiating break-ups, participants were frustrated by their ex-partner's inability or unwillingness to "hear the music," but resentful of their partner's failure in musicianship when they were the ones "facing the music."

Tenets of Naive Realism

The limitations in perspective taking that we have been discussing reflect a kind of worldview or lay epistemology that can appropriately be termed *naive realism*. That is, people persist in feeling that their own take on the world enjoys particular authenticity, and that other actors will, or at least should, share that take, if they are attentive, rational, and objective perceivers of reality and open-minded seekers of truth. It is not that people are unaware that their own views have been shaped by their own, perhaps atypical, experiences. On the contrary, there clearly are cases in which we recognize that our views and priorities reflect our unique status or our unique experiences. Yet in such cases, we are inclined to feel that our particular vantage point (e.g., that of a devout Christian, the child of an alcoholic, a volunteer at the local battered women's shelter, or the CEO of a Fortune 500 company) has been particularly *enlightening*. By contrast, we see others' unique status or unique experiences as a source of inevitable and understandable biases that distort their objectivity and lead them to unwise or unreasonable positions on the relevant issues.

This epistemological stance can be summarized in the form of the follow-ing three specific propositions or tenets (Ross & Ward, 1996) that, for ease of exposition, we express in first-person terms:

1. I see stimuli, issues, and events as they are in objective reality, and my social attitudes, beliefs, preferences, priorities, and the like follow from a relatively dispassionate (indeed, unmediated) apprehension of the infor-mation or evidence at hand.
2. Other rational social perceivers generally share my judgments and reac-tions – provided that they have had access to the same information that gave rise to my views, and provided that they too have processed that information in a reasonably thoughtful and open-minded fashion.
3. The failure of a given individual or group to share my judgments and reac-tions arises from one of three possible sources: (1) the individual or group in question may have been exposed to a different sample of information than I was (in which case, provided that the other party is reasonable and open-minded, the sharing or pooling of information will lead us to reach agreement); (2) the individual or group in question may be lazy, irrational, or otherwise unable or unwilling to proceed in a normative fashion from objective evidence to reasonable conclusions; and (3) the individual or group in question may be biased (either in interpreting the evidence or in proceeding from evidence to conclusions) by ideology, self-interest, or some other distorting influence.

Some Implications of Naive Realism

The first two tenets of naive realism deal with the tendency for people to believe that they see the world objectively, and that other reasonably attentive and objective perceivers will thus share their views. Relevant evidence is pro-vided by research (see Neale & Bazerman, 1983; Thompson & Lowenstein, 1992) showing that disputants are overly optimistic in predicting the assessments of third-party judges and arbitrators. The question of more immediate interest, however, involves the consequences that ensue when people come to recognize that others do not share their views; that is, what happens when it becomes ap-parent that others have accepted different evidence as credible, or interpreted ambiguous evidence differently? What happens when people discover that others hold very different priorities about which societal ills demand immediate attention no matter what the cost, and which ills are instead inevitable, bearable, or only appropriate to tackle after a careful cost–benefit analysis? How does the naive realist make sense of such differences in feelings and responses? It is to these questions, and to the implications of the third tenet of naive realism, that we now turn.

Overconfidence about Ability to Persuade Others

As naive realists, our initial interpretation of disagreements is apt to be relatively charitable. We are inclined to assume that the other party has not yet been exposed to the "way things are," or has not yet been privy to the "real" facts and considerations. Indeed, we may even be so charitable as to concede that the other party may be privy to additional facts and considerations that might actually change our own views. In either case, this charitable interpretation of disagreement leads us to be confident – indeed, *over*confident – that rational, open-minded dialog, in which information is freely exchanged, will lead to agreement or at least to an appreciable narrowing of disagreement. This optimism is likely to be short-lived, however, especially in the social and political arena. Repeated attempts at dialog with those on the other side make it quite clear that they rarely yield to our attempts to enlighten them, and that they rarely present new facts and arguments that persuade us to change our minds.

Given this state of affairs, less charitable interpretations of disagreement become inevitable, especially when our adversaries are persistent and outspoken and the issue is consequential. We conclude that our adversaries are biased by self-interest, ideology, or some other distorting top-down influence. We assume that these biases distort either their construal of relevant information or their capacity to proceed rationally and cogently from facts to conclusions. We feel that while we have proceeded in a logical bottom-up manner, from the available facts to reasonable construals and beliefs, those who hold opposing beliefs have done just the opposite (i.e., they have proceeded in top-down fashion, from preexisting motives and beliefs to biased interpretation). Indeed, a close examination of matters serves to sustain rather than allay such suspicions. We note that the rich favor lower taxes while the poor favor a higher minimum wage. We see the religious zealot interpret scientific evidence with injurious prejudice and an eye to the scriptures, while the atheist dismisses personal testimony about the power of prayer. What we fail to detect is the congruity between our own views and interests and the way *we* interpret evidence.

The Hostile Media/Mediator Effect

As noted at the outset of this chapter, opposing partisans exposed to the same set of "objective" facts interpret those facts differently as they fill in details of context and content, infer connections, and use idiosyncratic scripts and schemas in the search for coherence and meaning. Cognitive biases lead them to see and remember a reality that is consistent with their beliefs and expectations, while motivational biases cause them to see what is consistent with their needs, wishes, and self-interest. Through such information-processing biases, two opposing partisans who encounter the same facts, historical accounts, scientific evidence, or even witness the same events can find additional support for their preconceptions. Thus, advocates and opponents of capital punishment, asked by Lord, Ross, and Lepper (1979) to review a pair of studies providing mixed results on the deterrent effects of capital punishment, later reported themselves to be even more polarized in their views than before. Similarly, the Princeton and Dartmouth football fans in Hastorf and Cantril's (1954) study who viewed the film of a then-recent hard-fought contest between their teams, seemingly saw two different games – each with a different balance of misdeeds by the two teams.

Pursuing the theme of this chapter, it is worth considering how the relevant partisans in those two studies would have responded to each other's assessments of the evidence or events in question, or to the assessments of a supposedly neutral third party. Suppose that a capital punishment proponent in the Lord et al. study heard a capital punishment opponent claim that the balance of evidence in the two studies they had read justified an end to legal executions, or suppose that some social scientist claimed that the two studies were equally probative and urged both partisan groups to moderate their positions accordingly. By the same token, suppose that the Hastorf and Cantril partisans were asked about the assessment of the game offered by the other school's commentators, or to rate the impartiality of the referee who had tried to assess penalties in an evenhanded manner. In both studies, we suspect, the partisan groups would feel that their counterparts were either lying for strategic reasons or guilty of bias in their perceptions and recollections. We further suspect that, in both instances, the two opposing groups would perceive a lack of objectivity on the part of the supposedly neutral adjudicator.

The conjecture that partisans' biased information processing would lead them to perceive bias on the part of disinterested third parties led Vallone, Ross, and Lepper (1985) to explore the *hostile media effect*. Capitalizing on longstanding, passionately held, differences of opinion about the Arab–Israeli conflict, these investigators presented pro-Israeli and pro-Arab partisans with identical samples of major network television coverage of the Beirut massacre. The reactions of these viewers showed that biased perceptions can indeed give rise to perceptions of bias (Fig. 36.2A). Pro-Arab and pro-Israeli viewers alike were convinced that the media had favored the other side, that their own side had been treated unfairly, and that the media's biases reflected the self-interest and ideology of those responsible for the program. There was also evidence, reminiscent of Hastorf and Cantril, that the groups in effect "saw" different programs (see Fig. 36.2B). Whereas pro-Israeli viewers claimed that the reports contained a greater percentage of material that was hostile to Israel than favorable, pro-Arab viewers made just the opposite assessment. Perhaps the most telling result

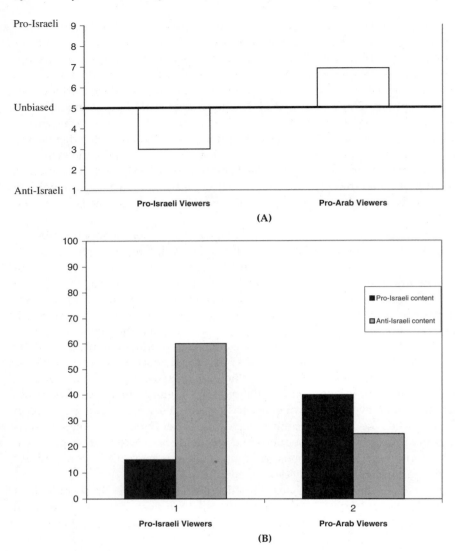

Figure 36.2. (A) Perceived bias in media sample. (B) Estimated percentage of pro-Israeli versus anti-Israeli content in media sample.

was both sides' concern that neutral viewers of the program would be swayed in the direction of their adversaries.

Could the same processes that lead partisans to perceive the media as hostile also lead them to hold a similarly jaundiced view of third-party mediators who are attempting to apply fair and consistent standards and give both sides a fair chance to make their case? A role-play study by Morris and Su (1999) confirmed this unhappy scenario. Neutral third parties trying to mediate a conflict between a "programming manager" and a "contract administrator" were perceived, by both parties, as having been more receptive and having devoted more time to the concerns of the other side.

The False Polarization Effect

In many contemporary social debates, such as those surrounding affirmative action, abortion policy, or welfare reform, the opposing partisans seem well aware that they construe facts and arguments differently from their adversaries. What exacerbates conflict, again, is the way the parties account for these differences. Both sides in the conflict believe that although their own views reflect the complexity, ambiguity, and contradictions of objective reality, the views of the other side have been dictated and distorted by ideology, self-interest, and other biases. These attributions in turn lead the conflicting partisans to see the other side as extreme, unreasonable, and unreachable. Assumptions about top-down processing may also lead partisans to overestimate the ideological consistency and extremity of those on their *own* side of the conflict. The result is an overestimation of the relevant construal gap between the modal views of the two sides and an underestimation of the amount of common ground that could serve as a basis for conciliation and constructive action. A schematic illustration of the relevant *false polarization effect*, one which uses circles and triangles to represent the views of opposing partisans, is presented in Fig. 36.3. This inaccurate and overly pessimistic assessment of differences in views becomes especially difficult to reverse when pessimism about the possibility of finding common ground makes the antagonists reluctant to engage in the type of frank dialogue that could reveal common interests and beliefs.

A pair of studies by Robinson, Keltner, Ward, and Ross (1995) has provided evidence for this false polarization effect. One study dealt with "pro-choice"

Figure 36.3. Actual versus perceived differences in partisan group views.

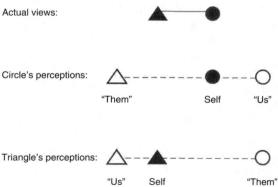

versus "pro-life" views relevant to the ongoing abortion rights debates (e.g., assumptions about which circumstances most often prompt decisions to abort and about the positive versus negative consequences likely to result from a tightening of abortion restrictions). The second study dealt with "liberal" versus "conservative" perceptions about specific events in the racially charged Howard Beach incident, in which an African American teenager was fatally injured by an automobile while running from a group of white pursuers (e.g., perceptions regarding the intentions and motives of the various participants in the incident).

Both studies, as one might expect, provided evidence of actual construal differences on the part of the "opposing" parties, and both studies further showed that the partisans greatly overestimated the magnitude of these differences. Nonpartisan respondents, it is worth noting, similarly tended to overestimate the ideological extremity and consistency of the two sides. They too underestimated the common ground in the opposing partisans' assumptions, beliefs, and values.

In one of several replications of the false polarization effect, Bastardi, Ross, and Lepper (1996) examined the real versus presumed "gender gap" in attitudes and beliefs concerning date rape, sexual harassment in the workplace, sex discrimination, and related concerns. As our conceptual analysis predicted, both men and women overestimated gender differences in attitudes; and both sexes overestimated the extremity and consistency not only of the views held by the opposite sex, but also of the views held by members of their same sex. Underestimation of common ground by opposing partisans was also demonstrated in a study by Robinson and Keltner (1996), which focused on instructors' views about the proper balance of traditional and nontraditional works in foundational English literature courses. They found that although "traditionalists," and to some extent "revisionists" as well, suspected that there would be little overlap in the reading lists they favored, the two groups' actual lists overlapped considerably. In other words, the chasm that they thought to be huge was actually rather narrow, and with some cooperation, easily bridgeable.

Thus far in accounting for the false polarization effect, we emphasized the role of naive realism and resulting presumptions of ideological consistency, extremism, and bias. Research in our laboratory suggests an additional, more social source of the phenomenon. During contentious discussions, many individuals choose to remain silent, and thereby leave misperceptions intact; those who do not remain silent generally hesitate to reveal any ambivalence in their beliefs. When addressing peers who seem to be on the other side of the issue, partisans seek mainly to defend their position rather than share doubts or complexities in their beliefs, lest their "concessions" give their adversaries "ammunition." When speaking with individuals whom they perceive to be on their own side, they similarly hesitate to reveal their doubts or appreciation for valid arguments of the other side – in this case, for fear that such ambivalence will be disapproved of by their peers, whom they (erroneously) assume to be fully resolved and free of ambivalence about the matter.

If such erroneous assumptions and self-presentation concerns play a role in perpetuating false polarization, a common prescription for helping adversaries move toward agreement may be ill-advised. Asking opposing partisans to sit down together, and inviting them to share their views and the reasons they hold them, might actually prove counterproductive, because such exchanges are apt to reinforce rather than weaken presumptions of extremity and intractability.

This hypothesis led us (Puccio & Ross, 1998) to conduct a series of studies contrasting two potential techniques for attenuating the false polarization bias. One technique simply invited partisans to express and defend their own position on a divisive issue, whereas the other technique essentially required them to express the best arguments they saw on the "other side." This *express-other-position* condition was designed to debias (or even counterbias) the partisans' social presentations, obliging them to reveal the very complexities, doubts, and uncertainties in their views that they might normally conceal, and in so doing to offer their peers and adversaries alike a more accurate portrait of their real views.

The results of our studies confirmed these predictions. Partisans in the express-own-position condition in these studies showed the expected false polarization effect, markedly overestimating the gap between the positions of the two sides. By contrast, participants in the express-other-position condition (and, in one study, those in a third condition in which they expressed both positions) hardly overestimated this gap at all. It is unsurprising, perhaps, that participants saw peers and adversaries as less extreme after those individuals had articulated and even acknowledged the other side's arguments. What is noteworthy, however, is that interpersonal assessments based on such artificially biased presentations proved to be more accurate than assessments based on the participants' unconstrained presentations of their actual views.

ACTOR–OBSERVER DIFFERENCE IN PERCEPTIONS OF BIAS

Implicit in our discussion of biases contributing to conflict and misunderstanding is the assumption that people recognize or presume the influence of such biases more readily when they are evaluating other actors' responses than when they are evaluating their own. While we have thus far emphasized attributions involving self-interest or ideological bias, the phenomenon in question is broader. That is, laypeople may be well aware of most of the biases that social psychologists and judgment and decision-making researchers have documented over the last few decades. But the sophistication that laypeople show as "intuitive psychologists" may make its influence felt primarily in social perception rather than self perception.

There is, of course, a long history of research comparing and contrasting the processes of social perception and self perception (Cooley, 1902; Mead, 1934; Bem, 1972; Nisbett & Ross, 1980, Chapter 9). Most relevant to present concerns, perhaps, is the suggestion by Jones and Nisbett (1971) that a variety of motivational, perceptual, and informational factors lead people to be more *dispositionist* – that is, more inclined to infer stable traits and dispositions while overlooking the determinative influence of situational or contextual factors – in the attributions they make about other people's behavior than in the attributions they make about their own behavior. Andersen (1984; also Andersen & Ross, 1984) suggests a source of actor–observer differences in attributions that is particularly relevant to our present concerns. That source involves the access that actors enjoy to their private thoughts, feelings, and interpretations of stimuli. In particular, Andersen showed that people give heavy weight to such nonobservable events in stipulating the characteristics that are most revealing or even defining of them, but not in stipulating the characteristics that are revealing or defining of others.

In a somewhat similar vein, Kahneman and Lovallo (1993) stressed the role of private experience in distinguishing between "inside" and "outside" perspectives in decision making. Actors' predictions about their outcomes and prospects are likely to be heavily influenced by the access they enjoy to their own plans, goals, level of motivation or commitment, and by their awareness of the countermeasures they will take should any of several obstacles arise. Observers who lack such insider information, by contrast, are likely to ignore particular features of the case at hand. They give little weight to the actors' expressions of confidence or even to the specifics of their plans and intentions, and give much heavier weight than the actor to base-rate information about the outcome of similar undertakings by this actor and others.

Consistent with this analysis, Buehler, Griffin, and Ross (1994, Study 5) found that although actors consistently commit the *planning fallacy* by underestimating how long it will take them to complete a given task, observers do not. Indeed, when provided with a description of a task and both the actor's self-predicted completion time and relevant base-rate data (i.e., the actor's memories of completion times for relevant previous tasks), observers tended to *over*estimate how long the actor would take. However, when the observers were exposed to the actor's insider perspective (i.e., actor's mental plans for completing the task), their estimates about completion time approached the actor's own (unduly optimistic) estimates.

We note again, however, that our present concern lies not with differences between actor and observer assessments, or even with actor–observer differences in accuracy. Rather, our concern lies with the perceptions that people have about the status of their own assessments versus those offered by other people. In particular, as implied in our account of naive realism, we contend that people perceive their own views and sentiments about the world, and its problems and opportunities, to be more on target – and less susceptible to the various biases that afflict human judgment – than the views and sentiments of their peers.

There is a sense in which this proposition about invidious comparison of own versus other's assessment of the world is a truism. In any particular assessment, one must feel that one's particular assessment is the most reasonable one given the information at hand (otherwise, one presumably would adjust that assessment to make it more reasonable). Furthermore, because other actors necessarily offer some assessments that differ from our own, we are bound to feel that they are less wise and realistic than we are, at least until unfolding events impose a more objective and data-based standard for such comparisons.

Assessments made about the self are particularly pertinent to our present discussion. In such assessments, we are apt to regard the products of our own insider perspective as a gold standard against which assessments made by others can be measured. By contrast, in the case of assessments made about others, we are not apt to regard those individuals' self-assessments as the standard against which our assessments or those of all other observers should be measured.

Consider the case of a female professor who gives the highest grade in the class to an unusually handsome young man who sat close to the front of the room, gazed intently at her throughout lectures, responded eagerly when she posed questions to the class, often came to her office to seek clarification of particular lecture points, and wrote an exceptionally long and interesting paper in fulfillment of the only formal course requirement. From the professor's insider perspective, the student deserved the highest grade both because of his paper and because of his exemplary in-class contributions. Moreover, she is aware of specific steps she took to guarantee objectivity in grading and of the strong value she places on fairness. Now consider another student in the same class, one who sat quietly toward the back of the room and earned a lower grade in spite of what she felt to be a great deal of effort, and who personally has been unimpressed with the professor's "star pupil" in a couple of conversations. This student is apt to be less certain about the professor's objectivity. Furthermore, if the unimpressed peer makes her views about the male student known to the professor, or complains that the professor is a "sucker" for a handsome face and sycophantic behavior, and has succumbed to the "halo effect" in her grading of essays, the professor is very likely to believe that she understands the *real* source of the female student's protests – perhaps better than the student herself.

Our characterization of naive realism and the biased assessments that people offer of their own and others' capacity to discern the "truth" goes beyond matters of perceived objectivity. Even when an individual recognizes that her views are in part the product of her unique status or particular set of life experiences, the individual is apt to feel that her status and experiences have been a source of *enlightenment* rather than error.

A female administrator who defends the university's decision to eliminate the men's wrestling team and add a woman's water polo team is apt to face a charge from her male colleagues that she has been biased by her gender. She, in turn, may acknowledge that her own experiences as a woman in university administration (and her earlier experiences as a star intramural softball player, with no opportunity to compete on a varsity team) played a role in shaping her present views and perhaps account for the passion with which she defends them. Yet she would vehemently deny that she is showing the kind of gender bias that her male counterparts showed for years in favoring an all-male athletic program. On the contrary, she would insist that her college and professional experiences help her to understand the magnitude of the disadvantages that women in general and women athletes in particular have faced. (At the same time, however, she may be relatively skeptical and sense the "same old" male gender bias when the wrestling coach talks of his own earlier frustrations as a student wrestler who received less support than athletes in revenue-producing sports, and insists that male wrestlers are currently being unfairly deprived of a valuable experience in order to meet an unfair gender quota.)

By the same token, members of various ethnic groups sometimes feel that only a member of their own group really understands the issues that affect them. However, they feel that members of other ethnic groups are hopelessly, if understandably, biased by their particular status and experiences, and cannot be given "veto power" over policies that affect them.

In concluding this chapter, we first review evidence that people make invidious distinctions between their ability to render enlightened judgments about others and others' ability to render enlightened judgments about them. We also explore some specific hypotheses about the source of such invidious distinctions. Then we turn our attention to lay perceptions about susceptibility of self and others to specific types or sources of bias – both in the context of everyday judgment and decision making and in the context of intergroup conflict.

Perceptions of Intrapersonal and Interpersonal Insight

Our discussion of naive realism and insider versus outsider perspectives gives rise to the following four hypotheses about lay perceptions of self-knowledge and knowledge of others (see Pronin, Kruger, Savitsky, & Ross, 2001):

1. People perceive their own self-knowledge and insight to be more accurate and complete than that of other people.
2. People perceive their knowledge of other people to be more accurate and complete than other people's knowledge of them.
3. People perceive the discrepancy between their self-knowledge and other people's knowledge of them to be greater than the corresponding discrepancy between other people's self-knowledge and their knowledge of those other people.
4. People perceive their group's knowledge of other groups to be more accurate and complete than other groups' knowledge of their group.

In an initial exploration of the first three of these hypotheses, Pronin et al. (2001) simply asked roommates to complete a survey. In this survey, respondents evaluated how well they knew themselves, how well they knew their roommate, how well their roommate knew them, and how well their roommate knew himself or herself, with respect to domains ranging from specific traits (e.g., competitiveness) and behaviors (e.g., frequency of looking in the mirror) to more general knowledge about thoughts, feelings, and motives. The results provided evidence for all three hypotheses. In virtually every domain, people rated their self-knowledge to be superior to their roommate's self-knowledge, and their knowledge about their roommate to be greater than vice versa. They also indicated that although they sometimes knew their roommates as well as, if not better than, their roommates knew themselves, there were no domains in which their roommates matched or exceeded the participants' own self-knowledge. Figure 36.4 shows a summary of results from this study and three related studies reported in the same article, which we describe later. Further analysis suggested that participants were most skeptical of the accuracy of their roommates' self-knowledge relative to their own when the traits in question were negative (e.g., messiness, susceptibility to flattery, inability to handle stress) rather than neutral or positive (e.g., risk-taking, giving weight to moral considerations), and when they pertained to private thoughts and feelings rather than overt behavior.

Subsequent studies by Pronin et al. (2001) revealed that people show this asymmetry not only in assessments of intrapersonal and interpersonal insight on the part of roommates with whom they interact on a daily basis, but also in assessments of how much they learn about strangers, and vice versa, from observing small, dubiously informative samples of behavior. In one such study, previously unacquainted individuals were given a chance to get to know each other by taking turns asking relatively innocuous personal questions of their choosing (e.g., "Where do you hope to see yourself in ten years?" or "What would your ideal vacation be?"). Participants generally believed that they learned more about the other person from the brief encounter than the other person learned about them. This perception was revealed both in ratings of how much each learned about the other (in terms of traits, preferences, etc.) and also in the length of written descriptions about what they had learned (see Fig. 36.4).

A similar result was obtained in a third study in which participants both furnished completions of word fragments and read the completions of another participant. Participants saw their "partner's" responses as more self-revealing than they did their own (see Fig. 36.4). They typically saw their own responses as either situationally determined (that is, as suggested by the fragment, or cued by a previous response) or as an essentially random and uninformative reflection of their momentary state of mind, while they saw their partners' responses as reflective of personal traits or dispositions. In other words, they seemed well aware of the folly involved in attaching much significance to their spontaneous and rather haphazard answers, but less aware of the folly involved in making inferences about their partners on the basis of the same type of information. As in the brief encounter study, they recognized their partners' susceptibility to bias, misinterpretation, and especially over-interpretation when their partners made inferences about them on the basis of the meager information provided,

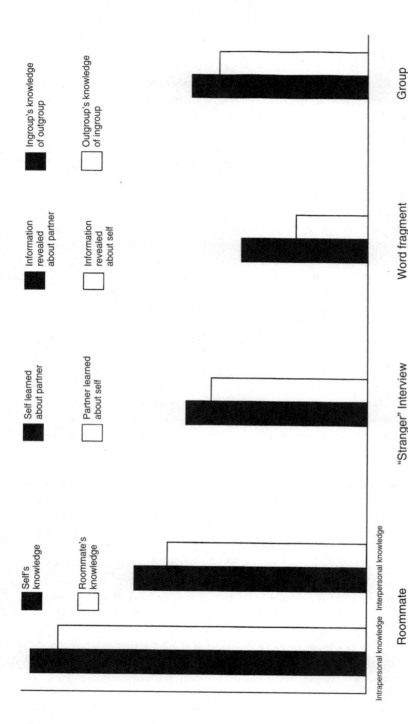

Figure 36.4. Asymmetric assessments of self and other knowledge across four studies. Different scales and different measures were used in the different studies. The histogram was adjusted to compensate for these differences, but otherwise reflects both the size of the relevant self–other differences and the absolute amounts of knowledge in the relevant domain. Pairs of bars are significantly different.

but they did not recognize the likelihood that they would be equally susceptible to those failings when they made inferences about their partners on a similar basis.

Interestingly, participants in this study showed this self–other asymmetry only when they assessed the diagnosticity of their partners' completions *before* providing and assessing their own completions. In other words, the tendency to make overly confident trait inferences about the actor whose responses one was considering seemed, at least in this study, to be forestalled by the prior opportunity to ponder the determinants of one's own responses.

In a final study, Pronin et al. (2001) found evidence for similar biases and asymmetries in perceptions of accuracy and bias at the *group* level. That is, individuals claimed that the political groups to which they belonged (e.g., liberals versus conservatives, pro-choice versus pro-life advocates) knew and understood their counterparts better than vice versa (see Fig. 36.4). The same tendency was also true for men's and women's perceptions about each other's insights, although the relevant asymmetry in this case was masked somewhat by the fact that both sexes agreed that women understood men better than men understood women. The women simply thought this gap was greater!

What accounts for the impression or belief that we know them better than vice versa? One possibility relevant to our present concerns, suggested by Quattrone and Jones (1980), is the conviction that the members of other groups (i.e., "they") are simply more homogeneous and therefore more easily characterized than the members of our group (i.e., "we"). This conviction, in turn, may arise from a tendency to view other groups' responses (just as we view other individuals' responses) as more dictated by self-interest, ideology, or other top-down influences than those of our own group. In any case, there is ample research evidence that individual group members believe that members of the other group fail to appreciate their group's diversity or variability, and see them in a stereotyped manner (Linville, Fischer, & Salovey, 1989; Park & Judd, 1990). Indeed, a pilot study conducted in our own laboratory (Pronin & Berger, 1999) suggests that students who live in two residences subject to campus-wide stereotypes (i.e., as the "jock frat" and "hippie house") each believed that their house would recognize the diversity in the responses of residents of the other house more than vice versa. A more specific source of the belief that they are more misinformed and less knowledgeable about us than vice versa, is further suggested by this pilot study. Respondents believed that inhabitants of the other house gave more credence to stereotypes and propaganda about their house than vice versa.

In the concluding section of this chapter, we essentially generalize the foregoing argument. We document the fact that people think that other people in general (and those who disagree with them in particular) are more subject than themselves not just to stereotyping and effects of propaganda, but to many of the other biases that psychologists and other social scientists have increasingly devoted attention to over the past few years. We also explore some sources of this perceived asymmetry in an attempt to understand why it occurs, and therefore when it is most likely to be pronounced and when it is likely to disappear.

Assessing Biases in Others versus Self

In a questionnaire study, we (Pronin, Lin, & Ross, 2002) asked Stanford students the extent to which they and the "average American" displayed a variety of different inferential or judgmental biases that our conceptual analysis led us to believe would be subject to invidious self–other comparisons. The list included self-serving or ego-defensive attribution of success versus failure, dissonance reduction after free choice, the halo effect, biased assimilation of information to preexisting beliefs or preconceptions, reactive devaluation of offers and compromises received from the "other side," unwarranted perception of media hostility to one's group or cause, and an inclination to underestimate the role of situational as opposed to dispositional determinants of behavior. Each bias was described in a couple of simple jargon-free sentences of the following sort:

Psychologists have claimed that people show a 'self-serving' tendency in the way they view their academic or job performance. That is, they tend to take credit for success but deny responsibility for failure; they see their successes as the result of personal qualities, like drive or ability, but their failures as the result of external factors, like unreasonable work requirements or inadequate instruction.

As anticipated (Fig. 36.5), the students claimed that they personally displayed each of the relevant biases to a lesser degree than the "Average American," with the average discrepancy constituting about one standard deviation on the relevant 9-point scale.

We further obtained survey evidence that the phenomenon in question was neither restricted to the perhaps atypically smug population of Stanford students nor a reflection of some highly general tendency for people to deny all personal shortcomings. This second survey used a sample of travelers awaiting flights at the San Francisco Airport. It included not only the items used in our Stanford survey, but also additional items pertaining to personal limitations or biases that would likely be at least as salient to the actor as the observer (e.g., fear of public speaking, procrastination, the planning fallacy) and therefore, according to our conceptual analysis, an unlikely source of invidious self-other comparisons. The results of this study both replicated our earlier results and supported our prediction about when the phenomenon should and should not occur. Thus, although our airport sample again made invidious self–other comparisons regarding the tendency to engage in ego-defensive attributions, commit the fundamental attribution error, act in a self-interested manner, and *overestimate* media hostility against the positions or causes they favor, they did not see themselves as less afraid of public speaking, less guilty of procrastination, or less susceptible to the planning fallacy.

The results of a third survey in this series further attest to the inability of people to perceive biases in themselves – even in the face of an explicit prompt about

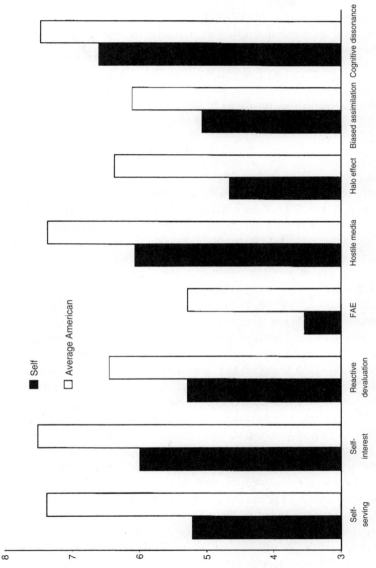

Figure 36.5. Perceptions of bias in self versus the "average American." Ratings were provided on 9-point scales (1 = no bias; 9 = strong bias). Pairs of bars are significantly different. FAE = Fundamental attribution error.

the prevalence of that bias. In this study, participants first rated themselves relative to their Stanford peers on a variety of dimensions (i.e., dependability, objectivity, consideration for others, snobbery, deceptiveness, and selfishness). As is generally the case in such studies, the great majority (87%) showed the familiar tendency to rate themselves more positively than their peers with respect to these characteristics (see Alicke et al., 1995).

After offering these ratings, however, participants were informed on the next page of the questionnaire that

Studies have shown that on the whole people show a "better than average" effect when assessing themselves relative to other members within their group. That is, 70–80% of individuals consistently rate themselves "better than average" on qualities that they perceive as positive and, conversely, evaluate themselves as having "less than average" amounts of characteristics that they believe are negative.

They were then asked to indicate what they thought the "most accurate, valid, and objective measures available" would show about them. Given this opportunity to acknowledge the likelihood that they had succumbed to the bias in question, only 24% of the participants who had shown the relevant self-enhancement bias did so. That means that 76% of the participants indicated that they expected the "most accurate and object measures available" to show either that they had rated themselves perfectly accurately, or that they had rated themselves too *modestly!*

Underestimating Bias in the Self. As Wilson, Hodges, and La Fleur (1995) provocatively noted, "People are often unaware of their own unawareness" (p. 17). Four biases that we mentioned earlier seem to hinge at least in part on such lack of awareness. The most general of these biases is the much researched and highly robust *false consensus effect* (Ross, Greene, & House, 1977). As noted earlier, this bias seems to depend on the individual's failure to recognize that his or her estimates of response consensus (and the appropriate interpretation to place on the two response alternatives) have been heavily influenced by the particular way in which those alternatives are construed. The individual who shows the false consensus effect fails to recognize that other respondents might construe those alternatives differently, and as a result make a different choice; indeed, the individual fails to recognize that any construal is involved.

Other more specific biases can be seen as special cases or by-products of the false consensus effect. One example is the *third-person effect* (Davidson, 1983; see also Gunther, 1995; Innes & Zeitz, 1988), which refers to the tendency for people to believe that other respondents, on average, are more influenced than they by "propaganda" or other types of information that they feel ought to be dismissed out of hand. Presumably, individuals who see a message as persuasive and reasonable are apt to assume that other recipients of the message will feel likewise (and deem acceptance of the relevant message as normative rather than indicative of susceptibility to bias). At the same time, individuals who see the message as unpersuasive and hateful may be inclined to fear that others, especially others who have a vested interest in accepting such a message, will view it uncritically and succumb to its influence. The net effect of combining estimates that others will be "appropriately" persuaded whenever we are persuaded, and estimates that at least some others will be "inappropriately" persuaded, even when we are not, should be clear – that is, an overall tendency to overestimate the message's impact. (See Hoorens & Ruiter, 1996, for evidence that people do not see themselves as less amenable to persuasion than their peers, just as more discerning in evaluating the value of the messages.)

Research by Armor (1998) provides more direct evidence about perceived and actual objectivity of self versus others. In one study, this investigator introduced participants to a number of problems used to demonstrate normative violations in judgment and inference (for example, "base-rate neglect" or violation of the "conjunction rule"). As predicted, participants both underestimated their susceptibility to the relevant inferential shortcomings and perceived themselves to be less susceptible than their peers. Once again, this tendency for people to overestimate their own objectivity is perhaps inevitable, because people would presumably change their assessment in the appropriate direction in any instance in which they recognized that the response of a peer (or any other particular response available to them) was more objective or normative than their own. To make accurate assessments of our objectivity, we must recognize and make allowance for the fact that (notwithstanding our impressions about individual assessments we are making) we are likely in many instances to be unobjective, and in error – in fact, to be in error just as often as our peers who seem to be making less reasonable assessments than we are every time their assessments differ from our own.

Overestimating Bias in Others.   There is ample evidence that people recognize that their peers are subject to a variety of biases. Researchers have demonstrated people's awareness of others' susceptibility to the actor versus observer bias in the attribution process (Krueger, Ham, & Linford, 1996), the false consensus effect (Krueger & Zeiger, 1993), the correspondence bias (Van Boven, Kamada, & Gilovich, 1999), the influence of self-interest (Epley & Dunning, 2000; Kruger & Gilovich, 1999; Miller & Ratner, 1998), and the motivating power of extrinsic rewards (Heath, 1999).

Not only are people aware of the judgmental biases we have listed, there is evidence that people may actually overestimate their magnitude, especially when the potentially biased judgments are being made about *them*. Thus, Van Boven, Kamada, and Gilovich (1999) found that actors in an experiment assumed that observers would make even more extreme dispositional inferences about them than proved to be the case. As the authors note, people assume that those evaluating their responses will be "no-holds-barred" dispositionalists, and that they alone assign appropriate weight to person and situation in their attributions.

A completely different and more motivational set of naive theories seem involved in lay assumptions and overestimations when it comes to assessing the impact of ego-defensive or self-serving biases. In one such set of studies, Kruger and Gilovich (1999) found that participants were overly "cynical" in their predictions about how others would allocate responsibility for successes and failures. That is, they believed others would claim too much credit for success and too little blame for failure, when in fact individuals tended to allocate too much personal responsibility for both types of outcomes (see also Ross & Sicoly, 1979).

This tendency for people to see others as more self-serving than they are may occur in part because lay explanations for attributions that seem congruent with the actor's self interest are overly motivational or at least overly simplistic. (See Nisbett & Ross, 1980 for an account of nonmotivational determinants of such bias; see also Dunning, Perie, & Story, 1991, and Kunda, 1987, for more sophisticated accounts of the sometimes subtle interaction between motivational and cognitive determinants.) In any case, introspection about our own assessments regarding our actions and attributes are apt to reveal no simple motive (or at least no simple conscious motive) to think well of ourselves at all costs, and the feedback most of us get from our friends is apt to suggest that we are just as inclined to be too hard on ourselves as too easy.

Evidence that people see themselves as less guilty of self-serving attributional biases than others comes from a study by Friedrich (1996), who simply described the self-serving bias and asked participants how subject they were to it relative to the average person. Participants rated themselves as significantly less prone than others to this bias. It is important to note, however, that people are not completely unaware that their own positive self-assessments reflect idiosyncratic cognitive processes. In a study by Krueger (1998), the positive correlation between people's assessments of the desirability of a particular trait and the extent to which they ascribed that traits to themselves (see also Dunning, Perie, & Story, 1991) was accompanied by the participants' recognition that their self-ascriptions would be *less* strongly correlated with *others'* ratings of trait desirability than their own ratings. Krueger's participants, we suspect, would have denied showing motivated self-enhancement, and have claimed that they simply try to behave in a manner consistent with the values they personally deem important. Indeed, by their own criteria, they may well have felt that other people were less enlightened than themselves about which traits are important (or even that other people's ratings of trait importance were biased by their knowledge of their own personal strengths and shortcomings).

Not only do we view others' attributions as more self-serving than our own, we have similar views about behavior and general motives for action. In a provocative set of experiments on the "myth of self-interest," Miller and Ratner (1998) demonstrated that individuals judge others according to a naive theory that attaches great weight to naked self-interest. For example, they found that participants overestimated other people's tendency to be influenced by economic incentives in deciding whether or not to donate blood and overestimated other people's tendency to be influenced by their group membership (as a woman or a smoker) in determining their views about abortion or smoking restrictions. Furthermore, they expected others to behave in a manner consistent with self-interest regardless of whether they reported that their own behavior would be similarly guided. In a related line of research, Heath (1999) has shown that people assume others' on-the-job motivation is rooted in extrinsic financial incentives, while they report their own motives to be more rooted in intrinsic incentives such as the opportunity to learn new skills.

In a final set of studies to be considered, Epley and Dunning (2000) showed that people judge others' pro-social behavior in given situations (e.g., cooperating in a Prisoner's Dilemma Game, donating money to a nonprofit organization) to be more self-serving and less purely altruistic than their own. Interestingly, and in contrast to the Miller and Ratner findings cited earlier, individuals showing this "holier than thou" effect were more accurate in their predictions regarding others than in predictions regarding themselves; that is, rather than underestimating others' altruism, they overestimated their own. Both sets of findings, however, seem to reflect the difference in insider versus outsider perspectives that we have discussed at several points in this chapter. In the Miller and Ratner study, the actors' insider perspective makes them aware that self-interest is not the sole or even the principal motive for their own choices, but this perspective offers no corresponding insight about the private feelings and motives of others. In the Epley and Dunning study, the actors apparently give too much weight to the "holy intentions" that underlie the resolution of their dilemmas, and in so doing these actors lack the objectivity of outside observers who consider other possibilities as well.

In a sense, the actor is like a detective with more clues than the observer, and with different clues enjoying high perceptual or cognitive salience. To the extent that the clues in question are in fact probative, the insider has the advantage over the outsider. To the extent that these clues are more salient than they are probative, the insider is at a disadvantage to any outsider who relies on simpler theories and more general base-rate assumptions. But in either case, the actor feels that his or her perspective is the one that affords greatest accuracy. And in either case, the actor is apt to feel frustrated or even angry with those who dispute the authenticity and special insight of his or her view of "reality."

37. Assessing Uncertainty in Physical Constants

Max Henrion and Baruch Fischhoff

Accurate estimates of the fundamental constants of physics, such as the velocity of light or the rest mass of the electron, are central to the enterprise of science (Pipkin & Ritter, 1983). Like any measurements, they are subject to uncertainties from a variety of sources. Reliable assessments of this uncertainty are needed (1) to compare the precision of different measurements of the same quantity; (2) to assess the accuracy of other quantities derived from them; and, most crucially, (3) to evaluate the consistency of physical theory with the current best measurements. Thus, as Eisenhart pointed out, "A reported value whose accuracy is entirely unknown is worthless" (1968, p. 1201).

It is not unusual to encounter individual examples of errors in measurements of physical quantities that turn out to be disconcertingly large relative to the estimated uncertainty. One well-known case was in Millikan's oil-drop experiment in 1912 to determine e, whose result turned out 15 years later to be off by 0.6%, or three standard deviations, due to reliance on a faulty value for the viscosity of air (Cohen, Crowe, & Dumond, 1957). A more recent example concerns measurements of $|v_{+-}|$, the parameter that measures the degree of violation of CP (charge–conjugation–parity) invariance. The six measurements prior to 1973 agreed reasonably, but more accurate measurements since then differ consistently by about seven standard deviations from the pre-1973 mean, a discrepancy that remains unexplained in terms of experimental procedure (Franklin, 1984). Such extreme cases may be exceptions, but they raise the more general question of how well on the average reported uncertainties reflect actual errors, an issue on which there has been little systematic study (Roos, Hietanen, & Luoma, 1975). Here, we present evidence from historical measurements of a range of physical constants to illustrate the scope of the problem of underestimation of uncertainty. A wider awareness of such results may help in interpreting reported uncertainties, and may have some important educational implications.

A comprehensive assessment of uncertainty cannot rest solely on statistical analysis. Unavoidably, it involves a considerable element of subjective judgment. Therefore, we first review some recent findings of cognitive psychology from laboratory studies of human judgment under uncertainty. After examining

This is an edited version of a paper that first appeared in the *American Journal of Physics*, 54, 791–798. Reprinted with permission. Copyright © 1986, American Association of Physics Teachers.

evidence from measurements of physical constants, we discuss possible explanations for these problems in the light of the psychological literature, and explore the prospects for alleviating them.

THE PSYCHOLOGY OF JUDGMENT UNDER UNCERTAINTY

The premise of laboratory studies of human judgment is that all judgments are governed by a set of core cognitive processes (Tversky & Kahneman, 1981; Kahneman, Slovic, & Tversky, 1982). If those can be understood in experimental settings, then reasonable speculations can be made about human performance in the real world (Fischhoff & Whipple, 1981; Morgan, Henrion, & Morris, 1981). This literature reveals both strengths and weaknesses. When people have the explicit training or there has been the opportunity to receive clear and prompt feedback, people can assess many aspects of uncertain processes. For example, weather forecasters in the United States provide assessments of the probability of precipitation that are probabilistically *well calibrated*: It rains on about 70% of the occasions on which they forecast a 70% probability of rain (Murphy & Katz, 1983). They have developed this ability through years of hands-on experience, with guidance from computer models, with ample feedback, and within an institution that rewards them for candor (rather than, say, for exuding confidence or avoiding firm commitments). In less favorable circumstances, however, people often lack an intuitive feel for probabilistic processes, relying instead on mental *heuristics* (deterministic rules of thumb) to guide their judgments. Although often useful, these rules can lead to predictable biases.

The intuitive assessment of uncertainty has proven to be especially problematic (Lichtenstein, Fischhoff, & Phillips, 1982). People seem insufficiently sensitive to how much they know, so that changes in knowledge are accompanied by inappropriate changes in confidence. The most common problem is *overconfidence*. A common way to assess the precision of an uncertain quantity is by a subjective confidence interval, indicating a range within which the assessor believes the true value has, say, a 98% chance of falling. The *probabilistic calibration* of a set of such judgments for different quantities may be measured by comparing the assessed probability for the interval with the fraction of times the true value lies within it. Cases in which the true value (once known) turns out to fall outside the assessed confidence interval may be termed "surprises." The *surprise index* is the percentage of 98% confidence intervals for which the true value is a surprise. Having significantly more than 2% surprises indicates overconfidence, in the sense of underestimating the range of possibilities. Conversely, too few surprises means underconfidence. Another measure of calibration is the *interquartile index*, the percent of judgments for which the true value lies between the assessed 25th and 75th percentiles. An interquartile index that is much less than 50% also indicates overconfidence. The overwhelming result in laboratory studies with nonspecialist assessors has been intervals that are too tight, reflecting overconfidence: Typically the surprise index is 20 to 40%

instead of the ideal 2%, and the interquartile index is 30 to 40% instead of 50% (Lichtenstein et al., 1982).

The important role of probabilistic judgment is coming to be recognized in several areas involving risk analysis, including medicine, toxicology, and nuclear safety [see, e.g., Raiffa, 1968; Greene & Bourne, 1972; U.S. Nuclear Regulatory Commission (USNRC), 1981; National Academy of Sciences (NAS), 1983]. The few studies of judgments in such real-world contexts outside the psychologist's laboratory suggest that the laboratory findings of overconfidence may generalize to situations of practical importance (see, e.g., Hynes & Vanmarcke, 1976). However, such evaluations have been rare. An evaluation of the uncertainty estimates for physical constants should therefore be of interest to the study of probabilistic judgment in general, as well as to the practice of physics. . . .

MEASURES OF CALIBRATION

One can obtain some empirical insights into the calibration of a set of assessments by comparing reported uncertainties with the variability among the measurements. Suppose each experiment i, for $i = 1, 2, \ldots N$, reports an estimate x_i with standard error σ_i, and $\bar{x}$ is the group mean, weighted inversely by the variances. The sum of the squares of the normalized residuals, $h_i = (x_i - \bar{x})/\sigma_i$, should be distributed as the chi-squared statistic with $(N - 1)$ degrees of freedom, assuming the errors are independent and normally distributed with the reported standard deviations. This statistic can then be used to test the appropriateness of these assumptions.

A related measure, the Birge ratio, R_B (Birge, 1932), assesses the compatibility of a set of measurements by comparing the variability among experiments to the reported uncertainties. It may be defined as the standard deviation of the normalized residuals:

$$R_B^2 = \sum_i h_i^2/(N - 1). \tag{1}$$

Alternatively, the Birge ratio may be seen as a measure of the appropriateness of the reported uncertainties. If the uncertainty assessments are independent and perfectly calibrated, the expectation of R_B is 1. If R_B is much greater than 1, then one or more of the experiments has underestimated its uncertainty and may contain unrecognized systematic errors. Such insensitivity to systematic error is a sign of overconfidence. If R_B is much less than 1, then either the uncertainties have, in the aggregate, been overestimated or the errors are correlated.

UNCERTAINTY IN c

The velocity of light, c, is perhaps the most measured fundamental physical constant (Pipkin & Ritter, 1983), starting with Galileo's unsuccessful attempts,

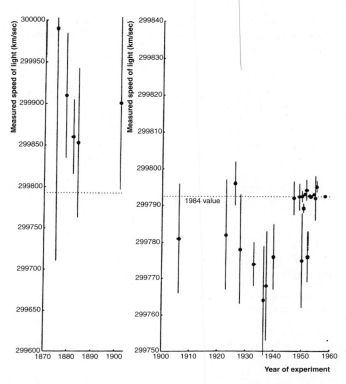

Figure 37.1. Measurements of the velocity of light; 1875–1958. Results are as first reported, with correction from air to vacuum where needed. The uncertainties are also as originally reported, where available, or as estimated by the earliest reviewers. Error bars show standard error (s.e. = 1.48 × probable error).

using assistants flashing lanterns on neighboring hills. Figure 37.1 displays the results of all measurements between 1875 and 1958 with reported uncertainty from several major surveys (Froome & Essen, 1969; Taylor, Parker, & Langenberg, 1969; Birge, 1932, 1942; Rush, 1955). The vertical bars represent the standard error according to the original experiment or earliest reviewer. The horizontal dashed line is the 1984 value of 299,792.458 km/s.

The Birge ratio for the entire set of 27 measurements with errors relative to the 1984 value is 1.42. The probability of finding such large variability by chance is less than 0.005, assuming that the errors were normally distributed with the reported standard deviations. If the standard deviations of the discrepant studies fully express the respective investigators' uncertainties regarding their estimates, then, on average, those uncertainties must be significantly underestimated.

Over time, both the reported uncertainty and the actual error of these estimates have been reduced enormously. There was, however, no significant

Table 37.1. Calibration Statistics for Measurements of Physical Constants

Quantity	Date	Statistic				
		N^a	R_B^b	Pr^c	IQ^d	SI^e
c	1875–1941	13	1.47	0.01	23%	8%
c	1947–1958	14	1.32	0.05	57%	14%
c	1875–1958	27	1.42	0.005	41%	11%
G	1798–1983	14	1.38	0.025	41%	29%
μ_p'/μ_n'	1949–1967	7	1.44	0.05	14%	14%
α^{-1} High accuracy		24	2.95	(0)	21%	38%
α^{-1} Low accuracy		14	1.26	0.10	64%	7%
$\Omega_{ABS}/\Omega_{NBS}$	1938–1968	7	0.40	0.995	100%	0%
Particle lives		92	1.26			9%
Particle masses		214	1.24			6%
Particle total		306	1.24			7%
$S_{10}(h/1.1)$			1.24		44%	6%
Recommended values	1928–1973	40	7.42	(0)	22%	57%
Well-calibrated normal distribution			1.00		50%	2%

[a] N Number of measurement analyzed.
[b] R_B Birge ratio (standard deviation of normalized residuals).
[c] Pr Probability of getting Birge ratio that large by chance if the normalized residuals have independent unit normal distributions.
[d] IQ Interquartile index: Percentage that falls between assessed 25th percentile and 75th percentile, or within 0.675σ.
[e] SI Surprise index: Percentage that falls outside assessed 98% confidence interval, or outside 2.33σ.

corresponding improvement in the Birge ratio, which was 1.47 for measurements up to 1941 and 1.32 since 1947 (top of Table 37.1). For both periods, the variability was significantly greater than one would expect, indicating unduly tight uncertainty estimates.

These changes in accuracy over time were accompanied by changes in the direction of error. From 1876 to 1902, the measurements overestimated the value by about 70 km/s on the average. From 1905 to 1950, they underestimated it by about 15 km/s on the average. This change in the mean caused deBray to suggest that the speed of light was not constant but decreasing by about 4 km/s/year. In 1934, Edmondson proposed that it might be varying sinusoidally with a period of 40 years. Discounting these claims, Birge (1942) argued c has a constant value that the overconfident uncertainty estimates too frequently failed to include. In 1941, he adjusted a set of recent estimates with untreated systematic error, producing corrected values with a Birge ratio of 0.544. Birge concluded, "Thus, after a long and, at times, hectic history, the value for c has at last settled down into fairly satisfactory 'steady' state" (1942, p. 101).

Unfortunately, as illustrated in Fig. 37.2, his confidence turned out to be premature. Just 8 years later, the recommended value had shifted by 2.4 of his 1941 standard deviations (Eisenhardt, 1968). This 1950 value, too, was soon

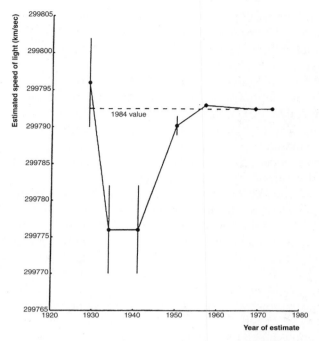

Figure 37.2. Recommended values for the velocity of light; 1929–1973.

supplanted, by a value different by more than 2 of its standard deviations. Once again, shifting estimates prompted the suggestion that c might be changing, this time increasing (Rush, 1955). One can only speculate whether better calibrated assessments of uncertainty (showing that the varied estimates were compatible with one another) would have forestalled such paradigm-shattering proposals. Table 37.1 summarizes these data in terms of various calibration statistics, including the Birge ratio, interquartile index, and surprise index. All indicate overconfidence. For measurements of c, there are too few values between the 0.25 and 0.75 quartiles (41% instead of 50%) and too many surprises (11% instead of 2%).

UNCERTAINTY IN OTHER CONSTANTS AND RECOMMENDED VALUES

The remainder of Table 37.1 summarizes similar analyses for other physical constants, including the gravitational constant G, the magnetic moment of the proton μ'_p / μ'_n, two sets of measures of the inverse fine structure constant, α^{-1}, and the ratio of the absolute ohm to the ohm maintained by the National Bureau of Standards, $\Omega_{ABS} / \Omega_{NBS}$. Table 37.1 reveals a similar pattern of overconfidence in all cases but the last. This shows a Birge ratio of significantly less than 1.0 and an interquartile ratio of 100%, results we return to later.

The "particle lives" and "particle masses" entries in Table 37.1 represent 92 measurements of Kaon and hyperon lifetimes and 214 measurements of meson resonance masses taken from the Particle Data Group's biennial *Review of Particle Properties* (Roos et al., 1975; Rosenfeld, 1975). Their thorough scrutiny of all published experimental measurements results in the rejection of about 40% on grounds of suspect assumptions, poor-quality work, unreported errors, or gross inconsistency with other results. Nonetheless, the Birge ratio of 1.24 and surprise index of 6% of the 306 combined results indicate a significant degree of overconfidence in the remaining uncertainty assessments.

Periodically, reviewers propose "recommended values" for physical constants after careful consideration of all the most precise measurements. The diligence of these analyses and the incumbent obligation to confront the inconsistencies among studies should make them particularly sensitive to uncertainty. Figure 37.2 showed the residual overconfidence in such reviews for the velocity of light. Figure 37.3 shows comparable results for five other fundamental constants derived from a series of six reviews between 1952 and 1973 (Cohen et al., 1955, 1957; Taylor et al. 1969; Dumond & Cohen, 1953; Cohen & Dumond 1965; Cohen & Taylor, 1973). In most cases, the best-guess value at each revision was well outside the range of possibilities defined by the uncertainty estimates for the preceding evaluation period. For example, the 1963–1969 shift was 3 to 5 1963 standard deviations for all five of these constants. Table 37.1 (next to last line) gives calibration indices for these same five constants for eight reviews from 1929 to 1969, with residuals calculated relative to 1973 estimates (Cohen et al., 1955, 1957; Taylor et al., 1969; Birge, 1929, 1942; Dumond & Cohen, 1953; Cohen & Dumond, 1965; Cohen & Taylor, 1973). The surprise index of 57% indicates that current estimates would have come as a surprise to earlier reviewers in more than half the cases. The 1969 review acknowledges these problems, and provides graphs similar to Fig. 37.3 to caution readers to be skeptical (Taylor et al., 1969).

SOURCES OF OVERCONFIDENCE

In several sets of carefully analyzed measurements of physical constants, we found consistent replication of a robust finding of laboratory studies of human judgement: Reported uncertainties are too small. How could this apparent overconfidence arise? Experimental studies of human judgment have shown that such biases can arise quite unintentionally from cognitive strategies used in processing uncertain information. However, there are two possible ways in which such effects might be caused by deliberate decisions by the scientist.

One concerns the procedures chosen to assess the uncertainty. The recommended practice in physics is to consider all possible sources of systematic uncertainty when reporting results. However, without specific guidelines regarding what to consider and explicit recognition of the subjective elements in uncertainty assessments, one cannot be sure how comprehensively individual

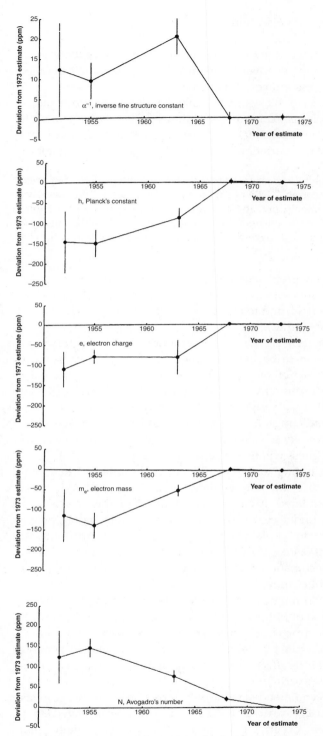

Figure 37.3. Recommended values for fundamental constants; 1952–1973.

scientists have examined the uncertainty surrounding their own experiments. Conceivably, some of the apparent overconfidence reflects a deliberate decision to ignore the harder-to-assess sources of uncertainty.

A second possible source of bias is that, unlike laboratory experiments on judgment, which can take great care to ensure that subjects are motivated to express their uncertainty candidly, real-world settings create other pressures. Taylor et al. (1969) suggest that variations in attitude leads some investigators to

cautiously assign unreasonably large errors so that a later measurement will not prove their work to have been "incorrect." Others tend to underestimate the sources of systematic error in their experiments, perhaps because of an unconscious (or conscious) desire "to have done the best experiments." Such variation in attitude, although out of keeping with scientific objectivity, is nevertheless unavoidable so long as scientists are also human beings. (p. 20)

In principle, none of these problems should affect the compilations of recommended values. These analyses are intended to be comprehensive, to consider reporting practices in the field, and to capture the state of knowledge (not just the precision of particular studies).

The factors that seem to have encouraged overconfidence in laboratory studies of judgement also seem to be likely candidates for having encouraged overconfidence in the estimation of physical constants. One such factor is the difficulty of thinking of reasons why one's best guess might be wrong (Koriat, Lichtenstein, & Fischhoff, 1980). Supporting reasons typically come to mind more readily than contradicting ones. If ease of recollection is taken as an indicator of frequency (Tversky & Kahneman, 1973), the preponderance of reasons supporting the best guess will tend to be overestimated.

A second factor contributing to overconfidence is the unequal treatment of such confirming and disconfirming evidence as is discovered. When discrepant results are encountered, it could mean that either the new data or the old database contain undetected systematic errors. Unfortunately, people have a considerable ability to "explain away" events that are inconsistent with their prior beliefs (Nisbett & Ross, 1980). The data elimination and adjustment procedures that precede estimation of recommended values are natural places for disproportionate skepticism regarding unexpected results to emerge. One documented example of "trimming" (i.e., excessive zeal in eliminating outliers) emerged in an examination of Millikan's laboratory notebooks for his oil-drop experiment. Of the 107 oil drops he observed, he excluded from publication 49 that seemed discrepant, despite his claim that he reported all his observations (Franklin, 1981). This had little effect on the best estimate of e, but increased the apparent precision of the experiment.

Having a preexisting recommended value may particularly encourage investigators to discard or adjust unexpected results, and so induce correlated errors in apparently independent experiments. The result would be initially small Birge ratios, unduly tight confidence intervals, and the exclusion of discrepant data that later prove to be more accurate than included ones. This can explain what Franklin (in press) has termed the *bandwagon effect* [e.g., the tendency for the measurements of the speed of light (in Fig. 37.1) to cluster around particular values at different periods]. In The large Birge ratio (2.95) for high accuracy measurements of α^{-1} (Table 37.1) may be due to the fact that those measurements were actually derived from experiments designed to measure other quantities, so that discrepancies in the implied value of α^{-1} would have been less obvious to the original investigators. However, measurements of the ratio of the absolute ohm to the as-maintained ohm ($\Omega_{ABS}/\Omega_{NBS}$) have a natural anchor at unity (i.e., assuming they are equal), which could explain the unusual degree of agreement, evidenced by the Birge ratio of 0.40.

IMPROVING UNCERTAINTY ASSESSMENT

In order to reduce the need for judgment in selecting data for producing recommended values, several attempts have been made to develop mathematical procedures for selecting and averaging measurements. Statisticians have long sought more robust estimators, such as trimmed means, that use all useful information without being unduly sensitive to outliers. However, in tests with real data, more sophisticated estimators provide only marginal improvements over simple averages (Stigler, 1977). Roos et al. (1975) describe a maximum likelihood technique based on their initial observation that the adjusted residual errors for particle properties had a broad tailed Student distribution. This was used in the *Review of Particle Properties* from 1976 to 1980, but was dropped after subsequent distributions of residuals differed in form (Trippe, 1983). There have also been attempts to develop algorithms for estimating the fundamental physical constants that deal better with apparently discrepant data. However, after tests with historical data, Taylor concluded that thoughtful and conscientious judgment about which data to exclude is still much more important than the choice of algorithm (Taylor, 1982).

It is no easy matter to eliminate judgmental biases (Lichtenstein et al., 1982). A categorical recommendation to treat all results equally would, on average, give undue credence to inaccurate observations and bad research. Nor is simple exhortation to "think harder" likely to prove any more useful here than it has in laboratory experiments on judgment. What is needed are ways to think more effectively. If the judgmental aspect of assessing uncertainty in physical measurements is explicitly acknowledged, then several techniques based on insights from psychological research may be helpful (Fischhoff & Whipple, 1981; Morgan et al., 1981, 1984; Spetzler & Staël von Holstein, 1975).

One approach is to encourage a broader search for relevant considerations, both supportive and disconfirming, and an unbiased evaluation of those considerations. For example, referees might be asked to scrutinize the account of an experiment blind before knowing its outcome and whether it affirmed prior expectations (Slovic & Fischhoff, 1977). To overcome the problem of anchoring on an initial best guess, investigators can be pressed to search for reasons why they might be wrong (Koriat, Lichtenstein, & Fischhoff, 1980). One device to encourage that search is to focus attention on extreme possibilities, for example, asking, "Imagine that, ten years hence, today's best estimate proves to be off by four standard deviations; how could you explain it?" Additional prompts may come from reading "horror stories": case studies describing major unsuspected errors in past experiments.

A second approach is to decompose the holistic judgement of overall uncertainty into its component sources of potential systematic errors, each to be estimated separately with the best available elicitation procedure (Fischhoff & Whipple, 1981; Morgan et al., 1981, 1984; Spetzler & Staël von Holstein, 1975). This can be aided by checklists covering each component of the measurement apparatus, each auxiliary quantity, and each theoretical assumption and approximation employed in the calculations.

Wherever analysis of reported uncertainties reveals a systematic bias, users of the measurements may use this information to readjust the original reports so as to improve calibration. Along these lines, the Particle Data Group expands the standard deviation whenever the Birge ratio is greater than unity among measurements of the same quantity (Rosenfeld, 1975; Particle Data Group, 1982). Their procedure usually produces stable recommended values for particle properties; however, it somewhat exaggerates the uncertainty by ignoring the possibility that some fluctuations of R_B above 1 are purely by chance. Roos et al. (1975) describe another procedure for readjusting the standard errors, based on the empirical distribution of the residuals they had observed for the particle properties.

The basis for such readjustments must be secondary analyses, such as those given here, showing probabilistic miscalibration in the estimates of uncertainty for previous similar measurements. In using such data, it is important to bear in mind that miscalibration reflects, not properties of the physical quantities themselves, but the nature of the procedures and judgmental processes used in selecting data and assessing uncertainty. Thus they are likely to vary with the training of the experimenter, the familiarity of the experimental techniques, and the maturity of the field, among other things. Compiling such data for wider classes of measurements can permit analysis of the importance of these factors. Even if uncertainty estimates are not explicitly readjusted, empirical calibration information could be helpful for anyone who uses measurements and recommended values for physical constants in their work. Even a rough estimate of overconfidence could help one interpret the significance of apparent discrepancies between measurements.

Another approach to improving uncertainty assessment is education designed to get better estimates in the first place. For example, in teaching experimental methods, greater exposure to the kind of results presented here should be helpful, together with attention to the role of judgment in the assessment process. Although one might hope that instructions in the processes and pitfalls of judgement would, by themselves, improve performance, the evidence to date suggests that people have difficulty in integrating an understanding of general principles with their own cognitive processes (see, e.g., Gaeth & Shanteau, 1984). What *has* proved more effective in other domains is task-specific training with personal feedback (Lichtenstein et al., 1982). For example, in laboratory classes, where students are required to measure the same quantities, it should be instructive to compile distributions of normalized residuals and measures of calibration for the class results and discuss together the reasons both for individual errors and for systematic miscalibration in reported uncertainties.

CONCLUSIONS

The underestimation of uncertainty in measurements of physical constants and compilations of recommended values seems to be pervasive. This evidence extends previous findings of overconfidence in laboratory studies of human judgment to a task domain of great practical importance. If reported uncertainties do not reflect the magnitude of actual errors, whether due to incomplete analysis or to judgmental biases, the usefulness of those measurements is significantly diminished. Measurements are then hard to compare, and are unlikely to produce "enduring values" (Youden, 1972), as we have illustrated in the repeated contradiction of accepted values by subseqent measurements. Recognizing that subjective judgment is an essential element in the assessment of systematic uncertainty enables us to use findings from cognitive research to help understand how these biases arise and suggest approaches for dealing with these problems more effectively.

38. Do Analysts Overreact?

Werner F. M. De Bondt and Richard H. Thaler

It has long been part of the conventional wisdom on Wall Street that financial markets overreact. Both casual observation and academic research support irrational exuberance (Shiller, 2000). For instance, Shiller's survey evidence relating to the 1987 stock market crash reveals that investors were reacting to each other's behavior rather than to hard economic news.

In prior research, we argued that mean reversion in stock prices is evidence of overreaction. In our 1985 paper, we showed that stocks that were extreme losers over an initial 3- to 5-year period earned excess returns over subsequent years. In the 1987 paper, we showed that these excess returns could not easily be attributed to changes in risk, tax effects, or the small firm anomaly. Rather, we argued that the excess returns to losers might be explained by biased expectations of future earnings. We found that the earnings for losing firms had fallen precipitously while their share prices were lagging market performance, but then rebounded strongly over the next few years. Perhaps, we speculated, "the market" did not correctly anticipate this reversal in earnings. This hypothesis, of excessive pessimism about the future prospects of companies that had done poorly, was suggested by the work of Kahneman and Tversky (1973). They found that people's intuitive forecasts have a tendency to overweight salient information such as recent news, and underweight less salient data such as long-term averages.

Of course, there are many reasons to be skeptical that actual investors and stock market professionals are subject to the same biases as student subjects in laboratory experiments. Those who follow the stock market for a living are experts in their field, have much at stake, and may be driven out of business if they are prone to systematic error (see Stickel, 1992). Therefore, we present here a study of the expectations of one important group of financial market professionals: security analysts who make periodic forecasts of individual company earnings.

The original version of this paper, "Do Security Analysts Overreact?" was published in the *American Economic Review*, 1990. By permission of the American Economic Association. Although the analyses we report here are the same as those shown in the original, for this book we updated the text and included some references to research that has appeared since our original article appeared.

This is an interesting group to study on three counts. First, other investigators have found repeatedly that earnings forecasts (and forecast revisions) have an important influence on stock prices (Brown, Foster & Noreen, 1985). Second, past work suggests that analysts are rather good at what they do. For example, analyst forecasts often outperform time series models (see Conroy & Harris, 1987). Finally, the precision of analyst expectations represents a natural upper bound to the quality of the earnings forecasts of less sophisticated agents. After all, most investors do not have the time or the skill to produce their own predictions and, accordingly, they buy (rather than sell) earnings forecasts. Thus, for all of the above reasons, it is particularly interesting to see whether market professionals display any of the biases discovered in studies of nonexpert judgment.

We test for a type of *generalized overreaction*, the tendency to make forecasts that are too extreme, given the predictive value of the information available to the forecaster. This tendency is well illustrated by an experiment conducted by Kahneman and Tversky. Subjects were asked to predict the future grade point average (GPA) for each of 10 students on the basis of a percentile score of some predictor. Three predictor variables in percentile form were used: GPA, a test of mental concentration, and a test of sense of humor. Obviously, a percentile measure of GPA is a much better predictor of actual GPA than is a measure of mental concentration that, in turn, is likely to be more reliable than information on sense of humor. Therefore, subjects should give forecasts that are much more regressive in the latter two conditions. That is, the forecasts should deviate less from the mean. The results indicated that people were not nearly sensitive enough to this consideration. Subjects that were given a nearly useless predictor (the *sense of humor* condition) made predictions that were almost as extreme in variation as those given a nearly perfect predictor (the *percentile GPA* condition). This pattern leads to a systematic bias: forecasts that diverge the most from the mean tend to be too extreme, implying that forecast errors are predictable.

Our study asks whether security analysts display similar biases. Our focus is on forecasted changes in earnings per share (EPS) for 1- and 2-year time horizons. We study two questions: The first is whether forecast errors in EPS are systematically linked to forecasted changes. In particular, are the forecasts too extreme? Are most forecast revisions "up" ("down") if the analysts initially projected large declines (rises) in EPS? Clearly, under rationality, neither forecast errors nor forecast revisions should ever be predictable from forecasted changes. The second question is whether the bias in the forecasts gets stronger as uncertainty grows and less is (or objectively can be) known about the future.

To investigate this question, we run regressions of the form $AC = \alpha + \beta \, FC$, where AC is the actual change in earnings and FC is the forecasted change. The null hypothesis of rational expectations is that $(\alpha, \beta) = (0, 1)$. If α is not equal to zero, then the forecasts are, on average, either too optimistic ($\alpha < 0$) or too pessimistic ($\alpha > 0$). If β is not equal to 1 then the forecasted changes are either too extreme (if $\beta < 1$) or not extreme enough ($\beta > 1$). Our primary focus is on the estimates of β because there are numerous explanations for the optimism we (and others) find. The two behavioral hypotheses sketched above make the following predictions for our estimates of β:

HYPOTHESIS 1 *Forecasted changes are too extreme, so actual changes are less (in absolute value) than predicted: $\beta < 1$.*

HYPOTHESIS 2 *The estimated β for the 2-year forecasts is less than the β for the 1-year forecasts.*

The next two sections describe the data and the empirical results. We find considerable support for the behavioral view. We then briefly discuss the sources of the systematic forecast error.

DATA

The analysts' earnings forecasts are taken from IBES International. We study forecasts between 1976 and 1984. IBES contacts individual analysts on a regular basis and computes summary data such as means or standard deviations. The data are sold to institutional investors. Updates are available each month. Here, we work with the April and December predictions of EPS for the current as well as the subsequent year. The April forecasts are approximately 1- and 2-year forecasts because we only consider companies with a fiscal year ending in December. For these firms, actually realized earnings are announced during the first few months of the following calendar year.

We match the earnings forecasts with stock returns and accounting numbers. The returns are provided by the Center for Research on Security Prices (CRSP) at the University of Chicago. The accounting data are listed on COMPUSTAT sold by Standard & Poor's. Because all data sources contain full historical records, no survivorship biases affect the sample selection. We further adjust the data for stock splits and stock dividends so that all current and past returns, earnings figures, and forecasts are expressed on a comparable basis. When necessary, forecasts of fully diluted earnings per share (EPS) are converted to forecasts of primary EPS (excluding extraordinary items).

Although some IBES data are available for approximately 2,300–2,800 companies each year, our annual sample contains many fewer observations. For example, for the 1-year forecasts, the number varies between 461 and 785. This follows from the data selection criteria. Companies only qualify if they have (1) records on IBES, CRSP, and COMPUSTAT; (2) returns for 3 years prior to the forecast month; (3) EPS numbers for 10 years prior to the forecast month; (4) a December fiscal year; and (5) the data needed to compute the variables in the regressions described later.

METHODS AND RESULTS

The empirical analysis is based on three sets of variables: forecasted changes in earnings per share (EPS), ($FC1$, $FC2$, and $FC12$), actual changes in EPS ($AC1$, $AC2$, and $AC12$), and forecast revisions ($FR1$, $FR2$, and $FR12$). The consensus 1- and 2-year forecasts of earnings per share [$FEPS(t)$ and $FEPS$ $(t+1)$] are defined as the cross-sectional means or medians of analyst forecasts reported in April of year t ($t = 1976 \ldots 1984$). Forecasted changes are computed as $FC1(t) = FEPS(t) - EPS(t-1)$, $FC2(t) = FEPS(t+1) - EPS(t-1)$, and $FC12(t) = FEPS(t+1) - FEPS(t)$, where $EPS(t)$ represents company announced earnings per share. We compute actual earnings changes in a way that is similar to the forecasted changes. For example, $AC1(t) = EPS(t) - EPS(t-1)$. Eight-month forecast revisions ($FR1$) subtract the April forecast of $EPS(t)$ from the equivalent forecast in December. Twenty-month forecast revisions ($FR2$) are the difference between the December forecast in year $t+1$ and the April forecast of $EPS(t+1)$. Similarly, $FR12$ subtracts the April $FC12(t)$ from the equivalent $FC12(t)$ in December of year t.

The regressions in Table 38.1 use mean consensus forecasts. All variables are normalized by the standard deviation of earnings per share between years $t-10$ and $t-2$. (We also tried other normalization procedures, such as dividing by company assets per share at the end of year $t-1$, the stock price on the last trading day of year $t-5$, or the standard deviation of EPS between $t-5$ and $t-2$. Results are qualitatively the same for all methods.) Even though

Table 38.1. Tests for the Rationality of Earnings per Share Forecasts

Equation	Variables	Constant	Slope	Adj. R^2
1	$AC1$, $FC1$	−.094	.648	.217
		(−3.7)	(−3.7)	[5736]
2	$FR1$, $FC1$	−.120	−.181	.041
		(−6.7)	(−15.6)	[5736]
3	$AC2$, $FC2$	−.137	.459	.071
		(−2.3)	(−19.5)	[3539]
4	$FR2$, $FC2$	−.192	−.381	.074
		(−3.9)	(−16.8)	[3538]
5	$AC12$, $FC12$	.153	−.042	.000
		(2.4)	(−16.9)	[3520]
6	$FR12$, $FC12$	.348	−.439	.153
		(19.4)	(−25.3)	[3562]

Note: All variables are as defined in the text. The dependent variable is listed first. T values appear in parentheses beneath the regression coefficients and test whether they differ from zero. However, for the slopes of Eqs. 1, 3, and 5, the t-statistics test whether the coefficients differ from one. Note that the number of observations is given in brackets in the far right column.

we also ran the regressions year by year, the results in Table 38.1 are based on the pooled samples. There are three main findings: Forecasts are too optimistic, too extreme, and even more extreme for 2-year forecasts than for single-year predictions.

Equation 1 refers to the 1-year forecasts. We regress the actual change in earnings on the April forecasted change. The intercept is significantly negative, indicating that the forecasts are too optimistic. This excessive optimism also appears in Eq. 3 for the 2-year forecasts. The negative intercepts in Eqs. 2 and 4 reveal that there is a tendency for forecasts to be revised downwards between April and December.

The finding of unrealistic optimism is consistent with the experimental research of Weinstein (1980) and others who find such biases in the expectations of individuals in everyday life. (See, e.g., Moore, Kurtzberg, Fox & Bazerman, 1999, on positive illusions in mutual fund investment decisions.) However, we do not want to push this argument too far for two reasons. First, if we consider the nine individual year-by-year regressions, the intercepts are positive four times. Second, the optimism bias also has other plausible explanations. For example, many analysts work for brokerage houses that make money by encouraging trading. Because every customer is potentially interested in a buy recommendation, whereas only current stockholders (and a few willing to go short) are interested in sell recommendations, optimistic forecasts may be preferable. Indeed, it is well known that buy recommendations issued by brokerage houses greatly exceed sell recommendations (Carleton, Chen, & Steiner, 1998; Michaely and Womack, 1999; Stickel, 1995).

All six regressions in Table 38.1 support the view that forecasts are too extreme. Ignoring the constant term in Eq. 1, the actual EPS changes average only 65% of the forecasted 1-year changes. For the 2-year forecasts (Eq. 3), this statistic falls to 46%. The 2-year regressions are open to criticism because the sampling interval (1 year) is shorter than the forecast interval (2 years), creating nonindependence across data points. To remove this problem, we break the sample in two, and replicate equation 3 using forecasts just from every other year, so that the time periods are nonoverlapping. Results are comparable. In the year-by-year regressions equivalent to Eqs. 1 and 3, the slope coefficients are less than 1 every single time.

Equations 1 and 3 may be rewritten with the forecast errors ($AC1$-$FC1$ and $AC2$-$FC2$) on the left side and with the forecasted changes as the regressors. The new slope coefficients then equal the betas in Table 38.1 minus 1, whereas the t-statistics remain the same. The new slopes have a straightforward interpretation: The larger the forecasted changes, the larger is the forecast error in the opposite direction. The R-squares of these regressions are .076 and .097.

The evidence suggests that forecast revisions should also be predictable from forecasted changes, and indeed they are, as shown in Eqs. 2 and 4. In these regressions, rationality implies that β should be equal to zero. In actuality, the slopes are significantly negative. By December, the average reversal of the 1-year forecasts made in April equals 18% of the original predicted changes. For the 2-year forecasts the reversal amounts to 38%.

As expected, the results are stronger for the 2-year forecasts. The 2-year results are clearly driven by the predicted changes for the second year (see Eqs. 5 and 6). With the R-square for Eq. 5 equal to zero, actual changes are simply unrelated to forecasted changes in EPS from year t to $t + 1$. On average, any nonzero prediction, either positive or negative, is pure error. By December, the analysts have reversed their April forecasted changes for the second year by 44%. Kang et al. (1994) and Lim (2001) confirm that the analyst bias increases with the forecast horizon.

In sum, these results are consistent with generalized overreaction. However, a different interpretation is based on the problem of errors in variables. If our measure of forecasted changes in earnings contains error, then the slope coefficients are biased downward. In evaluating this argument, one should consider the most likely sources of error. One possibility is IBES data entry errors. Following O'Brien (1988), we removed any data points for which the predicted change in EPS or the forecast revision was greater than $10. The results in Table 38.1 reflect this screen. In addition, we also recomputed regressions 1 and 3 using a smaller sample of firms for which the consensus forecast is based on the individual predictions of three analysts or more. We then used the median forecasted earnings change as the regressor. The βs increased but they were still significantly less than 1.

A second source of error stems form the fact that the forecasts on the IBES tape may be stale. In fact, O'Brien finds that the average IBES forecast is 34 days old. This is troublesome if the forecasters do not know the earnings for year $t - 1$ when they make their predictions for year t. For example, a forecaster who thinks that year t earnings will remain unchanged from year $t - 1$ will appear to be predicting a change in earnings if his estimate of $t - 1$ earnings is wrong. We selected April as the month to study with an eye toward minimizing the problem. We chose the longest possible forecast horizon where we could still be confident that the forecasters would know the previous year's earnings exactly or have a very good estimate. Thus it seems unlikely that such a large bias could be produced by errors of this type. (Keane and Runkle (1998) discuss further econometric refinements.)

Another reason for confidence in the notion of generalized overreaction is that others have obtained similar results in studies of professional forecasters. Using just the 1976–1978 years of the IBES data, Elton, Gruber, and Gultekin (1984) estimated regressions similar to ours, and obtained slope coefficients less than one in each year. More recently, Capstaff et al. (2001) find strong overreaction bias (as well as strong optimism bias) in analysts' EPS forecasts in nine European countries between 1987 and 1995. For regressions similar to Eq. 1, the average slope coefficient is .73. The slope is the lowest for Switzerland (.52) and the highest for the United Kingdom (.82). The findings are based on more than 500,000 forecasts made by individual analysts and listed on IBES. In a study of exchange rate expectations, Froot and Frankel (1989) also found evidence consistent with overreaction, or what they call *excessive speculation*. Forecast errors are regressed on forecasted changes in exchange rates. The slope coefficients are always significantly different from zero. Finally, Ahlers and Lakonishok (1983) studied economists' forecasts of ten macroeconomic variables. In regressions similar to our Eq. 1, they found that, for every variable, predicted changes were more volatile than actual changes, consistent with overreaction. As mentioned, analysts may have incentives to make biased forecasts (e.g., to support their employers' underwriting business; Williams et al., 1996; Carleton et al., 1998; Michaely & Womack, 1999), to maintain good relations with top executives (Francis & Philbrick, 1993), or to stimulate trading by customers (Hayes, 1998). Agency problems can produce an overreaction bias as well as an optimism bias. Whether this argument is plausible, the fact that the overreaction bias is observed for forecasters in domains in which the agency problem is not present suggests that the bias is produced by cognitive errors rather than faulty incentives.

We documented generalized overreaction. However, an interesting question remains: What causes excessive optimism or pessimism in earnings forecasts? Definitely, the forecast errors are large, whatever metric one uses (Dreman & Berry, 1995; Clayman & Schwartz, 1994). We considered several variables that might explain EPS forecast errors. Two variables that are of interest in light of our previous work include a measure of market valuation, MV/BV, the ratio of the market value of a company's equity to its book value (at the end of year $t-1$), and earnings trend (the growth rate of earnings over the years $t-6$ to $t-2$). Both variables were significantly related to forecast error in the expected direction, that is, excessive optimism for high MV/BV and high earnings growth firms, and excessive pessimism for firms low on these measures. Unfortunately, neither factor explained much of the variation in the forecast errors. [Even though Lakonishok et al. (1994) do not study analysts' earnings forecasts directly, their findings on investor extrapolation bias and contrarian investment are consistent with our results; see also Barth et al. (1998)].

We did not examine the links between earnings forecasts and recent earnings surprises from a time series point of view. However, research shows that, from this perspective, earnings forecasts often underreact to earnings news (Klein, 1990; Abarbanell & Bernard, 1992). In other words, analysts behave as if they do not believe the news. Their forecasts are not sufficiently revised in the direction of the surprise, especially when it is unfavorable. Dowen (1996), Amir and Ganzach (1998), Easterwood and Nutt (1999), Nutt, Easterwood, and Easterwood (1999), and Maines and Hand (1996) observe the same bias in an experimental setting.

Another aspect of the forecast process that we did not consider is the strategic interaction between analysts and company management (Loffler, 1998). Executives release their own earnings forecasts (Penman, 1980) and, more importantly, they manage the actual earnings numbers. Sometimes, they smooth accounting income and they want to avoid losses (Burgstahler & Dichev, 1997). At other times, they purposively take an earnings bath. Sloan (1996) and others find that investors are misled (and stock prices distorted) by accounting magic relating to accruals – as management tries to hit the earnings targets set by analyst forecasts (Degeorge, Patel, & Zeckhauser, 1999).

CONCLUSION

Formal economic models of financial markets typically assume that all agents in the economy are rational. Although most economists recognize that, in fact, not everyone is fully rational, the existence of an irrational segment of the economy is often dismissed as irrelevant with the claim that there will be enough rational arbitrageurs to assure that rational equilibria will still obtain. Whatever the theoretical merits of this position (for a critique, see Russell & Thaler, 1985), an interesting empirical question is whether the presumed smart money segment actually can be identified. This paper investigates one possible source of rationality in financial markets, namely security analysts.

The conclusion we reach from our examination of analysts' forecasts is that they are decidedly human. The same pattern of overreaction found in the predictions of naive undergraduates is replicated in the predictions of stock market professionals. Forecasted changes are simply too extreme to be considered rational. The fact that the same pattern is observed in economists' forecasts of changes in exchange rates and macroeconomic variables adds force to the conclusion that generalized overreaction can pervade even the most professional of predictions.

The proper inference from this, we think, is to take seriously the behavioral explanations of anomalous financial market outcomes. When practitioners describe market crashes as panics, produced by investor overreaction, perhaps they are right. After all, are not these practitioners the very same "smart money" that is supposed to keep markets rational?

39. The Calibration of Expert Judgment: Heuristics and Biases Beyond the Laboratory

Derek J. Koehler, Lyle Brenner, and Dale Griffin

The study of how people use subjective probabilities is a remarkably modern concern, and was largely motivated by the increasing use of expert judgment during and after World War II (Cooke, 1991). Experts are often asked to quantify the likelihood of events such as a stock market collapse, a nuclear plant accident, or a presidential election (Ayton, 1992; Baron, 1998; Hammond, 1996). For applications such as these, it is essential to know how the probabilities experts attach to various outcomes match the relative frequencies of those outcomes; that is, whether experts are properly "calibrated." Despite this, relatively few studies have evaluated how well descriptive theories of probabilistic reasoning capture the behavior of experts in their natural environment. In this chapter, we examine the calibration of expert probabilistic predictions "in the wild" and assess how well the heuristics and biases perspective on judgment under uncertainty can account for the findings. We then review alternate theories of calibration in light of the expert data.

Calibration and Miscalibration

Miscalibration presents itself in a number of forms. Figure 39.1 displays four typical patterns of miscalibrated probability judgments. The solid diagonal line, identity line, or line of perfect calibration, indicates the set of points at which judged probability and relative frequency coincide. The solid line marked *A*, where all judgments are higher than the corresponding relative frequency, represents *overprediction bias*. The solid line *B*, where all judgments are lower than the corresponding relative frequency, represents *underprediction bias*. The dotted line *C*, where judgments lower than 50% are too low and judgments higher than 50% are too high, represents *overextremity bias*. The dotted line *D*, where judgments lower than 50% are too high and judgments higher than 50% are too low, represents *underextremity bias*. Note that overextremity entails overly radical judgments (too close to 0 and 100) and underextremity entails overly conservative judgments (too far from 0 and 100). Combinations of under- or overprediction and either of the extremity biases are also possible, and result

Acknowledgments: The authors acknowledge the helpful comments of Roger Buehler, Tom Gilovich, Richard Gonzalez, and Yuval Rottenstreich. The research was partially supported by an NSERC grant to Derek Koehler and a SSHRC grant to Dale Griffin.

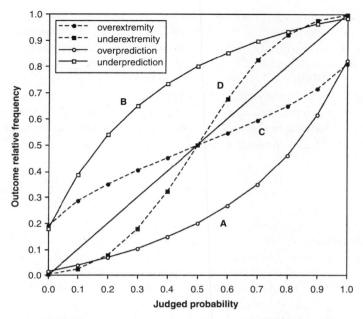

Figure 39.1. Calibration curves, generated by RST simulations, illustrating distinction between miscalibration due to overprediction (or underprediction) of target event versus that due to judgments which are overly (or insufficiently) extreme.

Note: Neglect model predictions based on RST simulation assuming no focal bias ($\beta = 0$) and fixed judgmental extremity ($\sigma = 1$). Over- and underprediction curves constructed assuming fixed discriminability ($\alpha = 1$) with varying target event base rate ($BR = 20\%$ for overestimation; $BR = 80\%$ for underestimation). Over- and underextremity curves constructed assuming fixed base rate ($BR = 50\%$) with varying discriminability ($\alpha = 2.0$ for overextremity; $\alpha = 0.5$ for underextremity).

in lines that cross the diagonal at points other than 50%. Overconfidence, the poster child of judgmental biases, is a simple summary term (average subjective probability minus overall outcome relative frequency) that does not uniquely identify any one of these patterns (Wallsten & Budescu, 1983). Nonetheless, when referring to previous research, we use the term *overconfidence*, as this simple bias measure is often the primary statistic reported.

Each of the four patterns illustrated in Fig. 39.1 is consistent with the use of judgmental heuristics (e.g., Kahneman & Tversky, 1973), and the pattern found depends on specific qualities of the judgmental task or situation and how they interact with the relevant heuristics (Griffin & Tversky, 1992; Griffin, Gonzalez, & Varey, 2000). The neglect of base rates that follows from reliance on judgmental heuristics leads to overprediction bias (*A*) when the outcome base rate is low and underprediction bias (B) when the outcome base rate is high. The neglect of evidence quality that follows from reliance on judgmental heuristics leads to overextremity bias (C) when the evidence quality is low and underextremity bias (D) when the evidence quality is high. The dependence of miscalibration upon the difficulty of the task and the knowledge of the judge (the difficulty or hard–easy effect) was established as the fundamental bias in general knowledge calibration by Lichtenstein, Fischhoff, and Philips (1982) in their comprehensive review. Nonetheless, general claims about the ubiquity of "overconfidence" continue to dominate managerial and academic textbooks.

THE MODEL

The predictions of the heuristics and biases perspective are typically qualitative in nature, but recently Brenner (1995) introduced a parametric model of calibration that makes precise quantitative predictions. Random support theory (RST; Brenner, 1995) combines elements of support theory (Rottenstreich & Tversky, 1997; Tversky & Koehler, 1994) and signal detection theory (e.g., Tanner & Swets, 1954) to fit calibration data and yield a set of psychologically meaningful parameters. Support theory itself is a "coherence theory" of subjective probability and evidence strength, describing when and why intuitive probability judgments depart from the syntactic rules of probability theory. RST extends the logic of support theory to the semantic question of the "correspondence" of the probability and the actual outcome (cf. Hammond, 1996). According to RST, probability judgments reflect the balance of evidence captured by underlying distributions of support for correct and incorrect hypotheses. Based on the observed probability judgments and the associated outcomes, RST provides an efficient summary of these underlying support distributions. We focus on three parameters of the model: Alpha (α) measures the judge's *discrimination ability*, defined as the difference in support for correct and incorrect hypotheses, indexing the quality or "weight" of the evidence. Sigma (σ) measures the *extremity* of the judge's responses, defined as the tendency to depart from the base-rate value, indexing the perceived strength of the evidence. Beta (β) measures the *differential support* received by the focal hypothesis; among other things, β can be viewed as an index of a judge's sensitivity to the outcome base rate.

   In this model, good calibration arises when σ is matched to α so that extremity of judgment is appropriate for the level of evidence quality, and when the outcome base rate is matched by the use of β. A zero response bias ($\beta = 0$) is appropriate when the base rate is 50%; an increasingly negative response bias maintains calibration as the base rate moves below 50%, and an increasingly positive response bias maintains calibration as the base rate moves above 50%. The patterns of miscalibration presented in Fig. 39.1 were generated by RST: overprediction was simulated by a low base rate (20% probability of focal outcome) with no bias adjustment ($\beta = 0$), and a balance between extremity and discriminability ($\sigma = \alpha$); underprediction was simulated by a high base rate (80% probability of focal outcome) with no bias adjustment ($\beta = 0$), and a balance between extremity and discriminability ($\sigma = \alpha$); overextremity was simulated by a moderate base rate (50%), and greater extremity than discriminability ($\sigma > \alpha$); and underextremity was simulated by a moderate base rate (50%), and less extremity than discriminability ($\sigma < \alpha$).

Support theory and RST are closely related to the strength–weight model of confidence and calibration (Griffin & Tversky, 1992), sharing an assumption that confidence or judged probability reflects the support or strength of evidence for the focal hypothesis relative to that for its alternative. These models all belong to a class we refer to as *direct support models* because of their common assumption that confidence (when measured via judged probability) reflects a direct translation of the support, or strength of evidence, of the focal outcome relative to that of its alternative. Direct support models naturally depict judgments of confidence as case-based, in the sense that support is based on an assessment of the available evidence regarding the case at hand. In case-based judgment, the impression conveyed by the evidence determines the degree of confidence, with little regard given to the reliability of the relationship between the evidence and the target event. Such an interpretation is consistent with the observation that people are often insensitive to characteristics of the larger set of events to which the specific case at hand belongs, such as base rates or evidence quality (e.g., Kahneman & Tversky, 1973). In certain instances, set-based characteristics may be treated by people as arguments in a case-based evaluation; for example, the base rate of a medical condition may be one argument considered by a physician ("There is a lot of that going around"). However, such usage typically leads to underweighting of the base rate compared to the ideal statistical model. The impact of a base-rate "argument" seems to be determined by its apparent relevance to the case at hand (Tversky & Kahneman, 1982) rather than by considerations of the reliability of the evidence, as in the Bayesian model. When base rates are used, as in a within-subjects design, they are used in an additive manner, rather than in the multiplicative manner required by the Bayesian model (Novemsky and Kronzon, 1999). This is consistent with the notion that when base rates are salient, they are used to adjust the case-based impression, which acts as an anchor (Griffin & Tversky, 1992).

An advantage of direct support models is that, in many cases, people can provide direct ratings of the extent to which the available evidence supports a given hypothesis. Consider as an example a study reported by Tversky and Koehler (1994, Study 3; for details, see Koehler, 1996), in which subjects assessed the probability that the home team would win in each of 20 upcoming basketball games among a set of five Pacific Division NBA teams. Subjects were asked to rate the strength of each of the five teams, which was assumed to be monotonically related to the team's support in the confidence assessment via a

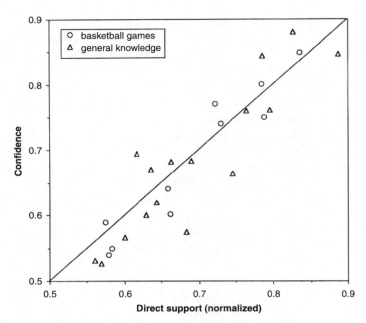

Figure 39.2. Confidence as predicted by normalized direct rat-
ings of support, for basketball game predictions (Koehler, 1996;
Tversky & Koehler, 1994) and general-knowledge questions
(Varey, Griffin, & James, 1998).

Note: Basketball data compares mean judged probability assigned to predicted winning team (inferred from full-range probability assigned to
home team) with normalized direct ratings of "team strength" obtained
from the same group of subjects. General-knowledge data compares
mean confidence in selected answer with direct ratings of "proportion of
evidence" supporting chosen alternative obtained from a separate group
of subjects.

power transformation. As shown in Fig. 39.2 (circles), the predictions based on
the team strength ratings fit the mean probability judgment data quite closely.
Koehler, Brenner, and Tversky (1997) report the results of a number of additional
studies in which direct ratings of support are used successfully to fit probability
judgments.

The triangles in Fig. 39.2 plot mean judgments of evidence strength against
mean probability judgments for general knowledge questions (Varey, Griffin, &
James, 1998). Subjects in a "support" condition were asked to report the proportion of evidence available to them supporting each alternative whereas subjects
in a "confidence" condition reported their subjective probability that each alternative was correct. For both sports predictions and general knowledge answers,
the slope of the best-fitting regression line is very close to 1.0, consistent with
the notion that respondents directly translated their impressions of support into
probability judgments (cf. Kahneman & Tversky, 1973).

Out of the Laboratory

Most theories of judgmental calibration were developed on the basis of laboratory data from the two-alternative (half-range) forced-choice (2 *AFC*) paradigm, usually with general knowledge questions as the object of judgment (see Lichtenstein et al., 1982). There are a number of reasons for this tradition. General knowledge or "almanac" studies are quick and efficient, producing hundreds of easy-to-score judgments from hundreds of subjects, whereas it is both difficult and time-consuming to assess the quality of judgments made in applied settings: Loftus and Wagenaar (1988), for example, took 3 years to collect judgments about self-reported wins and losses from 182 trial lawyers. The two-alternative paradigm is closely linked to research and theory on "meta-cognition," the study of how well people can monitor their own knowledge (e.g., Nelson, Leonesio, Landwehr, & Narens, 1986), and more generally has a long history in psychophysics. In addition, the half-range measure of probability fits the intuitive notion of "confidence," running from complete uncertainty (.5) to complete certainty (1.0).

This reliance on half-range studies, however, has obscured several important issues. For full-range judgments the focal hypothesis for a given domain can be defined in alternate ways (e.g., a set of basketball games can be assessed in terms of wins for the home team, or wins for the team higher in the standings), and many measures of judgmental calibration are sensitive to the choice of the designated event (Liberman & Tversky, 1993). This complication is avoided in half-range studies, but at the cost of losing some important information about human judgment. Most critically, half-range studies confound the role of outcome base rate and task difficulty. In a typical half-range study, the outcome can be summarized by the overall percent correct, which serves to define the expected outcome or base rate as well as the difficulty of the question set.

In a half-range study, the effects of base rate and difficulty or discriminability may be distinguished by designating one of the possible responses to each item as a target, implicitly creating a one-alternative judgment task (cf. Ferrell & McGoey, 1980). However, these manipulated targets are often arbitrary [e.g., P(True) versus P(False)]. In true one-alternative judgments (e.g., predicting the likelihood of a given disease, predicting the likelihood of winning a court case), the base rate of the positive outcome is clearly separable from the difficulty of discriminating positive outcomes from negative outcomes. Predicting a nuclear accident or a stock market bubble may be difficult either because the event is rare *or* because the available evidence is not diagnostic (or both) – a distinction that may make all the difference to understanding and debiasing such judgments.

Expert Judgment: A Question of Competence?

Many commentators have argued that expert judgments, at least those made in a naturalistic setting, may be immune from the systematic judgmental biases found in laboratory experiments. The prevalence of judgmental biases is often blamed on factors intrinsic to the psychology laboratory such as unmotivated subjects and misleading and unrepresentative questions (see, e.g., Shanteau, 1999). Thus, "decision heuristics ... appear more likely to create biases in the psychology laboratory than in the [medical] clinic" (Schwarz & Griffin, 1986, p. 82), and "biases found readily in other research are not evident in the judgements of professional auditors" (Smith & Kida, 1991, p. 485). By and large such conclusions are based on studies of domain experts completing pencil-and-paper measures in their domains of expertise, rather than from the observation and assessment of expert judges in their day-to-day activities.

There are many reasons to expect that the judgments of experts will depart systematically from the judgments of novices (Shanteau, 1999). Experts know more, they can organize cues into larger "chunks" (Chase & Simon, 1973), and they can recognize patterns more easily, more accurately and more quickly (Glaser, 1990; Klein, 1998). As Simon noted in his classic studies of expert judgment, experts seem particularly good at that part of recognition that consists of automatic pattern matching between a stimulus and a category (Chase and Simon, 1973; Simon, 1979). All these statements are consistent with a direct support account, and in terms of our guiding model imply that in well-ordered domains, expert judgments will have a higher α than novice judgments, reflecting experts' greater ability to correctly discriminate between different outcomes. However, the ability to order cases in terms of the likelihood of a given outcome (discrimination) does not necessarily correspond to the ability to assign the appropriate level of probability to that outcome (calibration) (Liberman & Tversky, 1993). Thus, depending on the problem environment, even the most knowledgeable and perceptive expert may nonetheless show the patterns of miscalibration portrayed in Fig. 39.1 (see Stewart, Roebber, & Bosart, 1997, and Wagenaar & Keren, 1986, for related arguments).

Previous Theories Applied to Experts

According to the confirmatory bias model of Koriat, Lichtenstein, and Fischhoff (1980), a general tendency toward overconfidence arises from people's inclination to recruit reasons from memory that confirm the focal hypothesis. The stronger and more numerous the reasons that are recruited, the greater is the confidence expressed in the selected answer. Because this process inclines the judge to overlook reasons against the selected answer, however, he or she is likely to be overconfident that the selected answer is correct. Consistent with this claim, Koriat et al. reported that asking subjects to generate reasons favoring and opposing both options in a $2\,AFC$ task reduced overconfidence relative to a control condition in which no such reasons were generated. Furthermore, asking subjects to generate reasons contradicting their preferred alternative reduced overconfidence relative to a control condition while generation of supporting reasons had no effect.

Experts might be more or less susceptible to confirmatory bias than novices. On the one hand, their extensive experience may help them learn to evaluate evidence in a more impartial manner, and could also lead them to spontaneously generate alternatives to the focal hypothesis. On the other hand, the broader knowledge base of experts might lead them to more readily generate a biased set of reasons favoring the focal hypothesis.

It should be noted that the results of Koriat et al.'s (1980) studies have proven somewhat difficult to replicate (e.g., Fischhoff & MacGregor, 1982). Biased recruitment of evidence may play a more pronounced role when the focal hypothesis is highly self-relevant such that the judge is motivated to confirm (or disconfirm) it. Hoch (1985), for example, reported results consistent with the confirmatory search model in a study of predictions made by business school students about the outcomes of their job searches, all of which were evaluatively positive (e.g., receiving more than three job offers). When compared to the actual job search outcomes, the students' predictions proved to be substantially overconfident in the sense of overestimating these positive events' likelihood of occurrence (the pattern of overprediction in Fig. 39.1); furthermore, overprediction was greater for low-baserate events. As predicted by the confirmatory search model, asking students to generate reasons why the target event would not occur substantially reduced this overconfidence, while asking them to generate reasons supporting the target event's occurrence had no influence. Confirmatory search processes, then, might be apparent only in the assessment of highly self-relevant outcomes, producing optimistic overconfidence (Kahneman & Lovallo, 1993; Kahneman & Tversky, 1995; Taylor & Brown, 1988). Experts may not generally exhibit such an optimistic bias, as the outcomes they assess do not typically concern themselves personally.

Some researchers have argued that the prevalence of overconfidence in two-alternative laboratory tasks is attributable to biased selection of particularly difficult or surprising items, a concern first raised by May (1986). Derived from a Brunswikian framework in which cue-based representations of the environment are constructed from experience (Brunswik, 1943, 1955), ecological models draw attention to the manner in which the events serving as the target of judgment in laboratory tasks are selected or constructed (Björkman, 1994; Gigerenzer et al., 1991; Juslin, 1994). Ecological models are based on an explicit or implicit assumption that people are able to accurately internalize cue-based environmental probabilities. According to the ecological models, people produce these ecological or cue validities when asked for confidence assessments, and should be expected to be well-calibrated as long as test items are selected from the reference class in an unbiased manner. Miscalibration, on this account, is a result of non-representative sampling of test items.

The ecological models predict perfect calibration for tasks in which judgment items are randomly selected from a natural reference class. Consistent with such claims, early comparisons between "selected" and "representative" tasks revealed substantial overconfidence for selected tasks but little or no overconfidence for the representative tasks (Gigerenzer et al., 1991; Juslin, 1994). Critics, however, have noted that such experiments confounded method of item selection with task difficulty (Griffin & Tversky, 1992): The easier, representative tasks would be expected to yield less overconfidence than the more difficult, selected tasks on the basis of difficulty alone. Moreover, a number of studies using representative sampling have nonetheless found overconfidence (e.g., Budescu, Wallsten, & Au, 1997; Griffin & Tversky, 1992; Paese & Sniezek, 1991; Suantak, Bolger, & Ferrell, 1996; Schneider, 1995; Sniezek, Paese & Switzer, 1990). A survey of 25 tasks employing representative sampling (Juslin, Olsson, & Björkman, 1997) reveals a clear pattern of overconfidence for difficult tasks and underconfidence for easy tasks, contrary to the predictions of the ecological models that no such effect should occur under representative sampling.

For full-range tasks, the ecological models imply that there should be no systematic effect of discriminability or target event base rate on calibration; indeed, as long as representative sampling is used, these models predict perfect calibration regardless of level of discriminability or base rate. Both of these variables have been found to influence full-range calibration for general knowledge items (e.g., Lichtenstein et al., 1982; Smith & Ferrell, 1983), contrary to the predictions of the ecological models. One might argue, however, that such laboratory studies fail to satisfy representative design. By contrast, representative sampling of items is essentially satisfied by definition in studies of on-the-job assessments of experts; the items judged by an expert in practice should reflect the natural reference class of items for which the judge's expertise is relevant. Ecological models, then, predict that experts should be uniformly well calibrated in the studies we review.

Although RST was developed in the heuristics and biases tradition, it can represent the predictions of a number of theories of judgment, based on how the parameters of the model vary with changes in base rate and evidence quality. The notion of case-based judgment from the heuristics and biases perspective suggests that as the outcome base rate varies across tasks and contexts, the bias parameter β will remain essentially constant (neglect of base rate), and that as the level of evidential weight or discriminability varies, the extremity parameter σ will remain essentially constant (neglect of evidence quality). Case-based judgment implies that support will reflect the evidence related to the particular case at hand, and will not be sensitive to aggregate properties of the set of judgment items. Consequently, the parameters of the RST model that ought to reflect these aggregate properties (β and σ) will remain roughly constant despite changes in base rate or evidence quality.

In contrast, the general confirmatory bias model implies a positive measure of focal bias (β) regardless of the task characteristics, and the special case of optimistic bias is characterized by a positive focal bias for positive events and a negative focal bias for negative events. Ecological models predict that, with representative sampling of items, calibration will be perfect, implying that in ecologically meaningful situations, β will track changes in base rate and σ will track changes in discriminability.

THE DATA

We review research on calibration from five applied domains: medicine, meteorology, law, business, and sports. Wherever possible, we restrict ourselves to studies where the judges were making predictions as part of their daily professional activities and where the stimuli were neither selected nor restricted by the researchers. Due to space limitations – and to limitations on data we were able to collect from secondary sources – we focus only on the shape of calibration curves relating outcome frequency to probability judgments, even though RST makes precise predictions about the expected distribution of judgments. Our approach is necessarily descriptive and we do not explore the variety of quantitative performance measures available to diagnose miscalibration (see e.g. Harvey, Hammond, Lusk, & Mross, 1992; Murphy & Winkler, 1992; Stewart & Lusk, 1994; Yates, 1992; Yates & Curley, 1985).

Expert Judges and Expert Judgments: Two Textbook Examples

Before we present the summaries of data collected across five domains of expertise, we first review two paradigmatic examples of excellent calibration. Few textbook discussions of calibration and prediction fail to mention the essentially perfectly calibrated predictions of expert bridge players (Keren, 1987) and meteorologists predicting rain in Chicago (Murphy & Winkler, 1977). These two striking case studies have been enough to convince many commentators of the intrinsic superiority of expert calibration in the field. It is useful to consider how these classic examples fit into our theoretical framework before continuing on to review less well-known data sets.

Perfect calibration is theoretically possible with various possible combinations of outcome base rate and discriminability or difficulty. Indeed, ecological models predict perfect calibration in any naturalistic or representative environment. Case-based or direct support models predict excellent calibration when the base rate is moderate (near 50%) and when evidence quality is moderate. These conditions are well met in the predictions of the world-class bridge players studied by Keren (1987). The probability of successfully obtaining a given contract (the focal outcome) was moderate (55%) and so no response bias was needed or found (observed $\beta = .05$). Furthermore, the players were moderately good at discriminating between successful and unsuccessful contracts ($\alpha = .96$, where $\alpha = 0$ represents no ability to discriminate, and α values above 1.3 represent excellent discrimination); and this level of discriminability was almost exactly matched by the moderate extremity of predictions ($\alpha = .90$). Thus, excellent calibration can be entirely consistent with a heuristic case-based account such as direct support theory.

The government meteorologists studied by Murphy and Winkler (1977) were also moderately good at discriminating between days with and without rain ($\alpha = 1.09$), and also showed moderate extremity of judgment ($\sigma = .94$). However, rain fell on only 26% of the days, so a substantially negative response bias was required (and obtained) to maintain calibration ($\beta = -.71$). Here, excellent calibration marks a distinct departure from the predictions of the heuristic case-based account. As we discuss below in our review of meteorologists' predictive judgment, it is difficult to know if this sensitivity is a tribute to clinical or actuarial judgment, as meteorologists combine statistical summary data with intuitive adjustments.

Not all published data sets reviewed below provided enough information to fit the full RST model. However, all provided a calibration curve or table relating subjective probabilities to actual outcomes, the base rate of the target or focal outcome, and some measure of discriminability (usually A_z, the area under the Receiver Operating Characteristics curve in SDT, which itself is a linear transformation of d' in SDT, of α in RST, and of the ordinal correlation of discrimination recommended by Liberman & Tversky, 1993). In the absence of complete data, we provide a graphical and qualitative comparison of the direct support predictions with the expert data. We create "direct support" calibration curves by setting the extremity parameter σ to 1, indicating a moderate level of judgmental extremity that is insensitive to evidence quality, and by setting the response bias parameter β to 0, indicating no sensitivity to outcome base rate, and allowing discriminability and base rate to vary from one data set to the next. We then examine the fit of the direct support curves to the observed judgments.

These direct support curves serve as "neglect models," indicating the pattern of judgments expected if base rate and discriminability are completely neglected. Observed curves that fall close to these predicted curves provide evidence consistent with the case-based neglect account. Observed curves that fall closer to the identity line than the predicted curves imply some sensitivity to base rate and discriminability.

Domain 1: Calibration in Medical Settings

We begin with the expert domain for which the widest variety of data sets is available. Since the early 1980s, there has been a growing interest in the quality of physicians' prognostic and diagnostic judgments and this interest is now reflected in a substantial body of empirical research (for reviews, see Dawson, 1993; Winkler & Poses, 1993). Data points from nine such studies are presented in Fig. 39.3, and Table 39.1 provides accompanying information such as the target event, base rate, and α, the RST measure of discriminability. Figure 39.3 also shows simulated curves based on random support theory with constant β and σ (i.e., our case-based "neglect model"), for three combinations of base rate and discriminability. The theoretical curves give a good qualitative fit to the data points.

The data summarized in Fig. 39.3 reveal that, across the different sets of medical events, physicians' judgments show marked underprediction (when base rate is high and discriminability is high), fair calibration (when base rate is low and discriminability is high), and marked overprediction (when base rate is very low and discriminability is low). These variations in calibration

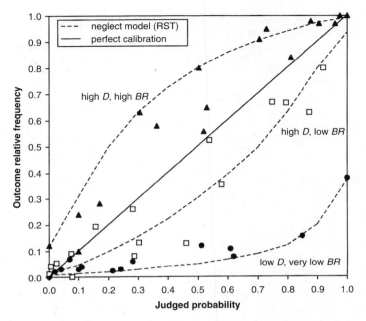

Figure 39.3. Physicians: Calibration of physicians' judgments, represented by circle (very low *BR*), square (low *BR*), and triangle points (high *BR*), compared with predictions of neglect model. (See Table 39.1 for details of these studies.)

Note: Neglect model predictions based on RST simulation assuming no focal bias ($\beta = 0$) and fixed judgmental extremity ($\sigma = 1$). Discriminability (D) and base rate (BR) are approximately matched to the empirical datasets as follows: For low D, $\alpha = 0.7$; for high D, $\alpha = 1.0$; very low $BR = 5\%$; low $BR = 30\%$; and high $BR = 80\%$.

are clearly inconsistent with ecological theories or the presence of an overall confirmatory bias in favor of the focal hypothesis. Nor are they consistent with the form of the confirmatory bias explanation that is most common in the medical decision making literature: the "value-induced bias" or "warning bias" (Edwards & von Winterfeldt, 1986). According to this account, summarized by Wallsten (1981), physicians tend to exaggerate the likelihood of very severe conditions, either because their utilities contaminate their probability estimates, or because they search for signs of a dangerous condition. This account implies that overprediction should increase with the severity of the event; in fact, both a very severe negative event (heart attack) and a positive event (surviving cancer for 5 years) show moderate overprediction whereas a rare but relatively mild negative event (streptococcal throat infection) shows gross overprediction.

The pattern of calibration across studies is also inconsistent with the many accounts that implicate regular feedback (whether event-based or in terms of probability scoring) as the key to good calibration (Keren, 1988; Edwards & von

Table 39.1. Target Event Description, Base Rate (BR), and Discriminability (α) for Medical Calibration Studies Depicted in Fig. 39.3

Study	Target Event	BR (%)	α
Low D, very low BR			
Christensen-Szalanski & Bushyhead (1981)	Pneumonia	2.7	0.23[a]
Poses, Cebul, Collins, & Fager (1985)	Streptococcal pharyngitis	4.9	0.33[a]
Poses & Anthony (1991)	Bacteremia	7.9	0.50
High D, low BR			
Tierney et al. (1986)	Myocardial infarction	12	1.13
Centor, Dalton, & Yates (1994)	Streptococcal throat infection	25	1.04
Mackillop & Quirt (1997)	Cancer survival	28	1.34
High D, high BR			
McClish & Powell (1989)	ICU survival	75	1.23
Poses et al. (1990)	ICU survival	77	1.04
Detsky et al. (1981)	ICU survival	91	1.04[a]

[a] Values of discriminability parameter α for these studies were computed based on relevant values estimated from published graphs, as the necessary values were not explicitly provided in the source article.

Winterfeldt, 1986). Because the physicians in all studies had clear, unambiguous event-based feedback regarding events that they could not control (Murphy & Brown, 1984), feedback cannot explain the marked variation in the calibration of their probability judgments. There is also no clear distinction in terms of quality of calibration between prognostic (predictive) judgments (where physicians might accept that the events truly are uncertain) and diagnostic judgments (where the correct answer is at least theoretically knowable), in contrast to suggestions by Winkler and Poses (1993; see also Wagenaar & Keren, 1985). There is considerable variation in calibration between studies within the category of prognostic judgments (e.g., between surviving cancer for several years and surviving as an in-patient in an intensive care ward for a few days or weeks) as well as between studies within the category of diagnostic judgments (e.g., between having streptococcal throat infection and having a heart attack).

Winkler and Poses (1993, p. 1537) noted that "many factors could have contributed to such differences, but one that seems to stand out is the base rate." Consistent with direct support models and more general heuristic models such as "prediction by evaluation" (Kahneman & Tversky, 1973), the pattern of over-prediction and underprediction is strongly related to the base rate likelihood of the target events, and to a lesser extent (particularly for the heart attack study) to the discriminability of the relevant hypotheses. This is exactly what would be expected if the physicians' judgments reflected the support for the relevant hypotheses with little regard for the base rate likelihood of the events or the discriminability of the hypotheses.

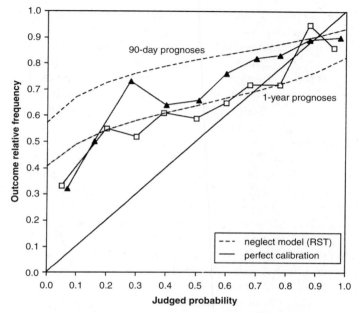

Figure 39.4. Physicians: Calibration curves for heart patient survival predictions reported by Poses et al. (1997) compared with predictions of neglect model. Triangles represent 90-day ($BR =$ 81%) prognoses; squares represent 1-year ($BR = 64\%$) prognoses. *Note*: Neglect model predictions based on RST simulation assuming no focal bias ($\beta = 0$) and fixed judgmental extremity ($\sigma = 1$). Discriminability ($\alpha = 0.41$ for 90-day prognoses and 0.33 for 1-year prognoses) and base rate are matched to values reported by Poses et al. (1997).

The outcomes represented in Fig. 39.3 differ in many ways other than base rate and discriminability. Figure 39.4, however, displays two calibration curves that are roughly matched for outcome and discriminability and differ only in time scale and hence base rate of survival. These data from Poses et al. (1997) represent survival predictions for cardiac patients over a 3-month and 1-year period. Although the shorter time frame seems intuitively "easier" to predict (and indeed yields a slightly higher value of the discriminability index α), consistent with the direct support account the three-month predictions show a more marked underprediction bias due to the more extreme base rate (i.e., 81% versus 64% survival rate).

The direct support account is consistent with the finding that personal experience with a patient (relative to written descriptions) increased overprediction in diagnosing cardiac failure (Bobbio et al., 1992). It is also consistent with the report that physicians' judgments of the probability of bacteremia were correlated with the availability of cases of bacteremia in their memory (Poses & Anthony, 1991). Both the vivid experience that comes with personal contact with a patient and easily accessible memories of a given outcome could give rise to stronger impressions of support for a hypothesis.

The apparent neglect of base rate across these studies fits the earlier observation that experienced physicians (sometimes) and medical students (frequently) neglected the prevalence rate of a disease when making a diagnosis, and tended to characterize uncertain hypotheses by "50–50" ratings rather than by their prevalence rate (Wallsten, 1981). Eddy's (1982) classic report on probabilistic thinking in medicine also highlighted many barriers to physicians' use of base rate information. It is unlikely that the present findings reflect ignorance on the part of the physicians as their judgments of prevalence rates have been found to be quite accurate (e.g., Bobbio, Deorsola, Pistis, Brusca, & Diamond, 1988; Christensen-Szalanski, 1982). For example, in a study on diagnosis of skull fractures (DeSmet, Fryback, & Thornbury, 1979), physicians' mean estimate of fracture incidence was 2.2% (with a range from 0 to 10%), when the actual rate was 2.9%. This study, which was not included in Fig. 39.3 because of space limitations, found dramatic overprediction similar to that documented by Christensen-Szalanski and Bushyhead (1981) in their study of pneumonia diagnosis (base rate 3.4%).

Not all instances of base rate effects on calibration represent neglect of known base rates; when the base rate varies across populations or cohorts, it can be very difficult for a judge to make appropriate adjustments. For example, Tape, Heckerling, Ornato and Wigdon (1991) investigated pneumonia diagnoses in three medical centers in different U.S. states. Both the base rate likelihood of pneumonia and the validity of common diagnostic cues varied markedly in the three centers. As Yates (1994) noted in his discussion of these data, if the more extreme base rate in Illinois (11% confirmed cases in the sample) was known and taken into account by the physicians, these judgments should have been easier than those in Nebraska (32% pneumonia cases). However, the probability judgments in Illinois showed much more overprediction than the probability judgments in Nebraska. These data were originally analyzed with the lens model equations (Hammond, Hursch & Todd, 1964; Tucker, 1964), which do not include base rate neglect as a possible source of judgmental bias. Stewart and Lusk (1994) presented a more inclusive model of forecasting skill that adds base rate bias and regression bias (insufficient adjustment for low predictability) to the lens model decomposition; this combination of calibration principles with the lens model approach is highly consistent with the RST approach we outline here.

In medical settings, it is instructive to consider the patient as an additional source of expert judgment, one with privileged access to internal states. Two recent studies have compared physician and patient judgments of survival for patients with metastatic colon and lung cancer (Weeks et al., 1998) and for "seriously ill" patients (Arkes et al. & SUPPORT Investigators, 1995). Surviving 6 months was considerably less common for the cancer patients (about 45% of whom survived 6 months) than for the mixture of seriously ill patients (about 70% of whom survived 6 months), and in both cases physicians were moderately

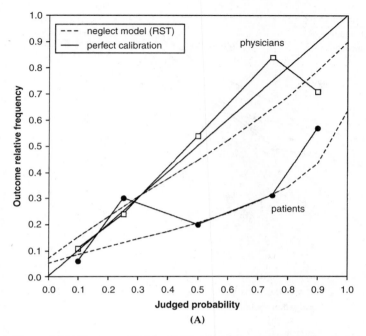

Figure 39.5. Cancer patients: Calibration curves from Weeks et al. (1998) study of yoked patient (circles) and physician (squares) predictions of patient survival ($BR = 44.7\%$), compared with neglect model predictions.

Note: Neglect model predictions based on RST simulations with fixed judgmental extremity ($\sigma = 1$). Discriminability ($\alpha = 0.82$ for physicians and $\alpha = 0.57$ for patients) and base rate are matched to values reported by Weeks et al. (1998), assuming positive ("optimistic") focal bias ($\beta = 2$) for patients but not for physicians ($\beta = 0$).

(*Continued on next page*)

good at discriminating those who would survive from those who would die (α's between .8 and .9). Thus, the direct support model implies that the physicians should be well calibrated for the cancer patients, and show distinct underprediction for the seriously ill patients. This pattern was indeed found, as displayed in Figs. 39.5A and B. Also displayed in Fig. 39.5 are the patients' self-predictions of survival. They are notably less discriminating than the physicians' judgments, and show a marked positive or "optimistic" bias that is absent from the physicians' judgments.

Domain 2: Calibration in Weather Forecasting

The calibration of American meteorologists predicting precipitation (e.g., Murphy & Winkler, 1977) has been described as "superb" (Lichtenstein et al., 1982), "champion" (Edwards & von Winterfeldt, 1986) and as an "existence proof" of good calibration (Wallsten & Budescu, 1983). There are at least five non-exclusive explanations for this excellent calibration: the use of sophisticated

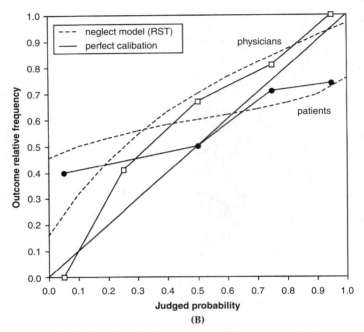

Figure 39.5. (*Continued*) (B) Seriously ill patients: Calibration curves from Arkes et al. (1995) study of yoked patient (circles) and physician (squares) predictions of patient survival ($BR = 70\%$), compared with neglect model predictions.

Note: Neglect model predictions based on RST simulations with fixed judgmental extremity ($\sigma = 1$). Discriminability ($\alpha = 0.87$ for physicians and $\alpha = 0.22$ for patients) and base rate are matched to values reported by Arkes et al. (1995), assuming positive ("optimistic") focal bias ($\beta = 2$) for patients but not for physicians ($\beta = 0$).

computer models and centrally provided forecasts that allow direct "pattern matching" of present cues to past outcomes (e.g., Fischhoff, 1988), the clear and unambiguous feedback received by the forecasters coupled with their knowledge that they cannot affect the outcome (Murphy & Winkler, 1984; Keren, 1991), training in probabilistic thinking (Murphy & Brown, 1984), the explicit presentation of base rates that allow their use as an "anchor" at the time of prediction, and, consistent with the direct support account, the combination of accurate cues (i.e., high discrimination) with moderate base rates.

Some historical information casts doubt on the necessary roles of computer models and training in probabilistic thinking. Murphy and Winkler (1984) present data collected by Hallenback (1920) on his probabilistic predictions of rain in the Pecos Valley in New Mexico. These predictions (base rate 42%), based on composite weather maps, show very good calibration, with only a small tendency towards underprediction in the middle and high ranges. However, they cannot be described as a triumph of intuitive judgment; they were really a triumph of early weather technology in the actuarial mode. Hallenback (1920) described a pattern-matching or "table look-up" strategy in which certain prototypical weather patterns were matched with the relative frequency of past outcomes: "The basis of this method is a series of composite weather maps showing the frequency of precipitation, in percentages, with different types of pressure distribution" (p. 645).

Winkler and Poses (1993) noted that the excellent calibration of modern American weather forecasters predicting rain may be related to the moderate base rate (about 25% in the Murphy & Winkler, 1977, analysis), and contrasted this with the poorer calibration of weather forecasters predicting extreme storms (base rate 13%). However, they cautioned that the forecasters also have more experience with forecasting precipitation than forecasting storms. A closer look at the moderate overprediction of storms indicates an intriguing pattern: "a strong tendency to overforecast existed for the smaller areas and . . . a tendency to underforecast existed for the larger areas" (Murphy, 1981, p. 72). That is, when storms are rare (as in smaller forecast areas) forecasters tend to overuse high probabilities; when storms are more common (as in larger forecast areas) forecasters tend to underuse high probabilities, consistent with base rate neglect and the direct support account.

Murphy and Daan (1984) reported another striking finding in their study of Dutch weather forecasters. The forecasters were given detailed probabilistic feedback based on one year's worth of predictions. Data collected during the second year of the study showed that this feedback served to reduce the overprediction observed in the first year so that the overall calibration curve (averaged across many prediction events) for the second year followed the identity line fairly closely. However, as Murphy and Daan (1984) noted, "the amount of overforecasting increases, in general, as the sample climatological probabilities of the events decrease in both years" (p. 416). Figure 39.6 displays this pattern for the prediction of various weather events along with the relevant direct support lines (representing complete neglect of base rates and evidence quality). Weather events have been categorized in terms of base rate and discriminability as shown in Table 39.2.

Consistent with the general predictions of direct support theory, when the meteorological event was common, calibration was very good, whereas when the event was rare, there was marked overprediction. Did this occur because the meteorologists were reporting the strength of their evidence for a given hypothesis without due regard for the base rate, or because the rarer events were also more severe and meteorologists were determined not to miss them? It is impossible to rule out the presence of a "warning bias" in this situation, but data from other types of forecasts cast doubt on this explanation. Much more overprediction is found for predictions of rainfall greater than 1.4 mm (base rate 9%) than predictions of rainfall greater than .2 mm (base rate 20%), although the former is by no means an extreme amount of rain. Similarly, there is more overprediction when judges evaluate whether visibility will be less than

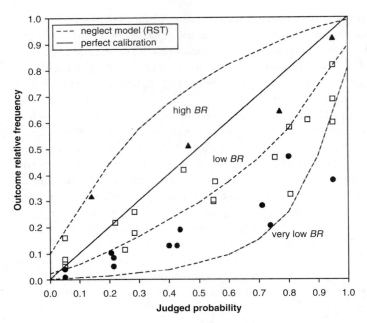

Figure 39.6. Meteorologists: Calibration of weather forecasts from Daan and Murphy's (1982) study, represented by circles (very low *BR*), squares (low *BR*), and triangles (high *BR*), compared with predictions of neglect model (derived from RST simulations). (See Table 39.2 for details of these forecasts).

Note: Neglect model predictions based on RST simulation assuming no focal bias ($\beta = 0$) and fixed judgmental extremity ($\sigma = 1$). Discriminability (D) and base rate (BR) is matched to average values from the Daan and Murphy (1982) study, with $\alpha = 1.19$, 0.86, and 0.96 in the very low ($BR = 6\%$), low ($BR = 29\%$), and high ($BR = 75\%$) base rate conditions, respectively.

4 km (base rate 17%) than when they evaluate whether visibility will be less than 10 km (base rate 44%). In this case, the 4-km prediction does not include extreme or dangerous events as these form another category, visibility less than 1 km (base rate 3%, with extreme overprediction). Although value-induced or warning biases may add to the tendency for overprediction, the evidence suggests that the base rate had a substantial and independent effect on miscalibration. Inspection of Fig. 39.6 reveals that the empirical points are somewhat closer to the line of perfect calibration than the RST prediction lines; this indicates that the meteorologists were giving more weight to the base rate than the "neglect" model predicted. As discussed, this discrepancy from the case-based support model may be a result of the considerable technical information provided to the weather forecasters or their training in statistical models.

Table 39.2. Target Event Description, Base Rate (BR), and Discriminability (α) for Daan & Murphy (1982) Weather Forecasting Data Depicted in Fig. 39.6.

Target Event	BR (%)	α
Low base rate (BR < 12%)		
visibility < 1 kilometer	3	1.17
windspeed > 31 knots	4	1.17
precipitation > 1.4 millimeter	11	0.71
Moderate base rate (18% ≤ BR ≤ 43%)		
Visibility < 4 kilometers	18	0.99
Precipitation > 0.3 millimeters	25	0.74
Windspeed > 21 knots	31	0.95
Visibility < 10 kilometers	43	0.81
High base rate (BR = 75%)		
Windspeed > 12 knots	75	0.95

Note: Values of discriminability parameter α for these data sets were estimated, as the necessary values were not explicitly provided in the Daan & Murphy (1982) source article.

Domain 3: The Calibration of Legal Judgments

The appropriateness of lawyers' probability judgments has important implications for the quality of their service – decisions about whether to sue, settle out of court, or plead guilty to a lesser charge all depend on a lawyer's judgment of the probability of success. Surprisingly, then, there is relatively little research assessing the calibration of lawyers' probability judgments in their day-to-day practice. Figure 39.7 presents calibration curves representing Dutch (Malsch, 1989) and American (Goodman-Delahunty, Granhag, & Loftus, 1998) lawyers' judgments of whether they would win their cases. Base rates in both studies were near 50%, but predictions of the Dutch lawyers were somewhat discriminating ($\alpha = .54$), whereas the American lawyers' judgments showed no predictive validity ($\alpha = .15$, hardly above chance). Malsch (1989) describes a number of differences in the Dutch and American legal systems that might explain the differential sensitivity to outcomes. In both data sets, there is surprisingly little evidence that lawyers' judgments show a confirmatory bias given the pressures of the adversarial system; if confirmatory biases were rife, then the calibration curves should fall largely under the identity line. Instead, consistent with the case-based model, both sets of judgments show an overextremity bias (underprediction of success for low probabilities and overprediction of success for high probabilities). As expected given their poorer discrimination, this bias is much more marked for the American than for the Dutch lawyers.

Goodman-Delahunty et al. (1998) found other interesting patterns within their data. When lawyers were surveyed close to their trial date (and had somewhat valid information about a given case, $\alpha = .33$) they were moderately

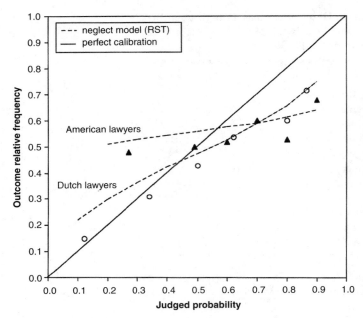

Figure 39.7. Lawyers: Calibration curves from Dutch lawyers (Malsch, 1989; represented by circles) and American lawyers (Goodman-Delahunty et al., 1998; represented by triangles), compared with predictions of neglect model.

Note: Neglect model predictions based on RST simulations assuming no focal bias ($\beta = 0$) and fixed judgmental extremity ($\sigma = 1$). Discriminability (D) and base rate (BR) are matched to values from original studies, with $\alpha = 0.54$ and $BR = 47.5\%$ for Malsch (1989), and $\alpha = 0.15$ and $BR = 56\%$ for Goodman-Delahunty et al. (1998). Neglect model curves are truncated for purposes of presentation.

well calibrated, and showed a moderate extremity bias; when surveyed far from the trial date (with completely nondiagnostic cues, $\alpha = .03$) they showed a strong extremity bias and outcomes were at the base rate level regardless of expressed probability. Again, this neglect of discriminability is consistent with the direct support account. There was also some evidence for optimistic overconfidence when the predictions were personally relevant: the subset of lawyers who were working for plaintiffs on a contingency fee basis were just as confident as other lawyers (generally about 65% confident) but won their cases much less often (42% compared to 56% overall).

Domain 4: Calibration in Business Settings

Indirect evidence implies that optimistic overconfidence, a focal bias towards the desirable outcome (Kahneman & Lovallo, 1993; Kahneman & Tversky, 1995), may be prevalent in business settings. Financial forecasts made over the last century have been consistently optimistic (Hogarth & Makridakis, 1981). For example, Wall Street analysts expected the Standard and Poors 500 Index to post average earnings growth of 21.9% per year from 1982 to 1997, whereas actual annual earnings growth averaged 7.6% (Cadsby, 2000). A survey of macroeconomic predictions from 14 OECD countries indicated that industrial firms were systematically over-optimistic in their production estimates (Madsen, 1994); further analyses implicated a search for confirming evidence, as it took more and stronger evidence to lead firms to predict decreased production than increased production. A series of laboratory studies by Bazerman and colleagues showed that people in negotiation settings overestimated the probability their final offer would be accepted and were overly optimistic that a third party would rule in their favor (Bazerman & Neale, 1982; Neale & Bazerman, 1983; Farber & Bazerman, 1986, 1989). A survey of almost 3000 new business owners revealed that they were unrealistically optimistic about their own business succeeding (81% probability of success for their own business versus 59% probability of businesses like theirs, whereas a realistic estimate is somewhere in the range of 30% to 70%; Cooper, Woo, & Dunkelberg, 1988).

Figure 39.8 displays the calibration of professional American economic forecasters predicting the likelihood of economic recession at various points in the future. The plot shows an overextremity bias that increases with an increasing time frame, as discriminability decreases (Braun & Yaniv, 1992). When the economists predicted the outcome of the current quarter, they had valid models and cues with which to work ($\alpha = 1.17$); however, the base rate of recession was relatively low (about 20%), and so marked overprediction occurred for subjective probabilities above .6. As the time horizon increased, the judges moderated the extremeness of their predictions but not enough to match the declining validity of their models and cues, and so for forecasts two quarters ahead ($\alpha = .58$), overprediction was found for subjective probabilities above .4. When the forecast horizon was four quarters ahead, the judges' cues and models were essentially worthless ($\alpha \approx 0$, indicating no discrimination), and so regardless of the judged probability of recession (which ranged from 0 to 90%) the observed frequency of recession was always close to the base rate value. The observed curves are generally consistent with the predictions of the random support model; however, the observed judgments are markedly higher (i.e., closer to the line of perfect calibration) than are the direct support lines, implying that the economists were at least somewhat sensitive to the base rate.

There are a number of studies on stock market prediction, although few lend themselves to calibration analyses. In an analysis of trading at large discount brokerage houses, Odean (1998) reported a bias towards overtrading, such that purchased stocks underperformed sold stocks, consistent with optimistic overconfidence in stock choice. In a laboratory study with real-life information, undergraduate and graduate students in finance courses were asked to predict the probability that a given stock (earning) would increase by more than 10%, increase by between 5% and 10%, and so on (Yates, McDaniel, & Brown, 1991).

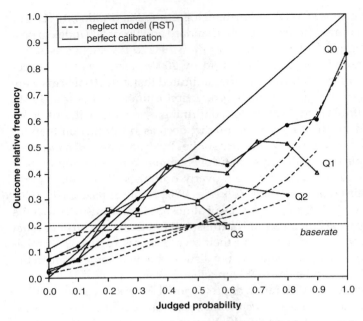

Figure 39.8. Economists: Calibration of economists' forecasts of recession (i.e., decrease in real gross national product) at varying forecast horizons of one to four quarters beyond time of prediction (Q0 to Q3, respectively; Braun & Yaniv, 1992), compared with predictions of neglect model.

Note: Neglect model predictions based on RST simulations assuming no focal bias ($\beta = 0$) and fixed judgmental extremity ($\sigma = 1$), assuming that discriminability decreases at longer forecast horizons ($\alpha = 1, 0.7, 0.4,$ and 0.1 for Q0 to Q3, respectively). Accuracy values of calibration curves estimated from Exhibit 1 of Braun and Yaniv (1992); data points representing 20 or fewer observations have been excluded, and neglect model curves truncated accordingly. Base rate line indicates approximate historical base rate probability of recession from 1947 to the time the forecasts were made (see Braun & Yaniv, 1992, pp. 224–227).

The primary finding was the graduate students ("experts") were more likely to attend to non-predictive cues and so were more poorly calibrated than the undergraduate students, who made less extreme and less variable predictions. In a series of follow-up studies, stock brokers and related financial professionals predicted changes in the Turkish stock market (Onkal & Muradoglu, 1994); the primary finding was that calibration became poorer with longer time intervals, and that the relative performance of experts and semi-experts depended on the time horizon. The bottom line in Fig. 39.9 represents the calibration of Turkish stockbrokers predicting whether the share price of each in a set of Turkish companies would increase or decrease over a 1-week period. Although

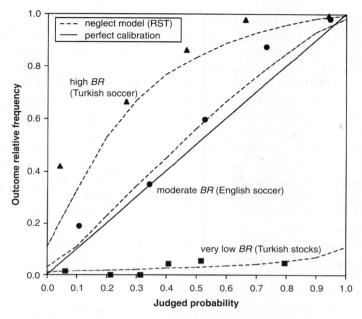

Figure 39.9. Sportswriters and stockbrokers. Calibration curves from Onkal and Ayton (1997) study of sportswriters predicting winners in upcoming English (moderate *BR*, represented by circles) and Turkish (high BR, represented by triangles) football (soccer) games, and from Onkal and Muradogui (1996) study of expert stock market predictions (very low *BR*, represented by squares), compared with neglect model predictions.

Note: Neglect model predictions based on RST simulations assuming no focal bias ($\beta = 0$) and fixed judgmental extremity ($\sigma = 1$). Base rate values for soccer predictions matched to those reported by Onkal and Ayton (1997) for English ($BR = 56\%$) and Turkish ($BR = 83\%$) games, assuming common discriminability ($\alpha = 1.07$). Base rate ($BR = 3\%$) and discriminability ($\alpha = 0.45$) for stock predictions matched to data reported by Onkal and Muradoglu (1996).

the stockbrokers showed some ability to discriminate successful from unsuccessful companies ($\alpha = .45$), only 1 of the 32 companies actually increased in price over the target week (presumably a bearish week on the newly deregulated Turkish market) and in the face of this very low base rate the traders showed a marked overprediction bias.

Domain 5: Calibration in Sports

In no other domain are predictions more ubiquitous – or arguably less important – than in sports. Commentators, fans, bookies, and bettors all have a reason for assessing the probability of a win, the chances of the champion surviving the first round, and the likelihood of setting a new world record. Sports events have been a major source of data for studies of predictive judgment, but few of these studies have used expert judges. An exception to this rule is the study of horserace odds by economists interested in the rationality of the aggregate market. Odds for horse races shift as a result of the money placed by large numbers of individual investors, so the unbiasedness of such odds is a test of the rationality of market forces. Many studies have revealed a small but systematic bias such that posted odds and wagered amounts for favorites (high-probability winners) are too low whereas posted odds and wagered amounts for longshots (low-probability winners) are too high (termed the *favorite-longshot bias* for obvious reasons; e.g., Snyder, 1978; Thaler & Ziemba, 1988). This has been explained by general risk-seeking in gamblers (the pleasure of the long-shot) and by loss aversion driving gamblers to try to turn their losses into gains by a big win. It has even been tied to an "overconfidence" bias, though the observed pattern is actually one of underextremity.

We know of one cross-national study of expert commentators (television and newspaper sports reporters) that offers a clear test case for the direct support account. Ayton and Onkal (1996) asked media commentators in England and Turkey to give probabilistic predictions for a set of football (soccer) Cup Matches in their own countries. The natural target hypothesis is a home team win. In fact, there was a marked home field advantage in the Turkish cup games and little home field advantage in the English cup games; in other words, the base rate for a home team win was high (80%) in Turkey and moderate (close to 50%) in England. The commentators in both countries were moderately (and equally) good at discriminating between winning and losing teams ($\alpha = 1.07$) leading to a situation in which the direct support account implies good calibration for the English commentators and substantial underprediction for the Turkish commentators. As the top lines in Fig. 39.9 attest, this pattern emerged very clearly.

Summary of the Data

In all domains of expert judgment surveyed, systematic miscalibration was observed. In each case, the observed patterns matched the qualitative predictions of the heuristics and biases perspective, as embodied by the direct support account. Nonetheless, there were notable differences among the domains in the magnitude of miscalibration, such that the judgments of experts with the greatest training and technical assistance in statistical modeling (meteorologists and economists) were less biased than the direct support account predicted. Judgments of experts with less training in normative judgmental models, such as physicians, stockbrokers, and sports commentators, were captured well by the direct support account.

OTHER STOCHASTIC MODELS

In this section, we briefly discuss two additional models of subjective probability calibration that, like RST, incorporate stochastic components in their attempt to reproduce calibration curves. With appropriate supplemental assumptions, both models are capable in theory of reproducing the patterns of miscalibration found in our review of expert judgments. We argue, however, that in most cases RST offers a more parsimonious account that yields more easily interpreted parameter values, providing a framework that allows insights into the psychological underpinnings of miscalibration.

Partition Model

At the time of the Lichtenstein et al. (1982) review, the only existing model precise enough to be fit to empirical data was the decision variable partition model (herein the *partition model*) of Ferrell and McGoey (1980). In the tradition of signal detection theory, this model describes confidence judgment as a process of partitioning an internal decision variable (which might be thought of as a feeling of confidence) into confidence categories, which are used in making the overt judgment or response. The decision variable itself is not scaled in terms of probability; instead, the judgment is assumed to arise from a partition of some underlying variable. The model successfully fits calibration curves found in general knowledge tasks, though it should be noted that in such applications the number of free parameters is relatively high when compared to the number of data points being fit. Perhaps more impressive is the partition model's performance when supplemented by the assumption that the judge's set of partition cutoffs is insensitive to changes in task difficulty in the absence of performance feedback (Ferrell & McGoey, 1980; Smith & Ferrell, 1983; Suantak, Bolger, & Ferrell, 1996). Although there exists, for any given level of proportion correct, a set of cutoffs that would ensure perfect calibration, Ferrell and colleagues have found that the miscalibration observed in experimental contexts is often well accounted for by a single set of cutoffs that is not changed over large variations in task difficulty. In this sense, the partition model with fixed cutoffs can be seen as a close relative of RST with fixed extremity and focal bias parameters.

Perhaps the single greatest weakness of the partition model is its agnosticism regarding the underlying determinants of the unobservable decision variable, that is, the feeling of confidence upon which the partition is constructed. The model makes no attempt to specify how evidence is evaluated to arrive at the feeling of confidence, or how the judge goes about partitioning the resulting decision variable. In this sense, the partition model might be construed rather narrowly as a model of the response stage of the confidence assessment process, as Ferrell has acknowledged (e.g., Ferrell, has 1994, p. 433). Although the partition model typically produces a good fit to empirical calibration curves (and response proportions), achieving such a fit requires estimation of a fairly large number of parameters. For example, to fit a full-range calibration dataset with 11 probability categories (0%, 10%, ... , 100%), the partition model requires discriminability and base-rate parameters comparable to those of RST, but in addition requires estimation of a set of 10 cutoff values, for which RST substitutes only two additional parameters (extremity and focal bias). Arguably, RST's parameter values are also more readily interpreted (e.g., in terms of case- vs. class-based reasoning) than those of the partition model.

Error Models

A number of researchers have considered the consequences of unreliability in confidence judgments for the assessment of calibration. Erev, Wallsten, and Budescu (1994; also Wallsten & Budescu, 1983) offered a Thurstonian "true score plus error" model in which an underlying feeling of confidence is subjected to some degree of stochastic variation prior to being translated into an overt judgment. They assumed, for demonstration purposes, that the underlying "true" judgment equals the actuarial probability of the event being judged, and investigated how error due to unreliability affected the resulting calibration analysis. To illustrate, suppose that a weather forecaster's true judgment based on a set of forecasting cues is equal to the actual probability of precipitation given those cues, but that his or her overt judgment is subject to some error. How does this error influence calibration? Erev et al. (1994; also Budescu, Erev, and Wallsten, 1997), assuming a particular instantiation of their general model, demonstrated using simulation data that calibration curves can indicate overextremity even when the confidence judgments themselves are unbiased estimates of the true probability subject to symmetric error. This result arises primarily from effects of regression, but may also be enhanced by boundary effects due to rounding at scale endpoints. Pfeifer (1994) independently developed a very similar thesis to that of Erev et al. Such error models generally produce greater overextremity as the degree of error increases, and in this sense can account for the difficulty effect.

The results of Erev et al. can be interpreted in two ways, as a methodological prescription or as a descriptive model of probability judgment. The methodological prescription highlights the perils of diagnosing overconfidence on the basis of the calibration curve because "error alone" can produce the appearance of overconfidence in such a curve even when underlying "true" judgments are unbiased. Brenner, Koehler, Liberman, and Tversky (1996) argued that the standard measure of overconfidence in $2AFC$ tasks, namely the difference between mean confidence and overall accuracy, provides an unbiased estimate of aggregate overconfidence which is not subject to the same kind of regression effect apparent in the calibration curve. In response to the more general methodological recommendations of Erev et al., Brenner (2000) raised questions about the appropriateness of evaluating calibration on hard-to-define true scores rather than well-defined actual judgments.

Budescu, Wallsten, and Au (1997) assess the relative contributions of measurement error and systematic bias (i.e., over- or underconfidence) to overall miscalibration, using Wallsten and González-Vallejo's (1994) statement verification model. The reliability of subjective probability judgments is assessed from replicate judgments and used to estimate the degree of miscalibration expected on the basis of error alone (i.e., in the absence of systematic bias), which is then used to construct a less strict standard of "ideal" performance than that which is usually employed (see also Klayman, Soll, González-Vallejo, & Barlas, 1999). Using this method, Budescu, Wallsten, and Au (1997) found substantial overextremity, even after correcting for the unreliability of the assessments, in a full-range task involving the relative populations of pairs of cities. As a descriptive model, then, the assumption of an unbiased "true score" subject to error is not a sufficient account of the miscalibration found in this and other laboratory tasks.

Several researchers (Björkman, 1994; Juslin et al., 1997; Juslin, Wennerholm, & Olsson, 1999; Soll, 1996) offered modified ecological models in which stochastic error components have been introduced as a way of improving the fit of such models to actual calibration data. In such models, the "internal" probability is only an estimate of the corresponding ecological probability, unbiased but subject to sampling error. Soll (1996), Juslin et al. (1997), and Budescu, Erev, and Wallsten (1997) have shown, using simulations, that a modified ecological model incorporating sampling error can produce overconfidence that increases with task difficulty (as determined by the uncertainty of the environment and the sample size, i.e., number of available previous cases matching the present one). Soll (1996) further demonstrated, in a cue-based task somewhat different from the typical calibration experiment, that subjects appeared to be able to produce unbiased estimates of the ecological conditional probabilities associated with a set of cues, even though in terms of calibration these subjects were substantially overconfident.

Sampling error alone, it should be noted, cannot produce underextremity (Juslin et al., 1997, p. 197). Given the number of empirical studies which have reported underconfidence for relatively easy tasks (e.g., Baranski & Petrusic, 1994; Björkman, Juslin, & Winman, 1993; Brake, Doherty, & Kleiter, 1997; Griffin & Tversky, 1992; Juslin et al., 1999; Suantak et al., 1996), it is clear that sampling error, by itself, cannot account for the full range of results from calibration experiments. Moreover, at a conceptual level, it is not entirely clear what it means to argue that a judge's confidence assessments are not systematically biased, but instead merely fail to account for the uncertainty associated with prediction based on the available evidence. Arguably, it is precisely such uncertainty which the judge is expected to convey in his or her confidence assessment. This issue highlights an apparent conflict of goals between proponents of error models, who are concerned with whether the judge says what she means (i.e., gives a confidence assessment that properly reflects the corresponding "internal" probability), and the typical "consumer" of such assessments in everyday life, who is more concerned with whether the judge means what she says (i.e., gives a confidence assessment that properly reflects the actual probability of being correct). The consumer of judgments by Soll's (1996) subjects, for example, is unlikely to take much comfort in the purported accuracy of these subjects' underlying judgments upon discovering that when they indicated confidence in the range of 90% to 100%, they were accurate approximately 60% of the time.

CONCLUSION

Our survey of the calibration of probabilistic judgments in applied settings has identified the discriminability of the hypotheses and the base rate likelihood of the outcome as major predictors of miscalibration in experts' everyday judgments. Consistent with direct support models and the partition model – and with the difficulty effect described by Lichtenstein et al. (1982) – good calibration is found when discriminability is high and base rates are moderate; overprediction is found when base rates are low; underprediction is found when base rates are high; and an extremity bias (what is usually meant by the term *overconfidence*) is found when discriminability is low and base rates are moderate. Apparently, the prevalence of overprediction and overconfidence in many domains is not a sign that people are intrinsically biased to give high or extreme probabilities, but that important domains are marked by low base rates and by relatively non-diagnostic information (e.g., identification of drug users in transport industries by personal interviews) (Griffin & Varey, 1996).

The observed pattern of miscalibration in expert judgment is consistent with the predictions of the case-based direct support models derived from the literature on judgmental heuristics. Other models fared less well. Contrary to the predictions of ecological models, expert judgments exhibited systematic miscalibration despite representative sampling of judgment items. In the expert data sets we examined, there is little or no indication of a general bias in favor of the focal hypothesis, as implied by the confirmatory bias model. In particular, there was little evidence of optimistic bias in these data sets. Note, however, that most of the judgments were generally not self-relevant. When the issues were extremely self-relevant, such as the patients' predictions of their own survival, there was considerable optimistic bias shown. Apparently, an optimistic bias can sometimes contribute to but is not a necessary condition for miscalibration of subjective probability. Other stochastic models, like RST, might be able to reproduce the pattern of miscalibration in expert judgments that we described (or any other pattern), with appropriate supplemental assumptions. We find the general framework of support theory in which RST is based, however, to provide a useful and psychologically plausible interpretation of the patterns that we found: Assessments of probability typically reflect a direct translation of the support provided by the evidence for the target hypotheses, with little regard to the reliability of the evidence or the base rate of the outcome.

The identification of subjective probability with psychological support or strength of evidence gives rise to two very different reactions. According to some scholars, personal or subjective probabilities are of little interest because they do not reflect the way that people naturally process uncertainty (which is presumed to be through frequency counts, Gigerenzer, 1994). A second approach is to accept that subjective probabilities are not only natural, but inescapable. A historical review of the use of concepts related to "chance" in more than 500 years of English literature noted that "With one exception, all quotations found ... are subjective probabilities. They all are expressions of degrees of belief, at least in a poetic sense, that an event will happen" (Bellhouse & Franklin, 1997, p. 80). Consider the following statement, taken from a recent financial column: "Three months ago, I might have put the risk of an Asia-wide credit crunch ... at less than 10%, now I'd say it is approaching 30% to 40%." How can this statement about a unique, not to say unprecedented, event be reworded in frequency terms?

Our guess is that there will always be judgments made in terms of subjective probability or odds about unique events, and many such judgments, even by experts, will fail the test of correspondence. Accepting this, these results imply that training in probability and statistics, and in particular, training in the distinction between intuitive support and extensional probability, is essential to improve judgmental calibration in applied fields (see Stewart & Lusk, 1994, for one useful categorization of the skills needed for proper calibration). The attainment of expertise may sometimes imply good discrimination, but it rarely ensures good calibration.

40. Clinical versus Actuarial Judgment

Robyn M. Dawes, David Faust, and Paul E. Meehl

A psychiatric patient displays ambiguous symptoms. Is this a condition best treated by psychotherapy alone or might it also require an antipsychotic medication with occasionally dangerous side effects? An elderly patient complains of memory loss but neurological examination and diagnostic studies are equivocal. The neuropsychologist is asked to administer tests to help rule out progressive brain disease. A medical work-up confirms a patient's worst fears: He has terminal cancer. He asks the doctor how long he has to put his life in order.

These three brief scenarios illustrate a few of the many situations in which experts are consulted to diagnose conditions or to predict human outcomes. Optimal planning and care often hinge on the consultant's judgmental accuracy. Whether as physicians, psychiatrists, or psychologists, consultants perform two basic functions in decision-making: they collect and interpret data. Our interest here is in the interpretive function, specifically the relative merits of clinical versus actuarial methods.

METHODS OF JUDGMENT AND MEANS OF COMPARISON

In the clinical method the decision-maker combines or processes information in his or her head. In the actuarial or statistical method the human judge is eliminated and conclusions rest solely on empirically established relations between data and the condition or event of interest. A life insurance agent uses the clinical method if data on risk factors are combined through personal judgment. The agent uses the actuarial method if data are entered into a formula, or tables and charts that contain empirical information relating these background data to life expectancy.

Clinical judgment should not be equated with a clinical setting or a clinical practitioner. A clinician in psychiatry or medicine may use the clinical or actuarial method. Conversely, the actuarial method should not be equated with automated decision rules alone. For example, computers can automate clinical judgments. The computer can be programmed to yield the description "dependency traits," just as the clinical judge would, whenever a certain response appears on a psychological test. To be truly actuarial, interpretations must be both automatic (that is, prespecified or routinized) and based on empirically established relations.

Virtually any type of data is amenable to actuarial interpretation. For example, interview observations can be coded quantitatively (patient appears withdrawn: [1] yes, [2] no). It is thereby possible to incorporate qualitative observations and quantitative data into the predictive mix. Actuarial output statements, or conclusions, can address virtually any type of diagnosis, description, or prediction of human interest. . . .

Although some research appeared on clinical and actuarial judgment before the mid-1950s, Meehl (1954) introduced the issue to a broad range of social scientists in 1954 and stimulated a flurry of studies. Meehl specified conditions for a fair comparison of the two methods.

First, both methods should base judgments on the same data. This condition does not require that clinical judgment and statistical method, before comparison, use the same data to derive decision strategies or rules. The clinician's development of interpretive strategies depends on prior experience and knowledge. The development of actuarial methods requires cases with known outcome. The clinical and actuarial strategies may thus be derived from separate or overlapping data bases, and one or the other may be based on more or fewer cases or more or less outcome information. For example the clinician may have interpreted 1,000 intelligence tests for indications of brain dysfunction and may know the outcome for some of these cases based on radiologic examination. The actuarial method may have been developed on the subset of these 1,000 cases for which outcome is known.

Second, one must avoid conditions that can artificially inflate the accuracy of actuarial methods. For example, the mathematical procedures (such as regression analysis or discriminant analysis) used to develop statistical actuarial decision rules may capitalize on chance (nonrepeating) relations among variables. Thus, derivation typically should be followed by cross-validation, that is, application of the decision rule to new or fresh cases, or by a standard statistical estimate of the probable outcome of cross-validation. Cross-validation counters artificial inflation in accuracy rates and allows one to determine, realistically, how the method performs. Such applications are essential because a procedure should be shown to work where it is needed, that is, in cases in which outcome is unknown. If the method is only intended for local use or in the setting in which it was developed, the investigator may partition a representative sample from that setting into derivation and cross-validation groups. If broader application is intended, then new cases should be representative of the potential settings and populations of interest.

RESULTS OF COMPARATIVE STUDIES

The three initial scenarios provide examples of comparative studies. Goldberg studied the distinction between neurosis and psychosis based on the Minnesota

Multiphasic Personality Inventory (MMPI), a personality test commonly used for such purposes (Goldberg, 1965, 1968). This differential diagnosis is of practical importance. For example, the diagnosis of psychosis may lead to needed but riskier treatments or to denial of future insurance applications. Goldberg derived various decision rules through statistical analysis of scores on 11 MMPI scales and psychiatric patients' discharge diagnoses. The single most effective rule for distinguishing the two conditions was quite simple: add scores from three scales and then subtract scores from two other scales. If the sum falls below 45, the patient is diagnosed neurotic; if it equals or exceeds 45, the patient is diagnosed psychotic. This has come to be known as the *Goldberg Rule.*

Goldberg next obtained a total of 861 new MMPIs from seven different settings, including inpatient and outpatient services from either medical school, private, or Veterans Administration hospital systems in California, Minnesota, and Ohio. The accuracy of the decision rules when applied to these new cases was compared with that of 29 judges who analyzed the same material and attempted the same distinction. Some of the judges had little or no prior experience with the MMPI and others were Ph.D. psychologists with extensive MMPI experience.

Across the seven settings, the judges achieved mean validity coefficients ranging from $r = 0.15$ to 0.43, with a total figure of 0.28 for all cases, or 62% correct decisions. The single best judge achieved an overall coefficient of 0.39, or 67% correct decisions. In each of the seven settings, various decision rules exceeded the judges' mean accuracy level. The Goldberg Rule performed similarly to the judges in three of the settings and demonstrated a modest to substantial advantage in four of the settings (where the rule's validity coefficient exceeded that of the judges by 0.16 to 0.31). For the total sample, the Goldberg Rule achieved a validity coefficient of 0.45, or 70% correct decisions, thereby exceeding both the mean accuracy of the 29 judges and that of the single best judge.

Rorer and Goldberg then examined whether additional practice might alter results. Judges were given MMPI training packets consisting of 300 new MMPI profiles with the criterion diagnosis on the back, thus providing immediate and concrete feedback on judgmental accuracy. However, even after repeated sessions with these training protocols culminating in 4,000 practice judgments, none of the judges equaled the Goldberg Rule's 70% accuracy rate with these test cases. Rorer and Goldberg finally tried giving a subset of judges, including all of the experts, the outcome of the Goldberg Rule for each MMPI. The judges were free to use the rule when they wished and knew its overall effectiveness. Judges generally made modest gains in performance but none could match the rule's accuracy; every judge would have done better by always following the rule.

In another study using the same 861 MMPI protocols, Goldberg constructed mathematical (linear) models of each of the 29 judges that reproduced their decisions as closely as possible (Goldberg, 1970). Modeling judges' decisions requires no access to outcome information. Rather, one analyzes relations between the information available to the judge and the judge's decisions. In principle, if a judge weights variables with perfect consistency or reliability (that is, the same data always lead to the same decision), the model will always reproduce that judge's decisions. In practice, human decision-makers are not perfectly reliable and thus judge and model will sometimes disagree. Goldberg found that in cases of disagreement, the models were more often correct than the very judges on whom they were based. The perfect reliability of the models likely explains their superior performance in this and related studies (Dawes & Corrigan, 1974).

Leli and Filskov studied the diagnosis of progressive brain dysfunction based on intellectual testing (Leli & Filskov, 1984). A decision rule derived from one set of cases and then applied to a new sample correctly identified 83% of the new cases. Groups of inexperienced and experienced clinicians working from the same data correctly identified 63% and 58% of the new cases, respectively. In another condition, clinicians were also given the results of the actuarial analysis. Both the inexperienced and experienced clinicians showed improvement (68% and 75% correct identifications, respectively), but neither group matched the decision rule's 83% accuracy. The clinicians' improvement appeared to depend on the extent to which they used the rule.

Einhorn (1972) studied the prediction of survival time following the initial diagnosis of Hodgkin's disease as established by biopsy. At the time of the study, survival time was negatively correlated with disease severity (Hodgkin's is now controllable). All of the 193 patients in the study subsequently died, thus tragically providing objective outcome information.

Three pathologists, one an internationally recognized authority, rated the patients' initial biopsy slides along nine histological dimensions they identified as relevant in determining disease severity and also provided a global rating of severity. Actuarial formulas were developed by examining relations between the pathologists' ratings and actual survival time on the first 100 cases, with the remaining 93 cases used for cross-validation and comparison. The pathologists' own judgments showed virtually no relation to survival time; cross-validated actuarial formulas achieved modest but significant relations. The study revealed more than an actuarial advantage. It also showed that the pathologists' ratings produced potentially useful information but that only the actuarial method, which was based on these ratings, tapped their predictive value.

Additional Research

These three studies illustrate key features of a much larger literature on clinical versus actuarial judgment. First, the studies, like many others, met the previously specified conditions for a fair comparison.

Second, the three studies are representative of research outcomes. Eliminating research that did not protect sufficiently against inflated results for actuarial methods, there remain nearly 100 comparative studies in the social sciences. In virtually every one of these studies, the actuarial method has equaled or surpassed the clinical method, sometimes slightly and sometimes substantially

(Meehl, 1986; Sawyer, 1966). For example, in Watley and Vance's (1974) study on the prediction of college grades the methods tied; in Carroll et al.'s (1982) study on the prediction of parole violation, the actuarial method showed a slight to modest advantage; and in Wittman's (1941) study on the prediction of response to electroshock therapy, the actuarial method was correct almost twice as often as the clinical method.

The earlier comparative studies were often met with doubts about validity and generalization. It was claimed, for example, that the studies misrepresented the clinical method either by denying judges access to crucial data sources such as interviews, by using artificial tasks that failed to tap their areas of expertise, or by including clinicians of questionable experience or expertise.

The evidence that has accumulated over the years meets these challenges. First, numerous studies have examined judgments that are not artificial but common to everyday practice and for which special expertise is claimed. Examples include the three studies described above, which involved the differential between less serious and major psychiatric disorder, the detection of brain damage, and the prediction of survival time. Other studies have examined the diagnosis of medical versus psychiatric disorder (Oskamp, 1962); the description or characterization of personality (Halbower, 1955); and the prediction of treatment outcome (Barron, 1953), length of psychiatric hospitalization (Dunham & Meltzer, 1946), and violent behavior (Werner, Rose, & Yesavage, 1983). These are decisions that general practitioners or specialists often address, and in a number of studies investigators did not introduce judgment tasks that clinicians then performed, but rather examined decisions already made in the course of everyday practice.

Other studies have provided clinicians or judges with access to preferred sources of information. Even in 1966, Sawyer was able to locate 17 comparisons between actuarial and clinical judgment based on the results of psychological testing and interview. Other investigators have allowed judges to collect whatever data they preferred in whatever manner they preferred. In Carroll et al.'s (1982) naturalistic study on the prediction of parolees' behavior after release, the parole board did not alter the data collection procedures. In Dawes's (1971) study on the prediction of graduate student performance, the admissions committee relied on the same data normally used to reach decisions. None of the 17 comparisons reviewed by Sawyer and neither of the studies by Carroll et al. or Dawes favored clinical over actuarial judgment.

Nor has the outcome varied within or across studies involving judges at various levels of experience or expertise. In Goldberg's (1965) study, novice and experienced MMPI interpreters performed similarly when using the clinical method and neither group surpassed the actuarial method, results parallel to those of Leli and Filskov (1984) in their study on the detection of brain damage. Other studies on the detection and localization of brain damage have yielded similar results (Leli & Filskov, 1981; Wedding, 1983). For example, Wedding found that neither clinicians with extensive experience interpreting the tests under study nor a nationally prominent neuropsychologist surpassed the overall accuracy of actuarial methods in determining the presence, location, and cause of brain damage.

The comparative studies often do not permit general conclusions about the superiority of one or another specific actuarial decision rule. Some studies, such as Goldberg's, do show application across settings, but much of the research has involved restricted samples. Investigators have been less interested in a specific procedure's range of application than in performing an additional test of the two methods and thereby extending the range of comparative studies.

The various studies can thus be viewed as repeated sampling from a universe of judgment tasks involving the diagnosis and prediction of human behavior. Lacking complete knowledge of the elements that constitute this universe, representativeness cannot be determined precisely. However, with a sample of about 100 studies and the same outcome obtained in almost every case, it is reasonable to conclude that the actuarial advantage is not exceptional but general and likely encompasses many of the unstudied judgment tasks. Stated differently, if one poses the query: "Would an actuarial procedure developed for a particular judgment task (say, predicting academic success at my institution) equal or exceed the clinical method?" The available research places the odds solidly in favor of an affirmative reply. "There is no controversy in social science that shows such a large body of qualitatively diverse studies coming out uniformly . . . as this one" (Meehl, 1986, p. 373).

Possible Exceptions

If fair comparisons consistently favor the actuarial method, one may then reverse the impetus of inquiry and ask whether there are certain circumstances in which the clinical judge might beat the actuary. Might the clinician attain superiority if given an informational edge? For example, suppose the clinic lacks an actuarial formula for interpreting certain interview results and must choose between an impression based on both interview and test scores and a contrary actuarial interpretation based on only the test scores. The research addressing this question has yielded consistent results (Sawyer, 1966; Wiggins, 1981). Even when given an information edge, the clinical judge still fails to surpass the actuarial method; in fact, access to additional information often does nothing to close the gap between the two methods.

It is not difficult to hypothesize other circumstances in which the clinical judge might improve on the actuarial method: (1) judgments mediated by theories and hence difficult or impossible to duplicate by statistical frequencies alone, (2) select reversal of actuarial conclusions based on the consideration of rare events or utility functions that are not incorporated into statistical methods and (3) complex configural relations between predictive variables and outcome (Meehl, 1957, 1959, 1976).

The potential superiority of theory-mediated judgments over conclusions reached solely on the basis of empirical frequencies may seem obvious to those in the "hard" sciences. Prediction mediated by theory is successful when the scientist has access to the major causal influences, possesses accurate measuring instruments to assess them, and uses a well-corroborated theory to make the transition from theory to fact (that is, when the expert has access to a specific model). Thus, although most comparative research in medicine favors the actuarial method overall, the studies that suggest a slight clinical advantage seem to involve circumstances in which judgments rest on firm theoretical grounds (Martin, Apostolakos, & Roazen, 1960).

The typical theory that underlies prediction in the social sciences, however, satisfies none of the needed conditions. Prediction of treatment response or violent behavior may rest on psychodynamic theory that permits directly contradictory conclusions and lacks formal measurement techniques. Theory-mediated judgments may eventually provide an advantage within psychology and other social sciences, but the conditions needed to realize this possibility are currently but a distant prospect or hope.

Clinicians might be able to gain an advantage by events that are not included in the actuarial formula (due to their infrequency) and that countervail the actuarial conclusion. This possibility represents a variation of the clinical-actuarial approach, in which one considers the outcome of both methods and decides when to supersede the actuarial conclusion. In psychology this circumstance has come to be known as the "broken leg" problem, on the basis of on an illustration in which an actuarial formula is highly successful in predicting an individual's weekly attendance at a movie but should be discarded upon discovering that the subject is in a cast with a fractured femur (Meehl, 1954, 1957). The clinician may beat the actuarial method if able to detect the rare fact and decide accordingly. In theory, actuarial methods can accommodate rare occurrences, but the practical obstacles are daunting. For example, the possible range of intervening events is infinite.

The broken leg possibility is easily studied by providing clinicians with both the available data and the actuarial conclusion and allowing them to use or countervail the latter at their disgression. The limited research examining this possibility, however, all shows that greater overall accuracy is achieved when clinicians rely uniformly on actuarial conclusions and avoid discretionary judgments (Goldberg, 1968; Sawyer, 1966).

When operating freely, clinicians apparently identify too many "exceptions," that is, the actuarial conclusions correctly modified are outnumbered by those incorrectly modified. If clinicians were more conservative in overriding actuarial conclusions they might gain an advantage, but this conjecture remains to be studied adequately.

Consideration of utilities raises a related possibility. Depending on the task, certain judgment errors may be more serious than others. For example, failure to detect a condition that usually remits spontaneously may be of less consequence than false identification of a condition for which risky treatment is prescribed. The adjustment of decision rules or cutting scores to reduce either false-negative or false-positive errors can decrease the procedure's overall accuracy but may still be justified if the consequences of these opposing forms of error are unequal. As such, if the clinician's counter-actuarial judgments, although less likely than the actuarial to be correct, were shown empirically to lower the probability of the rule's deliverances being correct (say, from 0.8 to 0.6), then in some contexts consideration of the joint probability-utility function might rationally reverse the action suggested by reliance on the formula alone. This procedure is formally equivalent to putting the clinician's judgment (as a new variable) into the actuarial equation, and more evidence on this process is needed to adequately appraise its impact. Here again, one cannot assume that the clinician's input helps. The available research suggests that formal inclusion of the clinician's input does not enhance the accuracy, nor necessarily the utility, of the actuarial formula and that informal or subjective attempts at adjustment can easily do more harm than good (Sawyer, 1966).

The clinician's potential capacity to capitalize on configural patterns or relations among predictive cues raises two related but separable issues that we will examine in order: the capacity to recognize configural relations and the capacity to use these observations to diagnose and predict. Certain forms of human pattern recognition still cannot be duplicated or equaled by artificial means. The recognition of visual patterns has challenged a generation of researchers in the field of artificial intelligence. Humans maintain a distinct advantage, for example, in the recognition of facial expressions. Human superiority also exists for language translation and for the invention of complex, deep-structure theories. Thus, for example, only the human observer may recognize a particular facial expression or mannerism (the float-like walk of certain schizophrenic patients) that has true predictive value. These observational abilities provide the potential for gathering useful (predictive) information that would otherwise be missed.

The possession of unique observational capacities clearly implies that human input or interaction is often needed to achieve maximal predictive accuracy (or to uncover potentially useful variables) but tempts us to draw an additional, dubious inference. A unique capacity to observe is not the same as a unique capacity to predict on the basis of integration of observations. As noted earlier, virtually any observation can be coded quantitatively and thus subjected to actuarial analysis. As Einhorn's (1972) study with pathologists and other research shows, greater accuracy may be achieved if the skilled observer performs this function and then steps aside, leaving the interpretation of observational and other data to the actuarial method.

FACTORS UNDERLYING THE SUPERIORITY OF ACTUARIAL METHODS

Contrasts between the properties of actuarial procedures and clinical judgment help to explain their differing success. First, actuarial procedures, unlike the human judge, always lead to the same conclusion for a given data set. In one study rheumatologist's and radiologists's reappraisals of cases they themselves had evaluated previously often resulted in different opinions (Fries et al., 1986). Such factors as fatigue, recent experience, or seemingly minor changes in the ordering of information or in the conceptualization of the case or task can produce random fluctuations in judgment (Hammond & Summers, 1965; Kahneman & Tversky, 1984). Random fluctuation decreases judgmental reliability and hence accuracy. For example, if the same data lead to the correct decision in one case but to a different, incorrect decision in the second case, overall accuracy will obviously suffer.

Perhaps more importantly, when properly derived, the mathematical features of actuarial methods ensure that variables contribute to conclusions based on their actual predictive power and relation to the criterion of interest. For example, decision rules based on multiple regression techniques include only the predictive variables and eliminate the nonpredictive ones, and they weight variables in accordance with their independent contribution to accurate conclusions. These achievements are essentially automatic with actuarial prediction but present formidable obstacles for human judges.

Research shows that individuals have considerable difficulty distinguishing valid and invalid variables and commonly develop false beliefs in associations between variables (Chapman & Chapman, 1967, 1969). In psychology and psychiatry, clinicians often obtain little or no information about the accuracy of their diagnoses and predictions. Consultants asked to predict violence may never learn whether their predictions were correct. Furthermore, clinicians rarely receive immediate feedback about criterion judgments (for example, diagnoses) of comparable validity to that physicians obtain when the pathologist reports at the end of a clinicopathological conference (Meehl, 1973). Lacking sufficient or clear information about judgmental accuracy, it is problematic to determine the actual validity, if any, of the variables on which one relies. The same problem may occur if actuarial methods are applied blindly to new situations or settings without any performance checks.

In other circumstances, clinical judgments produce "self-fulfilling prophecies." Prediction of an outcome often leads to decisions that influence or bias that outcome (Einhorn & Hogarth, 1978). An anecdote illustrates this problem. A psychiatrist in a murder trial predicted future dangerousness, and the defendant was sentenced to death. While on death row the defendant acted violently, which appeared to support the psychiatrist's predictive powers. However, once sentenced to death this individual had little to lose; he may have acted differently had the psychiatrist's appraisal, and in turn the sentence, been different.

Additionally, known outcomes seem more predictable than they are in advance (Fischhoff, 1975), and past predictions are mistakenly recalled as overly consistent with actual outcomes (Fischhoff, 1980; Fischhoff & Beyth-Marom, 1975). For example, Arkes et al. (1981) presented the same case materials to groups of physicians and asked them to assign probabilities to alternate diagnoses. When probabilities were assigned in foresight, each diagnosis was considered about equally likely. However, when the physicians were informed that one or another diagnosis had been established previously and they were then asked to state what initial diagnosis they likely would have made, they assigned the highest probability to whatever diagnosis they were told had been established. If one's view or recall of initial judgments is inadvertently shaped to fit whatever happens to occur, outcome information will have little or no corrective value.

The clinician is also exposed to a skewed sample of humanity and, short of exposure to truly representative samples, it may be difficult, if not impossible, to determine relations among variables. For example, suppose that about half of the adolescents appraised for a history of juvenile delinquency show subtle electroencephalographic (EEG) abnormalities. Based on these co-occurrences the clinician may come to consider EEG abnormality a sign of delinquency or may conclude that delinquency is associated with brain dysfunction. In fact, clinicians have often postulated these relations (Spreen, 1981).

One cannot determine, however, whether a relation exists unless one also knows whether the sign occurs more frequently among those with, versus those without, the condition. For example, to determine whether EEG abnormality is associated with delinquency, one must also know the frequency with which delinquents do not obtain EEG abnormalities and the frequencies with which nondelinquents do and do not obtain EEG abnormalities. Further, even should a valid relation exist, one cannot determine the sign's actual utility unless one knows: (1) how much more frequently it occurs when the condition is present than when it is absent and (2) the frequency of the condition. For example, a sign that is slightly more common among those with the condition may be of little diagnostic utility. If the condition is infrequent, then positive identifications based on the sign's presence can even be wrong in most cases, for most individuals who display the sign will not have the condition. If 10% of brain-damaged individuals make a particular response on a psychological test and only 5% of normals, but 9 of 10 clinic patients are not brain-damaged, most patients who show the feature will not be brain-damaged.

In practice, the clinician is far more likely to evaluate individuals with significant problems than those without them, and this skewed exposure hinders attempts to make all of the needed comparisons. In fact, empirical study shows that EEG "abnormalities" are common among normal children and further suggests that the incidence of delinquency is no greater among those with than without neurological disorder (Capute, Neidermeyer, & Richardson, 1968; Spreen, 1981). The formation of such false beliefs is further compounded by a decided human tendency to overattend to information consistent with one's hypotheses and to underattend to contradictory information (Greenwald, Pratkanis, & Leippe, 1986). The result is that mistaken beliefs or conclusions, once formed, resist counterevidence. . . .

The difficulty in separating valid and invalid variables on the basis of clinical experience or judgment is demonstrated in many studies examining diagnostic or predictive accuracy (Faust, 1984). Research shows that clinical judgments based on interviews achieve, at best, negligible accuracy or validity (Carroll et al., 1982). Other studies show that clinical judgments based on psychological test results may be of low absolute validity (Leli & Filskov, 1981, 1984; Wedding, 1983; Werner, Rose, & Yesavage, 1983). Although clinical interviews or psychological tests can produce useful information, the clinical judge often cannot distinguish what is useful from what is useless. In all studies cited immediately above, statistical analysis of the same data uncovered useful variables or enhanced predictive accuracy.

The optimal weighting of variables is a less important advantage of the statistical method than is commonly assumed. In fact, unit (equal) weights yield predictions that correlate highly with those derived from optimally weighted composites, the only provisos being that the direction in which each predictor is related to the criterion can be specified beforehand and the predictors not be negatively correlated with each other (Dawes & Corrigan, 1974; Einhorn & Hogarth, 1975; Wainer, 1978; Wilks, 1938). Further, optimal weights are specific to the population in which they were derived, and any advantage gained in one setting may be lost when the same method is applied in another setting. However, when optimal weighting adds meaningfully to predictive accuracy, the human judge is at a decided disadvantage. As Meehl (1986, p. 372) has stated:

Surely we all know that the human brain is poor at weighting and computing. When you check out at a supermarket you don't eyeball the heap of purchases and say to the clerk, "Well it looks to me as if it's about $17.00 worth; what do you think?" The clerk adds it up. There are no strong arguments . . . from empirical studies . . . for believing that human beings can assign optimal weights in equations subjectively or that they apply their own weights consistently.

It might be objected that this analogy, offered not probatively but pedagogically, presupposes an additive model that a proponent of configural judgment will not accept. Suppose instead that the supermarket pricing rule were, "Whenever both beef and fresh vegetables are involved, multiply the logarithm of 0.78 of the meat price by the square root of twice the vegetable price"; would the clerk and customer eyeball that any better? Worse, almost certainly. When human judges perform poorly at estimating and applying the parameters of a simple or component mathematical function, they should not be expected to do better when required to weight a complex composite of these variables.

LACK OF IMPACT AND SOURCES OF RESISTANCE

Research on clinical versus statistical judgment has had little impact on everyday decision making, particularly within its field of origin, clinical psychology. Guilmette et al.'s (1990) survey showed that most psychologists specializing in brain damage assessment prefer procedures for which actuarial methods are lacking over those for which actuarial formulas are available. The interview remains the *sine qua non* of entrance into mental health training programs and is required in most states to obtain a license to practice. Despite the studies that show that clinical interpretation of interviews may have little or no predictive utility, actuarial interpretation of interviews is rarely if ever used, although it is of demonstrated value.

Lack of impact is sometimes due to lack of familiarity with the scientific evidence. Some clinicians are unaware of the comparative research and do not even realize an issue exists. Others still refer to earlier studies and claim that the clinician was handicapped, unaware of the subsequent research that has rendered these arguments counterfactual.

Others who know the evidence may still dismiss it based on tendentiousness or misconception. Mental health professionals' education, training, theoretical orientations and identifications, and personal values may dictate against recognition of the actuarial advantage. Some psychologists, for example, believe that the use of a predictive equation dehumanizes their clients. The position overlooks the human costs of increased error that may result.

A common anti-actuarial argument, or misconception, is that group statistics do not apply to single individuals or events. The argument abuses basic principles of probability. Although individuals and events may exhibit unique features, they typically share common features with other persons or events that permit tallied observations or generalizations to achieve predictive power. An advocate of this anti-actuarial position would have to maintain, for the sake of logical consistency, that if one is forced to play Russian roulette a single time and is allowed to select a gun with one or five bullets in the chamber, the uniqueness of the event makes the choice arbitrary.

Finally, subjective appraisal may lead to inflated confidence in the accuracy of clinical judgment and the false impression that the actuarial method is inferior. Derivation and cross-validation of an actuarial method yields objective information on how well it does and does not perform (Dawes, 1979). When the clinician reviews research that shows, for example, that the Goldberg Rule for the MMPI achieved 70% accuracy in a comparable setting and exceeded the performance of 29 judges in the study, this may still seem to compare unfavorably to self-perceived judgmental powers. The immediacy and salience of clinical experience fosters the misappraisal. The clinician may recall dramatic instances in which his interpretations proved correct or in which he avoided error by countervailing an actuarial conclusion, failing to recognize or correctly tally counter-instances.

Ultimately, then, clinicians must choose between their own observations or impressions and the scientific evidence on the relative efficacy of the clinical and actuarial methods. The factors that create difficulty in self-appraisal of judgmental accuracy are exactly those that scientific procedures, such as unbiased sampling, experimental manipulation of variables, and blind assessment of outcome, are designed to counter. Failure to accept a large and consistent body of scientific evidence over unvalidated personal observation may be described as a normal human failing or, in the case of professionals who identify themselves as scientific, plainly irrational.

APPLICATION OF ACTUARIAL METHODS: LIMITS, BENEFITS AND IMPLICATIONS

The research reviewed in this article indicates that a properly developed and applied actuarial method is likely to help in diagnosing and predicting human behavior as well or better than the clinical method even when the clinical judge has access to equal or greater amounts of information. Research demonstrating the general superiority of actuarial approaches, however, should be tempered by an awareness of limitations and needed quality controls.

First, although surpassing clinical methods, actuarial procedures are far from infallible, sometimes achieving only modest results. Second, even a specific procedure that proves successful in one setting should be periodically reevaluated within that setting and should not applied to new settings mindlessly. Although theory and research suggest that the choice of predictive variables is often more important than their weighting, statistical techniques can be used to yield weights that optimize a procedure's accuracy when it is applied to new cases drawn from the same population. Moreover, accuracy can be easily monitored as predictions are made, and methods modified or improved to meet changes in settings and populations. Finally, efforts can be made to test whether new variables enhance accuracy.

When developed and used appropriately, actuarial procedures can provide various benefits. Even when actuarial methods merely equal the accuracy of clinical methods, they may save considerable time and expense. For example, each year millions of dollars and many hours of clinicians' valuable time are spent attempting to predict violent behavior. Actuarial prediction of violence is far less expensive and would free time for more productive activities, such as meeting unfulfilled therapeutic needs. When actuarial methods are not used as the sole basis for decisions, they can still serve to screen out candidates or options that would never be chosen after more prolonged consideration.

When actuarial methods prove more accurate than clinical judgment the benefits to individuals and society are apparent. Much would be gained, for example, by increased accuracy in the prediction of violent behavior and parole violation, the diagnosis of disorder and the identification of effective treatment. Additionally, more objective determination of limits in knowledge or predictive power can prevent inadvertent harm. Should a confident but incorrect clinical diagnosis of Alzheimer's disease be replaced by a far more cautious statement, or even better by the correct conclusion, we would avoid much unnecessary human misery.

Actuarial methods are explicit, in contrast to clinical judgment, which rests on mental processes that are often difficult to specify. Explicit procedures facilitate informed criticism and are freely available to other members of the scientific community who might wish to replicate or extend research.

Finally, actuarial methods – at least within the domains discussed in this article – reveal the upper bounds in our current capacities to predict human behavior. An awareness of the modest results that are often achieved by even the best available methods can help to counter unrealistic faith in our predictive powers and our understanding of human behavior. It may well be worth exchanging inflated beliefs for an unsettling sobriety, if the result is an openness to new approaches and variables that ultimately increase our explanatory and predictive powers.

The argument that actuarial procedures are not available for many important clinical decisions does not explain failure to use existent methods and overlooks the ease with which such procedures can be developed for use in special settings. Even lacking any outcome information, it is possible to construct models of judges that will likely surpass their accuracy (Dawes & Corrigan, 1974; Goldberg, 1970). What is needed is the development of actuarial methods and a measurement assurance program that maintains control over both judgment strategies so that their operating characteristics in the field are known and an informed choice of procedure is possible. Dismissing the scientific evidence or lamenting the lack of available methods will prove much less productive than taking on the needed work.

POSTSCRIPT

Two subsequent publications have greatly strengthened the arguments of this article. The first meta-analysis of clinical versus mechanical prediction (Grove, Zald, Lebow, Snitz, & Nelson, 2000) looked at 136 comparisons and found the mechanical procedure to be equal or superior in all but eight. That 6% of the studies had nothing in common except that the clinician had the advantage of more data, and those atypical studies may merely be unreplicable sampling error. Grove and Meehl (1996) examined the common persistent objections to adopting the mechanical method and showed them to be either empirically unsupported, logically or mathematically fallacious, or morally or economically unsound.

41. Heuristics and Biases in Application

Baruch Fischhoff

Heuristics and biases are in the public domain. They appear in texts, courses, books, and applications of many kinds. These endorsements speak to the persuasiveness of the basic research, the severity of the applied problems, and the face validity of debiasing as a possible solution. However, as the research itself shows, popularity alone proves little. Erroneous beliefs can be firmly and widely held even in applied fields with high stakes (Bunker, Barnes, & Mosteller, 1977; Byrne, 1986, Gilovich, 1991). One cannot expect practitioners to read the research literature. Moreover even peer-reviewed journals can be penetrated by vigorous advocates of flawed work. Nor can one expect them to extract simple lessons from individual applications. Coincidental events are always at play, in explanation, prediction, or prescription. Both radical skeptics and rabid enthusiasts can find ad hoc reasons for creating the picture that they seek regarding the applicability of research.

Achieving cumulative wisdom regarding the generalizability of heuristics-and-biases research requires interpreting the available evidence within a stable, comprehensive framework – one that identifies a set of potentially relevant contextual factors and provides bridging theories for characterizing actual situations in its terms. When those situations are in the lab, such a framework might reveal otherwise neglected complexity (when investigators manipulate one feature, without considering concurrent changes in others or the restricted circumstances in which their focal change is possible). With real-world situations, an interpretative framework might reduce otherwise bewildering complexity, by focusing attention on features whose influence (if any) will emerge over time. This chapter offers such a framework. It provides the subtext for reviewing applications of the heuristics-and-biases paradigm in many domains. These applications focus primarily on health, safety, and environmental decisions – arenas in which many choices rest on judgments of novel, uncertain events.

Having something to say in diverse cases demonstrates the range of the heuristics-and-biases perspective – and its ability to be tested in them. Its validity is affirmed by observing similar phenomena under comparable circumstances in the lab and the world. Each such application tests the validity of the theories emerging from the lab. It shows how clearly the research literature provides guidance on how heuristics are used and on what biases (if any) result.

Inevitably, each extension requires auxiliary hypotheses, mapping the abstract terms of the theory to the concrete complexities of the real world. Each application simultaneously tests both the theory and the auxiliary hypotheses. A framework allows for orderly, rather than ad hoc, tests of those hypotheses. This chapter critically examines the application of heuristics-and-biases research from these dual perspectives, asking what theory and practice can learn from each other. It focuses, in turn, on applications to (1) explaining past judgments, (2) predicting future judgments, and (3) improving future judgments.

THE CONTEXT OF HEURISTICS AND BIAS

Much experimental research proceeds incrementally. Perceiving a threat to a study's validity, investigators repeat it, deliberately varying one or two suspect features. Or, perceiving the opportunity to generalize a result, investigators extend it to a new domain, again, deliberately varying a feature or two. The modesty of these variations reflects that fact that even studies with partial factorial designs, sacrificing higher-order interactions, cannot manipulate more than a tiny fraction of the features that might, conceivably, influence behavior. Moreover, there may be many instantiations of a given feature (e.g., different incentive schemes, different kinds of group, different sorts of affect). As a result, most cells of the vast task-by-context matrix will always be empty or lightly populated.

Under these constraints, the best that one can do is to group studies whose tasks share common features. If a feature produces consistent results across otherwise diverse studies, then one can more confidently generalize those response patterns to other settings. Table 41.1 offers one partition of features that have been proposed as affecting the chances of observing biased judgments (Fischhoff, 1982). Its major sections ascribe bias to features of (1) the task, (2) the individuals performing it, or (3) a mismatch between the two. Table 41.1 was created to account for variation in performance among lab studies. If one believes in the reality of experimental contexts, features that matter there should also matter in applied settings (just as one should feel more comfortable ignoring features that have made no difference in the lab). Each category suggests ways to reduce bias, by changing that feature.

The original review (Fischhoff, 1982) applied this framework to all existing studies (subject to some screening criteria) of two biases: hindsight and overconfidence. Neither bias was much affected by most manipulations. The exceptions were (1) task restructuring (e.g., asking subjects to consider alternative explanations and contrary evidence) and (2) extensive training. The relative success of these two classes of manipulations affirms the theory of heuristics. Such task restructuring counters the naturally enhanced availability of reasons supporting initial beliefs. Training provides feedback that everyday life typically lacks, allowing people to test and refine judgmental skills. The limits to such instruction suggest which cognitive structures are particularly hard to acquire.

Table 41.1. Debiasing Strategies, According to Underlying Assumptions

Assumption	Strategies
Faulty Tasks	
Unfair tasks	Raise stakes
	Clarify instructions/stimuli
	Discourage second-guessing
	Use better response modes
	Ask fewer questions
Misunderstood tasks	Demonstrate alternative goal
	Demonstrate semantic disagreement
	Demonstrate impossibility of task
	Demonstrate overlooked distinction
Faulty Judges	
Perfectible individuals	Warn of problem
	Describe problem
	Provide personalized feedback
	Train extensively
Incorrigible individuals	Replace them
	Recalibrate their responses
	Plan on error
Mismatch between Judges and Tasks	
Restructuring	Make knowledge explicit
	Search for discrepant information
	Decompose problem
	Consider alternative situations
	Offer alternative formulations
Education	Rely on substantive experts
	Educate from childhood

Source: Fischhoff (1982).

The consistency of the results, across these two domains, involving some-what overlapping cognitive skills, makes them mutually reinforcing. A decade later, a review of some 100 hindsight studies showed the same general pattern, and some others, of varying practical usefulness (Christensen-Szalanski & Willham, 1991; also Koch & Loewenstein, 1989; Rachlinski, 1998). It found systemically stronger hindsight effects with occurrences than with non-occurrences (e.g., wars started versus wars averted), supporting the theoretical account of new information rapidly restructuring beliefs and retrieval processes, to the extent that it is noted. That review also found a mean difference of 10% between foresight and hindsight probabilities. Extrapolating that result to an applied context requires matching investigators' item-sampling processes to those in the real-world task. For example, there is little room for hindsight bias with easily predicted events. To what extent did investigators use such events? To what extent do practitioners face them? A bias of that magnitude might have more impact in changing a prediction from 0 to 10% (so that it is no longer a complete surprise) than from 40% to 50% (values that are relatively indistinct; Kahneman & Tversky, 1979).

Although there is no comparable metaanalysis of confidence studies, similar interpretative issues arise. Indeed, the term *overconfidence* itself incompletely represented the domain of studies. The fundamental phenomenon is "miscalibration," a mismatch between how confident people are and how confident they should be (given how much they know). This overall tendency typically emerges as overconfidence in hard tasks and as underconfidence in easy ones (Lichtenstein & Fischhoff, 1977). Researchers' tasks have tended to be hard, so that overconfidence has typically been observed. That selection bias might skew lab tasks toward those of greatest applied interest – if important real-world uncertainties concern hard questions. The same matching concerns remain when stimuli are created by artificial procedures, such as random sampling (In what frame?) or full factorial designs (How natural are the combinations?).

Thus, a complex inferential web connects the lab and the world. The remainder of this chapter focuses on the complexities arising in applied settings. It asks what those dealing with them can learn from and teach to researchers concerned with fundamental psychological processes. Scientists got to work on these problems because someone perceived biased judgments. That someone might be researchers, arguing "perhaps (even) we can help," or practitioners, sufficiently worried to tell researchers, "perhaps (even) you can help." Regardless of who starts this interplay, the collaboration should increase the chances that applications will be good for behavioral decision making (BDM), just as BDM tries to be good for the applications (Fischhoff, 1996).

Explanation

As part of a project attempting to derive responsible advice to women for reducing the risk of sexual assault (summarized in Fischhoff, 1992), Marcia Morgan, Lita Furby, and I reviewed a large sample of popular publications. These created a dismaying picture of confident, universal, yet contradictory recommendations. The most striking division was between experts strongly advising all women to undertake physical resistance and those telling women to avoid it. Experts proscribing such resistance were disproportionately from law enforcement sources – rather than, say, rape crisis centers or self-defense classes. Police predominately see women who resisted physically (hence, can better defend themselves in court), women whose resistance failed (meaning that rapes were completed), and women who suffered other injuries (which are easier to prosecute than coerced sexual acts). Thus, police samples are biased toward unsuccessful physical resistance. Police officers would be like other "victims of availability," if they remembered what they had seen and heard, perhaps in great detail, but lacked an appreciation of what they were not seeing.

If the police worried about such bias, undoing its effects would require understanding its sources, assessing their magnitude, and affording equal cognitive status to unseen events. The last of these steps would confront the difficulty of integrating case-specific and base-rate information, often attributed to reliance on the representativeness heuristic. Base-rate neglect has sometimes been reduced by presenting representative samples case-by-case (e.g., Manis et al., 1980). For police, that would mean meeting women who currently avoid the law-enforcement system. Doing so would require reducing the barriers to seeking police help after sexual assaults.

Judgmental biases can hamper such social change. Assessing the effectiveness of responses to sexual assault is a very difficult task (even for researchers). Overconfident experts have an exaggerated sense of having seen it all. One could hope that experts would systematically look for evidence contradicting their favored beliefs – therefore benefit from the debiasing that such searches produce in lab studies. That search should be particularly valuable when experts second-guess women's responses to assaults. Misfortunes may be disproportionately salient – hence, induce more hindsight bias – than the "nonevents" of avoiding harm. Unwilling to wait for spontaneous debiasing efforts, advocates for women's welfare have lobbied for better protection of victims' rights, dedicated "rape teams," and community-oriented policing. In addition to their direct value, these reforms create a new balance of evidence, broadening the sample of women coming to the police and the experiences that they are willing to share. Both trends should weaken the overconfidence of simplistic accounts, based on even the most conscientious summaries of biased samples of evidence.

Such explanations can (and, indeed, should) be applied to other advice providers. For example, what do self-defense trainers see vis-à-vis women's ability to resist sexual assaults physically? Indeed, how do these judgmental processes affect scientists working on the problem? They, too, have favored sources of evidence, and expectations regarding their results. Our project included a secondary analysis of all studies that we could find regarding the effectiveness of self-defense strategies. There were about three dozen, using varying methodologies and analytical procedures. Attempting to avoid some of the judgmental biases in impressionistic summaries (Rosenthal, 1994), we translated all studies into a common analytical framework and unit of effectiveness: the difference in the percentages of completed sexual assaults among women who did and who did not use each strategy. In so doing, we found that several authors had reversed the conditionality in this relationship, looking at the percentage of women who did and did not use a strategy, among those experiencing completed assaults. In effect, they had committed the "base-rate fallacy," ignoring the percentage using each strategy (Dawes, 1993). Eddy (1982) shows evidence and implications of such confusion among mammographers. We chose to make little note of these biases, in deference to the scientists conducting these very difficult studies.

Our review yielded a moderately consistent signal: Women who resisted physically experienced completed sexual assaults less frequently than women who used other self-defense strategies. That summary fits the preconceptions of some women and practitioners, but not others. For it to make sense to all, it would have to be integrated with their own anecdotal observations and "mental models" of how these processes work (Fischhoff, 1999; Furnham, 1988; Leventhal, Diefenbach, & Leventhal, 1992; Rouse & Morris, 1986). For example, they might be told how assaults can evolve over time and the role of physical resistance in them, as well as why appearances may be deceiving (in the sense of what gets seen and reported). Such debiasing falls into the general category of improving the match between individual and task. A specific category (not mentioned explicitly in Table 41.1) might be "integrating episodic and semantic beliefs." Doing so is part of the training in many professional fields, whose apprenticeship includes working through specific examples in the context of general theories.

Past events provide a natural (and essential) arena for evaluating theories of heuristic behavior. Finding a plausible role for a theory provides a minimal test of its relevance. The strength of that account increases to the extent that: (1) bridging theories show where and how heuristics should be invoked and (2) similar conditions produce bias in the lab and the world. This section examined these issues in one applied context, seemingly conducive to well-intended, but imperfect judgments. It raised speculations that could be examined empirically, by surveying the beliefs and information sources of advice givers. The results of such studies would have to be evaluated in the overall context of evidence regarding heuristic thinking. The next section considers the possibilities that arise with the chance to predict future behavior.

Prediction

The predictive use of heuristics requires an understanding of both psychology and circumstances. One must answer the following questions:

- Will heuristic thinking arise?
- Which heuristics will be invoked?
- How will they be interpreted?
- How accurate will the resulting judgments be?
- What debiasing processes will arise?
- How will those processes affect the judgments and individuals' confidence in them?

Possible Processes in Risk Estimation. One broad domain that invites heuristic thinking is estimating risks to health, safety, and the environment. Sexual assault is typical: People rarely get quantitative risk estimates. If they do, they still must integrate population values with the specifics of personal situations. Moreover, expert estimates are themselves but judgments – going beyond the realm of solid observation and robust theory. As a result, people must decide how far to trust the experts' beliefs, as well as their own.

Given the great variety of risks that people might consider, relying on general-purpose heuristics seems plausible. Some form of availability seems like a particularly reasonable choice: How often has one seen or heard about the risk occurring? How readily can one imagine it? If people follow this strategy, they should assign higher probabilities to events that they see or hear about more often. The accuracy of these estimates should depend on how well three conditions are met: (1) the exposures are proportional to actual frequencies; (2) the events are equally memorable; and (3) people have reliable mental mechanisms for converting the availability of instances into summary estimates. Predicting availability-based risk estimates requires predicting these component processes, as well as the impact of any attempted debiasing procedures (e.g., seeking multiple sources, discounting media sensationalism).

Such judgments should go astray in several predictable ways. Some causes of death are seldom, if ever, reported (e.g., suicide, in societies where it is proscribed; cancer, where it is not discussed; AIDS, where individuals hope to hide their route of exposure; smoking, where deaths are attributed to immediate causes, such as emphysema). Other deaths are routinely reported close to where they occur (e.g., fires, homicides, single-fatality auto accidents), around the country (e.g., tornadoes, multi-fatality auto accidents), or around the world (e.g., hate crimes, terror acts, earthquakes). Word of mouth creates other differential exposures. Whispers may fill in the blanks of some unreported events, reiterate some reported ones, and even invent some fictitious ones. Direct experience creates its own patterns of exposure to causes of death. These may depend on age (e.g., how many older people does one know?), culture (e.g., how isolated are different ages and classes?), and socioeconomic status (e.g., how well is violence hidden? how are deaths from lingering illnesses explained?).

Generating availability-based predictions requires understanding these exposure patterns. These are topics in anthropology, sociology, and communications research. They have methods, and perhaps even results, for estimating particular exposures. These include counting mentions of a topic in the news media and observing what people see (and notice) of what is mentioned (Combs & Slovic, 1979; Singer & Endreny, 1994; Slater, 1996; Tyler, 1990). A more psychological approach to measuring exposures is asking people what they remember having seen or heard (e.g., "Tell me about everyone you know who was murdered, killed in an auto accident."). These reports need not be taken as veridical, but could be interpreted in the light of research into the vagaries of time (e.g., telescoping), introspection, and encoding processes (e.g., Ericsson & Simon, 1994; Hasher & Zacks, 1984; Hintzman, 1976; Nisbett & Wilson, 1977).

Some Lay Estimates. Figure 41.1 shows a result of applying this perspective to predicting lay estimates of the annual frequency of 41 causes of death in the United States, as compared to public health statistics. It represents one of the first applications of heuristics-and-biases research to public policy. It has been widely cited in the debate over the public's competence to participate in decision-making regarding modern technologies. Although any hard evidence should be better than anecdote and rhetoric, the study has often been invoked to support preconceived notions. In particular, it has been cited as demonstrating lay ignorance, even irrationality, regarding risks. I have heard it used to "prove"

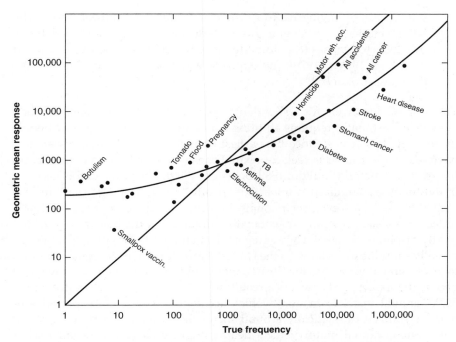

Figure 41.1. Geometric means (GM) of ratio judgments by motor vehicle accident group subjects as a function of true frequency (TF). (Curved line is best-fitting quadratic: log GM = .07 [log TF]² + .03 log TF + 2.27.) *Source:* Lichtenstein et al., (1978).

that citizens are hopelessly confused about nuclear power, which was not even in the stimulus set (and whose average-year fatality rate was judged to be quite low in a related study; Slovic, Fischhoff, & Lichtenstein, 1980). Such strong claims could hardly be demonstrated authoritatively with any single study. As with sexual assault advice, they reflect on the claimants as well as the evidence.

The two most salient patterns in the figure are consistent with availability (and were predicted before we saw the data):

1. The best-fit curve is too flat, relative to the perfect-prediction identity line. That would occur if respondents used the heuristic briefly (as the study required), allowing little opportunity to appreciate fully the differences between very large and very small risks. Such flattening is seen even in experimental studies with stimulus frequencies varying over one order of magnitude, rather than the present five (e.g., Jonides & Naveh-Benjamin, 1987). Brevity could be one source of measurement error producing regressive estimates.
2. The residuals, relative to the best-fit curve, are predictably correlated with several direct and indirect measures of availability. The former included

self-reports of having heard of the events causing death or injury. The latter included newspaper mentions of deaths from each cause. Relatively overreported causes (e.g., tornado, floods) were relatively overestimated (Combs & Slovic, 1979); the opposite was true for quieter killers (e.g., diabetes, stroke).

These predictions were for respondents' *relative* frequency estimates. Predicting *absolute* estimates requires additional assumptions regarding how people use quantitative scales. Since the earliest days of psychophysics, researchers have known that subjects seek contextual cues when confronted with unfamiliar response modes (Poulton, 1989; Schwarz, 1999). The terms in this task are, individually, all familiar: "number" of "deaths" in an "average year" in "the United States." However, their conjunction is unusual – except for risk buffs. Indeed, pretests, providing no context at all (and just the questions), elicited wildly disparate answers. The aggregate death toll for some subjects implied a brutally short life expectancy in the United States; for others, it implied halcyon days of miraculous longevity. Clearly, many subjects had little idea how many people die in a typical year. As a result, we introduced an anchor, noting the 50,000 annual deaths from motor vehicle accidents. As would be expected, estimates stabilized dramatically around the anchor. Because they are reported fairly often, annual motor vehicle deaths might be a relatively fair anchor for this task, already in some people's minds when predicting real-world risk estimates.

A second experimental condition tested the malleability of these judgments by reporting, instead, that 1,000 persons die annually from electrocution. (At the time, there was no death penalty, so "accidental" went without saying.) Electrocution was chosen because instances seemed proportionately reported and its death toll was a round number, far from the extremes of the range (Poulton, 1968). Reducing the anchor by a factor of 50 (relative to motor vehicle deaths) reduced respondents' estimates by a factor of 2–5. Having estimates vary by less than a tenth of the variation in anchors indicates the strength of these beliefs. Another sign of robustness was the strong correlation between estimates produced with the two anchors. That ordering was also strongly correlated with one implied by relative frequency judgments for 106 paired causes of death. Thus, despite the novelty of these tasks, subjects revealed consistent beliefs, moderately predicted by availability and anchoring, however the question was asked.

Some Interpretations of Observed Estimates. How satisfactory predictions are depends on the application. For predicting which causes of death most occupy people, an ordering might be adequate (Davies, 1996; Fischer et al., 1991). For predicting which risks people find acceptable, absolute estimates are needed (as are absolute estimates of the associated benefits). Such predictions require delineating the conditions under which real-world estimates are made. Which anchors do people see or generate naturally? Which anchors do others (e.g., advertisers) present, in order to shape judgments? Are risks and benefits viewed in a common framework, reducing the need for absolute estimates (e.g., looking at the cost-effectiveness of different ways to secure a fixed benefit)?

It takes even more delineation to answer the question that prompted this, and much other, research into risk perceptions: Do people know enough to assume a responsible role in managing risks, whether in their lives or in society as a whole? The picture of potential competence that evolved from that research is one of behavioral decision research's more visible impacts (e.g., Canadian Standards Association, 1997; Fischhoff, 1998; National Research Council, 1989, 1996; Slovic, 1987). The very act of conducting such research makes a political statement: claims regarding public competence need to be disciplined by fact. This is not welcome news to those hoping to create a particular image of the public, reflecting their own prejudices (see Okrent & Pidgeon, 1998). Some partisans would like to depict an immutably incompetent public, in order to justify protective regulations or deference to technocratic experts. Other partisans would like to depict an already competent public, able to fend for itself in an unfettered marketplace and participate in technological decisions.

In Fig. 41.1, the case for the glass being half-full rests on (1) the consistency of estimates elicited with different response modes; (2) the strong correlation (although not absolute correspondence) between lay and statistical estimates; and (3) the correlations between lay fatality estimates and measures of availability. The last of these relationships indicates that people can track what they see, even if they don't realize how unrepresentative the observed evidence is. The case for the glass being half-empty rests on (1) the enormous range of the statistical frequencies, making some correlation almost inevitable (could people get through life, without knowing that cancer kills more people than botulism?); (2) the malleability of the absolute estimates (which are what people need for making risk–benefit evaluations); and (3) the availability-related biases. The last of these weaknesses might be exploited by those (scaremongers or pacifiers) hoping to manipulate the availability of specific risks.

Choosing Predictive Criteria. These results inform the debate over public competence only to the extent that public responses to risk depend on perceived frequency of death. Subsequent research found, however, that *risk* has multiple meanings (Slovic, Fischhoff, & Lichtenstein, 1980). When asked to estimate risk (on an open-ended scale with a modulus of 10), lay subjects rank some sources similarly for risk and average year fatalities, but others quite differently. Lay subjects who made this distinction showed sensitivity to the task of Fig. 41.1 (hence, had avoided one of the pitfalls in Table 41.1's second section). However, a sample of technical experts treated the two definitions of risk as synonymous. A search ensued for additional factors that shape lay definitions of risk.

An early candidate for such a risk factor was *catastrophic potential*: Other things being equal, people might see greater risk in hazards that can claim many lives at once, as seen perhaps in special concern about plane crashes, nuclear power, and the like. Some experts even proposed raising the number of deaths in each possible accident sequence to an exponent (>1), when calculating expected fatalities (Fischhoff, 1984). That idea faded when they realized that, with large accidents, the exponent swamps the rest of the analysis. Moreover, the empirical research suggested that catastrophic potential per se was not a driving factor (Slovic, Lichtenstein, & Fischhoff, 1984). Rather, people worry about the uncertainty surrounding a technology's risks. It is often great with technologies able to produce catastrophic accidents. If so, then uncertain risk management may have scared audiences more than potential body counts in films like *The China Syndrome* and *A Civil Action*.

The correlation between catastrophic potential and uncertainty first emerged in behavioral research predicting risk preferences. Its impetus was Starr's widely cited (1969) claim that, for a given benefit, the public tolerates greater risk if it is incurred voluntarily (e.g., skiing) than if it is imposed. As evidence, he estimated fatality risks and economic benefits from eight sources. In a plot, he sketched two parallel "acceptable risk" lines, an order of magnitude apart, for voluntary and involuntary risks. Although seminal, the paper was technically quite rough, in terms of sources, estimates, and statistics (Fischhoff et al., 1981). More fundamentally, it assumed that people's risk and benefit perceptions matched their statistical estimates when determining acceptable trade-offs. The heuristics-and-biases literature made that assumption questionable. A straightforward way to test it was asking citizens to judge technologies in terms of risk, benefits, voluntariness and other potentially relevant risk factors (e.g., catastrophic potential, dread, controllability, scientific uncertainty) (Lowrance, 1976). A first study pursuing that strategy (Fischhoff et al., 1978) found:

1. Little correlation between estimates of current risks and current benefits from the different sources (so that subjects did not see societal institutions as having exacted greater benefit from riskier technologies).
2. No increase in the perceived risk-benefit correlation, after partialing out judgments of the various risk factors (so that subjects did not see society as having set a double standard for voluntary and involuntary technologies – or for any other factor).
3. A belief that the acceptable level of risk for many (but not all) technologies was lower than current levels (contrary to Starr's hypothesis of a socially determined balance).
4. A significant correlation between judgments of current benefits and *acceptable* risk levels (indicating a willingness to incur greater risk in return for greater benefit).
5. A large improvement in predicting acceptable risk from perceived benefits, when many risk factors were partialed out, indicating the desire for a double standard (e.g., with higher acceptable levels for voluntarily incurred risks).

This research has helped many institutions to realize that risk entails more than just average-year fatalities when setting their risk-management policies (e.g., Institute of Medicine, 1999; National Research Council, 1996). Predicting public responses to specific technologies requires research like that of the causes-of-death study: looking at how, and how accurately, people perceive the factors determining their judgments of risk (including which heuristics are invoked and where they lead). We (Fischhoff et al., 2001) found that how people perceive a technology on these risk factors predicts its chances of being the target of consumer boycotts or screened by socially responsible investment funds. If so, then the accuracy of those perceptions matters a lot, financially.

Prescription

Conditions for Manipulation. If biases seem plausible, even predictable, then it behooves researchers to help reduce them. The first step in that process is establishing that bias has, in fact, been demonstrated (the topic of Table 41.1's second section). Clear normative standards are essential to protecting the public from interventions that promote some belief, under the guise of correcting poor lay judgments. For example, a popular strategy for defending risky activities is comparing them with other, apparently accepted risks. Living next to a nuclear power plant has been compared to eating peanuts, which the carcinogenic fungus, aflatoxin, can contaminate (e.g., Cohen & Lee, 1979; Wilson, 1979). To paraphrase an ancient advertisement, the implication is that, "If you like Skippy (Peanut Butter), you'll love nuclear power." Such comparisons ignore both the multifactor character of risk (by looking just at fatality estimates) and the uncertainty surrounding the estimates (by considering only best guesses, rather than full probability distributions). Moreover, risky decisions are not about risks alone. People reasonably care about the associated benefits, as well as the societal processes determining risk-benefit tradeoffs. A given risk should be less acceptable if it provides less benefit or is imposed on those bearing it (eroding their rights and respect) (Fischhoff, 1995; Leiss, 1996).

When bias can be demonstrated, identifying the responsible heuristic has both applied and normative value. On the applied side, it points to debiasing opportunities. On the normative side, it clarifies the legitimacy of any such intervention. For example, invoking availability means attributing bias to systematic use of systematically unrepresentative evidence. Failing to adjust for biased sampling could reflect insufficient skepticism (taking observations at face value) or insufficient knowledge (about how to adjust). Being ignorant in these ways is quite different from being stupid or hysterical, charges that often follow allegations of bias. Indeed, Fig. 41.1 confuses this attribution, by labeling imperfect statistics as "True Frequency," reflecting our own incomplete understanding at the time (see also Shanteau, 1978). In this light, both citizens and scientists need the same thing: better information, along with better understanding of its limits.

Similarly, attributing concern over catastrophic potential to concern over the associated uncertainty shifts attention to whether people have the metacognitive skills for evaluating technical evidence. It reduces the importance of any biases induced by hearing worst-case analysis scenarios. It also implies a more easily defended normative principle: worrying about how well a technology is understood, rather than whether casualties occur at once or are distributed over time. These two principles imply very different public policies. Concern over catastrophic potential means creating incentives for locating technologies remotely and disincentives for investing in technologies that could affect many people at once. Concern over uncertainty means creating incentives for research that sharpens risk estimates and disincentives for highly innovative technologies (which cannot be known that well). Without direct research into what citizens want and believe, policies will be mistakenly created in their name (Fischhoff, 2000a, 2000b).

Improving Expert Judgment. The central role played by expert judgment in public policy has evoked a stream (although not quite a torrent) of concern regarding its quality (National Research Council, 1996). The heuristics-and-bias literature has persuaded some analysts that experts are like lay people, when forced to go beyond their data, historical records, and specialized procedures – and rely on judgment. In addition to advocating caution, these analysts have promoted procedures to improve judgment in fields such as decision analysis (Kleindorfer et al., 1993; Watson & Buede, 1990), risk analysis (Fischhoff, 1989; Kammen & Hassenzahl, 1999; Keeney, 1992; Morgan & Henrion, 1990), forecasting (Arkes, 2001; Armstrong, 2001; Wright, 1996), intelligence analysis (Beyth-Marom, 1982; Heuer, 1999; Vertzberger, 1998), negotiations (Bazerman & Neale, 1992), finance (Dreman, 1979, 1999; Thaler, 1993), and jurisprudence (Hanson & Kysar, 1999a,b; Rachlinski, 1998).

A Climate Example

A striking feature of the debates over many technical issues is the focus on best estimates, with uncertainties expressed, at best, in terms of verbal quantifiers (e.g., "rarely," "likely"). Such incomplete treatment of uncertainty might itself reflect incomplete statistical intuitions (Fischhoff & Beyth-Marom, 1983; Funtowicz & Ravetz, 1990; Phillips, 1973). In an effort to clarify disagreements over the climate changes caused by increased atmospheric CO_2, Morgan and Keith (1995) conducted daylong interviews with a dozen leading scientists. By focusing on uncertainties, they tried to introduce Bayesian thinking into a high-stakes domain where it was lacking – eliciting probability distributions over variables like "the change in mean global temperature at $40°$ N, assuming a doubling of atmospheric CO_2." Their introduction included a lecture on the psychology of judgment. In order to reduce the risk of overconfidence, the interviewers used cognitively informed procedures, such as starting with extreme fractiles (rather than anchoring on best estimates) and eliciting reasons why proposed values might be right and wrong. In order to improve the match between the task and respondents' natural ways of thinking, the experts were encouraged to redefine questions to forms that they were more accustomed to answering. (Experts who did so also provided the auxiliary assumptions needed to translate their answers to ones fitting the original questions, so that all respondents' judgments could be expressed in common terms.) Lest the experts become captive of a single perspective, the interviewers had them triangulate answers to related questions.

These interviews elicited sufficiently precise judgments to be evaluated, once events unfolded. Moreover, they documented the experts' reasons clearly enough for those events to teach something about the underlying theories. Unfortunately, a long time will pass before the critical events occur, and decisions need to be made now. Unless the beliefs of today's experts are used well, people of the future will have far worse worries than determining which cognitive processes led to fatefully wrong decisions. Appropriate usage means understanding not only what the experts believe, but also how far to trust them.

In the absence of external events for evaluating experts, there may be internal ones. For example, some experts' beliefs suggested incoherence, reminiscent of that seen in experimental studies. One form involved inconsistency between holistic judgments (e.g., mean temperature at 40°N) and estimates obtained by combining conditional judgments (e.g., mean temperature at 40°N, with and without the North Atlantic conveyor shutting down) with probabilities for the conditioning events (e.g., the conveyor shutting down, or not). A second form of incoherence involved believing that uncertainty could be greater in the future, despite the intervening research. Such beliefs might reflect the sort of second-order uncertainty that should be incorporated in probability distributions, according to some accounts of Bayesian inference, but might be withheld, according to others (Gärdenfors & Sahlin, 1989; Savage, 1955; Shafer & Tversky, 1985).

For policy purposes, an important result of the study was revealing hitherto undocumented consistency across the different experts' beliefs. That is, their probability distributions typically overlapped considerably, a fact obscured in discussions of best estimates. Even the distributions of a prominent skeptic (about global warming) typically lay within the ranges established by the other experts. The skeptic's distributions were, however, much narrower, reflecting much greater confidence (and perhaps overconfidence?). There is reason to believe that the interview process and the credibility of its results benefited from being grounded in psychological research. Time will tell whether the exercise led to better gambles with our environment.

Conditions for Expertise
Like the very wealthy (Mills, 1959), the very well trained are hard to study. Investigators face problems of access, as well as the challenge of learning enough about experts' specialties to understand how well they are doing. Occasionally, deliberate experiments provide useful evidence. A well-known judgment example is the training of weather forecasters (Murphy & Winkler, 1977, 1984). That experience confirms the experimental results: performance improves with good conditions for learning (i.e., prompt, unambiguous feedback, with incentives for performance). It can become excellent for short-term precipitation forecasts (clear, discrete, daily events), but remains poorer for

tornadoes (rare, not always observed) and wind velocities (variable, continuous events).

In addition to deliberate experiments, there are natural ones, exposing experts to conditions that should affect heuristics use. Naturally, these raise even greater interpretative challenges. For example, Henrion and Fischhoff (1986; Chapter 37, this volume) found great overconfidence in judgments akin to confidence intervals, assigned by physicists to estimates of fundamental values (e.g., speed of light, Planck's constant, rest mass of the electron). Shlyakhter et al. (1994) extended this result to other expert estimates (e.g., for population, energy consumption), also finding consistent overconfidence. Many of these estimates arose from group processes, such as the Particle Data Group or the Energy Modeling Forum.

Improving Lay Judgment. Nobody is perfect. Sometimes, no one needs to be. Some situations are forgiving of imperfect judgments. That can be a mixed blessing. Forgiving situations lack the sharp feedback often needed to improve judgment (or even to convince people that improvement is needed). As a result, individuals living in a forgiving world may be particularly vulnerable when they face novel and demanding situations, where they need to "get it right the first time." Thus, diminishing the local importance of judgmental biases increases the global plausibility of their existence.

One prominent analysis of the sensitivity of decisions to inaccuracy in judgment led to von Winterfeldt and Edwards's (1986) *flat maximum principle*. They described a broad class of choices with continuous options (e.g., invest X, respond in Y msec, travel at Z mph), whose expected utility varies little with estimates of any input parameter, as long as it is around the correct value. However, Lichtenstein et al. (1982) describe a class of choices with discrete options (e.g., operate/don't, sell/hold), where sensitivity can be much greater. Henrion (1982; also Morgan & Henrion, 1990) characterized decisions by their sensitivity to the appropriateness of confidence judgments (or *calibration*). Dawes and Corrigan (1974) and others (e.g., Camerer, 1981; Goldberg, 1968) identified conditions under which choices are insensitive to the weights assigned to different considerations. If specific decisions can be characterized in these general terms, then one has a prior probability for the need to improve judgments.

Better Products

Where needed, one can analyze the sensitivity of specific decisions to the accuracy of the beliefs guiding them. Table 41.2 shows the impact that learning about each of many side effects should have on patients' decisions about a surgical procedure. Only three side effects prove large enough to change many patients' choices, hence should be the focus of informed-consent procedures. This kind of analysis creates a *supply curve*, showing the optimal order for providing new facts. Effective communication must convey both the probability and the nature of each such event (Fischhoff, 1994). That will be easier for some events than for others. In this example, the probabilities of the three focal side effects

Table 41.2. A Materiality Standard for Prioritizing Information

Carotid endarterectomy involves scraping out the artery leading to the brain, reducing the risk of stroke for patients with arteriosclerosis. However, having a sharp object in one's neck can also cause problems, as can major surgery itself. Consider a population of patients, for all of whom the surgery would be a rational choice, if there were no risks (and money were no object). They vary in their physical condition, represented by probability distributions over possible consequences, and in their values, represented by distributions of tradeoffs across those consequences. Monte Carlo sampling produces a set of hypothetical patients, each characterized by a combination of physical states and personal values. Calculate the expected utility of the surgery decision for each such patient, ignoring all risks. Then recalculate it, including knowledge of the probability of each possible consequence. Information about a risk is material if it changes the expected utility of surgery from positive to negative.

The results of such an analysis are shown below. About 15% of such patients should decline the surgery on learning the probability of immediate death. Another 5% should decline if told the risk of iatrogenic stroke. An additional 3% should be dissuaded by hearing the risk of facial paralysis. Although many other side effects are possible, few would affect many choices. Thus, although the set of potentially relevant facts is large, the set of critically relevant ones is small.

The percentage of a simulated patient population that would decline carotid endarterectomy on learning of each risk:

Outcome	Percentage Declining (Standard Deviation)
Death	15.0 (0.3)
Stroke and neurologic deficit	5.0 (0.2)
Facial Nerve paralysis	3.0 (0.2)
(Myocardial infarction MI)	1.1 (0.1)
Lung damage	0.9 (0.06)
Headache	0.8 (0.1)
Resurgery	0.4 (0.03)
Tracheostomy	0.2 (0.03)
Gastrointestinal upset	0.09 (0.1)
Broken teeth	0.01 (0.01)
Liver damage	0.01 (0.01)
Parotiditis	0.01 (0.01)
Kidney dysfunction	0.01 (0.01)

Source: Merz et al., 1993.

are large enough to be readily comprehended (rather than, say, thousandths of a percent). The nature of the two top side effects (death, stroke) should be familiar, especially to candidates for the procedure, who face these possibilities already (and might even have had strokes). Thus, communication might focus on what the unfamiliar third side effect (facial nerve paralysis) is like.

The example assumes patients who know little, as might be the case with such a surgery. For patients with sharper (and potentially biased) priors, the analysis would consider the impact of each fact on updating them. Those priors could be elicited directly or derived theoretically. For example, patients relying on heuristics should underestimate risks that are either hard to imagine or not "representative" of the procedure (e.g., facial paralysis). Looking at potential messages from a cognitive perspective might also identify facts that are just too hard to communicate comprehensibly. Deemphasizing them saves time, while acknowledging that less overall understanding is possible. Priorities would also change if some facts proved redundant, in the sense that people who know one can predict others. With artificial tasks, any two features can occur together (e.g., the sizes and probabilities of outcomes in lab gambles), allowing no such efficiencies (although subjects may independently assume dependencies). However, people facing real-world prospects may already have many beliefs and quickly infer others.

The search for such cognitive connections has prompted the study of *mental models* in many domains (e.g., Bartlett, 1932; Furnham, 1988; Johnson-Laird, 1983; Tolman, 1937). A typical finding is that people organize diverse facts into highly flexible templates, in effect, *substantive heuristics* (e.g., how the circulatory system works, how the body processes toxins, how hazardous chemicals flow through groundwater, how risks mount up through repeated exposure). These studies typically contrast beliefs with a normative standard. For decisions regarding complex, loosely bounded problems, that standard can be captured in an *influence diagram*, showing the factors that determine the probabilities appearing in the associated decision tree (Clemen, 1991; Fischhoff et al., 1998; Howard, 1989). These diagrams show *what is worth knowing* about the problem, for individuals who otherwise know nothing. The contrast between them and lay beliefs shows *what is worth saying*, in order to make best use of individuals' limited attention. Such contrasts have guided the development of communications on many topics, including radon, climate change, industrial chemicals, electromagnetic fields, mammography, HIV/AIDS, other sexually transmitted diseases, and nuclear energy in space (Bostrom et al., 1992; Fischhoff, 1998, 1999; Morgan et al., 2001).

Determining what is worth knowing and saying seems like the obvious communication strategy. Yet it is often hard to see its impact on many public health brochures, drug package inserts, home appliance instructions, or the like. Riley et al. (2001) showed that individuals who did everything listed on the labels of some brands of paint stripper could still face very high exposures. For other brands, users' exposure depended on what they read (e.g., just first five items, the instructions, warnings, bolded items). Casman et al. (2000) found that standard warnings for outbreaks of the waterborne parasite, *Cryptosporidium*, provide little useful information. By the time an outbreak has been confirmed, it is too late to help consumers, even if they conscientiously follow instructions to use boiled or bottled water. Rather, immunocompromised individuals need to be told to avoid vulnerable water at all times. Determining the content of communications and rendering it comprehensible requires collaborations between psychologists and subject-matter specialists.

Better Processes

Conveying information should be easier as recipients' judgments improve. Skilled individuals should acquire new information more readily, as well as know more already (by observing their environment more effectively). Training programs, designed to improve judgment by redirecting heuristic processes, arose early in the research. By the mid-1970s, courses had been created for military and intelligence officers in the United States and Israel (Heuer, 1999; Lanir, 1978; Lipschitz, 1983). High school curricula followed (Baron & Brown, 1991; Beyth-Marom et al., 1985), fitting educators' increasing demand for critical thinking skills, as did a (UK) Open University course on "Risk" (Dowie, 1983), among others. Larrick et al. (1990) report an ambitious training program, whose impacts generalized to similar problems presented outside classroom settings. These courses represent complex debiasing interventions, with elements ranging from mere exhortation and warning (Table 41.1, middle) to attempts to change how individuals approach tasks (Table 41.1, bottom). Although the courses could grade participants' performance on textbook exercises, they could not evaluate effects on real-world performance.

One context where real-world training effects have been evaluated is with *social skills* programs, shown to reduce teens' rates of risk behaviors, such as smoking, unsafe sex, and driving after drinking (Dryfoos, 1990). These programs aim to help teens understand and resist temptations, in part by addressing judgmental biases. For example, course leaders explain how the availability of other teens' overt risk behaviors (and claims thereof) leads to overestimating their prevalence – whereas less salient avoidance of risk behavior is underestimated. That lesson is reinforced in group discussions of strategies for avoiding risk behaviors. These exercises attempt to make otherwise abstract base rates concrete – in addition to securing public commitment to better behavior. Showing students the (surprisingly) high rate of responsible drinking is part of social marketing approaches found to reduce binge drinking on college campuses (Wechsler et al., 2000).

Nonetheless, assessing the role of improved judgment in these complex interventions is difficult. That is true even for the many programs with decision-making modules. It would be nice to believe that these modules are critical to the programs' successes. However, their content is often rather general, akin to warning manipulations, with little attention to redirecting cognitive processes. A review of evaluations concluded that none allowed evaluating changes in decision-making competence (Beyth-Marom et al., 1991). A cynical possibility is that decision-making modules enhance programs' more manipulative elements by seemingly respecting teens' rights and abilities to make independent choices (Institute of Medicine, 1999). A more upbeat conclusion is found in the observation that teens who perform better on behavioral decision-making tasks are less likely to engage in antisocial behaviors, even after controlling for intelligence (verbal and non) and peer influence (Parker & Fischhoff, 2001). If those skills can be taught, then better real-world choices might result.

CONCLUSION

Academic psychology might be advanced by sweeping generalizations (e.g., people are bias prone, people act rationally, people learn what is important from experience). The ensuing research and controversy can help dispassionate observers achieve a balanced feeling for the boundary conditions for various behaviors. However, with applications, it is the specifics that matter: How much help do particular people need in particular situations? How (well) can it be provided?

Most of the applications described here were conducted in conjunction with subject matter specialists. Such collaborations help psychologists to identify the contextual factors shaping judgment and where help is most needed. They also encourage humility, by showing the stakes riding on the responsible use of psychological research. Reliance on heuristics can produce both good and bad performance. When the research shows people to be competent enough to perform the tasks facing them, it defends their autonomy. Where it shows otherwise, the research can increase that autonomy through process-based de-biasing procedures. By asking hard questions about performance standards, the heuristics-and-biases approach invites evaluating the competence of those making claims of authority (e.g., technocrats, physicians, parents). Unlike staunch proponents of rational-actor models, behavioral decision researchers can be driven by the facts, ready to allow whatever they observe to enrich their science.

42. Theory-Driven Reasoning about Plausible Pasts and Probable Futures in World Politics

Philip E. Tetlock

This chapter explores the applicability of the error-and-bias literature to world politics by examining experts' expectations for the future as well as their explanations of the past. One set of studies tracks the reactions of experts to the apparent confirmation or disconfirmation of conditional forecasts of real-world events in real time. Key issues become: (1) the extent to which experts who "get it wrong" resort to various belief-system defenses; (2) the effectiveness of these defenses in helping experts who got it wrong to preserve confidence in their prior world views; (3) the rationality of these defenses. The other set of studies examines retrospective reasoning: the tightness of the connection between experts' conceptions of what would have happened in "counterfactual worlds" and their general ideological outlook. The key issue becomes the extent to which counterfactual reasoning about historical possibilities is theory-driven (predictable from abstract preconceptions) as opposed to data-driven (constrained by the peculiar "fact situation" of each episode). In these studies of both prospective and retrospective reasoning, individual differences in cognitive style and in conceptual orientations are important moderator variables. Although there is a general tendency among our experts to rely on theory-driven modes of reasoning and to fall prey to theory-driven biases such as overconfidence and belief perseverance, these tendencies are systematically more pronounced among experts with strong preferences for parsimony and explanatory closure.

THEORY-DRIVEN DEFENSES OF CONDITIONAL FORECASTS

Assessing the "truth value" of conditional forecasts initially looks more promising than assessing that of historical counterfactuals. When I "retrodict" that "if X had occurred, Y would have," there is no way of decisively refuting me. But when I predict that "if X occurs, then Y will occur" and X indisputably occurs and Y equally indisputably does not, I am obliged to qualify or abandon my original claim. Closer analysis reveals, however, that judging conditional forecasts in world politics is typically far more controversial than this idealized example suggests. Experts have at least five logically defensible strategies for protecting conditional forecasts that run aground troublesome evidence:

1. The antecedent was never adequately satisfied – in which case, the conditional forecast becomes an historical counterfactual with the passage of time. Thus, experts might insist that "if we had properly implemented deterrence or reassurance, we could have averted war" or "if real shock therapy had been practiced, we could have averted this nasty bout of hyperinflation."

2. Although the specified antecedent was satisfied, key background conditions (covered by the ubiquitous *ceteris paribus* clause) took on unexpected values, thereby short-circuiting the otherwise reliably deterministic connection between cause and effect. Experts might defiantly declare that rapid privatization of state industries would have led to the predicted surge in economic growth but only if the government had exercised tight monetary control.

3. Although the predicted outcome did not occur, it "almost occurred" and would have but for some inherently unpredictable exogenous shock. Examples of close-call counterfactuals include "the hardliners almost overthrew Gorbachev" and "the EU almost disintegrated during the currency crises of 1992."

4. Although the predicted outcome has not yet occurred, it eventually will and we just need to be more patient (hardline communists may yet prevail in Moscow and the EU still might fall apart).

5. Although the relevant preconditions were satisfied and the predicted outcome never came close to occurring and now never will, this failure should not be held against the framework that inspired the forecast. Forecasting exercises are best viewed as light-hearted diversions of no consequence because everyone knows, or else should know, that politics is inherently indeterminate (Jervis, 1992). As Henry Kissinger wryly conceded to Daniel Moynihan after the fragmentation of the Soviet Union, "Your crystal ball worked better than mine" (Moynihan, 1993, p. 23). On close inspection, of course, this concession concedes nothing.

Tetlock (1999) demonstrated that expert observers of world politics draw on all five strategies of minimizing the conceptual significance of unexpected events. However, tempting though it is to dismiss such intellectual maneuvering as transparently defensive *post hocery*, it is wrong to issue automatic indictments for the judgmental bias of belief perseverance. Each defense highlights a potentially valid objection to viewing disconfirmation of the conditional forecast as disconfirmation of the underlying theory. Fortunately, it is not necessary here to stake out a detailed position on the merits of specific variants of falsificationism in the philosophy of science (Suppe, 1973). It is sufficient to specify a straightforward procedural test of bias that, if failed, would convince even the most forgiving falsificationist that something is awry. This *de minimis* test poses the question: When evidence arises bearing on a conditional forecast, do judges who "got it wrong" display much greater interest than judges who "got it right" in questioning whether the antecedent was satisfied, in generating close-call counterfactuals, and in otherwise challenging the probity of the exercise? If so, we still cannot determine who is biased (incorrect forecasters may be too quick to complain about the test or correct forecasters may be too quick to accept it) but we can say that some bias – in the form of theory-driven selectivity of information processing – does exist.

The normative analysis need not, moreover, stop here. With appropriate data, it is possible to construct Bayesian benchmarks for gauging experts' willingness to change their prior confidence in their beliefs in response to subsequent events. Key questions become: Do experts who "got it wrong" retain more confidence in their prior understanding of the underlying forces at work than they should, given their earlier assertions about the probability of particular events vis-à-vis particular hypotheses concerning underlying forces? Do experts who "got it right" take these confirmations too seriously, inflating their confidence in underlying forces at work even more than they should? And what cognitive mechanisms generate these effects? Is Bayesian underadjustment of "priors" among inaccurate experts mediated by reliance on the five belief-system defenses? These experts may see little reason to adjust their prior beliefs in accord with diagnosticity ratios provided long ago when they now believe that the *ceteris paribus* clause was not satisfied, the predicted consequences almost happened, and prediction is inherently impossible. By contrast, experts who made correct forecasts may "overadjust." They may be proud of their accomplishment and disinclined to question it too closely by raising awkward questions about whether their forecasts turned out right for the wrong reasons.

To test these hypotheses, Tetlock (1999) drew on a longitudinal data base of predictions of a wide array of outcomes from 1985 to 2010. This chapter considers the predictions that experts offered for the 5-year futures of the Soviet Union in 1988, of South Africa in 1989, of Kazakhstan in 1992, of the European Monetary Union in 1991, and of Canada in 1992. It also examines the predictions for the U.S. presidential race of 1992 in a 4-month time frame and for the Persian Gulf crisis/war of 1990–1991 in a 1-year frame. All participants received some graduate training in social science or history, specialized in one or more of the regions under examination, and earned their livelihoods either as advanced graduate students in comparative politics and international relations ($n = 58$), post-doctoral fellows in international security and related fields ($n = 25$), university professors ($n = 51$), policy analysts in think-tanks ($n = 17$), intelligence analysts in government service ($n = 39$), or journalists in the employ of the mass media ($n = 9$).

The Technical Appendix in Tetlock (1999) presents the detailed instructions, assurances, and questions given to experts. Among other things, experts responded to a working-style questionnaire (designed, in part, to assess individual differences in preferences for parsimony and explanatory closure) and also rated a number of probabilities necessary for comparing their belief updating with the normative Bayesian model. Respondents were given detailed guidance on how to use the subjective-probability scales that ranged from 0 to 1.0. Experts rated their probabilities that: (1) their interpretation of the underlying forces operating in the scenario was correct (e.g., that their theory or model of the Soviet Union was correct) (prior probability of H); (2) the most influential alternative interpretation of the underlying forces was correct (e.g., that a different theory or model of the Soviet Union was correct) (prior probability of $H\sim$); (3) various possible futures for [x] would occur, assuming that: (1) their own understanding of underlying forces shaping events was correct (conditional probability of outcome given H); and (2) the most influential alternative interpretation of the underlying forces shaping events was correct (conditional probability of outcome given $H\sim$). The "possible futures" were designed to be logically exclusive and exhaustive. For example, in the Soviet case, the scenarios included a strengthening, a reduction, or no change in communist party control.

After the specified forecasting interval had elapsed, 78% of the original forecasters were successfully contacted and questioned again. After exploring experts' ability to recall their original answers, experts were reminded of their original forecasts and confidence estimates. Experts rated their agreement with 9 propositions that could theoretically either cushion the disappointment of "disconfirmation" or deflate the euphoria of "confirmation." Experts also answered "retrospective-probability" questions that assessed the degree to which they updated their prior probabilities in an approximately Bayesian fashion (although this was done in only 4 of the 7 forecasting domains examined here). The retrospective probabilities were compared with the posterior probabilities derived by combining the relevant prior probabilities and conditional probabilities collected at the pre-test (described in the paragraph above).

Across all seven domains, experts were only slightly more accurate than one would expect from chance (the proverbial dart-throwing, blindfolded chimpanzee who poses such tough competition for financial forecasters – Malkiel, 1990). Almost as many experts as not thought that the Soviet Communist Party would remain firmly in the saddle of power in 1993, that Canada was doomed by 1997, that neo-fascism would prevail in Pretoria by 1994, that the EMU would collapse by 1997, that Bush would be reelected in 1992, and that the Persian Gulf crisis would be resolved peacefully. Moreover, although experts only sporadically exceeded chance predictive accuracy, they regularly assigned subjective probabilities that exceeded the scaling anchors for "just guessing." Most experts, especially those who valued parsimony and explanatory closure, thought they knew more than they did. Moreover, these margins of error were larger than those customarily observed in laboratory research on the calibration of confidence. Across all predictions elicited across domains, experts who assigned confidence estimates of 80% or higher were correct only 45% of the time, a hit rate not appreciably higher than that for experts who endorsed the "just-guessing" subjective probabilities of 0.50 and 0.33 (for 2 and 3 outcome scenarios, respectively). Expertise thus may not translate into

Table 42.1. Subjective Probabilities Experts Assigned to their Understanding
of the Underlying Forces at the Beginning and End of Forecasting Periods

Predicting the Future of	Status of Forecast	Judged Prior Probability (Before Outcome Known)	Judged Posterior Probability (After Outcome Known)	Bayesian Predicted Posterior Probability
Soviet Union	Inaccurate	0.74	0.70	0.49[a]
	Accurate	0.69	0.83[b]	0.80
South Africa	Inaccurate	0.72	0.69	0.42[a]
	Accurate	0.70	0.77	0.82
EMU	Inaccurate	0.66	0.68	0.45[a]
	Accurate	0.71	0.78	0.85
Canada	Inaccurate	0.65	0.67	0.39[a]
	Accurate	0.68	0.81[b]	0.79

[a] Indicates a significant deviation of expert-assigned posterior probabilities from the posterior probabilities that Bayes Theorem stipulates experts should endorse if they were correctly multiplying their subjective prior odds by the diagnosticity ratios provided at original forecast.
[b] Indicates significant shift in subjective probability assigned to one's understanding of underlying forces at beginning and end of forecasting (prior versus posterior).

predictive accuracy but it does translate into the ability to generate explanations for predictions that experts themselves find so compelling that the result is massive over-confidence.

Our principal interest is, however, in experts' reactions to the apparent confirmation or disconfirmation of their forecasts. A clear pattern emerges: experts do not change their minds nearly to the degree they should if they were true Bayesians committed to using the diagnosticity ratios they provided at the outset of the forecasting exercises. Table 42.1 shows that, across all four domains with measures of prior probabilities and diagnosticity ratios at the original forecasts, and of posterior probabilities at the follow-up session, experts whose most likely scenarios materialized were pretty good Bayesians; they *increased* their confidence in their prior understanding of underlying forces that led them to assign varying probabilities to scenarios at the outset of the forecasting period. And they did so in approximately the right amounts. By contrast, experts whose most likely scenarios failed to materialize did *not* decrease their estimates of the likelihood of the observed events given their prior understanding of underlying forces that led them to make the subjective forecasts they earlier advanced. They held their ground, notwithstanding that the Bayesian formula prescribed that they should have lost a great deal of confidence in their prior understanding (and should, in some cases, have outright converted to what they once called "the most influential alternative view of the underlying forces shaping events"). These findings replicate the well known "conservatism bias" in probabilistic reasoning: confronted by the unexpected, people do not change their minds as much as a good Bayesian would. It also merits note that cognitive

Table 42.2. Average Reactions of Experts to Confirmation and Disconfirmation of Their Conditional Forecasts

Predicting the Future of	Status of Forecast	Belief-System Defenses				
		Close-call Counter-factuals	Ceteris Paribus Did Not Hold	Antecedent Did Not Hold	Just Unlucky About Timing	Dismiss Forecasting Exercises in General
Soviet Union	Inaccurate	7.0^a	7.1^a	6.8^a	6.4	7.3^a
	Accurate	4.1	3.9	3.6	5.0	3.1
South Africa	Inaccurate	7.1^a	7.0^a	7.3^a	3.7	7.1^a
	Accurate	4.5	3.5	3.3	4.0	4.8
EMU	Inaccurate	7.2^a	5.9	6.2	7.8^a	7.0^a
	Accurate	5.1	4.6	4.9	3.8	4.3
Canada	Inaccurate	7.6	6.8^a	6.5^a	8.0^a	7.2^a
	Accurate	6.8	3.7	4.2	4.4	4.5
Kazakhstan	Inaccurate	6.5^a	7.2^a	6.9^a	7.3^a	6.8^a
	Accurate	2.8	2.9	3.5	3.6	5.0
Persian Gulf Crisis	Inaccurate	7.0	6.6	6.4	4.4	6.9^a
	Accurate	4.1	4.8	4.5	4.2	4.1
1992 Presidential Election	Inaccurate	7.5^a	6.7^a	6.6^a	3.5	6.9^a
	Accurate	5.8	3.2	3.1	3.6	5.2

[a] Indicates significantly stronger endorsements of the belief-system defense among inaccurate forecasters ($p < .05$).

style emerges again as a predictor among inaccurate (but not accurate) forecasters. Inaccurate experts who value parsimony and explanatory closure were more prone to "conservatism" – a result that is consistent with past laboratory work on both "need for closure" and "integrative complexity."

Defenders of the rationality of our experts (especially of the experts who valued parsimony and closure) are not, however, logically compelled to submit to the looming negative verdict. They can rightly point out that, in the intervening periods, experts may have quite sensibly changed their minds about the diagnosticity of various events vis-à-vis various hypotheses concerning the "underlying forces shaping events." Indeed, Table 42.2 itemizes the five belief-system defenses that experts invoked to neutralize the diagnosticity of unexpected events. These defensive strategies included: arguing that either the antecedent or *ceteris paribus* clauses underpinning the original forecasts were not satisfied, invoking close-call counterfactuals, claiming that the predicted event might still occur, and minimizing the conceptual significance of forecasting exercises. Table 42.2 shows that, in 26 of 35 cases, t-tests reveal that experts whose most likely scenarios did not occur showed significantly more enthusiasm ($p < .05$) for "defensive" cognitions than experts whose most likely scenarios did occur.

Each defense invokes a potentially defensible reason for why relatively inaccurate experts should not abandon prior probability assessments that were conditional on their original understanding of underlying forces. Why change one's mind about the validity of one's pre-forecast conceptual framework when the necessary antecedent conditions for applying that framework were never fulfilled, exogenous shocks vitiated the *ceteris paribus* requirement for all fair tests of hypotheses, the predicted event almost occurred despite all these obstacles and still might, and prediction exercises are so riddled with indeterminacy as to be meaningless? This analysis suggests that the focus on whether experts got their Bayesian arithmetic right is misplaced. The more fundamental question concerns the defensibility of each belief-system defense. Let's consider each in turn.

1) *Nonfulfillment of antecedent and ceteris-paribus clauses.* There are sound philosophy-of-science grounds for refusing to abandon a theory until one is convinced that the antecedent conditions for activating the relevant covering laws have been fulfilled and the ceteris paribus clause has been satisfied (Hempel, 1965). Experts often had reason for suspecting that the "fundamental forces" on which forecasts were initially predicated were not the same forces shaping events at the end of the forecasting period. Inherently unpredictable exogenous shocks had transformed the original meanings of key analytical concepts – rationality, economic determinism, the perceived interests of former apparatchiks or the white business elite – underlying forecasts. And background conditions – too numerous to specify in advance – occasionally took on extreme values that routed events down "unforeseeable" paths.

2) *Close-call counterfactuals.* Political outcomes often appear under the control of complex conjunctions of stochastic processes that could easily have yielded different effects. One's reaction to this defense hinges on one's metaphysical outlook. LaPlacean determinists reject it out of hand, but if one accepts Steven Jay Gould's (1995) provocative thought experiment in which, holding initial conditions constant, repeatedly re-running the tape of evolutionary history yields thousands of distinctive outcomes (with intelligent life one of the least likely), it is reasonable to talk about alternative histories "almost happening" and even to distinguish alternative histories on the basis of how "close" they came to happening. It is certainly not far-fetched to claim that the Parti Québecois almost won the second secessionist referendum. It is arguably not far-fetched to claim that hardline communists nearly reclaimed power in the late Gorbachev period (and might have had they been smarter and more cohesive) or that the European Monetary Union nearly collapsed in the wake of the 1992 currency crisis (and might have but for the obstinacy of key politicians such as Mitterand and Kohl) or that the Gulf War of 1991 was almost averted (and would have been but for Saddam Hussein's irrational unwillingness to undertake a partial preemptive withdrawal from Kuwait in the fall of 1990). Indeed, if we interpret the subjective-probability estimates attached to forecasts literally as "frequentist" claims about the distribution of possible worlds in repeated-simulations of history, experts who assigned 80% confidence to "incorrect" forecasts may quite literally have been correct. Strange though it sounds, in the ontology of Lewis' (1973) modal logic, it makes sense to say that in 80% of the Soviet Unions that were possible as of 1988, the predicted outcome occurred. We just happened to wind up in that unlikely subset of possible worlds in which communist control collapsed. Of course, this defense quickly wears thin: People will tire of hearing that the world they happen to inhabit is vanishingly improbable;

3) *Off-on-timing.* This defense is reminiscent of the probably apocryphal account of a Trotskyite rally at which the speaker declares Leon Trotsky to be a remarkably far-sighted man and offers as proof that "of all the predictions Trotsky has made not one has yet come true." That said, this defense still merits a hearing. The domains in which the defense was most frequently invoked – Russia, the EMU, and Canada – were those in which experts were especially unsure, *ex ante*, of the temporal boundaries to place on their forecasts. Even now, there is residual disagreement over whether the Russian communist party or some other authoritarian force will yet triumph, and over whether Canada and the EMU will dissolve. Posterity will ridicule us, not the experts, if we classify forecasts as categorically wrong that turn out to have been just a bit tardy.

4) *Conceptual Significance of Prediction.* This defense takes the indeterminacy argument to its ultimate extension. Rather than invoking indeterminacy in piecemeal fashion (a close-call counterfactual here or there), experts proclaim politics to be hopelessly "cloudlike," disparage those who look for lawful regularities as subscribing to a naive "clocklike" perspective, and dismiss forecasting exercises as trivial at best or deeply misleading at worst (the winners deserve no more credit for good judgment than does the lucky roulette player who repeatedly bets on his favorite nephew's birthdate). These experts are embracing a philosophical position with radical implications for the notion of good judgment. There should be as little consistency in who wins political forecasting tournaments as there is in forecasting tournaments for financial markets where random-walk models are widely held to hold (Malkiel, 1990).

Implications for Rationality

Converging evidence suggests that experts not only rely, but over-rely, on their preconceptions in generating expectations about the future (producing overconfidence) and in revising preconceptions in response to unexpected events (producing belief underadjustment by Bayesian standards). Moreover, we can identify several belief-system defenses that experts deploy to protect their worldviews from falsification and we can identify a characteristic cognitive-style profile for those experts most inclined to invoke these defenses and to display overconfidence in the original forecasts and underadjustment in response to unexpected events. The more value experts place on parsimony and explanatory closure, the more prone they are to overconfidence (*ex ante*) and Bayesian under-adjustment (*ex post*).

In complex natural settings, though, we need to be careful in rendering normative judgment. As already noted, the belief-system defenses may themselves be defensible, at least up to a point. Reliance on these defenses may also be compatible with several conceptions of learning from history. Indeed, the data shed light on when learning is likely and on the forms that it will take. It will often be stimulated by failure, and constrained by the cognitive and organizational principles of least resistance, to take incremental forms (Nye, 1988; Tetlock, 1991). Most experts initially respond to unexpected events by tinkering with peripheral cognitions that require minimal modification of their belief systems. Rather than conceding on "fundamentals," they argue that some new unforeseeable causal force emerged, thus nullifying the *ceteris paribus* clause, or that the predicted outcome "almost occurred." The cumulative effect of such tinkering should not be understated. Whenever experts argue that their predicted future would have occurred but for some historical accident or previously unacknowledged moderator variable, they have learned in a significant sense. Their belief systems now assign a more important role to chance and recognize causality to have been more complex than previously acknowledged. From this standpoint, the more defensive close-call counterfactuals one generates, the greater the likelihood that one is *learning*, both in the cognitive-structural meaning of the term (evolving differentiated and integrated knowledge structures for processing future evidence) and in the efficiency-enhancement sense of the term (acquiring the ability either to make more accurate forecasts or at least to attach more realistic confidence estimates to one's forecasts). This argument suggests a curious conclusion: the more experts are wrong, the wiser they become as they internalize more qualifications on when their expectations hold. The real threat to good judgment lies in the hubris that builds up from a succession of predictions that serendipitously turn out right. We thus have a substantive cognitive argument – in addition to the formal statistical argument invoking regression toward the mean – for expecting the poor predictive performers of yesterday to catch up to the superstar predictors of today.

RETROSPECTIVE REASONING: THEORY-DRIVEN INFERENCES ABOUT COUNTERFACTUAL WORLDS

Close-call counterfactuals play a central role in cushioning conditional forecasts from the logical sting of unexpected events. The more theory-driven an expert's style of reasoning, the more likely the expert was to endorse scenarios in which the predicted event (that did not occur) almost occurred: the "I-was-almost-right" defense. Shifting from prospective to retrospective reasoning, however, there are good reasons for expecting the opposite functional relationship to emerge: the more theory-driven the expert's style of reasoning, the more inclined the expert should be to dismiss close-call counterfactuals as whimsical and far-fetched. A good example of how close-call counterfactuals can undermine belief systems arises whenever experts offer confidently deterministic explanations of the past that portray what happened as inevitable but then confront plausible arguments that highlight how easily events might have gone down a different path. For instance, many students of world politics subscribe to some variant of the deterministic thesis that World War I was inevitable – perhaps because of the inherent instability of multiethnic empires and of multipolar balances of power or perhaps because of the widespread perception that the side that mobilized and struck first would possess a decisive advantage. Let's suppose that we challenge these experts with the argument, "If the assassination of Archduke Ferdinand on June 28, 1914, had been thwarted, then World War I would not have broken out in August, 1914." These experts have three distinct lines of defense:

1. They could challenge the mutability of the antecedent and insist that it is hard to undo the assassination because the Archduke was so detested in Sarajevo and the Serbian assassins were so determined. Few experts, however, endorse this defense in this case – perhaps because the assassination depends on a transparently improbable series of coincidences, each easily "undoable" by the standards of Kahneman and Miller's (1986) norm theory.
2. They could challenge the adequacy of the connecting principles linking antecedent to consequent. Counterfactual arguments are inherently elliptical; it is too exhausting to spell out the exhaustive lists of background assumptions that must be satisfied to sustain even the simplest antecedent-consequent linkages. To invoke the standard example, "If the match had been struck, it would have lighted" rests on an elaborate matrix of assumptions, including the presence of oxygen, the absence of water, sufficient friction, and the proper chemical composition of the match. In the Archduke counterfactual, experts could challenge the connecting principles by arguing that Austro-Hungary would have attacked Serbia anyway and the assassination merely provided a convenient *casus belli*.
3. They could concede both the mutability of the antecedent ("Yes, the Archduke could have escaped death on July 28, 1914") and the soundness of the connecting principles ("Yes, war probably would not have broken out that summer"), but insist that the war would not have been long delayed because some other match would have ignited the conflagration. This defense, the most popular of the three in this case, is designated a second-order counterfactual: It undoes the undoing of the original close-call counterfactual. Second-order counterfactuals allow for deviations from reality but minimize the significance of the deviations by invoking higher-order forces that soon bring events in the simulated world back toward the observed historical path.

Drawing on this analysis, Tetlock (1998) argued that individual differences in both theoretical outlook and cognitive style (especially in preferences for parsimony and explanatory closure) should predict resistance to close-call counterfactuals that erode favorite deterministic accounts of the past (*covering laws*; Hempel, 1965). Belief-system defense now requires invoking the "I-was-not-almost-wrong" defense: demonstrating that, although it might seem easy to derail a particular historical process, on close inspection it proves remarkably difficult. As soon as one cuts off one causal pathway to the observed outcome, another pathway arises, hydralike, in a second-order counterfactual.

To test these hypotheses, Tetlock (1998) constructed scales to measure four dimensions of beliefs about political causality: (1) the instability of the balance of power as a necessary and sufficient explanation for the outbreak of war in general and for World War I in particular; (2) the efficacy of classic balance-of-power mechanisms in preventing the emergence of hegemons on the European continent in the last few centuries; (3) the Soviet political system as an adequate explanation for both Stalinist tyranny in domestic policy and external expansion in foreign policy; and (4) the role played by nuclear weapons in preventing a third world war between the United States and the Soviet Union. Tetlock (1998) also constructed a composite (multimethod) indicator of cognitive style by combining responses to a truncated version of Kruglanski and Webster's (1996) need-for-closure scale with integrative complexity scores derived from coding experts' open-ended explanations for why the 20th century turned out to be as violent as it did. Henceforth, this measure is designated *strength of preferences for parsimony and explanatory closure*.

As Table 42.3 indicates, the predicted pattern emerged. The stronger their preconceptions about history, the more unequivocally experts rejected close-call counterfactuals that poked indeterminacy holes in the applicability of those

Table 42.3. Multiple Regression Analyses for Predicting Resistance to Close-Call Counterfactuals at Key Junctures in 20th Century History

Event	β	t	Significance
Undoing WWI			
Cognitive style	−.12	−.78	NS
Macro Causes of War	.80	9.38	.01
Interaction	−.40	−2.62	.01
Undoing Outcome of WWI			
Cognitive style	−.32	−2.05	.04
Neorealist balancing	.86	8.76	.01
Interaction	−.57	−2.75	.01
Undoing Outcome of WWII			
Cognitive style	−.28	−1.37	NS
Neorealist balancing	.73	10.69	.00
Interaction	−.35	−1.73	NS
Undoing Cold War			
Cognitive style	−.35	−1.49	NS
Essentialist view of USSR	.74	7.21	.01
Interaction	−.21	−.88	NS
Undoing Cold War Outcome			
Cognitive style	−.42	−1.93	NS
Efficacy of Nuclear Deterrence	.80	9.45	.01
Interaction	−.67	−3.10	.01

preconceptions to a particular historical episode – in the process, often invoking all three layers of belief-system defense. For example, experts whose essentialist outlook on the Soviet Union stressed the inherently expansionist character of the regime objected most forcefully to counterfactual claims that the Cold War could easily have been avoided by triggering Stalin's cerebral hemorrhage in 1945 instead of 1953 or by triggering FDR's stroke in 1944 instead of 1945, thereby replacing Truman with a relatively left-wing president (Wallace). Experts who believed in the inherent stability of nuclear deterrence and the rationality of policy makers were more skeptical of close-call counterfactuals that implied that we came precariously close to a nuclear Armageddon in the Cuban missile crisis or in other Cold-War confrontations. Perhaps most interesting, this skepticism was not limited to challenging the political logic connecting antecedents to consequents or to invoking the even more abstract second-order close-call-counterfactual defense. Many experts also challenged the mutability of medical antecedents (the health of leaders) and meteorologic antecedents (cloud cover over Cuba in October). Indeed, the three belief-system-defenses were sufficiently intercorrelated to aggregate them into a single index.

The individual-difference measure of cognitive style played a robust moderator-variable role. Experts with strong preferences for parsimony and explanatory closure were most dismissive of close-call counterfactuals that poked holes in favorite covering laws. The predicted interaction materialized in the clear majority of historical domains examined.

Here we confront an interesting choice of normative value spin to be placed on styles of reasoning. Academic observers can either (1) applaud the high-parsimony respondents for their logical rigor and taut belief systems and deplore their low-parsimony counterparts for their mental sloppiness and loose-linkage belief systems; or (2) criticize the high-parsimony respondents for their mental rigidity and lack of historical imagination and praise their low-parsimony counterparts for their cognitive flexibility and vision. Either way, the data reveal a belief-system continuum anchored at one end by theorists with great tolerance for ambiguity who acknowledge a multiplicity of possible histories of the twentieth century and anchored at the other end by theorists with strong preferences for explanatory closure who insist that things had to work out as they did and have little tolerance for counterfactual "parlor games." Toward the middle of the continuum is the bulk of our sample: theorists who acknowledge systemic constraints on what could have happened but who concede that it was often possible for history to stray, sometimes for prolonged periods, from the observed path. These latter theorists give their counterfactual imaginations freer rein than their high-parsimony counterparts but are more likely to rein in those imaginations than their low-parsimony counterparts.

SOME CLOSING OBSERVATIONS

How should we balance these seemingly endless arguments bearing on the "rationality" of professional observers of world politics? Here it is useful to recall the Faustian compromises underlying our research designs. The goal was to study how experts think about problems that arise naturally in their professional lives: extracting lessons from history, changing one's mind about historical causation in response to evidence, and responding to the apparent confirmation or disconfirmation of conditional forecasts. In making this choice, we sacrificed the precise normative benchmarks of error that laboratory researchers enjoy. Respondents did not randomly draw red or blue marbles from an urn and then judge the likelihood of various distributions of colors – a task with a clear right or wrong Bayesian answer. Rather, they dealt with subtly interrelated and constantly evolving path-dependent sequences of arguably unique events. As a result, even with *ex ante* diagnosticity ratios in hand, it is extraordinarily difficult to single out any given individual as biased. That said, there is still a strong circumstantial case that the results of these naturalistic studies are tapping into the same underlying processes documented in laboratory work on errors and biases in social judgment. Consider the following: (a) the overconfidence in political forecasts reaffirms a substantial early body of work on calibration of subjective probability estimates of knowledge (Fischhoff, 1982); (b) the selective activation of belief-system defenses dovetails nicely with the classic dissonance prediction that people would most need "defenses" when they appear to have been wrong about something in which they were originally quite confident (Festinger, 1964); (c) the skepticism that experts reserved for dissonant historical arguments extends the work on theory-driven assessments of evidence and on selective standards of proof in scientific hypothesis testing (Griffin & Ross, 1991); (d) the generation of close-call counterfactuals in response to unexpected events is consistent with experimental evidence on determinants of spontaneous counterfactual thinking (Kahneman & Miller, 1996); (e) the reluctance of experts to change their minds in response to unexpected events and in accord with earlier specified diagnosticity ratios parallels the excessive conservatism in belief revision often displayed by subjects in experiments that explicitly compare human judgment to Bayesian formulas (Dawes, 1998); (f) the cognitive-stylistic differences in belief-system defense and belief under-adjustment offer further evidence of the construct validity of the need for closure and integrative complexity measures (Kruglanski & Webster, 1996). In all six respects, the current results underscore the generalizability of laboratory-based demonstrations of bounded rationality in a more ecologically representative research design. The psychological findings hold up well when highly trained experts (as opposed to sophomore conscripts) judge complex, naturally occurring, political events (as opposed to artificial problems that the experimenter has often concocted with the intent of demonstrating bias).

In closing, let us assume – for sake of argument – that the current results highlight how easily even highly trained experts, especially those who uphold the classic scientific value of parsimony, can slip into tautological patterns of reasoning in which: (a) they rely on their preconceptions to fill in what would have happened in the missing counterfactual control conditions of history (the "I-was-not-almost-wrong" anti-close-call-counterfactual defense); (b) these counterfactual beliefs reinforce the lessons from history that experts were already conceptually predisposed to draw and shape their expectations about future events; and (c) once again, experts rely on their preconceptions, but this time, to shield conditional expectations from disconfirmation by invoking a battery of belief-system defenses (including the "I-was-almost-right" close-call-counterfactual defense). If this grim portrait does capture how many professional observers think about world politics, there is a compelling case for shifting the research agenda – from cursing the cognitive darkness to lighting methodological candles. Miscalculation in world politics is just too expensive – in lives as well as money – to comment calmly on how hard it is to avoid becoming prisoners of our preconceptions.

Our most recent work has indeed begun to explore potential remedies. It is far too early to announce "cures" but it is safe to make two cautionary observations, one about the limitations of psychological knowledge in diagnosing the problem and the other about the limitations of psychology in prescribing solutions. First, our psychological data base is skewed toward emphasizing the perils of closed-mindedness. The implicit message seems to be: the more dissonant, mind-stretching possibilities people can be induced to consider, the better off they are. This stance is, almost surely, too simplistic. Odd though it may sound, there may be perils of open-mindedness, an intriguing implication of several strands of research, including work on support theory that highlights the subjective-probability-inflating effects of unpacking sets of outcomes into their logically exclusive and exhaustive components (Tversky & Fox, 1995), work on dilution effects in prediction that highlights the dangers of incorporating too much information into one's assessments (Tetlock & Boettger, 1989), and work on cognitive styles that highlights the risks of excessive integrative complexity (Suedfeld & Tetlock, 2001). The relative costs and benefits of erring in the direction of open or closed-mindedness in different environments are just not yet well enough understood to justify confident normative prescriptions (Tetlock & Lebow, 2001). Second, social psychologists sometimes focus on accuracy as an end in itself, as though it were immaterial in which direction, false alarms or misses, the errors fall. As signal detection theorists have long appreciated, this position is also too simplistic. In politics, accuracy is valued only conditionally, as a means to higher ends such as deterring expansionism or preventing crisis escalation. The relative importance of Type I and Type II errors cannot be ignored, and these judgment calls ultimately hinge as much on our moral–political priorities as on technical psychological issues of fine-tuning cognitive processes.

References

Numbers in square brackets at the end of each entry refer to the chapter(s) in which that reference appears.

Abarbanell, J. S., & Bernard, V. L. (1992). Tests of analysts overreaction/underreaction to earnings information as an explanation for anomalous stock price behavior. *Journal of Finance, 47*, 1181–1207. **[38]**

Abell, G. O. (1981). Astrology. In *Science and the paranormal: Probing the existence of the supernatural* (pp. 70–94), G. O. Abell & B. Singer (Eds.). New York: Charles Scribner & Sons. **[34]**

Adams, E. W. (1975). *The logic of conditionals*. Dordrecht, The Netherlands: D. Reidel. **[3]**

Adelmann, P., & Zajonc, R. (1989). Facial efference and the experience of emotion. *Annual Review of Psychology, 40*, 249–280. **[5]**

Adler, J. E. (1984). Abstraction is uncooperative. *Journal for the Theory of Social Behaviour, 14*, 165–181. **[24]**

Adler, J. E. (1991). An optimist's pessimism: Conversation and conjunctions. In *Probability and rationality: Studies on L. Jonathan Cohen's philosophy of science* (pp. 251–282), E. Eells & T. Maruszewski (Eds.). Amsterdam: Editions Rodopi. **[24]**

Affleck, G., & Tennen, H. (1996). Construing benefits from adversity: Adaptational significance and dispositional underpinnings. *Journal of Personality, 64*, 899–922. **[16]**

Agnoli, F. (1991). Development of judgmental heuristics and logical reasoning: Training counteracts the representativeness heuristic. *Cognitive Development, 6*, 195–217. **[2]**

Agnoli, F., & Krantz, D. H. (1989). Suppressing natural heuristics by formal instruction: The case of the conjunction fallacy. *Cognitive Psychology, 21*, 515–550. **[2]**

Ahlers, D., & Lakonishok, J. (1983). A study of economists' consensus forecasts. *Management Science, 29*, 1113–1125. **[38]**

Ainslie, G. (1992). *Picoeconomics: The strategic interaction of successive motivational states within the person*. Cambridge, U.K.: Cambridge University Press. **[16]**

Ajzen, I. (1977). Intuitive theories of events and the effects of base rate information on prediction. *Journal of Personality and Social Psychology, 35*, 303–314. **[1, 24]**

Ajzen, I. (1991). The theory of planned behavior. *Organizational Behavior and Human Decision Processes, 50*, 179–211. **[14]**

Ajzen, I., & Madden, T. J. (1986). Prediction of goal-directed behavior: Attitudes, intentions, and perceived behavioral control. *Journal of Experimental Social Psychology, 22*, 453–474. **[14]**

Alhakami, A. S., & Slovic, P. (1994). A psychological study of the inverse relationship between perceived risk and perceived benefit. *Risk Analysis, 14*(6), 1085–1096. **[23]**

Alicke, M. D., Klotz, M. L., Breitenbecher, D. L., Yurak, T. J., & Vredenburg, D. S. (1995). Personal contact, individuation, and the better-than-average effect. *Journal of Personality and Social Psychology, 68*, 804–825. [27, 36]

Alker, H., & Hermann, M. (1971). Are Bayesian decisions artificially intelligent? The effect of task and personality on conservatism in information processing. *Journal of Personality and Social Psychology, 19*, 31–41. [24]

Allen, S. W., & Brooks, L. R. (1991). Specializing the operation of an explicit rule. *Journal of Experimental Psychology: General, 120*, 3–19. [22]

Allison, S. T., & Beggan, J. K. (1994). Estimating popular support for group decision outcomes: An anchoring and adjustment model. *Journal of Social Behavior & Personality, 9*, 617–638. [6]

Allison, S. T., & Messick D. M. (1990). Social decision heuristics and the use of shared resources. *Journal of Behavioral Decision Making, 3*, 195–204. [30]

Alpert, M., & Raiffa, H. (1982). A progress report on the training of probability assessors. In *Judgment under uncertainty: Heuristics and biases* (pp. 294–305), D. Kahneman, P. Slovic, & A. Tversky (Eds.). Cambridge, U.K.: Cambridge University Press. [13, 15]

Amir, E., & Ganzach, Y. (1998). Overreaction and underreaction in analysts' forecasts. *Journal of Economic Behavior & Organization, 37*, 333–347. [38]

Andersen, S. M., & Ross, L. (1984). Self knowledge and social inference: I. The impact of cognitive/affective and behavioral data. *Journal of Personality and Social Psychology, 46*, 280–293. [36]

Andersen, S. M. (1984). Self knowledge and social inference: II. The diagnosticity of cognitive/affective and behavioral data. *Journal of Personality and Social Psychology, 46*, 294–307. [36]

Anderson, C. A. (1983a). Abstract and concrete data in the perseverance of social theories: When weak data lead to unshakeable beliefs. *Journal of Experimental Social Psychology, 19*, 93–108. [20]

Anderson, C. A. (1983b). Imagination and expectation: The effect of imagining behavioral scripts on personal intentions. *Journal of Personality and Social Psychology, 45*, 293–305. [4, 17, 19]

Anderson, C. A., Lepper, M. R., & Ross, L. (1980). Perseverance of social theories: The role of explanation in the persistence of discredited information. *Journal of Personality and Social Psychology, 39*, 1037–1049. [4]

Anderson, J. R. (1983). A spreading activation theory of memory. *Journal of Verbal Learning and Verbal Behavior, 22*, 261–295. [20]

Anderson, N. H. (1968). Likableness ratings of 555 personality-trait words. *Journal of Personalility and Social Psychology, 9*, 272–279. [18]

Anderson, N. H. (1981). *Foundations of information integration theory.* New York: Academic Press. [20, 23]

Anderson, N. H. (1991). *Contributions to Information Integration Theory. Vol. I: Cognition.* Hillsdale, NJ: Lawrence Erlbaum Associates. [2]

Anderson, N. H. (1996). *A functional theory of cognition.* Mahwah, NJ: Lawrence Erlbaum Associates. [2]

Andrews, F. M., & Robinson, J. P. (1991). Measures of subjective well-being. In *Measures of personality and social psychological attitudes* (Vol. 1, pp. 61–114), J. P. Robinson, P. R. Shaver, & L. S. Wrightsman (Eds.), San Diego: Academic Press. [16]

Angier, N. (1999). *Woman: An intimate geography.* Boston: Houghton Mifflin Company. [30]

Appadurai, A. (1981). Gastro-politics in Hindu South Asia. *American Ethnologist, 8*, 494–511. [11]

Appley, M. H. (Ed.). (1971). *Adaptation-level theory: A symposium.* New York: Academic Press. **[20]**

Ariely, D. (1998). Combining experiences over time: The effects of duration, intensity changes and on-line measurements on retrospective pain evaluations. *Journal of Behavioral Decision Making, 11,* 19–45. **[2]**

Ariely, D. (2001). Seeing sets: Representation by statistical properties. *Psychological Science, 12*(2), 157–162. **[2]**

Ariely, D., Kahneman, D., & Loewenstein, G. (2000). Joint comment on "When does duration matter in judgment and decision making?" (Ariely & Loewenstein, 2000). *Journal of Experimental Psychology: General, 129,* 524–529. **[2]**

Ariely, D., & Loewenstein, G. (2000). When does duration matter in judgment and decision making? *Journal of Experimental Psychology: General, 129,* 508–523. **[2]**

Arkes, H. R. (1991). Costs and benefits of judgment errors: Implications for debiasing. *Psychological Bulletin, 110,* 486–498. **[6]**

Arkes, H. R. (2001). Overconfidence in judgmental forecasting. In *Principles of forecasting handbook* (pp. 495–515), J. S. Armstrong (Ed.). Boston: Kluwer. **[41]**

Arkes, H. R., & Blumer, C. (1985). The psychology of sunk cost. *Organizational Behavior and Human Decision Processes, 35,* 125–140. **[32]**

Arkes, H. R., Dawson, N. V., Speroff, T., Harrell, F. E., Jr., Alzola, C., Phillips, R., Desbiens, N., Oye, R. K., Knaus, W., Connors, A. F., Jr., & the SUPPORT Investigators (1995). The covariance decomposition of the probability score and its use in evaluating prognostic estimates. *Medical Decision Making, 15,* 120–131. **[39]**

Arkes, H. R., Faust, D., Guilmette, T. J., & Hart, K. (1988). Eliminating the hindsight bias. *Journal of Applied Psychology, 73,* 305–307. **[6, 14]**

Arkes, H. R., Wortmann, R. L., Saville, P. D., & Harkness, A. R. (1981). Hindsight bias among physicians weighing the likelihood of diagnoses. *Journal of Applied Psychology, 66,* 252–254. **[40]**

Arkin, R. A., & Duval, S. (1975). Effects of focus of attention on the causal attributions of actors and observers. *Journal of Experimental Social Psychology, 11,* 427–438. **[20]**

Armor, D. A. (1998). *The illusion of objectivity: A bias in the perception of freedom from bias.* Doctoral dissertation, University of California, Los Angeles. **[36]**

Armor, D. A., & Taylor, S. E. (1998). Situated optimism: Specific outcome expectancies and self-regulation. In *Advances in experimental social psychology* (Vol. 30, pp. 309–379), M. P. Zanna (Ed.). New York: Academic Press. **[14]**

Armor, D. A., & Taylor, S. E. (2000). *Mindset, prediction, and performance: Self-regulation in deliberative and implemental frames of mind.* Unpublished manuscript, Yale University. **[19]**

Armstrong, J. S. (Ed.). (2001). *Principles of forecasting handbook.* Boston: Kluwer. **[41]**

Aronson, E. (1969). The theory of cognitive dissonance: A current perspective. In *Advances in experimental social psychology* (Vol. 4, pp. 1–34), L. Berkowitz (Ed.). New York: Academic Press. **[36]**

Aronson, E., & Carlsmith, J. M. (1962). Performance expectancy as a determinant of actual performance. *Journal of Abnormal and Social Psychology, 65,* 178–186. **[19]**

Aronson, E., & Mills, J. (1959). The effect of severity of initiation on liking for a group. *Journal of Abnormal and Social Psychology, 59,* 177–181. **[Introduction]**

Ashby, F. G., Alfonso-Reese, L. A., Turken, A. U., & Waldron, E. M. (1998). A neuropsychological theory of multiple systems in category learning. *Psychological Review, 105,* 442–481. **[22]**

Ashby, F. G., Isen, A. M., & Turken, A. U. (1999). A neuropsychological theory of positive affect and its influence on cognition. *Psychological Review, 106,* 529–550. **[29]**

Ashton, R. H. (1992). Effects of justification and a mechanical aid on judgment performance. *Organizational Behavior and Human Decision Processes, 52*, 292–306. **[32]**

Aspinwall, L. G., Kemeny, M. E., Taylor, S. E., Schneider, S. G., & Dudley, J. P. (1991). Psychological predictors in gay men's AIDS risk-reduction behavior. *Health Psychology, 10*, 432–444. **[19]**

Aspinwall, L. G., & Richter, L. (1999). Optimism and self-mastery predict more rapid disengagement from unsolvable tasks in the presence of alternatives. *Motivation and Emotion, 23*, 221–245. **[19]**

Astington, J., Harris, P., & Olson, D. (Eds.). (1988). *Developing theories of mind*. New York: Cambridge University Press. **[8]**

Atkinson, J. W. (1964). *An introduction to motivation*. Princeton, NJ: Van Nostrand. **[19, 35]**

Au, T. K. (1993). Developing an intuitive understanding of conservation and contamination. *Developmental Psychology, 29*, 286–299. **[11]**

Ayton, P. (1992). On the competence and incompetence of experts. In *Expertise and decision support* (pp. 77–105), G. Wright & F. Bolger (Eds.). Plenum Press: New York. **[39]**

Ayton, P. (1997). How to be incoherent and seductive: Bookmakers' odds and support theory. *Organizational Behavior and Human Decision Processes, 72*, 99–115. **[27]**

Ayton, P. (1998). How bad is human judgment? In *Forecasting with judgment*, G. Wright & P. Goodwin (Eds.). West Sussex, England: John Wiley & Sons. **[2]**

Ayton, P., & Hardman, D. (1997). Are two rationalities better than one? *Current Psychology of Cognition, 16*, 39–51. **[24]**

Ayton, P., & Önkal, D. (1996). *Effects of expertise on forecasts and confidence in forecast*. Paper presented at the International Symposium on Forecasting, Istanbul, Turkey. **[39]**

Baker, L. A., & Emery, R. E. (1993). When every relationship is above average: Perceptions and expectations of divorce at the time of marriage. *Law and Human Behavior, 17*, 439–450. **[19]**

Baker, N. (1991). *Room temperature*. New York: Vintage. **[35]**

Bandura, A. (1977). Self-efficacy: Toward a unifying theory of behavioral change. *Psychological Review, 84*, 191–215. **[19, 36]**

Bandura, A. (1997). *Self efficacy: The exercise of control*. New York: W. H. Freeman and Company. **[19]**

Bankhart, C. P., & Elliot, R. (1974). Heart rate and skin conductance in anticipation of shocks with varying probability of occurrence. *Psychophysiology, 11*, 160–174. **[30]**

Bar-Hillel, M. (1973). On the subjective probability of compound events. *Organizational Behavior and Human Performance, 9*, 396–406. **[1]**

Bar-Hillel, M. (1980). The base-rate fallacy in probability judgments. *Acta Psychologica, 44*, 211–233. **[24]**

Bar-Hillel, M. (1983). The base rate fallacy controversy. In *Decision making under uncertainty* (pp. 39–61), R. W. Scholz (Ed.). Amsterdam: North-Holland. **[13]**

Bar-Hillel, M. (1990). Back to base rates. In *Insights into decision making: A tribute to Hillel J. Einhorn* (pp. 200–216), R. M. Hogarth (Ed.). Chicago: University of Chicago Press. **[24]**

Bar-Hillel, M., & Fischhoff, B. (1981). When do base-rates affect predictions? *Journal of Personality and Social Psychology, 41*(4), 671–680. **[2]**

Bar-Hillel, M., & Neter, E. (1993). How alike is it versus how likely is it: A disjunction fallacy in probability judgments. *Journal of Personality and Social Psychology, 65*, 1119–1131. **[Introduction, 2, 25, 26]**

Baranski, J. V., & Petrusic, W. M. (1994). The calibration and resolution of confidence in perceptual judgments. *Perception and Psychophysics, 55,* 412–428. **[39]**

Barefield, R. M., & Comiskey, E. E. (1975). The accuracy of analysts' forecasts of earnings per share. *Journal of Business Research, 3,* 241–252. **[19]**

Bargh, J. A. (1982). Attention and automaticity in the processing of self-relevant information. *Journal of Personality and Social Psychology, 43,* 425–436. **[9]**

Bargh, J. A. (1997). The automaticity of everyday life. In *The automaticity of everyday life.* R. S. Wyer, Jr. (Ed.). In *The automaticity of everyday life: Advances in social cognition* (Vol. 10, pp. 1–61). R. S. Wyer, Jr. (Ed.). Mahwah, NJ: Erlbaum. **[Introduction, 2, 30]**

Bargh, J. A., Bond, R. N., Lombardi, W. J., & Tota, M. E. (1986). The additive nature of chronic and temporary sources of construct accessibility. *Journal of Personality and Social Psychology, 50*(5), 869–878. **[2]**

Bargh, J. A., & Chartrand, T. L. (1999). The unbearable automaticity of being. *American Psychologist, 54,* 462–479. **[Introduction]**

Baron, J. (1992). The effect of normative beliefs on anticipated emotions. *Journal of Personality and Social Psychology, 63,* 320–330. **[16]**

Baron, J. (1993). *Morality and rational choice.* Dordrecht, The Netherlands: Kluwer. **[24]**

Baron, J. (1994a). Nonconsequentialist decisions. *Behavioral and Brain Sciences, 17,* 1–42. **[24]**

Baron, J. (1994b). *Thinking and Deciding,* 2nd ed. New York: Cambridge University Press. **[6]**

Baron, J. (1997). Confusion of relative and absolute risk in valuation. *Journal of Risk and Uncertainty, 14*(3), 301–309. **[23]**

Baron, J. (1998). *Judgment misguided: Intuition and error in public decision making.* New York: Oxford University Press. **[24, 39]**

Baron, J., & Brown, R. (Eds.). (1991) *Teaching decision making to adolescents.* Hillsdale, NJ: Lawrence Erlbaum. **[41]**

Barone, D. F., Maddux, J. E., & Snyder, C. R. (1997). *Social cognitive psychology: History and current domains,* New York: Plenum Press. **[Introduction]**

Barrett, S. (1987). Homeopathy: Is it medicine? *Skeptical Inquirer, 12,* 56–62. **[34]**

Barron, F. J. (1953). An ego-strength scale which predicts response to psychotherapy. *Journal Of Consulting and Clinical Psychology, 17,* 327–333. **[40]**

Barsalou, L. W. (1985). Ideals, central tendency, and frequency of instantiation as determinants of graded structure in categories. *Journal of Experimental Psychology: Learning, Memory, and Cognition, 11,* 629–654. **[20]**

Barsalou, L. W. (1987). The instability of graded structure: Implications for the nature of concepts. In *Concepts reconsidered: The ecological and intellectual bases of categories,* U. Neisser (Ed.). New York: Cambridge University Press. **[20]**

Barth, M. E., Elliot, J. A., & Finn, M. W. (1999). Market rewards associated with patterns of increasing earnings. *Journal of Accounting Research, 37,* 387–413. **[38]**

Bartlett, F. C. (1932). *Remembering.* Cambridge, U.K.: Cambridge University Press. **[41]**

Basil, R. (1989). Graphology and personality, "Let the buyer beware." *Skeptical Inquirer, 13,* 241–243. **[34]**

Bastardi, A., Ross, L., & Lepper, M. R. (1996). False polarization and the gender gap: Actual vs. assumed discrepancies in belief. Unpublished manuscript, Stanford University. **[36]**

Baumeister, R., Bratslavsky, E., Finkenauer, C., & Vohs, K. D. (in press). Bad is stronger than good. (Review of General Psychology.) **[11]**

Baumeister, R. F., & Leary, M. F. (1995). The need to belong: Desire for interpersonal attachments as a fundamental human motive. *Psychological Bulletin, 117*, 497–529. **[32]**

Baumeister, R. F., & Steinhilbm, A. (1984). Paradoxical effects of supportive audiences on performance under pressure: The home field disadvantage in sports championships. *Journal of Personality and Social Psychology, 47*, 85–93. **[35]**

Baumhart, R. (1968). *An honest profit.* New York: Prentice-Hall. **[18]**

Bazerman, M. H., & Neale, M. A. (1982). Improving negotiation effectiveness under final offer arbitration: The role of selection and training. *Journal of Applied Psychology, 67*, 543–548. **[39]**

Bazerman, M. H., & Neale, M. A. (1992). *Negotiating rationally.* New York: John Wiley & Sons. **[41]**

Beach, L. R. (1990). *Image theory: Decision making in personal and organizational contexts.* Chichester, England: John Wiley & Sons. Ltd. **[30]**

Beach, L. R., & Mitchell, T. R. (1987). Image theory: Principles, goals and plans in decision making. *Acta Psychologica, 66*, 201–220. **[30]**

Beattie, J., & Baron, J. (1988). Confirmation and matching biases in hypothesis testing. *Quarterly Journal of Experimental Psychology, 40A*, 269–297. **[6]**

Bechera, A., Damasio, H., Tramel, D., & Damasio, A. R. (1997). Deciding advantageously before knowing the advantageous strategy. *Science, 275*, 1293–1295. **[29]**

Beck, A. T., Ward, C. H., Mendelson, M., Mock, J. E., & Erbaum, J. K. (1961). An inventory for measuring depression. *Archives of General Psychology, 4*, 561–571. **[14]**

Becker, G. (1996). *The economic way of looking at behavior: The Nobel lecture.* Stanford, CA: Stanford University, Hoover Institution on War, Revolution, and Peace.

Begg, I., Anas, A., & Farinacci, S. (1992). Dissociation of processes in belief: Source recollection, statement familiarity, and the illusion of truth. *Journal of Experimental Psychology: General, 121*(4), 446–458. **[2]**

Begg, I., & Armour, V. (1991). Repetition and the ring of truth: Biasing comments. *Canadian Journal of Behavioural Science, 23*, 195–213. **[2]**

Bell, D. E. (1982). Regret in decision making under uncertainty. *Operations Research, 30*, 961–981. **[21]**

Bell, D. E. (1983). Risk premiums for decision regret. *Management Science, 29*, 1156–1166. **[21]**

Bell, D. E. (1985). Disappointment in decision making under uncertainty. *Operations Research, 33*, 1–27. **[21]**

Bellhouse, D. R., & Franklin, J. (1997). The language of chance. *International Statistical Review, 65*(1), 73–85. **[39]**

Bem, D. J. (1967). Self-perception: An alternative interpretation of cognitive dissonance phenomena. *Psychological Review, 74*, 183–200. **[9]**

Bem, D. J. (1972). Self-perception theory. In *Advances in experimental social psychology* (Vol. 6, pp. 1–62), L. Berkowitz (Ed.). New York: Academic Press. **[Introduction, 9, 10, 36]**

Benartzi, S., & Thaler, R. H. (2001). Naive diversification strategies in defined contribution saving plans. *American Economic Review, 91*(1), 79–98. **[30]**

Benthin, A., Slovic, P., Moran, P., Severson, H., Mertz, C. K., & Gerrard, M. (1995). Adolescent health-threatening and health-enhancing behaviors: A study of word association and imagery. *Journal of Adolescent Health, 17*, 143–152. **[23]**

Berkeley, D., & Humphreys, P. (1982). Structuring decision problems and the "bias heuristic." *Acta Psychologica, 50*, 201–252. **[24]**

Beyth-Marom, R. (1981). *The subjective probability of conjunctions* (Decision Research Report No. 81-12). Eugene, OR: Decision Research. **[1]**

Beyth-Marom, R. (1982). How probable is probable? Numerical translation of verbal probability expressions. *Journal of Forecasting, 1,* 257–269. **[41]**

Beyth-Marom, R., Dekel, S. K., Gombo, R., & Shaked, M. (1985). *An elementary approach to thinking under uncertainty.* Hillsdale, NJ: Erlbaum **[41]**

Beyth-Marom, R., Fischhoff, B., Quadrel, M. J., & Furby, L. (1991). Teaching adolescents decision making. In *Teaching decision making to adolescents* (pp. 19–60), J. Baron & R. Brown (Eds.). Hillsdale, NJ: Lawrence Erlbaum. **[41]**

Bierce, A. (1914). *The devil's dictionary.* New York: World Publishing Company. **[14]**

Biller, B., Bless, H., & Schwarz, N. (1992, April). *Die Leichtigkeit der Erinnerung als Information in der Urteilsbildung: der Einfluβder Fragenreihenfolge* (Ease of recall as information: The impact of question order). Tagung experimentell arbeitender Psychologen, Osnabrück, FRG. **[5]**

Birge, R. T. (1929). Probable Values of the General Physical Constants. *Reviews of Modern Physics, 1,* 1–73. **[37]**

Birge, R. T. (1932). The Calculation of Errors by the Method of Least Squares. *Physical Review, 40,* 207–227. **[37]**

Birge, R. T. (1941). The General Physical Constants: As of August 1941 with Details on the Velocity of Light Only. *Reports on Progress in Physics, 8,* 90–134. **[37]**

Birnbaum, M. H. (1983). Base rates in Bayesian inference: Signal detection analysis of the cab problem. *American Journal of Psychology, 96,* 85–94. **[24]**

Birnbaum, M. H. (1999). How to show that 9 > 221: Collect judgments in a between-subjects design. *Psychological Methods, 4*(3), 243–249. **[2]**

Birnbaum, M. H., & Mellers, B. A. (1983). Bayesian inference: Combining base rates with opinions of sources who vary in credibility. *Journal of Personality and Social Psychology, 45,* 792–804. **[2]**

Biswas, A., & Burton, S. (1993). Consumer perceptions of tensile price claims in advertisements: An assessment of claim types across different discount levels. *Journal of the Academy of Marketing Science, 21,* 217–229. **[6]**

Björkman, M. (1994). Internal cue theory: Calibration and resolution of confidence in general knowledge. *Organizational Behavior and Human Decision Processes, 58,* 386–405. **[39]**

Björkman, M., Juslin, P., & Winman, A. (1993). Realism of confidence in sensory discrimination: The underconfidence phenomenon. *Perception and Psychophysics, 54,* 75–81. **[39]**

Blalock, S. J., DeVellis, B. M., & Afifi, R. A. (1990). Risk perceptions and participation in colorectal cancer screening. *Health Psychology, 9,* 792–806. **[17]**

Blaney, P. H. (1986). Affect and memory: A review. *Psychological Bulletin, 99,* 229–246. **[29]**

Bless, H. (1997). *Stimmung und Denken.* (Mood and reasoning.) Bern, Switzerland: Huber. **[29]**

Bless, H. (2001). The consequences of mood on the processing of social information. In *Blackwell handbook of social psychology: Intraindividual processes* (pp. 391–421), A. Tesser & N. Schwarz (Eds.). Oxford, U.K.: Blackwell. **[29]**

Bless, H., Bohner, G., Schwarz, N., & Strack, F. (1990). Mood and persuasion: A cognitive response analysis. *Personality and Social Psychology Bulletin, 16,* 331–345. **[29]**

Bless, H., Clore, G. L., Schwarz, N., Golisano, V., Rabe, C., & Wolk, M. (1996). Mood and the use of scripts: Does a happy mood really lead to mindlessness? *Journal of Personality and Social Psychology, 71,* 665–679. **[2, 29]**

Bless, H., & Schwarz, N. (1999). Sufficient and necessary conditions in dual process models: The case of mood and information processing. In *Dual process theories in social psychology* (pp. 423–440), S. Chaiken & Y. Trope (Eds.). New York: Guilford. **[29]**

Bless, H., Schwarz, N., & Kemmelmeier, M. (1996). Mood and stereotyping: The impact of moods on the use of general knowledge structures. In M. Hewstone & W. Stroebe (Eds.). *European Review of Social Psychology, 7*, 63–93. **[29]**

Bless, H., Schwarz, N., & Wieland, R. (1996). Mood and stereotyping: The impact of category membership and individuating information. *European Journal of Social Psychology, 26*, 935–959. **[29]**

Block, R. A., & Harper, D. R. (1991). Overconfidence in estimation: Testing the anchoring-and-adjustment hypothesis. *Organizational Behavior and Human Decision Processes, 49*, 188–207. **[6]**

Bobbio M., Deorsola A., Pistis G., Brusca A., & Diamond G. A. (1988). Physician perception of exercise electrocardiography as a prognostic test after acute myocardial infarction. *American Journal of Cardiology, 62*, 675–678. **[39]**

Bobbio, M., Detrano, R., Shandling, A. H., Ellestad, M. H., Clark, J., Brezden, O., Abecia, A., & Martinezcaro, D. (1992). Clinical assessment of the probability of coronary-artery disease – Judgmental bias from personal knowledge. *Medical Decision Making, 12*, 197–203. **[39]**

Bodenhausen, G. V. (1990). Stereotypes as judgmental heuristics: Evidence of circadian variations in discrimination. *Psychological Science, 1*(5), 319–322. **[Introduction, 2]**

Bodenhausen, G. V., Gabriel, S., & Lineberger, M. (1999). *Sadness and susceptibility to judgmental bias: The case of anchoring.* Unpublished manuscript, Northwestern University. **[29]**

Bodenhausen, G. V., Kramer, G. P., & Süsser, K. (1994). Happiness and stereotypic thinking in social judgment. *Journal of Personality and Social Psychology, 66*, 621–632. **[29]**

Bodenhausen, G. V., & Wyer, R. S. (1987). Social cognition and social reality: Information acquisition and use in the laboratory and the real world. In *Social information processing and survey methodology* (pp. 6–41), H. J. Hippler, N. Schwarz, & S. Sudman (Eds.). New York: Springer Verlag. **[5]**

Bollnow, O. F. (1956). *Das Wesen der Stimmungen.* (The nature of moods.) Frankfurt: Klostermann. **[29]**

Bond, M. H., & Cheung, T. S. (1983). The spontaneous self-concept of college students in Hong Kong, Japan, and the United States. *Journal of Cross-Cultural Psychology, 14*, 153–171. **[15]**

Boneau, C. A. (1990). Short-term recognition memory under rehearsal instructions and imaging instructions. *Bulletin of the Psychonomic Society, 28*, 297–299. **[17]**

Borg, I. (1987). The effect of mood on different well-being judgments. *Archiv für Psychologie, 139*, 181–188. **[29]**

Borgida, E., & Nisbett, R. E. (1977). The differential impact of abstract vs. concrete information on decisions. *Journal of Applied Social Psychology, 7*, 258–271. **[28]**

Bornstein, R. F. (1989). Exposure and affect: Overview and meta-analysis of research, 1968–1987. *Psychological Bulletin, 106*, 265–289. **[23]**

Bostrom, A., Fischhoff, B., & Morgan, G. M. (1992). Characterizing mental models of hazardous processes: A methodology with an application to radon. *Journal of Social Issues, 48*(4), 85–100 **[41]**

Bower, G. H. (1981). Mood and memory. *American Psychologist, 36*, 129–148. **[29]**

Bower, G. H., & Mayer, J. D. (1985). Failure to replicate mood congruent retrieval. *Bulletin of the Psychonomic Society, 23,* 39–42. **[29]**

Brainard, R. W., Irby, T. S., Fitts, P. M., & Alluisi, E. (1962). Some variables influencing the rate of gain of information. *Journal of Experimental Psychology, 63,* 105–110. **[12]**

Braine, M. D. S. (1990). The "natural logic" approach to reasoning. In *Reasoning, necessity, and logic: Developmental Perspectives* (pp. 133–157), W. F. Overton (Ed.). Hillsdale, NJ: Erlbaum. **[22]**

Brake, G. L., Doherty, M. E., & Kleiter, G. D. (1997). *A Brunswikian approach to calibration of subjective probabilities.* Unpublished manuscript, Bowling Green State University. **[39]**

Brase, G. L., Cosmides, L., & Tooby, J. (1998). Individuation, counting, and statistical inference: The role of frequency and whole-object representations in judgment under uncertainty. *Journal of Experimental Psychology: General, 127,* 3–21. **[24]**

Braun, P. A., & Yaniv, I. (1992). A case study of expert judgment: Economists probabilities versus base-rate model forecasts. *Journal of Behavioral Decision Making, 5,* 217–231. **[39]**

Brehm, J. W. (1966). *A theory of psychological reactance.* New York: Academic Press. **[36]**

Brehm, J. W., & Cohen, A. R. (1962). *Explorations in cognitive dissonance.* New York: Wiley. **[36]**

Brehm, S. S., & Brehm, J. W. (1981). *Psychological reactance: A theory of freedom and control.* New York: Academic Press. **[36]**

Breiman, L., Friedman, J. H., Olshen, R. A., & Stone, C. J. (1984). *Classification and regression trees.* Belmont, CA: Wadsworth International Group. **[31]**

Brenner, L. (2000). Should observed overconfidence be dismissed as a statistical artifact? Critique of Erev, Wallsten, and Budescu (1994). *Psychological Review, 107,* 943–946. **[27, 39]**

Brenner, L. A. (1995). *A stochastic model of the calibration of subjective probabilities.* Unpublished Doctoral dissertation, Stanford University. **[27, 39]**

Brenner, L., & Koehler, D. J. (1999). Subjective probability of disjunctive hypotheses: Local-weight models for decomposition of evidential support. *Cognitive Psychology, 38,* 16–47. **[27]**

Brenner, L. A., Koehler, D. J., Liberman, V., & Tversky, A. (1996). Overconfidence in probability and frequency judgments: A critical examination. *Organizational Behavior and Human Decision Processes, 65,* 212–219. **[Introduction, 39]**

Brenner, L., & Rottenstreich, Y. (1999). Focus, repacking, and the judgment of grouped hypotheses. *Journal of Behavioral Decision Making, 12,* 141–148. **[27]**

Brenner, L., & Rottenstreich, Y. (2000). *Asymmetric support theory: Focus-dependence and context independence in likelihood judgment.* Unpublished manuscript. **[27]**

Brewer, M. B. (1988). A dual process model of impression formation. In *Advances in social cognition* (Vol. 1, pp. 1–36), T. K. Srull & R. S. Wyer (Eds.). Hillsdale, NJ: Lawrence Erlbaum Associates. **[29]**

Brickman, P., Coates, D., Janoff-Bulman, R. J. (1978). Lottery winners and accident victims: Is happiness relative? *Journal of Personality and Social Psychology, 36,* 917–927. **[16]**

Brier, G. W. (1950). Verification of forecasts expressed in terms of probability. *Monthly Weather Review, 78*(1), 1–3. **[15]**

Briggs, L. K., & Krantz, D. H. (1992). Judging the strength of designated evidence. *Journal of Behavioral Decision Making, 5,* 77–106. **[25, 26, 27]**

Brockner, J., Rubin, J. Z., & Lang, E. (1981). Face-saving and entrapment. *Journal of Experimental Social Psychology, 17*, 68–79. **[32]**

Brody, N. (1997). Intelligence, schooling, and society. *American Psychologist, 52*, 1046–1050. **[24]**

Brooks, L. R. (1978). Nonanalytic concept formation and memory for instances. In *Cognition and categorization* (pp. 169–215), E. Rosch & B. B. Lloyd (Eds.). Hillsdale, NJ: Erlbaum. **[20]**

Brooks, L. R. (1987). Decentralized control of categorization: The role of prior processing episodes. In *Concepts reconsidered: The ecological and intellectual bases of categories* U. Neisser (Ed.). New York: Cambridge University Press. **[20]**

Brooks, L. R., Norman, G. R., & Allen, S. W. (1991). Role of specific similarity in a medical diagnostic task. *Journal of Experimental Psychology: General, 120*, 278–287. **[22]**

Broome, J. (1990). Should a rational agent maximize expected utility? In *The limits of rationality* (pp. 132–145), K. S. Cook & M. Levi (Eds.). Chicago: University of Chicago Press. **[24]**

Brown & Williamson Tobacco Company (1999). **[23]**

Brown, P., Foster, G., & Noreen, E. (1985). *Security analyst multi-year earnings forecasts and the capital market.* Sarasota: American Accounting Association. **[38]**

Browne, T. (1642/1963). *Riligio. Medici.* Cambridge, U.K.: Cambridge University Press. **[16]**

Bruner, J. (1986). *Actual minds, possible worlds.* Cambridge, MA: Harvard University Press. **[24]**

Bruner, J. (1990). *Acts of meaning.* Cambridge, MA: Harvard University Press. **[24]**

Bruner, J. S. (1957). Going beyond the information given. In *Contemporary approaches to cognition* (pp. 41–69), H. Gruber, K. R. Hammond, & R. Jesser (Eds.). Cambridge, MA: Harvard University Press. **[36]**

Bruner, J. S. (1966). On the conservation of liquids. In *Studies in cognitive growth*, J. S. Bruner, R. R. Olver, & P. M. Greenfield, et al. (Eds.), New York: Wiley. **[1]**

Brunswik, E. (1943). Organismic achievement and environmental probability. *Psychological Review, 50*, 255–272. **[2, 39]**

Brunswik, E. (1955). Representative design and probabilistic theory in a functional psychology. *Psychological Review, 2*, 193–217. **[Introduction, 39]**

Brunswik, E. (1964). Scope and aspects of the cognitive problem. In *Contemporary approaches to cognition* (pp. 5–31), J. S. Bruner et al. (Eds.). Cambridge, MA: Harvard University Press. **[31]**

Buckley, T., & Sniezek, J. (1992). Passion, preference, and predictability in judgmental forecasting. *Psychological Reports, 70*, 1022. **[19]**

Budescu, D. V., Erev, I., & Wallsten, T. S. (1997). On the importance of random error in the study of probability judgment. Part I: New theoretical developments. *Journal of Behavioral Decision Making, 10*, 157–171. **[39]**

Budescu, D. V., Wallsten, T. S., & Au, W. T. (1997). On the importance of random error in the study of probability judgment. Part II: Applying the stochastic judgment model to detect systematic trends. *Journal of Behavioral Decision Making, 10*, 173–188. **[39]**

Buehler, R., & Griffin, D. (1996, August). *Getting things done: The impact of predictions on task completion.* Paper presented at the annual meeting of the American Psychological Association, Toronto, Canada. **[14, 19]**

Buehler, R., & Griffin, D. (2000a). *Dispositional, contextual, and cognitive underpinnings of the planning fallacy.* Unpublished manuscript, Wilfrid Laurier University, Waterloo, Ontario. [14]

Buehler, R., & Griffin, D. (2000b). *Motivated prediction for self and others.* Unpublished manuscript, Wilfrid Laurier University, Waterloo, Ontario. [14]

Buehler, R., Griffin, D., & MacDonald, H. (1997). The role of motivated reasoning in optimistic time predictions. *Personality and Social Psychology Bulletin, 23,* 238–247. [14, 19]

Buehler, R., Griffin, D., Otsubo, Y., Lehman, D., & Heine, S. (2000). *A cross-cultural comparison of the planning fallacy.* Unpublished manuscript, Wilfrid Laurier University, Waterloo, Ontario. [14]

Buehler, R., & McFarland, C. (in press). Intensity bias in affective forecasts: The role of temporal focus. *Personality and Social Psychology Bulletin.* [14]

Buehler, R., Griffin, D., & Ross, M. (1994). Exploring the "planning fallacy": Why people underestimate their task completion times. *Journal of Personality and Social Psychology, 67,* 366–381. [14, 19, 36]

Buehler, R., Griffin, D., & Ross, M. (1995). It's about time: Optimistic predictions in work and love. In *European Review of Social Psychology* (Vol. 6, pp. 1–32), W. Stroebe & M. Hewstone (Eds.). Chichester, U.K.: John Wiley & Sons. [14]

Bunker, J. P., Barnes, B. A., & Mosteller, F. (Eds.). (1977). *Costs, risks, and benefits of surgery.* New York: Oxford University Press. [41]

Bunn, D. W., & Salo, A. A. (1993). Forecasting with scenarios. *European Journal of Operational Research, 68,* 291–303. [14]

Burgstahler, D., & Dichev, I. (1997). Earnings management to avoid earnings decreases and losses. *Journal of Accounting and Economics, 24,* 99–126. [38]

Burros, O. K. (1978). *Mental measurement yearbook,* 8th ed. Highland Park, NJ: Gryphon Press. [34]

Busemeyer, J., Hastie, R., & Medin, D. L. (Eds.) (1995). *Decision making from a cognitive perspective,* San Diego: Academic Press. [23]

Busemeyer, J. R., & Goldstein, W. M. (1992). Linking together different measures of preference: a dynamic model of matching derived from decision field theory. *Organizational Behavior and Human Decision Processes, 52,* 370–396. [6]

Busemeyer, J. R., & Townsend, J. T. (1993). Decision field theory: A dynamic–cognitive approach to decision making in an uncertain environment. *Psychological Review, 100,* 432–459. [6]

Byram, S. J. (1997). Cognitive and motivational factors influencing time prediction. *Journal of Experimental Psychology: Applied, 3,* 216–219. [14]

Byrne, J. A. (1986). Business fads: What's in – and out: Executives latch on to any management idea that looks like a quick fix. *Business Week,* January 20, 52–61. [41]

Byrnes, J. P., & Overton, W. F. (1986). Reasoning about certainty and uncertainty in concrete, causal, and propositional contexts. *Developmental Psychology, 22,* 793–799. [24]

Cacciari, C., & Tabossi, P. (Eds.) (1993). *Idioms.* Hillsdale, NJ: Lawrence Erlbaum Associates. [8]

Cacioppo, J. T., Priester, J. R., & Berntson, G. G. (1993). Rudimentary determinants of attitudes. II. Arm flexion and extension have differential effects on attitudes. *Journal of Personality and Social Psychology, 65,* 5–17. [2, 7, 29]

Cadsby, T. (2000). *The ten biggest investment mistakes Canadians make and how to avoid them.* Toronto: Stoddart. [39]

Calderon, T. G. (1993). Predictive properties of analysts' forecasts of corporate earnings. *The Mid-Atlantic Journal of Business, 29*, 41–58. **[19]**

Camerer, C. (1981). General conditions for the success of bootstrapping models. *Organizational Behavior and Human Performance, 27*, 411–422. **[41]**

Camerer, C. (1990). Do markets correct biases in probability judgment? Evidence from market experiments. In *Advances in behavioral economics* (Vol. 2, pp. 125–172), L. Green & J. H. Kagel (Eds.). Northwood, NJ: Ablex. **[13]**

Camerer, C., & Hogarth, R. (1999). The effects of financial incentives in experiments: A review and capital-labor production framework. *Journal of Risk and Uncertainty, 19*, 7–42. **[Introduction]**

Camerer, C., & Lovallo, D. (1999). Overconfidence and excess entry: An experimental approach. *The American Economic Review, 89*, 306–318. **[19]**

Campbell, J. D., & Fairey, P. J. (1985). Effects of self-esteem, hypothetical explanations, and verbalization of expectancies on future performance. *Journal of Personality and Social Psychology, 48*, 1097–1111. **[19]**

Campbell, J. I. D. (1987). The role of associative interference in learning and retrieving arithmetic facts. In *Cognitive processes in mathematics*, J. A. Sloboda & D. Rogers (Eds.). Oxford: Oxford University Press. **[22]**

Canadian Standards Association. (1997). *Risk management* (CSA-850). Ottawa. **[41]**

Capute, A. J., Neidermeyer, E. F. L., & Richardson, F. (1968). Electroencephalogram in children with minimal cerebral dysfunction. *Pediatrics, 41*, 1104–1114. **[40]**

Carey, S. (1985). *Conceptual change in childhood*. Cambridge, MA: MIT Press. **[22]**

Carleton, W. T., Chen, C. R., & Steiner, T. L. (1998). Optimism biases among brokerage and nonbrokerage equity recommendations: Agency costs in the investment industry. *Financial Management, 27*, 17–30. **[38]**

Carlson, B. W. (1990). Anchoring and adjustment in judgments under risk. *Journal of Experimental Psychology: Learning, Memory, and Cognition, 16*, 665–676. **[6, 7]**

Carlson, S. (1985). A double-blind test of astrology. *Nature, 318*, 419–425. **[34]**

Carpenter, P. A., & Just, M. A. (1975). Sentence comprehension: A psycholoinguistic processing model of verification. *Psychological Review, 82*, 45–73. **[9]**

Carroll, J. B. (1993). *Human cognitive abilities: A survey of factor-analytic studies*. Cambridge, U.K.: Cambridge University Press. **[24]**

Carroll, J. B. (1997). Psychometrics, intelligence, and public perception. *Intelligence, 24*, 25–52. **[24]**

Carroll, J. S. (1978). The effect of imagining an event on expectations for the event: An interpretation in terms of the availability heuristic. *Journal of Experimental Social Psychology, 14*, 88–96. **[4, 17, 21]**

Carroll, J. S., Wiener, R. L., Coates, D., Galegher, J., & Alibrio, J. J. (1982). Evaluation, diagnosis, and prediction in parole decision making. *Law and Society Review, 17*, 199–228. **[40]**

Carson, T. P., & Adams, H. E. (1980). Acticity valence as a function of mood change. *Journal of Abnormal Psychology, 89*, 368–377. **[29]**

Carver, C. S., & Scheier, M. F. (1981). *Attention and self-regulation: A control-theory approach to human behavior*. New York: Springer Verlag. **[19]**

Carver, C. S., & Scheier, M. F. (1998). *On the self-regulation of behavior*. New York: Cambridge University Press. **[19]**

Casman, E., Fischhoff, B., Palmgren, C., Small, M., & Wu, F. (2000). Integrated assessment of Cryptosporidium risks. *Risk Analysis, 20*, 493–509. **[41]**

Casscells, W., Schoenberger, A., & Graboys, T. (1978). Interpretation by physicians of clinical laboratory results. *New England Journal of Medicine, 299,* 999–1001. **[24]**

Caverni, J.-P., & Pris, J. L. (1990). The anchoring–adjustment heuristic in an "information rich, real world setting": Knowledge assessment by experts. In *Cognitive biases,* J.-P. Caverni, J.-M. Fabre, & M. Gonzalez (Eds.). New York: North-Holland. **[6]**

Centor, R. M., Dalton, H. P., & Yates, J. F. (1984). *Are physicians' probability estimates better or worse than regression model estimates?* Paper presented at the Sixth Annual Meeting of the Society for Medical Decision Making, Bethesda, MD. **[39]**

Cervone, D., & Peake, P. K. (1986). Anchoring, efficacy, and action: the influence of judgmental heuristics on self-efficacy judgments and behavior. *Journal of Personality and Social Psychology, 50,* 492–501. **[6, 7]**

Chafe, W. L. (1976). Givenness, contrastiveness, definiteness, subjects, topics, and point of view. In *Subject and topic,* C. N. Li (Ed.). New York: Academic Press. **[8]**

Chaiken, S. (1980). Heuristic versus systematic information processing and the use of source versus message cues in persuasion. *Journal of Personality and Social Psychology, 39,* 752–766. **[32]**

Chaiken, S. (1987). The heuristic model of persuasion. In *Social influence: the Ontario symposium* (Vol. 5, pp. 3–39), M. P. Zanna, J. M. Olson, & C. P. Herman (Eds.). Hillsdale, NJ: Lawrence Erlbaum Associates. **[9]**

Chaiken, S., Liberman, A., & Eagly, A. H. (1989). Heuristic and systematic processing within and beyond the persuasion context. In *Unintended thought* (pp. 212–252), J. S. Uleman & J. A. Bargh (Eds.). New York: Guilford Press. **[Introduction, 22]**

Chaiken, S., & Trope, Y. (1999). *Dual-process theories in social psychology.* New York: Guilford Press. **[2, 5, 22, 23]**

Chapman, G. B., & Bornstein, B. H. (1996). The more you ask for the more you get: Anchoring in personal injury verdicts. *Applied Cognitive Psychology, 10,* 519–540. **[6]**

Chapman, G. B., & Johnson, E. J. (1994). The limits of anchoring. *Journal of Behavioral Decision Making, 7,* 223–242. **[6, 7]**

Chapman, G. B., & Johnson, E. J. (1999). Anchoring, activation and the construction of value. *Organizational Behavior and Human Decision Processes, 79,* 115–153. **[6]**

Chapman, L. J., & Chapman, J. P. (1967). Genesis of popular but erroneous psychodiagnostic observations. *Journal of Abnormal Psychology, 72,* 193–204. **[1, 40]**

Chapman, L. J., & Chapman, J. P. (1969). Illusory correlation as an obstacle to the use of valid psychodiagnostic signs. *Journal of Abnormal Psychology, 74,* 271–280. **[40]**

Chase, W. G., & Simon, H. A. (1973). Perception in chess. *Cognitive Psychology, 4,* 55–81. **[39]**

Cheng, P. W., & Holyoak, K. J. (1985). Pragmatic reasoning schemas. *Cognitive Psychology, 17,* 391–416. **[22]**

Cheng, P. W., & Holyoak, K. J. (1989). On the natural selection of reasoning theories. *Cognition, 33,* 285–313. **[24]**

Cherniak, C. (1986). *Minimal rationality.* Cambridge, MA: MIT Press. **[24]**

Christensen-Szalanski, J. J. J., & Beach, L. R. (1982). Experience and the base-rate fallacy. *Organizational Behavior and Human Performance, 29,* 270–278. **[39]**

Christensen-Szalanski, J. J. J., & Bushyhead, J. B. (1981). Physicians' use of probabilistic information in a real clinical setting. *Journal of Experimental Psychology: Human Perception and Performance, 7,* 928–935. **[39]**

Christensen-Szalanski, J. J. J., & Willham, C. F. (1991). The hindsight bias: A metaanalysis. *Organizational Behavior and Human Decision Processes, 48,* 147–173. **[41]**

Chwe, M. (1998). Culture, circles, and commercials: Publicity, common knowledge, and social coordination. *Rationality & Society, 10,* 47–75. [8]

Cialdini, R. B., Levy, A., Herman, C. P., Kozlowski, I. T., & Petty, R. E. (1976). Elastic shifts of opinion: Determinants of direction and durability. *Journal of Personality and Social Psychology, 34,* 663–672. [32]

Clark, D. M., & Teasdale, J. D. (1982). Diurnal variation in clinical depression and accessibility of memories of positive and negative experiences. *Journal of Abnormal Psychology, 91,* 87–95. [29]

Clark, H. H. (1979). Responding to indirect speech acts. *Cognitive Psychology, 11,* 430–474. [20]

Clark, H. H. (1996). *Using language.* Cambridge, U.K.: Cambridge University Press. [8]

Clark, H. H., & Carlson, T. B. (1981). Context for comprehension. In *Attention and Performance IX* (pp. 313–330), J. Long & A. Baddeley (Eds.). Hillsdale, NJ: Lawrence Erlbaum Associates. [8]

Clark, H. H., & Chase, W. G. (1972). On the process of comparing sentences against pictures. *Cognitive Psychology, 3,* 472–517. [9]

Clark, H. H., & Chase, W. G. (1974). Perceptual coding strategies in the formation and verification of descriptions. *Memory and Cognition, 2,* 101–111. [9]

Clark, H. H., & Haviland, S. E. (1977). Comprehension and the given new contract. In *Discourse production and comprehension* (pp. 1–40), R. O. Freedle (Ed.). Norwood, NJ: Ablex. [20]

Clark, H. H., & Marshall, C. R. (1981). Definite reference and mutual knowledge. In *Elements of discourse understanding* (pp. 10–63), A. H. Joshe, B. Webber, & I. A. Sag (Eds.). Cambridge, U.K.: Cambridge University Press. [8]

Clayman, M. R., & Schwartz, R. A. (1994). Falling in love again: Analysts' estimates and reality. *Financial Analysts Journal, 50,* 66–68. [38]

Clemen, R. (1991). *Making hard decisions.* Boston: PWS-Kent. [41]

Clore, G. L. (1992). Cognitive phenomenology: Feelings and the construction of judgment. In *The construction of social judgments* (pp. 133–163), L. L. Martin & A. Tesser (Eds.). Hillsdale, NJ: Lawrence Erlbaum Associates. [5]

Clore, G. L., & Byrne, D. (1974). A reinforcement affect model of attraction. In *Foundations of interpersonal attraction* (pp. 173–170), T. L. Huston (Ed.). New York: Academic Press. [29]

Clore, G. L., Schwarz, N., & Conway, M. (1994). Affective causes and consequences of social information processing. In *Handbook of social cognition* (2nd ed.; Vol. 1, pp. 323–418), R. S. Wyer & T. K. Srull (Eds.). Hillsdale, NJ: Erlbaum. [29]

Cohen, B., & Lee, I. S. (1979). A catalog of risks. *Health Physics, 36,* 707–722. [41]

Cohen, E. R., Crowe, K. M., & Dumond, J. W. M. (1957). *Fundamental constants of Physics.* New York: Interscience. [37]

Cohen, E. R., & Dumond, J. W. M. (1965). Our knowledge of the fundamental constants of physics and chemistry in 1965. *Review of Modern Physics, 37,* 537–594. [37]

Cohen, E. R., Dumond, J. W. M., Layton, T. W., & Rollett, J. S. (1955). Analysis of variance of the 1952 data on the atomic constants and a new adjustment, 1955. *Review of Modern Physics, 27,* 363–380. [37]

Cohen, E. R., & Taylor, B. N. (1973). The 1973 Least-Squares adjustment of the fundamental constants. *Journal of Physical and Chemical Reference Data, 2*(4), 663–734. [37]

Cohen, J. (1969). Statistical power analysis for the behavioral sciences. San Diego: Academic Press. [2]

Cohen, J. (1992). A power primer. *Psychological Bulletin, 112*(1), 155–159. **[2]**

Cohen, J., & Hansel, C. M. (1957). The nature of decision in gambling: Equivalence of single and compound subjective probabilities. *Acta Psychologica, 13*, 357–370. **[1]**

Cohen, L. J. (1977). *The probable and the provable.* Oxford, U.K.: Clarendon Press. **[1]**

Cohen, L. J. (1979). On the psychology of prediction: Whose is the fallacy? *Cognition, 7*, 385–407. **[24, 28]**

Cohen, L. J. (1981). Can human irrationality be experimentally demonstrated? *Behavioral and Brain Sciences, 4*, 317–370. **[Introduction, 24, 28]**

Cohen, L. J. (1982). Are people programmed to commit fallacies? Further thoughts about the interpretation of experimental data on probability judgment. *Journal for the Theory of Social Behavior, 12*, 251–274. **[24]**

Cohen, L. J. (1983). The controversy about irrationality. *Behavioral and Brain Sciences, 6*, 510–517. **[24]**

Cohen, L. J. (1986). *The dialogue of reason.* Oxford, U.K.: Oxford University Press. **[24]**

Coleman, J. S. (1990). *Foundations of Social Theory.* Cambridge, MA: Belknap Press.

College Board (1976–1977). *Student descriptive questionnaire.* Princeton, NJ: Educational Testing Service. **[18]**

Collins, R. L., Taylor, S. E., & Skokan, L. A. (1990). A better world or a shattered vision? Changes in life perspectives following victimization. *Social Cognition, 8*, 263–285. **[16]**

Combs, B., & Slovic, P. (1979). Newspaper coverage of causes of death. *Journalism Quarterly, 56*, 832–849. **[41]**

Conway, M., & Ross, M. (1984). Getting what you want by revising what you had. *Journal of Personality and Social Psychology, 47*, 738–748. **[19]**

Cooke, R. M. (1991). *Experts in Uncertainty.* New York: Oxford University Press.

Cooley, C. H. (1902). *Human nature and the social order.* New York: Scribner's. **[36]**

Cooper, A., Woo, C., & Dunkelberg, W. (1988). Entrepreneurs' perceived chances for success. *Journal of Business Venturing, 3*, 97–108. **[13, 39]**

Cooper, A. C., & Artz, K. W. (1995). Determinants of satisfaction for entrepreneurs. *Journal of Business Venturing, 10*, 439–457. **[19]**

Cooper, R., DeJong, D., Forsythe, B., & Ross, T. (1992). Forward induction in coordination games. *Economics Letters, 40*, 167–172. **[8]**

Cooper, R., DeJong, D., Forsythe, B., & Ross, T. (1994). Alternative institutions for resolving coordination problems: Experimental evidence on forward induction and preplay communication. In *Problems of coordination in economic activity* (pp. 129–146), J. Friedman (Ed.). Norwell, MA: Kluwer. **[8]**

Corneille, O., Leyens, J., Yzerbyt, V. T., & Walter, E. (1999). Judgeability concerns: The interplay of information, applicability, and accountability in the overattribution bias. *Journal of Personality and Social Psychology, 76*, 377–387. **[32]**

Cosmides, L. (1989). The logic of social exchange: Has natural selection shaped how humans reason? Studies with the Wason selection task. *Cognition, 31*, 187–276. **[24]**

Cosmides, L., & Tooby, J. (1994). Beyond intuition and instinct blindness: Toward an evolutionarily rigorous cognitive science. *Cognition, 50*, 41–77. **[24]**

Cosmides, L., & Tooby, J. (1996). Are humans good intuitive statisticians after all? Rethinking some conclusions from the literature on judgment and uncertainty. *Cognition, 58*(1), 1–73. **[Introduction, 2, 14, 24]**

Cowley, G., King, P., Hager, M., & Rosenberg, D. (1995, June 26). Going mainstream. *Newsweek*, 56–57. **[34]**

Crocker, J. (1982). Biased questions in judgment of covariation studies. *Personality and Social Psychology Bulletin, 8*, 214–220. **[7]**

Crosby, F. (1976). A model of egoistical relative deprivation. *Psychological Review, 83*, 85–113. **[35]**

Crosby, F. J., & Cordova, D. I. (1996). Words of wisdom: Toward an understanding of affirmative action. *Journal of Social Issues, 52*, 33–49. **[10]**

Cross, H., Holcomb, A., & Matter, C. G. (1967). Imprinting or exposure learning in rats given early auditory stimulation. *Psychonomic Science, 7*, 233–234. **[30]**

Cross, P. (1977). Not can but will college teaching be improved. *New Directions for Higher Education, 17*, 1–15. **[18]**

Cummings, K. M., Becker, M. H., & Maile, M. C. (1980). Bringing the models together: An empirical approach to combining variables used to explain health actions. *Journal of Behavioral Medicine, 3*, 123–145. **[17]**

Cummins, D. D. (1996). Evidence for the innateness of deontic reasoning. *Mind & Language, 11*, 160–190. **[24]**

Curley, S. P., Yates, J. F., & Abrams, R. A. (1986). Psychological sources of ambiguity avoidance. *Organizational Behavior and Human Decision Processes, 38*, 230–256.

Cvetkovich, G. (1978). Cognitive accommodation, language, and social responsibility. *Social Psychology, 2*, 149–155. **[32]**

Czaczkes, B., & Ganzach, Y. (1996). The natural selection of prediction heuristics: anchoring and adjustment. *Journal of Behavioral Decision Making, 9*, 125–139. **[6]**

Czerlinski, J. (1997). *Algorithm calculation costs measured by EIPs*. Manuscript, Max Planck Institute for Psychological Research, Munich. **[31]**

Damasio, A. R. (1994). *Descarte's error: Emotion, reason and the human brain*. New York: Grosset/Putnam **[23, 29]**

Damasio, A. R., Tranel, D., & Damasio, H. C. (1990). Individuals with sociopathic behavior caused by frontal damage fail to respond autonomically to social stimuli. *Behavioural Brain Research, 41*, 81–94. **[23]**

David, F. N. (1949). *Probability theory for statistical methods*. Cambridge, U.K.: Cambridge University Press. **[33]**

Davidson, W. P. (1983). The third person effect in communication. *Public Opinion Quarterly, 47*, 1–15. **[36]**

Davies, T. (Ed.), (1996). *Comparing environmental risks*. Washington, DC: Resources for the Future. **[41]**

Davis, H. L., Hoch, S. J., & Ragsdale, E. E. (1986). An anchoring and adjustment model of spousal predictions. *Journal of Consumer Research, 13*, 25–37. **[6]**

Davis, J. A. (1966). The campus as a frog pond: An application of the theory of relative deprivation to career decisions of college men. *American Journal of Sociology, 72*, 17–31. **[20]**

Dawes, R. (1998). Judgment and choice. In *Handbook of social psychology*, D. Gilbert, S. Fiske, & G. Lindzey (Eds.) (pp. 497–548). New York: McGraw Hill. **[42]**

Dawes, R. M. (1971). A case study of graduate admissions: Application of three principles of human decision making. *American Psychologist, 26*, 180–188. **[40]**

Dawes, R. M. (1979). The robust beauty of improper linear models in decision making. *American Psychologist, 34*, 571–582. **[13, 31, 40]**

Dawes, R. M. (1980). You can't systemize human judgment: Dyslexia. *New Directions for Methodology of Social and Behavioral Science, 4*, 67–78. **[28]**

Dawes, R. M. (1988). *Rational choice in an uncertain world*, New York: Harcourt Brace Jovanovich. **[Introduction, 13, 14]**

Dawes, R. M. (1989). Statistical criteria for establishing a truly false consensus effect. *Journal of Experimental Social Psychology, 25*, 1–17. **[24]**

Dawes, R. M. (1990). The potential nonfalsity of the false consensus effect. In *Insights into decision making* (pp. 179–199), R. M. Hogarth (Ed.). Chicago: University of Chicago Press. **[24]**

Dawes, R. M. (1993). Equating the inverse probabilities in implicit personality judgments. *Psychological Science, 6*, 396–400. **[41]**

Dawes, R. M. (1994). *House of cards: Psychology and psychotherapy built on myth.* New York: Free Press. **[34]**

Dawes, R. M., & Corrigan, B. (1974). Linear models in decision making. *Psychological Bulletin, 81*, 95–106. **[31, 40, 41]**

Dawes, R. M., Faust, D., & Meehl, P. E. (1989). Clinical versus actuarial judgment. *Science, 243*, 1668–1674. **[13]**

Dawson, S. (1993). Decision-making and leadership: Heller, F. *Journal of Management Studies, 30*(3), 479–481. **[39]**

De Bondt, W. F. M., & Thaler, R. H. (1985). Does the stock market overreact? *Journal of Finance, 40*, 793–805. **[38]**

De Bondt, W. F. M., & Thaler, R. H. (1987). Further evidence on investor overreaction and stock market seasonality. *Journal of Finance, 42*, 557–581. **[38]**

de Finetti, B. (1970). *Theory of probability* (Vol. 1). New York: John Wiley and Sons (republished 1990). **[Introduction, 24]**

Dean, G. (1987). Does astrology need to be true? Part II: The answer is no. *Skeptical Inquirer, Spring*, 257–273. **[34]**

Degeorge, F., Patel, J., & Zeckhauser, R. (1999). Earnings management to exceed thresholds. *Journal of Business, 72*, 1–33. **[38]**

DeKay, M. L., & McClelland, G. H. (1995). Probability and utility components of endangered species preservation programs. *Journal of Experimental Psychology: Applied, 2*, 60–83. **[2]**

Dellarosa, D., & Bourne, L. E. (1984). Decisions and memory: Differential retrievability of consistent and contradictory evidence. *Journal of Verbal Learning and Verbal Behavior, 23*, 669–682. **[6]**

DeMarco, T. (1982). *Controlling software projects: Management, measurement, and estimation.* New York: Yourdon. **[14]**

Dempster, A. P. (1967). Upper and lower probabilities induced by a multivalued mapping. *Annals of Mathematical Statistics, 38*, 325–339. **[1, 25]**

Denes-Raj, V., & Epstein, S. (1994). Conflict between intuitive and rational processing: When people behave against their better judgment. *Journal of Personality and Social Psychology, 66*, 819–829. **[23]**

Dennett, D. C. (1981). *Brainstorms: Philosophical essays on mind and psychology.* Cambridge, MA: Bradford/MIT Press. **[16, 28]**

Dennett, D. C. (1981). Three kinds of intentional psychology. In *Reduction, time and reality*, R. Healey (Ed.). Cambridge, U.K.: Cambridge University Press. **[28]**

Dennett, D. C. (1983). *True believers: The intentional strategy and why it works.* Unpublished manuscript, Tufts University. **[28]**

DePaulo, B. M., Stone, J. L., & Lassiter, G. D. (1985). Deceiving and detecting deceit. In *The self in social life* (pp. 323–370), B. R. Schlenker (Ed.). New York: McGraw-Hill. **[9]**

Descartes, R. (1984). Principles of philosophy. In *The philosophical writings of Descartes* (Vol. 1, pp. 193–291), J. Cottingham, R. Stoothoff, & D. Murdoch, (Eds. and Trans.).

Cambridge, U.K.: Cambridge University Press. (Original work published 1644.) **[9]**

DeSmet A. A., Fryback D. G., & Thornbury J. R. (1979). A second look at the utility of radiographic skull examination for trauma. *American Journal of Roentgenology, 132*(1), 95–99. **[39]**

Desvouges, W. H., Johnson, F., Dunford, R., Hudson, S., Wilson, K., & Boyle, K. (1993). Measuring resource damages with contingent valuation: Tests of validity and reliability. In *Contingent valuation: A critical assessment*. Amsterdam: North Holland. **[2]**

Deutsch, R. M. (1977). *The new nuts among the berries: How nutrition nonsense captured America*. Palo Alto, CA: Ball Publishing. **[34]**

Diamond, (1996). Testing the internal consistency of contingent valuation surveys. *Journal of Environmental Economics and Management, 28*, 155–173. **[2]**

Diener, E. (1984). Subjective well-being. *Psychological Bulletin, 95*, 542–575. **[16]**

Diener, E. (1994). Assessing subjective well-being: Progress and opportunities. *Social Indicators Research, 31*, 103–157. **[16]**

Diener, E., Emmons, R. A., Larsen, R. J., & Griffin, S. (1985). The Satisfaction With Life Scale. *Journal of Personality Assessment, 49*, 71–75. **[16]**

DiFranza, J. R., Rigotti, N. A., McNeill, A. D., Ockene, J. K., Savageau, J. A., St Cyr, D., & Coleman, M. (2000). Initial symptoms of nicotine dependence in adolescents. *Tobacco Control, 9*, 313–319. **[23]**

DiMatteo, M. R., & DiNicola, D. D. (1982). *Achieving patient compliance*. New York: Pergamon Press. **[4]**

Doleys, E. J., & Renzaglia, G. A. (1963). Accuracy of student prediction of college grades. *Personnel and Guidance Journal, 41*, 528–530. **[19]**

Dominowski, R. L. (1995). Content effects in Wason's selection task. In *Perspectives on thinking and reasoning* (pp. 41–65), S. E. Newstead & J. S. B. T. Evans (Eds.). Hove, England: Erlbaum. **[24]**

Donaldson, M. (1978). *Children's minds*. London: Fontana Paperbacks. **[24]**

Donaldson, M. (1993). *Human minds: An exploration*. New York: Viking Penguin. **[24]**

Dovidio, J. F., Kawakami, K., Johnson, C., & Johnson, B. (1997). On the nature of prejudice: automatic and controlled processes. *Journal of Experimental Social Psychology, 33*, 510–540. **[10]**

Dowen, R. J. (1996). Analyst reaction to negative earnings for large well-known firms. *Journal of Portfolio Management, 23*, 49–55. **[38]**

Dowie, J. (1983). *Risk*. Buckinghamshire, England: Open University. **[41]**

Downs, J. S., & Shafir, E. (1999). Why some are perceived as more confident and more insecure, more reckless and more cautious, more trusting and more suspicious, than others: Enriched and impoverished options in social judgment. *Psychonomic Bulletin and Review, 6*, 598–610. **[27]**

Dreman, D. (1979). *Contrarian investment strategy*. New York: Random House. **[41]**

Dreman, D. (1999). *Contrarian investment strategies: The next generation*. New York: Simon & Schuster. **[41]**

Dreman, D. N., & Berry, M. A. (1995). Analyst forecasting errors and their implications for security analysis. *Financial Analysts Journal, 51*, 30–41. **[38]**

Dryfoos, J. G. (1990). *Adolescents at risk: Prevalence and prevention*. New York: Oxford University Press. **[41]**

Dube-Rioux, L., & Russo, J. E. (1988). An availability bias in professional judgment. *Journal of Behavioral Decision Making, 1*, 223–237. **[25]**

Dubois, D., & Prade, H. (1988). Modelling uncertainty and inductive inference: A survey of recent non-additive probability systems. *Acta Psychologica, 68*, 53–78. **[25]**

Dulany, D. E., & Hilton, D. J. (1991). Conversational implicature, conscious representation, and the conjunction fallacy. *Social Cognition, 9*, 85–110. **[2, 24]**

Dumond, J. W. M., & Cohen, E. R. (1951). Least-Squares adjusted values of the atomic constants as of December, 1950. *Physical Review, 82*, 555–556. **[37]**

Dumond, J. W. M., & Cohen, E. R. (1952). Least-Squares adjustment of the atomic constants. *Reviews of Modern Physics, 25*, 691–708. **[37]**

Dun & Bradstreet. (1967). *Patterns of success in managing a business*. New York: Dun & Bradstreet. **[13]**

Dunham H. W., & Meltzer, B. M. (1946). Predicting length of hospitalization of mental patients. *American Journal of Sociology, 52*, 123–131. **[40]**

Dunning, D., Griffin, D. W., Milojkovic, J., & Ross, L. (1990). The overconfidence effect in social prediction. *Journal of Personality and Social Psychology, 58*, 568–581. **[13, 14, 16]**

Dunning, D., Meyerowitz, J. A., & Holzberg, A. D. (1989). Ambiguity and self-evaluation: The role of idiosyncratic trait definitions in self-serving assessments of ability. *Journal of Personality and Social Psychology, 57*, 1082–1090. **[19, 27]**

Dunning, D., Perie, A., & Story, A. L. (1991). Self-serving prototypes of social categories. *Journal of Personality and Social Psychology, 61*, 957–968. **[36]**

Durkheim, E. (1976). *The elementary forms of the religious life* (2nd ed.). London: Allen and Unwin. (Original work published 1925). **[32]**

Dutton, D. G, & Aron, A. P. (1974). Some evidence for heightened sexual attraction under conditions of high anxiety. *Journal of Personality & Social Psychology, 30*, 510–517. **[10]**

Duval, S., & Wicklund, R. A. (1972). *A theory of objective self-awareness*. New York: Academic Press. **[20]**

Dweck, C. S. (1986). Motivational processes affecting learning. *American Psychologist, 41*, 1040–1048. **[36]**

Eagly, A. H., & Chaiken, S. (1993). *The psychology of attitudes*. Fort Worth: Harcourt Brace Jovanovich. **[14, 22, 29]**

Eddy, D. M. (1982). Probabilistic reasoning in clinical medicine: Problems and opportunities. In *Judgment under uncertainty: Heuristics and biases* (pp. 249–267), D. Kahneman, P. Slovic, & A. Tversky (Eds.). Cambridge, U.K.: Cambridge University Press. **[39, 41]**

Edmonson, F. K. (1934). Velocity of Light. *Nature, 133*, 759–760. **[37]**

Edwards, A. L. (1957). *Techniques of attitude scale construction*. New York: Appleton-Century-Croft. **[23]**

Edwards, K., & Smith, E. E. (1996). A disconfirmation bias in the evaluation of arguments. *Journal of Personality and Social Psychology, 71*, 5–24. **[36]**

Edwards, W. (1954). The theory of decision making. *Psychological Bulletin, 51*, 380–417. **[31]**

Edwards, W. (1961). Behavioral decision theory. *Annual Review of Psychology, 12*, 473–498. **[31]**

Edwards, W. (1968). Conservatism in human information processing. In *Formal representation of human judgment* (pp. 17–52), B. Kleinmuntz (Ed.). New York: Wiley. **[Introduction, 13]**

Edwards, W. (1970). Comment. *Journal of the American Statistical Association, 70*, 291–293. **[1]**

Edwards, W., Lindman, H., & Savage, L. J. (1963). Bayesian statistical inference for psychological research. *Psychological Review, 70*, 193–242. **[Introduction]**

Edwards, W., & von Winterfeldt, D. (1986). Cognitive illusions and their implications for the law. *Southern California Law Review, 59*, 225–276. **[39]**

Einhorn, H. J. (1972). Expert measurement and mechanical combination. *Organizational Behavior and Human Decision Processes, 7*, 86–106. **[40]**

Einhorn, H. J., & Hogarth, R. M. (1975). Unit weighting schemes for decision making. *Organizational Behavior and Human Decision Processes, 13*, 171–192. **[40]**

Einhorn, H. J., & Hogarth, R. M. (1978). Confidence in judgment: Persistence of the illusion of validity. *Psychological Review, 85*, 395–416. **[28, 40]**

Einhorn, H. J., & Hogarth, R. M. (1981). Behavioral decision theory: Processes of judgment and choice. *Annual Review of Psychology, 32*, 53–88. **[1, 24, 28]**

Einhorn, H. J., & Hogarth, R. M. (1982). *A theory of diagnostic inference: Imagination and the psychophysics of evidence.* Center for Decision Research, Graduate School of Business, University of Chicago. **[20]**

Einhorn, H. J., & Hogarth, R. M. (1985). Ambiguity and uncertainty in probabilistic inference. *Psychological Review, 92*, 433–461. **[6]**

Einhorn, H. J., & Hogarth, R. M. (1986). Probable cause: A decision making framework. *Psychological Bulletin, 99*, 3–19. **[20]**

Eisenhardt, C. (1968). Expression of uncertainties of final results. *Science, 160*, 1201–1204. **[37]**

Elliott, R. (1975). Heart rate in anticipation of shocks which have different probabilities of occurrences. *Psychological Reports, 36*, 923–931. **[30]**

Ellis, H. D. (1986). Face recall: A psychological perspective. Human Learning. *Journal of Practical Research and Applications, 5*, 189–196. **[17]**

Elster, J. (1977). *Ulysses and the sirens.* Cambridge, U.K.: Cambridge University Press. **[16]**

Elster, J. (1983). *Sour grapes: Studies in the subversion of rationality.* Cambridge, U.K.: Cambridge University Press. **[24]**

Elster, J., & Loewenstein, G. (1992). Utility from memory and anticipation. In *Choice over time* (pp. 213–234), J. Elster & G. Loewenstein (Eds.). New York: Russell Sage Foundation. **[14]**

Elton, E. J., Gruber, M. J., & Gultekin, M. N. (1984). Professional expectations: Accuracy and diagnosis of errors. *Journal of Financial and Quantitative Analysis, 19*, 351–365. **[38]**

Englich, B., & Mussweiler, T. (in press). Legal judgment under uncertainty: Anchoring effects in the court room. *Journal of Applied Social Psychology.* **[6]**

Epley, N., & Dunning, D. (2000). Feeling "holier than thou": Are self-serving assessments produced by errors in self- or social prediction? *Journal of Personality and Social Psychology, 79*, 861–875. **[14, 36]**

Epley, N., & Gilovich, T. (2000a). Anchoring and effortful adjustment from self-generated anchors. Unpublished manuscript, Cornell University. **[7]**

Epley, N., & Gilovich, T. (2000b). Close but not quite: insufficient adjustment from self-generated anchors. Unpublished manuscript, Cornell University. **[7]**

Epley, N., & Gilovich, T. (2001). Putting adjustment back in the anchoring-and-adjustment heuristic: Self-generated versus experimenter provided anchors. *Psychological Science, 12*, 391–396. **[Introduction]**

Epstein, S. (1994). Integration of the cognitive and psychodynamic unconscious. *American Psychologist, 49*(8), 709–724. **[2, 23, 24]**

Epstein, S., Lipson, A., Holstein, C., & Huh, E. (1992). Irrational reactions to negative outcomes: Evidence for two conceptual systems. *Journal of Personality and Social Psychology, 62,* 328–339. **[22]**

Erber, R., Wegner, D. M., & Therriault, N. (1996). On being cool and collected: Mood regulation in anticipation of social interaction. *Journal of Personality and Social Psychology, 70,* 757–766. **[16]**

Erber, R., & Tesser, A. (1992). Task effort and the regulation of mood: The absorption hypothesis. *Journal of Experimental Social Psychology, 28,* 339–359. **[16]**

Erev, I., Wallsten, T. S., & Budescu, D. V. (1994). Simultaneous over- and underconfidence: The role of error in judgment processes. *Psychological Review, 101,* 519–527. **[15, 25, 26, 39]**

Ericsson, A., & Simon, H. (1994). *Verbal reports as data* (2nd ed.). Cambridge, MA: MIT Press. **[41]**

Erwin, P. G., & Calev, A. (1984). The influence of Christian name stereotypes on the marking of children's essays. *British Journal of Educational Psychology, 54,* 223–227. **[23]**

Evans, J. St. B. T. (1982). *The psychology of deductive reasoning.* London: Routledge. **[24]**

Evans, J. St. B. T. (1984). Heuristic and analytic processes in reasoning. *British Journal of Psychology, 75,* 451–468. **[24]**

Evans, J. St. B. T. (1989). *Bias in human reasoning: Causes and consequences.* London: Erlbaum Associates. **[24]**

Evans, J. St. B. T. (1996). Deciding before you think: Relevance and reasoning in the selection task. *British Journal of Psychology, 87,* 223–240. **[24]**

Evans, J. St. B. T., Barston, J., & Pollard, P. (1983). On the conflict between logic and belief in syllogistic reasoning. *Memory & Cognition, 11,* 295–306. **[22, 24]**

Evans, J. St. B. T., Handley, S. H., Perham, N., Over, D. E., & Thompson, V. A. (2000). Frequency versus probability formats in statistical word problems. *Cognition, 77,* 197–213. **[Introduction]**

Evans, J. St. B. T., & Lynch, J. S. (1973). Matching bias in the selection task. *British Journal of Psychology, 64,* 391–397. **[24]**

Evans, J. St. B. T., Newstead, S. E., & Byrne, R. M. J. (1993). *Human reasoning: The psychology of deduction.* Hove, England: Erlbaum. **[24]**

Evans, J. St. B. T., & Over, D. E. (1996). *Rationality and reasoning.* Hove, England: Psychology Press. **[Introduction, 22, 24]**

Evans, J., Handley, S. J., Perham, N., Over, D. E., & Thompson, V. A. (2000). Frequency versus probability formats in statistical word problems. *Cognition, 77,* 197–213. **[2]**

Evans-Pritchard, E. E. (1937). *Witchcraft, oracles and magic among the Azande.* Oxford: Clarendon. **[34]**

Falk, R. (1981). The perception of randomness. In *Proceedings, Fifth International Conference for the Psychology of Mathematics Education.* Grenoble, France. **[33]**

Falk, R. (1992). A closer look at the probabilities of the notorious three prisoners. *Cognition, 43,* 197–223. **[22]**

Farber, H. S., & Bazerman, M. H. (1986). The general basis of arbitrator behavior: An empirical analysis of conventional and final offer arbitration. *Econometrica, 54,* 1503–1528. **[39]**

Farber, H. S., & Bazerman, M. H. (1989). Divergent expectations as a cause of disagreement in bargaining: Evidence from a comparison of arbitration schemes. *Quarterly Journal of Economics, 104,* 99–120. **[39]**

Faust, D. (1984). *The limits of scientific reasoning.* Minneapolis, MN: University of Minnesota Press. **[40]**

Fazio, R. H. (1995). Attitudes as object-evaluation associations: Determinants, consequences, and correlates of attitude accessibility. In *Attitude strength: Antecedents and consequences* (pp. 247–282), R. E. Petty & J. A. Krosnick (Eds.). Mahwah, NJ: Erlbaum. [23]

Fazio, R. H., Jackson, J. R., Dunton, B. C., & Williams, C. J. (1995). Variability in automatic activation as an unobtrusive measure of racial attitudes: A bona fide pipeline? *Journal of Personality and Social Psychology, 69*, 1013–1027. [10]

Feather, N. T. (1967). Valence of outcome and expectation of success in relation to task difficulty and perceived locus of control. *Journal of Personality and Social Psychology, 7*, 372–386. [35]

Feather, N. T. (1969). Attribution of responsibility and valence of success and failure in relation to initial confidence and task performance. *Journal of Personality and Social Psychology, 13*, 129–144. [35]

Ferrari, J. R., Johnson, J. L., & McGown, W. G. (1995). *Procrastination and task avoidance: Theory, research, and treatment*. New York: Plenum Press. [14]

Ferrell, W. R. (1994). Discrete subjective probabilities and decision analysis: Elicitation, calibration, and combination. In *Subjective probability* (pp. 411–451), G. Wright & P. Ayton (Eds.). Chichester, U.K.: Wiley. [39]

Ferrell, W. R., & McGoey, P. J. (1980). A model of calibration for subjective probabilities. *Organizational Behavior and Human Performance, 26*, 32–53. [13, 27, 39]

Festinger, L. (1954). A theory of social comparison processes. *Human Relations, 7*, 117–140. [35]

Festinger, L. (1957). *A theory of cognitive dissonance*. Stanford, CA: Stanford University Press. [16, 36]

Festinger, L. (Ed.). (1964). *Conflict, decision, and dissonance*. Stanford, CA: Stanford University Press. [42]

Festinger, L., & Maccoby, N. (1964). On resistance to persuasive communications. *Journal of Abnormal and Social Psychology, 68*, 359–366. [9]

Fetherstonhaugh, D., Slovic, P., Johnson, S. M., & Friedrich, J. (1997). Insensitivity to the value of human life: A study of psychophysical numbing. *Journal of Risk and Uncertainty, 14*(3), 282–300. [23]

Fiedler, K. (1988). The dependence of the conjunction fallacy on subtle linguistic factors. *Psychological Research, 50*, 123–129. [24]

Fiedler, K., & Armbruster, T. (1994). Two halfs may be more than one whole. *Journal of Personality and Social Psychology, 66*, 633–645. [25]

Fiedler, K., Pampe, H., & Scherf, U. (1986). Mood an memory for tightly organized social information. *European Journal of Social Psychology, 16*, 149–164. [29]

Finucane, M. L., Alhakami, A., Slovic, P., & Johnson, S. M. (2000). The affect heuristic in judgments of risks and benefits. *Journal of Behavioral Decision Making, 13*, 1–17. [2, 23, 30]

Fischer, G. W., & Hawkins, S. A. (1988). Preference reversals in multiattribute decision making: Scale compatibility, strategy compatibility, and the prominence effect. Carnegie-Mellon University. Typescript. [12]

Fischer, G. W., Morgan, G. M., Fischhoff, B., Nair, I., & Lave, L. B. (1991). What risks are people concerned about? *Risk Analysis, 11*, 303–314. [41]

Fischer, P. M. (1991). Brand logo recognition by children ages 3 to 6 years: Mickey Mouse and Old Joe the Camel. *Journal of the American Medical Association, 266*, 3145. [23]

Fischhoff, B., Slovic. P., & Lichtenstein, S. (1981). Lay foibles and expert fables in judgments about risk. In *Progress in resource management and environmental planning* (Vol. 3, pp. 161–202), T. O'Riordan & R. K. Turner (Eds.). Chichester, U.K.: Wiley. **[33]**

Fischhoff, B. (1975). Hindsight is not equal to foresight: the effect of outcome knowledge on judgment under uncertainty. *Journal of Experimental Psychology: Human Perception and Performance, 1,* 288–299. **[5, 6, 8, 40, 42]**

Fischhoff, B. (1980). For those condemned to study the past. In *New Directions for Methodology of Social and Behavioral Science* (pp. 79–93), R. A. Schweder & D. W. Fiske (Eds.). San Francisco: Jossey-Bass. **[40]**

Fischhoff, B. (1982a). Debiasing. In *Judgment under uncertainty: Heuristics and biases* (pp. 422–444), D. Kahneman, P. Slovic, & A. Tversky (Eds.). Cambridge, U.K.: Cambridge University Press. **[5, 10, 13, 14, 41, 42]**

Fischhoff, B. (1982b). For those condemned to study the past: Heuristics and biases in hindsight. In *Judgment under uncertainty: Heuristics and biases* (pp. 201–208), D. Kahneman, P. Slovic, & A. Tversky (Eds.). Cambridge, U.K.: Cambridge University Press. **[5, 19]**

Fischhoff, B. (1984). Setting standards: A systematic approach to managing public health and safety risks. *Management Science, 30,* 823–843. **[41]**

Fischhoff, B. (1988). Judgment and decision making. In *The psychology of human thought* (pp. 153–187), R. Sternberg & E. E. Smith (Eds.). New York: Cambridge University Press. **[39]**

Fischhoff, B. (1989). Eliciting knowledge for analytical representation. *IEEE Transactions on Systems, Man and Cybernetics, 13,* 448–461. **[41]**

Fischhoff, B. (1992). Giving advice: Decision theory perspectives on sexual assault. *American Psychologist, 47,* 577–588. **[41]**

Fischhoff, B. (1994). What forecasts (seem to) mean. *International Journal of Forecasting, 10,* 387–403. **[41]**

Fischhoff, B. (1995). Risk perception and communication unplugged: Twenty years of process. *Risk Analysis, 15,* 137–145. **[41]**

Fischhoff, B. (1996). The real world: What good is it? *Organizational Behavior and Human Decision Processes, 65,* 232–248. **[41]**

Fischhoff, B. (1998). Communicate unto others. . . . *Reliability Engineering and System Safety, 59,* 63–72. **[41]**

Fischhoff, B. (1999). Why (cancer) risk communication can be hard. *Journal of the National Cancer Institute Monographs, 25,* 7–13. **[41]**

Fischhoff, B. (2000a). Informed consent in eliciting environmental values. *Environmental Science and Technology, 38,* 1439–1444 **[41]**

Fischhoff, B. (2000b). Need to know: Analytical and psychological criteria. *Roger Williams University Law Review.* **[41]**

Fischhoff, B., & Bar-Hillel, M. (1984). Focusing techniques: A shortcut to improving probability judgments? *Organizational Behavior and Human Performance, 34,* 175–194. **[13]**

Fischhoff, B., & Beyth, R. (1975). "I knew it would happen" – remembered probabilities of once-future things. *Organizational Behavior and Human Performance, 13,* 1–16. **[7, 8, 19, 40]**

Fischhoff, B., & Beyth-Marom, R. (1983). Hypothesis evaluation from a Bayesian perspective. *Psychological Review, 90,* 239–260. **[13, 41]**

Fischhoff, B., Slovic, P., & Lichtenstein, S. (1978). Fault trees: Sensitivity of estimated failure probabilities to problem representation. *Journal of Experimental Psychology: Human Perception and Performance, 4,* 330–344. **[14, 25]**

Fischhoff, B., Lichtenstein, S., Slovic, P., Derby, S. L., & Keeney, R. L. (1981). *Acceptable risk*. New York: Cambridge University Press. **[41]**

Fischhoff, B., & MacGregor D. (1982). Subjective confidence in forecasts. *Journal of Forecasting, 1*, 155–172. **[13, 39]**

Fischhoff, B., Nadaï, A., & Fischhoff, I. (2001). Investing in Frankenfirms. *Journal of Psychology and Financial Markets, 2*, 100–111. **[41]**

Fischhoff, B., Parker, A., Bruine de Bruin, W., Downs, J., Palmgren, C., Dawes, R. M., & Manski, C. (2000). Teen expectations for significant life events. *Public Opinion Quarterly, 64*, 189–205. **[41]**

Fischhoff, B., Riley, D., Kovacs, D., & Small, M. (1998). What information belongs in a warning? A mental models approach. *Psychology and Marketing, 15*, 663–686. **[41]**

Fischhoff, B., Slovic, P., & Lichtenstein, S. (1977). Knowing with certainty: The appropriateness of extreme confidence. *Journal of Experimental Psychology: Human Perception and Performance, 3*, 552–564. **[15]**

Fischhoff, B., Slovic, P., Lichtenstein, S., Reid, S., & Coombs, B. (1978). How safe is safe enough? A psychometric study of attitudes towards technological risks and benefits. *Policy Sciences, 9*, 127–152. **[23, 41]**

Fischhoff, B., & Whipple, C. (1981). Risk Assessment: Evaluating error in subjective estimates. *Environmental Professional, 3*, 277–291. **[37]**

Fishbein, M., & Ajzen, I. (1975). *Belief, attitude, intention, and behavior: An introduction to theory and research*. Reading, MA: Addison-Wesley. **[14]**

Fishburn, P. (1983). Nontransitive measurable utility. *Journal of Mathematical Psychology, 26*, 31–67. **[21]**

Fiske, A., & Tetlock, P. E. (1997). Taboo trade-offs: Reactions to transactions that transgrees spheres of justice. *Political Psychology, 18*, 255–297. **[32]**

Fiske, S. T., Kenny, D. A., & Taylor, S. E. (1982). Structural models for the mediation of salience effects on attribution. *Journal of Experimental Social Psychology, 18*, 105–127. **[20]**

Fiske, S. T., & Neuberg, S. L. (1990). A continuum of impression formation, from category-based to individuating processes: Influences of information and motivation on attention and interpretation. In *Advances in experimental social psychology* (Vol. 23, pp. 1–74), M. P. Zanna (Ed.). New York: Academic Press. **[Introduction, 29]**

Fiske, S. T., & Taylor, S. E. (1991). *Social cognition*, 2nd Ed. New York: McGraw-Hill. **[Introduction]**

Fitts, P. M., & Seeger, C. M. (1953). S–R compatibility: spatial characteristics of stimulus and response codes. *Journal of Experimental Psychology, 46*, 199–210. **[12]**

Flavell, J. (1986). The development of children's knowledge about the appearance–reality distinction. *American Psychologist, 41*, 418–425. **[11]**

Flavell, J. H. (1963). *The developmental psychology of Jean Piaget*. New York: Van Nostrand. **[27, 36]**

Flavell, J. H. (1985). *Cognitive development*, 2nd ed. Englewood Cliffs, NJ: Prentice Hall. **[36]**

Fleming, J., & Arrowood, A. J. (1979). Information processing and the perseverance of discredited self-perceptions. *Personality and Social Psychology Bulletin, 5*, 201–205. **[20]**

Fodor, J. A. (2000). *The mind doesn't work that way: The scope and limits of computational psychology*, Cambridge, MA: MIT Press. **[Introduction]**

Fodor, J. A., & Pylyshyn, Z. W. (1988). Connectionism and cognitive architecture: A critical analysis. *Cognition, 28*, 3–71. **[22]**

Fong, G. T., Krantz, D. H., & Nisbett, R. E. (1983). *Improving inductive reasoning through statistical training*. Unpublished manuscript, University of Michigan. **[28]**

Fong, G. T., Krantz, D. H., & Nisbett, R. E. (1986). The effects of statistical training on thinking about everyday problems. *Cognitive Psychology, 18*, 253–292. **[24]**

Fordyce, M. W. (1988). A review of research on the happiness measures: A sixty second index of happiness and mental health. *Social Indicators Research, 20*, 355–381. **[16]**

Forer, B. (1949). The fallacy of personal validation: A classroom demonstration of gullibility. *Journal of Abnormal and Social Psychology, 44*, 118–123. **[13]**

Forgas, J. P. (1995). Emotion in social judgments: Review and a new affect infusion model (AIM). *Psychological Bulletin, 117*, 39–66. **[29]**

Forgas, J. P., & Bower, G. H. (1987). Mood effects on person perception judgments. *Journal of Personality and Social Psychology, 53*, 53–60. **[29]**

Forster, J., & Strack, F. (1996). Influence of overt head movements on memory for valenced words: a case of conceptual-motor compatibility. *Journal of Personality and Social Psychology, 71*, 421–430. **[7]**

Forster, J., & Strack, F. (1997). Motor actions in retrieval of valenced information: a motor congruence effect. *Perceptual and Motor Skills, 85*, 1419–1427. **[7]**

Fox, C. R. (1999). Strength of evidence, judged probability, and choice under uncertainty. *Cognitive Psychology, 38*, 167–189. **[27]**

Fox, C. R., & Kahneman, D. (1992). Correlations, causes, and heuristics in surveys of life satisfaction. *Social Indicators Research, 27*, 221–234. **[27]**

Fox, C. R., Rogers, B. A., & Tversky, A. (1996). Options traders exhibit subadditive decision weights. *Journal of Risk and Uncertainty, 13*, 5–17. **[25, 26, 27]**

Fox, C. R., & Tversky, A. (1995). Ambiguity Aversion and comparative ignorance. *Quarterly Journal of Economics, 110*, 585–603. **[27]**

Fox, C. R., & Tversky, A. (1998). A belief-based account of decision under uncertainty. *Management Science, 44*, 879–895. **[26, 27]**

Frame, D. M. (transl.). (1943). *The complete essays of Montaigne*. Stanford, CA: Stanford University Press. **[8]**

Francis, J., & Philbrick, D. R. (1993). Analysts' decisions as products of multi-task environment. *Journal pf Accounting Research, 31*, 216–230.

Frank, M. G., & Gilovich, T. (1988). The dark side of self- and social perception: Black uniforms and aggression in professional sports. *Journal of Personality and Social Psychology, 54*, 74–85. **[35]**

Frank, R. H., & Cook, P. (1995). *The winner-take-all society*. New York: Free Press. **[35]**

Franklin, A. D. (1981). Millikan's Published and Unpublished Data on Oil Drops. *Historical Studies in Physical Science, 11*, 185–201. **[37]**

Franklin, A. D. (1984). Forging, cooking, trimming, and riding on the bandwagon. *American Journal of Physics, 52*, 786–793. **[37]**

Frazer, J. G. (1890/1959). *The golden bough: a study in magic and religion*. New York: Macmillan. (Reprint of 1922 abridged edition, edited by T. H. Gaster; original work published 1890) **[11]**

Frederick, S. W., & Fischhoff, B. (1998). Scope (in)sensitivity in elicited valuations. *Risk, Decision, and Policy, 3*, 109–124. **[2, 30]**

Fredrickson, B. L., & Kahneman, D. (1993). Duration neglect in retrospective evaluations of affective episodes. *Journal of Personality and Social Psychology, 65*, 45–55. **[2, 16]**

Freud, A. (1936). *Ego and the mechanisms of defense* (Rev. ed., 1966, trans., C. Baines). New York: International Universities Press. **[16]**

Freud, S. (1913). *The interpretation of dreams.* London: George Allen & Unwin. **[22]**

Freud, S. (1950). *Totem and taboo: some points of agreement between the mental lives of savages and neurotics.* (J. Strachey, Trans.). New York: W. W. Norton & Co. (Original work published 1913) **[11]**

Freud, S. (1966). The Dream Work. In *Introductory lectures on psychoanalysis* (Lecture XI, pp. 170–183), J. Strachey (Ed. & Trans.). New York: W. W. Norton & Co. (Original work published 1920) **[11]**

Friedman, N., & Goldszmit, L. (1996). *A software for learning Bayesian networks.* (Not released for public use.) **[31]**

Friedman, R. S., & Förster, J. (2000). The effects of approach and avoidance motor actions on the elements of creative insight. *Journal of Personality and Social Psychology, 79,* 477–492. **[29]**

Friedrich, J. (1996). On seeing oneself as less self serving than others: The ultimate self serving bias? *Teaching of Psychology, 23,* 107–109. **[36]**

Friedrich, J. Barnes, P., Chapin, K., Dawson, I., Garst, V., & Kerr, D. (1999). Psychophysical numbing: When lives are valued less as the lives at risk increase. *Journal of Consumer Psychology, 8*(3), 277–299. **[23]**

Fries, J. F., Bloch, D. A., Sharp, J. T., McShane, D. J., Spitz, P., Bluhm, G. B., Forrester, D., Genant, H., Gofton, P., Richman, S., et al. (1986). Assessment of radiologic progression in rheumatoid arthritis. A randomized, controlled trial. *Arthritis and Rheumatism, 29,* 1–9. **[40]**

Frisch, D. (1993). Reasons for froming effects. *Organizational Behavior Human Decision Processes, 54,* 399–429. **[24]**

Froome, & Essen. (1973). *The Velocity of Light and Radio Waves.* London: Academic. **[37]**

Froot, K. A., & Frankel, J. A. (1989). Forward discount bias: Is it an exchange risk premium? *Quarterly Journal of Economics, 104,* 139–161. **[38]**

Funder, D. C. (1982). On the accuracy of dispositional vs. situational attributions. *Social Cognition, 1,* 205–222. **[20]**

Funder, D. C. (1987). Errors and mistakes: Evaluating the accuracy of social judgment. *Psychological Bulletin, 101,* 75–90. **[24]**

Funtowicz, S., & Ravetz, J. (1990). *Uncertainty and quality in science for policy.* London: Kluwer. **[41]**

Furnham, A. F. (1988). *Lay theories.* London: Pergamon Press. **[41]**

Fussell, S. R., & Krauss, R. M. (1989). The effects of intended audience on message production and comprehension: reference in a common ground framework. *Journal of Experimental Social Psychology, 25,* 203–219. **[8]**

Gabrielcik, A., & Fazio, R. H. (1984). Priming and frequency estimation: A strict test of the availability heuristic. *Personality and Social Psychology Bulletin, 10,* 85–89. **[5]**

Gaeth, G. J., & Shanteau, J. (1984). Reducing the influence of irrelevant information on experienced decision makers. *Organizational Behavior and Human Performance, 33,* 263. **[37]**

Gallagher, D., & Clore, G. L. (1985, May). *Effects of fear and anger on judgments of risk and blame.* Paper presented at the meetings of the Midwestern Psychological Association, Chicago. **[29]**

Ganzach, Y. (1996). Preference reversals in equal-probability gambles: A case for anchoring and adjustment. *Journal of Behavioral Decision Making, 92,* 95–109. **[6]**

Ganzach, Y. (2000). Judging risk and return of financial assets. *Organizational Behavior and Human Decision Processes, 83,* 353–370. **[23]**

Ganzach, Y., & Krantz, D. H. (1990). The psychology of moderate prediction. I. Experience with multiple determination. *Organizational Behavior and Human Decision Processes, 47,* 177–204. **[2]**

Garner, W. R. (1962). *Uncertainty and structure as psychological concepts.* New York: Wiley. **[20]**

Garner, W. R. (1970). Good patterns have few alternatives. *American Scientist, 58,* 34–42. **[20]**

Gati, I., & Tversky, A. (1982). Representations of qualitative and quantitative dimensions. *Journal of Experimental Psychology: Human Perception and Performance, 8,* 325–340. **[1]**

Gerard, H. B., & Mathewson, G. C. (1966). The effects of severity of initiation on liking for a group: A replication. *Journal of Experimental Social Psychology, 2,* 278–287. **[Introduction]**

Gerrard, M., Gibbons, F. X., & Warner, T. D. (1991). Effects of reviewing risk-relevant behavior on perceived vulnerability among women Marines. *Health Psychology, 10,* 173–179. **[17]**

Gerrard, M., & Luus, C. A. E. (1995). Judgments of vulnerability to pregnancy: The role of risk factors and individual differences. *Personality and Social Psychology Bulletin, 21,* 160–171. **[19]**

Gettys, C. E., Mehle, T., & Fisher, S. (1986). Plausibility assessments in hypothesis generation. *Organizational Behavior and Human Decision Processes, 37,* 14–33. **[25]**

Gigerenzer, G. (1991a). How to make cognitive illusions disappear: Beyond "heuristics and biases." In *European Review of Social Psychology* (Vol. 2, pp. 83–115), W. Stroebe & M. Hewstone (Eds.). Chichester, U.K.: Wiley. **[2, 14]**

Gigerenzer, G. (1991b). From tools to theories: A heuristic of discovery in cognitive psychology. *Psychological Review, 98,* 254–267. **[Introduction, 24, 27]**

Gigerenzer, G. (1991c). How to make cognitive illusions disappear: Beyond heuristics and biases. *European Review of Social Psychology, 2,* 83–115. **[Introduction, 24]**

Gigerenzer, G. (1993). The bounded rationality of probabilistic mental models. In *Rationality: Psychological and philosophical perspectives* (pp. 284–313), K. Manktelow & D. Over (Eds.). London: Routledge. **[24]**

Gigerenzer, G. (1994). Why the distinction between single-event probabilities and frequencies is important for psychology (and vice versa). In *Subjective probability* (pp. 129–161), G. Wright & P. Ayton (Eds.). New York: Wiley. **[Introduction, 14, 39]**

Gigerenzer, G. (1996). On narrow norms and vague heuristics: A reply to Kahneman and Tversky (1996). *Psychological Review, 103,* 592–596. **[24]**

Gigerenzer, G. (1998). Ecological intelligence: An adaptation for frequencies. In *The evolution of mind* (pp. 9–29), D. Dellarosa Cummins & C. Allen (Eds.). New York: Oxford University Press. **[Introduction, 14]**

Gigerenzer, G., & Goldstein, D. G. (1996). Reasoning the fast and frugal way: Models of bounded rationality. *Psychological Review, 103,* 650–669. **[2, 24, 30, 31]**

Gigerenzer, G., & Hoffrage, U. (1995). How to improve Bayesian reasoning without instruction: Frequency formats. *Psychological Review, 102,* 684–704. **[2, 24]**

Gigerenzer, G., Hell, W., & Blank, H. (1988). Presentation and content – the use of base rates as a continuous variable. *Journal of Experimental Psychology – Human Perception and Performance, 14*(3), 513–525. **[2, 13]**

Gigerenzer, G., Hoffrage, U., & Kleinbolting, H. (1991). Probabilistic mental models: A Brunswikian theory of confidence. *Psychological Review, 98*, 506–528. **[13, 31, 39]**

Gigerenzer, G., Swijtink, Z., Porter, T., Daston, L., Beatty, J., & Krtiger, L. (1989). *The empire of chance: How probability changed science and even life.* Cambridge, U.K.: Cambridge University Press. **[31]**

Gigerenzer, G., Todd, P. M., & the ABC Research Group. (1999). *Simple heuristics that make us smart,* New York: Oxford University Press. **[Introduction, 2, 30, 31]**

Gilbert, D. (1989). Thinking lightly about others: Automatic components of the social inference process. In *Unintended thought* (pp. 189–211), J. Uleman & J. A. Bargh (Eds.). New York: Guilford. **[2, 7]**

Gilbert, D. T. (1990). Unbelieving the unbelievable: Some problems in the rejection of false information. *Journal of Personality and Social Psychology, 59*, 601–613. **[6]**

Gilbert, D. T. (1991). How mental systems believe. *American Psychologist, 46*, 107–119. **[2, 6, 9, 10, 16]**

Gilbert, D. T. (1993). The assent of man: Mental representation and the control of belief. In *The handbook of mental control* (pp. 57–87), D. M. Wegner & J. W. Pennebaker, (Eds.). Englewood Cliffs, NJ: Prentice-Hall. **[9, 10]**

Gilbert, D. T. (1999). What the mind's not. In *Dual process theories in social psychology* (pp. 3–11), S. Chaiken & Y. Trope (Eds.). New York: Guilford. **[2, 9]**

Gilbert, D. T., Giesler, R. B., & Morris, K. A. (1995). When comparisons arise. *Journal of Personality and Social Psychology, 69*, 227–236. **[9]**

Gilbert, D. T., Gill, M. J., & Wilson, T. D. (in press). The future is now: Temporal correction in affective forecasting. *Organizational Behavior and Human Decision Processes.* **[16]**

Gilbert, D. T., Krull, D. S., & Malone, P. S. (1990). Unbelieving the unbelievable: Some problems in the rejection of false information. *Journal of Personality and Social Psychology, 59*, 601–613. **[9]**

Gilbert, D. T., Krull, D. S., & Pelham, B. W. (1988). Of thoughts unspoken: Social inference and the self-regulation of behavior. *Journal of Personality and Social Psychology, 55*, 685–694. **[9]**

Gilbert, D. T., McNulty, S. E., Giuliano, T. A., & Benson, J. E. (1992). Blurry words and fuzzy deeds: The attribution of obscure behavior. *Journal of Personality and Social Psychology, 62*, 18–25. **[9]**

Gilbert, D. T., & Malone, P. S. (1995). The correspondence bias. *Psychological Bulletin, 117*, 21–38. **[9, 36]**

Gilbert, D. T., Miller, A. G., & Ross, L. (1998). Speeding with Ned: A personal view of the correspondence bias. In *Attribution and social interaction: the legacy of Edward E. Jones* (pp. 5–66), J. M. Darley & J. Cooper (Eds.). Washington, DC: American Psychological Association. **[6]**

Gilbert, D. T., & Osborne, R. E. (1989). Thinking backward: Some curable and incurable consequences of cognitive busyness. *Journal of Personality and Social Psychology, 57*, 940–949. **[8, 9]**

Gilbert, D. T., Pelham, B. W., & Krull, D. S. (1988). On cognitive busyness: When person perceivers meet person receivers. *Journal of Personality and Social Psychology, 54*, 733–740. **[6, 8, 9]**

Gilbert, D. T., Tafarodi, R. W., & Malone, P. S. (1993). You can't not believe everything you read. *Journal of Personality and Social Psychology, 65*, 221–233. **[6, 9]**

Gilbert, D. T., & Wilson, T. D. (2000). Miswanting: Some problems in the forecasting of future affective states. In *Feeling and thinking: The role of affect in social cognition* (pp. 178–198), J. Forgas (Ed.). Cambridge, U.K.: Cambridge University Press. **[14, 16]**

Gilboa, I., & Schmeidler, D. (1994). Additive representations of non-additive measures and the Choquet integral. *Annals of Operation Research, 51,* 43–65. **[25]**

Gill, M., & Gilbert, D. T. (1999). *Sequential operations in self-perception.* Unpublished data. **[9]**

Gillies, G. T. (1983). *The Newtonian Gravitational Constant: An Index of Measurements* (BIPM-83/1), Bureau International des Poids et Mesures. **[37]**

Gilovich, T. (1983). Biased evaluation and persistence in gambling. *Journal of Personality and Social Psychology, 44,* 1110–1126. **[18, 19, 33]**

Gilovich, T. (1990). Differential construal and the false consensus effect. *Journal of Personality and Social Psychology, 59,* 623–634. **[36]**

Gilovich, T. (1991). *How we know what isn't so: The fallibility of human judgment in everyday life,* New York: Free Press. **[Introduction, 34, 41]**

Gilovich, T. (2000, June). *Motivated skepticism and motivated credulity: Differential standards of evidence in the evaluation of desired and undesired propositions.* Address presented at the 12th Annual Convention of the American Psychological Society, Miami Beach, Florida. **[27]**

Gilovich, T., Kerr, M., & Medvec, V. H. (1993). Effect of temporal perspective on subjective confidence. *Journal of Personality and Social Psychology, 64,* 552–560. **[19]**

Gilovich, T., & Medvec, V. H. (1995). The experience of regret: What, when, and why. *Psychological Review, 102,* 379–395. **[16]**

Gilovich, T., Medvec, V. H., & Chen, S. (1995). Omission, commission, and dissonance reduction: Coping with regret in the "Monty Hall" problem. *Personality and Social Psychology Bulletin, 21,* 182–190. **[21]**

Gilovich, T., Medvec, V. H., & Savitsky, K. (2000). The spotlight effect in social judgment: An egocentric bias in estimates of the salience of one's own actions and appearance. *Journal of Personality and Social Psychology, 78,* 211–222. **[7]**

Gilovich, T., & Savitsky, K. (1999). The spotlight effect and the illusion of transparency: egocentric assessments of how we're seen by others. *Current Directions in Psychological Science, 8,* 165–168. **[7, 8]**

Gilovich, T., Savitsky, K., & Medvec, V. H. (1998). The illusion of transparency: Biased assessments of others' ability to read our emotional states. *Journal of Personality and Social Psychology, 75,* 332–346. **[7, 8]**

Gilovich, T., Vallone, R. P., & Tversky, A. (1985). The hot hand in basketball: On the misperception of random sequences. *Cognitive Psychology, 17,* 295–314. **[35]**

Girotto, V., & Gonzalez, M. (2001). Solving probabilistic and statistical problems: A matter of information structure and question form. *Cognition, 78,* 247–276. **[Introduction]**

Glaser, R. (1990). Expertise. In *The Blackwell dictionary of cognitive psychology* (p. 139), M. W. Eysenk, A. N. Ellis, E. Hunt, & P. Johnson-Laird (Eds.). Oxford, U.K.: Blackwell Reference. **[39]**

Gleicher, F., Boninger, D. S., Strathman, A., Armor, D., Hetts, J., & Ahn, M. (1995). With an eye toward the future: The impact of counterfactual thinking on affect, attitudes, and behavior. In *What might have been: The social psychology of counterfactual thinking* (pp. 283–304), N. J. Roese & J. M. Olson (Eds.). Mahwah, NJ: Lawrence Erlbaum Associates. **[21]**

Goldaper, S. (1990, June 9). Pistons put the game on the line. *The New York Times,* p. C46. **[21]**

Goldberg, J. H., Lerner, J. S., & Tetlock, P. E. (1999). Rage and reason: The psychology of the intuitive prosecutor. *European Journal of Social Psychology, 29,* 781–795. **[32]**

Goldberg, L. R. (1965). "Diagnosticians vs. diagnostic signs: The diagnosis of psychosis vs. neurosis from the MMPI," *Psychological Monographs, 79* (9, Whole No. 602). **[40]**

Goldberg, L. R. (1968). Simple models or simple processes? Some research on clinical judgment. *American Psychologist, 23,* 483–496. **[40, 41]**

Goldberg, L. R. (1970). Man versus model of man: A rationale, plus some evidence, for a method of improving on clinical inferences. *Psychological Bulletin, 73,* 422–432. **[40]**

Goldman, A. I. (1978). Epistemics: The regulative theory of cognition. *Journal of Philosophy, 55,* 509–523. **[24]**

Goldsmith, R. W. (1978). Assessing probabilities of compound events in a judicial context. *Scandinavian Journal of Psychology, 19,* 103–110. **[1]**

Goldstein, D. G., & Gigerenzer, G. (1996). Satisficing inference and the perks of ignorance. In *Proceedings of the Eighteenth Annual Conference of the Cognitive Science Society* (pp. 137–141), G. W. Cottrell (Ed.). Mahwah, NJ: Erlbaum. **[31]**

Goldstein, W. M. (1984). *The relationship between judgment and choice.* Unpublished Doctoral dissertation, University of Michigan, Ann Arbor. **[23]**

Goldstein, W. M., & Einhom, H. J. (1987). Expression theory and the preference reversal phenomena. *Psychological Review, 94,* 236–254. **[6, 12, 23]**

Gollwitzer, P. M. (1993). Goal achievement: The role of intentions. In *European review of social psychology* (Vol. 4, pp. 141–185), W. Stroebe & M. Hewstone (Eds.). London: John Wiley & Sons. **[16]**

Gollwitzer, P. M. (1999). Implementation intentions: Strong effects of simple plans. *American Psychologist, 54,* 493–503. **[14]**

Gollwitzer, P. M., & Brandstatter, V. (1997). Implementation intentions and effective goal pursuit. *Journal of Personality and Social Psychology, 73,* 186–199. **[14]**

Gollwitzer, P. M., Heckhausen, H., & Steller, B. (1990). Deliberative and implemental mindsets: Cognitive tuning toward congruous thoughts and information. *Journal of Personality and Social Psychology, 59,* 1119–1127. **[16]**

Gonzales, M., & Bonini, N. (1995). *Probability judgments in two-outcome situations: What induces a defect in complementarity?* Unpublished manuscript, Centre de Recherche en Psychologie Cognitive, University de Provence, Aix-en-Provence, France. **[26]**

Good, I. J. (1971). The probabilistic explication of information, evidence surprise, causality, explanation, and utility. In *Foundations of statistical inference: Proceedings on the foundations of statistical inference,* V. P. Godambe & D. A. Sprott (Eds.). Toronto, Ontario: Holt, Rinchart & Winston. **[1]**

Goodman-Delahunty, J., Granhag, P. A., & Loftus, E. F. (1998). *How well can lawyers predict their chances of success?* Unpublished manuscript, University of Washington. **[39]**

Gopnik, A., & Wellman, H. (1992). Why the child's theory of mind is really a theory. *Mind and Language, 7,* 145–171. **[8]**

Gough, P. B. (1965). Grammatical transformations and speed of understanding. *Journal of Verbal Learning and Verbal Behavior, 4,* 107–111. **[9]**

Gough, P. B. (1966). The verification of sentences: the effects of delay of evidence and sentence length. *Journal of Verbal Learning and Verbal Behavior, 5,* 492–496. **[9]**

Gould, S. J. (1991). *Bully for brontosaurus. Reflections in natural history.* New York: Norton. **[2, 22]**

Gould, S. J. (1995). *Dinosaur in a haystack: Reflections in natural history.* New York: Harmony Books. **[42]**

Gould, S. J. (1997). The pleasures of pluralism. *New York Review of Books*, June 26. **[Introduction]**

Grayson, C. E., & Schwarz, N. (1999). Beliefs influence information processing strategies: declarative and experiential information in risk assessment. *Social Cognition, 17*, 1–18. **[5]**

Green, A. E., & Bourne, A. J. (1972). *Reliability technology*. New York: Wiley. **[37]**

Green, D., Jacowitz, K. E., Kahneman, D., & McFadden, D. (1998). Referendum contingent valuation, anchoring, and willingness to pay for public goods. *Resource and Energy Economics, 20*, 85–116. **[6]**

Green, M., Visser, P., & Tetlock, P. E. (1999). Coping with accountability cross-pressures: Low-effort evasive tactics and high-effort quests for complex compromises. Unpublished manuscript, The Ohio State University. **[32]**

Greene, S. B., Gerrig, R. J., McKoon, G., & Ratcliff, R. (1994). Unheralded pronouns and management by common ground. *Journal of Memory and Language, 33*, 511–526. **[8]**

Greenwald, A. G. (1980). The totalitarian ego: Fabrication and revision of personal history. *American Psychologist, 35*, 603–618. **[16]**

Greenwald, A. G., & Banaji, M. R. (1995). Implicit social cognition: Attitudes, self-esteem, and stereotypes. *Psychological Review, 102*, 4–27. **[16]**

Greenwald, A. G., Carnot, C. G., Beach, R., & Young, B. (1987). Increasing voter behavior by asking people if the expect to vote. *Journal of Applied Psychology, 72*, 315–318. **[19]**

Greenwald, A. G., McGhee, D. E., & Schwartz, J. L. K. (1998). Measuring individual differences in implicit cognition: the Implicit Association Test. *Journal of Personality and Social Psychology, 74*, 1464–1480. **[10]**

Greenwald, A. G., Pratkanis, A. R., Leippe, M. R., & Baumgardner, M. H. (1986). Under what conditions does theory obstruct research progress? *Psychological Review, 93*, 216–229. **[40]**

Gregory, W. L., Cialdini, R. B., & Carpenter, K. M. (1982). Self-relevant scenarios as mediators of likelihood estimates and compliance: Does imagining make it so? *Journal of Personality and Social Psychology, 43*, 89–99. **[4, 17]**

Grether, D. M. (1980). Bayes' rule as a descriptive model: The representativeness heuristic. *The Quarterly Journal of Economics, 95*, 537–557. **[13]**

Grether, D. M. (1992). Testing Bayes' rule and the representativeness heuristic: Some experimental evidence. *Journal of Economic Behavior and Organization, 17*, 31–57. **[13]**

Grether, D. M., & Plott, C. R. (1979). Economic theory of choice and the preference reversal phenomenon. *American Economic Review, 69*, 623–638. **[Introduction, 12]**

Grice, H. P. (1975). Logic and conversation. In *Syntax and semantics*. Vol. 3. *Speech acts*, (pp. 41–58), P. Cole and J. L. Morgan (Eds.). New York: Academic Press. **[1, 6, 8, 20, 32]**

Griffin, D. W., & Buehler, R. (1999). Frequency, probability, and prediction: Easy solutions to cognitive illusions? *Cognitive Psychology, 38*, 48–78. **[Introduction, 14, 19]**

Griffin, D. W., Dunning, D., & Ross, L. (1990). The role of construal processes in overconfident predictions about the self and others. *Journal of Personality and Social Psychology, 59*, 1128–1139. **[14, 16]**

Griffin, D. W., Gonzalez, R., & Varey, C. (2001). *The heuristics and biases approach to judgment under uncertainty*. In *Blackwell handbook of social psychology: Intrapersonal processes*, N. Schwarz & A. Tesser (Eds.). Oxford, U.K.: Blackwell Publishers. **[8, 27, 34, 39]**

Griffin, D. W., & Kahneman, D. (in press). Judgmental heuristics: Human strength or human weakness? In *The Psychology of Human Strengths* (pp. 319–359), L. Aspinwall & U. Staudinger (Eds.). APA Books. **[Introduction]**

Griffin, D. W., & Ross, L. (1991). Subjective construal, social inference and human misunderstanding. In *Advances in Experimental Social Psychology* (Vol. 21, pp. 319–359), M. P. Zanna (Ed.). New York: Academic Press. **[Introduction, 8, 16, 42]**

Griffin, D. W., & Tversky, A. (1992). The weighing of evidence and the determinants of confidence. *Cognitive Psychology, 24,* 411–435. **[Introduction, 2, 6, 8, 14, 15, 27, 39]**

Griffin, D., & Varey, C. (1996). Towards a consensus on overconfidence. *Organizational Behavior and Human Decision Processes, 65,* 227–231. **[39]**

Griffith, R. M. (1949). Odds adjustments by American horse-race bettors. *American Journal of Psychology, 62,* 290–294. **[13]**

Griffth, R. W., & Rogers, R. W. (1976). Effects of fear-arousing components of driver education on students' safety attitudes and simulator performance. *Journal of Educational Psychology, 68,* 501–506. **[17]**

Griggs, R. A., & Cox, J. R. (1982). The elusive thematic-materials effect in Wason's selection task. *British Journal of Psychology, 73,* 407–420. **[24]**

Griggs, R. A., & Cox, J. R. (1983). The effects of problem content and negation on Wason's selection task. *Quarterly Journal of Experimental Psychology, 35,* 519–533. **[24]**

Grove, W. M., & Meehl, P. E. (1996). Comparative efficiency of informal (subjective, impressionistic) and formal (mechanical, algorithmic) prediction procedures: The clinical/statistical controversy. *Psychology, Public Policy, and Law, 2,* 1–31. **[40]**

Grove, W. M., Zald, D. H., Lebow, B. S., Snitz, B. E., & Nelson, C. (2000). Clinical vs. mechanical prediction: A meta-analysis. *Psychological Assessment, 12,* 19–30. **[40]**

Guilmette, T. J., Faust, D., Hart, K., & Arkes, H. R. (1990). A national survey of psychologists who offer neuropsychological services. *Archives of Clinical Neuropsychology, 5,* 373–392. **[40]**

Gunther, A. C. (1995). Overrating the X-rating: The third-person perception and support for censorship of pornography. *Journal of Communication, 45,* 26–39. **[36]**

Gur, R. C., & Sackheim, H. A. (1979). Self-deception: A concept in search of a phenomenon. *Journal of Personality and Social Psychology, 37,* 147–169. **[16]**

Gärdenfors, P., & Sahlin, N. E. (Eds.). (1989). *Decision, probability and utility.* Cambridge: Cambridge University Press. **[41]**

Haddock, G., Rothman, A. J., Reber, R., & Schwarz, N. (1999). Forming judgments of attitude certainty, importance, and intensity: the role of subjective experiences. *Personality and Social Psychology Bulletin, 25,* 771–782. **[5]**

Hagafors, R., & Brehmer, B. (1983). Does having to justify one's judgments change the nature of the judgment process? *Organizational Behavior and Human Performance, 31,* 223–232. **[32]**

Haidt, J., Koller, S., & Dias, M. (1993). Affect, culture, and morality: Or, is it wrong to eat your dog? *Journal of Personality and Social Psychology, 65,* 613–628. **[11]**

Haidt, J., McCauley, C. R., & Rozin, P. (1994). A scale to measure disgust sensitivity. *Personality and Individual Differences, 16,* 701–713. **[11]**

Hakmiller, K. L. (1966). Threat as a determinant of downward comparison. *Journal of Experimental Social Psychology,* Supplement 1, 32–39. **[17]**

Halbower, C. C. (1955). A comparison of actuarial vs. clinical prediction to classes discriminated by the Minnesota multiphasic personality inventory. Unpublished Doctoral Dissertation, University of Minnesota. **[40]**

Hall, P. (1980). *Great planning disasters.* London: Weidenfeld & Nicolson. **[14]**

Hallenback, C. (1920). Forecasting precipitation in percentages of probability. *Monthly Weather Review,* 645–647. **[39]**

References 795

Hamer, C. (1981). "Good-fishin!" (2nd ed.). St. Paul, MN: P. F., Inc. **[28]**

Hammond (1996). *Human Judgment and Social Policy: Irreducible Uncertainty, Inevitable Error, Unavoidable Injustice*. New York: Oxford. **[2, 39]**

Hammond, K. R. (1955). Probabilistic functioning and the clinical method. *Psychological Review, 62*, 255–262. **[2]**

Hammond, K. R., & Brehmer, B. (1973). Quasi-rationality and distrust: Implications for international conflict. In *Human judgment and social interaction*, L. Rappoport & D. A. Summers (Eds.). New York: Holt, Rinehart & Winston. **[1]**

Hammond, K., Hursch, C., & Todd, F. (1964). Analyzing the components of Clinical Inference. *Psychological Review, 71*, 438. **[39]**

Hammond, K. R., & Summers, D. A. (1965). Cognitive dependence on linear and nonlinear cues. *Psychological Review, 72*, 215–224. **[40]**

Hampson, S. E., John, O. P., & Goldberg. L. R. (1986). Category breadth and hierarchical structure in personality: Studies of asymmetries in judgments of trait implications. *Journal of Personality and Social Psychology, 51*, 37–54. **[18]**

Hansen, R. D., & Donoghue, J. M. (1977). The power of consensus: Information derived from one's own and other's behavior. *Journal of Personality and Social Psychology, 35*, 294–302. **[20]**

Hanslin, J. M. (1967). Craps and magic. *American Journal of Sociology, 73*, 316–330. **[34]**

Hanson, J. D., & Kysar, D. A. (1999a). Taking behavioralism seriously: Some evidence of market manipulation. *Harvard Law Review, 112*(7), 1420–1572. **[23, 41]**

Hanson, J. D., & Kysar, D. A. (1999b). Taking behavioralism seriously: The problem of market manipulation. *New York University Law Review, 74*(3), 630–749. **[23, 41]**

Hanson, J. D., & Kysar, D. A. (2001). The joint failure of economic theory and legal regulation. In *Smoking: Risk, perception, and policy* (pp. 229–276), P. Slovic (Ed.). Thousand Oaks, CA: Sage. **[23]**

Harari, H., & McDavid, J. W. (1973). Name stereotypes and teachers' expectations. *Journal of Educational Psychology, 65*, 222–225. **[23]**

Hare, R. D. (1965). Psychopathy, fear arousal and anticipated pain. *Psychological Reports, 16*, 499–502. **[23]**

Harman, G. (1995). Rationality. In *Thinking* (Vol. 3, pp. 175–211), E. E. Smith & D. N. Osherson (Eds.). Cambridge, MA: MIT Press. **[24]**

Harris, W., & Joyce, M. A. (1980). What's fair? It depends on how you ask the question. *Journal of Personality and Social Psychology, 38*, 165–170. **[30]**

Hart, H. L. A., & Honore, A. M. (1959). *Causation in the law*. London: Oxford University Press. **[20]**

Hartman, R. S., Doane, M. J., & Woo, C. K. (1991). Consumer rationality and the status quo. *Quarterly Journal of Economics, 106*(1), 142–162. **[30]**

Harvey, L. O., Jr., Hammond, K. R., Lusk, C. M., & Mross, E. F. (1992). Application of signal detection theory to weather forecasting behavior. *Monthly Weather Review, 120*, 863–883. **[39]**

Harvey, N. (1997). Confidence in judgment. *Trends in Cognitive Sciences, 1*, 78–82. **[27]**

Hasher, L., & Zacks, R. T. (1979). Automatic and effortful processes in memory. *Journal of Experimental Psychology: General, 108*, 356–388. **[9, 41]**

Hastie, R. (1984). Causes and effects of causal attribution. *Journal of Personality and Social Psychology, 46*, 44–56. **[20]**

Hastie, R., & Kumar, R. A. (1979). Person memory: Personality traits as organizing principles in memory for behaviors. *Journal of Personality and Social Psychology, 37,* 25–38. **[20]**

Hastorf, A., & Cantril, H. (1954). They saw a game: A case study. *Journal of Abnormal and Social Psychology, 49,* 129–134. **[36]**

Hausch, D. B., Ziemba, W. T., & Rubinstein, M. (1981). Efficiency of the market for racetrack betting. *Management Science, 27,* 1435–1452. **[13]**

Hawkins, S. A., & Hastie, R. (1990). Hindsight: biased judgment of past events after the outcomes are known. *Psychological Bulletin, 107,* 311–327. **[5, 6, 7]**

Hayes, R. M. (1998). The impact of trading commission incentives on analysts' stock coverage decisions and earnings forecasts. *Journal of Accounting Research, 36,* 299–320. **[38]**

Haynes, R. B., Taylor, D. W., & Sackett, D. L. (1979). *Compliance in health care.* Baltimore: Johns Hopkins University Press. **[4]**

Heath, C. (1999). On the social psychology of agency relationships: Lay theories of motivation overemphasize extrinsic incentives. *Organizational Behavior and Human Decision Processes, 78,* 25–62. **[36]**

Heath, C., Larrick, R. P., & Wu, G. (1999). Goals as reference points. *Cognitive Psychology, 38,* 79–109. **[14]**

Heath, F., & Tversky, A. (1991). Preference and belief: Ambiguity and competence in choice under uncertainty. *Journal of Risk and Uncertainty, 4,* 5–28. **[13]**

Heider, F. (1958). *The psychology of interpersonal relations,* New York: Wiley. **[Introduction, 9, 20]**

Heider, F. (1994). Social perception and phenomenal causality. *Psychological Review, 51,* 358–374. **[2]**

Heine, S., & Lehman, D. (1995). Cultural variation in unrealistic optimism: Does the West feel more invulnerable than the East? *Journal of Personality and Social Psychology, 68,* 595–607. **[14]**

Hejmadi, A., Rozin, P., & Siegal, M. (2000). Development of the concept of contagious essence in Indian and American children. Unpublished manuscript. **[11]**

Helmholtz, H. von (1903). *Popular lectures on scientific subjects* (E. Atkinson, trans.). New York: Green. (Originally published 1881.) **[1]**

Helmreich, W. B. (1992). *Against all odds: Holocaust survivors and the successful lives they made in America.* New York: Simon & Schuster. **[16]**

Helson, H. (1964). *Adaptation level theory: An experimental and systematic approach to behavior.* New York: Harper. **[20]**

Hempel, C. (1965). *Aspects of scientific explanation and other essays in the philosophy of science.* New York: Free Press. **[42]**

Hendrickx, L., Vlek, C., & Oppewal, H. (1989). Relative importance of scenario information and frequency information in the judgment of risk. *Acta Psychologica, 72,* 41–63. **[23]**

Henle, M. (1962). On the relation between logic and thinking. *Psychological Review, 69,* 366–378. **[24]**

Henrion, M. (1982). *The value of knowing how little you know: The advantages of a probabilistic approach to uncertainty in policy analysis.* Doctoral dissertation, Carnegie Mellon University. **[41]**

Herrnstein, R. J. (1990). Rational choice theory. *American Psychologist, 45,* 356–367. **[16]**

Herrnstein, R. J. (1969). Method and theory in the study of avoidance. *Psychological Review, 76,* 49–69. **[16]**

Hershey, J. C., & Schoemaker, P. J. H. (1985). Probability versus certainty equivalence methods in utility measurement: are they equivalent? *Management Science, 31,* 1213–1231. **[6, 8]**

Hertel, G., Neuhof, J., Theuer, T., & Kerr, N. L. (2000). Mood effects on cooperation in small groups: Does positive mood simply lead to more cooperation? *Cognition and Emotion, 14,* 441–472. **[29]**

Hertwig, R., & Gigerenzer, G. (1999). The "conjunction fallacy" revisited: How intelligent inferences look like reasoning errors. *Journal of Behavioral Decision Making, 12*(4), 275–305. **[2]**

Heuer, R. J. (1999). *The psychology of intelligence analysis.* Langley, VA: Center for the Study of Intelligence. **[41]**

Higgins, E. T. (1996). Knowledge: Accessibility, applicability, and salience. In *Social psychology: handbook of basic principles* (pp. 133–168), E. T. Higgins & A. Kruglanski (Eds.). New York: Guilford. **[5]**

Higgins, E. T., King, G. A., & Mavin, G. H. (1982). Individual construct accessibility and subjective impressions and recall. *Journal of Personality and Social Psychology, 43,* 35–47. **[Introduction]**

Higgins, E. T., & Brendl, C. M. (1995). Accessibility and applicability: Some "activation rules" influencing judgment. *Journal of Experimental Social Psychology, 31,* 218–243. **[2]**

Higgins, E. T., Rholes, W. S., & Jones, C. R. (1977). Category accessibility and impression formation. *Journal of Experimental Social Psychology, 13,* 141–154. **[Introduction]**

Higgins, E. T., & King, G. (1981). Accessibility of social constructs: Information-processing consequences of individual and contextual variability. In *Personality, cognition and social interaction* (pp. 69–121), N. Cantor & J. F. Kihlstrom (Eds.). Hillsdale, NJ: Erlbaum. **[20]**

Higgins, E. T., & Lurie, L. (1983). Context, categorization, and memory: The "change-of-standard" effect. *Cognitive Psychology, 15,* 525–547. **[20]**

Hilton, D. J. (1995). The social context of reasoning: Conversational inference and rational judgment. *Psychological Bulletin, 118,* 248–271. **[24]**

Hilton, D. J., & Slugoski, B. R. (1986). Knowledge-based causal attribution: The abnormal conditions focus model. *Psychological Review, 93,* 75–88. **[9]**

Hilton, D. J., & Slugoski, B. R. (2001). Conversational processes in reasoning and explanation. In *Blackwell handbook of social psychology. Vol. 1: Intraindividual processes,* (pp. 181–206), A. Tesser & N. Schwarz (Eds.). Oxford, U.K.: Blackwell. **[2]**

Hinds, P. J. (1999). The curse of expertise: The effects of expertise and debiasing methods on prediction of novice performance. *Journal of Experimental Psychology: Applied, 5,* 205–221. **[36]**

Hinton, G. E. (1990). Mapping part-whole hierarchies into connectionist networks. *Artificial Intelligence, 46,* 47–76. **[22]**

Hintzman, D. (1976). Repetition and memory. In *The psychology of learning and motivation* (Vol. 10, pp. 47–91), G. H. Bower (Ed.). New York: Academic Press. **[41]**

Hintzman, D. L. (1986). "Schema abstraction" in a multiple-trace memory model. *Psychological Review, 93*(4), 411–428. **[20]**

Hintzman, D. L., & Ludlam, G. (1980). Differential forgetting of prototypes and old instances: Simulation by an exemplar-based classification model. *Memory and Cognition, 8,* 378–382. **[20]**

Hiroto, D. S., & Seligman, M. E. P. (1975). Generality of learned helplessness in man. *Journal of Personality and Social Psychology, 31,* 311–327. **[19]**

Hirshleifer, D., & Shumway, T. (2001). *Good day sunshine: Stock returns and the weather.* Unpublished manuscript, Ohio State University. **[29]**

Hirt, E. R., & Markman, K. D. (1995). Multiple explanation: a consider-an-alternative strategy for debiasing judgments. *Journal of Personality and Social Psychology, 69,* 1069–1086. **[10]**

Hoch, S. J. (1984). Availability and inference in predictive judgment. *Journal of Experimental Psychology: Learning, Memory, and Cognition, 10,* 649–662. **[14, 17]**

Hoch, S. J. (1985). Counterfactual reasoning and accuracy in predicting personal events. *Journal of Experimental Psychology: Learning, Memory, and Cognition, 11,* 719–731. **[14, 19, 39]**

Hofstadter, D. R. (1979). *Godel, Escher, Bach: An eternal golden braid.* New York: Basic Books. **[20]**

Hofstadter, D. R. (1985). *Metamagical themas: Questing for the essence of mind and pattern.* New York: Basic Books. **[20]**

Hogarth, R. M. (1980). *Judgement and choice.* New York: Wiley. **[28]**

Hogarth, R. M., & Einhorn, H. J. (1992). Order effects in belief updating: the belief-adjustment model. *Cognitive Psychology, 24,* 1–55. **[6]**

Hogarth, R., & Makridakis, S. (1981). Beyond discrete biases: Functional and dysfunctional aspect of judgmental heuristics. *Psychology Bulletin, 90,* 115–137. **[39]**

Hoorens, V. (1995). Self-favoring biases, self-presentation, and the self-other asymmetry in social comparison. *Journal of Personality, 63,* 793–813. **[27]**

Hoorens, V., & Ruiter, S. (1996). The optimal impact phenomenon: Beyond the third person effect. *European Journal of Social Psychology, 26,* 599–619. **[36]**

Hoosain, R. (1986). Perceptual processes of the Chinese. In *The psychology of the Chinese people* (pp. 38–72), M. H. Bond (Ed.), Hong Kong: Oxford University Press. **[15]**

Horton, W. S., & Keysar, B. (1996). When do speakers take into account common ground? *Cognition, 59,* 91–117. **[8]**

House Subcommittee on Health and Long-Term Care (1984). *Quackery: A $10 billion scandal: A report by the chairman of the Subcommittee on Health and Long-Term Care.* Washington, DC: United States Government Printing Office. **[34]**

Howard, R. A. (1989). Knowledge maps. *Mananagement Science, 35,* 903–922. **[41]**

Howe, E. (1970). Astrology. In *Man, myth, & magic: An illustrated encyclopedia of the supernatural* (pp. 149–153), R. Cavendish (Ed.). New York: Marshall Cavendish Corporation. **[34]**

Hsee, C. K. (1995). Elastic justification: How tempting but task-irrelevant factors influence decisions. *Organizational Behavior and Human Decision Processes, 62,* 330–337. **[23]**

Hsee, C. K. (1996a). Elastic justification: How unjustifiable factors influence judgments. *Organizational Behavior and Human Decision Processes, 66,* 122–129. **[23]**

Hsee, C. K. (1996b). The evaluability hypothesis: An explanation for preference reversals between joint and separate evaluations of alternatives. *Organizational Behavior and Human Decision Processes, 67,* 242–257. **[23]**

Hsee, C. K. (1998). Less is better: When low-value options are valued more highly than high-value options. *Journal of Behavioral Decision Making, 11,* 107–121. **[23]**

Hsee, C. K., & Kunreuther, H. (2000). The affection effect in insurance decisions. *Journal of Risk and Uncertainty, 20,* 141–159. **[23]**

Hsee, C. K., & Menon, S. (1999). *Affection effect in consumer choices.* Unpublished study, University of Chicago. **[23]**

Hume, D. (1955). *An inquiry concerning human understanding.* Indianapolis, IN: Bobbs-Merrill. (Originally published 1748) **[28]**

Hunter, J. E., & Hunter, R. F. (1984). The validity and utility of alternative predictors of job performance. *Psychological Bulletin, 96,* 72–98. **[10]**

Huntley, J. (1990). *The elements of astrology*. Shaftesbury, Dorset, U.K.: Element Books Limited. [34]

Hurd, M., McFadden, D., Chand, H., Gan, L., Merrill, A., & Roberts, M. (1997). Consumption and savings balances of the elderly: Experimental evidence on survey response data. Paper presented at the National Bureau of Economics Research Conference on the Economics of Aging, April, 1997. [6]

Hynes, M., & Vanmarcke, E. (1976). Reliability of Embankment Performance Prediction. *Paper presented at the ASCE Engineering Mechanics Division Specialty Conference*, Waterloo, Ontario, Canada. [37]

Ichheiser, G. (1949). Misunderstandings in human relations: A study in false social perception. *American Journal of Sociology, 55* (Suppl.). [36]

Imada, S., Haidt, J., McCauley, C. R., & Rozin, P. (2000). Disgust sensitivity in Japan. (Unpublished data). [11]

Inhelder, B., & Piaget, J. (1958). *The growth of logical thinking from childhood to adolescence*. New York: Basic Books. [36]

Innes, J. M., & Zeitz, H. (1988). The public's view of the impact of the mass media: A test of the "third person" effect. *European Journal of Social Psychology, 18*, 457–463. [36]

Institute of Medicine. (1999). *Adolescent decision making*. Washington, DC: National Academy Press. [41]

Irwin, F. W. (1953). Stated expectations as functions of probability and desirability of outcomes. *Journal of Personality, 21*, 329–335. [19]

Isaacs, E. A., & Clark, H. H. (1987). References in conversation between experts and novices. *Journal of Experimental Psychology: General, 116*, 26–37. [8]

Isen, A. M. (1984). Toward understanding the role of affect in cognition. In *Handbook of social cognition* (Vol. 3, pp. 179–236), R. S. Wyer, Jr., & T. K. Srull (Eds.). Hillsdale, NJ: Erlbaum. [29]

Isen, A. M. (1987). Positive affect, cognitive processes, and social behavior. In *Advances in experimental social psychology* (Vol. 20, pp. 203–253), L. Berkowitz (Ed.). New York: Academic Press. [16, 29]

Isen, A. M. (1993). Positive affect and decision making. In Handbook of emotions (pp. 261–277), M. Lewis, & J. M. Haviland (Eds.). New York: Guilford Press. [23]

Isen, A. M., Nygren, T. E., & Ashby, F. G. (1988). Influence of positive affect on the subjective utility of gains and losses – it is just not worth the risk. *Journal of Personality and Social Psychology, 55*(5), 710–717. [2]

Isen, A. M., Shalker, T. E., Clark, M. S., & Karp, L. (1978). Affect, accessibility of material in memory, and behavior: A cognitive loop? *Journal of Personality and Social Psychology, 36*, 1–12. [29]

Izard, C. E. (1990). Facial expressions and the regulation of emotions. *Journal of Personality and Social Psychology, 58*, 487–498. [5]

Jacoby, L. L., & Brooks, L. R. (1984). Nonanalytic cognition: Memory, perception, and concept learning. In *The psychology of learning and motivation: Advances in research and theory* (Vol. 18, pp. 1–47), G. H. Bower (Ed.). New York: Academic Press. [20]

Jacoby, L. L., & Dallas, M. (1981). On the relationship between autobiographical memory and perceptual learning. *Journal of Experimental Psychology: General, 3*, 306–340. [2]

Jacowitz, K. E., & Kahneman, D. (1995). Measures of anchoring in estimation tasks. *Personality and Social Psychology Bulletin, 21*, 1161–1167. [6, 7]

James, W. (1890/1950). *The principles of psychology*. New York: Dover Publications. [22, 32]

James, W. (1892). *Psychology*. New York: Holt. **[35]**

James, W. (1897). *The will to believe and other essays in popular philosophy*. New York: Longman, Green. **[10]**

Janis, I. J., & Mann, L. (1977). *Decision making: A psychological analysis of conflict, choice, and commitment*. New York: Free Press. **[21, 32]**

Janoff-Bulman, R., & Brickman, P. (1982). Expectations and what people learn from failure. In *Expectations and actions: Expectancy-value models in psychology* (pp. 207–237), N. T. Feather (Ed.). Hillsdale, NJ: Erlbaum. **[19]**

Jenni, K. E., & Loewenstein, G. (1997). Explaining the "identifiable victim effect." *Journal of Risk and Uncertainty, 14*(3), 235–258. **[23]**

Jennings, D., Amabile, T., & Ross, L. (1982). Informal covariation assessment. In *Judgment under uncertainty: Heuristics and biases*, D. Kahneman, P. Slovic, & A. Tversky (Eds.). New York: Cambridge University Press. **[1]**

Jepson, C., Krantz, D. H., & Nisbett, R. E. (1983). Inductive reasoning: Competence or skill? *Behavioral and Brain Sciences, 6*, 494–501. **[28]**

Jervis, R. (1976). *Perception and misperception in international politics*. Princeton, NJ: Princeton University Press. **[8, 42]**

Jervis, R. (1992). The future of international politics: Will it resemble the past? *International Security, 16*, 39–73. **[42]**

John, R. S., Edwards, W., & Winterfeldt, D. von (n.d.). *Equal weights, flat maxima, and trivial decisions*. Research Report 80-2. Social Science Research Institute, University of Southern California. **[31]**

Johnson, E. J., Hershey, J., Meszaros, J., & Kunreuther, H. (1993). Framing, probability distortions, and insurance decisions. *Journal of Risk and Uncertainty, 7*, 35–51. **[25, 27, 30]**

Johnson, E. J., & Schkade, D. A. (1989). Bias in utility assessments: Further evidence and explanations. *Management Science, 35*, 406–424. **[6]**

Johnson, E. J., & Tversky, A. (1983). Affect generalization and the perception of risk. *Journal of Personality and Social Psychology, 45*, 20–31. **[21, 23, 29]**

Johnson, J. T. (1986). The knowledge of what might have been: Affective and attributional consequences of near outcomes. *Personality and Social Psychology Bulletin, 12*, 51–62. **[35]**

Johnson, M. (1987). *The body in the mind. The bodily basis of meaning, imagination, and reason*. Chicago: University of Chicago Press. **[11]**

Johnson, M. K., & Sherman, S. J. (1990). Constructing and reconstructing the past and the future in the present. In *Handbook of motivation and social cognition: Foundations of social behavior* (Vol. 2, pp. 482–526), E. T. Higgins & R. M. Sorrentino (Eds.). New York: Guilford Press. **[14]**

Johnson-Laird, P. N. (1983). *Mental models*. Cambridge, MA: Harvard University Press. **[22, 41]**

Johnson-Laird, P. N., & Byrne, R. M. J. (1991). *Deduction*. Hillsdale, NJ: Erlbaum. **[22]**

Johnson-Laird, P. N., & Wason, P. C. (1977). A theoretical analysis of insight into a reasoning task. In *Thinking*, P. N. Johnson-Laird & P. C. Wason (Eds.). Cambridge, U.K.: Cambridge University Press. **[1]**

Jones, B. B., & McGillis, D. (1976). Correspondent inference and the attribution cube: A comparative appraisal. In *New directions in attribution research* (Vol. 1, pp. 389–420), J. Harvey, W. Ickes, & R. Kidd (Eds.). Hillsdale, NJ: Erlbaum. **[20]**

Jones, E. E. (1979). The rocky road from acts to dispositions. *American Psychologist, 34*, 107–117. **[20, 36]**

Jones, E. E. (1990). *Interpersonal Perception*. New York: W. H. Freeman & Co., Publishers. [36]

Jones, E. E., & Davis, K. E. (1965). From acts to dispositions: The attribution process in person perception. In *Advances in experimental social psychology* (Vol. 2, pp. 219–266), L. Berkowitz (Ed.). New York: Academic Press. [9]

Jones, E. E., & Gerard, H. B. (1967). *Foundations of social psychology*. New York: Wiley. [16]

Jones, E. E., & Harris, V. A. (1967). The attribution of attitudes. *Journal of Experimental Social Psychology, 3*, 1–24. [9, 20]

Jones, E. E., & Nisbett, R. E. (1972). *The actor and the observer: Divergent perceptions of the causes of behavior*. In *Attribution: Perceiving the causes of behavior* (pp. 79–94), E. E. Jones, D. E. Kanouse, H. H. Kelley, R. E. Nisbett, S. Valins, & B. Weiner (Eds.). Morristown, NJ: General Learning Press. [13, 14, 20, 36]

Jones, E. E., Rhodewalt, F., Berglas, S. C., & Skelton, A. (1981). Effects of strategic self-presentation on subsequent self-esteem. *Journal of Personality and Social Psychology, 41*, 407–421. [9]

Jones, G. V. (1982). Stacks not fuzzy sets: An ordinal basis for prototype theory of concepts. *Cognition, 12*, 281–290. [1]

Jonides, J., & Naveh-Benjamin, M. (1987). Estimating frequency of occurrence. *Journal of Experimental Psychology: Learning, Memory* & Cognition, 13, 230–240. [41]

Joseph, J. G., Montgomery, S., B., Emmons, C. A., Kirscht, J. P., Kessler, R. C., Ostrow, D. G., Wortman, C. B., O'Brien, K., Eller, M., & Eshelman, S. (1987). Perceived risk of AIDS: Assessing the behavioral and psychological consequences in a cohort of gay men. *Journal of Applied Social Psychology, 17*, 231–250. [19]

Jungermann, H. (1986). The two camps on rationality. In *Judgment and decision making* (pp. 627–641), H. R. Arkes & K. R. Hammond (Eds.). Cambridge, U.K.: Cambridge University Press. [24]

Juslin, P. (1994). The overconfidence phenomenon as a consequence of informal experimenter guided selection of almanac items. *Organizational Behavior and Human Decision Processes, 57*, 226–246. [39]

Juslin, P., Olsson, H., & Björkman, M. (1997). Brunswikian and Thurstonian origins of bias in probability assessment: On the interpretation of stochastic components of judgment. *Journal of Behavioral Decision Making, 10*, 189–209. [39]

Juslin, P., Wennerholm, P., & Olsson, H. (1999). Format dependence in subjective probability calibration. *Journal of Experimental Psychology: Learning, Memory, and Cognition, 25*, 1038–1052. [39]

Kahana, E., Kahana, B., Harel, Z., Rosner, T. (1988). Coping with extreme trauma. In *Human adaptation to extreme stress: From the Holocaust to Vietnam* (pp. 55–79), J. P. Wilson, Z. Harel, & B. Kahana (Eds.), New York: Plenum. [16]

Kahneman, D. (1973). *Attention and effort*. Englewood-Cliffs, NJ: Prentice-Hall. [9]

Kahneman, D. (1981). Who shall be the arbiter of our intuitions? *Behavioral and Brain Sciences, 4*, 339–340. [24]

Kahneman, D. (1986). Valuing environmental goods: An assessment of the contingent valuation method. In *Valuing environmental goods: An assessment of the contingent valuation method*, R. Cummings, D. Brookshire, & W. Schulze (Eds.). Totowa, NJ: Rowman and Allanheld. [2]

Kahneman, D. (1991). Judgment and decision making: A person view. *Psychological Science, 2*, 142–145. [34]

Kahneman, D. (1992). Reference points, anchors, norms, and mixed feelings. *Organizational Behavior and Human Decision Processes, 51*, 296–312. [6]

Kahneman, D. (1995). Varieties of counterfactual thinking. In *What might have been: The social psychology of counterfactual thinking* (pp. 375–396), N. Roese & J. Olson (Eds.). Hillsdale, NJ: Erlbaum. **[35]**

Kahneman, D. (1997). New challenges to the rationality assumption. *Legal Theory, 3,* 105–124. **[23]**

Kahneman, D. (2000a). Evaluation by moments: Past and future. In *Choices, values, & Frames,* D. Kahneman & A. Tversky (Eds.). Cambridge, U.K.: Cambridge University Press. **[30]**

Kahneman, D. (2000b). Experienced utility and objective happiness: a moment-based approach. Ch. 37 in Kahneman, D., & Tversky, A. (Eds.) *Choices, Values, and Frames.* New York: Cambridge University Press and the Russell Sage Foundation. **[2]**

Kahneman, D. (2000c). A psychological point of view: Violations of rational rules as a diagnostic of mental processes (Commentary on Stanovich and West). *Behavioral and Brain Sciences, 23,* 681–683. **[2]**

Kahneman, D., Fredrickson, B. L., Schreiber, C. A., & Redelemeier, D. A. (1993). When more pain is preferred to less: Adding a better end. *Psychological Science, 4,* 401–405. **[2, 30]**

Kahneman, D., & Knetsch, J. (1993). Anchoring or shallow inferences: The effect of format. Unpublished manuscript, University of California, Berkeley. **[6]**

Kahneman, D., Knetsch, J. L., & Thaler, R. H. (1991). The endowment effect, loss aversion, and status quo bias. *Journal of Economic Perspectives, 5,* 193–206. **[27, 36]**

Kahneman, D., & Lovallo, D. (1993). Timid choices and bold forecasts. A cognitive perspective on risk taking. *Management Science, 39,* 17–31. **[13, 14, 36, 39]**

Kahneman, D. T., & Miller, D. (1986). Norm theory: Comparing reality to its alternatives. *Psychological Review, 93,* 136–153. **[2, 19, 21, 23, 35]**

Kahneman, D., & Ritov, I. (1994). Determinants of stated willingness to pay for public goods: a study in the headline method. *Journal of Risk and Uncertainty, 9,* 5–38. **[2, 23]**

Kahneman, D., Ritov, I., & Schkade, D. (1999). Economic preferences or attitude expressions? An analysis of dollar responses to public issues. *Journal of Risk and Uncertainty, 19,* 203–235. **[2]**

Kahneman, D., Schkade, D. A., & Sunstein, C. R. (1998). Shared outrage and erratic awards: the psychology of punitive damages. *Journal of Risk and Uncertainty, 16,* 49–86. **[2, 23]**

Kahneman, D., Slovic, P., & Tversky, A. (1982). *Judgment under Uncertainty: Heuristics and biases.* Cambridge, U.K.: Cambridge University Press. **[Introduction, 1, 2, 8, 11, 13, 23, 24, 25, 26, 27, 28, 33, 37]**

Kahneman, D., & Snell, J. (1990). Predicting utility. In *Insights in decision making* (pp. 295–310), R. Hogarth (Ed.). Chicago: University of Chicago Press. **[16]**

Kahneman, D., & Snell, J. (1992). Predicting a change in taste: Do people know what they will like? *Journal of Behavioral Decision Making, 5,* 187–200. **[14, 16, 23]**

Kahneman, D., & Tversky A. (1972). Subjective probability: A judgment of representativeness. *Cognitive Psychology, 3,* 430–454. **[1, 2, 3, 4, 11, 13, 28]**

Kahneman, D., & Tversky, A. (1973). On the psychology of prediction. *Psychological Review, 80,* 237–251. **[1, 2, 3, 13, 20, 28, 36, 38, 39]**

Kahneman, D., & Tversky, A. (1979a). Intuitive prediction: Biases and corrective procedures. *TIMS Studies in Management Science, 12,* 313–327. **[14, 19, 25]**

Kahneman, D., & Tversky, A. (1979b). Prospect theory: An analysis of decision under risk. *Econometrica, 47,* 263–291. **[11, 16, 27, 32, 36, 41]**

Kahneman, D., & Tversky, A (1982). On the study of statistical intuitions. *Cognition, 11*, 123–141. **[Introduction, 1, 2, 27, 28]**

Kahneman, D., & Tversky, A. (1982a). Intuitive prediction: Biases and corrective procedures. In *Judgment under uncertainty: Heuristics and biases* (pp. 414–421), D. Kahneman, P. Slovic, & A. Tversky (Eds.). Cambridge, U.K.: Cambridge University Press. **[13]**

Kahneman, D., & Tversky, A. (1982b). The psychology of preferences. *Scientific American, 246*(1), 160–173. **[21, 35]**

Kahneman, D., & Tversky, A. (1982). The simulation heuristic. In *Judgment under uncertainty: Heuristics and biases* (pp. 201–208), D. Kahneman, P. Slovic, & A. Tversky (Eds.). Cambridge, U.K.: Cambridge University Press. **[14, 19, 20, 21, 35]**

Kahneman, D., & Tversky, A. (1982c). Variants of uncertainty. *Cognition, 11*, 143–157. **[1, 14, 25]**

Kahneman, D., & Tversky, A. (1982d). Variants of uncertainty. In *Judgment under uncertainty: Heuristics and biases* (pp. 509–520), D. Kahneman, P. Slovic, & A. Tversky (Eds.). Cambridge, U.K.: Cambridge University Press. **[Introduction]**

Kahneman, D., & Tversky, A. (1983). Can irrationality be intelligently discussed? *Behavioral and Brain Sciences, 6*, 509–510. **[24]**

Kahneman, D., & Tversky, A. (1984). Choices, values, and frames. *American Psychologist, 39*, 341–350. **[11, 36, 40]**

Kahneman, D., & Tversky, A. (1995). Conflict resolution: A cognitive perspective. In *Barriers to Conflict Resolution*, K. Arrow et al. (Eds.). Chapter 3. New York: Norton. **[39]**

Kahneman, D., & Tversky, A. (1996). On the reality of cognitive illusions. *Psychological Review, 103*, 582–591. **[2, 24]**

Kahneman, D., & Varey, C. A. (1990). Propensities and counterfactuals: The loser that almost won. *Journal of Personality and Social Psychology, 59*(6), 1101–1110. **[Introduction, 2]**

Kahneman, D., Wakker, P. P., & Sarin, R. (1997). Back to Bentham? Explorations of experienced utility. *Quarterly Journal of Economics, 112*, 375–405. **[2]**

Kammann, R., & Flett, R. (1983). Affectometer 2: A scale to measure current level of general happiness. *Australian Journal of Psychology, 35*, 257–265. **[16]**

Kammen, D., & Hassendzahl, D. (1999). *Shall we risk it?* Princeton, NJ: Princeton University Press. **[41]**

Kang, S.-H., O'Brien, J., & Sivaramakrishnan, K. (1994). Analysts' interim earnings forecasts: Evidence on the forecasting process. *Journal of Accounting Research, 32*, 103–112. **[38]**

Katz, D. (1960). The functional approach to the study of attitudes. *Public Opinion Quarterly, 24*, 163–204. **[36]**

Keane, M. P., & Runkle, D. E. (1998). Are financial analysts' forecasts of corporate profits rational? *Journal of Political Economy, 106*, 768–805. **[38]**

Keeney, R. L. (1992). *Value focused thinking: A path to creative decisionmaking.* Cambridge, MA: Harvard University Press. **[41]**

Keeney, R. L., & Raiffa, H. (1993). *Decisions with multiple objectives.* Cambridge, U.K.: Cambridge University Press. **[31]**

Keil, F. C. (1989). *Concepts, kinds and cognitive development.* Cambridge, MA: MIT Press. **[22]**

Keller, J. B. (1985). The probability of heads. *American Mathematical Monthly, 93*, 191–197. **[33]**

Kelley, C. M., & Jacoby, L. L. (1996). Adult egocentrism: Subjective experience versus analytic bases for judgment. *Journal of Memory and Language, 35,* 157–175. **[Introduction]**

Kelley, H. H. (1967). Attribution theory in social psychology. In *Nebraska Symposium on Motivation* (Vol. 15, pp. 192–238), D. Levine (Ed.). Lincoln: University of Nebraska Press. **[9, 20]**

Kelley, H. H. (1972). *Causal schemata and the attribution process.* Morristown, NJ: General Learning Press. **[29]**

Keltner, D., Ellsworth, P., & Edwards, K. (1993a). Beyond simple pessimism: Effects of sadness and anger on social perception. *Journal of Personality and Social Psychology, 64,* 740–752. **[29]**

Keltner, D., Locke, K. D., & Audrain, P. C. (1993b). The influence of attributions on the relevance of negative feelings to satisfaction. *Personality and Social Psychology Bulletin, 19,* 21–30. **[29]**

Keren, G. (1987). Facing uncertainty in the game of bridge. A calibration study. *Organizational Behavior and Human Decision Processes, 39,* 98–114. **[13, 15, 39]**

Keren, G. (1988). On the ability of monitoring non-veridical perceptions and uncertain knowledge: Some calibration studies. *Acta Psychologica, 67,* 95–119. **[13, 39]**

Keren, G. (1991). Calibration and probability judgments: Conceptual and methodological issues. *Acta Psychologica, 77,* 217–273. **[39]**

Keren, G., & Wagenaar, W. A. (1985). On the psychology of playing blackjack: Normative and descriptive considerations with implications for decision theory. *Journal of Experimental Psychology: General, 114,* 133–158. **[21]**

Keynes, J. A. (1921). *A treatise on probability.* London: Macmillan. **[Introduction, 26]**

Keysar, B. (1989). On the functional equivalence of literal and metaphorical interpretations in discourse. *Journal of Memory and Language, 28,* 375–385. **[2]**

Keysar, B. (1993). Common sense and adult theory of communication. *Behavioral and Brain Sciences, 16,* 54. **[8]**

Keysar, B. (1994). The illusory transparency of intention: Linguistic perspective taking in text. *Cognitive Psychology, 26,* 165–208. **[8, 36]**

Keysar, B. (1998). Language users as problem solvers: just what ambiguity problem do they solve? In *Social and cognitive psychological approaches to interpersonal communication* (pp. 175–200), S. R. Fussell & R. J. Kreuz (Eds.). Hillsdale, NJ: Lawrence Erlbaum Associates. **[8]**

Keysar, B. (2000). The illusory transparency of intention: does June understand what Mark means because he means it? *Discourse Processes, 29,* 161–172. **[8]**

Keysar, B., Barr, D. J., Balin, J. A., & Brauner, J. S. (2000). Taking perspective in conversation: the role of mutual knowledge in comprehension. *Psychological Sciences, 11,* 32–38. **[8]**

Keysar, B., Barr, D. J., Balin, J. A., & Paek, T. S. (1998). Definite reference and mutual knowledge: process models of common ground in comprehension. *Journal of Memory and Language, 39,* 1–20. **[8]**

Keysar, B., Barr, D. J., & Horton, W. S. (1998). The egocentric basis of language use: Insights from a processing approach. *Current Directions in Psychological Science, 7,* 46–50. **[8]**

Keysar, B., & Bly, B. (1995). Intuitions of the transparency of idioms: Can one keep a secret by spilling the beans? *Journal of Memory and Language, 34,* 89–109. **[7, 8]**

Keysar, B., & Bly, B. (1999). Swimming against the current: Do idioms reflect conceptual structure? *Journal of Pragmatics, 31,* 1559–1578. **[8]**

Keysar, B., Ginzel, L., & Bazerman, M. H. (1995). States of affairs and states of mind:

The effect of knowledge of beliefs. *Organizational Behavior and Human Decision Processes, 64*, 283–293. **[36]**

Keysar, B., & Henly, A. S. (1998). Speakers overestimate the transparency of their intention. In *The 39th Annual Meeting of the Psychonomics Society*, November. Dallas, TX. **[8]**

Keysar, B., & Henly, A. S. (in press). Speakers' overestimation of their effectiveness. *Psychological Science.* **[8]**

Kidd, J. B. (1970). The utilization of subjective probabilities in production planning. *Acta Psychologica, 34*, 338–347. **[13]**

Kirkwood, C. W., & Pollock, S. M. (1982). Multiple attribute scenarios, bounded probabilities, and threats of nuclear theft. *Futures, 14*, 545–553. **[1]**

Klaaren, K. J., Hodges, S. D., & Wilson, T. D. (1994). The role of affective expectations in subjective experience and decision making. *Social Cognition, 12*, 77–101. **[16, 19]**

Klahr, D., Fay, A. L., & Dunbar, K. (1993). Heuristics for scientific experimentation: A developmental study. *Cognitive Psychology, 25*, 111–146. **[24]**

Klar, Y., & Giladi, E. E. (1997). No one in my group can be below the group's average: A robust positivity bias in favor of anonymous peers. *Journal of Personality and Social Psychology, 73*, 885–901. **[27]**

Klar, Y., & Giladi, E. E. (1999). Are most people happier than their peers, or are they just happy? *Personality and Social Psychology Bulletin, 25*, 585–594. **[27]**

Klar, Y., Medding, A., & Sarel, D. (1996). Nonunique vulnerability: Singular versus distributional probabilities and unrealistic optimism in comparative risk judgments. *Organizational Behavior and Human Decision Processes, 67*, 229–245. **[27]**

Klayman, J., & Ha, Y. (1987). Confirmation, disconfirmation, and information in hypothesis testing. *Psychological Review, 94*, 211–228. **[6, 9]**

Klayman, J., & Shoemaker, P. J. H. (1993). Thinking about the future: A cognitive perspective. *Journal of Forecasting, 12*, 161–168. **[14]**

Klayman, J., Soll, J. B., Gonzáles-Vallejo, C., & Barlas, S. (1999). Overconfidence: It depends on how, what, and whom you ask. *Organizational Behavior and Human Decision Processes, 79*, 216–247. **[39]**

Klein, G. (1998). *Sources of power: How people make decisions.* Cambridge, MA: MIT Press. **[24, 39]**

Klein, S. B., & Loftus, J. (1993). The mental representation of trait and autobiographical knowledge about the self. In *Advances in social cognition* (Vol. 5, pp. 1–50), T. K. Srull & R. S. Wyer (Eds.). Hillsdale, NJ: Erlbaum. **[9]**

Kleindorfer, P. R., Kunreuther, H. C., & Schoemaker, P. J. H. (1993). *Decision sciences: An integrative perspective.* New York: Cambridge University Press. **[41]**

Koch, S. J., & Loewenstein, G. F. (1989). Outcome feedback: Hindsight and information. *Journal of Experimental Psychology: Learning, Memory, and Cognition, 15*(4), 605–619. **[41]**

Koehler, D. J. (1991). Explanation, imagination, and confidence in judgment. *Psychological Bulletin, 110*, 499–519. **[14]**

Koehler, D. J. (1994). Hypothesis generation and confidence in judgment. *Journal of Experimental Psychology: Learning, Memory, and Cognition, 20*, 461–469. **[6, 25]**

Koehler, D. J. (1996). A strength model of probability judgments for tournaments. *Organizational Behavior and Human Decision Processes, 66*, 16–21. **[27, 39]**

Koehler, D. J. (2000). Probability judgment in three-category classification learning. *Journal of Experimental Psychology: Learning, Memory, and Cognition, 26*, 28–52. **[27]**

Koehler, D. J., Brenner, L. A., & Tversky, A. (1997). The enhancement effect in probability judgment. *Journal of Behavioral Decision Making, 10,* 293–313. **[Introduction, 25, 27, 39]**

Koehler, J. (1996). The base-rate fallacy reconsidered: Descriptive, normative, and methodological challenges. *Behavioral and Brain Sciences, 19,* 1–53. **[Introduction, 2, 24]**

Kopp, R. (1992). Why existence value should be used in cost–benefit analysis. *Journal of Policy Analysis and Management, 11,* 123–130. **[2]**

Koriat, A., Lichtenstein, S., & Fischhoff, B. (1980). Reasons for confidence. *Journal of Experimental Psychology: Human Learning and Memory, 6,* 107–118. **[5, 6, 13, 14, 15, 37, 39]**

Krantz, D. H. (1991). From indices to mappings: The representational approach to measurement. In *Frontiers of mathematical psychology: Essays in honor of Clyde Coombs* (pp. 1–52), D. R. Brown & E. K. Smith (Eds.). New York: Springer Verlag. **[26]**

Krantz, D. H., Fong, G. T., & Nisbett, R. E. (1983). *Formal training improves the application of statistical heuristics to everyday problems.* Unpublished manuscript. Murray Hill, NJ: Bell Laboratories. **[28]**

Krauss, R. M., & Fussell, S. R. (1991). Perspective-taking in communication: representations of others' knowledge in reference. *Social Cognition, 9,* 2–24. **[8]**

Kraut, R. E., & Higgins, E. I. (1984). Communication and social cognition. In *Handbook of social cognition* (Vol. 3, pp. 81–127), R. S. Wyer & I. K. Srull (Eds.). Hillsdale, NJ: Erlbaum. **[20]**

Kreps, D. M. (1990). *Game theory and economic modeling.* Oxford, U.K.: Clarendon Press. **[8]**

Krieger, L. H. (1995). The content of our categories: A cognitive bias approach to discrimination and equal employment opportunity. *Stanford Law Review, 47,* 1161–1248. **[10]**

Krosnick, J. A., Li, F., & Lehman, D. R. (1990). Conversational conventions, order of information acquisition, and the effect of base rates and individuating information on social judgment. *Journal of Personality and Social Psychology, 59,* 1140–1152. **[2]**

Krueger, J. (1998). Enhancement bias in descriptions of self and others. *Personality and Social Psychology Bulletin, 24,* 505–516. **[36]**

Krueger, J., & Clement, R. (1994). The truly false consensus effect: An ineradicable and egocentric bias in social perception. *Journal of Personality and Social Psychology, 65,* 596–610. **[24]**

Krueger, J., Ham, J. J., & Linford, K. M. (1996). Perceptions of behavioral consistency: Are people aware of the actor–observer effect? *Psychological Science, 7,* 259–263. **[36]**

Krueger, J., & Zeiger, J. S. (1993). Social categorization and the truly false consensus effect. *Journal of Personality and Social Psychology, 65,* 670–680. **[24, 36]**

Kruger, J. (1999). Lake Wobegon be gone! The "below-average effect" and the egocentric nature of comparative ability judgments. *Journal of Personality & Social Psychology, 77,* 221–232. **[6, 7, 27]**

Kruger, J., & Dunning, D. (1999). Unskilled and unaware of it: How difficulties in recognizing one's own incompetence lead to inflated self-assessments. *Journal of Personality and Social Psychology, 77,* 1121–1134. **[36]**

Kruger, J., & Gilovich, T. (1999). "Naive cynicism" in everyday theories of responsibility assessment: on biased assumptions of bias. *Journal of Personality and Social Psychology, 76,* 743–753. **[10, 36]**

Kruglanski, A., & Webster, D. (1996). Motivated closing of the mind: Seizing and freezing. *Psychological Review, 103*, 263–278. **[42]**

Kruglanski, A. W., & Freund, T. (1983). The freezing and unfreezing of lay inferences: Effects on impressional primacy, ethnic stereotyping, and numerical anchoring. *Journal of Experimental Social Psychology, 19*, 448–468. **[2, 32]**

Krull, D. S. (1993). Does the grist change the mill? The effect of the perceiver's inferential goal on the process of social inference. *Personality and Social Psychology Bulletin, 19*, 340–348. **[9]**

Krull, D. S., & Erickson, D. J. (1995). On judging situations: The effortful process of taking dispositional information into account. *Social Cognition, 13*, 417–438. **[9]**

Kuhberger, A. (1995). The framing of decisions: A new look at old problems. *Organizational Behavior and Human Decision Processes, 62*, 230–240. **[24]**

Kunda, Z. (1987). Motivated inference: Self-serving generation and evaluation of causal theories. *Journal of Personality and Social Psychology, 53*, 636–647. **[18, 36]**

Kunda, Z. (1990). The case for motivated reasoning. *Psychological Bulletin, 108*, 480–498. **[14, 16, 27]**

Kunda, Z. (1999). *Social cognition: Making sense of people.* Cambridge, MA: MIT Press. **[29]**

Kunda, Z., Fong, G. T., Sanitioso, R., & Reber, E. (1993). Directional questions direct self-conceptions. *Journal of Experimental Social Psychology, 29*, 63–86. **[27]**

Kyburg, H. E. (1983). Rational belief. *Behavioral and Brain Sciences, 6*(2), 231–273. **[1, 24]**

La France, M., & Hecht, M. A. (1995). Why smiles generate leniency. *Personality and Social Psychology Bulletin, 21*, 207–214. **[23]**

Laitin, D. D. (1993). The game theory of language regimes. *International Political Science Review, 14*, 227–239. **[8]**

Lakoff, G. (1972). Hedges: A study in meaning criteria and the logic of fuzzy concepts. In *Papers from the Eighth Regional Meeting, Chicago Linguistic Society* (pp. 183–228). Chicago: Chicago Linguistic Society. **[22]**

Lakoff, G. (1982). *Categories and cognitive models* (Cognitive Science Report No. 2). Berkeley: University of California. **[1]**

Lakoff, G. (1987). *Women, fire, and dangerous things.* Chicago: University of Chicago Press. **[20]**

Lakoff, G., & Johnson, M. (1980). *Metaphors we live by.* Chicago: University of Chicago Press. **[11]**

Lakonishok, J., Shleifer, A., & Vishny, R. (1994). Contrarian investment, extrapolation, and risk. *Journal of Finance, 49*, 1541–1578. **[38]**

Lalljee, M., & Abelson, R. R. (1983). The organization of explanations. In *Attribution theory: Social and functional extensions* (pp. 65–80), M. Hewstone (Ed.). Oxford, U.K.: Blackwell. **[20]**

Landman, J. (1987). Regret and elation following action and inaction: Affective responses to positive versus negative outcomes. *Personality and Social Psychology Bulletin, 13*, 524–536. **[20, 21]**

Langer, E. J. (1978). Rethinking the role of thought in social interaction. *New directions in attribution research.* Vol. 2. (Harvey, Ickes, & Kidd, Eds.), Potomac, MD: Lawrence Erlbaum Associates. **[2]**

Lanir, Z. (1978). *Critical reevaluation of the strategic intelligence methodology.* Tel Aviv: Center for Strategic Studies, Tel Aviv University. **[41]**

LaPiere, R. T. (1934). Attitudes and actions. *Social Forces, 13*, 230–237. **[14]**

Larrick, R. P. Morgan, J. N., & Nisbett, R. E. (1990). Teaching the use of cost-benefit reasoning in everyday life. *Psychological Science, 1*, 362–370. **[41]**

Larrick, R. P., Nisbett, R. E., & Morgan, J. N. (1993). Who uses the cost–benefit rules of choice? Implications for the normative status of microeconomic theory. *Organizational Behavior and Human Decision Processes, 56,* 331–347. **[24]**

Larrick, R. P., Smith, E. E., & Yates, J. F. (1992, November). *Reflecting on the reflection effect: Disrupting the effects of framing through thought.* Paper presented at the meetings of the society for Judgment and Decision Making, St. Louis, MO. **[24]**

Larwood, L. (1978). Swine flu: A field study of self-serving biases. *Journal of Applied Social Psychology, 18,* 283–289. **[18]**

Larwood, L., & Whittaker, W. (1977). Managerial myopia: Self-serving biases in organizational planning. *Journal of Applied Psychology, 62,* 194–198. **[18]**

Lau, L.-Y., & Ranyard, R. (1999). Chinese and English speakers' linguistic expression of probability and probabilistic thinking. *Journal of Cross-Cultural Psychology, 30,* 411–421. **[15]**

Lau, R. R., & Russell, D. (1980). Attributions in the sports pages: A field test of some current hypotheses about attribution research. *Journal of Personality and Social Psychology, 39,* 29–38. **[35]**

Law of averages a reality for ballplayers. (June 7, 1981). *Los Angeles Times.* Pt. 3, p. 6. **[28]**

Lay, C. H. (1986). At last, my research article on procrastination. *Journal of Research in Personality, 20,* 474–495. **[14]**

Lazarus, R. S. (1985). The costs and benefits of denial. In *Stress and coping: An anthology* (2nd ed., pp. 154–173), A. Monat & R. S. Lazarus (Eds.), New York: Columbia University Press. **[16]**

Leary, M. R. (1982). Hindsight distortion and the 1980 Presidential election. *Personality and Social Psychology Bulletin, 8,* 257–263. **[5]**

Lee, J. W., Yates, J. F., Shinotsuka, H., Singh, R., Onglatco, M. L. U., Yen, N. S., Gupta, M., & Bhatnagar, D. (1995). Cross-national differences in overconfidence. *Asian Journal of Psychology, 1,* 63–69. **[14, 15]**

Leedham, B., Meyerowitz, B. E., Muirhead, J., & Frist, W. H. (1995). Positive expectations predict health after heart transplantation. *Health Psychology, 14,* 74–79. **[19]**

Lehman, D. R., Davis, C. G., Delongis, A., Wortman, C. B., Bluck, S. Mandel, D. R., & Ellard, J. H. (1993). Positive and negative life changes following bereavement and their relations to adjustment. *Journal of Social and Clinical Psychology, 12,* 90–112. **[16]**

Lehnert, W. (1978). *The process of question answering.* Hillsdale, NJ: Erlbaum. **[20]**

Leiss, W. (1996). Three phases in the evolution of risk communication practice. *Annals of the American Academy of Political and Social Science, 545,* 85–94. **[41]**

Leli, D. A., & Filskov, S. B. (1981). Clinical-actuarial detection and description of brain impairment with the W-B Form I. *Journal of Clinical Psychology, 37,* 623–629. **[40]**

Leli, D. A., & Filskov, S. B. (1984). Clinical detection of intellectual deterioration associated with brain damage. *Journal of Clinical Psychology, 40,* 1435–1441. **[40]**

Lerner, J., & Tetlock, P. E. (1999). Accounting for the effects of accountability. *Psychological Bulletin, 125,* 255–275. **[32]**

Lerner, J. S., Goldberg, J. H., & Tetlock, P. E. (1998). Sober second thought: The effects of accountability, anger and authoritarianism on attributions of responsibility. *Personality and Social Psychology Bulletin, 24,* 563–574. **[32]**

Lerner, M. J. (1980). *The belief in a just world: A fundamental delusion.* New York: Plenum. **[20]**

Lerner, M. J., & Miller, D. I. (1978). Just world research and the attribution process: Looking back and ahead. *Psychological Bulletin, 85*, 1030–1051. [20]

Leslie, A. M. (1987). Pretence and representation: The origins of "theory of mind." *Psychological Review, 94*, 412–426. [8]

Levelt, W. J. M. (1989). *Speaking: from intention to articulation.* Cambridge, MA: MIT Press. [8]

Leventhal, H. (1970). Findings and theory in the study of fear communications. In *Advances in experimental social psychology (Vol. 5)*, L. Berkowitz (Ed.), New York: Academic Press. [4]

Leventhal, H., Diefenbach, M., & Leventhal, E. A. (1992). Illness cognition. *Cognitive Therapy and Research, 16*, 143–163. [41]

Levi, A. S., & Pryor, J. B. (1987). Use of the availability heuristic in probability estimates of future events: The effects of imagining outcomes versus imagining reasons. *Organizational Behavior and Human Decision Processes, 40*, 219–234. [17]

Levi, I. (1983). Who commits the base rate fallacy? *Behavioral and Brain Sciences, 6*, 502–506. [24]

Levin, I. P., Schnittjer, S. K., & Thee, S. L. (1988). Information framing effects in social and personal decisions. *Journal of Experimental Social Psychology, 24*, 520–529. [6]

Levinson, S. C. (1995). Interactional biases in human thinking. In *Social intelligence and interaction* (pp. 221–260), E. Goody (Eds.). Cambridge, U.K.: Cambridge University Press. [24]

Lewis, D. K. (1973). *Counterfactuals.* Cambridge: Harvard University Press. [20, 42]

Liberman, N., & Trope, Y. (1998). The role of feasibility and desirability considerations in near and distant future decisions: A test of temporal construal theory. *Journal of Personality and Social Psychology, 75*, 5–18. [14]

Liberman, V., & Tversky, A. (1993). On the evaluation of probability judgments: Calibration, resolution, and monotonicity. *Psychological Bulletin, 114*, 162–173. [39]

Lichtenstein, S., & Fischhoff, B. (1977). Do those who know more also know more about how much they know? The calibration of probability judgments. *Organizational Behavior and Human Performance, 20*, 159–183. [13, 15, 41]

Lichtenstein, S., Fischhoff, B., & Phillips, L. (1982). Calibration and probabilities: The state of the art to 1980. In *Judgment under uncertainty: Heuristics and biases* (pp. 306–334), D. Kahneman, P. Slovic, & A. Tversky (Eds.). Cambridge, U.K.: Cambridge University Press. [13, 14, 15, 24, 25, 27, 37, 41]

Lichtenstein, S., & Slovic, P. (1971). Reversals of preference between bids and choices in gambling decisions. *Journal of Experimental Psychology, 89*, 46–55. [6, 7, 12, 23]

Lichtenstein, S., & Slovic, P. (1973). Response-induced reversals of preference in gambling: An extended replication in Las Vegas. *Journal of Experimental Psychology, 101*, 16–20. [23]

Lichtenstein, S., Slovic, P., Fischhoff, B., Layman, M., & Combs, B. (1978). Judged frequency of lethal events. *Journal of Experimental Psychology: Human Learning and Memory, 4*, 551–578. [4, 19, 23, 41]

Lim, T. (2001). Rationality and analysts' forecast bias. *Journal of Finance, 56*, 369–385. [38]

Lindley, D. V., Tversky, A., & Brown, R. V. (1979). On the reconciliation of probability assessments. *Journal of the Royal Statistical Society, 142*, 146–180. [1, 25]

Linville, P. W., Fischer, G. W., & Salovey, P. (1989). Perceived distributions of the characteristics of in-group and out-group members: Empirical evidence and a computer simulation. *Journal of Personality and Social Psychology, 57*, 165–188. [36]

Lipschitz, R. (1983). Knowing and practicing: Teaching behavioral sciences at the Israel Defense Forces Command and General Staff College. *Journal of Management Studies, 20,* 121–140. **[41]**

Locke, E. A., & Latham, G. P. (1990). *A theory of goal setting and task performance.* Englewood Cliffs, NJ: Prentice Hall. **[14]**

Loewenstein, G. (1987). Anticipation and the valuation of delayed consumption. *Economic Journal, 97,* 666–684. **[23]**

Loewenstein, G. (1996). Out of control: Visceral influences on behavior. *Organizational Behavior and Human Decision Processes, 65,* 272–292. **[14, 30]**

Loewenstein, G. (1999). A visceral account of addiction. In *Getting hooked: Rationality and addiction,* J. Elster & O. J. Skog (Eds.). Cambridge, U.K.: Cambridge University Press. **[23]**

Loewenstein, G. & Adler, D. (1995). A bias in the prediction of tastes. *Economic Journal, 105,* 929–937. **[16, 30]**

Loewenstein, G., & Frederick, S. (1997). Predicting reactions to environmental change. In *Environment, ethics, and behavior: The psychology of environmental valuation and degradation* (pp. 52–72), M. H. Bazerman, D. M., Messick, A. E., Tenbrunsel, & K. A. Wade-Benzoni, (Eds.). San Francisco: The New Lexington Press. **[14, 16]**

Loewenstein, G., Nagin, D., & Paternoster, R. (1997). The effect of sexual arousal on expectations of sexual forcefulness. *Journal of Research in Crime & Delinquency, 34*(4). 443–473. **[30]**

Loewenstein, G., Prelec, D., & Shatto, C. (1998). Hot/cold empathy gaps and the underprediction of curiosity. Working paper (Carnegie Mellon University). **[30]**

Loewenstein, G., & Schkade, D. (1999). Wouldn't it be nice? Predicting future feelings. In *Well-being: The foundations of hedonic psychology* (pp. 85–105), D. Kahneman, E. Diener, & N. Schwarz (Eds.). New York: Russell Sage Foundation Press. **[14, 16, 23]**

Loewenstein, G., Weber, E., Hsee, C., & Welch, N. (2001). Risk as feelings. *Psychological Bulletin, 127,* 267–286. **[23, 30]**

Loffler, G. (1998). Biases in analysts' forecasts: Cognitive, strategic or second-best? *International Journal of Forecasting, 14,* 261–275. **[38]**

Loftus, E. (1975). Leading questions and the eyewitness report. *Cognitive Psychology, 7,* 560–572. **[27]**

Loftus, E. F., & Wagenaar, W. A. (1988). Lawyers' Predictions of Success. *Jurimetrics, 28,* 437. **[39]**

Logan, G. D. (1988). Toward an instance theory of automatization. *Psychological Review, 95,* 492–527. **[22]**

Loomes, G. (1988). Further evidence of the impact of regret and disappointment in choice and uncertainty. *Economica, 55,* 47–62. **[21]**

Loomes, G., & Sugden, R. (1982). Regret theory: An alternative theory of rational choice under uncertainty. *Economic Journal, 92,* 805–824. **[21]**

Loomes, G., & Sugden, R. (1987a). Some implications of a more general form of regret theory. *Journal of Economic Theory, 41,* 270–287. **[21]**

Loomes, G., & Sugden, R. (1987b). Testing for regret and disappointment in choice under uncertainty. *Economic Journal, 97,* 118–129. **[21]**

Lopes, L. L. (1982a). Doing the impossible: A note on induction and the experience of randomness. *Journal of Experimental Psychology: Learning, Memory, and Cognition, 8,* 626–636. **[24, 28]**

Lopes, L. L. (1982b). Toward a procedural theory of judgment. ONR final report, University of Wisconsin. [6]

Lopes, L. L., & Oden, G. C. (1991). The rationality of intelligence. In *Probability and rationality: Studies on L. Jonathan Cohen's philosophy of science* (pp. 199–223), E. Eells & T. Maruszewski (Eds.). Amsterdam: Editions Rodopi. [24]

Lord, C. G., Lepper, M. R., & Preston, E. (1984). Considering the opposite: A corrective strategy for social judgment. *Journal of Personality and Social Psychology, 47,* 1231–1243. [6, 10, 14]

Lord, C. G., Lepper, M. R., & Mackie, D. (1984a). Attitude prototypes as determinants of attitude–behavior consistency. *Journal of Personality and Social Psychology, 46,* 1254–1266. [14]

Lord, C. G., Ross, L., & Lepper, M. R. (1979). Biased assimilation and attitude polarization: The effects of prior theories on subsequently considered evidence. *Journal of Personality and Social Psychology, 37,* 2098–2109. [18, 27, 36]

Lovie, P. (1985). A note on an unexpected anchoring bias in intuitive statistical inference. *Cognition, 21,* 69–72. [6]

Lowrance, W. W. (1976). *Of acceptable risk: Science and the determination of safety.* Los Altos, CA: William Kaufman. [41]

Lubinski, D., & Humphreys, L. G. (1997). Incorporating general intelligence into epidemiology and the social sciences. *Intelligence, 24,* 159–201. [24]

Luce, M., Bettman, J., & Payne, J. W. (1997). Choice processing in emotionally difficult decisions. *Journal of Experimental Psychology: Learning, Memory, and Cognition, 23,* 384–405. [29]

Lusted, L. B. (1977). *A study of the efficacy of diagnostic radiologic procedures: Final report on diagnostic efficacy.* Chicago: Efficacy Study Committee of the American College of Radiology. [13]

Lycan, W. G. (1981). "Is" and "ought" in cognitive science. *Behavioral and Brain Sciences, 4,* 344–345. [28]

Lyon, D., & Slovic, P. (1976). Dominance of accuracy information and neglect of base rates in probability estimation. *Acta Psychologica, 40,* 287–298. [24]

Macchi, L. (1995). Pragmatic aspects of the base-rate fallacy. *Quarterly Journal of Experimental Psychology, 48A,* 188–207. **[Introduction, 2, 24]**

Macchi, L., Osherson, D., & Krantz, D. H. (1999). A note on superadditive probability judgment. *Psychological Review, 106,* 210–214. [27]

Macchi, L., Osherson, D., & Legrenzi, P. (1995, November). *Superadditivity with complementary pairs of hypotheses.* Paper presented at the annual meeting of the Society for Judgment and Decision Making, Los Angeles. [26]

Macdonald, R. R., & Gilhooly, K. J. (1990). More about Linda *or* conjunctions in context. *European Journal of Cognitive Psychology, 2,* 57–70. [24]

MacGregor, D. G., Slovic, P., Dreman, D., & Berry, M. (2000). Imagery, affect, and financial judgment. *Journal of Psychology and Financial Markets, 1*(2), 104–110. [23]

Mackie, D. M., & Worth, L. T. (1989). Cognitive deficits and the mediation of positive affect in persuasion. *Journal of Personality and Social Psychology, 57,* 27–40. [29]

Mackie, J. L. (1974). *The cement of the universe: A study of causation.* Oxford, U.K.: Clarendon Press. [20]

MacLeod, C. M. (1991). Half a century of research on the Stroop effect: An integrative review. *Psychological Bulletin, 109,* 163–203. [6]

Macrae, C. N., Milne, A. B., & Bodenhausen, G. V. (1994). Stereotypes as energy-saving devices: A peek inside the cognitive toolbox. *Journal of Personality and Social Psychology, 66,* 37–47. **[29]**

Madsen, J. B. (1994). Tests of rationality versus an "over optimist" bias. *Journal of Economic Psychology, 15*(4), 587–599. **[39]**

Maher, P. (1993). *Betting on theories.* Cambridge, U.K.: Cambridge University Press. **[24]**

Maines, L. A., & Hand, J. R. M. (1996). Individuals' perceptions and misperceptions of time series properties of quarterly earnings. *Accounting Review, 71,* 317–336. **[38]**

Malkiel, B. (1990). *A random walk down Wall Street.* New York: Norton. **[42]**

Malsch, M. (1989). *Lawyers' predictions of judicial decisions.* Doctoral thesis, University of Leiden, The Netherlands. **[39]**

Mandler, G., Hamson, C., & Dorfman, J. (1990). Tests of dual process theory – word priming and recognition. *Quarterly Journal of Experimental Psychology, 42*(4), 713–739. **[2]**

Manis, M., Dovalina, I., Avis, N. E., & Cardoze, S. (1980). Base rates can affect individual predictions. *Journal of Personality and Social Psychology, 38,* 321–248. **[41]**

Manktelow, K. I., & Evans, J. St. B. T. (1979). Facilitation of reasoning by realism: Effect or non-effect? *British Journal of Psychology, 70,* 477–488. **[24]**

Manktelow, K. I., & Over, D. E. (1991). Social roles and utilities in reasoning with deontic conditionals. *Cognition, 39,* 85–105. **[24]**

Maoz, I., Ward, A., Katz, M., & Ross, L. (2000). Reactive devaluation of an "Israeli" vs. "Palestinian" peace proposal. Unpublished manuscript, Stanford University. **[36]**

March, J. G. (1988). Bounded rationality, ambiguity, and the engineering of choice. In *Decision making: Descriptive, normative, and prescriptive interactions* (pp. 33–57), D. Bell, H. Raiffa, & A. Tversky (Eds.). Cambridge, U.K.: Cambridge University Press. **[24]**

March, J. G., & Olsen, J. P. (1989). *Rediscovering institutions.* New York: Free Press. **[32]**

March, J. G., & Olsen, J. P. (1995). *Democratic governance.* New York: Free Press. **[32]**

Margolis, H. (1987). *Patterns, thinking, and cognition.* Chicago: University of Chicago Press. **[24]**

Markman, A. B., & Gentner, D. (1993). Structural alignment during similarity comparisons. *Cognitive Psychology, 25,* 431–467. **[22]**

Markman, K. D., Gavanski, I., Sherman, S. J., & McMullen, M. N. (1993). The mental simulation of better and worse possible worlds. *Journal of Experimental Social Psychology, 29,* 87–109. **[35]**

Markovits, H., & Vachon, R. (1989). Reasoning with contrary-to-fact propositions. *Journal of Experimental Child Psychology, 47,* 398–412. **[24]**

Marks, R. W. (1951). The effect of probability, desirability and privilege on the stated expectations of children. *Journal of Personality, 19,* 431–465. **[19]**

Markus, H. R. (1977). Self-schemata and processing of information about the self. *Journal of Personality and Social Psychology, 35,* 63–78. **[5, 9]**

Marlatt, G. A. (1978). Craving for alcohol, loss of control, and relapse: a cognitive behavioral analysis. In *Alcoholism: new directions in behavioral research and treatment,* P. E. Nathan, G. A. Marlatt, & T. Loberg (Eds.). New York: Plenum. **[4]**

Martignon, L., Hoffrage, U., & Kriegeskorte, N. (1997). *Lexicographic comparison under uncertainty: A satisficing cognitive algorithm.* Submitted for publication. **[31]**

Martignon, L., & Laskey, K. (in press). Laplace's Demon meets Simon: The role of rationality in a world of bounded resources. In *Simple heuristics that make us smart,*

G. Gigerenzer, P. Todd, & the ABC group (Eds.). New York: Oxford University Press. **[31]**

Martin, L. L. (1986). Set/reset: use and disuse of concepts in impression formation. *Journal of Personality and Social Psychology, 51,* 493–504. **[10]**

Martin, L. L., Abend, T., Sedikides, C., & Green, J. D. (1997). How would it feel if . . . ? Mood as input to a role fulfillment evaluation process. *Journal of Personality and Social Psychology, 73,* 242–253. **[29]**

Martin, L. L., & Clore, G. L. (Eds.) (2001). *Theories of mood and cognition: A user's handbook.* Mahwah, NJ: Erlbaum. **[29]**

Martin, L. L., Harlow, T. F., & Strack, F. (1992). The role of bodily sensations in the evaluation of social events. *Personality and Social Psychology Bulletin, 18,* 412–419. **[7]**

Martin, L. L., Seta, J. J., & Crelia, R. A. (1990). Assimilation and contrast as a function of people's willingness and ability to expend effort in forming an impression. *Journal of Personality and Social Psychology, 59,* 27–37. **[22]**

Martin, L. L., & Stapel, D. A. (1998). Correction and metacognition: are people naive dogmatists or naive empiricist during social judgments? In *Metacognition: cognitive and social dimensions* (pp. 228–247), V. Yzerbyt, G. Lories, & B. Dardenne (Eds.). New York: Sage. **[10]**

Martin, L. L., Ward, D. W., Achée, J. W., & Wyer, R. S. (1993). Mood as input: People have to interpret the motivational implications of their moods. *Journal of Personality and Social Psychology, 64,* 317–326. **[29]**

Martin, W. B., Apostolakos, P. C., & Roazen, H. (1960). Clinical versus actuarial prediction in the differential diagnosis of jaundice. A study of the relative accuracy of predictions made by physicians and by a statistically derived formula in differentiating parenchymal and obstructive jaundice. *American Journal of Medical Science, 240,* 571–578. **[40]**

Masur, F. T. (1981). Adherence to health care regimens. In *Medical psychology: Contributions to behavioral medicine,* C. Prokop & L. A. Bradley (Eds.). New York: Academic Press. **[4]**

Mauss, M. (1902/1972). *A general theory of magic* (R. Brain, Trans.), (Esquisse d'une theorie generale de la magie. *L'Annee Sociologique*) New York: W. W. Norton. (Original work published 1902.) **[11]**

May, R. M. (1986). Inferences, subjective probability, and frequency of correct answers: A cognitive approach to the overconfidence phenomenon. In *New directions in research on decision making* (pp. 175–189), B. Brehmer, H. Jungermann, P. Lourens, & A. Sevoaan (Eds.). Amsterdam: North-Holland. **[13, 39]**

Mayer, J. D., Gaschke, Y. N., Braverman, D. L., & Evans, T. W. (1992). Mood-congruent recall is a general effect. *Journal of Personality and Social Psychology, 63,* 119–132. **[29]**

McAllister, D. W., Mitchell, T. R., & Beach, L. R. (1979). The contingency model for the selection of decision strategies: An empirical test of the effects of significance, accountability, and reversibility. *Organizational Behavior and Human Performance, 24,* 228–244. **[32]**

McArthur, L. A. (1972). The how and what of why: Some determinants and consequences of causal attribution. *Journal of Personality and Social Psychology, 22,* 171–193. **[20]**

McClelland, A. G. R., & Bolger, F. (1994). The calibration of subjective probabilities:

Theories and models 1980–94. In *Subjective probability* (pp. 453–482), G. Wright & P. Ayton (Eds.). Chichester, U.K.: Wiley. **[27]**

McClelland, J. L., & Rumelhart, D. E. (1985). Distributed memory and the representation of general and specific information. *Journal of Experimental Psychology: General, 114*, 159–188. **[20, 22]**

McCrae, R. R., & Costa, P. T. Jr. (1994). The stability of personality: Observations and evaluations. *Current Directions in Psychological Science, 6*, 173–175. **[16]**

McFadden, D. (1999). Rationality for economists? *Journal of Risk and Uncertainty, 19*, 73–105. **[Introduction]**

McFadden, D., & Leonard, G. K. (1993). Issues in the contingent valuation of environmental gods: methodologies for data collection and analysis. In *Contingent valuation. A critical assessment*, Hausman (Ed.). Amsterdam: North-Holland. **[2]**

McGeorge, P., Crawford, J., & Kelly, S. (1997). The relationships between psychometric intelligence and learning in an explicit and an implicit task. *Journal of Experimental Psychology: Learning, Memory, and Cognition, 23*, 239–245. **[24]**

McGlothlin, W. H. (1956). Stability of choices among uncertain alternatives. *American Journal of Psychology, 69*, 604–615. **[13]**

McGregor, D. (1938). The major determinants of the prediction of social events. *Journal of Abnormal and Social Psychology, 33*, 179–204. **[19]**

McKenzie, C. R. M. (1998). Taking into account the strength of an alternative hypothesis. *Journal of Experimental Psychology: Learning, Memory, and Cognition, 24*, 771–792. **[27]**

McKenzie, C. R. M. (1999). (Non)complementary updating of belief in two hypotheses. *Memory & Cognition, 27*, 152–165. **[27]**

McNeil, B. J., Pauker, S. G., Sox, H. C., & Tversky, A. (1982). On the elicitation of preferences for alternative therapies. *New England Journal of Medicine, 306*, 1259–1262. **[27]**

Mead, G. H. (1934). *Mind, self, and society*. Chicago: University of Chicago Press. **[32, 36]**

Mearsheimer, J. J. (1990). Back to the future: Instability in Europe after the Cold War. *International Security, 15*, 5–56. **[42]**

Medcof, J. W. (1990). PEAT: An integrative model of attribution processes. In M. P. Zanna (Ed.). *Advances in experimental social psychology, 23*, 111–209. **[9]**

Medin, D. L., Goldstone, R. L., & Gentner, D. (1993). Respects for similarity. *Psychological Review, 100*, 254–278. **[22]**

Medin, D. L., & Ross, B. H. (1997). *Cognitive psychology* (2nd ed.). Fort Worth: Harcourt Brace. **[5]**

Medin, D. L., & Schaffer, M. M. (1978). Context theory of classification learning. *Psychological Review, 85*, 207–238. **[20]**

Meehl, P. (1990). Appraising and amending theories: The strategy of Lakatosian defense and two principles that warrant it. *Psychology Inquiry, 1*, 108–141. **[32]**

Meehl, P. E. (1954). *Clinical versus statistical prediction*. Minneapolis: University of Minnesota Press. **[Introduction, 40]**

Meehl, P. E. (1957). When shall we use our heads instead of the formula? *Journal of Counseling Psychology, 4*, 268–273. **[40]**

Meehl, P. E. (1959). A comparison of clinicians with five statistical methods of identifying psychotic MMPI profiles. *Journal of Counseling Psychology, 6*, 102–109. **[40]**

Meehl, P. E. (1967). Wanted – A good cookbook. In *Problems in human assessment* (pp. 529–540), D. N. Jackson & S. Messick (Eds.). New York: McGraw-Hill. **[40]**

Meehl, P. E. (1973). *Psychodiagnosis: Selected papers*. Minneapolis, MN: University of Minnesota Press. **[40]**

Meehl, P. E. (1986). Causes and effects of my disturbing little book. *Journal of Personality Assessment, 50*, 370–375. **[40]**

Mehle, T., Gettys, C. F., Manning, C., Baca, S., & Fisher, S. (1981). The availability explanation of excessive plausibility assessment. *Acta Psychologica, 49*, 127–140. **[25]**

Meichenbaum, D. H., & Goodman, J. (1971). Training impulsive children to talk to themselves: a means of developing self-control. *Journal of Abnormal Psychology, 77*, 115–126. **[4]**

Meigs, A. S. (1984). *Food, sex, and pollution: A New Guinea religion.* New Brunswick, NJ: Rutgers University Press. **[11, 34]**

Mellers, B., Hertwig, R., & Kahneman, D. (2001). Do frequency representations eliminate conjunction effects? An exercise in adversarial collaboration. Forthcoming in *Psychological Science.* **[2]**

Mellers, B. A., Richards, V., & Birnbaum, J. H. (1992). Distributional theories of impression formation. *Organizational Behavior and Human Decision Processes, 51*, 313–343. **[23]**

Mervis, C. B., & Rosch, E. (1981). Categorization of natural objects. *Annual Review of Psychology, 32*, 89–115. **[1]**

Merz, J., Fischhoff, B., Mazur, D. J., & Fischbeck, P. S. (1993). Decision-analytic approach to developing standards of disclosure for medical informed consent. *Journal of Toxics and Liability, 15*, 191–215. **[41]**

Messer, W. S., & Griggs, R. A. (1993). Another look at Linda. *Bulletin of the Psychonomic Society, 31*, 193–196. **[24]**

Messick, D. M. (1993). Equality as a decision heuristic. In *Psychological prespectives on Justice*, B. A. Mellers & J. Baron (Eds.). New York: Cambridge University Press. **[30]**

Michaely, R., & Womack, K. (1999). Conflict of interest and the credibility of underwriter analyst recommendations. *Review of Financial Studies, 12*, 653–686. **[38]**

Michotte, A. (1963). *The perception of causality.* New York: Basic Books. **[Introduction, 2]**

Mikhail, M., Walther, B., & Willis, R. (1997). Do security analysts improve their performance with experience? *Journal of Accounting Research, 35*, 131–157. **[38]**

Mill, J. S. (1974). *A system of logic ratiocinative and inductive.* Toronto, Ontario: University of Toronto Press. (Originally published 1843.) **[28]**

Miller, A. G., Baer, R., & Schenberg, R. (1979). The bias phenomenon in attitude attribution: Actor and observer perspectives. *Journal of Personality and Social Psychology, 37*, 1421–1431. **[20]**

Miller, D. T. (1981, August). *Changes over time in the selection of causes and the definitions of effects.* Paper presented at the meeting of the American Psychological Association, Los Angeles. **[20]**

Miller, D. T., & Gunasegaram, S. (1990). Temporal order and the perceived mutability of events: Implications for blame assignment. *Journal of Personality and Social Psychology, 59*, 1111–1118. **[21]**

Miller, D. T., & McFarland, C. (1986). Counterfactual thinking and victim compensation: A test of norm theory. *Personality and Social Psychology Bulletin, 12*, 513–519. **[20, 21, 35]**

Miller, D. T., & Ratner, R. K. (1998). The disparity between the actual and assumed power of self-interest. *Journal of Personality and Social Psychology, 74*, 53–62. **[36]**

Miller, D. T., & Ross, M. (1975). Self-serving biases in the attribution of causality: Fact or fiction? *Psychological Bulletin, 82*, 213–225. **[Introduction, 14, 19]**

Miller, D. T., & Turnbull, W. (1990). The counterfactual fallacy: Confusing what might have been with what ought to have been. *Social Justice Research, 4*, 1–19. **[21]**

Miller, D. T., Turnbull, W., & McFarland, C. (1990). Counterfactual thinking and social perception: Thinking about what might have been. In *Advances in experimental social psychology* (Vol. 23, pp. 305–331), M. P. Zanna (Ed.). New York: Academic Press. **[21, 35]**

Miller, G. A., Galanter, E., & Pribram, K. H. (1960). *Plans and the structure of behavior.* New York: Holt, Rinehart & Winston. **[31]**

Miller, G. A., & Cantor, N. (1982). Book review of Nisbett, R., & Ross, L. Human inference: Strategies and shortcomings of social judgment. *Social Cognition, 1,* 83–93. **[28]**

Miller, N. E., & Dollard, J. (1946). *Social learning and imitation.* New Haven, CT: Yale University Press. **[32]**

Mills, C. W. (1959). *The sociological imagination.* New York: Oxford University Press. **[41]**

Mischel, W., Cantor, N., & Feldman, S. (1996). Principles of self-regulation: The nature of willpower and self-control. In *Social psychology: Handbook of basic principles* (pp. 329–360), E. T Higgins & A. W. Kruglanski (Eds.). New York: Guilford. **[16]**

Mita, T. H., Dermer, M., & Knight, J. (1997). Reversed facial images and the mere exposure hypothesis. *Journal of Personality and Social Psychology, 35,* 597–601. **[30]**

Mitchell, R., & Carson, R. (1989). *Using surveys to value public goods: the contingent valuation method.* Washington, DC: Resources for the Future. **[2]**

Mitchell, T. R., & Thompson, L. (1994). A theory of temporal adjustments of the evaluation of events: Rosy prediction and rosy retrospection. *Advances in Managerial Cognition and Organizational Information Processes, 5,* 85–114. **[16]**

Mitchell, T. R., Thompson, L., Peterson, E., & Cronk, R. (1997). Temporal adjustments in the evaluation of events: The "rosy view." *Journal of Experimental Social Psychology, 33,* 421–448. **[19]**

Monat, A., Averill, J. R., & Lazarus, R. S. (1972). Anticipatory stress and coping reactions under various conditions of uncertainty. *Journal of Personality and Social Psychology, 24,* 237–253. **[30]**

Mongin, P. (1994). Some connections between epistemic logic and the theory of nonadditive probability. In *Patrick Suppes: Scientific philosopher,* P. W. Humphreys (Ed.). Dordrecht, The Netherlands: Kluwer. **[25]**

Monson, I. C., & Snyder, M. (1977). Actors, observers and the attribution process: Toward a reconceptualization. *Journal of Experimental Social Psychology, 13,* 89–111. **[20]**

Montgomery, H. (1983). Decision rules and the search for a dominance structure: Towards a process model of decision making. In *Analysing and aiding decision processes* (pp. 343–369), P. Humphreys, O. Svenson & A. Vari (Eds.). Amsterdam: North Holland. **[23]**

Montgomery, S. B., Joseph, J. G., Becker, M. H., Ostrow, D. G., Kessler, R. C., & Kirscht, J. P. (1989). The health belief model in understanding compliance with preventative recommendations for AIDS: How useful? *AIDS Education and Prevention, 1,* 303–323. **[19]**

Moore, D. A., Kurtzberg, T. R., Fox, C. R., Bazerman, M. H. (1999). Positive illusions and forecasting errors in mutual fund investment decisions. *Organizational Behavior and Human Decision Processes, 79,* 95–114. **[38]**

Morgan, M. G., Fischhoff, B., Bostrom, A., & Atman, C. (2001). *Risk communication: The mental models approach.* New York: Cambridge University Press. **[41]**

Morgan, M. G., Henrion, M., & Morris, S. C. (1981). BNL No. 51358, Brookhaven National Laboratory. **[37]**

Morgan, M. G., Henrion, M., & Morris, S. C. (1984). Technical Uncertainty in Quantitative Policy Analysis – A Sulfur Air Pollution Example. *Risk Analysis, 4*, 201–216. **[37]**

Morgan, M. G., & Henrion, M. (1990). *Uncertainty: A guide to dealing with uncertainty in quantitative risk and policy analysis.* New York: Cambridge University Press. **[41]**

Morgan, M. G., & Keith, D. W. (1995). Subjective judgments by climate experts. *Environmental Science and Technology, 29*, 468A–476A. **[41]**

Morier, D. M., & Borgida, E. (1984). The conjunction fallacy: A task specific phenomenon? *Personality and Social Psychology Bulletin, 10*, 243–252. **[3]**

Morris, M. W., & Su, S. K. (1999). The hostile mediator phenomenon: Egocentric standards of fairness lead disputants to see mediators as favoring the opponent. Unpublished manuscript, Stanford University. **[36]**

Morris, M., Heath, C., & Jost, J. (1999). Agency misattributions and the curse of knowledge. Working paper, Stanford University. **[36]**

Morris, P. (1997). Communities of assent and descent. *Massah; Journey. Journal of the New Zealand Council of Christians and Jews, 3* (Winter), 2–4. **[11]**

Morris, W. N. (1989). *Mood: The frame of mind.* New York: Springer Verlag. **[29]**

Morwitz, V. G., Johnson, E., & Schmittlein, D. (1993). Does measuring intent change behavior? *Journal of Consumer Research, 20*, 46–61. **[19]**

Moshman, D., & Franks, B. (1986). Development of the concept of inferential validity. *Child Development, 57*, 153–165. **[24]**

Mowrer, O. H. (1960a). Learning theory and behavior. New York: Wiley. **[23]**

Mowrer, O. H. (1960b). Learning theory and the symbolic processes. New York: Wiley. **[23]**

Moynihan, D. P. (1993). *Pandemonium.* New York: Oxford University Press. **[42]**

Murphy, A. H. (1973). A new vector partition of the probability score. *Journal of Applied Meteorology, 12*, 595–600. **[15]**

Murphy, A. H. (1981). Subjective quantification of uncertainty in weather forecasts in the United States. *Meteorolgische Rudschau, 34*, 65–77. **[39]**

Murphy, A. H. (1985). Probabilistic weather forecasting. In *Probability, statistics, and decision making in the atmospheric sciences* (pp. 337–377), A. H. Murphy & R. W. Katz (Eds.). Boulder, CO: Westview Press. **[25]**

Murphy, A. H., & Brown, B. G. (1984). A comparative evaluation of objective and subjective weather forecasts in the United States. *Journal of Forecasting, 3*, 369–393. **[39]**

Murphy, A. H., & Daan, H. (1984). Impacts of feedback and experience on the quality of subjective probability forecasts: Comparison of results from the first and second years of the Zierikzee experiment. *Monthly Weather Review, 112*, 413–423. **[39]**

Murphy, A. H., & Katz, R. W. (Eds.). (1983). *Probability, Statistics and Decision-Making in the Atmospheric Sciences.* Boulder, CO: Westview Press. **[37]**

Murphy, A. H., & Winker, R. L. (1977a). Can weather forecasters formulate reliable probability forecasts of precipitation and temperature? *National Weather Digest, 2*, 2–9. **[13, 41]**

Murphy, A. H., & Winkler, R. L. (1977b). Reliability of subjective probability forecasts of precipitation and temperature. *Applied Statistics, 26*, 41–47. **[39]**

Murphy, A. H., & Winkler, R. L. (1984a). Probability forecasting in meteorology. *Journal of the American Statistical Association, 79*, 489–500. **[39]**

Murphy, A. H., & Winkler, R. L. (1984b). Probability of precipitation forecasts: A review. *Journal of the American Statistical Association, 79*, 391–400. **[41]**

Murphy, A. H., & Winkler, R. L. (1992). Diagnostic verification of probability forecasts. *International Journal of Forecasting, 7*, 435–455. **[39]**

Murphy, G. L. (1993). Theories and concept formation. In *Categories and concepts: Theoretical views and inductive data analysis* (pp. 173–200), I. Van Mechelen, J. Hampton, R. Michalski, & P. Theuns (Eds.). London: Academic Press. **[22]**

Murphy, R. (1994). The effects of task characteristics on covariation assessment: The impact of accountability and judgment frame. *Organizational Behavior and Human Decision Processes, 60*, 139–155. **[32]**

Mussweiler, T., & Strack, F. (1999). Hypothesis-consistent testing and semantic priming in the anchoring paradigm: A selective accessibility model. *Journal of Experimental Social Psychology, 35*, 136–164. **[Introduction, 6, 7, 29]**

Mussweiler, T., & Strack, F. (2000a). Comparing is believing: a selective accessibility model of judgmental anchoring. In *European Review of Social Psychology*, (Vol. 10, pp. 135–167), W. Stroebe & M. Hewstone (Eds.). Chichester, U.K.: Wiley. **[6]**

Mussweiler, T., & Strack, F. (2000b). The use of category and exemplar knowledge in the solution of anchoring tasks. *Journal of Personality and Social Psychology, 78*, 1038–1052. **[7]**

Mussweiler, T., Strack, F., & Pfeiffer, T. (2000). Overcoming the inevitable anchoring effect: considering the opposite compensates for selective accessibility. *Personality and Social Psychology Bulletin, 26*, 1142–1150. **[6]**

Nathanson, S. (1994). *The ideal of rationality.* Chicago: Open Court. **[24]**

National Academy of Sciences (1983). Priority Mechanisms for Toxic Chemicals, National Académy, (Washington, DC) **[37]**

National Research Council (1989). *Improving risk communication.* Washington, DC: National Academy Press. **[41]**

National Research Council (1996). *Understanding risk.* Washington, DC: The Council. **[41]**

Neale, M. A., & Bazerman, M. H. (1983). The effects of perspective taking ability under alternate forms of of arbitration on the negotiation process. *Industrial and Labor Relations Review, 36*, 378–388. **[36, 39]**

Neale, M. A., & Bazerman, M. H. (1990). *Cognition and rationality in negotiation.* New York: The Free Press. **[13]**

Neisser, U. (1963). The multiplicity of thought. *British Journal of Psychology, 54*, 1–14. **[22]**

Neisser, U., Boodoo, G., Bouchard, T., Boykin, A. W., Brody, N., Ceci, S. J., Halpern, D., Loehlin, J., Perloff, R., Sternberg, R., & Urbina, S. (1996). Intelligence: Knowns and unknowns. *American Psychologist, 51*, 77–101. **[24]**

Nelson, T., Leonesio, R., Landwehr, R., & Narens, L. (1986). A comparison of three predictors of an individual's memory performance: The individual's feeling of knowing vs. the normative feeling of knowing vs. base-rate item difficulty. *Journal of Experimental Psychology: Learning, Memory & Cognition, 21*, 279–287. **[39]**

Nemeroff, C. (1988). *Contagion and the transfer of essence.* Doctoral dissertation, University of Pennsylvania. **[11]**

Nemeroff, C. (1995). Magical thinking about illness virulence: conceptions of germs from "safe" versus "danderous" others. *Health Psychology, 14*, 147–151. **[11]**

Nemeroff, C., Brinkman, A., & Woodward, C. (1994). Magical cognitions about AIDS in a college population. *AIDS Education and Prevention, 6*, 249–265. **[11]**

Nemeroff, C., & Rozin P. (1989). "You are what you eat": Applying the demand-free impressions technique to an unacknowledged belief. *Ethos, 17*, 50–69. **[11, 34]**

Nemeroff, C., & Rozin, P. (1992). Sympathetic magical beliefs and kosher dietary practice: The interaction of rules and feelings. *Ethos, 20*, 96–115. **[11]**

Nemeroff, C., & Rozin, P. (1994). The contagion concept in adult thinking in the United States: Transmission of germs and interpersonal influence. *Ethos, 22*, 158–186. [11]

Nemeroff, C., & Rozin, P. (2000). The makings of the magical mind. In *Imagining the impossible: magical, scientific, and religious thinking in children* (pp. 1–34), K. S. Rosengren, C. N. Johnson, & P. L. Harris (Eds.). New York: Cambridge University Press. [11]

Neustadt, R. E., & May, E. R. (1986). *Thinking in time: The uses of history for decision-makers.* New York: Free Press. [42]

Nevo, B. (Ed.). (1986). *Scientific aspects of graphology: A handbook.* Springfield, IL: Charles C. Thomas. [34]

Newby-Clark, I. R., Ross, M., Buehler, R., Koehler, D., & Griffin, D. (2000). People focus on optimistic and disregard pessimistic scenarios while predicting task completion times. *Journal of Experimental Psychology: Applied, 6*, 171–182. [14, 19]

Newell, A., & Simon, H. A. (1972). *Human problem solving.* Englewood Cliffs, NJ: Prentice Hall. [31]

Newton, E. (1990). *Overconfidence in the communication of intent: Heard and unheard melodies.* Unpublished doctoral dissertation, Stanford University. [36]

Newton, E. L. (1990). *The rocky road from actions to intentions.* Stanford, CA: An unpublished doctoral dissertation. [8]

Nickerson, C. (1995). Does willingness-to-pay reflect the purchase of moral satisfaction? A reconsideration of Kahneman and Knetsch. *Journal of Environmental Economics and Management, 28*, 126–133. [2]

Nickerson, R. S. (1996). Hempel's paradox and Wason's selection task: Logical and psychological puzzles of confirmation. *Thinking and Reasoning, 2*, 1–31. [24]

Nickerson, R. S. (1999). How we know – and sometimes misjudge – what others know: imputing one's own knowledge to others. *Psychological Bulletin, 125*, 737–760. [8]

Nisbett, R. E., Borgida, E., Crandall, R., & Reed, H. (1976). Popular induction: Information is not always informative. In *Cognition and social behavior* (pp. 227–236), J. Carrol & J. Payne (Eds.). Hillsdale, NJ: Erlbaum. [20]

Nisbett, R. E., Caputo, C., Legant, P., & Maracek, J. (1973). Behavior as seen by the actor and as seen by the observer. *Journal of Personality and Social Psychology, 27*, 154–164. [20]

Nisbett, R. E., Krantz, D. H., Jepson, C., & Kunda, Z. (1983). The use of statistical heuristics in everyday inductive reasoning. *Psychological Review, 90*, 339–363. [1, 2, 14]

Nisbett, R. E., Peng, K., Choi, I., & Norenzayan, A. (2001). Culture and systems of thought: Holistic versus analytic cognition. *Psychological Review, 108*, 291–310. [15]

Nisbett, R. E., & Ross, L. (1980). *Human inference: Strategies and shortcomings of social judgment.* Englewood Cliffs, NJ: Prentice-Hall. [Introduction, 1, 5, 10, 11, 13, 20, 24, 28, 33, 34, 36, 37]

Nisbett, R. E., & Wilson, T. D. (1977a). Telling more than we can know: verbal reports on mental processes. *Psychological Review, 84*, 231–259. [7, 10, 16, 41]

Nisbett, R. E., & Wilson, T. D. (1977b). The halo effect: Evidence for unconscious alteration of judgments. *Journal of Personality and Social Psychology, 35*, 250–256. [10]

Nisbett, R. E., Zukier, H., & Lemley, R. (1981). The dilution effect: Nondiagnostic information. *Cognitive Psychology, 13*, 248–277. [32]

Norem, J. K., & Cantor, N. (1986a). Anticipatory and post-hoc cushioning strategies: Optimism and defensive pessimism in "risky" situations. *Cognitive Therapy and Research, 10*, 347–362. [19]

Norem, J. K., & Cantor, N. (1986b). Defensive pessimism: Harnessing anxiety as motivation. *Journal of Personality and Social Psychology, 51*, 1208–1217. [16]

Norman, D. A., & Bobrow, D. G. (1975). On data-limited and resource-limited processes. *Cognitive Psychology, 7*, 44–64. **[9]**

Northcraft, G. B., & Neale, M. A. (1987). Experts, amateurs, and real estate: An anchoring-and-adjustment perspective on property pricing decisions. *Organizational Behavior and Human Decision Processes, 39*, 84–97. **[6]**

Novemsky, N., & Kronzon, S. (1999). How are base-rates used, when they are used: A comparison of Bayesian and additive models of base-rate use. *Journal of Behavioral Decision Making, 12*, 55–69. **[2, 39]**

Nutt, S. R., Easterwood, J. C., & Easterwood, C. M. (1999). New evidence on serial correlation in analyst forecast errors. *Financial Management, 28*, 106–117. **[38]**

Nuttin, J. M. (1985). Narcissism beyond gestalt and awareness – the name letter effect. *European Journal of Social Psychology, 15*(3), 353–361. **[30]**

Nuttin, J. M. (1987). Affective consequences of mere ownership – the name letter effect in 12 European languages. *European Journal of Social Psychology, 17*(4), 381–402. **[30]**

Nye, J. (1988). Nuclear learning and U.S.-Soviet security regimes. *International Organizations, 41*, 121–166. **[42]**

O'Brien, P. C. (1988) Analysts' forecasts as earnings expectations. *Journal of Accounting and Economics, 10*, 53–83. **[38]**

Oaksford, M., & Chater, N. (1993). Reasoning theories and bounded rationality. In *Rationality: Psychological and philosophical perspectives* (pp. 31–60), K. Manktelow & D. Over (Eds.). London: Routledge. **[24]**

Oaksford, M., & Chater, N. (1994). A rational analysis of the selection task as optimal data selection. *Psychological Review, 101*, 608–631. **[24]**

Oaksford, M., & Chater, N. (1995). Theories of reasoning and the computational explanation of everyday inference. *Thinking and Reasoning, 1*, 121–152. **[24]**

Oaksford, M., & Chater, N. (1996). Rational explanation of the selection task. *Psychological Review, 103*, 381–391. **[24]**

Oaksford, M., & Chater, N. (1998). *Rationality in an uncertain world.* Hove, England: Psychology Press. **[24]**

Odean, T. (1998). Are investors reluctant to realize their losses? *Journal of Finance, 53*(5), 1775–98. **[39]**

Okrent, D., & Pidgeon, N. (Eds.) (1998). Actual versus perceived risk. Special issue of *Reliability Engineering and System Safety, 59.* **[41]**

Olson, C. L. (1976). Some apparent violations of the representativeness heuristic in human judgment. *Journal of Experimental Psychology: Human Perception and Performance, 2*, 599–608. **[25]**

Olson, D. R., & Torrance, N. (1987). Language, literacy, and mental states. *Discourse Processes, 10*, 157–168. **[8]**

Olson, J. M., Herman, P., & Zanna, M. P. (1986). *Relative deprivation and social comparison: The Ontario symposium* (Vol. 4). Hillsdale, NJ: Erlbaum. **[35]**

Onkal, D., & Muradoglu, G. (1994). Evaluating probabilistic forecasts of stock prices in a developing stock market. *European Journal of Operational Research, 74*, 350–358. **[39]**

Orbell, S., Hodgkins, S., & Sheeran, P. (1997). Implementation intentions and the theory of planned behavior. *Personality and Social Psychology Bulletin, 23*, 945–954. **[14]**

Ordóñez, L., & Benson, L., III. (1997). Decisions under time pressure: How time constraint affects risky decision making. *Organizational Behavior and Human Decision Processes, 71*(2), 121–140. **[2]**

Ortmann, A., & Hertwig, R. (2000). *Biases and heuristics in psychology and economics.* Article proposal for *The Journal of Economic Literature.* Posted on-line at http://195.113.12.52/ortmann/JELprospectus.html [Introduction]

Ortony, A., Clore, G. L., & Collins, A. (1988). *The cognitive structure of emotions.* London: Cambridge University Press. [29]

Osberg, T. M., & Shrauger, J. S. (1986). Self-prediction: Exploring the parameters of accuracy. *Journal of Personality and Social Psychology, 51,* 1044–1057. [14]

Osborne, R. E., & Gilbert. D. T. (1992). The preoccupational hazards of social life. *Journal of Personality and Social Psychology, 62,* 219–228. [9]

Osgood, C. E., Suci, G. J., & Tannenbaum, P. H. (1957). *The measurement of meaning.* Urbana: University of Illinois Press. [23]

Osherson, D. N. (1995). Probability judgment. In *Thinking* (Vol. 3, pp. 35–75), E. E. Smith & D. N. Osherson (Eds.). Cambridge, MA: MIT Press. [24]

Osherson, D. N., & Smith, E. E. (1981). On the adequacy of prototype theory as a theory of concepts. *Cognition, 9,* 35–38. [1]

Osherson, D. N., & Smith, E. E. (1982). Gradedness and conceptual combination. *Cognition, 12,* 299–318. [1]

Osherson, D., Smith, E. E., Wilkie, O., Lopez, A., & Shafir, E. (1990). Category-based induction. *Psychological Review, 97,* 185–200. [22]

Oskamp, S. (1962). The relation of clinical experience and training methods to several criteria of clinical prediction. *Psychological Monographs, 76* (28, Whole No. 547). [13, 40]

Oskamp, S. (1965). Overconfidence in case-study judgments. *The Journal of Consulting Psychology, 29,* 261–265. [13, 27]

Ouellette, J. A., & Wood, W. (1998). Habit and intention in everyday life: The multiple processes by which past behavior predicts future behavior. *Journal of Personality and Social Psychology, 124,* 54–74. [14]

Over, D. E. (2000). Ecological rationality and its heuristics. *Thinking and Reasoning, 6,* 182–192. [Introduction]

Paese, P. W., & Sniezek, J. A. (1991). Influences on the appropriateness of confidence in judgment: Practice, effort, information, and decision-making. *Organizational Behavior and Human Decision Processes, 48,* 100–130. [39]

Papineau, D. (2000). *The evolution of knowledge.* King's College, London technical report posted on http://www.kcl.ac.uk/kis/schools/hums/philosophy/staff/evoknow.html. [Introduction]

Parducci, A. (1965). Category judgment: A range-frequency model. *Psychological Review, 72,* 407–418. [2]

Park, B., & Judd, C. M. (1990). Measures and models of perceived group variability. *Journal of Personality and Social Psychology, 59,* 173–191. [36]

Parker, A., & Fischhoff, B. (2001). *An individual References approach decision-making competence.* Under editorial review. [41]

Parrott, W. G. (1993). Beyond hedonism: Motives for inhibiting good moods and for maintaining bad moods. In *Handbook of mental control* (pp. 278–305), D. M. Wegner & J. W. Pennebaker (Eds.). Englewood Cliffs, NJ: Prentice-Hall. [16]

Particle Data Group: Roos M., Porter F. C., Aguilar-Benitez, M., Montanet, L., Walck, C., Crawford, R. L., Kelly, R. L., Rittenberg, A., Trippe, T. G., Wohl, C. G., Yost, G. P., Shimada, T., Losty, M. J., Gopal, G. P., Hendrick, R. E., Scrock, R. E., Frosch, R., Roper, L. D., Armstrong, B., et al. (1982). Review of Particle Properties. *Physics Letters, 111B,* 1–21. [37]

Patrick, C. J. (1994). Emotion and psychopathy: startling new insights. *Psychophysiology, 31,* 415–428. **[23]**

Payne, J. W., Bettman, J. R., & Johnson, E. J. (1988). Adaptive strategy selection in decision making. *Journal of Experimental Psychology: Learning, Memory, and Cognition, 14,* 534–552. **[31]**

Payne, J. W., Bettman, J. R., & Johnson, E. J. (1990). The adaptive decision maker: Effort and accuracy in choice. In *Insights in decision making: A tribute to Hillel J. Einhorn* (pp. 129–153), R. M. Hogarth (Ed.). Chicago: The University of Chicago Press. **[31]**

Payne, J. W., Bettman, J. R., & Johnson, E. J. (1992). Behavioral decision research: a constructive processing perspective. *Annual Review of Psychology, 43,* 87–131. **[6]**

Payne, J. W., Bettman, J. R., & Johnson, E. J. (1993). *The adaptive decision maker.* New York: Cambridge University Press. **[5, 23, 30, 31]**

Peake, P. K., & Cervone, D. (1989). Sequence anchoring and self-efficacy: Primacy effects in the consideration of possibilities. *Social Cognition, 7,* 31–50. **[19]**

Pelham, B. W., Sumarta, T. T., & Myaskovsky, L. (1994). The easy path from many to much: The numerosity heuristic. *Cognitive Psychology, 26,* 103–133. **[25]**

Penman, S. H. (1980). An empirical investigation of the voluntary disclosure of corporate earnings forecasts. *Journal of Accounting Research, 18,* 132–160. **[38]**

Pennington, N., & Hastie, R. (1993). A theory of explanation-based decision making. In *Decision Making in Action: Models and Methods* (pp. 188–204), G. Klein, J. Orasano, R. Calderwood, & C. E. Zsambok (Eds.). Norwood, NJ: Ablex. **[23]**

Perloff, L. S., & Fetzer, B. K. (1986). Self-other judgements and perceived vulnerability to victimization. *Journal of Personality and Social Psychology, 50,* 502–510. **[17, 19, 27]**

Perner, J., Leekam, S., & Wimmer, H. (1987). Three-year-olds' difficulty with false belief: The case for a conceptual deficit. *British Journal of Developmental Psychology, 5,* 125–137. **[8]**

Peters, E., & Slovic, P. (1996). The role of affect and worldviews as orienting dispositions in the perception and acceptance of nuclear power. *Journal of Applied Social Psychology, 26*(16), 1427–1453. **[23]**

Peters, E., & Slovic, P. (2000). The springs of action: Affective and analytical information processing in choice. *Personality and Social Psychology Bulletin, 26,* 1465–1475. **[23]**

Peterson, C. R., Schneider, R. J., & Miller, A. J. (1965). Sample size and the revision of subjective probabilities. *Journal of Experimental Psychology, 69,* 522–527. **[13]**

Peterson, C. R., & Miller, A. J. (1965). Sensitivity of subjective probability revision. *Journal of Experimental Psychology, 70,* 117–121. **[13]**

Peterson, D. K., & Pitz, G. F. (1988). Confidence, uncertainty, and the use of information. *Journal of Experimental Psychology: Learning, Memory and Cognition, 14,* 85–92. **[25]**

Petty, R., & Cacioppo, J. (1986). *Communication and persuasion: Central and peripheral routes to attitude change.* New York: Springer Verlag. **[29]**

Petty, R. E., & Cacioppo, J. T. (1986). The elaboration likelihood model of persuasion. In *Advances in experimental social psychology,* (Vol. 19, pp. 123–205), L. Berkowitz (Ed.). San Diego: Academic Press. **[Introduction, 19, 22]**

Petty, R. E., & Wegener, D. T. (1993). Flexible correction processes in social judgment: Correcting for context-induced contrast. *Journal of Experimental Social Psychology, 29,* 137–165. **[6, 10]**

Petty, R. E., Wells, G. L., & Brock, T. C. (1976). Distraction can enhance or reduce yielding to propaganda: Thought disruption versus effort justification. *Journal of Personality and Social Psychology, 34,* 874–884. **[9]**

Pfeifer, P. E. (1994). Are we overconfident in the belief that probability forecasters are overconfident? *Organizational Behavior and Human Decision Processes, 58*, 203–213. **[39]**

Pham, L. B., & Taylor, S. E. (1999). From thought to action: Effects of process-versus outcome-based mental simulations on performance. *Personality and Social Psychology Bulletin, 25*, 250–260. **[14, 19]**

Pham, M. T. (1998). Representativeness, relevance, and the use of feelings in decision making. *Journal of Consumer Research, 25*, 144–159. **[23]**

Phillips, L. D. (1973). *Bayesian statistics for social sciences.* London: Nelson. **[41]**

Phillips, L. D., & Edwards, W. (1966). Conservatism in a simple probability inference task. *Journal of Experimental Psychology, 72*, 346–354. **[13, 24]**

Phillips, L. D., Hays, W. L., & Edwards, W. (1966). Conservatism in complex probabilistic inference. *IEEE Transactions on Human Factors in Electronics, 7*, 7–18. **[24]**

Phillips, L. D., & Wright, G. N. (1977). Cultural differences in viewing uncertainty in assessing probabilities. In *Decision making and change in human affairs* (pp. 507–519), H. Jungermann & G. de Zeeuw (Eds.). Dordrecht, The Netherlands: Reidel. **[15]**

Piaget, J. (1926). *The language and thought of the child.* London: Routledge and Kegan Paul. **[22, 36]**

Piaget, J. (1928). *Judgment and reasoning in the child.* New York: Harcourt, Brace. **[36]**

Piaget, J. (1983). *The child's conception of the world.* Totowa, NJ: Rowman & Allanheld (a division of Littlefield, Adams, & Co.). (Original work published 1929) **[11]**

Piaget, J., & Inhelder, B. (1975). *The origin of the idea of chance in children.* New York: Norton. (Originally published 1951) **[28]**

Piattelli-Palmarini, M. (1994). *Inevitable illusions: How mistakes of reason rule our minds.* New York: John Wiley. **[24]**

Pinker, S. (1997). *How the mind works.* New York: Norton. **[Introduction, 11, 24]**

Pipes, R. (1993). *Russia under the Bolshevik regime.* New York: A. A. Knopf. **[42]**

Pipkin, F. M., & Ritter, R. C. (1983). Precision measurements and fundamental constants. *Science, 219*, 4587. **[37]**

Plous, S. (1989). Thinking the unthinkable: the effect of anchoring on likelihood estimates of nuclear war. *Journal of Applied Social Psychology, 19*, 67–91. **[6, 7]**

Politzer, G., & Noveck, I. A. (1991). Are conjunction rule violations the result of conversational rule violations? *Journal of Psycholinguistic Research, 20*, 83–103. **[24]**

Pope, J. (1991). *How cultural differences affect multi-country research.* Minneapolis: Custom Research, Inc. **[15]**

Poses, R. M., & Anthony, M. (1991). Availability, wishful thinking, and physicians' diagnostic judgments for patients with suspected bacteremia. *Medical Decision Making, 11*, 159–168. **[39]**

Poses, R. M., Smith, W. R., McClish, D. K., Huber, E. C., Clemo, F. L. W., Schmitt, B. P., Alexander-Forti, D., Racht, E. M., Colenda, C. C. III, & Centor, R. M. (1997). Physicians' survival predictions for patients with acute congestive heart failure. *Archives of International Medicine, 157*, 1001–1007. **[39]**

Posner, M. I., & Snyder, C. R. R. (1975). Attention and cognitive control. In *Information processing and cognition: The Loyola symposium* (pp. 55–85), R. L. Solso (Ed.). Hillsdale, NJ: Lawrence Erlbaum Associates. **[9, 22]**

Poulton, E. C. (1968). The new psychophysics: Six models for magnitude estimation. *Psychological Bulletin, 69*, 1–19. **[41]**

Poulton, E. C. (1989). *Bias in quantifying judgments.* London: Erlbaum. **[2, 41]**

Poulton, E. C. (1994). *Behavioral decision theory: A new approach*. Cambridge, U.K.: Cambridge University Press. **[26]**

Powell, J. L. (1988). A test of the knew-it-all-along effect in the 1984 presidential statewide elections. *Journal of Applied Social Psychology, 18*, 760–773. **[5]**

Pratkanis, A. (1989). The cognitive representation of attitudes. In *Attitude structure and function* (pp. 71–98), A. R. Pratkanis, S. J. Breckler, & A. G. Greenwald (Eds.). Hillsdale, NJ: Erlbaum. **[Introduction, 23]**

Prelec, D., & Loewenstein, G. (1997). Beyond time discounting. *Marketing Letters, 8*, 97–108. **[16]**

Price, P. C., & Murphy, R. O. (1999). General-knowledge overconfidence: A comparison of Brazilian and American university students. *Mente Social, 5*, 55–74. **[15]**

Priester, J. R., Cacioppo, J. T., & Petty, R. E. (1996). The influence of motor processes on attitudes toward novel versus familiar semantic stimuli. *Personality and Social Psychology Bulletin, 22*, 442–447. **[7]**

Pronin, E., & Berger, J. (1999). Perceptions of intergroup knowledge: The "hippie house" versus the "jock frat." Unpublished manuscript, Stanford University. **[36]**

Pronin, E., Kruger, J., Savitsky, K., & Ross, L. (2001). You don't know me, but I know you: The illusion of asymmetric insight. *Journal of Personality and Social Psychology, 81*. **[36]**

Pronin, E., Lin, D. Y., & Ross, L. (2002). The bias blind spot: Perceptions of bias in self versus others. *Personality and Social Psychology Bulletin*. **[36]**

Pronin, E., & Ross, L. (1999). Two views of romantic break-ups: Biased perceptions of the clarity of intimate communications. Unpublished manuscript, Stanford University. **[36]**

Proust, M. (1949). *Remembrance of things past: the captive* (C. K. S. Moncrieff, Trans.). London: Chatto and Windus. (Original work published 1923.) **[9]**

Pruitt, J. Z., Rubin, D. G., & Kim, S. (1994). *Social conflict: Escalation, stalemate, and settlement*. New York: McGraw-Hill. **[36]**

Pryor, J. B., & Kriss, N. (1977). The cognitive dynamics of salience in the attribution process. *Journal of Personality and Social Psychology, 35*, 49–55. **[20]**

Puccio, C., & Ross, L. (1998). Real versus perceived ideological differences: Can we close the gap? Unpublished manuscript, Stanford University. **[36]**

Puccio, C., & Ross, L. (1999). Understanding "My World": Failures in perspective-taking in predicting performance on a new task. Unpublished manuscript, Stanford University. **[36]**

Pyszczynski, T. A., & Greenberg, J. (1981). Role of disconfirmed expectancies in the instigation of attributional processing. *Journal of Personality and Social Psychology, 40*, 31–38. **[19]**

Quattrone, G., & Jones, E. E. (1980). The perception of variability within in-groups and out-groups: Implications for the law of small numbers. *Journal of Personality and Social Psychology, 38*, 141–152. **[36]**

Quattrone, G. A. (1982). Overattribution and unit formation: when behavior engulfs the person. *Journal of Personality and Social Psychology, 42*, 593–607. **[6, 9]**

Quattrone, G. A. (1985). On the congruity between internal states and action. *Psychological Bulletin, 98*, 3–40. **[16]**

Quattrone, G. A., Lawrence, C. P., Finkel, S. E., & Andrus, D. C. (1981). Explorations in anchoring: The effects of prior range, anchor extremity, and suggestive hints. Manuscript, Stanford University. **[6]**

Quine, W. V. (1977). Natural kinds. In *Naming, necessity, and natural kinds* (pp. 155–175), S. P. Schwartz (Ed.). Ithaca, NY: Cornell University Press. **[22]**

Rabin, M. (1997). Psychology and economics. Berkeley Department of Economics Working Paper. No. 97–251. [30]

Rachlinski, J. (1994). *Prospect theory and the economics of litigation.* Unpublished Doctoral dissertation, Stanford University. [36]

Rachlinski, J. J. (1998). A positive psychological theory of judging in hindsight. *University of Chicago Law Review, 65,* 571–625. [41]

Rachman, S. (1994). The overprediction of fear: A review. *Behavior Research and Therapy, 32,* 683–690. [16]

Rachman, S., & Bichard, S. (1988). The overprediction of fear. *Clinical Psychology Review, 8,* 303–312. [16]

Rachman, S., Levitt, & Lopatka, C. (1988). III. Experimental analyses of panic: Claustrophobic subjects. *Behavior Research and Therapy, 26,* 41–52. [16]

Radhakrishnan, P., Arrow, H., & Sniezek, J. A. (1996). Hoping, performing, learning, and predicting: Changes in the accuracy of self-evaluations of performance. *Human Performance, 9,* 23–49. [19]

Raghunathan, R., & Pham, M. T. (1999). All negative moods are not created equal: Motivational influences of anxiety and sadness on decision making. *Organizational Behavior and Human Decision Performance, 79,* 56–77. [29]

Raiffa, H. (1968). *Decision analysis:* Introductory lectures on choice under uncertainty. Reading, MA: Addison-Wesley. [37]

Read, A. W. et al., (Eds.). (1978). *Funk & Wagnalls new comprehensive international dictionary of the English language.* New York: The Publishers Guild Press. [34]

Read, D. (1985). Determinants of relative mutability. Unpublished research, University of British Columbia, Vancouver, Canada. [20]

Read, D., & Loewenstein, G. (1995). Diversification bias: Explaining the discrepancy in variety seeking between combined and separated choices. *Journal of Experimental Psychology: Applied, 1,* 34–49. [16]

Read, D., & van Leeuwen, B. (1998). Predicting hunger: The effects of appetite and delay on choice. *Organization Behavior and human Decision Processes, 76,* 189–205. [30]

Read, S. J. (1984). Analogical reasoning in social judgment: The importance of causal theories. *Journal of Personality and Social Psychology, 46,* 14–25. [20]

Reber, A. S. (1993). *Implicit learning and tacit knowledge.* New York: Oxford University Press. [24]

Reber, R., Winkielman, P., Schwarz, N. (1998). Effects of perceptual fluency on affective judgments. *Psychological Science, 9,* 45–48. **[Introduction]**

Redding, S. G. (1978). Bridging the culture gap. *Asian Business and Investment, 4,* 45–52. [15]

Redelmeier, D., & Kahneman, D. (1996). Patients' memories of painful medical treatments: real-time and retrospective evaluations of two minimally invasive procedures. *Pain, 66,* 3–8. [2]

Redelmeier, D., Katz, J., & Kahneman, D. (2001). Memories of colonoscopy: A randomized trial. Working paper. [2]

Redelmeier, D., Koehler, D. J., Liberman, V., & Tversky, A. (1995). Probability judgment in medicine: Discounting unspecified alternatives. *Medical Decision Making, 15,* 227–230. [25, 27]

Reeder, G. D., & Brewer, M. B. (1979). A schematic model of dispositional attribution in interpersonal perception. *Psychological Review, 86,* 61–79. [9]

Reeves, T., & Lockhart, R. S. (1993). Distributional versus singular approaches to probability and errors in probabilistic reasoning. *Journal of Experimental Psychology: General, 122,* 207–226. [24, 25]

Regan, D. T., & Totten, J. (1975). Empathy and attribution: Turning observers into actors. *Journal of Personality and Social Psychology, 32*, 850–856. [20]

Rescher, N. (1988). *Rationality: A philosophical inquiry into the nature and rationale of reason*. Oxford, U.K.: Oxford University Press. [24]

Resnik, M. D. (1987). *Choices: An introduction to decision theory*. Minneapolis: University of Minnesota Press. [24]

Revlin, R., Leirer, V., Yopp, H., & Yopp, R. (1980). The belief-bias effect in formal reasoning: The influence of knowledge on logic. *Memory & Cognition, 8*, 584–592. [22]

Riley, D. M., Fischhoff, B., & Small, M., & Fischbeck, P. (2001). Evaluating the effectiveness of risk-reduction strategies for consumer chemical products. *Risk Analysis, 21*, 357–369. [41]

Rips, L. J. (1990). Reasoning. *Annual Review of Psychology, 41*, 321–353. [22]

Rips, L. J. (1994). *The psychology of proof: Deductive reasoning in human thinking*. Cambridge, MA: MIT Press. [22, 24]

Ritov, I. (1996). Anchoring in simulated competitive market negotiations. *Organizational Behavior and Human Decision Processes, 67*, 16–25. [6]

Ritov, I., & Baron, J. (1990). Reluctance to vaccinate: Commission bias and ambiguity. *Journal of Behavioral Decision Making, 3*, 263–277. [21]

Ritov, I., & Baron, J. (1992). Status-quo and omission biases. *Journal of Risk and Uncertainty, 5*, 49–61. [21]

Robins, R. W., & Craik, K. H. (1993). Is there a citation bias in the judgment and decision literature? *Organizational Behavior and Human Decision Processes, 54*, 225–244. [Introduction]

Robinson, L. B., & Hastie, R. (1985). Revision of beliefs when a hypothesis is eliminated from consideration. *Journal of Experimental Psychology: Human Perception and Performance, 4*, 443–456. [25]

Robinson, R. J., & Keltner, D. (1996). Much ado about nothing? Revisionists and traditionalists choose an introductory English syllabus. *Psychological Science, 7*, 18–24. [36]

Robinson, R. J., Keltner, D., Ward, A., & Ross, L. (1995). Actual versus assumed differences in construal: "Naïve realism" in intergroup perception and conflict. *Journal of Personality and Social Psychology, 68*, 404–417. [36]

Roch, S. G., Lane, J. A. S., Samuelson, C. D., Allison, S. T., & Dent, J. L. (2000). Cognitive load and the equality heuristic: A two-stage model of resource overconsumption in small groups. *Organizational Behavior and Human Decision Processes, 83*, 185–212. [30]

Rock, I., & Nijhawan, R. (1989). Regression to egocentrically determined description of form under conditions of inattention. *Journal of Experimental Psychology: Human Perception and Performance, 15*, 259–272. [9]

Roese, N. J. (1994). The functional basis of counterfactual thinking. *Journal of Personality and Social Psychology, 66*, 805–818. [14, 35]

Roese, N. J., & Olson, J. M. (1995). *What might have been: The social psychology of counterfactual thinking*. Hillsdale, NJ: Erlbaum. [35]

Rogers, R. W., & Mewborn, C. R. (1976). Fear appeals and attitude change. *Journal of Personality and Social Psychology, 34*, 54–61. [4]

Ronis, D. L., & Yates, J. F. (1987). Components of probability judgment accuracy: Individual consistency and effects of participant matter and assessment method. *Organizational Behavior and Human Decision Processes, 40*, 193–218. [15]

Roos, M., Hietanen, M., & Luoma, J. (1975). A New Procedure for Averaging Particle Properties. *Physics Fennica, 10*, 21–33. [37]

Rorty, R. (1970). Incorrigibility as the mark of the mental. *The Journal of Philosophy, 67*, 399–424. **[16]**

Rosch, E. (1978). Principles of categorization. In *Cognition and categorization*, E. Rosch & B. B. Lloyd (Eds.). Hillsdale, NJ: Erlbaum. **[1, 3]**

Rosen, A., & Rozin, P. (1993). Now you see it...Now you don't: The preschool child's conception of invisible particles in the context of dissolving. *Developmental Psychology, 29*, 300–311. **[11]**

Rosenberg, M. (1965). *Society and the adolescent self-image.* Princeton, NJ: Princeton University Press. **[14]**

Rosenfeld, H. (1975). The particle date group: Growth and operators. *Annual Review of Nuclear Science, 25*, 555–599. **[37]**

Rosenthal, R. (1994). Metaanalysis: A review. *Psychosomatic Medicine, 53*, 247–271. **[41]**

Ross, L. (1977). The intuitive psychologist and his shortcomings: Distortions in the attribution process. In *Advances in Experimental Social Psychology*, (Vol. 10, pp. 174–214), L. Berkowitz (Ed.). New York: Academic Press. **[Introduction, 20, 36]**

Ross, L. (1990). Recognizing the role of construal processes. In *The legacy of Solomon Asch: essays in cognition and social psychology*, I. Rock (Ed.). Hillsdale, NJ: Lawrence Erlbaum Associates. **[8]**

Ross, L. (1995). Reactive devaluation in negotiation and conflict resolution. In *Barriers to the negotiated resolution of conflict* (pp. 30–48), K. Arrow, R. Mnookin, L. Ross, A. Tversky, & R. Wilson (Eds.). New York: Norton. **[36]**

Ross, L., Amabile, T. M., & Steinmetz, J. L. (1977). Social roles, social control, and biases in social-perception processes. *Journal of Personality and Social Psychology, 35*, 485–494. **[9]**

Ross, L., & Anderson, C. A. (1982). Shortcomings in the attribution process: On the origins and maintenance of erroneous social assessments. In *Judgment under uncertainty: Heuristics and biases* (pp. 129–152), D. Kahneman, R. Slovic, & A. Tversky (Eds.). New York: Cambridge University Press. **[20]**

Ross, L., Greene, D., & House, P. (1977). The false consensus effect: An egocentric bias in social perception and attribution processes. *Journal of Personality and Social Psychology, 13*, 279–301. **[36]**

Ross, L., & Lepper, M. R. (1980). The perseverance of beliefs: Empirical and normative considerations. In *New directions for methodology of social and behavioral science: Fallible judgment in behavioral research* (pp. 17–36), R. A. Shweder & D. Fiske (Eds.). San Francisco: Jossey Bass. **[20, 36]**

Ross, L., Lepper, M. R., Strack, F., & Steinmetz, J. L. (1977). Social explanation and social expectation: the effects of real and hypothetical explanation upon subjective likelihood. *Journal of Personality and Social Psychology, 35*, 817–829. **[4]**

Ross, L., & Nisbett, R. E. (1991). *The person and the situation.* New York: McGraw-Hill. **[36]**

Ross, L., & Stillinger, C. (1991). Barriers to conflict resolution. *Negotiation Journal, 8*, 389–404. **[36]**

Ross, L., & Ward, A. (1995). Psychological barriers to dispute resolution. In *Advances in experimental social psychology*, (Vol. 27, pp. 255–304), M. Zanna (Ed.). San Diego: Academic Press. **[36]**

Ross, L., & Ward, A. (1996). Naïve realism in everyday life: Implications for social conflict and misunderstanding. In *Values and knowledge* (pp. 103–135), T. Brown, E. Reed, & E. Turiel (Eds.). Hillsdale, NJ: Erlbaum. **[36]**

Ross, M. (1989). The relation of implicit theories to the construction of personal histories. *Psychological Review, 96*, 341–357. **[16, 19]**

Ross, M., & Buehler, R. (2001). Identity through time: Constructing personal pasts and futures. In *Blackwell handbook of social psychology: Intraindividual processes* (Vol. 1, pp. 518–544), A. Tesser & N. Schwarz (Eds.). Oxford, U.K.: Blackwell. **[14]**

Ross, M., & Fletcher, G. J. O. (1985). Attribution and social perception. In *The handbook of social psychology* (3rd ed.; Vol. 2, pp. 73–122), G. Lindzey & A. Aronson (Eds.). Reading, MA: Addison-Wesley. **[14]**

Ross, M., & Sicoly, F. (1979). Egocentric biases in availability and attribution. *Journal of Personality and Social Psychology, 37*, 322–336. **[36]**

Rothbart, M., Fulero, S., Jenson, D., Howard, J., & Biffell, P. (1978). From individual to group impressions: availability heuristics in stereotype formation. *Journal of Experimental Social Psychology, 14*, 237–255. **[4]**

Rothman, A. J., Klein, W. M., & Weinstein, N. D. (1996). Absolute and relative biases in estimations of personal risk. *Journal of Applied Social Psychology, 26*, 1213–1236. **[19, 27]**

Rothman, A. J., & Schwarz, N. (1998). Constructing perceptions of vulnerability: personal relevance and the use of experiential information in health judgments. *Personality and Social Psychology Bulletin, 24*, 1053–1064. **[5]**

Rottenstreich, Y., Brenner, L., & Sood, S. (1999). Similarity between hypotheses and evidence. *Cognitive Psychology, 38*, 110–128. **[27]**

Rottenstreich, Y., Hsee, C. K. (2001). Money, kisses, and electric shocks: On the affective psychology of risk. *Psychological Science, 12*, 185–190. **[23, 30]**

Rottenstreich, Y., & Tversky, A. (1997). Unpacking, repacking, and anchoring: advances in support theory. *Psychological Review, 104*, 406–415. **[6, 14, 26, 27, 39]**

Rouse, W. B., & Morris, N. M. (1986). On looking into the black box: Prospects and limits in the search for mental models. *Psychological Bulletin, 100*, 349–363. **[41]**

Rozin, P. (1990). Social and moral aspects of eating. In *The legacy of Solomon Asch: Essays in cognition and social psychology* (pp. 97–110), I. Rock (Ed.). Potomac, MD: Lawrence Erlbaum Associates. **[11]**

Rozin, P. (1996). Towards a psychology of food and eating: from motivation to model to meaning, morality and metaphor. *Current Directions in Psychological Science, 5*, 1–7. **[11]**

Rozin, P., & Fallon, A. E. (1987). A perspective on disgust. *Psychological Review, 94*, 23–41. **[11]**

Rozin, P., Fallon, A. E., & Augustoni-Ziskind, M. (1985). The child's conception of food: the development of contamination sensitivity to "disgusting" substances. *Developmental Psychology, 21*, 1075–1079. **[11]**

Rozin, P., Fallon, A. E., & Augustoni-Ziskind, M. (1986). The child's conception of food: development of categories of accepted and rejected substances. *Journal of Nutrition Education, 18*, 75–81. **[11]**

Rozin, P., Fallon, A. E., & Mandell, R. (1984). Family resemblance in attitudes to food. *Developmental Psychology, 20*, 309–314. **[11]**

Rozin, P., Grant, H., Weinberg, S., & Parker, S. (2000). "Head versus heart": Effect of monetary frames on expression of sympathetic magical concerns. Unpublished manuscript. **[11]**

Rozin, P., Haidt, J., & McCauley, C. R. (1993). Disgust. In *Handbook of emotions* (pp. 575–594), M. Lewis & J. Haviland (Eds.). New York: Guilford. **[11]**

Rozin, P., Haidt, J., McCauley, C. R., Dunlop, L., & Ashmore, M. (1999). Individual differences in disgust sensitivity: comparisons and evaluations of paper-and-pencil versus behavioral measures. *Journal of Research in Personality, 33,* 330–351. **[11]**

Rozin, P., Haidt, J., McCauley, C. R., & Imada, S. (1997). The cultural evolution of disgust. In *Food preferences and taste: Continuity and change* (pp. 65–82), H. M. Macbeth (Ed.). Oxford, U.K.: Berghahn. **[11]**

Rozin, P., & Kalat, J. W. (1971). Specific hungers and poison avoidance as adaptive specializations of learning. *Psychological Review, 78,* 459–486. **[11]**

Rozin, P., Markwith, M., & McCauley, C. R. (1994). The nature of aversion to indirect contact with another person: AIDS aversion as a composite of aversion to strangers, infection, moral taint and misfortune. *Journal of Abnormal Psychology, 103,* 495–504. **[11]**

Rozin, P., Markwith, M., & Nemeroff, C. (1992). Magical contagion beliefs and fear of AIDS. *Journal of Applied Social Psychology, 22,* 1081–1092. **[11]**

Rozin, P., Markwith, M., & Ross, B. (1990). The sympathetic magical law of similarity, nominal realism and the neglect of negatives in response to negative labels. *Psychological Science, 1,* 383–384. **[11]**

Rozin, P., Millman, L., & Nemeroff, C. (1986). Operation of the laws of sympathetic magic in disgust and other domains. *Journal of Personality and Social Psychology, 50,* 703–712. **[11]**

Rozin, P., Nemeroff, C., Horowitz, M., Gordon, B., & Voet, W. (1995). The borders of the self: Contamination sensitivity and potency of the mouth, other apertures and body parts. *Journal of Research in Personality, 29,* 318–340. **[11]**

Rozin, P., Nemeroff, C., Wane, M., & Sherrod, A. (1989). Operation of the sympathetic magical law of contagion in interpersonal attitudes among Americans. *Bulletin of the Psychonomic Society, 27,* 367–370. **[11]**

Rozin, P., & Nemeroff, C. J. (1990). The laws of sympathetic magic: A psychological analysis of similarity and contagion. In *Cultural psychology: Essays on comparative human development* (pp. 205–232.), J. Stigler, G. Herdt & R. A. Shweder (Eds.). Cambridge, U.K.: Cambridge University Press. **[11]**

Rozin, P., & Royzman, E. (in press). Negativity bias, negativity dominance, and contagion. *Personality & Social Psychology Bulletin.* **[11]**

Rozin, P., Taylor, C. P., Ross, L., Bennett, G., & Hejmadi, A. (2000). Recognition of disgust and other emotional expressions, individual differences in obsessive and compulsive tendencies, and disgust sensitivity. Unpublished manuscript. **[11]**

Rubinstein, A. (1979). False probabilistic arguments vs. faulty intuition. *Israel Law Review, 14,* 247–254. **[1]**

Rumelhart, D. E. (1989). Towards a microstructural account of human reasoning. In *Similarity and analogical reasoning* (pp. 298–312), S. Vosniadou & A. Ortony (Eds.). Cambridge, U.K.: Cambridge University Press. **[22]**

Rumelhart, D. E., & Zipser, D. (1985). Feature discovery by competitive learning. *Cognitive Science, 9,* 75–112. **[22]**

Rush, H. (1955, August). The speed of light. *Scientific American,* 62–67. **[37]**

Russell, T., & Thaler, R. H. (1985). The relevance of quasi-rationality in competitive markets. *American Economic Review, 75,* 1071–1082. **[38]**

Russo, J. E., & Kolzow, K. (1994). Where is the fault in fault trees? *Journal of Experimental Psychology: Human Perception and Performance, 20,* 17–32. **[25]**

Russo, J. E., & Shoemaker, P. J. H. (1989). *Decision traps.* New York: Simon and Schuster. **[6]**

Rutledge, R. W. (1993). The effects of group decisions and group-shifts on use of the anchoring and adjustment heuristic. *Social Behavior and Personality, 21*, 215–226. **[6]**

Ryle, G. (1949). *The concept of mind.* London: Hutchinson. **[9, 16]**

Sackett, D. L., & Snow, J. S. (1979). The magnitude of compliance and noncompliance. In *Compliance in health care* (pp. 11–22), R. B. Haynes, D. W. Taylor, & D. L. Sackett (Eds.). Baltimore: Johns Hopkins University Press. **[4]**

Saks, M. J., & Kidd, R. F. (1981). Human information processing and adjudication: Trials by heuristics. *Law & Society Review, 15*, 123–160. **[1]**

Samuels, R., Stich, S., & Bishop, M. (in press). Ending the rationality wars: How to make disputes about human rationality disappear. In *Common sense, reasoning and rationality: Vancouver studies in cognitive science,* (Vol. 11) R. Elio (Ed.). New York: Oxford University Press. **[Introduction]**

Samuelson, W., & Zeckhauser, R. (1988). Status quo bias in decision making. *Journal of Risk and Uncertainty, 1*, 7–59. **[30, 32]**

Sanfey, A., & Hastie, R. (1998). Does evidence presentation format affect judgment? An experimental evaluation of displays of data for judgments. *Psychological Science* 9(2), 99–103. **[23]**

Sanna, L. J., Schwarz, N., & Stocker, S. L. (2001). When debiasing backfires: Accessible content and accessibility experiences in debiasing hindsight through mental simulations. Manuscript under review. **[5]**

Sargent, T. J. (1993). *Bounded rationality in macroeconomics.* Oxford, U.K.: Clarendon Press. **[31]**

Saunders S. (1993). Stock prices and Wall Street weather. *American Economic Review, 83*, 1337–45 **[29]**

Savage, L. J. (1954). *The foundations of statistics.* New York: Wiley. **[31, 41]**

Savitsky, K., Medvec, V. H., Charlton, A. E., & Gilovich, T. (1998). "What, me worry?" Arousal, misattribution and the effect of temporal distance on confidence. *Personality and Social Psychology Bulletin, 24*, 529–536. **[19, 29]**

Sawyer, J. (1966). Measurement and prediction, clinical and statistical. *Psychological Bulletin, 66*, 178–200. **[40]**

Scanlon, M., & Mauro J. (1992, November/December). The lowdown on handwriting analysis: Is it for real? *Psychology Today, 80*, 46–53. **[34]**

Schank, R. C. (1982). *Dynamic memory: Learning in computers and people.* New York: Cambridge University Press. **[20]**

Scheier, M. F., & Carver, C. S. (1985). Optimism, coping, and health: Assessment and implications of generalized outcome expectancies. *Health Psychology, 4*, 219–247. **[14]**

Scheier, M. F., & Carver, C. S. (1988). A model of behavioral self-regulation: Translating intention into action. In *Advances in Experimental Social Psychology* (Vol. 21, pp. 303–346), L. Berkowitz (Ed.). New York: Academic Press. **[19]**

Schelling, T. (1960). *The Strategy of Conflict.* Cambridge, MA: Harvard University Press. **[30]**

Schelling, T. (1984). Self-command in practice, in policy, and in theory of rational choice. *American Economic Review, 74*, 1–11. **[16]**

Schick, F. (1987). Rationality: A third dimension. *Economics and Philosophy, 3*, 49–66. **[24]**

Schick, F. (1997). *Making choices: A recasting of decision theory.* Cambridge, U.K.: Cambridge University Press. **[24]**

Schick, T., & Vaughn, L. (1999). *How to think about weird things: Critical thinking for a new age.* Mountain View, CA: Mayfield. **[Introduction, 34]**

Schifter, D. E., & Ajzen, I. (1985). Intention, perceived control, and weight loss: An application of the theory of planned behavior. *Journal of Personality and Social Psychology, 49*, 843–851. **[14]**

Schkade, D. A., & Johnson, E. J. (1989). Cognitive processes in preference reversals. *Organizational Behavior and Human Decision Processes, 44*, 203–231. **[6, 7]**

Schkade, D. A., & Kahneman, D. (1998). Does living in California make people happy? A focusing illusion in judgments of life satisfaction. *Psychological Science, 9*, 340–346. **[14, 16]**

Schkade, D. A., & Kilbourne, L. M. (1991). Expectation-outcome consistency and hindsight bias. *Organizational Behavior and Human Decision Processes, 49*, 105–123. **[19]**

Schlenker, B. R. (Ed.). (1985). *The self and social life.* New York: McGraw-Hill. **[32]**

Schneider, S. L. (1995). Item difficulty, discrimination, and the confidence-frequency effect in a categorical judgment task. *Organizational Behavior and Human Decision Processes, 61*, 148–167. **[39]**

Schneider, W., & Shiffrin, R. M. (1977). Controlled and automatic human information processing: Detection, search, and attention. *Psychological Review, 84*, 1–66. **[9, 22]**

Schoemaker, P. J. H. (1993). Multiple scenario development: Its conceptual and behavioral foundation. *Strategic Management Journal, 14*, 193–213. **[14]**

Schoenbach, V. J. (1987). Appraising the health risk appraisal. *American Journal of Public Health, 77*, 409–410. **[17]**

Schreiber, C., & Kahneman, D. (2000). Determinants of the remembered utility of aversive sounds. *Journal of Experimental Psychology: General, 129*, 27–42. **[2]**

Schul, Y., & Bernstein, E. (1985). When discounting fails: Conditions under which individuals use discredited information in making a judgment. *Journal of Personality and Social Psychology, 49*, 894–903. **[20]**

Schumacher, E. (1985, September 21). Death of "Yiyo" raises passions over bullfights. *The Globe and Mail*, p. B9. **[21]**

Schustack, M. W., & Sternberg, R. J. (1981). Evaluation of evidence in causal inference. *Journal of Experimental Psychology: General, 110*, 101–120. **[20]**

Schwarz, N. (1987). *Stimmung als Information: Untersuchungen zum Einfluß von Stimmungen auf die Bewertung des eigenen Lebens.* (Mood as information: Investigations into mood effects on the evaluation of one's life.) Heidelberg, FRG: Springer Verlag. **[29]**

Schwarz, N. (1990). Feelings as information: Informational and motivational functions of affective states. In *Handbook of motivation and cognition: Foundations of social behavior* (Vol. 2, pp. 527–561), E. T. Higgins & R. Sorrentino (Eds.). New York: Guilford Press. **[21, 29]**

Schwarz, N. (1994). Judgment in a social context: Biases, shortcomings, and the logic of conversation. In *Advances in experimental social psychology* (Vol. 26, pp. 123–162), M. P. Zanna (Ed.). San Diego: Academic Press. **[6, 32]**

Schwarz, N. (1995). Social cognition: Information accessibility and use in social judgment. In *Thinking.* (*An Invitation to Cognitive Science*, Vol. 3, 2nd ed., pp. 345–376), E. E. Smith & D. N. Osherson (Eds.). Cambridge, MA: MIT Press. **[5]**

Schwarz, N. (1996). *Cognition and communication: judgmental biases, research methods, and the logic of conversation.* Mahwah, NJ: Lawrence Erlbaum Associates. **[2, 24]**

Schwarz, N. (1998). Accessible content and accessibility experiences: the interplay of declarative and experiential information in judgment. *Personality and Social Psychology Review, 2*, 87–99. **[5]**

Schwarz, N. (1999). Self reports. *American Psychologist, 54*, 93–105. **[41]**

Schwarz, N. (2001). Feelings as information: Implications for affective influences on information processing. In *Theories of mood and cognition: A user's handbook* (pp. 159–176), L. L. Martin & G. L. Clore (Eds.). Mahwah, NJ: Lawrence Erlbaum Associates. **[29]**

Schwarz, N. (in press). Where are the unique predictions? *Psychological Inquiry.* **[29]**

Schwarz, N., & Bless H. (1992). Constructing reality and its alternatives: an inclusion/ exclusion model of assimilation and contrast effects in social judgment. In *The construction of social judgments* (pp. 217–245), L. L. Martin & A. Tesser (Eds.). Hillsdale NJ: Lawrence Erlbaum Associates. **[6]**

Schwarz, N., Bless, H., & Bohner, G. (1991). Mood and persuasion: Affective states influence the processing of persuasive communications. In *Advances in Experimental Social Psychology* (Vol. 24, pp. 161–199), M. Zanna (Ed.). San Diego, CA: Academic Press. **[29]**

Schwarz, N., Bless, H., Strack, F., Klumpp, G., Rittenauer-Schatka, H., & Simons, A. (1991). Ease of retrieval as information: Another look at the availability heuristic. *Journal of Personality and Social Psychology, 61*, 195–202. **[2, 5]**

Schwarz, N., & Clore, G. L. (1983). Mood, misattribution, and judgments of well-being: Informative and directive functions of affective states. *Journal of Personality and Social Psychology, 45*, 513–523. **[2, 5, 29]**

Schwarz, N., & Clore, G. L. (1988). How do I feel about it? Informative functions of affective states. In *Affect, cognition, and social behavior* (pp. 44–62), K. Fiedler & J. Forgas (Eds.). Toronto: Hogrefe International. **[23, 29, 30]**

Schwarz, N., & Clore, G. L. (1996). Feelings and phenomenal experiences. In *Social psychology: a handbook of basic principles* (pp. 433–465), E. T. Higgins & A. Kruglanski (Eds.). New York: Guilford. **[5, 29]**

Schwarz, N., & Schuman, H. (1997). Political Knowledge, attribution, and inferred political interest. *International journal of Public Opinion Research, 9*, 191–195. **[5]**

Schwarz, N., Servay, W., & Kumpf, M. (1985). Attribution of arousal as a mediator of the effectiveness of fear-arousing communications. *Journal of Applied Social Psychology, 15*, 74–78. **[29]**

Schwarz, N., & Skurnik, I. (in press). Feeling and thinking: Implications for problem solving. In *The nature of problem solving*, J. Davidson & R. Sternberg (Eds.). Cambridge, U.K.: Cambridge University Press. **[29]**

Schwarz, N., Strack, F., Hilton, D., & Naderer, G. (1991). Base rates, representativeness, and the logic of conversation: The contextual relevance of "irrelevant" information. *Social Cognition, 9*, 67–84. **[2]**

Schwarz, N., Strack, F., Kommer, D., & Wagner, D. (1987). Soccer, rooms and the quality of your life: Mood effects on judgments of satisfaction with life in general and with specific life-domains. *European Journal of Social Psychology, 17*, 69–79. **[29]**

Schwarz, S., & Griffin, T. (1986). *Medical thinking: The psychology of medical judgment and decision making.* New York: Springer Verlag. **[39]**

Schyns, P. G. (1991). A modular neural network model of concept acquisition. *Cognitive Science, 15*, 461–508. **[22]**

Seligman, M. E. P. (1975). *Helplessness: On depression, development, and death.* San Francisco: Freeman. **[16]**

Sen, S., & Johnson, E. J. (1997). Mere-possession effects without possession in consumer choice. *Journal of Consumer Research, 24,* 105–117. **[6]**

Sensenig, P. E., & Cialdini, R. B. (1984). Social psychological influences on the compliance process: implications for behavioral health. In *Behavioral health: A handbook of health enhancement and disease prevention,* J. D. Matarazzo, N. E. Miller, S. M. Weiss, J. A. Herd, & S. M. Weiss (Eds.). New York: John Wiley & Sons, Inc. **[4]**

Shafer, G. (1976). *A mathematical theory of evidence.* Princeton, NJ: Princeton University Press. **[1, 20, 25, 26]**

Shafer, G., & Tversky, A. (1983). *Weighting evidence: The design and comparisons of probability thought experiments.* Unpublished manuscript, Stanford University. **[1]**

Shafer, G., & Tversky, A. (1985). Languages and designs for probability judgment. *Cognitive Science, 9,* 309–339. **[41]**

Shafir, E. (1993). Choosing and rejecting: why some options are both better and worse. *Memory & Cognition, 21,* 546–556. **[6]**

Shafir, E., Osherson, D. N., & Smith, E. E. (1989). An advantage model of choice. *Journal of Behavioral Decision Making, 2,* 1–23. **[23]**

Shafir, E., Simonson, I., & Tversky, A. (1993). Reason-based choice. *Cognition, 49,* 11–36. **[23, 32]**

Shafir, E. B., Smith, E. E., & Osherson, D. N. (1990). Typicality and reasoning fallacies. *Memory and Cognnition, 18,* 229–239. **[3]**

Shaklee, H., & Fischhoff, B. (1982). Strategies of information search in causal analysis. *Memory and Cognition, 10,* 520–530. **[14]**

Shanteau, J. (1978). When does a response error become a judgmental bias? *Journal of Experimental Psychology: Human Learning and Memory, 4,* 579–581. **[41]**

Shanteau, J. (1999). Decision making by experts: The GNAHM effect. In *Decision research from Bayesian approaches to normative systems: Reflections on the contributions of Ward Edwards,* J. Shanteau, B. Mellers, & D. Schum (Eds.). Norwell, MA: Kluwer Academic Publishers. **[39]**

Sheeran, P., Orbell, S., & Trafimow, D. (1999). Does the temporal stability of behavioral intentions moderate intention–behavior and past behavior–future behavior relations? *Personality and Social Psychology Bulletin, 25,* 721–730. **[14]**

Shepperd, J. A., Ouellette, J. A., & Fernandez, J. K. (1996). Abandoning unrealistic optimism: Performance estimates and the temporal proximity of self-relevant feedback. *Journal of Personality and Social Psychology, 70,* 844–855. **[19]**

Sherif, C., Sherif, M., & Nebergall, R. (1965). *Attitude and attitude change: The social judgment–involvement approach.* Philadelphia: Saunders. **[6]**

Sherif, M., & Hovland, D. (1961). *Social judgment: Assimilation and contrast effects in communication and attitude change.* New Haven, CT: Yale University Press. **[6]**

Sherman, D. A., Kim, H., & Zajonc, R. B. (1998). Affective perseverance: Cognitions change but preferences stay the same. Paper presented at the annual meeting of the American Psychological Society, 1998. **[23]**

Sherman, R. S. (1982). *Decreasing premature termination from psychotherapy via an imagination/explanation procedure.* Unpublished Doctoral dissertation, Indiana University. **[4]**

Sherman, S. J. (1980). On the self-erasing nature of errors of prediction. *Journal of Personality and Social Psychology, 39,* 211–221. **[4, 14, 19]**

Sherman, S. J., Cialdini, R. B., Schwartzman, D. F., & Reynolds, K. D. (1985). Imagining can heighten or lower the perceived likelihood of contracting a disease: The mediating effect of ease of imagery. *Personality and Social Psychology Bulletin, 11,* 118–127. **[21]**

Sherman, S. J., & Corty, E. (1984). Cognitive heuristics. In *Handbook of social cognition* (Vol. 1, pp. 189–286), R. S. Wyer & T. K. Srull (Eds.). Hillsdale, NJ: Lawrence Erlbaum Associates. **[5]**

Sherman, S. J., Skov, R. B., Hervitz, E. F., & Stock, C. B. (1981). The effects of explaining hypothetical future events: From possibility to actuality and beyond. *Journal of Experimental Social Psychology, 17,* 142–158. **[14, 17, 19]**

Sherman, S. J., Zehner, K. S., Johnson, J., & Hirt, E. R. (1983). Social explanation: the role of timing, set, and recall on subjective likelihood estimates. *Journal of Personality and Social Psychology, 44,* 1127–1143. **[4]**

Shiffrin, R. M., Dumais, S. T., & Schneider, W. (1981). Characteristics of automatism. In *Attention and performance IX* (pp. 223–238), J. B. Long & A. Baddeley (Eds.). Hillsdale, NJ: Erlbaum. **[22]**

Shiffrin, R. M., & Schneider, W. (1977). Controlled and automatic human information processing: II. Perceptual learning, automatic attending, and a general theory. *Psychological Review, 84,* 127–190. **[22]**

Shiller, R. J. (1987). Investor behavior in the October 1987 stock market crash: Survey evidence. Working Paper, Cowles Foundation, Yale University. **[38]**

Shiller, R. J. (2000). *Irrational exuberance.* Princeton, NJ: Princeton University Press. **[38]**

Shimojo, S., & Ichikawa, S. (1989). Intuitive reasoning about probability: theoretical and experimental analyses of the "problem of three prisoners." *Cognition, 32,* 1–32. **[22]**

Shlyakhter, A. I., Kammen, D. M., Broido, C. L., & Wilson, R. (1994). Quantifying the credibility of energy projections from trends in past data: The U.S. energy sector. *Energy Policy, 22,* 119–131. **[41]**

Shrauger, J. S., Mariano, E., & Walter, T. J. (1998). Depressive symptoms and accuracy in the prediction of future events. *Personality and Social Psychology Bulletin, 24,* 880–892. **[14]**

Shrauger, J. S., & Osberg, T. M. (1981). The relative accuracy of self-predictions and judgments by others in psychological assessment. *Psychological Bulletin, 90,* 322–351. **[14]**

Shrauger, J. S., Ram, D., Greninger, S. A., & Mariano, E. (1996). Accuracy of self-predictions versus judgments by knowledgeable others. *Personality and Social Psychology Bulletin, 22,* 1229–1243. **[14]**

Shweder, R. A. (1977). Likeness and likelihood in everday thought: Magical thinking in judgments about personality. *Current Anthropology, 18*(4), 637–658. **[2, 11]**

Shweder, R. A. (1987). Comments on Plott and on Kahneman, Knetsch, & Thaler. In *Rational choice: The contrast between economics and psychology* (pp. 161–170), R. M. Hogarth & M. W. Reder (Eds.). Chicago: Chicago University Press. **[24]**

Sieck, W., & Yates, J. F. (1997). Exposition effects on decision making: Choice and confidence in choice. *Organizational Behavior and Human Decision Processes, 70,* 207–219. **[24]**

Siegal, M. (1988). Children's knowledge of contagion and contamination as causes of illness. *Child Development, 59,* 1353–1359. **[11]**

Siegal, M., & Share, D. L. (1990). Contamination sensitivity in young children. *Developmental Psychology, 26,* 455–458. **[11]**

Siegel, S. (1956). *Nonparametric statistics.* New York: McGraw-Hill. **[33]**

Siegel-Jacobs, K., & Yates, J. F. (1996). Effects of procedural and outcome accountability on judgment quality. *Organizational Behavior and Human Decision Processes, 1*, 1–17. **[32]**

Siemer, M., & Reisenzein, R. (1998). Effects of mood on evaluative judgment: Influence of reduced processing capacity and mood salience. *Cognition and Emotion, 12*, 783–805. **[29]**

Siero, S., Kok, G., & Pruyn, J. (1984). Effects of public education about breast cancer and breast self-examination. *Social Science and Medicine, 18*, 881–888. **[17]**

Simon, H. (1978). Rational decision making in organizations. *The American Economic Review, 69*(4), 493–513. **[30]**

Simon, H. (1982). *Models of bounded rationality.* Cambridge, MA: MIT Press. **[11, 31]**

Simon, H. A. (1956a). Dynamic programming under uncertainty with a quadratic criterion function. *Econometrica, 24*, 19–33. **[31]**

Simon, H. A. (1956b). Rational choice and the structure of the environment. *Psychological Review, 63*, 129–138. **[Introduction, 23]**

Simon, H. A. (1957). *Models of man: Social and rational.* New York: Wiley. **[Introduction, 28]**

Simon, H. A. (1979). *Models of thought*, Vol. 1. New Haven, CT: Yale University Press. **[39]**

Simon, H. A. (1983). *Reason in human affairs.* Stanford, CA: Stanford University Press. **[Introduction]**

Simon, H. A. (1992). *Economics, bounded rationality, and the cognitive revolution.* Aldershot Hants, England: Elgar. **[31]**

Simonson, I. (1989). Choice based on reasons: The case of attraction and compromise effects. *Journal of Consumer Research, 16*, 158–174. **[32]**

Simonson, I. (1992). The influence of anticipating regret and responsibility on purchase decisions. *Journal of Consumer Research, 19*, 105–118. **[21]**

Simonson, I., & Nye, P. (1992). The effect of accountability on susceptibility to decision errors. *Organizational Behavior and Human Decision Processes, 51*, 416–446. **[32]**

Simonson, I., & Staw, B. M. (1992). Deescalation strategies: A comparison of techniques for reducing commitment to losing courses of action. *Journal of Applied Psychology, 77*, 419–426. **[32]**

Sinclair, R. C., & Mark, M. M. (1992). The influence of mood state on judgment and action: Effects on persuasion, categorization, social justice, person perception, and judgmental accuracy. In *The construction of social judgment* (pp. 165–193), L. L. Martin & A. Tesser (Eds.). Hillsdale, NJ: Lawrence Erlbaum Associates. **[29]**

Sinclair, R. C., Mark, M. M., & Clore, G. L. (1994). Mood-related persuasion depends on misattributions. *Social Cognition, 12*, 309–326. **[29]**

Singer, E., & Endreny, P. M. (1994). *Reporting on risk.* New York: Russell Sage Foundation. **[41]**

Singer, J. A., & Salovey, P. (1988). Mood and memory: Evaluating the network theory of affect. *Clinical Psychology Review, 8*, 211–251. **[29]**

Skov, R. B., & Sherman, S. J. (1986). Information-gathering processes: Diagnosticity, hypothesis-confirmatory strategies, and perceived hypothesis confirmation. *Journal of Experimental Social Psychology, 22*, 93–121. **[6]**

Skyrms, B. (1986). *Choice & chance: An introduction to inductive logic* (3rd ed.). Belmont, CA: Wadsworth. **[22, 24]**

Slater, J. (1996). Theory and method in health audience segmentation. *Journal of Health Communication, 1*, 267–283. **[41]**

Sloan, R. G. (1996). Do stock prices fully reflect information in accruals and cash flows about future earnings? *Accounting Review, 71*, 289–315. **[38]**

Sloman, S. A. (1993). Feature-based induction. *Cognitive Psychology, 25,* 231–280. [22]

Sloman, S. A. (1996). The empirical case for two systems of reasoning. *Psychological Bulletin, 119,* 3–22. [Introduction, 2, 22, 23, 24]

Sloman, S. A. (1998). Categorical inference is not a tree: The myth of inheritance hierarchies. *Cognitive Psychology, 35,* 1–33. [22]

Sloman, S., & Over, D. E. (in press). Probability judgment: From the inside and out. To appear in D. E. Over (Ed.), *Evolution and the psychology of thinking: The debate.* Hove, U.K.: Psychology Press. [Introduction]

Sloman, S. A., Slovak, L., & Over, D. (2000). *Frequency illusions and other fallacies.* Manuscript under review, Brown University. [Introduction]

Slovic, P. (1967). The relative influence of probabilities and payoffs upon perceived risk of a gamble. *Psychonomic Science, 9,* 223–224. [6]

Slovic, P. (1987). Perception of risk. *Science, 236,* 280–285. [23, 41]

Slovic, P. (1995). The construction of preference. *American Psychologist, 50,* 364–371. [23, 24]

Slovic, P. (2000). Rational actors and rational fools: The influence of affect on judgment and decision making. *Roger Williams University Law Review, 6,* 167–216. [23]

Slovic, P. (2001). Cigarette smokers: Rational actors or rational fools. In *Smoking: Risk, perception, and policy* (pp. 97–124), P. Slovic (Ed.). Thousand Oaks, CA.: Sage. [23]

Slovic, P., & Fischhoff, B. (1977). On the psychology of experimental surprises. *Journal of Experimental Psychology: Human Perception and Performance, 3,* 544–551. [5, 6, 37]

Slovic, P., Fischhoff, B., & Lichtenstein, S. (1976). Cognitive processes and societal risk taking. In *Cognition and social behavior,* J. S. Carroll & J. W. Payne (Eds.). Potomac, MD: Erlbaum. [1]

Slovic, P., Fischhoff, B., & Lichtenstein, S. (1977). Behavioral decision theory. *Annual Review of Psychology, 28,* 1–39. [24]

Slovic, P., Fischhoff, B., & Lichtenstein, S. (1980). Facts and fears: Understanding perceived risk. In *Societal risk assessment: How safe is safe enough?* (pp. 181–214), R. Schwing & W. A. Albers, Jr. (Eds.). New York: Plenum Press. [41]

Slovic, P., Fischhoff, B., & Lichtenstein, S. (1982). Response mode, framing, and information-processing effects in risk assessment. In *New directions for methodology of social and behavioral science: Question framing and response consistency* (pp. 21–36), R. Hogarth (Ed.). San Francisco: Jossey-Bass. [12]

Slovic, P., Layman, M., Kraus, N., Flynn, J., Chalmers, J., & Gesell, G. (1991). Perceived risk, stigma, and potential economic impacts of a high-level nuclear waste repository in Nevada. *Risk Analysis, 11,* 683–696. [23]

Slovic, P., & Lichtenstein, S. (1968). Relative importance of probabilities and payoffs in risk-taking. *Journal of Experimental Psychology Monograph 78*(3, Pt. 2), 1–18. [6, 12, 23, 26]

Slovic, P., & Lichtenstein, S. (1971). Comparison of Bayesian and regression approaches to the study of information processing in judgment. *Organizational Behavior and Human Decision Performance, 6,* 649–744. [8, 12, 13]

Slovic, P., & Lichtenstein, S. (1983). Preference reversals: A broader perspective. *American Economic Review, 73,* 596–605. [6, 12]

Slovic, P., Lichtenstein, S., & Fischhoff, B. (1984). Modeling the societal impact of fatal accidents. *Management Science, 30,* 464–474. [41]

Slovic, P., MacGregor, D. G., Malmfors, T., & Purchase, I. F. H. (1999). *Influence of affective processes on toxicologists' judgments of risk* (Report No. 99–2). Eugene, OR: Decision Research. **[23]**

Slovic, P., & MacPhillamy, D. (1974). Dimensional commensurability and cue utilization in comparative judgment. *Organizational Behavior and Human Performance II,* 172–194. **[12]**

Slovic, P., Monahan, J., & MacGregor, D. M. (2000). Violence risk assessment and risk communication: The effects of using actual cases, providing instructions, and employing probability vs. frequency formats. *Law and Human Behavior, 24*(3), 271–296. **[23]**

Slovic, P., & Tversky, A. (1974). Who accepts Savage's axiom? *Behavioral Science, 19,* 368–373. **[24]**

Slugoski, B. R., & Wilson, A. E. (1998). Contribution of conversation skills to the production of judgmental errors. *European Journal of Social Psychology, 28,* 575–601. **[24]**

Smith, E. E., & Medin, D. L. (1981). *Categories and concepts.* Cambridge, MA: Harvard University Press. **[1, 20]**

Smith, G. (1997). *The political impact of name sounds.* Unpublished manuscript, Eastern Washington University, Ellensburg. **[23]**

Smith, J. F., & Kida, T. (1991). Heuristics and biases: Expertise and task realism in auditing. *Psychological Bulletin, 109,* 472–489. **[39]**

Smith, M., & Ferrell, W. R. (1983). The effect of base rate on calibration of subjective probability for true-false questions: Model and experiment. In *Analyzing and aiding decisions,* P. Humphreys, O. Svenson, & A. Vari (Eds.). Amsterdam: North-Holland. **[39]**

Smith, S. M., & Levin, I. P. (1996). Need for cognition and choice framing effects. *Journal of Behavioral Decision Making, 9,* 283–290. **[24]**

Smith, V. L. (1994). Economics in the laboratory. *Journal of Economic Perspectives, 8,* 113–132. **[42]**

Snell, J., Gibbs, B. J., & Varey, C. (1995). Intuitive hedonics: Consumer beliefs about the dynamics of liking. *Journal of Consumer Psychology, 4,* 33–60. **[16]**

Sniezek, J. A., Paese, P. W., & Switzer, F. S. (1990). The effect of choosing on confidence in choice. *Organizational Behavior and Human Decision Processes, 46,* 264–282. **[15, 39]**

Sniezek, J. A., & Switzer, F. S. (1989). *The over-underconfidence paradox: High pi's but poor unlucky me.* Paper presented at the Judgment and Decision Making Society Annual Meeting in Atlanta, Georgia. **[13]**

Snortum, J. R., & Wilding, F. W. (1971). Temporal estimation of heart rate as a function of repression sensitization score and probability of shock. *Journal of Consulting and Clinical Psychology, 37,* 417–422. **[30]**

Snyder, C. R. (1989). Reality negotiation: From excuses to hope and beyond. *Journal of Social and Clinical Psychology, 8,* 130–157. **[19]**

Snyder, C. R., & Higgins, R. L. (1988). Excuses: Their affective role in the negotiation of reality. *Psychological Bulletin, 104,* 23–35. **[14, 19]**

Snyder, C. R., Shenkel, R. J., & Lowery, C. R. (1977). Acceptance of personality interpretations: The "Barnum effect" and beyond. *Journal of Consulting and Clinical Psychology, 45,* 104–114. **[20]**

Snyder, M., & Swann, W. B., Jr. (1978a). Behavioral confirmation in social interaction: from social perception to social reality. *Journal of Experimental Social Psychology, 14,* 148–162. **[6]**

Snyder, M., & Swann, W. B., Jr. (1978b). Hypothesis-testing processes in social interaction. *Journal of Personality and Social Psychology, 36,* 1202–1212. **[Introduction, 7, 9]**

Snyder, W. (1978). Horse racing: Testing the efficient markets model. *Journal of Finance, 33*(4), 1109–1118. **[39]**

Soldat, A. S., & Sinclair, R. C. (2001). Colors, smiles, and frowns: External affective cues can directly affect responses to persuasive communications in a mood-like manner without affecting mood. Unpublished manuscript; University of Alberta. **[29]**

Soldat, A. S., Sinclair, R. C., & Mark, M. M. (1997). Color as an environmental processing cue: External affective cues can directly affect processing strategy without affecting mood. *Social Cognition, 15,* 55–71. **[29]**

Soll, J. B. (1996). Determinants of overconfidence and miscalibration: The roles of random error and ecological structure. *Organizational Behavior and Human Decision Processes, 65,* 117–137. **[39]**

Spearman, C. (1904). General intelligence, objectively determined and measured. *American Journal of Psychology, 15,* 201–293. **[24]**

Spearman, C. (1927). *The abilities of man.* London: Macmillan. **[24]**

Spinoza, B. (1982). *The Ethics and selected letters.* (S. Feldman, Ed.; S. Shirley, Trans.). Indianapolis: Hackett Publishing Co. (Original work published 1672) **[9]**

Spranca, M., Minsk, E., & Baron, J. (1991). Omission and commission in judgment and choice. *Journal of Experimental and Social Psychology, 27,* 76–105. **[21]**

Spreen, O. (1981). The relationship between learning disability, neurological impairment, and delinquency: Results of a follow-up study. *Journal of Nervous and Mental Disease,* 169, 791–799. **[40]**

Sprinchorn, E. (1964). *Ibsen: Letters and Speeches.* New York: Hill and Wang.

Springer, K., & Belk, A. (1994). The role of physical contact and association in early contamination sensitivity. *Developmental Psychology, 30,* 864–868. **[11]**

Sptezler, C. S., & Stael von Holstein, C. A. S. (1975). Probability encoding in decision analysis. *Management Science, 22,* 340–358. **[37]**

Srull, T. K. (1983). Affect and memory: The impact of affective reactions in advertising on the representation of product information in memory. In *Advances in consumer research* (Vol. 10), R. Bagozzi & A. Tybout (Eds.). Ann Arbor: Association for Consumer Research. **[29]**

Srull, T. K. (1984). The effects of subjective affective states on memory and judgment. In *Advances in consumer research* (Vol. 11, pp. 530–533), T. Kinnear (Ed.). Provo: Association for Consumer Research. **[29]**

Srull, T. K., & Wyer, R. S. (1979). The role of category accessibility in the interpretation of information about persons: Some determinants and implications. *Journal of Personality and Social Psychology, 37,* 1660–1672. **[Introduction]**

Srull, T. K., & Wyer, R. S. (1980). Category accessibility and social perception: Some implications for the study of person memory and interpersonal judgments. *Journal of Personality and Social Psychology, 38,* 841–856. **[Introduction]**

Stanovich, K. E. (1986). *How to think straight about psychology.* Glenview, IL: Scott, Foresman, & Co. **[Introduction]**

Stanovich, K. E. (1999). *Who is rational? Studies of individual differences in reasoning.* Mahwah, NJ: Lawrence Erlbaum Associates. **[2, 24]**

Stanovich, K. E., & West, R. F. (1997). Reasoning independently of prior belief and individual differences in actively open-minded thinking. *Journal of Educational Psychology,* 89, 342–357. **[24]**

Stanovich, K. E., & West, R. F. (1998a). Cognitive ability and variation in selection task performance. *Thinking and Reasoning, 4*, 193–230. **[24]**

Stanovich, K. E., & West, R. F. (1998b). Individual differences in framing and conjunction effects. *Thinking and Reasoning, 4*, 289–317. **[24]**

Stanovich, K. E., & West, R. F. (1998c). Individual differences in rational thought. *Journal of Experimental Psychology: General, 127*, 161–188. **[24]**

Stanovich, K. E., & West, R. F. (1999). Discrepancies between normative and descriptive models of decision making and the understanding/acceptance principle. *Cognitive Psychology, 38*, 349–385. **[24]**

Stanovich, K. E., & West, R. F. (2000). Individual differences in reasoning: Implications for the rationality debate. *Behavioral and Brain Sciences, 23*, 645–665. **[Introduction]**

Stapel, D. A., Martin, L. L., & Schwarz, N. (1998). The smell of bias: What instigates correction processes in social judgments? *Personality and Social Psychology Bulletin, 24*, 797–806. **[10]**

Starmer, C., & Sugden, R. (1993). Testing for juxtaposition and event-splitting effects. *Journal of Risk and Uncertainty, 6*, 235–254. **[25]**

Starr, C. (1969). Societal benefit versus technological risk. *Science, 165*, 1232–1238. **[41]**

Staw, B. (1980). Rationality and justification in organizational life. In *Research in organizational behavior* (Vol. 2, pp. 1–57), B. Staw & L. Cummings (Eds.). Greenwich, CT: JAI Press. **[32]**

Staw, B. M., & Ross, J. (1980). Commitment in an experimenting society: A study of the attribution of leadership from administrative scenarios. *Journal of Applied Psychology, 65*, 249-260. **[32]**

Staël von Holstein, C.-A. S. (1972). Probabilistic forecasting: An experiment related to the stock market. *Organizational Behavior and Human Performance, 8*, 139–158. **[13]**

Stazyk, E. H., Ashcraft, M. H., & Hamman, M. S. (1982). A network approach to mental multiplication. *Journal of Experimental Psychology: Learning, Memory, and Cognition, 8*, 320–335. **[22]**

Steele, C. (1988). The psychology of self-affirmation: Sustaining the integrity of the self. In *Advances in experimental social psychology* (Vol. 21, pp. 261–303), M. Zanna (Ed.), New York: Academic Press. **[16]**

Stein, E. (1996). *Without good reason: The rationality debate in philosophy and cognitive science*. Oxford, U.K.: Oxford University Press. **[24]**

Stein, R. I., & Nemeroff, C. J. (1995). Moral overtones of food: Judgements of other based on what they eat. *Personality & Social Psychology Bulletin, 21*, 480–490. **[11]**

Stepper, S., & Strack, F. (1993). Proprioceptive determinants of emotional and nonemotional feelings. *Journal of Personality and Social Psychology, 64*, 211–220. **[5]**

Sternberg, R. J., & Kaufman, J. C. (1998). Human abilities. *Annual Review of Psychology, 49*, 479–502. **[24]**

Stevens, S. S. (1957). On the psychophysical law. *Psychological Review, 64*, 153–181. **[2]**

Stevens, S. S. (1975). *Psychophysics: Introduction to its perceptual, neural, and social prospects*. New York: John Wiley & Sons. **[2]**

Stevenson, H. N. C. (1954). Status evaluation in the Hindu caste system. *Journal of the Royal Anthropological Institute of Great Britain and Ireland, 84*, 45–65. **[11]**

Stewart, T. R., & Lusk, C. M. (1994). Seven components of judgmental forecasting skill: Implications for research and the improvement of forecasts. *Journal of Forecasting, 13*, 575–599. **[39]**

Stewart, T. R., Roebber, P. J., & Bosart, L. F. (1997). The importance of the task in analyzing expert judgment. *Organizational Behavior and Human Decision Processes*, 69, 205–219. **[39]**

Stich, S. P. (1990). *The fragmentation of reason*. Cambridge, MA: MIT Press. **[24]**

Stich, S. P., & Nisbett, R. E. (1980). Justification and the psychology of human reasoning. *Philosophy of Science*, 47, 188–202. **[24]**

Stickel, S. E. (1992). Reputation and performance among security analysts. *Journal of Finance*, 47, 1811–1836. **[38]**

Stickel, S. E. (1995). The anatomy of the performance of buy and sell recommendations. *Financial Analysts Journal*, 51, 25–39. **[38]**

Stigler, S. M. (1977). *Annals of Statistics*, 5, 1055–1098. **[37]**

Storms, M. (1973). Videotape and the attribution process: Reversing actors' and observers' points of view. *Journal of Personality and Social Psychology*, 27, 165–175. **[20]**

Strack, F. (1992). The different routes to social judgment: Experiential versus informational strategies. In *The construction of social judgments* (pp. 249–276), L. L. Martin & A. Tesser (Eds.). Hillsdale, NJ: Lawrence Erlbaum Associates. **[5]**

Strack, F., Martin, L. L., & Schwarz, N. (1988). Priming and communication: the social determinants of information use in judgments of life-satisfaction. *European Journal of Social Psychology*, 18, 429–442. **[2]**

Strack, F., & Mussweiler, T. (1997). Explaining the enigmatic anchoring effect: mechanisms of selective accessibility. *Journal of Personality and Social Psychology*, 73, 437–446. **[6, 7, 29]**

Suantak, L., Bolger, F., & Ferrell, W. R. (1996). The hard–easy effect in subjective probability calibration. *Organizational Behavior and Human Decision Processes*, 67, 201–221. **[39]**

Sudman, S., Bradburn, N. M., & Schwarz, N. (1996). *Thinking about answers: The application of cognitive processes to survey methodology*. San Francisco: Jossey–Bass, Inc. **[6]**

Suedfeld, P. (1997). Reactions to societal trauma: Distress and/or eustress. *Political Psychology*, 18, 849–861. **[16]**

Suedfeld, P., & Tetlock, P. E. (2001). Cognitive styles. In *Blackwell international handbook of social psychology: Intra-individual processes*, (Vol. 1, pp. 284–304), A. Tesser & N. Schwartz. London: Blackwell Publishers. **[42]**

Sugden, R. (1985). Regret, recrimination and rationality. *Theory and Decision*, 19, 77–99. **[21]**

Suh, E., Diener, E., & Fujita, F. (1996). Events and subjective well-being: Only recent events matter. *Journal of Personality and Social Psychology*, 70, 1091–1102. **[16]**

Suinn, R. (1976). Body thinking: psychology for Olympic champs. *Psychology Today*, 10, 38–43. **[4]**

Suls, J. M., & Miller, R. L. (1977). *Social comparison processes: Theoretical and empirical perspectives*. New York: Wiley. **[20, 35]**

Suppe, F. (1973). *The structure of scientific theories*. Chicago: University of Chicago Press. **[42]**

Suppes, P. (1974). The measurement of belief. *Journal of the Royal Statistical Society, B*, 36, 160–191. **[25]**

Suppes, P. (1975). Approximate probability and expectation of gambles. *Erkenntnis*, 9, 153–161. **[1]**

Sutton, S. R., & Eiser, J. R. (1990). The decision to wear a seat belt: The role of cognitive factors, fear, and prior behavior. *Psychology and Health*, 4, 111–123. **[17]**

Svenson, O. (1981). Are we all less risky and more skillful than our fellow driver? *Acta Psychologica*, 47, 143–148. **[18, 27]**

Swann, W. B., Jr., & Predmore, S. C. (1985). Intimates as agents of social support: Sources of consolation or despair? *Journal of Personality and Social Psychology, 49,* 1607–1617. **[9]**

Swets, J. A. (1986). Form of empirical ROCs in discrimination and diagnostic tasks: Implications for theory and measurement of performance. *Psychological Bulletin, 99,* 181–198. **[15]**

Switzer, F., & Sniezek, J. A. (1991). Judgment processes in motivation: Anchoring and adjustment effects on judgment and behavior. *Organizational Behavior and Human Decision Processes, 49,* 208–229. **[6, 7, 8]**

Sá, W., West, R. F., & Stanovich, K. E. (1999). The domain specificity and generality of belief bias: Searching for a generalizable critical thinking skill. *Journal of Educational Psychology, 91,* 497–510. **[24]**

Tafarodi, R. W., & Swann, W. B., Jr. (1995). Self-liking and self-competence as dimensions of global self-esteem: Initial validation of a measure. *Journal of Personality Assessment, 65,* 322–342. **[16]**

Tait, R., & Silver, R. C. (1989). Coming to terms with major negative life events. In *Unintended thought* (pp. 351–382), J. S. Uleman & J. A. Bargh (Eds.). New York: Guilford Press. **[35]**

Takemura, K. (1994). Influence of elaboration on the framing of decision. *Journal of Psychology, 128,* 33–39. **[24]**

Tambiah, S. J. (1990). *Magic, science, religion, and the scope of rationality.* Cambridge, U.K.: Cambridge University Press. **[11]**

Tanenhaus, M. K., Spivey-Knowlton, M. J., Eberhard, K., & Sedivy, J. C. (1995). Integration of visual and linguistic information in spoken language comprehension. *Science, 268,* 1632–1634. **[8]**

Tanford, J. A. (1990). The law and psychology of jury instructions. *Nebraska Law Review, 69,* 71–111. **[10]**

Tanner, W. P. Jr., & Swets, J. A. (1954). A decision-making theory of visual detection. *Psychological Review, 61,* 401–409. **[39]**

Tape, T. G., Heckerling, P. S., Ornato, J. P., & Wigton, R. S. (1991). Use of clinical judgment analysis to explain regional variations in physicians' accuracies in diagnosing pneumonia. *Medical Decision Making, 11,* 189–197. **[39]**

Tauber, T. M. (1998). How to do business – Chinese and Western negotiation cultures. *Transition, 9*(6), 8–10. **[15]**

Taylor, B. N. (1982). NBSIR 81-2426, National Bureau of Standards. **[37]**

Taylor, B. N., Parker, W. H., & Langenberg, D. N. (1969). *The fundamental constants and quantum electrodynamics.* New York: Academic Press. **[37]**

Taylor, K. F., & Sluckin, W. (1964). Flocking in domestic chicks. *Nature, 201,* 108–109. **[30]**

Taylor, K. M., Shepperd, J. A. (1998). Bracing for the worst: Severity, testing, and feedback timing as moderators of the optimistic bias. *Personality and Social Psychology Bulletin, 24,* 915–926. **[19]**

Taylor, S. E. (1982). The availability bias in social perception and interaction. In *Judgment under uncertainty: heuristics and biases* (pp. 190–200), D. Kahneman, P. Slovic, & A. Tversky (Eds.). Cambridge, U.K.: Cambridge University Press. **[5]**

Taylor, S. E. (1983). Adjustment to threatening events: A theory of cognitive adaptation. *American Psychologist, 38,* 1161–1174. **[16]**

Taylor, S. E. (1991). Asymmetrical effects of positive and negative events: The mobilization–minimization hypothesis. *Psychological Bulletin, 110,* 67–85. **[16]**

Taylor, S. E., & Armor, D. A. (1996). Positive illusions and coping with adversity, *Journal of Personality, 64,* 873–898. **[16]**

Taylor, S. E., & Brown, J. (1988). Illusion and well-being: A social psychological perspective on mental health. *Psychological Bulletin, 103*, 193–210. **[10, 13, 14, 16, 17, 18, 36, 39]**

Taylor, S. E., & Fiske, S. T. (1978). Salience, attention and attribution: Top of the head phenomena. In *Advances in experimental social psychology* (Vol. 11, pp. 249–288), L. Berkowitz (Ed.). New York: Academic Press. **[20]**

Taylor, S. E., & Gollwitzer, P. M. (1995). The effects of mindset on positive illusions. *Journal of Personality and Social Psychology, 69*, 213–226. **[19]**

Taylor, S. E., Kemeny, M. E., Aspinwall, L. G., Schneider, S. C., Rodriguez, R., & Herbert, M. (1992). Optimism, coping, psychological distress, and high-risk sexual behavior among men at risk for AIDS. *Journal of Personality and Social Psychology, 63*, 460–473. **[17, 19]**

Taylor, S. E., & Lobel, M. (1989). Social comparison activity under threat: Downward evaluation and upward contacts. *Psychological Review, 96*, 569–575. **[19, 35]**

Taylor, S. E., Pham, L. B., Rivkin, I. D., & Armor, D. A. (1998). Harnessing the imagination: Mental simulation, self-regulation, and coping. *American Psychologist, 53*, 429–439. **[14]**

Taylor, S., & Rachman, S. J. (1994). Stimulus estimation and the overprediction of fear. *British Journal of Clinical Psychology, 33*, 173–181. **[16]**

Taylor, S. E., Wood, J. V., & Lichtman, R. R. (1983). It could be worse: Selective evaluation as a response to victimization. *Journal of Social Issues, 39*, 19–40. **[19]**

Teigen, K. H. (1974a). Overestimation of subjective probabilities. *Scandinavian Journal of Psychology, 15*, 56–62. **[25]**

Teigen, K. H. (1974b). Subjective sampling distributions and the additivity of estimates. *Scandinavian Journal of Psychology, 15*, 50–55. **[25]**

Teigen, K. H. (1983). Studies in subjective probability III: The unimportance of alternatives. *Scandinavian Journal of Psychology, 24*, 97–105. **[25]**

Telch, M. J., Valentiner, D., & Bolte, M. (1994). Proximity to safety and its effects in fear prediction bias. *Behavior Research and Therapy, 32*, 747–751. **[16]**

Tesser, A., & Campbell, J. (1983). Self-definition and self-evaluation maintenance. In *Social psychological perspectives on the self* (Vol. 2, pp. 1–31), J. M. Suls & A. Greenwald (Eds.). Hillsdale, NJ: Lawrence Erlbaum Associates. **[9]**

Tetlock, P. E. (1983a). Accountability and complexity of thought. *Journal of Personality and Social Psychology: Attitudes and Social Cognition, 45*, 74–83. **[32]**

Tetlock, P. E. (1983b). Accountability and perseverance of first impressions. *Social Psychology Quarterly, 46*, 285–292. **[32]**

Tetlock, P. E. (1985). Accountability: A social check on the fundamental attribution error. *Social Psychology Quarterly, 48*, 227–236. **[32]**

Tetlock, P. E. (1991). Learning in U.S. and Soviet foreign policy: In search of an elusive concept. In *Learning in U.S. and Soviet foreign policy*, (pp. 20–62). G. Breslauer & P. Tetlock (Eds.). Boulder, CO: Westview. **[42]**

Tetlock, P. E. (1992a). Good judgment in world politics: Three psychological perspectives. *Political Psychology, 13*, 517–540. **[42]**

Tetlock, P. E. (1992b). The impact of accountability on judgment and choice: Toward a social contingency model. In *Advances in experimental social psychology* (Vol. 25, pp. 331–376), M. P. Zanna (Ed.). New York: Academic Press. **[19, 32]**

Tetlock, P. E. (1998). Close-call counterfactuals and belief system defenses: I was not almost wrong but I was almost right. *Journal of Personality and Social Psychology, 75*, 230–242. **[42]**

Tetlock, P. E. (1998). Losing our religion: On the collapse of precise normative standards in complex accountability systems. In *Influence processes in organizations:*

Emerging themes in theory and research (pp. 121–145), R. Kramer & M. Neale (Eds.). Thousand Oaks, CA: Sage. **[32]**

Tetlock, P. E. (1999). Theory-driven reasoning about possible pasts and probable futures: Are we prisoners of our preconceptions? *American Journal of Political Science, 43,* 335–366. **[42]**

Tetlock, P. E. (2000). Cognitive biases and organizational correctives: Do both disease and cure depend on the political beholder? *Administrative Science Quarterly, 45,* 293–316. **[32]**

Tetlock, P. E. (in press). Social-functionalist metaphors for judgment and choice: The intuitive politician, theologian, and prosecuter. *Psychological Review.* **[32]**

Tetlock, P. E., & Belkin, A. (1996). *Counterfactual thought experiments in world politics: Logical, methodological, and psychological perspectives.* Princeton, NJ: Princeton University Press. **[42]**

Tetlock, P. E., & Boettger, R. (1989). Accountability: A social magnifier of the dilution effect. *Journal of Personality and Social Psychology, 57,* 388–398. **[32, 42]**

Tetlock, P. E., & Boettger, R. (1994). Accountability amplifies the status quo effect when change creates victims. *Journal of Behavioral Decision Making, 7,* 1–23. **[32]**

Tetlock, P. E., & Kim, J. (1987). Accountability and judgment in a personality prediction task. *Journal of Personality and Social Psychology: Attitudes and Social Cognition, 52,* 700–709. **[32]**

Tetlock, P. E., Kristel, O., Elson, B., Green, M., & Lerner, J. (2000). The psychology of the unthinkable: Taboo trade-offs, forbidden base rates, and heretical counterfactuals. *Journal of Personality and Social Psychology, 78,* 853–870. **[32]**

Tetlock, P. E., & Lebow, R. N. (in press). Poking counterfactual holes in covering laws: Cognitive styles and historical reasoning. *American Political Science Review.* **[42]**

Tetlock, P. E., Peterson, R., & Lerner, J. (1996). Revisiting the value pluralism model: Incorporating social content and context postulates. In *Ontario symposium on social and personality psychology: Values* (Vol. 8, pp. 25–51), C. Seligman, J. Olson, & M. Zanna (Eds.). Hillsdale, NJ: Earlbaum. **[32]**

Tetlock, P. E., Skitka, L., & Boettger, R. (1989). Social and cognitive strategies for coping with accountability: Conformity, complexity, and bolstering. *Journal of Personality and Social Psychology, 57,* 632–640. **[32]**

Thagard, P. (1982). From the descriptive to the normative in philosophy and logic. *Philosophy of Science, 49,* 24–42. **[24]**

Thagard, P., & Nisbett, R. E. (1982). Variability and confirmation. *Philosophical Studies, 42,* 379–394. **[28]**

Thaler, R. (1993). *Quasi-rational economics.* New York: Russell Sage. **[41]**

Thaler, R. H., & Ziemba, W. T. (1988). Parimutural betting markets: Racetracks and lotteries. *Journal of Economic Perspectives, 2*(2), 161–174. **[39]**

Thomas, K. (1983). *Man and the natural world.* New York: Pantheon Books. **[11]**

Thompson, L. (1995). They saw a negotiation: Partisanship and involvement. *Journal of Personality and Social Psychology, 68,* 839–853. **[32]**

Thompson, L., & Loewenstein, G. (1992). Egocentric interpretations of fairness and negotiation. *Organizational Behavior and Human Decision Processes, 51,* 176–197. **[36]**

Thurstone, L. L. (1928). Attitudes can be measured. *American Journal of Sociology, 33,* 529–554. **[23]**

Tice, D. M. (1992). Self-presentation and self-concept change: The looking glass self as a magnifying glass. *Journal of Personality and Social Psychology, 63,* 435–451. **[9]**

Tiedens, L. Z., & Linton, S. (in press). Judgment under emotional certainty and uncertainty: The effects of specific emotions on information processing. *Journal of Personality and Social Psychology.* [29]

Tolin, D. F., Brigidi, B. D., & Foa, E. B. (1999). Disgust sensitivity in obsessive compulsive disorder. Paper presented at meeting of Association for Advancement of Behavior Therapy. [11]

Tolman, E. C. (1937). *Purposive behavior in man and animals.* New York: Appleton-Century-Crofts. [41]

Tooby, J., & Cosmides, L. (in press). Ecological rationality and the multimodular mind. Grounding normative theories in adaptive problems. In *Evolutionary psychology: Foundational papers*, J. Tooby & L. Cosmides (Eds.). Cambridge, MA: MIT Press. [31]

Totterdell, P., Parkinson, B., Briner, R. B., & Reynolds, S. (1997). Forecasting feelings: The accuracy and effects of self-predictions of mood. *Journal of Social Behaviour and Personality, 12*, 631–650. [16]

Trabasso, T., Rollins, H., & Shaughnessey, E. (1971). Storage and verification stages in processing concepts. *Cognitive psychology, 2*, 239–289. [9]

Treadwell, J., & Nelson, T. O. (1996). Availability of information and the aggregation of confidence in prior decisions. *Organizational Behavior and Human Decision Processes, 68*, 13–27. [Introduction]

Trope, Y. (1986). Identification and inferential processes in dispositional attribution. *Psychological Review, 93*, 239–257. [9]

Trope, Y., & Bassok, M. (1982). Confirmatory and diagnosing strategies in social information gathering. *Journal of Personality and Social Psychology, 43*, 22–34. [7]

Trope, Y., & Liberman, N. (2000). Temporal construal and time-dependent changes in preference. *Journal of Personality and Social Psychology, 79*, 876–889. [14]

Tucker, L. R. (1964). A suggested alternative formulation in the developments by Hursch, Hammond, and Hursch, and by Hammond, Hursch, and Todd. *Psychological Review, 71*(6), 528–530. [39]

Tucker, W. (1987). Where do the homeless come from? *National Review*, Sept. 25, pp. 34–44. [31]

Turnbull, W. (1981). Naive conceptions of free will and the deterministic paradox. *Canadian Journal of Behavioural Science, 13*, 1–13. [35]

Tversky, A. (1972). Elimination by aspects: A theory of choice. *Psychological Review, 79*, 281–299. [23, 30, 31]

Tversky, A. (1975). A critique of expected utility theory: Descriptive and normative considerations. *Erkenntnis, 9*, 163–173. [24]

Tversky, A. (1977). Features of similarity. *Psychological Review, 84*, 327–352. [1, 3, 6, 12, 32]

Tversky, A., & Craig, F. (1995). "Weighting risk and uncertainty." *Psychological review, 102*(2), 269–283. [42]

Tversky, A., & Fox, C. R. (1995). Weighing risk and uncertainty. *Psychological Review, 102*, 269–283. [25, 27]

Tversky, A., & Griffin, D. (1991). Endowment and contrast in judgments of well-being. In *Strategy and choice* (pp. 297–318), R. J. Zeckhauser (Ed.). Cambridge, MA: MIT Press. [35]

Tversky, A., & Kahneman, D. (1971). Belief in the law of small numbers. *Psychological Bulletin, 76*, 105–110. [1, 2, 13, 20, 28, 33]

Tversky, A., & Kahneman, D. (1973a). Availability: A heuristic for judging frequency and probability. *Cognitive Psychology, 5*, 207–232. [Introduction, 1, 2, 4, 5, 20, 21, 28, 37]

Tversky, A., & Kahneman, D. (1973b). Response-induced reversals of preference in gambling: an extended replication in Las Vegas. *Journal of Experimental Psychology, 101*, 16–20. **[12]**

Tversky, A., & Kahneman, D. (1974). Judgement under uncertainty: Heuristics and biases. *Science, 185*, 1124–1131. **[2, 6, 7, 8, 9, 12, 13, 16, 18, 19, 23, 26, 28, 29, 32, 33, 34, 36]**

Tversky, A., & Kahneman, D. (1980). Causal schemas in judgments under uncertainty. In *Progress in social psychology*, M. Fishbein (Ed.). Hillsdale, NJ: Erlbaum. **[1]**

Tversky, A., & Kahneman, D. (1981). The framing of decisions and the psychology of choice. *Science, 211*, 453–458. **[1, 24, 37]**

Tversky, A., & Kahneman, D. (1982a). Causal schemas in judgments under uncertainty. In *Judgment under uncertainty: Heuristics and biases* (pp. 117–128), D. Kahneman, P. Slavic, & A. Tversky (Eds.). New York: Cambridge University Press. **[Introduction, 20]**

Tversky, A., & Kahneman, D. (1982b). Evidential impact of base rates. In *Judgment under uncertainty: Heuristics and biases* (pp. 153–160), D. Kahneman, P. Slovic, & A. Tversky (Eds.). Cambridge, U.K.: Cambridge University Press. **[24, 39]**

Tversky, A., & Kahneman, D. (1982c). Judgments of and by representativeness. In *Judgment under uncertainty: Heuristics and biases*, D. Kahneman, P. Slovic, & A. Tversky (Eds.). New York: Cambridge University Press. **[1, 2]**

Tversky, A., & Kahneman, D. (1983). Extensional versus intuitive reasoning: The conjunction fallacy in probability judgment. *Psychological Review, 90*, 293–315. **[Introduction, 2, 3, 14, 22, 24, 25, 26, 27, 28, 30, 33]**

Tversky, A., & Kahneman, D. (1986). Rational choice and the framing of decisions. Part 2. *Journal of Business, 59*, 251–278. **[2, 25, 27]**

Tversky, A., & Kahneman, D. (1992). Advances in prospect theory: Cumulative representation of uncertainty. *Journal of Risk and Uncertainty, 5*, 297–323. **[27]**

Tversky, A., & Koehler, D. J. (1994). Support theory: A nonextensional representation of subjective probability. *Psychological Review, 101*, 547–567. **[14, 25, 26, 27, 39]**

Tversky, A., & Sattath, S. (1979). Preference trees. *Psychological Review 86*, 542–573. **[25]**

Tversky, A., Sattath, S., & Slovic, P. (1988). Contingent weighting in judgment and choice. *Psychological Review, 95*, 371–384. **[6, 12]**

Tversky, A., Slovic, P., & Kahneman, D. (1990). The causes of preference reversal. *American Economic Review, 80*, 204–217. **[12, 23]**

Tversky, A., & Wakker, P. (1995). Risk attitudes and decision weights. *Econometrica, 63*, 1255–1280. **[27]**

Tyler, T. R. (1990). *Why people obey the law*. New Haven: Yale University Press. **[41]**

Tylor, E. B. (1871/1974). *Primitive culture: Researches into the development of mythology, philosophy, religion, art and custom*. New York: Gordon Press. (Original work published 1871.) **[11]**

U.S. Nuclear Regulatory Commission (1981). *Fault tree handbook* (Catalog No. NUREG-0492) Washington, DC: NRC. **[37]**

Vaillant, G. (1993). *The wisdom of the ego*. Cambridge, MA: Harvard University Press. **[16]**

Vallone, R. P., Griffin, D. W., Lin, S., & Ross, L. (1990). Overconfident prediction of future actions and outcomes by self and others. *Journal of Personality and Social Psychology, 58*, 582–592. **[13, 14]**

Vallone, R. P., Ross, L., & Lepper, M. R. (1985). The hostile media phenomenon: Biased perception and perceptions of media bias in coverage of the Beirut massacre. *Journal of Personality and Social Psychology, 49*, 577–585. **[36]**

Van Boven, L., Dunning, D., & Loewenstein, G. (2000). Egocentric empathy gaps between owners and buyers: misperceptions of the endowment effect. *Journal of Personality and Social Psychology, 79*, 66–76. **[7]**

Van Boven, L., Kamada, A., & Gilovich, T. (1999). The perceiver as perceived: Everyday intuitions about the correspondence bias. *Journal of Personality and Social Psychology, 77*, 1188–1199. **[36]**

van der Pligt, J., Eiser, J. R., & Spears, R. (1987). Comparative judgments and preferences: The influence of the number of response alternatives. *British Journal of Social Psychology, 26*, 269–280. **[25]**

Van Wallendael, L. R., & Hastie, R. (1990). Tracing the footsteps of Sherlock Holmes: Cognitive representations of hypothesis testing. *Memory & Cognition, 18*, 240–250. **[25]**

Varey, C. A., Griffin, D. W., & James, M. (1998) *The effect of context on confidence.* Unpublished manuscript, University of Sussex. **[39]**

Vargas Llosa, M. (1986). My son the Rastafarian. *The New York Times Magazine,* February 16, pp. 20–28, 30, 41–43, 67. **[30]**

Vaughn, L. A. (1997). *Effects of expertise on use of recall experiences and recalled information for social judgments.* Unpublished Doctoral dissertation, University of Michigan, Ann Arbor, MI. **[5]**

Verschoth, A. (1992, July 22). Who will win what. *Sports Illustrated.* **[35]**

Vertzberger, Y. (1998). *Risk taking and decision making.* Stanford: Stanford University Press. **[41]**

Viscusi, W. K. (1992). *Smoking: Making the risky decision.* New York: Oxford University Press. **[23]**

von Mises, R. (1928). *Probability, statistics and truth.* 1954 translation, New York: Macmillan. **[Introduction]**

von Winterfeldt, D., & Edwards, W. (1986). *Decision analysis and behavioral research.* New York: Cambridge University Press. **[13, 31, 41]**

Vygotsky, L. S. (1934/1987). Thinking and speech. In *The Collected Works of L. S. Vygotsky. Vol. 1: Problems of General Psychology* (pp. 101–120), R. W. Rieber & A. S. Carton (Eds.). New York: Plenum Press. **[22]**

Wagenaar, W. A. (1972). Generation of random sequences by human subjects. A critical survey of literature. *Psychological Bulletin, 77*, 65–72. **[33]**

Wagenaar, W. A., & Keren, G. B. (1985). Calibration of probability assessments by professional blackjack dealers, statistical experts, and lay people. *Organizational Behavior and Human Decision Processes, 36*, 406–416. **[39]**

Wagenaar, W. A., & Keren, G. B. (1986). Does the expert know? The reliability of predictions and confidence ratings of experts. In *Intelligent Decision Support in Process Environments* (pp. 87–103), E. Hollnagel, G. Manici, & D. D. Woods (Eds.). Berlin: Springer Verlag. **[13, 39]**

Wagener, J. J., & Taylor, S. E. (1986). What else could I have done? Patients' responses to failed treatment decisions. *Health Psychology, 5*, 481–496. **[19]**

Wainer, H. (1978). On the sensitivity of regression and regressors. *Psychological Bulletin, 85*, 267–273. **[40]**

Walley, P. (1991). *Statistical reasoning with imprecise probabilities.* London: Chapman & Hall. **[25]**

Wallsten, T. S. (1981). Physician and medical student bias in evaluating diagnostic information. *Medical Decision Making, 1*, 145–164. **[39]**

Wallsten, T. S., & Budescu, D. V. (1983). Encoding subjective probabilities: A psychological and psychometric review. *Management Science, 29*, 151–173. **[27, 39]**

Wallsten, T. S., Budescu, D. V., & Zwick, R. (1992). Comparing the calibration and coherence of numerical and verbal probability judgments. *Management Science, 39,* 176–190. **[25, 27]**

Wallsten, T. S., & Gonzáles-Vallejo, C. (1994). Statement verification: A stochastic model of judgment and response. *Psychological Review, 101,* 490–504. **[39]**

Walster, E., Walster, G. W., Piliavin, E., & Schmidt, L. (1973). Playing hard to get: Understanding an elusive phenomenon. *Journal of Personality and Social Psychology, 26,* 113–121. **[21]**

Wansink, B., Kent, R. J., & Hoch, S. J. (1998). An anchoring and adjustment model of purchase quantity decisions. *Journal of Marketing Research, 35,* 71–81. **[6]**

Ward, R. (1994, February). Maternity ward. *Mirabella,* 89–90. **[34]**

Wason, P. C. (1960). On the failure to eliminate hypotheses in a conceptual task. *Quarterly Journal of Experimental Psychology, 12,* 129–140. **[2, 6]**

Wason, P. C. (1966). Reasoning. In *New horizons in psychology* (pp. 135–151), B. Foss (Ed.). Harmonsworth, U.K.: Penguin. **[24]**

Wason, P. C., & Johnson-Laird, P. N. (1972). *The psychology of reasoning.* Cambridge, MA: Harvard University Press. **[9]**

Watley, D. J., & Vance, F. L. (1974). U.S. Office of Education Cooperative Research Project No. 2022. University of Minnesota, Minneapolis. **[40]**

Watson, S., & Buede, D. (1990). *Decision synthesis.* New York: Cambridge University Press. **[41]**

Wax, A. L. (1999). Discrimination as accident. *Indiana Law Journal, 74,* 1129–1236. **[10]**

Weber, M. (1978). *Economy and society.* G. Roth & K. Wittich (Eds.). Berkeley: University of California Press. **[32]**

Wechsler, H., Lee, J. E., Kuo, M. C. (2000). College binge drinking in the 1990s. *Journal of the American College Health Association, 48,* 199–210. **[41]**

Wedding, D. (1983). Comparison of statistical and actuarial models for predicting lateralization of brain damage. *International Journal of Clinical Neuropsychology, 5,* 15–20. **[40]**

Weeks, J. C., Cook, E. F., O'Day, S. J., Peterson, L. M., Wenger, N., Reding, D., Harrell, F. E., Kussin, P., Dawson, N. V., Connors, A. F., Jr., Lynn, J., & Phillips, R. S. (1998). Relationship between cancer patients' predictions of prognosis and their treatment preferences. *Journal of the American Medical Association, 279,* 1709–1714. **[39]**

Wegener, D. T., & Petty, R. E. (1994). Mood management across affective states: The hedonic contingency hypothesis. *Journal of Personality and Social Psychology, 66,* 1034–1048. **[16, 29]**

Wegener, D. T., Petty, R. E., & Smith, S. M. (1995a). Positive mood can increase or decrease message scrutiny: The hedonic contingency view of mood and message processing. *Journal of Personality and Social Psychology, 69,* 5–15. **[29]**

Wegener, D. T., & Petty, R. E. (1995b). Flexible correction processes in social judgment: The role of naïve theories in corrections for perceived bias. *Journal of Personality and Social Psychology, 68,* 36–51. **[22, 32]**

Wegener, D. T., & Petty, R. E. (1997). The flexible correction model: the role of naive theories of bias in bias correction. In *Advances in experimental social psychology* (Vol. 29, pp. 141–207), M. P. Zanna (Ed.). San Diego: Academic Press. **[10]**

Wegner, D. M., & Bargh, J. (1998). Automaticity and mental control. In *The handbook of social psychology* (4th ed. pp. 446–496), D. T. Gilbert, S. T. Fiske, & G. Lindzey (Eds.). New York: McGraw-Hill. **[9]**

Wegner, D. M., Coulton, G., & Wenzlaff, R. (1985). The transparency of denial: Briefing in the debriefing paradigm. *Journal of Personality and Social Psychology, 49*, 338–346. **[9]**

Wegner, D. M., Wenzlaff, R., Kerker, R. M., & Beattie, A. E. (1981). Incrimination through innuendo: Can media questions become public answers? *Journal of Personality and Social Psychology, 40*, 822–832. **[9]**

Weiner, B. (1985). "Spontaneous" causal thinking. *Psychological Bulletin, 97*, 74–84. **[19, 20]**

Weiner, B., Frieze, I., Kukla, A., Reed, L., Rest, S., & Rosenbaum, R. M. (1972). Perceiving the causes of success and failure. In *Attribution: Perceiving the causes of behavior* (pp. 95–120), E. E. Jones, D. E. Kanouse, H. H. Kelley, R. E. Nisbett, S. Valins, & B. Weiner (Eds.). Morristown, NJ: General Learning Press. **[9, 28]**

Weinstein, N. (1980). Unrealistic optimism about future life events. *Journal of Personality and Social Psychology, 39*, 806–820. **[14, 17, 18, 19, 27, 38]**

Weinstein, N. D. (1983). Reducing unrealistic optimism about illness susceptibility. *Health Psychology, 2*, 11–20. **[17]**

Weinstein, N. D. (1987). Unrealistic optimism about illness susceptibility: Conclusions from a community-wide sample. *Journal of Behavioral Medicine, 10*, 481–500. **[17, 19]**

Weinstein, N. D. (1993). Testing four competing theories of health protective behavior. *Health Psychology, 12*, 324–333. **[17]**

Weinstein, N. D. (1998a). Accuracy of smokers' risk perceptions. *Annals of Behavioral Medicine, 20*, 135–140. **[19]**

Weinstein, N. D. (1998b). *References on optimistic biases about risk, unrealistic optimism, and perceived invulnerability.* Unpublished manuscript, Rutgers University. **[19]**

Weinstein, N. D., & Klein, W. M. (1995). Resistance to personal risk perceptions to debiasing interventions. *Health Psychology, 14*, 132–140. **[19]**

Weinstein, N. D., & Lachendro, E. (1982). Egocentrism as a source of unrealistic optimism. *Personality and Social Psychology Bulletin, 8*, 195–200. **[27]**

Weinstein, N. D., Sandman, P. M., & Roberts, N. E. (1991). Perceived susceptibility and self-protective behavior: A field experiment to encourage home radon testing. *Health Psychology, 10*, 25–33. **[17]**

Weldon, E., & Gargano, G. M. (1988). Cognitive loafing: The effects of accountability and shared responsibility on cognitive effort. *Personality and Social Psychology Bulletin, 14*, 159–171. **[32]**

Wellman, H. M. (1990). *The child's theory of mind.* Cambridge, MA: MIT Press. **[8]**

Wells, G. L. (1993). What do we know about eyewitness identification? *American Psychologist, 48*, 553–571. **[10]**

Wells, G. L., & Gavanski, I. (1989). Mental simulation of causality. *Journal of Personality and Social Psychology, 56*, 161–169. **[35]**

Wells, G. L., & Petty, R. E. (1980). The effects of overt head movements on persuasion: compatibility and incompatibility of responses. *Basic and Applied Social Psychology, 1*, 219–230. **[7]**

Werner, P. D., Rose, T. L., & Yesavage, J. A. (1983). Reliability, accuracy, and decision-making strategy in clinical predictions of imminent dangerousness. *Journal of Consulting and Clinical Psychology, 51*, 815–825. **[40]**

Wetherick, N. E. (1971). Representativeness in a reasoning problem: A reply to Shapiro. *Bulletin of the British Psychological Society, 24*, 213–214. **[24]**

Wetherick, N. E. (1995). Reasoning and rationality: A critique of some experimental paradigms. *Theory & Psychology, 5*, 429–448. **[24]**

Whitcomb, K. M, Önkal, D., Curley, S. P., & Benson, P. G. (1995). Probability judgment accuracy for general knowledge: Cross-national differences and assessment methods. *Journal of Behavioral Decision Making, 8*, 51–67. **[15]**

Whitley, B. E., Jr., & Hern, A. L. (1991). Perceptions of vulnerability to pregnancy and the use of effective contraception. *Personality and Social Psychology Bulletin, 17*, 104–110. **[19]**

Wickens, C. D. (1984). *Engineering psychology and human performance*. Columbus, OH: Merrill. **[12]**

Wicklund, R. A. (1974). *Freedom and reactance*. Potomac, MD: Erlbaum. **[36]**

Wiggins, J. S. (1981). Clinical and statistical prediction: Where are we and where do we go from here? *Clinical Psychology Review, 1*, 3–18. **[40]**

Wilks, S. S. (1938). Weighting systems for linear functions of correlated variables when there is no dependent variable. *Psychometrika, 3*, 23–40. **[40]**

Williams, P. A., Moyes, G. D., & Park, K. (1996). Factors affecting earnings forecast revisions for the buy-side and sell-side analyst. *Accounting Horizons, 10*, 112–121. **[38]**

Wills, T. A. (1981). Downward comparison principles in social psychology. *Psychological Bulletin, 90*, 245–271. **[17]**

Wills, T. A. (1987). Downward comparison as a coping mechanism. In *Coping with negative life events: Clinical and social–psychological perspectives* (pp. 243–268), C. R. Snyder & C. Ford (Eds.). New York: Plenum Press. **[17]**

Wilson, J. Q. (1989). *Bureaucracy: What government agencies do and why they do it*. New York: Basic Books. **[32]**

Wilson, R. (1979). Analyzing the risks of everyday life. *Technology Review, 81*(4), 40–46. **[41]**

Wilson, T. D. (1985). Strangers to ourselves: The origins and accuracy of beliefs about one's own mental states. In *Attribution: Basic issues and applications* (pp. 9–36), J. H. Harvey & G. Weary (Eds.). Orlando, FL: Academic Press. **[16]**

Wilson, T. D. (2001). *Strangers to ourselves: self-insight and the adaptive unconscious*. Manuscript in preparation. **[10]**

Wilson, T. D., & Brekke, N. (1994). Mental contamination and mental correction: unwanted influences on judgments and evaluations. *Psychological Bulletin, 116*, 117–142. **[6, 10]**

Wilson, T. D., Dunn, D. S., Kraft, D., & Lisle, D. J. (1989). Introspection, attitude change, and attitude–behavior consistency: The disruptive effects of explaining why we feel the way we do. In *Advances in experimental social psychology* (Vol. 22, pp. 287–343), L. Berkowitz (Ed.). Orlando, FL: Academic Press. **[30]**

Wilson, T. D., Gilbert, D. T., & Wheatley, T. (1998). Protecting our minds: the role of lay beliefs. In *Metacognition: cognitive and social dimensions* (pp. 171–201), V. Yzerbyt, G. Lories, & B. Dardenne (Eds.). New York: Sage. **[10]**

Wilson, T. D., Hodges, S. D., & LaFleur, S. J. (1995). Effects of introspecting about reasons: Inferring attitudes from accessible thoughts. *Journal of Personality and Social Psychology, 69*, 16–28. **[36]**

Wilson, T. D., Houston, C., Etling, K. M., & Brekke, N. (1996). A new look at anchoring effects: Basic anchoring and it antecedents. *Journal of Experimental Psychology: General, 4*, 387–402. **[Introduction, 6, 8]**

Wilson, T. D., Lisle, D., Schooler, J., Hodges, S. D., Klaaren, K. J., & LaFleur, S. J. (1993). Introspecting about reasons can reduce post-choice satisfaction. *Personality and Social Psychology Bulletin, 10*, 331–339. **[30]**

Wilson, T. D., & Schooler, J. W. (1991). Thinking too much: introspection can reduce the quality of preferences and decisions. *Journal of Personality and Social Psychology, 60*(2), 181–192. **[30]**

Wilson, T. D., Wheatley, T., Meyers, Gilbert, D. T., & Axsom, D. (2000). Focalism: A source of durability bias in affective forecasting. *Journal of Personality and Social Psychology, 78*, 821–836. **[14, 16]**

Windschitl, P. D., & Weber, E. U. (1999). The interpretation of "likely" depends on the context, but "70%" is 70% – right?: The influence of associative processes on perceived certainty. *Journal of Experimental Psychology: Learning, Memory, and Cognition, 25*, 1514–1533. **[22]**

Winkielman, P., Zajonc, R. B., & Schwarz, N. (1997). Subliminal affective priming resists attributional interventions. *Cognition and Emotion, 11*(4), 433–465. **[23]**

Winkler, R. L., & Poses, R. M. (1993). Evaluating and combining physicians' probabilities of survival in an intensive care unit. *Management Science, 39*, 1526–43. **[39]**

Wittman, M. P. (1941). Mental efficiency levels before and after shock therapy. *Elgin Papers, 4*, 70–81. **[40]**

Wolford, G., Taylor, H. A., & Beck, J. R. (1990). The conjunction fallacy? *Memory and Cognition, 18*, 47–53. **[3]**

Wong, P. T. P., & Weiner, B. (1981). When people ask "why" questions, and the heuristics of the attributional search. *Journal of Personality and Social Psychology, 40*, 650–663. **[19]**

Wood, J. V. (1989). Theory and research concerning social comparisons of personal attributes. *Psychological Bulletin, 106*, 231–248. **[9, 17]**

Wood, J. V., Taylor, S. E., & Lichtman, R. R. (1985). Social comparison in adjustment to breast cancer. *Journal of Personality and Social Psychology, 49*, 1169–1183. **[19]**

Word, C. O., Zanna, M. P., & Cooper, J. (1974). The nonverbal mediation of self-fulfilling prophecies in interracial interaction. *Journal of Experimental Social Psychology, 10*, 109–120. **[Introduction]**

Wortman, C. B., & Silver, R. C. (1987). Coping with irrevocable loss. In *Cataclysms, crises, and catastrophes: Psychology in action* (pp. 185–235), G. R. VandenBos & B. K. Bryant (Eds.). Washington, DC: American Psychological Association. **[16]**

Wortman, C. B., & Silver, R. C. (1989). The myths of coping with loss. *Journal of Consulting and Clinical Psychology, 57*, 349–357 **[16]**

Wright, G., Lawrence, M. J., & Collopy, F. (1996). The role and validity of judgment in forecasting. *International Journal of Forecasting, 12*, 1–8. **[41]**

Wright, G., & Wisudha, A. (1982). Distribution of probability assessments for almanac and future event questions. *Scandinavian Journal of Psychology, 23*, 219–224. **[13, 15]**

Wright, G. N., & Phillips, L. D. (1980). Cultural variation in probabilistic thinking: Alternative ways of dealing with uncertainty. *International Journal of Psychology, 15*, 239–257. **[15]**

Wright, G. N., Phillips, L. D., Whalley, P. C., Choo, G. T., Ng, K. O., Tan, I., & Wisudha, A. (1978). Cultural differences in probabilistic thinking. *Journal of Cross-Cultural Psychology, 9*, 285–299. **[15]**

Wright, P. (1975). Consumer choice strategies: Simplifying versus optimizing. *Journal of Marketing Research, 12*, 60–67. **[23, 30]**

Wright, W. F., & Anderson, U. (1989). Effects of situation familiarity and financial incentives on use of the anchoring and adjustment heuristic for probability assessment. *Organizational Behavior and Human Decision Processes, 44*, 68–82. **[6, 7]**

Wu, G., & Gonzalez, R. (1999). Nonlinear decision weights in choice under uncertainty. *Management Science, 45*, 74–85. **[27]**

Wurtele, S. K. (1988). Increasing women's calcium intake: The role of health beliefs, intentions, and health value. *Journal of Applied Social Psychology, 18*, 627–639. [17]

Wurtele, S. K., & Maddux, J. E. (1987). Relative contributions of protection motivation theory components in predicting exercise intentions and behavior. *Health Psychology, 6*, 453–466. [17]

Wyer, R. S., & Carlston, D. (1979). *Social cognition, inference, and attribution.* Hillsdale, NJ: Erlbaum. [29]

Wyer, R. S., Jr. (1976). An investigation of the relations among probability estimates. *Organizational Behavior and Human Performance, 15*, 1–18. [1]

Wyer, R. S., & Gordon, S. E. (1984). The cognitive representation of social information. In *Handbook of social cognition* (Vol. 2, pp. 73–150), R. S. Wyer & T. K. Srull (Eds.). Hillsdale, NJ: Erlbaum. [20]

Wyer, R. S., & Srull, T. K. (1981). Category accessibility: Some theoretical and empirical issues concerning the processing of social stimulus information. In *Social cognition: The Ontario symposium* (Vol. 1, pp. 161–197), E. T. Higgins, C. R. Herman, & M. P. Zanna (Eds.). Hillsdale, NJ: Erlbaum. [20]

Wyer, R. S., & Srull, T. K. (1989). *Memory and cognition in its social context.* Hillsdale, NJ: Lawrence Erlbaum Associates. [5]

Wänke, M., Schwarz, N., & Bless, H. (1995). The availability heuristic revisited: experienced ease of retrieval in mundane frequency estimates. *Acta Psychologica, 89*, 83–90. [5]

Yadav, M. S. (1994). How buyers evaluate product bundles: a model of anchoring and adjustment. *Journal of Consumer Research, 21*, 342–353. [6]

Yamagishi, K. (1994). Consistencies and biases in risk perception. I. Anchoring processes and response-range effects. *Perceptual and Motor Skills, 79*(1, Pt. 2), 651–656. [6]

Yamagishi, K. (1997). When a 12.86% mortality is more dangerous than 24.14%: Implications for risk communication. *Applied Cognitive Psychology, 11*, 495–506. [23]

Yaniv, L., & Foster, D. (1990). Graininess of judgment: an accuracy–informativeness tradeoff. *Journal of Experimental Psychology: General, 21*, 1509–1521. [3]

Yates, J. F. (1982). External correspondence: Decompositions of the mean probability score. *Organizational Behavior and Human Performance, 30*, 132–156. [15]

Yates, J. F. (1990). *Judgment and decision making.* Englewood Cliffs, NJ: Prentice-Hall. [13, 14, 15]

Yates, J. F. (Ed.). (1992). *Risk-taking behavior.* Chichester, U.K.: Wiley. [39]

Yates, J. F. (1994). Subjective probability accuracy analysis. In *Subjective probability* (pp. 381–410), G. Wright & P. Ayton (Eds.), Chichester, U.K.: Wiley. [15, 39]

Yates, J. F. (1998). Conceptualizing, explaining, and improving accuracy: Process models of probability judgment. *Cognitive Studies, 5*(4), 49–64. [15]

Yates, J. F., Lee, J.-W., & Bush, J. G. (1997). General knowledge overconfidence: Cross-national variations, response style, and "reality." *Organizational Behavior and Human Decision Processes, 70*, 87–94. [15]

Yates, J. F., Lee, J.-W., Levi, K. R., & Curley, S. P. (1990). Measuring and analyzing probability judgment accuracy in medicine. *Philippine Journal of Internal Medicine, 28*(Suppl. 1), 21–32. [15]

Yates, J. F., Lee, J.-W., & Shinotsuka, H. (1996). Beliefs about overconfidence, including its cross-national variation. *Organizational Behavior and Human Decision Processes, 65*, 138–147. [15]

Yates, J. F., Lee, J.-W., Shinotsuka, H., Patalano, A. L., & Sieck, W. R. (1998). Cross-cultural variations in probability judgment accuracy: Beyond general knowledge overconfidence. *Organizational Behavior and Human Decision Processes, 74*, 89–117. **[15]**

Yates, J. F., Lee, J.-W., Shinotsuka, H., & Sieck, W. R. (2000). *The argument recruitment model: Explaining general knowledge overconfidence and its cross-cultural variations.* Working paper, Department of Psychology, University of Michigan, Ann Arbor. **[15]**

Yates, J. F., McDaniel, L. S., & Brown, E. S. (1991). Probabalistic forecasts of stock prices and earnings: The hazards of nascent expertise. *Organizational Behavior and Human Decision Processes, 49*, 60–79 **[39]**

Yates, J. F., Price, P. C., Lee, J.-W., & Ramirez, J. (1996). Good probabilistic forecasters: The "consumer's" perspective. *International Journal of Forecasting, 12*, 41–56. **[15]**

Yates, J. F., Zhu, Y., Ronis, D. L., Wang, D.-F., Shinotsuka, H., & Toda, M. (1989). Probability judgment accuracy: China, Japan, and the United States. *Organizational Behavior and Human Decision Processes, 43*, 145–171. **[15]**

Yates, J. F., & Curley, S. P. (1985). Conditional distribution analyses of probabilistic forecasts. *Journal of Forecasting, 4*, 61–73. **[39]**

Yates, J. F., & Lee, J.-W. (1996). Chinese decision making. In *The handbook of Chinese psychology* (pp. 338–351), M. H. Bond (Ed.), Hong Kong: Oxford University Press. **[15]**

Yates, J. F., & Patalano, A. L. (1999). Decision making and aging. In *Processing of medical information in aging patients: Cognitive and human factors perspectives* (pp. 31–54), D. C. Park, R. W. Morrell, & K. Shifren (Eds.), Mahwah, NJ: Lawrence Erlbaum Associates. **[15]**

Yik, M. S. M., Bond, M. H., & Paulhus, D. L. (1998). Do Chinese self-enhance or self-efface? It's a matter of domain. *Personality and Social Psychology Bulletin, 24*, 399–406. **[15]**

Youden, W. J. (1972). Enduring Values. *Technometrics, 14*, 1–11. **[37]**

Zadeh, L. A. (1978). Fuzzy sets as a basis for a theory of possibility. *Fuzzy Sets and Systems, 1*, 3–28. **[1, 25]**

Zadeh, L. A. (1982). A note on prototype theory and fuzzy sets. *Cognition, 12*, 291–297. **[1]**

Zajonc, R. B. (1968). Attitudinal effects of mere exposure. *Journal of Personality and Social Psychology Monograph, 9*(2, Pt. 2), 1–27. **[23, 30]**

Zajonc, R. B. (1980). Feeling and thinking: Preferences need no inferences. *American Psychologist, 35*, 151–175. **[Introduction, 2, 23, 29]**

Zajonc, R. B. (1997). Emotions. In *Handbook of social psychology, 4th Ed.* (pp. 591–632) D. T. Gilbert, S. T. Fiske, & G. Lindzey (Eds.). New York: Oxford University Press. **[2, 30]**

Zajonc, R. B., & Markus, H. (1982). Affective and cognitive factors in preferences. *Journal of Consumer Research, 9*, 123–131. **[23]**

Zarnowitz, V. (1985). Rational expectations and macroeconomic forecasts. *Journal of Business and Economic Statistics, 3*, 293–311. **[25]**

Zax, M., & Takahashi, S. (1967). Cultural influences on response style: Comparisons of Japanese and American college students. *Journal of Social Psychology, 71*, 3–10. **[15]**

Zentner, R. D. (1982). Scenarios, past, present and future. *Long Range Planning, 15*, 12–20. **[1]**

Zhang, B. (1992). *Cultural conditionality in decision making: A prospect of probabilistic thinking.* Unpublished Doctoral dissertation, Department of Information Systems, London School of Economics and Political Science, University of London, London. **[15]**

Zillman, D. (1978). Attribution and misattribution of excitatory reactions. In *New directions in attribution research* (Vol. 2, pp. 335–368), J. H. Harvey, W. I. Ickes, & R. F. Kidd (Eds.). Hillsdale, NJ: Erlbaum. **[5, 29]**

Zimbardo, P. G., & Lieppe, M. R. (1991). *The psychology of attitude change and social influence.* New York: McGraw-Hill. **[9]**

Zuckerman, M., DePaulo, B. M., & Rosenthal, R. (1981). Verbal and nonverbal communication of deception. In *Advances in experimental social psychology* (Vol. 14, pp. 1–59), L. Berkowitz (Ed.). New York: Academic Press. **[9]**

Zukier, H. (1986). The paradigmatic and narrative modes in goal-guided inference. In *Handbook of motivation and cognition: Foundations of social behavior* (Vol. 1, pp. 465–502), R. M. Sorrentino & E. T. Higgins (Eds.). New York: Guilford. **[14]**

Zusne, L., & Jones, W. H. (1982). *Anomalistic psychology.* Hillsdale, NJ: Lawrence Erlbaum Associates. **[34]**

Statistical abstract of the United States (1990). Washington, DC: U.S. Dept. of Commerce, Bureau of the Census. **[25]**

Index

ecological validity, 8
egocentrism, 152–157, 641–651
elimination by aspects, 548, 565
enhancement effect, 465–472
evaluability, 404–406
evidence strength versus weight, 231–232
   divergence from Bayesian analysis, 234
evolutionary psychology and judgmental
         heuristics, 9–11
expert judgment, 691–710
   doctors, 696–701
   lawyers, 705–706
   political experts, forecasts, 749–762
      confirmation vs. disconfirmation of
         predictions, reactions to
         Defensive strategies, 750–751, 752–762
         Individual differences, 754
   stock market analysts, 678–685, 707–708
   sports commentators, 709–710
   weather forecasters, 702–704
extension rule of probability, 20
   ways to encourage use, 41

false-belief paradigm, 151
false consensus effect, 642–643, 662
false polarization effect, 651–653
fast and frugal heuristics, 559–581
focalism, 266–267, 295–296, 303
forecasting, 251–253, 749–757
functionalist metaphors of judgment and
         decision making, 582–599
   intuitive politician, 583–593
   intuitive prosecutor, 598
   intuitive theologian, 595–597
fundamental attribution error, 361, 590, 598
fundamental computational bias, 436–439

gambler's fallacy, 601
Goldberg rule, 718–719
graphology, 622

heuristic elicitation design, 60–65
heuristics, statistical, 511–533
   factors influencing use, 516–530
   and generalization from instances, 513,
         516–522
   and domain specificity, 525–526
   and evolution, 532–533
hindsight bias, 112, 134, 158
homeopathy, 620
hostile media effect, 649–651
hot hand, 601–616
"how-do-I-feel-about-it" heuristic, 536–541

illusion of validity, 246–7
illusory transparency, 158–163
immune neglect, 296–297, 302–305, 308–309
inclusion fallacy, 387–388
individual differences in reasoning, 68
   and alternative construal of reasoning
         problems, 430–436
   dual process account, 436–438
   and normative/descriptive gap, 421–440
intensity bias, 266
interquartile index (of calibration), 667

law of small numbers, 49, 512, 601
legal experts, 705–706
loss aversion, 640

magical thinking, 201–202
   Freud's primary process, 203
   individual differences, 215
   Piaget's definition of, 203
medical experts, 696–701
Meliorists vs. Panglossians, 431, 422, 424, 425,
         439
mental contamination, 185–187, 192–198,
         199–200
"minimalist" heuristic, 562–571
Minnesota Multiphasic Personality Inventory
         (MMPI), 718–719
mood congruent memory, 535–536

naive realism, 641–653
natural assessments, underlying judgmental
         heuristics, 3–5, 17, 20
negativity bias, 207
norm theory, 348–366
   See also counterfactuals

optimistic bias, 168, 256, 262, 313–323, 336–345
overconfidence, 175, 230–239, 245, 248–9, 252,
         268–271, 277–280, 687
   and self-enhancement, 284–285
   and temporal proximity, 339–340
   cultural differences, 272–3, 275, 276
   difficulty as moderator, 242–3
   in assessments of ability, 324–333
   in probabilistic judgment of physical
         constants, 667–677
   in political forecasts, 749–762
   self versus other, 240–241

perceptions of bias
   actor-observer difference, 653–665
   and interpersonal conflict, 636–641